Microsoft®
OFFICE 2007

Introductory Course

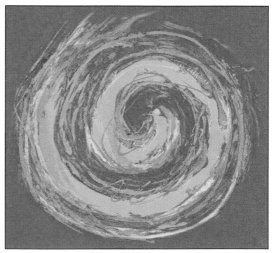

William R. Pasewark, Sr., Ph.D.
Professor Emeritus, Business Education, Texas Tech
University
Scott G. Pasewark, B.S.
Occupational Education, Computer Technologist
William R. Pasewark, Jr., Ph.D., CPA
Professor, Accounting, Texas Tech University
Carolyn Denny Pasewark, M.Ed.
National Computer Consultant, Reading and Math
Certified Elementary Teacher, K-12 Certified
Counselor
Jan Pasewark Stogner, MBA
Financial Planner
Beth Pasewark Wadsworth, B.A.
Graphic Designer
Rachel Biheller Bunin, **Jessica Evans**,
Katherine T. Pinard, **Robin M. Romer**
Contributing Authors

*Pasewark and Pasewark is a trademark of the
Pasewark LTD.

by Pasewark and Pasewark*

COURSE TECHNOLOGY
CENGAGE Learning™

Australia • Brazil • Japan • Korea • Mexico • Singapore • Spain • United Kingdom • United States

COURSE TECHNOLOGY
CENGAGE Learning™

Microsoft Office 2007 Introductory

Contributing Authors: Rachel Biheller Bunin, Jessica Evans, Ann Fisher, Katherine T. Pinard, Robin M. Romer, Barbara Waxer

Authors: William R. Pasewark, Sr., William R. Pasewark, Jr., Scott G. Pasewark, Jan Pasewark Stogner, Beth Pasewark Wadsworth, Carolyn Pasewark Denny

Managing Editor: Donna Gridley

Product Manager: Jennifer T. Campbell

Editorial Assistant: Amanda Lyons

Content Project Managers: Aimee Poirier, Jill Klaffky, Heather Furrow

Marketing Coordinator: Julie Schuster

Quality Assurance Testers: John Freitas, Christian Kunciw, GreenPenQA Tester, Serge Palladino, Jeff Schwartz, Marianne Snow, Teresa Storch

Developmental Editor: Custom Editorial Productions, Inc.

Composition: GEX Publishing Services

Art Director: Bruce Bond

Cover Designer: Joel Sadagursky

Cover Illustrator: Neil Brennan

For product information and technology assistance, contact us at
Cengage Learning Customer & Sales Support, 1-800-354-9706

For permission to use material from this text or product, submit all requests online at **cengage.com/permissions**
Further permissions questions can be emailed to
permissionrequest@cengage.com

ISBN-13: 978-1-4239-0396-3 (Hardcover)
ISBN-10: 1-4239-0396-X (Hardcover)

ISBN-13: 978-1-4239-0398-7 (Hardcover, spiral-bound)
ISBN-10: 1-4239-0398-6 (Hardcover, spiral-bound)

ISBN-13: 978-1-4239-0397-X (Softcover)
ISBN-10: 1-4239-0397-8 (Softcover)

Course Technology
25 Thomson Place
Boston, Massachusetts, 02210
USA

Cengage Learning is a leading provider of customized learning solutions with office locations around the globe, including Singapore, the United Kingdom, Australia, Mexico, Brazil, and Japan. Locate your local office at:
international.cengage.com/region

Cengage Learning products are represented in Canada by Nelson-Education, Ltd.

For your lifelong learning solutions, visit **course.cengage.com**

Visit our corporate website at **cengage.com**

*The Keyboarding Touch System Improvement Appendix is an excerpt from Keyboarding Skill Builder for Computers, Copyright 1996 by William R. Pasewark, Sr.

Some of the product names and company names used in this book have been used for identification purposed only and may be trademarks or registered trademarks of their respective manufacturers and sellers.

Microsoft and the Office logo are either registered trademarks or trademarks of Microsoft Corporation in the United States and/or other countries. Thomson Course Technology is an independent entity from the Microsoft Corporation, and not affiliated with Microsoft in any manner.

Printed in the United States of America
7 8 9 BM 11 10

Overview of This Book

Sample lesson pages

Objectives— Objectives are listed at the beginning of each lesson.

Vocabulary— Terms identified in blue throughout the lesson and summarized at the end.

SCANS— (Secretary's Commission on Achieving Necessary Skills)—The workplace competencies identified by the U.S. Department of Labor are identified in exercises where they apply. More information on SCANS can be found on the Instructor Resources CD.

Enhanced Screen Shots— Screen shots come to life on each page with color and depth.

Learning Boxes— These boxes expand and enrich learning with additional information or activities: Did You Know?, Computer Concepts, Net Tip, and more.

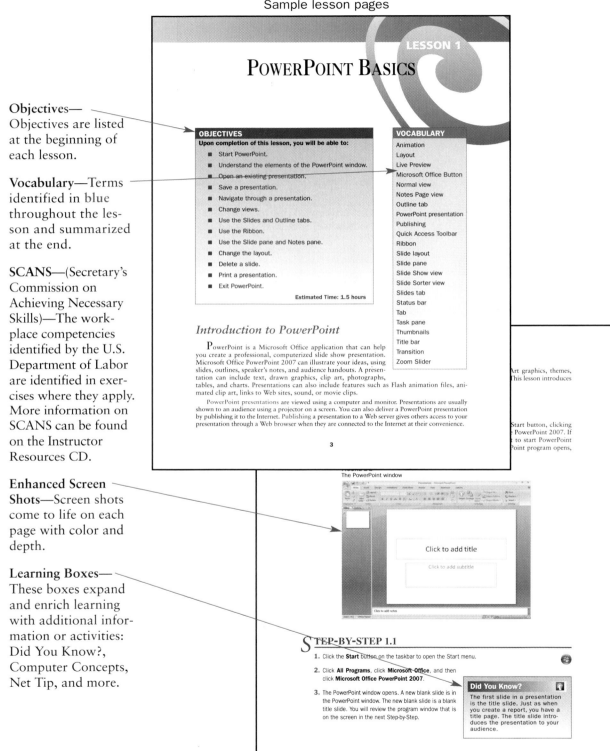

LESSON 1

POWERPOINT BASICS

OBJECTIVES

Upon completion of this lesson, you will be able to:

- Start PowerPoint.
- Understand the elements of the PowerPoint window.
- Open an existing presentation.
- Save a presentation.
- Navigate through a presentation.
- Change views.
- Use the Slides and Outline tabs.
- Use the Ribbon.
- Use the Slide pane and Notes pane.
- Change the layout.
- Delete a slide.
- Print a presentation.
- Exit PowerPoint.

Estimated Time: 1.5 hours

VOCABULARY

Animation
Layout
Live Preview
Microsoft Office Button
Normal view
Notes Page view
Outline tab
PowerPoint presentation
Publishing
Quick Access Toolbar
Ribbon
Slide layout
Slide pane
Slide Show view
Slide Sorter view
Slides tab
Status bar
Tab
Task pane
Thumbnails
Title bar
Transition
Zoom Slider

Introduction to PowerPoint

PowerPoint is a Microsoft Office application that can help you create a professional, computerized slide show presentation. Microsoft Office PowerPoint 2007 can illustrate your ideas, using slides, outlines, speaker's notes, and audience handouts. A presentation can include text, drawn graphics, clip art, photographs, tables, and charts. Presentations can also include features such as Flash animation files, animated clip art, links to Web sites, sound, or movie clips.

PowerPoint presentations are viewed using a computer and monitor. Presentations are usually shown to an audience using a projector on a screen. You can also deliver a PowerPoint presentation by publishing it to the Internet. Publishing a presentation to a Web server gives others access to your presentation through a Web browser when they are connected to the Internet at their convenience.

3

Art graphics, themes,
This lesson introduces

Start button, clicking
e PowerPoint 2007. If
t to start PowerPoint
Point program opens,

The PowerPoint window

Click to add title

Click to add subtitle

Click to add notes

STEP-BY-STEP 1.1

1. Click the **Start** button on the taskbar to open the Start menu.

2. Click **All Programs**, click **Microsoft Office**, and then click **Microsoft Office PowerPoint 2007**.

3. The PowerPoint window opens. A new blank slide is in the PowerPoint window. The new blank slide is a blank title slide. You will review the program window that is on the screen in the next Step-by-Step.

Did You Know?

The first slide in a presentation is the title slide. Just as when you create a report, you have a title page. The title slide introduces the presentation to your audience.

Overview of This Book

Sample end-of-lesson pages

Summaries—A recap of what you have learned.

Vocabulary/Review Questions—A list of new terms for the lesson and review questions such as multiple choice or true/false.

End-of-Lesson Projects—Hands-on exercises in which you apply the techniques learned in the lesson.

Critical Thinking Activities—An opportunity to use creative analysis and the Help system to solve problems.

End-of-Unit Projects—Hands-on application of concepts learned in the unit.

Unit Simulation—A realistic business simulation runs throughout the text at the end of each unit, reinforcing the material covered in the unit.

Capstone Simulation—A comprehensive business case at the end of the text gives students an opportunity to apply all of the skills they have learned.

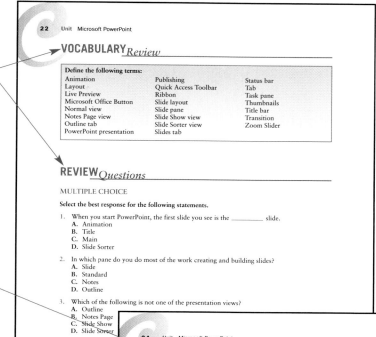

TEACHING AND LEARNING RESOURCES FOR THIS BOOK

Student Online Companion

The *Student Online Companion*, available at www.course.com, includes the Data Files, MCAS mapping grids, and Key Terms. CourseCasts and PowerPoint presentations allow students to learn more about the topics

Instructor Resources CD

The *Instructor Resources CD* contains the following teaching resources:

- The Data and Solution Files for this course.

- ExamView® tests for each lesson. ExamView is a powerful testing software package that allows instructors to create and administer printed, computer (LAN-based), and Internet exams.

- Instructor's Manual that includes lecture notes for each lesson, answers to the lesson and Unit Review questions, references to the solutions for Step-by-Step exercises, end-of-lesson activities, and Unit Review projects.

- Copies of the figures that appear in the student text.

- Grids that show skills required for the Microsoft Certification Application Specialist (MCAS) exam, SCANS workplace competencies and skills, and activities that apply to cross-curricular topics.

- Suggested Syllabus with block, two quarter, and 18-week schedule.

- Annotated Solutions and Grading Rubrics.

- PowerPoint presentations for each lesson.

- Spanish Glossary and a Spanish test bank.

- Models for Formatted Documents, such as a business letter, resume, research paper, etc.

- E-Mail Writing Guide, Letter Writing Guide, and Proofreader's Marks.

SCANS

The Secretary's Commission on Achieving Necessary Skills (SCANS) from the U.S. Department of Labor is a list of workplace competencies and foundation skills that can be used to ensure that students achieve the level of skills required to enter employment. The workplace competencies are identified as 1) ability to use resources, 2) interpersonal skills, 3) ability to work with information, 4) understanding of systems, and 5) knowledge and understanding of technology. The foundation skills are identified as 1) basic communication skills, 2) thinking skills, and 3) personal qualities.

Exercises in which students must use a number of these SCANS competencies and foundation skills are marked in the text with the SCANS icon.

Microsoft Certified Application Specialist Certification

This courseware, when used in conjunction with our *Microsoft Certification Application Specialist Office 2007 Workbook*, covers all of the necessary skills to prepare for the Microsoft Certification Application Specialist (MCAS) Program exams for Word, Excel, PowerPoint, and Access. To learn more about the MCAS program, go to www.microsoft.com/learning/exams/.

What is the Microsoft Business Certification Program?

The Microsoft Business Certification Program enables candidates to show that they have something exceptional to offer – proven experience in Microsoft Office programs. The two certification tracks allow candidates to choose how they want to exhibit their skills, either through validating skills within a specific Microsoft product or taking their knowledge to the next level and combining Microsoft programs to show that they can apply multiple skill sets to complete more complex office tasks. Recognized by businesses and schools around the world, over 3 million certifications have been obtained in over 100 different countries. The Microsoft Business Certification program is the only Microsoft-approved certification program of its kind.

What is the Microsoft Certified Application Specialist Certification?

The Microsoft Certified Application Specialist Certification exams focus on validating specific skill sets within each of the Microsoft® Office system programs. The candidate can choose which exam(s) they want to take according to the skills they want to validate. The available Application Specialist exams include:

Using Microsoft® Windows Vista™

Using Microsoft® Office Word 2007*

Using Microsoft® Office Excel® 2007*

Using Microsoft® Office PowerPoint® 2007*

Using Microsoft® Office Access® 2007*

Using Microsoft® Office Outlook® 2007

*Use this book along with the *Microsoft Certification Application Specialist Office 2007 Workbook* to practice the certification skills for this exam.

ASSESSMENT INSTRUMENTS

SAM 2007   *POWERED BY* **SAM**

SAM 2007 helps bridge the gap between the classroom and the real world by allowing students to train and test on important computer skills in an active, hands-on environment.

SAM 2007's easy-to-use system includes powerful interactive exams, training or projects on critical applications such as Word, Excel, Access, PowerPoint, Outlook, Windows, the Internet, and much more. SAM simulates the application environment, allowing students to demonstrate their knowledge and think through the skills by performing real-world tasks.

SAM 2007 includes built-in page references so students can print helpful study guides that match the textbooks used in class. Powerful administrative options allow instructors to schedule exams and assignments, secure tests, and run reports with almost limitless flexibility.

ExamView®

ExamView is a powerful objective-based test generator that enables you to create paper, LAN, or Web-based tests from test banks designed specifically for your Course Technology text. Utilize the ultra-efficient QuickTest Wizard to create tests in less than five minutes by taking advantage of Course Technology's question banks, or customize your own exams from scratch.

MESSAGE FROM THE AUTHORS

About the Pasewark Author Team

Pasewark LTD is a family-owned business with more than 90 years of combined experience authoring award-winning textbooks. They have written over 100 books about computers, accounting, and office technology. During that time, they developed their mission statement: *To help our students live better lives.*

Pasewark LTD authors are members of several professional associations that help authors write better books. The authors have been recognized with numerous awards for classroom teaching and believe that effective classroom teaching is a major ingredient for writing effective textbooks.

From the Contributing Authors

I would like to thank the good people at Course Technology for putting this terrific editorial and production team together to publish this landmark textbook. Special thanks to Donna Gridley the Managing Editor, and Jennifer Campbell the Project Manager. I am very grateful to my family for their support... a special shout out to David, Jennifer, Emily and Michael. – *Rachel Biheller Bunin*

I would like to thank Donna Gridley and Jennifer Campbell for the opportunity to work on this project and for their expert project management. I also want to thank my coauthors for their support and friendship while we were busy writing. Finally, thank you Richard and Hannah for your patience, understanding, support, and love while I tackled another book. When I count my blessings, you share the top spot on my list. – *Jessica Evans*

I'd like to thank Jennifer Campbell for inviting me to be part of this great team as well as Beckie Middendorf for her guidance throughout the production process. – *Ann Fisher*

As always, the talented team at Course Technology worked together to create a fantastic book under impossible deadlines. Thank you to Donna Gridley and Jennifer Campbell for giving me the opportunity to write, to Betsy Newberry for her editing skills, and to Jill Klaffky and Heather Furrow, my production editors. A special thank you to Andrew, Shelagh, Maura, and Helen for their support and patience. – *Katherine T. Pinard*

Many thanks to my talented coauthors and the dedicated editorial team at Course Technology. Much love to my family for their constant support. A special thank you to Brian for your patience and endurance, and to Jake, who just turned 5, for your help in writing all the As, Es, Js, and Ks. – *Robin M. Romer*

Kudos to a talented and gracious authoring and production team. – *Barbara Waxer*

Award-Winning Books by the Pasewarks

The predecessors to this book, *Microsoft® Office 2000: Introductory* and *Microsoft Office XP: Introductory*, by the Pasewarks, won the Text and Academic Authors Association *Texty Award* for the best el-hi computer book for the years 2000 and 2002.

Advisory Board

Thank you to the following instructors, who expertly reviewed the table of contents and provided valuable feedback to help guide the development of this book:

Jessica Sayer Hayes, Prince Edward County High School

Kimberly Webber, Oxford Area High School

Lynlee J. Caliguiri, South Fayette High School

Ralph Chianelli, Darien High School

GETTING STARTED

Start-Up Checklist

Minimum Hardware Configuration

✓ PC with Pentium processor.

✓ Hard disk with 400 MB free for typical installation.

✓ CD-ROM recordable drive or access to network drive for downloading and saving Data and Solution Files.

✓ Monitor set at 1024x768 or higher-resolution. *If your resolution differs, you will see differences in the Ribbon, and may have to scroll up or down to view the information on your screen. See the Office 2007 Basics lesson for more information.*

✓ Printer.

✓ Internet connection. If you are not connected to the Internet, see your instructor.

Software

This book was written and tested using the following settings:

✓ A typical installation of Microsoft Office 2007.

✓ Microsoft Windows Vista running with Aero off.

✓ Microsoft Internet Explorer 7 browser.

For Windows XP users

The screenshots in this book show Microsoft Office 2007 running on Windows Vista. If you are using Microsoft Windows XP, use these alternate steps.

Starting a program

1. Click the **Start** button on the taskbar.

2. Point to **All Programs,** point to **Microsoft Office,** and then click the application you want to use.

Saving a file for the first time

1. Click the **Office Button,** and then click **Save As.**

2. Type a name for your file in the File Name text box.

3. Click the **Save in** list arrow, and then navigate to the drive and folder where you store your Data Files.

4. Click **Save.**

Opening a file

1. Click the **Office Button,** and then click **Open.**

2. Click the **Look in** list arrow, and then navigate to the drive and folder where you store your Data Files.

3. Click the file you want to open.

4. Click **Open.**

DATA FILES GRID

APPLICATION	LESSON	DATA FILE	SOLUTION FILE
Office	1	Employees\Abbott	Employees\Abbott\June Work Schedule.xlsx
		Employees\Brown	Employees\Brown\June Work Schedule.xlsx
		Employees\Garner	Employees\Garner\June Work Schedule.xlsx
		Employees\Kamnani	Employees\Garner\Memo.docx
		Employees\Perez\Memo.docx	Employees\Kamnani\June Work Schedule.xlsx
		Employees\Perez\Schedule.xlsx	Employees\Perez\Memo.docx
		Employees\Reid	Employees\Perez\Schedule.xlsx
		Employees\Tab	Employees\Reid\June Work Schedule.xlsx
		Employees\Wong	Employees\Tab\June Work Schedule.xlsx
			Employees\Wong\June Work Schedule.xlsx
Word	1	Interview.docx	Cosmic Lecture.docx
		Lecture.docx	Holiday Clearance.docx
		Sale.docx	Interview Tips.docx
			Thank You Letter.docx
			To Do List.docx
	2	Golf Tournament.docx	Customer Letter.docx
		Job Interview.docx	Golf Tournament Notice.docx
		Letter.docx	Interview Preparation.docx
		Web Site.docx	Spelling List.docx
		Workshop.docx	Web Site Tips.docx
			Workshop Checklist.docx
	3	Application.docx	Application Letter.docx
		Lancaster Memo.docx	Club Minutes.docx
		Memo.docx	Driving School Memo.docx
		Minutes.docx	Lancaster Voting Memo.docx
		Museum.docx	Museum Visit.docx
	4	Certificate.docx	Break Room Poster.docx
		Checking Account.docx	Checking Account Info.docx
		Flyer.docx	Employee Certificate.docx
		Golf Tournament 2.docx	Employee Handbook.docx
		Handbook.docx	Formatted Golf Tournament Notice.docx
		Poster.docx	Race Track Flyer Final.docx
			Race Track Flyer.docx

APPLICATION	LESSON	DATA FILE	SOLUTION FILE
Word	5	Diet Guidelines.docx	Agenda.docx
		Diet.docx	American Diet Guidelines.docx
		Interview 2.docx	American Diet Title Page.docx
		Invitation.docx	American Diet.docx
		NADA Memo.docx	Break Room Poster 2.docx
		Poster 2.docx	Exercise Plan.docx
		Shipping.docx	Government.docx
			Health Plan.docx
			Interview Preparation Tips.docx
			NADA Office Supplies Memo.docx
			Overnight Shipping.docx
			Resume for Anna.docx
			Wedding Invitation.docx
	6	Invitation 2.docx	Garage Sale.docx
		Memo2.docx	HH Newsletter.docx
		Newsletter.docx	Holiday Invitation.docx
		Shelter.docx	Org Chart Memo.docx
			Park Map.docx
			Shelter News.docx
	7	Diet2.docx	Correspondence Guidelines.docx
		Guidelines.docx	Diet Final.docx
		References.docx	References Formatted.docx
		Sales.docx	References Unformatted.docx
			Sales Leaders.docx
	8	Bank Customers.docx	Bank Fax.docx
		Checking.docx	Bank Letter.docx
		Subscription.docx	Bank New Customer Letters.docx
		Telephone 2.docx	Bank Template.dotx
		Telephone.docx	Combined Bank Letter.docx
			Envelope.docx
			Final Bank Letter.docx
			Hodges Envelope.docx
			Hodges Labels.docx
			Journal Addresses.docx
			Journal Subscription.docx
			Journal Template.dotx
			Labels.docx
			Letter with Changes Accepted.docx
			Letter with Comments.docx
			Merged Journal Letters.docx
			My Resume.docx

APPLICATION	LESSON	DATA FILE	SOLUTION FILE
Word			Telephone Combined Solution.docx
			Telephone Etiquette 2.docx
			Telephone Etiquette.docx
	Unit Review	Bagels.docx	Bagel Mania.docx
		Baseball.docx	East Isle Properties.docx
		Menu.docx	Ergonomics.docx
		Properties.docx	Internet Terms.docx
		Recycling.docx	Java Menu.docx
		Tenses.docx	Pine Hill Baseball.docx
			Recycling Flyer.docx
			Star Contacts.docx
			Star Merge.docx
			Star Template.dotx
			Verb Tenses.docx
Excel	1	Frogs.xlsx	Activity 1-1 solution.docx
		Homes.xlsx	Activity 1-2 solution.docx
		Names.xlsx	Frogs Census.xlsx
		Neighborhood.xlsx	Homeownership.xlsx
			Last Names.xlsx
			Neighborhood Estimates.xlsx
	2	Balance.xlsx	Activity 2-1 solution.docx
		Basketball.xlsx	Activity 2-2 solution.docx
		Bird.xlsx	Basketball Standings.xlsx
		Budget.xlsx	Bird Census.xlsx
		Cell.xlsx	Cell Bill.xlsx
		Mileage.xlsx	Mileage Chart.xlsx
		Phone.xlsx	Nigel Budget.xlsx
			Phone shop solution.xlsx
			Techsoft Balance.xlsx
	3	Biology.xlsx	Biology Grades.xlsx
		Booster.xlsx	Booster Club.xlsx
		Imports.xlsx	Chimpanzee Behavior.xlsx
		Inventory.xlsx	Pool Attendance.xlsx
		Pool.xlsx	Store Assets.xlsx
		Store.xlsx	Supply Inventory.xlsx
		Time.xlsx	Time Record.xslx
		Utilities.xlsx	Trade Imports.xlsx
			Utilities Expenses.xlsx
	4	Drink.xlsx	Activity 4-2 solution.docx
		Formula.xlsx	Drink Sales.xlsx
		Investment.xlsx	Formula Practice.xlsx

APPLICATION	LESSON	DATA FILE	SOLUTION FILE
Excel		Prairie.xlsx	Investment Record.xlsx
		Results.xlsx	Job Offer.xlsx
		Zoo.xlsx	Prairie Development.xlsx
			Results of Formulas.xlsx
			Zoo Fundraiser.xlsx
	5	Finances.xlsx	Budget for *Student Name*.xlsx
		Functions.xlsx	Car Purchase.xlsx
		Golf.xlsx	Functions Worksheet.xlsx
		National.xlsx	Golf Tryouts.xlsx
		Occidental.xlsx	National Bank.xlsx
		Team.xlsx	Occidental Optical.xlsx
		Test.xlsx	Team Stats.xlsx
		Xanthan.xlsx	Test Grades.xlsx
			Xanthan Promotion.xlsx
	6	Botany.xlsx	Activity 6-1 solution.xlsx
		City.xlsx	Activity 6-2 solution.xlsx
		Compact.xlsx	Botany Florist.xlsx
		Employee.xlsx	City Facts.xlsx
		Expense.xlsx	Compact Cubicle.xlsx
		Impact.xlsx	Employee List.xlsx
		Oil.xlsx	Expense Report Web.mht
		Paper.xlsx	Expense Report 2003.xls
		Rose.tif	Expense Report.xlsx
		School bus.bmp	Impact Salaries.xlsx
		School.xlsx	Oil Production.xlsx
		Stock.xlsx	Paper Sales.xlsx
		Tax.xlsx	Roberts Statement.xlsx
		Top.xlsx	School Bus.xlsx
			Stock Quotes.xlsx
			Tax Estimate.xlsx
			Time Card.xlsx
			Top Movies.xlsx
	7	Alamo.xlsx	Activity 7-1.docx
		Annual.xlsx	Alamo Amalgamated.xlsx
		Continental.xlsx	Annual Statement.xlsx
		February.xlsx	Continental Sales.xlsx
		Rainfall.xlsx	February Statement.xlsx
		United.xlsx	Rainfall Records.xlsx
		Voting.xlsx	United Circuitry.xlsx
			Voting Tally.xlsx

APPLICATION	LESSON	DATA FILE	SOLUTION FILE
Excel	8	Chico.xlsx	Chico Temperatures.xlsx
		Concession.xlsx	Concession Sales.xlsx
		Coronado.xlsx	Coronado Foundries.xlsx
		Education.xlsx	Education Pays.xlsx
		Family.xlsx	Family Expenses.xlsx
		Grains.xlsx	Grains Sales.xlsx
		McDonalds.xlsx	McDonalds Restaurants.xlsx
		Populations.xlsx	Populations of Large Cities.xlsx
		Red.xlsx	Red Cross.xlsx
		Running.xlsx	Running Times.xlsx
		Study.xlsx	Sounds Good.xlsx
		Triangle.xlsx	Study and Grades.xlsx
			Triangle Growth.xlsx
	Unit Review	Gas.xlsx	Gas Sales.xlsx
		Organic.xlsx	Organic Financials.xlsx
		Club.xlsx	Club Members.xlsx
		CompNet.xlsx	CompNet Expenses.xlsx
		Computer.xlsx	Coffee Prices.xlsx
		Java.docx	Computer Prices.xlsx
			Java Menu.docx
			Java Menu Revised.docx
Access	1	Employees.accdb	Employees.accdb
		Members.accdb	Members.accdb
		Restaurants.accdb	Restaurants.accdb
		Stores.accdb	Stores.accdb
	2	Company.accdb	Company.accdb
			Interviews.accdb
			Music.accdb
			RetailStores.accdb
			Database.accdb (student supplies filename)
	3	Agents.accdb	Agents.accdb
		Listings.accdb	Listings.accdb
		Product.accdb	Product.accdb
		Properties.accdb	Properties.accdb
		Realtors.accdb	Realtors.accdb
	4	Broker.accdb	Broker.accdb
		Class.accdb	Class.accdb
		Recreation.accdb	Recreation.accdb
		Teacher.accdb	Teacher.accdb

APPLICATION	LESSON	DATA FILE	SOLUTION FILE
Access	5	Agencies.accdb	Agencies.accdb
		Office.gif	Sales.accdb
		Supplies.accdb	Staff.accdb
		Teacher.gif	Supplies.accdb
		Staff.accdb	
		Sales.accdb	
	6	Abbott.docx	Abbott.docx
		Clubs.txt	Club Officials.xlsx
		InfoTech.accdb	
		Inventory.accdb	
PowerPoint	1	Tornadoes.pptx	Tornado Report - Solution.pptx
		Network.pptx	Network Summary - Solution.pptx
			Critical Thinking 1-1 Sample Solution.pptx
			Critical Thinking 1-2 Sample Solution.pptx
	2	EMT Training.potx	EMT Training-Rosewood- Solution.pptx
		EMT Advanced Class.pptx	EMT Advanced Class Fall Session - Solution.pptx
		FirstAid.jpg	EMT Advanced Class Fall Session - Copy Solution.pptx
		TheRose.jpg	PowerPoint2007 Tour - Solution.pptx
		911.wav	Critical Thinking 2-1 Sample Solution.pptx
			Critical Thinking 2-2 Sample Solution.pptx
	3	Animals.pptx	Animal Shelter - Solution.pptx
		Cotton.pptx	Cotton Report - Solution.pptx
		Cotton Gin.jpg	Internet Company Research - Critical Thinking Sample Solution.pptx
		Highway.jpg	My New Company - Critical Thinking Sample Solution.pptx
		Potato Chip Plant.jpg	
		Sky.jpg	
		Truck.jpg	
		cribbedding.mpg	
	4	Planet Facts.docx	Astronomy Class - Solution.pptx
		Planet Number of Moons.docx	Many Moons - Solution.pptx
		The Moons of Jupiter.docx	The Solar System - Solution.pptx
		Planets.xlsx	The Solar System - Solution.docx
		Sun Facts.pptx	Critical Thinking 4-1 Description.pptx
			Critical Thinking 4-1 Description.pptx
Outlook	1	Alien Lecture.docx	

APPLICATION	LESSON	DATA FILE	SOLUTION FILE
Publisher	1	Yoga.pub	New Card solution.pub
		Coupon.pub	Yoga solution.pub
		Gift Certificate.pub	Coupon solution.pub
			My Card solution.pub
			Gift Certificate solution.pub
			Birthday Card solution.pub
	2	Ballet Classes.pub	Brochure solution.pub
		Flyer.pub	Ballet Classes solution.pub
		Layers.pub	Flyer solution.pub
			Guides solution.pub
			Layers solution.pub
			Airplane solution.pub
Capstone	1	Presentation.pptx	GWPresentation.pptx
		Potential Customers.txt	Neighbors.accdb
			Form Letter.docx
			Resident Letters.docx
			Billing.xlsx
			GWFlyer.pub
			Invoice.docx
			Income Statement.xlsx
			SNInvoice.docx
			Letterhead Template.dotx

TABLE OF CONTENTS

INTRODUCTION UNIT

MICROSOFT WORD UNIT

MICROSOFT EXCEL UNIT

MICROSOFT ACCESS UNIT

MICROSOFT POWERPOINT UNIT

MICROSOFT OUTLOOK UNIT

MICROSOFT PUBLISHER UNIT

PHOTO CREDITS

Photo Credits for Appendix A: Computer Concepts

- Figures A-1, A-5c1, A-5c2, A-7a, A-7b, A-8: Courtesy of Hewlett-Packard Company

- Figures A-2a, A2b, A-2e, A-12: Courtesy of Microsoft Corporation

- Figure A-2c: Photograph courtesy of Intermec Technologies

- Figures A-2d, A-2f: Courtesy of Logitech

- Figure A-3: Courtesy of Intel Corporation

- Figure A-4: Courtesy of Seagate Technology

- Figure A-5a: Courtesy of Memorex Products, Inc.

- Figure A-5b: Courtesy of Imation Corp.

- Figures A-5d, A-5e: Courtesy of SanDisk Corporation

- Figure A-6: ViewSonic Corporation

- Figure A-9: Courtesy of Nokia

- Figure A-10: Courtesy of Kingston Technology Company

- Figure A-13: Courtesy of Apple

- Figures A-14, A-15: Courtesy of IBM Archives

- Figure A-17a: © Jose Luis Pelaez, Inc./ Getty Images

- Figure A-17b: © Ryan McVay/ Getty Images

- Figure A-18: Courtesy of the Environmental Protection Agency

INTRODUCTION

Unit

Lesson 1
Windows Vista Basics

1 hr.

Lesson 1
Microsoft® Office 2007 Basics and the Internet

1.5 hrs.

Estimated Time for Unit: 2.5 hours

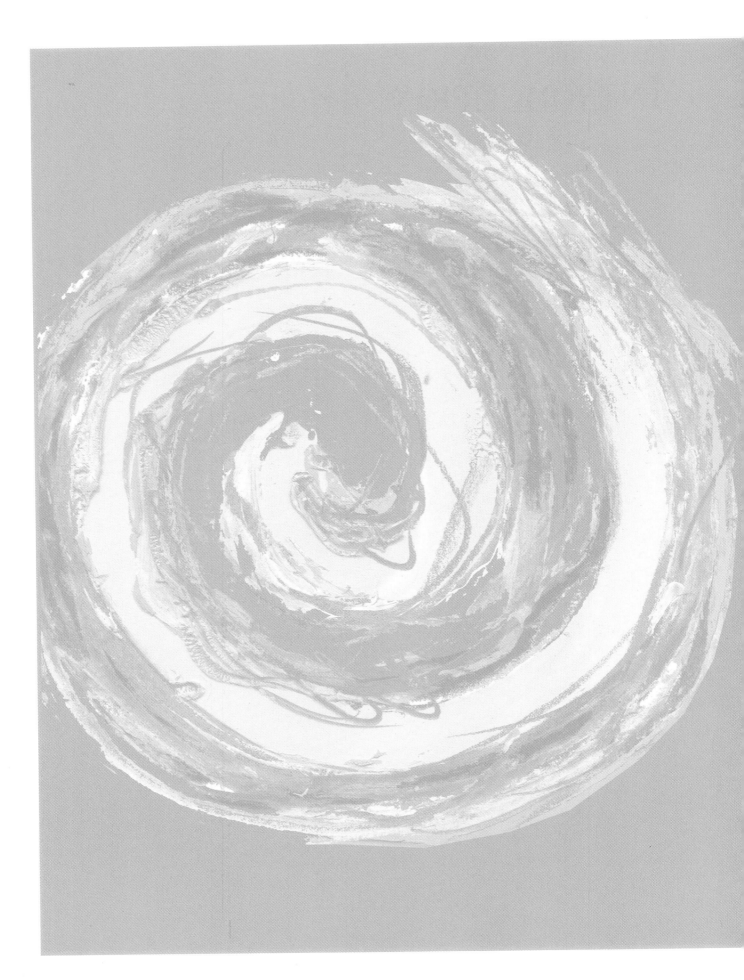

WINDOWS VISTA BASICS

This lesson will familiarize you with the Windows Vista operating system. An operating system is software that controls the basic operations of your computer. In this lesson, you will learn to control your computer's components, move around your desktop, and manage the files, folders, and other resources you work with every day. You will also learn about the Windows Help system and the basics of managing your computer.

Starting Windows

If Windows is already installed, it should start automatically when you turn on the computer. If your computer is on a network, you may need some help from your instructor. Remember that because there are many versions of Windows Vista available and not all educational institutions have hardware that supports all the Vista features, some tasks in this lesson may not be applicable, while other Vista features are intentionally not covered. For example, some editions of Windows Vista support Windows Aero, a graphic interface feature that gives a translucent quality to windows, dialog boxes, and other items. Aero allows you to see through one window to the next or scan through thumbnails and other miniatures in what is known as Flip or Flip 3D. For this lesson, Windows Aero is turned off.

STEP-BY-STEP 1.1

1. Turn on the computer and the monitor, if necessary.

2. After a few moments, the Windows Vista desktop appears.

3. If prompted for login information, type your **username** and **password**, and then click the **Next** button.

4. If the Welcome Center opens, click the **Close** button in the upper-right corner of the Welcome Center window.

Using a Pointing Device

A pointing device allows you to interact and communicate with your computer. A pointing device can be a mouse, trackball, touch pad or screen, pointing stick, digital pen, or even a joystick. All pointing devices share the ability to point to and manipulate graphics and text on the screen. The pointer, which appears as an arrow on the screen, indicates the position of the pointing device. Table 1-1 describes the five most common mouse operations.

TABLE 1-1
Common pointing device actions

ACTION	DESCRIPTION
Point	Positioning the pointing device on a specific object on the screen
Click	Pressing and releasing the left button once while pointing to an object on the screen
Double-click	Quickly pressing and releasing the left button twice to initiate an action
Drag	While pointing to an object on the screen, pressing and holding the left button and moving the object to a new location; releasing the button completes the drag operation
Right-click	Pressing and releasing the right button to view file properties or a menu of functions

Understanding the Desktop

When Windows starts up, icons, windows, folders, and files appear on the desktop. Files and folders, directories that contain files or other folders, are displayed in a small work area known as a window. The desktop is the main work area in Windows. It contains Windows program elements, other programs, and files. Figure 1-1

Did You Know?

Douglas Engelbart invented the first mouse in 1967 and was inducted into the Inventors Hall of Fame in 1998.

illustrates a typical desktop screen when Windows is first installed. Your desktop may contain different icons, shortcuts, or the Windows Sidebar. An **icon** is a small picture that represents a file, folder, program, or program shortcut. You use shortcuts to open files and folders and start applications. You can also drag icons to a new location on the desktop, copy, or delete them. The Windows Sidebar is a transparent panel that is attached to one side of the screen and contains gadgets. The **taskbar** displays icons of the programs you have open or that run in the background. You can customize and organize your desktop by creating files, folders, and shortcuts.

FIGURE 1-1
Typical Windows Vista desktop

The main features of the desktop screen are labeled on Figure 1-1 and discussed below:

1. The Recycle Bin stores the files you want to delete and allows you to restore them if needed.

2. Icons appear on the desktop and are visual representations of a program, file, or operation.

3. Wallpapers or themes use images, patterns, or colors as the background on the desktop.

4. The Start button brings up menus that give you a variety of options, such as starting a program, opening a document, searching for items on your computer, finding help, or shutting down the computer.

5. The Quick Launch toolbar on the taskbar contains buttons you can use to display the desktop or start frequently used programs.

6. The taskbar, located at the bottom of the screen, lets you access open programs and files.

7. Notification area task icons run in the background; you can use these to check the time and date, adjust speaker volume, and access other network or system features.

8. Gadgets on the Windows Sidebar are mini-programs that have specific functionality, such as displaying the time, weather, news feeds, slide shows, and other frequently accessed information.

Click the Start button to open the Start menu. The Start menu is divided into two panes. On the left, you can view recently opened programs, search for any file or folder, and easily access programs installed on your computer by pinning them to the menu. The right pane lists popular functions and features.

STEP-BY-STEP 1.2

1. On the taskbar, click the **Start** button. The Start menu appears in two panes, as shown in Figure 1-2.

FIGURE 1-2
Start menu

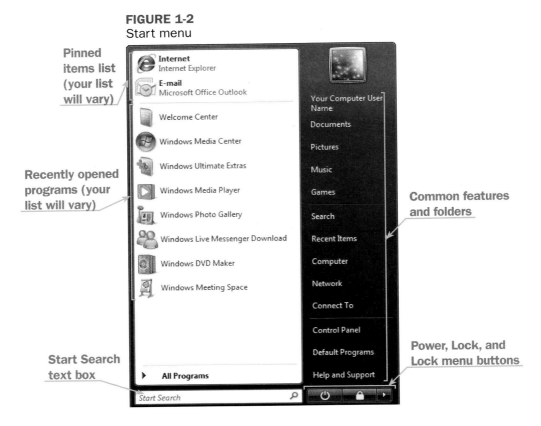

2. In the left pane, click **All Programs**. The list of programs installed on your computer appears in the left pane, as shown in Figure 1-3.

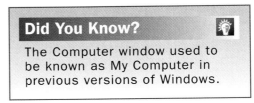

Did You Know?

The Computer window used to be known as My Computer in previous versions of Windows.

STEP-BY-STEP 1.2 Continued

FIGURE 1-3
Start menu showing list of All Programs

Installed programs (your list will vary)

Programs list

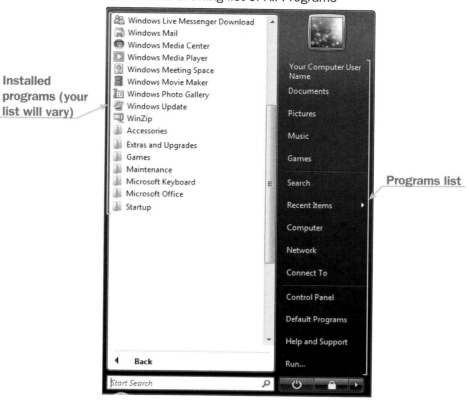

3. In the Programs list in the right pane, click **Computer**. The Computer window opens.

4. On the Quick Launch toolbar, click the **Launch Internet Explorer Browser** button.

5. In the upper-right corner of the Internet Explorer title bar, click the **Close** button to return to the open window on the desktop. Leave the Computer window open for the next Step-by-Step.

Navigating in Windows

Windows offers many features that allow you to easily locate and open the files you need. Explorer windows are used to navigate to items on your computer. Most windows share common navigation tools such as a Navigation pane, Address bar, or toolbar, even if their specific function varies.

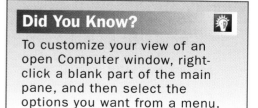

Did You Know?

To customize your view of an open Computer window, right-click a blank part of the main pane, and then select the options you want from a menu.

Switching to View Open Windows

Many windows you work with share common features, so you can work effortlessly and efficiently no matter the task you need to perform. Each window has a toolbar that contains functions specific to the window. Figure 1-4 shows common features in three different windows. You can move to an open window, program, or file by pressing and holding the Alt key, and then pressing the Tab key. As you press the Tab key, an icon representing the open window appears highlighted in a bar with icons of the other open windows. You can continue pressing the Tab key until the desired window is highlighted. When you release the Alt key, the selected window appears on the screen.

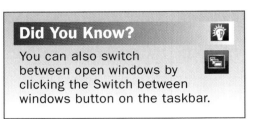

Did You Know?

You can also switch between open windows by clicking the Switch between windows button on the taskbar.

FIGURE 1-4
Viewing shared window features

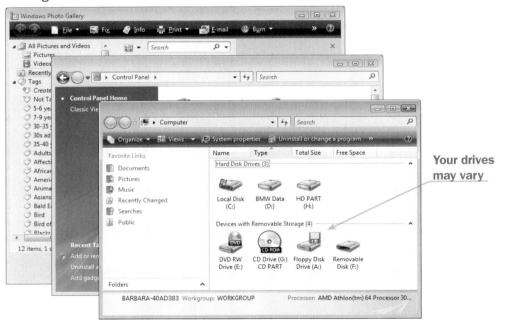

Your drives may vary

STEP-BY-STEP 1.3

1. Make sure the Computer button is on the taskbar, click the **Start** button, and then click **Control Panel** in the right pane. The Control Panel window opens.

2. Click the **Start** button, in the left pane click **All Programs**, and then click **Windows Photo Gallery**. The Windows Photo Gallery appears on top of the Control Panel. All three windows are open, but they overlap each other, making it difficult to view them all at once.

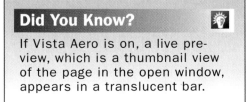

Did You Know?

If Vista Aero is on, a live preview, which is a thumbnail view of the page in the open window, appears in a translucent bar.

STEP-BY-STEP 1.3 Continued

3. Press and hold the **Alt** key, and then press the **Tab** key once. The Control Panel is on top.

4. Press and hold the **Alt** key, and then press the **Tab** key once. The Windows Photo Gallery is now on top.

5. Press and hold the **Alt** key, and then press the **Tab** key twice. The Computer window is on top. Compare your screen to Figure 1-5. Leave the windows open for the next Step-by-Step.

> **Did You Know?**
>
> Windows performs searches incrementally; it begins searching as soon as you type a character in the text box and refines the search as you add more text.

FIGURE 1-5
Viewing open windows

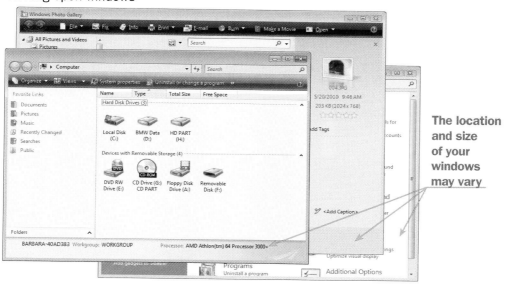

The location and size of your windows may vary

Navigating Using the Address Bar

The Address bar in Windows is a dynamic tool and shares some functionality with the Address bar in Internet Explorer. The Address bar identifies the path for the currently open folder, as shown in Figure 1-6. Each folder name in the path is a link that you can click to display that folder's contents, which is useful when working with subfolders within a main folder. To navigate to recently visited locations, click the Back button and the Forward button to the left of the Address bar. You can also view previous locations by clicking the Previous Locations arrow button at the end of the Address bar. The Search text box searches the contents of the open folder for the search term you entered.

FIGURE 1-6
Viewing a path in the Address bar

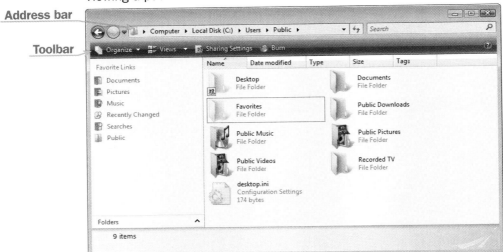

STEP-BY-STEP 1.4

1. Make sure the Computer window is open, and then double-click the **Local Disk (C:)** icon. (*Note*: Select another disk or device if this disk is not available. Because your computer setup may vary, read this Step-by-Step and complete as many steps as you can.)

2. In the Main pane, double-click **Users**, if necessary, double-click **Public**, and then compare your window to Figure 1-6. The Address bar shows the path to the Public folder.

3. In the Address bar, click **Computer**. The Main pane shows the disks and removable devices in the Computer folder.

4. Click the **Back** button next to the Address bar. The Main pane shows the files in the Public folder.

5. Click the **Forward** button next to the Address bar. The Main pane shows the files in the Computer folder. Keep this window open for the next Step-by-Step.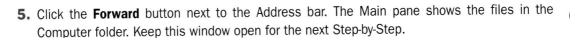

Navigating Using the Favorites and Folders List

Many Explorer windows have a Navigation pane to help you find your files, which you can also customize. The Navigation pane includes Favorite Links, which are links to folders containing the items you use the most, including recent searches. The Favorite Links contains popular default folders such as Documents, Pictures, and Music. You can add frequently used folders or files to the Favorite Links by dragging the file or folder from the Main pane to the Navigation pane. The Navigation pane also contains a Folders section that you can hide or show by clicking the Folders bar. Here you can view folders as a tree diagram, which provides an overview of the overall folder structure on your computer, as shown in Figure 1-7. You can display an individual folder in the Main pane by clicking it in the Folders section.

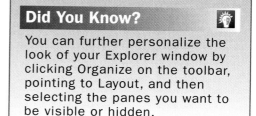

Did You Know?

You can further personalize the look of your Explorer window by clicking Organize on the toolbar, pointing to Layout, and then selecting the panes you want to be visible or hidden.

FIGURE 1-7
Viewing the Navigation pane

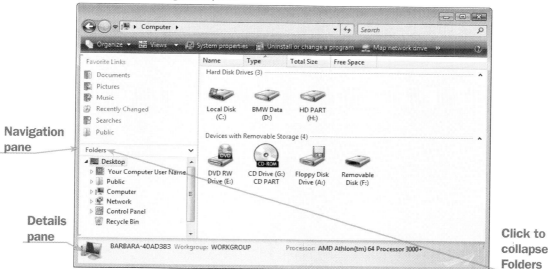

Navigation pane

Details pane

Click to collapse Folders

STEP-BY-STEP 1.5

1. Make sure the Computer window is open, and then in the Favorite Links section of the Navigation pane, click **Documents**. Files and folders in the Documents folder appear in the Main pane.

2. In the Favorite Links section of the Navigation pane, click **Pictures**, and then click a **photo** if one is available. Photos that you have downloaded to your computer appear in the Main pane, and a preview of the selected image appears in the Preview pane and in the Details pane, if those panes are visible.

Did You Know?

You can display a list of textual or graphic choices, known as a menu. To do so, click Organize on the toolbar, point to Layout, and then click Menu Bar.

STEP-BY-STEP 1.5 Continued

3. In the Navigation pane, click **Folders**, if necessary, and then click a folder to view its contents in the Main pane.

4. Click **Folders** to collapse the tree diagram, and then in the Address bar, click **Computer**. Close all open windows.

Using Windows

Windows are essential to using the Vista operating system. They display and store information and run programs. It is important to understand how to adjust and use them so you can optimize your efficiency.

Moving and Resizing Windows

Sometimes you will have several windows open on the screen at the same time. To work more effectively, you may need to move or change the size of a window. To move a window, click the title bar, the bar at the top of the window, and drag the window to another location. You can adjust the height, width, or overall size of a window by dragging a sizing handle on a window's border or corner. Depending where you position the pointer on a border or corner, the pointer changes to a two-headed arrow that is configured horizontally, vertically, or diagonally. When you adjust a corner border, the window is resized proportionately smaller or larger. You can also resize a window using the Maximize button, Minimize button, and Restore Down button, located in the upper-right corner of the window. See Figure 1-8. The Maximize button enlarges a window to the full size of the screen. The Minimize button reduces a window to an icon on the taskbar. The button on the taskbar is labeled, and you can click it any time to redisplay the window. When a window is maximized, the Maximize button is replaced by the Restore Down button. The Restore Down button returns the window to the size it was before the Maximize button was clicked. The Close button is used to close a window, which would include any file you have open in a program. If you are in a program, clicking the Close button will exit the program and you will be prompted to save or discard any changes in an open file.

FIGURE 1-8
Window resizing buttons

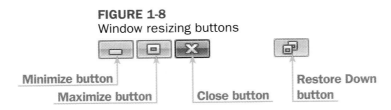

Minimize button

Maximize button

Close button

Restore Down button

STEP-BY-STEP 1.6

1. On the taskbar, click the **Start** button, and then click **Control Panel**. The Control Panel window opens.

2. Point to the title bar, click and hold the left mouse button, and then drag the **Control Panel window** until it appears to be centered on the screen. Release the mouse button.

3. Point to the border at the right side of the Control Panel window. When the pointer turns into a horizontal two-headed arrow, drag the right border farther to the right to expand the window.

4. Point to the lower-right corner of the window border. When the pointer turns into a two-headed diagonal arrow, drag the border up and to the left to resize both sides at the same time until the window appears similar to Figure 1-9.

FIGURE 1-9
Resizing a window

Sizing handle

5. Click the **Maximize** button in the upper-right corner of the window. The Control Panel window is maximized and you cannot adjust its borders.

6. Click the **Restore Down** button in the upper-right corner of the window. The Control Panel window returns to its previous size and approximate position on the desktop.

STEP-BY-STEP 1.6 Continued

7. Click the **Minimize** button in the upper-right corner of the window. The Control Panel window is no longer visible on the desktop, but it is still open. The minimized window is shown as an icon on the taskbar, as shown in Figure 1-10.

FIGURE 1-10
Minimized window

Control Panel minimized on the taskbar

8. On the taskbar, click the **Control Panel** button to restore the window. Leave the Control Panel open for the next Step-by-Step.

Scroll Bars

A scroll bar appears on the edge of a window any time there is more content than can appear in the window at its current size, as shown in Figure 1-11. A scroll bar can appear along the bottom edge (horizontal) and along the right side (vertical) of a window.

Scroll bars are a convenient way to bring another part of the window's contents into view. The scroll bar contains a scroll box and two scroll arrows. The scroll box is a slider that indicates your position within the window. When the scroll box reaches the bottom of the scroll bar, you have reached the end of the window's contents. Scroll arrows are located at the ends of the scroll bar. Clicking a scroll arrow moves the window content in that direction one line at a time. You can move to the end of a window's content by clicking a blank area of the scroll bar on either side of the scroll box.

FIGURE 1-11
Scroll bar, arrows, and boxes

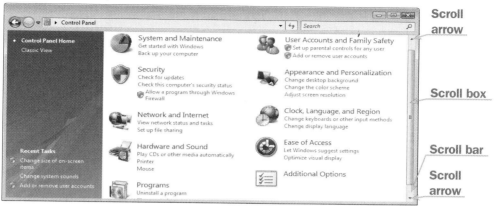

S TEP-BY-STEP 1.7

1. Make sure that the Control Panel window is open, and then, if necessary, resize the window vertically until the vertical scroll bar is visible on the right side of the window.

2. On the vertical scroll bar, click the **down scroll** arrow twice. The contents of the window shift downward one line at a time, as shown in Figure 1-11.

3. On the vertical scroll bar, drag the **scroll box** all the way up, and then the all the way down. You can drag the scroll box anywhere in the scroll bar to keep certain content in view.

4. Click the blank space above the vertical scroll box. The contents scroll all the way to the top.

5. Resize the Control Panel window until the scroll bar is no longer visible. Click the **Close** button in the Control Panel window.

> **Did You Know?**
>
> To scroll quickly through a window, point to a scroll arrow in a window, and then click and hold the mouse button.

Using Toolbars, Menus, and Dialog Boxes

You perform many tasks by clicking commands and buttons. These functions are usually contained on a menu, a toolbar, or in a dialog box. A toolbar contains buttons that execute a function or open a command menu. A menu contains commands for initiating certain actions or tasks. For example, when you click the Start button, a menu appears with a list of options. A dialog box, an interactive message window, appears when more information is required before the command can be performed. You may have to enter information, choose from a list of options, or simply confirm that you want the command to be performed. To back out of a dialog box without performing an action, press the Esc key, click the Close button, or choose Cancel (or No).

STEP-BY-STEP 1.8

1. On the taskbar, click the **Start** button, click **All Programs**, and then click **Windows Photo Gallery**. The Windows Photo Gallery window opens.

2. On the toolbar, click the **File** button. A list of commands appears, as shown in Figure 1-12.

FIGURE 1-12
Viewing a menu

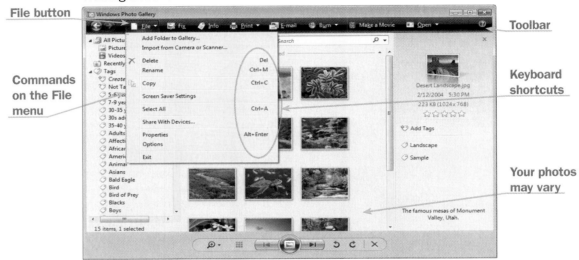

3. On the File menu, click **Options**. The Windows Photo Gallery Options dialog box opens, where you can change settings for managing photos on your computer, as shown in Figure 1-13.

STEP-BY-STEP 1.8 Continued

FIGURE 1-13
Windows Photo Gallery Options dialog box

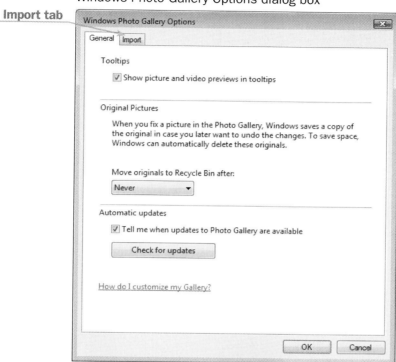

Import tab

4. Click the **Import** tab, click the **Settings for** list arrow to view the available options, and then click **CDs and DVDs**.

5. Click **Cancel** to close the Windows Photo Gallery Options dialog box.

6. On the toolbar, click the **File** button, and then click **Exit**. The Windows Photo Gallery program closes.

Using the Control Panel

The **Control Panel**, shown in Figure 1-14, is the command center for configuring Windows settings. You can customize settings for appearance, sounds, and performance. The number of icons and categories can be overwhelming and may not be descriptive enough for you to find exactly what you want. To find the settings you are interested in, enter a word or search term in the Search text box. For example, to find settings associated with sounds on your computer, type "sounds" in the Search text box. You can search in ordinary language without knowing the official or technical term.

FIGURE 1-14
Control Panel

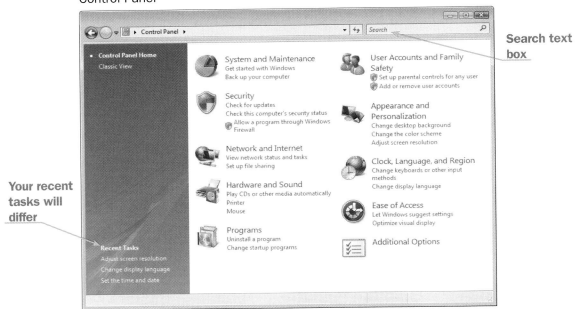

STEP-BY-STEP 1.9

1. On the taskbar, click the **Start** button, click **Control Panel**, and then resize the window so that the scroll bar is not visible.

2. Click **Appearance and Personalization**. Notice that topics pertaining to appearance and personalization appear.

3. In the Address bar, click **Control Panel** to return to Control Panel Home.

4. In the Search text box, type **sound**. Search results related to "sound" appear as you type the word, as shown in Figure 1-15. Your results may differ depending on your connection to the Internet.

STEP-BY-STEP 1.9 Continued

FIGURE 1-15
Viewing search results in the Control Panel

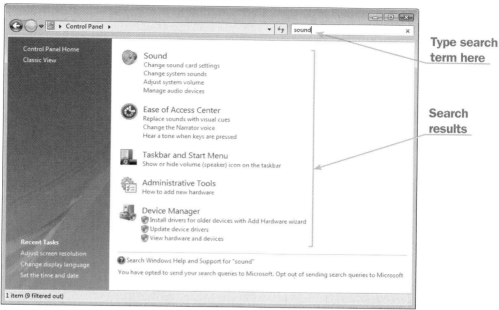

5. Click **Change system sounds**, review the options on the Sounds tab, and then click **Cancel** in the Sound dialog box to close it.

6. In the left pane, click **Control Panel Home**, and then click **Classic View**. The Control Panel changes to a collection of individual icons.

7. Scroll down, if necessary, and then double-click the **Sound** icon. The Sound dialog box opens, with the Playback tab active. Click the **Close** button in the Sound dialog box.

8. Close the Control Panel.

Managing Files and Folders

Windows Vista has several default folders, such as Music or Pictures. For example, the Computer folder is where you access hard disk drives, removable drives and media, CD and DVD drives, network locations, and other removable media such as cameras and scanners. The Documents folder stores the files you use for your projects, such as documents, presentations, and spreadsheets. Many programs use this folder as the default location for saving files. You use the Public folder to store the files you want to share with other users on the same computer or who are connected through a network. Note that you cannot restrict access to the Public folder.

> **Did You Know?**
>
> When you click the Views button on the toolbar of an Explorer window, you can select whether to view folder contents as Extra Large Icons, Large Icons, Medium Icons, Small Icons, List, Details, or Tiles.

The **Personal folder** stores your most frequently used folders and is by default named with the name you used to create your computer account. It appears on the Start menu under that name.

STEP-BY-STEP 1.10

1. On the taskbar, click the **Start** button, and then click **Computer**. The Computer window opens.

2. On the taskbar, click the **Start** button, and then click **Documents**. The Documents window opens, as shown in Figure 1-16.

FIGURE 1-16
Viewing folders in the Documents folder

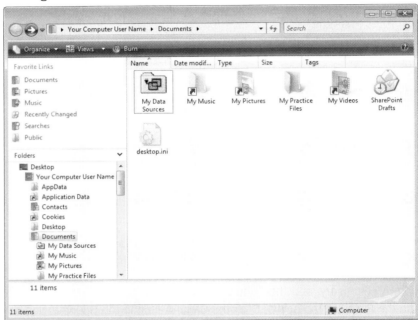

3. In the Navigation pane, click **Public** to display the Public folder and its contents.

4. Display the Folders section of the Navigation pane, scroll up, if necessary, and then click your **computer user name**. (*Note*: If you do not have an account on the computer, click the name that appears at the top of the folder list.)

5. Switch between each open window and note the contents of each folder window. When you are done, close each open window.

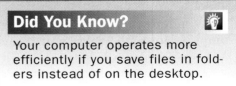

Did You Know?

Your computer operates more efficiently if you save files in folders instead of on the desktop.

Deleting Files Using the Recycle Bin

As you work with different files, there will always be some you no longer need and want to delete. When you delete a file from a window, its name is removed from the window's content and the file is physically moved to the Recycle Bin, the wastebasket icon on the desktop. However, while the item is stored for deletion, it is not permanently deleted. The Recycle Bin icon changes depending on whether or not it contains files, as shown in Figure 1-17. To permanently delete files in the Recycle Bin, right-click the Recycle Bin icon, and then click Empty Recycle Bin from the menu. Fortunately, just like a regular wastebasket, you can retrieve items before they're gone for good. To restore a deleted item from the Recycle Bin, you first open the Recycle Bin by double-clicking the icon, select the file you want to restore, and then click the Restore this item button on the toolbar. Note that once you permanently delete an item by emptying the Recycle Bin, you cannot restore it using another Vista function, although you can purchase third-party software that may be able to recover deleted files.

FIGURE 1-17
Comparing the Recycle Bin when it
has items or is empty

Items   Empty

Did You Know?

Emptying the Recycle Bin helps to keep your computer optimized and running more efficiently.

STEP-BY-STEP 1-11

1. On the desktop, double-click the **Recycle Bin** icon. If there are files in the Recycle Bin, it will look similar to Figure 1-18; if not, it will be empty.

FIGURE 1-18
Viewing an item in the Recycle Bin

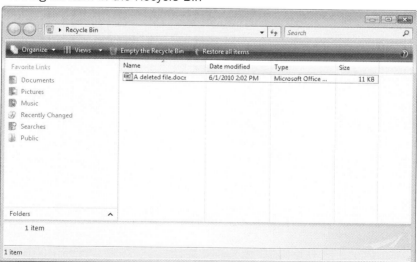

STEP-BY-STEP 1.11 Continued

2. On the toolbar, click **Empty the Recycle Bin** to delete the file, and then click **No** in the Delete File dialog box. (*Note*: Unless you work on your own computer, you should not make permanent deletions without first checking with your instructor or computer lab manager.)

3. Close the Recycle Bin.

Using Windows Help

This lesson has covered only a few of the many features of Windows. For additional information, Windows has an easy-to-use Help system. Use Help as a quick reference when you are unsure about a function. You can access Windows Help by clicking Help and Support on the Start menu. Then, from the Windows Help and Support window, you can choose a category in the Find an answer section, such as Windows Basics or Troubleshooting. You can continue to click topics or you can type a search term, just like you can in the Control Panel. You can also print topics, browse Help, and access online and other types of help. Note that if you are connected to the Internet, your searches can include Help results from the Windows Help online Web site. See Figure 1-19.

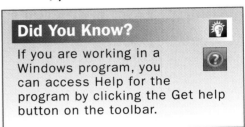

Did You Know?

If you are working in a Windows program, you can access Help for the program by clicking the Get help button on the toolbar.

FIGURE 1-19
Windows Help and Support window

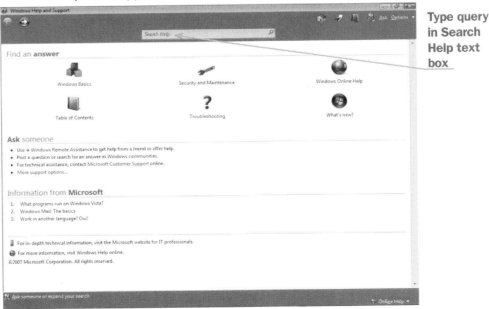

STEP-BY-STEP 1-12

1. On the taskbar, click the **Start** button, click **Help and Support**, and then maximize the window, if necessary. The Windows Help and Support window opens, as shown in Figure 1-19.

2. Click **Windows Basics**, on the Windows Basics: all topics page, scroll down, click **Exploring the Internet**, and then review the topic on the Exploring the Internet page.

3. Click the **Back** button twice to return to the main Help and Support page.

4. Click the **Search Help** text box, type **print photos**, and then click the **Search Help** button. A list of search results appears for the keywords you typed, as shown in Figure 1-20.

FIGURE 1-20
Viewing Help search results

5. Click a topic that interests you, read it, and then close the Windows Help and Support window.

Managing Your Computer

Like any machine, a computer requires maintenance to keep it running smoothly. Windows provides utilities designed to keep your computer optimized and safe.

Using Disk Cleanup

A computer handles thousands of files to do its job. Reducing the number of files on your hard disk frees up space and helps improve your computer's speed. Windows provides Disk Cleanup, a utility that deletes temporary files created when you surf the Web, edit files, or perform other actions, such as opening e-mail attachments from the message window instead of first saving the attachment to your hard disk. To run Disk Cleanup, click the Start button, click All Programs, click the Accessories folder in the left pane, click the System Tools folder, and then click Disk Cleanup. You can choose to clean up the files in your account or clean up all the files on the computer, and specify which drive(s) to clean. Disk Cleanup describes the categories of files it can delete and you check the boxes of the files you want to include, as shown in Figure 1-21. Click OK to begin the cleanup, and then click Delete Files to confirm the action.

FIGURE 1-21
Disk Cleanup

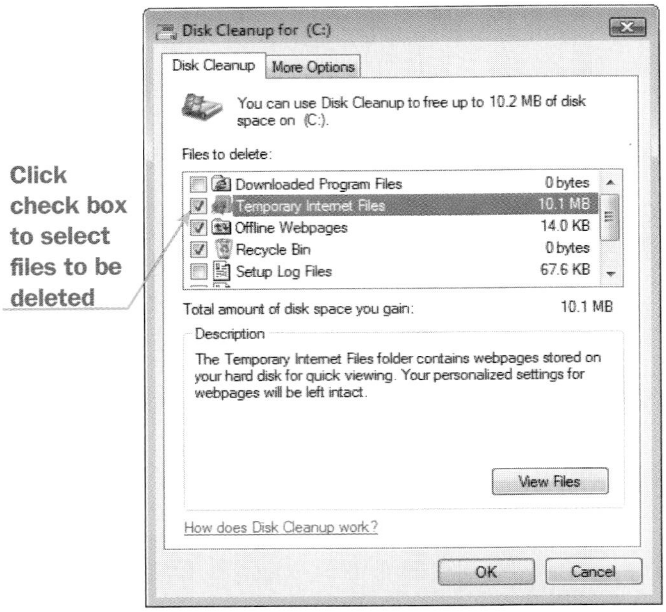

Click check box to select files to be deleted

Understanding the Windows Security Center

Windows Security Center monitors critical security components on your computer, such as the firewall, antivirus protection, spyware protection, and other features such as Windows updates and User Account Control. Protecting your computer from unauthorized access, malicious code, and software that collects information about your Web-surfing habits is essential. The components of the Windows Security Center are shown in Figure 1-22 and described in Table 1-2.

TABLE 1-2
Windows Security Center

COMPONENT	DESCRIPTION
Firewall	Monitors whether a firewall is installed and working properly
Automatic updating	Determines whether automatic updating is enabled and configured properly
Malware protection Antivirus Spyware	Verifies that your system is running antivirus software (third-party software) Verifies that your system is running antispyware software (Windows Defender or third-party software)
Other security settings Internet security settings User Account Controls	Determines whether Internet Explorer security settings are at recommended settings Requires explicit consent before allowing software changes to your computer

FIGURE 1-22
Windows Security Center

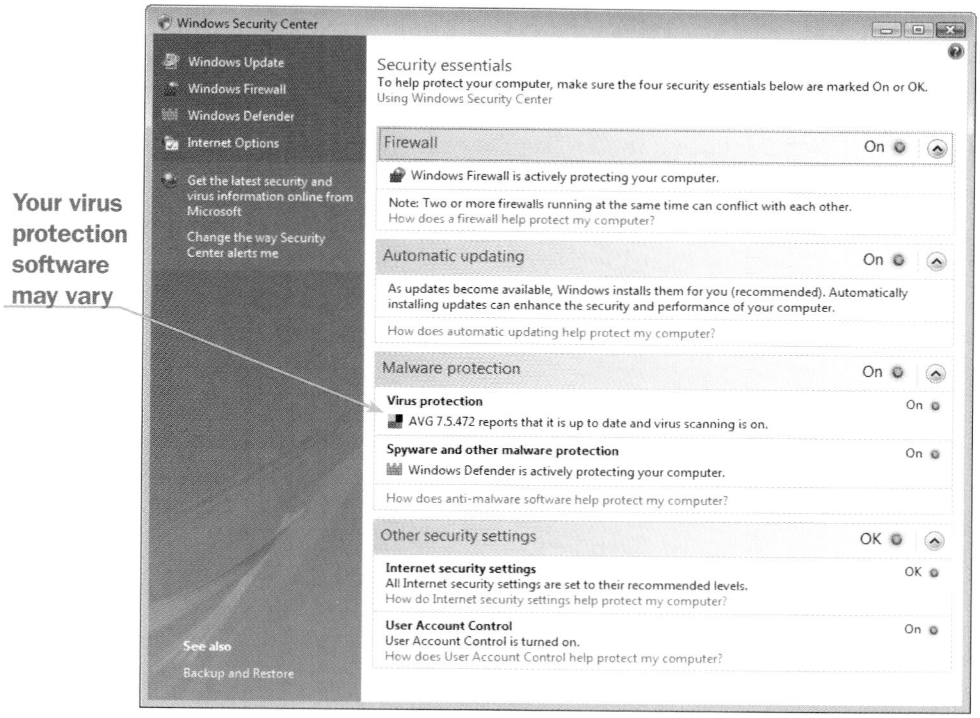

Your virus
protection
software
may vary

SUMMARY

In this lesson, you learned that:

- Starting Windows brings up the desktop, and possibly the Welcome Center window or other programs, depending on your settings. Several different versions of Windows Vista are available.

- A pointing device, such as a mouse, trackball, touch pad, or pointing stick, is a device you use to interact with and navigate your computer.

- The desktop is the main work area, and contains access to Windows elements such as files, folders, and programs, all of which are represented by icons. The main features of the desktop are the Start button, Recycle Bin, wallpaper or theme, Quick Launch toolbar, taskbar, notification area, and gadgets in the Windows Sidebar.

- Windows contain commands and buttons for a specific function. You can switch between open windows, open different folders by clicking folders in a path on the Address bar, and use the Navigation pane to open and organize favorite folders.

- Windows can be moved, resized, opened, and closed. If you are unable to display all the contents of a window as it is currently sized, scroll bars appear to allow you to move to the part of the window that you want to view. Windows can be maximized to fill the screen or minimized to appear as a button on the taskbar. You can use toolbars and menus in windows to perform tasks or actions, and input information in dialog boxes. The Control Panel contains searchable links for configuring Windows settings.

■ Windows provides several default folders for storing and organizing files on your computer and for viewing similar files, sharing files, or accessing frequently used files.

■ The Recycle Bin stores files you have deleted from your computer. You can restore deleted files that are placed in the Recycle Bin or delete them permanently from your computer.

■ The Windows Help and Support window provides additional information about the many features of Windows. You can access the Help program from Start menu or from any Windows program.

■ Windows provides several utilities you can use to clean up unnecessary files on your computer and check your computer's security settings.

VOCABULARY *Review*

Define the following terms:

Address bar	Icon	Restore Down button
Close button	Maximize button	Scroll arrows
Computer folder	Menu	Scroll bar
Control Panel	Minimize button	Scroll box
Desktop	Navigation pane	Taskbar
Dialog box	Operating system	Title bar
Disk Cleanup	Personal folder	Toolbar
Documents folder	Pointer	Window
Explorer windows	Pointing device	Windows Aero
Folder	Public folder	Windows Security Center
Gadgets	Recycle Bin	Windows Sidebar
Help and Support		

REVIEW *Questions*

TRUE/FALSE

Circle T if the statement is true or F if the statement is false.

T   F   1. You can view topics on adjusting your monitor in the Documents folder.

T   F   2. You can restore items moved to the Recycle Bin.

T   F   3. Pressing the Alt key and the Tab key minimizes all open windows.

T   F   4. You can use the path in the Address bar to navigate to a folder.

T   F   5. You can automatically share files in your Personal folder with other users.

WRITTEN QUESTIONS

Write a brief answer to each of the following questions.

1. What happens to a window when you minimize it?

2. Describe two ways you can find information in Windows Help and Support.

3. What does right-clicking a pointing device, such as a mouse, do?

4. How do you switch between open windows using the keyboard?

5. What is the difference between a toolbar and a menu?

PROJECTS

PROJECT 1-1

1. Start Windows.
2. Use the Start menu to open the Music window.
3. Use the Start menu to open Windows Calendar.
4. Make the Music window active, and then make Windows Calendar active.
5. Use the middle scroll bar to move to 11PM.
6. Minimize Windows Calendar.

7. Open the Pictures folder from the Music window.

8. Open the Control Panel from the Music window.

9. Close all open windows.

PROJECT 1-2

1. Open the Recycle Bin.

2. Double-click a file, if available, and then close the dialog box.

3. Restore the file.

3. Delete the contents of the Recycle Bin, if there are any, and if you are the sole user of the computer.

4. Use the toolbar to change the view to Details.

5. Close the Recycle Bin.

6. Exit Windows.

PROJECT 1-3

1. Open Windows Help and Support.

2. Find information about **print**, and then display search results for printing using Windows.

3. Print the page.

4. Open Windows Photo Gallery from the Start menu.

5. Search for photos using the term **ocean**. (*Hint*: Use another term if no ocean photos are available from the search.)

6. Right-click a photo, and then use the menu to rotate the photo counterclockwise.

7. Use the same menu to rotate the photo clockwise.

8. Open the Options dialog box from the File menu.

9. Cancel out of the dialog box, and then close Windows Photo Gallery.

CRITICAL*Thinking*

ACTIVITY 1-1

You want to add a photograph to your Web page, but first you need to edit the image. Use Windows Help and Support to find information about editing a photo and read several topics. Print the topic that lists tips for editing pictures.

ACTIVITY 1-2

Your supervisor has asked you to prepare a handout on how to create files and folders. Use Windows Help and Support to find a demo about Working with Files and Folders. Watch the demo, and then close the Windows Media Player window. Expand the transcript in the Help topic, and print the page.

ACTIVITY 1-3

You want to see how Windows can help you learn about burning a CD. Open Computer, Windows Help and Support, and the Control Panel. Search for "CD" in each window and write down the search results on a sheet of paper. Search for "burn CD" and compare the search results to the first search. Where possible, print the search results in each window.

MICROSOFT® OFFICE 2007 BASICS AND THE INTERNET

OBJECTIVES

Upon completion of this lesson, you will be able to:

■ Explain the concept of an integrated software package.

■ Start an Office program from Windows.

■ Explain the features of the program window.

■ Know how to use the Ribbon and contextual tools.

■ Open an existing Office file.

■ Save and close an Office file.

■ Know the shortcuts for opening recently used files.

■ Use the Office Help system.

■ Exit an Office program.

■ Use a Web browser to visit a Web site.

Estimated Time: 1.5 hours

VOCABULARY

Button

Contextual tab

Dialog box

File extension

Gallery

Group

Home page

Icon

Insertion point

Internet

Link

Live Preview

Menu

Microsoft Office 2007 (Office)

Mini toolbar

Office Button

Program window

Quick Access Toolbar

Ribbon

ScreenTip

Scroll bar

Shortcut menu

Sizing button

Status bar

Tab

Task pane

Title bar

Toolbar

Uniform Resource Locator (URL)

Web browser

Work area

World Wide Web (Web)

Introducing Microsoft Office 2007

Microsoft Office 2007 (or Office) is a collection of software programs. Word is the word-processing program. It enables you to create documents such as letters and reports. Excel, the spreadsheet program, lets you work with numbers to prepare items such as budgets or to calculate loan payments. Access, the database program, organizes information such as addresses or inventory items. The presentation program is PowerPoint. It is used to create electronic slides that usually accompany a verbal presentation. Outlook is the program used to send and receive e-mail messages and to organize information about people, appointments, and to-do lists. Publisher, the desktop

Net Tip

For more information on Microsoft Office and other Microsoft products, visit the Microsoft Web site at *www.microsoft.com*.

publishing program, helps you design professional-looking documents such as newsletters and brochures.

Office is available in many suites, each of which includes a different combination of programs. For example, the Professional suite includes Word, Excel, Access, PowerPoint, Outlook, and Publisher. Other Office suites include additional programs.

Because Office is an integrated program, the programs can be used together. For example, numbers from a spreadsheet can be included in a letter created in the word processor or in a presentation. This ability to share information between programs ensures consistency and accuracy. It also saves time because you don't have to reenter the same information in several programs.

> ### Did You Know?
>
> Many people call any file created on a computer a *document*. In Office, a *document* is created in Word, a *workbook* is created in Excel, a *database* is created in Access, and a *presentation* is created in PowerPoint.

Starting an Office Program

To start an Office program, click the Start button on the taskbar, click All Programs, and then click Microsoft Office. A list of the Office programs available on your computer appears, as shown in Figure 1-1. Click the name of the program you want to start.

FIGURE 1-1
Microsoft Office folder

Click the Microsoft Office folder to see all the programs

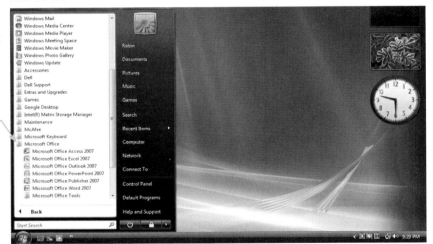

S TEP-BY-STEP 1.1

1. On the taskbar, click the **Start** button. The Start menu appears.

2. Click **All Programs**. The left side of the Start menu changes to show the All Programs menu.

3. Click **Microsoft Office**. The Microsoft Office folder expands to show all the Office programs installed on the computer, as shown in Figure 1-1.

4. Click **Microsoft Office PowerPoint 2007**. PowerPoint starts and opens a blank presentation.

STEP-BY-STEP 1.1 Continued

5. Click the **Start** button again, and then click **All Programs**.

6. Click **Microsoft Office**, and then click **Microsoft Office Word 2007**. Word starts and opens a blank document, as shown in Figure 1-2.

FIGURE 1-2
Blank document in Word

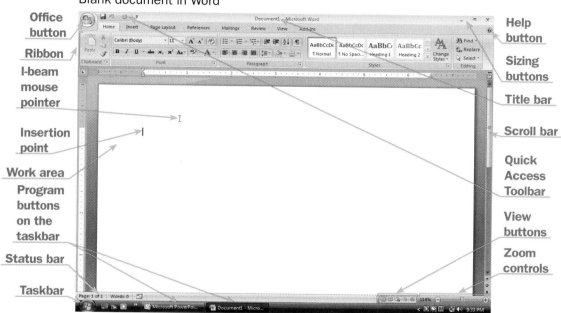

7. Leave Word and PowerPoint open for the next Step-by-Step.

Computer Concepts

When working in Office 2007 programs, you can open more than one file at a time. You can open multiple files in the same program. You can also open one or more files in different Office programs, such as Word and Excel. To move between the open files, just click the taskbar button for the file you want to display.

Careers

For help in choosing a career or college major, go to *www.careerkey.org*. You can take a test that measures your skills, abilities, talents, values, interests, and personality. A list of promising careers and jobs is identified based on the answers you provide.

Exploring the Program Window

A **program window** is the rectangle that contains the open program, tools for working with the file, and the work area. Look carefully at the parts of the Word program window labeled in Figure 1-2. These parts are similar in all of the Office programs and are described in Table 1-1.

TABLE 1-1
Items in the program window

ITEM	FUNCTION
Office Button	Contains commands for working with files, including commands for opening, saving, printing, and creating new files
Quick Access Toolbar	Provides access to commonly used commands
Title bar	Shows the names of the program and the current file
Sizing buttons	Change the size of the program window and exits the program
Ribbon	Contains tabs from which you can choose a variety of commands
Microsoft Office Help button	Opens the Help window for the program
Work area	Displays the file you are working on
Insertion point	Shows where text will appear when you begin typing
Scroll bars	Shifts other areas of the file into the work area
Status bar	Provides information about the current file and process
View buttons	Change how a file is displayed in the workspace

Using the Ribbon

The **Ribbon** is "command central" for the Office programs. The **tabs** on the Ribbon organize the commands into related tasks. The commands on each tab are organized into **groups**. Each group contains buttons that you click to choose a command. By clicking a **button** to choose a command, you give the program instructions about what you want to do. Each button has an **icon** (a small picture) or words to remind you of its function. Figure 1-3 labels the different parts of the Ribbon.

FIGURE 1-3
Parts of the Ribbon

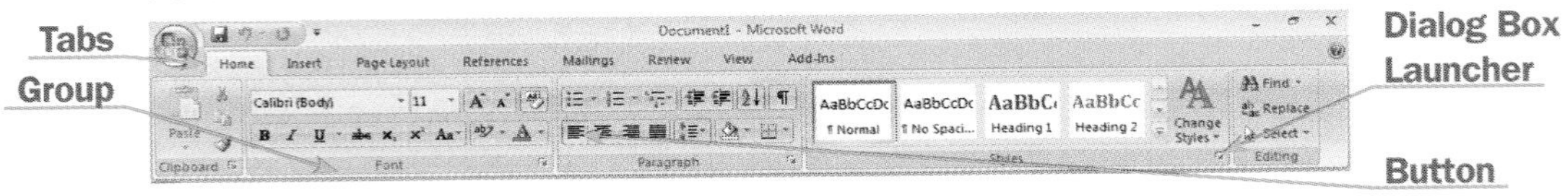

To use the buttons on the Ribbon, you need to click them. When a step instructs you to click a button or something else on the screen, it means to do the following: Move the mouse until the pointer is positioned on top of the item, press the left mouse button, and then release it.

Generally, when you click a button, something happens. Some buttons are like light switches: one click turns on the feature and the next click turns it off. This is often referred to as a *toggle*. Other buttons have two parts: a button that you can click to choose the command and an arrow that you can click to open a menu, or list, of other commands related to the button. Figure 1-4 compares these different types of buttons.

Did You Know?

You can shrink the Ribbon to one line that shows the tab names by double-clicking any tab. You can then see more of the work area. To redisplay the entire Ribbon, double-click any tab.

FIGURE 1-4
Buttons on the Ribbon

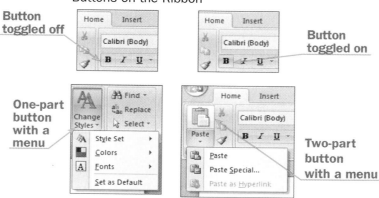

Button toggled off

Button toggled on

One-part button with a menu

Two-part button with a menu

Did You Know?

If you do not know the function of a button, move the pointer to the button, but do not click. A ScreenTip with the button's name and a short description of its function appears below the button. You'll learn more about ScreenTips later in this lesson.

Some buttons open galleries. A **gallery** shows the options available for a command. Galleries can also appear directly on the Ribbon. If a gallery on the Ribbon has more options than can be displayed on the Ribbon, you click its More button to open the full gallery. **Live Preview** lets you see how a gallery option affects your file without making the change. Point to an option in a gallery, but do not click it. Your file shows the results of selecting that option. After you find the option you want, you click that option to make the change in your file. See Figure 1-5.

FIGURE 1-5
Text Highlight Color gallery

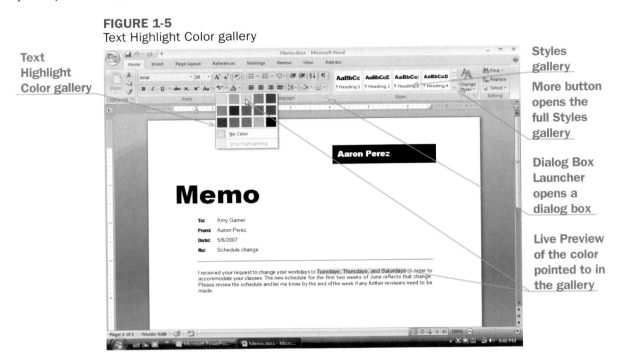

The Ribbon has one other type of button—the Dialog Box Launcher, which you click to open a dialog box or task pane to choose additional settings. A **dialog box** is a window that opens on top of the program window. A **task pane** is a pane, like a windowpane, that opens on the right or left side of the program window. The Dialog Box Launcher appears in the lower-right corner of any group that has a related dialog box or task pane. See Figure 1-5.

The buttons on the Ribbon change depending on settings in your computer and on how big the program window is. For example, the Home tab on the Ribbon in Word might look like the one shown in Figure 1-6a or the one shown in Figure 1-6b. If the Ribbon on your screen looks like the one shown in Figure 1-6b, you will need to make some adjustments as you follow the steps in this book. For example, look at the Editing group in both figures. A step might say "In the Editing group, click the Find button." If your screen looks like the one shown in Figure 1-6b, you will need to click the Editing button on the Ribbon first to expand the group, as shown in Figure 1-6b. Then you can click the Find button.

FIGURE 1-6
Ribbon with different computer settings

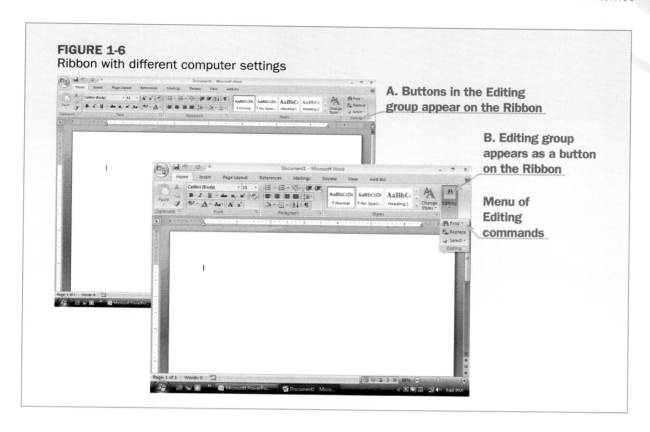

A. Buttons in the Editing group appear on the Ribbon

B. Editing group appears as a button on the Ribbon

Menu of Editing commands

Understanding Contextual Tools

Some tools appear as you work. Because they appear only when you need them, the work-space stays neat and uncluttered. This type of tool is called a contextual tool.

Contextual tabs appear on the Ribbon only when you select certain items in a file, and they contain commands related to that item. The contextual tabs work the same way as the standard tabs, but they disappear when you click somewhere else on the screen. Figure 1-7 shows the Drawing Tools contextual tabs. In this case, there is only one—the Format tab. This tab appears when you click a drawing in a Word document.

FIGURE 1-7
Drawing Tools Format contextual tab

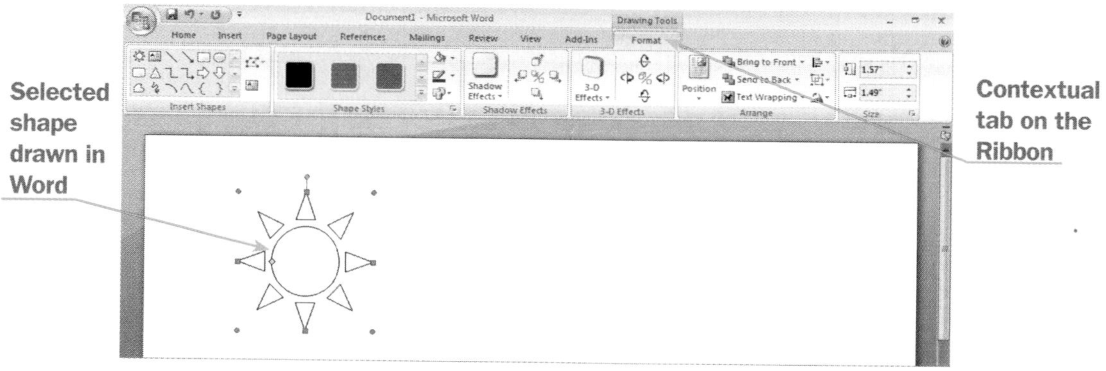

Selected shape drawn in Word

Contextual tab on the Ribbon

A toolbar contains buttons that you can click to perform common tasks. The Ribbon is actually a large toolbar. Office 2007 also has a special contextual toolbar called the Mini toolbar. It contains buttons you click to choose common formatting commands. The Mini toolbar appears in the work area after you drag the pointer over text while holding down the left mouse button. (This is called *selecting* text.) The Mini toolbar is transparent when you first select text. After you move the pointer over the Mini toolbar, it comes into full view and you can click buttons on it to format the selected text. The Mini toolbar disappears when you move the pointer off the toolbar, press a key, or press a button on your mouse. All of the commands on the Mini toolbar are also available on the Ribbon. Figure 1-8 shows the Mini toolbar in both transparent and full view.

FIGURE 1-8
Mini toolbar

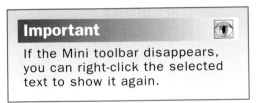

Transparent Mini toolbar   **Full view Mini toolbar**

Another contextual tool available in Office 2007 is the shortcut menu. **Shortcut menus** appear when you right-click something in the program window. They contain lists of commands that you are most likely to use with the item or text you right-clicked. The shortcut menu can be a faster way to get to these commands than the Ribbon. Figure 1-9 shows the shortcut menu

> **Important**
>
> If the Mini toolbar disappears, you can right-click the selected text to show it again.

that opens when you right-click selected text. Notice that the Mini toolbar appears at the top of this shortcut menu. (It does not appear on all shortcut menus; only on those shortcut menus that appear when you right-click selected text.)

FIGURE 1-9
Shortcut menu with the Mini toolbar

Using the Office Button to Open, Save, and Close Files

In all Office programs, you open, save, and close files in the same way—with the Office Button. *Opening* a file means loading a file from a disk into the program window. *Saving* a file stores it on a disk. *Closing* a file removes it from the program window.

Opening an Existing File

To open an existing file, you can click the Office Button to open the Office menu, and then click Open. The Open dialog box appears, as shown in Figure 1-10.

FIGURE 1-10
Open dialog box

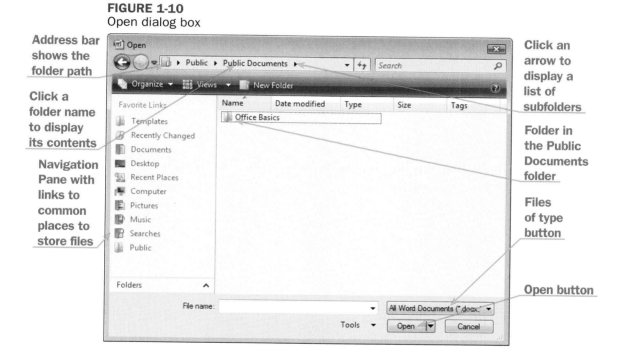

From the Open dialog box, you can open a file from any available disk or folder. You need to move to the location where the file you want to open is stored. The Address bar, near the top of the dialog box, shows the path of the drive and folders to your current location. Below the Address bar, a list shows the folders or files that are in the current location. The Navigation Pane, on the left side of the dialog box, provides links to common places on your computer to store files. To change the path, you can use a combination of the following methods:

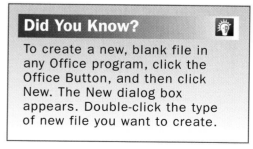

Did You Know?

To create a new, blank file in any Office program, click the Office Button, and then click New. The New dialog box appears. Double-click the type of new file you want to create.

■ Click a link in the Navigation Pane.

■ Click a location in the Address bar to see the folders and files in that location.

- Click a location arrow in the Address bar to see a list of folders in that location, and then click the folder you want to see.

- Double-click a folder to see its folders and files.

Did You Know?

In the Open dialog box, you can double-click a file to open it in the program without clicking Open.

The Open dialog box shows all the files in the folder that the active program can open. To see all the files in the folder, choose All Files from the Files of type button located above the Open button. After you have located the file you want to open, click the file to select it and then click Open.

The files you need for each lesson in this book are stored in a series of folders. The main folder shows the name of the program whose unit you are working on. For example, *Office Basics* is the main folder for this unit. The next folder lists the current lesson in the unit. For example, *Lesson1* is the subfolder for this lesson. Your instructor will tell you where to find the folders that store the Data Files you need for this book. The following Step-by-Step includes steps for moving to this location. All other lessons in this book instruct you to open the *File name* Data File.

S TEP-BY-STEP 1.2

1. In Word, click the **Office Button**, and then click **Open**. The Open dialog box appears, as shown in Figure 1-10.

2. Use the Navigation Pane and Address bar to move to the location of your Data Files.

3. Double-click the **Office Basics** folder, and then double-click the **Lesson1** folder. The *Employees* folder is stored in this folder, as shown in Figure 1-11.

STEP-BY-STEP 1.2 Continued

FIGURE 1-11
Employees folder

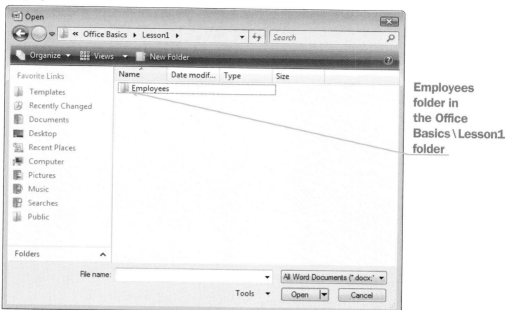

4. Double-click the **Employees** folder. The folders within the *Employees* folder appear, as shown in Figure 1-12.

FIGURE 1-12
Contents of the Employee folder

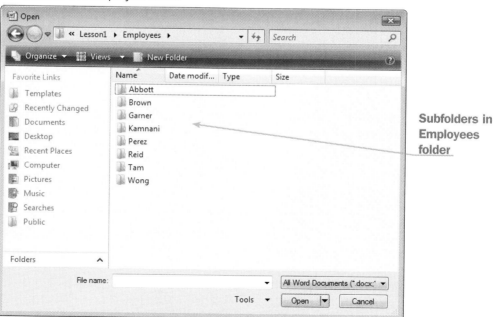

STEP-BY-STEP 1.2 Continued

5. Double-click the **Perez** folder. The Word document named *Memo.docx* appears in the *Perez* folder.

6. Click the **All Word Documents** button to display the list of file types. Click **All Files** to display all the files in the *Perez* folder. In addition to the *Memo.docx* file, there is also an Excel file named *Schedule.xlsx*.

7. Click **Memo.docx** to select it, and then click **Open**. The document appears in the work area of the Word program window, as shown in Figure 1-13.

FIGURE 1-13
Memo document

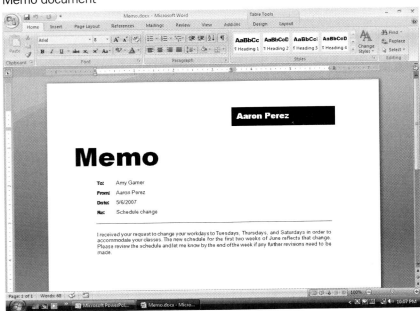

8. Leave the file open for the next Step-by-Step.

You can see how folders help organize and identify files. The *Perez* folder also contains the spreadsheet referenced in the memo that includes the work schedule for the first two weeks in June.

STEP-BY-STEP 1.3

1. On the taskbar, click the **Start** button, click **All Programs**, click **Microsoft Office**, and then click **Microsoft Office Excel 2007**. Excel starts and a blank spreadsheet appears.

2. Click the **Office Button**, and then click **Open**. The Open dialog box appears.

3. Use the Navigation Pane and Address bar to display the **Employees** folder.

4. Double-click the **Employees** folder, and then double-click the **Perez** folder.

STEP-BY-STEP 1.3 Continued

5. Double-click **Schedule.xlsx**. The *Schedule* workbook appears in the Excel work area, as shown in Figure 1-14.

FIGURE 1-14
Schedule workbook

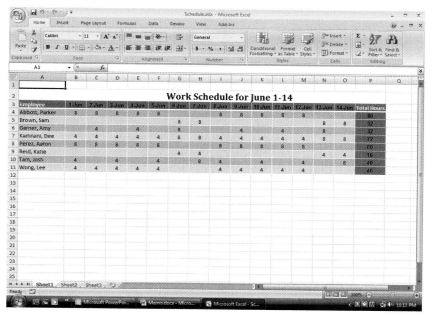

6. Leave the workbook open for the next Step-by-Step.

Saving a File

Saving is done using one of two methods. The Save command saves a file on a disk using its current name and save location. The Save As command lets you save a file with a new name. You can also use the Save As command to save a file to a new location.

Important

Whether or not you see the file extensions, you do not need to type one when you enter the descriptive name for a file. If you do type a file extension, you will create a duplicate, such as *June Schedule.xlsx.xlsx*.

Each program has a different file extension, which is a series of letters Office adds to the end of a file name that identifies in which program that file was created. Table 1-2 lists the file extensions for the four main Office programs. Depending on how your computer is set up, you might not see file extensions.

TABLE 1-2
File extensions for the Office programs

PROGRAM	FILE EXTENSION
Word	.docx
Excel	.xlsx
PowerPoint	.pptx
Access	.accdb

Computer Concepts

Earlier versions of Office used different file formats. The file extension for Word documents was .doc. The file extension for Excel workbooks was .xls. The file extension for PowerPoint presentations was .ppt. And, the file extension for Access databases was .mdb. If you want a file created in one of the Office 2007 programs to open in a program from an earlier version of Office, you need to save the file in one of these formats.

STEP-BY-STEP 1.4

1. Click the **Office Button**, and then click **Save As**. The Save As dialog box appears, as shown in Figure 1-15.

FIGURE 1-15
Save as dialog box

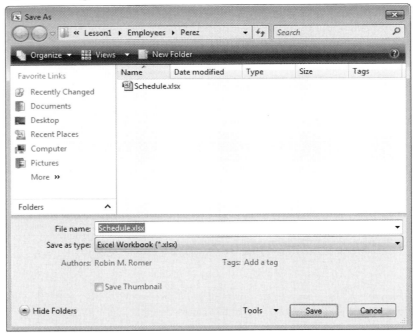

2. In the File name box, type **June Schedule** followed by your initials.

STEP-BY-STEP 1.4 Continued

3. In the Address bar, click the **Employees** location arrow. The list of folders in the *Employees* folder appears, as shown in Figure 1-16.

FIGURE 1-16
Employees subfolder list

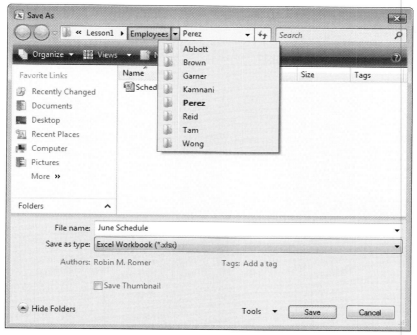

4. Click **Garner**.

5. Click **Save**. The workbook is saved with the new name in the Garner folder.

6. Leave the workbook open for the next Step-by-Step.

To save changes to a file using the same name and location, you can click the Save button on the Quick Access Toolbar.

Closing a File

You can close an Office file by clicking the Office Button and clicking Close. If you use the Close command on the Office menu to close a file, the program remains open and ready for you to work on another file. You can also close the file by clicking the Close button on the right side of the title bar. If you close a file with the Close button, and no other file is open in that program, the program also closes.

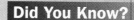

Did You Know?

If you try to close a file that contains changes you have not saved, a dialog box appears, asking whether you want to save the file. Click Yes to save and close the file. Click No to close the file without saving. Click Cancel to return to the program window without saving or closing the file.

STEP-BY-STEP 1.5

1. Click the **Office Button** to open the Office menu, and then click **Close**. The *June Schedule* workbook closes, and Excel remains open.

2. Click the **Memo - Microsoft Word** button on the taskbar to make the window active. The *Memo* document appears.

3. Click the **Office Button**, and then click **Close**. The *Memo* document closes, and Word remains open.

4. Leave Word, Excel, and PowerPoint open for the next Step-by-Step.

Using Shortcuts to Open Recently Used Files

Office provides two shortcuts for opening recently used files. The first shortcut is to click the Start button, and then click Recent Items on the Start menu. A menu opens listing the 15 most recently used files, similar to the menu shown in Figure 1-17. To open one of the recently used files, click the file you want to open.

FIGURE 1-17
Recent Items list on the Start menu

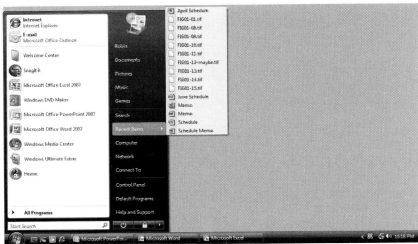

The second shortcut is to click the Office Button in any of the Office programs. The Recent Documents list appears on the right side of the Office menu and shows the file names of the 17 files that were most recently opened in that program. The most recently opened file appears at the top of the list, as shown in Figure 1-18. When a new file is opened, each file name moves down to make room for the new most recently opened file. To open one of the files, you simply click it as if it were a menu selection. You can click a pin next to a file in the Recent Documents list to keep that file "pinned" to the list. If the file you are looking for is not in the Recent Documents list on the Office menu, use the Open command to locate and select the file.

> **Important**
>
> If the file you want to open from a shortcut is on a disk, make sure that the correct disk is in the drive before you click the shortcut.

FIGURE 1-18
Recent Document lists on the Office menu

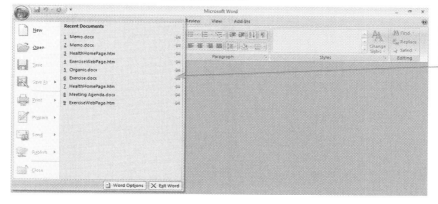

Click a pin
to keep the
file "pinned"
to the list

Getting Help in Office

This lesson has covered only a few of the many features of the Office programs. You will learn more about each of these programs in their individual units later in this text. But you can always learn more by using the Office Help system, which includes ScreenTips and the Help window.

Using ScreenTips

A ScreenTip is a box that appears when you point to a button. As shown in Figure 1-19, it contains the button's name and a description of its function. It can also include a link to more information and a keyboard shortcut if the command has one. To view a ScreenTip, you just point to a button—do not click it. If the ScreenTip includes a link to more information, you can press the F1 key to open the Help window with that topic displayed.

FIGURE 1-19
ScreenTip for the Show/Hide ¶ button

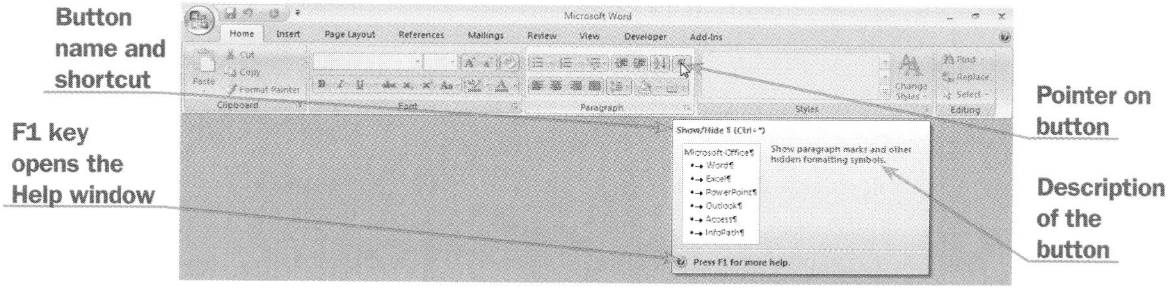

Button
name and
shortcut

F1 key
opens the
Help window

Pointer on
button

Description
of the
button

Using the Help Window

To get specific help about topics relating to the program you are using, you use the Help window, as shown in Figure 1-20. To open the Help window, click the Microsoft Office Help button located near the upper-right corner of the program window. Each program has its own Help window.

FIGURE 1-20
Word Help window with Table of Contents

You can search the Help system using the Table of Contents or keywords. The Table of Contents lists the general categories of topics and subtopics in the Help system. This is organized similarly to a table of contents in a book. To see the information in a category, click the text.

When you want to search for help on a particular topic, you can type a word or phrase in the *Type words to search for* box. After you click the Search button, a list of Help topics that include the keyword appears in the Help window, and you can click a topic to display it in the Help window.

STEP-BY-STEP 1.6

1. On the Ribbon, click the **Home** tab if it is not displayed.

2. In the Clipboard group, point to the **Show/Hide ¶** button, resting the pointer on the button. The button's ScreenTip appears, as shown in Figure 1-19.

3. Read the button's name and a description of its function in the ScreenTip.

4. On the Ribbon, point to the **Microsoft Office Word Help** button and read its ScreenTip.

5. Click the **Microsoft Office Word Help** button. If the Word Help window that appears does not fill the screen, click the **Maximize** button on the title bar.

STEP-BY-STEP 1.6 Continued

6. On the Help window toolbar, click the **Show Table of Contents** button to display a list of Help topic categories. If you have Internet access, this information is downloaded from Microsoft Office Online rather than only the Help topics stored on your computer.

7. In the Table of Contents pane, click the **Getting help** book, click the **Using Microsoft Office** book, and then click the **Use the Ribbon** topic. The topic appears in the right side of the Word Help window, as shown in Figure 1-20. If you are not connected to Microsoft Office Online, the list of topics and the topic content you see will differ.

8. Read the contents of the Help window.

9. On the Word Help window toolbar, click the **Hide Table of Contents** button to hide the pane.

10. In the Word Help window, click the **Type words to search for** box.

11. Type **print**, and then click the **Search** button to display the list of search results shown in Figure 1-21. If you are not connected to the Internet, your list of search results will differ.

FIGURE 1-21
Search results

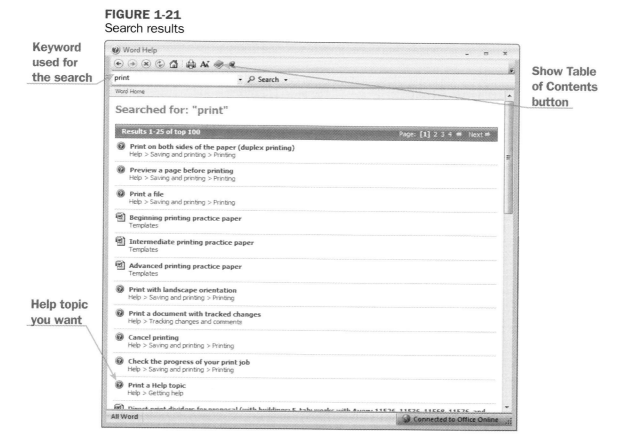

12. Search the list of results until you find **Print a Help topic**. Click it to display information in the Word Help window.

STEP-BY-STEP 1.6 Continued

13. Read the information, and then print the information by following the instructions.

14. On the Word Help window title bar, click the **Close** button. The Help window closes.

Exiting an Office Program

The Exit command, which is located on the Office menu, closes the open Office program. If you have only one file open in that program, you can also click the Close button on the right side of the title bar. If you have not saved the final version of your file, a dialog box opens, asking whether you want to save your changes. Click Yes to save and close the file and exit the program. When you exit an Office program, the program window closes.

STEP-BY-STEP 1.7

1. Click the **Office Button**. Notice the files listed on the right side of the menu. These are the most recently used files mentioned previously in this lesson.

2. Click **Exit Word**. Word closes and Excel appears on the screen.

3. On the Excel title bar, click the **Close** button. Excel closes, and PowerPoint appears on the screen.

4. Click the **Office Button**, and then click the **Exit PowerPoint** button. The desktop reappears on the screen.

Viewing a Web Page

The Internet is a vast network of computers located all over the world and linked to one another. The Internet allows people around the world to share information and ideas using Web pages, blogs, and e-mail as well as other services. Connecting to the Internet requires special hardware and software and an Internet service provider (ISP). Before you can use the Internet, your computer needs to be connected, and you should know how to access the Internet.

The World Wide Web (or Web) is a system of computers that share information by means of links on Web pages. A link is text (often colored and underlined) or a graphic that you click to "jump" to another location or Web page. A Web page is a document specially formatted to be displayed on computers connected to the Internet. To find a Web page, the Web uses an address system. Just like you have a home address, each Web

> **Net Tip**
>
> You can connect your computer to the Internet in a variety of ways. You might use a regular telephone line (also called a dial-up connection) or a high-speed connection through your local cable company or a special telephone service called DSL. You might also connect without any phone lines or cables by using a wireless connection. The connection you have depends on your service provider, how much you are willing to spend, and the way your computer is connected to the provider.

page has an address on the Web. The fancy name for these addresses is **Uniform Resource Locators** (URLs—you pronounce each letter separately: U-R-L or U-R-Ls). Examples of URLs are:

http://www.senate.gov

http://www.microsoft.com

http://www.course.com

To view Web pages, you need special software called a **Web browser**. Internet Explorer is the Web browser that is packaged with computers that run Windows. Figure 1-22 shows a Web page using Internet Explorer as a browser.

FIGURE 1-22
Internet Explorer Web browser

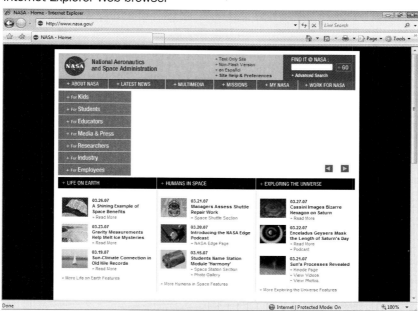

To go to a specific Web page, you click the Address bar in your browser, type the URL, and then click the Go button or press the Enter key. You can jump to other pages by clicking links on the page you are viewing. Click the Back button to move back to previous pages you viewed, and click the Forward button to move to subsequent pages you viewed. Click the Home Page button to load your **home page** (or *start page*), which is the first page that opens when you start your browser.

 **Careers**

You can use the Internet to research different careers in business. Find out about careers in business by typing the following URL in the Address bar in your browser: *www.careers-in-business.com.*

STEP-BY-STEP 1.8

1. On the taskbar, click the **Start** button, and then click **Internet Explorer**. The home page begins loading.

2. Click the Address bar, type **www.nasa.gov**, and then press the **Enter** key. The NASA home page appears in the browser, as shown in Figure 1-22.

3. Click a link to see more information.

4. Click the **Back** button to return to the previous page.

5. Click another link to display a different page.

6. Click the **Home** button to return to the home page for your computer.

7. On the title bar, click the **Close** button. Internet Explorer closes.

Net Tip

The length of time it takes to load a page depends upon the speed of your connection as well as the file size of the page you are viewing. If you want to go to a different address or click a link you can see on the page, you do not have to wait for the page to finish loading. Even when you cannot see the entire page, you can type a different URL in the Address bar or click a link on the partially loaded page.

Important

Because Web pages are updated frequently, the page you see might not look exactly like the one shown in Figure 1-22 even if you entered the same URL.

SUMMARY

In this lesson, you learned:

■ Microsoft Office 2007 is a combination of programs that can include a word-processor program, a spreadsheet program, a database program, a presentation program, a schedule/organizer program, and a desktop publishing program. The files of these programs can be used together.

■ Office programs can be started by clicking the Start button, clicking All Programs, clicking Microsoft Office, and then clicking the program name.

■ The basic parts of the program window are similar in all of the Office programs.

■ The Ribbon is "command central" for all the Office programs. Commands are organized in groups on tabs on the Ribbon. You click a button to choose the command you want. Some buttons open a menu of additional commands or a gallery of options.

■ Contextual tabs on the Ribbon, the Mini toolbar, and shortcut menus are tools that appear when you work with a specific object in the program window.

■ You can open an existing file from the Office menu. The Open dialog box appears, enabling you to open a file from any available disk or directory.

■ No matter which Office program you are using, the files are opened, saved, and closed the same way.

- You can open recently used files quickly by clicking the file name in the Recent Documents list on the right side of the Office menu. You can also click the Start button, and then click Recent Items to list the most recently used files.

- To exit an Office program, click the Office Button and click the Exit button, or click the Close button on the program window title bar.

- The Office Help system provides additional information about the many features of the Office programs. In the Help window, you can use the Table of Contents or the *Type word to search for* box to get information. If your computer is connected to the Internet, you see Help topics and additional information from Microsoft Office Online.

- Internet Explorer is a Web browser. You can use it to view Web pages.

VOCABULARY*Review*

Define the following terms:

Button	Menu	Sizing button
Contextual tab	Microsoft Office 2007	Status bar
Dialog box	(Office)	Tab
File extension	Mini toolbar	Task pane
Gallery	Office Button	Title bar
Group	Program window	Toolbar
Home page	Quick Access Toolbar	Uniform Resource Locator
Icon	Ribbon	(URL)
Insertion point	ScreenTip	Web browser
Internet	Scroll bar	Work area
Link	Shortcut menu	World Wide Web (Web)
Live Preview		

REVIEW*Questions*

WRITTEN QUESTIONS

Write a brief answer to each of the following questions.

1. List four of the programs that are included in Office 2007.

2. How do you start an Office program?

3. What is the location and the function of the following: title bar, Ribbon, and status bar?

4. What is the difference between the Save and Save As commands?

5. Describe two ways to get help in an Office program.

TRUE/FALSE

Circle T if the statement is true or F if the statement is false.

T F 1. Excel is the spreadsheet program in Office.

T F 2. You must type a file extension if you want to include it in the file name.

T F 3. To save a file with a different name and to a different location, click the Save button on the Quick Access Toolbar.

T F 4. Live Preview lets you see how an option affects your file without making the change.

T F 5. When you point to a button on the Ribbon, a gallery appears that shows the button's name and a description of its function.

PROJECTS

PROJECT 1-1

1. Start Word.

2. Start Excel. Use the Open dialog box to locate the **Employees** folder in the Data Files. Open the **Schedule.xlsx** Data File from the **Perez** folder.

3. Use the Save As command to save the workbook in the **Abbott** folder as **June Work Schedule** followed by your initials.

4. Repeat the process to save the file in the **Brown, Garner, Kamnani, Reid, Tam,** and **Wong** folders.

5. Close the **June Work Schedule** workbook and exit Excel. Word remains on the screen.

6. Use the Open dialog box to open the **Memo.docx** Data File from the **Perez** folder.

7. Save the document in the **Garner** folder with the same name followed by your initials.

8. Close the document, and then exit Word.

PROJECT 1-2

1. Start Word and open the Word Help window.

2. Search for how to minimize the Ribbon, and then open the *Minimize the Ribbon* Help topic.

3. Read the information in the Help topic, and then follow the directions to minimize the Ribbon.

4. Click the Insert tab to display the full Ribbon.

5. In the Pages group, click the Blank Page button. A new page is added to the document, and the Ribbon minimizes again.

6. Follow the directions in the Help topic to restore the Ribbon.

7. Close the Word Help window, and then exit Word. If prompted to save changes, click No.

PROJECT 1-3

1. Open your Web browser.

2. Go to the Microsoft Web site at *www.microsoft.com*.

3. Search for information about at least two Microsoft programs.

4. Return to your home page.

5. Close your Web browser.

CRITICAL *Thinking*

 ACTIVITY 1-1

The Office program can include Word, Excel, Access, PowerPoint, Outlook, and Publisher. Describe how you could use each of these Office programs in your personal life. Imagine you are a business owner. Describe how each of these Office programs would help you increase productivity. When you run a business, you need to correspond with clients, vendors, and employees; you need to track income and spending; you need to keep track of items, such as inventory, documents, and so on; and you need to market and advertise your business.

 ACTIVITY 1-2

Use the Office Help system to find out more about keyboard shortcuts. If you are connected to the Internet, you can click the Training Keyboard shortcuts in the 2007 Office system. Write a description of the different types of shortcuts. List one advantage of using shortcuts. Then list the three shortcuts you think you would use most frequently.

 ACTIVITY 1-3

Start your Web browser. Describe the function of all the buttons you see. Remember to point to each button to see its ScreenTip. Then describe the steps to print a Web page. Use the Help system as needed.

MICROSOFT WORD

Unit

 Estimated Time for Unit: 13 hours

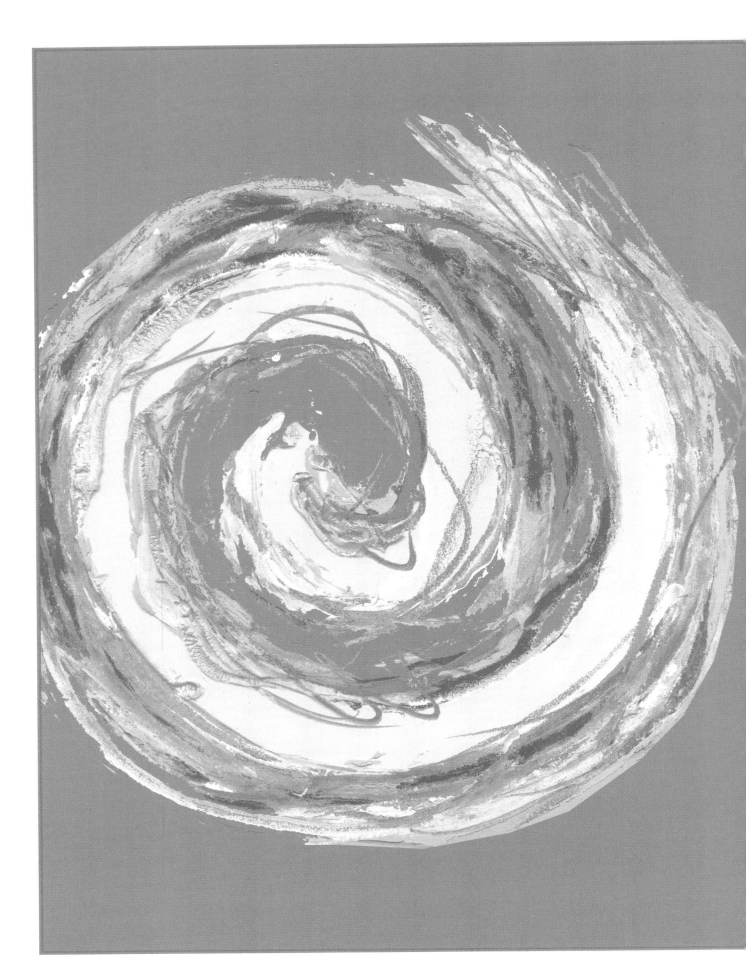

WORD BASICS

OBJECTIVES

Upon completion of this lesson, you will be able to:

- Start Word and identify the parts of the opening screen.
- Understand the five ways to view your document on the screen.
- Enter text in a document.
- Navigate a document.
- Use the Backspace and Delete keys to correct errors.
- Save a document.
- Create a folder in which to store your document.
- Locate and open an existing document.
- Create a new, blank document.
- Magnify and reduce the document using the Zoom feature.
- Use Full Screen Reading view and preview a document.
- Change the page orientation of a document.
- Print a document.
- Exit Word.

Estimated Time: 1 hour

VOCABULARY

Draft view

Full Screen
 Reading view

Insertion point

Landscape orientation

Office button

Outline view

Portrait orientation

Print Layout view

Print Preview

Quick Access Toolbar

Ribbon

Status bar

Toolbar

View buttons

Web Layout view

Word processing

Word wrap

Zoom

Zoom slider

Introduction to Word Processing

Word processing is the use of computer software to enter and edit text. When using word processing software such as Word, you can easily create and edit documents such as letters and reports. You can even create more complex documents such as newsletters with pictures and other graphics. These documents can be used in your school, career, personal, and business activities.

The lessons in this unit contain step-by-step exercises for you to complete using a computer and Word. After completing all of the exercises, you will be able to create and revise your own word-processing documents.

Starting Word

To start Word, click the Start button on the taskbar. Click All Programs on the Start menu, and then click Microsoft Office on the submenu. Click Microsoft Office Word 2007. A screen displaying copyright information appears briefly, followed by a window containing a blank page in which you can create and edit documents.

STEP-BY-STEP 1.1

1. Click the **Start** button on the taskbar.

2. Click **All Programs**. The Start menu changes to show all the programs installed on the computer.

3. On the Start menu, click the **Microsoft Office** folder. The list of programs in the folder appears. Click **Microsoft Office Word 2007** on the submenu. A blank document appears, as shown in Figure 1-1.

FIGURE 1-1
Opening screen in Word

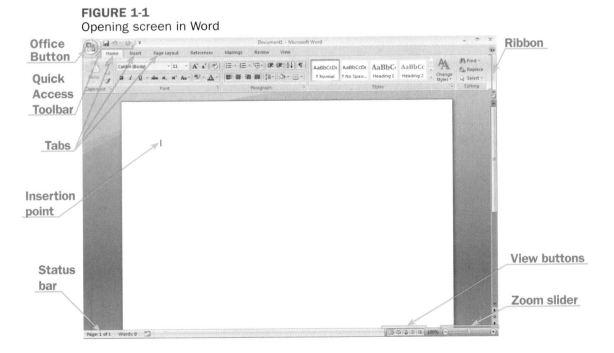

4. Leave the blank Word document open for the next Step-by-Step.

Identifying Parts of the Opening Screen

Look carefully at the parts of the opening screen labeled in Figure 1-1, and find them on your screen. Many of these elements appear in other Office applications. Table 1-1 describes some of the commonly used elements of the opening screen.

TABLE 1-1
Understanding the opening screen

ELEMENT	FUNCTION
Office Button	Click it to open a menu, which contains commands for working with files.
Ribbon	Contains commands for working with the document, organized by tabs.
Quick Access Toolbar	Contains buttons (icons) for three common commands; you can add additional buttons to it.
Insertion point	Shows where text will appear when you begin typing.
Status bar	Displays information about the current document and process.
View buttons	Allow you to change views quickly.
Zoom slider	Allows you to increase or decrease the size of the document on-screen.

When the pointer is in the document window, it looks like an uppercase letter *I* and is called the I-beam pointer. When you move the pointer out of the document window toward the Ribbon or the status bar, it turns into an arrow to allow you to point to and click the buttons. The pointer changes into other shapes for performing certain tasks.

Understanding Document Views

You have five ways to view a document on the screen: Print Layout, Full Screen Reading, Web Layout, Outline, and Draft. Table 1-2 describes each view.

TABLE 1-2
Document screen views

VIEW	DESCRIPTION
Print Layout	Shows how a document will look when it is printed; you can work with headers and footers, margins, columns, and graphics, which are all displayed.
Full Screen Reading	Shows text on the screen in a format that is easy to read; the Ribbon is replaced by a small bar called a toolbar that contains only a few relevant commands.
Web Layout	Simulates the way a document will look when it is viewed as a Web page; text and graphics appear the way they would in a Web browser.
Outline	Displays headings and text in outline form so you can see the structure of your document and reorganize easily; headers and footers, page boundaries, graphics, and backgrounds do not appear.
Draft	Shows only the text of a document; headers and footers, margins, columns, and graphics are not visible.

To switch between views, on the Ribbon, click the View tab, and then in the Document Views group, click the button that corresponds to the view you want. You can also click one of the view buttons at the bottom-right of the document window, to the left of the Zoom slider. You will work in Print Layout view most of the time.

Inserting Text and Understanding Word Wrap

To enter text in a new document, you begin typing. The text appears in the document window at the insertion point. As you type, the insertion point moves to the right and the word count indicator in the status bar changes to show the number of words in the document. If the text you are typing extends beyond the right margin, it automatically moves to the next line. This feature is called word wrap because words are "wrapped around" to the next line when they do not fit on the current line.

When you press the Enter key, a blank line is inserted automatically and you start a new paragraph. Most documents in the business world are typed with a blank line between paragraphs, rather than indenting the first line of each paragraph. The settings in Word 2007 help you do this easily.

STEP-BY-STEP 1.2

1. Type the following text. As you type, watch how the words at the end of lines wrap to the next line. If you type a word incorrectly, just continue typing. You learn how to correct errors later in this lesson.

   To help you meet your goals, you should take the time to plan and organize your work. It can be helpful to list the tasks you need to accomplish, and then you can rank them by importance.

2. Press the **Enter** key. The insertion point skips a line and appears blinking at the left margin, as shown in Figure 1-2.

FIGURE 1-2
Text entered in a Word document

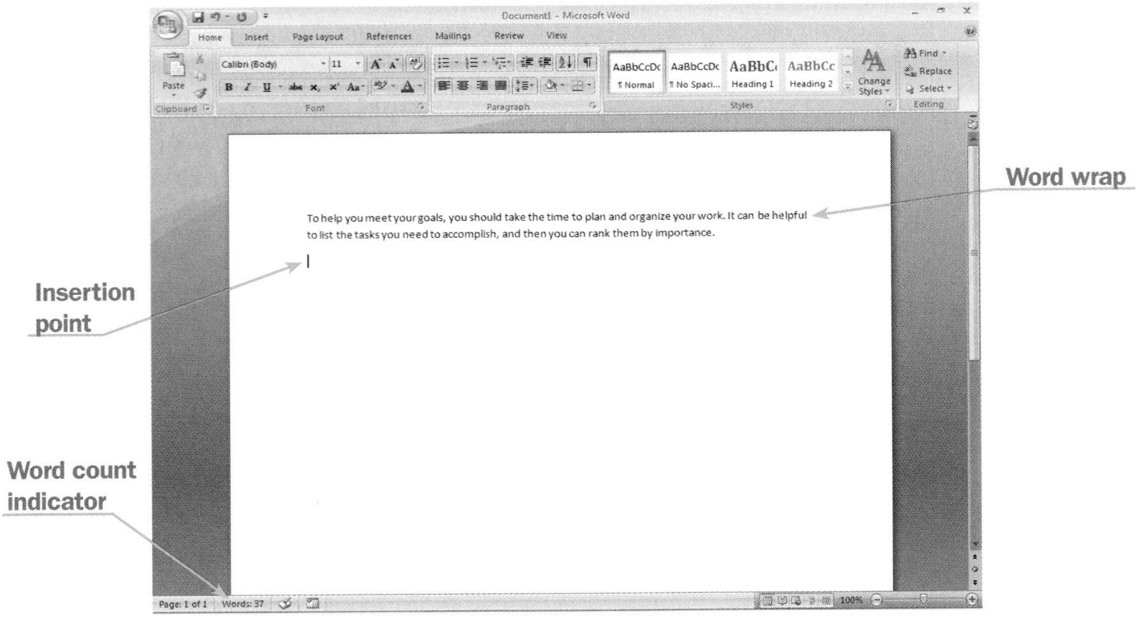

STEP-BY-STEP 1.2 Continued

3. Type the following text. Press the **Enter** key at the end of each paragraph.

Start by listing everything you need to accomplish today. Include both obligations (that is, tasks you must complete) and tasks you'd like to complete.

After you create your list, examine the items and number them in order of importance. Put the number 1 next to the most important task that must be completed today, number 2 next to the second most important task, and so on. Now you have a plan!

4. Leave the document open for the next Step-by-Step.

Navigating a Document

To correct errors, insert new text, or change existing text, you must know how to reposition the insertion point in a document. You can move the insertion point in a document by using the mouse or the keyboard. To reposition the insertion point using the mouse, move the mouse to the position where you want the insertion point to appear, and then click the left mouse button. The blinking insertion point appears at the point you clicked.

When working with a long document, it is faster to use the keyboard to move the insertion point. Table 1-3 lists the keys you can press to move the insertion point.

TABLE 1-3
Keyboard shortcuts for moving the insertion point

PRESS	TO MOVE THE INSERTION POINT
Right arrow	Right one character
Left arrow	Left one character
Down arrow	To the next line
Up arrow	To the previous line
End	To the end of the line
Home	To the beginning of the line
Page Down	To the next page
Page Up	To the previous page
Ctrl+right arrow	To the beginning of the next word
Ctrl+left arrow	To the beginning of the previous word
Ctrl+End	To the end of the document
Ctrl+Home	To the beginning of the document

In Table 1-3, two keys are listed for some of the movements. When you see an instruction to press two keys at once, press and hold the first key, press the second key, and then let go of both keys.

STEP-BY-STEP 1.3

1. Press the **Ctrl+Home** keys. The insertion point jumps to the beginning of the document.

2. Press the **Ctrl+right arrow** keys three times to move to the fourth word (*meet*) in the first line.

3. Press the **End** key. The insertion point moves to the end of the first line.

4. Press the **down arrow** key to move to the end of the next line.

5. Press the **Ctrl+End** keys. The insertion point jumps to the end of the document.

6. Press the **Ctrl+Home** keys to move back to the beginning of the document. Leave the document open for the next Step-by-Step.

Using the Backspace and Delete Keys

If you make a mistake typing, or you just want to change text, you might need to delete characters or words. There are two ways to delete characters: Use the Backspace key or use the Delete key. Pressing the Backspace key deletes the character to the left of the insertion point. Pressing the Delete key deletes the character to the right of the insertion point.

STEP-BY-STEP 1.4

1. Position the insertion point after the word *should* in the first sentence of the document.

2. Press the **Backspace** key until the words *you should* and the extra space are deleted.

3. In the second sentence of the first paragraph, position the insertion point before the second word *you* (after the word *then*).

4. Press the **Delete** key until the words *you can* and the space after *can* are deleted.

5. Look over the document. Position the insertion point as needed, and then use the Backspace key or Delete key to correct any typing errors you made.

6. Leave the document open for the next Step-by-Step.

Saving a Document

When you save a document for the first time, you can click the Save button on the Quick Access Toolbar, you can click the Office Button and then click Save, or you can click the Office Button and then click Save As. In all three cases, the Save As dialog box appears, as shown in Figure 1-3. This is where you name your file and choose a location to save it in.

Did You Know?

You can also press the Ctrl+S keys to save your file quickly.

FIGURE 1-3
Save As dialog box

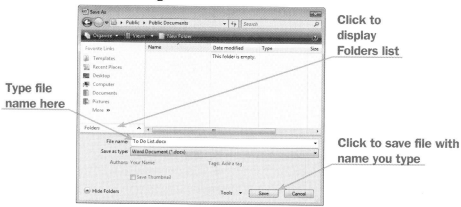

Click to
display
Folders list

Type file
name here

Click to save file with
name you type

Once you have saved a document for the first time, you can click the Save button on the Quick Access Toolbar or you can click the Office Button and then click Save, and Word saves the changes you made in the document by copying over the previous version. If you don't want to copy over the original version of your document, you can use the Save As command to open the Save As dialog box and save it using a different name or to a new location.

Creating Folders

Folders can help you organize files on your disks. You can create a new folder in the Save As dialog box. To create a new folder within your current folder, click the New Folder button on the toolbar in the Save As dialog box. A new folder appears in the list with the temporary name "New Folder" highlighted in blue, as shown in Figure 1-4. Because the name is highlighted,

Extra for Experts

You can rename a folder by right-clicking the folder, and then clicking Rename on the shortcut menu.

you can just type the new folder name, and the text you type will replace the old name. When you are finished, press the Enter key. The folder name is changed and the folder opens to become the current folder.

FIGURE 1-4
Save As dialog box after creating a new folder

New Folder
button

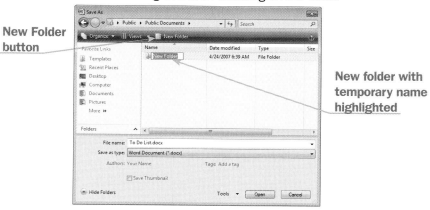

New folder with
temporary name
highlighted

STEP-BY-STEP 1.5

1. Click the **Office Button**, and then click **Save As**. The Save As dialog box appears.

2. In the Navigation pane on the left side of the dialog box, click the **Folders** bar to display the available disks and folders.

3. Click the drive and folder where you want to save the file.

4. On the toolbar, click the **New Folder** button. A new folder appears in the list in the dialog box with the name highlighted.

5. Type **Word Lesson 1**. Press the **Enter** key. The Address bar at the top of the Save As dialog box changes to indicate that Word Lesson 1 is the current folder.

6. In the File name box, select the entire name of the file, if necessary. Type **To Do List** followed by your initials.

7. Click **Save**. Word saves the file in the folder you created, and the dialog box closes. The new file name appears at the top of the document window.

8. Click the **Office Button**, and then click **Close** to close the document without exiting Word. Keep Word open for the next Step-by-Step.

Locating and Opening an Existing Document

You can open an existing document by clicking the Office Button, and then clicking Open. This displays the Open dialog box, as shown in Figure 1-5, where you can open a file from any available disk and folder. If you worked on the document recently, you can click the Office Button, and then click the name of the document in the list of Recent Documents on the right side of the menu.

FIGURE 1-5
Open dialog box

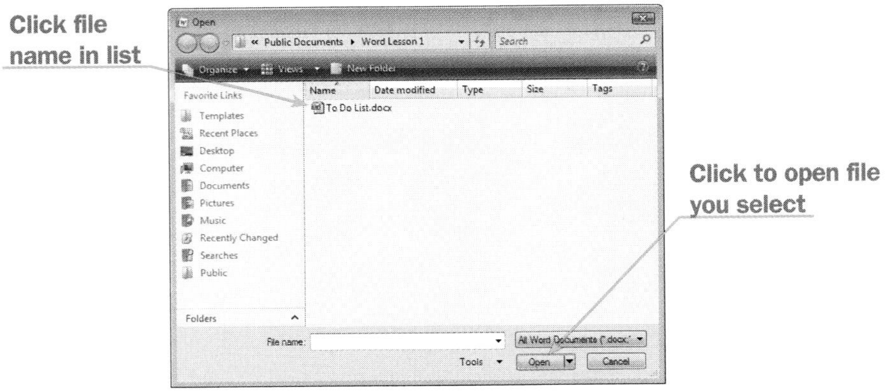

Click file name in list

Click to open file you select

Opening a New, Blank Document

You can open a new, blank document by clicking the Office Button, and then clicking New. This opens the New Document dialog box, as shown in Figure 1-6. In the Templates list on the left side of the dialog box, Blank and recent is selected, and at the top of the pane in the middle of the dialog box, Blank document is selected. Click Create. This closes the dialog box and opens a new, blank document.

FIGURE 1-6
New Document dialog box

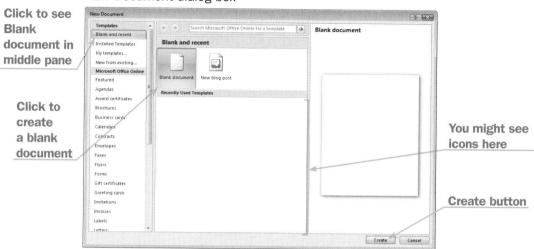

Click to see Blank document in middle pane

Click to create a blank document

You might see icons here

Create button

STEP-BY-STEP 1.6

1. With Word still running, click the **Office Button**, and then click **Open**. The Open dialog box appears.

2. In the Navigation pane on the left side of the dialog box, click the **Folders** bar to display the available disks and folders.

3. If necessary, click the disk and folder in which you created the Word Lesson 1 folder. Double-click the **Word Lesson 1** folder. The saved file **To Do List** appears in the dialog box.

> **Did You Know?**
>
> You can also open a file by double-clicking it in the Open dialog box.

4. Click **To Do List.docx** in the list. Click **Open**. The To Do List document appears on the screen.

5. Leave the document open for the next Step-by-Step.

Zooming a Document

You can use the zoom feature to magnify and reduce your document on the screen. Zoom is measured in percentage. A zoom percentage of 100% shows the document at its normal size. The higher the percentage, the larger the document appears; the lower the percentage, the smaller the document appears. The easiest way to change the percentage is to drag the Zoom slider at the bottom-right of the screen, or to click the Zoom In or Zoom Out buttons on either end of the Zoom slider. You can also click the Zoom level percentage to the left of the Zoom slider to open the Zoom dialog box. Finally, you can click the View tab on the Ribbon, and then click one of the buttons in the Zoom group to zoom to a preset percentage or click the Zoom button in the Zoom group to open the Zoom dialog box from there.

Switching to Full Screen Reading View

Full Screen Reading view removes the Ribbon and the status bar from the screen. It leaves only the document and, in place of the Ribbon, a small bar called a toolbar that contains buttons for performing commands. See Figure 1-7. Full Screen Reading view is useful for reading the document on the screen. It does not show how the document looks on a page.

To use Full Screen Reading view, click the View tab on the Ribbon, and then in the Document Views group, click the Full Screen Reading button. You can also click the Full Screen Reading button on the status bar to the left of the Zoom slider. To return to Print Layout view, click the Close button on the toolbar at the top of the screen.

FIGURE 1-7
Document in Full Screen Reading view

Toolbar

Close button

To help you meet your goals, take the time to plan and organize your work. It can be helpful to list the tasks you need to accomplish, and then rank them by importance.

Start by listing everything you need to accomplish today. Include both obligations (that is, tasks you must complete) and tasks you'd like to complete.

After you create your list, examine the items and number them in order of importance. Put the number 1 next to the most important task that must be completed today, number 2 next to the second most important task, and so on. Now you have a plan!

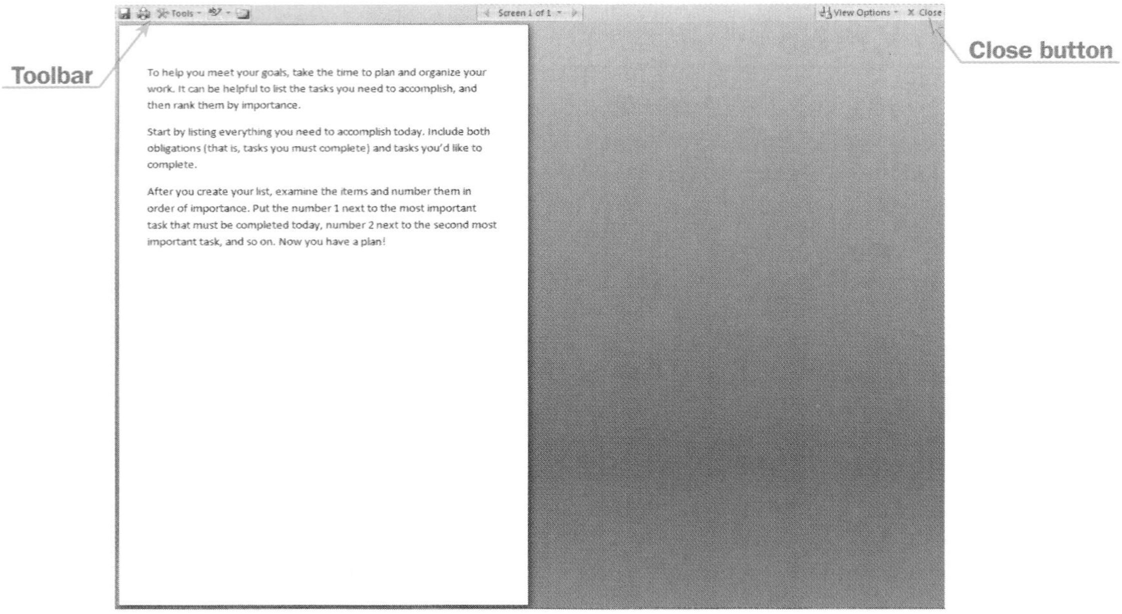

STEP-BY-STEP 1.7

1. At the lower-right of the document window, drag the **Zoom slider** all the way to the left. The zoom percentage is changed to 10% and the document appears as a small piece of paper in the upper-left of the document window.

2. At the right end of the Zoom slider, click the **Zoom In** button five times. The zoom percentage increases by 10 each time you click the Zoom In button. The zoom percentage is now 60%.

3. On the Ribbon, click the **View** tab. The Ribbon changes to show the View commands. In the Zoom group, click the **Page Width** button. The document just about fills the screen. See Figure 1-8.

FIGURE 1-8
View tab displayed on the Ribbon

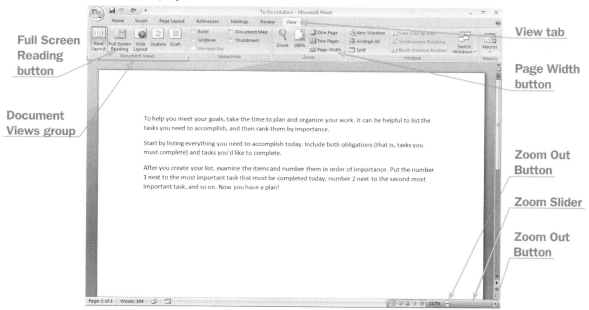

4. On the View tab, in the Zoom group, click the **100%** button. The document returns to 100% zoom.

5. On the View tab, locate the Document Views group. Click the **Full Screen Reading** button. The view changes to Full Screen Reading view.

6. At the right end of the toolbar, click the **Close** button. You return to Print Layout view.

7. Leave the document open for the next Step-by-Step.

Previewing a Document

The Print Preview command enables you to look at a document as it will appear when printed. To switch to Print Preview, click the Office Button, point to Print, and then click Print Preview in the list on the right side of the menu. The Print Preview window looks similar to the one shown in Figure 1-9.

FIGURE 1-9
Document in Print Preview

Print Preview tab

Close Print Preview button

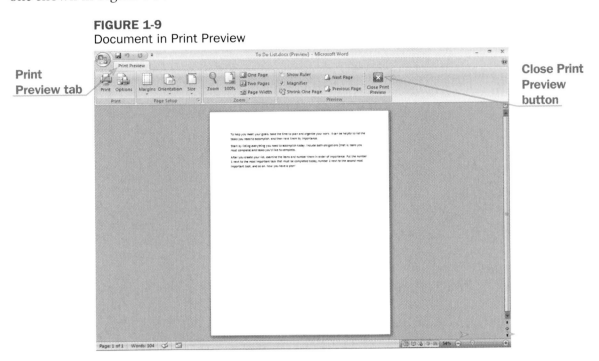

In Print Preview, the Ribbon changes to show only the Print Preview tab. The Print Preview tab contains commands for looking at your document. The commands let you print your document; change the margins, orientation (the direction of the paper), paper size, and zoom options; display the ruler; automatically shrink text to fit it on a page; and close Print Preview.

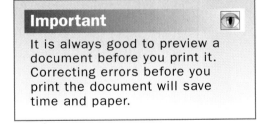

Important

It is always good to preview a document before you print it. Correcting errors before you print the document will save time and paper.

Selecting a Page Orientation

Word gives you two ways to print text on a page. Documents printed in portrait orientation, as shown in Figure 1-10, are longer than they are wide. By default, Word is set to print pages in portrait orientation. In contrast, documents printed in landscape orientation, as shown in Figure 1-11, are wider than they are long. Most documents are printed in portrait orientation. Some documents, such as documents with graphics or numerical information, look better when printed in landscape orientation.

FIGURE 1-10
Portrait orientation

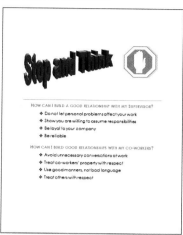

FIGURE 1-11
Landscape orientation

You can change the orientation of the document you want to print. To do this, click the Page Layout tab on the Ribbon, and then, in the Page Setup group, click the Orientation button, as shown in Figure 1-12.

FIGURE 1-12
Changing page orientation on the Page Layout tab

You can also change the orientation in Print Preview. After switching to Print Preview, locate the Page Setup group on the Ribbon, and then click the Orientation button. In both cases, after you click the Orientation button, you can click Portrait or Landscape on the menu.

STEP-BY-STEP 1.8

1. Click the **Office Button**, point to **Print**, and then click **Print Preview**. Notice that the page orientation of the document is portrait.

2. On the Ribbon in the Page Setup group, click the **Orientation** button. A menu opens.

3. On the menu, click **Landscape**. The page orientation of the document changes to landscape.

4. On the Ribbon in the Preview group, click the **Close Print Preview** button to return to Print Layout view.

5. On the Ribbon, click the **Page Layout** tab. The Page Layout commands appear on the Ribbon.

6. In the Page Setup group, click the **Orientation** button. Click **Portrait** on the menu.

7. On the Ribbon, click the **View** tab. In the Zoom group, click the **One Page** button. The document is in portrait orientation again.

8. On the Quick Access Toolbar, click the **Save** button. Leave the document open for the next Step-by-Step.

Printing a Document

At any time, you can print a full document, a single page, or multiple pages from a document on the screen. To print a document, click the Office Button and then click Print. The Print dialog box appears, as shown in Figure 1-13. You can also open the Print dialog box from Print Preview by clicking the Print button on the Print Preview tab.

FIGURE 1-13
Print dialog box

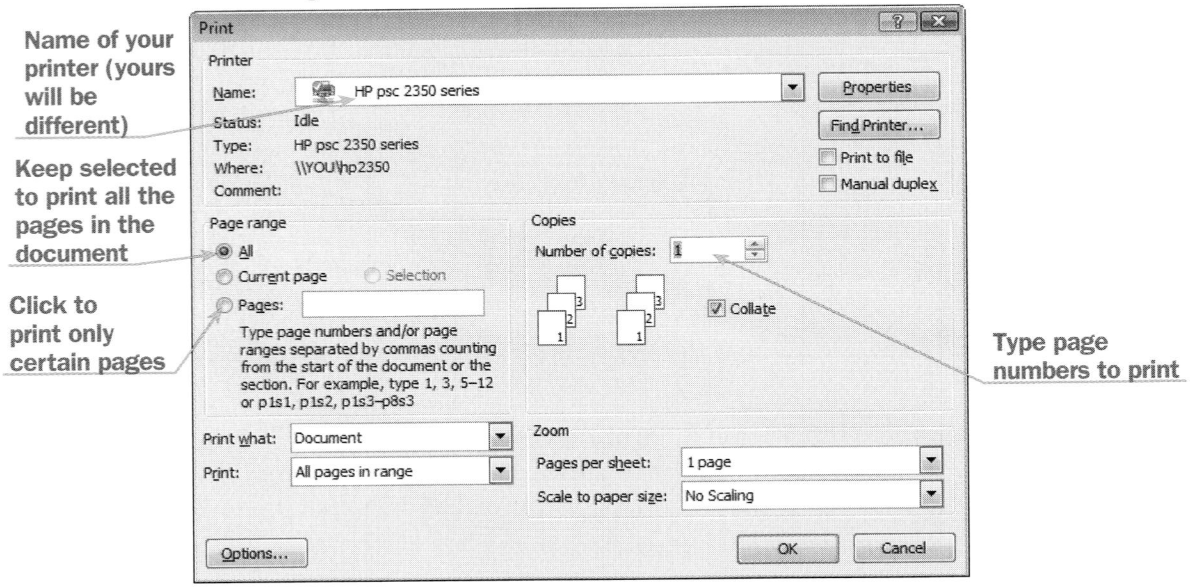

Name of your printer (yours will be different)

Keep selected to print all the pages in the document

Click to print only certain pages

Type page numbers to print

Print	
Printer	
Name:	HP psc 2350 series
Status:	Idle
Type:	HP psc 2350 series
Where:	\\YOU\hp2350
Comment:	

Properties
Find Printer...
☐ Print to file
☐ Manual duplex

Page range
◉ All
○ Current page   ○ Selection
○ Pages:

Type page numbers and/or page ranges separated by commas counting from the start of the document or the section. For example, type 1, 3, 5–12 or p1s1, p1s2, p1s3–p8s3

Print what: Document
Print: All pages in range

Copies
Number of copies: 1
☑ Collate

Zoom
Pages per sheet: 1 page
Scale to paper size: No Scaling

Options...   OK   Cancel

S TEP-BY-STEP 1.9

1. Use the Zoom slider to return to 100% view. Press the **Ctrl+End** keys to jump to the end of the document, press the **Enter** key, and then type your name.

2. Click the **Office Button**, and then click **Print**. The Print dialog box appears.

3. Click **OK** to print the document using the default settings. Leave the document open for the next Step-by-Step.

Exiting Word

When you are finished working, you can close your document and exit Word. To close the document without exiting Word, click the Office Button, and then click Close. To exit Word, click the Close button in the upper-right corner of the document window. You can also click the Office Button, and then click Exit Word.

S TEP-BY-STEP 1.10

1. Click the **Office Button**. Click **Close**. A dialog box opens asking if you want to save any changes. Click **Yes**. The document closes, but Word is still running.

2. In the upper-right corner of the window, click the **Close** button. Word exits and the Word program window closes.

SUMMARY

In this lesson, you learned:

- Word is a word-processing program that can be used to create documents such as letters, memos, forms, and even Web pages.

- The key elements of the screen in Print Layout view are the Ribbon, Quick Access Toolbar, insertion point, status bar, view buttons, and Zoom slider.

- You can view the document screen in Print Layout view, Full Screen Reading view, Web Layout view, Outline view, and Draft view.

- When text is entered, the word wrap feature automatically wraps words to the next line if they will not fit on the current line.

- When corrections or additions need to be made, you can place the insertion point anywhere within a document using the mouse or keyboard.

- You can delete text using the Backspace and Delete keys.

■ When you save a document for the first time, the Save As dialog box opens. This is where you name your file and choose a location in which to save it.

■ After you have saved a document the first time, you use the Save command to save your changes in the document or use the Save As command to save it with a different file name or to a new location.

■ You can create new folders for storing documents in the Save As dialog box.

■ You can locate and open an existing document using the Open dialog box.

■ You can use the Zoom slider to magnify or reduce the size of your document on the screen.

■ Full Screen Reading view makes it easier to view the entire document on the screen by removing the Ribbon and status bar and displaying only the text, not the layout, of the document.

■ The Print Preview command allows you to see a document as it will appear when printed.

■ You can use the Orientation command to change the page orientation to portrait orientation or landscape orientation.

■ You can print a document by using the Print command.

VOCABULARY *Review*

Define the following terms:

Draft view	Print Layout view	View buttons
Full Screen Reading view	Print Preview	Web Layout view
Insertion point	Quick Access Toolbar	Word processing
Landscape orientation	Ribbon	Word wrap
Office button	Status bar	Zoom
Outline view	Toolbar	Zoom slider
Portrait orientation		

REVIEW *Questions*

MULTIPLE CHOICE

Select the best response for the following statements.

1. In Print Layout view, you see all except which of the following?
   A. Ribbon
   B. Save As dialog box
   C. Zoom slider
   D. insertion point

2. Which dialog box do you use to save a file for the first time?
   A. Save File
   B. Locate File
   C. Save
   D. Save As

3. Dragging the Zoom slider to the right
   A. magnifies the document on-screen.
   B. reduces the size of the document on-screen.
   C. switches the document to Full Screen Reading view.
   D. changes the way the document will look when it is printed.

4. The feature that causes text you type to automatically move to the next line when it does not fit on the current line is called
   A. word processing.
   B. paragraphing.
   C. word wrap.
   D. jumping.

5. Commands for working with the document are organized into tabs on the
   A. status bar.
   B. Zoom slider.
   C. Ribbon.
   D. Quick Access Toolbar.

FILL IN THE BLANK

Complete the following sentences by writing the correct word or words in the blanks provided.

1. _____ view shows how a document will look when it is viewed as a Web page.

2. The blinking _____ shows where text will appear when you begin typing.

3. To insert a blank line and start a new paragraph in a document, press the _____ key.

4. _____ can help you organize files on your disks.

5. Documents printed in _____ orientation are taller than they are wide.

PROJECTS

PROJECT 1-1

Match the key or keys in the first column to the description in the second column.

Column 1	**Column 2**
___ 1. Right arrow	**A.** Moves to the previous page
___ 2. Left arrow	**B.** Moves to the end of the line
___ 3. Down arrow	**C.** Moves to the next word
___ 4. Up arrow	**D.** Moves to the end of the document
___ 5. End	**E.** Moves left one character
___ 6. Home	**F.** Moves to the beginning of a line
___ 7. Page Down	**G.** Moves to the previous word
___ 8. Page Up	**H.** Moves to the previous line
___ 9. Ctrl+right arrow	**I.** Moves to the beginning of the document
___ 10. Ctrl+left arrow	**J.** Moves right one character
___ 11. Ctrl+End	**K.** Moves to the next page
___ 12. Ctrl+Home	**L.** Moves to the next line

PROJECT 1-2

Create a flyer announcing an upcoming program at the planetarium.

1. Start Word. Open the **Lecture.docx** Data File.

2. Save the document as **Cosmic Lecture** followed by your initials.

3. Scroll down so you can see the lines of text below the drawing. Place the insertion point at the end of the first sentence, press the spacebar, and then type: **Dr. Jasmine Davis will present a program entitled "Cosmic Connections."**

4. Place the insertion point after the word *Park*, and then use the Backspace key to delete that word and the extra space.

5. Create a new paragraph after *Green Hills Planetarium*. Type the following: **Thursday, May 6, 7 p.m. to 8 p.m.**

6. Change the view to Full Screen Reading.

7. Close Full Screen Reading view.

8. Change the orientation of the document to landscape.

9. Preview the document.

10. In Print Layout view, press the Ctrl+End keys, press the Enter key, and then type your name.

11. Save, print, and close the document. Exit Word.

 PROJECT 1-3

Write a letter thanking Dr. Davis for the presentation.

1. Start Word. Click the Office Button, and then click New. The New Document dialog box opens. In the middle pane, make sure Blank document is selected. In the lower-right corner of the dialog box, click Create. A new, blank Word document opens.

2. Type the following text:

   Dear Dr. Davis,

   Thank you for participating in our lecture series. Your presentation was interesting as well as informative. Those who attended now understand much more about the origins of the galaxy. Because of your involvement, our lecture series continues to be a great success.

   Sincerely,

3. Press the Enter key twice to insert enough blank space after *Sincerely* for you to sign your name, and then type your name.

4. Change the document to Full Screen Reading view.

5. Close Full Screen Reading view.

6. Change the zoom to One Page.

7. Open the Save As dialog box. Navigate to the drive and folder where you want to save the file. Create a new folder in this location. Name the folder **Letters**.

8. Make sure the Letters folder is the current folder. Save the document as **Thank You Letter** followed by your initials.

9. Print and close the document. Exit Word.

 PROJECT 1-4

You are creating an advertisement for a department store sale. Before printing the advertisement, you need to add some text and change the orientation.

1. Open the **Sale.docx** Data File.

2. Save the document as **Holiday Clearance** followed by your initials.

3. Change the Zoom percentage to 110%.

4. Scroll down, and then position the insertion point in front of the sentence starting with *These great bargains.* Type: **Hurry down now to Seymour's for clearance prices on all holiday merchandise.** Press the spacebar.

5. Position the insertion point before the word *now* in the sentence you just typed, and then use the Delete key to delete that word and the space after it. Position the insertion point to the right of the word *Now* in the second line in the document. Use the Backspace key to delete that word and the space before it.

6. Press the Ctrl+End keys to move the insertion point to the end of the last sentence. Press the spacebar, and then type: **Don't miss out!**

7. Press the Enter key, and then type your name.

8. Change the orientation of the document to **portrait**.

9. Preview the document.

10. Save, print, and close the document. Exit Word.

 PROJECT 1-5

The Career Placement Center is preparing an informational pamphlet as a resource for people seeking employment. You need to revise a page in the pamphlet.

1. Start Word. Open the **Interview.docx** Data File. Save the document as **Interview Tips** followed by your initials.

2. Change the zoom to Page Width.

3. Change to Full Screen Reading view.

4. Read the document to become familiar with it.

5. Close Full Screen Reading view.

6. Press the Ctrl+Home keys to position the insertion point at the beginning of the document, if necessary.

7. Press the Ctrl+right arrow keys eight times to move the insertion point after the word *job* and before the comma. Press the spacebar, and then type **interview**.

8. Press the Ctrl+End keys to position the insertion point at the end of the document. Press the spacebar, and then type: **Third, prepare a list of questions about the position. Do not ask about salary at this point.**

9. Start a new paragraph and type: **After the interview, write a thank you note to the person who conducted the interview. In addition to being good manners, it reminds the interviewer who you are and sets you apart from the other candidates.**

10. Proofread the document. Use the Backspace or Delete keys to correct any errors.

11. Jump to the end of the document, insert a new paragraph, and then type your name.

12. Save, print, and close the document. Exit Word.

CRITICAL *Thinking*

 ACTIVITY 1-1

Thank you notes are easier to write when done promptly, preferably the day you receive a gift or attend an event. Using what you have learned in this lesson, start Word and write a thank you note to someone who has done something special for you recently. Save the document with a file name of your choice, print it, and then close the document and exit Word.

 ACTIVITY 1-2

With Windows, a file name may contain up to 255 characters and include spaces. You should use a descriptive file name that will remind you of what the file contains, making it easy to find.

Read each item below. From the information given, create a file name for each document. Create a new Word document and type the file name next to the appropriate number in a list. Each file must have a different name. Strive to develop descriptive file names. Choose a file name for the document you created, and then save the document. Print and close your document, and then exit Word.

1. A letter to Binda's Beautiful Clothing requesting a catalog.

2. A report entitled "Global Warming Controversies" written by the environmental foundation, EarthSave. The report will be used to develop a grant proposal.

3. A letter that will be enclosed with an order form used to place an order with Binda's Beautiful Clothing.

4. A letter of complaint to Binda's Beautiful Clothing for sending the wrong merchandise.

5. An announcement for a reception to be given in honor of a retiring executive, Jack Dawson.

6. A memo to all employees explaining new vacation time policies at Griffin Enterprises.

7. Minutes of the May board of directors' meeting of Lambert Insurance Company.

8. A press release written by EarthSave to the media about a one-day event called *Live in Harmony with Nature*.

9. A mailing list for sending newsletters to all employees of Griffin Enterprises.

10. An agenda for the June board of directors' meeting of Lambert Insurance Company.

SCANS ACTIVITY 1-3

By default, Word inserts new text to the left of the insertion point, and any text to the right of the insertion point "moves over" to make room for the newly typed text. You might want text you type to replace characters to the right of the insertion point. You can do this by switching to Overtype mode.

Use the Help system in Word to find out information about Overtype mode, and then turn it on. Create a new Word document, and then type the answer to the following questions. After you have finished answering the questions, turn Overtype mode off. Save the document you created, and then print it. Close the document and exit Word.

- How do you switch to Overtype mode?
- In the Advanced section of the Word Options dialog box, what do you think happens when you select the "Use the Insert key to control overtype mode" check box? (*Note*: If you select this option, make sure you deselect it when you are finished with this activity.)
- In which views can you use Overtype mode?

BASIC EDITING

VOCABULARY

Clipboard (system Clipboard)

Copy

Cut

Drag

Drag-and-drop

Find

Format

Go To

Office Clipboard

Paste

Paste Options

Quick Style

Redo

Repeat

Replace

Select

Show/Hide ¶

Toggle

Undo

Wildcard

Selecting Text

To select text means to highlight a block of text. Blocks can be as small as one character or as large as an entire document. After selecting a block of text, you can edit the entire block at once. You can select text using the mouse, using the keyboard, or using the keyboard in combination with the mouse.

To select text with the mouse, position the I-beam pointer to the left of the first character of the text you want to select. Hold down the left button on the mouse, drag the pointer to the end of the text you want to select, and release the button. This is called dragging. To remove the highlight, click the mouse button.

Did You Know?

To quickly select everything in a document, press and hold the Ctrl+A keys or on the Home tab, in the Editing group, click the Select button, and then click Select All.

To select text with the keyboard, press and hold down the Shift key, and then press an arrow key in the direction of the text you want to select. Pressing the Shift key extends the selection in the direction of the arrow key you press. To select a word at a time, press and hold the Shift+Ctrl keys, and then press the left or right arrow key. To select a paragraph at a time, press and hold the Shift+Ctrl keys, and then press the up or down arrow key. Table 2-1 summarizes additional ways to select text.

Extra for Experts

To select blocks of text that are not next to each other, select the first block of text, press and hold down the Ctrl key, and then use the mouse to select additional blocks of text.

TABLE 2-1
Selecting blocks of text

TO SELECT THIS	DO THIS
Characters	Click in front of the first character you want to select, press and hold the Shift key, and then click after the last character you want to select.
Word	Double-click the word.
Line	Position the pointer in the left margin next to the line so that it changes to ⇗, and then click.
Multiple lines	Position the pointer in the left margin next to the line so that it changes to ⇗, press and hold the left mouse button, and then drag down or up in the margin to select as many lines as you want.
Sentence	Press and hold down the Ctrl key, and then click anywhere in the sentence.
Paragraph	Triple-click anywhere in the paragraph. Or Position the pointer in the left margin next to the line so that it changes to ⇗, and then double-click.
Entire document	Triple-click in the left margin. Or Position the pointer in the left margin next to the line so that it changes to ⇗, press and hold down the Ctrl key, and then click in the left margin.

Showing Formatting Marks

Many times it is easier to select and edit sentences and paragraphs if you can view the paragraph marks and other formatting symbols. The Show/Hide ¶ command allows you to see these hidden formatting marks, as shown in Figure 2-1. To view the formatting marks, click the Show/Hide ¶ button in the Paragraph group on the Home tab. The formatting marks do not appear when you print your document.

FIGURE 2-1
Formatting marks displayed

Show/Hide ¶ button (selected)

Paragraph marker

Space markers

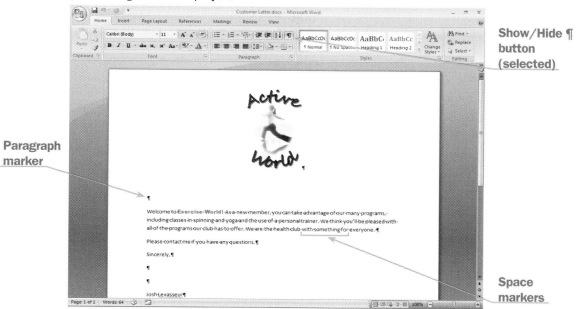

Understanding Toggle Commands

Clicking the Show/Hide ¶ button once displays paragraph and formatting marks; clicking the button again hides them. Switching between two options in this manner is known as toggling, so a command that you use by turning a feature on or off is sometimes known as a toggle command. Word 2007 contains several toggle commands that turn a feature on or off. When a toggle command on the Ribbon is selected, it is orange; when it is deselected, it is the normal blue color. Toggle commands can also appear on a menu. When a toggle command on a menu is selected, a check mark appears next to it.

S TEP-BY-STEP 2.1

1. Start Word. Open the **Letter.docx** Data File from the drive and folder in which your Data Files are stored. Save the document as **Customer Letter** followed by your initials.

2. On the Home tab, in the Paragraph group, click the **Show/Hide ¶** button. The paragraph marks and other hidden formatting marks appear on your screen, and the Show/Hide ¶ button on the Ribbon changes to orange to show that it is selected.

STEP-BY-STEP 2.1 Continued

3. Position the pointer in the left margin to the left of the word *Welcome* so that it changes to ⟨⟨. Click once. The first line in the document is selected, as shown in Figure 2-2.

FIGURE 2-2
Selecting a line

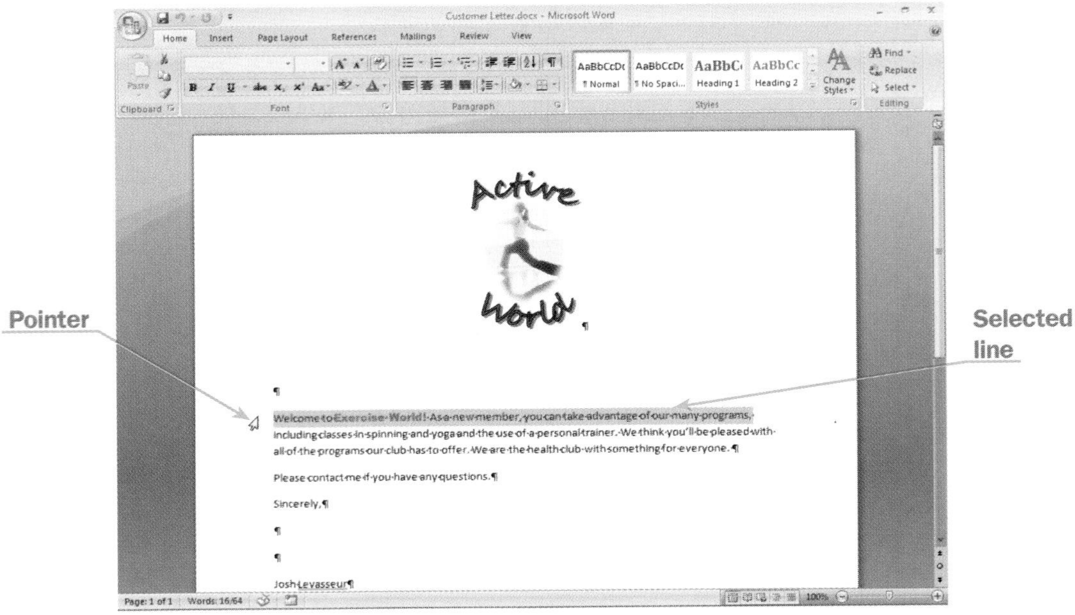

Pointer

Selected line

4. Click anywhere in the document. The text is deselected.

5. Double-click the word **Welcome** at the beginning of the first paragraph. The word is selected.

6. Click anywhere in the document to deselect the text.

7. Triple-click anywhere in the first paragraph. The entire paragraph is selected. Deselect the text.

8. In the first paragraph at the beginning of the second sentence, position the I-beam pointer before the *A* in the word *As*. Press and hold the left mouse button, and then drag to the right and down to just before the last sentence in the first paragraph (just before *We are the health club...*). Release the mouse button. The text you dragged the pointer over is selected.

9. On the Home tab, in the Editing group, click the **Select** button, and then click **Select All**. The entire document is selected. Deselect the text. Press the **Ctrl+A** keys. The entire document is selected again. Deselect the text.

10. Click the **Show/Hide ¶** button. The formatting characters are hidden again. Leave the document open for the next Step-by-Step.

Creating Paragraphs Without Blank Space Between Them

When you press the Enter key, you create a new paragraph. By default, paragraphs have blank space after them, so pressing the Enter key creates a new paragraph with blank space between it and the paragraph above it. The extra space is helpful when you are typing because you don't need to press the Enter key twice to insert space between paragraphs. But there may be times when you don't want that extra space to appear. For example, when you type a letter, extra space should not appear between the lines in the inside address.

To create a new paragraph without extra space before it, you can use the No Spacing button, which is located in the Styles group on the Home tab. To switch back to the normal paragraph style that includes space after each paragraph, you can click the Normal button, which also appears in the Styles group on the Home tab. When you click either of these buttons, the setting applies to the current paragraph and to each paragraph you create after that.

The No Spacing and the Normal buttons are called Quick Styles. Quick Styles are settings that affect the way text looks in the document and that you can apply by clicking a button on the Ribbon.

STEP-BY-STEP 2.2

1. Click the **Show/Hide ¶** button. The formatting marks are displayed.

2. Position the insertion point in the blank paragraph below the logo and above the first paragraph. Type **May 13, 2010**. Press the **Enter** key. A blank line is inserted and the insertion point is blinking at the beginning of a new paragraph.

STEP-BY-STEP 2.2 Continued

3. Type **Karen DeSimone**. On the Home tab, in the Styles group, click the **No Spacing** button. Press the **Enter** key. A new paragraph is created, but no space appears between the two paragraphs. See Figure 2-3.

FIGURE 2-3
Paragraphs with the No Spacing Quick Style applied

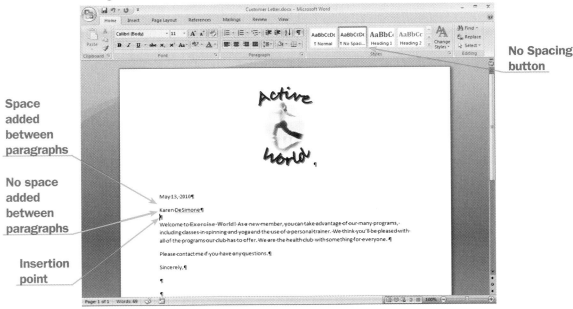

4. Type **47 Bradford St.**, press the **Enter** key, and then type **Salem, RI 02922**. The inside address is complete.

5. In the Styles group, click the **Normal** button. Space is inserted below the current paragraph. Press the **Enter** key. A new paragraph is created with a blank line above it.

6. Type **Dear Ms.**

7. On the Quick Access Toolbar, click the **Save** button to save your changes. Leave the document open for the next Step-by-Step.

Using the Undo, Redo, and Repeat Commands

When working on a document, you will sometimes delete text accidentally or change your mind about editing or formatting changes that you made. The Undo command is useful in these situations because it reverses recent actions. To use the Undo command, click the Undo button on the Quick Access Toolbar.

You can keep clicking the Undo button to continue reversing recent actions, or you can click the arrow next to the Undo button to see a list of your recent actions. The most recent action appears at the top of the list, as shown in Figure 2-4. Click an action in the list, and Word will undo that action and all the actions listed above it.

FIGURE 2-4
List of actions on the Undo button

The Redo command is similar to the Undo command. The **Redo** command reverses an Undo action. To use the Redo command, click the Redo button on the Quick Access Toolbar. Unlike the Undo command, you cannot open a list of actions to redo.

The Redo button does not appear on the Quick Access Toolbar until you have undone something. Until then, the Repeat button appears next to the Undo button. The **Repeat** command repeats the most recent action. For example, if you type something, and then click the Repeat button, the same text will appear on the screen. If you select text, delete it, and then select more text, clicking the Repeat button deletes the selected text. To use the Repeat command, click the Repeat button on the Quick Access Toolbar. The Repeat button is sometimes visible but dimmed, which means that it is unavailable; that is, you can't repeat the most recent action.

STEP-BY-STEP 2.3

1. On the Quick Access Toolbar, click the **arrow** next to the Undo button. The list of actions that can be undone appears.

2. Point to the third item in the list. The action you point to as well as all of the actions above it are selected. The command at the bottom of the list changes from *Cancel* to *Undo 3 Actions*.

3. Click the third item on the Undo list. The last three actions are "undone," and some of the text you typed disappears from the letter. Also note that the Redo button now appears next to the Undo button on the Quick Access Toolbar.

4. On the Quick Access Toolbar, click the **Redo** button three times. The actions you "undid" are "redone" and all the text is restored to the document. The Redo button on the Quick Access Toolbar changes to the Repeat button, which is dimmed.

5. Double-click the word **Ms.** in the salutation to select it. Press the **Delete** key. The word is deleted. On the Quick Access Toolbar, the Repeat button is now available.

6. Double-click the word **Dear** in the salutation to select it. On the Quick Access Toolbar, click the **Repeat** button. The last action is repeated and the selected word is deleted.

7. On the Quick Access Toolbar, click the **arrow** next to the Undo button. Click the second **Clear** in the list. The salutation is restored again.

8. Deselect the text, and then save the document. Leave the document open for the next Step-by-Step.

Using Drag-and-Drop to Move and Copy Text

At some point when you are editing a document, you will probably want to move or copy text to a different location. The easiest way to move text is to select it, position the pointer on top of the selected text, and then drag the selected text to the new location. This is called drag-and-drop. As you drag the selected text, a vertical line follows the pointer indicating where the text will be positioned when you release the mouse button, as shown in Figure 2-5. If you want to copy the text instead of move it, you must press and hold the Ctrl key while you drag it.

FIGURE 2-5
Using drag-and-drop to move selected text

Line indicates where dragged text will be positioned

Pointer

Selected text

STEP-BY-STEP 2.4

1. Press and hold the **Ctrl** key, and then click the last sentence of the first paragraph to select it.

2. Position the insertion point on top of the selected text. Press and hold the left mouse button, and then drag the pointer up to the first line in the first paragraph until the vertical line following the pointer is positioned just before the word *As*. Release the mouse button. The selected sentence no longer appears at the end of the first paragraph and is repositioned so that it is the second sentence in the first paragraph.

3. In the inside address, double-click **DeSimone**. The last name is selected.

4. Press and hold down the **Ctrl** key, and then drag the selected text to the salutation line so that the vertical indicator line is positioned between the period after *Ms.* and the paragraph mark. Release the mouse button. A copy of the selected text is positioned in the salutation line, and the original text is still in the inside address.

5. Press the **right arrow** key, and then type **:** (a colon).

6. Save your changes to the document. Leave it open for the next Step-by-Step.

Using the Clipboard to Move and Copy Text

Another way to move or copy text is to use the Clipboard. The Clipboard is a temporary storage place in the computer's memory. To use the Clipboard, you cut or copy text. When you cut selected text, it is removed from the document and placed on the Clipboard. When you copy selected text, it remains in its original location and a copy of it is placed on the Clipboard. Once you have placed text on the Clipboard, you can then paste into the document whatever is stored on the Clipboard.

The Clipboard can hold only one selection at a time, so each time you cut or copy text, the newly cut or copied text replaces the text currently stored on the Clipboard. The Clipboard is available to all the programs on your computer, and it is sometimes called the system Clipboard.

Moving Text

To move text from one location to another using the Clipboard, you need to use the Cut command and then the Paste command. First, select the text you want to move. Then, on the Home tab in the Clipboard group, click the Cut button.

To paste the text stored on the Clipboard to a new place in the document, position the insertion point at the location where you want the text to appear. On the Home tab in the Clipboard group, click the Paste button. The text currently stored on the Clipboard is pasted into the document. Moving text in this manner is referred to as *cutting and pasting*.

Computer Concepts

When you press the Delete or the Backspace key, the text you delete is not placed on the Clipboard; it is simply removed from the document.

Copying Text

To copy text in one location to another location, you need to use the Copy command. Select the text you want to copy. On the Home tab in the Clipboard group, click the Copy button.

To paste the copied text, you use the Paste command in the same manner as when you move text. This procedure is sometimes referred to as *copying and pasting*.

Did You Know?

Press the Ctrl+X keys to cut selected text; press the Ctrl+C keys to copy selected text; and press the Ctrl+V keys to paste text from the Clipboard into the document at the insertion point.

Using the Paste Options Button

When you use the Paste command, the Paste Options button appears below and to the right of the pasted text. Click this button to open a menu of options. You can choose to paste the text so its appearance matches the text in the location from where you cut or copied it. Or you can paste the text so its appearance matches the rest of the text in the location where you are pasting it. The appearance of text is called formatting.

Important

The options on the Paste Options button menu change depending on what you pasted in the document.

STEP-BY-STEP 2.5

1. Select the last sentence in the first paragraph. On the Home tab, in the Clipboard group, click the **Cut** button. The selected sentence disappears from the screen and is placed on the Clipboard.

2. Position the insertion point at the beginning of the second sentence in the first paragraph (immediately in front of *We are the health club...*). On the Home tab, in the Clipboard group, click the **Paste** button. The sentence you cut appears at the location of the insertion point.

3. In the first sentence in the first paragraph, select the green text **Exercise World**. On the Home tab, in the Clipboard group, click the **Copy** button. The text stays in the document and is also placed on the Clipboard, replacing the sentence that you had previously cut and placed on the Clipboard.

4. Press the **Ctrl+End** keys. The insertion point moves to the end of the document, in a blank paragraph below the closing.

> **Extra for Experts**
>
> You can also access the Cut, Copy, and Paste commands by right-clicking the mouse button on the selected text, and then choosing the commands from the shortcut menu.

5. On the Home tab, in the Clipboard group, click the **Paste** button. The text *Exercise World* appears in the last line of the document, below the closing. It is formatted green as in the first line of the first paragraph. The Paste Options button appears just below the pasted text.

6. Position the pointer on top of the **Paste Options** button. The button becomes orange and an arrow appears on it.

7. Click the **Paste Options** button. A menu appears with three options on it, as shown in Figure 2-6.

FIGURE 2-6
Menu on the Paste Options button

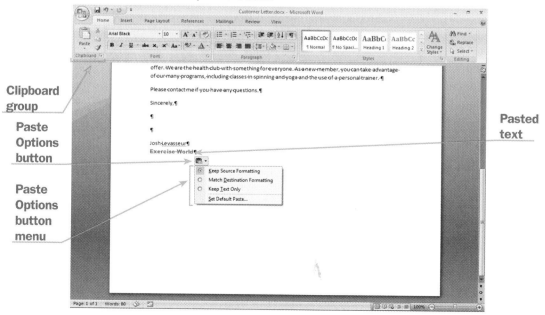

STEP-BY-STEP 2.5 Continued

8. Click the **Match Destination Formatting** option button. The menu closes, and the formatting of the pasted text changes to match the formatting of the text in the current paragraph.

9. Save your changes to the document. Leave it open for the next Step-by-Step.

Using the Office Clipboard

If you want to collect more than one selection at a time, you can use the Office Clipboard. The **Office Clipboard** is a special clipboard on which you can collect up to 24 selections. It is available only to Microsoft Office programs.

Unlike the system Clipboard, which is available all the time, you must activate the Office Clipboard in order to use it. On the Home tab in the Clipboard group, click the Clipboard Dialog Box Launcher. (Remember, the Dialog Box Launcher for a group is the small square with an arrow in the lower-right corner of the group.) This opens the Clipboard task pane on the left side of the window. Once the Clipboard task pane is open, each selection that you cut or copy is placed on it. The task pane displays up to 24 items. When you cut or copy a twenty-fifth item, it replaces the first item.

> **Extra for Experts**
>
> You can use the Office Clipboard in other Office programs, such as Excel. For example, you can copy a chart you created in Excel to a report you are writing in Word.

STEP-BY-STEP 2.6

1. Press the **Ctrl+Home** keys to jump to the beginning of the document. In the Clipboard group, click the **Clipboard Dialog Box Launcher**. The Clipboard task pane opens on the left side of the window. The item currently on the system Clipboard, *Exercise World*, is listed in the task pane.

2. In the first paragraph of the letter, at the beginning of the fourth sentence, select the text **As a new member,** (including the comma). On the Home tab, in the Clipboard group, click the **Cut** button. The text is deleted from the paragraph and appears in the Clipboard task pane, as shown in Figure 2-7.

> **Did You Know?**
>
> You can clear the Office Clipboard by clicking Clear All at the top of the Clipboard task pane, and you can paste all of the contents of the Office Clipboard at once by clicking Paste All.

STEP-BY-STEP 2.6 Continued

FIGURE 2-7
Clipboard task pane with items collected on it

Clipboard
Dialog Box
Launcher

Items on
the Office
Clipboard

Task pane
Close button

Text deleted
from letter

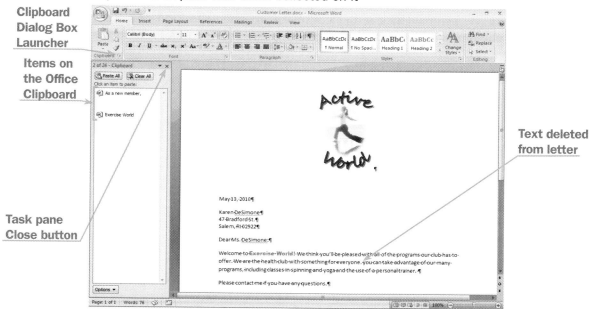

3. Position the insertion point in the first paragraph at the beginning of the second sentence (it begins with *We think you'll be pleased...*). In the Clipboard task pane, click **As a new member,**. The text is pasted at the location of the insertion point.

4. Press the **Delete** key, and then type **w**. If there is no space between the comma after *member* and *we*, press the **left arrow** key, and then press the **spacebar**.

> **Computer Concepts**
>
> Clicking the Paste button or pressing the Ctrl+V keys pastes the contents of the system Clipboard into the document, not the contents of the Office Clipboard.

5. Position the insertion point in the first paragraph at the beginning of the fourth sentence (it begins with *you can take advantage*). Type **At**, and then press the **spacebar.**

6. In the Clipboard task pane, click **Exercise World**. Press the **spacebar**.

7. In the title bar at the top of the Clipboard task pane, click the **Close** button. The task pane closes.

8. Save your changes to the document. Leave it open for the next Step-by-Step.

Using the Find and Replace Commands

Find and Replace are useful editing commands that let you find specific words in a document quickly and, if you wish, replace them instantly with new words. Both commands are located in the Editing group. Click either command to open the Find and Replace dialog box. The Find tab of the Find and Replace dialog box appears as shown in Figure 2-8; the Replace tab appears as shown in Figure 2-9.

FIGURE 2-8
Find tab in the Find and Replace dialog box

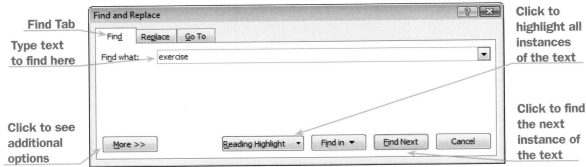

FIGURE 2-9
Replace tab in the Find and Replace dialog box

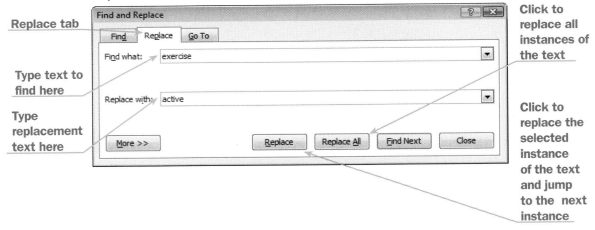

Using the Find command, you can quickly search a document for every occurrence of a specific word or phrase you type in the Find what box. When you click Find Next, the Find command moves the insertion point from its present position to the next occurrence of the word or phrase for which you are searching. When you click Reading Highlight, and then click Highlight All, all instances of the word or phrase in the document are highlighted.

Find locates the exact text you type in the Find what box, even if it's in the middle of another word. For example, you can find the word *all* or any word with *all* in it, such as *fall, horizontally,* or *alloy.* Find also ignores capitalization when finding words; for example, if you search for *run,* it will find *Run* as well as *run.*

You can further define your search criteria by clicking More in the Find and Replace dialog box. These additional search options are explained in Table 2-2.

TABLE 2-2
Find and Replace dialog box options

OPERATION	ACTION
Search	Lets you search from the location of the insertion point up to the top of the document, down to the end of the document, or through the entire document (all).
Match case	Searches for words that are capitalized the same as the text that you typed in the Find what box.
Find whole words only	Finds only the exact word or phrase you entered in the Find what box. (For example, choose this option if you want to find the word *all*, but not words with *all* in them, such as *fall, horizontally,* or *alloy.*)
Use wildcards	Makes it possible to search for words using **wildcards**, which are special characters that represent other characters. The most common wildcards are ? (the question mark), which represents any one character, and * (the asterisk), which represents any number of characters. For example, *a??* finds all three-letter words that begin with *a*, including *all* and *ask*, and a* finds all words of any length that begin with *a*, including *all*, *apple*, or *arithmetic.*
Sounds like	Locates homonyms—words that sound alike but are spelled differently. For example, if you type the word *so*, Word would also find the word *sew.*
Find all word forms	Lets you find different forms of words. For example, if you search for the word *run*, Word would also find *ran, runs*, and *running.*
Match prefix	Finds words that begin with the text you type in the Find what box.
Match suffix	Finds words that end with the text you type in the Find what box.
Ignore punctuation characters	Finds words that match the text in the Find what box, but ignores any punctuation in the words in the document. For example, if you type *its* in the Find what box, it will find *it's* as well as *its.*
Ignore white-space characters	Finds text that matches the text in the Find what box even if there is a space between some of the characters in the document. For example, if you type *Maryellen* in the Find what text box, it will also find *Mary Ellen.*
Format	Lets you search for formatting, such as bold, instead of searching for a specific word; or it allows you to search for the text in the Find what box with specific formatting applied, such as the word *active* in a green font.
Special	Lets you search for special characters that may be hidden, such as a paragraph mark.
No Formatting	Removes formatting you applied by clicking Format.

The **Replace** command has all the features of the Find command. In addition, the Replace command allows you to replace a word or phrase in the Find what box with another word or phrase you key in the Replace with box. The replacements can be made one at a time by clicking Replace, or all at once by clicking Replace All.

STEP-BY-STEP 2.7

1. Press the **Ctrl+Home** keys to position the insertion point at the beginning of the document. Scroll down until you can see the last line of the document.

2. On the Home tab, in the Editing group, click the **Find** button. The Find and Replace dialog box appears. The insertion point is blinking in the Find what box.

3. Type **exercise**.

4. Click the **Reading Highlight** button, and then click **Highlight All**. All three instances of the word *exercise* in the document are highlighted. (If the Find and Replace dialog box is covering the word, click the title bar at the top of the dialog box and drag the box out of the way.)

5. Click the **Reading Highlight** button, and then click **Clear Highlighting**. The highlighting is removed. Click **Find Next**. Word selects and stops on the first instance of *exercise*, in the first line of the first paragraph in the body of the letter.

6. At the top of the dialog box, click the **Replace** tab. The Replace tab appears on top in the dialog box. Click in the **Replace with** box, and then type **active**.

7. Click **Replace**. The first instance of the word *exercise* is replaced with *active*, and the next instance of the word *exercise* is selected. Notice that the first letter of the word *active* was automatically changed to an uppercase letter to match the case of the word it replaced. Also note that because this instance of the word *exercise* was formatted in green, the replacement word is formatted in the same way.

> **Did You Know?**
>
> To open the Find and Replace dialog box with the Replace tab on top, click the Replace button in the Editing group on the Home tab.

8. Click **Replace All**. The other two instances of *exercise* are replaced with the word *active*, and a dialog box opens telling you that Word has completed its search of the document and made two replacements. Click **OK** in this dialog box to close it. The Find and Replace dialog box is still open.

9. In the Find what box, select **exercise**, and then type **as**. In the Replace with box, select **active**, and then press the **Delete** key. With nothing in the Replace with box, instances of *as* will be deleted—that is, replaced with nothing.

STEP-BY-STEP 2.7 Continued

10. Click **Replace All**, and then click **OK** in the dialog box that opens telling you that six replacements were made. Scroll the document up so that you can see the body of the letter. Every instance of the letter combination *as* is deleted, as shown in Figure 2-10. However, notice that in addition to deleting the word *As* in the first paragraph at the beginning of the second sentence, *as* was deleted from the word *pleased* and *has* in the same sentence as well as everywhere else this letter combination appeared.

FIGURE 2-10
Unexpected results from using the Replace All command

The word "as" removed from here

The word "as" removed from these words as well

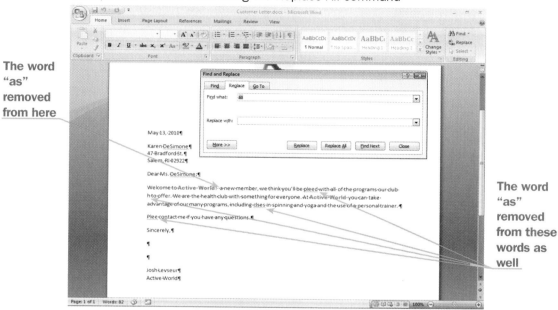

11. Click anywhere in the document. On the Quick Access Toolbar, click the **Undo** button. The letter combination *as* is restored to the document.

12. Click **Close** in the Find and Replace dialog box. The dialog box closes.

13. Save your changes to the document, and leave it open for the next Step-by-Step.

Using the Go To Command

One of the quickest ways to move through a long document is to use the Go To command. Go To allows you to jump to a specific part of a document. On the Home tab in the Editing group, click the arrow next to the Find button, and then click Go To on the menu. The Find and Replace dialog box opens with the Go To tab on top. See Figure 2-11. In the Go to what list, select the type of location you want to move to, and then enter the corresponding number or other information in the box on the right. After you click Next, Word moves the insertion point to the location you specified.

FIGURE 2-11
Go To tab in the Find and Replace dialog box

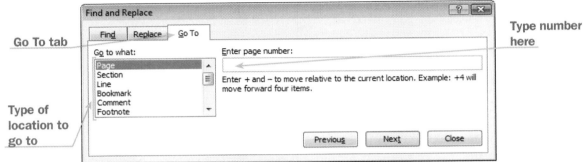

S TEP-BY-STEP 2.8

1. Press the **Ctrl+Home** keys to move the insertion point to the beginning of the document.

2. On the Home tab, in the Editing group, click the **arrow** next to the Find button. Click **Go To**. The Find and Replace dialog box appears with the Go To tab on top.

3. In the Go to what list, click **Line**. Click in the Enter line number box, and then type **11**.

4. Click **Go To**. The insertion point jumps to the eleventh line in the document (the paragraph above the closing).

5. In the dialog box, click **Close**. The Find and Replace dialog box closes.

6. Save your changes to the document, and leave it open for the next Step-by-Step.

Identifying the Number of Words in a Document or Selection

As you type and edit a document, you may want to know how many words it contains. The number of words in a document appears in the status bar and is updated as you type. If you select text, the status bar displays the number of words in the selection. You can also find out the number of characters, paragraphs, and lines in a document by opening the Word Count dialog box. To do this, you can click the number of words in the status bar, or you can click the Review tab, and then, in the Proofing group, click the Word Count button. See Figure 2-12.

FIGURE 2-12
Word count on the status bar and in the Word Count dialog box

Word
Count
button

Word Count
dialog box
with
statistics
for selected
text

Number of
words
currently
selected

Click here
to open the
Word Count
dialog box

Review tab

Total
number of
words in the
document

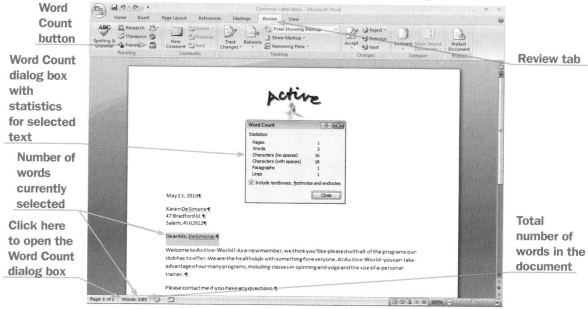

STEP-BY-STEP 2.9

1. Scroll to the top of the document. Look at the word count in the status bar. The document contains 83 words.

2. Select the entire salutation (*Dear Ms. DeSimone:*). The word count indicator in the status bar shows that three out of a total of 83 words are selected in the document.

3. In the status bar, click the word count indicator. The Word Count dialog box opens. Because text is currently selected, this dialog box displays information about the selected text. The selected text consists of 16 characters if you don't count spaces, and 18 if you do.

4. In the dialog box, click **Close**. The Word Count dialog box closes.

5. Deselect the text in the document. On the Ribbon, click the **Review** tab. In the Proofing group, click the **Word Count** button. The Word Count dialog box opens again. This time, because no text is selected, it tells you that the document contains 384 characters not including spaces, 458 characters if you do count the spaces, 10 paragraphs, and 16 lines. (Remember that a new paragraph is created every time you press the Enter key.) Because you might have inserted or removed a space when you cut or copied text, the character count with spaces in the dialog box on your screen might be slightly higher or lower than 458.

STEP-BY-STEP 2.9 Continued

6. In the Word Count dialog box, click **Close**. The dialog box closes.

7. On the Ribbon, click the **Home** tab. In the Paragraph group, click the **Show/Hide ¶** button. The button is deselected, and the formatting marks disappear from the screen.

8. At the bottom of the document, select the name **Josh Levasseur**, and then type your own name.

9. Save, print, and close the document.

SUMMARY

In this lesson, you learned:

■ You can select blocks of text to perform operations on the entire block of text at once, such as cutting, copying, and pasting.

■ The Show/Hide ¶ command allows you to view hidden formatting marks.

■ Toggle commands turn a feature on or off.

■ You can create a paragraph without space after it by using the No Spacing Quick Style. To change it back so that the paragraph has space after it, use the Normal Quick Style.

■ You can undo recent actions by using the Undo command. When you click the arrow next to the Undo button, a list of your recent actions appears. You can redo an action using the Redo button and repeat an action using the Repeat button.

■ You can drag selected text to a new location in the document. You can press and hold the Ctrl key to copy the selected text rather than move it when you drag.

■ You can send text to the Clipboard by using either the Cut or Copy command. You can paste text stored on the Clipboard by using the Paste command.

■ If you want to collect more than one item at a time to paste, you can use the Office Clipboard.

■ The Find command moves the insertion point from its present position to the next occurrence of the word or phrase for which you are searching.

■ Replace finds the next occurrence of the word or phrase for which you are searching and replaces it with the word or phrase you type in the Replace with box.

■ The Go To command moves the insertion point to a part of the document that you specify.

■ You can see the number of words in a document or a selection by checking the status bar. You can see the number of characters, paragraphs, and lines in a document or selection by opening the Word Count dialog box.

VOCABULARY *Review*

Define the following terms:

Clipboard (system Clipboard)	Format	Repeat
Copy	Go To	Replace
Cut	Office Clipboard	Select
Drag	Paste	Show/Hide ¶
Drag-and-drop	Paste Options	Toggle
Find	Quick Style	Undo
	Redo	Wildcard

REVIEW *Questions*

TRUE/FALSE

Circle T if the statement is true or F if the statement is false.

T   F   1. You cannot select a block of text using the keyboard.

T   F   2. You can undo more than one action at a time.

T   F   3. The Redo and Repeat commands are never available at the same time.

T   F   4. The Office Clipboard can store up to 24 items.

T   F   5. The only way to find out how many words are in a document or selection is to open the Word Count dialog box.

WRITTEN QUESTIONS

Write a brief answer to each of the following questions.

1. To use the keyboard to select text, what key must you press in combination with an arrow key?

2. How do the Cut and Copy commands differ?

3. Describe how to move and copy text using drag-and-drop.

4. Describe the difference between the system Clipboard and the Office Clipboard.

5. Which dialog box contains the Go To tab?

PROJECTS

 PROJECT 2-1

Create a list of commonly misspelled words.

1. Open a new Word document. Show hidden formatting marks. Change the Quick Style to No Spacing.

2. Type the list of commonly misspelled words shown below.

> **Committee**
> **Occurrence**
> **Occasional**
> **Separate**
> **Received**
> **Personnel**
> **Correspondence**
> **Judgment**
> **Absence**
> **Accommodate**

3. Type **Responsibility** below *Occurrence*.

4. Undo the last action. The word *Responsibility* disappears.

5. Redo the undone action. The word *Responsibility* appears again.

6. Use the Go To command to move the insertion point to line 5.

7. Use the drag-and-drop technique to alphabetize the word list.

8. Hide formatting marks.

9. Press the Ctrl+End keys, press the Enter key twice, and then type your name.

10. Save the document as **Spelling List** followed by your initials. Print and close the document.

 PROJECT 2-2

Create a checklist to send to candidates for a summer language workshop. The checklist should include the items missing from their applications.

1. Open the **Workshop.docx** Data File. Save the document as **Workshop Checklist** followed by your initials.

2. Show hidden formatting marks.

3. Use the Go To command to move the insertion point to line 2.

4. Type the following sentence at the beginning of line 2:

   We are pleased that you have applied to be part of the Summer Language Workshop at Granville University.

5. Use the drag-and-drop technique to move the line *Nonrefundable $15 application fee* to the end of the checklist.

6. Select the entire document. Copy the selection to the Clipboard.

7. Press the Ctrl+End keys to move to the end of the document. Paste the contents of the Clipboard.

8. Jump to the end of the document, and then type your name on a new line below the list. Delete any blank paragraphs. Hide formatting marks.

9. Preview the document. Print from the Print Preview window. Save and close the document.

 PROJECT 2-3

You own a Web site design business, and you have developed some tips for companies that now have Web sites. However, the document needs to be corrected before being distributed.

1. Open the **Web Site.docx** Data File. Save the file as **Web Site Tips** followed by your initials.

2. Highlight all instances of the word *sight* in the document. Replace them with the word **site**. There should be 10 replacements.

3. Make the insertions and deletions indicated by the proofreader's marks in Figure 2-13.

FIGURE 2-13

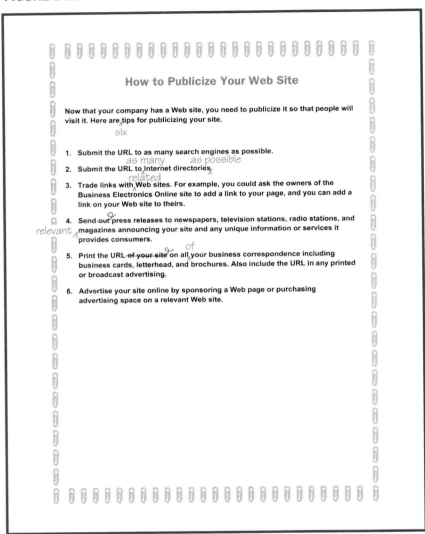

4. Display formatting marks. Move to the blank paragraph below tip number 6, type Document word count:, press the spacebar, and type the number of words currently in the document.

5. Change to the No Spacing Quick Style, and then press the Enter key. Type **Introductory paragraph word count:**, and then press the spacebar.

6. Insert another paragraph using the No Spacing Quick Style. Type **Introductory paragraph character count with spaces:**, and then press the spacebar.

7. Select all of the text in the introductory paragraph, and determine the number of words in the selection. Move to the end of the document, and then type this number after the phrase you typed in Step 5.

8. Determine the number of characters, including spaces, in the introductory paragraph, and then type this number after the phrase you typed in Step 6.

9. Jump to the end of the document, press the Enter key twice, and then type your name. Hide formatting marks.

10. Save, print, and close the document.

 PROJECT 2-4

Your business is sponsoring a golf tournament to benefit the local food pantry. Create an information sheet to post on a bulletin board.

1. Open the **Golf Tournament.docx** Data File. Save the document as **Golf Tournament Notice** followed by your initials.

2. Display formatting marks. Position the insertion point in the blank paragraph between the document heading and the first paragraph. Type the following text using the No Spacing Quick Style.

   Where: Forest Hills Golf Club
   When: June 26–27
   Time: Tee times begin at 8:00 a.m.
   Cost: $50 entry fee per person

3. With the insertion point in the last line that you typed, change the Quick Style back to Normal.

4. Select the word *Where*. Type **Location**.

5. Undo the change you made in Step 4.

6. Open the Office Clipboard. Cut the four lines you typed at the beginning of the document. Cut the last sentence in the first paragraph.

7. Copy all the text in the heading, but do not copy the paragraph marker in the paragraph.

8. Paste the four lines you typed below the paragraph in the document. Paste the *For more information* sentence in a paragraph below the four lines you typed.

9. Paste the heading at the end of the first sentence in the document, after *Sixth Annual*. Use the Paste Options button to match the format of the first paragraph.

10. In the last line, select the text *Robert Shade*, and then type your name.

11. Hide formatting marks and close the Clipboard task pane. Save, print, and then close the document.

PROJECT 2-5

The Career Placement Center is preparing informational pamphlets as a resource for people seeking employment. Edit the following page of the pamphlet.

1. Open the **Job Interview.docx** Data File. Save the document as **Interview Preparation** followed by your initials.

2. Replace all instances of the word *notes* with the word **information**. You should have two replacements.

3. In the last sentence, replace the word *these* with **this**.

4. In the second paragraph, in the first line, cut the text *be sure to*.

5. Use the Repeat command to cut the second paragraph.

6. Paste the paragraph you just cut below the last paragraph in the document.

7. At the end of the document, type your name in the empty paragraph.

8. Save, print, and close the document.

CRITICAL *Thinking*

 ACTIVITY 2-1

With a classmate, create a new Word document listing qualities employers look for in a job applicant. Some examples are a person who is responsible, detail-oriented, and cooperative. In another document, create a personal inventory of your own strengths and weaknesses as a potential applicant for a job of your choice.

ACTIVITY 2-2

A co-worker asks you the following questions about using the Office Clipboard to copy and paste items. Use Help to answer the questions.

■ Can I use the Office Clipboard without displaying the Clipboard task pane?

■ Is there another way to display the Office Clipboard?

■ How do I delete items from the Office Clipboard? How do I delete all the items from the Office Clipboard?

HELPFUL WORD FEATURES

OBJECTIVES

Upon completion of this lesson, you will be able to:

■ Use automatic features including AutoCorrect, AutoFormat As You Type, Quick Parts, and AutoComplete.

■ Insert the current date and time.

■ Check the spelling and grammar in a document.

■ Use the Thesaurus.

■ Insert symbols.

Estimated Time: 1 hour

VOCABULARY

AutoComplete

AutoCorrect

AutoFormat As You Type

Automatic grammar checking

Automatic spell checking

Building block

Contextual spell checking

Format

Quick Part

Quick Style

Superscript

Thesaurus

Understanding Automatic Features

Word offers many types of automated features that can help you create documents. The AutoCorrect feature corrects errors as you type, and AutoFormat As You Type, as the name implies, applies built-in formats as you type. You can create and use Quick Parts to insert frequently used text. The AutoComplete feature "guesses" days of the week and month names as you type, and then suggests the complete word.

Using AutoCorrect

AutoCorrect corrects common capitalization, spelling, grammar, and typing errors as you type. AutoCorrect is also useful for inserting text quickly. For example, you can specify that when you key the letters *nyc*, they will always be replaced with *New York City*.

The automatic correction occurs after you press the spacebar or the Enter key. If you hover the mouse pointer over text that has been automatically corrected, a small blue box appears just below the first character in the word. When you point to the box, it changes to the AutoCorrect Options button. You can click the button to open a menu of commands for changing the AutoCorrect action. In this way, Word "learns" what you want it to do in the future.

You can add or remove words from the AutoCorrect list and change the AutoCorrect options. To do this, you need to open the AutoCorrect dialog box. Click the Office Button, and then click Word Options at the bottom of the menu. This opens the Word Options dialog box. You can customize many Word features using this dialog box. Clicking a command on the left side of the Word Options dialog box changes the commands displayed on the right side of the dialog box. To open the AutoCorrect dialog box, click Proofing in the list on the left side of the dialog box. The right side of the dialog box changes to display commands for customizing proofing tools in Word. See Figure 3-1.

FIGURE 3-1
Proofing options in the Word Options dialog box

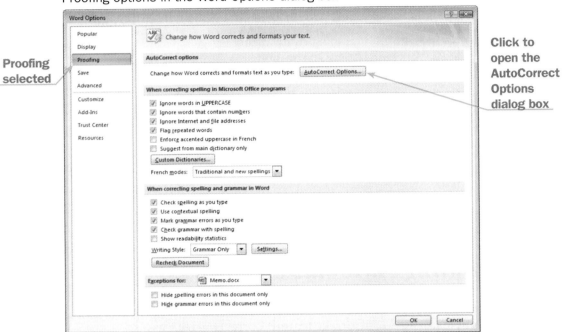

On the right side of the dialog box, click AutoCorrect Options. The AutoCorrect dialog box opens with the AutoCorrect tab on top, as shown in Figure 3-2.

FIGURE 3-2
AutoCorrect tab in the AutoCorrect dialog box

AutoCorrect options

Characters that represent symbols

Possible misspelled words

Symbols that automatically replace characters in the left column

Correct spellings

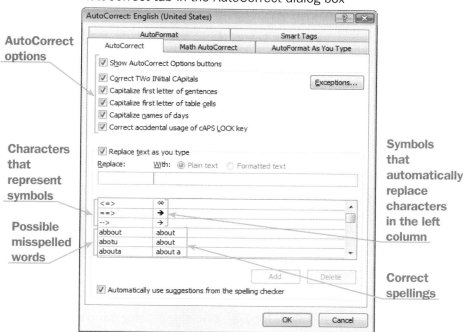

The check boxes at the top of the tab control the AutoCorrect options. Commonly misspelled or mistyped words are listed in the box at the bottom of the tab. The correct spellings that AutoCorrect inserts in the document when you press the Enter key appear on the right side of the list. Notice in the figure that the first few items listed in the box are not misspellings but characters that represent a symbol. If you type the sequence of characters, AutoCorrect automatically inserts the symbol in place of the characters.

Extra for Experts

You can click Exceptions in the AutoCorrect dialog box to add exceptions to the AutoCorrect options. For example, when the Capitalize first letter of sentences check box is selected, AutoCorrect automatically capitalizes the first word that follows the punctuation mark at the end of a sentence. Suppose you worked for a company that used *Ltd.* (the abbreviation for *Limited*) in its company name. You might want to specify that the next word following *Ltd.* is not capitalized, so you would add *Ltd.* to the Exceptions list.

STEP-BY-STEP 3.1

1. Start Word. Open the **Memo.docx** Data File from the drive and folder in which your Data Files are stored. Save the document as **Driving School Memo** followed by your initials. Ignore the words in the document that are misspelled for now.

2. Position the insertion point at the end of the second paragraph in the memo (immediately following the period after *time*). Press the **spacebar**, type **if**, and then press the **spacebar** again. Notice that as soon as you pressed the spacebar, the word *if* was capitalized because the AutoCorrect feature recognized it as the first word in a new sentence.

3. Type the following (with the lowercase *i* and the misspelled word *accomodate*): **possible, i will accomodate**, and then press the **spacebar**. AutoCorrect recognized that you meant to type *I* and automatically changed it, and automatically corrected the misspelled instance of *accommodate*.

4. Type **you.** (Be sure to type the period.)

5. Click the **Office Button**, and then click **Word Options** at the bottom of the Office menu. The Word Options dialog box opens.

6. In the list on the left, click **Proofing**. The right side of the dialog box changes to display commands for customizing proofing tools in Word.

7. On the right side of the dialog box, click **AutoCorrect Options**. The AutoCorrect dialog box opens.

8. In the Replace box, type your three initials in lowercase. Press **Tab** to move to the With box.

9. In the With box, type your name. Near the bottom of the dialog box, click **Add**. AutoCorrect is now customized with your name.

10. Click **OK** to close the AutoCorrect dialog box, and then click **OK** again to close the Word Options dialog box.

11. In the memo, next to the word *From:*, select **David Chofsky**. Type your three initials, and then press the **spacebar**. AutoCorrect replaces the initials with your name.

12. Move the pointer on top of your name. A small blue box appears below the first part of your name. Point to the **blue box**. The box changes to the AutoCorrect Options button.

13. Click the **AutoCorrect Options** button. A menu opens, as shown in Figure 3-3. The top two commands on the menu allow you to undo the correction or stop making that particular type of correction. The last command opens the AutoCorrect dialog box.

STEP-BY-STEP 3.1 Continued

FIGURE 3-3
AutoCorrect Options button in a document

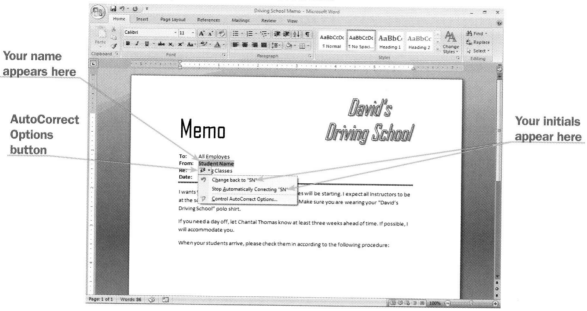

14. On the menu, click **Control AutoCorrect Options**. The AutoCorrect dialog box opens with the AutoCorrect tab on top.

15. In the list at the bottom, scroll down until you see your initials. (Note that the list is organized so that the Replace column is in alphabetical order.)

16. In the list, click your initials. The whole line is selected. Below the list, click **Delete**. Your initials and your name are removed from the list.

17. Click **OK** to close the AutoCorrect dialog box. Save the document and leave it open for the next Step-by-Step.

Understanding Formatting

Formatting means to change the look of text. You can format specific words or entire paragraphs. Examples of text formatting are adding bold, italics, or underlining to words to emphasize them. Examples of paragraph formatting are indenting the first line of a paragraph or double-spacing the lines of text in a paragraph. A paragraph format can also include text formatting. For example, a paragraph format for headings (like the preceding "Understanding Formatting" heading) can include extra space above and below it (paragraph formatting), as well as formatting the text as blue and in a larger font size.

Quick Styles are built-in formats for both text and paragraphs that you can apply by clicking a button in the Styles group on the Home tab. When you used the No Spacing Quick Style, you changed a paragraph format so there was no space after it. When you used the Normal Quick Style, you changed the paragraph format back to include the extra space after it.

Using AutoFormat As You Type

The AutoFormat As You Type feature automatically applies built-in formats to text as you type. In a new paragraph, for example, if you type the number *1* followed by a period, and then press the Tab key, Word assumes that you are trying to create a numbered list. The AutoFormat As You Type feature changes the Quick Style of the text you just typed and the new paragraph you just created to the List Paragraph Quick Style and formats it as a numbered list. If you type something in the list, and then press the Enter key, the number *2* followed by a period and a tab space is automatically inserted on the next line. Another example of text automatically formatted by the AutoFormat As You Type feature is certain fractions. For example, when you type *1/2*, it changes it to ½.

You can choose which automatic formatting options you want to use on the AutoFormat As You Type tab in the AutoCorrect dialog box, shown in Figure 3-4.

FIGURE 3-4
AutoFormat As You Type tab in the AutoCorrect dialog box

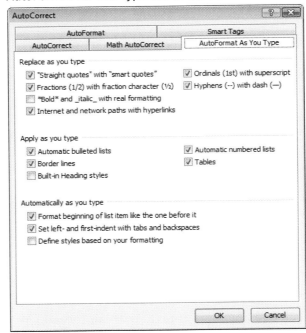

STEP-BY-STEP 3.2

1. On the Home tab, in the Paragraph group, click the **Show/Hide ¶** button. Formatting marks appear in the document. (Remember, this button is a toggle button, so if you don't see formatting marks in your document, click the button again to select it.) This will make it easier to see AutoFormat As You Type in action.

STEP-BY-STEP 3.2 Continued

2. Press the **Ctrl+End** keys to position the insertion point in the blank paragraph below the last paragraph. Type **1.**, and then press the **Tab** key. Pressing the Tab key moves the insertion point to the right approximately one-half inch. The formatting mark that indicates a tab is an arrow that points to the right. The AutoCorrect Options button appears to the left of the text you typed.

3. Point to the **AutoCorrect Options** button. It changes to the same AutoCorrect Options button you saw earlier. Click the **AutoCorrect Options** button to open the menu. The second command on the menu identifies the type of AutoCorrection that was made; in this case, the paragraph was changed to a numbered list. On the Ribbon, you can see in the Styles group that the Normal button is no longer selected, and in the Paragraph group, that the Numbering button is selected.

4. Press the **Esc** key to close the AutoCorrect Options menu without choosing a command. You want to create a numbered list.

5. Type **Check each student's name on the class list.** Press the **Enter** key. Because this text is formatted as a numbered list, the number *2* followed by a period and a tab mark automatically appears on the next line. The insertion point is blinking in the new line after the tab mark.

6. Type **On the 1st**. Press the **spacebar**. When you press the spacebar, the AutoFormat As You Type changed *st* to **superscript**—text that is formatted much smaller than the rest of the text and raised up to the top of the line.

7. Type **day of class, check the list from the accounting office to see if the student has paid for the class.** When this line wraps, the second line is automatically indented so that it aligns with words after the tab mark in the line above it. This formatting is part of the numbered list style.

8. Press the **Enter** key. The next line is formatted as part of the numbered list. Type **Give students who have not paid green slips and send them to the office.** Press the **Enter** key. The fourth item in the list is created.

9. Press the **Enter** key again. Because you didn't type any text as part of the fourth item, the item is removed, the numbered list is ended, and the insertion point moves back to the left margin.

> ### Did You Know?
>
> To change the paragraph from a numbered list to normal text, you also can click the Normal button in the Styles group on the Home tab.

10. Type **If you have any questions, refer to the Instructor's page on our Web site at www.davidsdriving.com.** Press the **Enter** key. A new paragraph is created and the Web page address you typed (www.davidsdriving.com) is formatted in blue and underlined. In addition, it is changed to a hyperlink to that Web site on the Internet.

11. Position the pointer over the blue underlined text. A ScreenTip appears telling you to press the Ctrl key and click to follow the link (which means to jump to that Web page on the Internet). The small blue AutoCorrect box appears just below the beginning of the URL.

STEP-BY-STEP 3.2 Continued

12. Point to the blue AutoCorrect box. The AutoCorrect Options button appears. Click the **AutoCorrect Options** button, and then click **Undo Hyperlink** on the menu. The link is removed and the text is no longer formatted as blue and underlined.

13. Save the document and leave it open for the next Step-by-Step.

> **Net Tip**
>
> The Web page address that you typed is not the address of a real Web page, so following the link will open a dialog box telling you that the page could not be opened.

Using Quick Parts

Building blocks are document parts that you can create, store, and reuse. **Quick Parts** are building blocks you create from frequently used text, such as a name, address, or slogan, and then save so that you can access them by clicking the Quick Parts button in the text group on the Insert tab.

Creating and Inserting a Quick Part

To create a Quick Part, select the text that you want to save as a Quick Part. Click the Insert tab on the Ribbon, and then, in the Text group, click the Quick Parts button. The Quick Parts menu opens. If any Quick Parts are stored on your computer or in your document, they will appear at the top of this menu. On the menu, click Save Selection to Quick Part Gallery. The Create New Building Block dialog box opens, as shown in Figure 3-5.

FIGURE 3-5
Create New Building Block dialog box

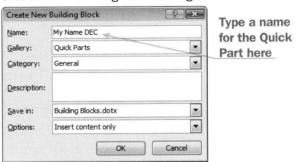

Type a name for the Quick Part here

The first few words of the selected text appear as the default name for the Quick Part in the Name box. You can change this name if you want. Click OK to save the Quick Part. After you create a Quick Part, it appears at the top of the Quick Parts menu.

STEP-BY-STEP 3.3

1. In the *From* line in the memo header, select your name. On the Ribbon, click the **Insert** tab. In the Text group, click the **Quick Parts** button, and then click **Save Selection to Quick Part Gallery**. The Create New Building Block dialog box opens.

STEP-BY-STEP 3.3 Continued

2. In the Name box, type **My Name** followed by your initials. You don't need to click in the box first because the text in the Name box is selected when the dialog box appears, and your typing automatically replaces the selected text.

3. Click **OK**. The dialog box closes.

4. In the first line of the second paragraph in the memo, select the text **Chantal Thomas**. Press the **Delete** key to delete her name.

5. On the Insert tab, in the Text group, click the **Quick Parts** button. The Quick Part you created appears at the top of the menu, similar to the one shown in Figure 3-6. If other *My Name* entries appear on this menu, scroll down until you see the one you created.

FIGURE 3-6
Inserting a Quick Part

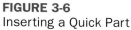

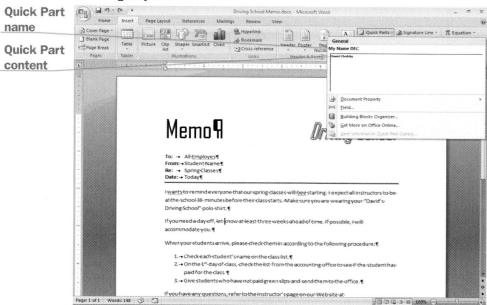

6. On the menu, click the **My Name** Quick Part that you created. The menu closes and your name appears in the document at the insertion point.

7. If there is no space between your last name and the word *know*, press the **spacebar** to insert a space.

8. Save the document and leave it open for the next Step-by-Step.

Did You Know?

A Quick Part can consist of text several paragraphs long. You can also format text that you want to save as a Quick Part so that it is inserted with the formatting.

Deleting a Quick Part

To delete a Quick Part, you need to open the Building Blocks Organizer dialog box. To do this, on the Ribbon, click the Insert tab. In the Text group, click the Quick Parts button, and then click Building Blocks Organizer. The Building Blocks Organizer dialog box opens, similar to the one shown in Figure 3-7.

FIGURE 3-7
Building Blocks Organizer dialog box

Click a column header to sort the list alphabetically by the entries in that column

Quick Part in the list

Preview of selected building block

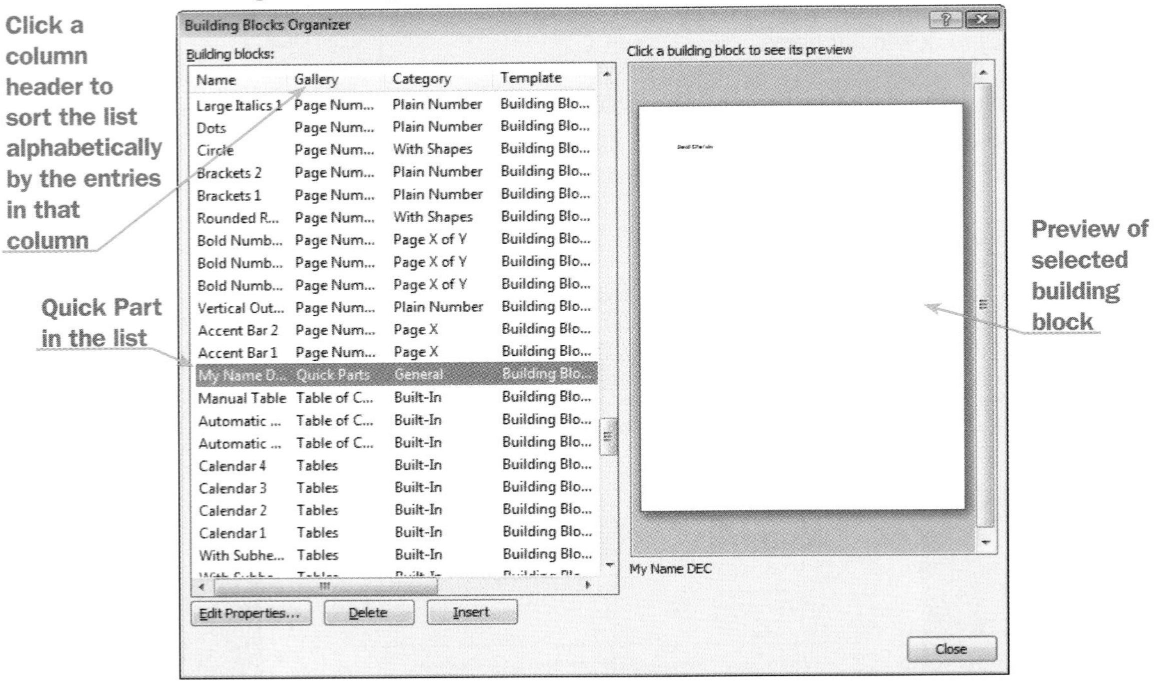

As you see, Word comes with quite a few built-in building blocks. Building blocks are organized into galleries. By default, the list is sorted alphabetically by gallery name. You can sort the building blocks in this list by any of the column headings in the dialog box. The Quick Part you created is stored in the Quick Parts gallery, so to see building blocks in the Quick Parts gallery, scroll down the list. To delete a Quick Part, select it, and then click Delete.

Extra for Experts

You can use the built-in building blocks just as you used the Quick Part you created. Click a building block in the list in the Building Blocks Organizer dialog box, and then click Insert. The building block is inserted into the document.

STEP-BY-STEP 3.4

1. If the Insert tab is not the active tab on the Ribbon, click the **Insert** tab. In the Text group, click the **Quick Parts** button, and then click **Building Blocks Organizer**.

2. If the list of building blocks is not sorted alphabetically by Gallery name (two Bibliographies entries should appear first, followed by several Cover Pages entries), click the **Gallery** column header.

3. Use the scroll bar to scroll down the list until you see Quick Parts in the Gallery column. Locate the Quick Part you created. Remember its name is *My Name* followed by your initials. Click the Quick Part you created to select it.

4. At the bottom of the dialog box, click **Delete**. A warning dialog box opens asking if you are sure you want to delete the selected building block. Click **Yes**. The selected Quick Part is deleted from the list.

5. Click **Close** to close the dialog box. Save the document and leave it open for the next Step-by-Step.

Using AutoComplete

AutoComplete is a feature in Word that automatically completes the spelling of days of the week and months of the year that have more than five letters in their names. After you type the first four letters, AutoComplete suggests the complete word. For example, if you type *Febr*, the word *February* appears in a ScreenTip above the insertion point. To insert the suggested word, press the Enter key, and AutoComplete automatically inserts the complete word for you. To ignore the suggested word, just keep typing.

STEP-BY-STEP 3.5

1. In the first paragraph, at the end of the first sentence, position the insertion point between the word *starting* and the period. Press the **spacebar**.

2. Type **Mond**. A ScreenTip appears telling you to press ENTER to insert *Monday*, as shown in Figure 3-8.

FIGURE 3-8
Inserting a day of the week with AutoComplete

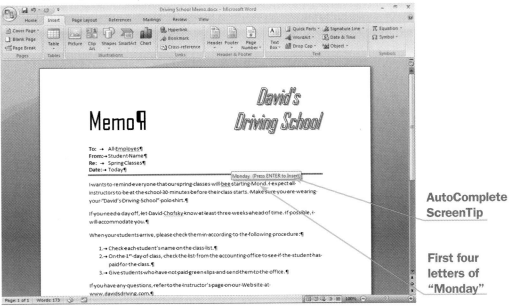

3. Press the **Enter** key to accept the AutoComplete suggestion. *Monday* appears in the document.

4. Save the document and leave it open for the next Step-by-Step.

Inserting the Date and Time

You can easily insert the current date and time into a word-processing document. To do this, on the Ribbon, click the Insert tab. Then, in the Text group, click the Date & Time button. The Date and Time dialog box opens, as shown in Figure 3-9. Select one of the available formats in the list. Some of the formats display only the date, and others display the date and time.

FIGURE 3-9
Date and Time dialog box

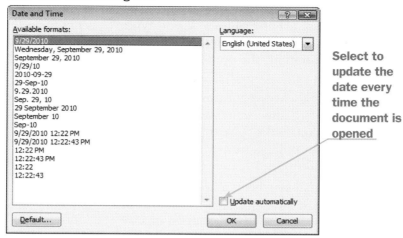

Select to update the date every time the document is opened

If you want to display the current date whenever you open the document, you would click the Update automatically check box to select it. For example, if you create a template or a report on a regular basis, you would probably want to have the current date displayed each time you opened the document. If you want a date inserted in the document to remain fixed, leave the Update automatically check box unselected. For example, when you create a letter or memo, you would want the date to remain fixed for recordkeeping purposes.

STEP-BY-STEP 3.6

1. In the *Date* line in the memo header, select the text **Today**. Press the **Delete** key.

2. If the Insert tab is not the active tab on the Ribbon, click the **Insert** tab. In the Text group, click the **Date & Time** button. The Date and Time dialog box opens.

3. In the Available formats list, click the third format, which shows today's date in a format similar to *September 29, 2010*. If the **Update automatically** check box has a check mark in it, click it to remove the check mark. This will prevent the date from updating to the current date every time this document is opened.

4. Click **OK**. The dialog box closes and the current date is inserted in the letter.

5. Save the document and leave it open for the next Step-by-Step.

Checking Spelling and Grammar as You Type

Word has the capability to identify misspelled or misused words or incorrect grammar. Automatic spell

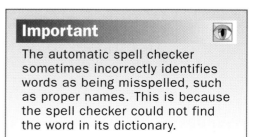

Important

The automatic spell checker sometimes incorrectly identifies words as being misspelled, such as proper names. This is because the spell checker could not find the word in its dictionary.

checking flags words that might be misspelled by underlining them with a red or blue wavy line immediately after you type them. A red, wavy underline indicates words that Word cannot find in its built-in dictionary—words that might be misspelled. A blue, wavy underline indicates a word that might be misused. For example, if you type *We came form the store*, the word *form* would be flagged with a blue, wavy underline as a word that might be misused. Word identifies possible misusage by examining the context in which the word is used. This feature is called **contextual spell checking**.

The **automatic grammar checking** feature checks your document for grammatical errors. When it finds a possible error, Word underlines the word, phrase, or sentence with a green, wavy line. The automatic grammar checker looks for capitalization errors, commonly confused words, misused words, passive sentences, punctuation problems, and other types of grammatical problems.

To correct an error that has been identified with a wavy underline, right-click the flagged word or phrase to open a shortcut menu with a list of suggestions to replace the possible error. Click a suggestion on the shortcut menu to select it and replace the flagged word or phrase.

Automatic spelling and grammar checking can be turned on and off or adjusted in the Proofing section of the Word Options dialog box. See Figure 3-10. The options and commands in the spelling and grammar section of the dialog box are described in Table 3-1.

> **Computer Concepts**
>
> Although automatic grammar checking is a helpful tool, you still need to have a good working knowledge of English grammar. The grammar checker can identify a possible problem, but you must decide if the change should be made depending on the context of the sentence.

FIGURE 3-10
Proofing options in Word Options dialog box

Select these to check spelling and grammar, including contextual spelling

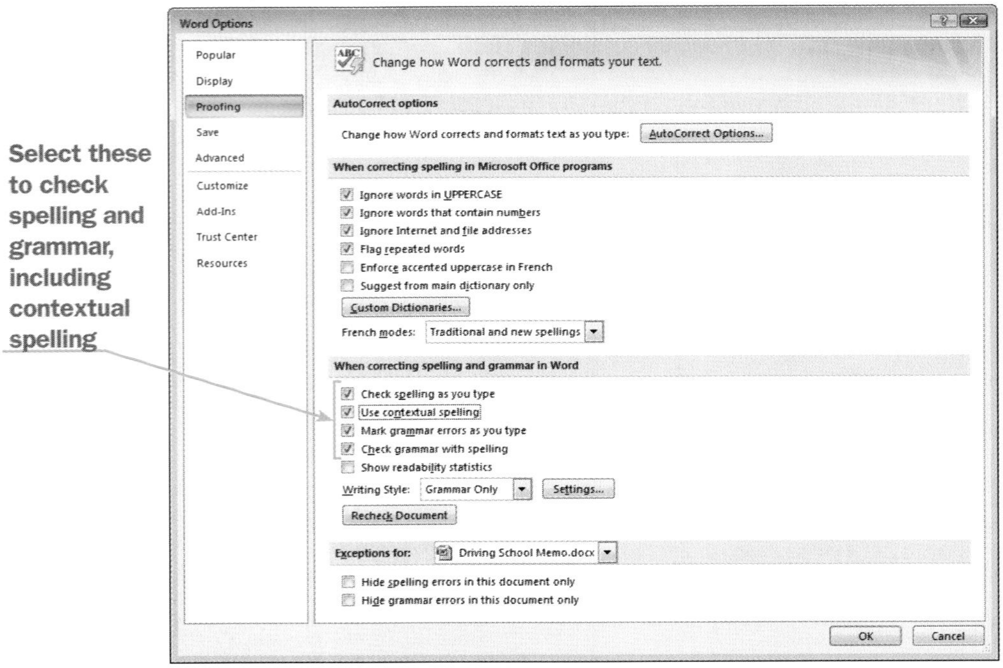

TABLE 3-1
Options and commands for correcting spelling and grammar errors in the Word Options dialog box

OPTION	ACTION
Check spelling as you type	Flags possible misspelled words in the document with a red, wavy underline; if the "Use contextual spelling" option is turned on, also flags possible misused words in the document with a blue, wavy underline.
Use contextual spelling	When checking the document for spelling errors, identifies possible misused words.
Mark grammar errors as you type	Flags possible grammatical errors in the document with a green, wavy underline.
Check grammar with spelling	When checking the document for spelling errors, also checks for grammatical errors.
Show readability statistics	Opens the Readability Statistics dialog box when the spelling and grammar check is complete. The Readability Statistics dialog box provides information about the reading level of the document.
Writing Style	If you enable the grammar checker, allows you to choose to check for grammar errors only or for writing style errors, such as use of the passive voice. The default is to check for grammar only.
Settings	Opens the Grammar Settings dialog box, in which you can select the grammar and writing style rules the grammar checker uses as it checks the document.
Recheck Document	Resets the spelling and grammar checker so that words you previously chose to ignore will be flagged again.

STEP-BY-STEP 3.7

1. Click the **Office Button**, and then click **Word Options**. In the list on the left side of the Word Options dialog box, click **Proofing**. The right side of the dialog box changes to display commands for customizing proofing tools in Word.

> **Computer Concepts**
>
> The options and commands in the "When correcting spelling in Microsoft Office programs" section (in the Proofing section of the Word Options dialog box) apply to all Microsoft Office programs installed on your computer, not just to Word.

2. In the section labeled "When correcting spelling and grammar in Word," the first four check boxes should be selected. If any of these check boxes does not contain a check mark, click it to insert a check mark. Click **OK** to close the dialog box.

3. Press the **Ctrl+End** keys. The insertion point moves to the end of the document. Type the following sentences *exactly* as they appear here: **If you have any other questions, plese call me. If there are no answer, leave a detailed message inn the voice mailbox.** The three obvious errors are flagged by Word with wavy underlines.

STEP-BY-STEP 3.7 Continued

4. Right-click **plese**, the word flagged with a red, wavy underline as a possible misspelled word. (Remember, right-click means to position the mouse pointer over the word or words specified, and then click the *right* mouse button.) A shortcut menu opens, as shown in Figure 3-11.

FIGURE 3-11
Correcting a spelling error using the shortcut menu

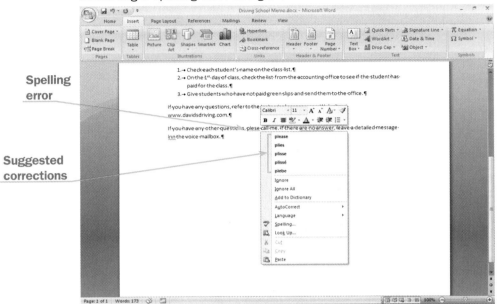

5. With the left mouse button, click **please** on the shortcut menu. The incorrect spelling is replaced with the correct spelling, and the red, wavy underline disappears.

6. Right-click anywhere on the words **are no answer**, which are flagged with a green, wavy underline as a possible grammatical error. On the shortcut menu that opens, click **is no answer**. This is the correct phrase to use in this instance. The incorrect phrase is replaced with the correct phrase, and the green, wavy underline disappears.

> **Extra for Experts**
>
> When you right-click a grammar error, you can click Grammar on the shortcut menu to learn more about the grammar error that has been identified.

7. Right-click **inn**, the word flagged with a blue, wavy underline. On the shortcut menu that opens, click **in**. The incorrectly used word is replaced with the correct word, and the blue, wavy underline disappears.

8. Save the document and leave it open for the next Step-by-Step.

Using the Spelling and Grammar Checker

In addition to checking your spelling and grammar as you type, you can use the Spelling and Grammar dialog box to check a document's spelling and grammar after you finish typing. You can check an entire document or a selected portion of a document. To do this, on the Ribbon, click the Review tab. Then, in the Proofing group, click the Spelling & Grammar button. The Spelling and Grammar dialog box opens, displaying the first flagged error identified in the document.

The options in the Spelling and Grammar dialog box change depending on the nature of the current error. When a spelling error is detected, the Spelling and Grammar dialog box appears similar to the one shown in Figure 3-12. When a contextual spelling error is detected, the dialog box that appears is the same as the one shown in Figure 3-12, but only the Ignore Once and Change commands are available. When a grammar error is identified, the Spelling and Grammar dialog box appears similar to the one shown in Figure 3-13.

FIGURE 3-12
Spelling error flagged in the Spelling and Grammar dialog box

FIGURE 3-13
Grammatical error flagged in the Spelling and Grammar dialog box

When an error is found, it is highlighted in the document and listed in the top box in the dialog box. Suggestions for correcting the error are listed in the bottom box in the dialog box. For some grammar errors, only a description of the type of error appears in the bottom box.

You can click in the document and correct the error, click in the top box in the dialog box and correct the error, or click a suggestion in the Suggestions box to correct the error. If you click in the document to correct the error, the Ignore Once command in the dialog box changes to Resume. If you correct the error by clicking in the top box in the dialog box, the Ignore Once command changes to Undo Edit. When you are finished working in the document, click in the dialog box, and then click Resume. Table 3-2 and Table 3-3 explain the options in the Spelling and Grammar dialog box.

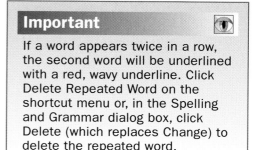

Important

If a word appears twice in a row, the second word will be underlined with a red, wavy underline. Click Delete Repeated Word on the shortcut menu or, in the Spelling and Grammar dialog box, click Delete (which replaces Change) to delete the repeated word.

TABLE 3-2
Spelling and Grammar dialog box options for spelling errors

OPERATION	ACTION
Ignore Once	Leaves the word in the document untouched and jumps to the next flagged error; changes to Resume if you click in the document to correct the error; and changes to Undo Edit if you correct a change in the top box.
Ignore All	Leaves all instances of the word untouched in the document and jumps to the next flagged error.
Add to Dictionary	Leaves all instances of the word untouched in the document, adds it to the built-in dictionary, and jumps to the next flagged error.
Change/Delete	The Change command changes the flagged word to the selected suggestion or to the correction you type in the top box in the dialog box, and then jumps to the next flagged error. The Delete command appears when a word appears twice in a row; click it to delete the repeated word.
Change All	Changes all instances of the flagged word in the document to the selected suggestion or to the correction you type in the top box in the dialog box, and then jumps to the next flagged error.
AutoCorrect	Changes the flagged word to the selected suggestion, adds the word and its correction to the AutoCorrect list, and jumps to the next flagged error.
Options	Opens the Proofing section in the Word Options dialog box to allow you to change default spelling and grammar check settings.
Undo/Undo Edit	Reverses the last decision you made in the dialog box.
Cancel/Close	Before you make a decision on the first spelling change, Cancel stops the spelling check. After you make a decision on the first error, it changes to Close, and clicking it stops the spelling and grammar check.

TABLE 3-3
Spelling and Grammar dialog box options for grammar errors

OPERATION	ACTION
Ignore Once	Leaves the flagged error untouched and jumps to the next flagged error; changes to Resume if you click in the document to correct the error; and changes to Undo Edit if you correct a change in the top box.
Ignore Rule	Leaves all instances of errors that violate the identified grammar rule untouched and jumps to the next flagged error.
Next Sentence	Leaves the flagged error untouched or changes the flagged error to the correction you type in the top box in the dialog box, and then jumps to the next flagged error.
Change	Changes the flagged error to the selected suggestion or to the correction you type in the top box in the dialog box, and then jumps to the next flagged error.
Explain	Opens a Word Help window with an explanation of the grammar or style rule being applied.
Options	Opens the Proofing section in the Word Options dialog box to allow you to change default spelling and grammar check settings.
Undo/Undo Edit	Reverses the last decision you made in the dialog box.
Cancel/Close	Before you make a decision on the first grammar change, Cancel stops the grammar check. After you make a decision on the first error, it changes to Close, and clicking it stops the spelling and grammar check.

STEP-BY-STEP 3.8

1. Press the **Ctrl+Home** keys. This ensures that the spelling and grammar check starts from the beginning of the document.

2. On the Ribbon, click the **Review** tab. The Ribbon changes to display the commands on the Review tab. In the Proofing group, click the **Spelling & Grammar** button. The Spelling and Grammar dialog box opens. The first error it finds in the document, *Employes*, is highlighted in the document and appears in red in the top box in the dialog box. The Suggestions list at the bottom of the dialog box contains several possible alternatives for the flagged word.

> **Did You Know?**
>
> To check only spelling in the document, click the Check grammar check box in the Spelling and Grammar dialog box to deselect it, or, in the Proofing section of the Word Options dialog box, click the Check grammar with spelling check box to deselect it.

3. In the Suggestions list, click **Employees**. Click **Change**. The word is corrected in the document, and the next possible error is flagged. If your first or last name is selected as the next error, click **Ignore All**, and then watch as the next error is flagged. It finds the misused word *too*.

4. Click in the box at the top of the dialog box, and then use the arrow keys to position the insertion point after the word *too*. Press the **Backspace** key to delete the second *o*. You also could have accepted the word in the Suggestions list.

STEP-BY-STEP 3.8 Continued

5. Click **Change**. Word replaces the misused word and continues checking. The word is corrected in the document and the next error, a Subject-Verb Agreement grammatical error in the first sentence, *wants*, is highlighted.

6. In the Suggestions list, make sure **want** is selected, and then click **Change**. If you made any typing errors, additional words might be highlighted next in the dialog box. If this happens, use the commands in the dialog box to correct these errors. When the spelling and grammar check is finished, the Spelling and Grammar dialog box closes and a dialog box opens telling you that the spelling and grammar check is complete.

7. Click **OK**. The dialog box closes. The insertion point returns to the beginning of the document.

8. Save the document and leave it open for the next Step-by-Step.

Using the Thesaurus

The Thesaurus is a useful feature for finding a synonym (a word with a similar meaning) for a word in your document. For some words, the Thesaurus also lists antonyms, or words with opposite meanings. Use the Thesaurus to find the exact word to express your message or to avoid using the same word repeatedly in a document.

To use the Thesaurus, select the word you want to look up. On the Ribbon, click the Review tab. Then, in the Proofing group, click the Thesaurus button. The Research task pane opens on the right side of the window, as shown in Figure 3-14. The word you selected in the document appears in the top box, and *Thesaurus: English (U.S.)* appears in the second box. A list of synonyms and antonyms appears below the box. The bold entries in the list are the main entries. To replace the selected text, point to a word underneath a main entry, click the arrow that appears, and then click Insert. If you click a word underneath a main entry, the Thesaurus looks that word up for you.

FIGURE 3-14
Using the Thesaurus

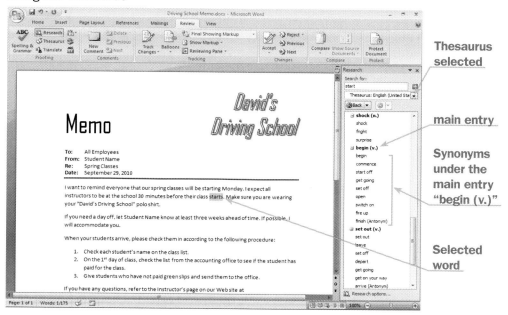

If you select a plural noun or a verb in a form other than its base form (the infinitive form), a list of related words appears in the list in the task pane. For example, if you select the word *walked* in the sentence *he walked to the park*, the Research task pane would display the word *walk* under the heading "Related Words" in the task pane. You click the correct related word in the list, and the task pane changes so that the related word appears in the top box and synonyms and antonyms appear in the task pane. If this happens, make sure you edit the word you insert in the document so it is in the same form as the original word.

> **Extra for Experts**
>
> To look up the definition of a word, select it, click the Thesaurus button to open the Research task pane, click the arrow in the second box in the task pane (the one that contains *Thesaurus: English (U.S.)*), and then click Encarta Dictionary: English (North America).

STEP-BY-STEP 3.9

1. In the first paragraph in the body of the memo, select the word **starts** at the end of the second sentence.

2. On the Ribbon, click the **Review** tab, if necessary. In the Proofing group, click the **Thesaurus** button. The Research task pane opens on the right side of the window with Thesaurus selected in the second box. The task pane displays a Related Words list with only one entry, *start*.

3. In the task pane under Related Words, click **start**. A list of synonyms for *start* appears in the task pane. Scroll down the list until you see the main entry *begin (v.)*. Point to **begin** under the main entry. Click the **arrow** that appears, then click **Insert**. The word *begin* replaces *starts* in the document.

> **Computer Concepts**
>
> Even synonyms can have different shades of meaning. Be sure a synonym makes sense in context before replacing a word with it.

STEP-BY-STEP 3.9 Continued

4. Click in the document at the end of the word *begin*, and then type **s** to change the word to *begins*.

5. In the task pane title bar, click the **Close** button to close the task pane.

6. Save the document and leave it open for the next Step-by-Step.

> **Extra for Experts**
>
> You can also look up a word in the Thesaurus or dictionary by right-clicking a selected word and choosing Look Up on the shortcut menu.

Inserting Symbols

At times, you may need to use a letter or symbol that is not on the keyboard. For example, you might want to insert a symbol used in a foreign language, such as the tilde over the *n* in Spanish (ñ), or a currency symbol such as the euro symbol (€) for currency in the European Union.

To insert a symbol, on the Ribbon, click the Insert tab. Then, in the Symbols group, click the Symbol button. Commonly used symbols appear on the menu. To insert a symbol located on the menu, click it. If you don't see the symbol you want on the menu, click More Symbols to open the Symbol dialog box, as shown in Figure 3-15.

FIGURE 3-15
Symbol dialog box

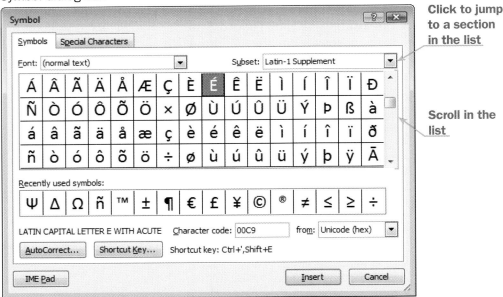

Click the symbol you want in the dialog box, and then click Insert. The symbol you selected appears in the document. You then need to click Close to close the dialog box. If the symbol you inserted from the dialog box was not on the Symbol menu, it will replace one of the other symbols on the menu to make it easier for you to insert it again.

STEP-BY-STEP 3.10

1. In the last line of the first paragraph in the body of the memo, position the insertion point between the *I* in *School* and the quotation marks.

2. On the Ribbon, click the **Insert** tab. In the Symbols group, click the **Symbol** button. Position the pointer on top of several of the symbols in the menu to see the ScreenTip identifying each of them.

3. Position the pointer over ™. This is the trademark symbol. The ScreenTip identifies it as TRADE MARK SIGN. Click ™. The menu closes and the trademark symbol is inserted into the document at the insertion point. (If you don't see the trademark symbol on the menu, click **More Symbols** to open the Symbol dialog box. In the Symbol dialog box, drag the scroll box to the bottom of the scroll bar, click the trademark symbol, click **Insert**, and then click **Close**.)

4. Turn off formatting marks.

5. Save, print, and close the document.

Extra for Experts

If you are writing a paper that includes mathematical equations, you can insert mathematical symbols and equations using the Equation button in the Symbols group.

SUMMARY

In this lesson, you learned:

- AutoCorrect automatically corrects common capitalization and spelling errors as you type. The AutoFormat As You Type feature automatically applies built-in formats to text as you type.

- You can create Quick Parts to store frequently used text so you don't have to retype the text each time. Quick Parts are a type of building block.

- AutoComplete automatically completes the spelling of days of the week and months with more than five letters in their names.

- You can automatically insert the date and time in a document using the Date & Time button.

- Automatic spell checking identifies misspelled words and words that are not in Word's dictionary by underlining them with a red, wavy underline immediately after you type them. Contextual spell checking identifies words that might be used incorrectly by underlining them with a blue, wavy line.

- Automatic grammar checking identifies grammatical errors by underlining the word, phrase, or sentence with a green, wavy line.

- The Spelling and Grammar dialog box contains options that allow you to check the spelling and grammar of words, make changes, and add words to your own custom dictionary.

- You can use the Thesaurus to find a synonym for a word in your document. For some words, the Thesaurus also lists antonyms.

- You can insert symbols and special characters not found on the keyboard using the Symbol button on the Insert tab.

VOCABULARY *Review*

Define the following terms:

AutoComplete	Automatic spell checking	Quick Part
AutoCorrect	Building block	Quick Style
AutoFormat As You Type	Contextual spell checking	Superscript
Automatic grammar checking	Format	Thesaurus

REVIEW *Questions*

FILL IN THE BLANK

Complete the following sentences by writing the correct word or words in the blanks provided.

1. Press the _____ key to accept a word suggested by AutoComplete.

2. To insert text you frequently use, you can create a(n) _____, which is a type of building block.

3. A blue, wavy underline in a document indicates a possible _____ error.

4. To check the entire document for spelling and grammar errors, use the _____ dialog box.

5. To insert letters, symbols, and characters not found on the keyboard, use the _____ button on the Insert tab.

MATCHING

Match the correct term in Column 2 to its description in Column 1.

Column 1	Column 2
___ 1. Document parts that you can store and reuse.	A. Thesaurus
___ 2. Changes fractions and numbers as you type, such as 3/4 to ¾.	B. Building blocks
___ 3. Corrects common capitalization, typing, spelling, and grammatical errors when you press the Enter key or the spacebar.	C. Automatic grammar checking
___ 4. Identifies possible grammatical errors with green wavy underlines.	D. AutoFormat As You Type
___ 5. Displays synonyms for a selected word.	E. AutoCorrect

PROJECTS

 PROJECT 3-1

The chairperson of the Lancaster Chamber of Commerce has asked you to send a memorandum to the members of the chamber reminding them to vote. Edit the memo before sending it to the members.

1. Open the **Lancaster Memo.docx** Data File. Save the document as **Lancaster Voting Memo** followed by your initials.

2. Turn on formatting marks, and then position the insertion point after the tab mark in the *From* line in the memo header.

3. Type **Dinah Muñoz**. (If the letter *ñ* is not on the Symbol menu, open the Symbol dialog box. Make sure the scroll box is at the top of the list, and then click the down scroll arrow eight times to see the row containing the character.)

4. Insert the current date after the tab mark in the *Date:* line in the format that looks like 9/29/10. Do not update the date automatically.

5. In the body of the memo, position the insertion point after the word *for* at the end of the first sentence. Use the AutoComplete and AutoFormat As You Type features to insert the text **January 31st**. Insert any necessary spaces. (*Hint*: You will need to press the spacebar after typing the date, and then remove the extra space before the period.)

6. Create a Quick Part named **Chamber** from the text *Chamber of Commerce* in the second sentence of the first paragraph. Insert the Chamber Quick Part at the end of the *To* line in the memo header.

7. Use the AutoFormat As You Type feature to create the following numbered list after the second paragraph in the body of the memo:
   1. **G. W. Carter Elementary School**
   2. **Jefferson Junior High School**
   3. **Lancaster High School**

8. Use the Thesaurus to replace the word *personal* in the last paragraph with a word that makes sense in context.

9. Delete the Chamber Quick Part.

10. Jump to the end of the document, press the Enter key twice, and then type your name.

11. Turn off formatting marks, and then save, print, and close the document.

 PROJECT 3-2

You are the assistant for East Hanover Business and Professionals Association. You need to make some changes to the minutes from last month's meeting before submitting them at the upcoming meeting.

1. Open the **Minutes.docx** Data File. Save the document as **Club Minutes** followed by your initials.

2. Check the document's spelling and grammar, and correct any errors.

3. Near the top of the document, insert the current date in the blank paragraph beneath *Minutes of the Business Meeting* in the format *Thursday, September 30, 2010.* Do not update the date automatically.

4. Insert your name at the beginning of the list of members who attended the meeting, and then create an AutoCorrect entry for your name.

5. In the second to last paragraph, position the insertion point between *recognized* and *as.* Use the AutoCorrect feature to insert your name. Insert any necessary spaces.

6. In the last sentence in the Old Business paragraph, find a synonym for the word *aim* that makes sense in context.

7. In the last sentence in the first New Business paragraph, find a synonym for the word *arrange* that makes sense in context.

8. At the end of the Announcements paragraph, type **The next meeting will be held on the 27th of next month.**

9. Delete the AutoCorrect entry you added.

10. Save, print, and close the document.

PROJECT 3-3

1. Open the **Museum.docx** Data File. Save the document as **Museum Visit** followed by your initials.

2. Use the Thesaurus to change as many words as you can without changing the meaning of the text.

3. Jump to the end of the document, press the Enter key twice, and then type your name.

4. Save, print, and close the document.

PROJECT 3-4

Robert Hartwell is graduating from his university with a degree in computer science. He is currently applying for an entry-level systems administration position at Ransom Resources, Inc. Help him edit his application letter before he mails it to the company.

1. Open the **Application.docx** Data File. Save the document as **Application Letter** followed by your initials.

2. Insert the current date in the format *September 29, 2010* in the blank paragraph above the inside address. Set the date to update automatically.

3. In the third paragraph in the body of the letter, position the insertion point in front of the last sentence (just before *These*), and then type the following sentence. (If you don't see the symbols on the Symbol menu, open the Symbol dialog box, click the Subset arrow, and then click Greek and Coptic to jump to the Greek alphabet.)

I have also been active on campus, holding various leadership positions in the service organization Omega Delta Psi (ΩΔΨ).

4. In the last line of the document, replace *Robert Hartwell* with your name.

5. Check the document's spelling and grammar, and correct any errors.

6. Save, print, and close the document.

CRITICAL *Thinking*

 ACTIVITY 3-1

It is important for students to begin to develop a personal portfolio for employment before they graduate from high school or college. A personal portfolio contains a resume, well-written application letters, a list of references, and a list of achievements. Write an application letter for a job that interests you. With a few classmates, edit and critique each other's application letters. Be careful to provide constructive criticism.

 ACTIVITY 3-2

You work for Candlelight Time, a regional chain of candle stores. A new store will be opening soon, and your supervisor asks you to type a letter to potential customers announcing the grand opening and offering a free candle to the first 100 customers. Make the letter at least three paragraphs long. Use any helpful automatic features. Insert the current date (set it to update automatically), and then check the spelling and grammar.

 ACTIVITY 3-3

Word has many helpful editing features. Some Word features are more helpful as you type your text, and some are more useful after you have finished typing. Make one list of the Word features you would use as you type a document, and then make another list of Word features you would use after you finished typing the document. When you have finished, save the file as **Editing Features**. Print and close the file.

FORMATTING TEXT

OBJECTIVES

Upon completion of this lesson, you will be able to:

- Change the font.
- Change the size, color, and style of text.
- Use different underline styles and font effects.
- Highlight text.
- Copy formatting using the Format Painter.
- Understand styles and apply Quick Styles.
- Change the theme.
- Create new Quick Styles.
- Clear formatting.

Estimated Time: 2 hours

VOCABULARY

Attribute

Color palette

Font

Font effect

Font size

Font style

Format Painter

Point

Style

Theme

Formatting Text

Once you have typed text in a document, Word provides many useful tools you can use to change the appearance of text and make an impact on the reader. You have used the Paste Options button to choose how to format pasted text and the No Spacing and Normal Quick Styles to change paragraph formatting. You also have used the AutoFormat As You Type feature to apply text and paragraph formats.

You can also format text directly. You can change the way text looks, its size, and its color, and you can use other Quick Styles to apply several formats at once.

To change the format of text, you must first select the text you want to change. If you are changing the format of a single paragraph, the insertion point must be located somewhere in that paragraph. You can also change the format before you start typing, and all the text you type from that point on will have the new format applied until you change to another format.

Changing the Font

Designs of type are called fonts. Just as clothing comes in different designs, fonts have different designs. For example, the font used for this text is Sabon and the font used for the blue *Changing the Font* heading above is BI Sabon.

Like clothing, fonts can be dressy or casual. When you are creating a document, you should consider what kind of impression you want the text to make. Do you want your document to look dressy and formal? Or do you want it to look casual and informal? Using the fonts shown in Figure 4-1 would result in very different looking documents.

FIGURE 4-1
Examples of different fonts

This font is called Calibri.

This font is called Times New Roman.

This font is called Arial.

This font is called Broadway.

𝔗𝔥𝔦𝔰 𝔣𝔬𝔫𝔱 𝔦𝔰 𝔠𝔞𝔩𝔩𝔢𝔡 𝔒𝔩𝔡 𝔈𝔫𝔤𝔩𝔦𝔰𝔥 𝔗𝔢𝔵𝔱 𝔐𝔗.

This font is called Comic Sans MS.

This font is called Lucida Handwriting.

To change the font, locate the Font group on the Home tab on the Ribbon. Click the arrow next to the Font box, as shown in Figure 4-2, and then scroll to the font of your choice. If you have selected text in the document first, you can point to each font to use Live Preview, the Microsoft Office feature that enables you to watch the selected text change in the document without actually making the change. When you find the font you want, click it. The menu closes and the new font is applied to the selected text.

| Calibri (Body) | ▼ |

FIGURE 4-2
Live Preview of the Algerian font

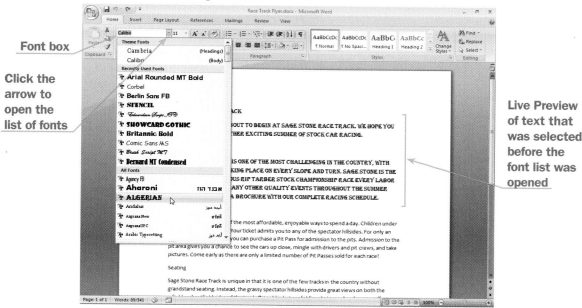

Font box

Click the
arrow to
open the
list of fonts

Live Preview
of text that
was selected
before the
font list was
opened

You can change the font of text already in the document by selecting it first, and then choosing a new font. To change the font of text not yet typed, first choose the font, and then type the text. The new font will be applied until you change to another font.

STEP-BY-STEP 4.1

1. Open the **Flyer.docx** Data File. Save the document as **Race Track Flyer** followed by your initials.

2. On the Home tab, in the Editing group, click the **Select** button, and then click **Select All**. All the text in the document is selected.

3. On the Home tab, in the Font group, click the **arrow** next to the Font box. The list of fonts opens. The current font, Calibri, is listed in the Font box and is selected at the top of the list.

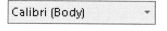

4. Point to **Algerian** (but don't click it). The Live Preview feature changes the selected text in the document to the Algerian font so you can see what it would look like.

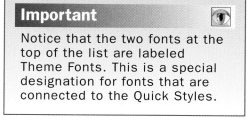

Important

Notice that the two fonts at the top of the list are labeled Theme Fonts. This is a special designation for fonts that are connected to the Quick Styles.

5. Point to a few other fonts in the list and watch the Live Preview.

6. Click a blank area of the document. The Font list closes and the font of the selected text stays the same.

7. Select the first line of text in the document. This is the title of the document.

STEP-BY-STEP 4.1 Continued

8. In the Font group, click the **arrow** next to the Font box. Click **Arial Rounded MT Bold**. The Font list closes and the selected text is changed to Arial Rounded MT Bold. Click a blank area of the document to deselect the text.

9. Save the document and leave it open for the next Step-by-Step.

Did You Know?

If you use the mouse to select text, the Mini toolbar will appear. To choose a different font using the Mini toolbar, move the mouse toward it to make it fully visible, and then click the arrow next to the Font box on the Mini toolbar.

Changing Font Attributes

Once you have decided on a font, you can change its attributes, or how it looks. For example, you can change the size of the font or change its style by making it bold, italic, or underlined. You can also add color and apply special effects.

Changing Font Size

Font size is determined by measuring the height of characters in units called points. Standard font sizes for text are 10, 11, and 12 points. Font sizes for headings are usually larger. For example, this text is 11 points, and the blue *Changing Font Attributes* heading above is 20 points. The higher the point size, the larger the characters. Figure 4-3 illustrates the Calibri font in different sizes. You can change font size by using the Font Size box on the Formatting toolbar or on the Mini toolbar.

Did You Know?

To increase or decrease the font size by small amounts, click the Grow Font or Shrink Font buttons in the Font group on the Home tab or on the Mini toolbar.

FIGURE 4-3
Examples of font sizes

This is 10-point Calibri.

This is 11-point Calibri.

This is 12-point Calibri.

This is 16-point Calibri.

This is 20-point Calibri.

STEP-BY-STEP 4.2

1. Select the first line of text in the document (the title). On the Home tab, in the Font group, look at the Font Size box. The selected text is 11 points. See Figure 4-4.

FIGURE 4-4
Identifying the font size of selected text

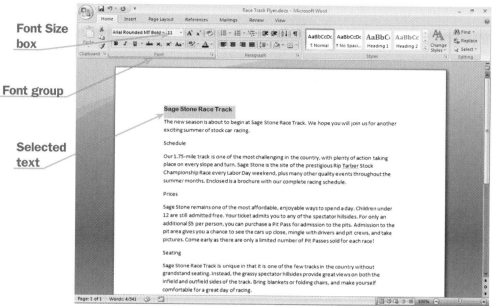

2. Select the second line of text in the document, and then look at the Font Size box again. This text is also 11 points. Although the characters in the first line of text look larger than the characters in the rest of the document, all of the text in the document is 11 points.

3. Select the first line of text again. Click the **arrow** next to the Font Size box. A list of font sizes appears.

4. Point to **72**. Live Preview shows the selected text in the document at 72 points.

5. Click **16**. The Font Size list closes, and the selected text is changed to 16 points. Deselect the text.

6. Save the document and leave it open for the next Step-by-Step.

Computer Concepts

Knowing the point size of text tells you the size of the text relative to text in other point sizes in the same font. As you can see, 11-point text in one font might be larger or smaller than 11-point text in another font.

Extra for Experts

If you want to use a font size that is not on the drop-down menu of the Font Size box, type the point size directly in the Font Size box, and then press the Enter key.

Changing the Color of Text

You can change the color of text to make it stand out or to add interest to a document. To change the color of text, click the arrow next to the Font Color button in the Font group on the Home tab. This opens a menu that includes the color palette, a coordinated set of colors available for use in the document. See Figure 4-5.

FIGURE 4-5
Font Color button palette

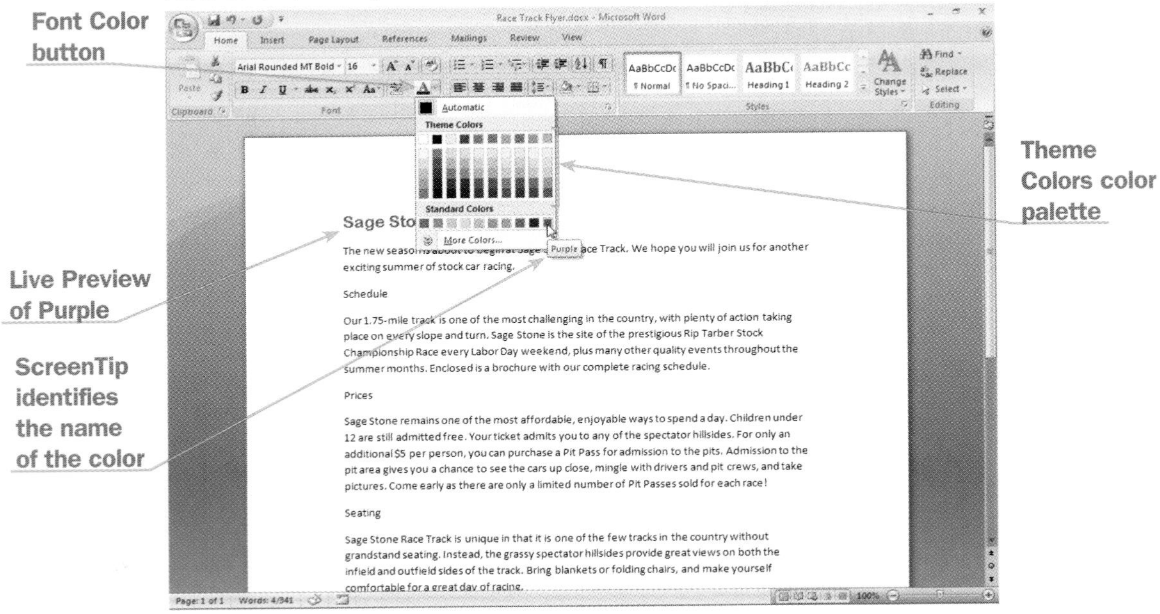

The menu has four sections. The top section contains the Automatic color for the current text; this is usually black. The middle section contains the color palette of Theme Colors, which are colors specifically designed to work with the current document. The bottom section contains the palette of Standard Colors, which are colors that are always available. Finally, the More Colors command at the bottom of the menu opens the Colors dialog box in which you can choose many more colors.

The colors in the palettes all have names. You can see the names by pointing to each color to see its ScreenTip, as shown in Figure 4-5. The Standard Colors have simple names, such as Red, Yellow, and Light Green. The Theme Colors have more complex names that identify the color, shade, and other information.

STEP-BY-STEP 4.3

1. Select the first line of text again.

2. In the Font group, click the **arrow** next to the Font Color button. A menu containing the color palette opens.

STEP-BY-STEP 4.3 Continued

3. In the Standard Colors row, point to the **Light Blue** color. Live Preview displays the selected text in light blue.

4. In the first row under Theme Colors, click the **Red, Accent 2** color. The color palette closes and the red color is applied to the selected text. Deselect the text.

5. In the bulleted list at the end of the document, in the second bulleted item, select **recycle**. Change the color to **Green** (located in the Standard Colors row).

6. Save the document and leave it open for the next Step-by-Step.

> **Did You Know?**
>
> The colored bar on the Font Color button changes to reflect the last color selected. If the colored bar is the color you want to apply, you can simply click the Font Color button to apply that color.

Changing Font Style

Font style is a formatting feature you can apply to a font to change its appearance. Common font styles are bold, italic, and underlining. These styles can be applied to any font. Figure 4-6 illustrates these styles applied to the Calibri font.

> **Did You Know?**
>
> When no style is applied to text, it is sometimes called *Roman*.

FIGURE 4-6
Examples of font styles

This text is bold.

This text is italic.

This text is underlined.

This text is bold, italic, and underlined.

The easiest way to change the font style is to select the text, and then click the Bold, Italic, or Underline buttons in the Font group on the Home tab. The Bold and Italic buttons are also available on the Mini toolbar. All three of the style commands are toggle commands, so to turn a style off, you click the button again.

Changing Underline Style and Color

When you underline text, you can underline with one line or change the style to multiple lines, dotted lines, dashed lines, or another style. You can also change the color of the underline. To change to another underline style or color, click the arrow next to the Underline button. See Figure 4-7.

FIGURE 4-7
Choosing an underline style and color

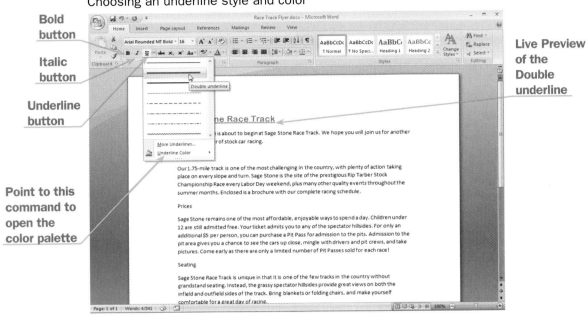

You can click one of the styles on the menu, or click More Underlines to open the Font dialog box. In the Font dialog box, click the Underline style arrow, and then scroll down the list to see additional underline styles. To change the color of the underline, click the arrow next to the Underline button, and then point to Underline Color. This opens the same palette of colors available when you click the Font Color button arrow.

STEP-BY-STEP 4.4

1. Near the beginning of the document, select the heading **Schedule**. On the Home tab, in the Font group, click the **Bold** button. The selected text becomes bold. The Bold button is orange to indicate that it is selected and bold formatting is turned on.

2. Make sure **Schedule** is still selected. In the Font group, click the **Italic** button. The selected text is italicized and the Italic button is selected.

Important

Remember that you create a new paragraph every time you press the Enter key, so a paragraph can be a single line or even one word.

STEP-BY-STEP 4.4 Continued

3. In the Font group, click the **Underline** button. Deselect the text. The heading *Schedule* is in bold italics and it is underlined. The Underline button is selected.

Did You Know?

To quickly change text to bold, press the Ctrl+B keys; to change text to italic, press the Ctrl+I keys; to underline text, press the Ctrl+U keys.

4. Select **Schedule** again. In the Font group, click the **Italic** button. The selected text is no longer italicized, and the Italic button is deselected.

5. In the Font group, click the **Underline** button. The selected text is no longer underlined.

6. In the paragraph under the *Schedule* heading, in the second sentence, select **Rip Tarber Stock Championship Race**. In the Font group, click the **arrow** next to the Underline button. The Underline menu opens.

Computer Concepts

Don't apply too many styles to text. Instead of focusing the reader's attention, it can make the text difficult to read.

7. Click the **Double underline**. The selected text is underlined with a double underline.

8. In the Font group, click the **arrow** next to the Underline button. Point to **Underline Color**. A menu containing the color palette opens.

9. In the first row under Theme Colors, click the **Red, Accent 2** color. The color palette closes and the underline color changes to red. Deselect the text.

Important

The next time you click the Underline button while working in this document, a red, double-underline will be applied because that was the last selection made using the Underline menu. You cannot tell which line style will be applied just by looking at the Underline button.

10. Save the document and leave it open for the next Step-by-Step.

Changing Font Effects

Font effects are similar to font styles and can help you enhance or clarify your text. Some font effects are available in the Font group on the Home tab, and others are available only in the Font dialog box. You open the Font dialog box by clicking the Dialog Box Launcher in the Font group on the Home tab. See Figure 4-8.

FIGURE 4-8
Font dialog box

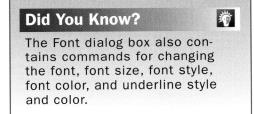

Font Dialog Box Launcher

Selected text

Effects section of the dialog box

Settings match the selected text

Preview box

To select a font effect, click the checkbox next to an effect in the Effects section of the dialog box. Like font styles, font effects are toggle commands—a font effect is either turned on or off.

Font effects are described in Table 4-1.

Did You Know?

The Font dialog box also contains commands for changing the font, font size, font style, font color, and underline style and color.

TABLE 4-1
Font effects

FONT EFFECT	RESULT
Strikethrough	~~No turning back~~
Double strikethrough	~~Caution: Hot~~
Superscript	$x^2 + x^2$
Subscript	H_2O
Shadow	By invitation only
Emboss	Fancy
Engrave	Invitation
Outline	Thursday
Small caps	CALYPSO STREET
All caps	GLENMERLE
Hidden	Hidden text is in the document, but doesn't print and can't be seen in the document unless formatting marks are turned on and the options are set to show Hidden text or all formatting.

STEP-BY-STEP 4.5

1. Select the first line of text in the document. On the Home tab, in the Font group, click the **Font Dialog Box Launcher**. The Font dialog box opens. A preview of the selected text with the font settings in the dialog box appears in the Preview box at the bottom.

2. In the Effects section, click the **Shadow** checkbox to select it. The text in the Preview box changes to reflect the selection.

3. In the Effects section, click the **Small caps** checkbox to select it. Click **OK**. The dialog box closes and the Shadow and Small caps effects are applied to the selected text. Deselect the text.

4. Save the document and leave it open for the next Step-by-Step.

Highlighting Text

When you read a paper document, you sometimes use a highlighting marker to draw attention to an important part of the document. You can highlight text in a Word document for the same effect. To highlight text, click the arrow next to the Text Highlight Color button in the Font group on the Home tab. A menu of colors opens. Click one of the colors.

If text is selected in the document, the text becomes highlighted with the color you chose. If no text is selected, the pointer changes to the Highlighter pointer, an I-beam pointer with a marker on it, when you position it on top of text in the document. You can drag the pointer over any text you want to highlight. When you are finished, click the Text Highlight Color button again to toggle this command off.

If text is highlighted and you want to remove the highlight, select the highlighted text, and then click the Text Highlight Button. If you'd rather drag over each selection of highlighted text to "erase" the highlighting, you can click the arrow next to the Text Highlight Color button, and then click No Color. The pointer changes to the Highlighter tool, and when you drag over highlighted text, you remove the highlight.

S TEP-BY-STEP 4.6

1. In the Font group, locate the Text Highlight Color button. The colored bar near the bottom of the button indicates what color the highlight will be. Click the **arrow** next to the Text Highlight Color button. A palette of colors opens. Click the **Yellow** box (even if the button already indicates that the current color is yellow). The Text Highlight Color menu closes. The colored bar on the Text Highlight Color button is yellow to reflect the color you chose, and the button is colored orange to indicate that it is selected.

2. Move the pointer so it is positioned anywhere on top of text. The pointer changes to the Highlighter tool.

3. In the paragraph under the *Prices* heading, position the pointer in front of the fourth sentence (in front of the word *For*). Click and drag the pointer through the entire sentence (finishing at *admission to the pits.*). Release the mouse button when you have selected the whole sentence. The fourth sentence is highlighted with yellow. See Figure 4-9.

FIGURE 4-9
Applying a Quick Style

Text Highlight
Color button

Highlighter
tool

STEP-BY-STEP 4.6 Continued

4. In the Font group, click the **Text Highlight Color** button. The button is no longer selected, and the pointer returns to normal.

5. In the same paragraph, select the last sentence (it starts with *Come early*). In the Font group, click the **arrow** next to the Text Highlight Color button. Click the **Bright Green** box. The selected text is highlighted with bright green. The pointer does not change to the Highlighter tool.

6. Select the green highlighted sentence. In the Font group, click the **arrow** next to the Text Highlight Color button. Click **No Color**. The highlighting is removed from the selected text.

7. Save the document and leave it open for the next Step-by Step.

Copying Formatting

Often you will spend time formatting text and then find that you need the same format in another part of the document. You can copy the format of selected text to other text by using the Format Painter button. The Format Painter button is located in the Clipboard group on the Home tab and on the Mini toolbar.

To use the Format Painter command, select the text with the format you want to copy, and then click the Format Painter button. When you move the pointer over text, it changes to the Format Painter tool, which is the I-beam pointer with a paintbrush to its left. Drag the Format Painter tool across the text you want to format. The text changes to the copied format. If you want to copy the format to more than one block of text, double-click the Format Painter button. The button will remain selected and the Format Painter tool stays active until you click the button again to deselect it.

> **Did You Know?**
>
> You can also press the Esc key to turn off the Highlighter or the Format Painter.

STEP-BY-STEP 4.7

1. Select the first line of text in the document (the title).

2. On the Home tab, in the Clipboard group, click the **Format Painter** button. The Format Painter button is selected. Move the pointer so it is on top of any text in the document. The pointer changes to the Format Painter tool.

3. Select the **Schedule** heading. The text is formatted with the same formats as the first line of text. Move the pointer on top of the text. It is the normal pointer again. The Format Painter button is no longer selected.

4. Make sure **Schedule** is still selected, and then, in the Clipboard group, double-click the **Format Painter** button.

STEP-BY-STEP 4.7 Continued

5. Select the **Prices** heading. The format of *Schedule* is copied to *Prices*. Move the pointer on top of the text to see that the Format Painter tool is still active. The Format Painter button is still selected.

6. Click the **Seating** heading. The format is copied again. See Figure 4-10.

FIGURE 4-10
Text after using Format Painter

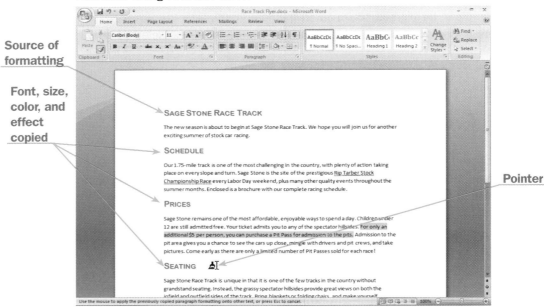

7. In the Clipboard group, click the **Format Painter** button. The button is no longer selected and the pointer returns to normal.

8. Jump to the end of the document, press the **Tab** key twice, and then type your name.

9. Save your changes to the document, and then print it. Leave it open for the next Step-by-Step.

Understanding Styles

In Word, a style is a set of formatting options that have been named and saved. The Normal and No Spacing buttons that you have used are examples of Quick Styles, which are styles available in the Quick Styles gallery on the Home tab. Character styles affect only selected text; paragraph styles affect entire paragraphs.

Using styles can save time and add consistency to a document. For example, if you are working on a long document, such as a research paper, that contains headings, you would want to format the headings to stand out from the regular (the Normal) text. You could do this manually by selecting each heading, changing the font size, and applying font styles, such as bold. You might also change the color of the headings. If your document contained many headings, you would need to do this for each heading, or use the Format Painter to copy the format to each heading. If you changed your mind about the look of the headings, for example, if you decide to use red text instead of bold purple text, you would need to change each heading again.

If you used a style to format your headings, the style could define this type of heading as 14-point bold, purple text. You could then apply that style with the click of the mouse to each heading. If you changed your mind and wanted the headings in red, you could change the style definition to format the text as red instead of purple, and the headings formatted with that style would change red to reflect the new definition.

> **Did You Know?**
>
> If you apply a style to the current paragraph and then press the Enter key, the new paragraph that you create has the same style as the original paragraph.

Applying Quick Styles

Word comes with many built-in Quick Styles. To apply a Quick Style, you click a button in the Styles group on the Home tab. If you want to see the additional Quick Styles available in the Quick Styles gallery, click the More button in the Styles group. This opens the Quick Styles gallery. See Figure 4-11.

FIGURE 4-11
Applying a Quick Style

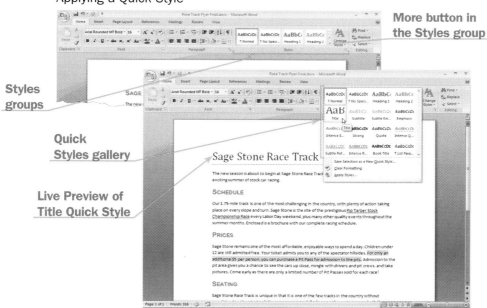

Like some of the direct formatting you applied using buttons in the Font group on the Home tab, you can see a Live Preview of Quick Styles. When the Quick Styles gallery is open, point to a Quick Style to see the effect in the document.

The default style for text is the Normal Quick Style. It is used for ordinary text.

> **Did You Know?**
>
> If you use the Format Painter to copy formatting from text that has a style applied to it, the style is copied to the new text.

STEP-BY-STEP 4.8

1. Save the Race Track Flyer document as **Race Track Flyer Final** followed by your initials.

2. Click anywhere in the first line of text. On the Home tab, locate the Styles group. The Normal style button has a yellow box around it indicating that it is selected.

3. In the Styles group, click the **More** button. The Quick Styles gallery opens. In the second row, first column, click the **Title** style button. The Quick Styles gallery closes and the Title Quick Style is applied to the current paragraph. The text is formatted with the font, color, and size defined by the Title Quick Style. The Title Quick Style also includes a light blue horizontal line under the paragraph.

4. Select the subheading **Schedule**. In the Styles group, click the **More** button to open the Quick Styles gallery. In the first row, third column, click the **Heading 1** style button. The Heading 1 Quick Style is applied to the paragraph. In addition to changing the text to medium-blue 14-point Cambria, the Heading 1 Quick Style removed the extra space after the paragraph.

5. Apply the **Heading 1** Quick Style to the **Prices** and **Seating** headings.

6. In the paragraph under the *Schedule* heading, select the underlined text **Rip Tarber Stock Championship Race**. In the Styles group, click the **More** button. Locate the button with the name *Intense E...*, and then point to it. The ScreenTip labels this button *Intense Emphasis*. Click the **Intense Emphasis** style button. The underline formatting you applied earlier is removed and the formats associated with the Intense Emphasis Quick Style are applied. The selected text is now light blue, bold, and italic.

> **Important**
>
> When you apply a Quick Style, any manual formatting that you've already applied to the text is overridden by the Quick Style formats.

7. Select the yellow-highlighted sentence. Open the Styles gallery. In the second row, last column, click the **Emphasis** style button. The text is formatted with the Emphasis Quick Style, which is the Normal style plus italics. Deselect the text. Note that the highlighting was not removed when you applied the Quick Style. Highlighting can be part of a style definition, but manual highlighting is not removed when you apply a different style.

8. Save the document and leave it open for the next Step-by Step.

Changing Themes

A theme is a coordinated set of fonts, styles, and colors. The theme determines the default font, the color of headings formatted in the Heading Quick styles, and other features of the document. To see the available themes, click the Page Layout tab, and then, in the Themes group, click the Themes button. A gallery of themes opens, as shown in Figure 4-12. Word comes with 20 built-in themes. The default theme is the Office theme.

FIGURE 4-12
Applying a theme

Themes button

Current theme

Themes gallery

Page Layout tab

The definitions of Quick Styles are tied to the themes. For example, in the previous section, the text that you formatted with the Heading 1 Quick Style appeared in bold, medium blue, 14-point Cambria. If you changed to the Apex theme, text formatted with the Heading 1 Quick Style would change to bold, yellow-brown, 14-point Lucida Sans, and if you changed to the Verve theme, Heading 1 text would change to bold, dark pink, 14-point Century Gothic.

> **Did You Know?**
>
> If you apply a style and then apply manual formatting, when you change to a new theme, the manual formatting will still be applied.

STEP-BY-STEP 4.9

1. On the Ribbon, click the **Page Layout** tab. In the Themes group, click the **Themes** button. The Themes gallery opens. The Office theme is the current theme, as indicated by the orange highlighting on the Office button.

> **Did You Know?**
>
> Point to the Themes button on the Page Layout tab to see a ScreenTip that identifies the current theme.

2. In the third row, last column, point to the **Opulent** theme button. Live Preview shows the changes to the document; the title, the headings, and the text you formatted with the Intense Emphasis Quick Style change to purple text, and the font used for all the text changes to Trebuchet MS.

3. Point to several other theme buttons, and watch the Live Preview to see each change.

STEP-BY-STEP 4.7 Continued

4. In the second row, first column, click the **Concourse** theme button. The Themes gallery closes and the Concourse theme is applied to the document. Notice that the document is now two pages long. This is because the Lucida Sans Unicode font used for the body text in the Concourse theme takes up more space than the Calibri font used in the Office theme.

5. Save the document and leave it open for the next Step-by Step.

Did You Know?

Notice in the status bar that the document is now two pages long. Although the font sizes in the new theme are the same as the font sizes in the old theme, the new font takes up more space than the old font.

Redefining an Existing Quick Style

What if none of the Quick Styles formats the text exactly the way you want it to look? You can create your own style. The easiest way to create your own style is to format text with an existing Quick Style, and then make changes until you are satisfied with the final look. To redefine an existing Quick Style, with the formatted text selected, right-click the Quick Style you want to redefine to open a shortcut menu. See Figure 4-13. In the example shown in Figure 4-13, you would click Update Intense Emphasis to Match Selection; for each Quick Style, *Intense Emphasis* in the menu command is replaced with the name of the Quick Style you right-click. The selected text doesn't change, but the Quick Style is redefined to match it. The redefined Quick Style is available only in the current document.

FIGURE 4-13
Redefining a Quick Style

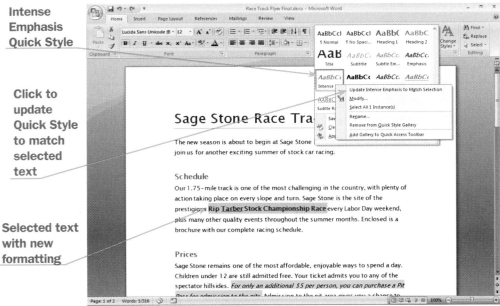

STEP-BY-STEP 4.10

1. In the paragraph under the *Schedule* heading, select the text **Rip Tarber Stock Championship Race**.

2. On the Ribbon, click the **Home** tab. In the Font group, click the **arrow** next to the Font Color button. In the color palette, note the red box around the turquoise color in the top row under Theme Colors. This is the color of the selected text.

3. In the last row of the color palette under Theme Colors, in the third column, click the **Light Turquoise, Background 2, Darker 90%** color.

4. In the Font group, click the **Italic** button to deselect it. In the Font group, click the **arrow** next to the Font Size box, and then click **12**. The selected text is changed to 12-point, dark turquoise text that is not italicized.

5. In the Styles group, click the **More** button. Right-click the **Intense Emphasis** style button. On the shortcut menu, click **Update Intense Emphasis to Match Selection**. The Quick Styles gallery closes. The selected text retains the formatting you applied, and the Intense Emphasis style is redefined to match the formatting of the selected text.

6. In the paragraph under the *Prices* heading, select the sentence highlighted in yellow. In the Styles group, click the **More** button and then click the **Intense Emphasis** style button. The sentence is reformatted with the modified Intense Emphasis style.

7. Save the document and leave it open for the next Step-by-Step.

Creating a New Quick Style

You can also create a brand new Quick Style. Again, the easiest way to do this is to first format text with the font, style, and any other characteristics that you want. To name your style and add it to the Quick Styles gallery, open the Quick Styles gallery, and then click Save Selection as a New Quick Style on the menu at the bottom of the gallery. This opens the Create New Style from Formatting dialog box. Type a name for your new Quick Style in the Name box, as shown in Figure 4-14. The new Quick Style is available only in your document.

FIGURE 4-14
Create New Style from Formatting dialog box

Name for new Quick Style

Extra for Experts

To make a redefined or new Quick Style available to other documents, right-click the Quick Style in the Styles group, click Modify on the shortcut menu to open the Modify Style dialog box, and then click the New documents based on this template option button.

S TEP-BY-STEP 4.11

1. Select the first paragraph in the document under the title. In the Font group, click the **Font Dialog Box Launcher** to open the Font dialog box. In the Font style list, click **Bold**. In the Effects section, click the **Small caps** checkbox to select it. Click **OK**. The dialog box closes and the selected text is reformatted to match the selections you made.

2. With the first paragraph still selected, in the Styles group, click the **More** button. On the menu below the gallery, click **Save Selection as a New Quick Style**.

3. In the Create New Style from Formatting dialog box, type **Important** in the Name box. Click **OK**. The dialog box closes. The new Quick Style appears as a button in the Styles group. If you don't see the new style, click the up arrow in the Styles gallery as many times as needed to scroll up and display the first row in the gallery on the Ribbon.

4. Scroll down to the bottom of the document. (Remember, this is now on page 2.) Position the insertion point in front of your name, and then press the **Enter** key. A new paragraph containing your name is created, and the insertion point is blinking at the beginning of the paragraph.

5. Select your name. In the Styles group, click the **Important** style button. The style is applied to all of the selected text.

6. Save the document and leave it open for the next Step-by Step.

Clearing Formatting

You can use the Clear Formatting command to clear manual formatting and styles. To do this, first select the formatted text to be cleared. You can then click the Clear Formatting button in the Font group on the Home tab. Or, you can open the Quick Styles gallery, and then click Clear Formatting on the menu at the bottom of the gallery, as shown in Figure 4-15. When you remove a style, the Normal Quick Style is automatically applied.

FIGURE 4-15
Locating the Clear Formatting command

Clear Formatting button

Clear Formatting command in Quick Styles gallery

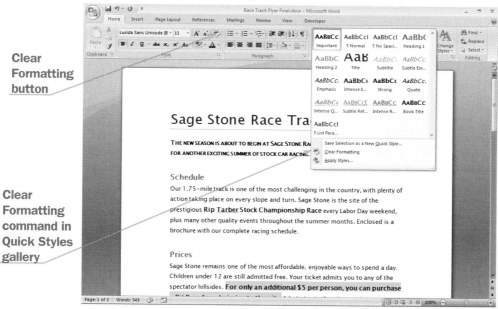

STEP-BY-STEP 4.12

1. Press the **Ctrl+Home** keys. Click anywhere in the first paragraph in the document under the title. In the Font group, click the **Clear Formatting** button. The Important Quick Style is removed from the current paragraph, and the Normal style button in the Styles gallery is selected.

2. Scroll the document down until you can see the second item in the bulleted list. Select **recycle**. In the Styles group, click the **More** button. At the bottom of the Quick Styles gallery, click **Clear Formatting**. The color is removed from the selected word.

3. Save, print, and close the document.

> **Important**
>
> To apply or clear a paragraph style, the insertion point can be located anywhere in the paragraph. To apply or clear a character style, all of the text that you want to affect must be selected.

SUMMARY

In this lesson, you learned:

- Fonts are designs of type that can be used to change the appearance of a document.

- Font size is measured in points. The higher the point size, the larger the characters.

- Common font styles are bold, italic, and underline. These styles can be applied to any font. You can change the color and style of underlines.

- The look of text can be changed by changing its color and adding font effects.

- Highlighting can be used to emphasize important text.

- Use the Format Painter to copy the format and style of blocks of text.

- Styles are predefined sets of formatting options that save time and add consistency to a document.

- A theme is a coordinated set of fonts, styles, and colors. When you change the theme, all text that has a Quick Style applied to it, including the Normal Quick Style, changes to the fonts, colors, and styles in the new theme.

- You can create new Quick Styles by redefining existing Quick Styles or by creating an entirely new Quick Style.

- The Clear Formatting command clears all formatting and styles from selected text.

VOCABULARY *Review*

Define the following terms:

Attribute	Font size	Point
Color palette	Font style	Style
Font	Format Painter	Theme
Font effect		

REVIEW *Questions*

TRUE/FALSE

Circle T if the statement is true or F if the statement is false.

T   F   1. Highlighting text has the same effect as using the Bold button.

T   F   2. The Format Painter command copies text but not the format of the text.

T   F   3. When you change the document theme, you change only the colors used for text.

T   F   4. Text that does not have any other Quick Style applied to it is actually formatted with the Normal Quick Style.

T   F   5. You can create a new Quick Style by redefining an existing one.

WRITTEN QUESTIONS

Write a brief answer to each of the following questions.

1. What is the unit of measurement for fonts?

2. What are three common font styles?

3. How do you open the Font dialog box?

4. Why would you use a style?

5. What are two ways to execute the Clear Formatting command?

PROJECTS

 PROJECT 4-1

You have been asked to prepare a certificate for the employee of the month at the hospital where you work.

1. Open the **Certificate.docx** Data File. Save the document as **Employee Certificate** followed by your initials.

2. Change all text to 20-point Bernard MT Condensed. If the font is not available, choose another appropriate font.

3. Change the color of all the text to the Dark Blue standard color.

4. Apply the Emboss font effect to all the text.

5. Select the first line of text and change it to 36 points and bold.

6. Create a new Quick Style named Certificate Heading based on the first line of text.

7. Change *Joe Harrington* to 36-point Brush Script MT. Replace *Joe Harrington* with your name.

8. Preview the document. Save, print, and close the document.

 PROJECT 4-2

You work as an assistant to the marketing director of Lighthouse Bank. You are making changes to a draft of a pamphlet for customers who are opening their first checking accounts.

1. Open the **Checking Account.docx** Data File. Save the document as **Checking Account Info** followed by your initials.

2. Change the theme to Civic.

3. Apply the Title Quick Style to the title *New Checking Account*.

4. Apply the Heading 2 style to the three headings in the document.

5. Near the bottom of the document, apply the No Spacing style to the first three lines of the bank's address (from *Lighthouse Bank* through *Box 875409*).

6. Highlight all four lines of the address with Gray-25% from the Text Highlight Color button palette.

7. In the last paragraph of the document, replace *the Customer Service Department* with your name. Highlight your name with yellow.

8. Preview the document. Save, print, and close the document.

 PROJECT 4-3

You have been asked to prepare a poster for the break room in your office building with tips about how to be a good employee.

1. Open the **Poster.docx** Data File. Save the document as **Break Room Poster** followed by your initials.

2. Apply the Title Quick Style to the first line of text.

3. Apply the Engrave font effect to the first line of text.

4. Apply the Book Title Quick Style to the second line of text.

5. Change the size of the second line of text to 16 points.

6. Change the color of the second line of text to Dark Blue, Text 2 (in the first row under Theme Colors in the color palette).

7. Use the Format Painter to copy the style of the second line of text to the sixth line of text

under the title (*How can I build good relationships with my co-workers?*).

8. Apply the List Paragraph Quick Style to the four lines of text under both headings.

9. Change the font size of the four lines of text under both headings to 14 points.

10. Change the theme to Verve.

11. Press the Ctrl+End keys, and then type your name. Format your name with italics.

12. Preview the document. Save, print, and close the document.

 PROJECT 4-4

You work as an assistant in a personnel department. Your supervisor has asked you to format the following document that will be included in the employee handbook.

1. Open the **Handbook.docx** Data File. Save the document as **Employee Handbook** followed by your initials.

2. Select all the text and clear the formatting.

3. Apply the Heading 1 Quick Style to the first line of text, *Employee Handbook*, and then change the font size to 22 points.

4. Add a Thick underline to the first line of text using the same color as the text.

5. Create a new Quick Style called Handbook Title based on the first line of text.

6. Apply the Heading 2 Quick Style to the other four headings in the document.

7. Select the heading *Regular Attendance*. Change the font size to 16 points. Change the color to Dark Red, Accent 2, Darker 50% (in the last row under Theme Colors in the color palette).

8. Redefine the Heading 2 Quick Style to match the *Regular Attendance* heading.

9. In the paragraph under the *Confidential Information* heading, italicize the word *Never* in the second to last line.

10. Jump to the end of the document, and then type your name on a new line. Format your name in bold.

11. Preview the document. Save, print, and close the document.

 PROJECT 4-5

You have been asked to format the information sheet for the golf tournament benefiting the local food bank.

1. Open the **Golf Tournament 2.docx** Data File. Save the document as **Formatted Golf Tournament Notice** followed by your initials.

2. Choose a different theme. Be sure your choice is appropriate for a golf tournament information sheet and that the colors go with the colors in the image at the top of the sheet.

3. In the four lines at the bottom of the sheet, change the format of the word in front of the colon to a different font, color, and style. (Use the same formatting for each of the four words.) Format all four lines in a larger text size.

4. Underline the title. Use the style and color of your choice, but do not underline with the same color as the title text and do not use the single underline style.

5. Apply a font effect to the title.

6. In the third line under the title, replace *Robert Shade* with your name.

7. Preview the document. Save, print, and close the document.

CRITICAL*Thinking*

 ACTIVITY 4-1

Create a certificate honoring a person in an organization to which you belong.

 ACTIVITY 4-2

You work for a photo lab. In addition to film developing, the lab also offers reprints, enlargements, slides, black-and-white prints, copies and restorations, posters, and passport photos. Your manager wants to include a list of services available with each customer's order, and he asks you to create it. List each service, how much it costs, and how much time it takes to complete. Choose an appropriate theme, and make effective use of Quick Styles, fonts, font sizes and style, colors, and effects. Save the document as **Photo Lab**. Print and close the document.

 ACTIVITY 4-3

Hidden text can be useful if you want to insert text in a document that won't print by default. But what if you forgot that you included hidden text in a file you sent to someone? Use Help to find out how to remove hidden data from a document.

FORMATTING PARAGRAPHS AND DOCUMENTS

OBJECTIVES

Upon completion of this lesson, you will be able to:

- Show and hide the ruler.
- Set the margins of a document.
- Align text.
- Adjust paragraph indents.
- Adjust line and paragraph spacing.
- Change vertical alignment.
- Set and modify tab stops.
- Create and modify bulleted and numbered lists.
- Create an outline numbered list.
- Organize a document in Outline view.

Estimated Time: 1 hour

VOCABULARY

Alignment

Bullet

Center

First-line indent

Hanging indent

Indent

Inside margin
(gutter margin)

Justify

Leader

Left-align

Margin

Mirrored margins

Multilevel list

Negative indent
(outdent)

Outline numbered list

Outside margin

Right-align

Tab stop (tab)

Vertical alignment

Formatting Paragraphs and Documents

Just as you apply formatting to text, you can also use Word features to format paragraphs and entire documents. Formatting presents a consistent and attractive style throughout a document, allowing readers to understand your message more easily.

Viewing the Ruler

Word provides rulers along the top and left margins to help you as you format your documents. The ruler is hidden by default. To display it, you can click the View Ruler button located at the top of the vertical scroll bar on the right side of the window. You can also click the View tab on the Ribbon, and then, in the Show/Hide group, click the Ruler check box.

Setting Margins

Margins are the blank areas around the top, bottom, and sides of a page. Word sets predefined, or default, margin settings, which you may keep or change. To change margin settings, click the Page Layout tab on the Ribbon, and then click the Margins button. You can choose from one of the preset margin settings, as shown in Figure 5-1, or you can click Custom Margins at the bottom to open the Margins tab of the Page Setup dialog box, as shown in Figure 5-2.

FIGURE 5-1
Margins menu

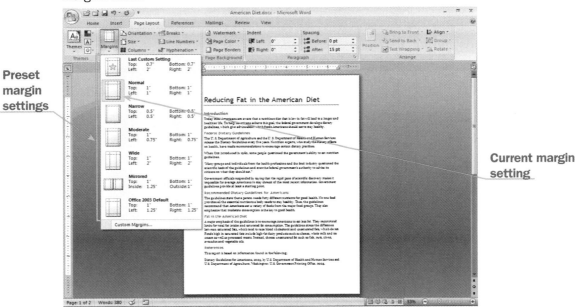

Preset margin settings

Current margin setting

FIGURE 5-2
Margins tab in the Page Setup dialog box

Margins tab

Margins section

Click arrows to change measurement one-tenth of an inch at a time

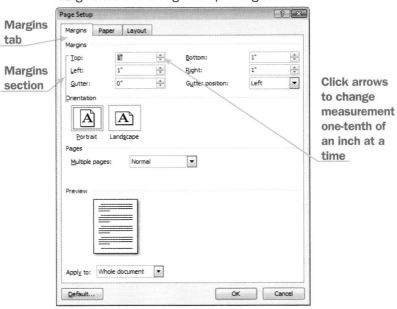

STEP-BY-STEP 5.1

1. Open the **Diet.docx** Data File. Save the document as **American Diet** followed by your initials.

2. If the ruler is not displayed below the Ribbon, above the vertical scroll bar, click the **View Ruler** button to display the ruler.

3. On the Ribbon, click the **View** tab. In the Zoom group, click the **One Page** button. Note that the current margins are one inch on all sides.

4. On the Ribbon, click the **Page Layout** tab. In the Page Setup group, click the **Margins** button. The current margin, Normal, is selected. Click **Wide**. The left and right margins increase to two inches.

5. In the Page Setup group, click the **Margins** button. Wide is selected on the menu. Click **Custom Margins** at the bottom of the menu. The Page Setup dialog box opens with the Margins tab on top.

6. In the Top box, click the **down arrow** three times to change the number to 0.7". Press the **Tab** key. The value in the Bottom box is selected. Type **.7**. Click **OK**. The dialog box closes and the top and bottom margins are changed.

7. In the Page Setup group, click the **Margins** button again. Notice that Last Custom Setting is selected at the top of the menu and that the settings match the custom settings you chose. Click a blank area of the document window to close the Margins menu without changing the current setting.

8. In the lower-right corner of the window, click the **Zoom In** button as many times as necessary to change the zoom to 100%.

9. Save the document and leave it open for the next Step-by-Step.

Extra for Experts

Pages in books and magazines are often formatted with **mirrored margins**, where instead of left and right margins, the page has inside and outside margins. The **inside margin** (also called the **gutter margin**) is the right margin on a left page and the left margin on the right page— the margins closest to the inside of the page, near the binding. The **outside margin** is the left margin on the left page and the right margin on the right page.

Aligning Text

 Alignment refers to the position of text between the margins. As Figure 5-3 shows, you can left-align, center, right-align, or justify your text. To align text, you click one of the Alignment buttons in the Paragraph group on the Home tab, as shown in Figure 5-4.

FIGURE 5-3
Examples of different text alignments

This paragraph is left-aligned.

This paragraph is centered.

This paragraph is right-aligned.

This text is justified because the text is aligned at both the left and right margins. This text is justified because the text is aligned at both the left and right margins.

FIGURE 5-4
Using Alignment buttons

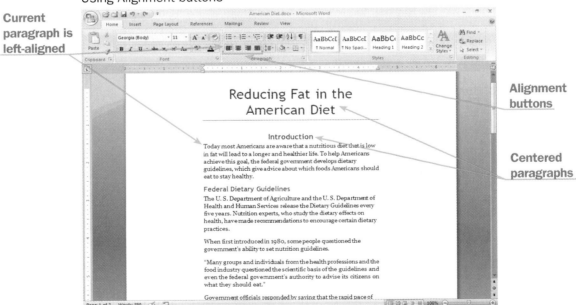

Left-aligned and justified are the two most commonly used text alignments in documents. For invitations, titles, and headings, text is often center-aligned. Page numbers and dates are often right aligned.

STEP-BY-STEP 5.2

1. Click anywhere in the title at the beginning of the document.

2. On the Ribbon, click the **Home** tab. In the Paragraph group, notice that the Align Text Left button is selected. Only one of the alignment buttons can be selected at a time.

3. In the Paragraph group, click the **Center** button. The title is centered. Alignment settings affect the current paragraph; you don't need to select all of the text.

> **Did You Know?**
>
> You can also click the Center button on the Mini toolbar.

4. Click anywhere in the **Introduction** heading. In the Paragraph group, click the **Center** button.

5. Click anywhere in the third paragraph under the *Federal Dietary Guidelines* heading (it starts with *"Many groups and individuals"*). In the Paragraph group, click the **Justify** button. The paragraph is justified.

6. Press the **Ctrl+End** keys. You jump to the end of the document. Select the last two paragraphs (*Prepared by Roberta Sanchez*).

7. In the Paragraph group, click the **Align Text Right** button on the toolbar. The last two paragraphs are right-aligned.

8. Save the document and leave it open for the next Step-by-Step.

Changing Indents

An indent is the space between text and a document's margin. You can indent text either from the left margin, from the right margin, or from both margins. You can also indent only the first line of a paragraph or all the lines in a paragraph *except* the first line.

Indenting Entire Paragraphs

To quickly change the indent of an entire paragraph one-half inch at a time, click the Increase Indent or Decrease Indent buttons in the Paragraph group on the Home tab. To change the indent by different amounts, you can drag the Left and Right Indent markers on the ruler. To change the left indent, you need to drag the Left Indent marker, which is the small rectangle at the bottom of the icon at the left margin. Note, however, that the entire icon will move when you drag it. See Figure 5-5. Indenting from both margins sets off paragraphs from the main body of text. You might use this type of indent for long quotations.

FIGURE 5-5
Setting paragraph indents

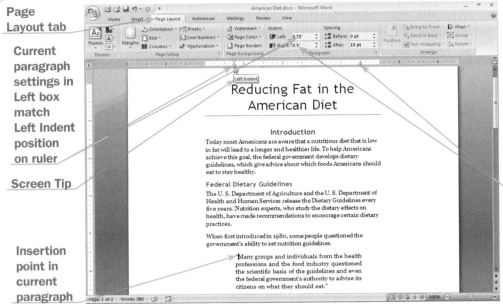

You can also change the left and right indents by clicking the Page Layout tab, and then setting the exact measurement of the indents in the Left and Right boxes in the Paragraph group, as shown in Figure 5-5.

STEP-BY-STEP 5.3

Extra for Experts

The Intense Quote Quick Style reformats paragraphs so they are indented from both margins, changes the color of the text to the Accent 1 color in the color palette, and adds a colored horizontal line under the last paragraph in the quote.

1. Scroll up in the document, if necessary, and then position the insertion point in the third paragraph under the *Federal Dietary Guidelines* section (it starts with *"Many groups and individuals*). In the Paragraph group, click the **Increase Indent** button twice. The entire paragraph indents one inch, and the Indent marker on the left end of the ruler moves to the one-inch mark on the ruler.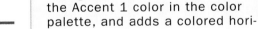

2. In the Paragraph group, click the **Decrease Indent** button. The paragraph indent moves back to the one-half inch mark.

3. On the ruler, position the pointer on top of the **rectangle** at the bottom of the Left Indent marker so that the Left Indent ScreenTip appears. Drag the **Left Indent** marker to the three-quarter-inch mark on the ruler. The paragraph indents another quarter of an inch.

STEP-BY-STEP 5.3 Continued

4. On the ruler, drag the **Right Indent** marker to the left to the 4-inch mark. The paragraph with the quote is indented three-quarters of an inch from the left margin and one-half inch from the right margin.

5. Save the document and leave it open for the next Step-by-Step.

Setting a First-Line Indent

A first-line indent is just what it sounds like— only the first line of a paragraph is indented. You are familiar with this because it is the normal format for paragraphs set in type in books, newspapers, and magazines. To indent the first line of a paragraph, you can drag the First Line Indent marker on the ruler, as shown in Figure 5-6. After you set a first-line indent in one paragraph, all subsequent paragraphs you type will have the same first-line indent.

> **Extra for Experts**
>
> If you've already typed a paragraph, you can click in front of the first line, and then press the Tab key. Instead of inserting a tab marker, this sets the first line indent to one-half inch. If you click in front of any other line in the paragraph and then press the Tab key, the entire paragraph is indented one-half inch. This behavior is controlled by the AutoFormat As You Type feature.

> **Computer Concepts**
>
> Some people indent the first line of a paragraph by pressing the Tab key before they start typing. It's better to set a first-line indent because each time you press the Enter key, the new paragraph will automatically have a first-line indent. Also, if you want to change the amount the paragraphs are indented or remove the indent completely, you can change the definition of the style or Quick Style applied to the paragraph, or just select all the paragraphs and reset the indent.

FIGURE 5-6
Setting a first-line indent

First-line indent set for selected paragraphs

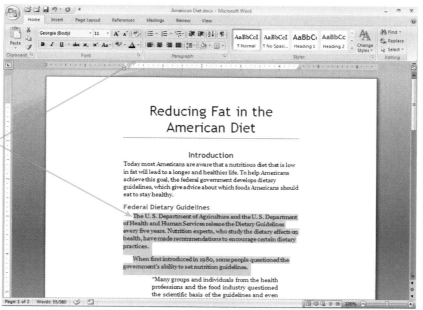

STEP-BY-STEP 5.4

1. Select the first two paragraphs under the *Federal Dietary Guidelines* heading.

2. On the ruler, position the pointer over the top triangle on the Left Indent marker so that the First Line Indent ScreenTip appears. Drag the **First Line Indent** marker to the one-quarter-inch mark on the ruler. The first line of the two selected paragraphs is indented one-quarter inch.

3. Select the paragraph above the *Recommended Dietary Guidelines for Americans* heading. Press and hold the **Ctrl** key. Use the mouse to select the paragraphs under the *Recommended Dietary Guidelines for Americans* and the *Fat in the American Diet* headings. Release the **Ctrl** key. The three paragraphs are selected.

4. On the ruler, drag the **First Line Indent** marker to the one-quarter-inch mark. The first line of the three selected paragraphs is indented one-quarter inch. Click a blank area of the document to deselect the text.

5. Save the document and leave it open for the next Step-by-Step.

> **Extra for Experts**
>
> You can also create a **negative indent**, sometimes called an **outdent**, by dragging the indent markers on the ruler to the left past the left margin, or by setting a negative number in the Left box in the Paragraph group on the Page Layout tab.

Setting a Hanging Indent

 You can also create hanging indents in which the first full line of text is not indented but the following lines are, as shown in Figure 5-7. To set a hanging indent, drag the Hanging Indent marker on the ruler to the right of the First Line Indent marker. Hanging indents appear commonly in lists and documents such as glossaries and bibliographies.

FIGURE 5-7
Hanging indent applied

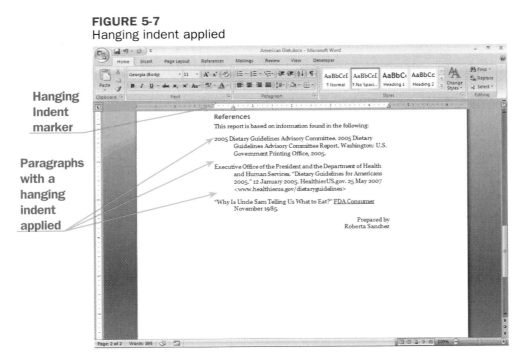

STEP-BY-STEP 5.5

1. Select the last three paragraphs in the document above the *Prepared by* line.

2. On the ruler, position the pointer over the bottom triangle on the Left Indent marker so that the Hanging Indent ScreenTip appears. Drag the **Hanging Indent** marker to the one-half-inch mark. All the lines except for the first line of the three selected paragraphs are indented one-half inch.

3. Save the document and leave it open for the next Step-by-Step.

Using the Paragraph Dialog Box to Set Indents

You can set indents on the Indents and Spacing tab in the Paragraph dialog box. You can open the Paragraph dialog box both from the Home tab and from the Page Layout tab by clicking the Paragraph Dialog Box Launcher in the Paragraph group. See Figure 5-8.

FIGURE 5-8
Paragraph dialog box

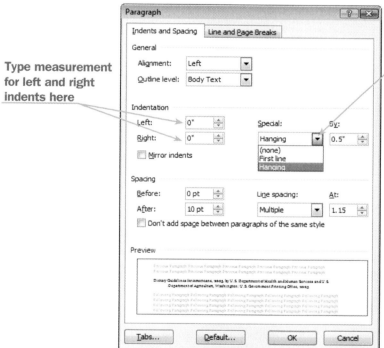

Type measurement for left and right indents here

Click to set regular (none), First Line, or Hanging indent

In the Indentation section on the Indents and Spacing tab, change the measurements in the Left and Right boxes to change the left and right indents. This is similar to using the Left and Right boxes in the Paragraph group on the Page Layout tab. To set a first-line or hanging indent, click the Special arrow, choose the type of indent you want, and then adjust the measurement in the By box.

Extra for Experts

If you are using mirror margins, you can use mirror indents. On the Indents and Spacing tab in the Paragraph dialog box, click the Mirror indents checkbox to select it.

Adjusting Line Spacing

You can adjust line spacing in a document, which is the amount of space between lines of text. Single-spaced text has no extra space between each line; double-spaced text has an extra line of space between each line of text. You might be surprised to learn that the default setting in a Word document is 1.15 lines, not single spaced. The little bit of extra space makes text easier to read on the screen. See Figure 5-9 for examples of different spacing.

FIGURE 5-9
Different line spacing

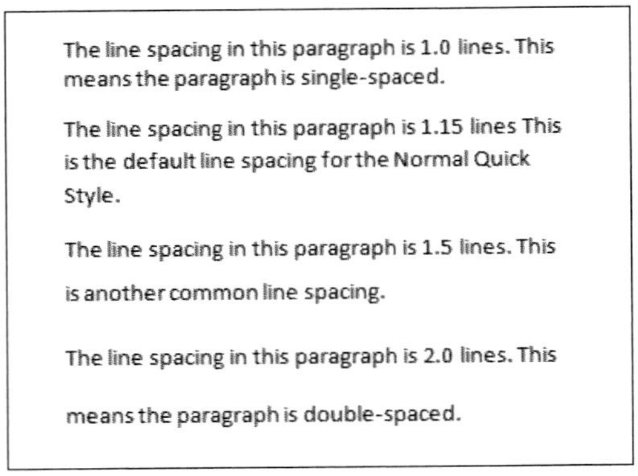

The line spacing in this paragraph is 1.0 lines. This means the paragraph is single-spaced.

The line spacing in this paragraph is 1.15 lines This is the default line spacing for the Normal Quick Style.

The line spacing in this paragraph is 1.5 lines. This is another common line spacing.

The line spacing in this paragraph is 2.0 lines. This

means the paragraph is double-spaced.

To change line spacing, you can click the Line spacing button in the Paragraph group on the Home tab, and then choose a new line spacing option on the menu.

Did You Know?

Although the default line spacing for the Normal Quick Style is 1.15 lines, the default spacing for the No Spacing Quick Style is 1.0 lines.

STEP-BY-STEP 5.6

1. Press the **Ctrl+Home** keys, and then click anywhere in the paragraph under the *Introduction* heading. Notice that the Normal Quick Style button is selected in the Styles group on the Home tab.

2. On the Home tab, in the Paragraph group, click the **Line spacing** button. A check mark appears next to 1.15, the current line spacing, as shown in Figure 5-10.

STEP-BY-STEP 5.6 Continued

FIGURE 5-10
Changing the line spacing

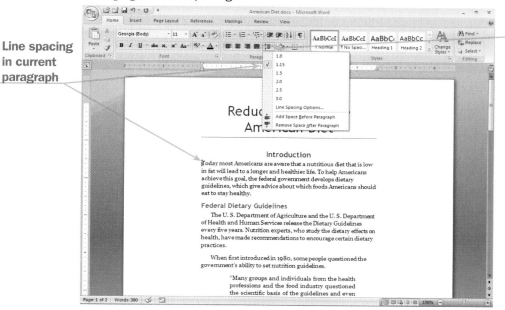

3. Click a blank area of the document to close the menu without making a selection. Click anywhere in the title. In the Styles group, click the **More** button. Notice that the Title Quick Style button is selected.

4. In the Paragraph group, click the **Line Spacing** button again. The line spacing for the title is 1.0 (single-spaced). Single spacing is part of the Title Quick Style definition. Click a blank area of the document to close the menu.

5. Press the **Ctrl+A** keys. All the text in the document is selected. In the Paragraph group, click the **Line Spacing** button. Click **1.0**. All the text in the document is single-spaced.

6. Save the document and leave it open for the next Step-by-Step.

Adjusting Paragraph Spacing

Another way to increase the readability of a page is to modify the paragraph spacing—the amount of space between paragraphs. You've seen this already because the default in Word is to add 10 points of space after each paragraph. Often heading styles include space before or after the heading paragraph as part of the style definition. For example, in this book, the format of the *Step-by-Step* headings include 29 points of space above them, and the format of the blue headings, such as the *Adjusting Paragraph Spacing* heading above, includes 42 points of space before and 27 points of space after. You can adjust the space before or after a paragraph in the Paragraph group on the Page Layout tab, as shown in Figure 5-11.

FIGURE 5-11
Examining paragraph spacing

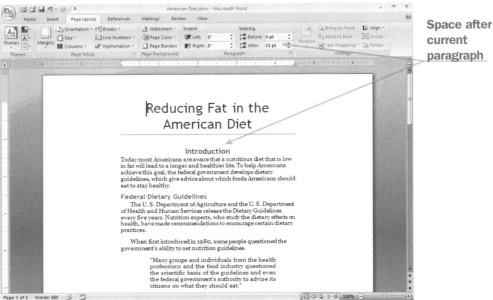

STEP-BY-STEP 5.7

1. Click anywhere in the paragraph under the *Introduction* heading. On the Ribbon, click the **Page Layout** tab. Locate the Spacing section in the Paragraph group, and notice that 10 pt appears in the After box. This is the default for the Normal style.

2. Click anywhere in the title, which is formatted with the Title Quick Style. The value in the After box changes to 15 pt. Click anywhere in the *Introduction* heading. This paragraph is formatted with the Heading 1 Quick Style. The value in the Before box changes to 24 pt and the value in the After box changes to 0 pt.

3. Click anywhere in the *Federal Dietary Guidelines* heading. This is formatted with the Heading 2 Quick Style. In the Paragraph group, click the **up arrow** next to the Before box twice to change the value to 18 pt.

STEP-BY-STEP 5.7 Continued

4. If necessary, scroll down in the document so that you can see both the *Federal Dietary Guidelines* and the *Recommended Dietary Guidelines for Americans* headings. The *Recommended Dietary Guidelines for Americans* heading is also formatted with the Heading 2 Quick Style, as are the other two headings in the document.

5. On the Ribbon, click the **Home** tab. Make sure the insertion point is still in the *Federal Dietary Guidelines* heading.

6. In the Styles group, right-click the **Heading 2** style button, and then click **Update Heading 2 to Match Selection**. Each paragraph formatted with the Heading 2 style is modified so that there are 18 points of space before it.

7. Click in the third paragraph under the *Federal Dietary Guidelines* heading (the paragraph that is indented from both the right and left margins). On the Ribbon, click the **Page Layout** tab. Change the space before and after the paragraph to **12 points**.

8. Press the **Ctrl+End** keys. Select **Roberta Sanchez**, and then type your name.

9. Save, print, and close the document, but leave Word open for the next Step-by-Step.

Changing Vertical Alignment

Vertical alignment refers to positioning text between the top and bottom margins of a document. You can align text with the top of the page, center the text, distribute the text equally between the top and bottom margins (justify), or align the text with the bottom of the page. To vertically align text, click the Page Setup Dialog Box Launcher and then click the Layout tab, as shown in Figure 5-12. In the Page section, click the arrow next to the Vertical alignment box and choose Top, Center, Justified, or Bottom.

FIGURE 5-12
Layout tab in Page Setup dialog box

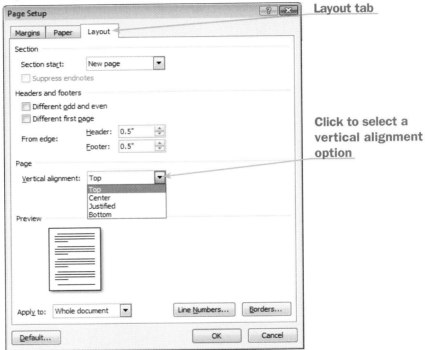

S TEP-BY-STEP 5.8

1. Create a new Word document. Save the document as **American Diet Title Page** followed by your initials.

2. Type your name, and then press the **Enter** key. Type the following:
Health and Nutrition 101
Reducing Fat in the American Diet

3. On the Ribbon, click the **View** tab. In the Zoom group, click the **One Page** button.

4. Select all the text. On the Ribbon, click the **Home** tab. In the Font group, click the **arrow** next to the Font Size button, and then click **20**. In the Paragraph group, click the **Center** button. Deselect the text.

STEP-BY-STEP 5.8 Continued

5. On the Ribbon, click the **Page Layout** tab. In the Themes group, click the **Themes** button, and then click **Urban**. This is the theme used in the American Diet document.

6. In the Page Setup group, click the **Page Setup Dialog Box Launcher**. The Page Setup dialog box opens with the Margins tab on top.

7. At the top of the dialog box, click the **Layout** tab. The dialog box changes to show the commands on the Layout tab.

8. In the Page section, click the **arrow** next to the Vertical alignment box, and then click **Center**. Click **OK**. The dialog box closes and the text is centered vertically on the page.

9. Save, print, and close the document, but leave Word open for the next Step-by-Step.

Understanding Tab Stops

Tab stops, or tabs, mark the place where the insertion point will stop when you press the Tab key. Tab stops are useful for creating tables or aligning numbered items. In Word, default tab stops are set every half inch and are left-aligned. Text alignment can be set with left, right, center, or decimal tab stops. See Figure 5-13 for examples of some of these tab stops. See Table 5-1 for a description of tab stops.

FIGURE 5-13
Types of tabs

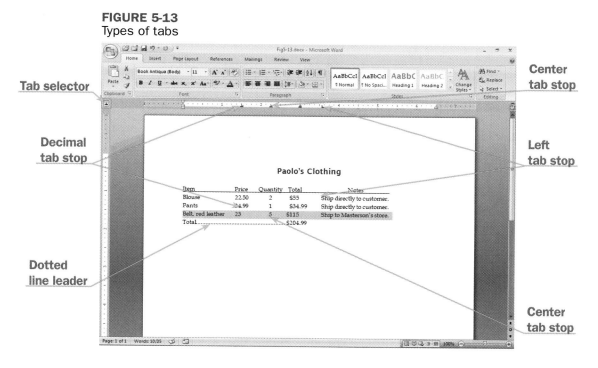

TABLE 5-1
Tab stops

TAB	TAB NAME	FUNCTION
⌞	Left Tab	Left-aligns selected text at the point indicated on the horizontal ruler. This is the default tab.
⌟	Right Tab	Right-aligns selected text at the point indicated on the horizontal ruler. This is useful for aligning page numbers in a table of contents.
⊥	Center Tab	Centers selected text at the point indicated on the horizontal ruler. This is used with titles and announcements.
⊥	Decimal Tab	Aligns selected text on the decimal point at the point indicated on the horizontal ruler. This is helpful when preparing price lists, invoices, and menus.

Setting, Modifying, and Clearing Tab Stops

To set a tab stop, select the paragraph, and then click the ruler at the location you want to set the tab. A tab stop marker appears on the ruler at the location you clicked. If you want to insert a tab stop other than a left tab stop, click the tab selector at the far left of the ruler. Each time you click, it changes to another type of tab—left, right, center, or decimal. To move a tab stop, drag the tab stop marker to a new location on the ruler. To remove a tab, drag the marker off the ruler.

> **Did You Know?**
>
> The tab selector has additional options—Bar ┃, First Line Indent ▽, and Hanging Indent ⌶. Keep clicking the tab selector to return to the Left Tab icon.

> **Extra for Experts**
>
> The Bar Tab ┃ is not a tab stop. It inserts a vertical line in the paragraph.

STEP-BY-STEP 5.9

1. Open the **NADA Memo.docx** Data File. Save the document as **NADA Office Supplies Memo** followed by your initials.

2. If paragraph marks are not displayed, in the Paragraph group on the Home tab, click the **Show/Hide ¶** button. If the ruler is not displayed, on the Ribbon, click the **View** tab. In the Show/Hide group, click the **Ruler** checkbox to select it. Notice that there are tab marks in each line in the memo header. The tab marks position the text after the tab mark at the next default tab stop. For all the lines except the *From* line, this is one-half inch. Because the text *From:* extends to the half-inch mark, the text after the tab mark is moved to the next default tab stop, one inch.

3. In the memo header, select all four paragraphs (from *To* through *Date*). Locate the tab selector to the left of the ruler below the Ribbon. If it is not displaying the Left Tab icon, click it as many times as necessary to display the Left Tab icon.

4. On the ruler, click the **three-quarter-inch** mark. A Left Tab marker is inserted on the ruler. In the selected paragraphs, the text after the tab mark moves over to left-align at the tab marker you inserted.

> **Did You Know?**
>
> Position the pointer over the tab selector or the tab stop marker on the ruler to see the type of tab.

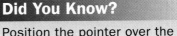

STEP-BY-STEP 5.9 Continued

5. Scroll down until you can see all the items in the list below the paragraph in the body of the memo (from *Surge protector* through *Total*). Select all of the items in the list. The items in the first column are left-aligned at the one-half inch mark, the first default tab stop. The items in the second column appear at the next available default tab stop in that line.

6. To the left of the ruler, click the **tab selector** twice. It changes to the Right Tab icon.

7. On the ruler, click the **3½-inch** mark. The first column in the list right-aligns at 3½ inches. You wanted the prices to right-align. Inserting a tab stop marker means that all the default tab stops before the tab stop marker are erased.

8. Click the **tab selector** five times to return to the Left Tab icon. On the ruler, click the **half-inch** mark. The first column in the list again left-aligns at one-half inch on the ruler, and the second column in the list right-aligns at the 3½-inch mark on the ruler. The price of the first item, *Surge protector*, doesn't have a decimal point, so the dollar amount doesn't align with the other dollar amounts.

9. On the ruler at the 3½-inch mark, drag the **Right Tab** stop marker down and off the ruler. The tab stop marker disappears and the prices are aligned at the next default tab stop marker in the line again.

10. Click the tab selector three times. It changes to the Decimal Tab icon.

11. On the ruler, click the **3½-inch** mark. The dollar amounts align on the decimal point, as shown in Figure 5-14. (The dollar amount for the first item in the list doesn't have a decimal point, but it is understood that it is the same as *29.00*.)

FIGURE 5-14
Left and decimal tab stops set for selected list

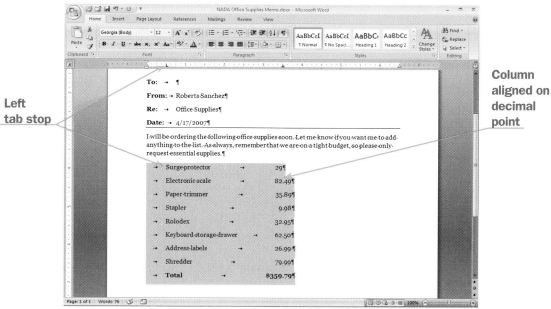

12. Save the document and leave it open for the next Step-by-Step.

Setting Leaders

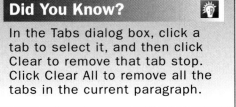

Leaders are solid, dotted, or dashed lines that fill the blank space before a tab setting. Leaders are often used in tables of contents. To insert a leader, open the Tabs dialog box, as shown in Figure 5-15. To do this, double-click a tab stop marker on the ruler, or on the Home or Page Layout tabs, click the Paragraph Dialog Box Launcher, and then click Tabs in the Paragraph dialog box. In the Leader section of the Tabs dialog box, click the option button next to the leader you want to use. If you want to set leaders for more than one tab stop, click Set, and then select the next tab stop and the leader you want to set.

Did You Know?

In the Tabs dialog box, click a tab to select it, and then click Clear to remove that tab stop. Click Clear All to remove all the tabs in the current paragraph.

FIGURE 5-15
Tabs dialog box

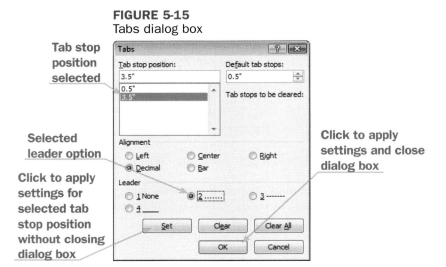

STEP-BY-STEP 5.10

1. Make sure the list under the first paragraph in the body of the memo is still selected. On the ruler, double-click the **tab stop marker** at the 3½ inch-mark. The Tabs dialog box opens. You want to set a leader in front of the tab at the 3½-inch mark. (If the Page Setup dialog box opened instead, click Cancel and try again. If you inserted a new tab stop marker on the ruler, drag it off the ruler, and then try again.)

2. In the Tab stop position list, click **3.5"**. The value is selected.

3. In the Leader section, click the **2 ....** option button. You are only setting the leader for one tab stop, so you do not need to click Set. Click **OK**. The dialog box closes and dotted leaders are inserted in front of the items aligned at the 3½-inch mark.

4. In the *To* line in the memo header, position the insertion point after the tab mark. Type your name.

5. Save, print, and close the document, but leave Word open for the next Step-by-Step.

Using Bulleted and Numbered Lists

Sometimes you may want to create a bulleted or numbered list in a document. A numbered list is useful when items appear sequentially, such as instructions. A bulleted list often is used when the order of items does not matter. A **bullet** is any small character that appears before an item. Small, solid circles are often used as bullets, but other symbols and icons, as well as pictures, may serve as bullets.

Creating Bulleted and Numbered Lists

You have already used the AutoFormat As You Type feature to create a numbered list. Another way to create a numbered list as you type is to create a new paragraph, and then, in the Paragraph group on the Home tab, click the Numbering button. Likewise, to create a bulleted list as you type, click the Bullets button in the Paragraph group.

When you are finished adding items to the list, press the Enter key twice. Pressing it the first time inserts a new bulleted or numbered item. When you press the Enter key a second time without typing anything, the AutoFormat As You Type feature assumes you are finished with the list and changes the new paragraph to a Normal paragraph. You can also click the Bullets or Numbering button in the Paragraph group to turn the feature off, or if the next paragraph is formatted with the Normal style, you can click the Normal style button in the Quick Styles gallery.

You can also change a list that you already typed to a bulleted or numbered list by selecting all the items in the list, and then clicking either the Bullets or Numbering button in the Paragraph group.

> **Did You Know?**
>
> You can also click the Bullets button on the Mini toolbar.

STEP-BY-STEP 5.11

1. Open the **Diet Guidelines.docx** Data File. Save the document as **American Diet Guidelines** followed by your initials.

2. Select the two paragraphs in the first indented list.

3. On the Home tab, in the Paragraph group, click the **Numbering** button. Numbers are inserted in front of each item, and the extra space after each paragraph is removed.

STEP-BY-STEP 5.11 Continued

4. In the list, click at the end of the first line (after *healthy weight*). Press the **Enter** key. A new numbered item 2 is created. Type **Be physically active each day**. See Figure 5-16.

FIGURE 5-16
Numbered list

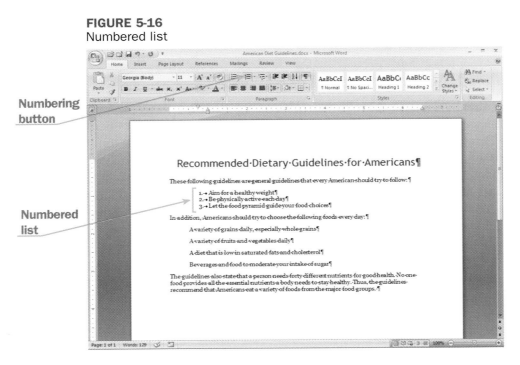

5. Select all the items in the second indented list. On the Home tab, in the Paragraph group, click the **Bullets** button. The paragraphs are changed to a bulleted list.

6. Click after the last item in the list (after *sugar*). Press the **Enter** key. A new bulleted item is created. Type **Food with less salt**. See Figure 5-17.

STEP-BY-STEP 5.11 Continued

FIGURE 5-17
Bulleted list

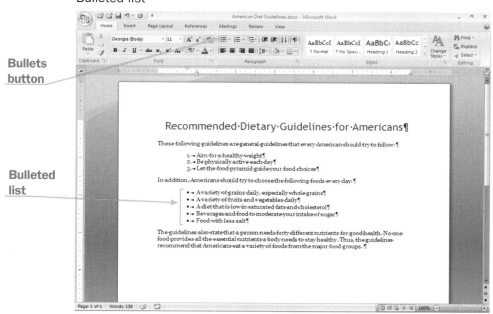

Bullets button

Bulleted list

7. Press the **Enter** key. A new bulleted item is created. Press the **Enter** key again. The bullet is removed and a new blank paragraph is created. Type **These guidelines emphasize that moderate consumption is the key to good health.**

8. Save the document and leave it open for the next Step-by-Step.

Customizing Bulleted and Numbered Lists

 You can customize bulleted and numbered lists. Lists are automatically indented and formatted with a hanging indent. You can change the indents by dragging the indent markers on the ruler.

You can also customize the bullets and the numbers in a list. To do this, click the arrow next to the Bullets or Numbering buttons in the Paragraph group to open a gallery of bullet or number styles, as shown in Figures 5-18 and 5-19. Click a different style in the gallery to change the bullets or numbers to that style.

FIGURE 5-18
Bulleted list styles

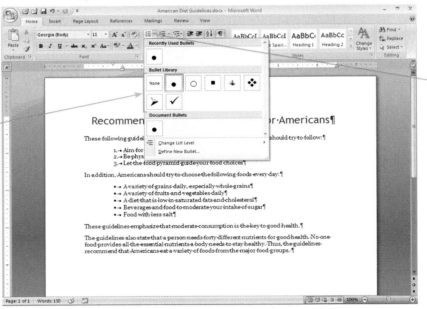

Arrow next to Bullets button

Bulleted list styles

FIGURE 5-19
Numbered list styles

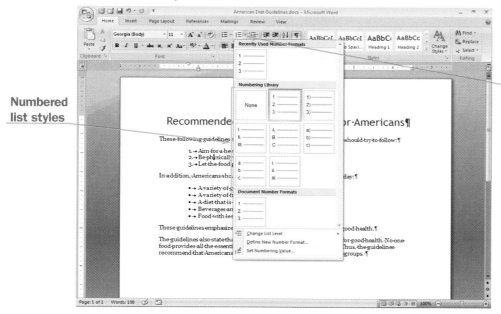

Numbered
list styles

Arrow next
to Numbering
button

STEP-BY-STEP 5.12

1. Select the three numbered list items. (The numbers themselves will not be selected.)

2. On the Home tab, in the Paragraph group, click the **arrow** next to the Numbering button. Click the **uppercase Roman numerals** button. The numbers in the list change to Roman numerals.

3. On the ruler, drag the **Left Indent** marker to the 1¼-inch mark. Notice that the other indent markers followed the Left Indent marker to keep the indents set the same distance apart. The indents change so that the numbers are aligned at the one-inch mark and the text after the numbers aligns at the 1¼-inch mark.

4. Select the bulleted list. (The bullets will not be selected.)

5. On the Home tab, in the Paragraph group, click the **arrow** next to the Bullets button. Click the **arrow** pointing to the right and shaded half black and half white. The bullets in the list change to right-pointing arrows.

6. Press the **Ctrl+End** keys, press the **Enter** key, and then type your name.

7. Save, print, and close the document, but leave Word open for the next Step-by-Step.

Creating a Multilevel List

A multilevel list is a list with two or more levels of bullets or numbering. A numbered multilevel list is sometimes called an **outline numbered list**. An easy way to create a multilevel list is to use the Multilevel List button in the Paragraph group. When you click it, a gallery of multilevel list styles opens, as shown in Figure 5-20. Click a style, and then start typing.

FIGURE 5-20
Multilevel list styles

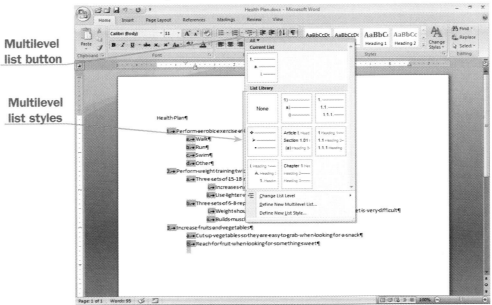

Multilevel list button

Multilevel list styles

You can create a lower-level item in a list in one of three ways: After pressing the Enter key to create the next item in the list, press the Tab key; click the Increase Indent button in the Paragraph group; or click the Multilevel List button in the Paragraph group, point to Change List Level, and then select the level you want in the submenu. Likewise, you can move up a level from an indented level in one of three ways: press the Shift+Tab keys, click the Decrease Indent button in the Paragraph group, or use the Change List Level submenu.

You can also create multilevel lists in an ordinary bulleted or numbered list using the same methods to change levels, but it's easier to choose the exact format you want when you use the Multilevel List button.

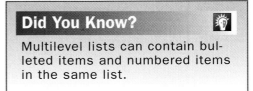

Did You Know?

Multilevel lists can contain bulleted items and numbered items in the same list.

STEP-BY-STEP 5.13

1. Create a new Word document. Save it as **Health Plan** followed by your initials.

2. Type **Health Plan**, and then press the **Enter** key.

3. On the Home tab, in the Paragraph group, click the **Multilevel List** button. In the gallery, click the list style that uses Arabic numbers (*1.*) as the first level, lowercase letters (*a.*) as the second level, and lowercase Roman numerals (*i.*) as the third level.

STEP-BY-STEP 5.13 Continued

4. Type **Perform aerobic exercise at least three times a week.**, and then press the **Enter** key. A second item at the first level is created.

5. On the Home tab, in the Paragraph group, click the **Increase Indent** button. The paragraph is changed to a second-level item.

6. Type the following, pressing the **Enter** key after you type each item:
Walk
Run
Swim
Other

7. If you didn't press the **Enter** key after entering the last item, press it now. In the Paragraph group, click the **Decrease Indent** button. The current paragraph is changed to a first-level item.

8. Type **Perform weight training twice a week.**, and then press the **Enter** key. Press the **Tab** key. The new item is changed to a second-level item.

9. Type **Three sets of 15–18 reps**, and then press the **Enter** key. Press the **Tab** key. The item is changed to a third-level item.

10. Type **Increases muscle tone**, and then press the **Enter** key. Type **Use lighter weights**, and then press the **Enter** key.

11. Press the **Shift+Tab** keys. The blank item is changed to a second-level item.

12. Type the rest of the items in the list, as shown below:
    b. Three sets of 5–8 reps
       i. Weight should be heavy enough that the last rep in each set is very difficult
      ii. Builds muscle
  3. Increase fruits and vegetables.
    a. Cut up vegetables so they are easy to grab when looking for a snack
    b. Reach for fruit when looking for something sweet

13. At the top of the vertical scroll bar, click the **View Ruler** button to hide the ruler.

14. At the top of the document, position the insertion point at the end of the first line (*Health Plan*), press the **Enter** key, and then type your name.

15. Save, print, and close the document, but leave Word open for the next Step-by-Step.

Organizing a Document in Outline View

In Outline view, you can type topic headings and subheadings for a document. You could use a multilevel list to do this, but when you use Outline view, you can switch to Normal view and the headings are all set up for you. To switch to Outline view, click the View tab on the Ribbon, and then in the Document Views group, click the Outline button. You can also click the Outline button to the left of the Zoom slider at the bottom-right of the document window.

When you switch to Outline view, a new tab, the Outlining tab, appears as the active tab on the Ribbon to the left of the Home tab. A round symbol with the minus sign in it appears in the document, as shown in Figure 5-21. When you type a heading, the text appears to the right of the circle. The minus sign indicates that there are no subheadings or body text below the heading. A plus sign in the circle before a heading indicates that there are subheadings or body text below the heading.

FIGURE 5-21
Text in Outline view

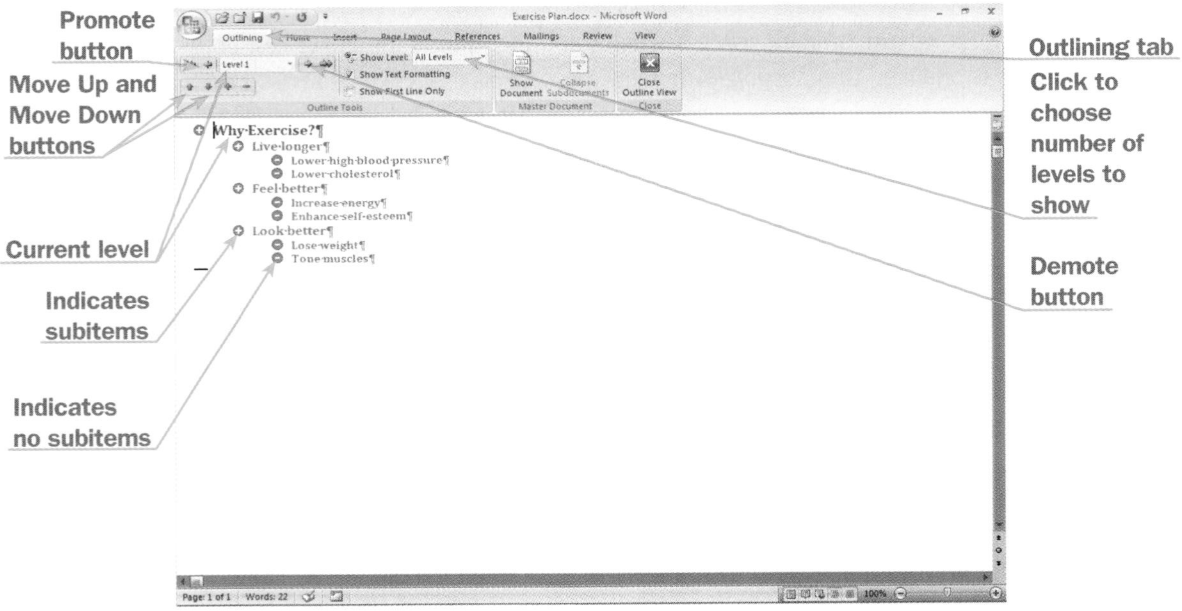

Promote button
Move Up and Move Down buttons
Current level
Indicates subitems
Indicates no subitems
Outlining tab
Click to choose number of levels to show
Demote button

Creating an Outline

When you switch to Outline view in a blank document, the first line of the document is ready for you to type the first heading. Word formats this heading with the Heading 1 style. When you press the Enter key, a new Level 1 heading, formatted with the Heading 1 style, is created. As with bulleted and numbered lists, if you press the Tab key, you create a Level 2 heading. In Outline view, you can also click the Demote button in the Outline Tools group to demote the text to Level 2. Likewise, if you want to change a heading from a lower level to a higher level, you can press the Shift+Tab keys or click the Promote button.

Did You Know?

If you like to switch back and forth from Print Layout view to Outline view, make sure you use the built-in Heading styles to format your headings in Print Layout view so that they show up in Outline view at the proper level. (You can modify the Heading styles, but keep the same names.)

STEP-BY-STEP 5.14

1. Create a new Word document. Save the document as **Exercise Plan** followed by your initials.

2. On the Ribbon, click the **View** tab. In the Document Views group, click the **Outline** button. The Outlining tab appears on the Ribbon to the left of the Home tab and is the active tab. The insertion point is blinking next to a circle containing a minus sign. In the Outline Tools group on the Outlining tab, the level is identified as Level 1 in the Outline Level box.

3. Type **Why Exercise?**. Press the **Enter** key. A new Level 1 paragraph is created.

4. In the Outline Tools group, click the **Demote** button to indent the paragraph to Level 2. The Outline Level box indicates that the item is a Level 2 item.

5. Type **Feel better**. Press the **Enter** key, and then press the **Tab** key. The next item indents more to become a Level 3 item.

6. Type **Enhance self-esteem**, and then press the **Enter** key. Type **Increase energy**, and then press the **Enter** key.

7. In the Outline Tools group, click the **Promote** button. The blank paragraph moves up to become a Level 2 item.

8. Type the following:
   Live longer
   　Lower high blood pressure

9. If you didn't press the Enter key after typing the last item, press the **Enter** key now. Press the **Shift+Tab** keys. The blank item moves up a level to Level 2.

10. Type the following:
    Look better
    　Lose weight
    　Tone muscles
    　Lower cholesterol

11. Save the document and leave it open for the next Step-by-Step.

Modifying an Outline

Once you have typed an outline, you can easily modify it. You can drag a heading to a different position in the outline by dragging the circle with the plus or minus sign in it. You can also click the Move Up and Move Down buttons in the Outline Tools group. When you move a heading, all the subordinate text underneath it moves too. To make it easier to reorganize the outline, you can click the Expand or Collapse buttons in the Outline Tools group or you can click the arrow next to Show Level in the Outline Tools group to view only the headings you want.

Closing Outline View

If you want to add text to your document below the headings you create in Outline view, it's easier to work in Print Layout view. To close Outline view, you click the Close Outline View button in the Close group on the Outlining tab.

STEP-BY-STEP 5.15

1. In the Outline Tools group, click the **arrow** next to the Show Level box. Click **Level 2**. The outline changes to display only the Level 1 and Level 2 items.

2. Double-click the **plus sign** next to *Live longer*. The item expands to display the subitem below it.

3. In the Outline Tools group, click the **arrow** next to the Show Level box. Click **All Levels**. All the levels are shown in the document again.

> **Did You Know?**
>
> You can also click the Expand button 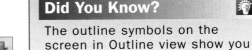 in the Outline Tools group to expand an item.

4. In the subitems under *Look better*, position the pointer on top of the **minus sign** next to *Lower cholesterol*. Press and hold the left mouse button and start dragging the minus sign up the list. As you drag, the pointer changes to a double-headed arrow ⇕ and a horizontal line appears. Drag until the line is above *Look better* and below *Lower high blood pressure*. Release the mouse button. The *Lower cholesterol* item is repositioned as the second subheading under *Live longer*.

5. Click the **minus sign** next to *Enhance self-esteem*. The item is selected.

6. In the Outline Tools group, click the **Move Down** button. The item moves down one line so it is the second Level 3 item in the *Feel better* section.

> **Did You Know?**
>
> The outline symbols on the screen in Outline view show you the document's structure. They will not appear when you print.

7. Click the **plus sign** next to the *Live longer* heading. The item and its subitems are selected.

8. In the Outline Tools group, click the **Move Up** button three times. The item and its subitems move up above the *Feel better* item.

> **Extra for Experts**
>
> To print only the headings (outline) of a document, switch to Outline view, display the level of headings you want to print, and then print the document.

9. Insert a new Level 1 heading at the end of the document, and then type your name.

10. In the Close group, click the **Close Outline View** button. Outline view closes and you are returned to Print Layout view. You can see that the headings are formatted with the Headings Quick Styles.

11. Switch back to Outline view. Save, print, and close the document.

SUMMARY

In this lesson, you learned:

■ You can show and hide the ruler to suit your working style by clicking the View Ruler button at the top of the vertical scroll bar, or by clicking the View tab, and then selecting the Ruler check box in the Show/Hide group.

■ Margins are the blank areas around the top, bottom, and sides of a page. You can change the margin settings by clicking the Margins button in the Page Setup group on the Page Layout tab.

■ You can align text by clicking one of the alignment buttons in the Paragraph group on the Home tab.

■ You can indent text either from the left margin, from the right margin, or from both margins. You can also set first-line and hanging indents.

■ You can change the line spacing of text from the default of 1.15 lines to 1.0 (single-spaced), 2.0 (double-spaced), or greater.

■ You can change the paragraph spacing by changing the measurements in the Before and After boxes in the Paragraph group on the Page Layout tab.

■ You can change the vertical alignment of text by opening the Page Setup dialog box, clicking the Layout tab, and selecting an alignment option from the Vertical alignment list in the Page section.

■ Text alignment can be set with left, right, centered, or decimal tabs. Leaders can be used with any kind of tab.

■ You can use the Bullets or Numbering buttons in the Paragraph group on the Home tab to create bulleted or numbered lists. To change the appearance of a list, click the arrow next to the Bullets or Numbering button to choose a different bullet or numbering style.

■ You can use the Multilevel list button in the Paragraph group on the Home tab to create a list with a hierarchical structure.

■ You can work in Outline view to set up the outline of a document.

VOCABULARY *Review*

Define the following terms:

Alignment	Justify	Outline numbered list
Bullet	Leader	Outside margin
Center	Left-align	Right-align
First-line indent	Margin	Tab stop (tab)
Hanging indent	Mirrored margins	Vertical alignment
Indent	Multilevel list	
Inside margin (gutter margin)	Negative indent (outdent)	

REVIEW *Questions*

TRUE/FALSE

Circle T if the statement is true or F if the statement is false.

T F 1. When you change the vertical alignment of text, you change the position of text between the top and bottom margins.

T F 2. Documents are normally left-aligned or justified.

T F 3. Line spacing is the amount of space between paragraphs.

T F 4. You cannot change the bullet used for bulleted lists.

T F 5. A hanging indent indents the lines that follow the first full line of text.

MULTIPLE CHOICE

Select the best response for the following statements.

1. What type of text has a full blank line between each line of text?
   A. indented
   B. aligned
   C. single-spaced
   D. double-spaced

2. Which of the following margins can you customize in a document?
   A. Top and bottom
   B. Right and left
   C. Top, bottom, right, and left
   D. You cannot customize margins in a document.

3. The upper triangle at the left edge of the ruler indicates the:
   A. left indent marker.
   B. first-line indent marker.
   C. hanging indent marker.
   D. decrease indent marker.

4. Text can be aligned using all of the following types of tab stops except:
   A. justified.
   B. decimal.
   C. right.
   D. center.

5. In Outline view, which button do you click to move an item up a level?
   A. Plus
   B. Promote
   C. Demote
   D. Expand

PROJECTS

 PROJECT 5-1

1. Open the **Poster 2.docx** Data File. Save the document as **Break Room Poster 2** followed by your initials.

2. Center the title and the two headings.

3. Change the line spacing of the four items after each heading to 1.5 lines.

4. Change the four items under each heading into a bulleted list. Use any bullet symbol except the solid, round bullet symbol.

5. Press the Ctrl+End keys, and then create a new paragraph that is not part of the second bulleted list. Type your name, press the Tab key, and then insert the current date. Display the ruler, if necessary, and then use a tab stop to right-align the date at the 6½-inch mark. (You'll have to click to position the tab stop near the 6½-inch mark on the ruler, and then drag the tab stop on top of the Right Indent marker.)

6. Vertically center the text on the page.

7. Preview the document. Hide the ruler, and then save, print, and close the document.

PROJECT 5-2

Your friend Anna recently graduated from high school and enrolled in a junior college. She wants a better paying part-time job while attending school. Before beginning her job search, she asked you to help her write her resume.

1. Create a new Word document. Save it as **Resume for Anna** followed by your initials.

2. Set all margins at .75 inch.

3. Type the resume shown in Figure 5-22. Use alignment commands, indenting, and tabs to format the text. The theme is the Office theme with the default font and font size. The name at the top is 14 points. All the text is single spaced. The text is centered vertically on the page.

FIGURE 5-22

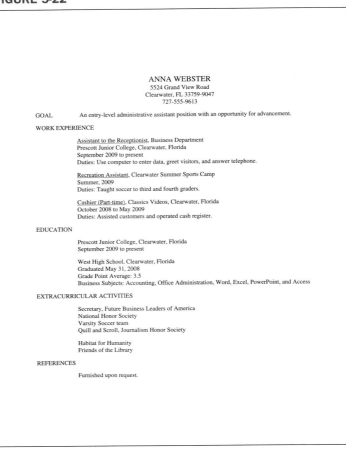

4. Preview the document.

5. Insert a new paragraph at the end of the document, type **Prepared by** followed by your name. Right-align this paragraph.

6. Save, print, and close the document.

PROJECT 5-3

A friend of yours will be married soon. She has asked you to help her design the wedding invitations.

1. Open the **Invitation.docx** Data File. Save the document as **Wedding Invitation** followed by your initials.

2. Change the font of all the text to 24-point, bold Edwardian Script ITC. (If this font is not available, choose another font.) Change the color to **Black, Text 1, Lighter 25%**.

3. Center the text vertically and horizontally on the page.

4. Create a new paragraph at the end of the document. Change the font to 11-point Calibri. Format the paragraph so that there are 36 points of space before it and 10 points after it. Type your name.

5. Preview the document. Save, print, and close the document.

 PROJECT 5-4

1. Open the **Interview 2.docx** Data File. Save the document as **Interview Preparation Tips** followed by your initials.

2. Change all the text except the title to double-spaced. Change the space after all the paragraphs except the title to 18 points.

3. Center the title. Justify the rest of the text.

4. Indent the first line of all the paragraphs except the title ½ inch.

5. At the end of the second paragraph, position the insertion point after the words *such as*. Insert a new paragraph and then type the following as a bulleted list. Use a bullet character of your choice.
   Social Security card
   Names and addresses of former employers
   Names and addresses of references
   A copy of your resume
   School records

6. Create a new paragraph at the end of the document, right-align it, and then type your name.

7. Preview the document. Save, print, and close the document.

PROJECT 5-5

1. Open the **Shipping.docx** Data File. Save the document as **Overnight Shipping** followed by your initials.

2. Jump to the end of the document, and then press the Enter key twice.

3. In the new paragraph, set left tabs at **1.75** inches, **3** inches, and **4.75** inches.

4. Type the headings **Company, Cost, Weight Limit,** and **Delivery Time,** using tabs to separate the four columns. Underline the headings.

5. Press the Enter key. In the new paragraph, remove all of the tabs from the ruler and turn off underlining.

6. Set a decimal tab at approximately **2** inches.

7. Set a center tab at **3.5** inches.

8. Set a right tab at **5.63** inches (the tick mark on the ruler between the 5½- and 5¾-inch marks).

9. Open the Tabs dialog box. In turn, select each of the measurements in the Tab stop position list, click the 2 .... option button, and then click Set. Click OK to close the dialog box after all three of the tab stops have been formatted with the dotted line leader.

10. Using the tabs you just set, type the following information:

Lightning	$11.75	1 lb., 4 oz.	1:00 p.m.
Pronto	$9.99	10 oz.	12:30 p.m.
Zippy	$14.50	2 lbs.	10:00 a.m.
Speed Air	$12.95	none	3:00 p.m.

11. Indent the first line of the paragraph under the *Overnight Shipping* heading one-quarter inch.

12. Change the spacing of the paragraph under the heading so that there are 6 points of space before it and 18 points of space after it.

13. Change the line spacing of the paragraph under the heading to 1.15 inches and change the line spacing of the paragraphs that make up the price list to 1.5 inches.

14. Create a new paragraph at the end of the document with 42 points of space before it. Type your name.

15. Preview the document. Save, print, and close the document.

PROJECT 5-6

As the student assistant to the superintendent of the Lancaster Independent School District, you have been asked to type the agenda for the next Board of Trustees meeting.

1. Create a new Word document. Save it as **Agenda** followed by your initials.

2. Set the top margin to 1.5 inches and the bottom, left, and right margins to 1 inch.

3. Type the agenda shown in Figure 5-23. Format all the paragraphs in the list so there is no space before or after them. Format the third paragraph in the heading (it starts with *4:00 p.m.*) so there are 36 points of space after it. All the lines are single spaced.

FIGURE 5-23

LANCASTER INDEPENDENT SCHOOL DISTRICT
Agenda for Board of Trustees Meeting
4:00 p.m., Monday, March 15, 2010

I. Verify quorum
II. Approve minutes for February 22, 2010 meeting
III. Approve the Tax Report for January, 2010
IV. Committee Reports
  A. Curriculum
  B. Textbooks
  C. Construction
  D. Building Maintenance
V. Old Business
  A. Maintenance Contracts
  B. Cafeteria
VI. New Business
  A. Recognition of students participating in School Clean-up Week
  B. Short-term Borrowing
VII. Next Meeting, Monday, April 19, 2010

4. Insert a new paragraph at the end of the document. Deselect the Multilevel List button. Format the new paragraph with 24 points of space above it, and then type your name.

5. Preview the document. Save, print, and close the document.

PROJECT 5-7

You need to write a five-page paper about the members in the three branches of the U.S. federal government. Create an outline for this paper.

1. Create a new Word document. Save it as **Government** followed by your initials.

2. In Outline view, type the following:

Executive Branch
  President
    Elected by Electoral College
    Term - Four years
Judicial Branch
  Supreme Court Justices
    Appointed by President
    Term - Life

Senators
       Elected by Direct Vote - Statewide
       Term - Six Years
Legislative Branch
   Representatives
       Elected by Direct Vote - Congressional District
       Term - Two Years

3. Move the Senators item so it is a Level 2 item with subitems and is the first item under *Legislative Branch*.

4. Press the Ctrl+Home keys. Type **U.S. Federal Government** as a new Level 1 heading. Insert your name as a new Level 2 heading.

5. Preview the document. Save, print, and close the document.

CRITICAL *Thinking*

 ACTIVITY 5-1

Create your own resume using the format of the resume in Project 5-2. Trade your resume with a classmate. Edit each other's resume, and then make corrections to your resume if you feel they are warranted.

 ACTIVITY 5-2

Make a bulleted list of your three favorite songs, three favorite books, and three favorite movies. Choose a different bullet symbol for each list by clicking Define New Bullet on the Bullets menu, and then click Symbol in the Define New Bullet dialog box. Click the arrow next to the Font box at the top of the dialog box, and then click one of the Wingdings fonts. Search for just the right bullet character for each list.

 ACTIVITY 5-3

Use Help to learn how to define a new multilevel list style.

WORKING WITH GRAPHICS

VOCABULARY

Aspect ratio

Callout

Chart

Clip art

Crop

Diagram

Floating object

Graphic

Inline object

Keyword

Object

Pull quote

Rotation handle

Selection rectangle

Sidebar

Sizing handle

SmartArt

Text box

WordArt

Working with Graphics

You can enhance documents by adding graphics. Graphics are pictures that help illustrate the meaning of the text and make the page more attractive. You can add predefined shapes, diagrams, and charts as well as photographs and drawings. You can also use Word's drawing tools to create your own graphics and add them to your documents.

Creating Columns

Sometimes a document can be more effective if the text is formatted in multiple columns. A newsletter is an example of a document that often has two or more columns. Columns are easy to create in Word. You click the Page Layout tab on the Ribbon, and then, in the Page Setup group, click the Columns button. The Columns menu appears, as shown in Figure 6-1.

FIGURE 6-1
Columns menu

Page Layout tab

Columns button

Click to open Columns dialog box

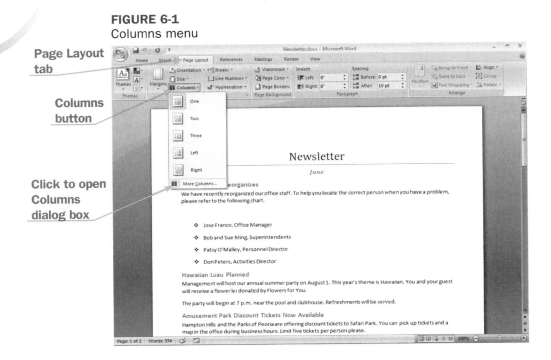

You can choose one, two, or three columns of equal width. You can also choose Left or Right, which creates two columns with either the left or the right column a little less than half the size of the other column. If none of these options suits you, you can click More Columns at the bottom of the Columns menu to open the Columns dialog box. See Figure 6-2. In this dialog box, you can create columns of custom widths, or you can add a vertical line between columns. You can also click the Apply to arrow and choose to apply the columns to the whole document (the default) or from the location of the insertion point to the end of the document.

After you create columns, you might need to change the point at which a new column starts. You can do this by inserting a column break. Position the insertion point immediately in front of the text you want to start the next column. Click the Page Layout tab, and then, in the Page Setup group, click the Breaks button. On the menu that opens, click Column. The menu closes and the text after the insertion point moves over to the top of the next column.

FIGURE 6-2
Columns dialog box

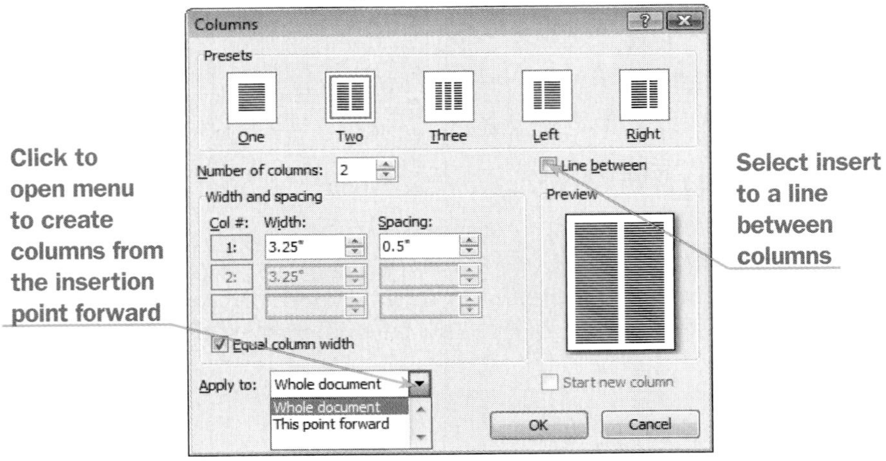

Click to open menu to create columns from the insertion point forward

Select insert to a line between columns

STEP-BY-STEP 6.1

1. Open the **Newsletter.docx** Data File. Save the document as **HH Newsletter** followed by your initials.

2. On the Ribbon, click the **Page Layout** tab. In the Page Setup group, click the **Columns** button. On the menu, click **Two**. The entire document is formatted in two columns. But you want the newsletter title and date to be centered across the page, not shifted into the first column.

3. On the Quick Access Toolbar, click the **Undo** button. The document returns to its original format.

4. Position the insertion point in front of the *Hampton Hills Reorganizes* heading. You want everything after this point to be formatted in two columns and everything before this point to remain formatted as one column.

5. In the Page Setup group, click the **Columns** button, and then click **More Columns**. The Columns dialog box opens. Notice that the Preview section shows one column.

6. In the Presets section at the top of the dialog box, click **Two**. Click the **Line between** check box to insert a check mark. The Preview section changes to show two columns with a line between the columns.

7. At the bottom of the dialog box, click the **Apply to** arrow, and then click **This point forward**. The Preview box changes to reflect this setting.

8. Click **OK**. The dialog box closes, all the text in the document from the first heading to the end is formatted in two columns, and a line appears between the two columns.

> ### Did You Know?
>
> To format only part of the document in columns without opening the Columns dialog box, select the paragraphs you want to format in columns. Then, click the Columns button in the Page Setup group on the Page Layout tab, and use any of the commands on this menu.

9. On the Ribbon, click the **View** tab. In the Zoom group, click the **One Page** button. The document appears in One Page view.

10. At the bottom of the first column, click immediately before the last heading in the column. On the Ribbon, click the **Page Layout** tab. In the Page Setup group, click the **Breaks** button, and then click **Column**. The text after the insertion point moves over to the top of the second column.

11. On the Ribbon, click the **Home** tab. In the Paragraph group, click the **Show/Hide ¶** button to display formatting marks. Notice at the top of the document, after *June*, a double dotted line and the words *Section Break* appear. This is the point in the document at which the two-column format starts. Notice at the bottom of the first column, a dotted line and the words *Column Break* appear. This is the manual column break you inserted.

12. In the Paragraph group, click the **Show/Hide ¶** button again to hide the formatting marks. Save your changes to the document. Leave it open for the next Step-by-Step.

Adding Borders and Shading to Paragraphs

Borders around a paragraph draw the reader's attention to the paragraph. You can specify whether the border appears on all four sides (like a box), on two sides, or on only one side of the paragraph. You can also specify the border style, for example, whether the border consists of a single or a double line, is thick or thin, or includes a shadow or a 3-D effect.

To add a border, first select the text around which you want the border to appear. On the Home tab on the Ribbon, click the arrow next to the Borders button in the Paragraph group. A menu of border choices opens, as shown in Figure 6-3. You can click a command on the menu to add a border. Note that you can then click the arrow next to the Borders button again and click another command to add a second border to the selected text. For example, if you wanted to add a border above and below a paragraph, you would click Bottom Border on the menu, open the menu again, and then click Top Border. If you opened the menu again, both commands would be selected. Note that the icon for the Borders button and the exact name of the ScreenTip changes to reflect the most recent choices made.

FIGURE 6-3
Borders menu

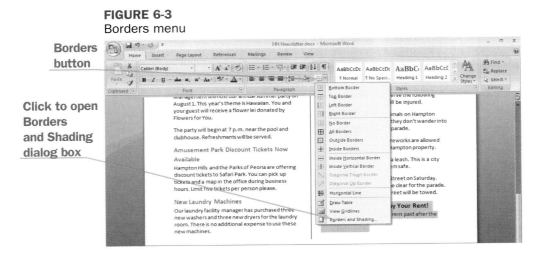

If you want to change the border style, you need to click Borders and Shading on the menu to open the Borders and Shading dialog box. In the dialog box, click the Borders tab if it is not the top tab. See Figure 6-4. Here you can specify the border setting, style, color, and width of the border line. To insert or remove borders, you click the sides of the paragraph preview on the right.

FIGURE 6-4
Borders tab in Borders and Shading dialog box

Places border on all four sides at once

Allows you to place border on each side individually

Click to change the width of the border line

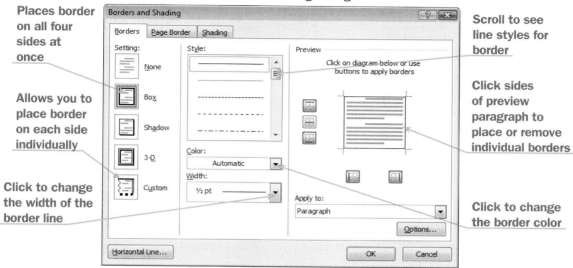

Scroll to see line styles for border

Click sides of preview paragraph to place or remove individual borders

Click to change the border color

You can also add shading or patterns to a paragraph or lines of text to emphasize the text. To do this, select the text you want to shade. In the Paragraph group on the Home tab, click the arrow beside the Shading button, and then click a color in the palette that opens.

To add a pattern, open the Borders and Shading dialog box, and then click the Shading tab, as shown in Figure 6-5. You can click the Fill arrow to choose a shading color from the same palette available on the Shading button. To add a pattern, click the Style arrow to choose a style or pattern for the shading (a percentage of the selected color, dots, or stripes), and then click the Color arrow to choose a color for the pattern. The Preview box shows you a sample of what your shading choices will look like.

Computer Concepts

Borders and shading add interest and emphasis to text, but you should use them sparingly. Too many borders or too much shading on a page can make it look cluttered and hard to read.

FIGURE 6-5
Shading tab in Borders and Shading dialog box

Shading tab

Color selected when you used shading button

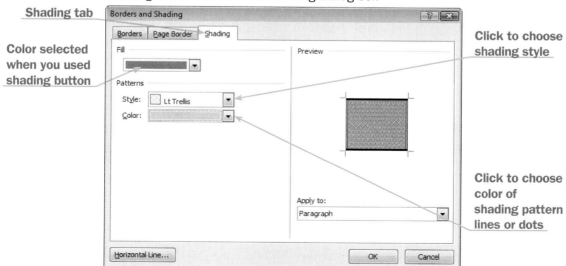

Click to choose shading style

Click to choose color of shading pattern lines or dots

STEP-BY-STEP 6.2

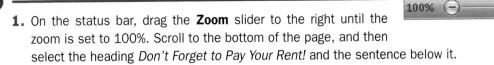

1. On the status bar, drag the **Zoom** slider to the right until the zoom is set to 100%. Scroll to the bottom of the page, and then select the heading *Don't Forget to Pay Your Rent!* and the sentence below it.

2. On the Ribbon, click the **Home** tab, if necessary. In the Paragraph group, click the **arrow** next to the Borders button. Notice that none of the border commands are selected on the menu. Click **Outside Borders**. The menu closes and borders are added on all four sides of the selected text.

3. In the Paragraph group, click the **arrow** next to the Shading button. In the palette, click the **Dark Blue, Text 2, Lighter 40%** box (fourth row, fourth column). The selected paragraphs are shaded with a medium blue color.

4. In the Paragraph group, click the **arrow** next to the Borders button. Notice that the top four commands as well as the Outside Borders command are selected on the menu. At the bottom of the menu, click **Borders and Shading**. The Borders and Shading dialog box opens, with the Borders tab on top. In the Setting section on the left, the Box button is selected. On the right, the Preview section shows the borders on all four sides of the paragraph.

5. In the center column in the dialog box, click the **Width** arrow, and then click **2 ¼ pt**. Because the Box button is selected, all four borders are changed to 2¼ points wide.

6. In the Setting section, click the **Custom** button. In the Style list, click the **down scroll arrow** twice, and then click the **double line** at the bottom of the list. In the Preview section, click the **left**, and then the **right** border. The borders you clicked change to double lines. When the Custom button is selected, you need to click a border in the Preview section to apply the new border.

7. Click the **Shading** tab. Notice that the Fill box is the same color you chose when you used the Shading button.

8. Click the **Style** arrow, scroll down to the bottom of the list, and then click **Lt Trellis**. The Preview section shows a trellis pattern.

9. Click the **Color** arrow, and then click the **White, Background 1, Darker 15%** box (third row, first column). Now the trellis pattern is much lighter.

10. Click **OK**. The selected paragraphs are formatted with the borders, shading, and pattern you chose.

11. Save your changes to the document. Leave it open for the next Step-by-Step.

Adding Borders and Shading to Pages

 Just as you can add borders to paragraphs, you can add borders and shading to entire pages. To do this, click the Page Layout tab on the Ribbon, and then, in the Page Background group, click the Page Borders button. This opens the Borders and Shading dialog box with the Page Border tab on top, as shown in Figure 6-6. This is the same Borders and Shading dialog box you opened to add borders and shading to paragraphs. Everything is the same except the default in the Apply to box is Whole document, and there is an additional box at the bottom of the middle section of the dialog box. This is the Art box, from which you can choose graphics to use as a border. As with a paragraph, you can add page borders to any or all sides of a page.

> **Extra for Experts**
>
> To specify the amount of space between the border and the text or edge of the page, click the Options button on the Borders tab or the Page Border tab in the Borders and Shading dialog box.

FIGURE 6-6
Page Border tab in Borders and Shading dialog box

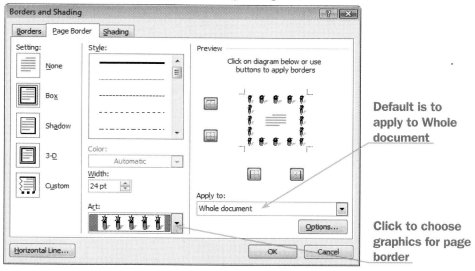

To add shading to an entire page, in the Page Background group on the Page Layout tab, click the Page Color button. The palette of theme colors opens. Click a color in the palette. The entire page is shaded with that color.

S TEP-BY-STEP 6.3

1. Switch to One Page view.

2. On the Ribbon, click the **Page Layout** tab. In the Page Background group, click the **Page Borders** button. The Borders and Shading dialog box opens, with the Page Border tab on top.

3. At the bottom of the middle section of the dialog box, click the **Art** arrow. Scroll down the list until you see the row of **red firecrackers**, and then click it. The Preview section changes to show a border of red firecrackers around the edge of the page.

STEP-BY-STEP 6.3 Continued

4. Click **OK**. The dialog box closes and the firecracker border appears around the page.

5. In the Page Background group, click the **Page Color** button. In the color palette, click the **Red**, **Accent 2**, **Lighter 80%** square (second row, sixth column). The page is shaded with a light red color.

6. Save your changes to the document. Leave it open for the next Step-by-Step.

Extra for Experts

To force a page border outside the header or footer on the page, click the Options button on the Page Border tab in the Borders and Shading dialog box, and then select the Surround header or Surround footer check boxes.

Understanding Objects

An **object** is anything that can be manipulated as a whole, such as clip art or another graphic that you insert in a document. You can insert, modify, resize, reposition, and delete objects in documents. You can cut, copy, and paste objects the same way you do text, using either the Cut, Copy, and Paste commands or by dragging and dropping the selected object.

Inserting Clip Art

Graphics that are already drawn or photographed and available for use in documents are called **clip art**. To insert clip art, click the Insert tab, and then, in the Illustrations group, click the Clip Art button. This opens the Clip Art task pane to the right of the document window. See Figure 6-7. In the Search for box, type a word or words that describe the type of clip art you wish to insert. These words are called **keywords**. By default, Word will search all clip art on your computer as well as on Microsoft Office Online, a Web site maintained by Microsoft that stores thousands of pieces of clip art. When Word finds clip art that matches the keywords you typed, it displays the images in the task pane. You can scroll to view the images and click the one you want. Word inserts the clip art at the insertion point in your document.

Did You Know?

The term *clip art* refers not only to drawn images, but also to photographs, movie clips, and sound files. To restrict your search to specific types of clip art, click the Results should be arrow in the Clip Art task pane, and then select the check boxes next to the type of clip art you want.

FIGURE 6-7
Inserting clip art

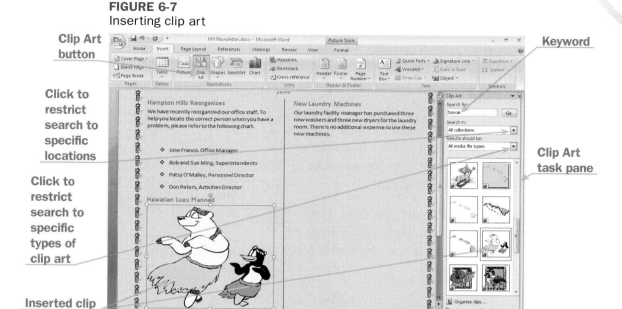

STEP-BY-STEP 6.4

1. Zoom the document to **100%**. Scroll back up to the top of the document.

2. In the first column, position the pointer after the word *Planned* in the heading *Hawaiian Luau Planned*. On the Ribbon, click the **Insert** tab. In the Illustrations group, click the **Clip Art** button. The Clip Art task pane appears to the right of the document window.

3. At the top of the Clip Art task pane, select the text in the Search for box. Type **Hawaii**, and then click **Go**. If a dialog box opens asking if you want access to clip art files online, click **Yes**. Clips relating to Hawaii appear in the task pane. (*Note*: If you are not connected to the Internet, you don't have access to Microsoft Office Online and you probably will not see

> **Did You Know?**
>
> You can press the Enter key instead of clicking Go in the task pane to search for clips matching the keywords.

any results when you search using *Hawaii* as the keyword. If this happens, replace the text in the Search for box with **party**, click the **Go** button, and then in the next steps, use any clip you like.)

4. In the task pane, scroll down until you see the clip of the polar bear and penguin dancing, and then point to it. (If you can't find this piece of clip art, click another clip that appropriately illustrates a luau.) An arrow appears on the clip. Click the **arrow**, and then on the menu, click **Insert**. The clip is inserted in the docu-

> **Did You Know?**
>
> You can also simply click a clip in the Clip Art task pane to insert it into the document.

ment. Because the clip is so large, the columns are adjusted and the second column is pushed onto the second page of the document.

STEP-BY-STEP 6.4 Continued

5. In the document window, scroll down until you see the heading *Independence Day Parade*. Position the insertion point immediately after that heading.

6. In the task pane, replace the text in the *Search for* box with **flag**, and then click **Go**. Clips of flags appear in the task pane.

7. In the task pane, scroll down until you see photos of American flags. Point to one, click the **arrow** on the clip, and then click **Insert**. The clip art photo of the flag is inserted into the document.

8. In the title bar of the Clip Art task pane, click the **Close** button. The task pane closes. Save the document and leave it open for the next Step-by-Step.

> **Extra for Experts**
>
> If you think you will use the clip art again, you can store it on your computer by clicking the arrow that appears when you point to the clip art in the task pane, and then clicking Make Available Offline.

Selecting an Object

To manipulate or modify an object, you must select it first. To select an object, position the pointer over the object, and then click. A box with small circles at the corners and small squares on each side appears around the object, as shown in Figure 6-8. The box appears when the object is selected and is called the selection rectangle. The squares and circles are called sizing handles; you drag the sizing handles to resize the object. The green circle is the rotation handle; you can drag it to rotate the object. To deselect an object, click a blank area of the document window, just as you would to deselect selected text.

FIGURE 6-8
Selected object

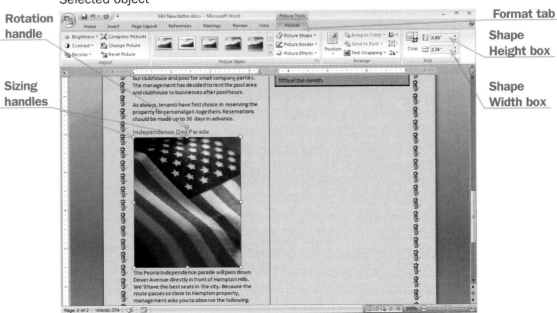

When you select a clip art image, the Picture Tools contextual tab called Format appears, as shown in Figure 6-8. Remember, contextual tabs contain commands that are available only when a particular type of object is selected. For example, after you insert clip art, you can change its height and width or recolor it. These commands appear on the contextual Format tab because you cannot perform either of these actions on regular text.

Resizing an Object

Once an object has been inserted, you can resize it to fit better on the page. To resize an object, first select it, and then drag a sizing handle. When you position the pointer directly on top of one of the sizing handles, it changes to a two-headed arrow. Drag the handle inward or outward to make the object smaller or larger.

The relationship of the object's height to its width is called the aspect ratio. If you drag a corner sizing handle (one of the circles), you change the size of the object without changing the aspect ratio; in other words, you change the object's height and width proportionately. If you drag a side sizing handle (one of the squares), you change the size of the object without maintaining the aspect ratio. You can also change the size of an object by selecting it, clicking the Format contextual tab, and then adjusting either of the measurements in the Size group. The default is to maintain the aspect ratio, so if you change the measurement in one box, the measurement in the other box adjusts automatically.

> **Did You Know?**
>
> To set precise height and width measurements in the Size group on the contextual Format tab without maintaining the aspect ratio, click the Size Dialog Box Launcher to open the Size dialog box, and then click the Lock aspect ratio check box to deselect it.

STEP-BY-STEP 6.5

1. If the clip art of the flag is not selected, click it.

2. If the rulers are not displayed on your screen, at the top of the vertical scroll bar, click the **View Ruler** button. The rulers are displayed. Using the ruler as a guide, drag the **upper-right sizing handle** on the flag down and to the left until the faint outline of the clip indicates that it is approximately two inches tall. Deselect the clip art.

3. Scroll up until you can see the clip art of the dancing animals, and then click the image to select it.

4. On the Ribbon, click the **Format** tab under Picture Tools, if necessary. In the Size group, click the **down arrow** in the Shape Width box (the bottom box) as many times as necessary until the measurement in the box is 3". Note that the measurement in the Shape Height box changed as well.

STEP-BY-STEP 6.5 Continued

5. In the Size group, click in the Shape Height box (the top box). The measurement is selected. Type **1.15**, and then press the **Enter** key. The height of the clip is changed to 1.15 inches, and the width automatically changed to 1.36 inches. (If you inserted a clip other than the dancing animals, this measurement might differ.) Now that both clips are resized smaller, the second column fits on the first page again. See Figure 6-9.

Extra for Experts

If you don't want part of a graphic to appear in the document, you can **crop** off (cut off) the part you don't want. Select the graphic, click the Format tab, and then, in the Size group, click the Crop button to change the pointer to the Crop pointer. Drag a sizing handle on the graphic toward the center of the graphic until the indicator box that appears includes only the section of the graphic you want to use. Click the Crop button again to turn off this feature.

FIGURE 6-9
Resizing objects

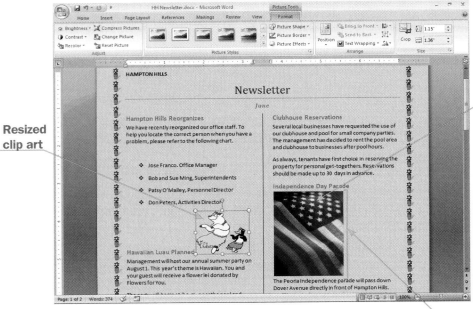

You might have chosen different clip art and it might be a different width

Resized clip art

Approximately two inches high

6. Save the document and leave it open for the next Step-by-Step.

Repositioning and Removing an Inline Object

When you insert an object, it is inserted as an inline object in the text, which means it is treated as if it were a character in the line of text. You can apply paragraph formatting commands to the paragraph that contains the inline object; for example, you can use the Align commands to change its alignment or set a specific amount of space before or after the paragraph. If you want to move or copy an inline object to another line in the document, click it to select it, and then use drag-and-drop or the Cut, Copy, and Paste commands to move or copy it, just as you would with text. If you want to delete an object, select it, and then press the Delete or the Backspace key, again, just as you would with text.

STEP-BY-STEP 6.6

1. In the second column, click the picture of the flag to select it.

2. On the Ribbon, click the **Home** tab. In the Paragraph group, click the **Center** button. The flag and the heading above it are centered in the column. Why did the heading become centered as well as the selected flag?

3. In the Paragraph group, click the **Show/Hide ¶** button. Because there is a paragraph mark after the flag but not after the heading, the flag is in the same paragraph as the heading, so any paragraph formatting you apply to the inline flag also applies to the heading.

4. In the Paragraph group, click the **Align Text Left** button. The paragraph, including the heading, is again left-aligned.

5. In the first column, click the image of the dancing animals to select it. Position the pointer directly on top of a selected object. The pointer changes to the Move pointer—a four-sided arrow attached to the arrow pointer.

6. Drag the selected image down until the indicator line is between the period at the end of the first paragraph under the *Hawaiian Luau Planned* heading and the paragraph mark, as shown in Figure 6-10, and then release the mouse button. The image is moved to the end of the first paragraph. It is the largest item in the line, so the space between the last line and the line above it increases to accommodate the image.

STEP-BY-STEP 6.6 Continued

FIGURE 6-10
Moving an object

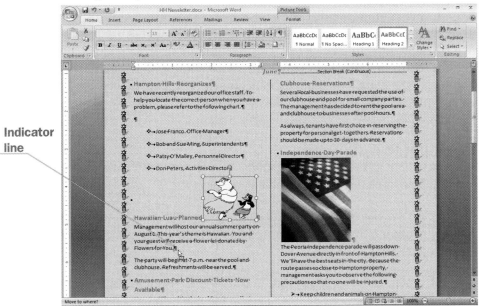

Indicator
line

---

7. Save the document and leave it open for the next Step-by-Step.

Wrapping Text Around an Object

To save space and make a document look more professional, you may want to wrap text around an object. To do this, you need to change the inline object to a floating object, an object that acts as if it were sitting in a separate layer on the page. You can drag a floating object anywhere on the page. To do this, click the contextual Format tab, and then in the Arrange group, click the Text Wrapping button to open a menu of wrapping options, as shown in Figure 6-11. Table 6-1 describes these options.

FIGURE 6-11
Wrapping text around an object

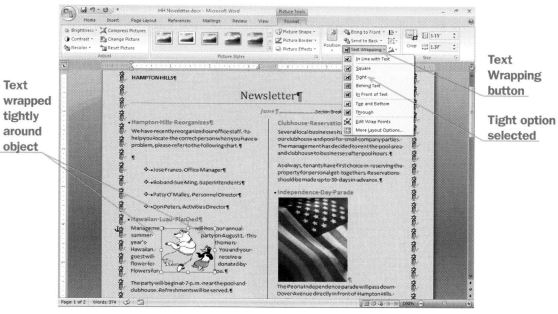

TABLE 6-1

COMMAND	ACTION
In Line with Text	Changes a floating object to an inline object
Square	Wraps text around top, bottom, and both sides of an object
Tight	Wraps text around all sides of an object no matter what shape the object is
Behind Text	Places the object behind the text
In Front of Text	Places the object in front of (on top of) the text
Top and Bottom	Wraps text around the top and bottom of an object and leaves the space on either side of the object empty
Through	Wraps text around all sides of an object—no matter what shape the object is—more tightly than the Tight command
Edit Wrap Points	Displays small squares around the perimeter of an object, which you can drag to change the perimeter for objects wrapped with the Tight or the Through option
More Layout Options	Opens the Advanced Layout dialog box with the Text Wrapping tab on top, displaying options for adjusting the distance between the text and the sides of the object

To change the object to a floating object that is positioned in a predetermined location on the page (centered in the top, middle, or bottom, one of the corners, or in the middle of the left or right side), click the Position button in the Arrange group on the Format tab, and then click one of the options in the gallery under With Text Wrapping. See Figure 6-12.

FIGURE 6-12
Positioning text in a predetermined position using the Position button

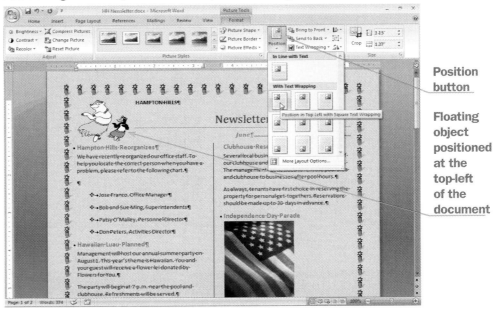

Position button

Floating object positioned at the top-left of the document

STEP-BY-STEP 6.7

1. If the clip art of the dancing animals is not already selected, click it.

2. On the Ribbon, click the Picture Tools **Format** tab. In the Arrange group, click the **Text Wrapping** button, and then click **Tight**. The text in the first column under the *Hawaiian Luau Planned* heading shifts and wraps around the clip art.

3. Drag the clip art up and to the left to approximately center it in the first paragraph so that all the text in the first paragraph wraps around the clip art.

4. In the second column, click the clip art of the **flag**. On the Ribbon, click the Picture Tools **Format** tab. In the Arrange group, click the **Text Wrapping** button, and then click **Behind Text**. Deselect the picture. The text in the second column under the *Independence Day Parade* heading flows on top of the picture.

5. Click the picture of the **flag**. The insertion point is placed in the paragraphs on top of the picture; the picture does not become selected. Press and hold the **Ctrl** key, and then click the picture of the **flag** again. Now the picture is selected.

STEP-BY-STEP 6.7 Continued

6. On the selected picture, drag the lower-right sizing handle down and to the right until the picture is as tall as all the text under the *Independence Day Parade* heading. If the picture is not as wide as or is wider than the text, drag the right-middle sizing handle as necessary to widen the picture or make it narrower. The picture should be approximately the same height and width as the text under the heading. See Figure 6-13.

FIGURE 6-13
Clip art behind text

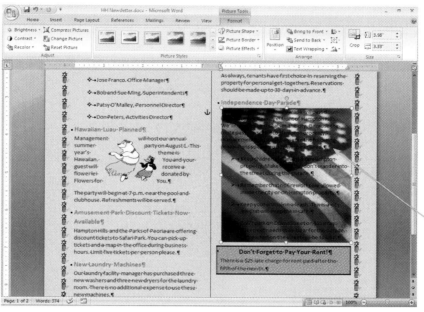

7. Save the document and leave it open for the next Step-by-Step.

Recoloring Pictures

Sometimes you need to adjust the color of an image. You can change the brightness or contrast, or recolor an image all in one shade or with a washout (very light) style. To do this, click the contextual Format tab. In the Adjust group, click the Brightness or Contrast button, and then click a percentage to adjust the settings. The Contrast menu is shown in Figure 6-14. Also in the Adjust group, you can click the Recolor button, and then click a style to recolor the image all in one shade. See Figure 6-15.

FIGURE 6-14
Contrast menu

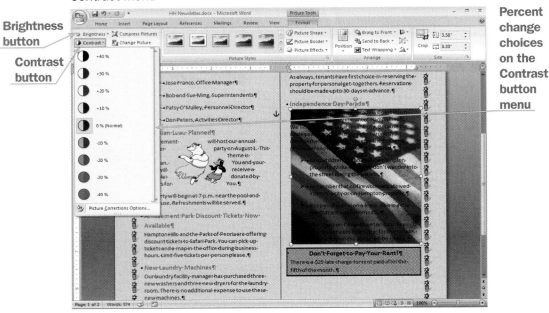

FIGURE 6-15
Recolor gallery

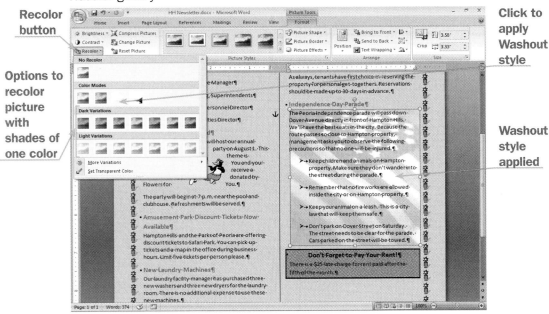

S TEP-BY-STEP 6.8

1. In the second column, select the picture of the **flag**, if necessary.

2. On the Ribbon, click the Picture Tools **Format** tab. In the Adjust group, click the **Brightness** button. Point to **+40%**, and watch the Live Preview of the picture. Point to **-30%**, and watch the Live Preview again. Press the **Esc** key to close the menu without selecting a command.

3. In the Adjust group, click the **Contrast** button. Point to **+40%**, and watch the Live Preview of the picture. Point to **-40%**, and watch the Live Preview again. Press the **Esc** key to close the menu without selecting a command.

4. In the Adjust group, click the **Recolor** button. Point to the **Grayscale** style under Color Modes (first style in the row). Point to several of the styles under Dark Variations and Light Variations. Under Color Modes, click the **Washout** style (third style in the row). The picture is recolored in the Washout style, and the text is now readable on top of the image.

5. Save the document and leave it open. You will not use it in the next Step-by-Step, but you will use it later.

Inserting Pictures

In Word, *pictures* are graphic files stored on your computer. To insert a picture in a document, click the Insert tab, and then in the Illustrations group, click the Picture button to open the Insert Picture dialog box. See Figure 6-16. This dialog box is similar to the Open and the Save As dialog boxes. You can navigate to the folder that contains the picture you want to insert, click the file, and then click Insert. The picture is inserted as an inline object at the location of the insertion point. You can then change the object to a floating object if you want, as well as resize and reposition it, in the same manner as clip art.

FIGURE 6-16
Insert Picture dialog box

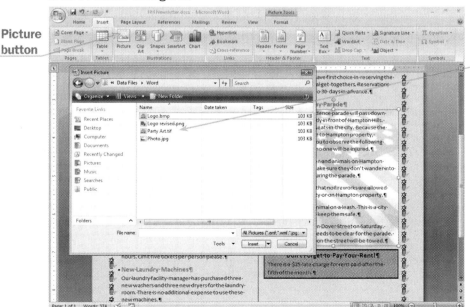

Picture button

Picture files of different file types

Drawing Shapes

Word provides tools for you to create your own graphic images. To access these tools, click the Insert tab, and then, in the Illustrations group, click the Shapes button to open a menu of choices. See Figure 6-17. Table 6-2 summarizes the types of drawing tools available on the menu.

FIGURE 6-17
Shapes menu

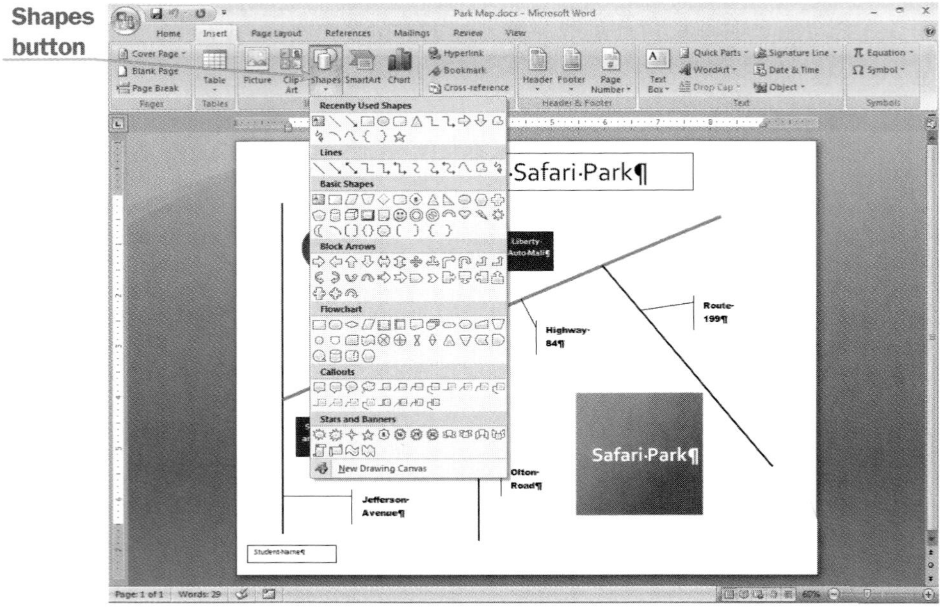

Shapes button

TABLE 6-2
Types of drawing tools

CATEGORY	DESCRIPTION
Lines	Draw straight or curved lines
Basic Shapes	Draw many basic shapes, including rectangles, ovals, triangles, and several more interesting shapes, such as a smiley face and a lightning bolt
Block Arrows	Draw various forms of block arrows
Flowchart	Draw shapes used to create a flow chart
Callouts	Draw boxes with lines that point to something to highlight or "call out" the item being pointed to
Stars and Banners	Draw star and banner shapes

Drawing Shapes

To draw a shape, click the shape you want to draw on the menu. The pointer changes to the crosshairs pointer. Drag the pointer on the document to draw the shape. Drawn shapes are inserted as floating objects by default. As with clip art objects, you can cut, copy, and paste drawn shapes as well as move and resize them.

STEP-BY-STEP 6.9

1. Create a new, blank Word document. Save it as **Park Map** followed by your initials. Study the map in Figure 6-18. You will be drawing a map similar to this one.

FIGURE 6-18
Map created with drawn shapes

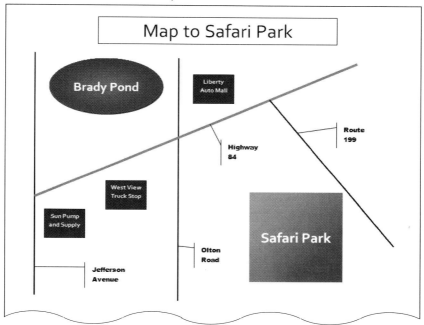

2. If formatting marks are showing, in the Paragraph group, click the Show/Hide ¶ button to hide them. If the ruler is not visible, at the top of the vertical scroll bar, click the View Ruler button to display the rulers. On the Ribbon, click the Page Layout tab. In the Page Setup group, click the Orientation button, and then click Landscape. On the Ribbon, click the View tab. In the Zoom group, click the One Page button. You're ready to draw the map now.

3. On the Ribbon, click the **Insert** tab. In the Illustrations group, click the **Shapes** button. The Shapes menu opens.

4. Under Basic Shapes on the menu, click the **Oval** button (top row under Basic Shapes, third from the right). The mouse pointer changes to a crosshairs pointer.

5. Position the pointer on the blinking insertion point, press and hold the mouse button, and then drag to draw an oval approximately 3 inches wide and 1½ inches high. When the oval is approximately the same size as the pond shown in Figure 6-18, release the mouse button. The Drawing Tools Format tab is active on the Ribbon.

STEP-BY-STEP 6.9 Continued

6. On the Ribbon, click the **Insert** tab. In the Illustrations group, click the **Shapes** button, and then under Lines, click the **Line** button (first button under Lines).

7. Position the pointer just above and about one-half inch to the left of the oval. Press and hold the Shift key, and then drag to draw a line down to the 6½-inch mark on the vertical ruler. Release the mouse button when your line is positioned similar to *Jefferson Avenue* in Figure 6-18.

8. Click the line you drew to select it. On the Ribbon, click the **Home** tab. In the Clipboard group, click the **Copy** button, and then click the **Paste** button. A copy of the line appears in the document. Drag the line to position it to the right of the circle you drew, similar to *Olton Road* in Figure 6-18.

9. Use the **Line** button to create the other two roads on the map.

10. Use the **Rectangle** button under Basic Shapes on the Shapes menu (first row, second column) to draw the rectangle labeled *Sun Pump and Supply* in Figure 6-18. Copy the rectangle twice, and then place one copy in the position labeled *West View Truck Stop* on the map and the other copy in the position labeled *Liberty Auto Mall* on the map.

11. Click the **Rectangle** button again, press and hold the **Shift** key, and then draw the square labeled *Safari Park* on the map.

12. Compare your document to the map shown in Figure 6-18. Resize and reposition any shapes as needed to make your drawing match the map as closely as possible. (Ignore the labels that identify the street names.)

13. Save the document and leave it open for the next Step-by-Step.

Adding Color and Style to Drawings

Color adds life to your drawings. Word has tools that you can use to fill objects with color and change the color of lines. To change the color, select the object you want to fill or the line you want to change, and then click the contextual Format tab under Drawing Tools. This tab contains the same Arrange group of commands as on the Picture Tools contextual Format tab as well as additional commands for working with a drawn object.

To fill the object with a different color, use the Shape Fill button on the contextual Format tab (see Figure 6-19). To change the line or outline color of a drawing, use the Shape Outline button on the contextual Format tab (see Figure 6-20). These buttons are similar to the Font Color button. You can click the arrow next to either of these buttons to open the color palette, or you can click the button itself to quickly apply the color that appears in the bar at the bottom of the button.

FIGURE 6-19
Applying a fill color to a shape

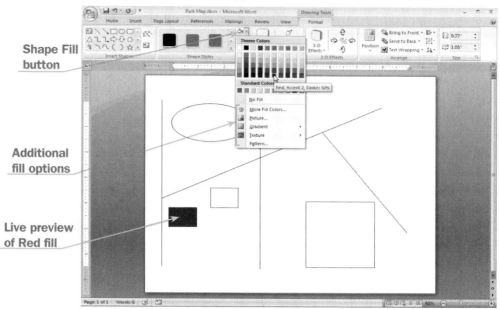

Shape Fill button

Additional fill options

Live preview of Red fill

FIGURE 6-20
Applying a line or outline color to a shape

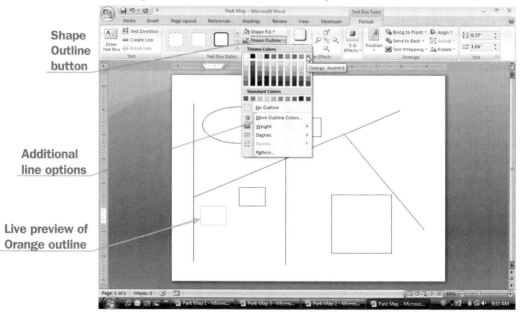

Shape Outline button

Additional line options

Live preview of Orange outline

You can also use the Shape Styles gallery to add color to your drawings. To open the Shape Styles gallery, in the Shape Styles group, click the More button. See Figure 6-21. The gallery provides various options for quickly formatting your shapes with styles and colors associated with the current theme.

Extra for Experts

Additional commands for modifying lines or shape outlines and the shape fill are available using the commands at the bottom of the menu that opens when you click the arrow next to either the Shape Outline or the Shape Fill button.

FIGURE 6-21
Shape Styles gallery

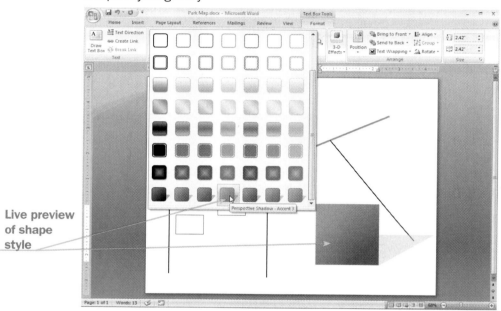

Live preview of shape style

Finally, you can also change the line weight, or thickness, of lines or shape outlines in your drawing. To do this, select the object. In the Shape Styles group, click the Shape Outline button, and then point to Weight on the menu. A submenu of line thicknesses measured in points opens. See Figure 6-22. Click the line weight you want to use.

FIGURE 6-22
Changing the thickness of a line

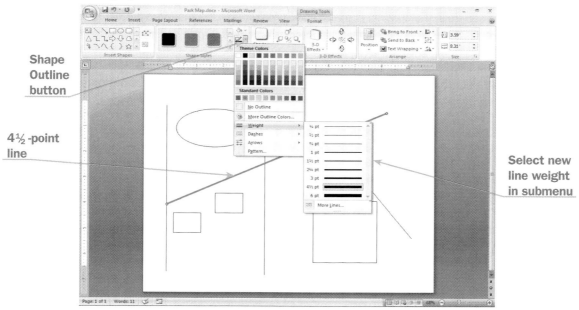

Shape Outline button

4½-point line

Select new line weight in submenu

STEP-BY-STEP 6.10

1. Click the line in the drawing that slants diagonally from the left edge of the page to the upper-right to select it.

2. If necessary, on the Ribbon, click the Drawing Tools **Format** tab. In the Shape Styles group, click the **arrow** next to the Shape Outline button. In the palette under Standard Colors, click the **Red** box. The selected line is recolored red.

3. Click one of the three rectangles in the drawing. In the Shape Styles group, click the **arrow** next to the Shape Fill button. In the palette under Theme Colors, click the **Red, Accent 2, Darker 50%** box (last row, sixth column). The selected rectangle is filled with a dark red color.

4. With the same rectangle selected, in the Shape Styles group, click the **arrow** next to the Shape Outline button. In the palette under Theme Colors, click the **Dark Blue, Text 2, Darker 50%** box (last row, fourth column). The outline color is changed to dark blue.

5. With the same rectangle selected, on the Ribbon, click the **Home** tab. In the Clipboard group, double-click the **Format Painter** button. Click the two other rectangles in the drawing. Press the **Esc** key to deselect the Format Painter button. All three rectangles are formatted the same way.

6. Select the oval in the drawing. Click the Drawing Tools **Format** tab. In the Shape Styles group, click the **More** button. The gallery of Shape Styles opens. Scroll to the bottom of the gallery, and then click the **Center Gradient – Accent 1** style (second-to-last row, second column). The oval is formatted with the selected style.

STEP-BY-STEP 6.10 Continued

7. Select the square in the drawing. In the Shape Styles group, click the **More** button, scroll to the bottom of the gallery, and then click the **Perspective Shadow – Accent 3** style (last row, fourth column). The square is formatted with the selected style. Notice that this style includes a shadow to the right of the shape.

8. On the Format tab, in the Shadow Effects group, click the **Shadow Effects** button. Under No Shadow Effect in the gallery, click the **No Shadow** style. The shadow effect is removed from the shape.

9. Click the red line in the drawing. In the Shape Styles group, click the **arrow** next to the Shape Outline button, point to **Weight**, and then click **4½ pt**. The weight of the red line is now 4½ points.

10. Click one of the other lines in the drawing, press and hold the **Shift** key, and then click the other two lines to select all three of them. Change the weight of the selected lines to **2¼ points**.

11. Select all three maroon rectangles, and then change the weight of the outline to **1½ points**.

12. Save the document and leave it open for the next Step-by-Step.

Adding Text to Your Drawings

Often your drawings will require labels. Word provides several ways to add text to a drawing. The easiest way is to right-click an object, and then click Add Text on the shortcut menu. Word places the insertion point inside the graphic. Type and format your text, and then click outside the object to deselect it.

Another way to add text to your drawing is to insert text boxes. A text box is a shape specifically designed to hold text. To add a text box, click the Insert tab, and then, in the Illustrations group, click the Shapes button. Click the Text Box button in the Basic Shapes section of the menu. Or, on the Insert tab, in the Text group, click the Text Box button, and then click Draw Text Box. The pointer changes to the crosshair pointer. Position the pointer where you want the text box to appear, and then click and drag to create a text box. An insertion point appears inside the text box so you can type the text you want. Text within a text box can be formatted in the same way you format ordinary text in a document.

A text box can be treated like any other object. You can format, resize, or change the position of a text box using the commands on the contextual Format tab that appears when you select the text box. (For text boxes, the label above the Format tab is Text Box Tools.)

Computer Concepts

Text copied from the document and set off in a text box is called a **pull quote**. Text that does not appear in a document but adds extra information for the reader and is set off in a text box is called a **sidebar**.

Did You Know?

To insert formatted text boxes, click the Text Box button on the Insert tab, and then click one of the text box styles in the gallery. The formatted text box appears as a floating object in the position indicated by the text box style in the gallery.

If you want to center the text horizontally in the text box, you use the Center command in the Paragraph group on the Home tab. However, when text is inserted in a text box, it is positioned at the top of the text box. If you want to center the text vertically within the text box or position it at the bottom of the text box, you need to use a dialog box. Click the Text Box Tools

Format tab on the Ribbon, and then, in the Text Box Styles group, click the Advanced Tools Dialog Box Launcher to open the Format AutoShape dialog box. Click the Text Box tab in this dialog box. See Figure 6-23. Use the options in the Vertical alignment section of the text box to adjust the vertical alignment.

FIGURE 6-23
Text Box tab in Format AutoShape dialog box

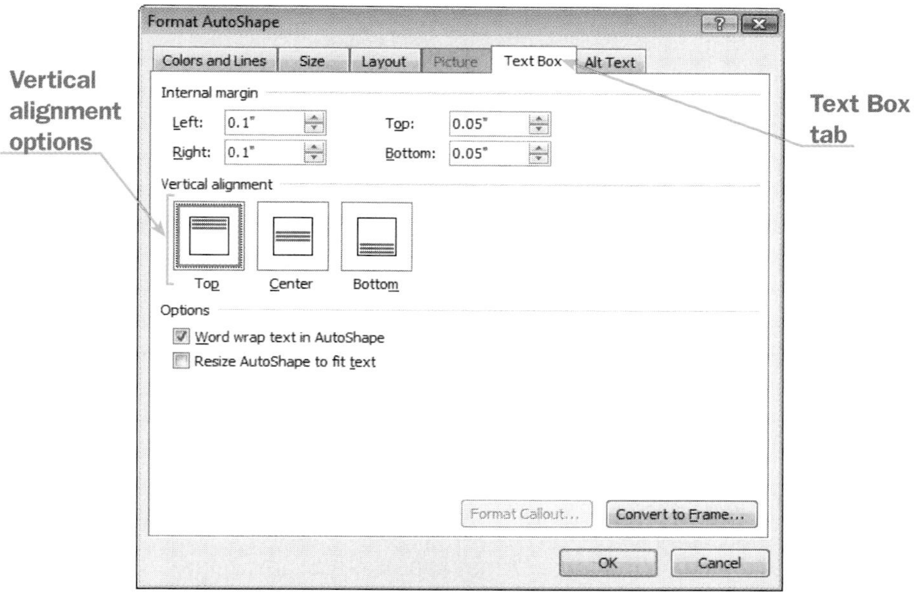

$\mathcal{S}$TEP-BY-STEP 6.11

1. Right-click the oval, and then on the submenu, click **Add Text**. A text box is created, and the insertion point appears in the oval.

2. Type **Brady Pond**. Change the style to **No Spacing**. Format the text as bold, white, 24-point Corbel, and then center it in the text box. The text is centered horizontally in the text box, but not vertically.

3. On the Ribbon, click the Text Box Tools **Format** tab, and then in the Text Box Styles group, click the **Advanced Tools Dialog Box Launcher**. The Format AutoShape dialog box opens with the Colors and Lines tab on top.

4. In the dialog box, click the **Text Box** tab. In the Vertical alignment section, click **Center**. Click **OK**. The dialog box closes and the text is centered in the oval.

5. Add the following text to the three maroon rectangles, using Figure 6-18 as a guide: **Sun Pump and Supply**, **West View Truck Stop**, and **Liberty Auto Mall**. Format the text as bold, white, 12-point Corbel, and then center it horizontally and vertically in the text boxes. (You cannot use the Format Painter to copy the format of the text because the Painter tries to copy the format of the shape instead.)

6. Add the text **Safari Park** to the large square. Change the style to **No Spacing**. Format the text as bold, white, 28-point Corbel, and then center it horizontally and vertically in the text box.

STEP-BY-STEP 6.11 Continued

7. On the Ribbon, click the **Insert** tab. In the Illustrations group, click the **Shapes** button. Under Basic Shapes, click the **Text Box** button (first row, first column under Basic Shapes). In the document, click at the top, above the drawing. A square text box appears with the insertion point inside it.

8. Type **Map to Safari Park**.

> **Did You Know?**
>
> You can quickly create a text box from existing text by selecting the text, clicking the Text Box button in the Text group on the Insert tab, and then clicking Draw Text Box. The selected text is removed from the document and placed inside the text box.

9. Drag the right, middle sizing handle to the right until the text box is approximately six inches wide. Change the style to **No Spacing**, format the text as 36-point Corbel, and then center the text horizontally in the text box.

10. Drag the bottom, middle sizing handle of the text box up to resize the text box so it is approximately one-half inch high.

11. Position the pointer on the edge of the text box so that it changes to the Move pointer, and then drag the text box to center it between the left and right margins.

12. On the Ribbon, click the **Insert** tab, if necessary. In the Text group, click the **Text Box** button. The Text Box gallery opens. At the bottom of the gallery, click **Draw Text Box**. Click in the document below the map, and then, in the text box that appears, type your name.

13. If necessary, resize the text box so that your name fits on one line. Reposition the text box so it appears in the lower-left corner of the map.

14. Save the document and leave it open for the next Step-by-Step.

Adding Callouts to Your Drawings

A **callout** is a special type of label in a drawing that consists of a text box with an attached line to point to something in the drawing. Many of the figures in this book have callouts identifying items on the screen. To add a callout, click one of the callout buttons on the Shapes menu, and then type the callout text in the callout shape.

STEP-BY-STEP 6.12

1. On the Ribbon, click the **Insert** tab. In the Illustrations group, click the **Shapes** button. Under Callouts, click the **Line Callout 2 (Accent Bar)** button (first row under Callouts, third button from the right).

> **Extra for Experts**
>
> To add an arrow to the end of a callout line (or any other drawn line), click the contextual Format tab. In the Styles group, click the Shape Outline button, point to Arrows, and then click the style of arrow you want to add.

STEP-BY-STEP 6.12 Continued

2. To create a label for Highway 84, place the crosshair pointer on the red diagonal line to the right of the center line, as shown on the map in Figure 6-18. Click and drag the mouse down approximately one-half inch, and then release the mouse button. A callout appears on the map, with the insertion point inside the text box.

3. Type **Highway 84**. Format the text as 12-point Arial Black.

4. Repeat Steps 2 and 3 to insert the callouts for **Jefferson Avenue**, **Olton Road**, and **Route 199** as shown on the map. Widen the Jefferson Avenue text box so that *Jefferson* fits on one line.

5. Compare your map to Figure 6-18. Make adjustments as needed.

6. Save, print, and close the document.

Creating Diagrams and Charts with SmartArt

Diagrams and charts are visual representations of data. They organize information in illustrations so readers can better understand relationships among data. In Word, you can insert diagrams and charts quickly using predesigned drawings called SmartArt. You can create many types of diagrams using SmartArt, including Cycle, Radial, Pyramid, Venn, and Target diagrams, and Organization Charts.

To create a SmartArt graphic, click the Insert tab, and then, in the Illustrations group, click the SmartArt button. The Choose a SmartArt Graphic dialog box opens, as shown in Figure 6-24. You can click a category in the list on the left to narrow the available choices in the middle pane in the dialog box. To insert a SmartArt graphic, click it in the pane in the middle of the dialog box, and then click OK. The graphic appears in the document with a border around it, and two SmartArt Tools tabs—Design and Format— appear on the Ribbon. You can use the commands on these tabs to add elements (shapes) and text to a diagram and to change its size and color.

Did You Know?

To change a SmartArt graphic to another shape, click the More button in the Layouts group on the SmartArtTools Design tab, and then click More Layouts to open the Choose a SmartArt Graphic dialog box again.

FIGURE 6-24
Choose a SmartArt Graphic dialog box

SmartArt categories

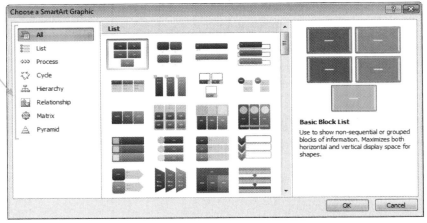

STEP-BY-STEP 6.13

1. If the **HH Newsletter.docx** document that you worked on earlier in this lesson is not open, open it now. If formatting marks are not visible, display them. Press the **Ctrl+Home** keys to jump to the top of the document.

2. In the first column in the newsletter, click in the blank paragraph above the bulleted list. On the Ribbon, click the **Insert** tab. In the Illustrations group, click the **SmartArt** button. The Choose a SmartArt Graphic dialog box opens.

3. In the category list on the left side of the dialog box, click **Hierarchy**. The middle section of the dialog box changes to display only charts that show hierarchical relationships. In the middle section of the dialog box, click the **Organization Chart** style (first row, first column). Click **OK**. An organization chart appears in the document as an inline object at the insertion point.

4. Save the document and leave it open for the next Step-by-Step.

Add Text to a SmartArt Graphic

When you create a SmartArt graphic, placeholder text appears in each shape. To insert text in a SmartArt graphic, click in each box in the graphic and start typing. The text you type replaces the placeholder text.

> **Did You Know?**
>
> You can click the Text pane control on the left side of the SmartArt graphic's border to open the Text pane, which displays the text of the SmartArt graphic as a bulleted list. You can add items to the list in the Text pane as you would to a bulleted list in a document.

STEP-BY-STEP 6.14

1. Click in the top box in the organization chart. The placeholder text disappears and the insertion point blinks in the box.

2. Type **Jose Franco**. Press the **Enter** key. Type **Office Manager**. Notice that the font size adjusted automatically as you typed so that all the text fits in the box.

STEP-BY-STEP 6.14 Continued

3. Replace the text in the three boxes in the third row in the chart with the names in the last three bullets in the bulleted list under the chart. Make sure you press the Enter key before typing the job titles. When you are finished, select the four items in the bulleted list below the chart, and then delete them.

4. Save the document and leave it open for the next Step-by-Step.

Modify a SmartArt Graphic

You can resize SmartArt graphics as you would resize any object. Instead of squares or circles, the sizing handles on a SmartArt graphic are three dots at each corner and in the middle of the sides of the selection rectangle. You can change a SmartArt graphic from an inline object to a floating object. You can also add an outline and a colored fill to the entire graphic.

In addition, you can change the look and structure of a SmartArt graphic by using some of the many commands available on the SmartArt Tools contextual tabs. On the Design tab (see Figure 6-25), you can add, move, or remove shapes to and from the diagram by using commands in the Create Graphic group. To change the layout of the graphic, click the More button in the Layouts group to display all the available layouts in the Layouts gallery. You can change the color scheme of the diagram by clicking the Change Colors button in the SmartArt Styles group. Or, you can change the style of the SmartArt, including choosing a 3-D look, by clicking the More button in the SmartArt Styles group to display the SmartArt Styles gallery.

FIGURE 6-25
Modifying SmartArt

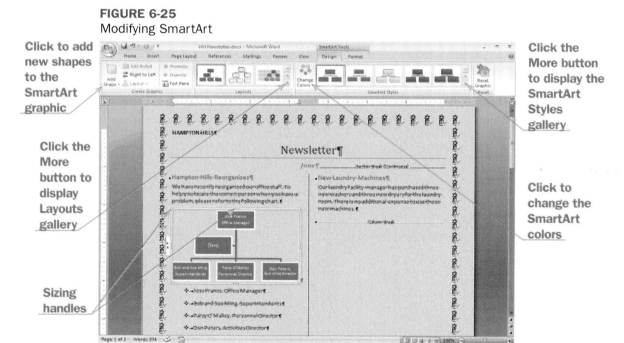

Click to add new shapes to the SmartArt graphic

Click the More button to display Layouts gallery

Sizing handles

Click the More button to display the SmartArt Styles gallery

Click to change the SmartArt colors

STEP-BY-STEP 6.15

1. In the organization chart, click the edge of the box in the second row. If a dashed line appears around the edge of the box, click the edge again to change it to a solid line. Press the **Delete** key. The box is deleted and the chart now contains only two rows of boxes.

STEP-BY-STEP 6.14 Continued

2. Click the **Patsy O'Malley** box. On the Ribbon, click the SmartArt Tools **Design** tab, if necessary. In the Create Graphic group, click the **bottom** of the Add Shape button. Make sure you click the words *Add Shape* and not the icon at the top of the button. If you click the icon, you add the default shape, which is a shape to the right of (after) the current shape.

3. On the menu, click **Add Shape Below**. A box appears in the chart below the Patsy O'Malley box. Type **Rosa Mendez**, press the **Enter** key, and then type **Assistant**.

4. On the Design tab, in the Layouts group, click the **More** button. Click the **Horizontal Hierarchy** style (second row, second column). The chart changes to the horizontal style.

5. In the SmartArt Styles group, click the **Change Colors** button. Under Accent 2 in the gallery, click **Colored Fill – Accent 2** (second style from the left). The chart colors change to dark red.

6. In the SmartArt Styles group, click the **More** button. Under Best Match for Document in the gallery, click **Intense Effect** (last style in the row under Best Match for Document). The chart style changes so that boxes have some shading.

7. Save the document and leave it open for the next Step-by-Step.

Creating WordArt

WordArt is stylized text that is treated as an object. To create WordArt, click the Insert tab, and then, in the Text group, click the WordArt button. A gallery of WordArt styles opens, as shown in Figure 6-26. Click one, and the Edit WordArt Text dialog box opens, as shown in Figure 6-27. In the Text box, type the text you want to use as the WordArt text. If the text you want to use as WordArt already exists in the document, you can select it first, and then click the WordArt button; the selected text appears in the Text box in the Edit WordArt Text dialog box.

FIGURE 6-26
Inserting WordArt

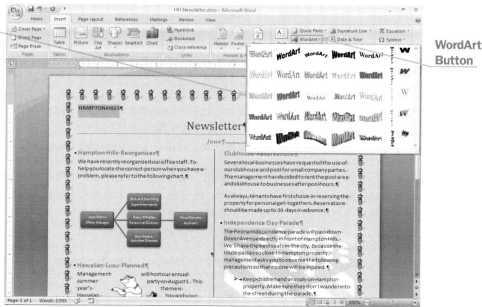

WordArt styles

WordArt Button

FIGURE 6-27
Edit WordArt Text dialog box

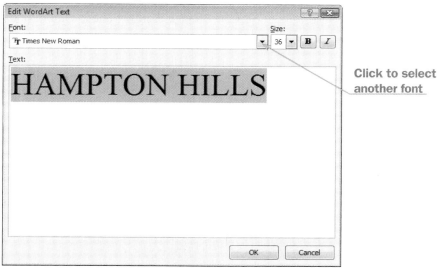

Click to select another font

After the text is entered in the Text box, click the OK button. The dialog box closes, the WordArt appears as an inline object in the document, and the WordArt Tools Format tab appears on the Ribbon. You can change the WordArt style, color, and outline color by clicking the appropriate buttons in the WordArt Styles group on the Format tab. In addition, you can change the WordArt shape by clicking the Change WordArt Shape button in the same group, and then choosing a shape from the gallery that appears. As with any other object, you can drag the sizing handles or use the boxes in the Size group on the Format tab to resize WordArt.

STEP-BY-STEP 6.16

1. Scroll to the top of the document, if necessary. Select **HAMPTON HILLS**. Do not select the paragraph mark.

2. On the Ribbon, click the **Insert** tab. In the Text group, click the **WordArt** button. Click **WordArt style 15** (third row, third column). The Edit WordArt Text dialog box opens with *HAMPTON HILLS* in the Text box.

3. Click the **Font** arrow, scroll up the list, and then click **Cambria**. Click **OK**. The dialog box closes and the selected text in the document is converted to an inline WordArt object in the style you selected—green text in front with a colored shadow behind it. The WordArt Tools Format tab is active on the Ribbon.

4. On the Format tab, in the WordArt Styles group, click the **arrow** next to the Shape Fill button. Click the **Dark Blue, Text 2, Lighter 40%** square (fourth column, fourth row). The text in the front changes to the blue color you selected.

5. In the WordArt Styles group, click the **arrow** next to the Shape Outline button. Click the **Red, Accent 2, Darker 25%** box (sixth column, fifth row). The outline of the text in front changes to the dark red color you selected.

6. In the Shadow Effects group, click the **Shadow Effects** button. At the bottom of the menu, point to **Shadow Color**. Click the **Red, Accent 2, Lighter 60%** box (sixth column, third row). The shadow text changes to a light red.

7. In the Word Art Styles group, click the **Change WordArt Shape** button. Under Warp, click the **Inflate Top** style (third row under Warp, first column). The WordArt changes shape. See Figure 6-28.

FIGURE 6-28
Modifying WordArt

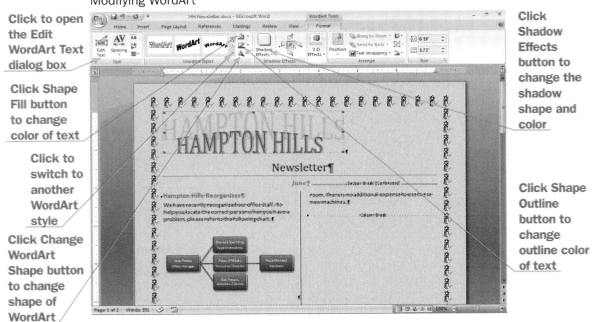

STEP-BY-STEP 6.16 Continued

8. On the Ribbon, click the **Home** tab. In the Paragraph group, click the **Center** button. The paragraph containing the inline WordArt object is centered in the line. Now you need to adjust the SmartArt graphic so the newsletter still fits on one page.

9. On the Ribbon, click the **View** tab. In the Zoom group, click the **One Page** button. In the first column, click the SmartArt graphic to select it. Drag the lower-right sizing handle up and to the left approximately one-half inch (using the rulers on the screen as a guide). The SmartArt graphic is smaller, and the newsletter now fits on one page. Deselect the SmartArt, compare your document to Figure 6-29, and make any adjustments necessary.

10. Press the **Ctrl+End** keys to jump to the end of the document, and then press the **Enter** key. On the Ribbon, click the **Home** tab, and then in the Styles group, click the **Normal** button (even though it is already selected). Type your name.

11. Hide formatting marks and the ruler. Save, print, and close the document.

FIGURE 6-29
Completed newsletter document

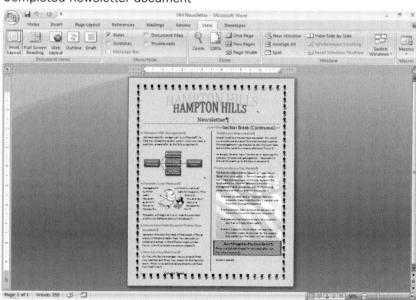

SUMMARY

In this lesson, you learned:

■ Graphics add interest to documents.

■ You can format all or part of a document in multiple columns.

■ You can add borders and shading to selected text to emphasize it. You can also add a page border and shading to the entire page.

■ An object is anything that can be manipulated as a whole. An inline object is inserted as if it were a character in a line of text. A floating object acts as if it is sitting in a separate layer on the page.

■ You can insert clip art and resize and recolor it to fit your document. You can also insert pictures in a document.

■ You can move objects anywhere in a document.

■ You can draw shapes in a document. Drawn objects can be resized, moved, and colored.

■ You can add text to drawn shapes or create a text box shape. Text boxes can be formatted, resized, or moved just like other drawn objects.

■ Callouts are special text boxes that have a line attached to them to point to specific items in a document.

■ Charts and diagrams organize your data in a manner that illustrates relationships among data. You can use SmartArt to add charts and diagrams to documents. You can change the structure and look of SmartArt.

■ You can insert WordArt to create stylized text objects. As with other objects, you can resize, reposition, and format WordArt.

VOCABULARY *Review*

Define the following terms:

Aspect ratio	Graphic	Sidebar
Callout	Inline object	Sizing handle
Chart	Keyword	SmartArt
Clip art	Object	Text box
Crop	Pull quote	WordArt
Diagram	Rotation handle	
Floating object	Selection rectangle	

REVIEW *Questions*

FILL IN THE BLANK

Complete the following sentences by writing the correct word or words in the blanks provided.

1. Choose the _____ tab on the Ribbon to add clip art, pictures, shapes, and WordArt to a document.

2. A(n) _____ is anything that can be manipulated as a whole.

3. A(n) _____ is an object that is inserted as if it were a character in the line of text.

4. To add text to a drawn object, right-click the object, and then click _____ on the shortcut menu.

5. The _____ is the relationship of an object's height to its width.

TRUE/FALSE

Circle T if the statement is true or F if the statement is false.

T   F   1.   To change the size of an object, you drag its sizing handles.

T   F   2.   Objects that you insert in a document can be placed only in a line of text in a paragraph.

T   F   3.   You must carefully choose the type of SmartArt to create because you cannot change it to another type later.

T   F   4.   To find an appropriate piece of clip art, you must scroll through an alphabetized list of all the available clip art.

T   F   5.   Borders can be placed on all four sides of a selected paragraph.

PROJECTS

 PROJECT 6-1

You volunteer at Plains Animal Shelter. The director has asked you to prepare a newsletter to be distributed to the community. She has given you some information and asked you to format it into a one-page newsletter.

1.   Open the **Shelter.docx** Data File. Save the document as **Shelter News** followed by your initials.

2.   Format the text in the document below the phone number as two columns. Do not add a line between the two columns.

3.   Center the headings in the columns.

4.   Insert a column break before the heading *Choosing a Puppy*.

5.   Near the bottom of the first column, apply a 2¼-point border at the top and the bottom of the paragraph that contains *Thank you for your help!*. Change the color of the border to Pink, Accent 2, Darker 50%. Add shading using the Pink, Accent 2, Lighter 40% theme color and add a 10% pattern, changing the color of the pattern to White, Background 1, Darker 15%.

6.   At the top of the second column, insert clip art of a person and a dog. Try using the keyword **pet** or **dog**. Use a photo or a drawing. Position the clip art to the left of the *Choosing a Puppy* heading.

7.   Change the clip art to a floating object so that the text wraps around it, and then resize it to approximately one-inch by one-inch. (If it is impossible to resize the clip art you chose to this size, click the Crop button in the Size group on the Format tab, and then drag one of the sizing handles on the side of the clip to crop off a portion of the clip so that the final size is close to one-inch by one-inch.)

8.   At the top of the newsletter, change *Plains Animal Shelter* to WordArt. Use WordArt style 9. Change the outline color to Teal, Accent 6, Darker 50%, and then change the fill color to Teal, Accent 6. If there is a blank paragraph below the WordArt, delete it.

9. View the document in One Page view. If necessary, adjust the clip art so that the entire newsletter fits on one page.

10. Insert a text box near the lower-right corner of the document. Type your name, and then resize the text box so your name fits on one line. Change the style to No Spacing, and then format it so the text is centered horizontally and vertically in the text box. Fill the text box with Yellow.

11. Save, print, and close the document.

PROJECT 6-2

A friend is having a garage sale. He asks you to create a flyer to distribute in the neighborhood.

1. Create the poster shown in Figure 6-30 using what you have learned in this lesson. The theme used is Solstice. Refer to the instructions shown in the figure.

FIGURE 6-30

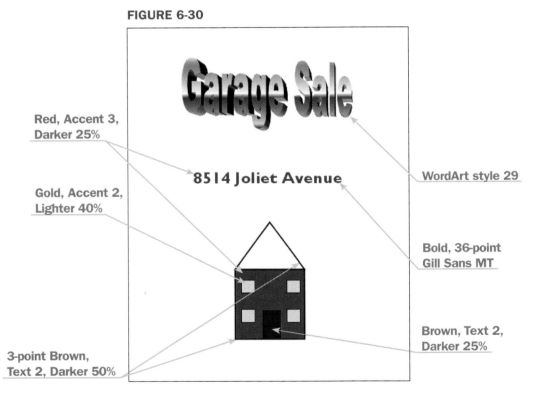

2. Insert a text box near the upper-right corner of the document. Type your name, then change the style to No Spacing. Change the outline of the text box so it is 4½ points wide.

3. Save the document as **Garage Sale** followed by your initials.

4. Print and close the document.

PROJECT 6-3

Your manager has asked you to create an invitation to the office holiday party.

1. Open the **Invitation2.docx** Data File. Save the document as **Holiday Invitation** followed by your initials.

2. Insert clip art with a holiday theme above the text. Resize and align the graphic to fit the document.

3. Change the text to a color, font, and size of your choice. The entire document should fit on one page.

4. Apply an appropriate page border and page color.

5. Insert a text box near the lower-right corner of the document. Type your name, and then resize the text box so that your name fits on one line. Format the text as bold, 12-point Calibri. Fill the text box with red.

6. Save, print, and close the document.

PROJECT 6-4

The vice president of finance for New World Marketing has asked each manager to submit an organization chart for his or her region. Vera Thomas has asked you to create the chart for the western region.

1. Open the **Memo2.docx** Data File from the location in which your data files are stored. Save the document as **Org Chart Memo** followed by your initials.

2. At the top of the document, change the color of *New World Marketing, Inc.* to Light Blue, Background 2, Darker 75%. Change the color of *MEMORANDUM* to the same color.

3. Add a border below *MEMORANDUM*. Choose a line style that has one thick line and one thin line. Apply the same color to the line as you used for *MEMORANDUM*.

4. At the top of the document, insert clip art. Use the keyword **world** to find an image of the earth.

5. Change the object to a floating object using the Tight text-wrapping option, and then resize it so it is approximately the same height as the header information at the top of the document (from the company name through the Web site address).

6. Change the object so that it appears behind the text. Recolor it or change the brightness or contrast so that the text is visible on top of the object.

7. At the end of the document, insert an organization chart using a SmartArt graphic.

8. Modify the organization chart and insert text so it matches the chart shown in Figure 6-31. The color is the Primary Theme Color Dark 2 Fill; the SmartArt style is Subtle Effect under Best Match for Document; and the Layout style is Hierarchy.

FIGURE 6-31

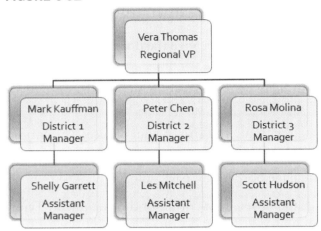

9. Add a callout in any style pointing to Rosa Molina's box. Type **Rosa was promoted to District Manager last week** as the text of the callout.

10. In the *From* line in the memo header, replace *Vera Thomas* with your name.

11. Save, print, and close your document.

CRITICAL *Thinking*

 ACTIVITY 6-1

You are having a birthday party for your friend. Create an invitation using clip art, borders, and shading. Use the drawing tools to create a map from your school to your house.

 ACTIVITY 6-2

With a classmate, create a newsletter about your class. Decide on a name for the newsletter, what information should be included, a page design, and attractive clip art. Have the class vote for their favorite.

 ACTIVITY 6-3

Use the Help system to find out how to insert a chart in a document. Create a new document, and insert a pie chart. Close the Excel window that opens, and then change the style to one that uses shades of all one color.

WORKING WITH DOCUMENTS

LESSON 7

OBJECTIVES

Upon completion of this lesson, you should be able to:

- Insert page breaks.
- Understand content controls.
- Insert and modify headers and footers.
- Insert page numbers.
- Modify document properties.
- Insert predesigned cover pages.
- Create a section with formatting that differs from other sections.
- Use the Research tool.
- Insert, modify, and format tables.
- Convert text into tables.
- Sort text.

Estimated Time: 2 hours

VOCABULARY

Cell

Content control

Document Information Panel

Footer

Gridline

Header

Orphan

Page break

Property

Section

Sort

Table

Widow

Inserting Page Breaks

In a multipage document, Word determines the place to end one page and begin the next. The place where one page ends and another begins is called a **page break**. Word automatically inserts page breaks where they are needed, but you can insert a page break manually. For example, you might want to do this to prevent an automatic page break from separating a heading from the text that follows, or you might want to start a new section of a document on a new page.

To insert a page break manually, click the Insert tab on the Ribbon, and then in the Pages group, click the Page Break button. You can also execute this command on the Page Layout tab—in the Page Setup group, click the Breaks button, and then click Page. Finally, you can also use the keyboard to insert a page break by pressing the Ctrl+Enter keys. If formatting marks are displayed, a manual page break appears immediately after the last line of text on the page. It is indicated by a dotted line with the words *Page Break* in the middle of the line, as shown in Figure 7-1. To delete manual page breaks, select the page break line, and then press the Backspace or Delete key.

FIGURE 7-1
Manual page break in a document

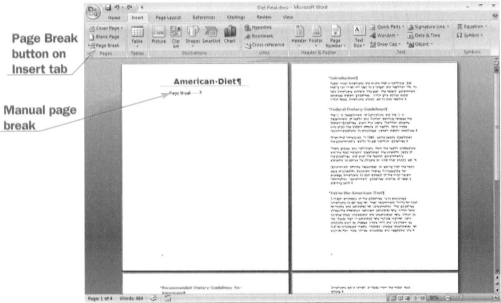

Page Break button on Insert tab

Manual page break

S TEP-BY-STEP 7.1

1. Open the **Diet2.docx** Data File. Save the document as **Diet Final** followed by your initials.

2. Display formatting marks. Position the insertion point at the beginning of the *Introduction* heading.

3. On the Ribbon, click the **Insert** tab. In the Pages group, click the **Page Break** button. A page break is inserted, and the document scrolls down so that the insertion point is blinking at the top of the new page 2. You created a new cover page for the document.

Extra for Experts

The style definition for headings usually includes a setting to keep the heading on the same page as the first line in the next paragraph. You can also specify that there is always a manual page break before a heading. To change these settings, in the Paragraph group on the Home tab or the Page Layout tab, click the Paragraph Dialog Box Launcher, and then click the Line and Page Breaks tab in the Paragraph dialog box. The settings are at the top in the Pagination section.

STEP-BY-STEP 7.1 Continued

4. Scroll up so that you can see the text near the top of page 1. The manual page break is indicated by a dotted line below the last line of text on the page with the words *Page Break* in the middle of it.

5. Scroll down so you can see the bottom of page 3 in the document. Position the insertion point in front of the heading *References*. Insert a page break.

6. Save your changes and leave the document open for the next Step-by-Step.

Computer Concepts

When you insert manual page breaks, you should try to avoid creating widows and orphans. A **widow** is the first line of a paragraph at the bottom of a page; an **orphan** is the last line of a paragraph at the top of a page. Widows and orphans are avoided when automatic page breaks are inserted.

Extra for Experts

Similar to a manual page break, you can also insert a manual line break to create a new line without creating a new paragraph. To do this, position the insertion point at the location in the line where you want the line to break, and then press the Shift+Enter keys.

Understanding Content Controls

Many predesigned elements in Word contain **content controls**, which are special placeholders designed to contain a specific type of text, such as a date or the page number. When you click a content control, the entire control is selected and a title tab appears at the top or to the left of the control. See Figure 7-2. The title tab can identify the type of information that appears in the control.

FIGURE 7-2
Content controls

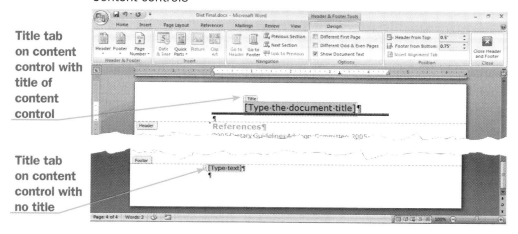

For most controls, you simply start typing, and the text you type replaces the placeholder text. For some controls, an arrow appears when you click the control, and you click the arrow to choose an item from a list or a date from a calendar. Sometimes the content control is removed when you enter text, and sometimes the content control remains in the document (although only the contents of the control will appear in the printed document). If you decide you don't want to use a content control, you can delete it. Click the title tab to select the entire control, and then press the Delete or Backspace key.

Inserting Headers, Footers, and Page Numbers

Headers and footers allow you to include the same information, such as your name and the page number, on each page of a document. A **header** is text that is printed at the top of each page. A **footer** is text that is printed at the bottom of each page. Figure 7-3 shows both a header and a footer.

FIGURE 7-3
Page with a header and footer

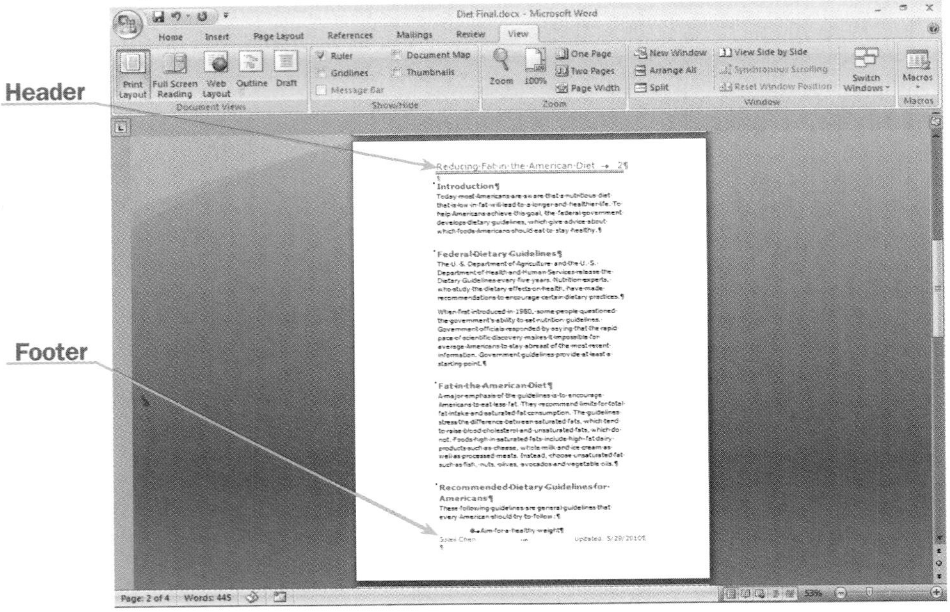

Inserting and Modifying Headers and Footers

Insert headers and footers by clicking the Insert tab, and then clicking the Header or Footer button in the Header & Footer group. When you click either of these buttons, a gallery of predesigned headers or footers opens, as shown in Figure 7-4. At the top of the list, two Blank styles are listed, and then additional styles are listed alphabetically. Each header and footer contains content controls.

FIGURE 7-4
Footer gallery

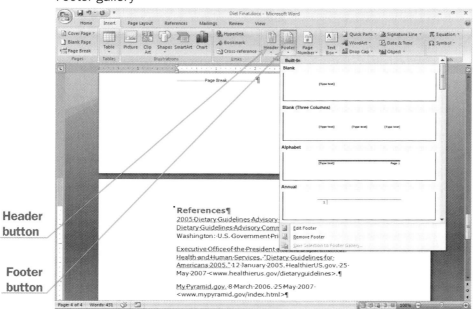

When the header or footer area is active, the Header & Footer Tools Design tab appears on the Ribbon, as shown in Figure 7-5. This tab contains buttons you can use to insert elements such as the date, time, and page numbers. Other buttons allow you to set formatting options. In the Options group, you can select the Different First Page check box to remove the header and footer from the first page of the document.

FIGURE 7-5
Footer with selected placeholder text

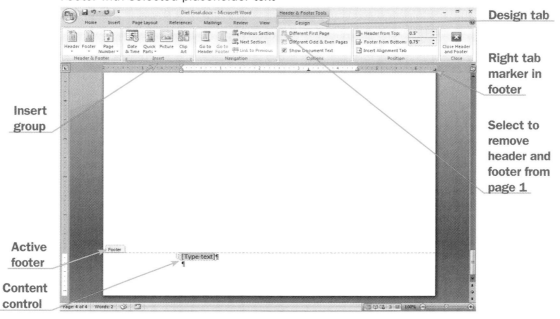

STEP-BY-STEP 7.2

1. Display the rulers, if necessary.

2. On the Insert tab, in the Header & Footer group, click the **Footer** button. A gallery of footer styles appears. Click **Blank**. The footer section appears at the bottom of the current page with placeholder text at the left margin. Notice that the footer contains a center tab marker at the 3¼-inch mark on the ruler and a right tab marker at the 6½-inch mark. The Header & Footer Tools Design tab appears on the Ribbon and is the active tab. The content control in the footer is selected, ready for you to enter text.

> **Did You Know?**
>
> To remove a header or footer, click the Header or Footer button on the Insert tab or the Header & Footer Tools Design tab, and then click Remove Header or Remove Footer.

3. In the footer section in the document, type your name. The text you type replaces the placeholder text in the content control. In this case, the content control is deleted as soon as you start typing.

4. On the ruler, drag the **right tab marker** positioned at the 6½-inch mark to the left so that it is directly on top of the right margin marker. Press **Tab** twice. The insertion point is at the right margin in the footer.

5. On the Design tab, in the Insert group, click the **Date & Time** button. In the Date and Time dialog box, deselect the Update automatically check box, if necessary, and then click **OK**. The current date is inserted in the footer in the format 5/25/2010.

6. On the Design tab, in the Header & Footer group, click the **Header** button, and then click the **Alphabet** style. The header section at the top of the page comes into view. The Alphabet style header with placeholder text is centered in the header. A blue border appears around the placeholder text and a title tab appears at the top, identifying this as a Title content control, that is, a content control that contains the document title. Type **American Diet Report**. The text you type replaces the placeholder text, but the content control stays in the document. See Figure 7-6.

STEP-BY-STEP 7.2 Continued

FIGURE 7-6
Header with text entered in Title content control

Active header

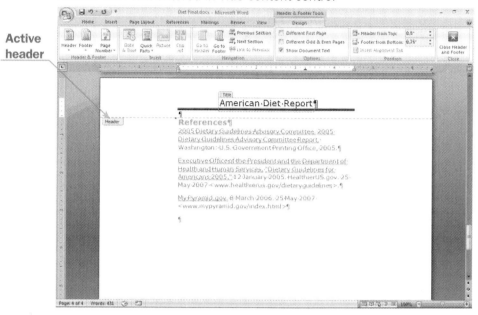

7. With the headers and footers still active, scroll up in the document so that you can see the top of page 2 and the bottom of page 1. Click in the header on page 2. On the Design tab, in the Options group, click the **Different First Page** check box, and then scroll up again so that you can see the bottom of page 1. The footer no longer appears on the first page of the document. The insertion point is still blinking in the header on page 2.

> **Extra for Experts**
>
> You can insert an empty header and footer with no content controls. In the Header & Footer group on the Insert tab, click the Header or Footer button, and then click Edit Header or Edit Footer on the menu.

8. On the Design tab, in the Navigation group, click the **Go to Footer** button. The footer on page 2 comes into view with the insertion point blinking at the beginning of the line.

9. Position the insertion point in front of the date. Type **Updated:**, and then press the **spacebar**.

10. Double-click the document window above the footer section. The section of the document that was active before you started working on the header and footer (page 4) jumps into view. The headers and footers appear faded, and the insertion point is blinking in the document window.

11. Save your changes and leave the document open for the next Step-by-Step.

Inserting Page Numbers

 Page numbers are included in some of the header and footer styles. If you choose a header or footer style that does not include page numbers, or if you want to insert page numbers without inserting anything else in a header or footer, you can use the Page Number button in the Header & Footer group on the Insert tab or on the Header & Footer Tools Design tab. A menu opens with choices for you to insert page numbers at the top or the bottom of the page, in the margin, or at the current position. When you point to any of these options, a gallery of choices appears. If you choose Top of Page or Bottom of Page, you automatically create a header or footer with only the page number as content. See Figure 7-7. If a header or footer already exists, the page number style you choose replaces it.

FIGURE 7-7
Top of Page gallery on Page Number menu

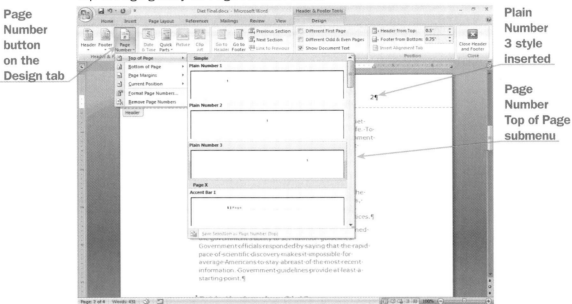

Page Number button on the Design tab

Plain Number 3 style inserted

Page Number Top of Page submenu

If you want to insert the page number in an existing header or footer, first position the insertion point in the header or footer at the location where you want the page number to appear. Click the Page Number button, point to Current Position, and then choose a style.

STEP-BY-STEP 7.3

1. Scroll so that you can see the top of page 2. Double-click anywhere in the header on page 2. The header becomes active and the insertion point blinks at the beginning of the content control.

2. On the Design tab, in the Header & Footer group, click the **Page Number** button, point to **Top of Page**, and then click **Plain Number 3**. Instead of adding the page number near the right margin, the page number header replaced the header you created.

3. On the Quick Access Toolbar, click the **Undo** button. The header you created reappears.

Did You Know?

To hide the margins and space between pages in a document, move the insertion point to the top of the page until it changes to a button with double arrows , and then double-click. To show the space again, position the insertion point on the top of the line between pages so that it changes to , and then double-click.

STEP-BY-STEP 7.3 Continued

4. On the ruler, drag the **right tab mark** positioned at the 6½-inch mark to the left so that it is directly on top of the right margin marker. Drag the **center tab mark** positioned at the 3¼-inch mark off the ruler to remove it. Press the **End** key, and then press the **right arrow** key. The insertion point is positioned between the content control and the paragraph mark. Press the **Tab** key. The insertion point is positioned at the right margin.

5. In the Header & Footer group, click the **Page Number** button. Point to **Current Position**, and then click **Plain Number**. The page number appears at the location of the insertion point, formatted in the same style as the rest of the header text.

6. On the Design tab, in the Close group, click the **Close Header and Footer** button.

7. Save your changes and leave the document open for the next Step-by-Step.

Modifying Document Properties

When you save a file, identifying information about the file is saved along with it, such as the author's name and the date the file was created. This information is known as the file properties.

To view or add properties to a document, click the Office button, point to Prepare, and then click Properties. The Document Information Panel appears at the top of the document window, as shown in Figure 7-8. To see additional properties, click the Document Properties button in the Document Information Panel, and then click Advanced Properties. The Properties dialog box for the current file opens. Click the Summary tab to see additional properties, as shown in Figure 7-9.

FIGURE 7-8
Document Information Panel open

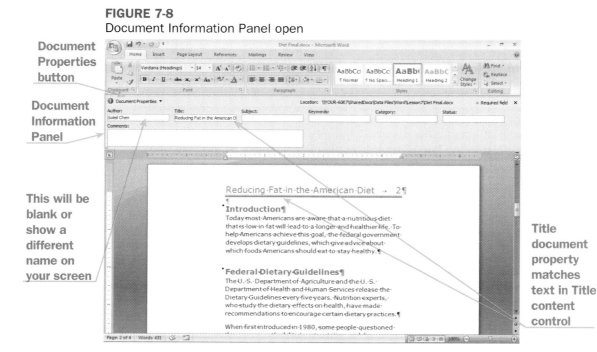

Document Properties button

Document Information Panel

This will be blank or show a different name on your screen

Title document property matches text in Title content control

FIGURE 7-9
Summary tab in Diet Final.docx Properties dialog box

Summary tab

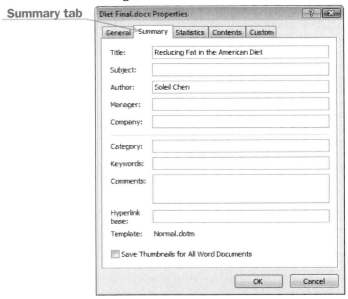

Content controls can be linked to document properties so that they pick up and display the information stored as a document property. For example, if a content control is tied to the Title document property, it displays the information stored in the Title box in the Document Information Panel. The connection works both ways, so that if you change the Title in the content control, the change appears in the Title box in the Document Information Panel and in every other Title content control in the document.

STEP-BY-STEP 7.4

1. If necessary, scroll up so you can see the header at the top of page 2. Click the **Office Button**, and then point to **Prepare**. In the right pane on the Office menu, click **Properties**. The Document Information Panel appears just below the Ribbon. Notice that *American Diet Report*, the title you typed in the Title content control in the header, appears in the Title box in the Document Information Panel.

2. In the Title box in the Document Information Panel, select all the text, and then type **Reducing Fat in the American Diet**. Click a blank area in the Document Information Panel. The text in the Title content control in the header on page 2 changes to the text you just typed.

3. If there is any text in the Author box in the Document Information Panel, select it. Type your name in the Author box.

4. In the upper-left of the Document Information Panel, click **Document Properties**, and then click **Advanced Properties**. The Diet Final.docx Properties dialog box opens. If necessary, click the **Summary** tab.

STEP-BY-STEP 7.4 Continued

5. If there is any text in the Company box, select it. Type your school name in the Company box. Click **OK**. In the upper-right of the Document Information Panel, click the **Close** button.

6. Save your changes and leave the document open for the next Step-by-Step.

Inserting a Cover Page

You can quickly create a cover page by inserting one of the many predesigned cover pages available with Word. To insert a predesigned cover page, click the Insert tab, and then, in the Pages group, click the Cover Page button. A gallery of cover pages opens, as shown in Figure 7-10.

FIGURE 7-10
Cover Page gallery

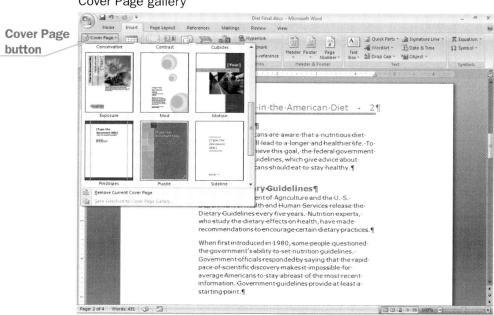

The cover pages contain content controls, as shown in Figure 7-11. As with the content controls that appear in headers and footers, you can use them or delete them, and then insert your own content.

FIGURE 7-11
Sideline cover page with information from document properties

Company content control picked up Company text from document properties

Title content control picked up Title text from document properties

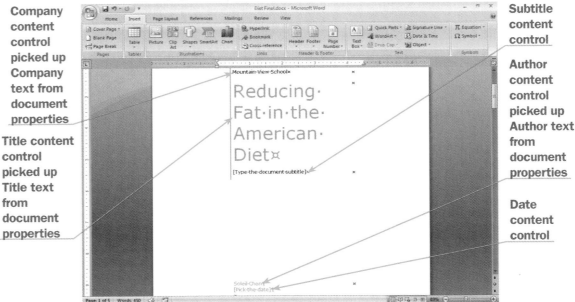

Subtitle content control

Author content control picked up Author text from document properties

Date content control

STEP-BY-STEP 7.5

1. If necessary, on the Ribbon, click the **Insert** tab. In the Pages group, click the **Cover Page** button. In the gallery, scroll down until you see Sideline, and then click **Sideline**. A cover page is inserted at the beginning of the document. At the top of the page, the Company content control is selected. *Company* in the title tab identifies this as a content control that picked up the Company name from the document properties. Notice that the title was picked up as well.

2. Click the **placeholder** that says *Type the document subtitle*. Click the **Subtitle** title tab. The title tab darkens. Press the **Delete** key. The content control is deleted.

3. Scroll to the bottom of the page. Notice that your name was picked up in the Author content control at the bottom of the page.

4. Click the **placeholder** that says *Pick the date*. The Date title tab appears, and an arrow appears to the right of the control.

5. Click the **arrow**. A calendar appears displaying the current month and year with today's date highlighted. See Figure 7-12.

> **Did You Know?**
>
> To insert a blank page, click the Blank Page button in the Pages group on the Insert tab.

STEP-BY-STEP 7.5 Continued

FIGURE 7-12
Selecting a date with a Date content control

Current date
(will differ
on your
screen)

Click
to open
calendar

Click arrows
to scroll to
new month

Click to insert
the current
date

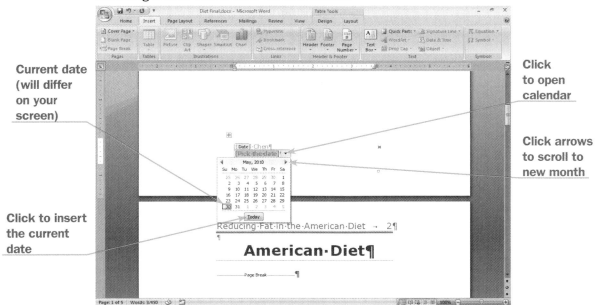

6. Click tomorrow's date in the calendar. Tomorrow's date appears in the document. (If you need to scroll to the next month, click the arrow to the right of the month name.)

7. Scroll down, if necessary, so that you can see the text and the page break on page 2. You don't need the temporary cover page any more. On page 2, select *American Diet*, the paragraph mark at the end of the line, the Page Break formatting mark, and the paragraph mark at the end of the line. Press the **Delete** key. The text on the page and the page break are deleted, removing the entire page from the document.

8. Save your changes and leave the document open for the next Step-by-Step.

> **Did You Know?**
>
> To split the document window and view two parts of a document at once, on the Ribbon, click the View tab. In the Window group, click the Split button. A horizontal gray line appears halfway down the window, and the pointer, which changed to a double-sided arrow, is on top of the gray line. Without pressing the mouse button, drag the bar to position it, and then click the left mouse button. To remove the split, click the Remove Split button in the Window group on the View tab.

Creating New Sections

You can divide a document into two or more sections. A section is a part of a document where you can create a different layout from the rest of the document. For example, you might want to format only part of a page with columns. You can also have different headers and footers, page numbers, margins, orientation, and other formatting features in different sections.

To create a new section, click the Page Layout tab, and then in the Page Setup group, click the Breaks button. A menu of choices for inserting breaks appears, as shown in Figure 7-13. The bottom half of the menu lists types of section breaks. To start the new section on the next page, choose Next Page. To start the new section on the same page, choose Continuous. To start the new section break on the next even-numbered or odd-numbered page, choose Even Page or Odd Page.

FIGURE 7-13
Breaks menu

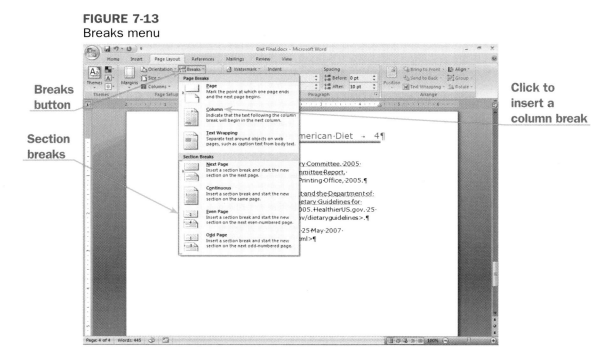

When formatting marks are displayed, a section break is indicated by a double dotted line across the page with the words *Section Break* in the middle, as shown in Figure 7-14. To delete a section break, select the section break line, and then press the Delete or Backspace key.

FIGURE 7-14
Continuous section break and column break in a document

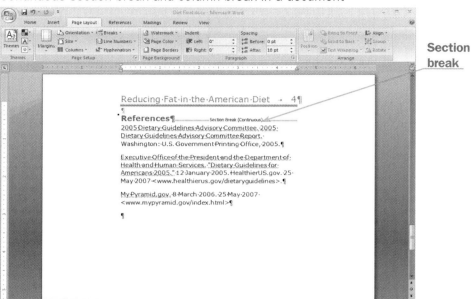

STEP-BY-STEP 7.6

1. Go to page 4 in the document. Position the insertion point in front of *2005 Dietary Guidelines Advisory Committee* in the first reference.

2. On the Ribbon, click the **Page Layout** tab. In the Page Setup group, click the **Breaks** button. Under Section Breaks, click **Continuous**. Because formatting marks are displayed, you can see that a continuous section break was inserted.

3. In the Page Setup group, click the **Columns** button, and then click **Two**. The current section is formatted in two columns. If the section break were not there, the entire document would have been formatted in two columns.

4. Position the insertion point in front of the third reference, *MyPyramid.gov*. In the Page Setup group, click the **Breaks** button, and then under Page Breaks, click **Column**. A column break is inserted below the last line in the *Executive Office of the President* reference.

5. Save your changes and leave the document open for the next Step-by-Step.

Using the Research Tool

Word provides online access to a dictionary, thesaurus, encyclopedia, and other resources to help you research information. You need an Internet connection for all research resources except the dictionary, thesaurus, and translation tool. To use the Research tool, click the Review tab on the Ribbon. In the Proofing group, click the Research button. The Research task pane opens to the right of the document window. Type the item to be researched in the Search for box, and then click the arrow in the box below the Search for box to select the reference that you want to use. The search executes and the results appear in the task pane. See Figure 7-15. If the reference you want to use already appears in the Search for box, you can click the Start searching button to execute the search.

FIGURE 7-15
Research task pane open with results from Encarta Encyclopedia

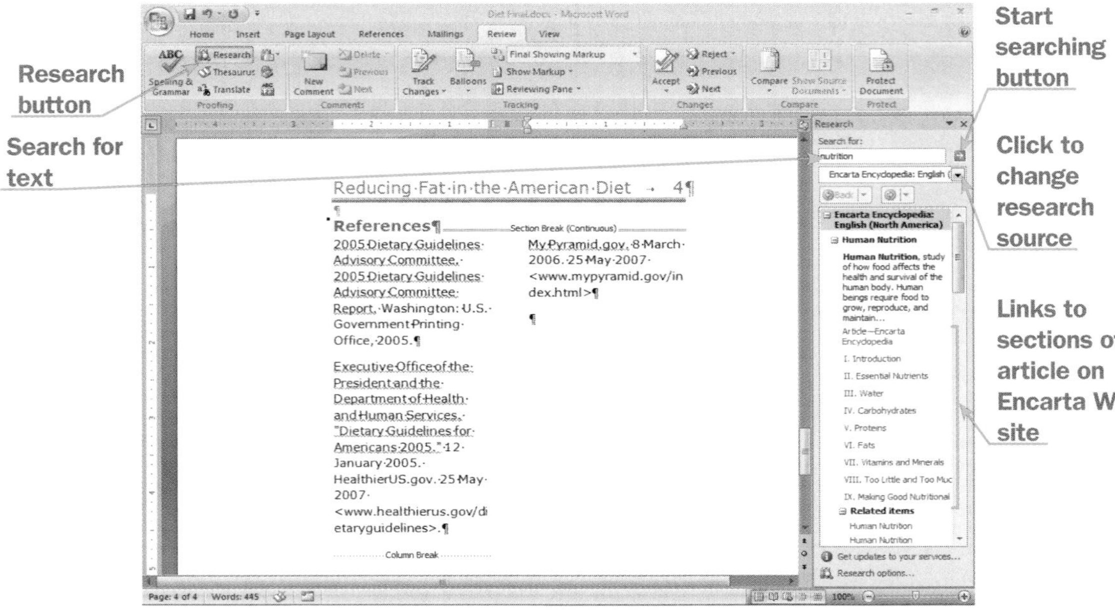

STEP-BY-STEP 7.7

1. On the Ribbon, click the **Review** tab. In the Proofing group, click the **Research** button. The Research task pane opens to the right of the document window. You'll find additional information about nutrition to add to the report.

2. In the Research task pane, select all the text in the Search for box if there is any, or simply click in the Search for box if it is empty. Type **nutrition**.

3. Click the **arrow** next to *All Reference Books* in the box below the Search for box. Click **Encarta Encyclopedia: English**. The search starts and, after a moment, results appear in the task pane. An outline of an article about human nutrition appears in the Research task pane. (*Note:* If you are not connected to the Internet, you will not get the same results. Use whatever results you get; if you do not get any results, read the rest of the steps in this section and only complete Steps 10 and 13.)

4. Click on the heading **VI. Fats**. Your browser starts, and the Web page containing information about fats on the MSN Encarta Web site appears in the browser window. See Figure 7-16. (If you don't see your browser window, look on the taskbar. The taskbar button for your browser should be blinking or appear orange. Click the browser taskbar button. If more than one button for your browser appears on the taskbar, click the orange button.)

STEP-BY-STEP 7.7 Continued

FIGURE 7-16
Web page with information about fats on the Encarta Web site

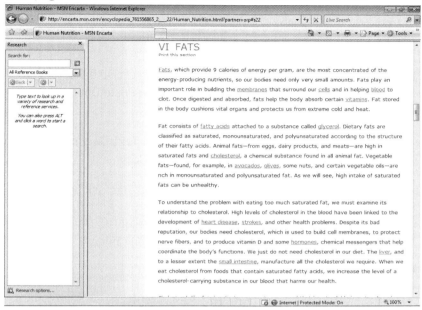

5. Scroll down several paragraphs, and then, in the last paragraph of the section about fats, drag to select the text beginning with *Health experts consider* to the end of the section. Right-click the selected text, and then click **Copy** on the shortcut menu. See Figure 7-17.

FIGURE 7-17
Copying information from the Encarta Web site

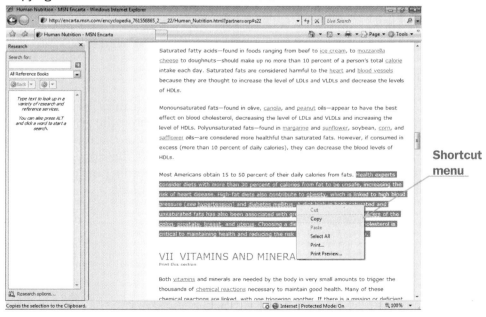

Shortcut menu

STEP-BY-STEP 7.7 Continued

6. In the upper-right corner of the browser window, click the **Close** button. The browser window closes. (If another browser window is open, click its Close button.)

7. Go to page 2. In the paragraph under the *Fat in the American Diet* heading, position the insertion point at the end of the last sentence. Press the **Enter** key.

8. On the Ribbon, click the **Home** tab. In the Clipboard group, click the **Paste** button. The selected text from the Encarta article appears in the document, and the Paste Options button appears just below the lower-right of the pasted text.

9. Click the **Paste Options** button, and then click the **Keep Text Only** option button. The Web page formatting, including the links, is removed from the document.

10. In the Research task pane title bar, click the **Close** button. The task pane closes.

11. Type **"**. Quotation marks appear after the period at the end of the text you just pasted. Position the insertion point at the beginning of the paragraph you just pasted. Type **"**.

12. Press the **left arrow** key. Type **According to the Encarta Encyclopedia,**. Press the **spacebar**.

13. Save your changes and leave the document open for the next Step-by-Step.

> **Important**
>
> Whenever you are using information from another source, it is important to document the source. If this were a real research paper, you would add the Encarta Encyclopedia to the References list at the end of the document.

Creating Tables

A table is an arrangement of text or numbers in rows and columns, similar to a spreadsheet. The intersection of a row and column is called a cell. Tables are sometimes easier to use than trying to align text with tabs.

Inserting a Table

To create a table, click the Insert tab, and then, in the Tables group, click the Table button. A menu opens with a grid in the top portion. As you move the pointer over the grid, the outline of the cells in the grid changes to orange, and the label at the top of the menu indicates the dimensions of the table. As you drag, the table appears in the document behind the grid. See Figure 7-18. Click when the grid and the label indicate the number of rows and columns you want to create. A table is inserted at the location of the insertion point.

FIGURE 7-18
Inserting a table

Table
button

Pointer

Dimensions of
inserted table

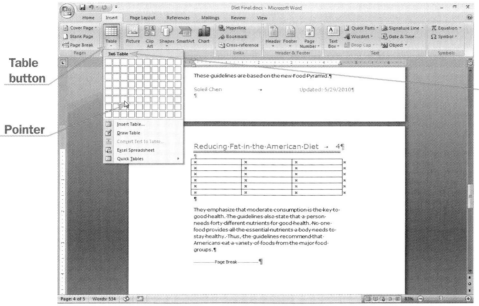

To enter text in a table, click in a cell, and then type. To move to the next cell to the right, press the Tab key or click in the cell. To move back one cell, press the Shift+Tab keys.

Did You Know?

If you know exactly how many rows and columns you want to create, you can also click the Table button in the Tables group on the Insert tab, and then click Insert Table on the menu. The Insert Table dialog box opens. Change the values in the Number of columns and the Number of rows boxes as needed.

S TEP-BY-STEP 7.8

1. Go to page 4. Position the insertion point in the empty paragraph at the top of the page. (If you were not able to complete the steps in Step-by-Step 7.7, go to page 3, and then below the bulleted list, position the insertion point in the empty paragraph below the sentence that starts *These guidelines are based.*)

2. On the Ribbon, click the **Insert** tab. In the Tables group, click the **Table** button. A menu opens with a grid at the top of it. *Insert Table* appears in the blue bar at the top of the grid.

3. Without clicking the mouse button, drag the pointer over the grid. As you drag, the squares change so they have orange outlines, and the text in the blue bar at the top of the grid changes to the number of squares you have selected.

4. Point to the cell that creates a **3x6 Table**, and then click. The menu closes and a table with three columns and six rows is inserted in the document. The insertion point is blinking in the first cell in the table.

5. Type **Food Groups**. The text you type appears in the first cell in the table. Press the **Tab** key. The insertion point moves to the next cell to the right. Type **Daily Recommendations**. Press the **Tab** key twice. The insertion point moves to the second cell in the first column.

STEP-BY-STEP 7.8 Continued

6. Type the rest of the data in the table as shown in Figure 7-19. Leave the third column blank.

FIGURE 7-19
Data in table

Food Groups	Daily Recommendations	
Grains	3 oz whole grains	
Vegetables	2 to 3 cups	
Fruits	1-1/2 to 2 cups	
Oils	5 to 7 teaspoons	
Milk	3 cups	

7. Click in the last cell in the table. Press the **Tab** key. A new row is created at the bottom of the table.

8. Type **Meat & beans**. Press the **Tab** key. Type **5 to 6-1/2 oz**.

9. Save your changes and leave the document open for the next Step-by-Step.

Modifying the Table Structure

You can modify the structure of a table by using commands on the Table Tools Layout tab on the Ribbon. To insert a row, click a cell in the table, and then in the Rows & Columns group, click the Insert Above or Insert Below button, depending on where you want the row to appear in relation to the insertion point. To insert a column, click the Insert Left or Insert Right button. To delete a row or column, position the insertion point in the row or column you want to delete. In the Rows & Columns group, click the Delete button, and then click the appropriate command to delete cells, columns, rows, or the entire table.

You can change the width of columns and the height of rows. Position the pointer on top of a gridline in the table so that it changes to a double-headed arrow. Drag the border line to resize the column or the row.

You can split cells to transform one column or row into two or more. You can merge cells to create one large cell out of several small cells. To merge cells, select the cells, and then click the Merge Cells button in the Merge group on the Table Tools Layout tab. To split cells, select a cell or cells, and then click the Split Cells button to open the Split Cells dialog box. Specify the number of columns and rows you want to create from the selected cell or cells, and then click OK. If the result is not what you expected, undo your change, open the Split Cells dialog box again, and then click the Merge cells before split check box.

> **Did You Know?**
>
> To select an entire row, click to the left of the row (outside the table). To select an entire column, position your pointer just above the column so that the pointer changes to a downward-pointing arrow, and then click.

STEP-BY-STEP 7.9

1. Position the insertion point in any cell in the last column of the table. On the Ribbon, click the Table Tools **Layout** tab, if necessary. In the Rows & Columns group, click the **Delete** button. Click **Delete Columns**. The current column is deleted.

2. Position the insertion point in any cell in the first row of the table. In the Rows & Columns group, click the **Insert Above** button. A new row is inserted above the row containing the insertion point.

3. Click in the first cell in the new row. Type **USDA Food Pyramid Guidelines**.

4. Position the pointer over the column divider between the two columns. The pointer changes to a double-headed arrow. Press and hold the mouse button, and then drag the column divider to the left until the left column is approximately 1¼ inches wide.

5. Drag the right border of the table to the right until the right column is approximately two inches wide and *Daily Recommendations* fits on one line.

6. Drag to select the two cells in the top row. On the Layout tab, in the Merge group, click the **Merge Cells** button. The two cells are merged into one cell. See Figure 7-20. (Remember, if you were not able to access the Internet and complete the steps in Step-by-Step 7.7, your table is on page 3, not page 4 as shown in Figure 7-20.)

FIGURE 7-20
Modified table

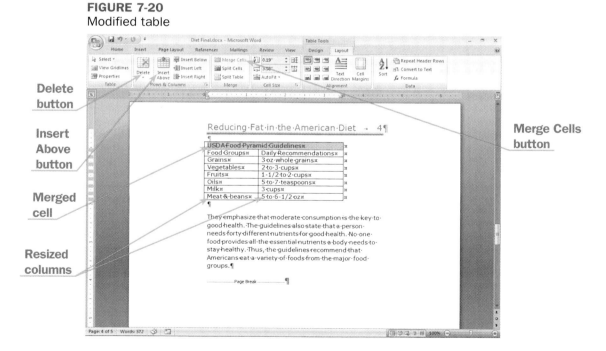

7. Save your changes and leave the document open for the next Step-by-Step.

Formatting Tables

The easiest way to format a table is to use one of the many predesigned formats in the Table Styles group on the Table Tools Design tab. See Figure 7-21. If you want to treat the first and last rows or the first and last columns differently than the rest of the rows and columns in the table, you can select the Header Row, Total Row, First Column, and Last Column check boxes in the Table Style Options group on the Table Tools Design tab. To add shading to every other row or every other column, select the Banded Rows or Banded Columns check boxes in the same group.

FIGURE 7-21
Live Preview of a table style

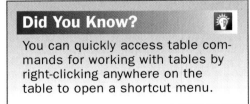

You can manually format text in a table as you would format any text in a document. You can select the entire table by positioning the pointer on top of the table and then clicking the table move handle that appears above the upper-right corner of the table. Then you can position the table on the page by clicking an alignment button in the Paragraph group on the Home tab. You can also change the color of the table lines and the fill color of the cells by using the Shading and Borders buttons in the Table Styles group on the Table Tools Design tab. To change the alignment of text in a cell, click one of the alignment buttons in the Alignment group on the Table Tools Layout tab.

> **Did You Know?**
>
> You can quickly access table commands for working with tables by right-clicking anywhere on the table to open a shortcut menu.

When you add color to borders, you need to make sure you are trying to format border lines, not table gridlines. Border lines are visible lines that print when you print your document. When a table is created, the **gridlines** form the structure of the table, the outline of the rows and columns. To make sure the table prints the way you expect, turn off the gridlines.

S TEP-BY-STEP 7.10

1. Click anywhere in the table. On the Ribbon, click the Table Tools **Design** tab. In the Table Style Options group, notice that the Header Row, First Column, and Banded Rows check boxes are selected.

2. On the Design tab, in the Table Styles group, click the **More** button, and then in the gallery, click the **Medium Shading 1 – Accent 6** style (fourth row, last column under Built-In). The gallery closes and the table is reformatted with that style.

3. In the Table Style Options group, click the **Banded Rows** check box to deselect it. The shading in every other row is removed. Click the **First Column** check box to deselect it. The bold formatting is removed from the first column.

4. Click in the first row of the table. On the Ribbon, click the Table Tools **Layout** tab. In the Alignment group, click the **Align Center** button. The text in the top row is centered in the cell.

5. Select all the text in the second row of the table. On the Ribbon, click the **Home** tab. In the Font group, click the **Bold** button. The text in the second row is bold, and *Daily Recommendations* might wrap to two lines.

6. If *Daily Recommendations* is now on two lines, click in the table to position the insertion point without selecting any text. Drag the right border of the table to the right just enough so that *Daily Recommendations* fits on one line again.

> **Did You Know?**
>
> You can double-click the right border of a column to automatically resize the column to accommodate the width of the longest entry in the column.

7. Position the pointer over the table. The table move handle appears above the upper-left cor- ner of the table. Position the pointer over the table move handle so that the pointer changes to a four-headed arrow, and then click the table move handle. The entire table is selected.

8. On the **Home** tab, in the Paragraph group, click the **Center** button. The table is centered on the page.

> **Did You Know?**
>
> Using the table move handle, you can drag a table anywhere in a document.

STEP-BY-STEP 7.10 Continued

9. Click anywhere in the table to position the insertion point in the table. On the Ribbon, click the Table Tools **Layout** tab. In the Table group, locate the View Gridlines button and determine if it is selected. If it is selected, it will be orange. See Figure 7-22. If it is selected, you will see a dotted gridline between the two columns in the table.

FIGURE 7-22
Formatted table with gridlines visible

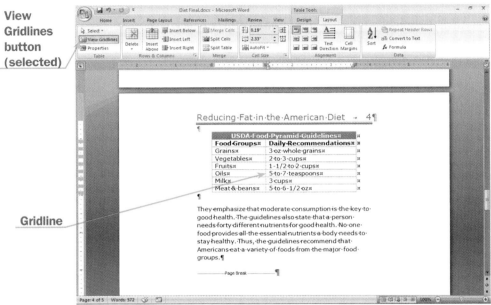

10. If the View Gridlines button is selected, click the **View Gridlines** button to deselect it. The dotted gridline between the two columns in the table disappears.

11. Drag to select all the rows in the table except the first row. On the Ribbon, click the Table Tools **Design** tab. In the Table Styles group, click the **arrow** next to the Borders button, and then click Borders and Shading. In the Setting list on the left, click the **All** button. Click **OK**. A vertical line appears between the first and second columns in the table.

12. Save your changes and leave the document open for the next Step-by-Step.

Converting Text into Tables

You can convert text you have already typed into a table. Select the text you want to convert to a table. On the Insert tab on the Ribbon, click the Table button in the Tables group, and then click Convert Text to Table on the menu. The Convert Text to Table dialog box opens. Word converts the text to a table by creating columns from text separated by a comma or a tab, and by creating rows from text separated by a paragraph marker.

Sorting Text

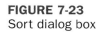 Sorting arranges a list of words in ascending order (*a* to *z*) or in descending order (*z* to *a*). Sorting can also arrange a list of numbers in ascending order (smallest to largest) or descending order (largest to smallest). Sorting is useful for putting lists of names or terms in alphabetical order.

To sort text in a table, click anywhere in the table, click the Table Tools Layout tab, and then in the Data group, click the Sort button. The Sort dialog box opens, as shown in Figure 7-23. In this dialog box, you can choose the options for the sort.

FIGURE 7-23
Sort dialog box

Click to change column on which data is sorted

Select to indicate that the selected data includes a header row

Options for changing sort order

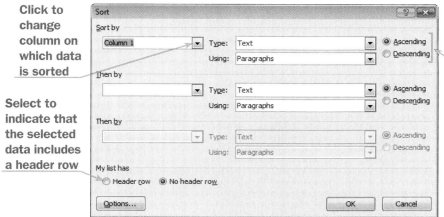

S TEP-BY-STEP 7.11

1. If necessary, drag to select all the rows in the table except the first row. On the Ribbon, click the Table Tools **Layout** tab. In the Data group, click the **Sort** button. The Sort dialog box opens.

2. Make sure **Column 1** appears in the Sort by box. Make sure that the **Ascending** option button at the top of the dialog box is selected. The table will be sorted in alphabetical order by the values in the first column.

3. At the bottom of the dialog box, click the **Header row** option button. This will exclude the first row of the selected rows from being included in the sort.

4. Click **OK**. The dialog box closes and the data in the table is sorted in alphabetical order by the values in the first column.

5. Deselect the table. Turn off the rulers and hide formatting marks.

6. Save, print, and close the document.

Did You Know?

You can also sort a list that is not organized in a table. Select the list, and then, in the Paragraph group on the Home tab, click the Sort button.

Did You Know?

If the table contains numbers, click the Type arrow in the Sort dialog box, and then click Number to sort the table numerically. Otherwise, it will sort the data using the first digit only, so that 10 would come before 2.

SUMMARY

In this lesson, you learned:

- Word automatically inserts page breaks where they are necessary. You also can insert page breaks manually.

- Content controls are special placeholders designed to contain a specific type of text. When you insert text, some content controls remain in the document and some are deleted.

- Headers appear at the top of every page in the document; footers appear at the bottom of every page. The Header & Footer Tools Design tab appears when a header or footer is active.

- You can insert page numbers in the header or footer area. The page number style can replace a header or footer, or you can use the Current Position command to insert a page number at the location of the insertion point.

- You can modify file properties in the Document Information Panel. Some types of content controls are linked to document properties.

- You can insert a predesigned cover page with content controls by clicking the Cover Page button in the Pages group on the Insert tab.

- To create different page layouts within one document, divide the document into sections.

- The Research tool allows you to access the Internet to explore different sources for information.

- Tables show data in columns and rows. You can modify tables by adding and removing rows and columns and merging and splitting cells. You can format a table with styles and manual formatting.

- You can convert text into a table with the Convert Text to Table command.

- You can sort text in a document alphabetically or numerically in ascending or descending order.

VOCABULARY *Review*

Define the following terms:

Cell	Header	Section
Content control	Orphan	Sort
Document Information Panel	Page break	Table
Footer	Property	Widow
Gridline		

REVIEW *Questions*

MULTIPLE CHOICE

Select the best response for the following statements.

1. When formatting marks are displayed, a manual page break is indicated in the document by a
    A. thick horizontal line.
    B. dotted line with the words *Page Break* in the middle of the line.
    C. row of paragraph marks.
    D. series of dashes.

2. To modify the document properties, you need to display the
    A. Summary dialog box.
    B. Document dialog box.
    C. Properties Panel.
    D. Document Information Panel.

3. A part of a document that is formatted with a different page layout than the rest of the document is called a(n)
    A. auto-orientation.
    B. table.
    C. section.
    D. manual break.

4. To find information on the Web using a variety of sources, what button do you click in the Proofing group on the Review tab?
    A. Research
    B. Proof
    C. Encyclopedia
    D. Resource

5. What is the intersection of a row and column in a table called?
    A. Cell
    B. Content control
    C. Grid
    D. Box

FILL IN THE BLANK

Complete the following sentences by writing the correct word or words in the blanks provided.

1. A special placeholder designed to contain a specific type of text, such as a date or the page number, is called a(n) _____ .

2. Document or file _____ are identifying information about the file, such as the author's name and the date the file was created, that is saved along with the file.

3. _____ form the structure of a table.

4. If a list of words is sorted alphabetically, it is listed in _____ order.

5. To select an entire table, click the _____ .

PROJECTS

PROJECT 7-1

Your supervisor has asked you to update the Guidelines for Outgoing Correspondence document.

1. Open the **Guidelines.docx** Data File. Save the document as **Correspondence Guidelines** followed by your initials.

2. Create a header using the Conservative style. Type **Guidelines** in the Title content control, and use the Date content control to insert the date for one week from today.

3. Insert the Stacks footer. Do not replace the placeholder text.

4. Do not display the header or footer on the first page of the document.

5. Open the Document Information Panel, and then open the Properties dialog box for the document. Delete any text in the Author box. Add your name as the Company name. In the Document Information Panel, change the title to **Guidelines for Correspondence**. Verify that the Title property is displayed in the header and that the Company name property is displayed in the footer.

6. Position the insertion point to the right of the content control in the footer, and then press the Tab key. Insert the Accent Bar 2 page number style at the current position.

7. On page 1, insert a page break before the *Check Spelling* heading.

8. Select the words *commonly misspelled words* in the *Check Spelling* section. Open the Research pane to find other lists of commonly misspelled words. Change the source for the research to MSN Search.

9. If you are connected to the Internet, open the Web page associated with one of the search results. Click in the Address bar at the top of the window to select the entire Web address. Right-click the selected address, and then click Copy on the shortcut menu. Close the browser window. Position the insertion point before the period at the end of the second sentence in the paragraph under the *Check Spelling* heading. Press the spacebar, type (and then paste the contents of the Clipboard (the Web site address). Type) and then close the Research task pane. (If you do not have access to the Internet, skip this step.)

10. Add the following words to the list of misspelled words: **laboratory, beginning, maintenance, cooperate,** and **friend.** Use the Sort button in the Paragraph group on the Home tab to sort the list in ascending order.

11. Insert a continuous section break before the spelling list. Format the second section (the one containing the spelling list) in three columns. Insert another continuous section break after the spelling list, and then format the last section of the document in one column.

12. Preview the document. Save, print, and close the document.

PROJECT 7-2

Robert Montgomery wants to create a list of references for his personal portfolio for employment.

1. Open the **References.docx** Data File. Save it as **References Formatted** followed by your initials.

2. Convert the text in the document into a table with two columns.

3. Use the Merge cells command to merge each cell containing a person's name with the two cells below it. Merge the three cells containing each address into one cell.

4. Enter the first and last row of information as shown in the table in Figure 7-24. Don't be concerned with the formatting yet.

FIGURE 7-24

Robert Montgomery References	
Dr. Kathy Bradford, Chairperson	State University Department of Computer Science Santa Fe, NM 87501
Joe Hernandez, President	Sierra Computer Consultants 1734 Water Street Santa Fe, NM 87505
Wayne Parks	Parks Electronics 8755 Arbor, Suite A Santa Fe, NM 87509

5. Format the table as shown in Figure 7-24. The table style is Medium Grid 3 – Accent 4. The text in the first row is 14 points. Notice that the names of the references in the first column are in bold, but the titles of the references are not. This means the first column is not formatted differently from the rest of the table; you need to format the names and titles manually. Also note that the first row is just tall enough to fit the text.

6. Resize the columns to the widths shown in Figure 7-24.

7. Change the name *Wayne Parks* to your name. Save your changes, and then print (but do not close) the document.

8. Select the entire table. On the Design tab, use the Shading and Borders buttons to remove the shading and the borders. The text in the first row is formatted in white, so it looks like there's nothing there. Change the color of the text in the first row to black. Save the revised document as **References Unformatted** followed by your initials.

9. Delete the first row in the document. If the new first row was reformatted as white text, select it, and then change the color of the text in the new first row to black. If necessary, correct the bold formatting in the first row.

10. Insert any style cover page you want. Insert **Robert Montgomery References** in the Title content control. If your cover page includes an Author content control, insert your name as the Author; if there is no Author content control, replace *Robert Montgomery* in the Title content control with your name. If the cover page includes a Date content control, insert the current date. Delete all other content controls in the cover page.

11. Preview the document. Save, print, and close the document.

 PROJECT 7-3

You have been asked to create a table for the leading salespersons for New World Marketing.

1. Open the **Sales.docx** Data File. Save the document as **Sales Leaders** followed by your initials.

2. Insert a new row at the top of the table. Type the following headings: **Name,** (skip the second column), **Region, Manager,** and **Year–to-Date Sales.**

3. Merge the cell containing *Name* and the cell to its right. Merge each of the cells containing first and last names so that each person's name appears in one cell. Remove the paragraph mark after each first name, and then insert a space between the first and last names.

4. Widen the fourth column so that *Year-to-Date Sales* fits on one line.

5. Format the table with the Colorful Grid - Accent 5 style. Add special formatting for the header row, and use banded columns.

6. Sort the table by year-to-date sales in descending order.

7. Center the table horizontally. Center the column headings and everything in the last column.

8. In the memo header, replace *All Employees* in the To line with your name.

9. Preview the document. Save, print, and close the document.

CRITICAL *Thinking*

 ACTIVITY 7-1

Using a table without borders, create your own list of references for your personal portfolio for employment.

 ACTIVITY 7-2

Use Help to learn how to insert a formula to add a column of numbers in a table. Use a formula to add the Year-to-Date Sales column in the Sales Leaders.docx document that you worked on in Project 7-3.

 ACTIVITY 7-3

You own a small company that sells used CDs and DVDs. To increase sales, you decide to develop a presence on the Web. To do this, you need to register a Web site address with a domain name registrar. Most registrars also offer to host your Web site, which means they store all the files that make up your Web site on a computer so that anyone using the Web can access your site.

Use the Internet to locate at least three registrars. (Try going to **www.internic.net** to find a list of registrars.) Create a table in Word to compare the data you find on the Internet regarding each registrar company's services provided, cost per month (per service, if available), and any convenience factors such as setup or installation requirements, fees, and customer service. Which company or companies offer the best package or services for your company?

After you have determined which registrar would be able to serve your needs, think of a possible Web site address for your company, and then use the registrar's search function to see if that Web site address is available. If the Web site address you want to register is already taken with *.com* as the top-level domain (the last three or four letters of a Web site address), try other top-level domains such as *.biz* or *.name*.

INCREASING EFFICIENCY USING WORD

OBJECTIVES

Upon completion of this lesson, you will be able to:

- Use and create templates.
- Use mail merge.
- Create and print envelopes and labels.
- Understand workgroup collaboration.
- Insert, view, edit, and print comments.
- Track changes.
- Accept and reject changes and delete comments.
- Combine different versions of a document.
- Customize Word.

Estimated Time: 3 hours

VOCABULARY

Data source

Mail merge

Main document

Merge field

Template

Track Changes

Workgroup collaboration

Using Templates

Suppose you are a sales representative, and you must file a report each week that summarizes your sales and the new contacts you have made. Parts of this report will be the same each week, such as the format and the headings. Re-creating the document each week would be time consuming. You can solve this problem by creating a template in Word or using an existing Word template for documents that you create frequently.

A template is a file that already contains the basic elements of a document, such as page and paragraph formatting, fonts, and text. You can customize the template to create a new document that is similar to but slightly different from the original. For example, a report template for a sales representative would save all formatting, font choices, and text that does not change, allowing you to fill in only the new information each week.

Using an Installed Template

Word contains many templates you can use to create documents. Some templates are installed on your computer, and others are available on the Microsoft Office Online Web site. To use an installed Word template, click the Office Button, and then click New. The New Document dialog box opens. In the Templates list on the left, click Installed Templates. The middle pane in the dialog box changes to show all the templates installed on your computer. You can scroll down to see the various templates installed. See Figure 8-1.

FIGURE 8-1
New Document dialog box with Installed Templates selected

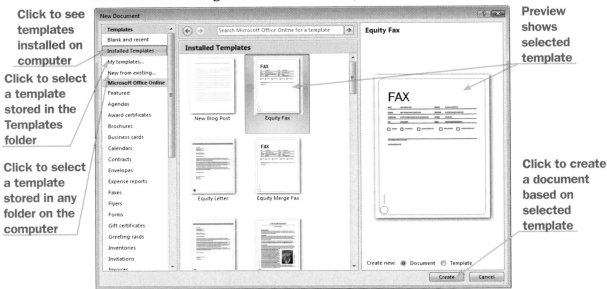

To create a new document based on one of the templates, click the template in the center pane, and then click Create. Word opens a new blank document with the settings and text specified by the template already in place. As with any new document, the file name in the title bar is *Document* followed by a number. Replace the data in the template with your own data and save it.

Net Tip

To create a document based on a template from Microsoft Office Online, click one of the categories under Microsoft Office Online in the list on the left, select a template in the middle pane, and then click Download. Click Continue to validate your copy of Microsoft Word or Office.

S TEP-BY-STEP 8.1

1. Click the **Office Button**, and then click **New**. The New Document dialog box opens.

2. In the list on the left under Templates, click **Installed Templates**. The installed templates appear in the middle pane. In the middle pane, click the **Equity Fax** icon. The preview in the right pane shows the Equity Fax template.

STEP-BY-STEP 8.1 Continued

3. In the lower-right corner of the dialog box, click **Create**. The Equity Fax template appears on your screen as a new, unsaved document. Note that the title in the title bar is *Document* followed by a number, like all new documents.

4. On the Quick Access Toolbar, click the **Save** button. Navigate to the drive and folder where you save your files. Replace the text in the File name box with **Bank Fax** followed by your initials, and then click **Save**.

5. To the right of *To*, click **[Type the recipient name]**. Notice that this is a content control. Type **Wyatt Brown, Marketing Assistant**. The text replaces the placeholder text, and the content control is deleted from the document.

6. Next to *From*, if placeholder text appears in the content control, click **[Type the sender name]**, and then type your name. If a name already appears in that location, select the name, and then type your name.

7. Replace the placeholder text next to each of the labels in the fax header, as indicated below:

Fax: **(914) 555-6409**
Pages: **2**
Phone: **(914) 555-6410**
Re: **New Account Campaign**
CC: **Angela Holden, Bank Manager**

8. Next to *Date*, use the Date content control to insert today's date.

9. Next to *Please Reply*, click inside the box, and then type **x**.

10. At the bottom of the memo, click the content control under *Comments*, and then type:

I reviewed the first draft of the checking account pamphlet. Please consider my comments as you revise the pamphlet. I would like to present the final version at the directors' meeting next month.

11. Save your changes. Print and close the document.

Creating a Template

You can create a customized template by modifying an existing template or document. To create a template, you need to save the document as a template. Click the Office Button, point to Save As, and then click Word Template. The Save As dialog box opens with Word Template (*.dotx) in the Save as type box. Type a file name, and then click Save. Your document will be saved as a template in the current folder.

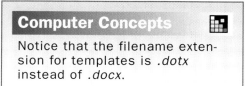

Computer Concepts

Notice that the filename extension for templates is *.dotx* instead of *.docx*.

S TEP-BY-STEP 8.2

1. Create a new, blank document.

2. Type the following:

   White Plains National Bank
   309 Third Street
   White Plains, NY 10610
   (914) 555-7534
   www.whiteplainsnationalbank.com

3. Press the **Enter** key. Type **<Replace with current date>**. Press the **Enter** key again.

4. Change the theme to **Verve**. Change the style of all the paragraphs above the *<Replace with current date>* placeholder text to **No Spacing**, and then center those paragraphs.

5. Change the paragraph spacing of the *<Replace with current date>* paragraph so that it has 36 points of space before it and 10 points of space after it.

6. Right-click the Web site address at the top of the document, and then click **Remove Hyperlink** on the shortcut menu.

7. Format the first line in the header as **14-point Engravers MT**. Change the font size of the rest of the lines in the header to **12 points**.

8. Position the insertion point in front of the word *White* in the first line of the header, and then search for clip art using the keyword **bank**. Insert a clip of a key with a dollar sign. If you can't find that clip, use another appropriate clip. If you do not have access to Microsoft Office Online, try the search using the keyword *money* instead, and use the clip with the dollar sign.

9. Change the size of the image to approximately 1 inch by 1 inch.

10. With the image still selected, on the Ribbon, click the **Format** tab, if necessary. In the Arrange group, click the **Position** button, and then click the first icon in the first row under With Text Wrapping. The image changes to a floating graphic and moves to the top-left corner of the document. Deselect the image. See Figure 8-2.

11. Add your name in a paragraph below the date placeholder.

12. Click the **Office Button**, and then point to **Save As**. On the right side of the menu, click **Word Template**. The Save As dialog box opens with Word Template (.dotx) listed in the Save as type box.

13. Select the text in the File name box, type **Bank Template** followed by your initials. Click **Save**.

14. Close the file, but do not exit Word.

Extra for Experts

To store your templates so that others can easily locate them, in the Save As dialog box, click Templates in the Favorite Links list, and then save the template in that folder. To access these templates, in the New Document dialog box, click My templates in the Templates list on the left, and then select the template in the New dialog box that opens.

STEP-BY-STEP 8.2 Continued

FIGURE 8-2
Completed Bank Template document

Image positioned at top-left corner of the document

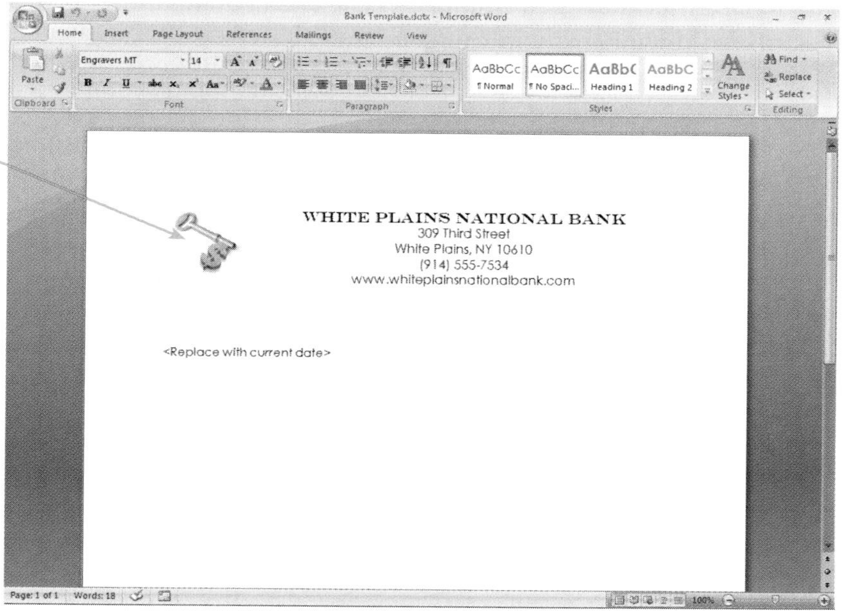

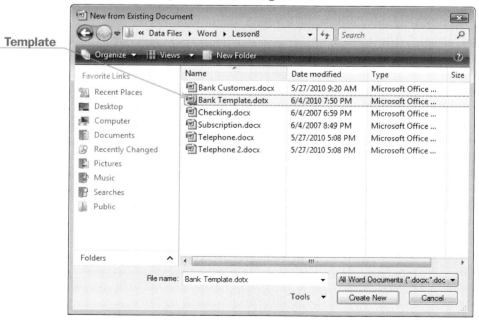

Creating a Document Using a Custom Template

You can use the template you created as many times as needed. To create a new document based on your template, open the New Document dialog box. In the list on the left, under Template, click New from existing. The New from Existing Document dialog box opens, as shown in Figure 8-3.

FIGURE 8-3
New from Existing Document dialog box

Template

Click your template name, and then click Create New. A new document opens with all the text and formatting from the template. As with the new document you created from the installed template, the file name in the title bar is *Document* followed by a number. After you make changes to this document, you can save the document as you normally would.

Did You Know?

If you double-click a Word document in an Explorer window, the document opens in a Word window with the document name in the title bar. If you double-click a template in an Explorer window, it opens as a new document in a Word window. Changes you make to the new document will not be saved in the template file.

STEP-BY-STEP 8.3

1. Click the **Office Button**, and then click **New**. The New Document dialog box opens. In the list on the left, under Templates, click **New from existing**. The New from Existing Document dialog box opens. Notice that the command button on the left in the lower-right corner of the dialog box is Open.

2. Click **Bank Template.dotx**. The Open button changes to Create New. Click **Create New**. The template opens as a new document.

3. Save the document as **Bank Letter** followed by your initials.

4. Move to the end of the document, and then press the **Enter** key to insert a blank paragraph between the *<Replace with current date>* line and the insertion point.

5. Open the **Checking.docx** Data File. Select all the text in the document, and then copy it to the Clipboard. Close the Checking.docx document.

6. Select your name in the Bank Letter document. In the Clipboard group, click the **Paste** button. On the right end of the status bar, click **100%** to open the Zoom dialog box. In the Percent box, select the value, and then type **77**. Click **OK**. Scroll down so that you can see the entire letter on the screen. Your screen should match Figure 8-4.

7. Change the zoom back to 100%. In the closing, replace *Marc Jacobsen* with your name.

8. Save your changes, and leave the document open for the next Step-by-Step.

Did You Know?

You can use *any* document as the basis for another document. In the list on the left in the New Document dialog box, click New from existing to open the New from Existing Document dialog box. Click the file you want to use as the basis for your new document, and then click Create New. Even if the file is a normal Word document rather than a template, the document opens as a new document.

STEP-BY-STEP 8.3 Continued

FIGURE 8-4
Text for Bank Letter document

Blank paragraph

Zoom percentage

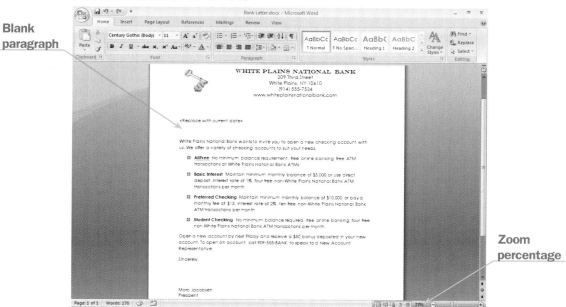

Using Mail Merge

Mail merge combines a document with information that personalizes it. For example, you might send a letter to each member of a professional organization. In each letter, the text is the same but the names of the recipients are different. For example, a letter may begin *Dear Mr. Montgomery* or *Dear Ms. Jansen*. The document with the information that does not change is called the **main document**. The **data source** is the file containing the information that varies in each document.

To perform a mail merge, you use the commands on the Mailings tab on the Ribbon. You start by clicking the Start Mail Merge button in the Start Mail Merge group, and then clicking the type of mail merge you want to do. The most common type is a letter. The second step is to choose the data source by clicking the Select Recipients button in the Start Mail Merge group. Next, you need to insert merge fields. **Merge fields** are placeholders that are replaced with data from the data source when you perform the merge. See Figure 8-5.

After you have inserted all the merge fields, you can click the Preview Results button in the Preview Results group. You can then click the Next Record and Previous Record buttons to scroll through the results preview. To finish the merge, click the Finish & Merge button in the Finish group. On the menu, you can click Print Documents to print the merged documents or Edit Individual Documents to create a new document consisting of all the merged documents.

FIGURE 8-5
Mailings tab on the Ribbon

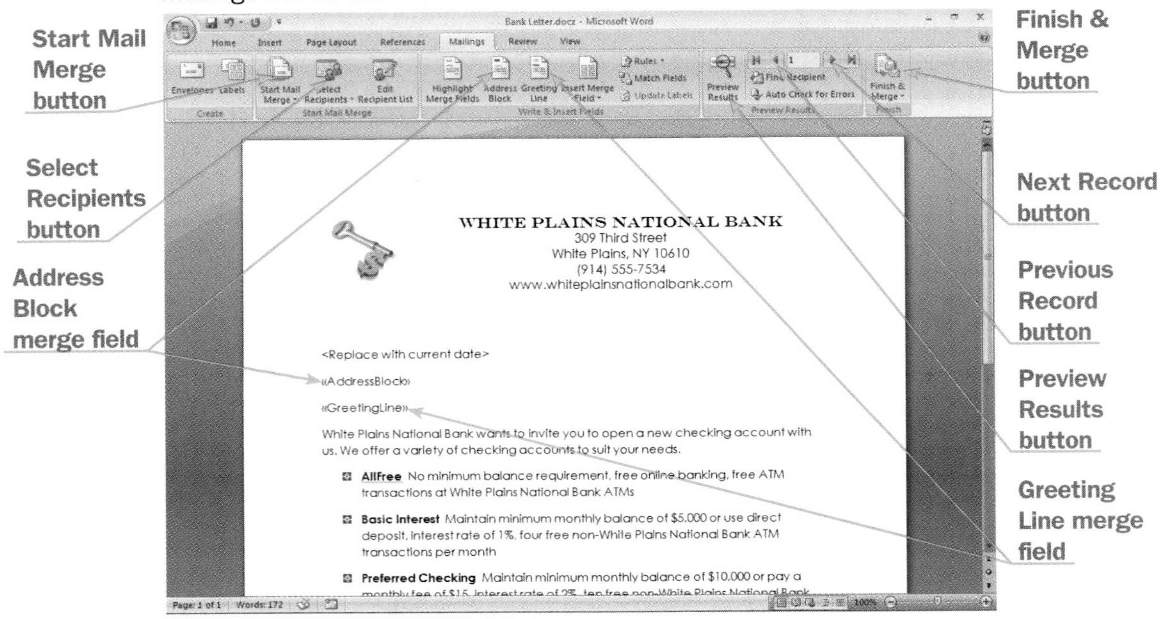

Start Mail
Merge
button

Select
Recipients
button

Address
Block
merge field

Finish &
Merge
button

Next Record
button

Previous
Record
button

Preview
Results
button

Greeting
Line merge
field

WHITE PLAINS NATIONAL BANK
309 Third Street
White Plains, NY 10610
(914) 555-7534
www.whiteplainsnationalbank.com

<Replace with current date>

«AddressBlock»

«GreetingLine»

White Plains National Bank wants to invite you to open a new checking account with us. We offer a variety of checking accounts to suit your needs.

☑ **AllFree** No minimum balance requirement, free online banking, free ATM transactions at White Plains National Bank ATMs

☑ **Basic Interest** Maintain minimum monthly balance of $5,000 or use direct deposit. Interest rate of 1%, four free non-White Plains National Bank ATM transactions per month

☑ **Preferred Checking** Maintain minimum monthly balance of $10,000 or pay a monthly fee of $15. Interest rate of 2%, ten free non-White Plains National Bank

S TEP-BY-STEP 8.4

1. Open the **Bank Customers.docx** Data File. This file contains a table with a list of names and addresses. This is the data source for the merge. Notice that each person's title, first name, and last name are in separate columns. Close this file.

2. On the Ribbon, click the **Mailings** tab. In the Start Mail Merge group, click the **Start Mail Merge** button. Click **Letters**. The current document is identified as a letter you will merge with a data source. Notice that none of the buttons in the Write & Insert Fields, Preview Results, or Finish groups are available.

3. In the Start Mail Merge group, click the **Select Recipients** button. Click **Use Existing List**. The Select Data Source dialog box opens. This dialog box is similar to the Open dialog box.

4. Navigate to the drive and folder where you store your Data Files. Click **Bank Customers.docx**, and then click **Open**. Now the rest of the buttons on the Mailings tab are available.

5. Position the insertion point in the blank paragraph below the date placeholder text. First, you need to insert the Address Block merge field, which will be replaced with the inside address in the letter. In the Write & Insert Fields group, click the **Address Block** button. The Insert Address Block dialog box opens.

Extra for Experts

If a list of recipients doesn't already exist, you can click the Select Recipients button and then click Type New List to open the New Address List dialog box. Click in the boxes under the column headings you want to include in your data source, and then type your data. Click OK when you are finished. In the Save Address List dialog box, navigate to the folder in which you want to save the data source, type a file name, and then click Save. The Save as type is Microsoft Office Address Lists (*.mdb).

STEP-BY-STEP 8.4 Continued

6. If necessary, in the list on the left, scroll down and then click the **Mr. Joshua Randall Jr.** name format, as shown in Figure 8-6.

FIGURE 8-6
Insert Address Block dialog box

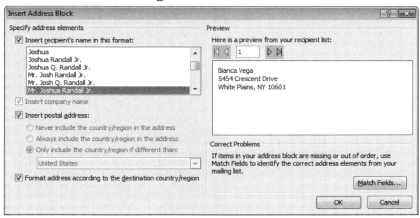

7. Click **OK**. The Address Block merge field is inserted in the document.

8. Press the **Enter** key. In the Write & Insert Fields group, click the **Greeting Line** button. The Insert Greeting Line dialog box opens.

9. If necessary, click the **arrow** next to the middle box in the row under Greeting line format, and then click **Mr. Randall** in the list. Click the **arrow** next to the comma (next to the rightmost box), and then click **:** (the colon). See Figure 8-7.

Extra for Experts

If your data source contains columns that Word might not recognize as part of the inside address, click Match Fields in the Insert Address Block dialog box to open the Match Fields dialog box. If any column in your data source is not listed in the boxes on the right, click the arrow in the box next to the part of the address that it should match, and then click OK.

FIGURE 8-7
Insert Greeting Line dialog box

Click to select form of salutation in greeting line

Click to select the punctuation after the greeting line

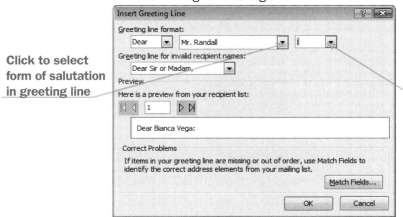

STEP-BY-STEP 8.4 Continued

10. Click **OK**. The Greeting Line merge field is inserted in the document.

Computer Concepts

To use a title in the Address Block or Greeting Line, titles must be included in the data source.

11. On the Mailings tab, in the Preview Results group, click the **Preview Results** button. The merge fields in the document are replaced with data in the first row in your data source (Bianca Vega's information). Notice that each line in the inside address has extra space after it. This is not normal formatting for the inside address.

12. In the Preview Results group, click the **Preview Results** button. The preview turns off and you see the merge fields again.

13. Click anywhere in the line containing the Address Block merge field, and then change the style to **No Spacing**. The blank line below the Address Block merge field disappears. Position the insertion point at the end of the Address Block line, and then press the **Enter** key. This inserts a single blank line (a paragraph formatted with the No Spacing style) between the last line of the inside address and the salutation.

14. On the Ribbon, click the **Mailings** tab, and then, in the Preview Results group, click the **Preview Results** button. Bianca Vega's information appears in the letter properly formatted. In the Preview Results group, to the right of the number *1*, click the **Next Record** button. The data from the recipient in the second row in the table in the data source (George Corrigan) appears in the document.

Extra for Experts

You can insert customized information in the body of the letter. Add the data to the data source, and then use the Insert Merge Field button on the Mailings tab to insert the custom data.

15. Replace the date placeholder text with the current date in the form *June 27, 2010*.

16. On the Ribbon, click the **Mailings** tab. In the Finish group, click the **Finish & Merge** button, and then click **Print Documents**. The Merge to Printer dialog box opens, in which you can specify the records you want to print. Click the **Current record** option button. This tells Word to print only the current letter (the letter addressed to George Corrigan) rather than all three letters. Click **OK**. The Print dialog box opens.

17. Click **OK**. The Print dialog box closes and the current letter prints.

18. In the Preview Results group, click the **Preview Results** button to display the merge fields again. In the Finish group, click the **Finish & Merge** button, and then click **Edit Individual Documents**. The Merge to New Document dialog box opens. Click the **All** option button, if necessary, and then click **OK**. A new document opens with the temporary name "Letters" followed by a number. This document contains one letter for each of the recipients listed in the data source.

19. Save the document as **Bank New Customer Letters** followed by your initials. Close the document. Close the Bank Letter document, and when the dialog box opens asking if you want to save changes, click **No**.

Creating and Printing Envelopes

Addressing envelopes is easy using Word. Click the Mailings tab on the Ribbon. In the Create group, click the Envelopes button to open the Envelopes and Labels dialog box with the Envelopes tab on top, as shown in Figure 8-8.

FIGURE 8-8
Envelopes tab in the Envelopes and Labels dialog box

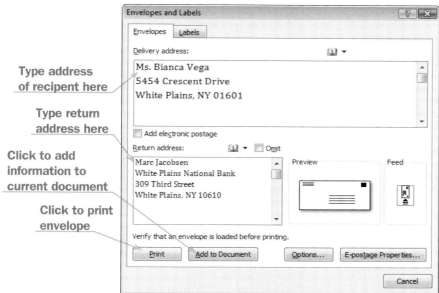

If you select an address (such as the inside address in a letter) before you open the dialog box, the address appears in the Delivery address box in the dialog box, although you can replace the text in the address box with any address you like. If there is any text in the Return address box, select it, and then type your own name and address. To print the envelope, insert an envelope in your printer, click Print, and then click OK in the Print dialog box. To see the envelope layout before you print, click Add to Document. The envelope appears at the top of the current document, as shown in Figure 8-9. Then you can print the envelope as you would any document.

FIGURE 8-9
Completed envelope

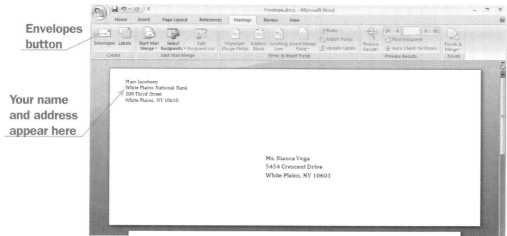

STEP-BY-STEP 8.5

1. Create a new, blank Word document.

2. On the Ribbon, click the **Mailings** tab. In the Create group, click the **Envelopes** button. The Envelopes and Labels dialog box opens with the Envelopes tab on top.

3. In the Delivery address box, type the following:

   Ms. Bianca Vega
   5454 Crescent Drive
   White Plains, NY 10601

4. Click in the Return address box, and then type your name and address.

5. Click **Add to Document**. A dialog box opens asking if you want to save the return address as the default return address. Click **No**. The dialog box closes and the setup of the document is changed to an envelope with the addresses you typed in the correct locations.

6. If you have an envelope, insert it into the printer; otherwise you can print on plain paper. Print the document.

7. Save the document as **Envelope** followed by your initials.

8. Close the document, but do not exit Word.

Did You Know?

You can also perform a mail merge with a data source to print envelopes and labels. In the Start Mail Merge group on the Mailings tab, click the Start Mail Merge button, and then click Envelopes or Labels.

Extra for Experts

To change the envelope size from the standard business-sized envelope, click Options on the Envelopes tab in the Envelopes and Labels dialog box.

Creating and Printing Labels

Creating labels is similar to creating envelopes. On the Mailings tab, click the Labels button in the Create group. The Envelopes and Labels dialog box opens with the Labels tab on top, as shown in Figure 8-10.

FIGURE 8-10
Labels tab in the Envelopes and Labels dialog box

Type address of recipient here

Click option to print one label or a sheet of labels with the same address

Click to print labels

Click to create a new document with labels

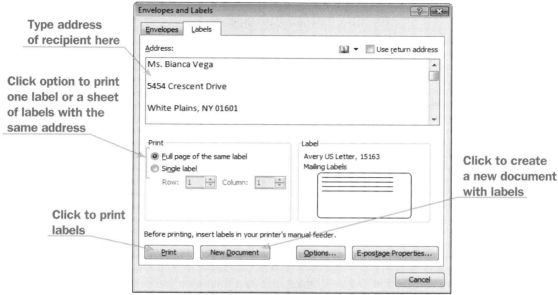

Type the address you want to appear on the labels. The default is to print a full page of the same label. If you want to print just one label, in the Print section, click the Single label option button.

The dimensions of the label are listed in the Label section. To print the labels, insert a sheet of labels in your printer, click Print, and then click OK in the Print dialog box. To see the layout of the labels before you print, click New Document. A new document opens with the labels, as shown in Figure 8-11. Then you can format and print the document as you would any document.

FIGURE 8-11
Completed Labels document

Table move handle

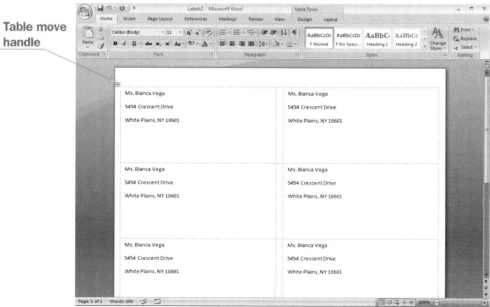

To choose a label type other than the one listed, click Options on the Label tab in the Envelopes and Labels dialog box. The Label Options dialog box opens. You can buy labels at an office supply store. Click the Label vendors arrow, and then click the manufacturer of the labels you purchased. Scroll down the Product number list, and then click the product number of the labels you bought (it will be on the box of labels).

STEP-BY-STEP 8.6

1. Create a new, blank Word document.

2. On the Ribbon, click the **Mailings** tab. In the Create group, click the **Labels** button. The Envelopes and Labels dialog box opens with the Labels tab on top.

3. In the Address box, type your name and address. The address is inserted with either the No Spacing or the Normal style applied.

4. In the Print section, make sure the **Full page of the same label** option button is selected.

5. Click **Options** to open the Label Options dialog box, and then click the Label vendors **arrow**. A list of label manufacturers opens. Each manufacturer sells labels of different sizes. If you have labels that you bought at an office supply store, you could click the name of the manufacturer of your labels, and then, in the Product number list, scroll down if necessary and click the product number of your labels. For now, you'll print on ordinary paper.

6. Click **Avery US Letter** in the Label vendors list, scroll down the Product number list until you see 15163, and then click **15163**. The Label information on the right indicates that the document will be set up for mailing labels two inches high and four inches wide on 8.5" × 11" paper.

7. Click **OK**. The Label Options dialog closes. Click **New Document**. The Envelopes and Labels dialog box closes and a document opens with the name and address you typed inserted into cells in a table. Dotted lines indicate the borders of the table.

8. If the addresses have the Normal style applied rather than the No Spacing style, position the pointer over the table so that the table move handle appears. Click the **table move handle** to select the entire table. Change the style to **No Spacing**.

9. Save the document as **Labels** followed by your initials. Print the document.

10. Close the document, but do not exit Word.

Collaborating with a Workgroup Using Comments and Tracked Changes

The process of working together in teams, sharing comments, and exchanging ideas for a common purpose is called workgroup collaboration. When you work in groups, the tasks are often divided among the team members. The team meets to review each other's work, comment on it, and suggest changes.

Word provides several ways team members can collaborate. Team members can circulate a document and add comments to the document. Each member can also make changes to the document and have those changes tracked so that it is easy for the owner of the document to see suggested insertions, deletions, and moved text.

Changing the User Name

When you make certain changes to a document, Word identifies the changes with the user name. To change the user name that appears for these changes, you need to open the Word Options dialog box. Click the Office Button, and then click Word Options at the bottom of the Office menu. The Word Options dialog box opens with Popular selected in the list on the left, as shown in Figure 8-12.

FIGURE 8-12
Word Options dialog box with Popular selected

Popular options are displayed

Information in User name and Initials boxes on your screen will differ

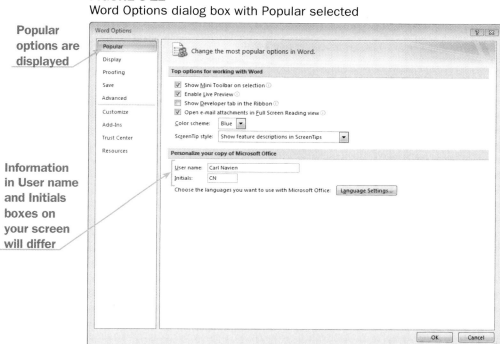

Under Personalize your copy of Microsoft Office, the User name and Initials boxes appear. You can change the name and initials in these boxes. When you are finished, click OK to close the dialog box and save your changes.

Using Comments

One way you can collaborate with others is to send a document out for review. Each person who reviews the document can insert comments in the document. To insert a comment, either position the pointer or select the text about which you wish to comment. On the Ribbon, click the Review tab, and then in the Comments group, click the New Comment button. A comment balloon appears to the right of the text. The comment balloon is connected to the text by a line. The initials from the Popular section of the Word Options dialog box and the comment number appear in the comment balloon. If you position the pointer on top of the comment balloon or the highlighted text in the document, the name of the person who made the comment as well as the date and time the comment was made appear in a ScreenTip, as shown in Figure 8-13. If you send the same version of the document to another person for review and that person inserts comments, their comments appear in a different color.

FIGURE 8-13
Comment in a document

Initials and user name are the same as in the Word Options dialog box

Line connects comment to document

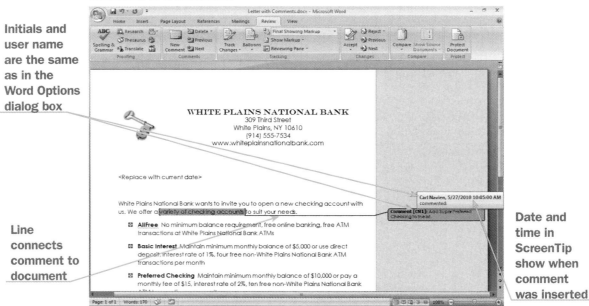

Date and time in ScreenTip show when comment was inserted

After you have inserted your comments in a document, you can go back and make changes to them. To move from comment to comment, click the Next or Previous button in the Comments group on the Review tab. To edit a comment, click inside the comment balloon, and then make your changes.

STEP-BY-STEP 8.7

1. Open the **Bank Letter.docx** file that you created earlier in this lesson. Save it as **Letter with Comments** followed by your initials.

2. Click the **Office Button**, and then click **Word Options**. The Word Options dialog box opens with Popular selected in the list on the left. Write down the name and initials that appear in the User name and Initials boxes.

3. Select all the text in the User name box, and then type **Carl Navien**. Select the text in the Initials box, and then type **CN**. Click **OK**. The dialog box closes.

Extra for Experts

If a comment is very long, or if there are many comments on a page, only the first part of the comment appears in the comment balloon, and a button with three small dots appears in the lower-right corner of the comment balloon. To see the entire comment, click the button to open the Reviewing pane to the left of or below the document window. You can also click the Reviewing Pane button in the Tracking group on the Review tab.

STEP-BY-STEP 8.7 Continued

4. Position the insertion point at the beginning of the first paragraph in the body of the letter. On the Ribbon, click the **Review** tab. In the Comments group, click the **New Comment** button. The first word in the paragraph is highlighted in color and a comment balloon appears off to the right. The initials *CN* appear in the balloon, and the insertion point is blinking in the balloon.

5. Type **Make sure you send this to the list of potential customers.**

6. In the second sentence of the first paragraph in the body of the letter, select the phrase *variety of checking accounts*. In the Comments group, click the **New Comment** button. The phrase you selected is highlighted with your comment color, and another comment balloon appears.

7. In the comment balloon, type **Add Super Preferred Checking to the list.**

8. Click in the first comment balloon. Position the insertion point immediately in front of the word *list*. Type **new**, and then press the **spacebar**.

9. Click the **Office Button**, and then click **Word Options**. Change the name in the User name box to **Stefanie E. Riposa**. Change the initials in the Initials box to **SER**. Click **OK**.

10. In the second item in the bulleted list (the *Basic Interest* item), select the word *four*. On the Review tab, in the Comments group, click the **New Comment** button. A new comment is inserted with Stefanie's initials and in a color different from the color used for Carl's comments. Type **This is now three transactions per month.**

11. Position the pointer over the first comment. A ScreenTip appears identifying Carl Navien as the person who inserted the comment. See Figure 8-14. The date and time the comment was inserted also appear in the ScreenTip.

FIGURE 8-14
Document with comments from two people

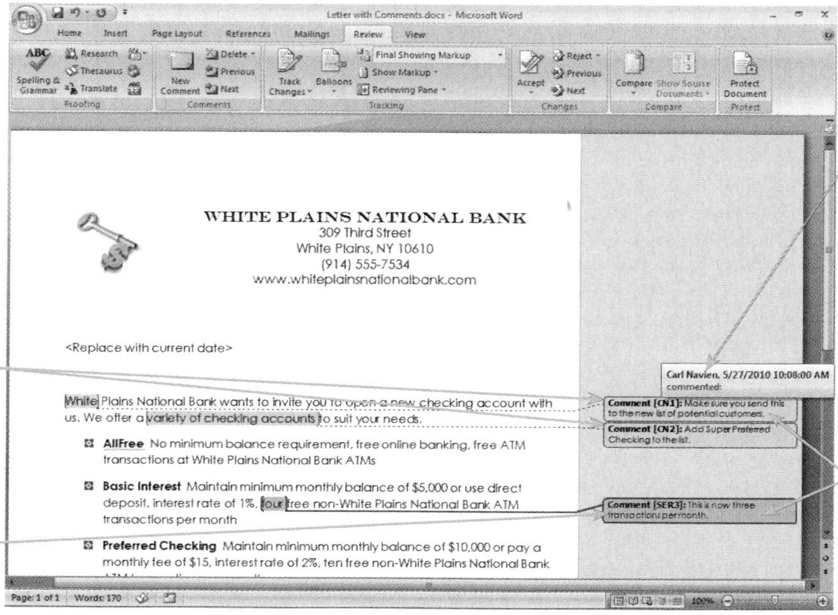

STEP-BY-STEP 8.7 Continued

12. Position the pointer over the last comment in the document. The ScreenTip identifies Stefanie E. Riposa as the author of this comment.

13. Save the document. Leave it open for the next Step-by-Step.

Tracking Changes

Word provides a tool called Track Changes that keeps a record of any changes you or a reviewer makes in a document. If you turn this feature on, any changes made are marked in the document. Text that you insert is underlined and colored with the same color as your comments. Text you delete is put into a Deleted balloon similar to a comment balloon.

If you move text and it is at least a sentence long, the text you cut is marked with a Moved balloon. The pasted text is also marked with a Moved balloon and appears in green with a green double underline. Both Moved balloons have a Go button in them. You can click the Go button to jump back and forth between the cut and paste locations. The two Moved balloons associated with the first moved selection both have the number *1* in them. If you move a second selection, the two Moved balloons for the second move will have the number *2* in them.

You can position the pointer on top of inserted, deleted, or moved text, and as with comments, a ScreenTip identifies the person who made the change and the date and time the change was made.

To turn on the Track Changes feature, click the Review tab on the Ribbon, and then, in the Tracking group, click the Track Changes button.

> **Extra for Experts**
>
> To show the document with all the changes, in the Tracking group, click the Final Showing Markup arrow, and then click Final. The insertions appear as normal text, and the Moved and Deleted balloons are removed.

STEP-BY-STEP 8.8

1. On the Review tab, in the Tracking group, click the **Track Changes** button to turn on the Track Changes feature.

2. In the first item in the bulleted list (the *AllFree* item), delete the phrase *free online banking,*. Make sure you delete the comma and the space after the comma. A Deleted balloon appears to the right of the document, showing the deleted text. As with the comment balloons, a line connects the balloon to the location of the deleted text in the document. The line and the outline of the balloon are the same color as Stefanie Riposa's comment. (*Note:* If the deleted text appears with a line through it instead of in a Deleted balloon, in the Tracking group, click the **Balloons** button, and then click **Show Revisions in Balloons**.)

3. In the last paragraph at the bottom of the letter, select *New Account*, and then type **Customer Service**. Note that the new text is underlined and shown in the color of Stefanie's comment.

STEP-BY-STEP 8.8 Continued

4. In the last paragraph, select the first sentence. (It starts with *Open a new account.*) Use drag-and-drop or the Cut and Paste commands to move the selected sentence to the end of the first paragraph. The moved text appears in green with a double underline, and a Moved balloon with a Go button appears next to the moved text and next to the paragraph where the text was located before you moved it. The two Moved balloons both have the number *1* in them. See Figure 8-15.

FIGURE 8-15
Document with tracked changes

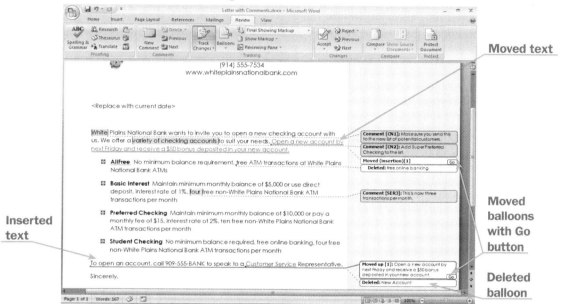

5. In the Moved balloon next to the first paragraph, click **Go**. The other Moved balloon associated with this Moved balloon is selected.

6. Click the **Office Button**, and then click **Word Options**. Select the text in the User name box, and then replace it with the original name that you wrote down when you first opened the Word Options dialog box. Select the text in the Initials box, and then replace it with the original initials. Click **OK**.

7. Save the document and leave it open for the next Step-by-Step.

Accepting and Rejecting Changes and Deleting Comments

Now that the changes have been made to the document, you have an opportunity to either accept or reject them. To accept or reject a change in the document, click the text that has been changed to select it, and then click the Accept or Reject button in the Changes group on the Review tab. The change is accepted or rejected, and the insertion point jumps to the next change in the document. If you don't want to jump to the next change in the document, click the arrow below the Accept or Reject button, and then click Accept Change or Reject Change.

S TEP-BY-STEP 8.9

1. Move the insertion point to the beginning of the document. On The Review tab, in the Comments group, click the **Next** button. The first comment in the document, Carl Navien's first comment, is selected. This comment is a reminder to send the letter to the new list of potential customers, so it would be helpful to leave it in the letter.

2. In the Comments group, click the **Next** button. The next comment is selected. You'll add the information requested after deleting the comment. In the Comments group, click the **Delete** button. The comment is deleted.

> **Did You Know?**
>
> To delete all comments in a document, in the Comments group, click the arrow next to the Delete button, and then click Delete All Comments in Document.

3. In the document, click after the last word in the *Preferred Checking* bullet (after *month*). Press the **Enter** key. Type **Super Preferred Checking**. Press the **Ctrl+B** keys to turn off the automatic bold formatting that was picked up from the previous item in the list. Press the **spacebar** twice. Type **Maintain minimum monthly balance of $25,000 or pay a monthly fee of $25, interest rate of 3.75%, free transactions at all ATMs**. Because you changed the User name and Initials back to their originals, the inserted text appears in a third color.

4. Press the **left arrow** key to position the insertion point in the new bulleted item. In the Changes group, click the **Accept** button. The inserted text is accepted and changes to the normal black color, and the next change, the Moved balloon, is selected.

5. In the Changes group, click the **arrow** below the Accept button, and then click **Accept Change**. Both Moved balloons disappear, and the green underlined moved text in the first paragraph changes to black. The insertion point stays at the location of the Moved balloon that was selected.

> **Did You Know?**
>
> To reject a tracked change, in the Changes group, click the Reject button or the arrow next to the Reject button, and then click Reject Change.

6. In the Comments group, click the **Next** button. A dialog box opens asking if you want to start searching from the beginning of the document. Click **OK**. The first comment is selected again.

7. Click the second comment in the document, Stefanie's comment. In the Comments group, click the **Delete** button. In the Tracking group, click the **Track Changes** button to turn off the Track Changes feature. In the *Basic Interest* bullet, replace the word *four* with **three**.

8. In the Changes group, click the **Next** button. The deletion *New Account* is selected. In the Changes group, click the **Accept** button. Click the Accept button again to accept the insertion of *Customer Service*. In the dialog box, click **OK** to continue searching from the beginning of the document. The comment is highlighted again.

9. In the Changes group, click the **Next** button. The space between the second and third sentences in the first paragraph is highlighted. When you moved the sentence, Word automatically inserted the space. The space wasn't accepted when you accepted the Moved text because the inserted space wasn't part of the moved text.

STEP-BY-STEP 8.9 Continued

10. In the Changes group, click the **arrow** below the Accept button, and then click **Accept All Changes in Document**. The inserted space and the deletion in the bulleted list are accepted.

11. Save the document as **Letter with Changes Accepted** followed by your initials. Leave it open for the next Step-by-Step.

Print Comments and Tracked Changes

You can print a document with comments and tracked changes. To do this, click the Office Button, and then click Print. In the Print what box in the Print dialog box, Document showing markup is selected. Click OK to print the document with the changes, exactly as it looks on-screen.

Did You Know?

If you click the Print what arrow in the Print dialog box, and then click Document, the document prints as if all changes were accepted and without any comments.

STEP-BY-STEP 8.10

1. Click the **Office Button**, and then click **Print**. The Print dialog box opens. Make sure the Print what box indicates that Document showing markup is selected.

2. Click **OK**. The document prints with the comment.

3. Delete the comment in the document.

4. Save the document as **Final Bank Letter** followed by your initials. Print the document. Leave the document open for the next Step-by-Step.

Combine Different Versions of a Document

The Compare and Combine commands are useful ways to see differences between documents. Suppose you send your document to several colleagues for review. They return their copies with changes and suggested revisions. Using the Compare or Combine command, you can merge their comments and changes into one document for easy review.

To combine documents, click the Review tab on the Ribbon. In the Compare group, click the Compare button. On the menu that opens, click Combine. The Combine Documents dialog box opens. The dialog box can display many or few options. The command button in the lower-left corner of the dialog box is *More* when no options are displayed in the dialog box, and *Less* when the dialog box is expanded. Figure 8-16 shows the expanded dialog box.

FIGURE 8-16
Combine Documents dialog box

Button changes to More button when bottom part of dialog box isn't visible

Combined document will be created in a new document

Click to open a dialog box and browse for document

Click to select documents from list of recently opened documents

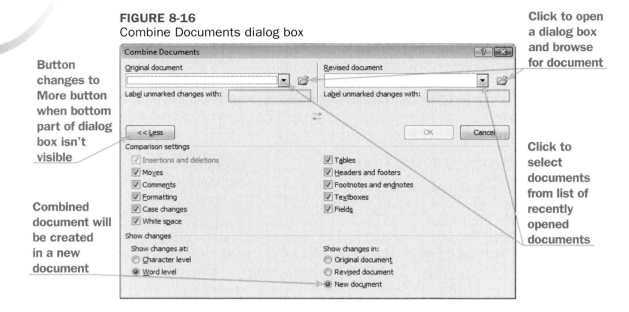

Click the Original document arrow to display a list of recently opened documents or click the Browse button in the dialog box to use a dialog box similar to the Open dialog box to locate the original document. Click the original document in the list or double-click it in the Browse dialog box. Do the same in the Revised document section. The name that appears in the Label unmarked changes with box below the Original document box is the name that was in the User name box in the Word Options dialog box when the document was saved.

When you click OK, the dialog box closes, and a new document is created with the changes from the revised document marked. You can then choose to view just the combined document or view the combined document along with the original, the revised, or both the original and revised documents in a pane to the right of the combined document with the Revision pane open to the left. You should always look over the combined document carefully because the results might not be what you expect.

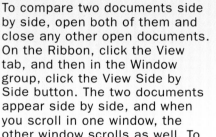

Extra for Experts

To compare two documents side by side, open both of them and close any other open documents. On the Ribbon, click the View tab, and then in the Window group, click the View Side by Side button. The two documents appear side by side, and when you scroll in one window, the other window scrolls as well. To be able to scroll each window independently, click the Window button in either window, and then click Synchronous Scrolling.

STEP-BY-STEP 8.11

1. On the Review tab, in the Compare group, click the **Compare** button, and then click **Combine**. The Combine Documents dialog box opens. If the More button appears instead of the Less button, click **More** to expand the dialog box.

2. Click the Original document **arrow**. Locate and click **Bank Letter.docx**.

3. Click the Revised document **arrow**. Locate and click **Final Bank Letter.docx**. Notice that the New document option button is selected under Show changes in at the bottom of the dialog box.

STEP-BY-STEP 8.11 Continued

4. Click **OK**. A new document with *Combine Result* or *Document* in the document window title bar, followed by a number, opens.

5. In the Compare group, click the **Show Source Documents** button. Click **Show Both** (even if it's already selected). The combined document appears in the middle pane in the window. On the right, the original document appears at the top and the revised document appears on the bottom. The Revision pane appears on the left.

6. Scroll through the combined document in the middle pane. Note that the changes made to create the Final Bank Letter document are indicated in the combined document. The author of the changes is the name that currently appears in the Word Options dialog box.

7. Save the document as **Combined Bank Letter** followed by your initials. Print the document showing markup, and then close the document. Close the Final Bank Letter document.

Customizing Word

You can customize many features of Word by using the Word Options dialog box. You have already used this dialog box when you checked the spelling and grammar settings and when you changed the user name and initials.

To customize Word, click the Office Button, and then click Word Options. The Word Options dialog box displays different options and commands depending on the category selected in the list on the left. The options that appear when Popular is selected are some of the most common options for customizing Word, including the User name and Initials boxes. The options that appear when Display is selected (see Figure 8-17) affect how the document looks on the screen and when printed.

FIGURE 8-17
Word Options dialog box with Display selected

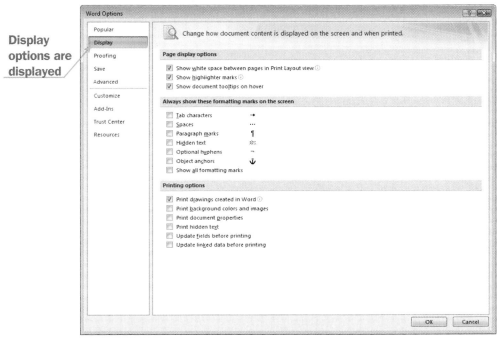

Display options are displayed

The Proofing options (see Figure 8-18) affect the spelling and grammar checker. You can also open the AutoCorrect dialog box when Proofing is selected in the list on the left.

FIGURE 8-18
Word Options dialog box with Proofing selected

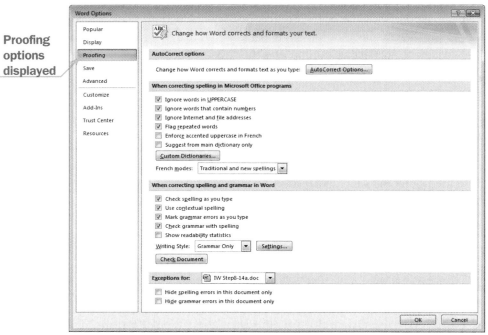

Clicking Save in the list on the left (see Figure 8-19) changes the dialog box so that you can change default save locations and behaviors. Clicking Advanced in the list on the left (see Figure 8-20) changes the dialog box so that it shows several categories of advanced options.

FIGURE 8-19
Word Options dialog box with Save selected

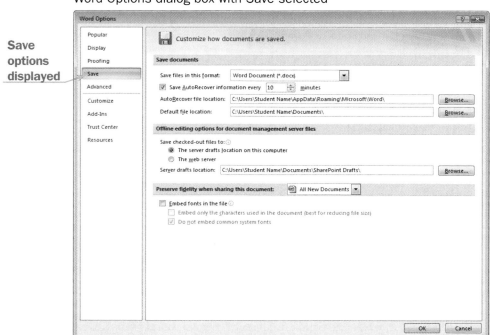

FIGURE 8-20
Word Options dialog box with Advanced selected

Advanced options displayed

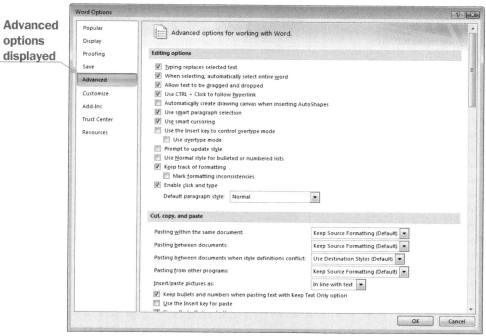

The last option for customizing Word is to customize the Quick Access Toolbar. To do this, click Customize in the list on the left of the Word Options dialog box. The dialog box changes to show two lists of commands. See Figure 8-21.

FIGURE 8-21
Word Options dialog box with Customize selected

Click to change list of available commands

Customize options displayed

Commands that appear on the Quick Access Toolbar

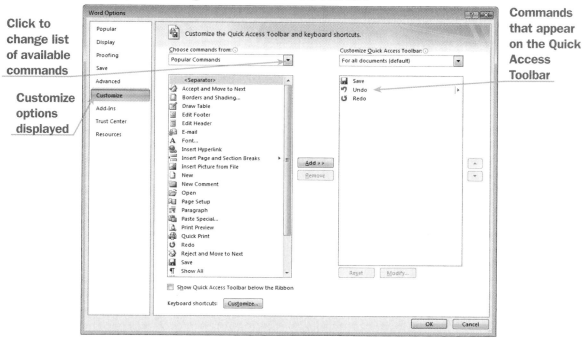

The commands currently on the Quick Access Toolbar are listed in the list on the right in the order they appear on the Quick Access Toolbar. All of the commands available in Word appear in the list on the left. To filter the commands, click the Choose commands from arrow at the top of the list, and then click a category of commands. The default is the set of Popular Commands. You can also choose to list all the commands. The commands appear alphabetically in the list. To add a command to the Quick Access Toolbar, in the list on the left, click the command you want to add, and then click Add. To remove a command from the toolbar, click the command in the list on the right, and then click Remove.

To open the Word Options dialog box with Customize already selected in the list on the left, click the Customize Quick Access Toolbar button to the right of the Quick Access Toolbar, and then click More Commands. To remove a button on the Quick Access Toolbar without opening the Word Options dialog box, right-click the button on the toolbar, and then click Remove from Quick Access Toolbar on the shortcut menu.

SUMMARY

In this lesson, you learned:

■ Templates allow you to save the format, font choices, and text of commonly produced documents. You can use installed templates, templates available on Microsoft Office Online, or you can create your own.

■ Mail merge lets you insert changing information into a standard document.

■ You can quickly create envelopes and labels in Word.

■ When working in a group, suggesting changes to a document is easily done by inserting comments, which are labeled with the person's name and the date and time the comment was made.

■ Changes made by each person can be identified and labeled by using the Track Changes feature.

■ You can accept or reject tracked changes and delete comments.

■ You can print a document with tracked changes and comments, or you can print the document without the comments and as if all the tracked changes were accepted.

■ You can combine documents with comments and changes into one document for easy review.

■ You can customize Word by changing the options in the Word Options dialog box.

VOCABULARY*Review*

Define the following terms:

Data source	Merge field	Track Changes
Mail merge	Template	Workgroup collaboration
Main document		

REVIEW *Questions*

WRITTEN QUESTIONS

Write a brief answer to each of the following questions.

1. How will using a template increase your efficiency?

2. How do you create a custom template?

3. How does Word indicate each of the following when the Tracked Changes feature is turned on?
   A. Inserted text

   B. Deleted text

   C. Moved text

4. Under what circumstances would you use Mail Merge?

5. Describe two ways to remove commands from the Quick Access Toolbar.

TRUE/FALSE

Circle T if the statement is true or F if the statement is false.

T   F   1. A template file can be used only once.

T   F   2. If you want to create a sheet of labels with different names and addresses on each label, you should use the Labels button on the Mailings tab.

T   F   3. In a mail merge, the data source contains the information that changes.

T   F   4. The name that appears in the ScreenTip for a comment balloon is the same as the Author name in the Document Information Panel.

T   F   5. You cannot print comments.

PROJECTS

PROJECT 8-1

1. Create a new document based on the installed template **Urban Resume**. (This template might be named **Resume (Urban Theme)** on your computer.) Save the document as **My Resume** followed by your initials.

2. Replace the name at the top of the document with your name, if necessary. Replace the appropriate placeholders with your address and phone number.

3. Delete the fax number placeholder.

4. If you have a Web site, type the Web site address in the *Type your website* placeholder; otherwise, type **www.websiteplaceholder.com**. Press the spacebar after typing the Web site address. Remove the hyperlink formatting from the Web site address.

5. Next to the *Education* heading, replace the placeholder with the name of your school.

6. Save, print, and close the document.

PROJECT 8-2

1. Open the **Subscription** Data File. Save the document as a template named **Journal Subscription** followed by your initials.

2. Create a new blank document. Save it as **Journal Addresses** followed by your initials. Create a table with seven columns and four rows. Type as the column names **First Name**, **Last Name**, **Company**, **Address**, **City**, **State**, and **Zip**. Enter the following data in the table:

Ben Hodges
Unisource Marketing, Inc.
1908 Queens Street
Los Angeles, CA 90025

David Norris
Pillar Shipping Company
6421 Douglas Road
Coral Gables, FL 33134

Charlotte Buckner
Accent Wireless
717 Pacific Parkway
Honolulu, HI 96813

3. Save and close the document.

4. Insert the current date in the appropriate position in the Journal Subscription template. On the Mailings tab, select the Journal Addresses document as the recipient list. Insert the Address Block merge field with the recipient's name in the format *Joshua Randall Jr.* Insert the Greeting Line merge field with the greeting in the format *Dear Joshua,*. Adjust the spacing for the Address Block field.

5. In the closing, replace *Alan Dunn* with your name. Save your changes and close the document.

6. Create a new document based on the Journal Subscription template. When the dialog box opens asking if you want to continue using data from the database *Journal Addresses.docx*, click the Yes button.

7. Preview the results of the merge. Scroll through the three documents. Print the third document (the letter addressed to Charlotte Buckner). Merge the documents in a new document, and then save the merged document as **Merged Journal Letters** followed by your initials. Close the document. Close the Journal Subscription document without saving changes.

8. Create a new document, and then create and print an envelope for Ben Hodges. Use your name and address as the return address. Save it as **Hodges Envelope**, and then print and close the document.

9. Create and print a sheet of labels with Ben Hodges's information. In the labels document, replace the name in the first cell with your name. Adjust the paragraph spacing, if necessary. Save it as **Hodges Labels**. Print and close the document.

 PROJECT 8-3

1. Open the **Telephone.docx** Data File. Save the document as **Telephone Etiquette** followed by your initials.

2. Turn on the Tracked Changes feature. Change the User name and Initials in the Word Options dialog box to your own.

3. Click at the end of the first numbered item, after the text *Answer the telephone promptly.* Insert the following as a comment: **Add a note to answer the phone after the first ring.**

4. In the third sentence in the third item, delete the words **using** and **terms**.

5. In item 5, delete the last sentence. (Make sure you do not delete the paragraph mark.)

6. Move the sixth item under *Answering the Telephone* so it is the third item under *Taking Messages*. Change its number accordingly.

7. In the second item under *Taking Messages*, add the prefix **pre** to the word *determined*.

8. In a blank paragraph at the end of the document, type your name.

9. Print the document showing changes and comments.

10. Turn the Track Changes feature off. Change the User name and Initials in the Word Options dialog box back to their original values.

11. Save and close the document.

 PROJECT 8-4

1. Open the **Telephone 2.docx** Data File. Save it as **Telephone Etiquette 2** followed by your initials.

2. Turn on the Tracked Changes feature. Change the User name and Initials in the Word Options dialog box to your own.

3. Make the changes suggested in the two comments.

4. Delete the comments.

5. In a blank paragraph at the end of the document, type your name.

6. Accept the changes in the first numbered item. Reject the changes in the third numbered item. Accept the rest of the changes in the document.

7. Save, print, and close the document, but do not exit Word.

8. Use the Combine command to combine the **Telephone 2.docx** Data File with the **Telephone Etiquette 2.docx** file you created.

9. Save the combined document as **Telephone Combined**. Print the document showing the changes and comments. Close the document.

CRITICAL *Thinking*

 ACTIVITY 8-1

Write an application letter for a job that interests you. Save the document on a USB drive or other removable media and give it to a classmate. Have your classmate use Track Changes to add comments and propose changes. Review your classmate's suggestions, and accept or reject the changes and delete the comments.

 ACTIVITY 8-2

Create a letterhead for an organization to which you belong. Save it as a template.

 ACTIVITY 8-3

It is career week at your school, which gives students an opportunity to explore possible careers. Your faculty advisor asks you to prepare a list of jobs that interest you. Next, follow the steps outlined below.

1. Set up appointments with at least two people who currently are working in the field(s) that interest you.

2. Interview each person. Ask leading questions, such as:
   A. Why did you choose this career?
   B. What did you have to do to prepare for this career?
   C. What work habits did you have to form to succeed in your job?

Listen attentively to the answers. Make sure you take notes as well. Before leaving the interview, read back your responses to the person you are interviewing to make sure you captured the appropriate information.

3. Write a report in a Word document explaining the job responsibilities of the people you interviewed and disclose whether you would consider a career in that field.

4. Present your findings to the class.

INTRODUCTION TO MICROSOFT WORD

REVIEW *Questions*

MATCHING

Match the correct term in Column 2 to its description in Column 1.

Column 1

_____ 1. Formatting you can apply by clicking a button in the Styles group on the Home tab

_____ 2. Designs of type

_____ 3. Text printed at the bottom of each page

_____ 4. Building block you create from frequently used text

_____ 5. File that contains formatting with text you can customize

Column 2

A. fonts

B. Quick Part

C. taskbar

D. Quick Style

E. header

F. footer

G. template

WRITTEN QUESTIONS

Write a brief answer to the following questions.

1. What are two ways to check the spelling in a document?

2. How do you align text? What are the four text alignment positions?

3. Describe how to redefine an existing Quick Style, and then describe how to create a new Quick Style.

4. What does the Track Changes command do?

5. What is the difference between the system Clipboard and the Office Clipboard?

PROJECTS

PROJECT 1

1. Open the **Properties.docx** Data File.

2. Save the document as **East Isle Properties** followed by your initials.

3. Check the document for spelling and grammar errors. Make changes as needed.

4. Find the word *Property* and replace it with **Properties** each time it occurs in the document.

5. Move the heading *How do I get more information?* and the paragraph that follows to the end of the document.

6. Use the Find command to locate the word *excellent*, and then replace it with a synonym that makes sense in context.

7. Change the theme to Aspect.

8. Change the orientation to landscape.

9. Add an appropriate page border.

10. Center align the text vertically on the page.

11. Change the title to 28 point, centered. Change the font of the title to one of your choice. Change the color to one that coordinates with the page border.

12. Change each of the headings to the Heading 1 Quick Style. Change the color to coordinate with the page border. Update the definition of the Heading 1 Quick Style to match the revised format.

13. Center the last heading. Indent the last heading and paragraph one inch on each side.

14. Create a 3-point border around the last heading and paragraph. Change the color of the border and shade the paragraphs with colors that match the page border.

15. Add your name in a blank paragraph under the paragraphs with the border around them. Preview the document. Save, print, and close the document.

PROJECT 2

1. Open the **Tenses.docx** Data File. Save the document as **Verb Tenses** followed by your initials.

2. Display the ruler if it is not already showing.

3. Apply any appropriate Quick Style to the title except for the Heading 1 Quick Style, and then, if necessary, center it and apply bold formatting. Change the font size to 20.

4. Select all the text in the document, set a left tab marker at the one-inch mark on the ruler, and then set a right tab marker at the five-inch mark.

5. Modify the right tab so that there is a dashed line leader in front of it.

6. Format the *Present* heading so it is 16 points, centered, and bold.

7. Redefine the Heading 1 Quick Style to match the style of the heading you just formatted, and then apply the new Heading 1 Quick Style to the other two headings.

8. Insert a formatted header that contains a date content control, and then insert a footer that has a content control that contains the company name. Add your name as the Company name in the document properties. Select the current date in the Date content control in the header. Delete any other content controls (including the page number) that appear in the header or footer.

9. Preview the document. Save, print, and close the document.

 PROJECT 3

1. Open the **Bagels.docx** Data File.

2. Save the document as **Bagel Mania** followed by your initials.

3. Change the theme to Apex, change the size of all the text to 14 points, and change the color of all the text to Aqua, Accent 3, Darker 25%.

4. Format the title *Bagel Mania* with the Title Quick Style. Center the title, change it to 24-point Arial Black, and add the shadow and small caps font effects. Define a new Quick Style named Bagel Title based on this formatting.

5. Center the subtitle *"The Best Bagels in Town"*. Change it to Arial, 16-point, bold, and italic.

6. Indent the first line of the first paragraph under the subtitle one-half inch.

7. Change the list of bagels (from *Rye* to *Cinnamon-Raisin*) to a bulleted list, and then sort it in alphabetical order. Make all the text in the list bold.

8. Format the list of bagels in three columns. The rest of the document should remain one column.

9. Format the *Breakfast Bagels* heading with the Heading 2 Quick Style. Change it to small caps, with a double underline in the same color as the text. Redefine the Heading 2 Quick Style based on this formatting.

10. Apply the redefined Heading 2 Quick Style to the *Lunch Bagels* heading.

11. Change the left margin of the entire document to 1.25 inches, and the right margin to .75 inches.

12. Change the items in the breakfast and lunch bagel lists to numbered lists.

13. Change the line spacing of the paragraph under the subtitle to single-spacing and the types of bagels list to 1.5 lines.

14. Format the last line, *Come again!*, as 18-point, bold, italic Arial.

15. Add your name in 10-point type in a new line at the end of the document. Save and preview the document. Print from the Preview screen.

16. Save and preview the document. Print from the Preview screen, and then close the document.

 PROJECT 4

1. Open a new Word document. Switch to Outline View.

2. Type the outline shown in Figure UR-1. (Note that the zoom in the figure is set at 130% zoom so that you can more easily read the text.)

FIGURE UR-1

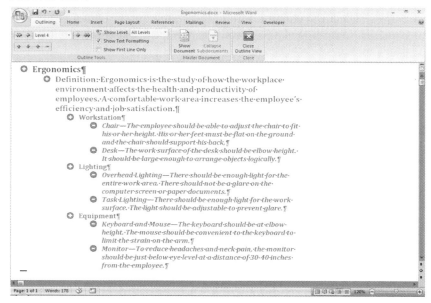

3. Collapse the outline to show only the heading levels 1-3.

4. Move the *Equipment* heading above the *Lighting* heading.

5. Expand the outline.

6. Move the *Desk* heading (and its text) above the Chair heading.

7. Add your name in a new blank Level 1 paragraph at the end of the document. Save the document in Outline view as **Ergonomics** followed by your initials.

8. Preview the document. Print and close the document.

PROJECT 5

1. Open a new Word document. Create letterhead for Star Financial Group, as shown in Figure UR-2

FIGURE UR-2

Use different clip art if you can't find this one

12-point Engravers MT

WordArt Style 11 with the font changed to Engravers MT and filled with Orange, Accent 6 Darker 50% and outlined with orange, accent 6, Lighter 40%

2. Save the document as a Word Template named **Star Template** followed by your initials.

3. Insert four blank lines below the letterhead. (*Hint*: Remember that with the Normal Quick Style, each paragraph has a blank line inserted after it automatically.) Insert the current date so that it is updated automatically.

4. Press the Enter key twice, type **Sincerely,** press the Enter key three times, and then type your name. Save this as a Quick Part named **Closing** in the template only. Delete the text from the document.

5. Save your changes. Close the file.

6. Create a new document based on the **Star Template** followed by your initials.

7. After the date, press the Enter key three times. Type the letter shown in Figure UR-3.

FIGURE UR-3

This is to let you know that I have recently joined the professionals at the Star Financial Group. I am happy to be working with such a highly regarded company.

I would like to set up a meeting with you to discuss the type of services I can provide. This brief visit will not obligate you in any way, and it could result in an exchange of worthwhile ideas regarding your general financial strategy.

I plan to call you within the next few days to arrange an appointment at your convenience. Thank you for your consideration.

8. In a new paragraph below the body of the letter, insert four blank lines at the end of the letter. Insert the Closing Quick Part that you created.

9. Save the document as a Word document named **Star Letter**.

10. Create a new document. Create a table and type the following names as the contact list. Include columns for the title, first name, last name, address, city, state, and zip code. Format the table with a table style (choose any style you like). Save the contact list as **Star Contacts** followed by your initials, and then close the file.

Ms. Katherine McGuire
717 Oakridge Avenue
Indianapolis, IN 46225

Mr. Alex Novak
5506 Douglas Street
Indianapolis, IN 46216

Mr. Michael Vincent
1908 Cameron Road
Indianapolis, IN 46206

11. Use the mail merge process to merge the Star Letter document with the Star Contacts data source. Use the recipient's title in the greeting line. Complete the merge to a new document, and then print the letter to Katherine McGuire.

12. Save the document as **Star Merge**, and then close the document. Close the Star Letter document without saving changes.

13. Create an envelope in a new document addressed to Katherine McGuire for the letter using your address as the return address. Save it as **Star Envelope**, and then print and close the document.

 PROJECT 6

1. Open the **Recycling.docx** Data File. Save the document as **Recycling Flyer** followed by your initials.

2. Format all the text in the document as a multilevel list. Indent items so they make sense.

3. Switch to the theme of your choice. Add **Recycling at Sage Stone Race Track** as the document title, and format it appropriately.

4. Add the title you typed in Step 3 as the Title document property. Add your name as the Author document property. Add **Draft** as the Status document property.

5. Insert the Stacks footer, and then type **Sage Stone Race Track** in the Company name content control. Insert one of the Cubicles headers. Delete the empty content control in the header.

6. Save, print, and close the document.

 PROJECT 7

You want to create your own greeting card. You can do this using a template from Microsoft Office Online. You need to have access to the Internet and Microsoft Office Online in order to complete this project.

1. Open the New Document dialog box, click Greeting cards under Microsoft Office Online, and then scroll through the greeting card templates in the middle pane in the dialog box.

2. To see a preview of a template, click it to select it and then look at the preview in the pane on the right.

3. When you find a greeting card you like, select it, and then click Download. Follow the instructions that appear in dialog boxes to verify your copy of Microsoft Office and to download the template, clicking Yes or OK as needed. The template appears in a new document window.

4. Replace the placeholder text with your own text.

5. If you don't like the colors used, adjust the text and page background colors.

6. Add clip art if you like. Resize and reposition the clip art to fit nicely on the page. Change it to a floating object if necessary.

7. Add your name in a text box in an appropriate place in the card. Use a font that looks like script (handwriting).

8. Save the document with a name of your choice, and then print and close it.

SIMULATION

You work at the Java Internet Café, which has been open only a few months. The café serves coffee, other beverages, and pastries, and offers Internet access. Seven computers are set up on tables along the north side of the store. Customers can come in, have a cup of coffee and a Danish, and explore the World Wide Web.

Because of your Microsoft Office experience, your manager asks you to create and revise many of the business's documents.

 JOB 1

Some customers at Java Internet Café do not have much experience using computers or accessing the Internet. Your manager asks you to create a poster with definitions of the most common terms users encounter while surfing the Internet. The poster will hang near each computer.

1. Open a new Word document.

2. Create the poster shown in Figure UR-4. Use the Technic theme.

FIGURE UR-4

Title Style, 48 points

Clip art is recolored with Accent color 2 Light style

16 points

Internet Terminology

Browser: A program used on a computer connected to the Internet that provides access to the World Wide Web. The browser translates the documents stored on the World Wide Web into a format you can read on your screen.

Download: To transfer a file from a remote computer to your computer through a modem and a telephone line, cable, or wirelessly.

E-mail (Electronic Mail): Electronic mail messages you send over the Internet from one computer to another.

FAQ (Frequently Asked Questions): On a Web site, a list of questions commonly asked by users and the answers to those questions to assist people using the site.

Internet: A worldwide system of linked computers that allows users to send and receive e-mail and documents from one computer to another.

URL (Universal Resource Locator): The address of a Web page on the World Wide Web.

Web (World Wide Web or WWW): A subset of the Internet that allows people to view documents called Web pages using a browser. You can click items called links on a Web page to open another Web page anywhere on the Web identified by the link.

3. Add your name in a text box at the bottom of the document. Save the document as **Internet Terms** followed by your initials.

4. Print and close the document.

 JOB 2

Many customers become curious when they see computers through the window of the coffee shop. The café servers are often too busy to explain the concept to customers entering the store. Your manager asks you to revise the menu to include a short description of the café. These menus will be printed and placed near the entrance.

1. Open the **Menu.docx** Data File. Save the document as **Java Menu** followed by your initials.

2. Jump to the end of the document, and then type the following text:

   Java Internet Café offers customers computers with high-speed Internet access as well as free Wi—Fi. Each of our computers has a special interface for new users to help you get started exploring the World Wide Web. You have heard about it; now you need to try it! Ask your server to help you get started.

3. Change the font of the paragraph you just keyed to Arial, 11 point, if necessary.

4. Change the left and right margins to 1 inch.

5. Insert a new paragraph with the Normal style, and then type the title **Menu**.

6. Format *Menu* with the Title Quick Style. Center it, and then redefine the Title Quick Style to reflect the modified format.

7. Save, print, and close the document. Close Word.

MICROSOFT EXCEL

Unit

 Estimated Time for Unit: 16.5 hours

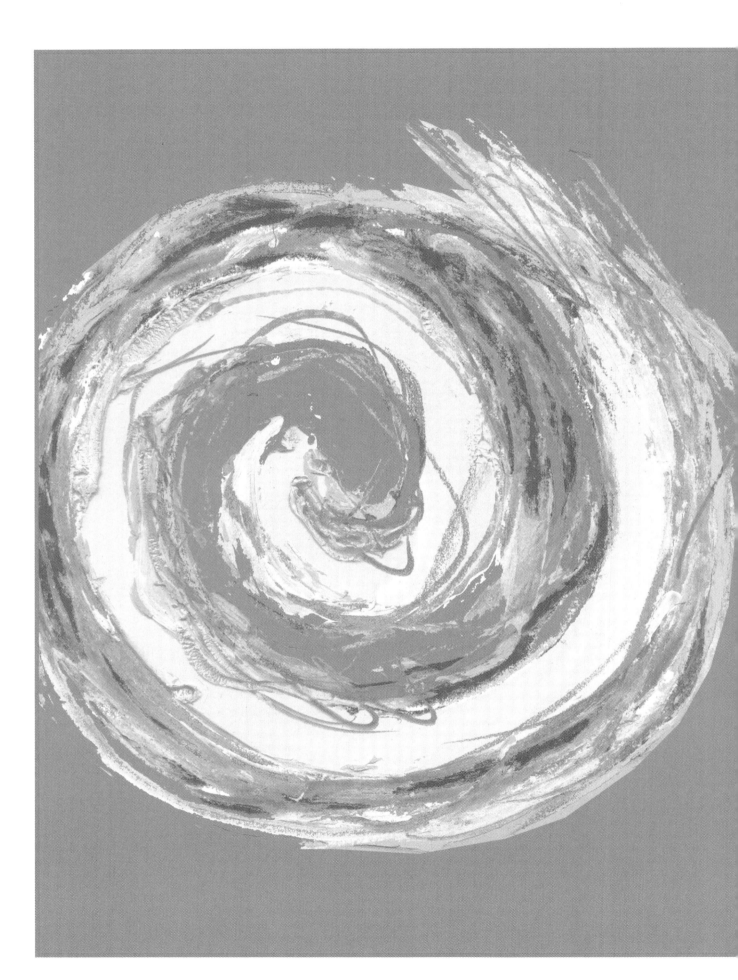

EXCEL BASICS

OBJECTIVES

Upon completion of this lesson, you will be able to:

- Define the terms *spreadsheet* and *worksheet.*
- Identify the parts of a worksheet.
- Open an existing workbook.
- Save a workbook.
- Move the active cell in a worksheet.
- Select cells and enter data in a worksheet.
- Edit data in cells.
- Find and replace data.
- Zoom in a worksheet.
- Preview and print a worksheet.
- Close a workbook.

Estimated Time: 1.5 hours

VOCABULARY

Active cell

Active worksheet

Cell

Cell reference

Column

Formula

Formula Bar

Microsoft Office Excel 2007 (Excel)

Name Box

Range

Range reference

Row

Sheet tab

Spreadsheet

Workbook

Worksheet

Introduction to Spreadsheets

Microsoft Office Excel 2007 (or Excel) is the spreadsheet program in Microsoft Office 2007. A spreadsheet is a grid of rows and columns in which you enter text, numbers, and the results of calculations. The purpose of a spreadsheet is to solve problems that involve numbers. Without a computer, you could try to solve these types of problems by creating rows and columns on paper and using a calculator to determine the results (see Figure 1-1). Spreadsheets have many uses. For example, you can use a spreadsheet to calculate grades for students in a class, to prepare a budget for the next few months, or to determine payments for repaying a loan.

FIGURE 1-1
Spreadsheet prepared on paper

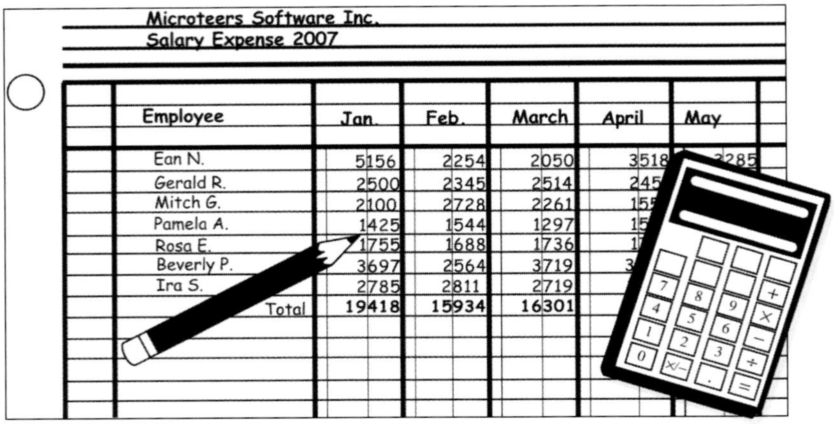

Computer spreadsheets also contain rows and columns with text, numbers, and the results of calculations. But, computer spreadsheets perform calculations faster and more accurately than you can do with spreadsheets you create on paper, using a pencil and a calculator. The primary advantage of computer spreadsheets is their ability to complete complex and repetitious calculations quickly and accurately.

Computer spreadsheets are also flexible. Making changes to an existing computer spreadsheet is usually as easy as pointing and clicking with the mouse. Suppose, for example, you use a computer spreadsheet to calculate your budget (your monthly income and expenses) and overestimate the amount of money you need to pay for electricity. You can change a single entry in the computer spreadsheet, and the entire spreadsheet will be recalculated to determine the new budgeted amount. Think about the work this change would require if you were calculating the budget by hand on paper with a pencil and calculator.

In Excel, a computerized spreadsheet is called a worksheet. The file used to store worksheets is called a workbook. Usually, workbooks contain a collection of related worksheets.

Starting Excel

Y ou start Excel from the Start menu in Windows. Click the Start button, click All Programs, click Microsoft Office, and then click Microsoft Office Excel 2007. When Excel starts, the program window displays a blank workbook titled *Book1*, which includes three blank worksheets titled *Sheet1*, *Sheet2*, and *Sheet3*. The Excel program window has the same basic parts as all Office programs: the title bar, the Quick Access Toolbar, the Office Button, the Ribbon, and the status bar. However, as shown in Figure 1-2, Excel also has additional buttons and parts.

FIGURE 1-2
Excel program window

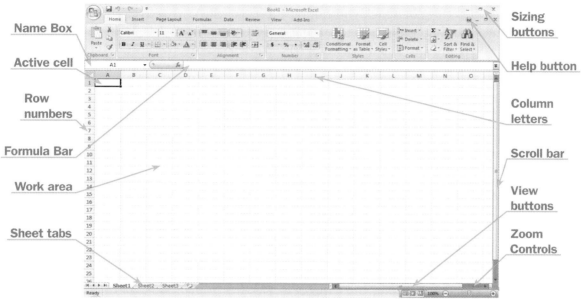

STEP-BY-STEP 1.1

1. With Windows running, click the **Start** button, click **All Programs**, click **Microsoft Office**, and then click **Microsoft Office Excel 2007**. Excel starts and a blank workbook titled *Book1* appears, as shown in Figure 1-2.

2. If the Excel program window does not fill your screen, click the **Maximize** button in the title bar.

3. Leave the workbook open for the next Step-by-Step.

Exploring the Parts of the Worksheet

Each new workbook contains three worksheets by default. The name of each worksheet appears in the **sheet tab** at the bottom of the worksheet window. **Columns** of the worksheet appear vertically and are identified by letters at the top of the worksheet window. **Rows** appear horizontally and are identified by numbers on the left side of the worksheet window. A **cell** is the intersection of a row and a column. Each cell is identified by a unique **cell reference**, which is formed by combining the cell's column letter and row number. For example, the cell that intersects at column C and row 4 has the cell reference C4.

The pointer becomes a thick white plus sign when it is in the worksheet. If you move the pointer up to the Ribbon, the pointer changes to a white arrow.

The cell in the worksheet in which you can type data is called the **active cell**. The active cell is distinguished from the other cells by a dark border. In your worksheet, cell A1 has the dark border, which indicates that cell A1 is the active cell. You can move the active cell from one cell to another. The **Name Box**, or cell reference area located below the Ribbon, displays the cell reference of the active cell.

The **Formula Bar** appears to the right of the Name Box and displays a formula when the cell of a worksheet contains a calculated value (or the results of the formula). A **formula** is an equation that calculates a new value from values currently in a worksheet, such as adding the numbers in cell A1 and A2.

Opening an Existing Workbook

Opening a workbook means loading an existing workbook file from a disk into the program window. You can open a workbook stored on any available disk or folder. To open an existing workbook, you click the Office Button to display the Office menu, and then click Open. The Open dialog box appears. The Open dialog box shows all the workbooks in the displayed folder that were created with Excel.

You need to display the location where the workbook you want to open is stored. In the Open dialog box, use the Address bar, Navigation pane, and Folders list to display the drive and folder containing the workbook you want to open. After you have located the file you want to open, double-click the file. When you start Excel, the program displays a new workbook titled *Book1*. This blank workbook disappears when you open another workbook.

STEP-BY-STEP 1.2

1. Click the **Office Button**, and then click **Open**. The Open dialog box appears.

2. Use the Address bar, Navigation pane, and Folders list to display the location of the Data Files for this lesson.

3. Open the **Frogs.xlsx** Data File. Depending on how Windows is set up on your computer, you might not see the file extension after the file name; in that case, open **Frogs**. The workbook appears in the program window, as shown in Figure 1-3.

FIGURE 1-3
Open workbook

Current workbook name (you may not see the file extension)

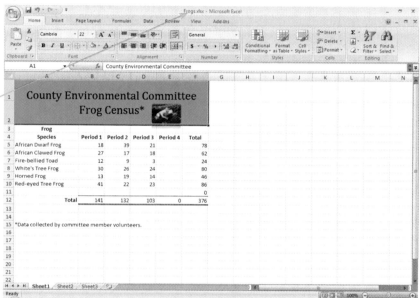

4. Leave the workbook open for the next Step-by-Step.

Saving a Workbook

Saving is done two ways. The Save command saves an existing workbook on a disk, using its current name and save location. The Save As command lets you save a workbook with a new name or to a new location.

The first time you save a new workbook, the Save As dialog box appears, as shown in Figure 1-4, so you can give the workbook a descriptive name and choose a save location. After you have saved the workbook, you can use the Save command on the Office menu or the Save button on the Quick Access Toolbar to periodically save the latest version of the workbook with the same name in the same location. To save a copy of the workbook with a new name or save location, you need to use the Save As dialog box. You'll use this method to save the Data File you opened with a new name, leaving the original workbook intact.

Important

Save frequently (at least every 10 minutes) to ensure that you always have a current version of the file available in case of an unexpected power outage or computer shutdown. You can press the Ctrl+S keys to quickly save your workbook.

FIGURE 1-4
Save As dialog box

Use the Navigation pane to change the current save location

Address bar shows the current drive and folder path

Workbooks already in the displayed save location

Depending on your Windows set up, file names might not include the file extension

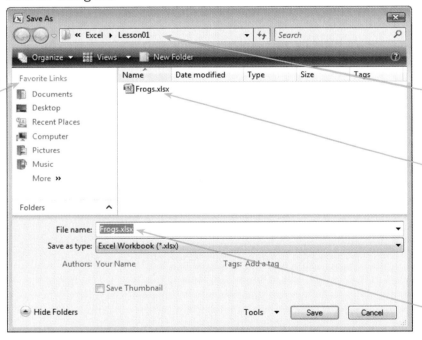

Did You Know?

You can create a new folder in which to save a file by clicking the New Folder button in the Save As dialog box. Type a name for the new folder, and then press the Enter key.

STEP-BY-STEP 1.3

1. Click the **Office Button**, and then click **Save As**. The Save As dialog box appears.

2. Change the save location to the drive and folder where you store the Data Files for this lesson.

3. In the File name box, type **Frog Census** followed by your initials.

4. Click **Save**.

5. Leave the workbook open for the next Step-by-Step.

Moving the Active Cell in a Worksheet

The easiest way to change the active cell in a worksheet is to move the pointer to the cell you want to make active and click. The dark border surrounds the cell you clicked, and the Name Box shows its cell reference. When working with a large worksheet, you might not be able to see the entire worksheet in the program window. You can display different parts of the worksheet by using the mouse to drag the scroll box in the scroll bar to another position. You can also move the active cell to different parts of the worksheet using the keyboard or the Go To command.

> **Did You Know?**
>
> The column letter and row number of the active cell are shaded in orange for easy identification.

Using the Keyboard to Change the Active Cell

You can change the active cell by pressing the keys or keyboard shortcuts shown in Table 1-1. When you press an arrow key, the active cell moves one cell in that direction. When you press and hold down an arrow key, the active cell shifts in that direction repeatedly and quickly.

TABLE 1-1
Keys for moving the active cell in a worksheet

TO MOVE	PRESS
Left one column	Left arrow key
Right one column	Right arrow key
Up one row	Up arrow key
Down one row	Down arrow key
To the first cell of a row	Home key
To cell A1	Ctrl+Home keys
To the last cell of the column and row that contain data	Ctrl+End keys
Up one window	Page Up key
Down one window	Page Down key

Using the Go To Command to Move the Active Cell

You might want to change the active cell to a cell in a part of the worksheet that you cannot see in the work area. The fastest way to move to that cell is with the Go To dialog box. On the Home tab of the Ribbon, in the Editing group, click the Find & Select button, and then click Go To. The Go To dialog box appears, as shown in Figure 1-5. Type the cell reference in the Reference box, and then click OK. The cell you specified becomes the active cell.

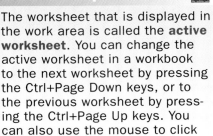

Extra for Experts

The worksheet that is displayed in the work area is called the **active worksheet**. You can change the active worksheet in a workbook to the next worksheet by pressing the Ctrl+Page Down keys, or to the previous worksheet by pressing the Ctrl+Page Up keys. You can also use the mouse to click the sheet tab of the worksheet you want to make active.

FIGURE 1-5
Go To dialog box

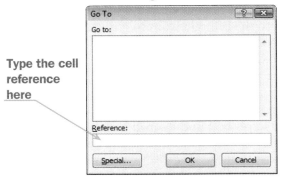

Type the cell reference here

STEP-BY-STEP 1.4

1. Press the **Ctrl+End** keys. The active cell moves from cell A1 to cell F15, which is the cell that intersects the last column and row that contain data in the worksheet.

2. Press the **Home** key. The active cell moves to the first cell of row 15—cell A15, which contains the words *Data collected by committee member volunteers*.

3. Press the **Up arrow** key six times to move the active cell up six rows. The active cell is cell A9, which contains the words *Horned Frog*.

4. On the Ribbon, click the **Home** tab, if the tab is not already active.

5. In the Editing group, click the **Find & Select** button to open a menu of commands, and then click **Go To**. The Go To dialog box appears, as shown in Figure 1-5.

Did You Know?

You can also open the Go To dialog box by pressing the Ctrl+G keys or by pressing the F5 key.

STEP-BY-STEP 1.4 Continued

6. In the Reference box, type **B4**.

7. Click **OK**. The active cell moves to cell B4.

8. On the Quick Access Toolbar, click the **Save** button to save the workbook.

9. Leave the workbook open for the next Step-by-Step.

Selecting a Group of Cells

Often, you will perform operations on more than one cell at a time. A group of selected cells is called a **range**. In an adjacent range, all cells touch each other and form a rectangle. The range is identified by its **range reference**, which is the cell in its upper-left corner and the cell in its lower-right corner, separated by a colon (for example, A3:C5). To select an adjacent range, click the cell in one corner of the range, drag the pointer to the cell in the opposite corner of the range, and then release the mouse button. As you drag, the range of selected cells becomes shaded (except for the first cell you selected), and the dark border expands to surround all the selected cells. In addition, the column letters and row numbers of the range you select change to orange. The active cell in a range is white; the other cells are shaded.

You can also select a range that is non-adjacent. A non-adjacent range includes two or more adjacent ranges and selected cells. The range reference for a non-adjacent range separates each range or cell with a semi-colon (for example, A3:C5;E3:G5). To select a non-adjacent range, select the first adjacent range or cell, press the Ctrl key as you select the other cells or ranges you want to include, and then release the Ctrl key and the mouse button.

> ### Teamwork
>
> Have a classmate call out cell references so you can practice moving the active cell in a worksheet using the methods you have learned.

STEP-BY-STEP 1.5

1. Click cell **B4**.

2. Press and hold the left mouse button as you drag the pointer to the right until cell **F4** is selected.

STEP-BY-STEP 1.5 Continued

3. Release the mouse button. The range B4:F4 is selected, as you can see from the shaded cells and the dark border. Also, the column letters B through F and the row number 4 are orange. See Figure 1-6.

FIGURE 1-6
Selected range

Column letters and row numbers included in the range are orange

Active cell in the range is white

Dark border surrounds the range

Selected cells in the range are shaded

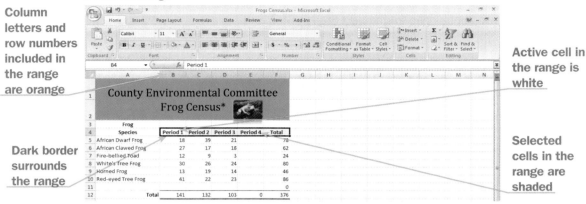

4. Click cell **B5**.

5. Press and hold the left mouse button as you drag down and to the right until cell **F12** is selected.

6. Release the mouse button. The range B5:F12 is selected.

7. Leave the workbook open for the next Step-by-Step.

Entering Data in a Cell

Worksheet cells can contain text, numbers, or formulas. Text is any combination of letters and numbers and symbols, such as headings, labels, or explanatory notes. Numbers are values, dates, or times. Formulas are equations that calculate a value.

You enter data in the active cell. First, type the text, numbers, or formula in the active cell. Then, click the Enter button on the Formula Bar or press the Enter or Tab key on the keyboard. The data you typed is entered in the cell. If you decide not to enter the data you typed, you can click the Cancel button on the Formula Bar or press the Esc key to delete the data without making any changes to the cell.

If you have already entered the data in the cell, you can undo, or reverse, the entry. On the

Did You Know?

If a cell is not long enough to display all the cell's contents, extra text extends into the next cells, if they are blank. If not, only the characters that fit in the cell appear, and the rest are hidden from view, but they are still stored. Numbers that extend beyond a cell's width appear as #### in the cell.

Did You Know?

After you type data in a cell, the active cell changes, depending on how you enter the data. If you click the Enter button on the Formula Bar, the cell you typed in remains active. If you press the Enter key, the cell below the cell you typed in becomes active. If you press the Tab key, the cell to the right of the cell you typed in becomes active.

Quick Access Toolbar, click the Undo button to reverse your most recent change. To undo multiple actions, click the arrow next to the Undo button. A list of your previous actions appears, and you can choose how many actions you want to undo.

STEP-BY-STEP 1.6

1. Click cell **E5** to make it active.

2. Type **15**. As you type, the numbers appear in the cell and in the Formula Bar.

3. Press the **Enter** key. The number is entered in cell E5, and the active cell moves to cell E6. The totals in cells F5, E12, and F12 change as you enter the data.

4. Type **22**.

5. On the Formula Bar, click the **Enter** button. The totals in cells F6, E12, and F12 change as you enter the data.

6. On the Quick Access Toolbar, next to the Undo button, click the **arrow**. A menu appears listing the actions you have just performed.

7. Click **Typing '22' in E6**, as shown in Figure 1-7. The data is removed from cell E6, and the data in cells F6, E12, and F12 return to their previous totals.

FIGURE 1-7
Undo menu

Click the arrow next
to the Undo button to
open the menu

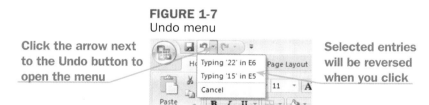

Selected entries
will be reversed
when you click

8. Click cell **A11**, and then enter **Pac Frog**. The Pac Frog species is added to the Frog Census.

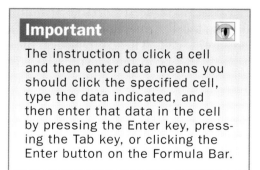

Important

The instruction to click a cell and then enter data means you should click the specified cell, type the data indicated, and then enter that data in the cell by pressing the Enter key, pressing the Tab key, or clicking the Enter button on the Formula Bar.

STEP-BY-STEP 1.6 Continued

9. In the range **E6:E11**, enter the data, as shown in Figure 1-8, to include the number of frogs sighted for each species in Period 4.

FIGURE 1-8
Data entered in the Frog Census

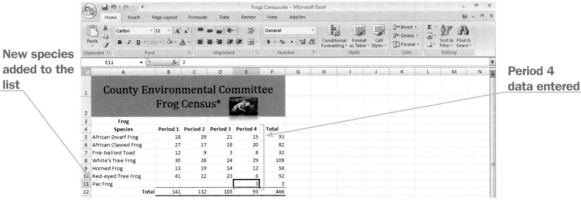

New species added to the list

Period 4 data entered

10. Save the workbook, and leave it open for the next Step-by-Step.

Changing Data in a Cell

After you enter data in cells in the worksheet, you might change your mind or discover a mistake. If so, you can edit, replace, or clear the data.

Editing Data

When you need to make a minor change to data in a cell, you can edit it in the Formula Bar or in the cell. The contents of the active cell always appear in the Formula Bar. To edit the data in the Formula Bar, click in the Formula Bar and then drag to select the text you want to edit. You can also use the arrow keys to position the insertion point. Then, press the Backspace or Delete key to remove data, or type the new data. To edit the data directly in a cell, make the cell active and then press the F2 key or double-click the cell. A blinking insertion point appears in the cell, and you can make changes to the data. When you are done, click the Enter button in the Formula Bar or press the Enter or Tab key.

> **Did You Know?**
>
> If you need help while working with any of the Excel features, use the Excel Help feature. Click the Microsoft Office Excel Help button. In the Excel Help window, type a word or phrase about the feature you want help with, and then click the Search button. A list of Help topics related to the word or words you typed appears. Click the appropriate Help topic to learn more about the feature.

Replacing Data

When you need to make significant changes to cell data, you can replace the entire cell contents. To replace cell contents, select the cell, type the new data, and then enter the data by clicking the Enter button on the Formula Bar or by pressing the Enter or Tab key. This is the same method used to enter data in a blank cell. The only difference is that you overwrite the existing cell contents.

Clearing Data

Clearing a cell removes all the data in the cell. To clear the active cell, you can use the Ribbon, the keyboard, or the mouse. On the Ribbon, on the Home tab, in the Editing group, click the Clear button to display a menu with options to clear the cell's format, contents, comments, or all of these. To use the keyboard, press the Delete or Backspace key. To use your mouse, right-click the active cell and then click Clear Contents on the shortcut menu.

S TEP-BY-STEP 1.7

1. Click cell **A11** to make it the active cell.

2. Press the **F2** key. A blinking insertion point appears in cell A11.

3. Press the **left arrow** key five times to move the insertion point after *Pac*.

4. Type **Man**, and then press the **Enter** key. The contents of cell A11 are edited to *PacMan Frog*.

5. Click cell **D10**, and then type **18**.

6. On the Formula Bar, click the **Enter** button. The number 18 is entered in cell D10, replacing the previous contents.

7. Click cell **A3**, and then press the **Delete** key. The contents are cleared from cell A3. Your screen should look similar to Figure 1-9.

8. Save the workbook, and leave it open for the next Step-by-Step.

FIGURE 1-9
Data in cells changed and cleared

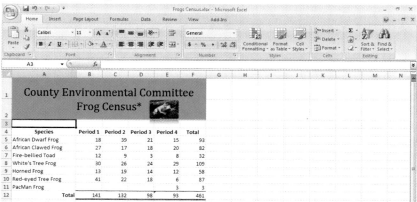

Searching for Data

The Find and Replace dialog box enables you to locate specific words or numbers in a worksheet. If you like, you can then change data you find.

Finding Data

The Find command locates data in a worksheet, which is particularly helpful when a worksheet contains a large amount of data. You can use Find to locate words or parts of words. For example, searching for *emp* finds the words *employee* and *temporary*. Likewise, searching for *85* finds the numbers *85, 850,* and *385*. On the Home tab of the Ribbon, in the Editing group, click the Find & Select button, and then click Find. The Find and Replace dialog box appears, with the Find tab active.

Replacing Data

The Replace command is an extension of the Find command. Replacing data substitutes new data for the data found. In the Editing group on the Home tab of the Ribbon, click the Find & Select button, and then click Replace. The Find and Replace dialog box appears, with the Replace tab active. If the Find and Replace dialog box is already open, click the Replace tab in the dialog box.

You can perform more specific searches by clicking the Options button in the dialog box. Figure 1-10 shows the Replace tab in the expanded Find and Replace dialog box. Table 1-2 lists the options you can specify in the Find and Replace dialog box.

FIGURE 1-10
Expanded Find and Replace dialog box

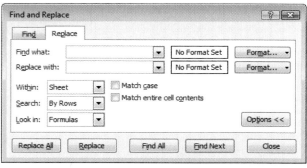

TABLE 1-2
Find and Replace options

SEARCH OPTION	SPECIFIES
Find what	The data to locate
Replace with	The data to insert in place of the located data
Format	The format of the data you want to find or replace
Within	Whether to search the worksheet or the entire workbook
Search	The direction to search: across rows or down columns
Look in	Whether to search cell contents (values) or formulas
Match case	Whether the search must match the capitalization you used for the find or search data
Match entire cell contents	Whether the search should locate cells whose contents exactly match the find data

STEP-BY-STEP 1.8

1. Click cell **A1**.

2. On the Home tab of the Ribbon, locate the **Editing** group.

3. Click the **Find & Select** button, and then click **Find**.

4. In the Find what box, type **Period**.

5. Click **Find Next**. The active cell moves to cell B4, the first cell with the search data.

6. In the Find and Replace dialog box, click the **Replace** tab. A Replace with box appears.

7. In the Replace with box, type **Month**.

8. Click **Replace**. The word *Period* is replaced by *Month* in cell B4, and the active cell moves to cell C4, which is the next cell that contains the search data.

9. Click **Replace All**. A dialog box appears, indicating that Excel has completed the search and made three additional replacements of the word *Period* with the word *Month*.

10. Click **OK**.

11. In the Find and Replace dialog box, click **Close**.

12. Save the workbook, and leave it open for the next Step-by-Step.

Zooming Worksheets

You can magnify or reduce the view of a worksheet with the Zoom controls on the status bar. The default magnification for the workbooks is 100%, which you can see in the Zoom level button. For a closer view of a worksheet, click the Zoom In button or drag the Zoom slider to the right to increase the zoom percentage. The entire worksheet looks larger, and you see fewer cells in the work area. If you want to see more cells in the work area, click the Zoom Out button or drag the Zoom slider to the left to decrease the zoom percentage. The entire worksheet looks smaller. To select a specific magnification, click the Zoom level button to open the Zoom dialog box, type the zoom percentage you want in the Custom box, and then click OK. Figure 1-11 shows the Zoom dialog box and the zoom controls.

FIGURE 1-11
Zoom dialog box and controls

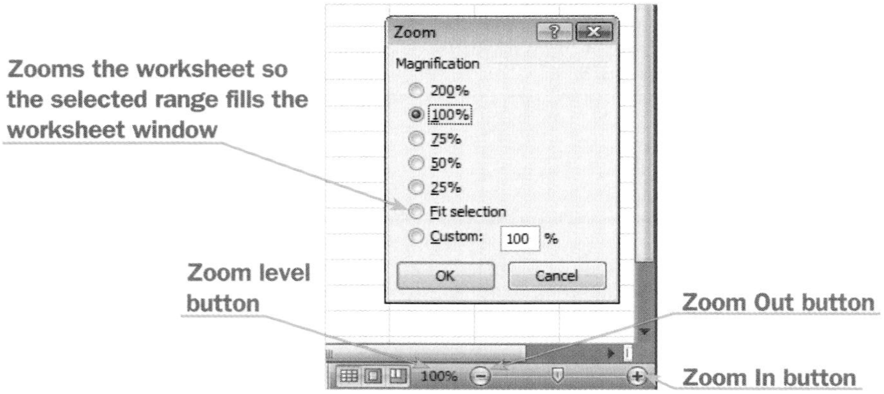

STEP-BY-STEP 1.9

1. On the status bar, click the **Zoom In** button three times. The worksheet zooms to 130%, and you see a close-up view of fewer cells.

2. On the status bar, drag the **Zoom slider** right to approximately 200%. The view of the worksheet is magnified even more.

3. On the status bar, click the **Zoom level** button. The Zoom dialog box appears, as shown in Figure 1-11.

4. Click **50%**, and then click **OK**. The view of the worksheet is reduced to half of its default size, and you see a long-distance view of more cells.

5. On the status bar, click the **Zoom In** button five times. The worksheet returns to its original zoom level of 100%.

Did You Know?

Zoom controls are also available on the Ribbon. On the View tab, in the Zoom group, click the Zoom button to open the Zoom dialog box. Click the 100% button to zoom the worksheet to 100% magnification. Click the Zoom to Selection button to zoom the worksheet so the selected range fills the worksheet window.

STEP-BY-STEP 1.9 Continued

6. Click cell **A16**, and then enter your name.

7. Save the workbook, and leave it open for the next Step-by-Step.

Previewing and Printing a Worksheet

Sometimes you need a printed copy of a worksheet to give to another person or for your own files. You can print a worksheet by clicking the Office Button, and then clicking Print to open the Print dialog box (see Figure 1-12). The Print dialog box enables you to select a printer, the number of copies to print, the parts of the worksheet to print, and the way the printed worksheet will look. For now, you will print the entire worksheet using the default settings.

> **Did You Know?**
>
> You can print a worksheet without opening the Print dialog box. Click the Office Button, point to Print, and then click Quick Print. The workbook is printed using the default settings in the Print dialog box. Use this method only if you have previously verified that the default printer and settings are the ones you want to use.

FIGURE 1-12
Print dialog box

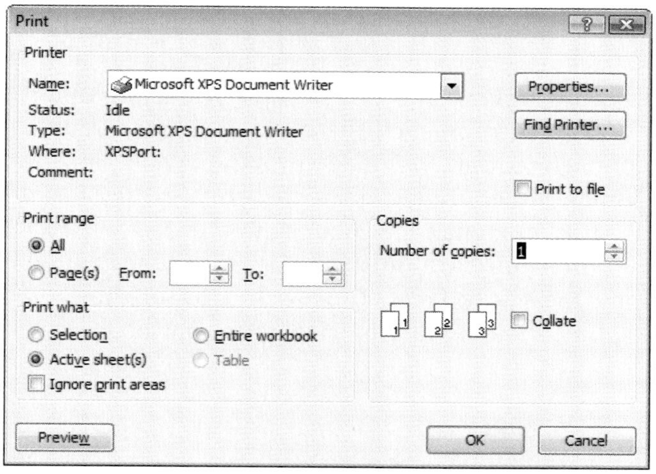

Before you use the resources to print a worksheet, you should use Print Preview to see how the printed pages will look. To switch to Print Preview (see Figure 1-13), click Preview in the Print dialog box. You can also click the Office Button, point to Print to open a menu with options to preview and print the document, and then click Print Preview.

FIGURE 1-13
Worksheet in Print Preview

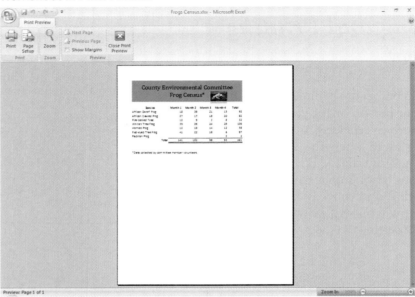

On the Ribbon, the Print Preview tab has groups of buttons for printing, zooming, and previewing. In the Preview group, click the Next Page and Previous Page buttons to display other pages of your worksheet. In the Zoom group, click the Zoom button or click the pointer (which becomes a magnifying glass in Print Preview) on the page to magnify or reduce the view. In the Print group, click the Page Setup button to open the Page Setup dialog box and select other options. When you have finished previewing the printed pages, you can return to the worksheet by clicking the Close Print Preview button in the Preview group. Or, you can return to the Print dialog box by clicking the Print button in the Print group.

STEP-BY-STEP 1.10

1. Click the **Office Button**, and then click **Print**. The Print dialog box appears, as shown in Figure 1-12.

2. Click **Preview**. The worksheet appears in Print Preview, as shown in Figure 1-13.

3. Move the pointer over the page in Print Preview, and then click. The previewed page becomes larger so you can examine it in more detail.

4. On the Print Preview tab of the Ribbon, locate the **Print** group. Click the **Print** button. The active worksheet is printed.

5. Leave the workbook open for the next Step-by-Step.

Closing a Workbook

You can close a workbook by clicking the Office Button to display the Office menu and clicking Close. If you use the Close command on the Office menu to close a workbook, Excel remains open and ready for you to open or create another workbook.

If you try to close a workbook that contains changes you haven't saved, a dialog box opens, asking whether you want to save the file. Click Yes to save and close the workbook. Click No to close the workbook without saving. Click Cancel to return to the Excel program window without saving or closing the workbook.

> **Did You Know?**
>
> You can also close the workbook and leave Excel open by clicking the Close Window button located below the sizing buttons in the title bar. To close the workbook and exit Excel, you can click the Close button in the title bar.

STEP-BY-STEP 1.11

1. Click the **Office Button**, and then click **Close**.

2. If you are asked to save changes, click **Yes**. The workbook closes.

SUMMARY

In this lesson, you learned:

- The purpose of a spreadsheet is to solve problems involving numbers. The advantage of using a computer spreadsheet is that you can complete complex and repetitious calculations quickly and accurately.

- A worksheet consists of columns and rows that intersect to form cells. Each cell is identified by a cell reference, which combines the letter of the column and the number of the row.

- The first time you save a workbook, the Save As dialog box opens so you can enter a descriptive name and select a save location. After that, you can use the Save command on the Office menu or the Save button on the Quick Access Toolbar to periodically save the latest version of the workbook.

- You can change the active cell in the worksheet by clicking the cell with the pointer, pressing keys, or using the scroll bars. The Go To dialog box lets you quickly move the active cell anywhere in the worksheet.

- A group of selected cells is called a range. A range is identified by the cells in the upper-left and lower-right corners of the range, separated by a colon. To select an adjacent range, drag the pointer across the rectangle of cells you want to include. To select a nonadjacent range, select the first adjacent range, hold down the Ctrl key, select each additional cell or range, and then release the Ctrl key.

- Worksheet cells can contain text, numbers, and formulas. After you enter data or a formula in a cell, you can change the cell contents by editing, replacing, or deleting it.

- You can search for specific characters in a worksheet. You can also replace data you have searched for with specific characters.

- Zoom enables you to enlarge or reduce the view of the worksheet in the worksheet window.

- You can print a worksheet to create a hard copy. Before you print, you should use Print Preview to see how the printed pages will look.

- When you finish your work session, you should save your final changes and close the workbook.

VOCABULARY *Review*

Define the following terms:

Active cell	Formula Bar	Row
Active worksheet	Microsoft Office Excel 2007	Sheet tab
Cell	(Excel)	Spreadsheet
Cell reference	Name Box	Workbook
Column	Range	Worksheet
Formula	Range reference	

REVIEW *Questions*

TRUE/FALSE

Circle T if the statement is true or F if the statement is false.

T   F   1. The primary advantage of the worksheet is the ability to solve numerical problems quickly and accurately.

T   F   2. A range is the intersection of a row and a column.

T   F   3. You use the Go To command to preview a worksheet before you print it.

T   F   4. You can use the Replace command to substitute *Week* for all instances of *Period* in a worksheet.

T   F   5. Each time you save a worksheet, you must open the Save As dialog box.

WRITTEN QUESTIONS

Write a brief answer to the following questions.

1.   What term describes a cell that is ready for data entry?

2.   How are columns identified in a worksheet?

3.   What term describes a group of cells?

4.   What key(s) do you press to move the active cell to the first cell of the row?

5.   If you decide not to enter data you just typed in the active cell, how do you delete the data without making any changes to the cell?

PROJECTS

PROJECT 1-1

In the blank space, write the letter of the key or keys from Column 2 that correspond to the movement of the active cell in Column 1.

Column 1	**Column 2**
___ 1. Left one column	**A.** Ctrl+Home keys
___ 2. Right one column	**B.** Page Up key
___ 3. Up one row	**C.** Left arrow key
___ 4. Down one row	**D.** Home key
___ 5. To the first cell of a row	**E.** Down arrow key
___ 6. To cell A1	**F.** Right arrow key
___ 7. To the last cell containing data	**G.** Ctrl+End keys
___ 8. Up one window	**H.** Up arrow key
___ 9. Down one window	**I.** Page Down key

PROJECT 1-2

1. Open the **Homes.xlsx** Data File.

2. Save the workbook as **Homeownership** followed by your initials.

3. In cell A15, enter **Colorado**.

4. In cell B15, enter **67.3**.

5. In cell C15, enter **62.2**.

6. In cell A16, edit the data to **Connecticut**.

7. In cell B16, edit the data to **66.8**.

8. In cell A5, delete the data.

9. In cell H1, enter your name.

10. Save, preview, print, and then close the workbook.

PROJECT 1-3

1. Open the **Neighborhood.xlsx** Data File.

2. Save the workbook as **Neighborhood Estimates** followed by your initials.

3. Enter the square footages in the following cells to estimate the home costs. The estimated home cost in each neighborhood will change as you enter the data.

Cell	Enter
C6	1250
C7	1500
C8	2200
C9	1500

4. After selling several houses in the Lake Side neighborhood, Neighborhood Properties has determined that the cost per square foot is $71, rather than $68.75. Edit cell B7 to **$71**.

5. In cell B1, enter your name.

6. Save, preview, print, and then close the workbook.

PROJECT 1-4

1. Open the **Names.xlsx** Data File.

2. Save the workbook as **Last Names** followed by your initials.

3. Use the Find command to locate the name *CHAVEZ*. The active cell should be cell A199.

4. Click in the worksheet outside the dialog box, and then press the Ctrl+Home keys to return to cell A1.

5. Click in the Find and Replace dialog box, and then locate the name *YORK*. The active cell should be cell A618. (*Hint*: The Find and Replace dialog box remains on-screen from Steps 3 and 4. You can simply enter the new search in the Find what box.)

6. Click in the worksheet, and then press the Ctrl+Home keys to return to cell A1.

7. Click in the Find and Replace dialog box, click the Replace tab, and then replace the name *FORBES* with **FABERGE**. The active cell should be cell A988.

8. Undo the last change you made to the workbook.

9. Save and close the workbook.

> **Extra Challenge**
>
> Try to find your last name, or the last names of three of your friends, in the LastNames.xlxs workbook you just worked on.

CRITICAL *Thinking*

 ACTIVITY 1-1

The purpose of a spreadsheet is to solve problems that involve numbers. Identify two numerical problems in each of the following categories that might be solved by using a spreadsheet.

1. Business

2. Career

3. Personal

4. School

 ACTIVITY 1-2

You have selected a large range of adjacent cells that extends over several screens. You realize that you incorrectly included one additional column of cells in the range.

To reselect the range of cells, you must page up to the active cell (the first cell of the range) and drag through several screens to the last cell in the range. Is there a better way to remove the column from the range, without having to reselect the entire range? Also, is there a faster way to select such a large range—one that doesn't include dragging through several screens?

Click the Microsoft Office Excel Help button to open the Excel Help window. Research how to select fewer cells without canceling your original selection. Then research how to select a large range without dragging. In your word processor, write a brief explanation of the steps you would take to change the selected range and to select a large range without dragging. (*Hint*: The answer appears in the topic "Select cells and their contents on a worksheet.")

CHANGING THE APPEARANCE OF A WORKSHEET

VOCABULARY

Alignment
AutoFit
Border
Cell style
Clear
Column heading
Editing mode
Fill
Font
Font size
Font style
Format Painter
Indent
Live Preview
Merge
Number format
Orientation
Points
Row heading
Style
Theme
Truncate
Wrap text

Changing the Size of a Cell

Worksheets are most valuable when the information they present is simple for the user to understand. Data in a worksheet must be accurate, but it is also important that the data be presented in a way that is visually appealing.

Changing Column Width

Sometimes the data you enter in a cell does not fit in the column. When you enter information that is wider than the column, one of the following happens:

- Text that fits in the cell is displayed. The rest is stored but hidden if the next cell contains data.
- Text that does not fit in the cell extends into the next cell, if that cell is empty.
- Numbers are converted to a different numerical form (for example, long numbers change to exponential form).
- Numbers that do not fit in the cell are shown as a series of number signs (######).

You can resize the column to fit a certain number of characters. Place the pointer on the right edge of the **column heading** (the column letter) until the pointer changes to a double-headed arrow. Click and drag to the right until the column expands to the width you want. Drag to the left to make the column width smaller. As you drag, a ScreenTip appears near the pointer, displaying the new column width measurement.

If you want to specify a precise column width, use the Column Width dialog box shown in Figure 2-1. To access the dialog box, click any cell in the column you want to change. On the Home tab of the Ribbon, in the Cells group, click the Format button, and then click Column Width. In the Column width box, type the width you want, and then click OK. The column resizes to fit the number of characters you specified.

> **Did You Know?**
>
> You can also open the Column Width dialog box with the mouse. Right-click the column heading of the column you want to resize, and then click Column Width on the shortcut menu.

FIGURE 2-1
Column Width dialog box

Type the number of characters you want to display

Changing Row Height

The process for changing row height is similar. Place the pointer below the row heading (the row number) until the pointer changes to a double-headed arrow. Click and drag down until the row has the number of lines you want. You can also use the Row Height dialog box to specify an exact row height. Click a cell in the row you want to resize. In the Cells group on the Home tab of the Ribbon, click the Format button, and then click Row Height to open the Row Height dialog box. In the Row height box, type the height you want, and then click OK.

Using AutoFit to Change Column Width or Row Height

Columns often contain data of varying widths. To make the worksheet easier to read, a column should be wide enough to display the longest entry, but no wider

> **Did You Know?**
>
> You can change the width of several columns at one time. Select the columns you want to resize. Then, use the pointer to click and drag the right edge of one of the selected column headings. You can use the same process to change the height of several rows. Select the rows you want to resize. Then, use the pointer to click and drag the bottom edge of one of the selected row headings.

than necessary. **AutoFit** determines the best width for a column or the best height for a row, based on its contents. Place the pointer on the right edge of the column heading (or below the row heading) until the pointer changes to a double-headed arrow. Then, double-click to resize the column or row to the best fit.

STEP-BY-STEP 2.1

1. Open the **Budget.xlsx** Data File.

2. Save the workbook as **Nigel Budget** followed by your initials. Notice that the text in some cells extends into the empty cells in the next column; for example, the month name in cell D3 extends into column E. Some text is hidden because the adjacent cell contains data, such as the month name in cell C3.

3. Place the pointer on the right edge of the column D heading. The pointer changes to a double-headed arrow.

4. Click and drag to the right until the ScreenTip reads *Width: 10.00 (75 pixels)*, as shown in Figure 2-2. Release the mouse button. The entire word *December* now fits within column D.

FIGURE 2-2
Column width ScreenTip

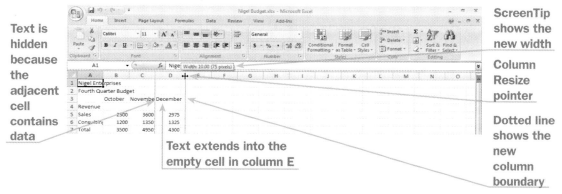

5. Select columns **B** and **C**. You want these two columns to be the same width as column D.

6. On the Ribbon, click the **Home** tab, and then locate the **Cells** group.

7. Click the **Format** button, and then click **Column Width**. The Column Width dialog box appears, as shown in Figure 2-1.

8. In the Column width box, type **10**.

9. Click **OK**. The widths of the selected columns change to 10.

10. Place the pointer on the bottom edge of the row 18 heading. The pointer changes to a double-headed arrow.

11. Click and drag down until the ScreenTip reads *Height: 18.00 (24 pixels)*.

12. Look at the data in column A. Some cells are not wide enough to display all the contents.

13. Click cell **A20**. You see only a portion of the words *Cumulative Profit* in the cell. The Formula Bar shows the complete contents of the cell.

STEP-BY-STEP 2.1 Continued

14. Double-click the right edge of the column A heading. Column A widens so you can see all of its data.

15. Save the workbook, and leave it open for the next Step-by-Step.

Positioning Data Within a Cell

Unless you specify otherwise, text you enter in a cell is lined up along the bottom-left side of the cell, and numbers you enter in a cell are lined up along the bottom-right side of the cell. However, you can position data within a cell in a variety of ways, as described in Table 2-1. All of these positions are available on the Home tab of the Ribbon, in the Alignment group.

TABLE 2-1
Positioning data within a cell

Position	Description	Example
Alignment	Specifies where data is lined up within the cell	Align Text Left is the default for text Align Text Right is the default for numbers Center is used for column headings
Indent	Changes the space between the cell border and its content	Increase Indent adds space; used for subheadings Decrease Indent removes space
Orientation	Rotates cell contents to an angle or vertically	Labels in a narrow column
Wrap Text	Moves data to a new line when the cell is not wide enough to display all the contents	Long descriptions
Merge	Combines multiple cells into one cell	Title across the top of a worksheet Merge & Center centers contents in the merged cell

Aligning Text

You can align the contents of a cell horizontally and vertically within the cell. Horizontal alignments are left, centered, or right. Vertical alignments are top, middle, or bottom, as shown in Figure 2-3. Excel left-aligns all text and right-aligns all numbers. All data is bottom-aligned. You can select a different horizontal and/or vertical alignment for any cell.

FIGURE 2-3
Horizontal and vertical alignments

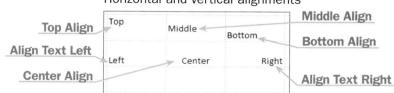

To change the alignment of a cell, select the cell and then click an alignment button in the Alignment group on the Home tab of the Ribbon. For other alignment options, click the Format Cells: Alignment Dialog Box Launcher to display the Alignment tab in the Format Cells dialog box. In the Text alignment section, click the alignment you want in the Horizontal or Vertical boxes, and then click OK.

Merging and Centering Data

You can also center cell contents across several columns. Select the cells, and then click the Merge & Center button in the Alignment group on the Home tab of the Ribbon. The selected cells merge, or combine into one cell, and the contents from the upper-left cell are centered in the newly merged cell.

> **Important**
>
> When you click the Merge & Center button, the selected cells are merged, and only the contents from the cell in the upper-left corner of the range are kept. All other content is deleted from the worksheet.

Indenting Data

Data can be indented (or shifted to the right) within cells to help distinguish categories or set data apart. Instead of trying to indent data with spaces, you should use the Increase Indent button in the Alignment group on the Home tab of the Ribbon. This way, all cells' contents are indented evenly. To move the indent in the other direction, click the Decrease Indent button.

S TEP-BY-STEP 2.2

1. Select the range **B3:D3**.

2. On the Home tab of the Ribbon, locate the **Alignment** group. All the positioning buttons are located in this group.

3. Click the **Center** button. The headings are centered.

4. Click cell **A7**.

5. On the Home tab, in the Alignment group, click the **Align Text Right** button. *Total Revenue* is aligned at the right of the cell.

6. Click cell **A17**, press and hold the **Ctrl** key, click cells **A19** and **A20**, and then release the **Ctrl** key. The nonadjacent range is selected.

STEP-BY-STEP 2.2 Continued

7. On the Home tab, in the Alignment group, click the **Align Text Right** button. The contents of the three cells are right-aligned.

8. Select the range **A1:D1**.

9. On the Home tab, in the Alignment group, click the **Merge & Center** button. Cells A1 through D1 are combined into one cell, and the title *Nigel Enterprises* is centered in the merged cell.

10. Select the range **A2:D2**. On the Home tab, in the Alignment group, click the **Merge & Center** button. Cells A2 through D2 are merged, and the subtitle *Fourth Quarter Budget* is centered in the merged cell.

11. Click cell **A5**. On the Home tab, in the Alignment group, click the **Increase Indent** button. The content of cell A5 shifts to the right.

12. Click cell **A6**. On the Home tab, in the Alignment group, click the **Increase Indent** button. The contents of cell A6 shift the same distance to the right and line up with the contents of cell A5.

13. Select the range **A10:A16**. On the Home tab, in the Alignment group, click the **Increase Indent** button. The contents of the cells in the range shift right.

14. Save the workbook, and leave it open for the next Step-by-Step.

Changing Text Orientation

Sometimes labels that describe the column data, or the data itself, are longer than the column widths. To save space in the worksheet, you can change each cell's text orientation to rotate its data to any angle. Changing the text orientation of some cells can also help give your worksheet a more professional look.

To change text orientation, select the cells whose contents you want to rotate. Click the Orientation button in the Alignment group on the Home tab of the Ribbon. A menu of orientation options appears, with commands for angling the text at 45-degree angles clockwise or counterclockwise, stacking the text vertically, or rotating the text up or down.

If you want to use a different angle, you need to use the Alignment tab in the Format Cells dialog box, as shown in Figure 2-4. Click the Format Cells: Alignment Dialog Box Launcher to display the Alignment tab in the Format Cells dialog box. In the Orientation box, click a degree point, drag the angle indicator, or type the angle you want in the Degrees box. Click OK.

> **Computer Concepts**
>
> Rotated text is often used for labels on charts. Angled or vertical text fits more data in a label, while remaining readable.

FIGURE 2-4
Alignment tab in the Format Cells dialog box

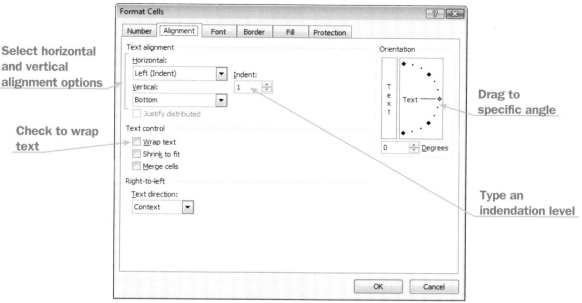

Select horizontal and vertical alignment options

Check to wrap text

Drag to specific angle

Type an indendation level

STEP-BY-STEP 2.3

1. Select the range **B3:D3**.

2. On the Home tab, in the Alignment group, click the **Orientation** button. A menu appears with the most common orientations.

3. Click **Angle Counterclockwise**. The text in cells B3 through D3 shifts to a 45-degree angle, and the height of row 3 increases to accommodate the angled text, as shown in Figure 2-5.

FIGURE 2-5
Alignments modified

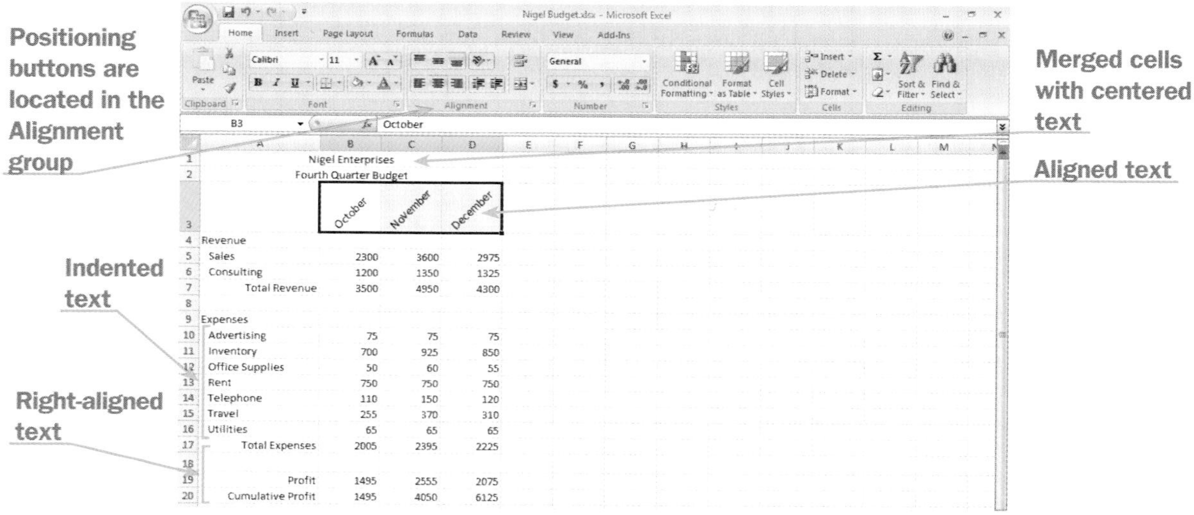

Positioning buttons are located in the Alignment group

Merged cells with centered text

Aligned text

Indented text

Right-aligned text

STEP-BY-STEP 2.3 Continued

4. If the width of columns B through D changed, set their widths to **10**.

5. Save the workbook, and leave it open for the next Step-by-Step.

Wrapping Text

Text that is too long to fit within a cell is displayed in the next cell, if it is empty. If the next cell already contains data, any text that does not fit in the cell is truncated, or hidden from view. One way to see all the text stored in a cell is to wrap text. The row height adjusts automatically to include additional lines until all the text is visible. When you wrap text, the column width is not changed.

To wrap text, select the cells in which you want to wrap text. Then, click the Wrap Text button in the Alignment group on the Home tab of the Ribbon. If the cells already contain text, the row height increases as needed to display all the content. If you enter text after you turn on Wrap Text, the row height expands to fit the text as you type.

STEP-BY-STEP 2.4

1. Click cell **A22**. Type **Budget submitted for approval**. Click the **Enter** button on the Formula Bar.

2. On the Home tab, in the Alignment group, click the **Wrap Text** button. The text wraps in the cell, and the row height adjusts to fit all the lines of text. The Wrap Text button remains selected.

3. Save the workbook, and leave it open for the next Step-by-Step.

Changing the Appearance of Cells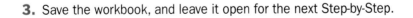

You can change the appearance of cells to make them easier to read, to differentiate sections in a worksheet, or to create a specific look and feel for the worksheet. To do this, you can modify the cell's default font, font size, font style, font and fill colors, and borders.

The fonts and colors used in each workbook are part of a theme. A theme is a preset collection of design elements, including fonts, colors, and other effects. By default, the Office theme is applied to each workbook. To change a workbook's appearance, you can select a different theme, or you can format cells with other fonts and colors. If you select another theme font or theme color, it will change when you apply a different theme. Or, you can choose non-theme or standard fonts and colors that stay the same no matter which theme is applied to the workbook.

As you format cells, Live Preview shows the results of the different formatting options you can choose. Select the cell or range you want to format, and then point to the formatting option you are considering. The cell or range changes to reflect that option. To accept that format, click the option.

Changing Fonts and Font Sizes

A font is the design of text. The default font for cells is Calibri. Font size determines the height of characters, as measured in points. The default font size for cells is 11 points. You can choose different fonts and font sizes in a worksheet to emphasize part of a worksheet or to distinguish worksheet titles and column headings from other data. The fonts and font sizes you use can significantly affect the readability of the worksheet. Office 2007 comes with a variety of fonts and sizes. However, the available fonts and sizes can change from one computer to another, depending largely on what fonts are installed on that computer.

To change fonts and sizes, you must first select the cells you want to change. Then, on the Home tab of the Ribbon, in the Font group, click the arrow next to the Font box to display a gallery of available fonts, or click the arrow next to the Font Size box to display a menu of available font sizes. When you point to a font or a size, Live Preview changes the cell contents to reflect that selection. Click the font or size you want to use.

> **Did You Know?**
>
> You can also use the Mini toolbar to change the font, font size, font style, and font color. Double-click the cell to enter **editing mode**, which places the insertion point within the cell contents, and then select the text you want to format. The transparent Mini toolbar appears above the selected text. Move the pointer to the Mini toolbar to bring it into full view, and then click the appropriate buttons to apply the formatting.

Applying Font Styles

Bold, *italic*, and underlining can add emphasis to the contents of a cell. These features are referred to as **font styles**. You can also combine font styles to change the emphasis, such as ***bolditalic***. To apply a font style, select the cell or range you want to change. Click the appropriate style button in the Font group on the Home tab of the Ribbon. To remove a font style from the cell contents, simply click the button again.

B
I
U

> **Did You Know?**
>
> You can quickly apply a font style to a selected cell or range. Press the Ctrl+B keys to apply bold. Press the Ctrl+I keys to apply italics. Press the Ctrl+U keys to apply underlining. Use the shortcut keys again to remove that font style from the selected cell or range.

 Careers

Excel workbooks are helpful to people and businesses in sales. Salespeople use worksheets to determine what items are available in inventories, analyze sales performance, and track customer orders.

S TEP-BY-STEP 2.5

1. Select the range **B3:D3**.

2. On the Home tab, in the Font group, next to the Font box, click the **arrow**. A menu appears, listing the fonts available on your computer, as shown in Figure 2-6.

FIGURE 2-6
Font menu

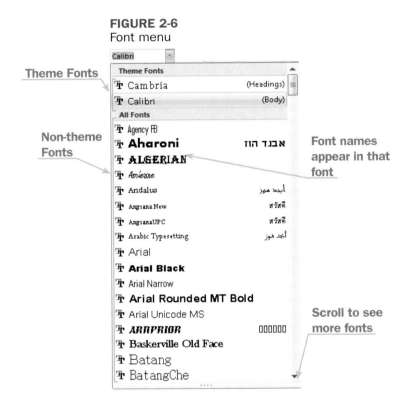

3. Scroll down the list and click **Times New Roman** (or a similar font). The font of the month names in cells B3, C3, and D3 changes from Calibri to Times New Roman.

4. On the Home tab, in the Font group, next to the Font Size box, click the **arrow**. A menu appears, listing the available font sizes.

5. Click **8**. The font of the month names in cells B3, C3, and D3 is reduced in size from 11 points to 8 points.

6. Click cell **A1** (which is the cell you merged from the range A1:D1). On the Home tab, in the Font group, next to the Font box, click the **arrow**. Click **Times New Roman**. The font of the company name in cell A1 changes to Times New Roman. Cell A1 remains active.

7. On the Home tab, in the Font group, next to the Font Size box, click the **arrow**. Click **14**. The font size of the company name in cell A1 increases to 14 points. Cell A1 remains active.

8. On the Home tab, in the Font group, click the **Bold** button. The text in cell A1 changes to bold, and the button remains selected to show it is toggled on.

STEP-BY-STEP 2.5 Continued

9. Click cell **A2**. On the Home tab, in the Font group, click the **Bold** button. The text in cell A2 changes to bold.

10. Apply bold to cells A4, A7, A9, A17, A19, and A20.

11. Reduce the width of column A to **18**.

12. Select the range **A5:A6**. In the Font group, click the **Italic** button. The revenue items are italicized.

13. Apply italic to the range A10:A16.

14. Select cell **A4**. In the Font group, click the **Underline** button. *Revenue* is underlined.

15. Click the **Underline** button. The underlining is removed from the text.

16. Save the workbook, and leave it open for the next Step-by-Step.

> ### Extra Challenge
> Experiment by changing the font, font size, and font style of data in the worksheet. When you are done, use the Undo button on the Quick Access Toolbar to undo changes you made.

Choosing Font and Fill Colors

You can use color to emphasize cells or distinguish them from one another. The default font color is black, but you can select a different color to make the cell contents stand out. The default **fill** (or background) color of cells is white, but you can change this background color to help accentuate certain cells, such as descriptive labels or totals.

To change the color of text in a cell, select the cell you want to change. In the Font group on the Home tab of the Ribbon, click the arrow next to the Font Color button. A gallery appears showing a palette of colors, as shown in Figure 2-7. Click the color you want. The cell contents change to that color.

> ### Did You Know?
> You can also change font and fill colors with the Format Cells dialog box. Press the Ctrl+1 keys to open the dialog box. On the Font tab, click the Color arrow, and then click the font color you want to use. On the Fill tab, click a color in the Background Color section to select a solid color. You can also select a pattern: click the Pattern Style arrow, and then click the pattern you want. To select a color for the pattern, click the Pattern Color arrow, and then click the color you want the pattern to appear in.

FIGURE 2-7
Font colors

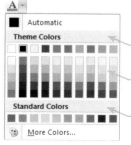

Theme colors change when you select a new theme

Theme colors are available in different shades

Standard colors are available in all themes

To change the background color of a cell, select the cell you want to change. In the Font group on the Home tab of the Ribbon, click the arrow next to the Fill Color button. A gallery appears with a palette of colors, as shown in Figure 2-8. Click the color you want. The cell is filled with that color.

FIGURE 2-8
Fill colors

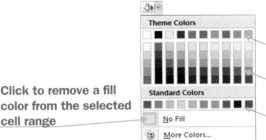

Theme colors change when you select a new theme

Theme colors are available in different shades

Click to remove a fill color from the selected cell range

Standard colors are available in all themes

STEP-BY-STEP 2.6

1. Click cell **A1**.

2. On the Home tab, in the Font group, next to the Font Color button, click the **arrow**. A gallery appears with a palette of colors, as shown in Figure 2-7.

3. Point to the **Orange** color (the third color in the Standard Colors section). A ScreenTip displays the name of the color, and *Nigel Enterprises*, the text in cell A1, changes to orange, showing you a Live Preview of that selection.

4. Point to the **Aqua, Accent 5** color (the ninth color in the first row of the Theme Colors section). A ScreenTip displays the name of the color, and Live Preview shows the company name in aqua.

5. Click the **Aqua, Accent 5** color. The gallery closes and the company name remains aqua. Cell A1 is still the active cell.

6. On the Home tab, in the Font group, next to the Fill Color button, click the **arrow**. A gallery appears with a palette of colors, as shown in Figure 2-8.

7. Click the **Aqua, Accent 5, Lighter 80%** color (the ninth color in the second row of the Theme Colors section). The cell background becomes light aqua. Cell A1 is still the active cell.

8. Save the workbook, and leave it open for the next Step-by-Step.

Inserting Cell Borders

You can add emphasis to a cell by placing a border (or line) around its edges. You can place the border around the entire cell or only on certain sides of the cell. You can also select different border styles, such as a thick border or a double border.

To insert a border, select a cell or range, and then, in the Font group on the Home tab of the Ribbon, click the arrow next to the Borders button. A menu appears with border styles, as shown in Figure 2-9. Click the border style you want to add. You can remove the borders from a selected cell by clicking No Border in the border style menu.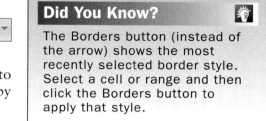

Did You Know?

The Borders button (instead of the arrow) shows the most recently selected border style. Select a cell or range and then click the Borders button to apply that style.

FIGURE 2-9
Borders menu

Preset border styles you can select

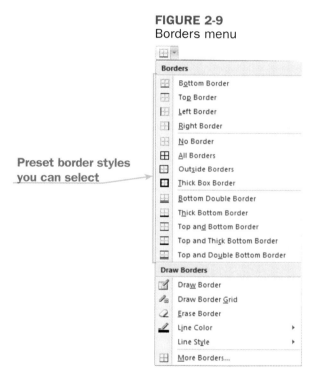

STEP-BY-STEP 2.7

1. Select the range **B7:D7**.

2. On the Home tab, in the Font group, next to the Borders button, click the **arrow**. A menu of border styles appears, as shown in Figure 2-9.

3. Click **Top and Double Bottom Border**. A single border appears above the range, and a double border appears below the range. The Borders button changes to Top and Double Bottom Border.

4. Select the range **B17:D17**.

STEP-BY-STEP 2.7 Continued

5. On the Home tab, in the Font group, click the **Top and Double Bottom Border** button. A single border appears above the range, and a double border appears below the range.

6. Save the workbook, and leave it open for the next Step-by-Step.

 Careers

Standard accounting format uses a single border below a column of numbers and a double border below the total.

Selecting Number Formats

Number formats change the way data looks in a cell. The actual content you entered is not changed. The default number format is General, which displays numbers the way you type them. However, you can select any of the number formats described in Table 2-2. Be aware that changing a number format affects only the appearance of the data in the cell. The actual value is not affected. The Formula Bar shows the actual value of the contents you see in the active cell. For example, the actual value shown in the Formula Bar might be 1000, whereas the number you see in the active cell is $1,000.00.

TABLE 2-2
Number formats

Format	Example	Description
General	1000	The default format; displays numbers as typed. If the number doesn't fit in the cell, decimals are rounded, or the number is converted to scientific notation.
Number	1000.00	Displays numbers with a fixed number of places to the right of the decimal point; the default is two decimal places
Currency	$1,000.00	Displays numbers preceded by a dollar sign with a thousands separator and two decimal places
Accounting	$1,000.00 $ 9.00	Displays numbers in the Currency format but lines up the dollar signs and the decimal points vertically within a column
Date	6/8/02	Displays text and numbers as dates
Time	7:38 PM	Displays text and numbers as times
Percentage	35.2%	Displays numbers with two decimal places followed by a percent sign
Fraction	35 7/8	Displays decimal numbers as fractions
Scientific	1.00E+03	Displays numbers in exponential (or scientific) notation
Text	45-875-33	Displays text and numbers exactly as you type them

TABLE 2-2 CONTINUED
Number formats

Format	Example	Description
Special	79410-1234 (503) 555-4567	Displays numbers with a specific format: zip codes, zip+4 codes, phone numbers, and Social Security numbers
Custom	000.00.0	Displays data in the format you create, such as with commas or leading zeros

To change the number format, select the cell or range. Then, click the appropriate buttons in the Number group on the Home tab of the Ribbon. You can also click the arrow next to the Number Format box to open a menu of number formats. The accounting and percentage number formats also have buttons you can click to quickly apply these common number formats. The other buttons let you choose whether the number includes a thousands separator (a comma) and how many decimal places to show.

Copying Cell Formatting

Format Painter enables you to copy formatting from one worksheet cell to another without copying the cell's contents. This is especially helpful when the cell formatting you want to copy includes several formats. For example, after formatting a cell as a percentage with a white font, a green fill, and a double bottom border, you can use the Format Painter to quickly format other cells the same way.

To copy a cell's formatting, select the cell that has the format you want to copy. Click the Format Painter button in the Clipboard group on the Home tab of the Ribbon. Then, click another cell or drag to select the range of cells you want to format in the same way.

> **Did You Know?**
>
> You can use the Format Painter to copy the same formatting to non-adjacent cells or ranges. Double-click the Format Painter button in the Clipboard group on the Home tab of the Ribbon. Select the cells or ranges you want to format. When you are done, click the Format Painter button again.

S TEP-BY-STEP 2.8

1. Select the range **B5:D5**, press and hold the **Ctrl** key, select the range **B7:D7**, and then release the **Ctrl** key. The non-adjacent range is selected.

2. On the Home tab, in the Number group, next to the Number Format box, click the **arrow**. A menu of number formats appears.

3. Click **Accounting**. The numbers in the selected ranges include a dollar sign, a thousands separator, and two decimal places, which is the standard Accounting number format.

4. Click cell **B5**. Compare the value in the Formula Bar with the value in the active cell. The Formula Bar shows *2300*, which is the actual value stored in cell B5. Cell B5 shows *$2,300.00*, which is the stored value formatted for display.

STEP-BY-STEP 2.8 Continued

5. On the Home tab, in the Clipboard group, click the **Format Painter** button. The pointer changes to a paintbrush next to the white plus pointer. A flashing dashed border surrounds cell B5 to remind you that the formatting from this cell is being copied.

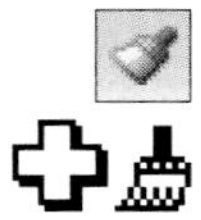

6. Click and drag from cell **B10** to cell **D10**. The format of the range B10:D10 changes to the Accounting number format.

7. Select the range **B11:D16**.

8. On the Home tab, in the Number group, next to the Number Format box, click the **arrow**, and then click **Number**. The cells in the range are formatted with two decimal places.

9. On the Home tab, in the Number group, click the **Comma Style** button. A thousands separator is added to numbers with four digits and the decimals points align with the values in the Accounting number format that appear in the cells above them.

10. On the Home tab, in the Clipboard group, click the **Format Painter** button. The range B11:D16 is surrounded by a blinking border.

11. Click and drag from cell **B6** to cell **D6**. The format of the range B6:D6 is formatted with both the Number and Comma Style number formats.

12. Apply the **Accounting** number format to the ranges B17:D17 and B19:D20.

13. Click cell **A1** to deselect the range. Your screen should look similar to Figure 2-10.

FIGURE 2-10
Formatted worksheet

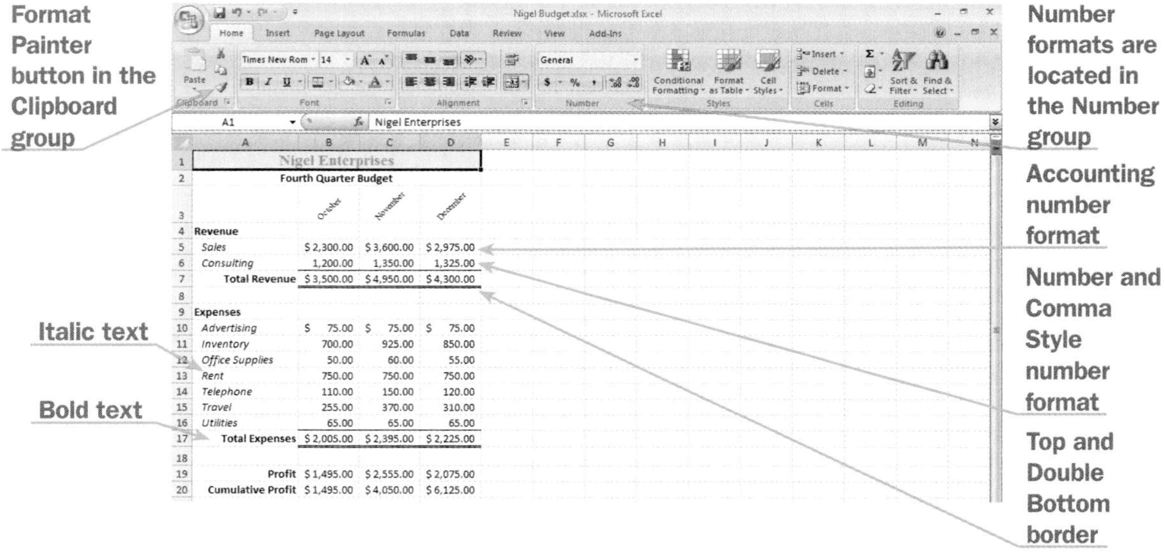

Format Painter button in the Clipboard group

Italic text

Bold text

Number formats are located in the Number group

Accounting number format

Number and Comma Style number format

Top and Double Bottom border

14. Save the workbook, and leave it open for the next Step-by-Step.

Using the Format Cells Dialog Box

The Format Cells dialog box provides access to all the formatting options available on the Ribbon, as well as some additional formatting options. To open the Format Cells dialog box, you can click the Dialog Box Launcher in the Font, Alignment, or Number group on the Home tab of the Ribbon, or you can press the Ctrl+1 keys. As shown in Figure 2-11, the Format Cells dialog box has Number, Alignment, Font, Border, and Fill tabs. You can use these tabs to change the number format, position of data, font options, borders, and cell background color as you have done so far.

FIGURE 2-11
Format Cells dialog box

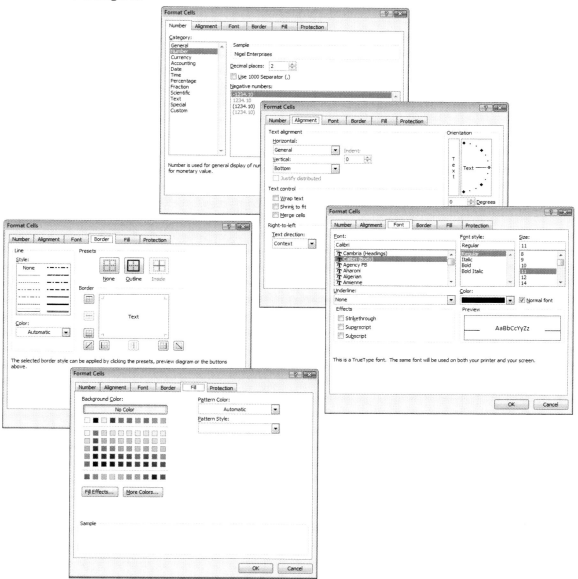

Using Styles

A style is a combination of formatting characteristics such as alignment, font, font size, font color, fill color, and borders. When you apply a style to a cell, you apply all the formatting characteristics simultaneously, saving you the time of applying the formats individually. Styles also help you format a worksheet consistently. When you use a style, you know that each cell with that style is formatted the same way.

Applying Cell Styles

A cell style is a collection of formatting characteristics you apply to a cell or range of data. To apply a cell style, select the cells you want to format. In the Styles group on the Home tab of the Ribbon, click the Cell Styles button. The Cell Style gallery appears, as shown in Figure 2-12. Point to a cell style in the gallery to see a Live Preview of that style on the selected cell or range in the worksheet. When you find a style you like, click the style to apply it. To remove a style from the selected cell, simply click Normal in the Good, Bad and Neutral section of the Cell Styles gallery.

FIGURE 2-12
Cell Styles gallery

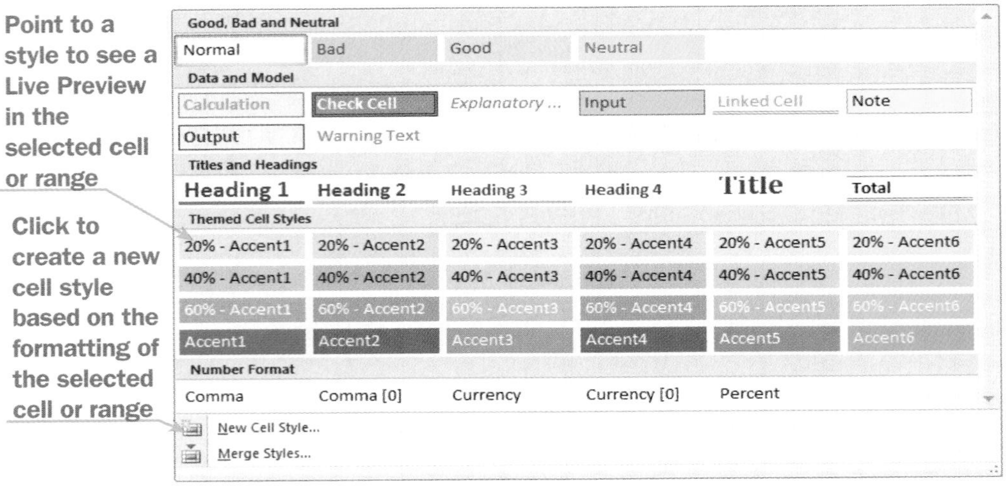

Point to a style to see a Live Preview in the selected cell or range

Click to create a new cell style based on the formatting of the selected cell or range

The Cell Styles gallery includes many predefined styles. However, if none of these styles meets your needs, you can define styles of your own. First, format a cell with the exact combination of formats you want. Then, select the formatted cell, and click New Cell Style at the bottom of the Cell Styles gallery. In the Style dialog box that opens, shown in Figure 2-13, type a descriptive name for the style in the Style name box, verify the formatting in the Style Includes section (uncheck any format you don't want to include), and then click OK. The style you created appears at the top of the Cell Styles gallery in the Custom section.

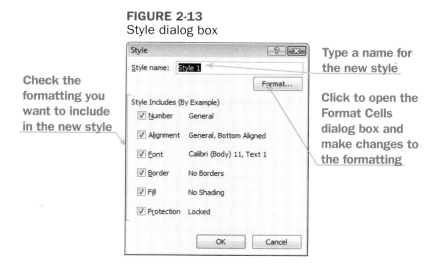

FIGURE 2-13
Style dialog box

Check the formatting you want to include in the new style

Type a name for the new style

Click to open the Format Cells dialog box and make changes to the formatting

Clearing Cell Formats

You have learned how to change the appearance of cells in a worksheet by applying individual formats as well as cell styles. At times, you might need to remove, or clear, all the formatting applied to a cell or range of cells. Select the cell or range, click the Clear button in the Editing group on the Home tab of the Ribbon, and then click Clear Format. Only the cell formatting is removed; the cell content remains unchanged.

STEP-BY-STEP 2.9

1. Select the range **A4:D4**.

2. On the Home tab, in the Styles group, click the **Cell Styles** button. The Cell Styles gallery appears, as shown in Figure 2-12.

3. In the Titles and Headings section, point to **Heading 2**. Live Preview shows the selected range with the font, font size, color, and border in that style.

4. In the Titles and Headings section, point to **Accent5** to see the Live Preview, and then click **Accent5**. Aqua fill and white font colors are applied to the cells in the selected range.

5. Select the range **A9:D9**.

6. On the Home tab, in the Styles group, click the **Cell Styles** button.

7. In the Cell Styles gallery, in the Titles and Headings section, click **Accent5**. Aqua fill and white font are applied to the cells in the selected range.

8. Click **A1**. On the Home tab, in the Styles group, click the **Cell Styles** button.

STEP-BY-STEP 2.9 Continued

9. In the Cell Styles gallery, in the Titles and Headings section, click **Heading 1**. The formatting for this style is added to the formatting you already applied to the cell.

10. Click **A22**. On the Home tab, in the Styles group, click the **Cell Styles** button.

11. In the Cell Styles gallery, in the Titles and Headings section, click **Accent2**. The cell is formatted with the selected style.

12. On the Home tab, in the Editing group, click the **Clear** button. A menu appears with the Clear commands.

13. Click **Clear Formats**. All the formatting applied to cell A22 disappears. The cell returns to the default font color and fill color and text wrap.

14. Click cell **A23**, and then enter your name.

15. Save, print, and close the workbook.

Finding and Replacing Cell Formatting

You have already learned to find and replace data in a workbook. You can also find and replace specific formatting in a workbook. For example, you might want to replace all italicized text with bolded text, or you might want to change all cells with a yellow fill color to another color.

STEP-BY-STEP 2.10

1. Open the **Basketball.xlsx** Data File.

2. Save the workbook as **Basketball Standings** followed by your initials.

3. On the Home tab, in the Editing group, click the **Find & Select** button, and then click **Replace**. The Find and Replace dialog box appears, with the Replace tab displayed.

4. Click the **Options** button to expand the Find and Replace dialog box, if it is not already expanded.

5. Delete any entries that appear in the Find what or Replace with boxes.

6. Click the top **Format** button. The Find Format dialog box appears. This dialog box has all the same tabs and options as the Format Cells dialog box.

7. Click the **Font** tab if it is not the active tab. In the Font style list, click **Italic**. This is the formatting you want to find.

8. Click **OK**. The Find Format dialog box disappears, and the Find and Replace dialog box reappears. The Find what Preview box shows the italic formatting you want to find.

STEP-BY-STEP 2.10 Continued

9. Click the lower **Format** button. The Replace Format dialog box appears. This dialog box has all the same tabs and options as the Format Cells dialog box.

10. On the Font tab, in the Font style list, click **Bold**.

11. Click **OK**. The Replace Format dialog box disappears, and the Find and Replace dialog box reappears. The Replace with Preview box shows the bold formatting you want to use instead of the italics.

12. Click **Replace All**. A dialog box appears, stating that Excel has completed the search and 5 replacements were made.

13. Click **OK**. The dialog box closes.

14. Click **Close**. The Find and Replace dialog box closes. Your screen should look similar to Figure 2-14.

FIGURE 2-14
Worksheet with formatting replaced

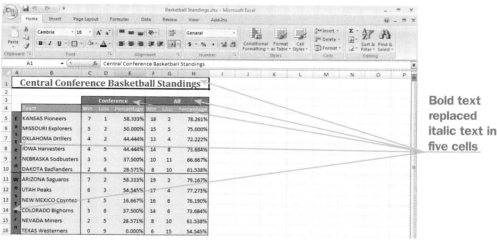

Bold text replaced italic text in five cells

15. Click cell B2, and then enter your name.

16. Save, print, and close the workbook.

SUMMARY

In this lesson, you learned:

■ If data does not fit in a cell, you can resize the columns and rows to make the data easier to read.

■ You can align, indent, rotate, wrap text, and merge cells to reposition data in worksheet cells.

■ You can change the appearance of cells to make the worksheet easier to read or to create a specific look and feel. Choose the appropriate fonts, font sizes, font styles, font and fill colors, and borders.

- A variety of number formats enable you to change how a number is displayed in the cell. No matter which number format you select, the actual value stored in the cell does not change. You can see this by comparing the formatted value in the active cell with the stored value in the Formula Bar.

- Format Painter copies all the formatting from one cell to another cell or range without copying the contents of the cell.

- The Format Cells dialog box provides all the number, alignment, font, border, and fill formatting options available on the Ribbon, as well as some additional ones.

- A style is a combination of formatting characteristics, such as alignment, font, font size, font color, fill color, and borders, that you can apply simultaneously. The Cell Styles gallery lets you quickly apply a style to selected cells.

- The Find and Replace dialog box can be used to change cell formatting.

VOCABULARY *Review*

Define the following terms:

Alignment	Font	Orientation
AutoFit	Font size	Points
Border	Font style	Row heading
Cell style	Format Painter	Style
Clear	Indent	Theme
Column heading	Live Preview	Truncate
Editing mode	Merge	Wrap text
Fill	Number format	

REVIEW QUESTIONS

TRUE/FALSE

Circle T if the statement is true or F if the statement is false.

T   F   1. A series of number signs (######) in a cell indicates that the data entered in the cell is longer than the width of the cell.

T   F   2. Wrapped text is truncated within the cell when the data exceeds the width of a column.

T   F   3. The Merge & Center button combines several cells into one cell and places the data in the center of the merged cell.

T   F   4. You can place a border around the entire cell or only on certain sides of the cell.

T   F   5. The default number format for data in a cell is Text.

WRITTEN QUESTIONS

Write a brief answer to the following questions.

1. Which cell formats display numerical data preceded by a dollar sign?

2. How can you have Excel determine the best width of a column?

3. What is one reason for changing the orientation of text in a cell?

4. What is the difference between fill color and font color?

5. What is an advantage of using cell styles?

PROJECTS

PROJECT 2-1

Write the letter of the cell format option in Column 2 that matches the worksheet format described in Column 1.

Column 1

___ 1. Displays data as typed

___ 2. Displays numbers with a fixed number of decimal places

___ 3. Displays numbers preceded by a dollar sign with a thousands separator and two decimal places; however, dollar signs and decimal points do not necessarily line up vertically within a column

___ 4. Displays numbers preceded by a dollar sign with a thousands separator and two decimal places; dollar signs and decimal points are lined up vertically within a column

___ 5. Displays text and numbers as dates

___ 6. Displays text and numbers as times

___ 7. Displays numbers with two decimal places followed by a percent sign

___ 8. Displays the value of 0.5 as 1/2

___ 9. Displays numbers in exponential notation

___ 10. Displays numbers with a specific format, such as zip codes, phone numbers, and Social Security numbers

___ 11. Displays data in the format you design

Column 2

A. Accounting

B. Time

C. Scientific

D. Fraction

E. Special

F. General

G. Date

H. Number

I. Percentage

J. Custom

K. Currency

PROJECT 2-2

1. Open the **Bird.xlsx** Data File.

2. Save the workbook as **Bird Census** followed by your initials.

3. Change the width of column A to 24.

4. Merge and center the range A1:F1 and the range A2:F2.

5. Format cell A1 with the Title cell style. Change the fill color of the range A1:A2 to Orange, Accent 6.

6. Bold the range A4:F4.

7. Angle the data in the range B4:F4 counterclockwise.

8. Change the width of column B through column E to 6.

9. Bold the range A12:F12.

10. Indent and italicize the range A5:A11.

11. Right-align the data in cell A12.

12. Format the range B12:F12 with a top and double bottom border.

13. Change the font color of the range F4:F12 to Orange, Accent 6.

14. In cell A3, type **Prepared by:** followed by your name.

15. Save, print, and close the workbook.

 PROJECT 2-3

1. Open the **Phone.xlsx** Data File.

2. Save the workbook as **Phone Shop** followed by your initials.

3. AutoFit column A.

4. Change the width of columns B, C, and D to 10.

5. Bold and center the text in the range B4:D5.

6. Bold the text in cell A5.

7. Indent the range A6:A9.

8. Change the text in cell A1 to 14-point Cambria. Merge and center the range A1:D1.

9. Change the fill color of cell A1 to the Standard Color Green.

10. Change the fill color of the range A2:D2 to the Standard Color Yellow.

11. Format the range C6:D9 and cell D10 as Currency with two decimal places.

12. Format cell D10 with the Total cell style. Change the fill color of cell D10 to Standard Color Yellow.

13. Add a thick bottom border to the range A5:D5.

14. In cell C2, enter your name.

15. Save, print, and close the workbook.

 PROJECT 2-4

1. Open the **Cell.xlsx** Data File.

2. Save the workbook as **Cell Bill** followed by your initials.

3. In cell A1, type **Cell Phone Bill Estimate**.

4. Bold the text in cell A1.

5. In cell A1, change the font size of the text to 14.

6. Merge and center the range A1:D1.

7. Change the fill color of cell A1 to Blue, Accent 1.

8. Change the font color of cell A1 to White, Background 1.

9. Underline the contents of cell A1.

10. Center the contents of the range B3:C3.

11. Format the range C4:D7 in the Currency number format with two decimal places.

12. Add a bottom border to cell D6.

13. Widen column A to 17. In cell A4, wrap text.

14. Middle-align the range B4:D4.

15. Apply the 20% - Accent 1 cell style to the range D4:D7.

16. In cell A2, enter your name.

17. Save, print, and close the workbook.

 PROJECT 2-5

1. Open the **Balance.xlsx** Data File.

2. Save the workbook as **TechSoft Balance** followed by your initials. This workbook contains a *balance sheet*, which is a financial statement that lists a corporation's assets (resources available), liabilities (amounts owed), and equity (ownership in the company).

3. Change the column width of column C to 5.

4. Format cell A1 with the Heading 1 cell style.

5. Format the range A2:A3 with the 20% - Accent 1 cell style.

6. Merge and center the ranges A1:E1, A2:E2, and A3:E3.

7. Bold cells A5, A6, A20, D5, D6, D17, and D21.

8. Apply a bottom border to cells B8, B13, E11, and E19. Apply a top and double bottom border to cells B20 and E21.

9. Format cells B7, E7, B20, and E21 in the Accounting number format with no decimal places.

10. Format the ranges B8:B19, E8:E15, and E18:E20 in the Number format with a thousands separator and no decimal places.

11. In cell A4, enter your name. Italicize the text in cell A4.

12. Save, print, and close the workbook.

 PROJECT 2-6

1. Open the **Mileage.xlsx** Data File.

2. Save the workbook as **Mileage Chart** followed by your initials.

3. Change the font size of the range A1:O15 to 8 points.

4. Format the range B2:O15 in the Number format with a thousands separator and no decimal places.

5. Bold the ranges B1:O1 and A2:A15.

6. Change the width of column A to 10.

7. Right-align the content of the range A2:A15.

8. Change the orientation of the range B1:O1 to Angle Clockwise.

9. Change the width of columns B through O to 5.

10. In cell A1, enter your name, and then change the font size to 12 points and wrap text.

11. Save, print, and close the workbook.

CRITICAL *Thinking*

 ACTIVITY 2-1

To be useful, worksheets must convey information clearly, both on-screen and on the printed page. Identify ways to accomplish the following:

1. Emphasize certain portions of a worksheet.

2. Make data in a worksheet easier to read.

3. Distinguish one part of a worksheet from another.

4. Format similar elements in a worksheet consistently.

 ACTIVITY 2-2

You have been spending a lot of time formatting worksheets. A friend tells you that you could save some time by using the Mini toolbar to apply formatting. Use Excel Help to research the following:

1. How do you access the Mini toolbar?

2. What formatting can you apply from the Mini toolbar?

3. How do you use the Mini toolbar to apply formatting to text in a cell?

4. Why might the Mini toolbar save you time formatting?

ORGANIZING THE WORKSHEET

OBJECTIVES

Upon completion of this lesson, you will be able to:

- Copy and move data to other cells.
- Use the drag-and-drop method and Auto Fill options to add data to cells.
- Insert and delete rows, columns, and cells.
- Freeze panes in a worksheet.
- Split a worksheet window.
- Check spelling in a worksheet.
- Prepare a worksheet for printing.
- Insert headers and footers.

Estimated Time: 2 hours

VOCABULARY

Automatic page break

Copy

Cut

Fill

Fill handle

Footer

Freeze pane

Header

Landscape orientation

Manual page break

Margins

Normal view

Office Clipboard (Clipboard)

Page Break Preview

Page Layout view

Paste

Portrait orientation

Print area

Print title

Scale

Split

Data in a worksheet should be arranged so that it is easy to locate, read, and interpret. You can reorganize data by moving it to another part of the worksheet. You can also reduce data entry time by copying data to another part of the worksheet. If you no longer need certain data, you can delete entire rows or columns. If you want to include additional information within existing data, you can insert another row or column.

Copying and Moving Cells

When creating or editing a worksheet, you might want to use the contents of one or more cells in another part of the worksheet. Rather than retype the same content, you can copy or move a cell or range, including its contents and formatting, to another area of the worksheet. Copying duplicates the cell's or range's contents in another location, while also leaving the content in its original location. Moving places the

Important

Data moved or copied to a cell replaces any content already in that cell. Be sure to check the destination cells for existing data before moving or copying.

contents of the cell or range in another location, and removes that content from its original position in the worksheet. In this lesson, you learn to use the Copy, Cut, and Paste buttons, the drag-and-drop method, and AutoFill to copy and move data in a worksheet.

Copying Cell Contents

When you want to copy the contents of a cell or range, you first select the cell or range. Then, you use buttons in the Clipboard group on the Home tab of the Ribbon. To duplicate the cell's contents without affecting the original cell, you click the **Copy** button. The selected cell contents are placed as an item on the Office Clipboard. The **Office Clipboard** (or **Clipboard**) is a temporary storage area for up to 24 selections you copy or cut. A flashing border appears around the copied selection, as shown in Figure 3-1.

FIGURE 3-1
Range copied to the Clipboard

Clipboard group contains the Copy, Cut, and Paste buttons

Selected cell is where the Clipboard item will be pasted

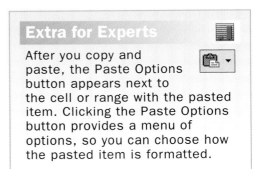

Flashing border surrounds selected cells copied or cut to the Clipboard

Next, you select the cell or upper-left cell of the range where you want the copied item to appear in the worksheet. Click the Paste button in the Clipboard group on the Home tab. The Clipboard item is pasted into the selected cell or range. Pasting places the last item from the Clipboard into the cell or range selected in the worksheet. You can continue to paste that item in the worksheet, as long as the flashing border appears around the cell. Just select the new destination cell or range, and then click the Paste button again.

Extra for Experts

After you copy and paste, the Paste Options button appears next to the cell or range with the pasted item. Clicking the Paste Options button provides a menu of options, so you can choose how the pasted item is formatted.

Moving Cell Contents

The process for moving cell contents is similar. First, select the cell or range whose contents you want to move. Then, click the Cut button in the Clipboard group on the Home tab of the Ribbon. A flashing border appears around the selection, and the selected cell contents are placed as an item on the Clipboard. Next, select the cell or upper-left cell of the range where you want to move the cut item. Click the Paste button in the Clipboard group on the Home tab. The cell contents are removed from the original position and placed in the new location. The flashing border disappears from the worksheet.

Computer Concepts

You can use shortcut keys to quickly cut, copy, and paste cells. Click the Ctrl+X keys to cut selected cells. Click the Ctrl+C keys to copy selected cells. Click the Ctrl+V keys to paste the selected cells.

S TEP-BY-STEP 3.1

1. Open the **Utilities.xlsx** Data File.

2. Save the workbook as **Utilities Expenses** followed by your initials. Some words in the workbook are misspelled. Ignore them for now.

3. Select the range **A3:D7**.

4. On the Home tab of the Ribbon, locate the **Clipboard** group. This group includes all the buttons for cutting, copying, and pasting.

5. Click the **Copy** button. A flashing border surrounds the selected range to indicate that it has been placed on the Clipboard.

6. Click cell **A9**. Cell A9 is the upper-left cell of the range in which you want to paste the copied cells, as shown in Figure 3-1.

7. On the Home tab, in the Clipboard group, click the **Paste** button. The range A3:D7 is copied from the Clipboard to the range A9:D13. All the formatting from the range A3:D7 is copied along with the data. The flashing border surrounds the range A3:D7 until you click another button on the Ribbon or type in a cell.

8. Click cell **A9**, and then enter **Natural Gas**. The flashing border disappears from the range A3:D7.

9. Click cell **B9**, and then enter **100 cf** to indicate the number of cubic feet in hundreds.

10. Click cell **C9**, and then enter **Cost/100 cf** to indicate the cost per hundred cubic feet.

11. Select the range **A9:D13**.

12. On the Home tab, in the Clipboard group, click the **Cut** button. A flashing border surrounds the range you selected.

13. Click cell **A8**.

14. On the Home tab, in the Clipboard group, click the **Paste** button. The data moves to the range A8:D12.

15. Save the workbook, and leave it open for the next Step-by-Step.

Extra for Experts

You can paste any of the last 24 items you cut or copied to the Clipboard. On the Home tab of the Ribbon, click the Clipboard Dialog Box Launcher. The Clipboard task pane appears in a separate pane along the left side of the worksheet. In the worksheet, click the cell where you want to paste an item. In the Clipboard task pane, click the item you want to paste. When you are done, click the Close button in the task pane title bar.

Did You Know?

Sometimes you might need to paste only part of the item you copy or cut. On the Home tab, in the Clipboard group, click the arrow below the Paste button. The Paste menu provides additional commands. The Formulas command pastes the actual formulas entered in the cells, whereas the Paste values command pastes the formula results. The Transpose command pastes a row of cells into a column, or a column of cells into a row. For even more options, click the Paste Special command to open the Paste Special dialog box.

Using the Drag-and-Drop Method

You can quickly move or copy data using the drag-and-drop method. First, select the cell or range you want to move or copy. Then, position the pointer on the top border of the selected cells. The pointer changes from a white cross to a four-headed arrow. To move the selected cells, drag them to a new location. A dashed border shows where the selected cells will be positioned after you release the mouse button, and a ScreenTip lists the destination cell or range address, as shown in Figure 3-2. When the destination you want is selected, release the mouse button.

Computer Concepts

The drag-and-drop method is the fastest way to copy or move data short distances in a worksheet. For longer distances, especially when you want the data in an area of the worksheet not currently visible, copy and paste or cut and paste the data.

To copy the cells, press and hold the Ctrl key to include a plus sign above the pointer as you drag the cells to a new location, and then release the Ctrl key and mouse button.

FIGURE 3-2
Range ready to drag and drop

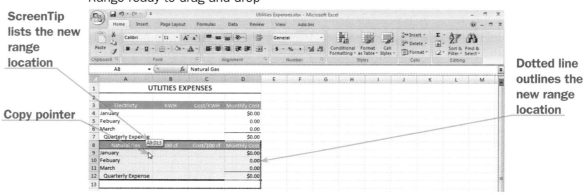

ScreenTip lists the new range location

Copy pointer

Dotted line outlines the new range location

STEP-BY-STEP 3.2

1. Select the range **A8:D12**.

2. Move the pointer to the top edge of cell A8 until it changes to a four-headed arrow.

3. Click the top border of cell **A8**, press and hold the **left mouse button**, and then drag down to cell **A9** until the ScreenTip reads *A9:D13*, as shown in Figure 3-2.

4. Release the mouse button. The data moves to range A9:D13 and remains selected.

5. Move the pointer to the top edge of cell A9 until it changes to a four-headed arrow.

6. Press and hold the **Ctrl** key. The pointer changes to a white arrow with a plus sign.

7. Click and drag down to cell **A15** until the ScreenTip reads *A15:D19*.

8. Release the mouse button, and then release the **Ctrl** key. The data is copied from range A9:D13 to range A15:D19.

STEP-BY-STEP 3.2 Continued

9. Click cell **A15**, and then enter **Water**.

10. Click cell **B15**, and then enter **1000 gallons**.

11. Click cell **C15**, and then enter **Cost/1000 gal** to indicate the cost per 1000 gallons of water.

12. Save the workbook, and leave it open for the next Step-by-Step.

Using the Fill Handle

Filling copies a cell's contents and/or formatting into an adjacent cell or range. Select the cell or range that contains the content and formatting you want to copy. The fill handle appears in the lower-right corner of the active cell or range. When you place the pointer over the fill handle, it changes to a black cross. Click and drag the fill handle over the cells you want to fill. Then, release the left mouse button. The cell contents and formatting are duplicated into the range you selected, and the Auto Fill Options button appears below the filled content. Click the Auto Fill Options button to open the menu shown in Figure 3-3. You choose whether you want to fill both the cell's formatting and the cell's contents, only the cell's contents, or only the cell's formatting. Be aware that you can fill data only when the destination cells are adjacent to the original cell.

Did You Know?

You can also use the fill handle to continue a series of text items, numbers, or dates. For example, you might want to enter column labels of months, such as January, February, March, and so on, or row labels of even numbers, such as 2, 4, 6, and so forth. First, enter data in at least two cells to establish the pattern you want to use. Then, select the cells that contain the series pattern. Finally, drag the fill handle over the range of cells you want to fill. Excel enters appropriate data in the cells to continue the pattern.

FIGURE 3-3
Auto Fill Options menu

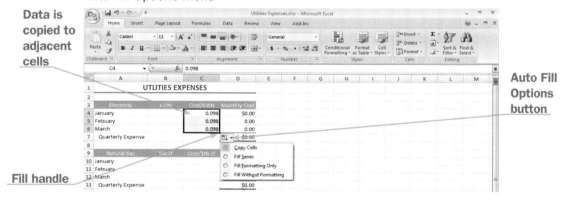

STEP-BY-STEP 3.3

1. Click cell **C4**, and then enter **.098** to record the cost of electricity. The cost of electricity for all three months is $0.098 per kilowatt hour.

2. Click cell **C4**. You want to fill this amount in cells C5 and C6.

3. Point to the **fill handle** in the lower-right corner of cell C4. The pointer changes to a black cross.

4. Drag the fill handle down to cell **C6**. The contents of C4 are copied to cells C5 and C6.

5. Click cell **C10**, and then enter **1.64** to record the cost per 100 cubic feet of natural gas.

6. Drag the fill handle in the lower-right corner of cell C10 down to cell **C12**. The data from cell C10 is copied to cells C11 and C12.

7. Click cell **C16**, and then enter **1.98** to record the cost per 1000 gallons of water.

8. Drag the fill handle in the lower-right corner of cell C16 down to cell **C18**. The data from cell C16 is copied to cells C17 and C18.

9. In column B, enter the utility usage data shown in Figure 3-4. The monthly costs are calculated based on the data you entered.

FIGURE 3-4
Utility usage data

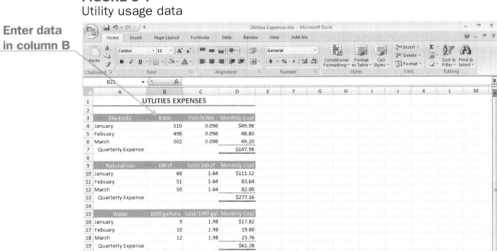

10. Save the workbook, and leave it open for the next Step-by-Step.

Inserting and Deleting Rows, Columns, and Cells

As you build a worksheet, you may discover that you need to add another row or column to store more data. Sometimes, you may find you need to remove a row or column of data that is no longer needed. At other times, you may need to insert or delete specific cells. On the Home tab of the Ribbon, the Cells group includes buttons for inserting and deleting rows, columns, and cells.

Inserting Rows and Columns

To insert a row, click the row number to select the row where you want the new row to appear. Then, click the Insert button in the Cells group on the Home tab. A blank row is added, and the existing rows shift down. To insert a column, click the column letter to select the column where you want the new column to appear. Then, click the Insert button in the Cells group. A blank column is added, and the existing columns shift to the right.

> **Did You Know?**
>
> If you select more than one row or column, the same number of rows or columns you selected is inserted in the worksheet.

Deleting Rows and Columns

The process is similar when you want to delete a row or column. First, click the row number or column letter of the row or column you want to delete. Then, in the Cells group on the Home tab, click the Delete button. The selected row or column disappears, erasing all its data and formatting. The existing rows shift up, or the existing columns shift left.

If you accidentally delete the wrong column or row, you can click the Undo button on the Quick Access Toolbar to restore the data. You can click the Redo button on the Quick Access Toolbar to cancel the Undo action.

> **Did You Know?**
>
> You can select one or more rows or columns, right-click the selected rows or columns, and then click Insert on the shortcut menu to insert an equal number or rows or columns in that location. To remove one or more rows or columns, right-click the selected rows or columns, and then click Delete on the shortcut menu.

Inserting and Deleting Cells

When entering a long column of data, it is not unusual to discover an omitted number near the top of the column. Rather than move the existing data to make room for entering the omitted data, you can insert a new, blank cell. First, select the cell where you want to insert the new cell. Then, in the Cells group on the Home tab, click the arrow next to the Insert button, and then click Insert Cells. The Insert dialog box appears, as shown in Figure 3-5. In this dialog box, you choose whether to shift the existing cells down or to the right.

FIGURE 3-5
Insert dialog box

Inserts a new row in the selected cell's row

Inserts a new column in the selected cell's column

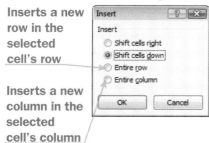

> **Did You Know?**
>
> You can also right-click a cell or selected range, and then, on the shortcut menu, click Insert to open the Insert dialog box or click Delete to open the Delete dialog box. In the dialog box, you can decide which way to shift cells. In addition, you can click the Entire row or Entire column option button, to add or remove the row or column that includes the selected cell.

Another common scenario is accidentally entering a number twice in a long column of data. To eliminate the duplicate data and reposition the rest of the data correctly, you can delete the individual cell. Select the cell you want to delete. Then, in the Cells group on the Home tab, click the arrow next to the Delete button, and then click Delete Cells. The Delete dialog box appears so you can choose whether to shift the remaining cells up or to the left.

S TEP-BY-STEP 3.4

1. Click the row **3** heading. The entire row 3 is selected.

2. On the Home tab, in the Cells group, click the **Insert** button. A new, blank row appears as row 3. The original row 3 becomes row 4.

3. Click cell **B3**, and then enter **Units Used**. Click cell **C3**, and then enter **Unit Cost**. Click cell **D3**, and then enter **Billed**.

4. Select the range **B3:D3**, and then apply the **20% - Accent3** cell style to the range.

5. Click the column **B** heading. The entire column B is selected.

6. On the Home tab, in the Cells group, click the **Insert** button. A new, blank column appears as column B. The original column B becomes column C.

7. Click cell **B3**, and then enter **Date Paid**. The active cell is cell B4.

8. On the Home tab, in the Cells group, next to the Delete button, click the **arrow**, and then click **Delete Sheet Columns**. Column B is deleted, and the remaining columns shift left.

9. Click the row **4** heading. The entire row 4 is selected.

10. In the Cells group, click the **Delete** button. Row 4 disappears, and the remaining rows shift up.

11. On the Quick Access Toolbar, click the **Undo** button. Row 4 reappears in the worksheet.

12. Click cell **B18**.

13. In the Cells group, next to the Insert button, click the **arrow**, and then click **Insert Cells**. The Insert dialog box appears, as shown in Figure 3-5.

Careers

Business managers use Excel worksheets in a variety of ways. For example, human resource managers use spreadsheets to conduct performance reviews and keep track of employee records. Production managers use spreadsheets to track machine production efficiency and to keep machine maintenance records.

STEP-BY-STEP 3.4 Continued

14. Click the **Shift cells down** option button, if it is not selected. Click **OK**. The data in the range B18:B19 shifts to the range B19:B20.

15. Click cell **B18**, if it is not already the active cell.

16. On the Home tab, in the Cells group, next to the Delete button, click the **arrow**, and then click **Delete Cells**. The Delete dialog box appears.

17. Click the **Shift cells up** option button, if it is not selected. Click **OK**. The data in the range B19:B20 shifts back to the range B18:B19.

18. Save the workbook, and leave it open for the next Step-by-Step.

Freezing Panes in a Worksheet

Often a worksheet includes too much data to view on the screen at one time. As you scroll to other parts of the worksheet, titles and labels at the top or side of the worksheet might shift out of view, making it difficult to identify the contents of particular columns. For example, the worksheet title *Utilities Expenses* in the previous Step-by-Step might have scrolled off the screen when you were working in the lower part of the worksheet.

You can view two parts of a worksheet at once by freezing panes. When you **freeze panes**, you select which rows and/or columns of the worksheet remain visible on the screen as the rest of the worksheet scrolls. For example, you can freeze the row or column titles so they appear on the screen no matter where you scroll in the worksheet. As shown in Figure 3-6, rows 1, 2, and 3 are frozen so they remain on-screen even when you scroll down to row 16 (hiding rows 4 through 15).

FIGURE 3-6
Worksheet with rows 1 through 3 frozen

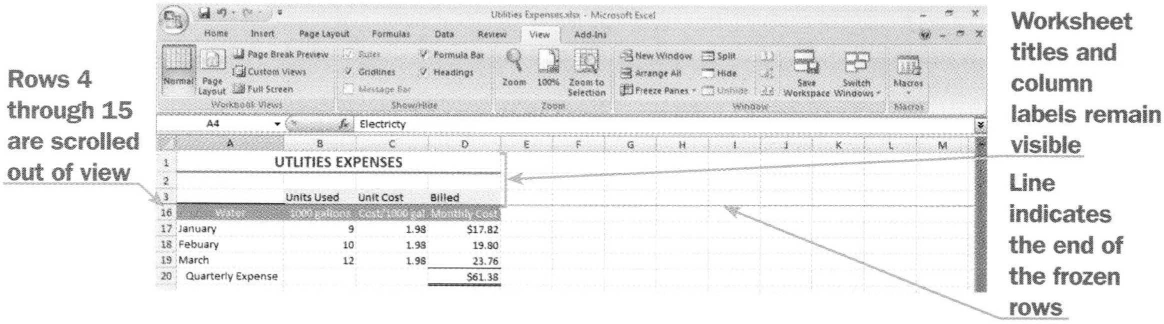

Rows 4 through 15 are scrolled out of view

Worksheet titles and column labels remain visible

Line indicates the end of the frozen rows

When you freeze panes in a worksheet, the rows and columns that remain locked on-screen depend on the location of the active row, column, or cell. Table 3-1 describes the different selection options. On the View tab of the Ribbon, in the Window group, click the Freeze Panes button, and then click Freeze Panes. A black gridline appears between the frozen and unfrozen panes of the worksheet.

TABLE 3-1
Freeze panes options

TO FREEZE	DO THE FOLLOWING
Rows	Select the first row below the row(s) you want to freeze
Columns	Select the first column to the right of the column(s) you want to freeze
Rows and columns	Select the first cell below and to the right of the row(s) and column(s) you want to freeze

When you want to unlock all the rows and columns to allow them to scroll, you need to unfreeze the panes. On the View tab of the Ribbon, in the Window group, click the Freeze Panes button, and then click Unfreeze Panes. The black gridline disappears, and all rows and columns are unfrozen.

Splitting a Worksheet Window

You might want to view different parts of a large worksheet at the same time. Splitting divides the worksheet window into two or four panes that you can scroll independently. This enables you to see distant parts of a worksheet at the same time. Splitting is particularly useful in a large worksheet when you want to copy data from one area to another. You can click in one pane and scroll the worksheet as needed while the other part of the worksheet remains in view in a different pane.

You can split the worksheet window into horizontal panes, as shown in Figure 3-7, vertical panes, or both. Select a row to split the window into horizontal panes. Select a column to split the worksheet into vertical panes. Select a cell to split the worksheet into both horizontal and vertical panes. Then, on the View tab of the Ribbon, in the Window group, click the Split button. The Split button remains selected, and a split bar separates the panes you created. If you want to resize the panes, drag the split bar. When you want to return to a single pane, click the Split button in the Window group again.

Did You Know?

You can also use the mouse to add, resize, and remove panes. Drag the split box above the vertical scroll bar down to create horizontal panes. Drag the split box that appears to the right of the horizontal scroll bar to the left to create vertical panes. Drag a split bar to resize the panes. Double-click a split bar to remove it.

FIGURE 3-7
Worksheet window split into horizontal panes

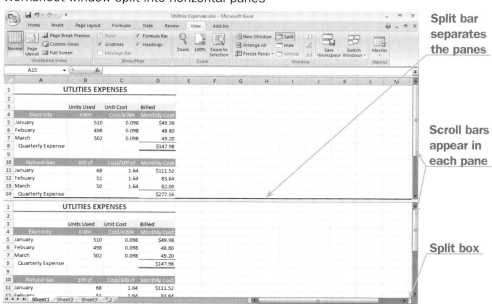

Split bar separates the panes

Scroll bars appear in each pane

Split box

STEP-BY-STEP 3.5

1. Click cell **A4**.

2. Click the **View** tab on the Ribbon, and then locate the **Window** group. This group contains the buttons for freezing and splitting panes.

3. Click the **Freeze Panes** button, and then click **Freeze Panes**. The title and column headings in rows 1 through 3 are locked. A black gridline appears between rows 3 and 4.

4. Scroll the worksheet down until row 16 is at the top of the worksheet window. The worksheet title and column headings remain locked at the top of the screen, even as other rows scroll out of view, as shown in Figure 3-6.

5. On the View tab, in the Window group, click the **Freeze Panes** button, and then click **Unfreeze Panes**. The title and column headings are no longer frozen.

6. Click the row **15** heading.

7. On the View tab, in the Window group, click the **Split** button. A split bar appears above row 15, dividing the worksheet into two horizontal panes.

8. Click in the lower pane and scroll up to row **1**. The same part of the worksheet appears in both panes, as shown in Figure 3-7.

9. Double-click the **split bar**. The split is removed, and worksheet is again one pane.

10. Save the workbook, and leave it open for the next Step-by-Step.

Checking Spelling in a Worksheet

An important step in creating a professional workbook is to correct any misspelling. Typographical errors can be distracting at best, and can cause others to doubt the accuracy of the rest of the workbook's content at worst. To help track down and correct spelling errors in a worksheet, you can use the Spelling command, which checks the spelling in the entire active worksheet against the dictionary that comes with Microsoft Office. To check the spelling in a worksheet, click the Review tab on the Ribbon, and then, in the Proofing group, click the Spelling button. The Spelling dialog box appears, as shown in Figure 3-8, with the first potential spelling error shown in the Not in Dictionary box.

FIGURE 3-8
Spelling dialog box

The Spelling dialog box provides many options for dealing with a possible misspelling. If the word is mistyped, you can correct the spelling yourself or click the correct word in the Suggestions box. Then, click Change to replace the current instance of the misspelling with the corrected word, or click Change All to replace every instance of the misspelling. If the word is correct (as often happens with company and product names), you can click Ignore to move to the next potential spelling error without making a change to the word, or click Ignore All to skip every instance of this word in the worksheet. After you have addressed all the possible misspellings in the worksheet, a dialog box appears to let you know that the spelling check is complete for the entire sheet.

Be aware that the spelling checker is not foolproof. As a final check, you should also proofread the worksheet for any misspellings that the spelling checker might have missed. You might find words that are spelled correctly, but used incorrectly (such as *they're*, *their*, and *there*, or *hour* and *our*). In addition, you might discover a missing word or two (*and* or *the*, for instance). This final check helps ensure your worksheet is free from errors.

Extra for Experts

If Excel incorrectly flags a word that you use frequently as a misspelling, you can add the word to a custom dictionary that resides on your computer by clicking the Add to Dictionary button. If the misspelling is a typo you make often, you can select the correct word in the Suggestions box, and then click the AutoCorrect button. Excel will automatically correct this mistake whenever you type it.

S TEP-BY-STEP 3.6

1. Press the **Ctrl+Home** keys. Cell A1 is the active cell in the worksheet.

2. Click the **Review** tab on the Ribbon, and then locate the **Proofing** group. The Spelling button is located here.

3. Click the **Spelling** button. The Spelling dialog box appears, as shown in Figure 3-8. The word *Electricty* is identified as a misspelled word. One correction appears in the Suggestions box.

4. In the Suggestions box, click **Electricity** if it is not selected, and then click **Change**. The spelling of the word in the workbook is corrected, and *Febuary* appears in the dialog box as the next possible misspelled word.

5. In the Suggestions box, click **February**, if it is not selected, and then click **Change All**. All three instances of this misspelling are corrected, and *cf* appears in the Not in Dictionary box as the next possible misspelling. However, *cf* is being used as an abbreviation for cubic feet, so you will ignore all instances of this abbreviation in the worksheet.

6. Click **Ignore All**. A dialog box appears, indicating the spelling check is complete for the entire sheet. (If the spelling checker flags other possible misspellings, change or ignore them as necessary, until the dialog box appears.)

7. Click **OK**.

8. Proofread the worksheet. In cell A1, the word *UTLITIES* is misspelled.

9. Click cell **A1**, and then, in the formula bar, click after *UT* to place the insertion point.

10. Type **I** to insert the missing letter in the word, and then press the **Enter** key.

11. Save the workbook, and leave it open for the next Step-by-Step.

Preparing a Worksheet for Printing

So far, you have used Normal view when entering and formatting data in a worksheet. Excel has other views as well. Page Layout view is helpful when you prepare a worksheet for printing. Excel has many options for changing how a worksheet appears on a printed page.

Setting Margins

Margins are blank spaces around the top, bottom, and sides of a page. The margins determine how many of a worksheet's columns and rows fit on a printed page. You can make the margins wider to leave extra blank space for jotting notes in the printed copy. Or, you can make the margins narrower when you want to print more columns and rows on a page. To change the margins of a worksheet, click the Page Layout tab on the Ribbon, and then, in the Page Setup group, click the Margins button. You can then choose among three pre-set margins—Normal (the default), Wide, and Narrow, as shown in Figure 3-9.

Extra for Experts

If the preset margins do not fit your needs, you can enter custom measurements for margins. Click the Margins button in the Page Setup group on the Page Layout tab, and then click Custom Margins. In each margin box, type the appropriate measurement, in inches, for the individual margins. Click OK when you are done.

FIGURE 3-9
Margins menu

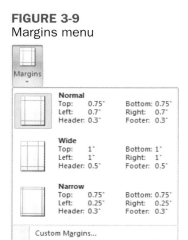

Changing the Page Orientation

Excel has two ways to print on a page. Worksheets printed in portrait orientation are longer than they are wide. In contrast, worksheets printed in landscape orientation are wider than they are long. By default, Excel is set to print pages in portrait orientation. Many worksheets, however, include more columns of data than fit on pages in portrait orientation. These pages look better and are easier to understand when printed in landscape orientation. You can change the orientation of the worksheet by clicking the Page Layout tab on the Ribbon, and then, in the Page Setup group, clicking the Orientation button. As shown in Figure 3-10, you can then click Portrait or Landscape on the menu.

FIGURE 3-10
Orientation menu

Setting the Print Area

When you print a worksheet, Excel assumes all of the data entered in that worksheet is to be printed. If you want to print only a portion of the data found in a worksheet, you will need to set the print area. The print area consists of the cells and ranges designated for printing. For example, you might want to print only the range A1:A19, which shows the utility and month data, and the range D3:D19 (billed amount). To do this, first select the range. Then, click the Page Layout tab on the Ribbon. In the Page Setup group, click the Print Area button, and then click Set Print Area. Each time you print, only the cells in the print area appear on the page. You must clear the print area to print the entire worksheet again. In the Page Setup group on the Page Layout tab, click the Print Area button, and then click Clear Print Area.

Inserting, Adjusting, and Deleting Page Breaks

When a worksheet or the print area doesn't fit on one printed page, page breaks indicate where the next page begins. Excel inserts an automatic page break whenever it runs out of room on a page. You can also insert a manual page break to start a new page. To insert a manual page break, select the row below where you want to insert a horizontal page break, or select the column to the left of where you want to insert a vertical page break. Then, click the Breaks button in the Page Setup group on the Page Layout tab, and then click Insert Page Break.

Did You Know?

You can center the worksheet on the printed page. Click the Page Layout tab on the Ribbon, and then click the Page Setup Dialog Box Launcher. Click the Margins tab in the Page Setup dialog box. In the Center on page section, check the Horizontally box to center the worksheet between the left and right margins. Check the Vertically box to center the worksheet between the top and bottom margins. Check both boxes to center the worksheet in both directions.

Extra for Experts

A print area can include multiple ranges and/or non-adjacent cells. For example, you might want to print the utility and month data as well as the bill amount. Select the cells and ranges you want to print, and then set the print area. The selected cells and ranges will print until you clear the print area.

The simplest way to adjust page breaks in a worksheet is in Page Break Preview, as shown in Figure 3-11. On the status bar, click the Page Break Preview button to switch the worksheet to this view. Dashed lines appear for automatic page breaks, and solid lines appear for manual page breaks. You can drag any page break to a new location.

FIGURE 3-11
Page Break Preview

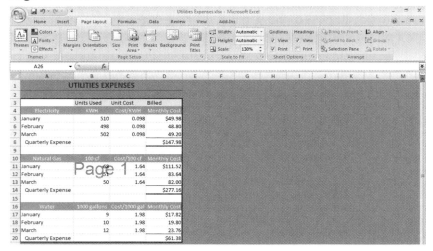

When you no longer want a manual page break, you can delete it. Click below or to the left of the page break you want to remove. Click the Page Layout tab on the Ribbon. In the Page Setup group, click the Breaks button, and then click Remove Page Break.

✳Scaling to Fit

Scaling enables you to resize a worksheet to print on a specific number of pages. The Scale to Fit group on the Page Layout tab contains three options for resizing a worksheet, as shown in Figure 3-12. You can fit the worksheet on the number of pages you specify for its width or height. Just click the arrow next to the Width or Height box and select the maximum pages for the printed worksheet's width or height. Another option is to set the percentage by which you want to shrink or enlarge the worksheet on the printed page. Click the arrows next to the Scale box to set the percentage.

FIGURE 3-12
Scale to Fit group

Choosing Sheet Options

By default, gridlines, row numbers, and column letters appear in the worksheet—but not on the printed page—to help you as you enter and format data. You can choose to show or hide gridlines and headings in a worksheet, as well as on the printed page. The Sheet Options group, shown in Figure 3-13, contains check boxes for viewing and printing gridlines and headings. Check and uncheck the boxes as needed.

FIGURE 3-13
Sheet Options group

Specifying Print Titles

Print titles are designated rows and/or columns in a worksheet that print on each page. Specified rows print at the top of each page. Specified columns print on the left of each page. To set print titles, click the Page Layout tab on the Ribbon, and then, in the Page Setup group, click the Print Titles button. The Page Setup dialog box appears with the Sheet tab displayed, as shown in Figure 3-14 (left). Click the Collapse button next to the Rows to repeat at top box to shrink the dialog box, as shown in Figure 3-14 (right). Click the row or rows to use as the print title. Then, click the Expand button to restore the dialog box to its full size. You use the same process to select columns to repeat at left. Click OK to add the print titles to the worksheet.

> **Extra for Experts**
>
> The Page Setup dialog box also provides tabs for the Page, Margins, and Header/Footer options available on the Ribbon, as well as a few additional options. To open the Page Setup dialog box, click the Dialog Box Launcher in the Page Setup, Scale to Fit, or Sheet Options group on the Page Layout tab of the Ribbon.

FIGURE 3-14
Sheet tab in the Page Setup dialog box

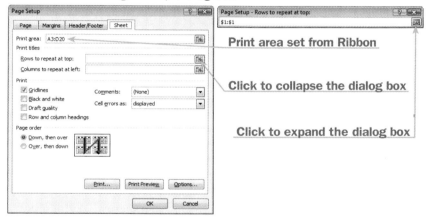

S TEP-BY-STEP 3.7

1. Click the **Page Layout** tab on the Ribbon. This tab contains many commands for preparing a worksheet for printing.

2. In the Page Setup group, click the **Margins** tab to open the menu shown in Figure 3-9, and then click **Wide**. The margins are set for 1 inch on all sides. A dashed line, indicating an automatic page break, appears after column F.

3. On the Page Layout tab, in the Page Setup group, click the **Orientation** button to open the menu shown in Figure 3-10, and then click **Landscape**. The automatic page break moves after column J, indicating that the printed workbook will be wider than it is tall.

4. Select the range **A3:D20**.

5. On the Page Layout tab, in the Page Setup group, click the **Print Area** button, and then click **Set Print Area**. Only the selected range will print on the page.

STEP-BY-STEP 3.7 Continued

6. On the Page Layout tab, in the Scale to Fit group, click the **up arrow** next to the Scale box, shown in Figure 3-12, until **130** appears in the box. The printed data will enlarge to take up more of the page.

7. On the Page Layout tab, in the Sheet Options group, click the **Gridlines Print** check box to insert a check mark. The gridlines will print on the page.

8. On the Page Layout tab, in the Page Setup group, click the **Print Titles** button. The Page Setup dialog box appears, as shown in Figure 3-14 (left).

9. On the Sheet tab, in the Print titles section, click the **Collapse** button after the Rows to repeat at the top box.

10. In the worksheet, click row **1** as the row to repeat at the top of each printed page. The row reference is added to the dialog box, as shown in Figure 3-14 (right).

11. In the collapsed Page Setup dialog box, click the **Expand** button.

12. Click **OK**.

13. Save the workbook, and leave it open for the next Step-by-Step.

Inserting Headers and Footers

Headers and footers are useful for adding identifying text to a printed page. A header is text that prints in the top margin of each page, as shown in Figure 3-15. A footer is text that prints in the bottom margin of each page. Text that is commonly included in a header or footer is your name, the page number, the current date, the workbook file name, and the worksheet name. Headers and footers are each divided into three sections, which you can use to organize the text.

FIGURE 3-15
Completed Header section

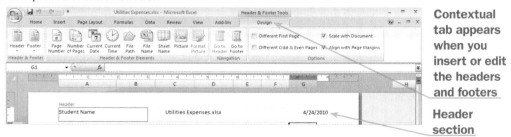

Contextual tab appears when you insert or edit the headers and footers

Header section

To create a header or footer for a printed worksheet, click the Insert tab on the Ribbon, and then in the Text group, click the Header & Footer button. The worksheet switches to Page Layout view, and the Header & Footer Tools appear on the Ribbon with one contextual tab—the Design tab. The insertion point is in the center header box, but you can easily move to the left or right section by clicking a different box. Type the text you want to enter, or click a button in the Header & Footer Elements group on the Design tab under Header & Footer Tools on the Ribbon. To enter a preset header or footer, in the Header & Footer group on the Design tab, click the Header or Footer button, and then click the header or footer you want to use. Click anywhere on the worksheet to close the headers and footers.

> **Did You Know?**
>
> You can enter, edit, delete, and format the text in each header and footer section the same way you do for text in worksheet cells.

S TEP-BY-STEP 3.8

1. Click the **Insert** tab on the Ribbon, and then locate the **Text** group.

2. Click the **Header & Footer** button. The Header & Footer Tools appear on the Ribbon with the Design contextual tab. The worksheet changes to Page Layout view. The insertion point is in the center header box.

3. On the Design contextual tab, in the Header & Footer Elements group, click the **File Name** button. The code *&[File]* appears in the center header box.

4. Press the **Tab** key to move to the right header box. The code *&[File]* in the center header box is replaced with *Utilities Expenses.xlsx*, which is the current file name of the workbook. Remember, if your computer is not set to show file extensions, you see *Utilities Expenses* without the file extension in the center header box.

5. On the Design contextual tab, in the Header & Footer Elements group, click the **Current Date** button. The code *&[Date]* appears in the right header box.

6. Press the **Tab** key to move the insertion point to the left header box. The code *&[Date]* in the right header box is replaced with the current date.

7. In the left header box, type your name. The header is complete, as shown in Figure 3-15.

8. On the Design contextual tab, in the Navigation group, click the **Go to Footer** button. The insertion point moves to the left footer box.

9. Click the center footer box.

10. On the Design contextual tab, in the Header & Footer Elements group, click the **Page Number** button. The code *&[Page]* appears in the center footer box. After you move the insertion point out of the center footer box, the actual page number will appear.

STEP-BY-STEP 3.8 Continued

11. Click the worksheet to close the headers and footers. The worksheet appears in Page Layout view, as shown in Figure 3-16, giving a good sense of how it will print on the page.

FIGURE 3-16
Worksheet in Print Layout view

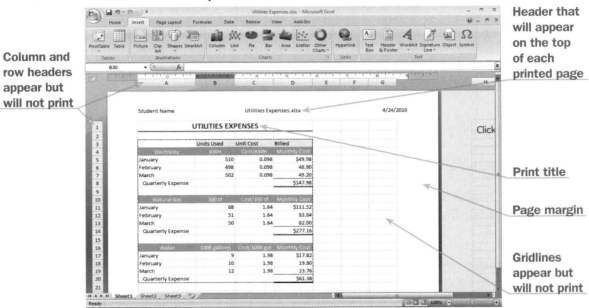

Column and row headers appear but will not print

Header that will appear on the top of each printed page

Print title

Page margin

Gridlines appear but will not print

12. Save the workbook.

13. Click the **Office Button**, point to **Print**, and then click **Print Preview**. The worksheet appears in Print Preview, as shown in Figure 3-17.

FIGURE 3-17
Worksheet in Print Preview

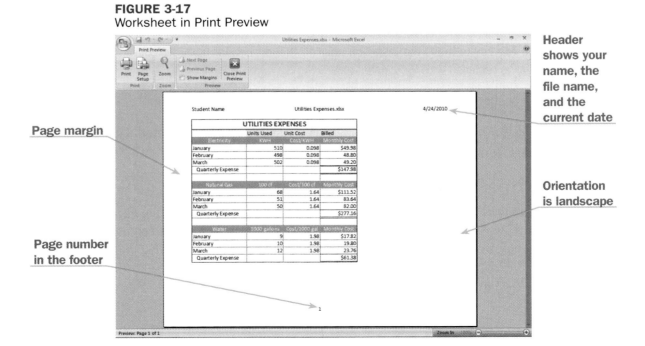

Page margin

Page number in the footer

Header shows your name, the file name, and the current date

Orientation is landscape

14. On the Print Preview tab, click the **Print** button. The Print dialog box opens.

15. Click **OK** to print the worksheet, and then close the workbook.

Use the formatting skills you learned in earlier lessons to make the worksheet more attractive.

SUMMARY

In this lesson, you learned:

- Worksheet data can be moved or copied to another part of the worksheet. You can use the Copy, Cut, and Paste buttons, the drag-and-drop method, and the fill handle to copy and move data in a worksheet. These tools save time by eliminating the need to retype data.

- As you build a worksheet, you may need to insert a row or column to enter more data, or delete a row or column of unneeded data. You can also insert or delete specific cells within a worksheet.

- When a worksheet becomes large, the column or row labels can scroll out of view as you work on other parts of the worksheet. To keep select rows and columns on the screen as the rest of the worksheet scrolls, you can freeze panes.

- Splitting a large worksheet enables you to view and work in different parts of a worksheet at once, in two or four panes that you can scroll independently.

- You can check a worksheet for possible misspellings and correct them using the Spelling dialog box.

- When you are ready to print a worksheet, switching from Normal view to Page Layout view can be helpful. You can modify how a worksheet appears on the printed page by increasing or decreasing the margins, changing the page orientation, designating a print area, inserting page breaks, scaling, showing or hiding gridlines and headings, and specifying print titles.

- Headers and footers are useful for adding identifying text at the top and bottom of the printed page. Common elements include your name, the page number, the current date, the workbook file name, and the worksheet name.

VOCABULARY *Review*

Define the following terms:

Automatic page break	Header	Page Layout view
Copy	Landscape orientation	Paste
Cut	Manual page break	Portrait orientation
Fill	Margins	Print area
Fill handle	Normal view	Print title
Footer	Office Clipboard (Clipboard)	Scale
Freeze pane	Page Break Preview	Split

REVIEW *Questions*

TRUE/FALSE

Circle T if the statement is true or F if the statement is false.

T   F   1. If you paste data into cells with existing data, the pasted data appears after the existing data.

T   F   2. The Fill commands are available only if you are copying data to cells adjacent to the original cell.

T   F   3. Deleting a row or column erases the data in that row or column.

T   F   4. Splitting creates two, three, or four panes in the worksheet.

T   F   5. The spelling checker might not find all the misspellings or incorrectly used words in a worksheet.

WRITTEN QUESTIONS

Write a brief answer to the following questions.

1. What key do you press to copy data using the drag-and-drop method?

2. How do you make multiple copies of data that has been copied to the Clipboard?

3. What should you do if you accidentally delete a column or row?

4. How do you keep the titles and column labels of a worksheet on the screen, no matter where the worksheet is scrolled?

5. What is the difference between a header and a footer?

PROJECTS

PROJECT 3-1

Match the correct command in Column 2 to the action indicated in Column 1.

Column 1	**Column 2**
____ 1. You are tired of typing repetitive data.	**A.** Print
____ 2. A portion of the worksheet would be more useful in another area of the worksheet.	**B.** Cut, Paste
____ 3. You forgot to type a row of data in the middle of the worksheet.	**C.** Insert Sheet Rows
____ 4. You no longer need a certain column in the worksheet.	**D.** Delete Sheet Columns
____ 5. Column headings scroll out of view when you are working in the lower part of the worksheet.	**E.** Fill or Copy
	F. Print Area
____ 6. You want to be sure that all words are spelled correctly in the worksheet.	**G.** Spelling
	H. Freeze Panes
____ 7. Your boss would rather not view your worksheet on the screen and has requested a copy on paper.	
____ 8. You want to print only a selected area of the worksheet.	

PROJECT 3-2

1. Open the **Store.xlsx** Data File.

2. Save the workbook as **Store Assets** followed by your initials.

3. Insert a column to the left of column B.

4. Change the width of column A to 45.

5. Move the contents of the range D3:D16 to the range B3:B16.

6. Change the width of columns B and C to 10.

7. Indent the contents of A9, A13, and A16.

8. Underline the contents of B3:C3.

9. Insert a footer that includes your name in the left footer box and the current date in the right footer box.

10. Save, preview, and print the worksheet, and then close the workbook.

PROJECT 3-3

1. Open the **Imports.xlsx** Data File.

2. Save the workbook as **Trade Imports** followed by your initials.

3. Freeze rows 1 through 6.

4. Check the spelling of the countries listed in the worksheet. (*Hint*: You will need to make four corrections.)

5. Change the orientation of the worksheet to portrait.

6. Scale the worksheet to 80% of its original size.

7. Change the margins to Wide.

8. In cell A5, enter your name.

9. Save, preview, and print the worksheet, and then close the workbook.

PROJECT 3-4

1. Open the **Inventory.xlsx** Data File.

2. Save the workbook as **Supply Inventory** followed by your initials.

3. Organize the worksheet so inventory items are grouped by supplier, as shown below. Be sure to insert suitable headings and format them appropriately. Some of the data is out of order and needs to be moved.

Item	Ordering Code	Quantity
Mega Computer Manufacturers		
Mega X-39 Computers	X-39-25879	20
Mega X-40 Computers	X-40-25880	24
Mega X-41 Computers	X-41-25881	28
Xenon Paper Source		
Xenon Letter Size White Paper	LT-W-45822	70
Xenon Letter Size Color Paper	LT-C-45823	10
Xenon Legal Size White Paper	LG-W-45824	40
Xenon Legal Size Color Paper	LG-C-45825	5
MarkMaker Pen Company		
MarkMaker Blue Ball Point Pens	MM-Bl-43677	120
MarkMaker Black Ball Point Pens	MM-Bk-43678	100
MarkMaker Red Ball Point Pens	MM-R-43679	30

4. The following inventory item has been accidentally excluded from the worksheet. Add the item by using the Fill command and then editing the copied data.

Item	Ordering Code	Quantity
MarkMaker Green Ball Point Pens	MM-G-43680	30

5. Delete the following item.

Item	Ordering Code	Quantity
Mega X-39 Computers	X-39-25879	20

6. Change the page orientation to landscape.

7. Hide the gridlines from view.

8. Insert a header that includes your name in the center header box and the current date in the right header box.

9. Save, preview, and print the worksheet, and then close the workbook.

PROJECT 3-5

1. Open the **Time.xlsx** Data File.

2. Save the workbook as **Time Record** followed by your initials.

3. Delete rows 4 and 5.

4. Enter the following data in the time record.

Date	From	To	Admin. Meetings	Phone	Work Description
9-Dec	8:15 AM	12:00 PM	1.00	2.75	Staff meeting and called clients
10-Dec	7:45 AM	11:30 AM	2.00	1.75	Paperwork and called clients
11-Dec	7:45 AM	11:30 AM		3.75	Called clients
13-Dec	8:00 AM	12:00 PM	2.00	2.00	Mailed flyers and met w/KF

5. Freeze headings above row 8.

6. Insert a blank row above row 16. Enter the following information:

Date	From	To	Admin. Meetings	Phone	Work Description
12-Dec	7:45 AM	11:30 AM	2.00	1.75	Paperwork and called clients

7. Change the orientation of the worksheet to landscape.

8. In the range B1:D1, enter your name. Save the workbook.

9. Preview the worksheet and zoom in to see the total hours worked.

10. Print the worksheet, and then close the workbook.

 PROJECT 3-6

1. Open the **Biology.xlsx** Data File.

2. Save the workbook as **Biology Grades** followed by your initials.

3. Merge and center the range A1:H1. Merge and center the range A2:H2.

4. Insert a column between the current columns A and B.

5. In the range B3:B9, enter the following data:

Cell	Data
B3	First Name
B4	Mike
B5	Owen
B6	Cindy
B7	Raul
B8	Alice
B9	Cameron

6. Change the worksheet to landscape orientation.

7. Switch to Page Layout view. Click in the left header box and type your name.

8. Go to the footer, and insert *Page 1* in the center footer box. (*Hint*: Under the Header & Footer tools, on the Design contextual tab, in the Header & Footer group, click the Footer button, and then click Page 1.)

9. Save, preview, and print the worksheet, and then close the workbook.

 PROJECT 3-7

1. Open the **Booster.xlsx** Data File.

2. Save the workbook as **Booster Club** followed by your initials.

3. Bold and center the column headings in row 2.

4. Insert a row above row 3.

5. Freeze the column headings in row 2.

6. Insert a row above row 8, and then, in cell A8, enter **Bats**.

7. Copy cell E4 to the range E5:E11.

8. Format the Cost (D4:D11) and Total (E4:E12) columns as currency with two decimal places.

 Did You Know?

As you type, the AutoComplete function displays the full text entered in other cells that begins with the same letters you have typed. To make a different entry, keep typing the new data. To accept the entry, press the Enter key.

9. In the Sport and Cost columns, enter the following data, and then widen the columns as needed to display all of the data:

Item	Sport	Cost
Basketballs	Basketball	28
Hoops	Basketball	40
Backboards	Basketball	115
Softballs	Softball	5
Bats	Softball	30
Masks	Softball	35
Volleyballs	Volleyball	25
Nets	Volleyball	125

10. In the Quantity column, enter the following data.

Basketballs	5	Bats	5
Hoops	2	Masks	1
Backboards	2	Volleyballs	7
Softballs	20	Nets	1

11. You have $1210 to spend on equipment. Use any remaining cash to purchase as many basketballs as possible. Increase the number of basketballs and watch the dollar amount in the total. You should use $1203.00 and have $7.00 left over.

12. In cell A16, enter **Prepared by:** followed by your name.

13. Save, preview, and print the worksheet, and then close the workbook.

 PROJECT 3-8

1. Open the **Pool.xlsx** Data File. The workbook contains attendance data for a neighborhood swimming pool.

2. Save the workbook as **Pool Attendance** followed by your initials.

3. Move data as needed to better organize the worksheet.

4. Format the worksheet in an appropriate and appealing way.

5. Insert your name, the workbook file name, and the current date in the appropriate header and footer boxes.

6. Save, preview, and print the worksheet, and then close the workbook.

CRITICAL*Thinking*

 ACTIVITY 3-1

As a zoo employee, you have been asked to observe the behavior of a chimpanzee during a three-day period. You need to record the number of minutes the animal displays certain behaviors during the time that the zoo is open to visitors. Set up a worksheet to record the number of minutes that the chimpanzee participates in the following behaviors during each of the three days.

- Sleeping

- Eating

- Walking

- Sitting

- Playing

Format the worksheet to make it attractive and easy to read. Change margins, orientation, and other page setup options to prepare the worksheet for printing. Include appropriate headers and footers, including at least your name in one of the boxes. Save the workbook with the file name **Chimpanzee Behavior** followed by your initials.

ENTERING WORKSHEET FORMULAS

OBJECTIVES

Upon completion of this lesson, you will be able to:

- Enter and edit formulas.
- Distinguish between relative, absolute, and mixed cell references.
- Use the point-and-click method to enter formulas.
- Use the Sum button to view summary calculations.
- Preview a calculation.
- Display formulas instead of results in the worksheet.
- Manually calculate formulas.

Estimated Time: 2.5 hours

VOCABULARY

Absolute cell reference

Formula

Manual calculation

Mixed cell reference

Operand

Operator

Order of evaluation

Point-and-click method

Relative cell reference

Sum button

What Are Formulas?

One of the main advantages of Excel is that you can use numbers entered in cells to make calculations in other cells. The equation used to calculate values in a cell is called a formula. Each formula begins with an equal sign (=). The results of the calculation appear in the cell in which the formula is entered. The formula itself appears in the formula bar. For example, if you enter the formula =8+6 in cell B3, the value 14 appears in the cell, and the formula =8+6 appears in the formula bar when cell B3 is the active cell, as shown in Figure 4-1.

FIGURE 4-1
Formula and formula results

Formula results appear in the cell

Formula in the active cell appears in the formula bar

Entering a Formula

Worksheet formulas consist of two components: operands and operators. An operand is a constant (text or number) or cell reference used in a formula. You can type cell references in uppercase (A1) or lowercase (a1). An operator is a symbol that indicates the type of calculation to perform on the operands, such as a plus sign (+) for addition. Table 4-1 shows the different mathematical operators you can use in formulas. Consider the formula =B3+5. In this formula, the cell reference B3 and the constant 5 are operands, and the plus sign (+) is an operator. This formula tells Excel to add the value in cell B3 to the value 5. After you finish typing a formula in a cell, you must enter it by pressing the Enter or Tab key or by clicking the Enter button on the formula bar.

TABLE 4-1
Mathematical operators

OPERATOR	OPERATION	EXAMPLE	MEANING
+	Addition	B5+C5	Adds the values in cells B5 and C5
−	Subtraction	C8−232	Subtracts 232 from the value in cell C8
*	Multiplication	D4*D5	Multiplies the value in cell D4 by the value in cell D5
/	Division	E6/4	Divides the value in cell E6 by 4
^	Exponentiation	B3^3	Raises the value in cell B3 to the third power

STEP-BY-STEP 4.1

1. Open the **Formula.xlsx** Data File.

2. Save the worksheet as **Formula Practice** followed by your initials.

3. Click cell **C3**. You'll enter a formula in this cell.

4. Type **=A3+B3**, and then press the **Enter** key. The formula result 380 appears in the cell. Cell C4 is the active cell.

5. Click cell **C4**, type **=A4–B4**, and then press the **Enter** key. The formula result –246 appears in the cell. Cell C5 is the active cell.

6. Click cell **C5**, type **=A5*B5**, and then press the **Enter** key. The formula result 18850 appears in the cell. Cell C6 is the active cell.

7. Click cell **C6**, type **=A6/B6**, and then press the **Enter** key. The formula result 2 appears in the cell. Compare your results to Figure 4-2.

> **Computer Concepts**
>
> The cell references you use in formulas are color-coded. Each cell reference in the formula appears in a specific color. The cell itself in the worksheet is outlined in the same color. You can change a cell reference in a formula by dragging the outlined cell to another location in the worksheet. You can also change which cells are included in a reference by dragging any corner of the colored outline to resize the selected range.

STEP-BY-STEP 4.1 Continued

FIGURE 4-2
Formulas entered in worksheet

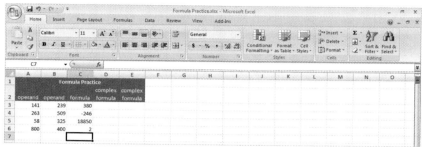

8. Save the workbook, and leave it open for the next Step-by-Step.

Order of Evaluation

Formulas can include more than one operator. For example, the formula =C3*C4+5 includes two operators and performs both multiplication and addition to calculate the value in the cell. The sequence used to calculate the value of a formula is called the order of evaluation.

Formulas are evaluated as follows:

1. Contents within parentheses are evaluated first. You can use as many pairs of parentheses as you want. The innermost set of parentheses is evaluated first.

2. Mathematical operators are evaluated in the order of priority shown in Table 4-2.

3. If two or more operators have the same order of evaluation, the equation is evaluated from left to right. For example, in the formula =20–15–2, first the number 15 is subtracted from 20, then 2 is subtracted from the difference (5).

TABLE 4-2
Order of evaluation priority

ORDER OF EVALUATION	OPERATOR	SYMBOL
First	Exponentiation	^
Second	Positive or negative	+ or –
Third	Multiplication or division	* or /
Fourth	Addition or subtraction	+ or –

STEP-BY-STEP 4.2

1. Click cell **D3**, and then type **=(A3+B3)*20**. This complex formula adds the values in cells A3 and B3, and then multiplies the result by 20.

2. Press the **Enter** key. The formula results in the value 7600, which appears in cell D3.

STEP-BY-STEP 4.2 Continued

3. Click cell **E3**, and then type **=A3+B3*20**. This formula is the same as the one you entered in cell D3, but without the parentheses. The lack of parentheses changes the order of evaluation and the resulting value.

4. Press the **Enter** key. As you see in cell E3, the formula results in the value 4921. This differs from the formula results in cell D3 because Excel multiplied the value in cell B3 by 20 before adding the value in cell A3. In cell D3, Excel added the values in cells A3 and B3, and then multiplied the sum by 20.

5. Save the workbook, and leave it open for the next Step-by-Step.

Editing Formulas

You cannot enter a formula with an incorrect structure in Excel. If you attempt to do so, a dialog box appears, explaining the error and providing a possible correction. You can accept that correction or choose to correct the formula yourself. For example, if you enter a formula with an opening parenthesis but no closing parenthesis, a dialog box appears, as shown in Figure 4-3, indicating that Excel found an error and proposing a correction that adds a closing parenthesis to the formula. Click Yes to accept the proposed correction. Click No to see a description of the error in another dialog box, and then click OK to return to the formula. You can correct the formula by editing it directly in the worksheet cell or by clicking in the formula bar.

FIGURE 4-3
Formula error message

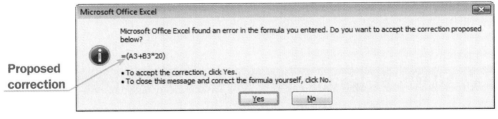

Proposed correction

Although Excel checks that the formula has the correct structure, it does not check that the formula contains the correct values or cell references. If you discover that you need to make a correction, you can edit the formula. Click the cell with the formula you want to edit. Press the F2 key or double-click the cell to enter editing mode. Move the insertion point as needed to edit the entry. Then, press the Enter key or click the Enter button on the formula bar to enter the formula.

> **Did You Know?**
>
> When you move the pointer into the formula bar or edit directly in a worksheet cell, the pointer changes to an I-beam.

S TEP-BY-STEP 4.3

1. Click cell **E3**. The formula is shown in the formula bar.

2. In the formula bar, click after = (the equal sign).

3. Type **(** (an opening parenthesis). You will intentionally leave out the closing parenthesis.

4. Press the **Enter** key. The dialog box shown in Figure 4-3 indicates that Excel found an error and offers a possible correction.

5. Read the message, and then click **No**. You will correct the error yourself. A dialog box appears, describing the specific error Excel found, as shown in Figure 4-4.

FIGURE 4-4
Formula error description message

Description
of the error
Excel found
in the
formula

6. Read the message, and then click **OK**.

7. Move the insertion point in the formula bar between the 3 and the *.

8. Type **)** (a closing parenthesis).

9. Press the **Enter** key. The value changes to 7600.

10. Save the workbook, and leave it open for the next Step-by-Step.

...ng *Relative, Absolute, and Mixed Cell*

...*:es*

...types of cell references are used in formulas: relative, absolute, and mixed. A relative
...ference adjusts to its new location when copied or moved. For example, when the formula ... +A4 is copied from cell A5 to cell B5, the formula changes to =B3+B4, as shown in
Figure 4-5. How does Excel know how to change a relative cell reference? It creates the same relationship between the cells in the new location. In other words, the formula =A3+A4 in cell A5
instructs Excel to add the two cells directly above it. When you move this formula to another cell,
such as cell B5, Excel uses that same instruction: to add the two cells directly above the cell with
the formula. Notice that only the cell references change; the operators remain the same.

FIGURE 4-5
Relative cell references

Original
formula with
relative
references

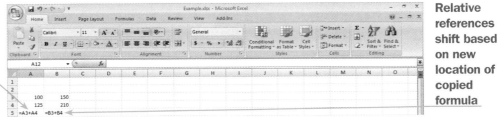

Relative
references
shift based
on new
location of
copied
formula

Absolute cell references do not change when copied or moved to a new cell. To create an
absolute cell reference, you insert a dollar sign ($) before the column letter and before the row
number. For example, when the formula =$A$3+$A$4 in cell A5 is copied to cell B7, the formula
remains unchanged, as shown in Figure 4-6.

FIGURE 4-6
Absolute cell references

Original
formula with
absolute
references

Absolute
references
remain
unchanged in
new location
of copied
formula

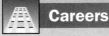
Careers

Engineers use Excel worksheets to perform complex calculations in areas such as
construction, transportation, and manufacturing. For example, Excel worksheets are
used to fit equations to data, interpolate between data points, solve simultaneous
equations, evaluate integrals, convert units, and compare economic alternatives.

Cell references that contain both relative and absolute references are called mixed cell references. When formulas with mixed cell references are copied or moved, the row or column references preceded by a dollar sign do not change; the row or column references not preceded by a dollar sign adjust to match the cell to which they are moved. As shown in Figure 4-7, when the formula =A$3+A$4 is copied from cell A5 to cell B7, the formula changes to =B$3+B$4.

FIGURE 4-7
Mixed cell references

Original
formula with
mixed
references
(relative
column
references
and absolute
row
references)

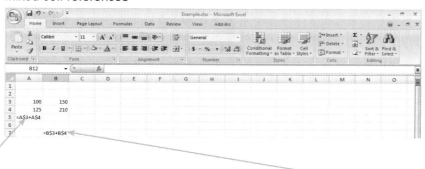

Relative
column
references
shift based
on new
location
of copied
formula;
absolute row
references
remain
unchanged

STEP-BY-STEP 4.4

1. Click cell **D3**. The formula =(A3+B3)*20 (shown in the formula bar) contains only relative cell references.

2. Drag the fill handle to cell **D4** to copy the formula from cell D3 to cell D4.

3. Click cell **D4**. The value in cell D4 is 15440, and the formula in the formula bar is =(A4+B4)*20. The operators in the formula remain the same, but the relative cell references change to reflect the new location of the formula.

4. Click cell **D5**, type **=$A$3*($B$3–200)**, and then press the **Enter** key. The value in cell D5 is 5499. The formula contains absolute cell references, which are indicated by the dollar signs that precede the row and column references.

> **Extra for Experts**
>
> You can press the F4 key to cycle a selected cell reference from a relative reference to an absolute reference to a mixed reference with an absolute row to a mixed reference with an absolute column and back to a relative reference.

5. Copy the formula in cell **D5** to cell **D6**. The value in cell D6 is 5499, the same as in cell D5.

6. Click cell **D5** and look at the formula in the formula bar.

7. Click cell **D6** and look at the formula in the formula bar. The formula in cell D5 is exactly the same as the formula in cell D6, because the formula you copied from cell D5 contains absolute cell references.

8. Click cell **E4**, type **=$A$4+B4**, and then press the **Enter** key. This formula contains mixed cell references (relative and absolute). The value in cell E4 is 772.

9. Copy the formula in cell **E4** to cell **E5**, and then click cell **E5**. The relative cell reference B4 changes to B5, but the absolute reference $A$4 stays the same. The value in cell E5 is 588.

STEP-BY-STEP 4.4 Continued

10. Copy the formula in cell **E5** to cell **F5**, and then click cell **F5**. The relative cell reference B5 changes to C5, but the absolute reference $A$4 stays the same. The value in cell F5 is 19113.

11. Click cell **A8**, and then enter your name. Save, print, and close the workbook.

Creating Formulas Quickly

So far, you have created formulas by typing the formula or editing an existing formula. You can also create formulas quickly by using the point-and-click method and the Sum button.

Using the Point-and-Click Method

Earlier, you constructed formulas by typing the entire formula directly in a worksheet cell. You can include cell references in a formula more quickly by using the point-and-click method to click each cell, rather than typing cell references. The point-and-click method is particularly helpful when you need to enter long formulas that contain multiple cell references.

To use the point-and-click method, simply click the cell instead of typing the cell reference. For example, to use the point-and-click method to enter the formula =A3+B3, click the cell in which you want to enter the formula, press =, click cell A3, press +, click cell B3, and then press the Enter key.

STEP-BY-STEP 4.5

1. Open the **Drink.xlsx** Data File.

2. Save the workbook as **Drink Sales** followed by your initials.

3. Click cell **F6**, type **=(** to begin the formula, and then click cell **B6**. A flashing blue border surrounds cell B6 to indicate it is selected, and its cell reference in the formula is also blue.

4. Type ***.** The flashing border disappears, but the cell border and reference remain blue.

5. Click cell **C6**. A flashing green border appears around cell C6, and its cell reference in the formula is the same color.

6. Type **)+(** and then click cell **D6**. The cell and formula reference are purple.

7. Type ***** and then click cell **E6**. The cell border and reference are red. Figure 4-8 shows the color-coded formula and cell references.

> **Did You Know?**
>
> A flashing colored border indicates that you can replace the current reference in the formula by clicking another cell or selecting a range. When the border is no longer flashing, the cell reference is "locked," and you must select the reference in the formula to replace it.

STEP-BY-STEP 4.5 Continued

Each cell reference in the formula is color-coded to match the selected cell border

FIGURE 4-8
Color-coded formula

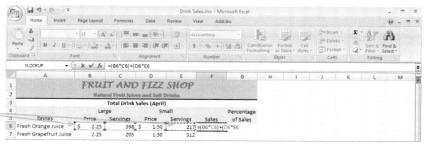

8. Type **)** and then press the **Enter** key. The amount $1,221.00 appears in cell F6.

9. Use the fill handle to copy the formula in cell **F6** to the range **F7:F11**. All the monthly sales are calculated for each type of drink, as shown in Figure 4-9.

FIGURE 4-9
Monthly drink sales

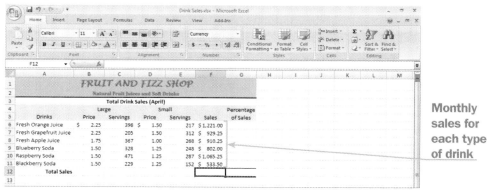

Monthly sales for each type of drink

10. Save the workbook, and leave it open for the next Step-by-Step.

Using the Sum Button

 Worksheet users frequently need to add long columns or rows of numbers. The **Sum button**, located in the Editing group on the Home tab of the Ribbon, makes this operation simple. To use the Sum button, click the cell where you want the total to appear, and then click the Sum button. Excel scans the worksheet to determine the most logical adjacent column or row of cells with numbers to add. An outline appears around the range it selects, and the range reference appears in the active cell. If you want to add the numbers in a different range, drag to select those cells. Press the Enter key to complete the formula. The active cell displays the sum.

Extra for Experts

Other commonly used functions find the AVERAGE, MAX (maximum), and MIN (minimum) of a range, as well as COUNT NUMBERS, to determine how many entries are included in the range. You can enter these from the Sum button menu. Click the cell in which you want to enter the function. On the Home tab, in the Editing group, click the arrow next to the Sum button. A menu lists these common functions. Click the function you want to use. Verify the range, and then press the Enter key.

The Sum button enters a formula with the SUM function, which is a shorthand way to specify adding numbers in a range. The SUM function that adds the numbers in the range D5:D17, for example, is =SUM(D5:D17). Functions are discussed in greater detail in the next lesson.

S TEP-BY-STEP 4.6

1. Click cell **F12**.

2. On the Home tab, in the Editing group, click the **Sum** button. The range F6:F11 is outlined, which is the range of cells you want to add. The formula =SUM(F6:F11) appears in the formula bar. See Figure 4-10.

FIGURE 4-10
Sum function in the formula

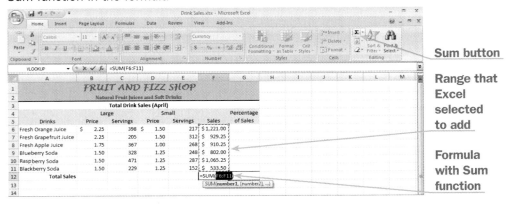

Sum button

Range that Excel selected to add

Formula with Sum function

3. Press the **Enter** key. Cell F12 displays $5,461.25, the sum of the numbers in column F.

4. Click cell **G6**, and then type **=**.

5. Click cell **F6**, and then type **/**.

6. Click cell **F12**, press the **F4** key, and then press the **Enter** key. You used an absolute reference to cell F12 because you want the cell reference to remain unchanged when you copy it to the rest of the range.

7. Copy the formula in cell **G6** to the range **G7:G11**. The Percentage of Sales is entered for all of the drinks.

8. Click cell **G12**. On the Home tab, in the Editing group, click the **Sum** button. Press the **Enter** key. The total percentage of sales is 100%. See Figure 4-11.

STEP-BY-STEP 4.6 Continued

FIGURE 4-11
Percentage of Sales calculated

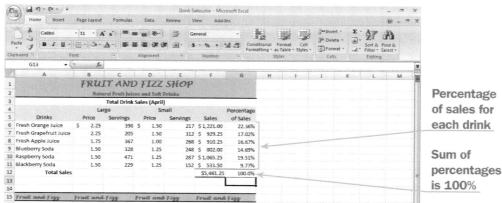

Percentage of sales for each drink

Sum of percentages is 100%

9. Save the workbook, and leave it open for the next Step-by-Step.

Previewing Calculations

Whenever you select a range, the status bar shows the results of common calculations for the selected cells. These summary calculations appear without your having to enter a formula. By default, Average, Count, and Sum appear in the status bar. You can also display Numerical Count, Minimum, and Maximum. Table 4-3 describes each of these options.

TABLE 4-3
Summary calculation options for the status bar

CALCULATION	DESCRIPTION
Average	Averages all the numbers in the selected cells
Count	Lists how many cells are selected
Numerical Count	Lists how many of the selected cells contain numbers
Minimum	Shows the smallest number in the selected cells
Maximum	Shows the largest number in the selected cells
Sum	Adds all the numbers in the selected cells

To display the default calculations in the status bar, just select a range. You can change which summary calculations appear in the status bar. Right-click the status bar to open the Customize Status Bar menu shown in Figure 4-12. Options that are preceded by a check mark appear in the status bar. Options without a check mark are hidden. You can choose which calculations you want to show or hide. Click a checked option to hide it, or click an unchecked option to show it. Click anywhere in the worksheet to close the menu. The checked summary calculations appear in the status bar for selected ranges until you change the displayed options.

FIGURE 4-12
Customize Status Bar menu

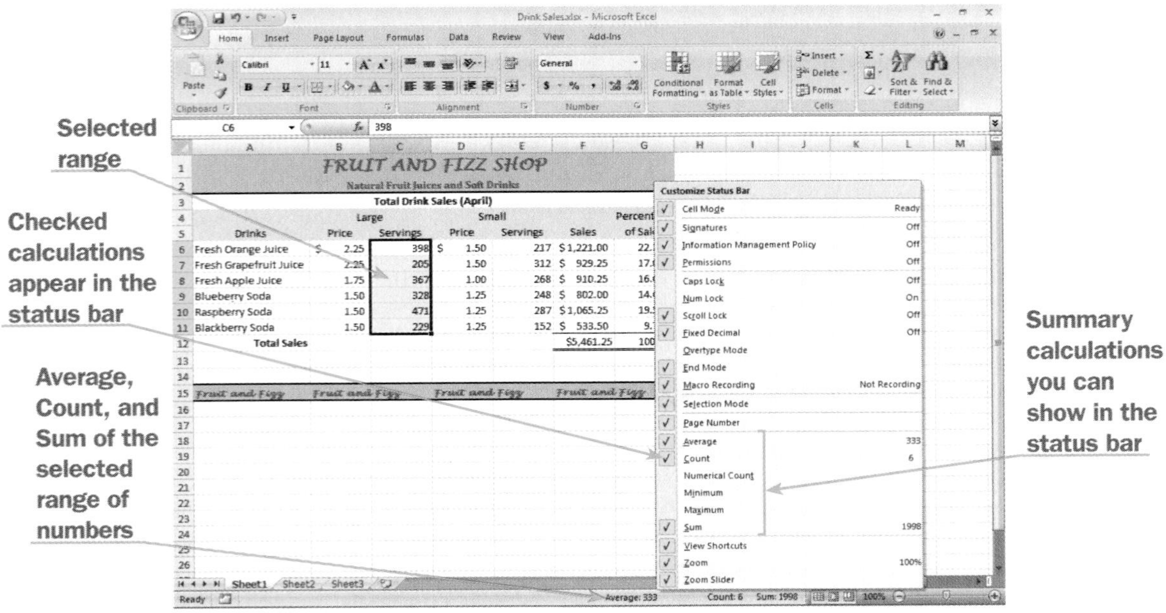

STEP-BY-STEP 4.7

1. Select the range **C6:C11**. Summary calculations for the large servings appear in the status bar, showing an Average of 333, a Count of 6, and the Sum of 1998.

2. Right-click the **status bar**. The Customize Status Bar menu appears, as shown in Figure 4-12.

3. Click **Minimum**. A check mark precedes Minimum on the menu, and the menu remains open so you can click additional options. The smallest number of large drinks served, 205, appears in the status bar.

4. Click **Minimum** to hide the calculation from the status bar, and then press the **Esc** key to close the menu.

5. Select the range **E6:E11**. Summary calculations for the small servings appear in the status bar, showing an Average of 247.333, a Count of 6, and the Sum of 1484.

Extra Challenge

You can use the summary calculations in the status bar to check formula results. Cell F12 contains the SUM function formula that adds the values in the range F6:F11. To confirm these results, select the range F6:F11, then compare the Sum value in the status bar with the value in cell F12. The sum in the status bar should equal the value in cell F12.

STEP-BY-STEP 4.7 Continued

6. Click cell **A13** to deselect the range.

7. Save the workbook, and leave it open for the next Step-by-Step.

Showing Formulas in the Worksheet

In previous Step-by-Steps, you viewed formulas in the formula bar or directly in worksheet cells as you typed or edited the formulas. After you enter the formulas, the cells show the formula results rather than the formulas themselves. Typically, this is what you want to view. However, when creating a work-sheet with many formulas, you may find it simpler to organize formulas and detect formula errors when all formulas are visible. To do this, click the Formulas tab on the Ribbon, and then click the Show Formulas button in the Formula Auditing group. The formulas replace the formula results in the work-sheet. If a cell does not contain a formula, the data entered in the cell remains displayed. The Show Formulas button remains selected until you click it again to redisplay the formula results. It can be helpful to print the worksheet showing formulas for reference.

> **Did You Know?**
>
> You can use also switch between showing formulas and showing formula results in a worksheet by pressing the Ctrl+` keys (the grave accent is located in the upper-left area of most standard keyboards).

Calculating Formulas Manually

Excel calculates formula results when you enter the formula and recalculates the results whenever the cells used in that formula change. However, the calculation and recalculation process can take a long time when a worksheet contains many formulas. When you need to edit a worksheet with many formulas, you can specify **manual calculation**, which lets you determine when Excel calculates the formulas.

The Formulas tab on the Ribbon contains all the buttons you need when working with manual calculations. To switch to manual calculation, click the Calculation Options but-ton in the Calculation group on the Formulas tab, and then click Manual. When you want to calculate the formula results for the entire workbook, click the Calculate Now button. To calculate the formula results for only the active worksheet, click the Calculate Sheet button. To return to automatic calculation, click the Calculation Options button in the Calculation group on the Formulas tab, and then click Automatic.

STEP-BY-STEP 4.8

1. Click the **Formulas** tab on the Ribbon. In the Formula Auditing group, click the **Show Formulas** button. All formulas appear in the worksheet cells instead of the formula results.

2. Scroll to the right as needed so that columns F and G appear on the screen.

3. On the Formulas tab, in the Calculation group, click the **Calculation Options** button. A menu of options appears, as shown in Figure 4-13.

FIGURE 4-13
Worksheet with formulas showing

Button is a toggle; click it again to redisplay the formula results

Text and numbers remain unchanged

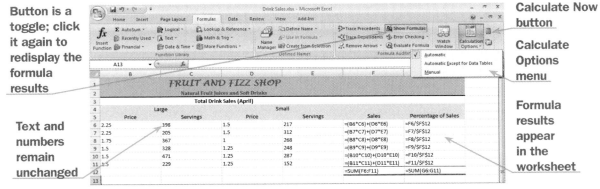

Calculate Now button

Calculate Options menu

Formula results appear in the worksheet

4. Click **Manual**. Automatic calculation is turned off.

5. Press the **Ctrl+`** keys. The formula results reappear.

6. Click cell **C6**, and then enter **402**. Click cell **C7**, and then enter **220**. Click cell **E10**, and then enter **305**. The worksheet values change, but Excel does not recalculate the formula results.

7. On the Formulas tab, in the Calculation group, click the **Calculate Now** button while watching the worksheet. Excel recalculates the formulas when you click the button. The total sales amount in cell F12 is $5,526.50.

8. On the Formulas tab, in the Calculation group, click the **Calculation Options** button, and then click **Automatic**.

9. Insert a header with your name in the left section and the current date in the right section.

10. Save, print, and close the workbook.

Extra Challenge

In the *Drink Sales.xlsx* workbook, the current sales amount for large and small orange juices sold is $1230. Determine how many large orange juices must sell to achieve more than $1700 in sales. Do this by entering larger amounts in cell C6. When you have determined the amount, close the workbook without saving.

SUMMARY

In this lesson, you learned:

■ Formulas are equations used to calculate values in a cell, based on values referenced in other cells of the worksheet. Each formula begins with an equal sign and contains at least two operands and one operator.

■ Formulas can include more than one operator. The order of evaluation determines the sequence used to calculate the value of a formula.

■ You cannot enter a formula with an incorrect structure. Excel can correct the error for you, or you can choose to edit it yourself. To edit a formula, click the cell with the formula and then make changes in the formula bar. You can also double-click a formula and then edit the formula directly in the cell.

■ Relative references adjust to a new location when copied or moved. Absolute references do not change, regardless of where they are copied or moved. Mixed references contain both relative and absolute references.

■ Formulas can be created quickly using the point-and-click method. With this method, you insert a cell reference in a formula by clicking the cell rather than typing its column letter and row number.

■ The Sum button in the Editing group on the Home tab inserts a formula with the SUM function, which adds the value of cells in the specified range.

■ The status bar shows a preview of common formulas, including Average, Count, and Sum, when you select a range of cells. You can choose which formula previews to show or hide.

■ You can view the formulas in a worksheet, instead of the formula results, by clicking the Show Formulas button in the Formula Auditing group on the Formulas tab.

■ Excel calculates formula results in a worksheet when you enter the formula, and recalculates the results whenever the cells used in that formula change. When you need to edit a worksheet with many formulas, you can click the Calculations Options button in the Calculation group on the Formulas tab, and then click Manual. When you want to calculate the formula results, click the Calculate Now button.

VOCABULARY *Review*

Define the following terms:		
Absolute cell reference	Operand	Point-and-click method
Formula	Operator	Relative cell reference
Manual calculation	Order of evaluation	Sum button
Mixed cell reference		

REVIEW *Questions*

TRUE/FALSE

Circle T if the statement is true or F if the statement is false.

T   F   1. An operand is a constant or cell reference used in formulas.

T   F   2. In a formula, subtraction is performed before multiplication.

T   F   3. In a formula, operations within parentheses are performed after operations outside parentheses.

T   F   4. An absolute reference does not change if the formula is copied or moved.

T   F   5. Manual calculation lets you determine when Excel calculates formula results.

WRITTEN QUESTIONS

Write a brief answer to the following questions.

1. Which operator has the highest priority in the order of evaluation in a worksheet formula?

2. What type of cell reference adjusts to its new location when it is copied or moved?

3. Write an example of a formula with a mixed cell reference.

4. Explain how to enter the formula =C4+B5+D2 using the point-and-click method.

5. How do you display formulas in the worksheet cells rather than the formula results?

PROJECTS

PROJECT 4-1

Match the letter of the worksheet formula in Column 2 to the description of the worksheet operation performed by the formula in Column 1.

Column 1	**Column 2**
_____ 1. Adds the values in cells A3 and A4	**A.** =A3/(27+A4)
_____ 2. Subtracts the value in cell A4 from the value in cell A3	**B.** =A3/27+A4
_____ 3. Multiplies the value in cell A3 times 27	**C.** =A3^27/A4
_____ 4. Divides the value in cell A3 by 27	**D.** =A3–A4
_____ 5. Raises the value in cell A3 to the 27th power	**E.** =A3/27
_____ 6. Divides the value in cell A3 by 27, and then adds the value in cell A4	**F.** =A3^27
_____ 7. Divides the value in cell A3 by the result of 27 plus the value in cell A4	**G.** =(A3*27)/A4
_____ 8. Multiplies the value in cell A3 times 27, and then divides the product by the value in cell A4	**H.** =A3+A4
	I. =A3*(27/A4)
_____ 9. Divides 27 by the value in cell A4, and then multiplies the result by the value in cell A3	**J.** =A3*27
_____ 10. Raises the value in A3 to the 27th power, and then divides the result by the value in A4	

 ## PROJECT 4-2

1. Open the **Results.xlsx** Data File.

2. Save the workbook as **Results of Formulas** followed by your initials.

3. Enter formulas in the specified cells that perform the operations listed below. After you enter each formula, write the resulting value in the space provided.

Resulting Value	Cell	Operation
_____ a.	C3	Add the values in cells A3 and B3.
_____ b.	C4	Subtract the value in cell B4 from the value in cell A4.
_____ c.	C5	Multiply the value in cell A5 by the value in cell B5.
_____ d.	C6	Divide the value in cell A6 by the value in cell B6.
_____ e.	B7	Sum the values in the range B3:B6.
_____ f.	D3	Add the values in cells A3 and B3, and then multiply by 3.
_____ g.	D4	Add the values in cells A3 and A4, and then multiply by cell B3.
_____ h.	D5	Copy the formula in cell D4 to cell D5.
_____ i.	D6	Subtract the value in cell B6 from the value in cell A6, and then divide by 2.
_____ j.	D7	Divide the value in cell A6 by 2, and then subtract the value in cell B6.

4. In cell A1, enter your name. Save, print, and close the workbook.

PROJECT 4-3

1. Open the **Zoo.xlsx** Data File.

2. Save the workbook as **Zoo Fundraiser** followed by your initials.

3. In cells D6, D7, D8, and D9, enter formulas that multiply the values in column B by the values in column C.

4. In cell D10, enter a formula to sum the totals in the range D6:D9.

5. In cell D11, enter a formula to calculate a 7% sales tax of the subtotal in cell D10.

6. In cell D12, enter a formula to add the subtotal and sales tax.

7. Change the worksheet to manual calculation.

8. Format the range D6:D12 in the Accounting number format. The worksheet is ready to accept customer data.

9. A customer purchases two tiger T-shirts, three dolphin T-shirts, one sweatshirt, and four coffee mugs. Enter these quantities in column C and press the F9 key to calculate.

10. Verify the formulas to ensure you have entered them correctly. If any of the formulas are incorrect, edit them and recalculate the worksheet. Repeat this process until you are confident that the worksheet is calculating results as intended.

11. Insert a footer with your name in the left section and the current date in the right section.

12. Save the workbook, print the customer's invoice, and then close the workbook.

PROJECT 4-4

1. Open the **Investment.xlsx** Data File.

2. Save the workbook as **Investment Record** followed by your initials.

3. In cells D6 through D8, enter formulas to calculate the values of the stocks. The formulas should multiply the number of shares in column B by the price of the shares in column C.

4. In cells D10 and D11, enter formulas to calculate the values of the mutual funds. As with the stocks, the formulas should multiply the number of shares in column B by the price of the shares in column C.

5. In cell D12, enter a formula that sums the values in cells D4 through D11. Format cell D12 by adding a Top and Double Bottom Border.

6. In cell E4, enter the formula **=D4/$D$12**. This formula determines the percentage of each investment value with respect to the total investment value.

7. Copy the formula in cell E4 to the ranges E6:E8 and E10:E11. Notice that the absolute reference to cell D12 in the formula remains unchanged as you copy the formula.

8. In cell E12, enter a formula that sums the percentages in cells E4 through E11. Format cell E12 by adding a Top and Double Bottom Border.

9. Save the workbook.

10. Change the worksheet to manual calculation in preparation for updating the investment values.

11. Enter the following updated share price amounts in the appropriate cells:

Investment	Price
MicroCrunch Corp.	$16.25
Ocean Electronics, Inc.	$21.25
Photex, Inc.	$13.50
Prosperity Growth Fund	$ 6.50
Lucrative Mutual Fund	$18.00

12. Perform the manual calculation.

13. Insert a footer with your name in the left section and the current date in the right section.

14. Save, print, and close the workbook.

 PROJECT 4-5

1.   Open the **Prairie.xlsx** Data File.

2.   Save the workbook as **Prairie Development** followed by your initials.

3.   Before considering other factors, the cost of a home is approximately $105 per square foot. In cell D5, enter a formula that multiplies the amount of square footage in cell B5 by the value per square foot in cell C5.

4.   The cost of a home is increased by $3,500 for each bathroom in the house. In cell D6, enter a formula that multiplies the number of bathrooms in cell B6 by the value per bathroom in cell C6.

5.   The cost of a home is increased by $3,250 for each car garage. In cell D7, enter a formula that multiplies the number of car garages in cell B7 by the value per car garage in cell C7.

6.   The cost of a home is increased by $3,000 if the house is located on a cul-de-sac. In cell D8, enter a formula that calculates the increase in value in cell C8 if 1 is entered in cell B8.

7.   The cost of a home is increased by $6,000 if the house has a swimming pool. In cell D9, enter a formula that calculates the increase in value in cell C9 if 1 is entered in cell B9.

8.   In cell D10, use the Sum button to calculate the sum of the numbers in the range D5:D9.

9.   A potential buyer inquires about the price of a home with the following qualities:

Square feet:	2000
Number of bathrooms:	3
Number of car garages:	2
On a cul-de-sac?	No
With a swimming pool?	Yes

In the range B5:B9, enter this data to determine the estimated price of the house.

10.   Insert a footer with your name in the left section and the current date in the right section.

11.   Save, print, and close the workbook.

CRITICAL *Thinking*

 ACTIVITY 4-1

You have been offered three jobs, each with a different salary. You know the gross pay (the amount before taxes), but not your net pay (the amount after taxes have been taken out). Assume you will have to pay 10% income tax and 7% Social Security tax. Develop a worksheet with formulas to determine your net pay. The format should be similar to that shown in Figure 4-14.

FIGURE 4-14
Format for net worksheet

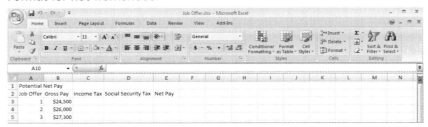

Your worksheet should include the following:

■ In the range C3:C5, formulas that multiply the gross pay in column B by .10.

■ In the range D3:D5, formulas that multiply the gross pay in column B by .07.

■ In the range E3:E5, formulas that subtract the amounts in columns C and D from the amount in column B.

Format the worksheet appropriately and attractively. Insert a header with your name and the current date. Save the workbook as **Job Offer** followed by your initials. Then print and close the workbook.

 ACTIVITY 4-2

One of the most difficult aspects of working with formulas in a worksheet is getting them to calculate the proper value after they are copied or moved. This requires an understanding of the differences between relative and absolute cell references. Research the differences between absolute and relative cell references in the Excel Help system. Write a brief explanation of the differences in your own words, and give an example of a situation in which you would use each type of cell reference. List the name(s) of the Help topics you used for reference.

USING FUNCTIONS

What Are Functions?

In the previous lesson, you created formulas that used cell references and constants. A formula can also contain a function. A function is a shorthand way to write an equation that performs a calculation. For example, the SUM function adds values in a range of cells. Functions often simplify formulas that are long or complex. Excel includes functions to perform complex calculations in specialized areas of mathematics, including statistics, logic, trigonometry, accounting, and finance. Function formulas are also used to display and determine dates and times.

A formula with a function has three parts: an equal sign, a function name, and at least one argument. The equal sign identifies the cell contents as a formula. The function name identifies the operation to be performed. The argument is the value the function uses to perform a calculation, including a number, text, or a cell reference that acts as an operand. The argument follows the function name and is enclosed in parentheses. If a function contains more than one argument, commas separate the arguments.

Equal sign → **=SUM(F6:F11)**
Function name ↗   ↖ Argument

In the previous lesson, you used the Sum button to enter a formula with the SUM function, =SUM(F6:F11). The equal sign specifies that the cell entry is a formula. The function name SUM identifies the operation. Parentheses enclose the argument, which is the range of cells to add—in this case, cells F6 through F11. The function provides a simpler and faster way to enter the formula =F6+F7+F8+F9+F10+F11.

Entering Formulas with Functions

To enter a formula with a function, you need to do the following. First, start the formula with an equal sign. Second, select the function you want to use. Third, enter the arguments. Finally, enter the completed formula. The results appear in the cell.

Because Excel includes so many functions, the best way to select a function is from the Insert Function dialog box. Click the Insert Function button on the Formula Bar to open the Insert Function dialog box. From this dialog box, you can browse all of the available functions to select the one you want. First, click a category in the Or select a category box, and then click the function you want in the Select a function box. A brief description of the selected function appears near the bottom of the dialog box, as shown in Figure 5-1. Click OK. The Function Arguments dialog box then appears.

> ### Did You Know?
>
> If you know the function you want to enter, you can click the appropriate category button in the Function Library group on the Formulas tab of the Ribbon. Then, click the function you want in the menu that appears. The Function Arguments dialog box appears.

FIGURE 5-1
Insert Function dialog box

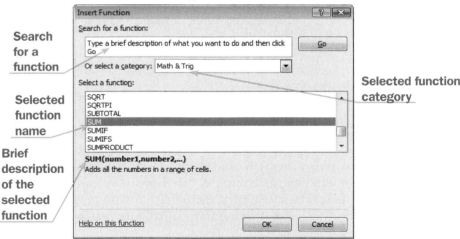

The Function Arguments dialog box, shown in Figure 5-2, provides a description of each argument you need to enter for the selected function. When an argument requires a cell or range, you can choose one of two ways to enter the reference. You can type the range directly in the appropriate argument box of the Function Arguments dialog box. Or, you can click in the appropriate argument box and then select the cell or range directly in the worksheet. When you select a range in the worksheet, the dialog box shrinks to show only the title bar and the argument box, so you can see more of the worksheet. It expands to the full size when you release the mouse button. You can also click the Collapse Dialog Box button at the end of

an argument box to shrink the dialog box so only its title bar and the argument box are displayed, and then click the Expand Dialog Box button to return the Function Arguments dialog box to its full size. After all the arguments are complete, click OK. The function is entered in the active cell.

FIGURE 5-2
Function Arguments dialog box

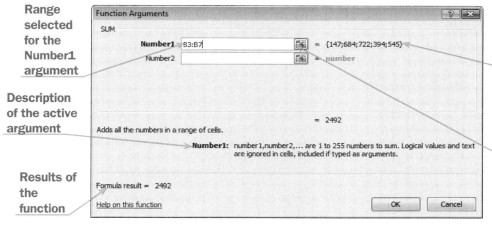

Entering a Function Directly in a Cell Using Formula AutoComplete

You can also enter a formula with a function directly in a cell by typing an equal sign, the function name, and the argument. **Formula AutoComplete** helps you enter a formula with a valid function name and arguments, as shown in Figure 5-3. As you begin to type the function name, a list of function names appears below the active cell. The functions listed match the letters you have typed. For example, when you type *=s*, all functions that begin with the letter s appear in the list box, such as SEARCH, SECON, and SERISSUM. When you type *=su*, the list narrows to show only functions that begin with the letters *su*, such as SUBSTITUTE, SUBTOTAL, and SUM. Continue typing until you see the function you want. Then, double-click the name of the function you want to use. The function and its arguments appear in a ScreenTip below the cell. You can use the ScreenTip as a guide to enter the necessary arguments.

FIGURE 5-3
Formula AutoComplete

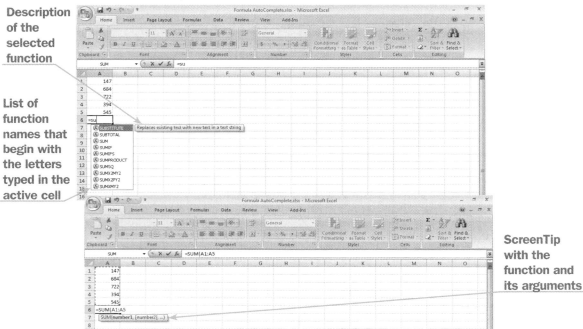

Description of the selected function

List of function names that begin with the letters typed in the active cell

ScreenTip with the function and its arguments

STEP-BY-STEP 5.1

1. Open the **Functions.xlsx** Data File.

2. Save the workbook as **Functions Worksheet** followed by your initials.

3. Click cell **B10**.

STEP-BY-STEP 5.1 Continued

4. On the Formula Bar, click the **Insert Function** button. The Insert Function dialog box appears.

5. Next to the Or select a category box, click the **arrow**, and then click **Math & Trig**.

6. Scroll down the **Select a function** list, and then click **SUM**. The SUM function and a description of its purpose appear below the Select a function box, as shown in Figure 5-1.

7. Click **OK**. The Function Arguments dialog box appears with a range reference selected in the Number1 box. The Number1 argument is the range of cells whose values you want to add. Excel tried to "guess" which cells you want to add. You want to add a different range.

8. In the worksheet, select the range **B3:B7**. The Function Arguments dialog box collapses when you click a cell in the worksheet and expands when you release the mouse button. The value that will appear in cell B10, 2492, appears below the SUM function section and at the bottom of the dialog box, as shown in Figure 5-2.

9. Click **OK**. The formula in cell B10 is =SUM(B3:B7).

10. Save the workbook, and leave it open for the next Step-by-Step.

Extra for Experts

You can also use the SUM function to total the values stored in up to 255 non-adjacent cells or ranges. You enter additional ranges in the Number2 through Number255 boxes.

Did You Know?

You can also enter the formula with the SUM function in cell B10 by typing *=SUM(B3:B7)* or clicking the Sum button in the Editing group on the Home tab.

Types of Functions

Excel provides many functions you can use in formulas. Each function has a different purpose. The functions are organized by category, such as Math & Trig, Statistical, Financial, Logical, Date & Time, and Text. The next sections introduce some of the most common functions in each of these categories.

Mathematical and Trigonometric Functions

Mathematical functions and trigonometric functions manipulate quantitative data in a worksheet. Some mathematical operations, such as addition, subtraction, multiplication, and division, do not require functions. However, mathematical and trigonometric functions are particularly useful when you need to determine values such as logarithms, factorials, sines, cosines, tangents, and absolute values.

You already used a mathematical and trigonometric function when you created a formula with the SUM function. Table 5-1 describes two other mathematical functions, the square root and rounding functions, as well as a trigonometric function, the natural logarithm. Notice that the rounding operation requires two arguments, which are separated by a comma.

TABLE 5-1
Mathematical and trigonometric functions

FUNCTION	RETURNS
SQRT(number)	The square root of the number in the argument. For example, =SQRT(C4) returns the square root of the value in cell C4.
ROUND(number,num_digits)	The number in the first argument rounded to the number of decimal places designated in the second argument. For example, =ROUND(14.23433,2) returns 14.23, which rounds the number in the first argument to two decimal places. If the second argument is a negative number, the first argument is rounded to the left of the decimal point. For example, =ROUND(142.3433,–2) returns 100.
LN(number)	The natural logarithm of a number. For example, =LN(50) returns 1.69897.

STEP-BY-STEP 5.2

1. Click cell **B11**. On the Formula Bar, click the **Insert Function** button. The Insert Function dialog box appears.

2. Next to the Or select a category box, click the **arrow**, and then click **Math & Trig**, if it is not already selected.

3. Click the **Select a function** box, and then press the **S** key five times until *SQRT* is selected. Read the description of the function.

4. Click **OK**. The Function Arguments dialog box appears. Read the description of the argument.

5. In the Number box, type **B10**. You want to calculate the square root of the value in cell B10, which is 2492, as shown to the right of the Number box. The number that will appear in cell B11, 49.9199359, appears under the function and at the bottom of the dialog box next to Formula result =, as shown in Figure 5-4.

FIGURE 5-4
SQRT funtction arguments

Cell with the
number you
want the
square root for

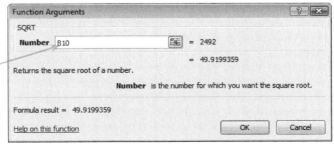

STEP-BY-STEP 5.2 Continued

6. Click **OK**. The formula entered in cell B11 is =SQRT(B10).

7. Click cell **B12**. On the Formula Bar, click the **Insert Function** button. The Insert Function dialog box appears with Math & Trig selected in the Or select a category box.

8. Click the **Select a function** box, and then press the **R** key five times to select *ROUND*.

9. Read the function's description. Click **OK**. The Function Arguments dialog box appears.

10. Read the description of the first argument. In the Number box, type **B11**.

11. Press the **Tab** key to place the insertion point in the Num_digits box. Read the description of the second argument.

12. Type **2**. The formula results appear below the function and at the bottom of the dialog box, as shown in Figure 5-5.

FIGURE 5-5
ROUND function arguments

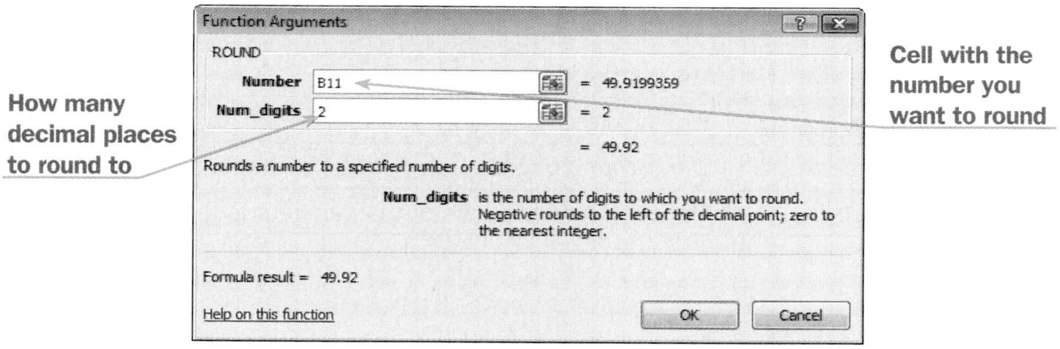

13. Click **OK**. The formula in cell B12 is =ROUND(B11,2), which displays the results of 49.92.

14. Save the workbook, and leave it open for the next Step-by-Step.

Statistical Functions

Statistical functions are used to describe large quantities of data. For example, statistical functions can determine the average, standard deviation, or variance of a range of data. Statistical functions can also determine the number of values in a range, the largest value in a range, and the smallest value in a range. Table 5-2 describes some of the statistical functions available in Excel. All the statistical functions contain a range for the argument. You can include multiple ranges by entering additional arguments. The range is the body of numbers the statistics will describe.

TABLE 5-2
Statistical functions

FUNCTION	RETURNS
AVERAGE(number1,number2...)	The average (or mean) of the range; for example, =AVERAGE(E4:E9) returns the average of the numbers in the range E4:E9
COUNT(value1,value2...)	The number of cells in the range that contain numbers; for example, =COUNT(D6:D21) returns 16 if all the cells in the range contain numbers
COUNTA(value1,value2...)	The number of cells in the range that contain data; for example, =COUNT(B4:B15) returns 11 if all the cells in the range contain data
MAX(number1,number2...)	The largest number in the range
MIN(number1,number2...)	The smallest number in the range
STDEV(number1,number2...)	The estimated standard deviation of the numbers in the range
VAR(number1,number2...)	The estimated variance of the numbers in the range

STEP-BY-STEP 5.3

1. Click cell **B15**. On the Formula Bar, click the **Insert Function** button. The Insert Function dialog box appears. You want to find the average of values in the range B3:B7.

2. Next to the Or select a category box, click the **arrow**, and then click **Statistical**. The Statistical functions appear in the Select a function box.

3. In the Select a function box, click **AVERAGE**, and then click **OK**. The Function Arguments dialog box appears.

4. Next to the Number1 box, click the **Collapse Dialog Box** button. The Function Arguments dialog box shrinks to its title bar and Number1 box.

5. In the worksheet, drag to select the range **B3:B7**. The range reference appears in the Number1 box, as shown in Figure 5-6.

> **Did You Know?**
>
> You can also enter a formula with the AVERAGE, COUNT, MAX, or MIN function in a selected cell by clicking the arrow next to the Sum button in the Editing group on the Home tab, clicking the function name in the list of functions, selecting the appropriate range, and then pressing the Enter key.

STEP-BY-STEP 5.3 Continued

FIGURE 5-6
Collapsed Function Arguments dialog box

Only the
Number1 box
is visible

Button to
expand the
dialog box to
its full size

6. Click the **Expand Dialog Box** button. The Function Arguments dialog box expands to its full size, as shown in Figure 5-7.

FIGURE 5-7
Expanded Function Arguments dialog box

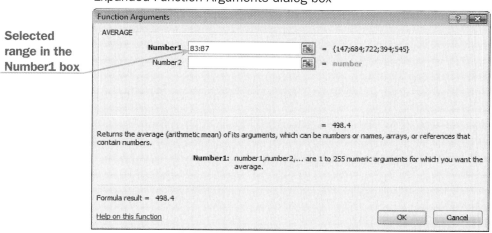

Selected
range in the
Number1 box

7. Click **OK**. The average of the values in the range B3:B7, which is 498.4, appears in cell B15.

8. Click cell **B16**. On the Formula Bar, click the **Insert Function** button. You want to find how many cells in the range B3:B7 contain numbers.

9. In the Or select a category box, click **Statistical**, if it is not already selected. In the Select a function box, double-click **COUNT**. The Function Arguments dialog box appears.

10. In the Value1 box, enter **B3:B7**, and then click **OK**. The number of cells in the range B3:B7 that contain numbers is 5.

11. Click cell **B17**, and then enter **=MAX(B3:B7)**. The largest number in the range B3:B7 is 722.

12. Click cell **B18**, and then enter **=MIN(B3:B7)**. The smallest number in the range B3:B7 is 147.

13. Click cell **B19**, and then enter **=STDEV(B3:B7)**. The standard deviation of the range B3:B7 is 235.0517.

14. Click cell **B20**, and then enter **=VAR(B3:B7)**. The variance of the range B3:B7 is 55249.3.

15. Save the workbook, and leave it open for the next Step-by-Step.

Financial Functions

Financial functions are used to analyze loans and investments. The primary financial functions are future value, present value, and payment, which are described in Table 5-3. Note that for these functions to return the correct value, the payment and the interest rate must have the same time period. For example, the payment period is usually expressed in months, whereas interest rates are commonly expressed in years. So, if the payment period is monthly, you must divide the annual interest rate by 12 to determine the monthly rate.

TABLE 5-3
Financial functions

FUNCTION	RETURNS
FV(rate,nper,pmt,pv,type)	The future value of an investment based on equal payments (third argument), at a fixed interest rate (first argument), for a specified number of periods (second argument). (The fourth and fifth arguments for the present value of the investment and the timing of the payments are optional.) For example, =FV(.08,5,100) determines the future value of five $100 payments earning an 8% interest rate at the end of five years.
PV(rate,nper,pmt,fv,type)	The present value of a loan or an investment based on equal payments (third argument), at a fixed interest rate (first argument), for a specified number of payments (second argument). (The fourth and fifth arguments for the future value of the investment and the timing of the payments are optional.) For example, =PV(.1,5,500) displays the current value of five payments of $500 at a 10% interest rate.
PMT(rate,nper,pv,fv,type)	The equal payments needed to repay a loan (third argument), at a fixed interest rate (first argument), in a specified number of periods (second argument). (The fourth and fifth arguments for the future value of the loan and the timing of the payments are optional.) For example, =PMT(.01,36,10000) displays the monthly payment needed to repay a $10,000 loan at a 1% monthly interest rate (12% annual interest rate divided by 12 months) for 36 months (three years divided by 12 months).

 Careers

Scientists use Excel workbooks to help them as they conduct research. They record collected data in worksheets. Then they use statistical function formulas to analyze experimental results.

STEP-BY-STEP 5.4

1. Click cell **B24**, and then enter **.035**. The annual interest rate of 3.5% appears in the cell.

2. Click cell **B25**, and then enter **6**, which is the number of payment periods—one payment each year for six years.

3. Click cell **B26**, and then enter **–150**. The annual payment of $(150.00) appears in the cell. (A negative number indicates a payment, whereas a positive number indicates income. In this case, you use a negative number because you are making a payment to the bank.)

4. Click cell **B27**. On the Formula Bar, click the **Insert Function** button. The Insert Function dialog box appears.

5. Next to the Or select a category box, click the **arrow**, and then click **Financial**. In the Select a function box, click **FV**. Click **OK**.

6. In the Rate box, type **B24**, the cell with the annual interest rate. In the Nper box, type **B25**, the cell with the number of payment periods. In the Pmt box, type **B26**, the cell with the annual payment you plan to make (see Figure 5-8).

FIGURE 5-8
FV function arguments

Cell
references
entered
for each
argument

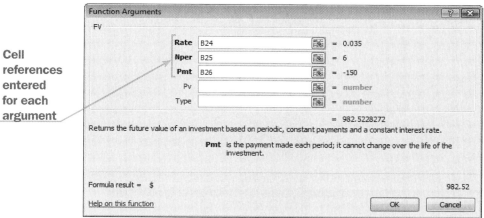

7. Click **OK**. As you can see in cell B27, the amount in the savings account will have grown to $982.52 after six years.

8. Click cell **B29**, and then enter **3**. The annual interest rate of 3.0% appears in the cell.

9. Click cell **B30**, and then enter **8**, which is the number of payment periods—one payment each year for eight years.

10. Click cell **B31**, and then enter **–210**. The annual payment of $(210) appears in the cell. (Remember, a negative number indicates a payment, whereas a positive number indicates income. In this case, you use a negative number because you are making a payment.)

STEP-BY-STEP 5.4 Continued

11. Click cell **B32**, and then enter **=PV(B29,B30,B31)**, using Formula AutoComplete to help you enter the function accurately. The delayed payments are more profitable because the present value, $1,474.14, is greater than the immediate lump sum of $1,200.

12. Click cell **B34**, and then enter **1**. The monthly interest rate of 1.0% appears in the cell. The monthly interest rate is determined by dividing the annual interest rate of 12% by 12 months.

13. Click cell **B35**, and then enter **=5*12** to determine the number of monthly payment periods (the number of years, 5, multiplied by 12 months). The number of monthly payment periods, 60, appears in the cell.

14. Click cell **B36**, and then enter **5000**, which is the amount of the loan.

15. Click cell **B37**, and then enter **=PMT(B34,B35,B36)**, using Formula AutoComplete to help you enter the function accurately. The monthly payment ($111.22) appears in the cell in red. The number is negative to indicate that it is a payment.

16. Click cell **B38**, and then enter **=(B37*B35)+B36** to determine the interest you will pay over the life of the loan. The formula multiples the monthly payment returned by the PMT function in cell B37 by the number of monthly payments calculated in cell B35, and then adds the loan amount in cell B36. Because the payments are negative, you need to add the loan amount to calculate the difference between the total payments and the total principal. Under the conditions of this loan, you will pay a total of $1,673.33 in interest over the life of the loan, as shown in Figure 5-9.

FIGURE 5-9
Financial functions

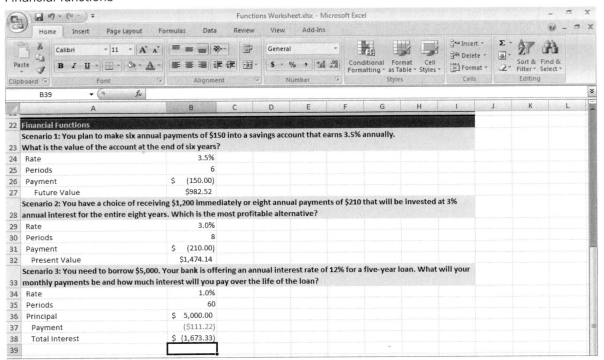

17. Insert a header with your name and the current date. Save, print, and close the workbook.

Logical Functions

 Logical functions, such as the IF function, display text or values if certain conditions exist. In the IF function, the first argument sets a condition for comparison, called a *logical test*. The second argument determines the value that appears in the cell if the logical test is true. The third argument determines the value that appears in the cell if the logical test is false.

> **Did You Know?**
>
> You must use quotation marks to enclose the text you want the IF function to return in the second and third arguments. For example, =IF(B10<100,"Low Result","High Result").

For example, a teacher might use the IF function to determine whether a student has passed or failed a course. The formula =IF(C4>60,"PASS","FAIL") returns *PASS* if the value in cell C4 is greater than 60. The formula returns *FAIL* if the value in cell C4 is not greater than 60.

Table 5-4 describes the IF, AND, NOT, OR, and IFERROR functions.

TABLE 5-4
Logical functions

FUNCTION	RETURNS
IF(logical_test,value_if_true,value_if_false)	One value if the condition in the logical test is true, and another value if the condition in the logical test is false; for example, =IF(2+2=4, Over, Under) returns *Over*
AND(logical1,logical2,…)	TRUE if all of the arguments are true, and FALSE if any or all of the arguments are false; for example, =AND(1+1=2,1+2=3) returns *TRUE*, but =AND(1+1=2,1+2=4) returns *FALSE*
OR(logical1,logical2,…)	TRUE if any of the arguments are true, and FALSE if none of the arguments is true; for example, =OR(1+1=2,1+2=3) returns *TRUE*, and =OR(1+1=2,1+2=4) returns *TRUE*, but =OR(1+1=3,1+2=4) returns *FALSE*
NOT(logical)	TRUE if the argument is false, and FALSE if the argument is true; for example, =NOT(2+2=1) returns *TRUE*, but =NOT(2+2=4) returns *FALSE*
IFERROR(value,value_if_error)	The formula results if the first argument contains no error, and the specified value if the argument is incorrect; for example, =IFERROR(2+2=1, "Error in calculation") returns *Error in calculation*

S TEP-BY-STEP 5.5

1. Open the **Occidental.xlsx** Data File.

2. Save the workbook as **Occidental Optical** followed by your initials.

3. Click cell **D6**, and then type **=IF(B6<5,25,0)**. This formula returns 25 (the shipping fee) if the quantity in cell B6 is less than 5. If the quantity in cell B6 is not less than 5, then the formula returns 0.

STEP-BY-STEP 5.5 Continued

4. Press the **Enter** key. This order has no shipping fee because the order quantity is 6, more than the 5 cartons needed for free shipping.

5. Copy the formula in cell **D6** to the range **D7:D15**, and then click cell **A18**. The shipping fee is calculated for all the orders, as shown in Figure 5-10.

FIGURE 5-10
Shipping fee calculated with the IF function

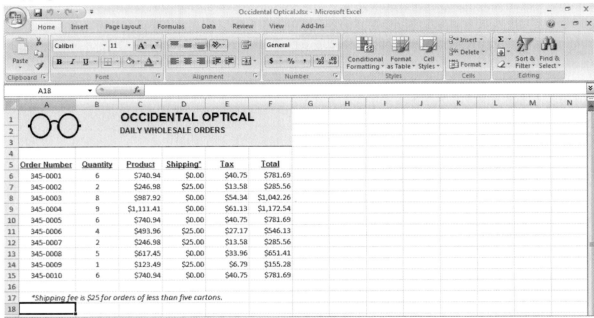

6. Insert a footer that includes your name and the current date. Save, print, and close the workbook.

Date and Time Functions

Functions can also be used to insert dates and times in a worksheet. For example, date and time functions can be used to convert serial numbers to a month, a day, or a year. A date function can also be used to insert the current date or the current date and time. Table 5-5 describes the DATE, NOW, and TODAY functions.

TABLE 5-5
Date and time functions

FUNCTION	RETURNS
DATE(year,month,day)	The date specified in the year, month, and day arguments, which are entered as numbers. For example, =DATE(2010,5,23) returns 5/23/2010.
NOW()	The current date and time based on the computer's date and time settings. For example, =NOW() returns the current date and time, such as 5/23/2010 22:05. This function has no arguments.
TODAY()	The current date based on the computer's date setting and formatted as a date. For example, =TODAY() returns the current date, such as 5/23/2010. This function has no arguments.

Text Functions

Text functions are used to format and work with cell contents. A text function can be used to convert text in a cell to all uppercase or lowercase letters. Text functions can also be used to repeat data contained in another cell. These functions are described in Table 5-6.

TABLE 5-6
Text functions

FUNCTION	OPERATION
PROPER(text)	Converts the first letter of each word in the specified cell to uppercase and the rest to lowercase.
LOWER(text)	Converts all letters in the specified cell to lowercase.
UPPER(text)	Converts all letters in the specified cell to uppercase.
SUBSTITUTE(text,old_text,new_text,instance_num)	Replaces existing text (the second argument) in a specified cell (the first argument) with new text (the third argument). If you omit the optional fourth argument, instance_num, every occurrence of the text is replaced. For example, =SUBSTITUTE(C2,"Income","Revenue") replaces every instance of the word Income in cell C2 with the word *Revenue*.
REPT(text,number_times)	Repeats the text (first argument) in the specified cell a specified number of times (second argument). For example, =REPT(B6,3) repeats the text in cell B6 three times.

STEP-BY-STEP 5.6

1. Open the **Finances.xlsx** Data File.

2. Click cell **A1**, and then replace the word *NAME* with your name.

3. Click cell **B13**, and then enter **=NOW()**. The current date and time appear in the cell.

4. Click cell **B13**. Click the **Home** tab on the Ribbon. In the Number group, next to the Number Format box, click the **arrow**, and then click **General**. The date changes to the serial number Excel uses to express the current date and time.

5. On the Home tab, in the Number group, next to the Number Format box, click the **arrow**, and then click **Short Date**. The date changes to the form 5/23/2010.

6. On the Quick Access Toolbar, click the **Undo** button twice. The current date and time reappear in cell B13.

7. Click cell **B14**. You want to repeat the text in cell A1 in cell B14.

8. Click the **Formulas** tab on the Ribbon. In the Function Library group, click the **Text** button, and then click **REPT**. The Function Arguments dialog box appears.

9. In the Text box, enter **A1**. In the Number_times box, enter **1**. The contents of cell A1 will be repeated one time in cell B14.

10. Click **OK**. The title in cell A1 is repeated in cell B14.

11. Save the workbook using the contents of cell B14 as the file name. Your screen should look similar to Figure 5-11.

> **Extra Challenge**
>
> Edit the contents of cell A1 by replacing your name with a friend's name. The REPT function in cell B14 updates the contents in that cell. On the Quick Access Toolbar, click the Undo button to return to your name.

FIGURE 5-11
Date & Time and Text functions

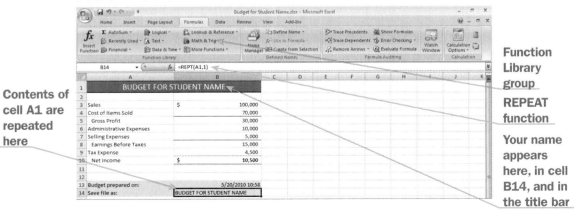

Contents of cell A1 are repeated here

Function Library group

REPEAT function

Your name appears here, in cell B14, and in the title bar

12. Print and close the workbook.

SUMMARY

In this lesson, you learned:

■ A function is a shorthand way to write an equation that performs a calculation. A formula with a function has three parts: an equal sign, a function name, and at least one argument, which acts as an operand.

■ The best way to select a function is from the Insert Function dialog box. The Function Arguments dialog box provides a description of each argument you enter for the function.

■ When you type a formula with a function directly in a worksheet cell, Formula AutoComplete helps you enter a formula with a valid function name and arguments.

■ Functions can be used to perform mathematical, statistical, financial, and logical operations. They can also be used to insert and calculate dates and times and to format text.

VOCABULARY *Review*

Define the following terms:

Argument	Function	Statistical functions
Date and time functions	Logical functions	Text functions
Financial functions	Mathematical functions	Trigonometric functions
Formula AutoComplete		

REVIEW *Questions*

TRUE/FALSE

Circle T if the statement is true or F if the statement is false.

T F 1. Formulas with functions have three parts: an equal sign, a function name, and an argument.

T F 2. The argument identifies the function to be performed.

T F 3. You select the function you want to use in the Insert Function dialog box.

T F 4. The NUMBER function returns the number of cells in the range identified in the argument that contain data.

T F 5. The IF function displays one value if the specified condition is true and a different value if the condition is false.

FILL IN THE BLANK

Complete the following sentences by writing the correct word or words in the blanks provided.

1. The _____ is enclosed in parentheses in a formula with a function.

2. The _____ dialog box specifies elements to be included in the function.

3. _____ functions manipulate quantitative data in a worksheet.

4. _____ functions describe large quantities of data, such as by determining the average, standard deviation, or variance of a range of data.

5. _____ functions are used to analyze loans and investments.

PROJECTS

PROJECT 5-1

Write the appropriate formula to perform each of the described operations. Refer to Tables 5-1 through 5-6 to help you determine the function and its arguments.

_____ 1. Determine the average of the values in the range B9:B45.

_____ 2. Determine the smallest value in the range S14:S90.

_____ 3. Determine the standard deviation of the values in the range K4:K27.

_____ 4. Determine the yearly payments on a $4,500 loan at 10% for 8 years.

_____ 5. Determine the value of a savings account at the end of 5 years, after making $450 yearly payments; the account earns 9%.

_____ 6. Round the value in cell D3 to the tenths place.

_____ 7. Determine the present value of a pension plan that will pay you 20 yearly payments of $5,000; the current rate of return is 7.5%.

_____ 8. Determine the square root of 275.

_____ 9. Determine the variance of the values in the range F9:F35.

_____10. Add all the values in the range F4:F19.

_____11. Determine how many cells in the range H7:H21 are filled with data.

_____12. Determine the largest value in the range E45:E92.

PROJECT 5-2

1. Open the **Test.xlsx** Data File.

2. Save the workbook as **Test Grades** followed by your initials.

3. In cell B25, enter a formula with a function to determine the number of students taking the examination.

4. In cell B26, enter a formula with a function to determine the average exam grade.

5. In cell B27, enter a formula with a function to determine the highest exam grade.

6. In cell B28, enter a formula with a function to determine the lowest exam grade.

7. In cell B29, enter a formula with a function to determine the standard deviation of the exam grades.

8. Format cells B26 and B29 to display one digit to the right of the decimal.

9. Insert a header with your name and the current date. Save, print, and close the workbook.

 PROJECT 5-3

1. Open the **National.xlsx** Data File.

2. Save the workbook as **National Bank** followed by your initials.

3. In cell B11, enter the PMT function to calculate the yearly payment for borrowers. The lending rate will be entered in cell B7, the term of the loan will be entered in cell B9, and the loan principal (or present value) will be entered in cell B5. (The formula results are *#DIV/0!*, indicating an error due to division by zero, because no data is entered in the argument's cell references.)

4. A potential borrower inquires about the payments on a $5,500 loan for four years. The current lending rate is 8%. Determine the yearly payment on the loan. (The number in cell B11 appears as a negative, because this amount must be paid.)

5. Insert a header with your name and the current date.

6. Print the portion of the worksheet that pertains to the loan (the range A1:C14) to give to the potential borrower.

7. In cell B24, enter the FV function to calculate the future value of periodic payments for depositors. The interest rate will be entered in cell B22, the term of the payments will be entered in cell B20, and the yearly payments will be entered in cell B18. (The formula results show *$0.00*, because no data is entered in the argument's cell references.)

8. A potential depositor is starting a college fund for her child. She inquires about the value of yearly deposits of $2,550 at the end of 15 years. The current interest rate is 4.5%. Determine the future value of the deposits. (Remember to enter the deposit as a negative because the depositor must pay this amount.)

9. Print the portion of the worksheet that pertains to the investment (the range A14:C26) to give to the potential depositor.

10. Save and close the workbook.

PROJECT 5-4

The Tucson Coyotes have just completed seven preseason professional basketball games. Coach Patterson will soon be entering a press conference in which he is expected to talk about the team's performance for the upcoming season. Coach Patterson wants to be well informed about player performance before entering the press conference.

Part 1

1. Open the **Team.xlsx** Data File.

2. Save the workbook as **Team Stats** followed by your initials.

3. In cell J6, enter a function that adds the values in the range B6:I6.

4. Copy the formula in cell J6 to the range J7:J12.

5. In cell J19, enter a function that adds the values in the range B19:I19.

6. Copy the formula in cell J19 to the range J20:J25.

7. In cell B13, enter a function that averages the game points in the range B6:B12.

8. In cell B14, enter a function that determines the standard deviation of the game points in the range B6:B12.

9. In cell B15, enter a function that counts the number of entries in the range B6:B12.

10. Copy the formulas in the range B13:B15 to the range C13:I15.

11. In cell B26, enter a function that averages the rebounds in the range B19:B25.

12. In cell B27, enter a function that determines the standard deviation of the rebounds in the range B19:B25.

13. In cell B28, enter a function that counts the number of entries made in the range B19:B25.

14. Copy the formulas in the range B26:B28 to the range C26:I28.

15. Insert a footer with your name and the current date. Save and print the workbook, and leave it open.

Part 2

Based on the Basketball Stats workbook you prepared, indicate in the blanks the names of the players who are likely to be mentioned in the following interview. When you have finished filling in the blanks, close the workbook.

Reporter: You have had a very successful preseason. Three players seem to be providing the leadership needed for a winning record.

Patterson: Basketball teams win by scoring points. It's no secret that we rely on (1) _____, (2) _____, and (3) _____ to get those points. All three average at least 10 points per game.

Reporter: One player seems to have a problem with consistency.

Patterson: (4) _____ has his good games and his bad games. He is a young player and we have been working with him. As the season progresses, I think you will find him to be a more reliable offensive talent.

(*Hint*: One indication of consistent scoring is the standard deviation. A high standard deviation might indicate high fluctuation of points from game to game. A low standard deviation might indicate that the scoring level is relatively consistent.)

Reporter: What explains the fact that (5) _____ is both an effective scorer and your leading rebounder?

Patterson: He is a perceptive player. When playing defense, he is constantly planning how to get the ball back to the other side of the court.

Reporter: Preseason injuries can be heartbreaking. How has this affected the team?

Patterson: (6) _____ has not played since being injured in the game against Kansas City. He is an asset to the team. We are still waiting to hear from the doctors whether he will be back soon.

Reporter: It is the end of the preseason. That is usually a time when teams make cuts. Of your healthy players, (7) _____ is the lowest scorer. Will you let him go before the beginning of the regular season?

Patterson: I don't like to speculate on cuts or trades before they are made. We'll just have to wait and see.

PROJECT 5-5

1. Open the **Golf.xlsx** Data File.

2. Save the workbook as **Golf Tryouts** followed by your initials. A player must average a score of less than 76 to qualify for the team.

3. In cell I5, enter a function that displays *Made* if the average score in cell H5 is less than 76 and *Cut* if the score is not less than 76. (*Hint*: The IF function has three arguments. The first argument is the logical test that determines whether the value in cell H5 is less than 76. The second argument is the text that appears if the statement is true. The third argument is the text that appears if the statement is false. Because the items to be displayed are words rather than numbers, they must be entered within quotation marks.)

4. Copy the formula from cell I5 to the range I6:I16.

5. In cell B21, enter a function that displays today's date.

6. Format cell B21 so that the date appears as the month followed by the day and year, such as March 14, 2010.

7. Click cell B22, and then enter your name. Save, print, and close the workbook.

PROJECT 5-6

You have worked for Xanthan Gum Corp. for several years and are now eligible for promotion. Promotions at Xanthan are determined by supervisor ratings and a written examination. To be promoted, employees must score an average of 80 or above in the following four categories:

- Supervisor rating of leadership potential
- Supervisor rating of understanding of duties
- Supervisor rating of willingness to work hard
- Written test score

After receiving your supervisor ratings, you prepare a worksheet to determine the minimum written test score you need to be promoted.

1. Open the **Xanthan.xlsx** Data File.

2. Save the workbook as **Xanthan Promotion** followed by your initials.

3. In cell B7, enter **70** as the supervisor rating of leadership potential. In cell B8, enter **85** as the supervisor rating of understanding of duties. In cell B9, enter **80** as the supervisor rating of willingness to work hard.

4. In cell B12, enter a function that determines the average of the values in the range B7:B10.

5. Format cell B12 as a Number with no decimal places.

6. In cell B13, enter an IF function that displays *PROMOTION* if the average score in cell B12 is greater than 80 and *NO PROMOTION* if the average score is less than 80.

7. Format the contents of cell B13 as bold and centered.

8. In cell B10, enter each of the following test scores: **75, 80, 85, 90,** and **95.** Which scores will result in a promotion?

9. Insert a footer with your name and the current date. Save, print, and close the workbook.

CRITICAL *Thinking*

 ACTIVITY 5-1

 You are considering purchasing a car and want to compare prices offered by different dealerships. Some dealerships have cars that include the accessories you want; others need to add the accessories for an additional price. Prepare a worksheet similar to that shown in Figure 5-12.

FIGURE 5-12

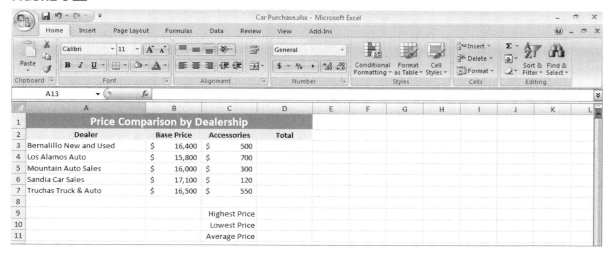

Perform the following operations to provide information that will be useful to making the car purchase decision.

- In the range D3:D7, enter formulas that add the values in column B to the values in column C.

- In cell D9, enter a function that determines the highest price in the range D3:D7.

- In cell D10, enter a function that determines the lowest price in the range D3:D7.

- In cell D11, enter a function that determines the average price in the range D3:D7.

Create a footer with your name and the current date. Save the workbook as **Car Purchase** followed by your initials. Print and close the workbook.

 ## ACTIVITY 5-2

The Insert Function dialog box contains a Search for a function box. When you enter a brief description of what you want to do and click Go, Excel will list functions best suited for the task you want to perform.

FIGURE 5-13
Insert Function dialog box

Search for a function

Suppose you are preparing a large worksheet in which all cells in a range should contain data. You want to enter a function near the end of a range that displays the number of cells in the range that are blank. If a number other than zero appears as the function result, you will know that you must search for the cell or cells that are empty and enter the appropriate data.

Open a new workbook, and then click the Insert Function button on the Formula Bar to open the Insert Function dialog box. Enter a description in the Search for a function box that will find a function to count the number of empty cells in a range. If more than one function is suggested, click each function in the Select a function box and read the description of the function that appears below the box. Which function is most appropriate to complete this task?

SCANS ACTIVITY 5-3

A manufacturing company prepares a budget each month. At the end of the month, the Accounting Department prepares a report similar to the one shown in Figure 5-13, which compares the actual amount spent to the budgeted amount.

FIGURE 5-14

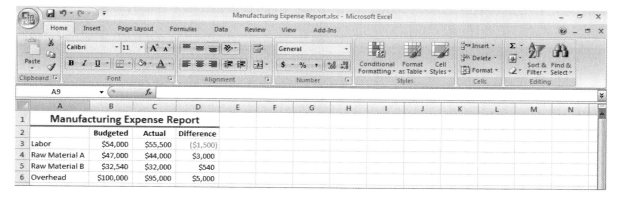

Write an IF function you can use to draw attention to an item that exceeded its budget.

ENHANCING A WORKSHEET

Sorting Data

Data entry often occurs in an order that is not necessarily best for understanding and analysis. Sorting rearranges data in a more meaningful order. For example, you might want to sort a list of names in alphabetical order. In an ascending sort, data with letters is arranged in alphabetical order (A to Z), data with numbers is arranged from lowest to highest, and data with dates is arranged from earliest to latest. The reverse order occurs in a descending sort, which arranges data with letters from Z to A, data with numbers from highest to lowest, and data with dates from oldest to newest. When you sort data contained in columns of a worksheet, Excel does not include the column headings.

To sort data, you first click a cell in the column by which you want to sort a range of data. Click the Data tab on the Ribbon. In the Sort & Filter group, click the Sort A to Z button for an ascending text sort or click the Sort Z to A button for a descending text sort. The button names change depending on what type of data you selected for sorting. For numerical data, the buttons are Sort Smallest to Largest and Sort Largest to Smallest. For date and time data, the buttons are Sort Oldest to Newest and Sort Newest to Oldest.

You can sort by more than one column of data. For example, you might want to sort a list of names in alphabetical order by last name and then within last names by first name. You set up a sort with multiple levels in the Sort dialog box, which is shown in Figure 6-1. To open the Sort

dialog box, on the Data tab of the Ribbon, in the Sort & Filter group, click the Sort button. You set up the first-level sort in the Sort by row in the Sort dialog box. The Column box indicates the column that will be used for the top-level sort, such as Last Name. The Sort On box indicates the type of data to be sorted, which is usually Values. If data is formatted with different font or fill colors, you can sort the data by color. The Order box specifies whether the sort is ascending or descending. To create an additional sort level, such as for the First Name column, click Add Level. The Then by row appears. You set up the next-level sort by selecting the sort column, the data type, and the sort order, just as you did for the top-level sort. When all sort levels are created, click OK. The data is rearranged in the order you specified.

Did You Know?

The Sort commands are also available on the Home tab of the Ribbon and on a shortcut menu. On the Home tab, in the Editing group, click the Sort & Filter button to open a menu with the Sort commands. Or, right-click the cell by which you want to sort the data, and then point to Sort in the shortcut menu to open a submenu with the Sort commands. In either case, click the appropriate Sort command.

FIGURE 6-1
Sort dialog box

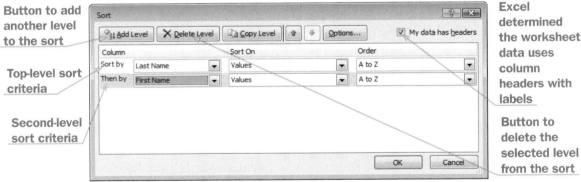

Button to add another level to the sort

Top-level sort criteria

Second-level sort criteria

Excel determined the worksheet data uses column headers with labels

Button to delete the selected level from the sort

STEP-BY-STEP 6.1

1. Open the **Employee.xlsx** Data File.

2. Save the workbook as **Employee List** followed by your initials.

3. Click cell **D4**. Clicking in the cell indicates that you want to sort by the Salary data in column D.

STEP-BY-STEP 6.1 Continued

4. Click the **Data** tab on the Ribbon, and then locate the **Sort & Filter** group. This group includes the buttons for sorting in ascending or descending order and opening the Sort dialog box.

5. In the Sort & Filter group, click the **Sort Smallest to Largest** button. The data in the range A4:D29 is sorted in ascending order by the numerical values in column D.

6. On the Data tab, in the Sort & Filter group, click the **Sort** button. The Sort dialog box appears. The sort you just created appears as the first-level sort in the Sort by row.

7. Next to the Column box, click the **arrow**, and then click **Last Name**. Values is already selected in the Sort On box.

8. Next to the Order box, click the **arrow**, and then click **A to Z**, if it is not already selected.

9. Click **Add Level**. A Then by row is added so you can specify the second sort level.

10. In the Then by row, next to the Column box, click the **arrow**, and then click **First Name**. Values is already selected in the Sort On box.

11. In the Then by row, next to the Order box, click the **arrow**, and then click **A to Z**, if it is not already selected. Your Sort dialog box should match Figure 6-1.

12. Click **OK**. The data is sorted by last name and then by first name, as shown in Figure 6-2.

FIGURE 6-2
Data sorted by last name and then by first name

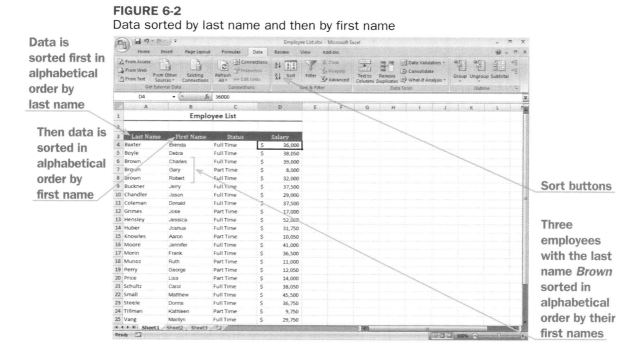

Data is sorted first in alphabetical order by last name

Then data is sorted in alphabetical order by first name

Sort buttons

Three employees with the last name *Brown* sorted in alphabetical order by their first names

13. Save the workbook, and leave it open for the next Step-by-Step.

Filtering Data

Filtering displays a subset of the data that meets certain criteria and temporarily hides the rows that do not meet the specified criteria. For example, you could filter a list of employees to show only those employees who work full time. The rows that contain part-time employees are then hidden, but not deleted from the worksheet.

You can filter by value, by criteria, or by color. On the Data tab of the Ribbon, in the Sort & Filter group, click the Filter button. **Filter arrows** appear in the lower-right corners of the column heading cells. When you click a filter arrow, the AutoFilter menu for that column appears, as shown in Figure 6-3. The **AutoFilter** menu displays a list of all the values that appear in that column along with additional criteria and color filtering options. Select one of the values to display only those rows in the worksheet in which that value is entered.

Did You Know?

Unlike sorting, filtering does not rearrange the order of the data. But, you can sort, copy, format, and print filtered data.

Did You Know?

The Filter commands are also available on the Home tab of the Ribbon and on a shortcut menu. On the Home tab, in the Editing group, click the Sort & Filter button to open a menu with the Filter commands. Or, right-click the cell by which you want to sort the data, and then point to Filter in the shortcut menu to open a submenu with the Filter commands. In either case, click the appropriate command.

FIGURE 6-3
Auto Filter menu

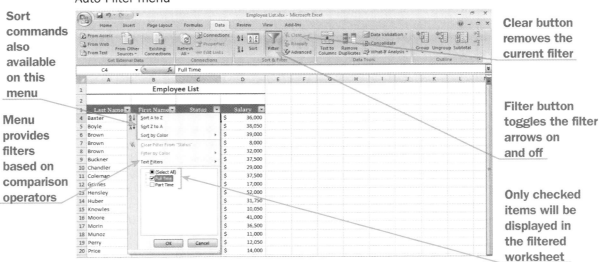

Sort commands also available on this menu

Menu provides filters based on comparison operators

Clear button removes the current filter

Filter button toggles the filter arrows on and off

Only checked items will be displayed in the filtered worksheet

The Number, Text, and Data AutoFilters provide different filtering options. For example, you can use comparison operators, such as equals, between, and begins with, to select data. You can also filter numbers based on their relative values, such as the top 10 and above or below average. If you select the Top 10 number filter, the Top 10 AutoFilter dialog box appears, as shown in Figure 6-4. In the Top 10 AutoFilter dialog box, you can choose to show the highest (top) or lowest (bottom) values in the column. For example, you might show the rows with the 10 largest values in that column of the worksheet. However, you can change the specifications in the dialog box to show a different number of items or a percentage, such as the Bottom 50 Items or the Top 10 Percent.

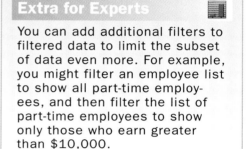

FIGURE 6-4
Top 10 AutoFilter dialog box

Rank of items to show

Items can be changed to Percent

Number of items or percentages to show

If data is formatted with different font or fill colors, you can filter the data by color. When a column is filtered, the filter arrow icon changes to [icon].

When you want to see all the data in a worksheet again, you can restore all the rows by clearing the filter. Click the filter arrow, and then click the Clear Filter From command or click the Clear button in the Sort & Filter group on the Data tab of the Ribbon. To turn off the filter arrows, click the Filter button in the Sort & Filter group.

> **Extra for Experts**
>
> You can add additional filters to filtered data to limit the subset of data even more. For example, you might filter an employee list to show all part-time employees, and then filter the list of part-time employees to show only those who earn greater than $10,000.

STEP-BY-STEP 6.2

1. Click cell **C4**.

2. On the Data tab, in the Sort & Filter group, click the **Filter** button. Filter arrows appear in cells A3 through D3.

3. In cell C3, click the **filter arrow**. The AutoFilter menu appears.

4. Click the **(Select All)** check box. All of the column values are deselected.

5. Click the **Full Time** check box. The Part Time check box remains deselected on the AutoFilter menu, as shown in Figure 6-3.

6. Click **OK**. The list of employees is filtered to show only the full-time workers. All of the part-time employees are hidden.

7. In cell D3, click the **filter arrow**. You'll add a second filter to show the 10 full-time employees who earn the highest salaries.

STEP-BY-STEP 6.2 Continued

8. On the AutoFilter menu, point to **Number Filters**, and then click **Top 10**. The Top 10 AutoFilter dialog box appears, as shown in Figure 6-4.

9. Click **OK**. The worksheet is filtered to show the 10 employees who work full time and earn the highest salaries.

10. Insert a footer that includes your name and the current date. Save and print the workbook.

11. Click the **Data** tab on the Ribbon. In the Sort & Filter group, click the **Clear** button. The filter is removed from the worksheet, and all of the employees are visible.

12. On the Data tab, in the Sort & Filter group, click the **Filter** button. The filter arrows disappear from the column labels.

13. Save the workbook, and leave it open for the next Step-by-Step.

Applying Conditional Formatting

Conditional formatting highlights worksheet data by changing the look of cells that meet a specified condition. Conditional formatting helps you analyze and understand data by providing answers to questions, such as, "Which employees have worked for the company for more than three years?" The Highlight Cells Rules format cells based on comparison operators such as greater than, less than, between, and equal to. You can also highlight cells that contain specific text, a certain date, or even duplicate values. The Top/Bottom Rules format cells based on their rank, such as the top 10 items, the bottom 15%, or those that are above average. You specify the number of items or the percentage to include.

To add conditional formatting, select the range you want to analyze. In the Styles group on the Home tab, click the Conditional Formatting button, point to Highlight Cells Rules or Top/Bottom Rules, and then click the condition you want. In the dialog box that appears, enter the appropriate criteria, select the formatting you want, and then click OK. The conditional formatting is applied to the selected range. To remove the conditional formatting, click the Conditional Formatting button, point to Clear Rules, and then click Clear Rules from Selected Cells or Clear Rules from Entire Sheet.

Did You Know?

If you update the data in a range, the conditional formatting changes to reflect the new values. Consider a worksheet that conditionally formats employee salaries to highlight the top 5 salaries. If an employee receives a raise that changes her salary rank from 6 to 5, this employee's salary is conditionally formatted and the salary previously ranked as 5 is cleared of conditional formatting.

STEP-BY-STEP 6.3

1. Select the range **D4:D29**. These cells contain the salaries for each of the 28 employees.

2. Click the **Home** tab on the Ribbon. In the Styles group, click the **Conditional Formatting** button. The Conditional Formatting menu appears, as shown in Figure 6-5.

FIGURE 6-5
Conditional formatting menu

Range to conditionally format

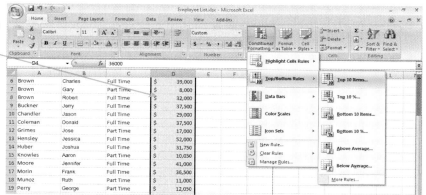

3. Point to **Top/Bottom Rules**, and then click **Top 10 Items**. The Top 10 Items dialog box appears, as shown in Figure 6-6.

FIGURE 6-6
Top 10 Items dialog box

Number of cells to format

Button to open the Conditional Formatting menu

Formatting to apply to the cells

Red highlights the cells with the 10 highest salaries

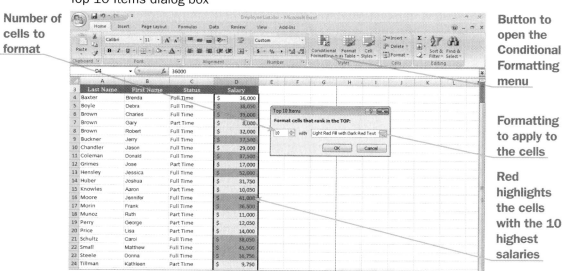

4. Type **5** in the left box to reduce the number of salaries to the top five.

STEP-BY-STEP 6.3 Continued

5. Click **OK**. The five highest salaries appear in red text on a red background.

6. On the Home tab, in the Styles group, click the **Conditional Formatting** button. On the Conditional Formatting menu, point to **Top/Bottom Rules**, and then click **Bottom 10 Items**. The Bottom 10 Items dialog box appears.

7. Type **5** in the left box, click the **arrow**, and then click **Yellow Fill with Dark Yellow Text**.

8. Click **OK**. The five lowest salaries appear in yellow text on a yellow background.

9. Save, print, and close the workbook.

Hiding Columns and Rows

Hiding temporarily removes a row or column from view. Hiding rows and columns enables you to use the same worksheet to emphasize different data. For example, you can hide monthly data to leave only the total values visible. Select how many rows or columns you want to hide, and then right-click the selection. On the shortcut menu that appears, click Hide to remove the selection from view in the worksheet. You can repeat this process to hide as many rows and columns in the worksheet as you like. Hidden rows and columns remain out of sight until you redisplay them. Select the row or column on each side of the hidden rows or columns you want to redisplay. Right-click the selection, and then click Unhide on the shortcut menu.

> **Did You Know?**
>
> You can also hide and unhide selected rows and columns from the Ribbon. Click the Home tab on the Ribbon. In the Cells group, click the Format button. On the Format menu that appears, in the Visibility section, point to Hide & Unhide. This sub-menu contains the Hide Columns and Hide Rows commands as well as the Unhide Columns and Unhide Rows commands.

STEP-BY-STEP 6.4

1. Open the **Oil.xlsx** Data File.

2. Save the workbook as **Oil Production** followed by your initials.

3. Select columns **B** through **G**. You'll hide the monthly data for the oil wells.

4. Right-click the selected columns. On the shortcut menu that appears, click **Hide**. Columns B through G are hidden.

5. Click cell **A19** to deselect the range. The worksheet shows the six-month production total for each well in the field, as shown in Figure 6-7.

STEP-BY-STEP 6.4 Continued

FIGURE 6-7
Worksheet with hidden columns

Columns B
through G
are hidden

6. Insert a footer with your name and the current date. Save and print the workbook.

7. Select columns **A** and **H**. These columns surround hidden columns.

8. Right-click the selected columns. On the shortcut menu that appears, click **Unhide**. Columns B through G reappear.

9. Select rows **6** through **14**. You'll hide individual oil well data, leaving only the monthly totals.

10. Right-click the selected rows, and then click **Hide** on the shortcut menu. Rows 6 through 14 are hidden.

11. Click cell **A19** to deselect the range. The worksheet shows only the field production totals for each month.

12. Save and print the workbook.

13. Select rows **5** and **15**. These rows surround the hidden rows.

14. Right-click the selected rows, and then click **Unhide** on the shortcut menu. Rows 6 through 14 reappear in the worksheet.

15. Save the workbook, and leave it open for the next Step-by-Step.

Adding Shapes to a Worksheet

Shapes, such as rectangles, circles, arrows, lines, flowchart symbols, and callouts, can help make a worksheet more informative. For example, you might use a rectangle or circle to create a corporate logo. Or, you might use a callout to explain a value in the worksheet. Excel has a gallery of shapes you can use.

Inserting a Shape

To open the Shapes gallery, click the Insert tab on the Ribbon, and then, in the Illustrations group, click the Shapes button. In the Shapes gallery that appears, as shown in Figure 6-8, click the shape you want to insert. The pointer changes to a crosshair, which you click and drag in the worksheet to draw the shape. The shape is inserted in the worksheet.

FIGURE 6-8
Shapes gallery

Up Arrow
Callout

Extra for Experts

You can make a perfect square or circle by pressing and holding the Shift key as you drag in the worksheet to draw the shape.

Did You Know?

The Format Shape dialog box has additional formatting options. Select the shape object you want to format. On the Drawing Tools Format tab, in the Shape Styles group, click the Dialog Box Launcher. The Format Shape dialog box appears. Use the different categories to select line color, line style, shadow, 3-D format and rotation, picture, and text box options.

Modifying Shapes

Shapes are inserted in the worksheet as objects. An **object** is anything that appears on the screen that you can select and work with as a whole, such as a shape, picture, or chart. When the shape is selected, the Drawing Tools appear on the Ribbon and contain the Format contextual tab, as shown in Figure 6-9. You use the tools on the Format tab to modify the shape. For example, you can change the shape's style, fill, and outline as well as add special effects, such as shadows. You can also move and resize the selected shape.

FIGURE 6-9
Formatted shape in the worksheet

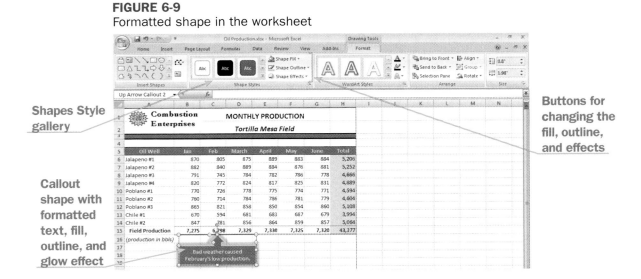

Shapes Style
gallery

Callout
shape with
formatted
text, fill,
outline, and
glow effect

Buttons for
changing the
fill, outline,
and effects

Deleting Objects

When you no longer need a shape or any other object in a worksheet, you can delete it. First click the object to select it. Then press the Delete key. The object is removed from the worksheet.

S TEP-BY-STEP 6.5

1. Click the **Insert** tab on the Ribbon. In the Illustrations group, click the **Shapes** button. The Shapes gallery appears, as shown in Figure 6-8.

2. In the Block Arrows section, click the **Up Arrow Callout** button (the last button in the second row). The pointer changes shape to a crosshair.

3. Click cell **B17** and drag to cell **E20**. The callout appears. The Format contextual tab appears under Drawing Tools on the Ribbon.

4. Type **Bad weather caused February's low production.** (including the period). The text is inserted in the callout.

5. Point to the middle-right sizing handle until the pointer changes to the Horizontal Resize pointer, and then drag left to column D. The callout is narrower.

6. Point to the callout to display the four-headed move pointer, and then drag the callout until its arrow points to cell **C15**. The callout points to the correct cell and remains selected.

7. Under Drawing Tools, on the Format tab, in the Shape Styles group, next to the Shape Fill button, click the **arrow**. A color palette appears.

8. In the Theme Colors section, click **Red, Accent 2** (the sixth color in the first row). The callout background color changes to red.

9. Under Drawing Tools, on the Format tab, in the Shape Styles group, next to the Shape Outline button, click the **arrow**. A color palette appears.

10. In the Standard Colors section, click **Orange** (the third color). The line around the callout changes to orange.

11. Under Drawing Tools, on the Format tab, in the Shape Styles group, click the **Shape Effects** button.

12. On the Shapes Effects menu, point to **Glow**. In the Glow Variations section, click **Accent color 2, 8 pt glow** (the second effect in the second row). The callout is formatted as shown in Figure 6-9.

13. Click any cell in the worksheet to deselect the shape. The Drawing Tools Format tab disappears from the Ribbon.

14. Save the workbook, and leave it open for the next Step-by-Step.

> ### Extra Challenge
> Add other shapes to the workbook, and then format them using the tools on the Format tab under Drawing Tools. When you are done, click the Undo button on the Quick Access Toolbar to undo your changes.

Adding SmartArt Graphics to a Worksheet

SmartArt graphics enhance worksheets by providing a visual representation of information and ideas. SmartArt graphics are often used for organizational charts, flowcharts, and decision trees.

Inserting a SmartArt Graphic

To insert a SmartArt graphic, click the SmartArt button in the Illustrations group on the Insert tab. The Choose a SmartArt Graphic dialog box appears, as shown in Figure 6-10. You can select from a variety of layouts, including list, matrix, and pyramid. Click the SmartArt graphic you want to use in the center pane and read its description in the right pane. Click OK to insert the graphic in the worksheet as an object.

FIGURE 6-10
Choose a SmartArt Graphic dialog box

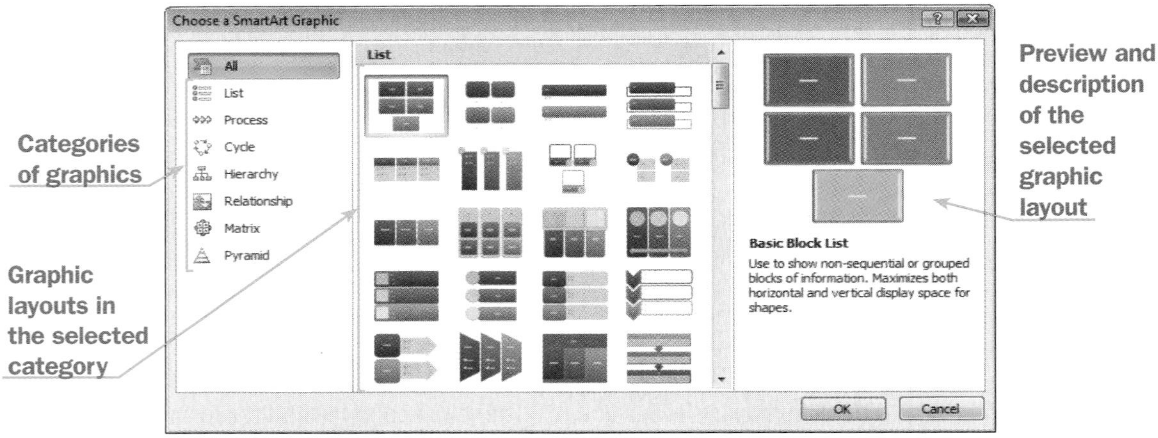

Modifying a SmartArt Graphic

When the SmartArt graphic is selected, SmartArt Tools appear on the Ribbon and contain the Design and Format contextual tabs, as shown in Figure 6-11. You use the tools on the Design tab to select a different layout, apply a style, and change the layout's color. The Format tab has tools to modify the shapes used in the selected layout, by changing shape, size, fill color, and outline color, and tools to apply shape styles and special effects, such as shadows. You can also move and resize the selected shapes.

FIGURE 6-11
Formatted SmartArt graphic

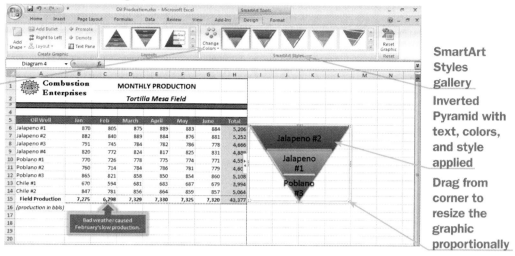

Button to select a different color for the graphic

SmartArt Styles gallery

Inverted Pyramid with text, colors, and style applied

Drag from corner to resize the graphic proportionally

S TEP-BY-STEP 6.6

1. Click the **Insert** tab on the Ribbon. In the Illustrations group, click the **SmartArt** button. The Choose a SmartArt Graphic dialog box appears, as shown in Figure 6-10.

2. In the left pane, click **Pyramid**.

3. In the center pane, click **Inverted Pyramid** (the second graphic).

4. Click **OK**. The SmartArt graphic appears in the worksheet. The SmartArt Tools appear on the Ribbon.

5. Click **[Text]** in the top level of the pyramid, if it is not already selected, and then type **Jalapeno #2**.

6. Click **[Text]** in the second level of the pyramid, and then type **Jalapeno #1**.

7. Click **[Text]** in the bottom level of the pyramid, and then type **Poblano #3**.

8. Drag the lower-right sizing handle up until the graphic is about 4 columns wide. Dragging from the corner resizes the graphic proportionally.

9. Drag the picture over the range **I6:L15**.

10. Under SmartArt Tools, on the Design tab, in the SmartArt Styles group, click the **Change Colors** button. The gallery of colors appears.

STEP-BY-STEP 6.6 Continued

11. In the Colorful section, click **Colorful – Accent Colors** (the first color option). Each of the top three oil well producers is a different color in the pyramid.

12. Under SmartArt Tools, on the Design tab, in the SmartArt Styles group, click the **More** button. The gallery of SmartArt Quick Styles appears.

13. Point to each style to see its Live Preview. In the 3-D section, click **Polished** (the first style in the top row). The pyramid changes to reflect the Quick Style, as shown in Figure 6-11.

14. Change the Orientation to **Landscape**. Save, print, and close the workbook.

Adding Pictures to a Worksheet

You might want to use a picture to make the appearance of a worksheet more attractive. A picture is a digital photograph or other image file. Some organizations like to include their corporate logo on their worksheets. Pictures can also be used to illustrate data in a worksheet. For instance, you might want to insert pictures of each product in an inventory list.

Inserting a Picture

You can insert a picture you have stored as a file, or you can use a picture from the Clip Art collection that comes with Excel. If you have access to the Internet, you can also download pictures from Office Online to insert in your worksheets.

To insert a picture from a file, click the Picture button in the Illustrations group on the Insert tab of the Ribbon. The Insert Picture dialog box, which looks and functions like the Open dialog box, appears. Change the location to the folder with the stored picture folder, and then double-click the picture file you want to use.

The Clip Art task pane provides a wide variety of clip art, photographs, movies, and sounds that you can use in a worksheet. To access the Clip Art task pane, click the Clip Art button in the Illustrations group on the Insert tab of the Ribbon. The Clip Art task pane appears on the right side of the program window, as shown in Figure 6-12. In the Search for box, type a brief description of the clip you want to find, and then click Go. Clips that fit the search words appear in the results box. Click an image to insert it in the worksheet.

> **Did You Know?**
>
> You can place a background pattern or picture in a worksheet. On the Page Layout tab, in the Page Setup group, click the Background button. In the Sheet Background dialog box, select the picture you want in the background of the worksheet, and then click Open.

> **Important**
>
> All images are protected by copyright law. You cannot download and reuse a picture you find on a Web site without permission. Contact the copyright holder to obtain permission. Some Web sites offer free images for non-commercial use. Others offer images you purchase for a fee.

FIGURE 6-12
Clip Art task pane

Keywords that describe the clip you want to find

The types of files you want to find—clip art, photographs, movies, and/or sounds

Search results; click a clip to insert it in the workbook

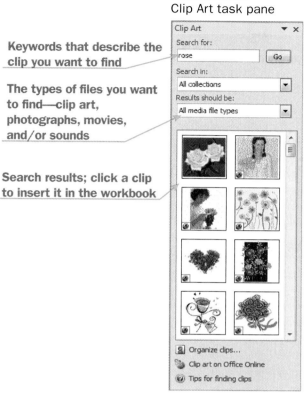

Modifying a Picture

A picture is inserted in the workbook as an object. As with shapes, you can move, resize, or format the picture to fit your needs. Click a picture to select it. The Picture Tools appears on the Ribbon, as shown in Figure 6-13. The Format contextual tab contains tools to edit and format the picture. The tools in the Adjust group enable you to change the look of the picture, including its brightness, contrast, and color. The Picture Styles group includes the Picture Styles gallery as well as tools to change the picture's shape and border, and effects such as shadows and rotation. The Size group includes the Crop button, which you use to cut out parts of the picture you do not want to use.

FIGURE 6-13
Formatted picture

Buttons for changing the brightness, contrast, and color

Picture with increased brightness and style applied

Buttons for changing the shape, border, and effects

Picture Styles gallery

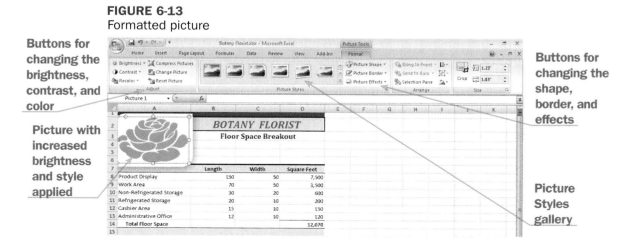

STEP-BY-STEP 6.7

1. Open the **Botany.xlsx** Data File.

2. Save the workbook as **Botany Florist** followed by your initials.

3. Click the **Insert** tab on the Ribbon. In the Illustrations group, click the **Picture** button. The Insert Picture dialog box appears.

4. Click the **Rose.tif** Data File. This is the picture you want to insert.

5. Click the **Insert** button. The picture of a rose is inserted in the worksheet. The Picture Tools appears on the Ribbon.

6. Drag the lower-right sizing handle up until the dark line at the bottom of row 6 is visible.

7. Drag the picture to the range **A2:A6**, if it is not already in that location.

8. Under Picture Tools, on the Format tab, in the Adjust group, click the **Brightness** button, and then click **+40%**. The picture's brightness increases, and the rose color is pinker.

9. Under Picture Tools, on the Format tab, in the Picture Styles group, click the **More** button. The gallery of Picture Styles appears.

10. Point to different picture styles to see the Live Preview, and then click **Rounded Diagonal Corner, White** (the second style in the third row). The picture's overall style changes, as shown in Figure 6-13.

11. Insert a footer with your name and the current date. Save, print, and close the workbook.

Using Templates

Templates are predesigned workbook files that you can use as the basis or model for new workbooks. The template includes all the parts of a workbook that will not change, such as text labels, formulas, and formatting. You save a copy of the template as a workbook and enter the variable data. You can use a template again and again, entering different data each time. For example, suppose your employer requires all employees to submit a weekly time sheet. Each week you use the same worksheet format, but the number of hours you enter in the worksheet changes. You can use a template file to save the portion of the worksheet that is the same every week. Then, each week, you need to add only the data that is pertinent to that week.

Excel comes with a variety of templates, which you access from the New Workbook dialog box, as shown in Figure 6-14. The Installed Templates are template files stored on your computer. If your computer is connected to the Internet, you also see templates available from Microsoft Office Online, organized by categories, such as Budgets, Expense Reports, Forms, and Invoices. Click a template category in the left pane. The center pane displays the templates available for that category. Click a template in the center pane to display a preview and description of the selected template in the right pane. To open a new workbook based on the selected template, click Create. Templates have the file extension .xltx to differentiate them from regular Excel workbook files. After you open a workbook based on a template file, you need to save it with a descriptive name to the appropriate location.

FIGURE 6-14
New Workbook dialog box

Templates installed on your computer

Categories of templates available on Microsoft Office Online if your computer is connected to the Internet

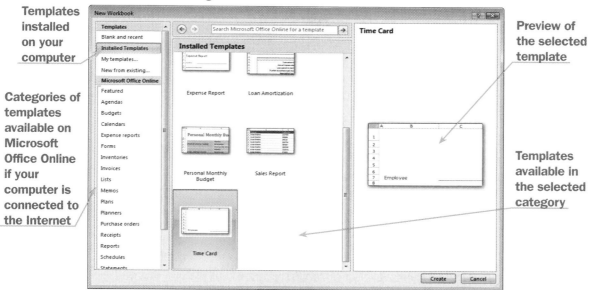

Preview of the selected template

Templates available in the selected category

You can also create a workbook based on an existing file. In the New Workbook dialog box, click the New from existing button in the left pane. The New from Existing Workbook dialog box, which looks and functions like the Open dialog box, appears. Select the workbook you want to use as a model for another workbook, and then click Create New. A copy of the selected workbook appears in the program window. You can modify the file as needed, and then save the file with an appropriate name and location.

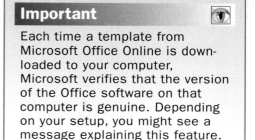

Important

Each time a template from Microsoft Office Online is downloaded to your computer, Microsoft verifies that the version of the Office software on that computer is genuine. Depending on your setup, you might see a message explaining this feature.

S TEP-BY-STEP 6.8

1. Click the **Office Button**, and then click **New**. The New Workbook dialog box appears.

2. In the left pane, click **Installed Templates**. A list of templates installed on your computer appears in the center pane.

3. Scroll down the Installed Templates list in the center pane, and then click **Time Card**. A preview of the Time Card template appears in the right pane, as shown in Figure 6-14.

4. Click **Create**. A workbook based on the Time Card template appears in the program window. The workbook is titled *TimeCard1*.

5. Save the workbook as **Time Card** followed by your initials.

6. Zoom the worksheet to **85%** so you can see the entire width of the time card.

STEP-BY-STEP 6.8 Continued

7. Click cell **C7**, if it is not already selected, and then enter your name.

8. Click cell **C16**, and then enter **5/25/2010** as the week ending date. The dates for the specified week appear in the range C21:C27, the Date column in the time card.

9. Click cell **D21**, and then enter **8**. The total hours for the day appear in cell H21, and the total regular hours for the week appear in cell D28.

10. Click cell **D29**, and then enter **10**. The rate of $10 per hour for regular hours is entered. The total regular pay for the day appears in cell D30, and the total pay for the week appears in cell H30.

11. Click cell **E21**, and then enter **1.5**. The total hours for the day in cell H21 are updated to include the overtime hours, and the total overtime hours for the week appear in cell E28.

12. Click cell **E29**, and then enter **15**. The rate of $15 per hour for overtime hours is entered. The total overtime pay for the day appears in cell E30, and the updated total pay for the week appears in cell H30. Your worksheet should look similar to Figure 6-15.

FIGURE 6-15
Worksheet created from a template

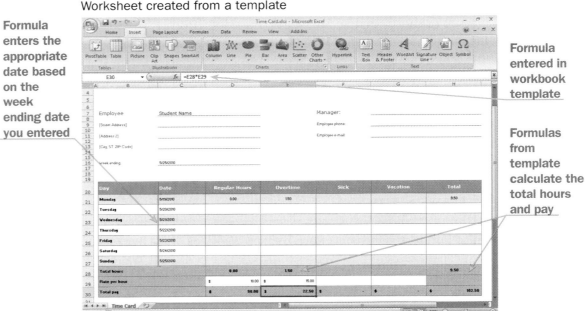

Formula enters the appropriate date based on the week ending date you entered

Formula entered in workbook template

Formulas from template calculate the total hours and pay

13. Save, print, and close the workbook.

Inserting Hyperlinks

 A hyperlink is a cell in a worksheet that opens another file or page when you click it. You can create hyperlinks to another Web page, another file, a specific location in the current workbook, a new document, and an e-mail address. For example, you might want to create a link to another Excel file that contains the source data for information used in the current worksheet. You might also create a link to a Web page that contains information related to items in the worksheet.

To create a hyperlink, first click the cell you want to use for the hyperlink, or select an object, such as a picture. On the Insert tab of the Ribbon, in the Links group, click the Hyperlink button (or right-click the cell or object, and then click Hyperlink on the shortcut menu). The Insert Hyperlink dialog box appears, as shown in Figure 6-16. Type the filename or Web page address in the Address box, and then click OK. The hyperlink is added to the worksheet, and the pointer appears as a hand when you point to the hyperlink.

> **Did You Know?**
>
> You can enter a custom ScreenTip that appears when a user points to a hyperlink. In the Insert Hyperlink dialog box, click ScreenTip. In the Set Hyperlink ScreenTip dialog box that appears, enter the text you want for the ScreenTip in the ScreenTip text box, and then click OK. Complete the Insert Hyperlink dialog box, and then click OK.

FIGURE 6-16
Insert Hyperlink dialog box

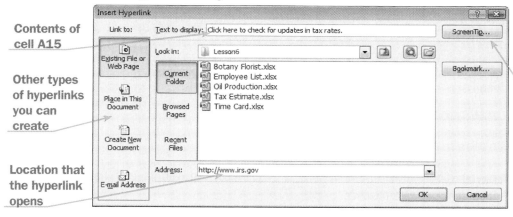

To use the hyperlink, click the cell or object. If you created a hyperlink to a file, that file opens when you click the hyperlink. If you created a hyperlink to a Web page, that page is opened in your Web browser when you click the hyperlink.

You can edit a hyperlink to change its displayed text, ScreenTip, and even link. Click the cell or object with the hyperlink, and then click the Edit Hyperlinks button in the Links group on the Insert tab. The Edit Hyperlink dialog box appears, and looks and functions just like the Insert Hyperlink dialog box. In addition, it contains the Remove Link button, which you can click to delete the hyperlink from the cell but leave its contents unaffected.

> **Important**
>
> The worksheet cell is the hyperlink, not the contents entered in that cell. If the contents extend beyond the cell's border, the hyperlink will not work if the user clicks the text that extends into the next cell. The actual cell must be clicked.

STEP-BY-STEP 6.9

1. Open the **Tax.xlsx** Data File.

2. Save the workbook as **Tax Estimate** followed by your initials.

3. Click cell **A15**. You want to use this cell as the hyperlink.

4. Click the **Insert** tab on the Ribbon. In the Links group, click the **Hyperlink** button. The Insert Hyperlink dialog box appears.

5. In the Address box, type **www.irs.gov**. This is the Web page you want to open when a user clicks the hyperlink. Excel precedes the Web address with *http://*, as shown in Figure 6-16.

6. Click **OK**, and then click cell **A17**. Cell A15 is a hyperlink with blue and underlined text, which is a common format for indicating a hyperlink, as shown in Figure 6-17.

FIGURE 6-17
Hyperlink added to the worksheet

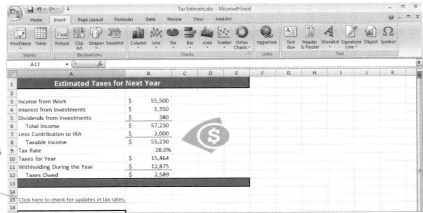

Blue, underlined text indicates cell A15 is a hyperlink

7. If your computer is connected to the Internet, click cell **A15**. The Web page of the Internal Revenue Service appears in your Web browser.

8. Exit your browser and return to the worksheet.

9. Insert a header with your name and the current date. Save, print, and close the workbook.

Saving a Workbook in a Different Format

Excel workbooks can be saved in different file formats so that they can be opened in other programs. For example, if you want to share data with a coworker or friend who uses an earlier version of Excel, you can save your Excel file in a format that is readable by Excel 2003. You can also save the file in a format that can be viewed as a Web page on the Internet. Table 6-1 describes some of the different types of formats in which you can save workbooks.

TABLE 6-1
Common file formats in which to save workbooks

FILE TYPE	DESCRIPTION	FILE EXTENSION
CSV (Comma delimited)	Data separated by commas	.csv
Excel Template	File used to create other similar files	.xltx
Formatted Text (Space delimited)	Data separated by spaces	.prn
Microsoft Excel 97-2003	Data created in an earlier version of Excel	.xls
Text (Tab delimited)	Data separated by tabs	.txt
Single File Web Page	File to be displayed on the Internet	.mhtm, .mhtml
Web Page	File to be displayed on the Internet	.htm, .html
XML Data	Data in Extensible Markup Language	.xml

STEP-BY-STEP 6.10

1. Open the **Expense.xlsx** Data File.

2. Save the workbook as **Expense Report** followed by your initials.

3. Click the **Office Button**, and then click **Save As**. The Save As dialog box appears.

4. In the File name box, type **Expense Report 2003** followed by your initials.

5. Click the **Save as type** button. A list of file types you can use to save the workbook appears.

6. Click **Excel 97-2003 Workbook (*.xls)**. You want to save the Excel 2007 workbook as an Excel 2003 workbook.

STEP-BY-STEP 6.10 Continued

7. Click **Save**. The Microsoft Office Excel – Compatibility Checker dialog box appears, as shown in Figure 6-18, listing elements of the workbook that are not supported by earlier versions of Excel. In this case, some of the formatting cannot be saved in the earlier file format. These formats will be converted to match the earlier format.

FIGURE 6-18
Microsoft Office Excel – Compatibility Checker dialog box

Level of incompatibility

Description of elements in the workbook that are incompatible with Excel 2003

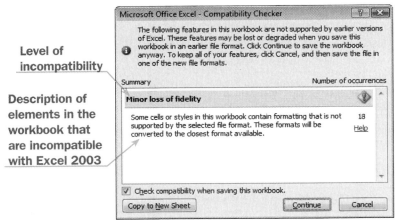

8. Click **Continue**. The workbook is saved as a file that can be opened in Excel 2003.

9. Close the **Expense Report 2003** workbook.

10. Open the workbook **Expense Report** followed by your initials that you created in Step 2.

11. Click the **Office Button**, and then click **Save As**. The Save As dialog box appears.

12. Click the **Save as type** button, and then click **Single File Web Page**. The dialog box expands.

13. Click **Change Title**. The Set Page Title dialog box appears.

14. In the Page title box, type **Expense Report for Sales Staff**, and then click **OK**. The page title will appear in the title bar of the browser.

15. Click **Publish**. The Publish as Web Page dialog box appears.

16. Next to the Choose box, click the **arrow**, and then click **Items on Sheet1**, if it is not already selected.

17. Click **Change**. The Set Title dialog box appears.

18. Press the **Delete** key to delete the text in the Title box, and then click **OK**. You do not want the same text to appear in both the browser title bar and the browser window centered over the worksheet content.

STEP-BY-STEP 6.10 Continued

19. In the File name box, change the file name to **Expense Report Web** followed by your initials. The full path shows the drive and folders in which the file will be saved.

20. Click the **Open published web page in browser** check box, if it is not already checked. The Publish as Web Page dialog box should match Figure 6-19.

FIGURE 6-19
Publish as Web Page dialog box

Items that will appear on the Web page

Click to set a title that appears in the browser window

Drive and folders path where the file will be saved

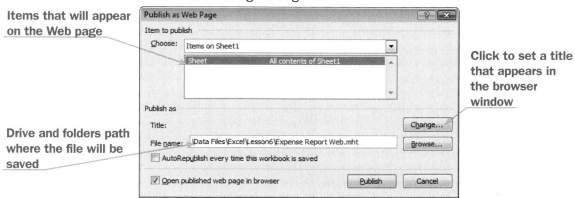

21. Click **Publish**. The Web page appears in your browser, as it would if it were published on the Web. If you use Internet Explorer as your Web browser, your screen should look similar to Figure 6-20.

FIGURE 6-20
Web page in Internet Explorer

Worksheet content saved as a Web page

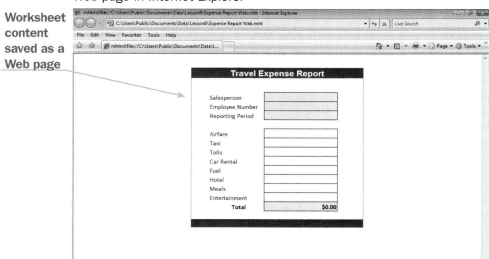

22. Close the browser. Save the workbook, and leave it open for the next Step-by-Step.

Working with Comments

A comment is a note attached to a cell that is usually used to explain or identify information contained in the cell. For example, you might use comments to provide the full text of abbreviations entered in cells. You might also use comments to explain the calculations in cells that contain formulas. Also, you can use comments to provide feedback to others without altering the worksheet structure. For example, a supervisor might use comments to offer suggestions to an employee on how to improve the worksheet format.

Inserting a Comment

All of the comments tools are located on the Review tab of the Ribbon in the Comments group. The New Comment button inserts a comment in the active cell. A comment box appears to the right of the selected cell with the user name followed by a colon at the top of the box. Type the comment, and then click outside the comment box to close it. A red triangle appears in the upper-right corner of the cell to indicate that it contains a comment. The comment box appears whenever you point to the cell that contains it. It disappears when you move the pointer to another cell. You can keep a specific comment onscreen by clicking the Show/Hide Comment button in the Comments group on the Review tab.

Editing and Deleting a Comment

To edit a comment, click the cell that contains the comment. Then click the Edit Comment button in the Comments group on the Review tab. Edit the text as usual. To delete a comment, click the cell that contains the comment. Then click the Delete button in the Comments group on the Review tab. The comment is removed from the cell.

Did You Know?

You can show and hide all the comments in a worksheet by toggling the Show All Comments button in the Comments group on the Review tab. The Comments group also has the Previous and Next buttons for moving between comments in the worksheet.

Computer Concepts

The user name that appears in the comment box matches the user name entered for that copy of Excel. To change the user name, click the Office Button, and then click Excel Options. The Excel Options dialog box appears with the Popular options displayed. In the Personalize your copy of Microsoft Office section, type the name you want to appear in comments in the User name box. Click OK.

STEP-BY-STEP 6.11

1. Click cell **A4**. You want to add a comment to this cell.

2. Click the **Review** tab on the Ribbon. In the Comments group, click the **New Comment** button. The comment box appears to the right of the active cell.

3. In the comment box, type the following comment: **Please change to Employee ID**.

4. Click cell **A13**. The comment box disappears, and a small red triangle appears in the upper-right corner of cell A4 to indicate that the cell contains a comment.

STEP-BY-STEP 6.11 Continued

5. On the Review tab, in the Comments group, click the **New Comment** button.

6. In the comment box, type the following comment: **The per diem maximum is $50**.

7. Click cell **A16**. The comment box disappears, and a small red triangle appears in the upper-right corner of cell A13, indicating that the cell contains a comment.

8. Point to cell **A13**. The cell comment appears, as shown in Figure 6-21.

FIGURE 6-21
Comments added to the worksheet

Button to insert a new comment in the active cell

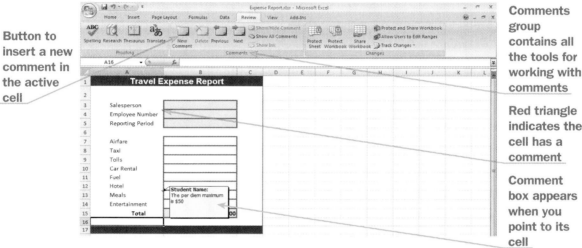

Comments group contains all the tools for working with comments

Red triangle indicates the cell has a comment

Comment box appears when you point to its cell

9. Click cell **B3**, and then enter your name. Save, print, and close the workbook.

Using the Research Task Pane

The Research task pane provides access to information typically found in references such as dictionaries, thesauruses, and encyclopedias. In Excel, the Research task pane also provides numerical data typically used in a worksheet, such as statistics or corporate financial data.

To open the Research task pane, click the Review tab on the Ribbon, and then, in the Proofing group, click the Research button. The Research task pane appears along the right side of the program window. In the task pane, select a reference book, a research site, or a business and financial site, and then search for a subject or topic. Your computer must be connected to the Internet to use the Research task pane.

STEP-BY-STEP 6.12

1. Open the **Stock.xlsx** Data File.

2. Save the workbook as **Stock Quotes** followed by your initials.

3. Click the **Review** tab on the Ribbon. In the Proofing group, click the **Research** button. The Research task pane appears on the right side of the program window.

4. In the Search for box, type **AMZN**.

5. Click the **arrow** next to the All Reference Books box, and then click **MSN Money Stock Quotes**. The search results appear in the task pane. The Last amount is the most recent price for that stock.

6. Click cell **C5**, and then enter the amount that appears for *Last*. The current price is entered in cell C5. Excel returns the total value in cell E5 by multiplying the value in cell C5 by the value in cell D5.

7. On the Research task pane, in the Search for box, type **HD**. Click the **Start searching** button. The most recent price for The Home Depot stocks appears in the search results box.

8. Click cell **C6**, and then enter the Last amount. The current price is entered in cell C6, and the value amounts are calculated.

9. Repeat the process in Steps 6 and 7 to find the current prices for the ticker symbols INTC, JNJ, and MSFT, and then enter the Last amounts in the range C7:C9. Your worksheet should be similar to Figure 6-22; however, the actual amounts in the Price and Values columns will differ, because they are based on the most recent stock prices.

FIGURE 6-22
Research task pane

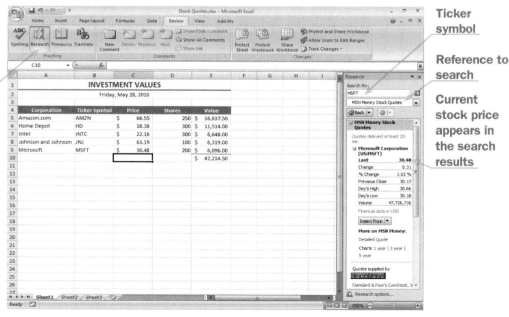

Button to toggle the Research task pane open and closed

Ticker symbol

Reference to search

Current stock price appears in the search results

STEP-BY-STEP 6.12 Continued

10. Click the **Review** tab on the Ribbon. In the Proofing group, click the **Research** button. The Research task pane closes.

11. Insert a header with your name and the current date. Save, print, and close the workbook.

SUMMARY

In this lesson, you learned:

- Sorting rearranges worksheet data in ascending or descending alphabetical, numerical, or chronological order.

- Filtering displays a subset of data in a worksheet that meets specific criteria.

- Conditional formatting highlights worksheet data by changing the look of cells that meet a specified condition, such as a comparison or rank.

- Hiding rows and/or columns lets you use the same worksheet to emphasize different data. You can unhide the hidden rows and columns at any time.

- Shapes, such as rectangles, circles, arrows, lines, flowchart symbols, and callouts, can help make a worksheet more informative. Excel has a gallery of shapes you can insert.

- SmartArt graphics enhance worksheets by providing a visual representation of information and ideas. Excel has a variety of layouts you can select.

- Pictures can make a worksheet's appearance more attractive. You can insert a picture you have stored as a file, or one from the Clip Art collection that comes with Excel.

- Templates are predesigned workbook files that can be used as the basis or model when creating a new workbook. A template includes all parts of the workbook that will not change, such as labels, formulas, and formatting.

- A hyperlink in a worksheet open another file or page when clicked. You can create hyperlinks to another Web page, another file, a specific location in the current workbook, a new document, or an e-mail address.

- You can save workbooks in different file formats, so they can be opened in other programs or earlier versions of Excel.

- Comments are notes that can be added to cells to provide additional information or feedback.

- The Research task pane provides access to information typically found in references such as dictionaries, thesauruses, and encyclopedias. In Excel, it also provides numerical data, such as current stock prices.

VOCABULARY *Review*

Define the following terms:

Ascending sort	Filter	Research task pane
AutoFilter	Filter arrows	SmartArt graphic
Comment	Hyperlink	Sort
Conditional formatting	Object	Template
Descending sort	Picture	

REVIEW *Questions*

TRUE/FALSE

Circle T if the statement is true or F if the statement is false.

T   F   1. Sorting always arranges data in a worksheet with the smallest values listed first.

T   F   2. Filtering reorganizes data so it appears in a different order.

T   F   3. Hiding deletes a row or column from a worksheet.

T   F   4. Inserting a comment in a cell affects the results of a formula contained in that cell.

T   F   5. Excel workbooks can be saved in other file formats.

MATCHING

Match the correct term in Column 2 to its description in Column 1.

Column 1	**Column 2**
___ 1. Workbook used as a model to create other workbooks	A. AutoFilter
___ 2. Changes the look of cells that meet a specific condition	B. Template
___ 3. Organizes data in a more meaningful order	C. Conditional formatting
___ 4. A cell or graphic that opens another file or Web page when clicked	D. Comment
___ 5. Displays a subset of data that meet certain criteria	E. Hyperlink
___ 6. A message that explains or identifies information in a cell	F. Sorting

PROJECTS

 PROJECT 6-1

1. Open the **Impact.xlsx** Data File. Save the workbook as **Impact Salaries** followed by your initials. The worksheet contains the annual salaries and ratings of Level 10 employees.

2. Sort the data in the range A6:E20 by the Performance Rating in descending numerical order (largest to smallest).

3. In cell F5, enter **Salary Category** as the label.

4. In cell F6, enter the following formula to indicate the employee's salary category (low or high) based on his annual salary: **=IF(D6<32001,"Low","High")**.

5. Copy the formula in cell F6 to the range F7:F20.

   The Level 10 management is concerned that employee salaries do not reflect the annual performance ratings. If salaries are allocated based on annual ratings, employees with higher performance ratings should appear near the top of the worksheet and have *High* in the Category column. Employees with lower ratings should appear near the bottom of the worksheet and have *Low* in the Category column. When a salary does not reflect the employee's annual rating, the word in column F might appear to be out of place.

6. Based on the data in the worksheet, which employees do you believe are underpaid? Why?

7. Insert a header with your name and the current date. Save, print, and close the workbook.

 PROJECT 6-2

1. Open the **Top.xlsx** Data File. Save the workbook as **Top Movies** followed by your initials.

2. Conditionally format the data to highlight the top 10 highest grossing films with a light green fill with dark green text. Column D contains the number of dollars that the film grossed.

3. Conditionally format the data to highlight the bottom 10 lowest grossing films with a yellow fill with dark yellow text.

4. Sort the data by Release Date in ascending order (oldest to newest) and then by Movie in ascending order (A to Z).

5. Insert a header with your name and the current date. Save, print, and close the file.

 SCANS PROJECT 6-3

1. Open the **City.xlsx** Data File. Save the workbook as **City Facts** followed by your initials.

2. Click cell B2 and turn on the filter arrows.

3. Run the following AutoFilters to answer the following questions. Remember to restore the records after each filter by clearing the filter.

Column	AutoFilter	Criterion
B	Top 10 Items	4 items
C	Bottom 10 Items	4 items
D	Top 10 %	10 percent
G	0	(not needed)

A. What are the four largest cities in the United States?

_____   _____   _____   _____

B. What are the four coldest cities in the United States during January?

_____   _____   _____   _____

C. What cities are in the top 10 percentile of average July temperatures?

_____   _____   _____   _____

D. How many of the 30 largest cities are at sea level (have altitudes of 0)?

4. Save and close the workbook.

PROJECT 6-4

1. Open the **Paper.xlsx** Data File. Save the workbook as **Paper Sales** followed by your initials.

2. Hide columns B through E to remove the quarterly data from view.

3. Unhide columns B through E to restore the quarterly data.

4. Hide rows 7 through 14 to remove the regional data from view.

5. Insert a header with your name and the current date. Print the worksheet.

6. Unhide rows 7 through 14 to restore the regional data.

7. Save and close the workbook.

PROJECT 6-5

1. In the New Workbook dialog box, display the templates installed on your computer, and open the **Billing Statement** template file.

2. Save the workbook as **Roberts Statement** followed by your initials.

3. Zoom the worksheet so you can see the entire statement, if it is not already in view.

4. Enter the following data in the worksheet.

Cell	Data
B1	(your name)
C8	15679
C10	EX6-5
F2	(504) 555-8796
F3	(504) 555-8797

F8	**Anita Roberts**
F9	**4509 Lumpton Road**
F10	**New Orleans, LA, 70135**
F11, F12	(delete cell contents)
B15	**10/8/10**
C15	**Event Planning**
D15	**013**
E15	**Graduation Party**
F15	**350**
G15	**50**

5. Save, print, and close the workbook.

 PROJECT 6-6

1. Open the **School.xlsx** Data File. Save the workbook as **School Bus** followed by your initials.

2. On the Insert tab, in the Illustrations group, click the Picture button. The Insert Picture dialog box appears.

3. Insert the **School Bus.bmp** Data File.

4. Under Picture Tools on the Format tab, in the Size group, click the Dialog Box Launcher. The Size and Properties dialog box appears.

5. On the Size tab, in the Scale section, in the Height box, type **41%**. Click Close.

6. Drag the picture so that it fits within the range E1:E3.

7. Under Picture Tools on the Format tab, in the Picture Styles group, click the Picture Effects button, point to Glow, and then click Accent color 6, 18 pt glow.

8. Insert a header with your name and the current date. Save, print, and close the workbook.

 PROJECT 6-7

1. Open the **Compact.xlsx** Data File. Save the workbook as **Compact Cubicle** followed by your initials.

2. In cell C8, insert the following comment: **Shut down for two hours for maintenance.**

3. In cell C9, insert the following comment: **Production time increased two hours to make up for maintenance on Machine 102.**

4. In cell G9, insert the following comment: **Shut down for major repairs.**

5. Insert a cube shape in the upper-left corner of the workbook.

6. On the Drawing Tools Format tab, in the Size group, enter **0.5"** in the Shape Height box and the Shape Width box.

7. Change the Shape Fill to Orange.

8. Change the Shape Effects so the 3-D Rotation is set to Off Axis 1 Right.

9. Copy and paste the cube shape, and then drag the copy so it overlaps the lower-right corner of the first cube.

10. Insert a header with your name and the current date. Save, print, and close the workbook.

CRITICAL*Thinking*

 ACTIVITY 6-1

Additional clip art is available on Microsoft Office Online. You can access the site by clicking *Clip art on Office Online* in the Clip Art task pane. If you have Internet access, use Office Online to locate the following clip art items:

■ Lion

■ Valentine heart

■ Doctor

■ Cactus

Copy each clip art item to the worksheet. Resize and format it appropriately. Insert a header with your name and the current date. Save and close the workbook.

 ACTIVITY 6-2

SmartArt graphics are a simple way to present hierarchical information or relationships, such as for a team, club, school, family, or organization. For example, your school probably has a principal, teachers, and students. In a worksheet, insert a SmartArt graphic to illustrate at least three levels of that hierarchy. Format the SmartArt graphic appropriately.

WORKING WITH MULTIPLE WORKSHEETS AND WORKBOOKS

OBJECTIVES

Upon completion of this lesson, you will be able to:

- Move between worksheets in a workbook.
- Rename worksheets.
- Change the color of sheet tabs.
- Reposition worksheets.
- Hide and unhide worksheets.
- Insert and delete worksheets.
- Create cell references to other worksheets.
- Create 3-D references.
- Print all or part of workbooks.
- Arrange multiple workbooks in the program window.
- Move and copy worksheets between workbooks.

Estimated Time: 2 hours

VOCABULARY

3-D reference

Active sheet

Destination

Sheet tab

Source

Worksheet range

Moving Between Worksheets

A workbook is a collection of worksheets. The worksheets within the workbook are identified by sheet tabs that appear at the bottom of the workbook window. The name of the worksheet appears on the tab. Until the worksheets are named, they are identified as Sheet1, Sheet2, and so on, as shown in Figure 7-1.

FIGURE 7-1
Default sheet tabs in a workbook

Sheet tab for the active worksheet

Tab scrolling buttons

Sheet tabs for the inactive worksheets

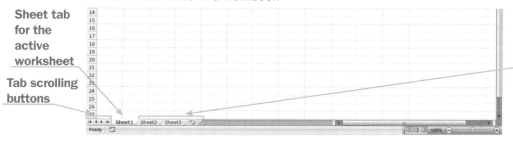

To view a specific worksheet, simply click its sheet tab. The worksheet that appears in the workbook window is called the active sheet. The active sheet has a white sheet tab. If you don't see the sheet tab for the worksheet you want to display, use the tab scrolling buttons to display the sheet tab.

Identifying Worksheets

 To better distinguish worksheets, you can give them more descriptive names. You can also change the color of each sheet tab.

Renaming Worksheets

Although you can leave the default worksheet names (Sheet1, Sheet2, and so forth), a good practice is to use descriptive names to help identify the contents of each worksheet. For example, the worksheet name *Quarter 1 Budget* is a better reminder of the worksheet contents than *Sheet1*. To rename a worksheet, double-click its sheet tab, type the new name, and then press the Enter key.

> **Did You Know?**
>
> To rename a worksheet, you can also right-click its sheet tab, and then click Rename on the short-cut menu. The worksheet name in the sheet tab is selected. Type a new name, and then press the Enter key.

Changing the Color of Sheet Tabs

Another way to categorize worksheets is by changing the color of the sheet tabs. For example, a sales manager might use different colors to identify each sales region. To change the tab color of a worksheet, right-click the sheet tab you want to recolor, point to Tab Color on the shortcut menu, and then click the color you want for that tab.

STEP-BY-STEP 7.1

1. Open the **Continental.xlsx** Data File. Save the workbook as **Continental Sales** followed by your initials.

2. Click the **Sheet3** sheet tab. The Sheet3 worksheet appears as the active sheet. It will summarize the sales data stored in other worksheets.

3. Double-click the **Sheet3** sheet tab. The worksheet name is highlighted.

4. Type **Corporate**, and then press the **Enter** key. The name *Corporate* appears on the third sheet tab.

STEP-BY-STEP 7.1 Continued

5. Double-click the **Sheet1** sheet tab, type **Western**, and then press the **Enter** key. The Sheet1 worksheet is renamed as *Western*.

6. Rename the Sheet2 worksheet as **Eastern**.

7. Rename the Sheet4 worksheet as **Northern**.

8. Right-click the **Corporate** sheet tab, and then point to **Tab Color**. A palette of colors appears, as shown in Figure 7-2.

FIGURE 7-2
Shortcut menu for the selected sheet tab

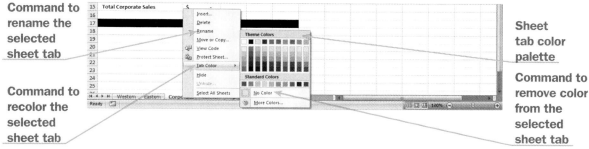

Command to
rename the
selected
sheet tab

Command to
recolor the
selected
sheet tab

Sheet
tab color
palette

Command to
remove color
from the
selected
sheet tab

9. In the Theme Colors section, click **Black, Text 1** (the second color in the first row). A black line appears at the bottom of the Corporate sheet tab.

10. Click the **Northern** sheet tab. The Northern worksheet becomes the active sheet, and you can see the black sheet tab for the Corporate worksheet.

11. Right-click the **Northern** sheet tab, point to **Tab Color** to open the color palette, and then, in the Theme Colors section, click **Orange, Accent 6** (the last color in the first row).

12. Right-click the **Western** sheet tab, point to **Tab Color**, and then click **Aqua, Accent 5** (the ninth color in the first row).

13. Right-click the **Eastern** sheet tab, point to **Tab Color**, and then, in the Theme Colors section, click **Purple, Accent 4** (the eighth color in the first row).

STEP-BY-STEP 7.1 Continued

14. Click the **Corporate** sheet tab. The Corporate worksheet is active, and the colored sheet tabs are visible for the regional worksheets, as shown in Figure 7-3.

FIGURE 7-3
Renamed and colored sheet tabs

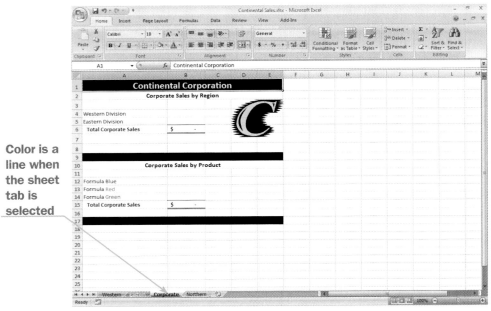

Color is a line when the sheet tab is selected

15. Save the workbook, and leave it open for the next Step-by-Step.

Managing Worksheets Within a Workbook

Often, data and analysis are best organized on multiple worksheets. For example, you could enter financial data for each quarter of the year in four different worksheets, and then summarize the annual data in a fifth worksheet. Another common workbook organization is to place sales data for each sales territory or region in its own worksheet, and then summarize the total sales in another worksheet.

Repositioning Worksheets

To make it simpler to find information, you can position worksheets in a logical order, such as placing a summary worksheet first, followed by actual data. You can reposition a worksheet by dragging its sheet tab to a new location. A placement arrow indicates the new location, as shown in Figure 7-4. When you release the mouse button, the worksheet moves to that position.

FIGURE 7-4
Sheet tab being repositioned

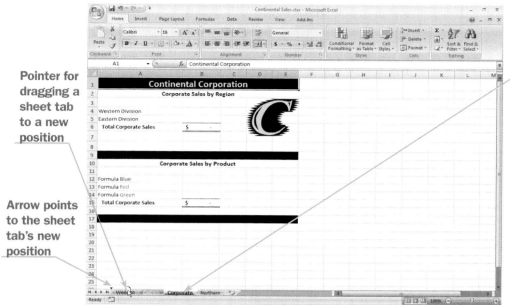

Pointer for dragging a sheet tab to a new position

Arrow points to the sheet tab's new position

Selected sheet tab is being moved

Hiding and Unhiding Worksheets

Some workbooks include many worksheets. Some might contain data you do not need to see, but still want to save, such as a list of employee names or data from past months. You can keep the sheet tabs streamlined by hiding the worksheets to which you do not need immediate access. Right-click the worksheet you want to hide, and then click Hide on the shortcut menu. To unhide a worksheet, right-click any sheet tab, and then click Unhide on the shortcut menu. The Unhide dialog box appears, as shown in Figure 7-5. Click the worksheet you want to unhide, and then click OK.

Extra for Experts

You can create a copy of a worksheet by pressing the Ctrl key as you drag and drop its sheet tab. When you release the mouse button, an exact copy of the selected worksheet is added in the location indicated by the arrow and the original worksheet remains in its same location. The sheet tab has the same name as the original worksheet followed by a number in parentheses.

FIGURE 7-5
Unhide dialog box

Worksheet hidden in the active workbook

Inserting and Deleting Worksheets

Each workbook opens with three worksheets. But, you can always add or delete worksheets as needed to accommodate your data. To insert a blank worksheet, click the Insert Worksheet tab next to the existing sheet tabs. A new worksheet is added after the other worksheets. You can drag the new worksheet to the position you want. Another option is to click the sheet tab of the worksheet that will *follow* the new sheet. On the Home tab of the Ribbon, in the Cells group, click the arrow to the right of the Insert button, and then click Insert Sheet. A new worksheet is inserted before the sheet you selected.

Deleting permanently removes a worksheet and all its contents from the workbook. You cannot undo the action. To delete a worksheet, click the sheet tab for the worksheet you want to remove. On the Home tab of the Ribbon, in the Cells group, click the arrow to the right of the Delete button, and then click Delete Sheet. A dialog box might appear to confirm that you want to permanently delete the data that might exist in the worksheet. Click Delete to continue the action, or click Cancel to leave the worksheet in the workbook. You can also right-click a sheet tab, and then click Delete on the shortcut menu. The worksheet is permanently removed from the workbook without confirmation.

S TEP-BY-STEP 7.2

1. Click and drag the **Corporate** sheet tab to the left until the arrow points to the left of the Western sheet tab, as shown in Figure 7-4.

2. Release the mouse button. The sheet tab for the Corporate worksheet is first.

3. Right-click the **Northern** sheet tab, and then click **Hide** on the shortcut menu. The Northern worksheet and its sheet tab disappear.

4. Right-click any sheet tab, and then click **Unhide** on the shortcut menu. The Unhide dialog box appears, as shown in Figure 7-5, listing the names of the worksheets that are currently hidden.

5. Click **Northern**, if it is not already selected, and then click **OK**. The Northern worksheet and its sheet tab reappear.

6. On the Home tab of the Ribbon, in the Cells group, to the right of the Delete button, click the **arrow**, and then click **Delete Sheet**.

7. If a dialog box appears warning that any data in the worksheet will be permanently deleted, click **Delete**. The Northern worksheet is deleted, and its sheet tab no longer appears at the bottom of the worksheet.

8. Save the workbook, and leave it open for the next Step-by-Step.

Consolidating Workbook Data

In some cases, you might need several worksheets to solve one numerical problem. For example, a business that has several divisions might keep the financial results of each division in a separate worksheet. Then another worksheet might combine those results to show summary results for all divisions.

Creating Cell References to Other Worksheets

Rather than retyping data and formulas, you can create a reference to existing data and formulas in other worksheets. For example, you would use this type of reference to display regional sales totals on a summary sheet. The location the data is being transferred from is the source. The location where the data will appear is the destination.

To display data or formula results from one worksheet in another worksheet of the same workbook, you use a formula. First, click the destination cell where you want to display the data or formula results from another worksheet. Type an equal sign to begin the formula. Click the sheet tab for the worksheet that contains the source cell or range you want to reference, and then click the source cell or select the source range to include it in the formula. Finally, press the Enter key to complete the formula. The contents of the source cell appear in the destination cell. Any change you make to the source cell also changes the value in the destination cell. For example, the reference *Sheet2!B3* refers to the value contained in cell B3 on Sheet 2.

Northern!A1:C3

Worksheet name

Exclamation point

Cells on the specified worksheet

Creating 3-D References

A 3-D reference is a reference to the same cell or range in multiple worksheets that you use in a formula. You can use 3-D references to incorporate data from other worksheets into the active worksheet. You use a 3-D reference with 18 different functions, including SUM, AVERAGE, COUNT, MIN, MAX, and PRODUCT. For example, you might want to enter the SUM function in a summary worksheet to add several numbers contained in other worksheets, such as with quarterly or regional sales data. In general, to use 3-D references, worksheets should have the same organization and structure.

A 3-D reference lists the worksheet range, an exclamation point, and a cell or range. A worksheet range is a group of adjacent worksheets. In a worksheet range, as in a cell range, a colon separates the names of the first worksheet and the last worksheet in the group. An exclamation mark separates the worksheet range from its cell or range reference. For example, the reference *Sheet2:Sheet4!B3* refers to the values contained in cell B3 on Sheet2, Sheet3, and Sheet4.

Because a worksheet range is a group of adjacent worksheets, moving a worksheet into the range or removing a worksheet from the range affects the formula results. In the previous example, if you move Sheet1 between Sheet3 and Sheet4, the value in cell B3 of Sheet1 is also included in the 3-D reference.

Eastern:Western!C3

Worksheet range

Exclamation point

Cell in each worksheet of the range

Table 7-1 gives other examples of how 3-D references might be used.

TABLE 7-1
Formulas that reference other worksheets

FORMULA	DESCRIPTION
=Sheet4!D9	Displays the value from cell D9 in the Sheet4 worksheet
=Sheet1!D10+Sheet2!D11	Adds the value from cell D10 in the Sheet1 worksheet and the value from cell D11 in the Sheet2 worksheet
=SUM(Sheet2!D10:D11)	Adds the values from cells D10 and D11 in the Sheet2 worksheet
=SUM(Sheet2:Sheet4!D12)	Adds the value from cell D12 in the Sheet2, Sheet3, and Sheet4 worksheets

STEP-BY-STEP 7.3

1. Click the **Corporate** sheet tab. You will enter formulas in this worksheet that reference cells in the Western and Eastern worksheets.

2. Click cell **B4**, and then type **=** to begin the formula.

3. Click the **Western** sheet tab. The worksheet name is added to the formula in the Formula Bar, which is =Western!. The Western worksheet appears in the workbook window so you can select a cell or range.

4. Click cell **B6**. The cell address is added to the reference in the Formula Bar, which is =Western!B6. The Western worksheet remains visible so you can select additional cells.

5. Press the **Enter** key. The formula is entered, and the Corporate worksheet is active again. The formula results $543,367 appear in cell B4.

6. Click cell **B5**, if it is not the active cell in the Corporate worksheet, and then type **=** to begin the formula.

7. Click the **Eastern** sheet tab, and then click cell **B6**. The formula =Eastern!B6 appears in the Formula Bar.

8. Press the **Enter** key. The formula is entered in cell B5 of the Corporate worksheet.

9. In the Corporate worksheet, click cell **B12**, and then type **=** to begin the formula.

10. Click the **Western** sheet tab, and then click cell **B3**. The formula =Western!B3 appears in the Formula Bar.

11. Type **+** to enter the operator, click the **Eastern** sheet tab, and then click cell **B3**. The formula =Western!B3+Eastern!B3 appears in the Formula Bar.

12. Press the **Enter** key. The formula is entered in cell B12 of the Corporate worksheet, which shows the formula results $306,744.

STEP-BY-STEP 7.3 Continued

13. Click cell **B13**, if it is not already selected, and then type **=SUM(** to begin the formula.

14. Click the **Western** sheet tab, press and hold the **Shift** key, and then click the **Eastern** sheet tab. Release the Shift key. The formula with the worksheet range reference =SUM('Western:Eastern'! appears in the Formula Bar.

15. Click cell **B4**, and then press the **Enter** key. The cell reference is added to the 3-D reference in the formula, which is =SUM('Western:Eastern'!B4). The formula results $566,399, which add the value from cell B4 in the Eastern and Westerns worksheets, appear in cell B13.

16. Copy the formula in cell B13 to cell B14. The value in cell B15 is the same as the value in cell B6, as shown in Figure 7-6.

FIGURE 7-6
Data summarized on one worksheet

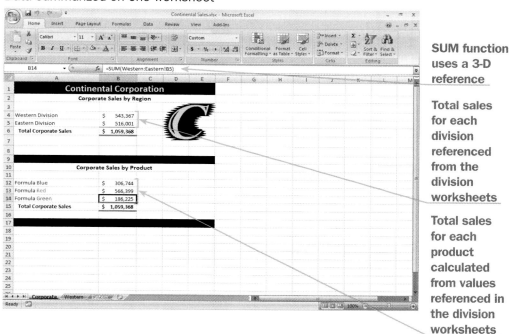

SUM function uses a 3-D reference

Total sales for each division referenced from the division worksheets

Total sales for each product calculated from values referenced in the division worksheets

17. Save the workbook, and leave it open for the next Step-by-Step.

 **Careers**

Excel workbooks are extremely useful in areas of business that have a quantitative orientation, such as accounting and finance. In accounting, formulas are used to build financial statements. Financial officers in corporations use spreadsheets to project sales and control costs.

Printing a Workbook

So far, you have printed an active worksheet or selected areas of an active worksheet. You can also print an entire workbook, selected worksheets, or selected areas of a workbook. You designate the portion of the workbook to print in the Print what section of the Print dialog box, as shown in Figure 7-7. The print options are described in Table 7-2.

FIGURE 7-7
Print dialog box

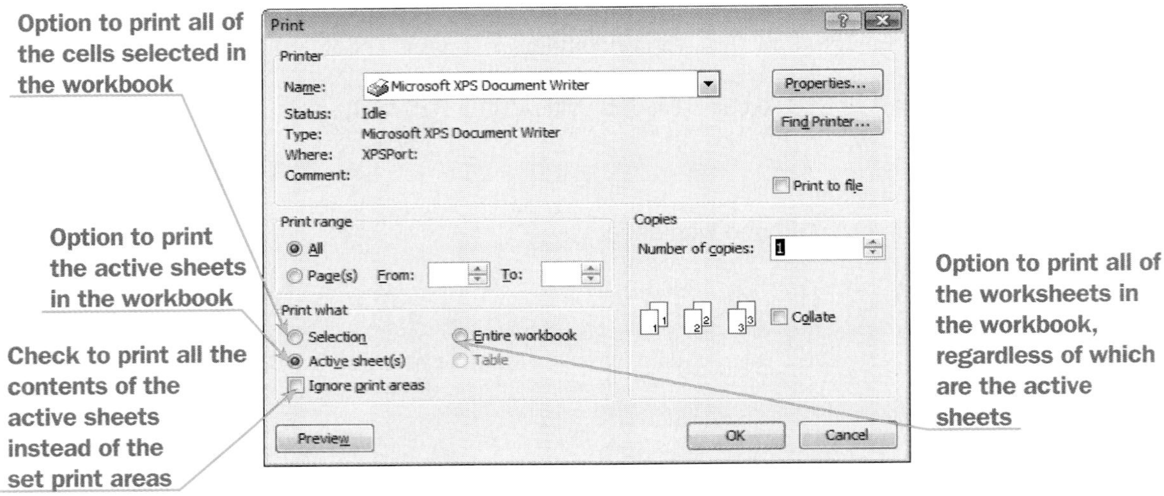

Option to print all of the cells selected in the workbook

Option to print the active sheets in the workbook

Check to print all the contents of the active sheets instead of the set print areas

Option to print all of the worksheets in the workbook, regardless of which are the active sheets

TABLE 7-2
Print what options

OPTION	PRINTS
Selection	The range or ranges selected within a single worksheet
Active sheet(s)	The worksheet that appears on-screen, or a group of selected worksheets (Ctrl+click sheet tabs to select multiple worksheets)
Entire workbook	All of the worksheets in a workbook

Printing Non-adjacent Selections of a Worksheet

You have already learned how to set a print area for a specific range in a worksheet. However, at times you might want to print more than one part of a worksheet on a page. For example, you might want to print the top and bottom sections of a worksheet, but not the middle portion. To do this, you need to select multiple ranges in the worksheet. To select more than one cell or range in a worksheet, select the first cell or range, hold down the Ctrl key, select each additional cell or range, and then release the Ctrl key. You can set the print area to include the non-adjacent range, and then print the active sheet as usual. Another alternative is to click the Selection option in the Print what section of the Print dialog box.

Printing More Than One Worksheet

When a workbook includes multiple worksheets, you will often want to print more than one worksheet at a time. To print all of the worksheets in the workbook, click the Entire workbook option in the Print what section of the Print dialog box. To print specific worksheets in a workbook, you must first select the worksheets. To select multiple worksheets in a workbook, hold down the Ctrl key as you click the sheet tab of each worksheet you want to include in the group, and then release the Ctrl key. In the Print dialog box, select the Active sheet(s) option in the Print what section.

STEP-BY-STEP 7.4

1. Insert a header with your name and the current date.

2. In the Corporate worksheet, select the range **A4:B6**.

3. Hold down the **Ctrl** key and select the range **A12:B15**. Non-adjacent ranges are selected in the Corporate worksheet.

4. Click the **Office Button**, and then click **Print**. The Print dialog box appears, as shown in Figure 7-7.

5. In the Print what section, click the **Selection** option button.

6. Click **Preview**. The range A4:B6 will print on page 1 and the range A12:B15 will print on page 2, as shown in Figure 7-8.

FIGURE 7-8
Print Preview of the selected ranges

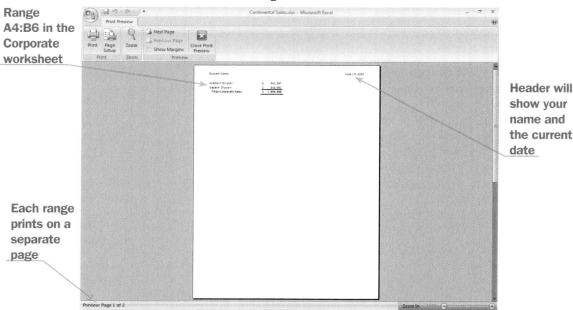

Range A4:B6 in the Corporate worksheet

Header will show your name and the current date

Each range prints on a separate page

7. Click **Print**. The selected areas print.

STEP-BY-STEP 7.4 Continued

8. Click the **Western** tab.

9. Hold down the **Ctrl** key and click the **Eastern** tab. The two sheet tabs are selected.

10. Click the **Office Button**, and then click **Print**. The Print dialog box appears.

11. In the Print what section, click the **Active sheet(s)** option button, if it is not already selected.

12. Click **Print**. The worksheets with the data for each division print on separate pages.

13. Save and close the workbook.

Working with Multiple Workbooks

So far, you have worked with worksheets in the same workbook. Sometimes you might want to use data from worksheets in different workbooks. You can view these worksheets on the screen by arranging the workbooks. If you want to use the data from a worksheet in one workbook in another workbook, you can move or copy the worksheet to the new workbook.

Arranging Workbooks

Arranging lets you view more than one workbook on the screen at the same time. To arrange all the open workbooks, click the Arrange All button in the Window group on the View tab of the Ribbon. The Arrange Windows dialog box appears, as shown in Figure 7-9. Click the arrangement in which you want to view the workbooks: Tiled, Horizontal, Vertical, or Cascade.

FIGURE 7-9
Arrange Windows dialog box

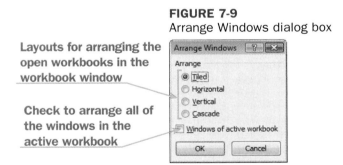

Layouts for arranging the open workbooks in the workbook window

Check to arrange all of the windows in the active workbook

You can tell which workbook is active by looking at its title. The active workbook has a blue title bar with the sizing buttons. Also, the active workbook contains scroll bars. To make a workbook active, just click its title bar or anywhere in the worksheet. All of the buttons and commands are available as usual.

Moving and Copying Worksheets Between Workbooks

When you need to use a worksheet from one workbook in another, you can copy or move the worksheet. Right-click the sheet tab of the worksheet you want to move or copy, and then click Move or Copy on the shortcut menu. The Move or Copy dialog box appears. Click the arrow next to the To book box and click the workbook in which you want the selected worksheet to appear. After you select the destination workbook, the names of all of its worksheets appear in the Before sheet box. Click the worksheet that you want to appear after the copied or moved worksheet. If you want to move the worksheet, click OK. If you want to copy the worksheet, click the Create a copy check box and then click OK.

STEP-BY-STEP 7.5

1. Open the **Annual.xlsx** Data File. Save the workbook as **Annual Statement** followed by your initials.

2. Open the **February.xlsx** Data File. Save the workbook as **February Statement** followed by your initials.

3. Click the **View** tab on the Ribbon. In the Window group, click the **Arrange All** button. The Arrange Windows dialog box appears, as shown in Figure 7-9.

4. Click the **Horizontal** button, and then click **OK**. Both workbooks appear on the screen, as shown in Figure 7-10.

FIGURE 7-10
Workbooks arranged horizontally

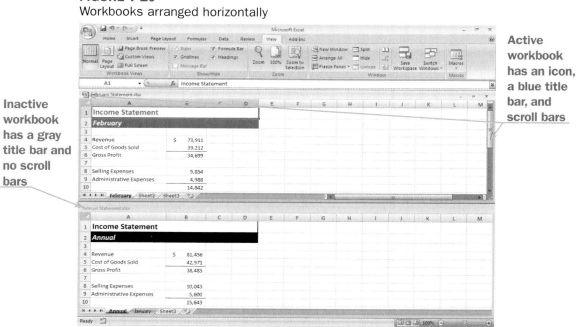

Inactive workbook has a gray title bar and no scroll bars

Active workbook has an icon, a blue title bar, and scroll bars

5. In the February Statement workbook, right-click the **February** sheet tab, and then click **Move or Copy** on the shortcut menu. The Move or Copy dialog box appears.

6. Click the **arrow** next to the To book box, and then click **Annual Statement.xlsx**. The worksheets in the Annual Statement workbook appear in the Before sheet box.

7. In the Before sheet box, click **Sheet3** so the February worksheet will follow the January worksheet.

STEP-BY-STEP 7.5 Continued

8. Click the **Create a copy** check box. The dialog box settings should appear similar to those in Figure 7-11.

FIGURE 7-11
Move or Copy dialog box

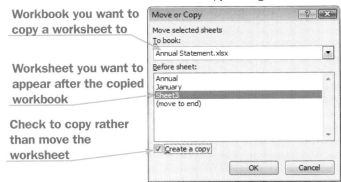

Workbook you want to copy a worksheet to

Worksheet you want to appear after the copied workbook

Check to copy rather than move the worksheet

9. Click **OK**. A copy of the February worksheet appears in the Annual Statement workbook.

10. Click in the **February Statement** workbook to make it the active workbook, and then close the workbook.

11. Click the **Maximize** button on the title bar of the Annual Statement workbook. The workbook expands to fill the program window.

12. Click the **Annual** tab. Notice that the totals include the values from the February worksheet, because of the 3-D references in the formulas.

13. Insert a header with your name and the current date. Print the January and February worksheets.

14. Save and close the workbook.

SUMMARY

In this lesson, you learned:

■ Sheet tabs identify the names of worksheets. You click a sheet tab to make a worksheet the active sheet.

■ You can rename worksheets with more descriptive names to better distinguish them. You can also change the color of the sheet tabs.

■ Data is often best organized in multiple worksheets. You can drag a sheet tab to a new position to organize the worksheets in a more logical order. You can hide worksheets from view and then unhide them when needed. You can also insert and delete worksheets to accommodate the data.

■ Rather than retyping data, you can create references to cells in another worksheet. You can also create formulas with 3-D references to the same cell or range in multiple worksheets.

■ Entire workbooks, selected worksheets, or selected ranges in a worksheet can be printed.

■ Arranging multiple workbooks in the program window lets you view their contents at the same time. Worksheets can be moved or copied from one workbook to the location you specify in the same or another workbook.

VOCABULARY *Review*

Define the following terms:

3-D reference	Destination	Source
Active sheet	Sheet tab	Worksheet range

REVIEW *Questions*

MATCHING

Match the correct formula result in Column 2 to its formula in Column 1.

Column 1

_____ 1. =Sheet2!D10

_____ 2. =Sheet2!D10+Sheet3!D11

_____ 3. =SUM(Sheet2:Sheet4!D10)

_____ 4. =SUM(Sheet2!D10:D11)

_____ 5. =Sheet3!D10+Sheet3!D11

Column 2

A. Adds the values in cells D10 and D11 of the Sheet2 worksheet

B. Adds the values in cells D10 and D11 of the Sheet3 worksheet

C. Adds the values in cell D10 of the Sheet2 worksheet and cell D11 of the Sheet3 worksheet

D. Inserts the value in cell D10 of the Sheet2 worksheet

E. Adds the values in cell D10 in the Sheet2, Sheet3, and Sheet4 worksheets

FILL IN THE BLANK

Complete the following sentences by writing the correct word or words in the blanks provided.

1. A(n) _____ is a collection of worksheets.

2. The worksheet that appears in the workbook window is the _____.

3. _____ identify worksheets within a workbook at the bottom of a workbook window.

4. You can create formulas with _____ to the same cell or range in multiple worksheets.

5. _____ multiple workbooks in the program window lets you view their contents at the same time.

PROJECTS

 PROJECT 7-1

1. Open the **Rainfall.xlsx** Data File. Save the workbook as **Rainfall Records** followed by your initials.

2. Rename the worksheets and change the sheet tab colors as listed below:

Worksheet	New Name	Tab Color
Sheet1	Annual	Blue, Accent 1
Sheet2	January	Blue, Accent 1, Lighter 80%
Sheet3	February	Blue, Accent 1, Lighter 60%
Sheet4	March	Blue, Accent 1, Lighter 40%

3. In the Annual worksheet, in cell B3, display the total rainfall recorded in the January worksheet in cell B34.

4. In the Annual worksheet, in cell B4, display the total rainfall recorded in the February worksheet in cell B31.

5. In the Annual worksheet, in cell B5, display the total rainfall recorded in the March worksheet in cell B34.

6. Insert a header with your name and the current date, and then save the workbook.

7. Print the Annual worksheet, and then close the workbook.

 PROJECT 7-2

1. Open the **Voting.xlsx** Data File. Save the workbook as **Voting Tally** followed by your initials.

2. Rename the worksheets and change the sheet tab colors as listed below:

Worksheet	New Name	Tab Color
Sheet1	District 5	Red
Sheet2	P107	Yellow
Sheet3	P106	Purple
Sheet4	P105	Green

3. Reposition the worksheets so they appear in the following order: District 5, P105, P106, and P107.

4. In the District 5 worksheet, in cell D7, enter a formula that adds the values in cell C5 of each of the precinct worksheets.

5. In the District 5 worksheet, in cell D9, enter a formula that adds the values in cell C7 of each of the precinct worksheets.

6. In the District 5 worksheet, in cell D11, enter a formula that adds the values in cell C9 of each of the precinct worksheets.

7. In the District 5 worksheet, in cell D13, enter a formula that adds the values in cell C11 of each of the precinct worksheets.

8. Insert a header with your name and the current date, and then save the workbook.

9. Print the District 5 worksheet, and then close the workbook.

 PROJECT 7-3

1. Open the **Alamo.xlsx** Data File. Save the workbook as **Alamo Amalgamated** followed by your initials.

2. Change the sheet tab colors as listed below:

Worksheet	Tab Color
Consolidated	Green
Alamogordo	Light Green
Artesia	Light Blue

3. In the Consolidated worksheet, in cell D6, enter a formula that adds the values in cell B6 of the Alamogordo and Artesia worksheets.

4. In the Consolidated worksheet, in cell D7, enter a formula that adds the values in cell B7 of the Alamogordo and Artesia worksheets.

5. In the Consolidated worksheet, in cell D9, enter a formula that adds the values in cell B9 of the Alamogordo and Artesia worksheets.

6. In the Consolidated worksheet, in cell D10, enter a formula that adds the values in cell B10 of the Alamogordo and Artesia worksheets.

7. Insert a header with your name and the current date, and then save the workbook.

8. Print all of the worksheets in the workbook, and then close the workbook.

 PROJECT 7-4

1. Open the **United.xlsx** Data File. Save the workbook as **United Circuitry** followed by your initials.

2. Change the worksheet tab colors as listed below:

Worksheet	Tab Color
Year	Red
January	Purple, Accent 4
February	Orange, Accent 6
March	Blue, Accent 1

3. In the Year worksheet, in cells B5, B6, and B7, display the total January monthly production for Circuits 370, 380, and 390. These values are recorded in the January worksheet in the range F4:F6.

4. In the Year worksheet, in cells C5, C6, and C7, display the total February monthly production for each circuit. These values are recorded in the February worksheet in the range F4:F6.

5. In the Year worksheet, in cells D5, D6, and D7, display the total March monthly production for each circuit. These values are recorded in the March worksheet in the range F4:F6.

6. Insert a header with your name and the current date, and then save the workbook.

7. Print the entire Year worksheet, and then close the workbook.

CRITICAL*Thinking*

 ACTIVITY 7-1

Suppose you manage a local clothing store chain. Each of the three stores has sent you a workbook in the same format that contains inventory data. You want to use the data you received to create a summary workbook with totals from all three stores. Use Excel Help to find out how you can create an external reference to a cell or range in another workbook. Write a brief description of what you learn.

LESSON 8

WORKING WITH CHARTS

OBJECTIVES

Upon completion of this lesson, you will be able to:

- Identify the purpose of charting worksheet data.
- Identify the types of charts you can create in Excel.
- Create a chart embedded in a worksheet.
- Move a chart to a chart sheet.
- Update a data source.
- Select chart elements.
- Choose a chart layout and style.
- Create a 3-D chart.
- Display or hide chart elements.
- Format and modify a chart.
- Edit and format chart text.
- Change the chart type.

Estimated Time: 2.5 hours

VOCABULARY

Axis
Chart
Chart area
Chart layout
Chart sheet
Chart style
Column chart
Data label
Data marker
Data series
Data source
Data table
Embedded chart
Exploded pie chart
Legend
Line chart
Pie chart
Plot area
Scatter chart
Selection box
Sizing handles

What Is a Worksheet Chart?

A chart is a graphical representation of data. Charts make the data in a worksheet easier to understand by providing a visual picture of the data. For example, the left side of the worksheet in Figure 8-1 shows the populations of three major American cities for three years. You might be able to detect the population changes by carefully examining the table. However, the population increases and decreases in each city are easier to see when the data is illustrated in a chart, such as the one shown on the right side of the worksheet in Figure 8-1.

FIGURE 8-1
Worksheet data and chart

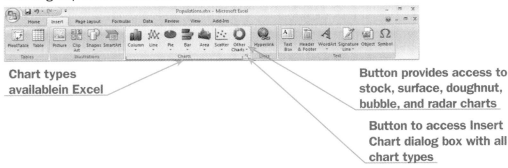

Chart based on the worksheet data

Data in the worksheet

Comparing Chart Types

You can create a variety of charts in Excel. Each type of chart has a different look and works best for certain types of data. In this lesson, you create four of the most commonly used charts: column chart, line chart, pie chart, and scatter chart. These charts and several other types of charts are available from the Insert tab on the Ribbon, in the Charts group, as shown in Figure 8-2.

FIGURE 8-2
Charts group on the Insert tab of the Ribbon

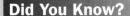

Chart types availablein Excel

Button provides access to stock, surface, doughnut, bubble, and radar charts

Button to access Insert Chart dialog box with all chart types

Column Chart

A column chart uses bars of varying heights to illustrate values in a worksheet. It is useful for showing relationships among categories of data. For example, the column chart in Figure 8-1 has one vertical column to show the population of a city for each of four years, and shows how the population of one city compares to populations of other cities.

Did You Know?

Businesses often use column, bar, and line charts to illustrate growth over several periods. For example, the changes in yearly production or income over a 10-year period can be shown easily in a column chart.

Line Chart

A line chart is similar to the column chart, but columns are replaced by points connected by a line. The line chart is ideal for illustrating trends over time. For example, Figure 8-3 is a line chart that shows the growth of the federal budget debt from 1990 to 2006. The vertical axis represents the amount of debt in billions of dollars, and the horizontal axis shows the years. The line chart makes it easy to see how the federal debt has grown over time. You can include multiple lines to compare two or more sets of data. For example, you could use a second line to chart the tax revenue received during the same time period.

FIGURE 8-3
Line chart

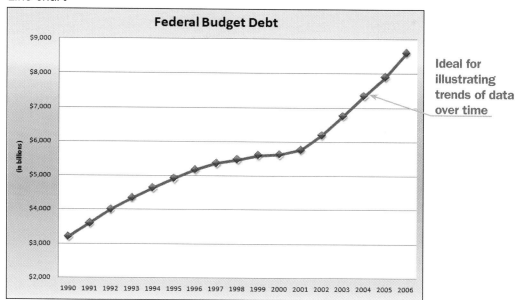

Ideal for illustrating trends of data over time

Pie Chart

A pie chart shows the relationship of a part to a whole. Each part is shown as a "slice" of the pie. For example, a teacher could create a pie chart of the distribution of grades in a class, as shown in Figure 8-4. Each slice represents the portion of grades given for each letter grade.

FIGURE 8-4
Pie chart

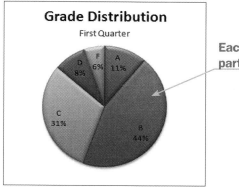

Each slice represents a part of the larger group

Scatter Chart

A **scatter chart**, sometimes called an XY chart, shows the relationship between two categories of data. One category is represented on the vertical axis, and the other category is represented on the horizontal axis. It is not practical to connect the data points with a line because points on a scatter chart usually do not relate to each other, as they do in a line chart. For example, the scatter chart in Figure 8-5 shows a data point for each of 12 individuals, based on the person's height and weight. In most cases, a tall person tends to be heavier than a short person. However, because some people are tall and skinny and others are short and stocky, the relationship between height and weight cannot be represented by a line.

FIGURE 8-5
Scatter chart

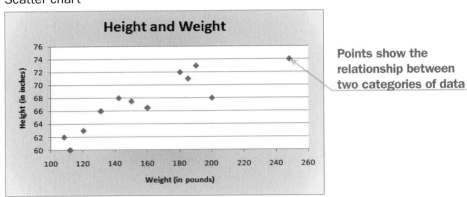

Points show the relationship between two categories of data

Creating Charts

The process for creating a chart is similar no matter which chart type you want to create. First, you select the data you want to use for the chart. Second, you select a chart type. Finally, you select the chart location. In this section, you will create a column chart.

Selecting Chart Data

Charts are based on data. In Excel, the chart data, called the **data source**, is stored in a range of cells in the worksheet. When you select the data source for a chart, you should also include the text you want to use as labels in the chart. You can also choose whether to chart more than one series of data. A **data series** is a group of related information in a column or row of a worksheet that is plotted on the chart.

Selecting a Chart Type

The next step is to select the type of chart you want to create, such as a column chart, a pie chart, or a line chart. Each type of chart has a variety of subtypes you can choose from. The chart types are available on the Insert tab in the Charts group. You can click the button for a specific chart type and then select the style you want. The Insert Chart dialog box, shown in Figure 8-6, provides access to all of the chart subtypes for each chart type. You open the Insert Chart dialog box by clicking the Dialog Box Launcher in the Charts group on the Insert tab.

FIGURE 8-6
Insert Chart dialog box

Chart types available in Excel

Chart subtypes are organized in sections by chart types

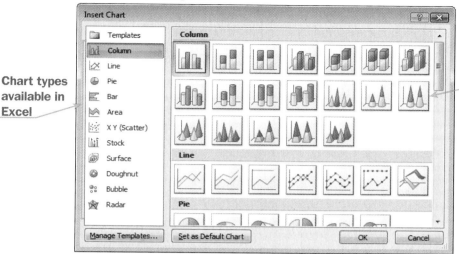

Choosing the Chart Location

After you select a chart type and style, the chart is inserted as an **embedded chart** in the center of the worksheet, as shown in Figure 8-7. The Chart Tools appear on the Ribbon with three contextual tabs: Design, Layout, and Format. The primary advantage of an embedded chart is that it can be viewed at the same time as the data from which it is created. When you print the worksheet, the chart is printed on the same page.

Computer Concepts

Embedded charts are useful when you want to print a chart next to the data the chart illustrates. When a chart will be displayed or printed without the data used to create the chart, a separate chart sheet is usually more appropriate.

FIGURE 8-7
Embedded chart

Data source for the column chart

Selection box appears around the selected column chart

Button to move the chart between a chart sheet and a worksheet

Chart Tools appear on the Ribbon when the chart is selected

Sizing handles

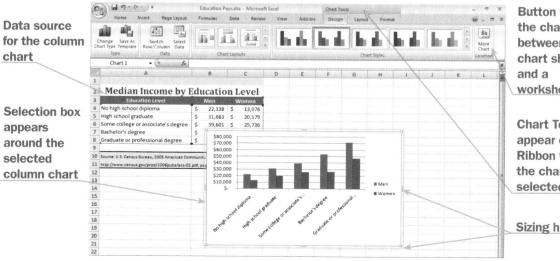

An embedded chart might cover the data source or other information in the worksheet. You can quickly move and resize the embedded chart. You move an embedded chart by dragging the selected chart to a different part of the worksheet. You resize the chart by dragging one of the **sizing handles**, which are indicated by the black dots at the corners and sides of the selected chart.

You can also choose to move the chart to a **chart sheet**, which is a separate sheet in the workbook that stores a chart. A chart sheet does not have worksheet cells and cannot contain data or formulas. A chart sheet displays the chart without its data source, and is convenient when you plan to create more than one chart from the same data or want to focus on the chart rather than its underlying data.

To move an embedded chart to a chart sheet, click the Design contextual tab under the Chart Tools on the Ribbon. Then, in the Location group, click the Move Chart button. The Move Chart dialog box appears, as shown in Figure 8-8. You can choose to move the chart to a new sheet that you name or to embed the chart in any worksheet in the workbook. You can use the same process to move a chart from a chart sheet to any worksheet as an embedded object.

Extra for Experts

You can keep a chart's height and width in the same proportion by pressing the Shift key as you drag a corner sizing handle.

Did You Know?

You can rename a chart sheet like any other worksheet. Right-click its sheet tab, and then click Rename on the shortcut menu. Type a descriptive name for the chart sheet, and then press the Enter key.

Did You Know?

A chart, whether embedded in a worksheet or on a chart sheet, is considered part of a workbook. When you save the workbook, you also save the charts you have created.

FIGURE 8-8
Move Chart dialog box

Option to create a new chart sheet

Option to embed the chart in a worksheet

Name for the new chart sheet

Name of the worksheet in which the chart will be embedded

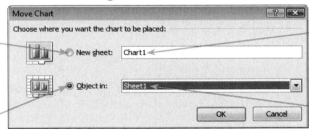

S TEP-BY-STEP 8.1

1. Open the **Education.xlsx** Data File. Save the workbook as **Education Pays** followed by your initials. Column A contains educational levels, and columns B and C contain the median incomes of men and women with corresponding levels of education.

2. Select the range **A3:C8**. This is the data you want to chart.

3. Click the **Insert** tab on the Ribbon. In the Charts group, click the **Column** button. A menu of available column chart subtypes appears.

4. In the 2-D Column section, point to **Clustered Column** (the first chart in the first row). A ScreenTip appears with a description of the selected chart: *Clustered Column. Compare values across categories by using vertical rectangles.*

5. Click the **Clustered Column** button. The 2-D clustered column chart is embedded in the worksheet. A selection box with sizing handles appears around the chart, as shown in Figure 8-7.

6. Drag the selected chart so that the upper-left corner of the chart is in cell E1. The chart is repositioned in the worksheet.

7. Drag the lower-right sizing handle to cell **K13**. The chart is sized to cover the range E1:K13.

8. On the Ribbon, under Chart Tools, click the **Design** tab, if it is not already selected.

9. In the Location group, click the **Move Chart** button. The Move Chart dialog box appears, as shown in Figure 8-8.

10. Click the **New sheet** option button. The text in the New sheet box is selected so you can type a descriptive name for the chart sheet.

11. In the New sheet box, type **Column**.

Careers

Excel worksheets are used in education to evaluate and instruct students. Instructors use worksheets to track student grades and to organize the number of hours spent on certain topics. Charts help illustrate numerical relationships for students.

STEP-BY-STEP 8.1 Continued

12. Click **OK**. The chart moves to a chart sheet named *Column*, as shown in Figure 8-9. The chart illustrates the value of education in attaining higher income. The columns get higher on the right side of the chart, indicating that those who stay in school are rewarded with higher incomes.

FIGURE 8-9
Chart sheet

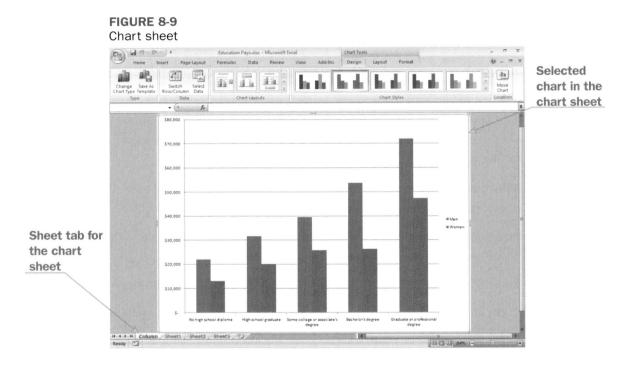

Selected chart in the chart sheet

Sheet tab for the chart sheet

13. Save the workbook, and leave it open for the next Step-by-Step.

Updating the Data Source

Charts are closely related to their underlying data stored in a worksheet. If you need to change the data in the worksheet, the chart is automatically updated to reflect the new data. You switch between a chart sheet and a worksheet by clicking the appropriate sheet tab.

STEP-BY-STEP 8.2

1. Click the **Sheet1** sheet tab. The worksheet with the data source appears.

2. Click cell **A5**, and then enter **High school diploma**. The label is updated.

STEP-BY-STEP 8.2 Continued

3. Click the **Column** sheet tab. The chart sheet appears. The label for the second column reflects the edit you made to the data source.

4. Save the workbook, and leave it open for the next Step-by-Step.

Designing a Chart

Charts have some basic elements, which you can choose to include or hide. You can also choose a chart style and layout to give the chart a cohesive design. Finally, you can add labels and other elements to make the chart easier to understand and interpret and more attractive.

Selecting Chart Elements

Charts are made up of different parts, or elements. The common chart elements are identified in Figure 8-10 and described in Table 8-1. Not all elements appear in every type of chart. For example, a pie chart does not have axes. Also, you can choose which chart elements to use in a chart.

FIGURE 8-10
Chart elements

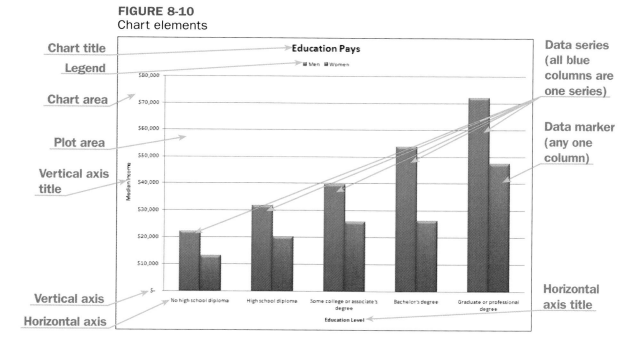

TABLE 8-1
Chart elements

ELEMENT	DESCRIPTION
Chart area	The entire chart and all other chart elements
Plot area	The graphical representation of all of the data series
Data series	Related information in a column or row that is plotted on a chart; many charts can include more than one data series
Data marker	A symbol (such as a bar, line, dot, slice, and so forth) that represents a single data point or value from the corresponding worksheet cell
Data label	Text or numbers that provide additional information about a data marker, such as the value from the worksheet cell (not shown in Figure 8-10)
Axes	Lines that establish a relationship between data in a chart; most charts have a horizontal x-axis and a vertical y-axis
Titles	Descriptive labels that identify the contents of the chart and the axes
Legend	A list that identifies patterns, symbols, or colors used in a chart
Data table	A grid that displays the data plotted in the chart (not shown in Figure 8-10)

The quickest way to select a chart element is to click it with the pointer. You can tell that you are clicking the right element by first pointing to the element to display a ScreenTip with its name. A selected chart element is surrounded by a **selection box**. You can also use the Ribbon to select chart elements. Click the Format tab under Chart Tools on the Ribbon. In the Current Selection group, click the arrow next to the Chart Elements box. A menu of chart elements for the selected chart appears. Click the name of the element you want to select.

After you select a chart element, you can modify it. For example, you can select the chart title or an axis title, and then enter new text for the title. You can also use the standard text formatting tools to change the font, font size, font color, and so forth of the selected title.

Choosing a Chart Layout and Style

You can quickly change the look of any chart you created by applying a layout and style. A **chart layout** specifies which elements are included in a chart and where they are placed. Figure 8-11 shows the chart layouts available for column charts. For example, the legend appears above, below, to the right of, or to the left of the chart in different layouts.

FIGURE 8-11
Chart Layouts gallery for column charts

Layouts include different
elements and placements

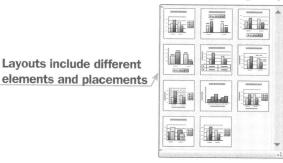

A chart style formats the chart based on the colors, fonts, and effects associated with the workbook's theme. Figure 8-12 shows the chart styles available for column charts.

FIGURE 8-12
Chart Styles gallery for column charts

Styles include
different colors
and effects

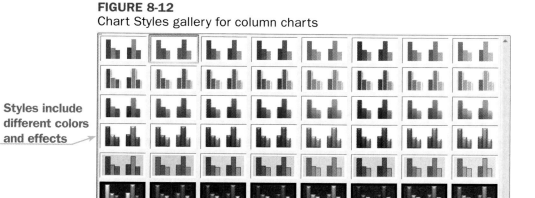

You can quickly choose a layout and styles for a selected chart from the Ribbon. Click the Design tab under Chart Tools on the Ribbon. In the Chart Layouts group, click the chart layout you want to use. In the Chart Styles group, click the chart style you want to use.

Arranging Chart Elements

You can also create a specific look for a chart by specifying which chart elements appear in the chart and where they are located. For example, you can choose when and where to display the chart title, axis titles, legend, data labels, data table, axes, gridlines, and the plot area. Select the chart. Then, click the Layout tab under Chart Tools on the Ribbon. The Labels, Axes, and Background groups contain buttons for each element. Use the commands on the appropriate button to display the element in a particular location in the chart area or to hide the element from the chart.

S TEP-BY-STEP 8.3

1. On the Ribbon, under Chart Tools, click the **Design** tab, if it is not already selected.

2. In the Chart Layouts group, click the **More** button. A gallery of chart layouts appears, as shown in Figure 8-11.

3. Click **Layout 9** (the third layout in the third row). Placeholders for the chart title and axes titles are added to the chart.

4. Click the **Chart Title** to select it.

5. Type **EDUCATION PAYS**, and then press the **Enter** key. The chart title is updated.

6. Click the vertical **Axis Title** to select it, type **Median Income**, and then press the **Enter** key.

7. Click the horizontal **Axis Title** to select it, type **Education Level**, and then press the **Enter** key.

8. On the Design tab under Chart Tools, in the Chart Styles group, click the **More** button. A gallery of chart styles appears, as shown in Figure 8-12.

9. Click **Style 26** (the second style in the fourth row). The chart changes to match the selected style.

10. On the Ribbon, under Chart Tools, click the **Layout** tab.

11. On the Layout tab under Chart Tools, in the Labels group, click the **Legend** button. A menu appears with different placement options for the legend.

12. Click **Show Legend at Top**. The legend moves to below the chart title, as shown in Figure 8-10.

13. Insert a header with your name and the current date, and then print the chart sheet.

14. Save and close the workbook.

> **Did You Know?**
>
> You can delete a selected chart by pressing the Delete key. You can delete chart sheets by right-clicking the chart sheet tab, and then clicking Delete on the shortcut menu.

Creating a 3-D Chart

A pie chart shows the relationship of a part to a whole. Each part is shown as a "slice" of the pie. The slices are different colors to distinguish each data marker. Pie charts, as with many chart types, can be either 2-D or 3-D. When you select the chart style, click a 3-D chart subtype to create a 3-D chart.

> **Computer Concepts**
>
> Businesses often use pie charts to indicate the magnitude of certain expenses in comparison to other expenses. Pie charts are also used to illustrate the company's market share in comparison to its competitors'.

STEP-BY-STEP 8.4

1. Open the **Grains.xlsx** Data File. Save the workbook as **Grains Sales** followed by your initials.

2. Select the range **A7:B10**. This range contains the data that shows the sales for each product segment.

3. Click the **Insert** tab on the Ribbon. In the Charts group, click the **Pie** button.

4. In the 3-D Pie section, click **Pie in 3-D** (the first chart in the first row). The pie chart is embedded in the worksheet.

> **Extra for Experts**
>
> You can pull one or more slices away from the pie to distinguish them, creating what is called an **exploded pie chart**. Click the data markers to select the series. Then, click the individual slice you want to explode to select just that one data marker. Finally, drag the selected slice away from the pie.

5. On the Ribbon, under Chart Tools, click the **Design** tab, if the tab is not already selected. In the Chart Layouts group, click the **More** button. A gallery of chart layouts appears.

6. Click **Layout 1** (the first layout in the first row). The legend disappears, and each slice of the pie shows the segment name and the percentage of the whole it comprises.

7. Click the **Chart Title**, type **Annual Sales by Segment**, and then press the **Enter** key. The new chart title is entered above the chart.

8. Move and resize the chart to fit within the range **D1:H15**. The 3-D pie chart, shown in Figure 8-13, illustrates that corn accounts for the largest percentage of sales.

FIGURE 8-13
3-D pie chart

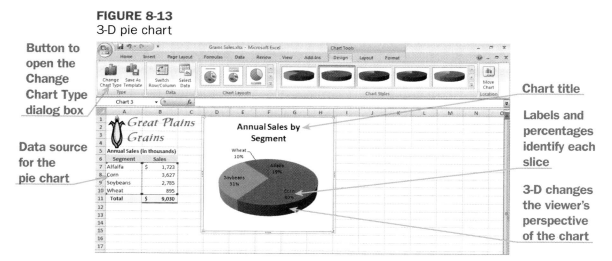

9. Insert a header with your name and the current date, and then print the worksheet.

10. Save and close the workbook.

Formatting and Modifying a Chart

Scatter charts are sometimes referred to as XY charts because they place data points between an x- and y-axis. Scatter charts can be harder to prepare because you must designate which data should be used as a scale on each axis.

STEP-BY-STEP 8.5

1. Open the **Coronado.xlsx** Data File. Save the workbook as **Coronado Foundries** followed by your initials.

2. Select the range **B6:B16**. Press and hold the **Ctrl** key as you select the range **D6:D16**. This nonadjacent range contains the data you want to chart.

3. Click the **Insert** tab on the Ribbon. In the Charts group, click the **Scatter** button. In the Scatter section, click **Scatter with only Markers** (the first chart in the first row). The scatter chart is embedded in the worksheet.

4. On the Ribbon, under Chart Tools, click the **Layout** tab.

5. In the Labels group, click the **Chart Title** button to open the menu of placement options, and then click **Above Chart**. The chart title appears above the scatter chart and is selected.

6. Type **Production and Scrap Report**, and then press the **Enter** key.

7. On the Layout tab under Chart Tools, in the Labels group, click the **Axis Titles** button, point to **Primary Horizontal Axis Title**, and then click **Title Below Axis**. The axis title appears below the horizontal axis and is selected.

8. Type **Units Produced**, and then press the **Enter** key. The horizontal axis title is updated.

9. On the Layout tab under Chart Tools, in the Labels group, click the **Axis Titles** button, point to **Primary Vertical Axis Title**, and then click **Rotated Title**. The axis title appears rotated along the vertical axis and is selected.

10. Type **Units of Scrap**, and then press the **Enter** key. The vertical access title is updated.

11. Click the **Legend** to select it, and then press the **Delete** key. The legend is removed from the chart.

12. Right-click the selected chart, and then click **Move Chart** on the shortcut menu. The Move Chart dialog box appears.

13. Click the **New sheet** option button. In the New sheet box, type **Scatter Chart**.

14. Click **OK**. The scatter chart appears on a chart sheet. The chart illustrates that factories with larger production tend to generate more scrap.

15. Save the workbook, and leave it open for the next Step-by-Step.

Formatting a Chart

The Chart Tools provide a simple way to create professional-looking charts. However, you might want to fine-tune a chart's appearance to better suit your purposes. For example, you might want to change the color of a data marker or the scale used for the axis. To make changes to an element's fill, border color, border style, shadow, 3-D format, alignment, and so forth, you need to open the Format dialog box. The Format dialog box for each element of a chart contains options for editing specific characteristics of that element.

To access the Format dialog box, select the chart you want to edit. Then, on the Format tab under Chart Tools on the Ribbon, in the Current Selection group, click the Format Selection button. The Format dialog box for the selected element appears. You can also right-click the part you want to edit, and then click the Format command on the shortcut menu.

STEP-BY-STEP 8.6

1. On the Ribbon, under Chart Tools, click the **Format** tab.

2. In the Current Selection group, next to the Chart Elements box, click the **arrow** to open a menu of elements on the selected chart, and then click **Horizontal (Value) Axis**.

3. In the Current Selection group, click the **Format Selection** button. The Format Axis dialog box appears with the Axis Options active, as shown in Figure 8-14.

FIGURE 8-14
Format Axis dialog box

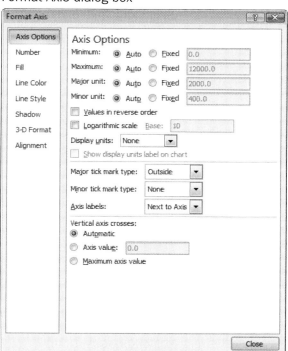

4. Next to Minimum, click the **Fixed** option button. In the Minimum Fixed box, type **4000**.

STEP-BY-STEP 8.6 Continued

5. Click **Close**. The section of the chart to the left of 4,000 on the x-axis, which did not have any data points, disappears.

6. Right-click the **Vertical (Value) Axis** on the chart, and then click **Format Axis** on the shortcut menu. The Format Axis dialog box appears with the Axis Options active.

7. Next to Maximum, click the **Fixed** option button. In the Maximum Fixed box, type **250**.

8. Click **Close**. The section of the chart above 250 on the y-axis, which did not have any data points, disappears.

9. Select the **Chart Area** (see Figure 8-15).

FIGURE 8-15
Scatter chart

Button to open the Format dialog box for the selected element

Scale changed to a maximum of 250

Scale changed to a minimum of 4,000

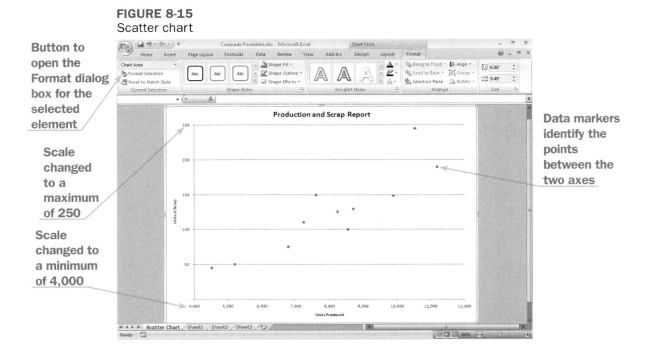

Data markers identify the points between the two axes

10. Insert a header with your name and the current date, and then print the worksheet.

11. Save and close the workbook.

Editing and Formatting Chart Text

You might want to change a title font or color to make a chart more attractive and interesting. You use the standard text formatting tools to make changes to the fonts used in the chart.

STEP-BY-STEP 8.7

1. Open the **Red** Data File. Save the workbook as **Red Cross** followed by your initials.

2. Click the **Bar Chart** sheet tab. The bar chart illustrates the operating expenses for each year.

3. Click **American Red Cross** to select chart title.

4. Click to the right of the last **s** in the title. An insertion point appears at the end of the title.

5. Press the **Enter** key. The insertion point is centered under the first line of the title.

6. Type **Operating Expenses**, and then click the **Chart Area**. The chart resizes to accommodate the new subtitle.

7. Click the **Horizontal (Value) Axis** to select it.

8. On the Home tab, in the Font group, next to the Font Size box, click the **arrow**, and then click **12**. The horizontal axis labels change to 12 points.

9. Click the **Vertical (Category) Axis** to select it.

10. On the Home tab, in the Font group, next to the Font Size box, click the **arrow**, and then click **12**. The vertical axis labels change to 12 points.

11. Save the workbook, and leave it open for the next Step-by-Step.

Changing the Chart Type

 You can change a chart type or subtype at any time. On the Design tab, under Chart Tools on the Ribbon, in the Type group, click the Change Chart Type button. The Change Chart Type dialog box appears, and has the same options as the Insert Chart Type dialog box. The only difference is that the chart type and subtype you select affect the selected chart and do not create a new chart.

> **Computer Concepts**
>
> Not all charts are interchangeable. For example, data suitable for a pie chart is often not logical in a scatter chart. However, most line charts are easily converted into column or bar charts.

STEP-BY-STEP 8.8

1. On the Ribbon, under Chart Tools, click the **Design** tab.

2. In the Type group, click the **Change Chart Type** button. The Change Chart Type dialog box appears with the Bar chart type selected.

3. In the Line section, click the **Line with Markers** (the fourth line chart subtype).

4. Click **OK**. The bar chart changes to a new line chart.

STEP-BY-STEP 8.8 Continued

5. Rename the chart sheet as **Line Chart**. The line chart should appear, as shown in Figure 8-16.

FIGURE 8-16
Line chart

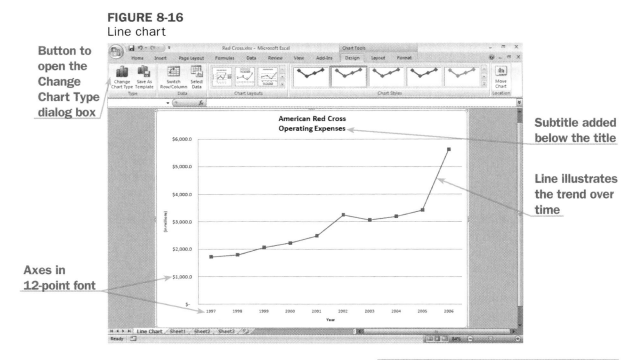

Button to open the Change Chart Type dialog box

Subtitle added below the title

Line illustrates the trend over time

Axes in 12-point font

6. Insert a header with your name and the current date, and then print the chart sheet.

7. Save and close the workbook.

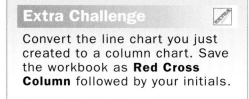

Extra Challenge

Convert the line chart you just created to a column chart. Save the workbook as **Red Cross Column** followed by your initials.

SUMMARY

In this lesson, you learned:

- A chart is a graphical representation of data. You can create several types of worksheet charts, including column, line, pie, and scatter charts.

- Charts can be embedded within a worksheet or created on a chart sheet.

- The process for creating a chart is the same for all chart types. Select the data for the chart. Select a chart type. Move, resize, and format the chart as needed.

- Any changes made to a data source automatically appear in the chart based on that data.

- Charts are made up of different parts, or elements. You can apply a chart layout and a chart style to determine which elements appear in the chart, where they appear, and how they look.

- If the data in a chart's data source is changed in the worksheet, the chart is automatically updated to reflect the new data.

■ You can fine-tune a chart by clicking a chart element and then opening its Format dialog box. You can also edit and format the chart text, using the standard text formatting tools.

■ You can change the type of chart in the Change Chart Type dialog box.

VOCABULARY *Review*

Define the following terms:

Axis	Data label	Legend
Chart	Data marker	Line chart
Chart area	Data series	Pie chart
Chart layout	Data source	Plot area
Chart sheet	Data table	Scatter chart
Chart style	Embedded chart	Selection box
Column chart	Exploded pie chart	Sizing handles

REVIEW *Questions*

TRUE/FALSE

Circle T if the statement is true or F if the statement is false.

T   F   1. Charts are a graphical representation of data.

T   F   2. Pie charts are the best way to represent data that are parts of a whole.

T   F   3. Scatter charts are good for representing trends over a period of time.

T   F   4. When the data source changes, charts created from that data also change.

T   F   5. After you create a chart, you cannot change the chart type or subtype.

FILL IN THE BLANK

Complete the following sentences by writing the correct word or words in the blanks provided.

1. A(n) _____ chart is represented by a circle divided into portions.

2. A(n) _____ chart is inserted on the same sheet as the data being charted.

3. In a chart, the _____ shows the patterns or symbols that identify the different types of data.

4. A(n) _____ formats the chart based on the colors, fonts, and effects associated with the workbook's theme.

5. Charts are made up of different parts, or _____ .

PROJECTS

 PROJECT 8-1

1. Open the **Populations.xlsx** Data File. Save the workbook as **Populations of Large Cities** followed by your initials.

2. Select the data in the range A5:B14, and then insert a column chart using the 2-D clustered column subtype.

3. Move the chart to a chart sheet named **Column Chart**.

4. Apply Layout 6 and Style 30 to the chart. Delete the Series 1 Data Labels from the chart if it appears over the Jakarta column.

5. Enter the chart title as **World's 10 Largest Cities**.

6. Enter the vertical axis title as **Population in Millions**.

7. Insert a header with your name and the current date, and then print the chart sheet. Save and close the workbook.

 PROJECT 8-2

1. Open the **Running.xlsx** Data File. Save the workbook as **Running Times** followed by your initials.

2. Using the data in the range A5:B14, insert a line chart with markers embedded in the worksheet.

3. Apply chart Style 39.

4. In the range A5:A14, delete the word *Week*, leaving only the week number.

5. Add a horizontal axis title below the axis with the text **Week**.

6. Add a rotated vertical axis with the text **Time in Minutes**.

7. Do not include a chart title. Do not include a legend in the chart.

8. Resize and move the chart to fill the range C4:H18.

9. Insert a header with your name and the current date. Print the worksheet with the embedded chart, and then save and close the workbook.

 PROJECT 8-3

1. Open the **McDonalds** Data File. Save the workbook as **McDonalds Restaurants** followed by your initials.

2. Using the data in the range A3:B5, create a pie chart using the Pie in 3-D subtype.

3. Apply the Layout 6 chart layout and the Style 26 chart style.

4. Enter the chart title **Total Restaurants**.

5. Show the legend above the chart.

6. Move the chart to a chart sheet named **Pie Chart**.

7. Format the font sizes of the chart title to 28 points, the slice percentages to 18 points, and the legend to 12 points.

8. Insert a header with your name and the current date. Print the chart sheet. Save and close the workbook.

 PROJECT 8-4

1. Open the **Family** Data File. Save the workbook as **Family Expenses** followed by your initials.

2. Using the data in the range A6:B13, create a pie chart using the Pie in 3-D subtype.

3. Move the chart to a chart sheet named **3-D Pie Chart**.

4. Choose the chart layout that includes a chart title and data labels with percentages, but does not include a legend.

5. Change the chart title to **Where Our Money Goes**.

6. Apply the Style 10 chart style.

7. Change the font size of the chart title to 24 points.

8. Change the font size of the data labels to 14 points.

9. Based on the chart, in what area(s) does the family spend the most?

10. Insert a header with your name and the current date. Print the chart sheet. Save and close the workbook.

 PROJECT 8-5

1. Open the **Study.xlsx** Data File. Save the workbook as **Study and Grades** followed by your initials.

2. Using the data in the range B4:C21, create a scatter chart with only markers.

3. Move the chart to a chart sheet named **Scatter Chart**.

4. Apply the Layout 4 chart layout to the chart.

5. Add the following chart title above the chart: **Relationship Between Exam Grades and Study Time**.

6. Add the following horizontal axis title below the axis: **Hours of Study**.

7. Add the following rotated vertical axis title: **Exam Grades**.

8. Change the font size of the chart title to 20 points.

9. Change the font size of the axis titles to 14 points.

10. Delete the legend.

11. Format the vertical axis so its minimum value is fixed at 50.

12. What relationship, if any, does the chart show between exam grades and study time?

13. Insert a header with your name and the current date. Print the chart sheet. Save and close the workbook.

 PROJECT 8-6

1. Open the **Concession.xlsx** Data File. Save the workbook as **Concession Sales** followed by your initials.

2. Using the data in the range A4:E9, create a 2-D clustered column chart.

3. Move the chart to a chart sheet named **Column Chart**.

4. Apply the Layout 1 chart layout to the chart.

5. Apply the Style 26 chart style to the chart.

6. Change the chart title to **Concession Sales**. Change the font size of the chart title to 24 points.

7. Add the following rotated vertical axis title: **Sales in Dollars**. Change the font size of the axis title to 14 points.

8. Change the font size of the horizontal and vertical axis labels to 12 points and make them bold.

9. Move the legend above the chart.

10. Change the font size of the legend to 12 points.

11. Right-click the plot area of the chart, and then click Format Plot Area on the shortcut menu. In the Format Plot Area dialog box that appears, click the Solid fill option button. Click the Color button arrow, and then click White, Background 1, Darker 15% (the first color in the third row). Click the Close button.

12. Which product has decreased in sales over the last four games? Which product has increased in sales over the last four games?

13. Insert a header with your name and the current date. Print the chart sheet. Save and close the workbook.

PROJECT 8-7

1. Open the **Triangle.xlsx** Data File. Save the workbook as **Triangle Growth** followed by your initials.

2. Using the data in the range A5:F7, create a 2-D line chart with markers.

3. Move the chart to a chart sheet named **Line Chart**.

4. Apply the Layout 1 chart layout to the chart.

5. Apply the Style 26 chart style to the chart.

6. Change the chart title to **Triangle Software Revenue and Income**.

7. Change the vertical axis title to (**Dollars in Thousands**).

8. Show the legend at the top of the chart.

9. Have the company's sales decreased, increased, or remained stable?

10. Insert a header with your name and the current date. Print the chart sheet.

11. Press and hold the Ctrl key as you drag the Line Chart tab to the right to make a copy. Rename the copied chart sheet **Clustered Column Chart**.

12. Change the chart type to a clustered column chart.

13. Print the chart sheet. Save and close the workbook.

 PROJECT 8-8

1. Open the **Chico.xlsx** Data File. Save the workbook as **Chico Temperatures** followed by your initials.

2. Using the data in the range A3:M5, create a 2-D line chart with markers.

3. Move the chart to a chart sheet named **Line Chart**.

4. Apply the Layout 5 chart layout to the chart.

5. Apply the Style 34 chart style to the chart.

6. Change the chart title to **Temperatures for Chico, California**.

7. Change the vertical axis title to **Temperatures in Fahrenheit**.

8. Under Chart Tools on the Ribbon, click the Layout tab. In the Current Selection group, use the Chart Elements box to select Series "High" in the chart.

9. Click the Format Selection button to open the Format Data Series dialog box. Make the following changes:
   A. Click Marker Fill to display the options. Click the Solid fill option button. Click the Color button, and then click Dark Red in the Standard Colors section.
   B. Click Line Color to display the options. Click the Solid line option button. Click the Color button, and then click Dark Red in the Standard Colors section.
   C. Click Marker Line Color to display the options. Click the Solid line option button. Click the Color button, and then click Dark Red in the Standard Colors section.

10. Click Close to close the Format Data Series dialog box.

11. On the Layout tab under Chart Tools on the Ribbon, in the Current Selection group, use the Chart Elements box to select Series "Low" in the chart.

12. Click the Format Selection button to open the Format Data Series dialog box. Make the following changes:
   A. Click Marker Fill to display the options. Click the Solid fill option button. Click the Color button, and then click Blue in the Standard Colors section.
   B. Click Line Color to display the options. Click the Solid line option button. Click the Color button, and then click Blue in the Standard Colors section.
   C. Click Marker Line Color to display the options. Click the Solid line option button. Click the Color button, and then click Blue in the Standard Colors section.

13. Click Close to close the Format Data Series dialog box.

14. Insert a header with your name and the current date. Print the chart sheet. Save and close the workbook.

CRITICAL *Thinking*

 ACTIVITY 8-1

 For each scenario, which chart type would be the most appropriate to illustrate the data? Justify your answer.

Scenario 1. A scientist has given varying amounts of water to 200 potted plants. Over 35 days, the height of the plant and the amount of water given to the plant are recorded in a worksheet. What is the best chart type to illustrate the connection between water and plant growth?

Scenario 2. A corporation developed a new product last year. A manager in the corporation recorded the number of units sold each month. He noticed that sales in summer months were much higher than sales in the winter months. What chart type can he use to illustrate this to other sales managers?

Scenario 3. Students entering a high school come from five middle schools. The principal has recorded the name of the middle school and the number of students from each middle school. What chart type can she use to show which middle schools supply significantly more students than other middle schools?

 ACTIVITY 8-2

You recently opened a store that buys and sells used CDs. As a small business owner, you are responsible for budgets and inventory. Initially, you tracked the inventory and budget data by hand in a paper notebook. Now that the business is growing, this method has become too cumbersome. You decide to transfer the data into an electronic format.

Create a new workbook and save it as **Sounds Good** followed by your initials. Create and format one worksheet to track inventory and one worksheet to track the budget. Both worksheets should contain the name of your store—Sounds Good CDs—and a title describing the data.

For the inventory worksheet, include (a) the title of the CD or DVD, (b) the artist, (c) the quantity of each, and (d) the cost per item. Enter the data shown in Figure 8-17 in the worksheet. Rename the worksheet as **Inventory**.

FIGURE 8-17

Title	Artist	Quantity	Cost
Nerve Net	Brian Eno	4	$ 6.95
Thursday Afternoon	Brian Eno	2	$ 7.95
Geometry	Robert Rich	3	$ 5.95
On This Planet	Steve Roach	3	$ 8.95
Possible Planet	Steve Roach	5	$ 6.95

The budget worksheet records the expected income and expenses for the month. Include rows for (a) sales revenue, (b) purchases of used CDs, (c) rent expense, (d) utilities expense, (e) tax expense, and (f) net income. Include columns for (a) budgeted amounts and (b) actual amounts. Then, enter the data shown in Figure 8-18.

FIGURE 8-18

	Actual	Budgeted
Sales Revenue	$ 12,875	$ 11,950
Purchases of CDs	5,500	4,800
Rent	575	575
Utilities	350	350
Taxes	817	667
Net Income		

For the Actual Net Income, enter a formula that subtracts the purchases and expenses from revenue. For the Budgeted Net Income, enter a formula that subtracts the purchases and expenses from revenue. Rename the worksheet as **Budget**.

Using the data you entered in the Budget worksheet, create a chart that compares the actual and budgeted values in each category. Use an appropriate chart type. Choose which chart elements to display, where they should be located, and how the chart is formatted.

For all worksheets, insert a header with your name and the current date, and then print the worksheets. Save the workbook as **Sounds Good** followed by your initials.

MICROSOFT EXCEL

REVIEW *Questions*

TRUE/FALSE

Circle T if the statement is true or F if the statement is false.

T F 1. The active cell reference appears in the Name Box.

T F 2. To select a group of cells, you must click each cell individually until all cells in the range are selected.

T F 3. The Save As dialog box appears every time you save a worksheet.

T F 4. The formula =$B$4+C9 contains mixed cell references.

T F 5. After you edit the data source in the worksheet, the chart is also updated to reflect the changes.

MATCHING

Match the description in Column 2 with the text position function in Column 1.

Column 1	Column 2
___ 1. Wrapping	A. Moves the text several spaces to the right or left
___ 2. Orientation	B. Aligns the text to the right, left, or center
___ 3. Indenting	C. Combines several cells into one and places the contents in the middle of the cell
___ 4. Alignment	D. Displays cell contents on multiple lines
___ 5. Merge and Center	E. Displays text at an angle, vertically, up, or down

FILL IN THE BLANK

Complete the following sentences by writing the correct word or words in the blanks provided.

1. A(n) _____ cell reference changes when copied or moved.

2. _____ formatting is used to highlight cells that meet specific criteria.

3. The _____ function adds a range of numbers in a worksheet.

4. A(n) _____ chart uses vertical rectangles to represent values in a worksheet.

5. The _____ is information that will appear at the top of every printed page.

MATCHING

Match the correct result in Column 2 to the formula in Column 1. Assume the following values appear in the worksheet:

Cell	Value
B2	5
B3	6
B4	4
B5	7

Column 1	Column 2
___1. =12+B5	A. 22
___2. =B2*B4	B. 5
___3. =(B3+B4)/B2	C. 20
___4. =AVERAGE(B3:B4)	D. 19
___5. =SUM(B2:B5)	E. 2

PROJECTS

 PROJECT 1

1. Open the **Gas.xlsx** Data File. Save the workbook as **Gas Sales** followed by your initials.

2. Format cell A1 with the Title cell style. Format the range A2:A3 with bold.

3. Change the width of column A to 15. Change the widths of columns B through D to 12.

4. Merge and center the range A1:D1.

5. In cell B2, enter the current date, and then apply the Long Date format.

6. Merge and center the range A2:D2.

7. In cell B3, enter 7:55 PM for time, and then apply the Time format.

8. Merge and center the range B3:D3.

9. Format the text in the range A2:D3 in 12-point Cambria.

10. Wrap the text in cell C5.

11. Format range A5:D5 with the Accent 1 cell style, and then bold and center the cells.

12. Format the range B6:B9 in the Number format with a comma separator and no decimal places.

13. Format the range C6:D9 in the Currency format with 2 decimal places.

14. In cell B10, use the SUM function to add the total number of gallons sold, and then format the cell with the Total cell style.

15. In cell D10, use the SUM function to add the total sales, and then format the cell with the Total cell style. Compare your worksheet to Figure UR-1, which shows the completed worksheet.

FIGURE UR-1

	A	B	C	D
1		Daily Sales Report		
2	Report Date		Wednesday, March 10, 2010	
3	Report Time		7:55:00 PM	
4				
5		Gallons	Price Per Gallon	Sales
6	Unleaded	3,170	$ 2.99	$ 9,478.30
7	Plus	3,975	$ 3.15	$ 12,521.25
8	Premium	2,240	$ 3.35	$ 7,504.00
9	Diesel	1,150	$ 2.79	$ 3,208.50
10		10,535		$ 32,712.05

16. Insert a header with your name and the current date. Save, print, and close the workbook.

PROJECT 2

1. Open the **Organic.xlsx** Data File. Save the workbook as **Organic Financials** followed by your initials.

2. Format the company name and other headings in bold and in a larger font than the items in the body of the financial statement.

3. Merge and center each of the first four rows across columns A and B.

4. Separate the headings from the body of the financial statement by one row.

5. Resize the columns so you can view all of their contents, wrapping text as appropriate.

6. Format the first (revenue) and last (net income) numbers in the financial statement to display dollar signs and thousands separators, but no decimal places.

7. Format all the other numbers to include a thousands separator but no dollar sign and no decimal places. Compare your worksheet to Figure UR-2.

FIGURE UR-2

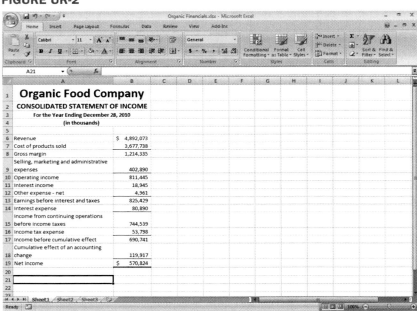

8. Format the worksheet to make it visually attractive and appealing, such as by adding borders, font colors, fill colors, alignments, cell styles, and so forth as appropriate.

9. Insert a header with your name and the current date. Save, print, and close the workbook.

PROJECT 3

1. Open the **Club.xlsx** Data File. Save the workbook as **Club Members** followed by your initials.

2. Sort the range A2:B20 by the values in column B in order from largest to smallest.

3. Resize the columns as needed to so that all the content is displayed.

4. Format the worksheet title with the Title cell style to distinguish it from the other text in the workbook.

5. Enter the title **Exceptional and Outstanding Members** above William Griffin's name, and then format the title in bold italics and in a font larger than the other text in the worksheet.

6. Enter the text **Exceptional Members** above William Griffin's name and bold it.

7. Enter the text **Outstanding Members** above Matthew Carcello's name and bold it.

8. Add the subtitle **Other Active Members** above Mohamed Abdul's name and bold it.

9. Format the service points in the Number format with a thousands separator and no decimal places. Compare your worksheet to Figure UR-3.

FIGURE UR-3

	A	B	C	D	E	F	G	H	I	J	K	L	M	N
1	**Computer Science Club**													
2	*Exceptional and Outstanding Members*													
3	**Exceptional Members**													
4	Griffin, William	1,150												
5	Atiase, Allen	1,020												
6	**Outstanding Members**													
7	Carcello, Matthew	980												
8	Anderson, George	970												
9	Santos, Jose	970												
10	Hill, Debra	950												
11	Smith, Marsha	920												
12	Davis, John	890												
13	Witt, Terry	870												
14	**Other Active Members**													
15	Abdul, Mohamed	780												
16	Doan, Arlette	740												
17	Porter, Sandra	680												
18	Mullin, Richard	630												
19	Vinson, Rhonda	630												
20	Squires, Judith	610												
21	Estes, Susan	570												
22	Tse, Allen	530												
23	Kermit, Paul	480												
24	Edwards, Alice	470												
25														
26	Exceptional members have earned 1,001 or more service points.													

10. Format the worksheet using cell styles, alignments, font styles, colors, and so forth to make the worksheet visually appealing.

11. Insert a header with your name and the current date. Save, print, and close the workbook.

PROJECT 4

1. Open the **CompNet.xlsx** Data File. Save the workbook as **CompNet Expenses** followed by your initials.

2. Create a pie chart in 3-D based on the data in the range A12:B18. Move the chart to chart sheet named **Expenses Chart**.

3. Apply the chart layout that includes a chart title above the chart and labels and percentages on the slices.

4. Apply the Style 10 chart style.

5. Enter **Expenses for 2010** as the chart title, and then change the font size to 24 points.

6. Change the font size of the data labels to 12 points. Compare your worksheet with Figure UR-4.

FIGURE UR-4

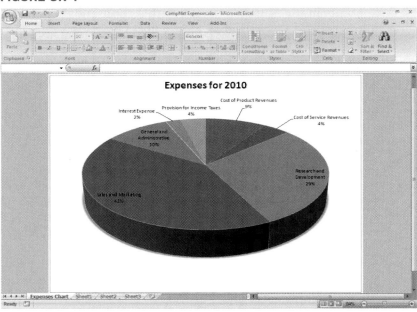

7. Based on the chart, what is the largest expense category? What is the smallest expense category?

8. Insert a header with your name and the current date. Save, print, and close the workbook.

SIMULATION

You work at the Java Internet Café, which has been open only a few months. The café serves coffee, other beverages, and pastries, and offers Internet access. Seven computers are set up on tables along the north side of the store. Customers can come in, have a cup of coffee and a pastry, and explore the World Wide Web.

Your manager asks you to create a menu of coffee prices and computer prices. You will do this by integrating Microsoft Excel and Microsoft Word.

 JOB 1

1. Create a new workbook. Save the workbook as **Coffee Prices** followed by your initials.

2. Enter the data shown in Figure UR-5 in the worksheet.

FIGURE UR-5

	A	B	C	D	E
1	Coffee Prices				
2					
3	House coffee	$1.00		Café latte	$3.50
4	Refills	$0.50		Cappucino	$3.50
5	Espresso	$2.00		Café breve	$3.25
6	Extra shot	$0.55		Café con panna	$3.75
7					

3. Change the widths of columns A and D to 20. Change the widths of columns B and E to 10. Change the width of column C to 4.

4. Left-align data in columns B and E.

5. Indent the text in cells A4 and A6.

6. Change the font of all data to Arial, 11 points.

7. Format the data in columns B and E as Currency with two decimal places.

8. Merge and center the range A1:E1. Change the font of the text in the merged cell A1 to Arial, 14 points. Format the merged cell A1 with a bottom border.

9. Hide the Gridlines from view. Copy the data in the range A1: E6. Save the workbook.

10. Start Word and open the **Java.docx** Data File. Save the document as **Java Menu** followed by your initials.

11. Insert one blank line below the *Menu* heading, center the blank line, and then paste a link to the worksheet data you copied. On the Home tab, in the Clipboard group, under the Paste button, click the arrow to open the Paste menu, and then click Paste Special. The Paste Special dialog box appears. In the Paste Special dialog box, click the Paste link option button, and then click Microsoft Office Excel Worksheet Object, as shown in Figure UR-6. Click OK.

FIGURE UR-6

Paste Special	? X
Source: Microsoft Office Excel Worksheet Sheet1!R7C1:R13C2	

As:

○ Paste: | Microsoft Office Excel Worksheet Object | ☐ Display as icon
● Paste link: | Formatted Text (RTF)
 | Unformatted Text
 | Picture (Windows Metafile)
 | Bitmap
 | Word Hyperlink
 | HTML Format
 | Unformatted Unicode Text

Result

Inserts the contents of the Clipboard as a picture.

Paste Link creates a shortcut to the source file. Changes to the source file will be reflected in your document.

OK Cancel

12. Switch to Excel, and then open the **Computer.xlsx** Data File. Save the workbook as **Computer Prices** followed by your initials.

13. Copy the data in the range A1:B13.

14. Switch to the **Java Menu** document.

15. Insert one blank line after the Coffee Prices menu items, center the line if it is not already centered, and then paste a link to the worksheet data you copied. On the Home tab, in the Clipboard group, under the Paste button, click the arrow to open the Paste menu, and then click Paste Special. In the Paste Special dialog box, click the Paste link option button, click Microsoft Office Excel Worksheet Object, and then click OK.

16. Insert your name and the current date in the blank line of the footer.

17. Preview the document. Adjust the placement of data if necessary so that all data fits on one page.

18. Save, print, and close the **Java Menu** document.

19. Close the **Coffee Prices** and **Computer Prices** workbooks without saving changes.

 **JOB 2**

The menu you created has been very successful. However, your manager asks you to make a few changes.

1. Open the **Coffee Prices** and **Computer Prices** workbooks you saved in Job 1.

2. Edit the **Coffee Prices** and **Computer Prices** workbooks as shown in Figure UR-7.

FIGURE UR-7

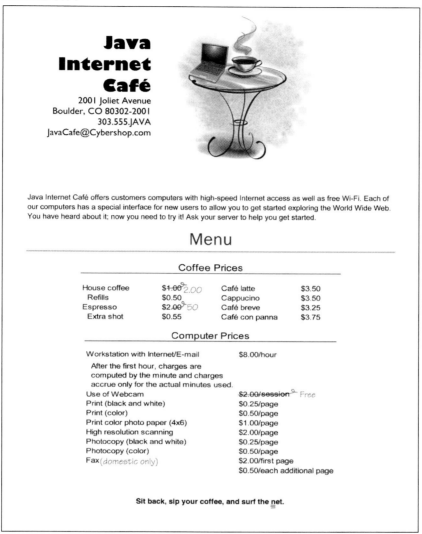

3. Save and close the **Coffee Prices** and **Computer Prices** workbooks.

4. Open the **Java Menu** document you created in Job 1.

5. Update the document when prompted because you revised the linked files since you saved and closed the Java Menu document.

6. Make the correction in the footer, as shown in Figure UR-7.

7. Save the document as **Java Menu Revised** followed by your initials.

8. Print and close the document.

MICROSOFT ACCESS

Unit

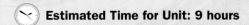 **Estimated Time for Unit: 9 hours**

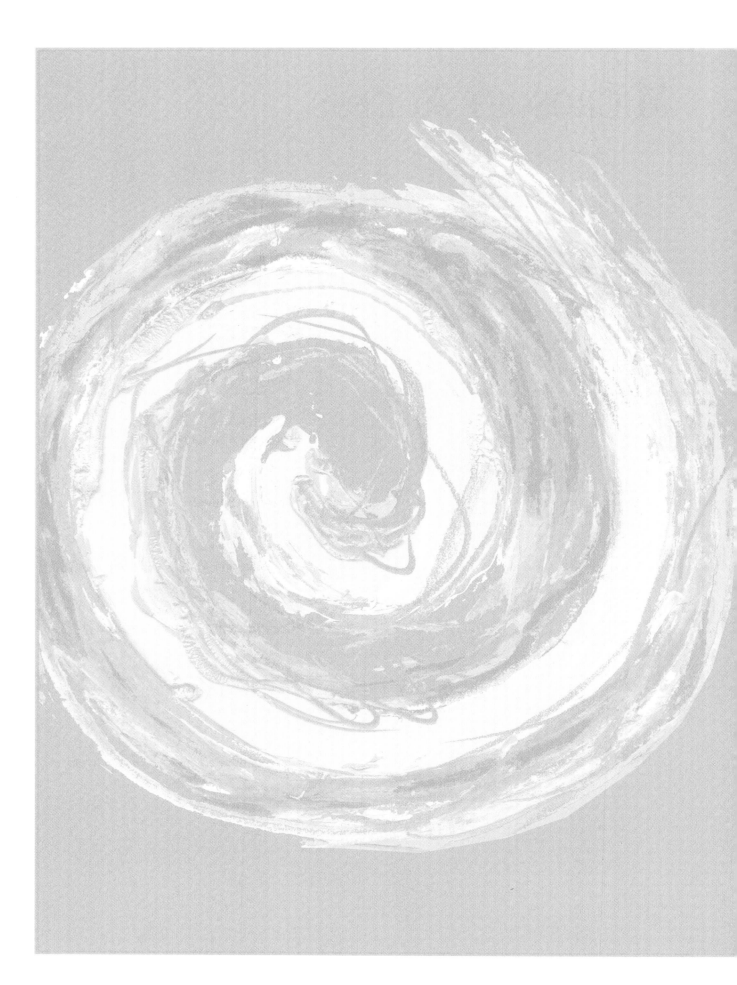

ACCESS BASICS

OBJECTIVES

Upon completion of this lesson, you will be able to:

- Understand databases and database terminology.
- Start Access, open a database, and open an object.
- Identify the parts of the Access screen.
- Navigate a datasheet.
- Edit a record and undo a change.
- Select records and fields.
- Delete a record.
- Cut, copy, and paste data.
- Change the appearance of a datasheet.
- Preview and print a table.
- Close an object and exit Access.

Estimated Time: 1.5 hours

VOCABULARY

Best fit

Compacting

Database

Database management system (DBMS)

Datasheet

Datasheet selector

Datasheet view

Field

Field name

Field selector

Field value

Navigation Pane

Record

Record selector

Database Basics

Access is a program known as a database management system (DBMS). A DBMS allows you to store, retrieve, analyze, and print information. You do not, however, need a computer to have a DBMS. A set of file folders or any system for managing data can be a DBMS. There are distinct advantages, however, to using a computerized DBMS.

A computerized DBMS is much faster, more flexible, and more accurate than using file folders. A computerized DBMS is also efficient and cost effective. A DBMS such as Access can store thousands of pieces of data that users can quickly search and sort, helping them to save time otherwise spent digging through file folders. For example, a computerized DBMS can find all the people with a certain zip code faster and more accurately than you could by searching through a large list or through folders.

Starting Access

To start Access, click the Start button on the taskbar, click All Programs, click Microsoft Office, and then click Microsoft Office Access 2007. After a few seconds, the Getting Started with Microsoft Office Access page opens, as shown in Figure 1-1. This page contains options for creating a new database, opening an existing database, and getting Help while using Access.

FIGURE 1-1
Getting Started with Microsoft Office Access page

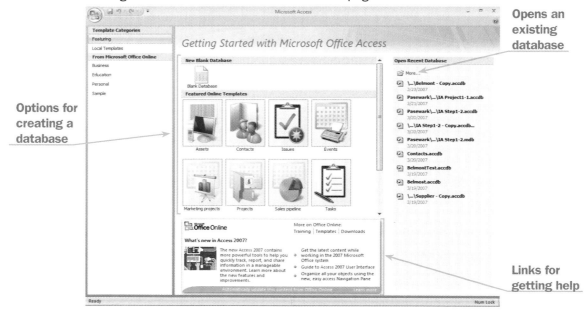

S TEP-BY-STEP 1.1

1. With Windows running, click the **Start** button on the taskbar.

2. Click **All Programs**, click **Microsoft Office**, then click **Microsoft Office Access 2007**. Access opens the Getting Started with Microsoft Office Access page, as shown in Figure 1-1. Leave this page open for the next Step-by-Step.

Opening a Database

A database is a collection of objects. The objects work together to store, retrieve, display, and summarize data and also to automate tasks. The object types are tables, queries, forms, reports, macros, and modules. You can open an existing database from the Open Recent Database pane displayed on the right side of the Getting Started with Microsoft Office Access page. To open a database from the Open Recent Database pane, click the database name in the list or click the More command to open the Open dialog box so you can select a database to open.

When you open an existing database, the Navigation Pane opens on the left side of the screen, as shown in Figure 1-2. The Navigation Pane lists the objects in the database.

FIGURE 1-2
Navigation Pane

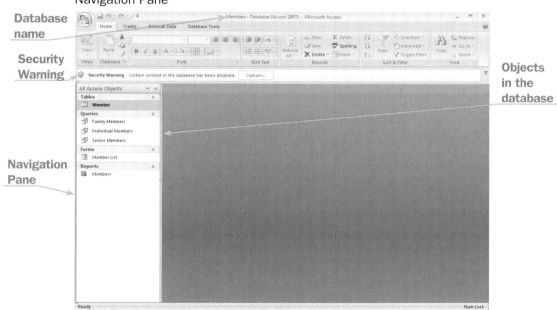

STEP-BY-STEP 1.2

1. Click the **More** command in the Open Recent Database pane of the Getting Started with Microsoft Office Access page. The Open dialog box appears.

2. Navigate to the drive and folder where your Data Files are stored, open the **Access** folder, then open the **Lesson1** folder.

3. Double-click the data file **Members.accdb** in the Lesson1 folder. Access opens the Members database. The Navigation Pane displays the objects in the database, as shown in Figure 1-2.

4. If the Security Warning opens, as shown in Figure 1-2, click **Options** on the Security Warning, click the **Enable this content** option button in the Microsoft Office Security Options dialog box, then click **OK**. Leave the database open for the next Step-by-Step.

The Access Screen

Like other Office 2007 programs, the Access screen has a title bar, Quick Access Toolbar, and Ribbon. The status bar is located at the bottom of the screen. As you use Access, various windows and dialog boxes will appear on the screen based on how you interact with the database.

Database Objects

When you create a database, you create a file that will store all of the objects in the database. As you create objects in the database, the Navigation Pane displays them in a list. You can change the way that the Navigation Pane displays objects, so you might see them organized differently.

Each object has a different icon to identify its function. Table 1-1 describes each type of object that you can create in a database and shows the icon used to identify the object in the Navigation Pane.

TABLE 1-1
Database objects

OBJECT	ICON	DESCRIPTION
Table	▦	Stores all the data in the database in a format called a datasheet. A datasheet is similar in appearance to a worksheet. A database usually contains many tables.
Query	▦	Used to search for and retrieve data from tables using conditions. A query is a question you ask the database.
Form	▦	Displays data from one or more tables or queries in a format that might be similar in appearance to a paper form.
Report	▦	Displays data from one or more tables or queries in a format that is usually customized for on-screen viewing or printing. A report is commonly used to summarize data and to calculate totals.
Macro	▨	Automates database operations by allowing you to issue a single command to perform a task, such as opening a form or closing a database.
Module	▨	Similar to a macro, but allows more complex programming of database operations. Creating a module requires the use of a programming language.

The Navigation Pane

When you open a database, the Navigation Pane displays the objects contained in the database. The database might contain any or all of the database objects described in Table 1-1 or just a single table. When you double-click a table, query, form, or report object in the Navigation Pane, the object opens in the main part of the Access screen so you can view its contents. The object name appears on a tab at the top of the window to identify its name and object type, as shown in Figure 1-3. When many objects are open, clicking a tab displays the object. If you want to display more of the open object, you can close the Navigation Pane by clicking the Shutter Bar Open/Close Button at the top of the Navigation Pane. To open it again, click the Shutter Bar Open/Close Button on the left side of the screen.

FIGURE 1-3
Open database objects

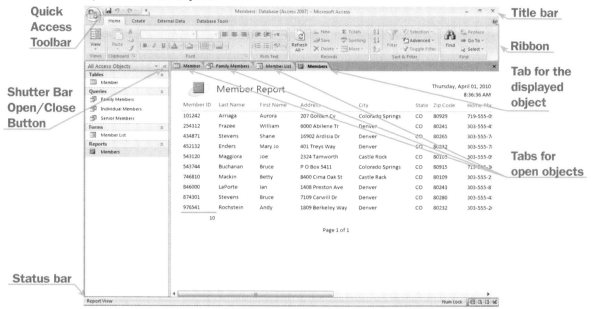

S TEP-BY-STEP 1.3

1. In the Navigation Pane, double-click **Member**. The Member table opens in Datasheet view.

2. In the Navigation Pane, double-click **Family Members**. The Family Members query opens in Query Datasheet view.

3. In the Navigation Pane, double-click **Member List**. The Member List form opens in Form view.

4. In the Navigation Pane, double-click **Members**. The Members report opens in Report view, as shown in Figure 1-3.

5. Click the **Member** tab to display the Member table datasheet.

6. Click the **Shutter Bar Open/Close Button** at the top of the Navigation Pane. The Navigation Pane closes. Leave the objects open for the next Step-by-Step.

Working with Records

Some terms are essential to know when working with databases. These terms relate to the way data is organized in a table. A record is a complete set of data. In the Member table, the data about each member is stored as a record. In a table, a record appears as a row, as shown in Figure 1-4.

FIGURE 1-4
Records and fields in a table

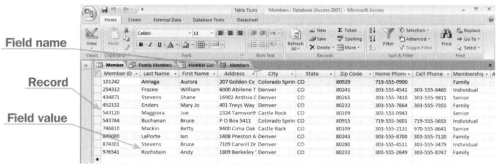

Each record is made up of one or more fields. For example, the first name of each member is placed in a field that stores first names. In a table, fields appear as columns. To identify the fields, each field has a field name. The data entered into a field is called a field value. In the Members table, for example, the first record has *Aurora* as the field value in the First Name field.

You can enter records directly into the table using Datasheet view. In Datasheet view, the table displays its data in rows and columns in a datasheet.

The techniques used to enter records in the table should be familiar to you. Press the Enter or Tab keys to move to the next field as you enter data. The field names describe the data that you enter in each field. For example, a Zip Code field might be designed to accept only numbers, or a State field might only accept entries consisting of two letters. If you enter an improper field value, an error message appears and tells you what to do to correct your mistake.

After entering records in a table, you do not need to save the changes as you do in other Office programs. Access automatically saves the changes you make to records.

Navigating Records in Datasheet View

You can use the pointer to move the insertion point to any field in a table by clicking in the desired field. You can also use the keys shown in Table 1-2 to navigate a table.

TABLE 1-2
Navigating in Datasheet view

KEY	DESCRIPTION
Enter, Tab, or right arrow	Moves to the next field in the current record
Left arrow or Shift+Tab	Moves to the previous field in the current record
End	Moves to the "Add New Field" column in the current record
Home	Moves to the first field in the current record
Up arrow	Moves up one record and stays in the same field
Down arrow	Moves down one record and stays in the same field
Page Up	Moves up one screen for the current field
Page Down	Moves down one screen for the current field
Ctrl+Home	Moves to the first field in the first record
Ctrl+End	Moves to the last field in the last record

STEP-BY-STEP 1.4

1. Click the **Member ID** field for the second record, which contains the field value *254312*. The insertion point appears in the field value.

2. Press the **Tab** key. The Last Name field for the second record is selected.

3. Press the **down arrow** key twice. The insertion point moves to the Last Name field for the fourth record, as shown in Figure 1-5.

FIGURE 1-5
Navigating a table datasheet

Last Name
field value
selected

Current
record
number 4 of
10 records
total

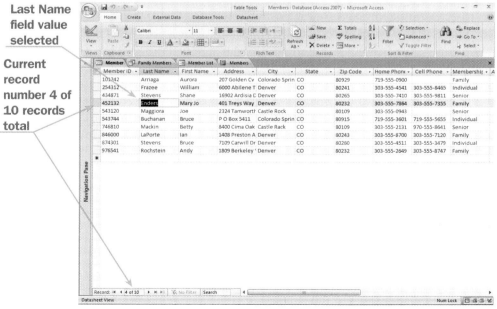

STEP-BY-STEP 1.4 Continued

4. Press the **Home** key. The Member ID field for the fourth record is selected.

5. Press the **Page Down** key. The first field in the blank row at the bottom of the datasheet is selected.

6. Press the **Ctrl+Home** keys. The first field value in the first record is selected. Leave the Member table open for the next Step-by-Step.

Editing Records

To make editing records easier, Access includes navigation buttons on the record navigation bar at the bottom of the datasheet. These buttons let you select records. They are very helpful when a table contains hundreds or thousands of records because they make it easy to move to the record you need. Figure 1-6 shows the navigation buttons.

FIGURE 1-6
Record navigation bar in Datasheet view

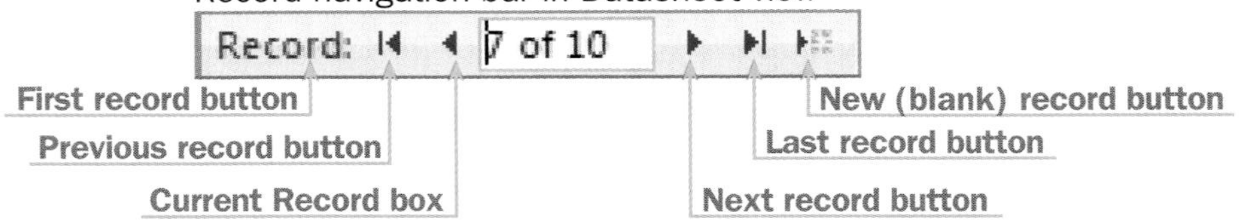

```
Record: |◄   ◄   7 of 10      ►   ►|  ►⦂
```

First record button
Previous record button
Current Record box

New (blank) record button
Last record button
Next record button

Clicking the First record button selects the first record in the table, and clicking the Last record button selects the last record in the table. The Next record and Previous record buttons select the next or previous record in the table. To select a specific record in a table, click in the Current Record box, select the value it contains, and then type the number of the record you want to select. Press the Enter key to move to the specified record. To add a new record to the table, click the New (blank) record button on the record navigation bar.

If you use the Enter or Tab key to move to a field, Access selects the contents of the field. When a field value is selected, you can replace the contents of the field by typing a new value. If you click a field with the pointer, the insertion point appears in the field. When an insertion point appears in a field, you can use the arrow keys to move through the field value. Use the Backspace key to delete characters to the left of the insertion point, or use the Delete key to delete characters to the right of the insertion point. When a record is selected, the record selector changes color from blue to orange. In Figure 1-5, the fourth record is selected, as indicated by the orange record selector for that row and the "4 of 10" that appears in the Current Record box.

Undoing Changes to a Cell

If you make a mistake when typing a field value, you can click the Undo button on the Quick Access Toolbar to undo your typing and restore the field value to its original state. You can also press the Esc key to restore the contents of the entire field.

S TEP-BY-STEP 1.5

1. Click the **Last record** button on the record navigation bar to move to the last record in the table.

2. Press the **Tab** key to move to the Last Name field.

3. Type **Richman**, then press the **Tab** key. The First Name field is the current field.

4. Click the **First record** button on the record navigation bar to move to the First Name field in the first record. Click the **Next record** button to move to the next record.

5. Click in the **Current Record** box on the navigation bar, select the text **2**, then type **7**. Press the **Enter** key. Record 7 is the current record.

6. Click the **Address** field value (*8400 Cima Oak*) for the seventh record. Press the **Tab** key to move to the City field. The field value *Castle Rack* is selected.

7. Click the insertion point to the right of the letter "R" in *Rack*. Press the **Delete** key, type **o**, then press the **Tab** key twice.

8. Type **11111**, then press the **Enter** key.

9. Click the **Undo** button on the Quick Access Toolbar. The field value *11111* returns to its original state (80109).

10. Press **Ctrl+Home**. Leave the Member table open for the next Step-by-Step.

Selecting Records and Fields

You can quickly select entire records and fields by clicking a record or field selector. A field selector appears at the top of each column in a table and contains the field name. When you click a field selector, the entire column is selected. A record selector appears to the left of the first field for each record. When you click a record selector, the entire record is selected. You can also select all of the records and fields in a table by clicking the datasheet selector, which is the box in the upper-left corner of a datasheet.

You can select more than one field by clicking the field selector in one field, holding down the Shift key, and clicking the field selector in another column. The two fields, and all the fields between them, will be selected. Figure 1-7 shows five selected fields. You can use the same method to select multiple records. You can also select multiple fields or records by clicking and dragging across the field or record selectors.

FIGURE 1-7
Selected fields in a datasheet

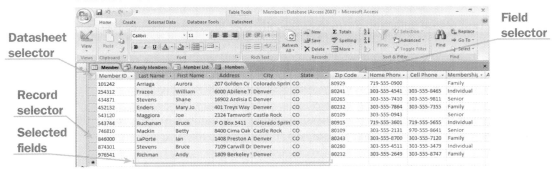

STEP-BY-STEP 1.6

1. Click the **Last Name** field selector to select the entire column.

2. Press and hold down the **Shift** key, click the **State** field selector, then release the **Shift** key. Five columns are selected, as shown in Figure 1-7.

3. Click the **Member ID** field selector. The Member ID field is selected, and the five columns are deselected.

4. Click the **Member ID** field value for the first record (*101242*) to deselect the column.

5. Click the **record selector** for the third record, with the Member ID field value *434871*. The entire record for Shane Stevens is selected.

6. Click the **datasheet selector** in the upper-left corner of the datasheet. All fields and records in the table are selected.

7. Click the **Member ID** field value for the first record (*101242*) to deselect the datasheet. Leave the table open for the next Step-by-Step.

Deleting Records

To delete a record from a table, select the record and then press the Delete key. A message box opens, as shown in Figure 1-8, warning you that you are about to delete a record. Click Yes to permanently delete the record or No to cancel the deletion. After you've deleted a record, you cannot use the Undo command or press the Esc key to restore it. Deleting a record is permanent.

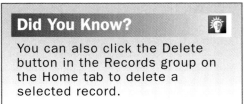

Did You Know?

You can also click the Delete button in the Records group on the Home tab to delete a selected record.

FIGURE 1-8
Message warning that you are about to delete a record

STEP-BY STEP 1.7

1. Click the **row selector** for the record with the Member ID *846000*.

2. Press the **Delete** key. A dialog box opens, as shown in Figure 1-8, warning that you are about to delete one record.

3. Click **Yes**. Leave the table open for the next Step-by-Step.

Cutting, Copying, and Pasting Data

The Cut, Copy, and Paste commands in Access work the same way as they do in other Office programs. You can use the commands to copy and move data within a table or into other tables. To cut or copy an entire record, select the record and click the Cut or Copy button in the Clipboard group on the Home tab.

Using the Cut, Copy, and Paste commands can sometimes be tricky, because data pasted in a table might overwrite the existing data. If you cut or copy an entire record and want to paste it into a table as a new record, click the arrow at the bottom of the Paste button in the Clipboard group on the Home tab, and then click Paste Append. When you select a record and click the Cut button, you will get the same warning message as when you press the Delete key. However, using the Cut button copies the record to the Clipboard, so you can paste it back into the table or into another table.

> **Extra for Experts**
>
> You can copy objects and paste copies of them into the same database or into another database. In the Navigation Pane, select the object (table, query, form, or report) that you want to copy, click the Copy button in the Clipboard group on the Home tab, then click the Paste button in the Clipboard group. Use the Paste As dialog box to type the name of the new object, then click OK.

STEP-BY-STEP 1.8

1. Click the **record selector** for the record for Shane Stevens (with the Member ID *434871*).

2. In the Clipboard group on the Home tab, click the **Copy** button.

3. In the Clipboard group on the Home tab, click the **arrow** at the bottom of the Paste button. Click **Paste Append**. A copy of the record for Shane Stevens is pasted at the bottom of the datasheet.

STEP-BY-STEP 1.8 Continued

4. In the Member ID field for the pasted record for Shane Stevens, change the Member ID field value to **457900**, then press the **up arrow** key.

5. Click the **record selector** for the original record for Shane Stevens (with the Member ID *434871*).

6. In the Clipboard group on the Home tab, click the **Cut** button. A dialog box opens and warns that you are about to delete one record.

7. Click **Yes**. The record is deleted.

8. On the record navigation bar, click the **New (blank) record** button. A new record is added to the table. The first field in the new record is selected.

9. Click the **arrow** at the bottom of the Paste button in the Clipboard group on the Home tab, then click **Paste Append**. The original record for Shane Stevens is pasted at the bottom of the datasheet.

10. Click the **record selector** for the record for Shane Stevens (with the Member ID *457900*), then press **Delete**. Click **Yes**.

11. Press the **Page Up** key. Leave the Member table open for the next Step-by-Step.

Changing Datasheet Layout

You can make many changes to the datasheet layout, including changing row height and column width, rearranging columns, freezing columns, and changing the background color of rows in the datasheet.

Changing Row Height

When you change the row height in a datasheet, the change affects all the rows. To change the row height, point to the bottom of any record selector. The pointer changes shape to a double arrow, as shown in Figure 1-9. Click and drag the row border up or down to adjust the row height.

FIGURE 1-9
Changing the row height

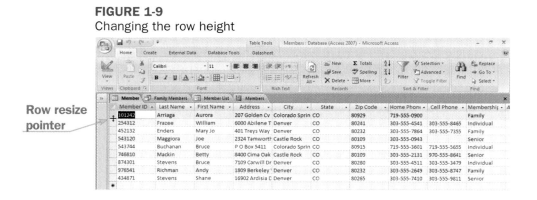

You can also specify an exact row height. In the Records group on the Home tab, click the More button, and then click Row Height. The Row Height dialog box opens, as shown in Figure 1-10. The standard (default) row height is 14.25 points. To change the row height to another value, select the value in the Row Height text box, type a new value, and then click OK.

FIGURE 1-10
Row Height dialog box

STEP-BY-STEP 1.9

1. Point to the bottom border of the record selector for the first record in the table (with the Member ID *101242*). The pointer is correctly positioned when it changes to a double-arrow shape.

2. Drag the row border down until it appears on top of the bottom of the record selector for the second record. When you release the mouse button, the change affects all rows in the table, as shown in Figure 1-11.

FIGURE 1-11
Datasheet after increasing the row height

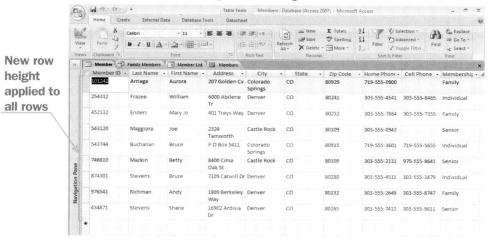

New row
height
applied to
all rows

3. In the Records group on the Home tab, click the **More** button, then click **Row Height**. The Row Height dialog box opens.

4. In the Row Height dialog box, click the **Standard Height** check box to add a check mark to it. The value in the Row Height text box changes to 14.25.

5. Click **OK**. The row height returns to the default setting. Leave the table open for the next Step-by-Step.

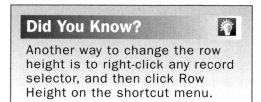

Did You Know?

Another way to change the row height is to right-click any record selector, and then click Row Height on the shortcut menu.

Changing Column Width

Often, the default column widths are too wide or too narrow for the data in the field. Adjusting column width is similar to adjusting row height. To change the column width, point to the right edge of the field selector for the column that you want to resize. The pointer changes to a double arrow, as shown in Figure 1-12. Click and drag the border to the right to make the column wider or to the left to make the column narrower. Unlike rows, which must all have the same height, each column can have a different width.

FIGURE 1-12
Changing the column width

Datasheet selector

Column resize pointer

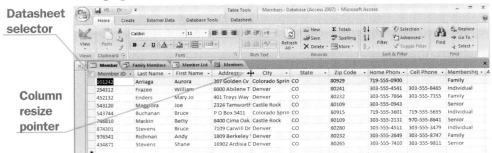

Another way of resizing a column is to change it to best fit, which automatically resizes the column to the best width for the data contained in the column. To resize a column to best fit, point to the right edge of the field selector for the column that you want to resize, and then double-click the pointer.

Did You Know?

To resize all of the columns on the screen to best fit, click the **datasheet selector** to select all columns, point to the right edge of any column, and then double-click the pointer.

S TEP-BY-STEP 1.10

1. Point to the right border of the **Address** field selector so the pointer changes to a double-arrow shape, as shown in Figure 1-12.

2. Drag the right edge of the **Address** field selector to the right about one-half inch, and release the mouse button. All of the data in the Address field should be visible.

3. Point to the right edge of the **City** field selector so the pointer changes to a double-arrow shape, then double-click. The City field is resized to best fit the data it contains.

4. Click the **datasheet selector** to select all columns in the datasheet.

5. Point to the right edge of the **Member ID** field selector so the pointer changes to a double-arrow shape, then double-click. All columns in the datasheet are resized to best fit.

6. Click the **Member ID** field value for the first record (*101242*) to deselect the columns. Leave the table open for the next Step-by-Step.

Rearranging Columns in a Datasheet

In Datasheet view, you can rearrange the order of the fields in a datasheet by dragging them to a new location. First, click the field selector for the column you want to move. Then, click and hold down the mouse button on the field selector and drag the column to the new location. A black vertical line follows the pointer to show where the column will be inserted. Release the mouse button to insert the column in its new location.

S TEP-BY-STEP 1.11

1. Click the **First Name** field selector.

2. Click and drag the **First Name** field selector to the left until the black vertical line appears between the Member ID and Last Name fields.

3. Release the mouse button. The First Name column appears between the Member ID and Last Name columns, as shown in Figure 1-13. Leave the table open for the next Step-by-Step.

FIGURE 1-13
Moving a column in a datasheet

First Name column after moving it to the left

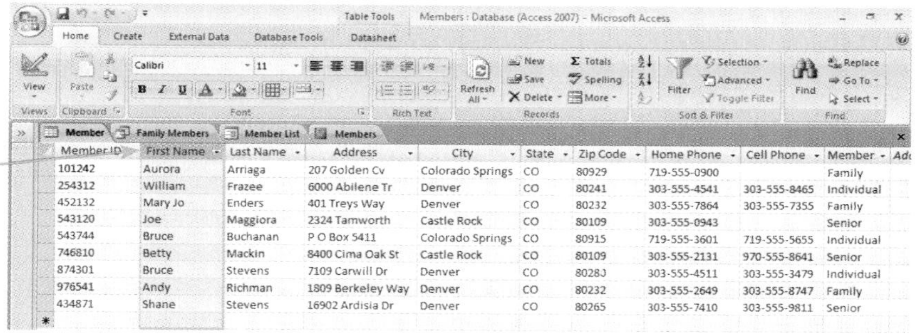

Freezing Columns

If a table has many columns, you might want to freeze one or more columns so you can still see them on the screen when you scroll the datasheet.

To freeze columns, select the field selectors for the columns that you want to freeze, click the More button in the Records group on the Home tab, and then click Freeze. To unfreeze columns, click the field selector for the frozen column, click the More button in the Records group on the Home tab, and then click Unfreeze.

S TEP-BY-STEP 1.12

1. Click the **field selector** for the Member ID field.

2. In the Records group on the Home tab, click the **More** button, then click **Freeze**. Press the **Home** key to deselect the Member ID field.

STEP-BY-STEP 1.12 Continued

3. Slowly drag the horizontal scroll bar at the bottom of the window to the right and notice that the Member ID field remains visible as you scroll the other columns. (Note: If you do not see a horizontal scroll bar, your screen is wide enough to display all of the columns. Continue to Step 4.)

4. Click the **field selector** for the Member ID field, click the **More** button in the Records group on the Home tab, then click **Unfreeze**.

5. Press the **Home** key to deselect the Member ID field. Leave the table open for the next Step-by-Step.

Changing the Background Row Color

By default, the rows in a datasheet are displayed with alternating light and dark background colors to make the data in the records easier to read. You can change the colors used by clicking the arrow on the Alternate Fill/Back Color button in the Font group on the Home tab. As shown in Figure 1-14, a gallery of colors opens and displays different themes and color selections. Pointing to a color in the gallery displays its name in a ScreenTip. Clicking a color in the gallery applies it to the row background.

FIGURE 1-14
Gallery with color choices for the background row color

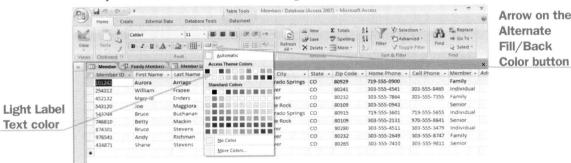

STEP-BY-STEP 1.13

1. In the Font group on the Home tab, click the **arrow** on the Alternate Fill/Back Color button.

2. In the Access Theme Colors section, click the **Light Label Text** color (the second color in the first row). The gallery closes and the new background color appears in every other row in the datasheet. Leave the table open for the next Step-by-Step.

Previewing and Printing a Table

Before printing a datasheet or any other database object, you should view it in Print Preview so you can check the print settings. To view an object in Print Preview, click the Office Button, point to Print, and then click Print Preview. Figure 1-15 shows the Print Preview window for the Member table. You can use the options on the Ribbon to change the printer, to change the page layout (portrait or landscape and the page margins), or to change the zoom setting on the report so you can view the entire page or a close-up of its contents. You can use the page navigation bar at the bottom of the Print Preview window to display additional pages when the object contains them. After previewing the object and making any adjustments, click the Close Print Preview button in the Close Preview group to return to Datasheet view.

FIGURE 1-15
Print Preview window

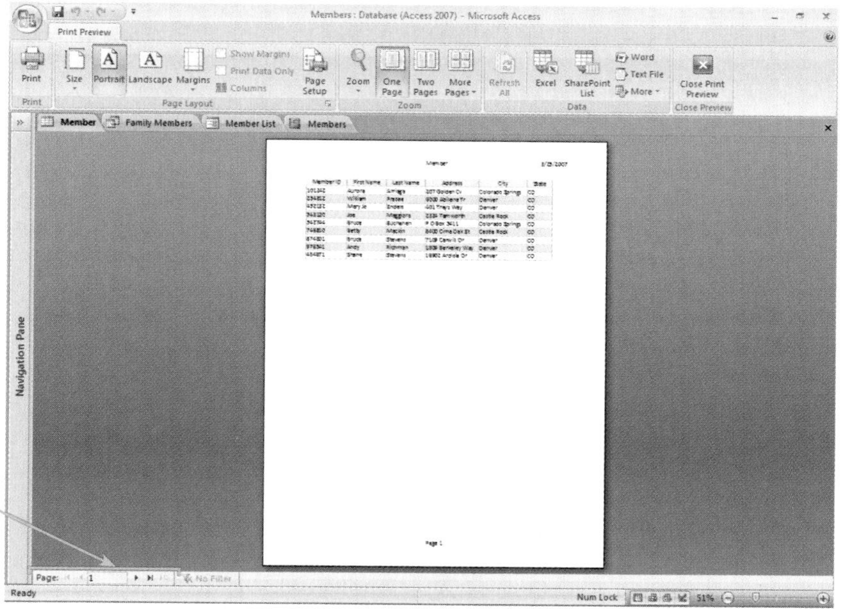

Page navigation bar

You can print a datasheet by clicking the Office Button, pointing to Print, and then clicking the Print command to select a printer and adjust the print settings. As shown in Figure 1-16, you can choose to print all the records, only the selected records, or certain pages. If you don't need to make any changes to the printer or print settings, click the Quick Print command to print the datasheet immediately.

FIGURE 1-16
Print dialog box

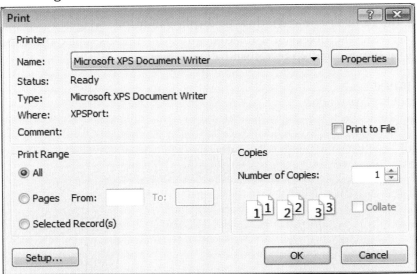

STEP-BY-STEP 1.14

1. Click the **Office Button**, point to **Print**, then click **Print Preview**. The datasheet appears in Print Preview, as shown in Figure 1-15.

2. In the Page Layout group on the Print Preview tab, click the **Landscape** button.

3. On the page navigation bar, click the **Next Page** button to view the second page of the datasheet.

4. In the Zoom group on the Print Preview tab, click the **Zoom** button. The zoom settings for the page change so that you can read the data in the datasheet.

5. In the Close Preview group on the Print Preview tab, click the **Close Print Preview** button. The datasheet is displayed again.

6. Click the **Office Button**, point to **Print**, then click **Print**. The Print dialog box opens, as shown in Figure 1-16. (Note: The printer for your computer will appear in the Printer section.)

7. Make sure that your printer appears in the Name box and that the **All** option button in the Print Range section is selected. Click **OK**. Leave the table open for the next Step-by-Step.

Saving and Closing Objects

As you are entering and changing data in a table, Access saves your changes to the data automatically. When you make changes to the layout or appearance of a datasheet, such as changing row height or column widths or changing the background row colors, you must save your changes by clicking the Save button on the Quick Access Toolbar. If your table already has a name, Access saves the table when you click the Save button. If you haven't given your table a name, the Save As dialog box opens first and requests a name.

You can close an object by clicking the Close button on the object window, as shown in Figure 1-17.

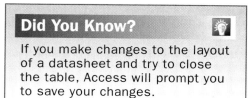

Did You Know?

If you make changes to the layout of a datasheet and try to close the table, Access will prompt you to save your changes.

FIGURE 1-17
Closing a database object

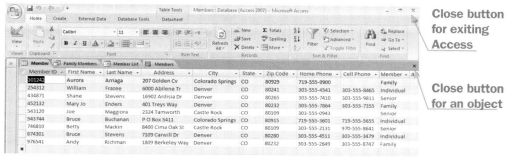

Close button for exiting Access

Close button for an object

STEP-BY-STEP 1.15

1. On the Quick Access Toolbar, click the **Save** button. The layout changes you made in the table are saved.

2. Click the **Close 'Member'** button on the table window. The table closes.

3. Click the **Close 'Members'** button on the report window. The report closes.

4. Click the **Close 'Member List'** button on the form window. The form closes.

5. Click the **Close 'Family Members'** button on the query window. The query closes. Leave the database open for the next Step-by-Step.

Compacting and Repairing a Database

 As you add and delete data or objects in a database, the database can become fragmented and use disk space inefficiently. Compacting a database rearranges how the database is stored on the disk and optimizes the performance of the database. Access combines compacting and repairing into one process. Depending on the size of the database and your computer's settings, it might take only a second or up to a minute to compact and repair a database. If the database you are compacting is small in size, like the Members database, you might not even notice that Access is compacting it because it will happen quickly.

STEP-BY-STEP 1.16

1. Click the **Office Button**, point to **Manage**, then click **Compact and Repair Database**.

2. Leave the database open for the next Step-by-Step.

Closing a Database and Exiting Access

When you are finished working in a database, you can close it by clicking the Office Button, and then clicking Close Database. After Access closes the database, the Getting Started with Microsoft Office Access page opens.

As in other Office 2007 programs, you exit Access by clicking the Office Button and then clicking Exit Access. You can also close Access by clicking the Close button on the title bar. Exiting Access takes you back to the Windows desktop.

STEP-BY-STEP 1.17

1. Click the **Office Button**, then click **Close Database**. The database closes.

2. On the Access title bar, click the **Close** button. Access closes.

SUMMARY

In this lesson, you learned:

■ Access is a program known as a database management system (DBMS). A computerized DBMS allows you to store, retrieve, analyze, and print information.

■ A database is a collection of objects. The objects work together to store, retrieve, display, and summarize data and also to automate tasks. The object types are tables, queries, forms, reports, macros, and modules. You can open an object by double-clicking it in the Navigation Pane.

■ You can open an existing database from the Open Recent Database pane displayed on the right side of the Getting Started with Microsoft Office Access page or by clicking the Office Button, clicking the Open command, and then double-clicking the database you want to open. The Access screen has a title bar, Quick Access Toolbar, and Ribbon.

■ A record is a complete set of data. Each record is made up of one or more fields. Each field is identified by a field name. The data entered into a field is called a field value.

- You can use the keys on the keyboard to move through the records and fields in a datasheet. You can also use the buttons on the record navigation bar in Datasheet view to move around the datasheet. The record navigation bar buttons allow you to select the first record, the last record, the previous record, or the next record. You can also use a button to add a new record or use the Current Record box to select a specific record.

- To select an entire row in a datasheet, click the record selector for the row. To select an entire field in a datasheet, click the field selector at the top of the column. To select multiple fields, click the field selector for the first field, press and hold down the Shift key, and then click a field selector in another column. To select all fields and rows in a datasheet, click the datasheet selector.

- To delete a record from a table, select the record and then press the Delete key. Use the Cut, Copy, and Paste buttons in the Clipboard group on the Home tab to move and copy data. Clicking the arrow at the bottom of the Paste button and then clicking Paste Append appends a record to the bottom of the datasheet.

- You can make many layout changes to a datasheet, such as changing the row height or column width, freezing columns, and changing the background row color of every other row.

- Before printing a database object, use Print Preview to check the print settings and to adjust the way the object is printed.

- You can close an object by clicking its Close button. To exit Access, click the Close button on the title bar.

VOCABULARY _Review_

Define the following terms:

Best fit	Datasheet	Field selector
Compacting	Datasheet selector	Field value
Database	Datasheet view	Navigation Pane
Database management system (DBMS)	Field	Record
	Field name	Record selector

REVIEW _Questions_

TRUE/FALSE

Circle T if the statement is true or F if the statement is false.

T F 1. A DBMS allows you to store, retrieve, analyze, and print information.

T F 2. The object that stores data in the database is a form.

T F 3. Clicking a record selector in a datasheet selects an entire row.

T   F   4. Holding down the Alt key allows you to select more than one column in a
            datasheet.

T   F   5. Changing the height of one row in a datasheet changes the height of all rows.

WRITTEN QUESTIONS

Write a brief answer to each of the following questions.

1. How do you delete a record in Datasheet view?

2. What does the Paste Append command do?

3. Why would you want to freeze columns in a datasheet?

4. Why should you preview an object before printing it?

5. Which database object allows you to search for and retrieve data?

PROJECTS

 PROJECT 1-1

1. Start Access.

2. Open the **Restaurants** database from the Data Files.

3. Open the **Favorites** table in Datasheet view.

4. Enter the records shown in Figure 1-18. (The first record was added for you.)

FIGURE 1-18

Name	Address	Phone	Specialty	Favorite Dish
Rosie's	8722 University Ave	817-555-6798	Mexican	Chicken fajitas
Health Hut	3440 Slide Rd	817-555-8971	Healthy foods	Fruit salad
Tony's BBQ	2310 S Lamar	817-555-7410	BBQ	Pulled pork sandwich
Stella's	7822 Broadway	817-555-7144	Italian	Lasagna
Westside Inn	5845 S 1st St	817-555-8200	American	Curry chicken salad
Alamo Diner	451 San Jacinto	817-555-0120	American	Chili cheese fries

5. Resize the columns in the datasheet to best fit.

6. Preview the datasheet in Print Preview. Change the page layout to landscape.

7. Print the datasheet. Close Print Preview.

8. Save the table and then close it.

9. Close the database, then exit Access.

PROJECT 1-2

1. Open the **Employees** database from the Data Files.

2. Open the **Department** table in Datasheet view.

3. Go to record 7 and change the first name to **Natalie**.

4. Go to record 11 and change the title to **Account Executive**.

5. Go to record 14 and change the department to **Marketing**.

6. Go to record 1 and change the last name to **Abraham**.

7. Undo your last change.

8. Select record 5. Delete record 5.

9. Select the datasheet (all rows and all columns). Change all columns to best fit.

10. Change the row height to **15**.

11. Move the First Name column so it appears between the Employee ID and Last Name columns.

12. Change the alternate fill/background color in the datasheet to Dark Blue 1 (in the Standard Colors section, second row, fourth column).

13. Preview the datasheet in Print Preview. Change the page layout to landscape.

14. Print the datasheet, then close Print Preview.

15. Save the Department table, then close it.

16. Compact and repair the database.

17. Close the database, then exit Access.

 **PROJECT 1-3**

1. Open the **Stores** database from the Data Files.

2. Open the **Manager** table in Datasheet view.

3. Copy record 4 and paste it at the bottom of the datasheet.

4. In the pasted record, change the Name to **Vision Eyewear**, the Address to **7500 Hwy 15 West**, the Zip Code to **43601**, the Phone to **419-555-0122**, the Specialty to **Contemporary eyewear**, and the Manager to **Trent Rodriguez**. Press the Tab key.

5. Move the Phone field so it appears between the Name and Address fields.

6. Freeze the Name column.

7. Scroll to the right until the Specialty field appears to the right of the Name field.

8. Unfreeze the Name column.

9. Change the alternate fill/back color of the datasheet to Medium Gray (in the Standard Colors section, the third color in the first row).

10. Resize the Specialty and Manager columns to best fit.

11. Preview the datasheet in Print Preview. Change the page layout to landscape.

12. Print the datasheet, then close Print Preview.

13. Save the Manager table, then close it.

14. Compact and repair the database.

15. Close the database, then exit Access.

CRITICAL *Thinking*

ACTIVITY 1-1

If you are working in Access and need help to complete a task, the Access Help window can help you find an answer. Start Access and click the Microsoft Office Access Help button below the Access Close button. In the Type words to search for text box, type **Navigation Pane,** and then click the Search All Access button. Review the links that you find and click ones that you believe will give you more information about customizing and using the Navigation Pane. Read the information that appears. After following several links and reading their contents, write a brief summary of two new things that you learned about the Navigation Pane. When you are finished with your report, close the Access Help window and exit Access.

ACTIVITY 1-2

You can use the Clipboard to collect and paste multiple items from the various Office programs. The Office Clipboard automatically copies multiple items when you do any of the following:

1. Copy or cut two different items in succession in the same program.

2. Copy one item, paste the item, then copy another item in the same program.

3. Copy one item twice in succession.

Using Access Help, find the steps to collect and paste multiple items. Briefly write the steps in numbered order. When you are finished with your report, close the Access Help window and exit Access.

CREATING A DATABASE

OBJECTIVES

Upon completion of this lesson, you will be able to:

- Create a database.
- Design, create, and save a table in Datasheet view.
- Set a field's data type in Datasheet view.
- Add, delete, rename, and move fields in Design view.
- Change field properties in Design view.
- Set field properties in Design view.

Estimated Time: 1.5 hours

VOCABULARY

Alphanumeric data

AutoNumber

Blank Database template

Data type

Default Value property

Description property

Design grid

Design view

Field Properties pane

Field property

Field Size property

Format property

Primary key

Required property

Template

Creating a Database

The first step in creating a database is to create the file that will store the database objects. You can choose to create a database using one of the many templates that are installed with Access. These templates contain objects that you can use to organize data about events, projects, tasks, and other categories of data. When you use a template to create a database, the template creates the database and one or more table, query, form, and report objects that you use to enter and view data. Another option is to use the Blank Database template, which creates a database with no objects in it.

To create a database, start Access. On the Getting Started with Microsoft Office Access page, double-click the icon for the template you want to use. Access will ask you to specify a file name to use and a location in which to store the database, as shown in Figure 2-1.

FIGURE 2-1
Saving a new, blank database

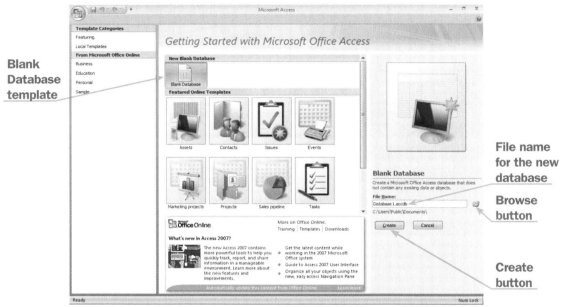

After specifying the file name and the location in which to store the database, click Create to create the new database and open it in Access. When you create a blank database, Access opens a blank table in Datasheet view so that you can start entering data, as shown in Figure 2-2.

FIGURE 2-2
New, empty table created

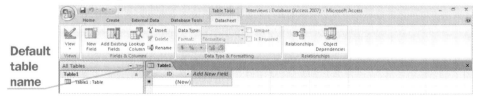

S TEP-BY-STEP 2.1

1. With Windows running, click the **Start** button on the taskbar. Click **All Programs**, click **Microsoft Office**, then click **Microsoft Office Access 2007**.

2. In the New Blank Database section, click the **Blank Database** template. See Figure 2-1.

3. In the Blank Database pane, click the **Browse** button. The File New Database dialog box opens.

STEP-BY-STEP 2.1 Continued

4. Navigate to the drive and folder where your Data Files are stored, then open the **Lesson2** folder. Click **OK**.

5. With the default database name *Database1.accdb* selected in the File Name text box in the Blank Database pane, type **Interviews** followed by your initials.

6. Click **Create**. Access creates the Interviews database and opens it. Access also opens a new, empty table, as shown in Figure 2-2. Leave the table open for the next Step-by-Step.

Did You Know?

Access adds the file name extension "accdb" to your file name automatically. You do not need to type it.

Creating and Saving a Table

When you create a blank database, Access creates the first table in the database for you and gives it the name *Table1*. You can change this name when you save the table for the first time. To save a table, click the Save button on the Quick Access Toolbar. In the Save As dialog box, type the name of the table, and then click OK. The new table name appears on the tab for the table and also as an object in the Navigation Pane, as shown in Figure 2-3. In many databases, data is stored in more than one table.

Another Way

You can create a new table in a database by clicking the Create tab on the Ribbon, and then clicking the Table button in the Tables group. You can also create a table using a table template by clicking the Table Templates button.

FIGURE 2-3
Table after saving it

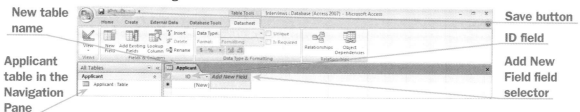

S TEP-BY-STEP 2.2

1. On the Quick Access Toolbar, click the **Save** button. The Save As dialog box opens. The default name *Table1* is selected.

2. In the Table Name text box, type **Applicant**.

3. Click **OK**. The tab for the table now displays the table name *Applicant*. The Applicant table appears in the Navigation Pane, as shown in Figure 2-3. Leave the table open for the next Step-by-Step.

> **Important**
>
> If you do not see a tab with the table name Applicant on it, click the Office Button, click Access Options, and then click Current Database in the Access Options dialog box. In the Application Options section, click the Tabbed Documents option button to select it, and then click OK. In the dialog box that opens, click OK. Close the Interviews database, and then reopen it.

Designing a Table

ⓒAfter creating a table in a database, you need to tell Access which fields to include in the table. When you create a blank database, the table that Access creates for you contains one field named *ID*. Access sets the ID field as the table's primary key. In a table, the primary key is the field that contains a unique field value for each record in the table. In some tables, this field is called an **AutoNumber** because it automatically adds a unique number to the primary key field for each record in the table. You can tell that Access created an AutoNumber for the ID field because of the word *(New)* in the first record's field. When you add the first record to the table, Access will change *(New)* to a unique number.

In some tables, your data might already have a field that stores unique numbers for each record. This unique field might store student identification numbers, employee numbers, or Social Security numbers. These types of values are also good candidates to use as a table's primary key field. The advantage of setting a primary key is that Access will not let you enter duplicate values for this field in different records. In other words, if you enter the student ID 1001 in the record for a student named John Hooper, Access will not let you enter the same student ID number in a record for another student. You'll learn more about primary key fields later in this lesson.

Entering Field Names in Datasheet View

To enter a field name in Datasheet view, double-click the "Add New Field" field selector. The "Add New Field" text is replaced by the insertion point (see Figure 2-4), so you can type the name that you want to use for the field. The field name is added to the field selector when you press the Tab key. You can continue typing field names and pressing the Tab key until you have entered all the fields that you plan to use in your table. When you have finished entering the field names, press the Tab key twice to enter the last field and move to the first row in the table. The last column in the table contains the "Add New Field" column in case you need to add another field later.

FIGURE 2-4
Creating a new field

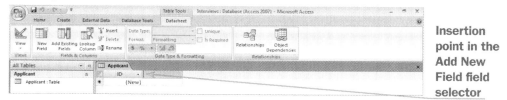

Insertion
point in the
Add New
Field field
selector

STEP-BY-STEP 2.3

1. Double-click the **Add New Field** field selector in the table. The Add New Field text is replaced by the insertion point blinking in the field selector, as shown in Figure 2-4.

2. Type **First Name** and press the **Tab** key. The First Name field is created and the insertion point appears in the third column.

3. Type **Last Name** and press the **Tab** key.

4. Type **Phone** and press the **Tab** key.

5. Type **Appointment Date** and press the **Tab** key.

6. Type **Job Number** and press the **Tab** key.

7. Type **Notes** and press the **Tab** key *twice*. Leave the table open for the next Step-by-Step.

Understanding Data Types

After creating all the fields for your table, you can enter the first record. As you enter each field value, Access assigns the field a data type based on the field value you enter. A field's data type determines the kind of data that you can enter in the field, such as numbers or text, or a combination of numbers and text (also called alphanumeric data). Table 2-1 describes the different data types that you can use in Access.

TABLE 2-1
Data types in Access

DATA TYPE	DESCRIPTION
Text	Accepts field values containing letters, numbers, spaces, and certain symbols such as an underscore (_). A Text field can store up to 255 characters and is used to store data such as names and addresses.
Memo	Accepts field values containing alphanumeric data, but can store field values containing up to 65,535 characters. Memo fields usually store long passages of text, such as detailed notes about a person or product.
Number	Stores numbers. Number fields are usually values that will be used in calculations, such as multiplying the cost of an item by the number of items ordered to get a total. Number fields are sometimes used to restrict the entered field values to numbers.
Date/Time	Stores dates, times, or a combination of both.
Currency	Accepts monetary values and displays them with a dollar sign and decimal point.
AutoNumber	Adds a unique numeric field value to each record in a table. AutoNumber fields are often used for primary key fields.
Yes/No	Stores Yes/No, True/False, or On/Off values.
OLE Object	Stores graphics, sound, and objects such as spreadsheets in a field. Objects can be embedded or linked.
Hyperlink	Stores a value that contains a hyperlink. Clicking the value activates the link and opens a Web page or other location, or addresses a message to an e-mail address.
Attachment	Stores graphics, sound, and movie files as attachments.
Lookup Wizard	Creates a field that lets you "look up" a value from another table or from a list of values.

Entering Records in Datasheet View

As you enter data in the first record, Access will assign each field a data type. For example, if you enter a person's name in a field, Access will choose the Text data type for the field because a person's name contains a small number of characters and no numbers. Figure 2-5 shows the table after creating all the fields. Figure 2-5 also shows the Table Tools Datasheet tab. You use this tab to add, delete, and insert fields. Notice that the ID field is selected. The options in the Data Type & Formatting group on the Table Tools Datasheet tab show that the current field has the AutoNumber data type. All the other fields that you created have the Text data type, unless you enter a value that needs a different data type. For example, when you type a date in the Appointment Date field, Access will change the data type for this field from Text to Date/Time.

FIGURE 2-5
Table after creating all the fields

AutoNumber
in the Data
Type box

ID field is the
selected
field

The First Name, Last Name, and Phone fields will contain alphanumeric data with less than 255 characters. These fields will use the Text data type. The Appointment Date field will store a date, so it will use the Date/Time data type. To make sure that all Job Numbers contain only digits, this field will use the Number data type. Finally, the Notes field might store field values that are longer than 255 characters, so it will use the Memo data type.

Because the ID field has the AutoNumber data type, you do not need to type a value in this field. While you are entering the record, the value *(New)* appears in the ID field. When you finish entering the record, Access will enter a unique value in the ID field automatically.

STEP-BY-STEP 2.4

1. With the ID field for the first record active, press the **Tab** key.

2. In the First Name field, type **Adam**. Press the **Tab** key.

3. In the Last Name field, type **Hoover**. Press the **Tab** key.

4. In the Phone field, type **505-555-7844**. Press the **Tab** key.

5. In the Appointment Date field, type **9/22/2010**. Press the **Tab** key.

6. In the Job Number field, type **5492**. Press the **Tab** key. Leave the table open for the next Step-by-Step.

Changing a Field's Data Type in Datasheet View

If you need to change the data type for a field, you can do so by clicking the Data Type arrow in the Data Type & Formatting group on the Table Tools Datasheet tab. The Notes field has the Text data type, but it needs to use the Memo data type. You can click the Data Type arrow in the Data Type & Formatting tab to display a list of data types for fields, as shown in Figure 2-6. Clicking a data type in the list changes the data type for the current field and also closes the list.

FIGURE 2-6
Data Type list for the Notes field

Data Type arrow

Notes field is selected

STEP-BY-STEP 2.5

1. With the Notes field for the first record active, click the **Data Type arrow** in the Data Type & Formatting group on the Table Tools Datasheet tab. Figure 2-6 shows the list that opens.

2. In the Data Type list, click **Memo**.

3. Press the **Tab** key.

4. Use Figure 2-7 to enter the remaining records in the table. Leave the table open for the next Step-by-Step.

FIGURE 2-7
Records added to the Applicant table

ID	First Name	Last Name	Phone	Appointmer	Job Number	Notes	Add New Field
7	Adam	Hoover	505-555-7844	9/22/2010	5492		
8	Julie	Hunter	505-555-9012	9/22/2010	5492		
9	Claire	Jeffries	303-555-4122	9/23/2010	5411		
10	Ruby	Sherman	505-555-0321	9/24/2010	5486		
*	(New)						

Working in Design View

When you are working on a table in Datasheet view, you can change the data type of a field. However, sometimes you need to make certain types of changes to a field that you cannot make in Datasheet view. In **Design view**, you can add, delete, and make changes to the way that fields store data. To change to Design view, click the View button in the Views group on the Table Tools Datasheet tab. Figure 2-8 shows the Applicant table in Design view. Notice that the field names and data types appear in the **design grid** in the top half of the Table window. The bottom half of the Table window is called the **Field Properties pane**. The properties for a field depend on the field's data type. For example, the selected field has the AutoNumber data type. The Field Properties pane displays the properties for AutoNumber fields. If the selected field has another data type, the Field Properties pane displays only those properties for that field's data type.

FIGURE 2-8
Applicant table in Design view

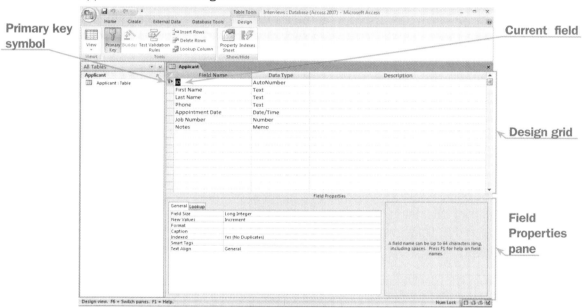

Notice that the record selector for the ID field has a key symbol in it. This key indicates that the field is the table's primary key. The record selector for the ID field is also orange. Just like when you select a record selector in a datasheet, the record selector for a selected field in the design grid changes color to orange when the field is selected.

Another Way

You can open a table directly in Design view from the Navigation Pane. Right-click the table name in the Navigation Pane, and then click Design View on the shortcut menu.

Adding, Deleting, Renaming, and Rearranging Fields in Design View

You can use the options in the Tools group on the Table Tools Design tab to add and delete fields. You can also drag fields in the design grid to new locations. To insert a new field between two existing rows in a table, click the record selector for the row *below* where you want the new field to appear. Then click the Insert Rows button in the Tools group on the Table Tools Design tab. If you want to add a new field at the end of the table, click in the first empty row in the design grid, and then type the field's name. You can delete a field by clicking the record selector for the field you want to delete, and then clicking the Delete Rows button in the Tools group on the Table Tools Design tab. To rename a field, edit the field name in the design grid and press the Tab key. To change a field's data type, click the Data Type box for the field. An arrow appears on the right side of the box. Clicking the arrow displays a list of data types so you can click the data type you want from the list. Any changes that you make in Design view are automatically updated in Datasheet view when you save the table.

> ### Did You Know?
> The Primary Key button in the Tools group on the Table Tools Design tab is a toggle button. For a primary key field, clicking the Primary Key button removes the key symbol from the field. For a field that is not the table's primary key, clicking the Primary Key button adds the key symbol to the field.

STEP-BY-STEP 2.6

1. In the Views group on the Table Tools Datasheet tab, click the **View** button. The Applicant table opens in Design view, as shown in Figure 2-8.

2. Click the **record selector** for the Last Name field. The field is selected.

3. Drag the **record selector** for the Last Name field up one row, so the black line appears between the First Name and ID fields. When the black line is between the First Name and ID fields, release the mouse button. The Last Name field now appears between the ID and First Name fields.

4. In the design grid, double-click the word **Appointment** in the Appointment Date field.

5. Type **Appt** and press the **down arrow** key. The field name changes to *Appt Date*. The Job Number field is selected.

STEP-BY-STEP 2.6 Continued

6. With the Job Number field selected, click the **Insert Rows** button in the Tools group on the Table Tools Design tab. A new row is inserted above the Job Number field.

7. Type **Confirmed** and press the **Tab** key.

8. Click the **Data Type arrow** for the Confirmed field. Figure 2-9 shows the list of data types.

FIGURE 2-9
Data Type list for the Confirmed field

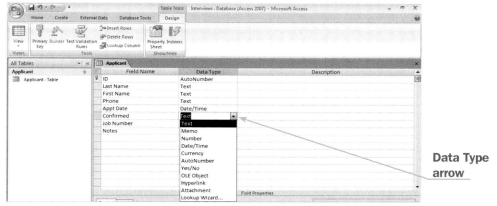

9. Click **Yes/No**.

10. On the Quick Access Toolbar, click the **Save** button. Leave the table open for the next Step-by-Step.

Description

The Description property in the design grid is an optional field property that you can use to describe what to enter in the field. If you give your fields descriptive names, you'll easily remember the field values to enter in them. For example, the Last Name field name easily communicates what field values to enter in the field. When you are entering data in the field, the Description property can remind you what field value to enter. For example, Figure 2-10 shows that the Description property for the Confirmed field in the Applicant table was set to "Has the interview been confirmed?" In this case, the Description property makes it easier to enter a field value. Because this field uses the Yes/No data type, the field value is "Yes" if you confirmed the interview; otherwise, the field value is "No."

FIGURE 2-10
Description property for the Confirmed field

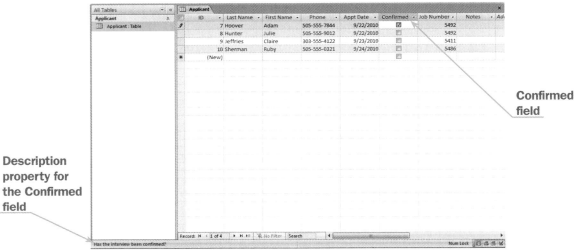

Confirmed field

Description property for the Confirmed field

STEP-BY-STEP 2.7

1. Press the **Tab** key. The insertion point moves to the Description property for the Confirmed field.

2. Type **Has the interview been confirmed?**

3. Press the **Enter** key. The Description property for the Confirmed field is set, as shown in Figure 2-11. Leave the table open for the next Step-by-Step.

Did You Know?

When you update certain field properties, the Property Update Options button might appear. Clicking this button and then clicking the Update option in the list lets you update the field property in certain database objects that use it.

FIGURE 2-11
Setting the Description property for the Confirmed field

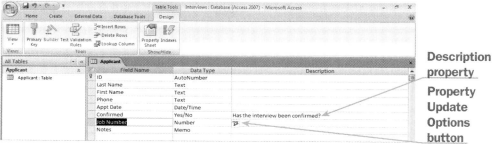

Description property

Property Update Options button

Changing Field Properties in Design View

When you created the fields in the Applicant table in Datasheet view, you assigned each field a name. Each field was also given a data type. When you set a field's data type, the field is given certain properties that help you to define and maintain the data you enter in the field. A field property describes a field's contents beyond the field's basic data type, such as indicating the number of characters the field can store or the allowable values that you can enter in the field. For example, Figure 2-12 shows the field properties for a Text field. Sometimes you won't need to change a field's properties at all. You can view and change field properties in Design view. Remember that the field properties for a field will vary depending on the field's data type.

FIGURE 2-12
Field properties for a Text field

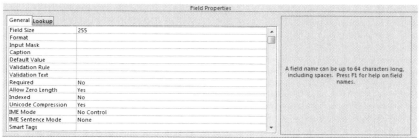

Changing the Field Size

The Field Size property sets the number of characters you can store in a Text, Number, or AutoNumber field. For Text fields, the default value is 255 characters. This means that every field value must have 255 or fewer characters. You can change the Field Size property for a Text field to store fewer characters. For example, if you create a field that stores state abbreviations, you might set the Field Size property to two characters, because all state abbreviations contain two characters. This change will ensure that no one can enter a three-character state abbreviation, which would be an incorrect field value. Also, when you decrease the Field Size property, the field requires less disk space to store the field values. All fields are given the default field properties for the data type assigned to them, unless you change the default field properties.

For Number fields, the Field Size property uses a different way of expressing the length. The default Field Size property for a Number field is Long Integer, which stores very large positive and negative whole numbers. Other field sizes for Number fields store numbers with decimals (such as 101.24), positive whole numbers only, and numbers that are less than or equal to 255. You select the field size by evaluating the numbers that you plan to store in the field and choosing the one that takes the smallest amount of disk space. The field sizes for Number fields are Byte, Integer, Long Integer, Single, Double, Replication ID, and Decimal. If you have computer programming experience, the available field sizes might be familiar to you. If the options mean nothing to you, don't worry. There is an easy way to select the appropriate field size. If your field stores whole numbers only, use the Integer or Long Integer field size. If your field stores numbers with decimal places, choose the Single or Double field size. To change the Field Size property for a Number field, click in the Field Size box. An arrow appears, as shown in Figure 2-13. Click the arrow to display the field sizes for a Number field, and then click the one you want to use.

FIGURE 2-13
Setting the Field Size property for a Number field

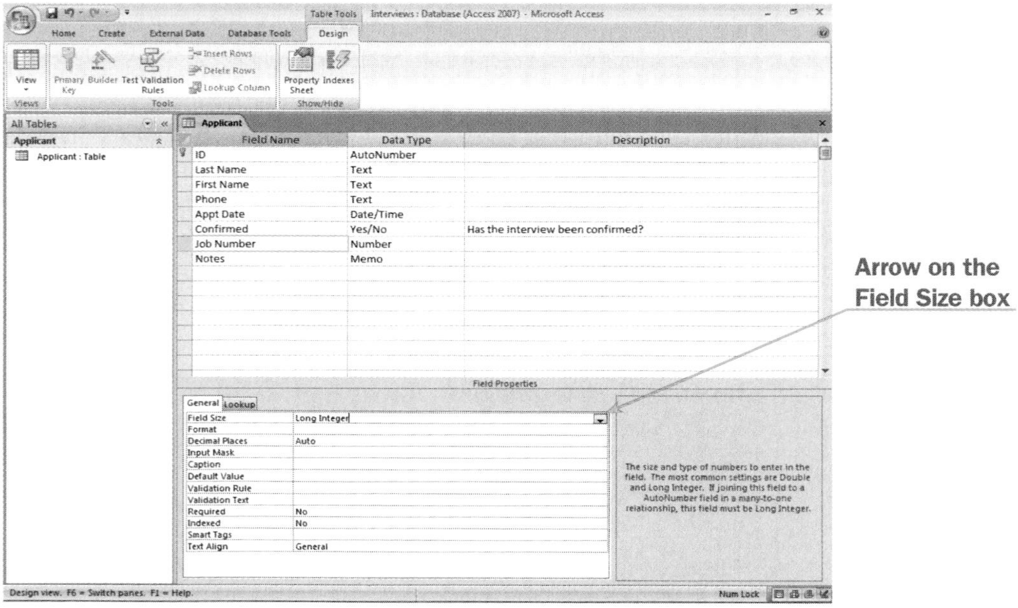

Arrow on the
Field Size box

After you change the Field Size property, Access might open the dialog box shown in Figure 2-14 to warn you that your changes might affect the data that is already stored in your table. For example, when you change the Field Size property for a Text field from 255 characters to 20 characters, Access decreases the number of characters in the field from 255 to 20. This means that any field values in the table that have 21 or more characters will be changed to 20 characters, resulting in a loss of data. After you change the Field Size property and save the table, you cannot undo your changes.

Did You Know?

Always be careful when changing a Field Size property to make sure that you will not lose any data in your fields. If a field value is 30 characters, and you reduce the Field Size to 20 characters, the last 10 characters of the field value will be deleted.

FIGURE 2-14
Dialog box that opens when you change a field size

Setting a Field's Format

Use the Format property to specify how you want Access to display numbers, dates, times, and text. For example, the default format for dates is *10/28/2010*. Using the Format property, you can change the format to *28-Oct-2010* or *Sunday, October 28, 2010*. When you set a field's Format property, Access displays the field value using the format you specify, even if it is not stored that way in the table. So, if you enter a date in the table as *10-28-10* but the Format property is set to display the date as *Sunday, October 28, 2010*, that's the way the date will be displayed.

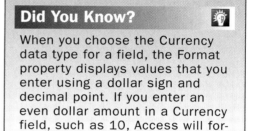

Did You Know?

When you choose the Currency data type for a field, the Format property displays values that you enter using a dollar sign and decimal point. If you enter an even dollar amount in a Currency field, such as 10, Access will format the 10 as $10.00.

S TEP-BY-STEP 2.8

1. In the design grid, click the **Last Name** field.

2. In the Field Properties pane, double-click the value **255** in the Field Size box to select it. Type **20**.

3. In the design grid, click the **First Name** field.

4. In the Field Properties pane, double-click the value **255** in the Field Size box to select it. Type **20**.

5. In the design grid, click the **Phone** field. Double-click the value **255** in the Field Size box in the Field Properties pane. Type **15**.

6. In the design grid, click the **Job Number** field.

7. In the Field Properties pane, click in the **Field Size** box. An arrow appears on the right side of the box, as shown in Figure 2-13.

8. On the Field Size box, click the **arrow**. A list of field sizes for Number fields opens.

9. In the Field Size list, click **Integer**.

10. In the design grid, click the **Appt Date** field.

11. In the Field Properties pane, click in the **Format** box. An arrow appears on the right side of the box.

12. On the Format box, click the **arrow**. In the Format list, click **Short Date**.

STEP-BY-STEP 2.8 Continued

13. On the Quick Access Toolbar, click the **Save** button. The dialog box shown in Figure 2-14 opens.

14. Click **Yes**.

15. In the Views group on the Table Tools Design tab, click the **View** button. The table is displayed in Datasheet view.

16. Click the **checkbox** in the Confirmed field for the first record (Adam Hoover). A check mark appears in the check box, indicating a "Yes" response. Notice the Description value on the status bar in the lower-left corner of the screen (see Figure 2-10). The other changes that you made to the fields in the table aren't readily visible in Datasheet view.

17. In the Views group on the Home tab, click the **View** button. The table is displayed in Design view. Leave the table open for the next Step-by-Step.

Setting a Field's Default Value

The Default Value property enters the same field value in a field every time a new record is added to the table. For example, if most of the customers in a database of names and addresses live in California, you can enter CA as the Default Value property for the State field. When you add a new record, the State field will automatically contain the field value CA. If you need to change the default value when you enter a new record, select the default value and type a new value.

> **Did You Know?**
>
> When you enter a default value for a Text field, Access adds quotation marks around the field value. Text fields can contain spaces; adding quotation marks is how Access defines the entire value. When you enter a default value for a Number field, Access does not add the quotation marks.

Using the Required Property

The Required property specifies whether you must enter a field value in a record. For example, in an employee database, you might set the Required property for a Phone field to "Yes" so that you must enter a phone number for each employee. If you try to enter a record for a new employee without entering a phone number, Access will open a dialog box similar to the one shown in Figure 2-15 stating that you must enter a phone number before Access will add the record to the table.

FIGURE 2-15
Dialog box that opens when you don't enter a required field value

When you click in the Required box for a field, an arrow appears on the right side of the box. Clicking the arrow displays the values "Yes" and "No" in a list. The default Required property for most fields is No.

After you change a field's Required property to Yes, the dialog box shown in Figure 2-16 opens when you save the table. This dialog box opens when you change the Required property because Access will test all of the existing field values in the column to make sure that they contain a field value. When you click Yes, Access will close the dialog box if there are no problems. If problems do exist, Access will help you decide what to do.

> **Did You Know?**
>
> Because the primary key field in a table must contain a value, its Required property is set to Yes automatically. You must enter a value in a primary key field or Access will not save the record.

FIGURE 2-16
Dialog box that opens when you require a field value

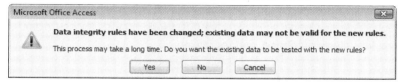

STEP-BY-STEP 2.9

1. In the design grid, click the **Notes** field.

2. In the Field Properties pane, click in the **Default Value** box.

3. In the Default Value box, type **Elise McDonnell will be the interviewer.** (Be sure to type the period.)

4. In the design grid, click the **Appt Date** field.

5. In the Field Properties pane, click in the **Required** box. An arrow appears on the right side of the box.

6. In the Required box, click the **arrow**. In the list that opens, click **Yes**.

7. On the Quick Access Toolbar, click the **Save** button. The dialog box shown in Figure 2-16 opens.

8. Click **Yes**.

9. In the Views group on the Table Tools Design tab, click the **View** button.

10. At the top of the Navigation Pane, click the **Shutter Bar Open/Close Button**. The Navigation Pane closes.

11. In the upper-left corner of the datasheet, click the **datasheet selector**. Double-click the right edge of the **ID** column heading. All columns in the datasheet are resized to best fit.

12. In the Records group on the Home tab, click the **New** button. A new record is added to the table. The ID field is the current field.

13. Press the **Tab** key, type **Peters**, press the **Tab** key, type **James**, press the **Tab** key, and type **970-555-6721**.

14. Press the **Tab** key *five times* to skip entering a field value in the Appt Date field and go to the next record. The dialog box shown in Figure 2-15 opens. Because this field's Required property is set to Yes, you must enter a field value in this field.

STEP-BY-STEP 2.9 Continued

15. Click **OK**. Click in the **Appt Date** field, then type **09/24/10**. Press the **Tab** key. Notice that the Format property for the Appt Date field changed the field value you entered to the Short Date format, 9/24/2010, even though you entered the field value as 09/24/10.

16. In the Confirmed field, press the **spacebar**. Access adds a check mark to the field.

17. Press the **Tab** key, then type **5486** in the Job Number field.

18. Press the **Tab** key. The Default Value property entered the value in the Notes field automatically.

19. Save the table. On the Access title bar, click the **Close** button. Access closes the Applicant table and the Interviews database, and then exits.

SUMMARY

In this lesson, you learned:

■ Creating a database creates a file that will store database objects. You can create a database using a template that creates one or more table, query, form, and report objects. You can also create a database using the Blank Database template, which creates a database with no objects in it.

■ You can create a table in Datasheet view by entering the field names you plan to use in your table. After entering the field names, you enter the first record. As you enter each field value, Access uses the data you entered to assign the field a data type. Access also creates an ID field to serve as the table's primary key. The primary key is the field that contains unique field values for each record in the table.

■ To save a table, click the Save button on the Quick Access Toolbar. Type the table name in the Table Name text box in the Save As dialog box, and then click OK. The table name appears on the tab for the table and also in the Navigation Pane.

■ A field's data type determines the kind of data that you can enter in the field, such as numbers or text, or a combination of numbers and text (also called alphanumeric data). The data types for Access are Text, Memo, Number, Date/Time, Currency, AutoNumber, Yes/No, OLE Object, Hyperlink, Attachment, and Lookup Wizard.

■ When you are working in Design view, you can add new fields to a table by clicking the Insert Rows button in the Tools group on the Table Tools Design tab. After adding a field, type its name and set its data type. You can delete a field from a table by selecting it in the design grid, and then clicking the Delete Rows button in the Tools group. To rename a field, click its name in the Field Name box, and then type the new name. To move a field, click its record selector in the design grid, and then drag it to the new position.

■ A field property describes a field's contents beyond the field's basic data type. The properties you can set for a field depend on the field's data type. You can add an optional Description property to identify the data to enter in a field. You can also change the Field Size property to set the number of characters in a Text field or to select the type of numbers to store in a Number field. The Format property lets you specify how to display numbers, dates, times, and text. When a field uses a commonly entered value, you can set the Default Value property to enter that value in new records automatically. Use the Required property when a field must contain a value.

VOCABULARY *Review*

Define the following terms:

Alphanumeric data	Description property	Field Size property
AutoNumber	Design grid	Format property
Blank Database template	Design view	Primary key
Data type	Field Properties pane	Required property
Default Value property	Field property	Template

REVIEW *Questions*

TRUE/FALSE

Circle T if the statement is true or F if the statement is false.

T   F   1. When you use the Blank Database template to create a new database, Access opens a table named *Table1* for you.

T   F   2. A table's primary key might be an AutoNumber field.

T   F   3. A field with the Text data type can store up to 65,535 characters.

T   F   4. To insert a new field in a table in Design view, click the row above where you want the new field to appear in the design grid.

T   F   5. The Description property is an optional field property that helps users understand what data to enter in a field.

WRITTEN QUESTIONS

Write a brief answer to each of the following questions.

1. What steps do you take to create a new database?

2. How do you create a new field in a table in Datasheet view?

3. How do you change a field's data type in Datasheet view?

4. What is the Field Size property?

5. What is the Format property?

PROJECTS

 PROJECT 2-1

1. Start Access. Use the Blank Database template to create a new database. Store the database in the Lesson2 folder with your Data Files. Use the file name **Music** followed by your initials.

2. Save the table that Access opens using the name **1980s Albums**.

3. In Datasheet view, create the following fields in columns 2 through 4: **Artist**, **Title**, and **Release Year**.

4. Use Figure 2-17 to enter three records in the table. (Remember, the ID field value is added automatically. Do not type it. Your ID field values might differ from the ones shown in Figure 2-17.)

FIGURE 2-17

1980s Albums				
ID	Artist	Title	Release Year	Add New Field
4	10,000 Maniacs	Blind Man's Zoo	1989	
5	Billy Joel	Glass Houses	1980	
6	The Police	Synchronicity	1983	
* (New)				

5. Resize all columns in the datasheet to best fit.

6. Save the table. Change to Design view.

7. Change the data type for the Release Year field to Text. Set the Field Size property to **4**.

8. Change the Field Size property for the Artist field to **25**.

9. Change the Field Size property for the Title field to **50**.

10. Add a new field named **Publisher** to the table so it appears between the Title and Release Year fields. Use the Text data type and change the Field Size property to **30**. Set the Description property to **Label that released the album.**

11. Set the Required property for the Artist field to Yes.

12. Save the table. When the dialog box opens and warns about data loss, click Yes. When the dialog box opens and warns about testing the data with the new rules, click Yes.

13. Change to Datasheet view. Print the datasheet in landscape orientation.

14. Close the table and database, and then exit Access.

 PROJECT 2-2

1. Start Access. Use the Blank Database template to create a new database. Store the database in the Lesson2 folder with your Data Files. Use the file name **RetailStores** followed by your initials.

2. Save the table that Access opens using the name **Retailers**.

3. In Datasheet view, create the following fields in columns 2 through 7: **Store Name, Address, Phone Number, Credit Card, Date Opened,** and **Outlet Number.**

4. Resize all columns in the datasheet to best fit.

5. Use Figure 2-18 to enter the first record in the table. (Remember, the ID field value is added automatically. Do not type it. Your ID field values might differ from the ones shown in Figure 2-18.)

FIGURE 2-18

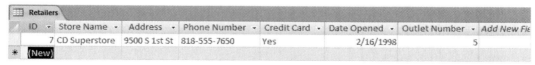

ID	Store Name	Address	Phone Number	Credit Card	Date Opened	Outlet Number	Add New Fie
7	CD Superstore	9500 S 1st St	818-555-7650	Yes	2/16/1998	5	
* (New)							

6. Click the Credit Card field for the first record. Use the Data Type arrow to change the data type to Yes/No. When the dialog box opens and warns about data loss, click Yes.

7. Save the table. Change to Design view.

8. Enter the Description property **Does the store accept credit cards?** for the Credit Card field.

9. Change the Field Size property for the Store Name field to **30**.

10. Change the Field Size property for the Address field to **30**.

11. Change the Field Size property for the Phone Number field to **15**.

12. Move the Outlet Number field so it appears between the Store Name and Address fields.

13. Save the table. When the dialog box opens and warns about data loss, click Yes.

14. Change to Datasheet view. Print the datasheet in landscape orientation.

15. Close the table and database, and then exit Access.

 PROJECT 2-3

1. Open the **Company** database from the Data Files.

2. Open the **Staff** table in Datasheet view. Change to Design view.

3. Move the Last Name field so it appears between the Employee ID and Title fields.

4. Move the First Name field so it appears below the Last Name field.

5. Change the name of the SS Number field to **SSN**.

6. Delete the Department field from the table. When asked if you want to permanently delete the field, click Yes.

7. Change the data type of the Salary field to Currency.

8. Set the Format property for the Birth Date field to Short Date.

9. Set the Default Value property for the Title field to **Sales Representative**.

10. Change the Employee ID field so it is the table's primary key.

11. Change the Required property for the SSN field to Yes.

12. Set the Description property for the Salary field to **Employee's monthly salary**.

13. Save the table. When asked if you want to test the data with the new rules, click Yes.

14. Change to Datasheet view. In a new record, enter the following field values: Employee ID: **2746**, Last Name: **Wells**, First Name: **Wendy**, Title: **Sales Representative**, SSN: **657-57-1600**, Address: **2610 21st St**, Zip Code: **79832-2610**, Birth Date: **2-15-72**, Salary: **2150**.

15. Print the datasheet in portrait orientation.

16. Close the table and database, and then exit Access.

 Careers

For information on careers, access the Occupational Outlook Handbook at www.bls.gov/oco. Web sites and addresses change frequently. If you can't find the information at this site, use your favorite search engine to search for other career sites.

CRITICAL *Thinking*

 ACTIVITY 2-1

Organize a group of contact information that you might have, such as people in your family or in your class. Use the Blank Database template to create a database to organize it. Give the database a name that accurately reflects the data, and add your initials to the end of the file name. Store the database in the Lesson2 folder with your Data Files.

Create and design a table for your data using a table template. To use a table template, close the Table1 table that Access created by clicking its Close button. On the Ribbon, click the Create tab. In the Tables group on the Create tab, click the Table Templates button. In the list that opens, click Contacts.

Save the table that opens as **My Contacts**. On the Ribbon, click the Home tab, then change to Design view. Use Design view to edit, move, add, and delete the fields you want to use to store your data. Save the table.

In Datasheet view, enter at least two records in the table. Print the table. Close the table and exit Access.

 ACTIVITY 2-2

In this lesson, you learned about using the Format property to control the way that Access displays field values. Another way to format field values is by using an input mask. Use Access Help to search for information about input masks. On a sheet of paper, describe what an input mask does, provide one example of how you might use it, and list the steps for entering an input mask in a field.

CREATING QUERIES

Creating a Query with the Simple Query Wizard

A query is a database object that lets you ask the database about the data it contains. The result of a query is a datasheet that includes the records you asked to see. For example, you might want to see all orders placed after a certain date or all customers who live in a certain zip code. In a query, the parts of the question that specify a certain date or zip code are called conditions. A condition (also called a criterion) is a way of telling the query which data you are interested in seeing. For example, when you ask to see customers living in a certain zip code, the zip code *78001* is a condition. When the condition has two or more parts to it, such as customers who have ordered a specific part *and* live in a certain zip code, the two conditions are called criteria. You can also create a query that doesn't contain any conditions, but that still displays any or all of the fields that you want to see.

A query is based on a table, and some queries are based on more than one table. When you say that a query is based on a table, it means that the data in the query datasheet is really data that is stored in a table. When you open a query object, you run the query.

Running a query displays a datasheet that is similar in appearance to the datasheet you see when you open a table. However, the query uses the conditions to display only the records and fields that you asked to see. When you run a query, the data in the table on which the query is based still exists in the table. A query is just another way of viewing the table's data.

An easy way to create a query is to use the **Simple Query Wizard**, which asks you what data you want to see by letting you select options in dialog boxes. To start the Simple Query Wizard, click the Create tab on the Ribbon. The Create tab contains options for creating different database objects. In the Other section on the Create tab, click the Query Wizard button. The New Query dialog box opens, as shown in Figure 3-1.

FIGURE 3-1
New Query dialog box

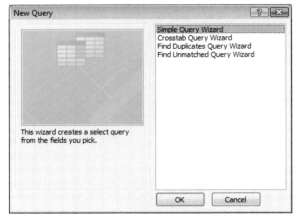

Make sure that the Simple Query Wizard option is selected, and then click OK. The first Simple Query Wizard dialog box opens, as shown in Figure 3-2. You use this dialog box to select the table that contains the data you want your query to display. You click a field in the Available Fields box, and then click the Select Single Field button to add one field at a time to the query. To add all fields to the query, click the Select All Fields button. When you add a field to a query, the field moves from the Available Fields list box to the Selected Fields list box.

FIGURE 3-2
First Simple Query Wizard dialog box

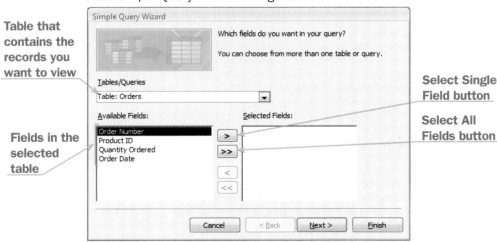

When you click Next, the second Simple Query Wizard dialog box gives you the option of creating a detail query or a summary query. A detail query shows every field in each record. A summary query lets you summarize relevant data, such as adding the field values in a column that stores price data. Access only gives you the choice of creating a summary query when the data you selected could be used for calculations.

In the last Simple Query Wizard dialog box, Access suggests a name for your query by using the object name on which the query is based, plus the word "Query," as shown in Figure 3-3. You can edit the default query name or use the name Access suggests. When you click Finish, the query datasheet is displayed.

> **Did You Know?**
>
> The Tables/Queries list box displays all the table and query objects in the database. The table objects are listed first (in alphabetical order), followed by the query objects (also in alphabetical order). To select a table or query in the list, click the Tables/Queries arrow.

FIGURE 3-3
Final Simple Query Wizard dialog box

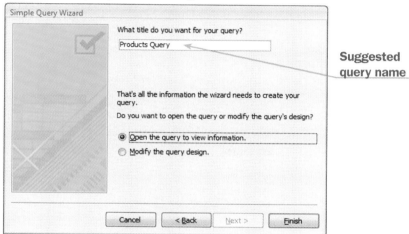

Suggested query name

STEP-BY-STEP 3.1

1. Start Access. Open the **Product.accdb** database from your Data Files.

2. If the Security Warning appears below the Ribbon, click **Options**, click the **Enable this content** option button, then click **OK**.

3. On the Ribbon, click the **Create** tab.

4. In the Other group on the Create tab, click the **Query Wizard** button. The New Query dialog box opens, as shown in Figure 3-1.

5. Make sure **Simple Query Wizard** is selected, then click **OK**. The first Simple Query Wizard dialog box opens, as shown in Figure 3-2.

6. Click the **Tables/Queries** arrow, then click **Table: Products**. The fields in the Products table appear in the Available Fields list box.

STEP-BY-STEP 3.1 Continued

7. In the Available Fields list box, click **Product Name**, then click the **Select Single Field** button. The Product Name field moves to the Selected Fields list box.

8. In the Available Fields list box, click **Retail Price**, then click the **Select Single Field** button.

9. Click **Next**. The second Simple Query Wizard dialog box asks if you want to create a detail query or summary query. Make sure the **Detail** option button is selected.

10. Click **Next**. The final Simple Query Wizard dialog box asks you for a title, as shown in Figure 3-3.

11. Select the text **Products Query** in the text box. Type **Price List**.

12. Make sure that the **Open the query to view information** option button is selected.

13. Click **Finish**. The query datasheet opens, as shown in Figure 3-4. The datasheet contains the Product Name and Retail Price fields from the Products table. Leave the query open for the next Step-by-Step.

FIGURE 3-4
Query datasheet

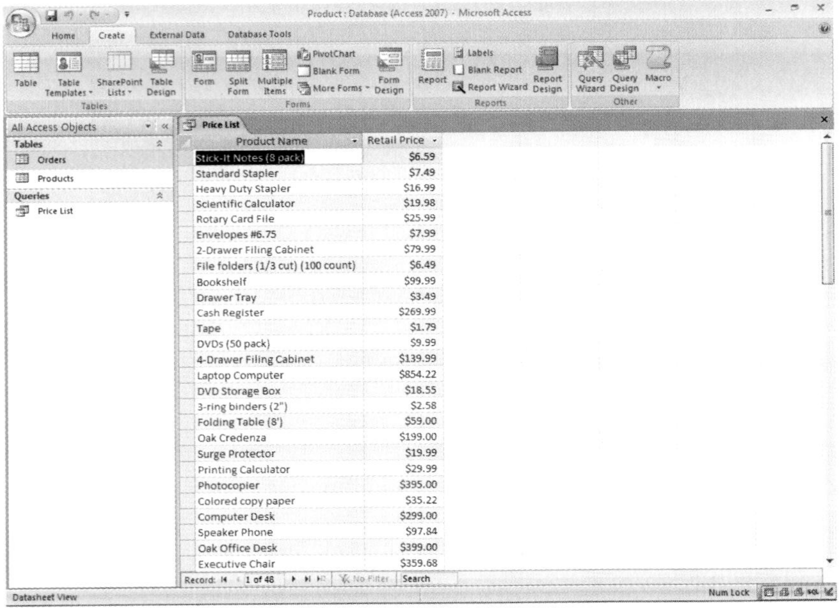

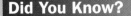

Sorting Data

When you view a table or query datasheet, the records might not appear in the order that you need. For example, you might want to list customers in alphabetical order or prices in order from least expensive to most expensive. When you view field values in ascending or descending order from A to Z or from

Did You Know?

Sorting a field in **ascending** order arranges records from A to Z, or smallest to largest. Sorting a field in **descending** order arranges records from Z to A, or largest to smallest.

smallest to largest, you apply a sort to the field. An easy method to change the way data is sorted is to click any field value in the field you want to sort, and then click the Ascending or Descending buttons in the Sort & Filter group on the Home tab.

STEP-BY-STEP 3.2

1. In the Retail Price column, click the value in the first row (*$6.59*). The Retail Price field is selected.

2. On the Ribbon, click the **Home** tab.

3. In the Sort & Filter group, click the **Ascending** button. The records are sorted in ascending order by retail price.

4. In the Sort & Filter group, click the **Descending** button. The records are sorted in descending order by retail price, as shown in Figure 3-5. Leave the query open for the next Step-by-Step.

Did You Know?

When a field is sorted, an arrow appears on the field selector to indicate the way records are sorted. In Figure 3-5, the Retail Price field selector has a small down arrow to indicate a descending sort order. An ascending sort order displays a small up arrow on the field selector.

FIGURE 3-5
Records sorted in descending order by retail price

Indicates a descending sort order for this field

Filtering Data

When you are viewing a table or query datasheet, you might want to display records that contain a certain value, such as products that have a retail price of $9.99. You can use a filter to view the data in this way. A filter temporarily displays records in a datasheet based on the condition that you specify. You can think of a filter as "filtering out" the records that do not match the condition.

You can use different types of filters to display the data you need. When you use Filter By Selection, you select a field value (or part of a field value) in a datasheet, and then click the Selection button in the Sort & Filter group on the Home tab. A menu opens with a list of options for filtering the field. For numerical data, the options let you filter records that have the same field value as the one you selected, field values that do not equal the selected field value, field values that are less than or equal to or greater than or equal to the selected field value, and in other ways. For fields defined with the Text data type, the options let you filter records that have the same field value, have different field values, contain the field value, or do not contain the field value. Clicking an option in the list displays only those records in the datasheet that match the filter condition.

You can use Filter By Form when you need to display records that contain one or more values based on the values stored in one or more fields. To use Filter By Form, click the Advanced button in the Sort & Filter group on the Home tab. In the menu that opens, click Filter By Form. The datasheet temporarily hides all the records it contains and displays a list box for a selected field, as shown in Figure 3-6. Clicking an arrow in a field displays the field values in a list. When you click a value in the list, you set the filter. Click the Toggle Filter button in the Sort & Filter group on the Home tab to display the records that match the filter. You can set the filter for one or more fields in the datasheet.

FIGURE 3-6
Price List datasheet after selecting Filter By Form

An easy way to sort and filter data using these same options is to use an AutoFilter. An AutoFilter is a menu that opens when you click the arrow on the right side of a field selector. The menu contains options for sorting data and clearing any filters that you have already applied. It also contains options for using Filter By Selection and Filter By Form. Figure 3-7 shows the AutoFilter that opens when you click the arrow on the Product Name field selector and then point to Text Filters. This menu shows the Filter By Selection options for the field.

FIGURE 3-7
AutoFilter for the Product Name field

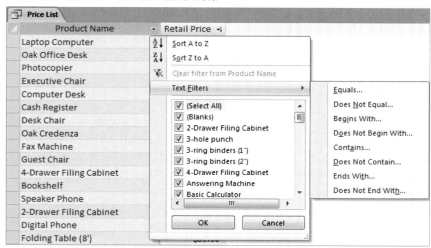

Figure 3-8 shows the AutoFilter that opens when you click the arrow on the Retail Price field selector, and then point to Number Filters. This menu shows the Filter By Selection options for the field.

FIGURE 3-8
AutoFilter for the Retail Price field

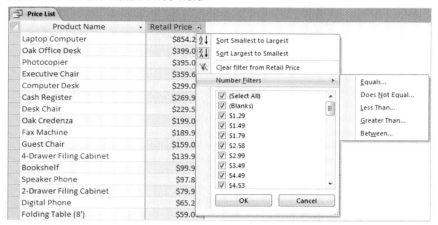

After applying any filter to a field, clicking the Toggle Filter button in the Sort & Filter group on the Home tab removes it and displays all records again. To remove all previously applied filters, click the Advanced button, and then click Clear All Filters.

STEP-BY-STEP 3.3

1. In the datasheet, click the second value in the Product Name field (*Oak Office Desk*).

2. In the Sort & Filter group on the Home tab, click the **Selection** button. In the menu that opens, click **Contains "Oak Office Desk"**. The filter is applied and one record is displayed.

3. In the Sort & Filter group, point to the **Toggle Filter** button. The Toggle Filter button has a "Remove Filter" ScreenTip because clicking it will remove the filter. Click the **Toggle Filter** button. The filter is removed and all records are displayed.

4. In the Product Name field in the second row in the datasheet, double-click **Desk**.

5. Click the **Selection** button, then click **Contains "Desk"**. Records that contain the word "Desk" in the Product Name field are displayed, as shown in Figure 3-9.

FIGURE 3-9
Using Filter By Selection to display records that
contain the word "Desk"

6. Click the **Toggle Filter** button. The filter is removed.

STEP-BY-STEP 3.3 Continued

7. In the Sort & Filter group on the Home tab, click the **Advanced** button. In the menu that opens, click **Clear All Filters**.

8. In the Sort & Filter group on the Home tab, click the **Advanced** button, then click **Filter By Form**. The data in the datasheet is hidden and an arrow appears in the Product Name field.

9. Click in the first row of the Retail Price field. An arrow appears in the first record for the Retail Price field. See Figure 3-6.

10. Click the **arrow** for the Retail Price field. In the list that opens, click **9.99**.

11. Point to the **Toggle Filter** button. The Toggle Filter button has an "Apply Filter" ScreenTip because clicking the button will apply the filter. Click the **Toggle Filter** button. Two records are displayed in the datasheet, both containing the value $9.99 in the Retail Price field.

12. Click the **Toggle Filter** button. The filter is removed.

13. Click the **arrow** on the Retail Price field selector. The AutoFilter opens. In the AutoFilter, click **Sort Smallest to Largest**.

14. Click the **Close 'Price List'** button to close the query. Click **Yes** to save the query. Leave the database open for the next Step-by-Step.

> **Did You Know?**
>
> You can identify a field that uses a filter by looking at the field selector. Figure 3-9 shows a filter icon on the Product Name field selector, indicating a filter has been applied. To remove the filter, click the Toggle Filter button in the Sort & Filter group on the Home tab. You can also click the filter icon on the field selector, and then click the Clear filter option on the AutoFilter.

Creating a Query in Design View

You might wonder if using a sort or a filter is the only method to change the way that data is displayed in a table or query datasheet. For a table datasheet, these are your only options. For a query datasheet, however, you have more sorting and filtering options if you create a query in Design view. In the Query Design window, you build and change the query using the query design grid. To create a query in Design view, click the Create tab on the Ribbon. In the Other group on the Create tab, click the Query Design button. A new query opens in Design view and the Show Table dialog box opens, as shown in Figure 3-10.

FIGURE 3-10
Show Table dialog box in Query Design view

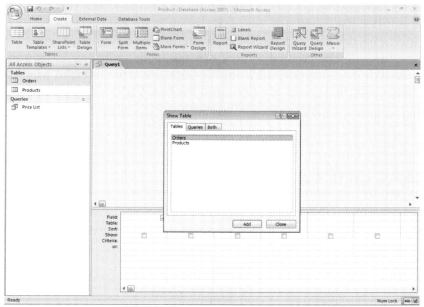

Because databases often include more than one table, you can select the table in the Show Table dialog box that contains the data you want to see in the query datasheet, and then click Add. After adding a table to the query design, click Close to close the Show Table dialog box. After adding the Orders table to the query design, the fields in the Orders table appear in a field list, as shown in Figure 3-11.

FIGURE 3-11
Orders table field list added to the query design

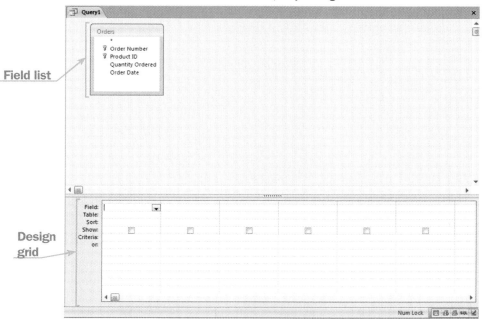

The Query window is divided into two parts. The top part of the window shows the field list for the table you included in the query design. The bottom part of the window contains a design grid that allows you to specify the fields to include in the query datasheet, any conditions that you want to use to filter data, and any sort orders you want to use in the query datasheet. You add fields to a query by double-clicking them in the table's field list. A query can contain one, some, or all of the fields in the table. You can add the fields in any order to the design grid. To add all of the fields to a query in one step, double-click the table name at the top of the field list to select all the fields, and then drag any field into the first Field box in the design grid.

After creating a query, you can save it by clicking the Save button on the Quick Access Toolbar.

STEP-BY-STEP 3.4

1. On the Ribbon, click the **Create** tab. In the Other group on the Create tab, click the **Query Design** button. The Query window opens in Design view, and the Show Table dialog box opens on top of the Query window. See Figure 3-10.

2. In the Show Table dialog box, make sure **Orders** is selected. Click **Add**. The Orders table field list is added to the Query window.

3. In the Show Table dialog box, click **Close**. The Show Table dialog box closes. See Figure 3-11.

4. At the top of the Orders table field list, double-click **Orders**. The fields are selected.

5. In the Orders table field list, drag any selected field to the Field box in the first column of the design grid. Release the mouse button. The fields from the Orders table appear in the design grid, as shown in Figure 3-12.

FIGURE 3-12
Fields added to the design grid

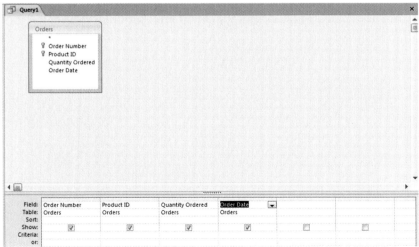

STEP-BY-STEP 3.4 Continued

6. On the Quick Access Toolbar, click the **Save** button. The Save As dialog box opens. The default query name, *Query1*, is selected.

7. In the Query Name text box, type **Orders List**. Click **OK**. Leave the query open for the next Step-by-Step.

Moving and Sorting Fields in Design View

You can select a sort order for a field by setting the sort order in the field's Sort box in the design grid. When you click in a field's Sort box, an arrow appears on the right side of the box. Clicking the arrow displays the Ascending, Descending, and (not sorted) options in a list. Click the Ascending or Descending option to set the sort order. To clear a sort from a field, click the (not sorted) option.

> **Another Way**
>
> Clicking the right side of the Sort box in the design grid selects the box, displays the arrow, and opens the list in one step.

When you need to sort data first based on the values in one field, and then by the values in a second field, you can set the sort orders for the two fields using the Sort boxes in the design grid. For example, you might sort customer names first by last name and then by first name. To sort on two or more fields, the field that you want to sort first (for example, Last Name) must be to the *left* of the field that you want to sort next (for example, First Name). Sorts on more than one field are applied in left-to-right order, so this is why the first sort field must be to the left of the second sort field. You can move a field in the design grid by clicking the bar above the field (see Figure 3-13), and then dragging the field to the new location. As you drag the field, a black vertical line shows you where the field will appear when you release the mouse button.

FIGURE 3-13
Selected Order Date field

Black vertical bar indicates where the field will be moved

Click at the top of the column to select it

STEP-BY-STEP 3.5

1. In the design grid, click the **bar** at the top of the Order Date column. The field is selected, as shown in Figure 3-13.

2. Click and drag the **bar** at the top of the Order Date column to the left. When the black vertical line appears to the left of the Order Number column (see Figure 3-13), release the mouse button.

> **Another Way**
>
> You can add a column to the design grid by clicking to select the column to the right of where you want to insert a new column, and then clicking the Insert Columns button in the Query Setup group on the Query Tools Design tab. To delete a column from the design grid, click the column to select it, and then click the Delete Columns button.

STEP-BY-STEP 3.5 Continued

3. Click in the **Sort** box for the Order Date field. The Order Date field is deselected, and an arrow appears on the right side of the field's Sort box.

4. Click the **arrow**. A list appears, as shown in Figure 3-14.

FIGURE 3-14
Sort options for the Order Date field

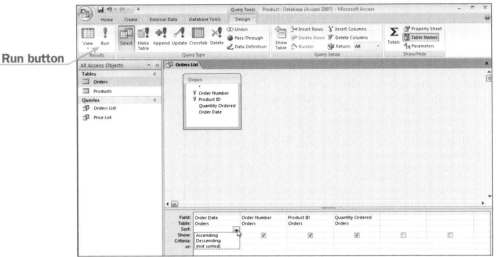

5. Click **Ascending** in the list.

6. Click the right side of the **Sort** box for the Order Number field to display the arrow and the list in one step. Click **Descending**. Leave the query open for the next Step-by-Step.

Adding a Condition to a Field

You could click the Run button, shown in Figure 3-14, to run the Orders List query and see all records in the Orders table, sorted in ascending order first by Order Date and then in descending order by Order Number. You already learned that queries usually contain conditions that help to answer a question about the data in the table. If the question is "Which orders contain an order for Product ID 1701?" then you need to add a condition to the query design before you run it. To add a condition to a field, click in the field's Criteria box, and then type the condition. If the field has the Text or Memo data type, Access will add quotation marks around the condition after you type it and go to another field or run the query. You can type the quotation marks if you like, but it's not necessary to do so.

> **Did You Know?**
>
> When you want to run a query and do not need to see the values in a field in the query datasheet, clear the field's Show check box in the design grid. The field is still part of the query design, but its field values will not be displayed in the query datasheet. To add the field back to the query datasheet, click the field's Show checkbox to add a check mark to it.

STEP-BY-STEP 3.6

1. In the design grid, click in the **Criteria** box for the Product ID field.

2. Type **1701**.

3. Press the **Tab** key. The condition for the Product ID field is set. Because the Product ID field has the Text data type, Access adds quotation marks around the condition. Leave the query open for the next Step-by-Step.

Running a Query

Before running a query, it is a good idea to save it. You can run the query by clicking the Run button in the Results group on the Query Tools Design tab. When you run a query, the results appear in a query datasheet. To return to the query in Design view, click the View button in the Views group on the Home tab.

STEP-BY-STEP 3.7

1. On the Quick Access Toolbar, click the **Save** button.

2. In the Results group on the Query Tools Design tab, click the **Run** button. The query datasheet shows the records containing orders for Product ID 1701. In addition, the records are sorted first in ascending order by Order Date, and then in descending order by Order Number. See Figure 3-15.

FIGURE 3-15
Orders List query datasheet

Calendar picker

3. In the Views group on the Home tab, click the **View** button. The query is displayed in Design view.

4. Click the **Close 'Orders List'** button to close the query. Leave the database open for the next Step-by-Step.

Did You Know?

When working with date field values, you might see a calendar picker like the one show in Figure 3-15. Clicking this icon opens a monthly calendar. You can enter date values in the field by clicking them on the calendar.

Creating Table Relationships

When a database contains more than one table, as most databases do, the feature of the database management system that lets you connect the data in the tables is a relationship. To create a **relationship** between two tables, you must design the tables so they contain a matching field. A **matching field** is a field that appears in both tables, has the same data type, and contains the same values. A matching field is also called a **common field** because it is *common* in both tables involved in the relationship. The common field usually has the same field name in the related table, but this requirement is not essential. It does, however, make it easier to identify the common field in a relationship when the common field has the same name in both tables.

When you relate the tables in a database, you can create queries and other objects that display information from several tables at once. For example, suppose you relate a table containing information about students (student ID number, name, address, and phone number) to a table containing information about classes (class ID number, class name, and room). As designed, these two tables do not have a common field. However, if you add the field from the Student table that contains the student ID number to the Classes table, the Student ID field becomes a common field in both tables. After relating the tables, you can use the Student ID field in the Classes table to identify the names of the students enrolled in the class. Without this common field, you wouldn't have a way to use a query to display the names of the students in each class.

You can create different types of relationships depending on the data used in the tables you are relating. The most common relationship is a one-to-many relationship. (The other types of relationships are one-to-one and many-to-many.) In a **one-to-many relationship**, *one* record in the first table (called the **primary table**) can match *many* (actually, zero, one or many) records in the second table (called the **related table**). The common field in the related table is called a **foreign key** when it is used in a relationship. In the primary table, the common field is usually the table's primary key.

When you relate tables, Access uses a set of rules to ensure that there are matching values in the common field used to form the relationship, both at the time you create the relationship and as you enter data in the tables after you create the relationship. This set of rules is called referential integrity. **Referential integrity** protects the data in the tables to make sure that data is not accidentally deleted or changed, resulting in inconsistent data. To enforce referential integrity between tables, choose the Enforce Referential Integrity option when creating the relationship. If you break one of the rules when relating tables or entering data into related tables, Access displays a message telling you about the problem and doesn't update the database.

To create a relationship between tables, click the Database Tools tab on the Ribbon. In the Show/Hide group, click the Relationships button. The Relationships window opens. In the Relationships group on the Relationships Tools Design tab, click the Show Table dialog box. Add the tables to the Relationships window, and then close the Show Table dialog box. The field lists for the tables are added to the Relationships window, just as you saw in Query Design view. After adding the field lists, drag the primary key in the primary table to the foreign key in the related table. When you release the mouse button, Access opens the Edit Relationships dialog box, where you select options for relating the tables.

S TEP-BY-STEP 3.8

1. On the Ribbon, click the **Database Tools** tab.

2. In the Show/Hide group on the Database Tools tab, click the **Relationships** button. The Relationships window opens.

3. In the Relationships group on the Relationship Tools Design tab, click the **Show Table** button. The Show Table dialog box opens.

4. In the Show Table dialog box, make sure **Orders** is selected, then click **Add**. Click **Products**, click **Add**, then click **Close**. The field lists for the Orders and Products tables are added to the Relationships window, and the Show Table dialog box closes.

5. Click and drag the **Product ID** field from the Products field list to the Product ID field in the Orders field list, then release the mouse button. The Edit Relationships dialog box opens, as shown in Figure 3-16.

FIGURE 3-16
Edit Relationships dialog box

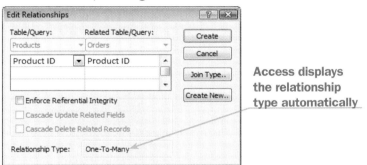

6. Click the **Enforce Referential Integrity** checkbox.

7. Click **Create**. Figure 3-17 shows the relationship between the tables.

FIGURE 3-17
Relationships window after creating a one-to-many relationship

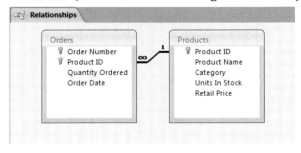

8. In the Relationships group on the Relationship Tools Design tab, click the **Close** button. In the dialog box, click **Yes** to save the changes you made. Leave the database open for the next Step-by-Step.

Viewing Related Records

After creating a one-to-many relationship between two tables, you can view the data in the related table by opening the datasheet for the primary table. In the relationship you just created, the Products table is the primary table. Figure 3-18 shows a column with indicators in each row. Clicking the expand indicator opens a subdatasheet, which contains the related records in the Orders table (the related table). You can use the subdatasheet to make changes to the related records.

> **Did You Know?**
>
> A one-to-many relationship has a "1" on the side of the primary table and an infinity symbol (the number 8 turned on its side) on the side of the related table. The key symbol next to a field name in a field list indicates the table's primary key. When you see two keys in a single table, the primary key is the combination of those fields.

FIGURE 3-18
Subdatasheet in the Products table

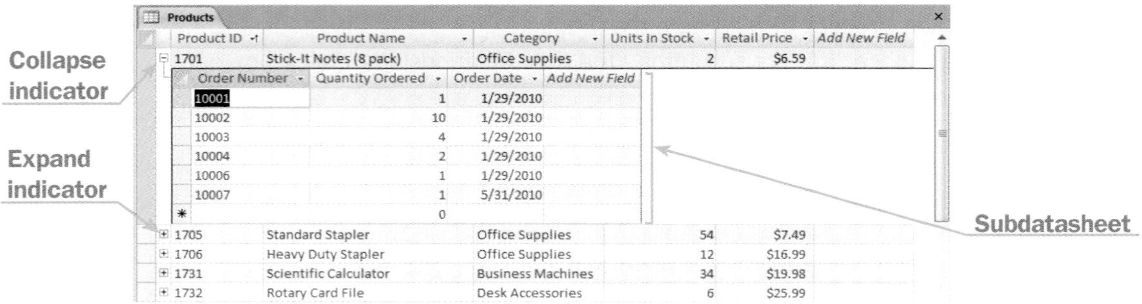

STEP-BY-STEP 3.9

1. In the Navigation Pane, double-click the **Products** table. The table opens in Datasheet view.

2. Click the **expand indicator** to the left of the record with Product ID 1701. Figure 3-18 shows that there are *many* related records from the Orders table for Product ID 1701.

3. Click the **expand indicator** for Product ID 1733. The subdatasheet is empty, which means that there are *zero* related records in the Orders table for Product ID 1733.

4. Click the **expand indicator** for Product ID 1705. The subdatasheet contains *one* related record from the Orders table for Product ID 1705.

5. Click the **collapse indicator** to the left of the record with Product ID 1701. The subdatasheet closes.

6. Click the **Close 'Products' button** to close the Products table. Leave the database open for the next Step-by-Step.

> **Careers**
>
> List three careers that would require using a database. For each career, describe the database and its contents.

Creating a Multitable Query

After defining relationships in a database, you can create a query that is based on more than one table. Queries that are based on more than one table are sometimes called multitable queries. For example, you might want to view customer information with the orders placed by the customers. To do this, you would need data from the table that stores customer information and the table that stores order information.

Creating a query based on more than one table simply requires you to add another table's field list to the query design. After you add two related tables to the query design, a join line shows the relationship between the tables, as shown in Figure 3-19. The join line connects the common field used to relate the tables. It also defines the type of relationship by using the "1" to represent the "one" side of the relationship and the infinity symbol to represent the "many" side of the relationship. Keep in mind that you can add the common field to the query design from either table—after all, the common field contains *matching* values, so it doesn't matter which one you choose.

FIGURE 3-19
Joined tables in the Query window

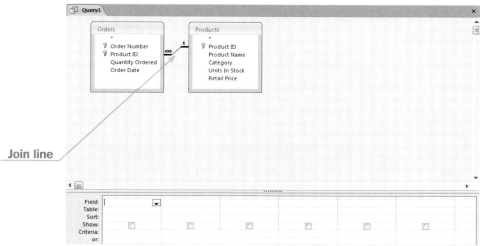

The skills for adding a table's field list, adding fields to the query design, sorting fields, and specifying conditions are the same for a multitable query as they are for a query based on a single table.

S TEP-BY-STEP 3.10

1. On the Ribbon, click the **Create** tab. In the Other group on the Create tab, click the **Query Design** button.

2. In the Show Table dialog box, make sure **Orders** is selected, then click **Add**.

3. In the Show Table dialog box, click **Products**, click **Add**, then click **Close**. The Query window displays the field lists for the Orders and Products tables. The join line connects the tables using the common field, Product ID. See Figure 3-19.

STEP-BY-STEP 3.10 Continued

4. In the Orders field list, double-click **Order Number**. The Order Number field is added to the first column in the design grid.

5. In the Products field list, double-click the following fields to add them to the design grid in the order shown: **Product ID**, **Product Name**, **Units In Stock**, and **Retail Price**.

6. Click the right side of the **Sort** box for the Product Name field, then click **Ascending** in the list. (If you don't see the list right away, click the arrow to display it.)

> **Did You Know?**
>
> When you add a table's field list to the query design, the field list initially displays a limited number of fields. If a table contains more fields, you can view the other fields by using the scroll bar that appears on the field list. You can also use the pointer to resize the field list so you can see more fields at once.

7. Click in the **Criteria** box for the Units In Stock field. Type **0** (a zero, not the capital letter O), then press the **Tab** key.

8. On the Quick Access Toolbar, click the **Save** button. In the Save As dialog box, type **Product Prices**, then click **OK**.

9. In the Results group on the Query Tools Design tab, click the **Run** button. Figure 3-20 shows the query datasheet. Only one item (Oak Office Desk) is out of stock.

FIGURE 3-20
Datasheet for a query based on two tables

Product Prices

Order Number	Product ID	Product Name	Units In Stock	Retail Price
10010	2002	Oak Office Desk	0	$399.00
*				

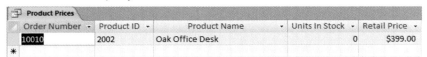

10. In the Views group on the Home tab, click the **View** button. The query is displayed in Design view. Leave the query open for the next Step-by-Step.

Using Operators in a Condition

The Product Prices query selects records for products that are out of stock (the Units In Stock field value is zero). This is called an exact match condition because the records must contain the value 0 in the Units In Stock field to be displayed in the query datasheet. The query selects only one record, for an Oak Office Desk.

Another type of condition that you can create causes a record to be displayed in the query datasheet when the record matches a range of values. This is called a range-of-values condition. For example, you might use a condition to find orders with a Units In Stock value of 2 (an exact match) or a Units In Stock value of 5 or more (a range-of-values match).

To create a range-of-values condition, you need to include a relational operator in the condition. You can use the relational operators listed in Table 3-1 in a condition.

TABLE 3-1
Relational operators

OPERATOR	DESCRIPTION
>	Greater than
<	Less than
=	Equal to
>=	Greater than or equal to
<=	Less than or equal to
<>	Not equal

You can also use the And or Or logical operators in a query. The **And operator** selects records that match all of two or more conditions in a query. For example, if you want to find records that meet more than one condition, such as employees who earn more than $30,000 a year *and* who have been with the company for less than two years, you can use the And operator. To create a query with the And operator, enter the condition for the first field and the condition for the second field on the *same* Criteria row in the design grid.

The **Or operator** selects records that match at least one of two or more conditions in a query. For example, if you want to find records for employees who earn more than $30,000 a year *or* who have been with the company for less than two years, you can use the Or operator. To create a query with the Or operator, enter the condition for the first field in the Criteria row in the design grid and the condition for the second field in the "or" row—a *different* row—in the design grid.

S TEP-BY-STEP 3.11

1. Select the **0** in the Criteria box for the Units In Stock field, then press the **Delete** key.

2. Type **>5** in the Units In Stock Criteria box.

3. Run the query. The datasheet displays 15 records that have more than five units in stock.

4. In the Views group on the Home tab, click the **View** button.

STEP-BY-STEP 3.11 Continued

5. Click in the **Criteria** box for the Retail Price field, then type **<20**. This condition will select records that have a value of less than $20.00. It is not necessary to type the dollar sign, decimal point, or decimal places. See Figure 3-21.

FIGURE 3-21
Query design that uses an And condition

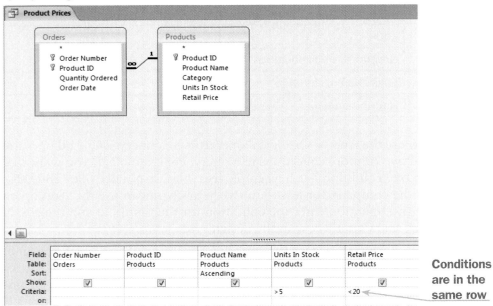

6. Run the query. Figure 3-22 shows the results of the query with the And condition.

FIGURE 3-22
Datasheet for a query with an And condition

Order Number	Product ID	Product Name	Units In Stock	Retail Price
10004	5192	Clipboard	32	$1.29
10003	5943	Envelopes #10 (500 count)	11	$11.99
10005	5421	Envelopes (9" x 12") (100 count)	41	$6.49
10005	3406	Scissors	6	$4.99
10003	3406	Scissors	6	$4.99
10002	3406	Scissors	6	$4.99
10001	1705	Standard Stapler	54	$7.49
10002	5912	Tape Dispenser	44	$5.99

7. Change to Design view. Select the condition **<20** in the Criteria row for the Retail Price field, then press the **Delete** key.

8. Press the **down arrow** key. The insertion point moves to the "or" row for the Retail Price field.

9. Type **<20**. Figure 3-23 shows the query design.

STEP-BY-STEP 3.11 Continued

FIGURE 3-23
Query design that uses an Or condition

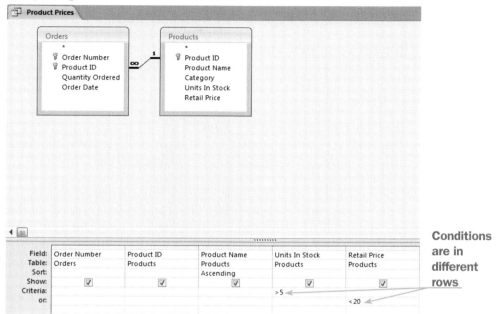

10. Run the query. Figure 3-24 shows the results of the query with the Or condition. Leave the query open for the next Step-by-Step.

FIGURE 3-24
Datasheet for a query with an Or condition

Order Number	Product ID	Product Name	Units In Stock	Retail Price
10000	1734	2-Drawer Filing Cabinet	32	$79.99
10010	5917	Answering Machine	53	$49.99
10004	5192	Clipboard	32	$1.29
10010	5465	Desk Accessory Set	8	$21.99
10006	5465	Desk Accessory Set	8	$21.99
10006	5918	Digital Phone	57	$65.29
10003	5943	Envelopes #10 (500 count)	11	$11.99
10005	5421	Envelopes (9" x 12") (100 count)	41	$6.49
10008	2010	Fax Machine	15	$189.95
10009	1996	Printing Calculator	221	$29.99
10003	3406	Scissors	6	$4.99
10005	3406	Scissors	6	$4.99
10002	3406	Scissors	6	$4.99
10001	1705	Standard Stapler	54	$7.49
10001	1701	Stick-It Notes (8 pack)	2	$6.59
10007	1701	Stick-It Notes (8 pack)	2	$6.59
10006	1701	Stick-It Notes (8 pack)	2	$6.59
10004	1701	Stick-It Notes (8 pack)	2	$6.59
10003	1701	Stick-It Notes (8 pack)	2	$6.59
10002	1701	Stick-It Notes (8 pack)	2	$6.59
10008	1995	Surge Protector	5	$19.99
10002	5912	Tape Dispenser	44	$5.99

Calculating Data

You can use a query to do more than just select records based on conditions. You can also use a query to perform calculations on the data selected by the query. Access provides two ways to calculate data in a query: using the Total row and creating a calculated field.

Did You Know?

When you use a date in a condition, Access puts number signs (#) around the date after you go to another field in the design grid or run the query. For example, when you enter the condition >=9/16/2010, Access changes it to >=#9/16/2010# when you go to another field or run the query.

Using the Total Row

When you are viewing a table or query datasheet, you can use the Total row to get a quick count of the number of values in a column. When the field contains numeric data, such as numbers or currency values, the Total row also includes functions that calculate the total of the values in a column or the average, minimum, or maximum value in a column. To use the Total row, display the datasheet, and then click the Totals button in the Records group on the Home tab. The Total row is added at the bottom of the datasheet, as shown in Figure 3-25. When you click in the Total row for a field, an arrow appears on the left side of the field. Clicking the arrow displays a list of functions that you can use in the field. The functions vary based on the field's data type. To hide the Total row, click the Totals button a second time.

FIGURE 3-25
Total row added to a query datasheet

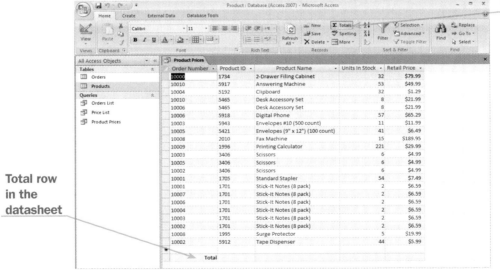

STEP-BY-STEP 3.12

1. In the Records group on the Home tab, click the **Totals** button. The Total row is added to the datasheet, as shown in Figure 3-25.

2. Click in the **Total** row for the Product Name field. An arrow appears on the left side of the field.

STEP-BY-STEP 3.12 Continued

3. Click the **arrow**, then click **Count**. The Count function counts the number of values. The value 22 in the Total row indicates that there are 22 products.

4. Click in the **Total** row for the Units In Stock field, click the **arrow**, then click **Sum**. The Sum function adds the values in the field. The value 611 in the Total row indicates the total number of units in stock.

5. Click in the **Total** row for the Retail Price field, click the **arrow**, then click **Average**. The Average function calculates the average value and displays $25.77 in the Total row.

6. In the Records group on the Home tab, click the **Totals** button. The Totals row is hidden.

7. Click the **'Close Product Prices'** button to close the query, then click **Yes** to save it. Leave the database open for the next Step-by-Step.

> ### Did You Know?
>
> The Minimum function finds the lowest value in a field. The Maximum function finds the highest value in a field. Two other functions for fields that contain numeric data—Standard Deviation and Variance—are used to compute statistical values.

Creating a Calculated Field

Because Access can use mathematical operators (+, -, *, and /) to perform calculations on numeric and date data, you do not need to include fields in your tables that store the *result* of a calculation. For example, creating a table with a field that stores a person's age would be considered poor table design because this value changes once a year. A better table design includes a field that stores a person's birth date. If you need to display a person's age, you can calculate age by subtracting the person's birth date from the current date. The result will always be the person's age.

To perform a calculation in a query, you add a new field to the query and enter the calculation you need to perform. When a field displays a value that is calculated using other fields in the query, it is called a **calculated field**. The calculation itself, such as *[Current Date] – [Birth Date]*, is called an **expression**. Notice that the field names *Current Date* and *Birth Date* are enclosed in square brackets, which is required when a field name containing spaces is used in an expression. Access uses the expression in the calculated field to display the result in the datasheet. For example, if today's date is June 16, 2010, and your birth date is May 31, 1996, then the result of the expression (your age) is 14.

How do you create a calculated field? You can type it directly into an empty column in the query design grid. This method works fine, but it is difficult to read the expression because the default column width in the design grid only displays about 20 characters. For this reason, it's worth the extra step to right-click the empty Field box in the design grid, and then click Zoom on the shortcut menu. The Zoom dialog box provides plenty of space to see your expression as you type it. When you have entered the expression, click OK to close the Zoom dialog box. Then you can run the query as usual.

S TEP-BY-STEP 3.13

1. On the Ribbon, click the **Create** tab. In the Other group on the Create tab, click the **Query Design** button.

2. In the Show Table dialog box, add the **Orders** and **Products** tables to the query design, then click **Close**.

3. In the Products table field list, double-click the **Product ID** field to add it to the design grid.

4. In the Products table field list, double-click the **Product Name** field to add it to the design grid.

5. Add the **Quantity Ordered** field from the Orders table to the design grid, then add the **Retail Price** field from the Products table to the design grid.

6. On the Quick Access Toolbar, click the **Save** button. In the Save As dialog box, type **Order Line Totals**, then click **OK**. The query design is shown in Figure 3-26.

FIGURE 3-26
Order Line Totals query design

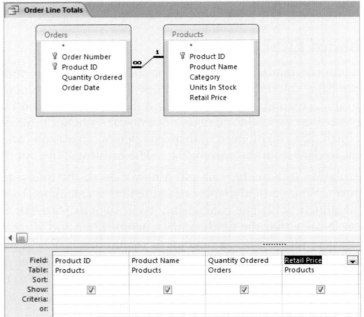

7. Right-click the empty **Field** box to the right of the Retail Price field in the design grid to open the short-cut menu.

8. On the shortcut menu, click **Zoom**. The Zoom dialog box opens.

9. Type **[Quantity Ordered] * [Retail Price]** in the Zoom dialog box, as shown in Figure 3-27.

STEP-BY-STEP 3.13 Continued

FIGURE 3-27
Zoom dialog box

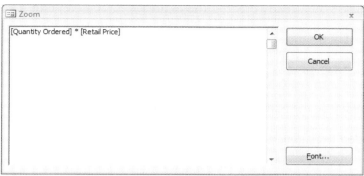

10. Click **OK**. The Zoom dialog box closes. The expression appears in the design grid in the column to the right of the Retail Price field.

11. Save the query. In the Results group on the Query Tools Design tab, click the **Run** button. The datasheet includes the calculated field, as shown in Figure 3-28. Leave the query open for the next Step-by-Step.

FIGURE 3-28
Order Line Totals query datasheet

Product ID	Product Name	Quantity Ordered	Retail Price	Expr1
1701	Stick-It Notes (8 pack)	1	$6.59	$6.59
1701	Stick-It Notes (8 pack)	10	$6.59	$65.90
1701	Stick-It Notes (8 pack)	4	$6.59	$26.36
1701	Stick-It Notes (8 pack)	2	$6.59	$13.18
1701	Stick-It Notes (8 pack)	1	$6.59	$6.59
1701	Stick-It Notes (8 pack)	1	$6.59	$6.59
1705	Standard Stapler	1	$7.49	$7.49
1734	2-Drawer Filing Cabinet	2	$79.99	$159.98
1995	Surge Protector	10	$19.99	$199.90
1996	Printing Calculator	1	$29.99	$29.99
2002	Oak Office Desk	6	$399.00	$2,394.00
2005	Desk Chair	1	$229.54	$229.54
2010	Fax Machine	2	$189.95	$379.90
3406	Scissors	3	$4.99	$14.97
3406	Scissors	1	$4.99	$4.99
3406	Scissors	3	$4.99	$14.97
5192	Clipboard	1	$1.29	$1.29
5421	Envelopes (9" x 12") (100 count)	1	$6.49	$6.49
5465	Desk Accessory Set	6	$21.99	$131.94
5465	Desk Accessory Set	2	$21.99	$43.98
5912	Tape Dispenser	1	$5.99	$5.99
5917	Answering Machine	2	$49.99	$99.98
5918	Digital Phone	10	$65.29	$652.90
5943	Envelopes #10 (500 count)	2	$11.99	$23.98

Calculated field

When you create a calculated field in a query, Access gives it a name using the letters "Expr" and a number (in this case, 1) to indicate the first expression in the query. The field name *Expr1* isn't meaningful. You can change the name of a calculated field by preceding the expression with the field name you want to use and a colon (such as *Order Line Total: [Quantity Ordered] * [Retail Price]*). Because you already created the expression, you can edit it to replace the default *Expr1* with *Order Line Total*.

STEP-BY-STEP 3.14

1. In the Views group on the Home tab, click the **View** button.

2. In the calculated field, double-click the text **Expr1**. Do not select the colon or any other text in the Field box.

3. Type **Order Line Total** and press the **Tab** key. Figure 3-29 shows the revised expression in the last column of the design grid.

FIGURE 3-29
Renaming the calculated field

Field:	Product ID	Product Name	Quantity Ordered	Retail Price	Order Line Total: [Qua
Table:	Products	Products	Orders	Products	
Sort:					
Show:	✓	✓	✓	✓	✓
Criteria:					
or:					

4. Save and run the query. Resize the Order Line Total column to best fit. Figure 3-30 shows the datasheet with the new calculated field name.

FIGURE 3-30
Query datasheet with the revised calculated field name

Product ID	Product Name	Quantity Ordered	Retail Price	Order Line Total
1701	Stick-It Notes (8 pack)	1	$6.59	$6.59
1701	Stick-It Notes (8 pack)	10	$6.59	$65.90
1701	Stick-It Notes (8 pack)	4	$6.59	$26.36
1701	Stick-It Notes (8 pack)	2	$6.59	$13.18
1701	Stick-It Notes (8 pack)	1	$6.59	$6.59
1701	Stick-It Notes (8 pack)	1	$6.59	$6.59
1705	Standard Stapler	1	$7.49	$7.49
1734	2-Drawer Filing Cabinet	2	$79.99	$159.98
1995	Surge Protector	10	$19.99	$199.90
1996	Printing Calculator	1	$29.99	$29.99
2002	Oak Office Desk	6	$399.00	$2,394.00
2005	Desk Chair	1	$229.54	$229.54
2010	Fax Machine	2	$189.95	$379.90
3406	Scissors	3	$4.99	$14.97
3406	Scissors	1	$4.99	$4.99
3406	Scissors	3	$4.99	$14.97
5192	Clipboard	1	$1.29	$1.29
5421	Envelopes (9" x 12") (100 count)	1	$6.49	$6.49
5465	Desk Accessory Set	6	$21.99	$131.94
5465	Desk Accessory Set	2	$21.99	$43.98
5912	Tape Dispenser	1	$5.99	$5.99
5917	Answering Machine	2	$49.99	$99.98
5918	Digital Phone	10	$65.29	$652.90
5943	Envelopes #10 (500 count)	2	$11.99	$23.98

STEP-BY-STEP 3.14 Continued

5. Save the query, then close it.

6. Click the **Office Button**, point to **Manage**, then click **Compact and Repair Database**.

7. Click the **Close** button on the Access title bar to close the database and to exit Access.

SUMMARY

> ### Did You Know?
>
> When you create a calculated field that displays numbers, you can change the way values are formatted in the calculated field. Select the field in the design grid in Query Design view, and then click the Property Sheet button in Show/Hide group on the Query Tools Design tab. Click the right side of the field's Format text box on the General tab, and then click the desired format. For example, to format numbers as currency, click Currency in the list. Click the Property Sheet button again to close the Property Sheet.

In this lesson, you learned:

■ A query is a database object that lets you ask the database about the data it contains. You can create a query quickly and easily using the Simple Query Wizard, which asks you about the data you want to see and lets you select options in dialog boxes.

■ You can change the way data is sorted in a datasheet by applying an ascending or a descending sort order to one of the fields.

■ You can use a filter in a datasheet to temporarily display records in a datasheet based on a condition that you specify. Filter By Selection lets you select a field value or part of a field value in a datasheet and then filter out all records that do not match the filter. Filter By Form lets you display records that match a value you select in a field. An AutoFilter opens when you click the arrow on a field selector. You can use an AutoFilter to sort and filter data. You can also move and sort fields in Design view. To run a query, click the Run button in the Results group on the Query Tools Design tab.

■ When you need to create a query that uses conditions to select records, create the query in Query Design view.

■ Use the Relationships window to create relationships between tables in a database by joining tables with a field that contains matching field values. A one-to-many relationship exists when one record in the primary table matches zero, one, or many records in the related table. Referential integrity is the set of rules that Access uses to protect data in the tables and to make sure that data is not accidentally deleted or changed.

■ A multitable query is a query that is based on two or more tables.

■ When you need to use a query to search for records that match a range of values, use a relational operator in the query design. When you need to select records that match all of two or more conditions in a query, use the And operator by placing the criteria in the same Criteria row in the design grid. When you need to select records that match at least one of two or more conditions in a query, use the Or operator by placing the criteria in different Criteria rows in the design grid.

■ In Access, you can perform calculations by using the Total row in a datasheet or by creating a calculated field in the design grid.

VOCABULARY *Review*

Define the following terms:

And operator	Expression	Query
Ascending	Filter	Range-of-values condition
AutoFilter	Filter By Form	Referential integrity
Calculated field	Filter By Selection	Related table
Common field	Foreign key	Relationship
Condition	Join line	Run
Criteria	Matching field	Simple Query Wizard
Criterion	Multitable query	Sort
Descending	One-to-many relationship	Subdatasheet
Detail query	Or operator	Summary query
Exact match condition	Primary table	Total row

REVIEW *Questions*

TRUE/FALSE

Circle the T if the statement is true or F if the statement is false.

T   F   1. When you sort a field that contains text values in ascending order, data is arranged from A to Z.

T   F   2. Applying a filter is a temporary way of selecting records in a datasheet.

T   F   3. To remove a filter from a datasheet, click the Cancel Filter button.

T   F   4. A common field used to relate tables must have the same field name in the related tables.

T   F   5. The >= relational operator selects records that are greater than or equal to the value in the condition.

WRITTEN QUESTIONS

Write a brief answer to each of the following questions.

1. What information do you specify when you run the Simple Query Wizard?

2. What steps do you follow to use Filter By Form in a datasheet?

3. How do you add all fields to the design grid in Query Design view in one step?

4. When a relationship exists between two tables in a database, what name is given to the matching field in the related table?

5. What is a subdatasheet?

PROJECTS

 PROJECT 3-1

1. Open the **Agents.accdb** database from the Data Files.

2. Use the Simple Query Wizard to create a query that includes all fields from the Agents table. Name the query **Agents Listing**.

3. Sort the records in alphabetical order by Last Name.

4. Use the Affiliation field and Filter By Selection to apply a filter that selects records for agents who do *not* work for Keller McCormack.

5. Remove the filter, then clear all filters.

6. Use Filter By Form to select records for agents who work for Keller McCormack. Apply the filter, then change the First Name and Last Name field values in the first record to your first and last names. Print the datasheet in landscape orientation.

7. Remove the filter.

8. Save the query, close the query, then exit Access.

PROJECT 3-2

1. Open the **Listings.accdb** database from the Data Files.

2. Create a new query in Query Design view. Add the Agents table field list to the query design.

3. Add all fields from the Agents table to the query design in the order that they appear in the field list.

4. In the design grid, move the Last Name field so it appears between the Agent ID and First Name fields.

5. Sort the records alphabetically first by Last Name, then alphabetically by First Name.

6. Add a condition to the query design so that only those agents who work for Montglow Real Estate appear in the query datasheet. (The Affiliation field stores the agent's employer.)

7. Save the query as **Montglow Realtors**.

8. Run the query. In the first record, change the Last Name and First Name field values to your last and first names. Print the datasheet in landscape orientation.

9. Close the Montglow Realtors query, then exit Access.

 PROJECT 3-3

1. Open the **Realtors.accdb** database from the Data Files.

2. In the Relationships window, create a relationship between the Agents and Houses tables. Use the Agent ID field in the primary Agents table and the Agent ID field in the related Houses table as the common field. (Use the scroll bar on the Houses table field list to see the Agent ID field in the list.)

3. Enforce referential integrity in the relationship. Close the Relationships window and save your changes.

4. Create a new query in Query Design view. Add the Agents and Houses field lists to the query design.

5. Add the following fields from the Agents table field list to the design grid in the order listed: Agent ID, Affiliation, and Last Name.

6. Add the following fields from the Houses table field list to the design grid in the order listed: Listing ID, Date Listed, and Price.

7. Save the query as **Listings By Agent**, then run the query.

8. Change to Design view. Add a condition to the Date Listed field so the datasheet selects records for properties that were listed after 9/16/2010. Save and run the query.

9. Change to Design view. Change the query design to select records for properties that were listed after 9/16/2010 *and* that have a price that is less than $100,000. Save and run the query.

10. Change to Design view. Change the query design to select records that were listed after 9/16/2010 *or* that have a price that is less than $100,000. Save and run the query. In the first record in the datasheet, change the value in the Last Name field to your last name. Print the datasheet in landscape orientation.

11. Close the Listings By Agent query, then exit Access.

 PROJECT 3-4

1. Open the **Properties.accdb** database from the Data Files. Close the Navigation Pane.

2. In the Relationships window, create a relationship between the Agents and Houses tables. Use the Agent ID field in the primary Agents table and the Agent ID field in the related Houses table as the common field. (Use the scroll bar on the Houses table field list to see the Agent ID field in the list.)

3. Enforce referential integrity in the relationship. Close the Relationships window and save your changes.

4. Create a new query in Query Design view. Add the Agents and Houses field lists to the query design.

5. Add the following fields from the Agents table field list to the design grid in the order listed: Agent ID, Last Name, and Affiliation.

6. Add the following fields from the Houses table field list to the design grid in the order listed: Listing ID, Bedrooms, Bathrooms, Garages, and Price.

7. Save the query as **Detailed Listings**, then run the query.

8. Change to Design view. Click in the Field box to the right of the Price field in the design grid. (You might need to scroll the design grid to see the new field.) Open the Zoom dialog box. In the Zoom dialog box, enter the following expression to calculate the estimated real estate commission for each listing: **Price * 0.06**. Save and run the query.

9. In Design view, change the default field name *Expr1* for the calculated field to **Estimated Commission**. Save and run the query. Resize the Estimated Commission field to best fit.

10. Change to Design view. Click the Field box for the Estimated Commission field, then click the Property Sheet button in the Show/Hide group on the Query Tools Design tab. On the General tab in the Property Sheet, change the Format property to Currency. Click the Property Sheet button again to close the Property Sheet. Save and run the query.

11. Use the datasheet to calculate the average price of all properties and the total (sum) of all estimated commissions.

12. In the first record in the datasheet, change the Affiliation field value to your first and last names. Print the datasheet in portrait orientation.

13. Save and close the query, then exit Access.

CRITICAL *Thinking*

 ACTIVITY 3-1

You are a realtor with three new clients who are ready to buy homes. List on paper each client's requirements for purchasing a home. For example, Buyer #1 might want a three-bedroom house with a brick exterior and have a budget of $90,000.

Using the **Realtors.accdb** database, create a query to locate the information for each client. Save the queries using the names **Buyer 1**, **Buyer 2**, and **Buyer 3**. After running each query, print the results in landscape orientation.

 ACTIVITY 3-2

Referential integrity is the set of rules that Access uses to check for valid relationships between tables. It also ensures that related data is not accidentally deleted or changed. Use the Help system to search for topics about **referential integrity**. In the list of links that opens, click "Guide to table relationships" and read the information in the section entitled "Understanding referential integrity." Determine which conditions must be met before you can enforce referential integrity in a relationship. Write a brief essay that explains the importance of referential integrity in a relational database and identifies some of the problems that referential integrity is designed to prevent and control.

 ACTIVITY 3-3

In addition to the Simple Query Wizard, Access includes other wizards that can help you create queries. One is the Find Unmatched Query Wizard, which finds records in one table that have no matching records in a second table. For example, this type of query is useful when you need to find students who are not enrolled in any classes, or realtors who have no listings.

Open the **Realtors.accdb** database from the Data Files. On the Create tab, click the Query Wizard button. In the New Query dialog box, click Find Unmatched Query Wizard, then click OK. The Find Unmatched Query Wizard starts and opens the first dialog box, in which you select the table that you want to search for unmatched records. Make sure that Table: Agents is selected, then click Next.

In the second dialog box, choose the table that contains the matching (related) records. Make sure that Table: Houses is selected, then click Next.

In the third dialog box, choose the fields that contain matching records. (If the tables are already related, then you won't need to complete this step.) Scroll the Houses field list until you see Agent ID at the bottom of the list, then click Agent ID. Click the Match Fields button between the field lists. The text *Agent ID < = > Agent ID* appears in the Matching fields box to indicate the matching fields. Click Next.

In the fourth dialog box, click the Select All Fields button to add all fields from the Agents table to the query datasheet. Click Next.

In the final dialog box, click Finish to accept the default query name and display the datasheet. Change the Affiliation field value for the first record to your first and last names, print the datasheet, then close the Agents Without Matching Houses query and the database. Which realtor in the database has no listings?

CREATING AND MODIFYING FORMS

VOCABULARY

AutoFormat

Bound control

Control

Control layout

Datasheet tool

Detail section

Field List pane

Find

Form

Form Footer section

Form Header section

Form tool

Form view

Form Wizard

Layout view

Multiple Items tool

Record source

Split Form tool

Unbound control

Creating a Form

A form is a database object that displays data from one or more tables or queries in a format that has a similar appearance to a paper form. The tables or queries that contain the data used in a form are called the record source. Most database experts agree that users should make all database updates by using a form, instead of by using table datasheets, because forms provide more control over the way data is displayed, updated, and entered. In addition, most users find that working in a form is easier than working in a table datasheet. The form can contain messages about how to enter data, format data in different ways to call attention to it, or include features that prevent users from updating data that should not be changed.

Access includes tools that you can use to create different kinds of forms. After selecting the table or query in the Navigation Pane on which to base the form, click the Create tab on the Ribbon. The different options for creating forms are located in the Forms group on the Create tab. The Form tool creates a simple form that includes all the fields in the selected table or query, uses a simple format, and includes a title with the same name as the record source. Figure 4-1 shows a form created using the Form tool. Each field in the record source appears in the form. In Figure 4-1, the "Listing ID" text appears in a label, and the field value for the first record (2042) appears in a text box. When fields appear in a form, they appear in controls. In this form, the Listing ID label and the Listing ID text box are controls. You can click the buttons on the record navigation bar at the bottom of the Form window to navigate the records in the record source and display them in the form.

FIGURE 4-1
Form created by the Form tool

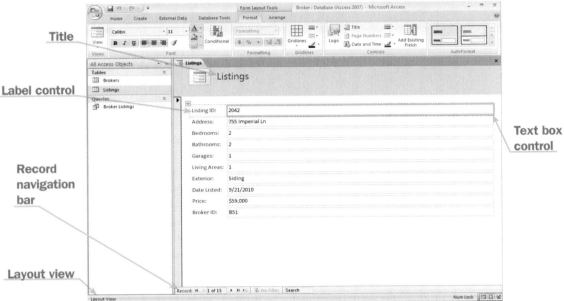

When you use a tool to create a form, the form opens in Layout view. In Layout view, you can view the controls in the form and data from the record source at the same time. You can also make certain types of changes to the form's format and appearance, such as resizing a control. When you click a text box control in Layout view, an orange border appears around the text box and a dotted border appears around its attached label to indicate that the control is selected.

The Split Form tool creates a form using all the fields in the selected table or query and splits the window into two panes, as shown in Figure 4-2. In the top pane, you see a form that is similar to the one created by the Form tool. In the bottom pane, you see a datasheet that contains the form data. The two views are synchronized—when you select a field in the top pane, it is also selected in the bottom pane.

FIGURE 4-2
Form created by the Split Form tool

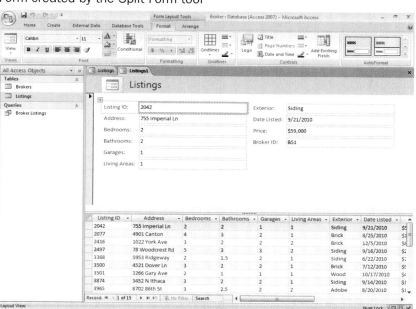

 The **Multiple Items** tool creates a form that lists all the fields in a datasheet format, but using a style that is similar to the form created by the Form tool. The **Datasheet** tool creates a form that looks just like a datasheet. All of these tools create forms quickly and easily.

STEP-BY-STEP 4.1

1. Open the **Broker.accdb** database from the Data Files.

2. If the Security Warning appears below the Ribbon, click **Options**, click the **Enable this content** option button, then click **OK**.

3. In the Navigation Pane, click the **Listings** table to select it.

4. On the Ribbon, click the **Create** tab. In the Forms group on the Create tab, click the **Form** button. The Form tool creates a form using all the fields in the Listings table. See Figure 4-1.

5. On the Ribbon, click the **Create** tab. In the Forms group, click the **Split Form** button. Access creates the split form shown in Figure 4-2.

6. On the Ribbon, click the **Create** tab. In the Forms group, click the **Multiple Items** button. Access creates a multiple items form, which displays the data in a form with a format similar to a datasheet.

> **Extra for Experts**
>
> Table, form, and report objects in the database can have the same name. For example, the Broker database contains a Listings table and a Listings form. However, you cannot give the same name to a table and a query object in the same database.

STEP-BY-STEP 4.1 Continued

7. On the Ribbon, click the **Create** tab. In the Forms group, click the **More Forms** button. In the menu, click **Datasheet**. Access creates a form that looks like a table or query datasheet.

8. Use the **Close** button to close each form that you created. Save each form using the form name that Access suggests. Leave the database open for the next Step-by-Step.

 When you need to create a simple form quickly, you can use the **Form Wizard**, which helps you create a form by letting you select options in dialog boxes to specify the form's record source, layout, and style. The Form Wizard provides four form layouts from which to choose. The Columnar layout displays fields in a stacked column format, with labels to the left of their controls. The Tabular layout displays fields with the labels at the top of a column that contains the field values. The Datasheet layout displays fields in a datasheet format. The Justified layout displays fields across the screen in the order in which they occur. A form's style, also called an **AutoFormat**, formats the form and its controls using a predefined color, font, and design scheme. After creating a form with any of these tools, you can use the tools and features in Access to customize the form.

STEP-BY-STEP 4.2

1. In the Forms group on the Create tab, click the **More Forms** button, then click **Form Wizard**. The first dialog box of the Form Wizard opens.

2. Click the **Tables/Queries** arrow, then click **Table: Brokers** in the list. The fields in the Brokers table appear in the Available Fields list box.

3. Click the **Select All Fields** button to move all fields to the Selected Fields list box, then click **Next**. The second Form Wizard dialog box opens, as shown in Figure 4-3.

FIGURE 4-3
Form Wizard dialog box for selecting a layout

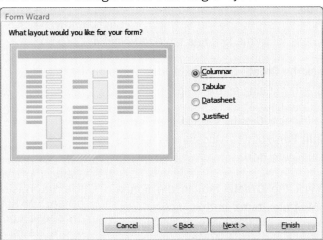

4. Make sure that the **Columnar** option button is selected, then click **Next**. In the third dialog box, you choose a style for the form.

STEP-BY-STEP 4.2 Continued

5. Click several of the styles in the dialog box, and watch the formatting that is applied to the sample form to the left of the list.

6. Click **Office** in the list, then click **Next**. In the final Form Wizard dialog box, enter a title for the form or accept the default name.

7. Click **Finish**. The form appears in Layout view, as shown in Figure 4-4. Leave the form open for the next Step-by-Step.

FIGURE 4-4
Brokers form in Form view

Navigating a Form

When you create a form using the Form Wizard, the form opens in Form view. When a form is displayed in Form view, you will see each record in the record source in a form. Form view includes a record navigation bar at the bottom of the Form view window that you can use to navigate the records. This record navigation bar has the same buttons with the same functions as the record navigation bar you used to navigate records in a table or query datasheet.

STEP-BY-STEP 4.3

1. On the record navigation bar, click the **Last record** button. The last record in the Brokers table appears in the form.

2. On the record navigation bar, click the **Previous record** button. Record 8 is displayed in the form.

3. On the record navigation bar, click in the **Current Record** text box, select the **8** in the text box, type **2**, then press the **Enter** key. The second record is displayed in the form.

4. On the record navigation bar, click the **First record** button. The first record is displayed in the form. Leave the Brokers form open for the next Step-by-Step.

Using a Form to Find and Replace Data

You have used filters and queries to find data in a database. Another option for finding data quickly is to use the **Find** command, which is available when you are using a table or query datasheet, form, or report. Using the Find command is an easy way to locate data in a database quickly. When you click the Find button in the Find group on the Home tab, the Find and Replace dialog box shown in Figure 4-5 opens.

FIGURE 4-5
Find and Replace dialog box

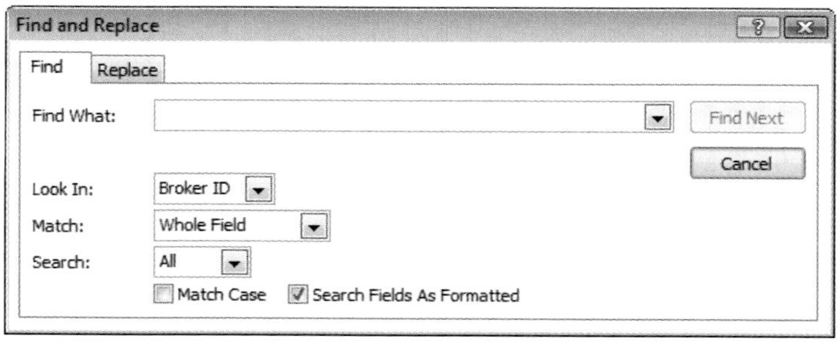

You have several options for finding data, including finding and replacing data. If you select part of a field value in the form (one or more characters or a single word) before clicking the Find button, the selected text appears in the Find What list box automatically. If nothing is selected or more than one word is selected before clicking the Find button, the Find What list box is empty, in which case you type the value you want to find in the text box.

When a field is selected in the form, its name appears in the Look In list box when you open the Find and Replace dialog box. If you want to search the entire table for a matching field value, click the Look In arrow, and then click the form name. You can use the options in the Match menu to search any part of the field, the whole field, or the start of the field as follows:

- If you type *S* in the Find What list box, and then select the Any Part of Field option in the Match menu, you'll find values that contain the letter *S* anywhere in the value.

- If you select the Whole Field option, you'll find values that contain *only* the letter *S*.

- If you select the Start of Field option, you'll find values that *begin* with the letter *S*.

The Search feature lets you search the entire form, or up and down from the location of the insertion point. The two check boxes—Match Case and Search Fields As Formatted—let you search for a matching value that has the same case as the entry in the Find What list box and search for formatted values, respectively. When the Match Case check box is selected, typing *Stars* in the Find What list box will find a record that contains the word *Stars* but will not select a record that contains the word *stars*. To start searching the form for matching records, click Find Next.

If you click the Replace tab in the Find and Replace dialog box, you will see additional options for finding text and replacing it with different text. The only difference is that you type the value that you want to find in the Find What list box and type the value that you want to replace it with in the Replace With list box. Figure 4-6 shows the Replace tab. Notice the Replace and Replace All buttons. When you start searching the form for matching values by clicking Find Next, you'll find the first matching value. Clicking Replace replaces that instance and resumes searching for the Find What value; clicking Replace All replaces that instance and all others that match.

FIGURE 4-6
Replace tab in the Find and Replace dialog box

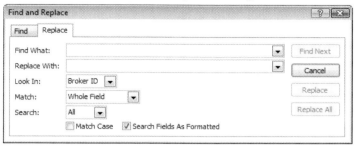

STEP-BY-STEP 4.4

1. Double-click the word **McCormack** in the Affiliation field in the first record to select it.

2. In the Find group on the Home tab, click the **Find** button. The Find and Replace dialog box opens. Notice that the selected field value *McCormack* in the Affiliation field appears in the Find What list box. See Figure 4-7.

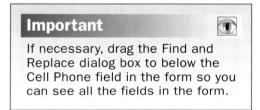

Important

If necessary, drag the Find and Replace dialog box to below the Cell Phone field in the form so you can see all the fields in the form.

FIGURE 4-7
Find and Replace dialog box with selected Find What value

3. Make sure that the options in your dialog box match the ones shown in Figure 4-7. Click **Find Next**. Because the Match option is set to Whole Field, and there is no field value in the Affiliation field that contains only the word *McCormack*, Access opens a dialog box indicating that it found no items.

4. Click **OK** to close the dialog box.

5. Click the **Match** arrow in the Find and Replace dialog box, then click **Any Part of Field**. Click **Find Next**. The Find command locates the word *McCormack* in the fourth record and selects it.

6. Click **Find Next**. The Find command displays the first record and selects the word *McCormack* in the record.

7. In the Find and Replace dialog box, click the **Replace** tab.

STEP-BY-STEP 4.4 Continued

8. In the Replace With list box, type **Greene**.

9. Make sure that the Look In value is **Affiliation** and the Match value is **Any Part of Field**. Click **Replace**. The word *McCormack* in the first record is replaced with the word *Greene*. The next record containing the Find What value is selected (record 4).

10. Click **Replace**. The word *McCormack* is replaced with the word *Greene* in the fourth record. Click **Replace**. Because record 4 contains the last occurrence of the word *McCormack* in the Affiliation field, a dialog box opens and indicates that Access cannot find any more matches.

11. Click **OK** to close the dialog box.

12. Click **Cancel** to close the Find and Replace dialog box. Leave the Brokers form open for the next Step-by-Step.

You need to be careful when replacing text, because you might accidentally replace text that you didn't intend to change. For example, if you want to replace the word *Green* with the word *Red*, your Find What value is *Green* and your Replace With value is *Red*. When you replace the text, you'll replace the word *Green* with the word *Red* as you intended. However, you'll also change the word *Greenfield* or *Greenley* to *Redfield* and *Redley*, which are changes that you did not intend to make. If you find a word that you don't want to replace, click Cancel to skip it.

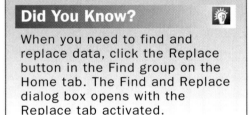

Did You Know?

When you need to find and replace data, click the Replace button in the Find group on the Home tab. The Find and Replace dialog box opens with the Replace tab activated.

Using a Form to Update Data

You can also use a form to update the record source, add new records, or delete existing records. Because you can customize a form to display data in different ways, most database experts recommend using a form instead of a table datasheet to make changes. To change a field value, select it and type the new value. To add a new record, click the New button in the Records group on the Home tab to open a blank form, into which you can type the field values for the new record. When you are finished adding the new record, tab to a new record or close the form.

STEP-BY-STEP 4.5

1. On the record navigation bar, click the **First record** button to display the first record.

2. In the form, double-click **Armbruster** in the Last Name field to select it.

3. Type **Arlington** then press the **Tab** key. The record is updated.

4. In the Records group on the Home tab, click the **New** button. A blank form is displayed. The insertion point is blinking in the Broker ID text box, ready for you to type the field value.

STEP-BY-STEP 4.5 Continued

5. Type **E99** then press the **Tab** key. The insertion point moves to the next text box (field).

6. Type **Hector** in the First Name text box, then press the **Tab** key.

7. Type the values shown in Figure 4-8. Remember to press the Tab key to move to the next field. Do not press the Tab key after typing the field value in the Cell Phone text box.

FIGURE 4-8
Adding a record in Form view

8. Press the **Tab** key. Record 10 is added to the Brokers table and a blank form appears.

9. On the Navigation Pane, double-click the **Brokers** table in the Tables group. The Brokers table opens in Datasheet view. Notice that the record you added, with the Broker ID E99, appears in the datasheet. Leave the Brokers table and the Brokers form open for the next Step-by-Step.

You might be wondering why the record for Hector Marques appears in record 4 in the table, instead of in record 10 as shown in the form. When you use a form to add a record, it is added in a blank form at the end of the record source. However, when you display the datasheet for the table or query on which the form is based, the new record appears in order based on the values in the primary key field. In the Brokers table, the Broker ID field is the table's primary key, and values in this column are alphabetical. That's why record E99 is listed fourth. Hector's record will be record 10 in the form until you close it and then reopen it, and then it will also appear as record 4 in the form.

Using a Form to Delete Data

Access provides two important options when using a form to delete a field value or record. When you click the Delete button in the Records group on the Home tab, you'll delete the selected field value. If you click the arrow on the Delete button, and then click Delete Record, you'll delete the record that is currently displayed in the form. Be careful when deleting data. You can use the Undo button on the Quick Access Toolbar to restore a deleted field value, but deleting a record permanently deletes it from the record source.

S TEP-BY-STEP 4.6

1. Click the **Close 'Brokers'** button to close the Brokers table.

2. On the record navigation bar, click the **Previous record** button. Hector's record is still record 10 in the form.

3. Close the Brokers form.

4. Double-click **Brokers** in the Forms group in the Navigation Pane to reopen the form.

5. Navigate to record **4**, which contains Hector's record.

6. Press the **Tab** key to select the value in the First Name text box.

7. In the Records group on the Home tab, click the **Delete** button. The field value in the First Name field is deleted.

8. On the record navigation bar, click the **Previous record** button.

9. On the record navigation bar, click the **Next record** button. The First Name field contains no value.

10. On the Quick Access Toolbar, click the **Undo** button. The field value *Hector* is added back to the First Name text box.

11. In the Records group on the Home tab, click the **arrow** on the Delete button. In the list, click **Delete Record**. The dialog box shown in Figure 4-9 opens.

FIGURE 4-9
Dialog box that opens when you delete a record

12. In the dialog box, click **Yes**. Hector's record is deleted from the Brokers table and is no longer displayed in the form. Notice that the Undo button on the Quick Access Toolbar is not available; you cannot restore a deleted record.

13. Close the Brokers form. Leave the database open for the next Step-by-Step.

Did You Know?

Similar to changing records in a table datasheet, you do not need to save your changes when adding or updating records using a form. You only need to save a form when you change its design.

Creating and Modifying a Form in Layout View

When you need to create a form to match a paper form that you are already using—or when you need to create a form that doesn't match the appearance of a form that you can create with a form tool or the Form Wizard—you can create a blank form in Layout view. To create a blank form, click the Create tab on the Ribbon, and then click the Blank Form button in the Forms group. A blank form opens in Layout view, and the Field List pane opens on the right side of the screen. The Field List pane contains the tables in the database and displays the fields they contain. When you double-click a field in the Field List, Access adds the field to the form. The fields are added to a control layout. A control layout is a "container" that groups together the controls in a form so that you can change them as a group. As you add fields to a form in Layout view, Access adds them to the control layout. You can change the way the controls are arranged by changing the control layout, or you can remove controls from the layout to work with individual controls.

The first task when creating a form from scratch is to create the form in Layout view, and then to use the Field List to add fields to the form.

STEP-BY-STEP 4.7

1. On the Ribbon, click the **Create** tab. In the Forms group, click the **Blank Form** button. A blank form opens. The Field List pane opens on the right side of the screen. See Figure 4-10.

> **Important**
>
> If you do not see the Field List pane, click the Add Existing Fields button in the Controls group on the Format tab. If you see "Show all tables" in the Field List pane instead of the tables shown in Figure 4-10, click Show all tables.

FIGURE 4-10
Blank form in Layout view

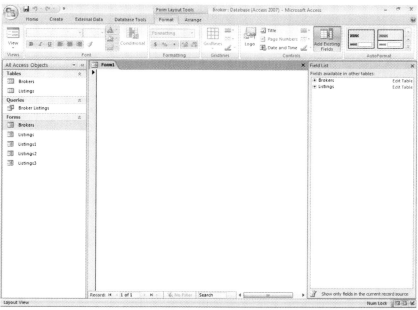

STEP-BY-STEP 4.7 Continued

2. If necessary, click the **expand indicator** to the left of the Listings table in the Field List pane to see the fields in the table.

3. In the Listings field list, double-click **Listing ID**. The label and text box controls for the Listing ID field are added to the upper-left corner of the form. When you add a field from one table, its related table moves to the "Fields available in related tables" section. See Figure 4-11.

FIGURE 4-11
Form after adding one field

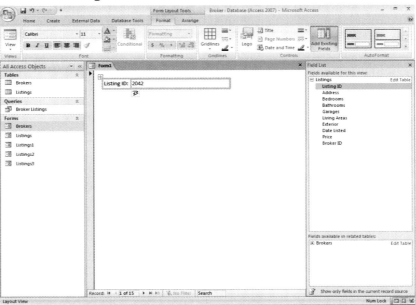

4. In the Field List pane, double-click **Address**. The label and text box controls for the Address field are added to the form in the control layout. See Figure 4-12.

FIGURE 4-12
Form after adding two fields

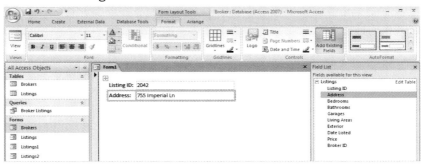

5. Double-click the following fields in the order listed: **Bedrooms**, **Bathrooms**, **Garages**, **Living Areas**, **Date Listed**, and **Price**.

STEP-BY-STEP 4.7 Continued

6. In the Fields available in related tables pane, click the **expand indicator** to the left of the Brokers table to display the fields.

7. In the Brokers table field list, double-click the **First Name** field. The Brokers table and its fields move to the top of the Field List pane. The First Name field is added to the form as a combo box control and not as a text box control because this field is in a related table. You can use the Property Update Options button to change it to a text box control.

8. Click the **Property Update Options** button, then click **Change to Text Box** in the menu that opens. The First Name control is changed to a text box control.

9. In the Brokers table field list, double-click the following fields in the order listed: **Last Name** and **Cell Phone**.

10. Click the **Add Existing Fields** button in the Controls group on the Format tab to close the Field List pane.

11. On the Quick Access Toolbar, click the **Save** button, type **Listings and Agents**, then click **OK**. See Figure 4-13. Leave the form open for the next Step-by-Step.

FIGURE 4-13
Form after adding all fields

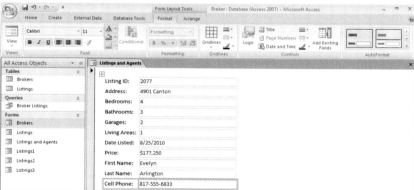

Adding a Title to a Form and Changing its Format

When you create a form, it contains one section called the Detail section. The form you just created contains a Detail section with controls that display one record at a time from the record source. When your form design includes other features, such as a title or a page number, you can add two additional sections to the form. The Form Header section displays information at the top of each form, and the Form Footer section displays information at the bottom of each form. You can add these sections to a form by clicking a tool in the Controls group on the Format tab. When you add a control to one of these sections, the Form Header and Form Footer sections are added to the form as a pair, even when you add a control to the form that appears in only one of the two sections.

The Controls group on the Format tab in Layout view shown in Figure 4-13 includes buttons that add different types of controls to a form. For example, the Logo tool adds a picture to a form, and the Title tool adds a title control in the Form Header section. You can add two types of controls to a form. A **bound control** is connected to a field in the record source and is used to display, enter, and update data. An **unbound control** is not connected to a record source and is used to display information, lines, rectangles, and pictures.

To add a title to a form, which adds an unbound control to the form, click the Title button in the Controls group on the Format tab. Access will add the Form Header and Form Footer sections to the form and add a title control to the Form Header section. The default form title is the form's name. Because you already saved the form as "Listings and Agents," this is the form title that will be added when you add a title control to the form. You can edit the title by clicking and editing text just like you would in a document. You can also change the default font size, color, and style of the title text using the buttons in the Font group on the Format tab.

STEP-BY-STEP 4.8

1. In the Controls group on the Format tab, click the **Title** button. Access adds the Form Header and Form Footer sections to the form, and adds a title control to the Form Header section. The text in the title control is "Listings and Agents," which is the same as the form object's name.

2. In the Font group on the Format tab, click the **Bold** button. The title changes to bold. The text is deselected, and the title control is selected, as indicated by its orange border shown in Figure 4-14.

FIGURE 4-14
Title control added to form

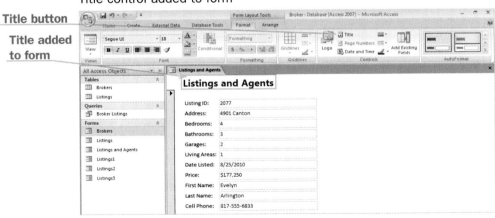

3. With the title control still selected, click the **arrow** on the Font Color button in the Font group on the Format tab. A gallery of colors opens.

4. In the gallery, click the **Dark Red** color (the first color in the last row of the Standard Colors section). The gallery closes and the text in the title control is dark red. Leave the form open for the next Step-by-Step.

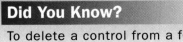
Did You Know?

To delete a control from a form, click the control to select it, and then press the Delete key.

Resizing a Control in a Form

When you add controls to a form, you might need to adjust their widths to display the text they contain correctly. For the Listings and Agents form, the text box controls are much wider than the data they contain. When you resize controls in a control layout in Layout view, reducing the width of *one* control reduces all the widths of all *other* controls in the control layout at the same time. When resizing the controls, be sure to resize them with the longest data value displayed in the form, so you don't accidentally resize a control too narrowly and limit what users can see. You can resize a control by dragging its edge to a new location. You can also resize a control precisely by watching the lower-left corner of the status bar to see the width of the control in characters as you drag it.

S TEP-BY-STEP 4.9

1. Use the record navigation bar to display record **11** in the form. This record contains the longest Address field value in the record source.

2. Click the **Address** text box to select it. An orange border appears around the text box, and a dotted border appears around the attached label.

3. Point to the right edge of the Address text box control. When the pointer changes shape to a ↔ double arrow, click and slowly drag the right edge of the Address text box control to the left. When the Characters value on left side of the status bar is 16, release the mouse button. Figure 4-15 shows the resized text box controls. Because all of the text boxes in the form are part of a control layout, they are all resized to the same size.

FIGURE 4-15
Resized text box controls in a control layout

4. Save the form. Leave the form open for the next Step-by-Step.

Moving a Control in a Form

When controls are grouped in a control layout, moving one control moves all the controls in the group. When you need to move one or more controls in a form, you'll need to remove them from the control layout first. To select one control, you click it. To select a group of controls, click the first control, press and hold down the Shift key, click the other controls, and then release the Shift key. Some people call this "Shift-Click" because you hold down the Shift key while clicking the other controls.

S TEP-BY-STEP 4.10

1. Click the **First Name** text box to select it. An orange border appears around the text box, and a dotted border appears around the attached label.

2. Press and hold down the **Shift** key.

3. Click the **Last Name** text box and the **Cell Phone** text box. Release the **Shift** key. Figure 4-16 shows the three selected controls.

FIGURE 4-16
Selected controls in a form

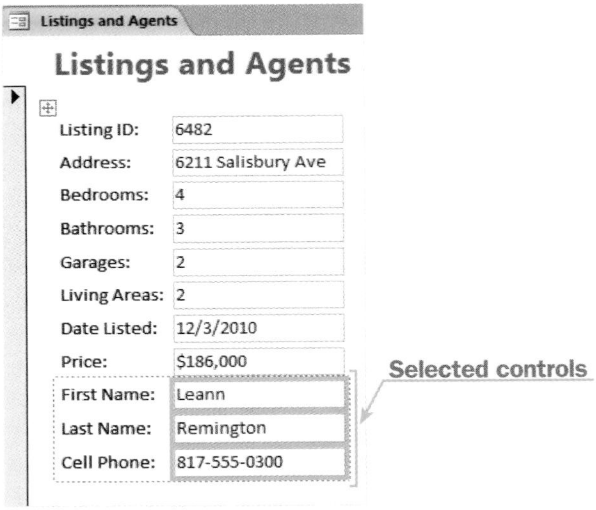

Listings and Agents

Listing ID:	6482
Address:	6211 Salisbury Ave
Bedrooms:	4
Bathrooms:	3
Garages:	2
Living Areas:	2
Date Listed:	12/3/2010
Price:	$186,000
First Name:	Leann
Last Name:	Remington
Cell Phone:	817-555-0300

Selected controls

4. On the Ribbon, click the **Arrange** tab. In the Control Layout group, click the **Remove** button. The selected controls are removed from the control layout. An orange border appears around the label and text box controls for the First Name, Last Name, and Cell Phone fields.

5. Point to the **First Name** label so the pointer changes shape to four arrows.

6. Click and drag the selected controls to the top of the form, so the three selected controls are to the right of and aligned with the Listing ID, Address, and Bedrooms controls, as shown in Figure 4-17.

STEP-BY-STEP 4.10 Continued

FIGURE 4-17
Controls removed from layout and moved to new position

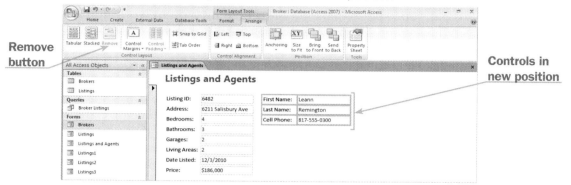

7. Save the form.

8. On the Ribbon, click the **Format** tab.

9. In the Views group on the Format tab, click the **arrow** at the bottom of the View button, then click **Form View**. The form is displayed in Form view. Leave the form open for the next Step-by-Step.

Extra for Experts

When you create a form in Layout view, you can click the More button in the AutoFormat group on the Format tab to change the form's style. After clicking the More button, click an AutoFormat in the gallery to apply it to the form.

Adding an Unbound Control to a Form in Design View

Some changes that you need to make to a form require you to work in the third form view, Design view. In Design view for a form, you see the controls that you added to the form on a grid, as shown in Figure 4-18. Unlike when working in Layout view, the controls do not display data from the record source. You must be in Design view to add controls such as lines, rectangles, and labels to a form. You add controls to the form by clicking the button for the desired control in the Controls group on the Design tab, and then clicking to position the control in the form. Another difference when working in Design view is that you see the Form Header, Detail, and Form Footer sections in the form. Each section contains a section bar at the top that you can click and select. You adjust the size of a section by clicking the bottom edge of the section and dragging it up or down to change its height. When you do not see a grid below a section, like the Form Footer section shown in Figure 4-18, the section height is set to zero. To expand a section, click the bottom edge of the section bar and then drag the border down to the desired height. You can see the position of objects in Design view as you are moving them, and you can position controls precisely by looking at the horizontal and vertical rulers that appear on the top and left sides of the form.

FIGURE 4-18
Form in Design view

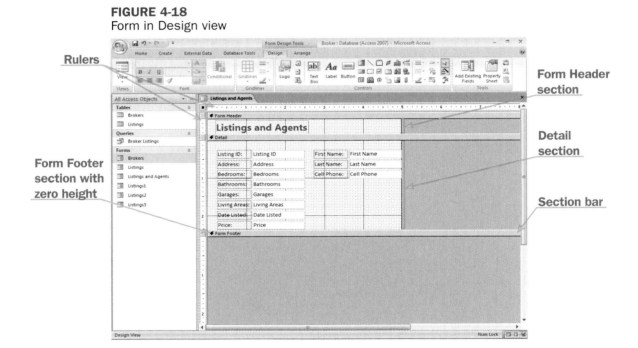

S TEP-BY-STEP 4.11

1. In the Views group on the Home tab, click the **arrow** at the bottom of the View button, then click **Design View**. The form is displayed in Design view, as shown in Figure 4-18.

2. Point to the bottom edge of the Form Footer section so the pointer changes shape to a double pointer ✛ with arrowheads pointing up and down, then drag the section bar down until the outline of the bottom edge of the section bar is at the one-half inch mark on the vertical ruler. Release the mouse button. The height of the Form Footer section increases, as shown in Figure 4-19.

FIGURE 4-19
Form Footer section with increased height

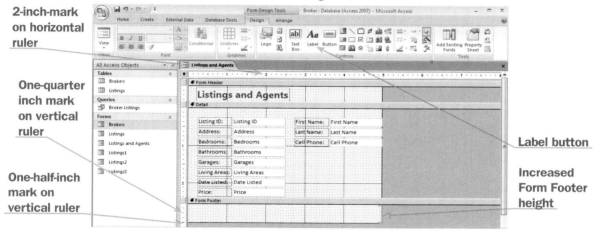

3. In the Controls group on the Design tab, click the **Label** button. The Label tool is selected.

STEP-BY-STEP 4.11 Continued

4. Move the pointer into the Form Footer section so the plus sign in the pointer is at the 2-inch mark on the horizontal ruler and the one-quarter-inch mark on the vertical ruler, then click. Figure 4-20 shows the label control added to the Form Footer section. The insertion point is blinking inside the control, which will expand in size when you start typing.

FIGURE 4-20
Form Footer section with label control added

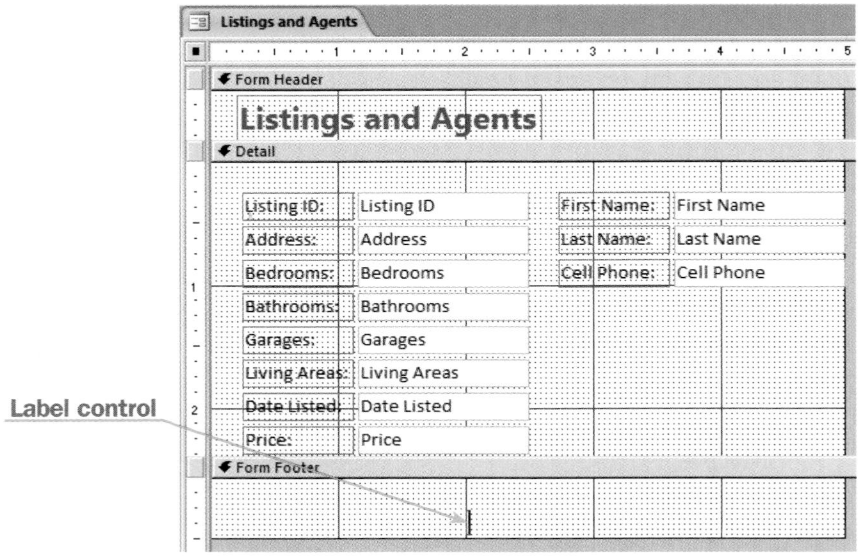

5. Type your first and last names, then press the **Enter** key.

6. Save the form.

7. On the Views group on the Design tab, click the **arrow** at the bottom of the View button, then click **Form View**. The form is displayed in Form view, and the label control in the Form Footer section displays your name. Leave the form open for the next Step-by-Step.

Previewing and Printing a Form

You can preview and print a form. To preview a form, click the Office Button, point to Print, and then click Print Preview. Each record in the record source appears in a miniature version of the form, one after the other, on the page. To print all records in the form from Print Preview, click the Print button in the Print group on the Print Preview tab.

To print the form with the current record displayed, you must be in Form view and navigate to the desired record. Click the Office Button, point to Print, and then click Print. The Print dialog box opens. Click the Selected Records option button, and then click OK.

STEP-BY-STEP 4.12

1. Click the **Office Button**, point to **Print**, then click **Print Preview**. The form is displayed in Print Preview.

2. Use the buttons on the page navigation bar to display each page of the form. Notice that each record appears in a form, and the forms for each record are stacked on top of each other. The title appears once at the top of the first page, and your name appears once at the bottom of the last page.

3. In the Close Preview group on the Print Preview tab, click the **Close Print Preview** button.

4. Navigate to record **3** in the form.

5. Click the **Office Button**, point to **Print**, then click **Print**. In the Print dialog box, make sure your printer is selected in the Name text box, click the **Selected Record(s)** option button, then click **OK**. The current record in the form is printed.

6. Close the **Listings and Agents** form.

7. Click the **Office Button**, point to **Manage**, then click **Compact and Repair Database**.

8. Close the database, then exit Access.

SUMMARY

In this lesson, you learned:

■ A form is a database object that displays data from a record source. You can create a form using a form tool or the Form Wizard, or you can create a blank form from scratch.

■ You can use the record navigation bar in Form view to navigate the records displayed in a form.

■ The Find command is used to locate records in a table or query datasheet, form, or report. When finding data in a form, you need to identify the text to find, the field in which to search (or to search the entire form), the type of search to conduct (whole field, any part of field, or start of field), the desired case of the search text, and the direction to search or to search the entire form. You can also find and replace data using the Replace tab in the Find and Replace dialog box.

■ You can use a form to update records and to add and delete records. When you make changes to data in a form, the changes are made in the record source on which the form is based.

■ You can create a blank form and add fields to it by double-clicking the fields in the Field List pane in Layout view. When you add fields to a form, they are added to the form as controls in a control layout. You can resize and change the controls in a control layout as a group. You can also remove controls from a control layout so you can work with individual controls.

- A form has one default section, called the Detail section, that contains the controls that display the data in a form. Two other sections, which are added when the form's design uses controls that appear in these sections, are the Form Header section and the Form Footer section. The Form Header section usually contains the form's title, and the Form Footer section might contain labels that describe the form.

- You can add two types of controls to a form. A bound control is connected to a field in the record source and is used to display, enter, and update data. An unbound control is not connected to a record source and is used to display information, lines, rectangles, and pictures.

- You can preview and print all the records in a form, or you can use the Print dialog box to print only selected records in a form.

VOCABULARY*Review*

Define the following terms:

AutoFormat	Find	Form Wizard
Bound control	Form	Layout view
Control	Form Footer section	Multiple Items tool
Control layout	Form Header section	Record source
Datasheet tool	Form tool	Split Form tool
Detail section	Form view	Unbound control
Field List pane		

REVIEW*Questions*

TRUE/FALSE

Circle T if the statement is true or F if the statement is false.

T   F   1. The table or query on which a form is based is called a record source.

T   F   2. The Multiple Items tool creates a form with multiple windows that display a form and a datasheet in separate panes.

T   F   3. Many database experts agree that updates to the data in a database should be made using forms.

T   F   4. When you click the Delete button in the Records group on the Home tab, the record displayed in Form view is deleted.

T   F   5. When you add fields to a form in Layout view, the fields are added to a control layout.

WRITTEN QUESTIONS

Write a brief answer to each of the following questions.

1. What are the three options for finding data in a form when selecting how to match data? What do these three options do?

2. Can you undo deleting a record using a form? Why or why not?

3. How do you add fields to a blank form in Layout view?

4. How do you remove a field from a control layout in a form displayed in Layout view?

5. What is a bound control? What is an unbound control?

PROJECTS

 PROJECT 4-1

1. Open the **Recreation.accdb** database from the Data Files.

2. Use the Form tool to create a form based on the Class table. Save the form as **Class Listing**.

3. Navigate the records in the record source until you find the one that you think has the longest field value in the Class Name text box.

4. Resize the width of the text boxes so the longest Class Name field value is displayed correctly.

5. Remove the Teacher ID field from the control layout.

6. Move the Teacher ID field to the right of the Class ID text box, so the bottom edges of the Class ID and Teacher ID controls are aligned.

7. Change the text in the title control to **Class Listing**. Press the Enter key.

8. Change the text in the title control to bold and Green (last row of the Standard Colors gallery, sixth column).

9. Change to Form view, then navigate to record 8. Change the field value in the Location text field to your first and last names.

10. Print record 8.

11. Use the Class Listing form to add a new record using the following information: Class ID: **201**, Class Name: **Masters Swimming**, Location: **Swim Center**, Start Date: **6/1/2010**, End Date: **6/30/2010**, Fee: **100.00**, and Teacher ID: **12910**.

12. Save and close the form, close the Recreation database, then exit Access.

 PROJECT 4-2

1. Open the **Teacher.accdb** database from the Data Files.

2. Use the Split Form tool to create a form based on the Teacher table.

3. In the datasheet, select the First Name field value for the second record. Type your first name. Press the Tab key, then type your last name in the Last Name field for record 2. Save the form as **Teacher Split Form**.

4. Change the text in the title control to **Teacher Information**, then change the font style to italic. Save and close the form.

5. Use the Multiple Items tool to create a form based on the Class table. Save the form as **Class Information**.

6. In Layout view, resize the columns in the Class Information form so that each column is just wide enough to display the widest field value it contains.

7. Change the text in the title control to **Class Information**. Then change the font style to bold and the font color to Dark Blue (last row, column 9 in the Standard Colors gallery).

8. Change to Design view. Click below the Form Footer section to deselect any selected controls. Increase the height of the Form Footer section so it is one-half inch. Add a label to the Form Footer section at the 3-inch mark on the horizontal ruler and the one-quarter-inch mark on the vertical ruler. Type your first and last names in the label control.

9. Save the Class Information form, then change to Form view.

10. Preview the Class Information form. Print the page in landscape orientation.

11. Close the Class Information form, close the Teacher database, then exit Access.

PROJECT 4-3

1. Open the **Class.accdb** database from the Data Files.

2. Create a blank form and save it as **Teachers and Classes**.

3. Add the following fields from the Class table to the form in the order listed: Class ID, Class Name, Location, Start Date, End Date, and Fee.

4. Use the Teacher table field list to add the Teacher ID field to the form, use the Property Update Options button to change the Teacher ID control to a text box control, then add the following fields from the Teacher table to the form in the order listed: First Name, Last Name, and Phone. Close the Field List pane.

5. Remove the Teacher ID, First Name, Last Name, and Phone controls from the control layout.

6. Move the Teacher ID, First Name, Last Name, and Phone controls to the right of the Class ID, Class Name, Location, and Start Date fields so the top of the Teacher ID text box is aligned with the top of the Class ID text box.

7. Add a title control to the form and use the default title.

8. Click the More button in the AutoFormat group on the Format tab. Use the ScreenTips to find the Opulent AutoFormat, then click the Opulent AutoFormat to apply it to the form. (You'll fix the overlapping problem with the Class ID and Teacher ID fields in Design view.)

9. Save the form and change to Design view.

10. Click the bottom edge of the Form Header section and drag the bottom edge down until you can see the gray bar and two grid dots with a purple background color in the Form Header section.

11. Increase the height of the Form Footer section to one-half inch. Then add a label to the Form Footer section at the 2-inch mark on the horizontal ruler and the one-quarter-inch mark on the vertical ruler that contains your first and last names.

12. Save the form and change to Form view.

13. Navigate to record 9 in the form (Class ID 123). Change the End Date field value to **6/30/2010**. Print record 9.

14. Close the Teachers and Classes form, close the Class database, then exit Access.

CRITICAL *Thinking*

 ACTIVITY 4-1

Open the **Broker.accdb** database from the Data Files. Use the Form Wizard to create a form based on the Broker Listings query. Include all fields from the Broker Listings query in the form, view the data by broker in a form with a subform, use a Tabular layout, use the Foundry AutoFormat, and use the name **Brokers Form** for the main form and **Listings Subform** for the subform. Click Finish. The form opens in Form view. Use the buttons on the record navigation bar at the bottom of the Form window to scroll through the records. How is the data in the subform related to the data in the main form? Explain your answer. Display record 5 in the main form, change the field value in the Affiliation field to your first and last names, then print record 5. Close the form, close the Broker database, then exit Access.

 ACTIVITY 4-2

Open the **Broker.accdb** database from the Data Files. Open the **Listings** form in Layout view, examine the form's contents, then change to Design view. Drag the bottom edge of the Detail section down approximately one inch to increase the height of this section. In the Controls group on the Design tab, click the Text Box button. Move the pointer to the Detail section, and click the plus sign in the pointer at the 4-inch mark on the horizontal ruler, approximately two rows of grid dots below the Broker ID text box control. A text box control and attached label are added to the form. Click in the text box control (which contains the word *Unbound*), then type **= Price * 0.06** and press the Enter key. Click the label control (which contains the word *Text*, a number, and a colon) to select it, double-click the text in the label control to select it, then type **Commission**. Click the text box control (which contains the expression you entered), click the Property Sheet button in the Tools group on the Design tab to open the Property Sheet, click the All tab (if necessary), then set the Format property to Currency. Close the Property Sheet, save the form, then change to Form view. What kind of text box control did you create? What value is displayed in the Commission text box? Close the form, close the Broker database, then exit Access.

CREATING AND MODIFYING REPORTS

OBJECTIVES

Upon completion of this lesson, you will be able to:

■ Create a report using the Report tool, the Label Wizard, and the Report Wizard.

■ Modify a report in Layout view.

■ Modify a report in Design view.

■ Add a line, label, and picture to a report.

■ Move a control in a report.

■ Set a report's properties.

Estimated Time: 1.5 hours

VOCABULARY

Grouping level

Label Wizard

Line tool

Print Preview

Read-only

Report

Report selector

Report tool

Report Wizard

Creating a Report Using the Report Tool

A report is a database object that displays data from one or more tables or queries in a format that has an appearance similar to a printed report. Just as with forms, the tables or queries that contain the data used in a report are called the record source. You can use a report to create a formatted list of information or to summarize information in different ways. You can even use reports to print form letters and mailing labels.

Access includes tools that you can use to create different kinds of reports. After selecting the table or query in the Navigation Pane on which to base the report, click the Create tab on the Ribbon. The different options for creating reports are located in the Reports group on the Create tab. The Report tool creates a simple report that includes all the fields in the selected table or query, uses a simple columnar format, and includes a title with the same name as the record source. In addition, Access adds the current date and time at the top of the report and a page number at the bottom of the report. Figure 5-1 shows a report created using the Report tool. Each field in the record source appears in the report. When fields appear in a report, they appear in controls. For example, in this report, the Teacher ID label and the records shown below the labels appear in controls.

FIGURE 5-1
Report created by the Report tool

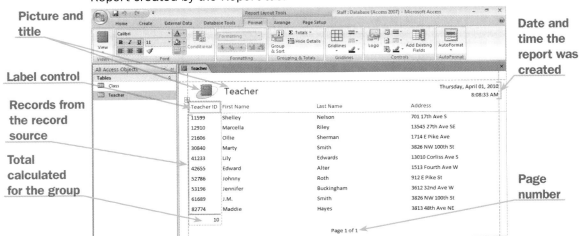

When you use the Report tool to create a report, the report opens initially in Layout view. In Layout view, you can view the controls in the report and records from the record source at the same time. In Layout view, you can make certain types of changes to the report's format and appearance, such as resizing a control. When you click a text box control in Layout view, an orange border appears around the text box and a dotted border appears around its attached label to indicate that the control is selected.

STEP-BY-STEP 5.1

1. Open the **Staff.accdb** database from the Data Files.

2. If the Security Warning appears below the Ribbon, click **Options**, click the **Enable this content** option button, then click **OK**.

3. In the Navigation Pane, click the **Teacher** table to select it.

4. On the Ribbon, click the **Create** tab.

5. In the Reports group on the Create tab, click the **Report** button. Access creates a report using all the fields in the Teacher table. See Figure 5-1.

STEP-BY-STEP 5.1 Continued

6. On the Quick Access Toolbar, click the **Save** button. Save the report as **Teacher List**.

7. Click the '**Close Teacher List**' button to close the report. Leave the database open for the next Step-by-Step.

Creating a Report Using the Label Wizard

The Label Wizard lets you create a report that you can use to print standard or custom labels. To create labels, select the record source in the Navigation Pane, click the Create tab on the Ribbon, and then click the Labels button in the Reports group on the Create tab. You use the Label Wizard dialog boxes to select the label you are using; to choose the font name, style, size, and color to use when printing the labels; to select the fields to include from the record source and their arrangement when printed on the label; to select an optional sort order; and to choose a name for the report. Figure 5-2 shows a report of mailing labels, printed three labels across the page and sorted in alphabetical order by the values in the Last Name field.

FIGURE 5-2
Report created by the Label Wizard

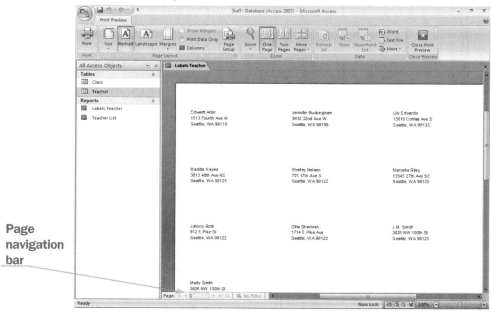

Page navigation bar

When you use a wizard to create a report, the report opens in Print Preview. When a report contains more than one page, you can click the buttons on the page navigation bar at the bottom of the Print Preview window to view additional pages in the report. You can also use the options on the Print Preview tab to change the page layout or zoom settings for the report.

Extra for Experts

You can use the buttons in the Data group on the Print Preview tab to save the data in the report in another file format, such as a Microsoft Word document.

STEP-BY-STEP 5.2

1. In the Navigation Pane, make sure the **Teacher** table is selected.

2. On the Ribbon, click the **Create** tab. In the Reports group, click the **Labels** button. The Label Wizard starts and opens the first dialog box, in which you choose a label. See Figure 5-3.

FIGURE 5-3
Using the Label Wizard to choose a label

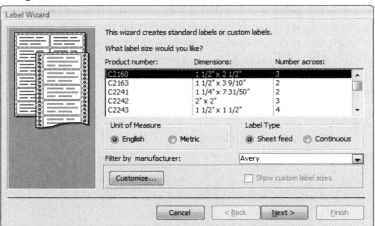

3. Make sure that **Avery** is selected in the Filter by manufacturer list box and that **C2160** is selected in the Product number column, then click **Next**. Figure 5-4 shows the second Label Wizard dialog box, in which you specify the font name, size, weight, and color that you want to use.

STEP-BY-STEP 5.2 Continued

FIGURE 5-4
Using the Label Wizard to choose the font

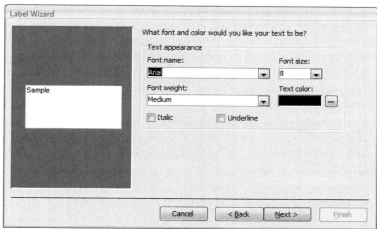

4. Make sure that the settings in your dialog box match the ones shown in Figure 5-4, then click **Next**. The third dialog box contains the Available fields list box, which contains the fields in the record source you selected. See Figure 5-5.

FIGURE 5-5
Using the Label Wizard to add fields to the label

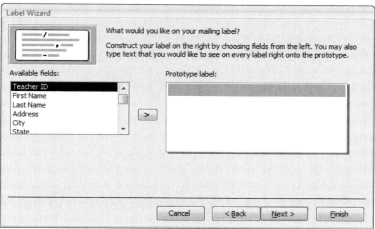

5. Double-click **First Name** in the Available fields box. The First Name field is added to the Prototype label section. Notice that the First Name field is enclosed in curly brackets. This is how Access indicates a field name used in a label.

6. Press the **spacebar**, then double-click **Last Name** in the Available fields box. You need to press the spacebar to insert a space between the field values when they are printed on the label.

7. Press the **Enter** key to start a new line on the label, then double-click **Address**.

STEP-BY-STEP 5.2 Continued

8. Press the **Enter** key, double-click **City**, type a **comma**, press the **spacebar**, double-click **State**, press the **spacebar**, then double-click **Zip**. Figure 5-6 shows the completed prototype of the label.

FIGURE 5-6
Completed prototype of the label

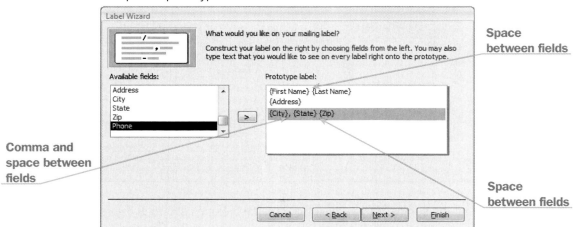

9. Make sure that your prototype label matches the one shown in Figure 5-6, then click **Next**.

10. In the Available fields list box in the fourth dialog box, double-click **Last Name** to add it to the Sort by box, then click **Next**. The labels will be printed in alphabetical order based on the values in the Last Name field.

11. In the final dialog box, make sure **Labels Teacher** appears in the text box and that the **See the labels as they will look printed** option button is selected, then click **Finish**. Figure 5-2 shows the report in Print Preview.

12. Click the **Close 'Labels Teacher'** button to close the Labels Teacher report. Leave the database open for the next Step-by-Step.

Creating a Report Using the Report Wizard

When you need to create a report quickly, you can use the Report Wizard, which asks you about the report you want to create and lets you select options in dialog boxes to specify the report's record source, layout, and style. Another option for reports is to select a grouping level. A grouping level organizes data based on one or more fields. For example, in a customer report, you might choose to group records using the State field so the records will be listed by the state in which customers live. You can also choose an optional sort order for the report, so records in one or more fields are sorted in ascending or descending order. The layout options for reports are Stepped,

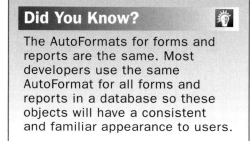

Did You Know?

The AutoFormats for forms and reports are the same. Most developers use the same AutoFormat for all forms and reports in a database so these objects will have a consistent and familiar appearance to users.

Block, and Outline, which arrange data in different ways. You can also choose the page orientation for the report (portrait or landscape). After choosing a layout, you can select a style for the report. A report's style, also called an AutoFormat, formats the report and its controls using a predefined color, font, and design scheme. After using the Report Wizard or a report tool to create a report, you can use the tools and features in Access to customize the report.

S TEP-BY-STEP 5.3

1. On the Ribbon, click the **Create** tab. In the Reports section on the Create tab, click the **Report Wizard** button. The Report Wizard starts and opens the first dialog box, in which you choose the record source for the report and the fields to print in the report.

2. Click the **Tables/Queries** arrow, then click **Table: Class** in the list. The fields for the Class table appear in the Available Fields list box.

3. Double-click the following fields in the order listed to add them to the Selected Fields list box: **Class ID**, **Class Name**, **Location**, **Start Date**, **End Date**, and **Fee**.

4. Click the **Tables/Queries** arrow, then click **Table: Teacher** in the list. The fields for the Teacher table appear in the Available Fields list box.

5. Double-click the following fields in the order listed to add them to the Selected Fields list box below the selected Fee field from the Class table: **Teacher ID**, **First Name**, and **Last Name**.

6. Click **Next**. The dialog box shown in Figure 5-7 asks how you want to view your data. Leave the Report Wizard open for the next Step-by-Step.

FIGURE 5-7
Report Wizard dialog box that asks how you want to view your data

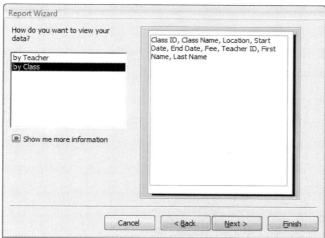

The dialog box shown in Figure 5-7 opens because you added fields from two related tables to the report's design. The sample page on the right of the dialog box illustrates how the data will be grouped in the report if it is grouped by the selected option (in this case, data is grouped by the Class table). You can also choose to group data by the Teacher table. In this case, you'll see the teacher's ID, first name, and last name and the classes he or she teaches in a group. You'll choose this option. After selecting a grouping option based on a table, you can use the next dialog box to add an additional grouping level to the report by choosing a field.

STEP-BY-STEP 5.4

1. In the dialog box, click **by Teacher**. The sample page changes to show the data grouped by teacher. See Figure 5-8.

FIGURE 5-8
Report Wizard dialog box that shows data grouped by teacher

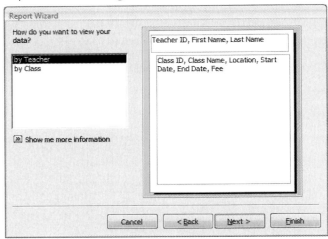

2. Click **Next**. You won't add an additional grouping level field to the report.

3. Click **Next**. A dialog box opens and asks if you want to add a sort order to the report.

4. Click the **arrow** on the first text box, click **Class Name** in the list, then click **Next**. The next dialog box requests information about the layout and page orientation that you would like to use in the report. A preview of the selected Stepped layout appears on the left side of the dialog box, as shown in Figure 5-9.

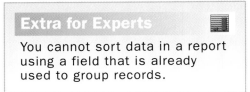

Extra for Experts

You cannot sort data in a report using a field that is already used to group records.

STEP-BY-STEP 5.4 Continued

FIGURE 5-9
Report Wizard dialog box that requests page layout information

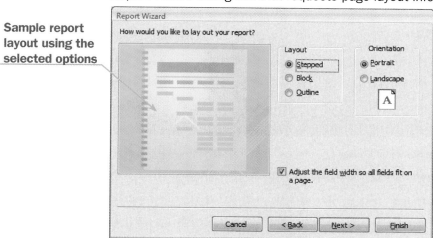

Sample report layout using the selected options

5. Click the **Block** option button to view a sample of this layout.

6. Click the **Outline** option button to view a sample of this layout.

7. Click the **Landscape** option button, click the **Block** option button, then click **Next**. The next dialog box asks you to select a style (AutoFormat) for the report.

8. In the list, click **Office**, then click **Next**. The final dialog box lets you accept the default name or enter a new one.

9. Select the default report name in the text box, type **Teachers and Classes**, make sure the **Preview the report** option button is selected, then click **Finish**.

STEP-BY-STEP 5.4 Continued

10. Click the **Shutter Bar Open/Close Button** to close the Navigation Pane. Figure 5-10 shows the report in Print Preview.

FIGURE 5-10
Report created by the Report Wizard

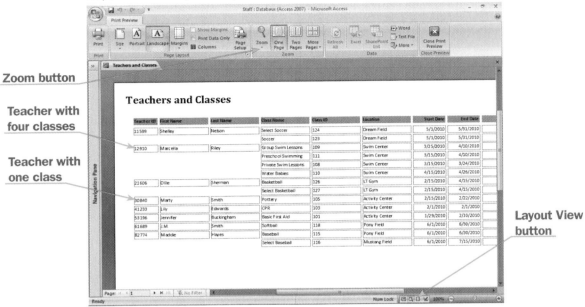

Zoom button

Teacher with four classes

Teacher with one class

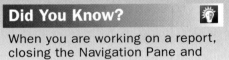

Layout View button

11. Use the horizontal scroll bar to scroll the report to the left so you can see the right edge of the page.

12. In the Zoom group on the Print Preview tab, click the **arrow** at the bottom of the Zoom button, then click **Fit to Window**. Leave the report open for the next Step-by-Step.

> **Did You Know?**
>
> When you are working on a report, closing the Navigation Pane and other on-screen features, such as the Field List and Property Sheet panes, gives you more room to see the entire report.

The report created by the Report Wizard opens in Print Preview because you chose the default "Preview the report" option in the final dialog box. In many cases, the report will need some adjustments to display the data in the desired manner. For example, in the Teachers and Classes report, you can resize the columns in the report to better fit the data they display. This change will also make the report's complete contents visible on a single page. Notice that the report is grouped by teachers, with the classes taught by each teacher appearing in a group with each teacher's ID, first name, and last name.

Modifying a Report in Layout View

Most developers use reports to provide on-screen displays or paper printouts of data in the database. An easy way to create a report is to use the Report Wizard to specify the report's record source, fields, grouping and sorting levels, layout, and style. However, you might find that the

Report Wizard doesn't create the *exact* report that you need, but you can use Layout view to make adjustments. If you close the report in Print Preview, Access will display the report in Design view. To change directly to Layout view, click the Layout View button on the status bar.

> **Extra for Experts**
>
> You can remove a control from a control layout in a report just like you can for forms. Display the report in Report Design view, click the control to select it, and then click the Remove button in the Control Layout group on the Arrange tab.

When the controls in a report exceed the page width that you selected for the report, you can usually resize the fields to make them fit on the page. Controls in reports are grouped in control layouts, just like they are in forms. When resizing a control, you can use the outline of the control as you drag it with the pointer to see the actual width of the control. You can also look at the status bar to see the control's width in characters and size a control exactly.

STEP-BY-STEP 5.5

1. On the status bar, click the **Layout View** button. The report is displayed in Layout view, as shown in Figure 5-11.

> **Important**
>
> If the Field List pane opens when you change to Layout view, click the Add Existing Fields button in the Controls group on the Format tab to close it.

FIGURE 5-11
Teachers and Classes report in Layout view

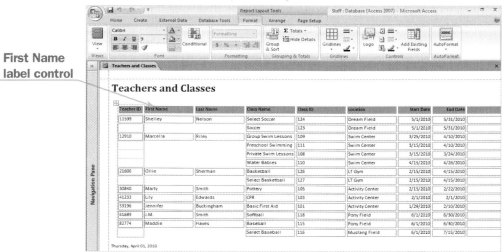

First Name label control

2. Click the **First Name** label control (at the top of the column) to select the column.

STEP-BY-STEP 5.5 Continued

3. Point to the right edge of the **First Name** label control. When the pointer changes to a double-arrow shape, click and slowly drag the right edge of the **First Name** label control to the left. When the lower-left corner of the status bar shows the width as 11 characters, release the mouse button. Figure 5-12 shows the resized First Name column. Because all of the text boxes in the column are part of a control layout, they are all resized to the same size. ↔

FIGURE 5-12
Resized First Name column

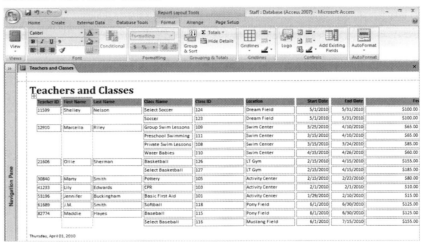

4. Use the technique described in Step 3 to resize the **Last Name** column to 13 characters.

5. Use the technique described in Step 3 to resize the **Class ID** column to 9 characters.

6. Use the technique described in Step 3 to resize the **Fee** column to 10 characters. Figure 5-13 shows the report with the resized columns. Leave the report open for the next Step-by-Step.

FIGURE 5-13
Report with resized columns

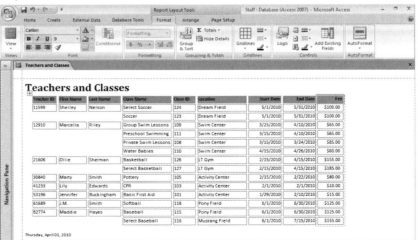

Modifying a Report in Design View

Similar to working with forms, there are certain types of changes for reports that you must make in Design view. When you view a report in Design view, you'll see the different sections of the report.

Extra for Experts

In Layout view, you can change the font, size, style, and other attributes of label and text box controls. Click a control to select it, and then use the options in the Font and Formatting groups on the Format tab to change the way data is displayed.

STEP-BY-STEP 5.6

1. On the Quick Access Toolbar, click the **Save** button to save the report.

2. On the status bar, click the **Design View** button. The report is displayed in Design view, as shown in Figure 5-14. Leave the report open for the next Step-by-Step.

FIGURE 5-14
Teachers and Classes report in Design view

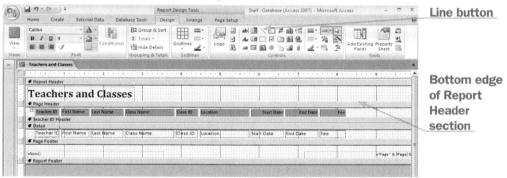

Table 5-1 identifies and describes the sections in a report. Just like in Form Design view, you can adjust the height of a section by dragging its bottom edge up or down, and you can select a section in a report by clicking its section bar.

TABLE 5-1
Report sections

SECTION	DESCRIPTION
Report Header	This section is printed once at the top of the first page of the report, and usually includes the report title.
Page Header	Because this section is printed at the top of every page of the report, you can use it to print a title or other information that is required on every page.
Group Header	This section is printed at the beginning of each new group of records. The section name includes the field name that is used to group records.
Detail	This section is printed once for each row in the record source and contains the main body of the report.
Group Footer	This section is printed at the end of each group of records and usually includes summary options, such as totals. The section name includes the field name that is used to group records.
Page Footer	Because this section is printed at the bottom of every page of the report, you can use it to include page numbers or other information that you want to print at the bottom of every page.
Report Footer	This section is printed once at the bottom of the last page of the report, and usually includes summary information for the entire report, such as grand totals.

The Controls group on the Design tab in Report Design view looks similar to the Controls group that you see in Form Design view. To add a control to a report, click the button in the Controls group, and then click the desired location in which to add the control in the report.

Adding a Line to a Report

 The Line tool lets you add a line to a report. Adding lines to a report makes it easier for users to identify the report sections and also adds visual interest. To insert a line, click the Line button in the Controls group on the Design tab. Move the pointer to the report, click the plus sign in the pointer where you want the line to begin, and then drag the pointer to the location where you want the line to end. When you release the mouse button, the line will appear in the report. To draw a straight line, press and hold down the Shift key while drawing the line.

> **Did You Know?**
>
> You use the horizontal and vertical rulers at the top and left side of the report in Report Design view to place controls in the report, just like you do in Form Design view.

STEP-BY-STEP 5.7

1. Point to the bottom edge of the **Report Header** section. When the pointer changes shape to a double pointer with a set of vertical arrowheads, click and drag the **Report Header** section down to the ¾-inch mark on the vertical ruler.

STEP-BY-STEP 5.7 Continued

2. In the Controls group on the Design tab, click the **Line** button.

3. Move the pointer to the Report Header section. Position the plus sign in the pointer at the ½-inch mark on the vertical ruler and in the second column of grid dots (just below the "T" in the Teachers and Classes title).

4. Press and hold down the **Shift** key. Click the pointer, then drag it to the 8.5-inch mark on the horizontal ruler. Release the mouse button, then release the **Shift** key. A line appears in the Report Header section, as shown in Figure 5-15.

FIGURE 5-15
Line in Report Header section

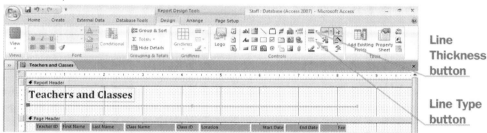

Line Thickness button

Line Type button

5. In the Controls group on the Design tab, click the **arrow** on the Line Thickness button, then point to the fourth line style in the list. Notice that the ScreenTip identifies the line style as "3 pt," which indicates a line thickness of three points.

6. Click the line with the ScreenTip "3 pt."

7. Click the **arrow** on the Line Type button, then click the first line type in the list, which has the ScreenTip "Solid."

8. Click anywhere in the Report Header section to deselect the line control. Figure 5-16 shows the line with the style and thickness you selected. Leave the report open for the next Step-by-Step.

FIGURE 5-16
Line in Report Header section with new thickness and style

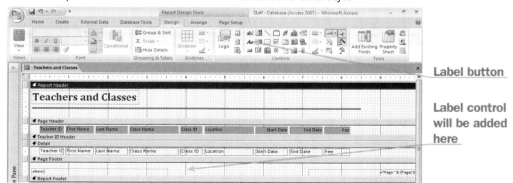

Label button

Label control will be added here

Adding a Label Control to a Report

You can add new controls to a report by using the tools in the Controls group. Just like when used in forms, you can add text to a report by adding it in the label control.

STEP-BY-STEP 5.8

1. In the Controls group on the Design tab, click the **Label** button.

Aa

2. Move the pointer to the Page Footer section. Move the plus sign in the pointer to the 4-inch mark on the horizontal ruler, in the fourth row of grid dots from the top of the Page Footer section. (See Figure 5-16 for the location to click.) Click the mouse button to insert the label control.

3. Type your first and last names, then press the **Enter** key.

4. On the Quick Access Toolbar, click the **Save** button to save the report.

5. On the status bar, click the **Print Preview** button. Figure 5-17 shows the report with the line and label controls added to it. Leave the report open for the next Step-by-Step.

FIGURE 5-17
Teachers and Classes report in Print Preview

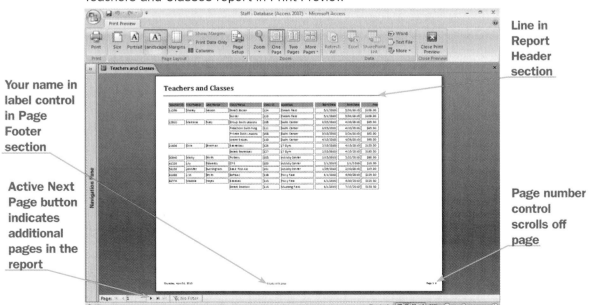

Moving a Control in Design View

The report's controls all fit on the page, with the exception of the control in the Page Footer section, which was added by the Report Wizard and contains the page number. You can drag the control to the left so it fits on the printed page. When you have controls that scroll off the page, additional pages are added to the report, causing blank pages or pages with very little content.

STEP-BY-STEP 5.9

1. On the page navigation bar, click the **Next Page** button. Depending on your printer, the next page might be blank or contain part of the page number in the lower-left corner of the page.

2. On the status bar, click the **Design View** button.

3. In the Page Footer section, click the control on the right, which contains the text that begins ="Page " &. The control is selected when it has an orange border.

4. Point to the top edge of the selected control so the pointer changes to a double-arrow shape.

5. Drag the selected control to the left, so the left edge of the control is at the 5-inch mark on the horizontal ruler and the top edge of the control is aligned with the top of the label control that contains your name. Figure 5-18 shows the new position of the control. Leave the report open for the next Step-by-Step.

FIGURE 5-18
Control in new position

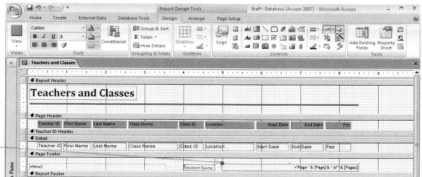

Drag control's left edge to here

Setting a Report Property

One final change that you will need to make is to check the width of the report, to make sure that the entire report fits on the printed page. You'll know that you need to make this change when you switch to Print Preview and get an error message that tells you that your report contains blank pages or when you see blank pages in the report. To change the report's width, you use the Property Sheet for the report. An easy way to access the report's Property Sheet is to click the report selector in the upper-left corner of the report where the horizontal and vertical rulers intersect. When you click the Property Sheet button in the Tools group on the Design tab, you'll see the report's properties. The Width property shows the width of the report in inches. Be careful when resizing a report—you need to make sure that it is wide enough to contain the data you want to display. Because your widest control is at the 8.5-inch mark on the horizontal ruler, and a page in landscape orientation can print content up to 11 inches wide, setting the Width property to 9 inches is a good adjustment.

Did You Know?

A green report error indicator appears on the report selector when the report's width exceeds the width of a page.

STEP-BY-STEP 5.10

1. In the upper-left corner of the report, where the horizontal and vertical rulers intersect, click the **report selector**.

2. In the Tools group on the Design tab, click the **Property Sheet** button. In the Property Sheet pane, click the **Format** tab. Figure 5-19 shows that the Width property for the form is 21", which is too wide to print on the page.

FIGURE 5-19
Property Sheet for the report

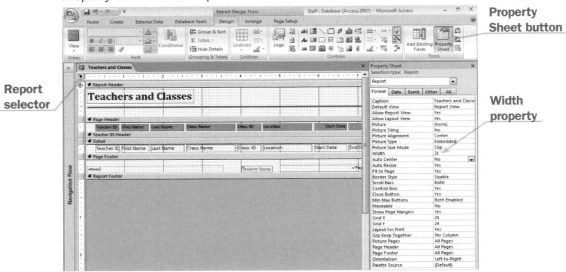

3. Select the text in the Width box, type **9**, then press the **Tab** key. The Width property changes to 9" and the report is resized.

4. On the Quick Access Toolbar, click the **Save** button.

5. In the Tools group on the Design tab, click the **Property Sheet** button to close the Property Sheet pane.

STEP-BY-STEP 5.10 Continued

6. On the status bar, click the **Print Preview** button. The report is displayed in Print Preview. Figure 5-20 shows the report, which now prints correctly on the page. Leave the report open for the next Step-by-Step.

FIGURE 5-20
Report in Print Preview

Inactive
Next Page
button
indicates
that there
are no
additional
pages

Page
number in
correct
position

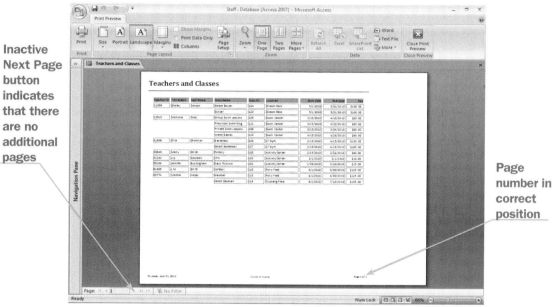

Adding a Picture to a Report

Reports are usually printed or viewed on the screen. Although the default appearance of a report is adequate, sometimes you might want to enhance a report by adding a picture. You can add any type of picture to a report, including a clip-art image, a graphic that you create using another program, or a digital image. To add a picture to a report, click the Logo button in the Controls group on the Design tab. In the Insert Picture dialog box, browse to and select the file that contains the picture you want to insert in the report. After selecting the file, click OK. An image control is added on the left side of the Report Header section by default. You can move the image control anywhere in the report. You can also use the sizing handles on the selected image control to resize the picture to the desired size and shape.

S TEP-BY-STEP 5.11

1. On the status bar, click the **Design View** button. The report is displayed in Design view.

2. In the Controls group on the Design tab, click the **Logo** button. The Insert Picture dialog box opens.

3. Browse to the **Lesson5** folder with your Data Files.

STEP-BY-STEP 5.11 Continued

4. Click the **Teacher.gif** file to select it, then click **OK**. The Insert Picture dialog box closes, and an image control containing the Teacher.gif picture is inserted in the report, as shown in Figure 5-21.

FIGURE 5-21
Image control added to Teachers and Classes report

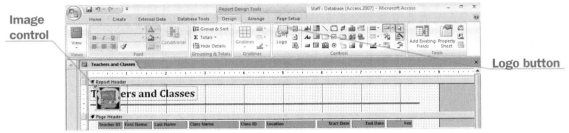

5. Drag the selected image control to the right of the Report Header section so that the right edge of the image control is aligned at the 8.5-inch mark on the horizontal ruler. There should be one row of grid dots above the picture. Figure 5-22 shows the image control in the new location.

FIGURE 5-22
Image control moved to new location

6. On the Quick Access Toolbar, click the **Save** button.

7. On the status bar, click the **Print Preview** button. Figure 5-23 shows the completed report.

STEP-BY-STEP 5.11 Continued

FIGURE 5-23
Completed report in Print Preview

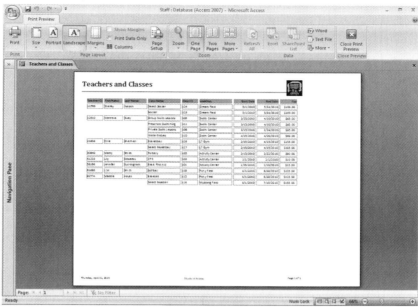

8. In the Close Preview group on the Print Preview tab, click the **Close Print Preview** button.

9. Close the Teachers and Classes report.

10. Click the **Office Button**, point to **Manage**, then click **Compact and Repair Database**.

11. Click the **Close** button on the Access title bar to exit Access.

SUMMARY

In this lesson, you learned:

■ A report is a database object that displays data from one or more tables or queries in a format that has an appearance similar to a printed report. You can use the Report tool or the Report Wizard to create a report. You can also use the Label Wizard to create a report that is used to print labels.

■ When used in a report, a field that is used as a grouping level organizes data into groups. You can also choose to sort data within the groups based on a field.

■ When working in Layout view, you can resize the controls in a control layout by selecting the control and dragging its edge to increase or decrease its width.

■ You can use Design view to change the height of a report section. You can also add a line, label, or picture to a report. You can change the location of a control in a report by dragging it to a new location.

■ To set a report's properties, click the report selector to select the report, then click the Property Sheet button in the Tools group on the Design tab.

VOCABULARY *Review*

Define the following terms:

Grouping level	Print Preview	Report selector
Label Wizard	Read-only	Report tool
Line tool	Report	Report Wizard

REVIEW *Questions*

TRUE/FALSE

Circle T if the statement is true or F if the statement is false.

T   F   1. When you use the Report tool to create a report, you can base it on two or more tables.

T   F   2. When a report is displayed in Layout view, you can use it to change the data the report contains.

T   F   3. When you use the Report Wizard to create a report, you can base it on two or more tables.

T   F   4. If you want to print something at the bottom of the last page of a report, add the content in the Page Footer section.

T   F   5. To draw a straight line in a report, press and hold down the Shift key while you draw the line.

WRITTEN QUESTIONS

Write a brief answer to each of the following questions.

1. List the steps for using the Report tool to create a report based on a table.

2.   List the steps for using the Label Wizard to create a report based on a table.

3.   What information might you include in the Report Header section of a report?

4.   How do you set the properties for a report?

5.   Which tool do you use to add a picture to a report?

PROJECTS

 PROJECT 5-1

1.   Open the **Sales.accdb** database from the Data Files.

2.   Use the Report tool to create a report based on the Brokers table.

3.   In Layout view, use the label controls to resize each column so that each column is just wide enough to display the longest value in the column.

4.   In Design view, add a label control at the top of the Report Footer section and at the 4-inch mark on the horizontal ruler. Type your first and last names in the label control.

5.   Save the report using the name **Brokers**.

6.   Display the report in Print Preview. Change the page orientation to landscape. Make sure that the report is displayed on a single page. If necessary, change to Design view and move any control that prints outside the page margin. Save the report, then close it.

7.   Use the Report tool to create a report based on the Listings table.

8.   In Layout view, use the label controls to resize each column so that each column is just wide enough to display the longest value in the column.

9.   In Design view, add a label control at the top of the Report Footer section and at the 1-inch mark on the horizontal ruler. Type your first and last names in the label control.

10. Change the Width property for the report to **9** (inches).

11. Save the report using the name **Listings**.

12. Display the report in Print Preview and make sure that it is displayed on a single page. If necessary, change to Design view and move any control that prints outside the page margin. Save the report if you make any changes, then close it.

13. Close the database and exit Access.

 PROJECT 5-2

1. Open the **Supplies.accdb** database from the Data Files.

2. Use the Report tool to create a report based on the Products table.

3. In Layout view, use the label controls to resize each column so that each column is just wide enough to display the longest value in the column. Scroll down the page and check to be sure that all values in each column are displayed.

4. In Design view, add a label control at the top of the Report Footer section and at the 1-inch mark on the horizontal ruler. Type your first and last names in the label control.

5. Click the control in the Report Footer section that displays a sum of the values in the Retail Price field and remove it from the control layout.

6. Press the Delete button to delete the control in the Report Footer section that displays a sum of the values in the Retail Price field.

7. Move the two controls in the Report Header section that print the current date and time to the left, so their right edges are aligned at the 6.5-inch mark on the horizontal ruler.

8. Delete the image control to the left of the Products title.

9. Insert the **Office.gif** file as a picture in the report. If necessary, move the image control that contains the Office.gif picture to the left of the title in the Report Header section.

10. Save the report using the name **Products**.

11. Preview the report and note any changes that you need to make so the content doesn't scroll off the edge of the page. If necessary, return to Layout view or Design view and make any required adjustments. Save the report, then print it.

12. Close the database, then exit Access.

 PROJECT 5-3

1. Open the **Agencies.accdb** database from the Data Files.

2. Use the Report Wizard to create a new report based on the Brokers and Listings tables.

3. Add the following fields from the Brokers table to the report in the order listed: Affiliation, Broker ID, First Name, Last Name, Office Phone, and Cell Phone.

4. Add the following fields from the Listings table to the report in the order listed: Price, Listing ID, Address, and Date Listed.

5. View the data by broker.

6. Use the Affiliation field as a grouping level.

7. Sort the data in ascending order by Price.

8. Choose the Stepped layout and the Landscape orientation.

9. Choose the Office style.

10. Use the report name **Brokers and Listings**.

11. In Layout view, use the label controls to resize each column so that the column is just wide enough to display the longest value in the column.

12. Change to Print Preview and make sure that all the data in the main body of the report fits on one page. If necessary, return to Layout view and continue resizing the label controls.

13. In Design view, move the control in the Page Footer section that contains the page number to the left, so that its right edge is aligned at the 9-inch mark on the horizontal ruler.

14. Add a label control anywhere in the Report Header section that contains your first and last names. Press the Enter key after typing your name, then move the label control so its right edge is aligned at the 9-inch mark on the horizontal ruler.

15. Change the Width property for the report to **9.5** (inches).

16. Close the report, close the database, and exit Access.

CRITICAL *Thinking*

 ACTIVITY 5-1

Open the **Sales.accdb** database from the Data Files. Open the Brokers report that you created in Project 5-1 in Print Preview. Why does the label control that contains your name print above the page number? What change would you need to make to print your name below the page number? Write your answer on a sheet of paper. Your answer should be specific to the Brokers report. Close the report, close the database, and exit Access.

 ACTIVITY 5-2

Open the **Sales.accdb** database from the Data Files. Open the Listings report that you created in Project 5-1 in Print Preview. A line and a number appear at the bottom of the Price column. What does the number represent? What do you call this? What was used to create this number? You used the Report tool to create the Listings report. Why do you think that the Report tool added this number to the report? Write your answer on a sheet of paper. Your answer should be specific to the Listings report. Close the report, close the database, and exit Access.

SCANS ACTIVITY 5-3

In this lesson, you learned how to use the Label Wizard to create labels that you might use to address envelopes or packages. What other uses can you think of for creating labels from a database? On a sheet of paper, give one example of the kind of labels that you might need and how you would use Access to create a record source and print the labels.

INTEGRATING ACCESS

OBJECTIVES

Upon completion of this lesson, you will be able to:

- Import data from other Office programs into a database.

- Export data from a database to other Office programs.

- Create a form letter.

- Merge a form letter with a data source.

- Edit a data source to print specific form letters.

Estimated Time: 1.5 hours

VOCABULARY

Comma-separated values (CSV)

Data source

Delimited data

Delimiter

Export

Form letter

Import

Main document

Merge field

Importing and Exporting Data

Sometimes you might find that you need to use the data stored in an Access database in other programs. For example, when providing information stored in a database to other people who do not have Access, you can share the information with them by saving it in another file format. When you save database data in another file format, you **export** the data from the database. You can export data to many other formats, including a Word document, an Excel workbook, or a text file. Access also exports data to another Access database, another database format, or an HTML document (which creates a Web page).

You might also find yourself in a situation where you need to add data stored in a different format to an Access database. Instead of entering the records one at a time, you can **import** the new data into the database. When you import data, you copy it from another Access database, an Excel workbook, a text file, or some other file format into an existing or new table in the current database. Importing saves you time and effort by adding records to a new or existing table automatically. Fortunately, Access includes features that make it easy to import and export data to and from a database.

Importing and Exporting Documents

When you need to export data from a database table to a Word document, click the External Data tab on the Ribbon, and then click the Word button in the Export group. When you export the data, it will be saved as an RTF file, which stands for Rich Text Format. Most word processors, including Word, can open files with the .rtf file name extension.

STEP-BY-STEP 6.1

1. Open the **School.accdb** database from the Data Files.

2. If the Security Warning appears below the Ribbon, click **Options**, click the **Enable this content** option button, then click **OK**.

3. On the Ribbon, click the **External Data** tab. In the Export group on the External Data tab, click the **Word** button. The Export – RTF File dialog box opens, as shown in Figure 6-1.

FIGURE 6-1
Export – RTF File dialog box

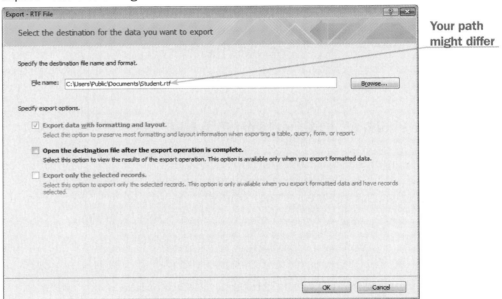

4. If necessary, click **Browse** and navigate to the drive and folder where your Data Files are stored, double-click the **Lesson6** folder, then click **Save** in the File Save dialog box to close it.

5. Click the **Open the destination file after the export operation is complete** check box to add a check mark to it.

6. Click **OK** to export the data. Word starts and opens the file that you created, which has the file name Student.rtf. The data appears in a table format when viewed in Word. See Figure 6-2.

STEP-BY-STEP 6.1 Continued

FIGURE 6-2
Exported data in Word

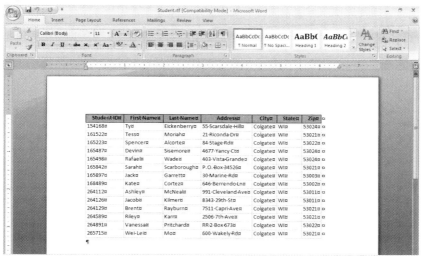

7. Click the **Close** button on the Word title bar to close Word.

8. If necessary, click **Close** to close the Export – RTF File dialog box. (You do not need to save the export steps.) Leave the database open for the next Step-by-Step.

You can import data from a Word document into an existing database table when the data has the same number of columns and the same *type* of data as the database table. For example, if the Access table has a field that is defined using the Number data type, you cannot import text data (containing letters) into the field. In this case, Access will display an error message. When you import data from a Word document, it is usually best to store it in a Word table. The Word table must contain the same number of columns as the database table.

When data is stored in another format, you can import the data and create a new table in a database in one step. When importing data from a text file, the data might be stored in a file format called comma-separated values (CSV). Most word processing, spreadsheet, and database programs can read and save CSV files. In a CSV file, commas separate the field values of each record in the data source. When data is formatted using comma separators, it is called delimited data and the comma is called a delimiter. A paragraph mark indicates the end of a record. To import data and create a new table, click the External Data tab on the Ribbon, and then click the Text File button in the Import group. Browse to and select the file that contains the data you want to import, and then choose the option to import the source data into a new table in the current database. Follow the steps in the Import Text Wizard to create a new table in the database using the file name of the text file.

> **Extra for Experts**
>
> Most programs have converters to separate the values in a CSV file into the columns of a worksheet or the cells of a table. When you convert a CSV file to another format, the program removes the commas that separate the field values. Sometimes you'll see quotation marks around text values in a text file. The conversion process also removes quotation marks.

$\mathcal{S}$TEP-BY-STEP 6.2

1. In the Import group on the External Data tab, click the **Text File** button. The Get External Data – Text File dialog box opens, as shown in Figure 6-3.

FIGURE 6-3
Get External Data – Text File dialog box

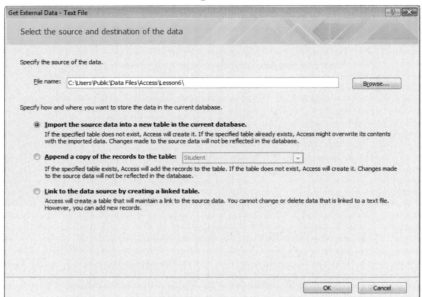

2. Click **Browse**. If necessary, navigate to and open the **Lesson6** folder, click **Student.txt** to select it, then click **Open** in the File Open dialog box.

3. Make sure that the **Import the source data into a new table in the current database** option button is selected, then click **OK**. The Import Text Wizard starts and opens the first dialog box, as shown in Figure 6-4.

STEP-BY-STEP 6.2 Continued

FIGURE 6-4
First Import Text Wizard dialog box

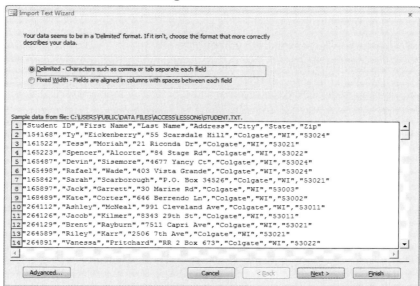

4. Make sure that the **Delimited** option button is selected, then click **Next**. The second dialog box requests information about the delimiter that separates the fields in the data source, as shown in Figure 6-5.

FIGURE 6-5
Second Import Text Wizard dialog box

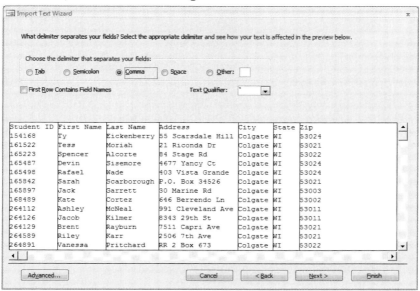

STEP-BY-STEP 6.2 Continued

5. Make sure that the **Comma** option button is selected, then click the **First Row Contains Field Names** check box to add a check mark to it. If you fail to identify the first row as having field names, the field names will be added in a record, instead of as field names.

6. Click **Next**. The third dialog box asks you about the data types you want to use for each field. If you do not choose any data types for the fields, they will all have the Text data type.

7. Click **Next**. The fourth dialog box lets you set or create a primary key field, as shown in Figure 6-6. Leave the Wizard open for the next Step-by-Step.

FIGURE 6-6
Fourth Import Text Wizard dialog box

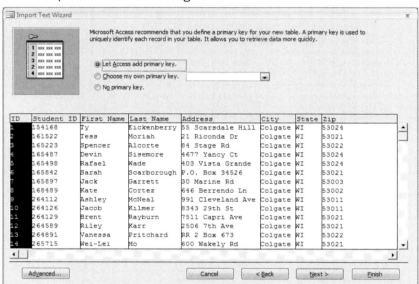

Recall that the primary key field stores unique values for each record in a table. The Student ID field already contains unique field values, so you can use the arrow on the list box to the right of the "Choose my own primary key" option button to select the Student ID field as your table's primary key. You can also choose not to set a primary key, or you can let Access create a primary key. If you select the option for Access to create a primary key, Access will create a field named ID at the beginning of the table and assign it the AutoNumber data type.

STEP-BY-STEP 6.3

1. Click the **Choose my own primary key** option button. Because the Student ID field is the first field in the table, it is selected automatically in the list box.

2. Click **Next**. The final dialog box asks you for a table name.

3. In the Import to Table text box, type **Student Word**, then click **Finish**.

STEP-BY-STEP 6.3 Continued

4. If necessary, click **Close** in the Get External Data – Text File dialog box to close it. (Do not save the import steps.)

5. In the Navigation Pane, double-click **Student Word** to open the table. Leave the Student Word table open for the next Step-by-Step.

The table contains the imported data. The field names are from the first row of the text file because you chose the option to import the field names. All the fields in the table have the Text data type because you didn't set them to other data types using the Import Text Wizard. The Text fields have the default properties as well, which includes a default Field Size property of 255 characters. To finish creating this table, you would change to Design view and reevaluate the data types and field properties for each field, to make sure that you are using the correct settings.

Importing and Exporting Workbooks

When you need to export data from a database table to an Excel workbook, click the External Data tab on the Ribbon, and then click the Excel button in the Export group. When you export the data, it will be saved in Excel format, with each field in the table stored in a worksheet column and each record in the table stored as a row in the worksheet.

> **Extra for Experts**
>
> You can export data from a database to a specific version of Excel by selecting a different file format in the Export – Excel Spreadsheet dialog box. The default file format is Excel 2007.

STEP-BY-STEP 6.4

1. In the Export group on the External Data tab, click the **Excel** button. The Export – Excel Spreadsheet dialog box opens, as shown in Figure 6-7.

FIGURE 6-7
Export – Excel Spreadsheet dialog box

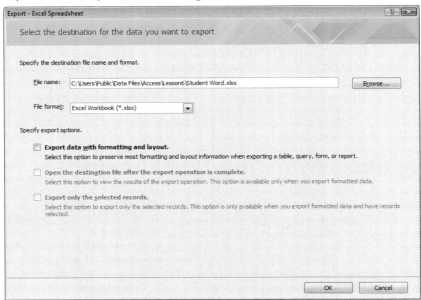

2. If the path to the Lesson6 folder for your Data Files does not appear in the File name text box, click **Browse**, navigate to and open the **Lesson6** folder, then click **Save** in the File Save dialog box.

3. Click the **Export data with formatting and layout** check box to add a check mark to it.

4. Click the **Open the destination file after the export operation is complete** check box to add a check mark to it.

5. Click **OK**. Excel starts and opens the file that contains the data you exported. See Figure 6-8.

STEP-BY-STEP 6.4 Continued

FIGURE 6-8
Excel worksheet with the exported data

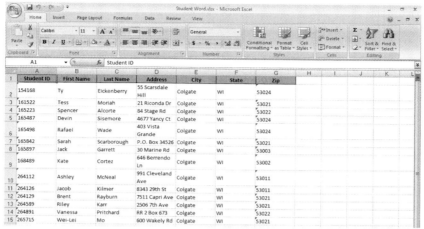

6. Click the **Close** button on the Excel title bar to close Excel.

7. If necessary, click **Close** to close the Export – Excel Spreadsheet dialog box. (Do not save the export steps.)

8. Click the **Close 'Student Word'** button to close the Student Word table. Leave the database open for the next Step-by-Step.

You can also import data stored in a workbook into a new or existing database table. When you use the data in a workbook to add records to a database table, the columns in the worksheet must be the same as the fields in the database and contain the same type of data. When you need to create a new table using the data in a workbook, the Import Spreadsheet Wizard will guide you through the process.

STEP-BY-STEP 6.5

1. In the Import group on the External Data tab, click the **Excel** button. The Get External Data – Excel Spreadsheet dialog box opens. See Figure 6-9.

FIGURE 6-9
Get External Data – Excel Spreadsheet dialog box

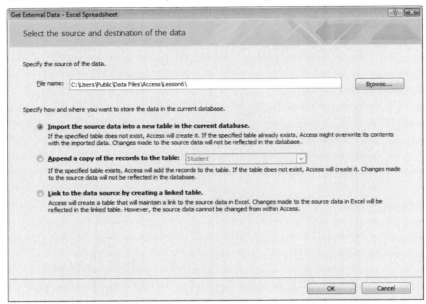

2. Click **Browse**, if necessary navigate to and open the **Lesson6** folder, click **Student Excel.xlsx**, then click **Open**.

3. Make sure that the **Import the source data into a new table in the current database** option button is selected.

4. Click **OK**. The Import Spreadsheet Wizard dialog box opens, as shown in Figure 6-10.

Careers

Databases are helpful in the sales business. Salespersons can create a database to store detailed information about their customers. They can then create queries and filters to search the database for specific information. They can also use the database to create reports, form letters, and mailing labels.

STEP-BY-STEP 6.5 Continued

FIGURE 6-10
First Import Spreadsheet Wizard dialog box

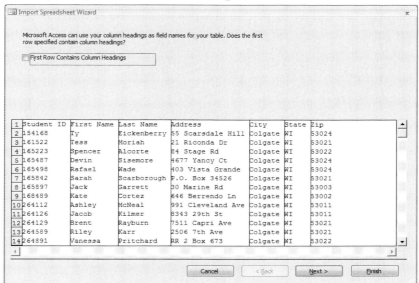

5. Click the **First Row Contains Column Headings** check box to add a check mark to it, then click **Next**. The second dialog box lets you set data types for fields. As when importing a text file, you can set the data types now or do so after creating the table. If you choose not to change the data types, all fields will have the Text data type and the default property settings for Text fields.

6. Click **Next**. The third dialog box asks you about the table's primary key.

7. Click the **Choose my own primary key** option button. Make sure that **Student ID** appears in the list box to the right of the Choose my own primary key option button, then click **Next**. The final dialog box asks you for the table name.

8. In the Import to Table text box, type **Student Excel**, then click **Finish**.

9. If necessary, in the Get External Data – Excel Spreadsheet dialog box, click **Close**. (Do not save the import steps.)

10. In the Navigation Pane, double-click **Student Excel** to open the table in Datasheet view. The table contains the data that was stored in the columns and rows in the worksheet.

11. Click the **Close 'Student Excel'** button to close the Student Excel table. Leave the database open for the next Step-by-Step.

Creating Form Letters

Another way to integrate Access and Word is to create form letters. A form letter is a document that includes codes that print information from a data source. The data source might be information stored in a Word document, Excel workbook, Access database, or another file format. When you merge the data source with the form letter, one letter is printed for each record in the data source. In this case, the form letter is also called the main document. Form letters are used to customize letters and other printed materials. When used with a data source, Word does the work of addressing letters or customizing forms, so you don't need to type the information directly and print each letter individually.

For example, suppose a fourth grade teacher wants to send a letter to the parents of students in her class to welcome them to the new school year. Instead of typing each recipient's name, mailing address, salutation (such as Dear Mr. and Mrs. Peterson), and child's name in each letter and printing it, she can create a form letter with the basic information she wants to include in the letter. Then she can create a data source that stores the mailing address and student information for each child in her class. When she merges the main document with the data source, Word will print letters using the specific address and student information from each record in the data source. All the teacher needs to do is set up the process and load the printer with paper.

Creating a Form Letter

A form letter is a document that you create using Microsoft Word and that contains codes to tell Word where to insert the record from the data source. The codes are the same as the field names used in the data source. When you insert the codes in a main document, they are called merge fields. When you insert a merge field in a Word document, the field name is enclosed in angle brackets. For example, the merge field for a First Name field is displayed as <<First_Name>> in the Word document. When you merge the main document and the data source, Word replaces <<First_Name>> with the First Name field value in the first record of the data source, and prints a first name.

You can use any document as a form letter, including documents that you create from scratch or a template. You can start a mail merge from Word or from Access. To start a mail merge using Access, open the database that contains the data source for the form letters, and then click the data source (table or query) in the Navigation Pane to select it. Click the External

> **Did You Know?**
>
> When a field name in the data source contains a space, the merge field in Word replaces the space with an underscore character. For example, the field name First Name becomes <<First_Name>>.

Data tab on the Ribbon. In the Export group on the External Data tab, click the More button. In the list, click Merge it with Microsoft Office Word. The Microsoft Word Mail Merge Wizard starts and asks if you want to link your data to an existing document or create a new document. If you click the option to use an existing document, the Select Microsoft Word Document dialog box opens. Use the options to browse to and select the document, and then click Open. Word starts and opens the document you selected, and sets the data source to the object you selected in the database. If you choose the option to create a new document, Word starts and opens a new document. In either case, after Word starts, the Mailings tab is selected on the Ribbon and the Mail Merge pane opens on the right side of the window, as shown in Figure 6-11.

FIGURE 6-11
Existing document selected for mail merge

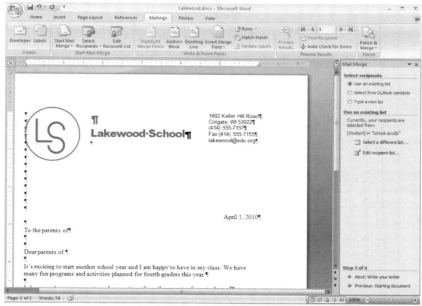

You can type or edit content in the document and use the tools in Word to make any changes to the letter, such as changing the font style or adding graphics. If you are creating a document from scratch, the first step is to select the type of document you are creating (letter, e-mail message, envelope, label, or a directory). For a form letter, choose the Letters option button. The second step asks you to select the document you want to use or to create a new document. After making your selection, click the Next: Select Recipients link at the bottom of the Mail Merge pane to select the data source.

In the third step, shown in Figure 6-11, you select the data source that contains the records for the recipients. This data source might be an existing list, an Outlook contact, or data that you type. When you start the mail merge from Access, Word sets the data source for you automatically.

If you want to merge all the records in the data source, then you don't need to do anything else. If you want to merge selected records in the data source, click the Edit recipient list link in the Mail Merge pane to open the Mail Merge Recipients dialog box, shown in Figure 6-12. The name of the data source appears in the first column, and the fields in the data source appear to the left of the Data Source column in the order in which they appear in the data source. In Figure 6-12, the data source is an Access database.

FIGURE 6-12
Mail Merge Recipients dialog box

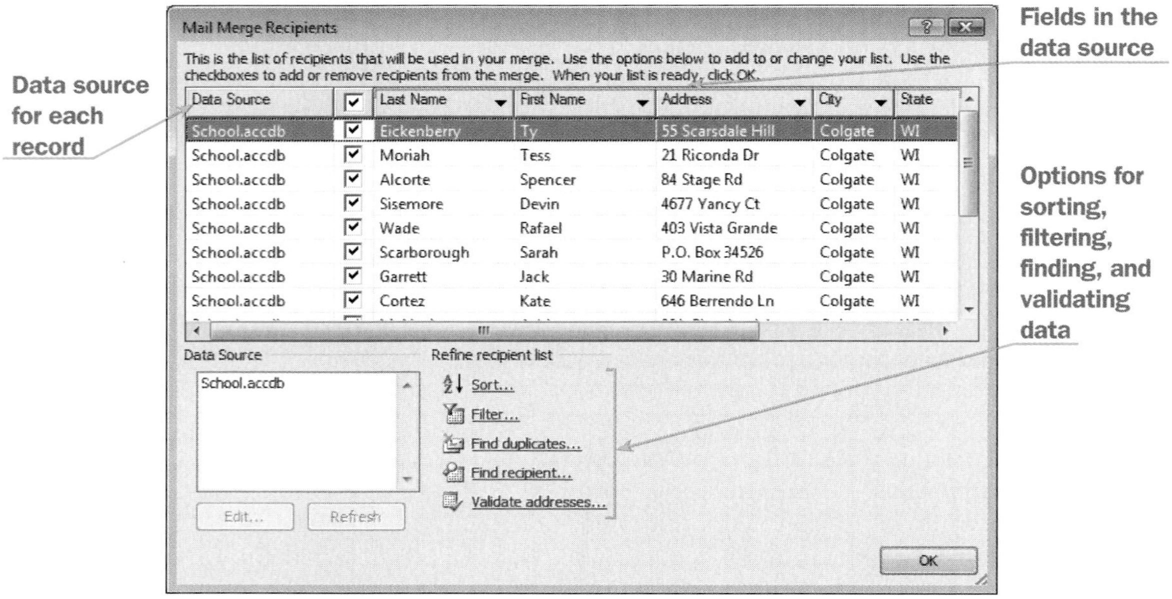

A check box is shown to the left of the first field for each record; a check mark indicates that the record will be printed. If you want to remove a record from the mail merge, clear its check box. Also notice the "Refine recipient list" section, which provides options for sorting and filtering data, finding duplicate records, locating a specific recipient, and validating addresses. You can use these options when you need to change how letters are printed when you complete the mail merge. For example, if you want to print form letters in alphabetical order based on a specific field, you can click the Sort link to open the Filter and Sort dialog box with the Sort Records tab selected, as shown in Figure 6-13. To sort on a specific field, click the Sort by arrow, and then select the field that you want to sort. Figure 6-13 shows that the mail merge will be printed in ascending order based on the values in the Last Name field.

FIGURE 6-13
Sort Records tab

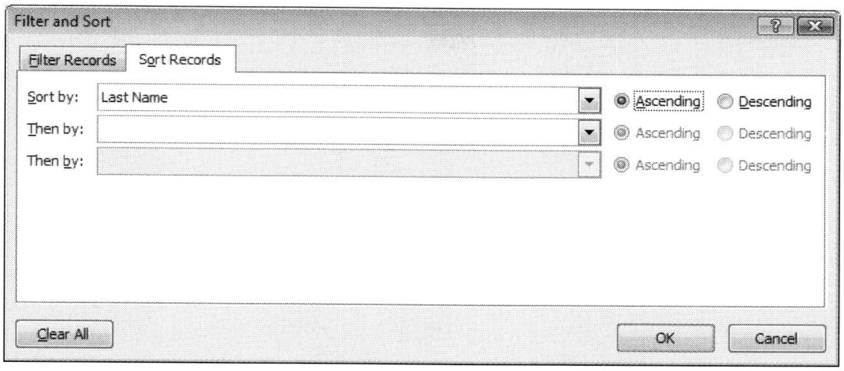

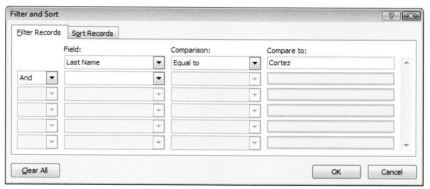

You can also filter records by clicking the Filter link in the Refine recipient list section, which opens the Filter and Sort dialog box with the Filter Records tab selected. To create a filter, use the Field list arrow to select the field to filter, use the Comparison arrow to choose the filter operator, and then type a value in the Compare to text box. Figure 6-14 shows a filter to select records with the last name *Cortez*.

FIGURE 6-14
Filter Records tab

When you click OK to close the Filter and Sort dialog box, you'll apply the new settings to the form letters. However, the changes you make are not reflected in the data source. Click OK to close the Mail Merge Recipients dialog box, and then click the Next: Write your letter link at the bottom of the Mail Merge pane. If necessary, make any changes to the content of the letter, just like you would in any other document.

Word provides several options for adding merge fields to a document. You can use the Address block link in the Mail Merge pane to add an address to the letter in the location of the insertion point. You can also add merge fields individually at the location of the insertion point by clicking the Insert Merge Field button in the Write & Insert Fields group on the Mailings tab. If you click the Address block link in the Mail Merge pane, the Insert Address Block dialog box opens and shows a preview of the address information that you will be inserting, as shown in Figure 6-15.

FIGURE 6-15
Insert Address Block dialog box

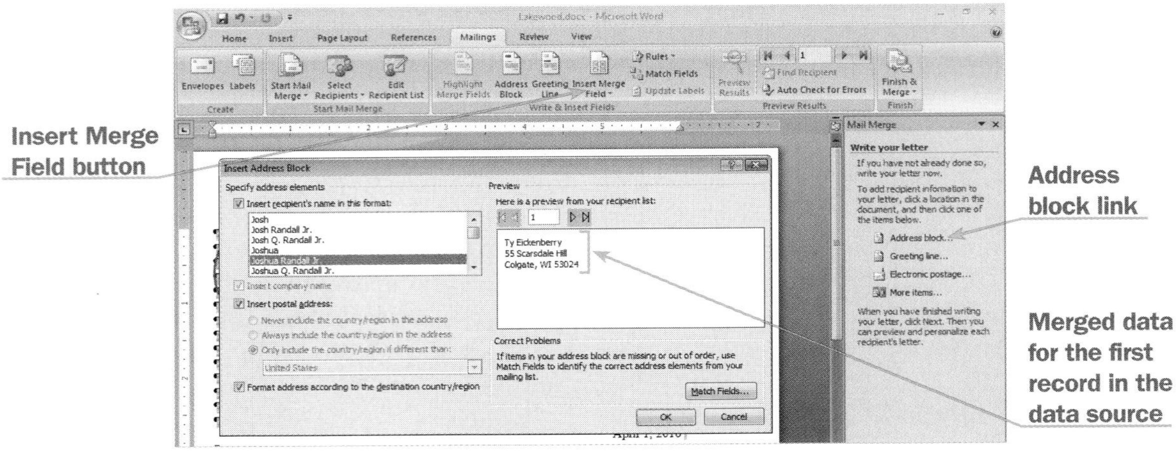

If the preview of the address block is correct, click OK. (If it is incorrect, click Match Fields to make adjustments.) After inserting the address block, it appears as <<AddressBlock>> in the main document.

You can insert individual fields from the data source wherever necessary in the main document. For example, you can include a first name in the middle of a sentence to customize the content. Figure 6-16 shows the first and last names added to the salutation and the first name inserted in the first sentence of the first paragraph. Be careful when inserting fields individually—you will need to type any surrounding punctuation, such as inserting a space between field names so the first and last names print as "Riley Karr" instead of as "RileyKarr" and typing a comma or colon after the salutation.

FIGURE 6-16
Document with merge fields inserted

Merge field to insert the address

Merge fields to insert the first name and last name, with a space between names

Merge field to insert the first name, with a space on each side

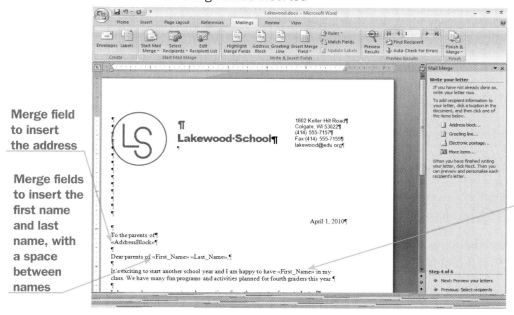

After adding the merge fields to the letter, click the Next: Preview your letters link at the bottom of the Mail Merge pane. The main document displays one letter for each record in the data source. Figure 6-17 shows the first letter. Notice that the <<AddressBlock>> merge field was replaced by the address information for Ty Eickenberry. Ty's first and last names replaced the <<First_Name>> and <<Last_Name>> fields in the salutation. Ty's first name replaced the <<First_Name>> field in the first sentence of the first paragraph. If you click the next and previous buttons in the Preview your letters section of the Mail Merge pane, you'll see the next and previous records as they will appear in the final letter.

FIGURE 6-17
Merged letter for the first record

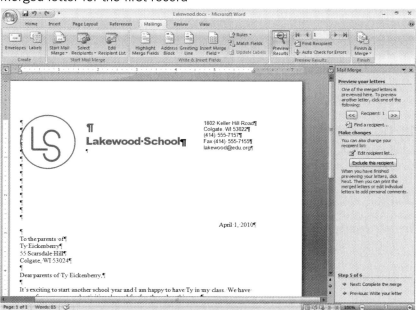

After verifying that your form letters are correct, click the Next: Complete the merge link at the bottom of the Mail Merge pane. Click the Print link in the Merge section of the Mail Merge pane to print the letters.

STEP-BY-STEP 6.6

1. In the Navigation Pane, click the **Student** table to select it as the data source.

2. In the Export group on the External Data tab, click the **More** button. In the list, click **Merge it with Microsoft Office Word**. The Microsoft Word Mail Merge Wizard opens.

3. If necessary, click the **Link your data to an existing Microsoft Word document** option button, then click **OK**. The Select Microsoft Word Document dialog box opens.

4. If necessary, navigate to and open the **Lesson6** folder, click **Lakewood.docx**, then click **Open**. The Select Microsoft Word Document dialog box closes. Word starts and opens the document you selected.

5. If necessary, click the **Lakewood.docx** program button on the taskbar to switch to Word.

6. If necessary, click the **Maximize** button on the Word title bar to maximize the program window. See Figure 6-11. Leave Word open for the next Step-by-Step.

Because you started the mail merge from Access, the Mail Merge pane opens with the Step 3 of 6 task displayed. The data source is already set to the Student table in the School database because you selected the data source in Access.

STEP-BY-STEP 6.7

1. At the bottom of the Mail Merge pane, click the **Next: Write your letter** link. The Step 4 of 6 Mail Merge pane is displayed.

2. In the document, click the blank line below the paragraph that contains the text *To the parents of*.

3. In the Mail Merge pane, click the **Address block** link. The Insert Address Block dialog box opens, as shown in Figure 6-15. Make sure the settings in your dialog box match the ones shown in Figure 6-15, then click **OK**.

4. In the document, click to the right of the line that contains the text *Dear parents of*.

5. In the Write & Insert Fields group on the Mailings tab, click the **arrow** at the bottom of the Insert Merge Field button. In the list, click **First_Name**.

6. Press the **spacebar**.

STEP-BY-STEP 6.7 Continued

7. In the Write & Insert Fields group on the Mailings tab, click the **arrow** at the bottom of the Insert Merge Field button. In the list, click **Last_Name**.

8. Type a comma.

9. In the first paragraph of the document, click after the word *have* in the first sentence. Use the **arrow** at the bottom of the Insert Merge Field button to insert the **First_Name** field in the sentence.

10. Press the **spacebar** and make sure that the <<First_Name>> field that you just inserted has a space on each side of it, so the text will be printed correctly.

11. At the bottom of the Mail Merge pane, click the **Next: Preview your letters** link. The data source is merged with the letter. See Figure 6-17.

12. In the Mail Merge pane, click the button to display the next merged letter.

13. In the Mail Merge pane, click the button to display the previous merged letter.

14. At the bottom of the Mail Merge pane, click the **Next: Complete the merge** link. The options on the Mail Merge pane change to let you print the letters or to edit individual letters.

15. On the Quick Access Toolbar, click the **Save** button. Leave Word open for the next Step-by-Step.

Editing the Recipient List

The default setting for a mail merge is to print all the records in the data source. If you want to restrict the printout to certain records, you can set a filter or choose specific records individually.

STEP-BY-STEP 6.8

1. At the bottom of the Mail Merge pane, click the **Previous: Preview your letters** link. The Step 5 of 6 Mail Merge pane is displayed. See Figure 6-17.

2. In the Mail Merge pane, click the **Edit recipient list** link. The Mail Merge Recipients dialog box opens. See Figure 6-12.

3. Click the **check box** next to the Data Source column heading at the top of the column of check boxes. The check marks are removed from all check boxes.

4. Click the **check box** to the left of the record for Rafael Wade to add a check mark to it.

5. Click **OK** to close the Mail Merge Recipients dialog box.

6. In the Preview your letters section of the Step 5 of 6 Mail Merge pane, click the button to display the next record. Because you set the mail merge to print only one record, there are no "next" letters.

STEP-BY-STEP 6.8 Continued

7. On the Quick Access Toolbar, click the **Save** button.

8. Click the **Close** button on the Word title bar to close Word.

9. Click the **Close** button on the Access title bar to close the Student database and Access.

SUMMARY

In this lesson, you learned:

■ You can import and export data from a database and use it in other programs. When importing data, you can append records to an existing table or create a new table. When appending records to an existing table, the data source must have the same number of fields and contain the same type of data as the existing table.

■ Delimited data contains commas or other separators to separate the fields in a data source. When the delimiter is a comma, the data is called comma-separated values (CSV). Access, Excel, and other programs can read and process CSV files.

■ A form letter is a document that includes codes that print information from a data source. The data source might be information stored in a Word document, an Excel workbook, an Access database, or another file format. When you merge the data source with the form letter, one letter is printed for each record in the data source.

■ A merge field tells Word where to print data from the data source.

■ To print certain records from a data source in a form letter, edit the recipient list by applying a filter or by selecting individual records.

VOCABULARY *Review*

Define the following terms:

Comma-separated values (CSV)	Delimiter	Import
	Export	Main document
Data source	Form letter	Merge field
Delimited data		

REVIEW *Questions*

TRUE/FALSE

Circle T if the statement is true or F if the statement is false.

T   F   1. When importing data from a Word document into an existing Access database table, the Word document data must contain the same number of columns and type of data as the database table.

T   F   2. When importing data into a database using the Import Text Wizard, you cannot specify a primary key for a new table.

T   F   3. When importing data into a new database table, the fields will have the default property settings for a Text field unless you choose new data types for the fields.

T   F   4. When creating a mail merge in Word, the data source must be a table in an Access database.

T   F   5. You can insert a merge field anywhere in a form letter.

WRITTEN QUESTIONS

Write a brief answer to each of the following questions.

1. List three file formats that you can use to import data into a database.

2. List three file formats that you can use to export data from a database.

3. In a comma-separated values file, what is the delimiter that separates fields? What is the delimiter that separates records?

4. How do you insert a merge field into a Word document?

5. How would you insert the city, state, and zip code fields from a data source in a letter? Use the field names City, State, and Zip in your answer. The data should be printed on a single line in the format *City, State Zip*.

PROJECTS

 PROJECT 6-1

1. Open the **Inventory.accdb** database from the Data Files.

2. Choose the option to import data from an Excel workbook.

3. Choose the Products.xlsx file in the Lesson6 folder as the data source.

4. Choose the option to append the records in the workbook to the existing Products table in the database.

5. Complete the steps in the Import Spreadsheet Wizard and accept the default settings. In the last dialog box, make sure that the Products table is listed in the Import to Table text box.

6. If necessary, close the Get External Data - Excel Spreadsheet dialog box without saving the import steps.

7. Close the database and exit Access.

 PROJECT 6-2

1. Open the **Items.accdb** database from the Data Files.

2. Choose the option to export data from the Products table to a text file. The delimiter is a comma and the first row contains field names.

3. Save the exported text file as **Products.txt** in the Lesson6 folder. Do not save the export steps.

4. Import the data in the Products.txt file into a new table in the Items database. The delimiter is a comma and the first row contains field names. Do not set the data types for any of the fields. Choose the Product ID field as the table's primary key. Change the default table name to **Products Import**.

5. If necessary, close the Get External Data - Text File dialog box without saving the import steps.

6. Close the database and exit Access.

PROJECT 6-3

1. Open the **InfoTech.accdb** database from the Data Files.

2. Start a mail merge using the Abbott.docx document from the Data Files.

3. In the main document, on the second line below the date, insert an address block.

4. On the line that contains the word *Dear*, type a space, insert the First_Name field, then type a comma.

5. Preview the letters.

6. Exclude Donna Abbott from the mail merge by displaying her record and using a button in the Mail Merge pane.

7. Save the document and close Word.

8. Close the database and exit Access.

PROJECT 6-4

1. Open the **InfoTech.accdb** database from the Data Files.

2. Start a mail merge using the Sales.docx document from the Data Files.

3. In Word, set a filter to select only those records that have the field value *Sales* in the Department field in the data source.

4. Sort the records in alphabetical (ascending) order by Last Name.

5. On the second line below the date, insert an address block.

6. On the line that contains the word *Dear*, type a space, insert the First_Name field, then type a comma.

7. Preview the letters.

8. Save the document and close Word.

9. Close the database and exit Access.

CRITICAL *Thinking*

 ACTIVITY 6-1

Word includes options to merge records from a data source with e-mail messages. Use the Help system to learn more about this process. On a sheet of paper, describe how you might use this feature to send information to your contacts about an upcoming event or function that is planned for your family or school.

 ACTIVITY 6-2

Start Access and use the Blank Database template to create a new database named **Swimming.accdb** in the Lesson6 folder with your Data Files. Close the default table that opens (Table1). Import the data in the Clubs.txt text file in the Lesson6 folder into a new table in the Swimming database. The delimiter is a comma and the first row contains field names. Do not change the data types of any fields. Choose the Club Code field as the table's primary key. Import the data into a new table named **Clubs**. Do not save the import steps.

Import the data in the Officials.xlsx Excel workbook in the Lesson6 folder into a new table in the Swimming database. The first row contains column headings. Do not change the data types of any fields. Choose the Official ID field as the table's primary key. Import the data into a new table named **Officials**. Do not save the import steps.

Create a relationship between the primary Clubs table and the related Officials table, using the Club Code field. Choose the option to enforce referential integrity. Save the Relationships window.

Use the Simple Query Wizard to create a query that includes the Club Code and Club Name fields from the Clubs table and the First Name, Last Name, and Position fields from the Officials table. Use the query name **Club Officials**.

Export the data in the Club Officials query to an Excel workbook named **Club Officials.xlsx** in the Lesson6 folder.

You created a new database and imported data from a text file and a workbook into the database to create two new tables. You related the tables using a common field, and then you created a query that includes data from both tables. Finally, you exported the data in the query to an Excel workbook.

How could you continue improving the database that you created? (*Hint:* Think about the fields in the tables and their data types and field properties.) When other swim teams need to add officials to the database, what advice would you give them about sending their data to you? (*Hint:* Consider the rules you learned about importing data into existing tables.)

Close the database and exit Access.

INTRODUCTORY MICROSOFT ACCESS

REVIEW *Questions*

TRUE/FALSE

Circle T if the statement is true or F if the statement is false.

T   F   1. A database is a collection of objects that store, retrieve, display, and summarize data.

T   F   2. A field's data type identifies the type of data that a field can store.

T   F   3. A query must contain a condition.

T   F   4. Forms are always based on tables.

T   F   5. The data in a report is read-only.

WRITTEN QUESTIONS

Write a brief answer to each of the following questions.

1. What data type would you choose for a field that stores alphanumeric data?

2. What field property do you use to change the number of characters that can be stored in a Text field?

3. What is a filter?

4. Describe how to delete a record using a form.

5. Define the term *comma-separated values* and explain how a CSV file is used when importing data into an Access database.

PROJECTS

 PROJECT 1

1. Open the **Favorites.accdb** database from the Data Files.

2. Open the **Stores** table in Design view.

3. Move the Hours field between the Specialty and Credit Cards fields.

4. Insert a field between the Hours and Credit Cards fields. Use the field name **Last Visit** and assign the field the Date/Time data type. Change the field's Format property to Short Date.

5. Change the Field Size property for the Specialty field to **30**.

6. Change the data type of the Credit Cards field to Yes/No.

7. Change the Required field property for the Name field to Yes.

8. Set the Store ID field so it is the table's primary key.

9. Save the table, change to Datasheet view, then resize the columns in the datasheet to best fit.

10. Enter today's date in the Last Visit field for the Electronics Plus record.

11. Change the Specialty field value for the Electronics Plus record to your first and last names.

12. Preview the datasheet, then print it in landscape orientation.

13. Compact and repair the database.

14. Close the database, then exit Access.

PROJECT 2

1. Open the **Dining.accdb** database from the Data Files.

2. Open the **Restaurants** table in Design view.

3. Change the Restaurant ID field so it is the table's primary key.

4. Change the Field Size property for the Name field to **30**, and change its Required property to Yes.

5. Change the Format property of the Last Visit field to Short Date.

6. Change the data type of the Reservations field to Yes/No.

7. Change the data type of the Meal Cost field to Currency.

8. Save the table, then change to Datasheet view.

9. In Datasheet view, change the Format property for the Last Visit field to Long Date. Resize the Last Visit column to best fit.

10. Preview the datasheet, print it in landscape orientation, then save and close the table.

11. Compact and repair the database.

12. Close the database, then exit Access.

 **PROJECT 3**

1. Open the **Personnel.accdb** database from the Data Files.

2. In the Relationships window, create a relationship using the Employee ID field in the primary Employees table and the Employee ID field in the related Personal Data table. Choose the option to enforce referential integrity. Save your changes, then close the Relationships window.

3. Use the Simple Query Wizard to create a query based on the Employees and Personal Data tables. Include the following fields in the order listed from the Employees table in the query: Employee ID, First Name, and Last Name. Include the following fields in the order listed from the Personal Data table in the query: Title, Department, Date of Birth, and Salary.

4. Choose the option to create a detail query and use the query name **Employee Data**.

5. In the query datasheet, sort the records from smallest to largest using the Salary field.

6. Filter the records so that only those employees working in the Marketing department are displayed.

7. Use the Total row to calculate the average salary for employees working in the Marketing department.

8. In the record with Employee ID 1007, change the First Name and Last Name field values to your first and last names.

9. Preview and print the Employee Data query in landscape orientation, then save and close the Employee Data query.

10. In Query Design view, create a new query using the Employees and Personal Data tables. Add the Employee ID, First Name, and Last Name fields from the Employees table to the query design. Then add the Salary field from the Personal Data table to the query design.

11. Use a condition to select the records for only those employees with salaries greater than $2,000.

12. Save the query as **High Salaries**, then run the query.

13. In the record with Employee ID 1099, change the First Name and Last Name field values to your first and last names.

14. Preview and print the High Salaries query, then close the High Salaries query.

15. Compact and repair the database.

16. Close the database, then exit Access.

 PROJECT 4

1. Open the **Meals.accdb** database from the Data Files.

2. Use the Form tool to create a form based on the Restaurants table.

3. Resize the width of the text boxes in the control layout in the form to 17 characters.

4. Apply the Flow AutoFormat to the form.

5. Change the form title to **My Favorite Restaurants**.

6. Delete the picture from the top-left corner of the form.

7. Change to Form view and delete the record with the Restaurant ID SAL2.

8. Display the record with the Restaurant ID TON1 in the form. Change the Name field value to your first and last names. Print the form for this record only.

9. Save the form using the name **My Favorite Restaurants**.

10. Close the form, close the database, then exit Access.

 PROJECT 5

1. Open the **Price.accdb** database from the Data Files.

2. Use the Report Wizard to create a report based on the Products table. Include all fields in the report.

3. Group the report by Category and sort the records in ascending order based on the Retail Price field.

4. Choose the Block layout and Landscape orientation.

5. Choose the Office style.

6. Change the report title to **Products by Category**, then choose the option to preview the report.

7. Change to Layout view. Resize each column to best fit the data it contains. Be sure to scroll down the page to check and make sure that the field values in each column are completely visible.

8. Change to Design view and move the text box control that contains the page number to the left, so its right edge is at the 8-inch mark on the horizontal ruler.

9. Open the property sheet for the report, then change the report's Width property to **9** (inches).

10. Save the report, preview the report, then print it.

11. Close the report, close the database, then exit Access.

SIMULATION

You work at the Java Internet Café, which has been open for a few months. The café serves coffee and pastries and offers clients the opportunity to use one of the café's computers to gain Internet access. Seven computers are set up on tables in quiet areas of the café. The café has many regular customers who grab a cup of coffee and a pastry in the mornings and then use one of the computers to browse the Internet before going to work or school.

The café charges a $10 monthly fee for Internet service. All membership fees for March were due on March 1. A few members have not paid their monthly fees. Your manager asks you to send out a reminder letter to customers with outstanding balances.

JOB 1

1. Open the **Java.accdb** database from the Data Files.

2. Open the **Members** table in Datasheet view.

3. Scott Payton just paid his membership fee for March. Update his record to show his $10 payment.

4. The café has a new member who paid her dues for April. Use Figure 1 to add the record for Halie Shook to the Members table.

FIGURE UR-1

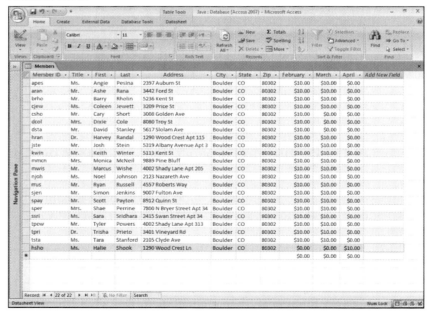

5. Close the Members table.

6. Merge the records in the Members table with the **Reminder.docx** letter from the Data Files.

7. Edit the recipient list so letters are merged only for those clients who have not paid their dues for March. (Use a filter to select records for members who have March field values of zero [0].) Use the Mail Merge Recipients dialog box to remove Halie Shook from the recipient list (she was not a member in March and should not receive a letter).

8. On the second line below the date field, add an address block.

9. On the second line below the address block you just inserted, add a greeting line in the format *Dear Mr. Stanley* followed by a comma.

10. Preview the merged letters.

11. Change the manager's name (Trace Green) in the closing to your first and last names. Exclude the first and second recipients and print the third recipient's letter only.

12. Save the document and close Word.

13. Close the database, then exit Access.

 JOB 2

You need to create mailing labels so you can mail the member statements for April.

1. Open the **Java.accdb** database from the Data Files.

2. Use the Label Wizard to create mailing labels for the Members table.

3. Use the Avery C2160 label and accept the default font settings. Add the Title, First, and Last fields on the first line of the label, separated by spaces; add the Address field on the second line of the label; and the City, State, and Zip fields on the last line of the label. There should be a comma and space between the City and State fields and a space between the State and Zip fields.

4. Save the report as **Labels Members**, then preview it.

5. Close the report, close the database, and exit Access.

MICROSOFT POWERPOINT

Unit

Estimated Time for Unit: 7 hours

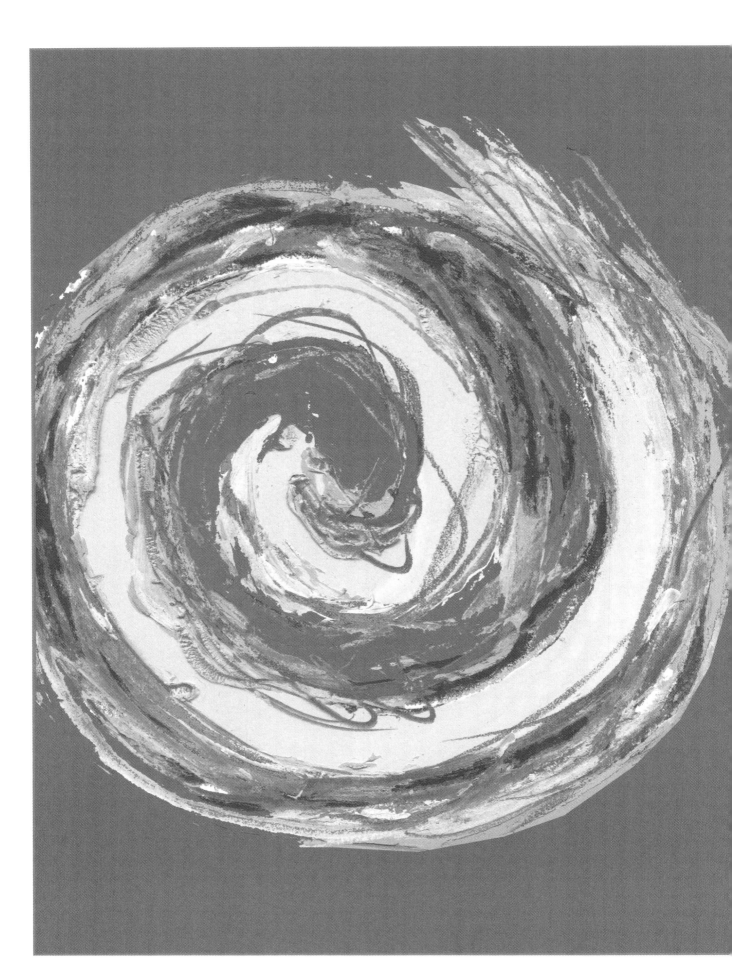

POWERPOINT BASICS

OBJECTIVES

Upon completion of this lesson, you will be able to:

- Start PowerPoint.
- Understand the elements of the PowerPoint window.
- Open an existing presentation.
- Save a presentation.
- Navigate through a presentation.
- Change views.
- Use the Slides and Outline tabs.
- Use the Ribbon.
- Use the Slide pane and Notes pane.
- Change the layout.
- Delete a slide.
- Print a presentation.
- Exit PowerPoint.

Estimated Time: 1.5 hours

VOCABULARY

Animation
Layout
Live Preview
Microsoft Office Button
Normal view
Notes Page view
Outline tab
PowerPoint presentation
Publishing
Quick Access Toolbar
Ribbon
Slide layout
Slide pane
Slide Show view
Slide Sorter view
Slides tab
Status bar
Tab
Task pane
Thumbnails
Title bar
Transition
Zoom Slider

Introduction to PowerPoint

PowerPoint is a Microsoft Office application that can help you create a professional, computerized slide show presentation. Microsoft Office PowerPoint 2007 can illustrate your ideas, using slides, outlines, speaker's notes, and audience handouts. A presentation can include text, drawn graphics, clip art, photographs, tables, and charts. Presentations can also include features such as Flash animation files, animated clip art, links to Web sites, sound, or movie clips.

PowerPoint presentations are viewed using a computer and monitor. Presentations are usually shown to an audience using a projector on a screen. You can also deliver a PowerPoint presentation by publishing it to the Internet. **Publishing** a presentation to a Web server gives others access to your presentation through a Web browser when they are connected to the Internet at their convenience.

Microsoft Office PowerPoint 2007 provides features, such as SmartArt graphics, themes, templates, and Quick Styles, that help make creating a presentation easier. This lesson introduces you to some of the features available in PowerPoint 2007.

Starting PowerPoint

Like other Office applications, you start PowerPoint by clicking the Start button, clicking All Programs, clicking Microsoft Office, and then clicking Microsoft Office PowerPoint 2007. If the Microsoft PowerPoint icon is on the desktop, you can double-click it to start PowerPoint rather than locating the command on the All Programs menu. The PowerPoint program opens, as shown in Figure 1-1.

FIGURE 1-1
The PowerPoint window

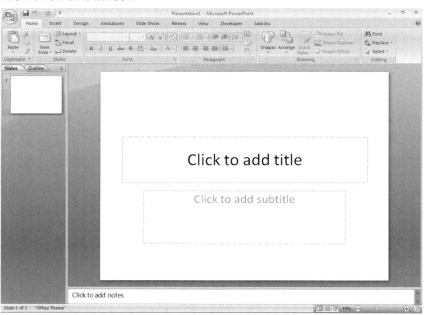

STEP-BY-STEP 1.1

1. Click the **Start** button on the taskbar to open the Start menu.

2. Click **All Programs**, click **Microsoft Office**, and then click **Microsoft Office PowerPoint 2007**.

3. The PowerPoint window opens. A new blank slide is in the PowerPoint window. The new blank slide is a blank title slide. You will review the program window that is on the screen in the next Step-by-Step.

Did You Know?

The first slide in a presentation is the title slide. Just as when you create a report, you have a title page. The title slide introduces the presentation to your audience.

Reviewing the PowerPoint Window

The PowerPoint window shares several common elements and tools with other Office applications. PowerPoint also has several views that you will learn about. You work with these elements and tools in the different views to create presentations. Refer to Figure 1-2, which shows a simple presentation with two slides and identifies the elements in Normal view.

FIGURE 1-2
Normal view

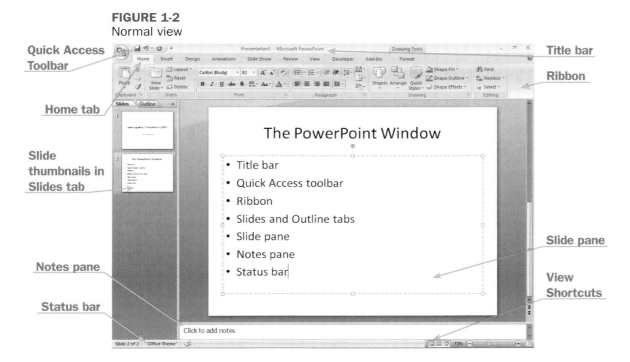

The **title bar**, at the top of the window, identifies the window as a PowerPoint window and lists the name of the open presentation. For a new presentation, the name is simply Presentation until you give it a name when you save the file. The title bar also includes the control buttons for restoring, maximizing, minimizing, or closing the window.

The Microsoft Office Button and the Quick Access Toolbar are on the left side of the title bar. The **Microsoft Office Button** opens the Office menu, which has commands common to all Office applications, such as New, Save, and Print. The **Quick Access Toolbar** has buttons for frequently used commands. You can add or remove buttons on the Quick Access Toolbar.

The **Ribbon** is the graphic collection of command buttons that are organized by tabs and in groups. The Home tab is the default tab on the Ribbon and includes many of the commands you will use most often when creating the slides.

The work area is divided into three panes: the Slides tab, the Outline tab, and the Slide pane. The Slides tab and the Outline tab contain **thumbnails** or small images of the selected slide that you are working on. The **Slides tab** shows the graphics on the slides; the **Outline tab** shows the text or words on the slides. The main section of the window, the Slide pane, is where you do most of the work to put text and graphics on the slide. Beneath the Slide pane is the Notes pane where you enter speaker notes that you can use while delivering the presentation to an audience. For some tasks, such as inserting clip art and animations, a **task pane** opens on the right side of the Slide pane.

The status bar appears at the bottom of your screen. The area on the left side of the status bar shows which slide is displayed in the Slide pane and tells you the total number of slides in the presentation. The next area indicates the theme currently in use. The center section is used to indicate various options, such as signatures, language options, permissions, and tracking. These options can be customized by right-clicking the status bar. The View Shortcuts buttons are buttons that you click to change between Normal, Slide Sorter, and Slide Show view. The Zoom Slider adjusts the zoom percentage of the window. The Fit slide to current window button is useful for quickly adjusting the selected slide to best fit in the current window.

S TEP-BY-STEP 1.2

1. On the Ribbon, click the **Insert** tab to view the different commands. You can see that the buttons have images to show what each button does. The buttons are organized into the Tables, Illustrations, Links, Text, and Media Clips groups.

2. On the Ribbon, click the **View** tab to view the different commands. PowerPoint has several views that you will learn about as you learn to create presentations.

3. On the Ribbon, click the **Design** tab to view the different commands. Themes are very decorative. You can see how the Theme buttons will help you create exciting presentations.

4. On the status bar, click the **Zoom In** button two times, and then click the **Zoom Out** button as many times as necessary so the Zoom percentage is 40%. See Figure 1-3.

FIGURE 1-3
Zooming in and out

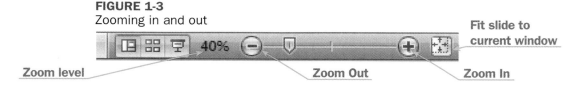

Fit slide to current window

Zoom level   Zoom Out   Zoom In

5. On the status bar, click the **Fit slide to current window** button.

Opening and Viewing an Existing Presentation

When you want to open an existing presentation that you have recently viewed, you can choose the presentation from the Recent Documents list. You can view the Recent Documents list by clicking the Microsoft Office Button. If the presentation is not on that list, click Open on the Office menu, and then locate the file name for the presentation in the Open dialog box. The Open dialog box is shown in Figure 1-4. The files and folders will differ for each computer system.

FIGURE 1-4
Open dialog box

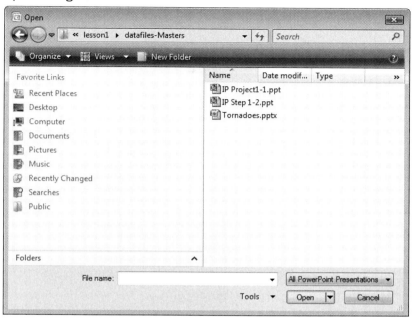

Click the presentation you want to open, and then click the Open button. The presentation you selected appears on the screen in the PowerPoint window. To view the presentation as a slide show, click the Slide Show button on the status bar. You can also click the View tab on the Ribbon, and then, in the Presentation Views group, click the Slide Show button. The presentation opens on the screen, and you can view it as it would appear if you were presenting it. You can press the right arrow key or the spacebar on the keyboard to advance the slides and the left arrow key to review a previous slide. You can also click the mouse button to advance a slide.

A slide show is a series of slides. Transition refers to the way each new slide appears on the screen. You can select from many exciting transition effects, such as checkerboards, swirls, dissolves, wipes, and cuts, to make your slide show fun to watch.

You can animate objects on a slide. Animation is text, objects, graphics, or pictures that have motion. You can set up a slide to advance automatically through the animation or to pause and allow users to start the animation effect manually when it is most convenient. When giving a presentation, you may find it necessary to speak further about a particular point on a slide. PowerPoint allows you to delay the animation on a slide by not starting the animation until you click your mouse or press the right arrow key or spacebar.

As you view the presentation in Step-by-Step 1.3, you can press the right arrow key to advance to the next animation or slide.

STEP-BY-STEP 1.3

1. Click the **Microsoft Office Button** and then click **Open**.

2. In the Open dialog box, locate the drive and folder where you have stored the Data Files for this course, click **Tornadoes.pptx**, and then click **Open**. The presentation file appears, as shown in Figure 1-5. The title slide is in the Slide pane. This slide uses several interesting elements, including animation, sound, and movies.

FIGURE 1-5
Tornadoes presentation

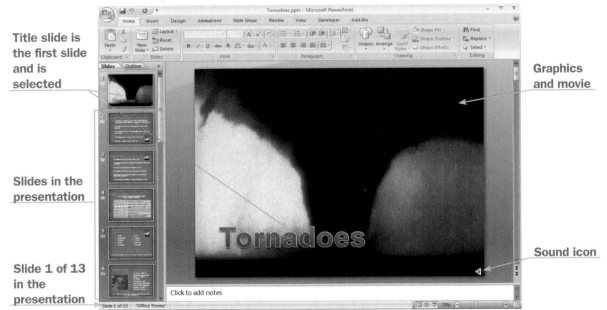

Title slide is the first slide and is selected

Slides in the presentation

Slide 1 of 13 in the presentation

Graphics and movie

Sound icon

3. On the status bar, click the **Slide Show** button. The title slide fills the screen, as shown in Figure 1-6. A movie of a tornado appears on the screen, and the word Tornadoes becomes animated. If your computer has a sound card and speakers, you should also hear a thunderstorm.

FIGURE 1-6
Title slide fills the screen

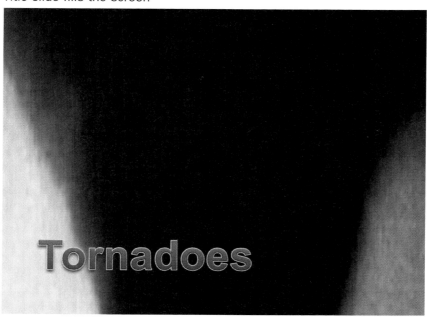

4. Click the mouse to advance to the next slide. Notice that the text animation on the slide advances automatically.

5. Click the mouse again to advance to the next slide. The title of this slide appears automatically. The slide show is set up to advance automatically, or when you click the mouse.

6. Continue to click the mouse to advance the slides. As each slide in the presentation continues, notice the different examples of animation. Some slides include pictures. Some pictures are animated. The next to last slide includes several hyperlinks. If your computer is connected to the Internet, you can click a link to open the Web site in the default browser.

7. The presentation ends with a black slide. The black slide lets you know the slide show is over. Click the mouse to return to Normal view. Leave the presentation open for the next Step-by-Step.

Saving a Presentation

 To save a new presentation the first time, you use the Save As command. You can also use the Save As command to give an existing presentation a new name. If the presentation does not have a name, click the Save button on the Quick Access Toolbar to open the Save As dialog box, as shown in Figure 1-7. You can open the Save As dialog box by clicking the Microsoft Office Button on the Quick Access Toolbar and then clicking Save As. In the Save As dialog box, click the Folders or Favorite Links to find the drive and folder where you will save your presentation. Click in the File name text box to select the default name, such as Presenation1, type a new file name, and then click Save.

FIGURE 1-7
Save As dialog box

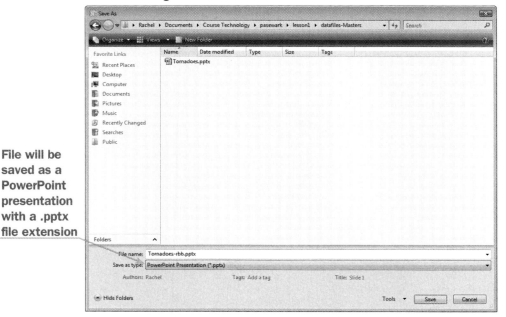

File will be
saved as a
PowerPoint
presentation
with a .pptx
file extension

The next time you want to save changes to your presentation, click the Save button on the Quick Access Toolbar or press the Ctrl+S keys. These commands update the file without opening the dialog box.

> **Computer Concepts**
>
> To save a presentation as an HTML file that can be viewed using a Web browser, click the Save as type arrow in the Save As dialog box, then click Web Page from the list of types. You can add a tag and a title to the Web page from within the dialog box.

S TEP-BY-STEP 1.4

1. Click the **Microsoft Office Button** and then click **Save As**. The Save As dialog box opens.

2. Click the **Folders** list in the left pane and locate the folder where you want to save the presentation.

3. In the File name box, type **Tornado Report**, followed by your initials.

4. Click **Save**. Leave the presentation open for the next Step-by-Step.

Changing Views

Y ou can view a presentation four different ways, using buttons found in the Presentation Views group of the View tab on the Ribbon: Normal, Slide Sorter, Notes Page, and Slide Show. (See Figure 1-8.) You can also change to Slide Sorter view, Normal view, or Slide Show view quickly by clicking one of the View Shortcut buttons on the status bar, shown in Figure 1-9.

FIGURE 1-8
Presentation Views group

FIGURE 1-9
View Shortcuts

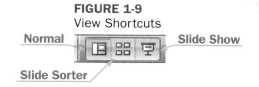

Normal View

You do most work creating slides in Normal view. This view can have up to four panes: the Slides tab and Outline tab, the Slide pane, the Notes pane, and the Task pane.

> **Did You Know?**
>
> Click and drag the pane borders to adjust the size of the different panes.

Using the Slides Tab and Outline Tab

When you are working with the slides in a presentation, PowerPoint displays all the slides in a pane on the left side of your screen. This pane has two tabs at the top, the Outline tab and the Slides tab. The Outline tab displays all the text on your slides in outline form. The Slides tab displays your slides as small pictures or thumbnails. See Figure 1-10. This pane lets you see the order of your slides and gives you a quick overview of the slides. It's a good way to see which slides come before and after other slides. Depending on the Zoom factor, you will see more slides (with smaller thumbnails) or less slides (with larger thumbnails). To switch between these modes, click the Slides tab or the Outline tab.

> **Did You Know?**
>
> You can also press the Page Down key to view the next slide or press Page Up to view the previous slide in any view.

FIGURE 1-10
Slides Tab

To select any slide in a presentation, click the thumbnail in the Slides tab or click the text in the Outline tab. You can use the Outline tab to add or edit text on the slide.

> **Did You Know?**
>
> While the Slides tab can show you several slides as thumbnails at one time, Slide Sorter view gives you an overview of all the slides in a presentation.

You can reorder slides by dragging the thumbnail in the Slides or Outline tab. You can close the pane by clicking the Close button in the upper-right corner of the pane. Click the Normal button on the status bar to restore this pane.

S TEP-BY-STEP 1.5

1. If it is not already selected, click the **Outline** tab.

2. Use the scroll bar to scroll down to select **slide 8**.

STEP-BY-STEP 1.5 Continued

3. Double-click **75,000** to select the number in the second bullet point in the Outline tab, type **93,000**, then press the **spacebar**. Notice the number also changes on the slide in the Slide pane.

4. Click the **Slides** tab. Leave the presentation on the screen for the next Step-by-Step.

Using the Ribbon

The Ribbon on the top of the screen contains commands for the various tasks you will use when creating presentations. It is located conveniently so you can use the commands while still working on your slides. The Home tab contains the most common commands. All commands are grouped to help you easily find the feature you need at any time. When clicked, some buttons open galleries. A gallery shows you thumbnails of the theme or effect that will be applied. For example, on the Ribbon, you can click the Design tab to view themes. You can then click the More button in the Themes group to see all the thumbnails, as shown in Figure 1-11. The Live Preview feature lets you see the effect before you apply it in your presentation. If you select a slide, you can see how the theme will change the slide as you move the mouse over each thumbnail.

FIGURE 1-11
Themes gallery

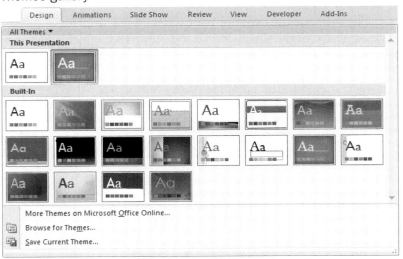

STEP-BY-STEP 1.6

1. On the Ribbon, click the **Design** tab, and then click **slide 3** in the Slides tab.

2. On the Design tab, in the Themes group, slowly move the pointer over each of the **Theme thumbnails** to preview the different theme effects on the slide.

Extra for Experts

On the Ribbon, on the Design tab, in the Themes group, click the More button to open the Themes gallery and try out more themes for the slides.

STEP-BY-STEP 1.6 Continued

3. In the Themes group, click the **Colors** button to open the Built-in Theme Colors gallery, and then slowly move the pointer over each of the Color Themes thumbnails to preview the different color theme effects on the slide.

4. In the Themes group, click the **Fonts** button to open the Built-in Fonts gallery, and then slowly move the pointer over each of the Font Themes thumbnails to preview the different font effects on the slide.

5. On the Ribbon, click the **Home** tab. Leave the presentation on the screen for the next Step-by-Step.

> **Extra for Experts**
>
> You can apply a theme or font to one slide or to all the slides. Right-click any theme and then click the appropriate command.

Using the Slide Pane

The Slide pane is the workbench for PowerPoint presentations. It displays one slide at a time and is useful for adding and editing text, inserting and formatting illustrations or objects, or generally modifying a slide's appearance. The Slide pane displays your slides in an area large enough for you to easily work on a slide. You can select the slide to view in the slide pane by clicking the thumbnail in the Slides tab, by scrolling the Slide pane, or by pressing the Page Up or Page Down keys on the keyboard.

If you drag and select text, then move the mouse back over the selected text, the Mini toolbar appears. The Mini toolbar has buttons for common formatting commands, such as font color, font style, font size, text alignment, and styling. Although buttons for these commands also appear in the Font group on the Ribbon, it is sometimes quicker to use the Mini toolbar. See Figure 1-12.

FIGURE 1-12
The Mini toolbar

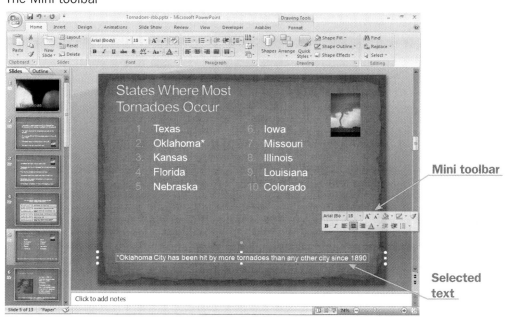

STEP-BY-STEP 1.7

1. Click **slide 5** in the Slides tab.

2. Drag to select the text **Oklahoma City has been hit by more tornadoes than any other city since 1890** in the text box.

3. Move the mouse so the Mini toolbar appears, click the **Font Color** button arrow, and then click the **Orange, Accent 2** color box in the first row in the Theme Colors section. The text is formatted for the new color.

4. Leave the presentation on the screen for the next Step-by-Step.

Inserting a New Slide with a New Slide Layout

The slide layout is how objects are placed on a slide. Objects are text, graphics, illustrations, tables, and charts. When you create a slide, you determine the layout. The default layout includes placeholders for different objects on a slide. There are placeholders for slide titles, text, and content. When you insert a new slide, you can select the layout. You can also change the layout for a slide that already has content. On the Home tab, in the Slides group, click the Layout button to view the different default layouts. See Figure 1-13.

FIGURE 1-13
Default layouts

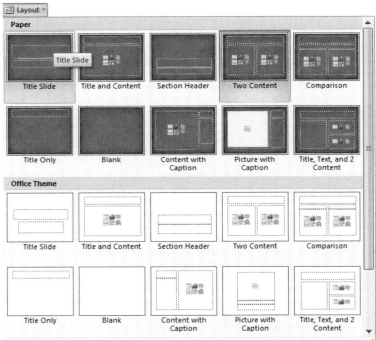

The layout placeholders are on the new slide. The Title and Content layout provides two placeholders, one for a title and one for content. Content can be text or any object. You click the placeholder and begin to type text, or you can click any one of the content icons to add an object. You will learn how to add text and content to slides in the next lesson.

STEP-BY-STEP 1.8

1. Use the scroll bar to scroll, and then click **slide 7** in the Slides tab.

2. On the Ribbon, on the Home tab, in the Slides group, click the lower part of the **New Slide** button. A gallery of layouts for the new slide opens.

3. Click the **Title and Content** thumbnail on the Layout gallery. You added a new slide with the Title and Content layout to the presentation.

4. Leave the presentation on the screen for the next Step-by-Step.

> **Did You Know?**
>
> The Theme used in this presentation is Paper; the layouts are for the Paper theme.

Notes Page View

The Notes Page view displays your slides on the top portion of the page, with any speaker notes that have been entered for each slide appearing in the Notes pane on the bottom of the page. You can use these notes to help you as you make a presentation. Notes are also helpful if you print a handout for your audience to guide them through your presentation. To add speaker notes, click in the Notes pane and begin typing. You can enter notes in Notes Page view. On the Ribbon, click the View tab, in the Presentation Views group, click the Notes Page button, then click in the Click to add text placeholder. You will learn more about the Notes pane and how to use it effectively in Lesson 2.

Using Slide Sorter View

Slide Sorter view, as shown in Figure 1-14, displays thumbnails of the slides on the screen so that you can move and arrange slides easily by clicking and dragging. Slide Sorter view gives you an overview of the entire presentation. You use Slide Sorter view to set slide timings, transitions, and animations. To switch to Slide Sorter view, on the status bar, click the View Shortcuts Slide Sorter button. You can also click the Slide Sorter button on the View tab in the Presentation Views group.

STEP-BY-STEP 1.9

1. Click the **Slide Sorter View** button. The screen appears, as shown in Figure 1-14.

FIGURE 1-14
Slide Sorter view

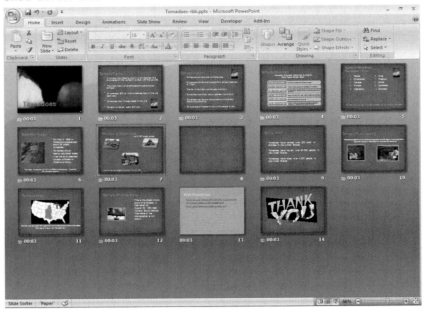

2. Click **slide 11** so that it is selected and outlined in gold.

3. Drag **slide 11** between slide 5 and slide 6. A line appears between the two slides. Release the mouse button. Slide 11 moves to become slide 6, and all other slides are moved forward and renumbered.

4. Click **slide 1**.

5. Leave the presentation on the screen for the next Step-by-Step.

Using Slide Show View

In Slide Show view, you run your presentation on the computer as if it were a slide projector to preview how it will look to your audience. When you run the slide show, each slide fills the screen. Any animations, sounds, and videos will play in Slide Show view. To switch to this view, on the Ribbon, click the Slide Show button in the Presentation Views group, or click the Slide Show button on the status bar, or press F5.

If you move the mouse to the lower-left corner of the screen as the slide show runs, a Slide Show menu appears. This menu, which has four buttons, helps you control the slide show. Table 1-1 describes the menu. You can also right-click any slide to open the shortcut menu, which includes the same commands. See Figure 1-15.

FIGURE 1-15
Slide show shortcut menu

TABLE 1-1
Slide Show menu

BUTTON	COMMAND ON SHORTCUT MENU	DESCRIPTION	NOTES
➡	Next	Advances to the next slide	
⬅	Previous	Displays the previous slide	
	Pointer Options	Allow you to annotate a slide	Options include Ballpoint pen, Felt tip pen, Highlighter, Arrow and Arrow options for Automatic, hidden, and visible
▤		Displays the shortcut menu	
	Screen	Changes screen	Can display a black or white screen or switch to another open program
	Go to Slide	Displays a list of all slides in the presentation	Click to advance to any specific slide in the presentation

STEP-BY-STEP 1.10

1. Click the **Slide Show** button on the status bar. Slide 1 appears on the screen.

2. Click the **mouse** to advance through all the slides. Once you've advanced through all the slides, a black screen displays.

3. Click to exit the presentation and return to the PowerPoint Slide Sorter view window.

4. Save the presentation and leave it open for the next Step-by-Step.

Did You Know?

You can press the Esc key any-time during a presentation to return to the view displayed prior to viewing the show.

Deleting Slides

 If you decide that a slide does not fit your presentation, you can easily delete it. In Normal view, with the particular slide displayed, press the Delete key on the keyboard. You can also delete a slide, using the Ribbon, on the Home tab, in the Slides group, by clicking the Delete button. If you accidentally delete the wrong slide, immediately click the Undo Delete Slide button on the Quick Access Toolbar to restore the slide.

Extra for Experts

If you make a mistake while using an Office program, you can press Ctrl+Z to undo the last entry. By default, you can undo up to 20 entries in PowerPoint. You can change the number of actions you can undo by changing the PowerPoint Options. Click the Microsoft Office Button, click PowerPoint Options, click Advanced in the left pane, then change the number in the Maximum number of undos box as needed. See Figure 1-16. Note, more undos requires more memory on your computer.

FIGURE 1-16
PowerPoint options

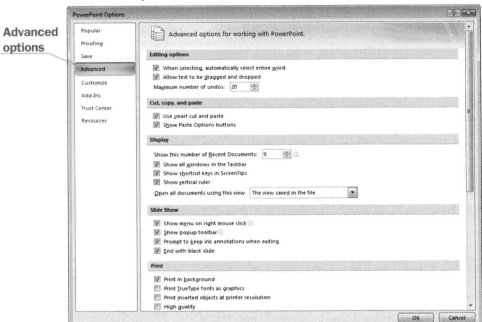

S TEP-BY-STEP 1.11

1. If not already in Slide Sorter view, click the **Slide Sorter** button on the status bar.

2. Click **slide 9**, the new blank slide you inserted in a previous Step-by-Step.

STEP-BY-STEP 1.11 Continued

3. On the Ribbon, on the Home tab, in the Slides group, click the **Delete** button. The slides renumber, and now there are 13 slides in the presentation.

4. Click **slide 1**.

5. Save the presentation and leave it open for the next Step-by-Step.

Printing a Presentation

PowerPoint offers several print options that can enhance your presentation for an audience. You can print handouts that contain small pictures or thumbnails of your slides, along with an area for taking notes. Click the Microsoft Office Button, then click Print to open the Print dialog box, as shown in Figure 1-17. You can choose to print your presentation as slides using the Slides option, with notes using the Notes Pages option, or as an outline using the Outline View option. Using the Handouts option, you can print handouts with two, three, four, six, or nine slides per page and choose whether they are ordered horizontally or vertically.

FIGURE 1-17
Print dialog box

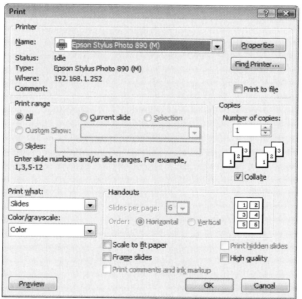

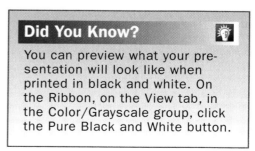

Did You Know?

You can preview what your presentation will look like when printed in black and white. On the Ribbon, on the View tab, in the Color/Grayscale group, click the Pure Black and White button.

You can choose to print all the slides, only the current slide, or any combination of slides in your presentation. If you aren't printing your presentation in color, you can choose either the Grayscale or Pure black-and-white option. To make sure the slides print on the page correctly, there is a Scale to fit paper option. With the Frame slides option, you can choose whether the border of the slides appears when printed.

Did You Know?

You do not have to switch views in order to print a view different from the one you are currently using. Instead, you can select the view you want to print from the Print dialog box.

STEP-BY-STEP 1.12

1. Click the **Microsoft Office Button** and then click **Print**. The Print dialog box opens. (Refer to Figure 1-17.)

2. In the Print range section, click the **Current slide** option button.

3. Click the **Print what** arrow, then click **Slides**, if it is not already selected.

4. Click the **Preview** button. The slide appears in the Print Preview tab window, as it would if you printed it.

5. To help distinguish your work from your classmates, enter your name in the presentation. On the Preview Ribbon, in the Print group on the Print Preview tab click the **Options** button, click **Header and Footer**, click the **Footer check box**, type your name, click the **Notes and Handouts tab**, click the **Footer check box**, type your name, and then click **Apply to All**.

6. Click the **Print** button, and then click **OK** in the Print dialog box to print the slide.

7. Click the **Microsoft Office Button** and then click **Print** to open the Print dialog box again, click the **Print what** arrow, and then click **Outline View**.

8. Click the **Scale to fit paper** check box.

9. Click the **Preview** button. The slide appears in the Print Preview tab window as an outline, as it would if you printed it.

10. Click **Print**, then click **OK**. The presentation prints as an outline on one page.

11. Open the Print dialog box again, click the **Print what** arrow, and then click **Handouts**.

12. In the Handouts section, click the **Slides per page** down arrow, and then click **9**.

13. In the Handouts Order section, click the **Horizontal** option button, if it is not already selected.

14. Click the **Preview** button. The slide appears in the Print Preview tab window, as it would if you printed it.

15. Click the **Print button** on the Print Preview tab, then click **OK**. The presentation prints as a handout.

16. Leave the presentation open for the next Step-by-Step.

Closing a Presentation and Exiting PowerPoint

When you want to close a presentation, click the Microsoft Office Button, then click Close on the Office menu, or click the presentation window Close button. To exit PowerPoint, click the Microsoft Office Button, then click Exit PowerPoint. You can also click the Close button in the upper-right corner of the title bar in the program window. If there are any unsaved changes to a presentation you have been working on, you will be asked if you want to save them before exiting.

STEP-BY-STEP 1.13

1. Click the **Microsoft Office Button** and then click **Close** on the Office menu to close the presentation.

2. Click **Yes** if prompted to save your changes.

3. Click the **Close** button in the upper-right corner of the program window to exit PowerPoint.

SUMMARY

In this lesson, you learned:

■ PowerPoint is an Office application that can help you create a professional presentation. When you start PowerPoint, you have the choice of opening an existing presentation or creating a new one.

■ You can view your presentation in four different ways: Normal view, Slide Sorter view, Slide Show view, and Notes Page view. Each view has its own advantages.

■ You can insert slides, add text and objects to slides, and delete slides as you work to create the presentation.

■ Using the Print dialog box, you can print your presentation as slides using the Slides option, with notes using the Notes Pages option, or as an outline using the Outline View option. You can also choose to print handouts with two, three, four, six, or nine slides per page.

■ To exit PowerPoint, click the Microsoft Office Button, and then click Exit PowerPoint.

VOCABULARY *Review*

Define the following terms:

Animation	Publishing	Status bar
Layout	Quick Access Toolbar	Tab
Live Preview	Ribbon	Task pane
Microsoft Office Button	Slide layout	Thumbnails
Normal view	Slide pane	Title bar
Notes Page view	Slide Show view	Transition
Outline tab	Slide Sorter view	Zoom Slider
PowerPoint presentation	Slides tab	

REVIEW *Questions*

MULTIPLE CHOICE

Select the best response for the following statements.

1. When you start PowerPoint, the first slide you see is the _____ slide.
   A. Animation
   B. Title
   C. Main
   D. Slide Sorter

2. In which pane do you do most of the work creating and building slides?
   A. Slide
   B. Standard
   C. Notes
   D. Outline

3. Which of the following is not one of the presentation views?
   A. Outline
   B. Notes Page
   C. Slide Show
   D. Slide Sorter

4. How do you delete a selected slide?
   A. Click the Delete Slide button.
   B. Click the Erase Slide button.
   C. Click the New Slide button.
   D. Click the Zoom Out button.

5. Which option in the Print dialog box lets you print the slides with notes for your audience?
   A. Grayscale
   B. Handouts
   C. Scale to fit
   D. Frame slides

FILL IN THE BLANK

Complete the following sentences by writing the correct word or words in the blanks provided.

1. The _____ appears when you select text, using the mouse, and has buttons you can click to format the text.

2. When you view a presentation in _____ view, the slides fill the screen.

3. The _____ tab in Normal view displays all of the text on your slides in outline form.

4. _____ view displays miniature versions of the slides on the screen so that you can move and arrange slides easily by dragging.

5. You can print _____ that contain small pictures or thumbnails of your slides.

PROJECTS

PROJECT 1-1

1. Open **Network** from the Data Files.

2. Save the presentation as **Network Summary**, followed by your initials.

3. Run the presentation as a slide show. Click to advance each slide.

4. Leave the presentation open for the next project.

PROJECT 1-2

1. View the presentation in Slide Sorter view.

2. Select and move slide number 6 so that it is the second slide in the presentation.

3. Print the presentation as audience handouts with four slides per page.

4. Run the presentation as a slide show.

5. Save and close the presentation.

PROJECT 1-3

1. Search the Internet for a PowerPoint project about a subject that interests you.

2. Save the project to your computer.

3. Run the presentation as a slide show.

4. Print the presentation as audience handouts with four slides per page.

5. Save and close the presentation.

CRITICAL *Thinking*

 ACTIVITY 1-1

You can change the way that PowerPoint displays when you initially open the program. Start PowerPoint, click the Microsoft Office Button, and then click PowerPoint Options. Review the Popular, Proofing, Save, and Advanced options that are available. Click Cancel to not save any changes.

 ACTIVITY 1-2

It is helpful to plan a presentation before you actually create it on the computer. Sketch out ideas on paper for a presentation on one of the topics below, or make up your own. The presentation should have at least four slides. Include a title slide and indicate where you would put clip art, a video, and animation.

- Help start a community campaign to keep your city clean.

- Encourage people to donate blood in the blood drive campaign next week.

- Explain the procedure for some safety technique (performing CPR, fire prevention, how to baby-proof a house, performing first-aid).

- Offer the opportunity to be involved in a community project or volunteer organization.

- Explain the advantages of adopting an animal from the local shelter.

- Provide information about a new class that will be available in the fall.

CREATING AND ENHANCING POWERPOINT PRESENTATIONS

OBJECTIVES

Upon completion of this lesson, you will be able to:

- Create presentations.
- Insert headers and footers.
- Apply themes.
- Use the Slide master.
- Use the Notes and Handout Master.
- Edit pictures.
- Add slides.
- Find and replace text.
- Add text to slides.
- Add notes to slides.
- Change alignment, spacing, case, and tabs.
- Work with bullets.
- Change font attributes.
- Check spelling, style, and usage.
- Format slides.
- Add clip art and sounds to slides.
- Insert hyperlinks.
- Apply custom animation.
- Apply slide transitions.

Estimated Time: 2 hours

VOCABULARY

Animation

Blank presentation

Design template

Effects Options

Handout Master

Hyperlink

Layout master

Live Preview

Motion Paths

Notes Master

Placeholder

Slide Master

Slide transitions

Creating Presentations

When you start PowerPoint, a new **blank presentation** appears on the screen. You can begin a new presentation from a blank presentation, or you can use any of the several features to help you start to create a new presentation. You can use slides from an existing presentation, or you can use a template or theme. Click the Office Button, and then click Open to open an existing presentation, or click New to open the New Presentation dialog box, as shown in Figure 2-1. Blank Presentation is the first option; however, you can select from Installed Templates, Installed Themes, My Templates, and New from existing. The list of Recently Used Templates contains the template files that were last opened.

FIGURE 2-1
New Presentation dialog box

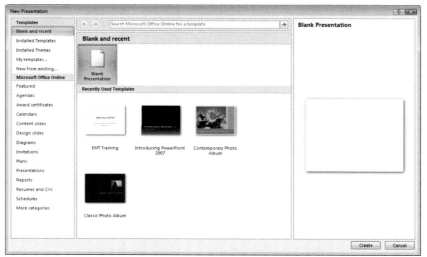

Creating New Presentations

The Blank Presentation option in the New Presentation dialog box lets you create a presentation from scratch, using the layout, format, colors, and styles you prefer. If you decide to create a presentation using the Template option, you can choose a template that is right for the presentation you have planned. The templates that come with PowerPoint are already formatted with certain themes, graphics, colors, fonts, and layouts. The Installed templates are shown in Figure 2-2.

FIGURE 2-2
Installed Templates

Templates installed on this computer

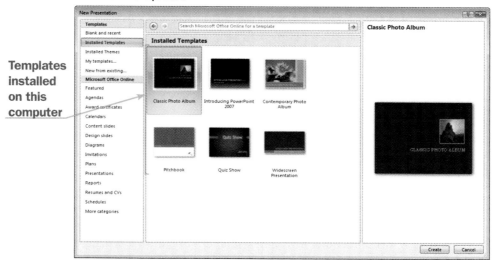

If your computer is connected to the Internet, you can select from professional design templates that are posted on Microsoft Office Online Web site. To choose a template from Microsoft's Web site, click the type of template you would like in the Microsoft Office Online section, and then click any thumbnail in the center pane. The right pane will show a larger thumbnail and give you additional information about the template, including a rating by user votes. Once you find the template you want, click Download, as shown in Figure 2-3.

FIGURE 2-3
Award certificates from Microsoft Office Online

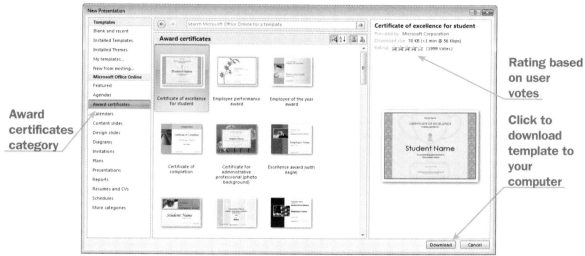

Unless you have a particular reason for creating a presentation from a blank document, it is easier and less time consuming to use a template. You can always modify the presentation as you go along.

If you cannot find a template that you like, you can choose one from another location or download one from the Internet.

S TEP-BY-STEP 2.1

1. Start PowerPoint. Click the **Office Button** and then click **New**. The New Presentation dialog box opens.

2. Click **Installed Templates** in the left pane, and then click **Introducing PowerPoint 2007** in the center pane.

3. Click **Create**.

STEP-BY-STEP 2.1 Continued

A presentation that includes 18 slides, complete with sample content, is created, as shown in Figure 2-4. The text is formatted, and many of the slides include graphics. You can view, edit, and modify this presentation just as you would any presentation. You can add and delete slides as necessary for your purposes.

FIGURE 2-4
New slide show from template

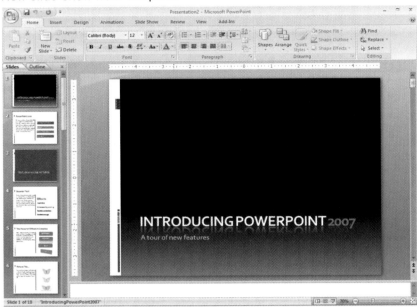

4. On the Quick Access Toolbar, click the **Save** button, and then save the presentation as **PowerPoint2007 Tour**, followed by your initials, to your Data Files.

5. Click the **Slide Show** button on the status bar, and then press the **spacebar** to advance through all of the slides in the presentation.

6. Click the **Office Button**, and then click **Close** to close the presentation. Leave PowerPoint on your screen for the next Step-by-Step.

Creating Presentations from Existing Templates

If you cannot find a template that you like on the Internet or that came with PowerPoint, you can use one created by yourself or a colleague. In the New Presentation dialog box, click My Templates in the left pane to view a list of templates that you have used before and saved. Click New from existing to search for templates that are on the computer.

Did You Know?

Templates have a .potx file extension. PowerPoint presentations have a .pptx file extension.

Inserting Headers and Footers

You can add text to the top or bottom of a slide by inserting a header or footer. You can also add the slide number, date, or time in a header or footer. Click the Insert tab on the Ribbon; in the Text group, click the Header & Footer button. The Header and Footer dialog box has two tabs. You can add headers and footers to the slides or the notes and handouts.

S TEP-BY-STEP 2.2

1. Click the **Office Button** and then click **New**. In the New Presentation dialog box, under the Templates section, click **New from existing**. Locate the folder that has the Data Files for this course, click **EMT Training.potx**, and then click **Create New**.

   EMT Training.potx is a template that was created for you. You created a new presentation from that template. You plan to customize it and use themes to enhance the presentation.

2. On the Quick Access Toolbar, click the **Save** button, and then save the presentation as **EMT Training-Rosewood**, followed by your initials, to the folder where you store your Data Files.

3. On the Ribbon, click the **Insert** tab, and then click the **Header & Footer** button in the Text group to open the Header and Footer dialog box. The Slide tab should be selected, as shown in Figure 2-5.

FIGURE 2-5
Header and Footer dialog box

4. Click the **Footer** check box, and then, in the Footer text box, type **This presentation is not intended as a substitute for professional medical training.**.

STEP-BY-STEP 2.2 Continued

5. Click the **Apply to All** button. On your screen, the footer appears on the title slide of the presentation, as well as all the slides in the presentation. See Figure 2-6.

FIGURE 2-6
Presentation created by using a template

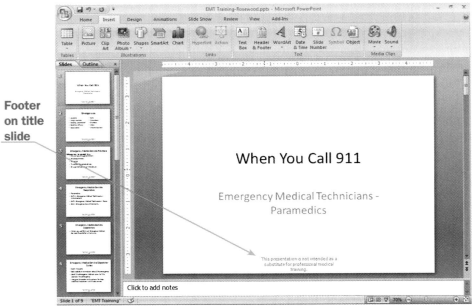

Footer on title slide

6. View the slide show. There are several slides in the presentation, but they do not have color, graphics, or any enhancements that would make a presentation fun and interesting to watch. Leave PowerPoint on your screen for the next Step-by-Step.

Applying Themes

You can use a theme to change the appearance of your slides without changing the content. Themes are predesigned graphic styles that you can apply to existing slides. You can change the color scheme, font, formatting, and layout of your slides to create a different look. You can also begin a new presentation with a theme. Open the New Presentation dialog box, click Installed Themes in the left pane, click the theme you want to use, and then click Create.

Applying Themes to the Entire Presentation

To apply a theme to an existing presentation, click the Design tab on the Ribbon. The Design tab displays all the available themes in the Themes group. When you hover over (place your mouse pointer over an object without clicking) a theme, the name of the theme appears, and the selected slide will show a **Live Preview** of the effect of the theme on the slide. If you right-click the theme thumbnail, the shortcut menu options let you apply the theme to all of the slides in your presentation or to only select slides. There are other options that you can use to set the default theme or add the Gallery to the Quick Access Toolbar. Click Apply to All Slides on the shortcut menu to change all your slides to the new theme.

STEP-BY-STEP 2.3

1. On the Ribbon, click the **Design** tab, and then click the **More** button in the Themes group to open the Themes gallery.

2. Move the mouse pointer over several of the themes to use Live Preview to see the effect on the slides, and then click the **Civic** theme thumbnail. PowerPoint applies the Civic theme to all of the slides in the presentation, as shown in Figure 2-7.

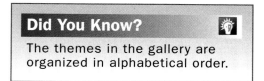

> **Did You Know?**
>
> The themes in the gallery are organized in alphabetical order.

FIGURE 2-7
Civic theme applied

You see that the theme made some changes to formatting that you will have to adjust. For example, the footer no longer fits on the slide.

3. Save the presentation and leave it open for the next Step-by-Step.

Changing Theme Color

The Civic theme, as do all themes, comes with default fonts and colors. You can change the theme fonts and colors at any time. To apply a different color scheme to your presentation, on the Ribbon, click the Design tab; in the Themes group, click the Colors button. You see the list of all colors for each theme, as shown in Figure 2-8. Live Preview is available as you move the mouse pointer over the colors. To apply the different theme colors to all of the slides, click the theme colors. You can apply the colors to specific slides by selecting the slides in the Slides tab. You can select more than one slide by holding down the Ctrl key while clicking the slides. To apply color schemes to only the selected slides, click the Colors button, right-click the Theme colors in the gallery, and then click Apply to Selected Slides on the shortcut menu.

FIGURE 2-8
Built-in Colors gallery

Civic theme

Changing Theme Fonts

To apply different fonts to your presentation, on the Ribbon, click the Design tab; in the Themes group, click the Fonts button. You see the list of all Fonts for each theme. Live Preview is available as you move the mouse pointer over the fonts in the list. You will see a change in the body text and title text on the slide. To apply the font theme to all of the slides, click the theme.

> **Did You Know?**
>
> You can use different colors to show a change of topics in your presentation.

Applying Themes to Individual Slides

You can use a theme to change the appearance of a single slide without changing the rest of the slides in the presentation. Click the Design tab on the Ribbon to display the Themes group. Previously, you learned how to apply these features to an entire presentation. In this Step-by-Step you apply themes and formatting to a single slide.

S TEP-BY-STEP 2.4

1. Click **slide 6**, *Emergency Medical Service Dispatcher Duties*.

2. On the Ribbon, click the **Design** tab, and then click the **More** button in the Themes group to open the Themes gallery.

3. In the Built-In Themes group, point to the **Verve** theme thumbnail, see the effect on the slide, right-click the **Verve** theme thumbnail, and then click **Apply to Selected Slides**.

The current slide is displayed on your screen with a new design.

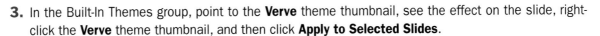

STEP-BY-STEP 2.4 Continued

4. In the Themes group, click the **Colors** button to open the Built-In Colors gallery, right-click **Metro**, and then click **Apply to Selected Slides**.

5. View the presentation to see your changes. Save the presentation and leave it open for the next Step-by-Step.

> **Did You Know?**
>
> The Apply to Matching Slides option applies the selected theme to all slides in the presentation that have the same layout as the selected slide.

Using the Slide Master

The slide master controls the formatting for all the slides in the presentation. Each slide master has layout masters. There is a slide master and associated layout masters for each theme in the presentation. You can use the slide master to change such items as the font, size, color, style, alignment, spacing, and background. Changing the slide master affects the appearance of all of the slides in a presentation associated with that master slide or master layout, and gives all slides associated with the master a consistent look. You can add headers and footers to slides. You can also place an object, such as a logo or graphic, on every slide by placing the object on the slide master.

To view the slide master and layout masters, as shown in Figure 2-9, click the View tab on the Ribbon. In the Presentation Views group, click the Slide Master button. When you are in Slide Master view, the Slide/Outline pane displays the slide master as the first thumbnail and the layout masters for each slide master. The layout masters are nested beneath each slide master. As you point to a slide or layout master in the Slide/Outline pane, the name of the layout and the slide numbers where it is applied appears. To make changes to a slide or title master, click the correct master to display it in the Slide pane.

FIGURE 2-9
Slide Master view

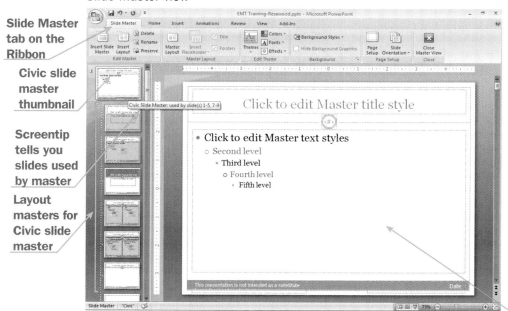

The Slide Master tab on the Ribbon is organized into groups to help you work with the slide master. Use the buttons in the Edit Master group to insert a new layout or insert a new slide master. The Master Layout group buttons help you change the master layout, including headers and footers. The Edit Theme buttons change the theme characteristics for the entire slide show. The Background group buttons work to change the graphics behind the objects, and open the Format Background dialog box to change the Fill or Picture on the background of the selected layouts. The Page Setup group changes the slide orientation from Portrait to Landscape and changes margins for the entire slide show. Click the Close Master View button to return to Normal view.

S TEP-BY-STEP 2.5

1. On the Ribbon, click the **View** tab, and then click the **Slide Master** button in the Presentation Views group to open Slide Master view.

2. Scroll to the top of the slide layout thumbnails, and then click the first thumbnail – **Civic Slide Master**. (Refer to Figure 2-9.)

3. Click the **second thumbnail** to view the **Title Slide Layout** master, and then click the **third thumbnail** to view the **Title and Content Layout** master. The ScreenTip tells you which slides are used by the Title and Content Layout. You continue to work using Slide Master view.

4. On the Ribbon, click the **Insert** tab, and then click the **Picture** button in the Illustrations group to open the Insert Picture dialog box.

5. Locate and click the file **FirstAid.jpg** in the folder where you store your Data Files, and then click **Insert**. The image of a red cross on a black background appears on the center of the slide layout master.

6. Click and drag the **picture** to the lower-right corner of the slide.

7. Drag the **upper-left sizing handle**, using the ⬉ pointer down and to the right to resize the picture so it is aligned with the dashed line for the content placeholder. See Figure 2-10.

STEP-BY-STEP 2.5 Continued

FIGURE 2-10
Resized graphic on Title and Content Layout master

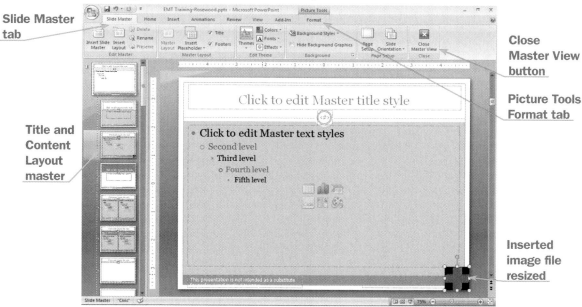

Slide Master tab

Title and Content Layout master

Close Master View button

Picture Tools Format tab

Inserted image file resized

8. Click the first thumbnail, the **Civic slide master**, click the **This presentation is not intended...** footer to select the text box, and then drag the **right-middle sizing handle**, using the ⟷ pointer to the right so the box fills the bottom of the slide and the text is fully visible.

9. On the Ribbon, click the **Close Master View** button, and then view the slides in the presentation. Slides 3–5 and 7–9, which have the Civic theme and the Title and Content layout, have the image in the lower-right corner of the slide. Slide 6 has its own Slide Master and associated Layout Masters with the Verve theme.

10. Save the presentation and leave it open for the next Step-by-Step.

> **Did You Know?**
>
> Display the slide master by pressing the Shift key and clicking the Normal button on the status bar in the lower-right corner of your screen. Press the Shift key and click the Slide Sorter button on the status bar in the lower-right corner of your screen to display the handout master.

Using the Notes Master and Handout Master

PowerPoint has other masters that work like the slide master. The handout master lets you add items that you want to appear on all your handouts, such as a logo, the date, the time, and page numbers. On the notes master, include any text or formatting that you want to appear on all your speaker notes. Click the View tab on the Ribbon, and in the Presentation Views group, click the Handout Master button to view the handout master, as shown in Figure 2-11. Click the Notes Master button to view the notes master, as shown in Figure 2-12.

FIGURE 2-11
The handout master

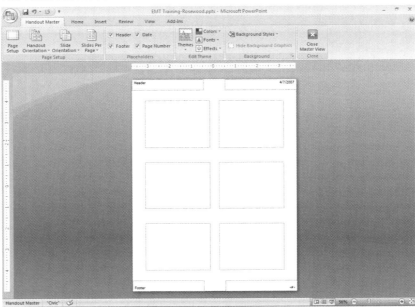

FIGURE 2-12
The notes master

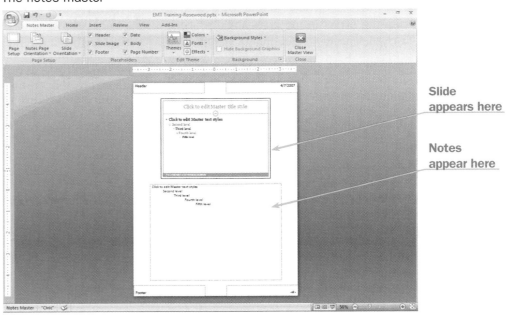

Editing Pictures in PowerPoint

PowerPoint contains picture editing tools that allow you to edit, format, and stylize a picture to get the exact effect you need for a slide. Select the picture you want to edit to open the Picture Tools Format tab on the Ribbon. The Picture Tools Format tab includes buttons that allow you to adjust the picture's contrast, color and brightness, set a transparent color, or compress the picture. You can apply a picture style and add a border or a professional picture effect. You can arrange the picture with the other objects on the slide. You can also crop, rotate, or resize the picture as needed to best fit the slide. The Reset Picture feature will undo all changes you made and display the picture as it originally appeared.

> **Did You Know?**
>
> You can override the formats applied to the presentation by the slide master by making changes directly to individual slides.

STEP-BY-STEP 2.6

1. Click **slide 1** in the Slides tab. On the Ribbon, click the **Insert** tab, and then click the **Picture** button in the Illustrations group to open the Insert Picture dialog box.

2. Locate the **TheRose.jpg** file in the folder where you store your Data Files, click the file **TheRose.jpg**, and then click **Insert**. The picture of a red rose appears on the center of the slide and fills the entire slide.

3. On the Ribbon, on the Format tab in the Size group, click the **Height down arrow** until the Height text box is **2** and the Width text box is **3**. The width will adjust proportionally because Lock Aspect Ratio is in effect.

4. Drag the **image of the rose** to below the word Paramedics.

5. In the Arrange group, click the **Align** button, and then click **Align Center**.

6. In the Picture Styles group, click the **More** button to open the Picture Styles gallery, point to several Picture Styles to see the effect on the picture, and then click **Bevel Perspective**.

7. In the Adjust group, click the **Recolor** button. In the Light Variations section, click **Accent color 1 Light**.

STEP-BY-STEP 2.6 Continued

8. In the Adjust group, click the **Compress Pictures** button, click the **Apply to selected pictures only** check box, and then click **OK**. Click to deselect the picture and compare your slide to Figure 2-13.

FIGURE 2-13
Formatted picture

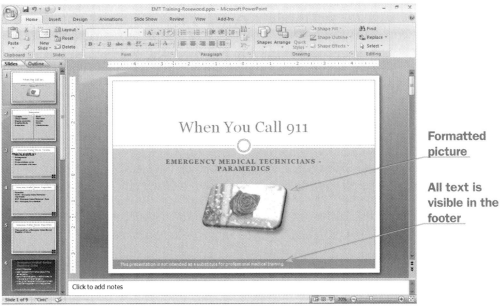

Formatted picture

All text is visible in the footer

9. Save the presentation and leave it open for the next Step-by-Step.

Adding Slides

You can add a slide to a presentation. On the Ribbon, on the Home tab, in the Slides group, click the New Slide button or right-click the slide thumbnail in the Slides tab or in Slide Sorter view, and click New Slide from the shortcut menu. You can also click Duplicate Slide on the shortcut menu to insert a new slide that is the same as the selected slide. In Normal view, PowerPoint places the new slide after the selected slide, using the same layout as the selected slide. Clicking the New Slide button arrow opens the Slide Layout gallery, which allows you to choose a layout for the new slide. The Slide Layout gallery has many layouts; the layouts available depend on the theme that has been applied and if any new slide layout masters have been added to the presentation. Click a layout to insert a new slide with that layout.

Did You Know?

You can reuse slides from other presentations. In the Slides group, click the New Slide button arrow, click the Reuse Slides command to open the Reuse Slides task pane, select the presentation that has the slides, and then select each slide you want to reuse.

S TEP-BY-STEP 2.7

1. Click **slide 9**, *Features of Emergency Departments*.

2. In the Slides group, click the **New Slide** button arrow to open the Slide Layout gallery. Layouts for both the Civic and Verve themes are in the gallery.

3. In the Civic section, click the **Two Content layout** to insert a new slide with the Civic theme. The new slide 10 has a title placeholder and two content placeholders. Your slide should look similar to Figure 2-14.

FIGURE 2-14
New slide with Two Content layout

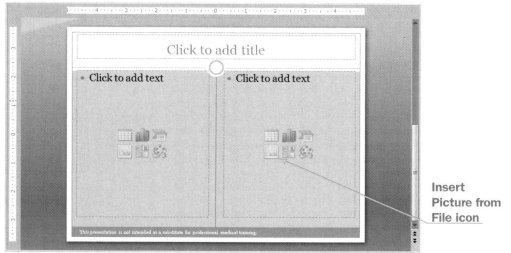

Insert
Picture from
File icon

4. In the right content placeholder, click the **Insert Picture from File** icon to open the Insert Picture dialog box. Locate and insert the Data File **FirstAid.jpg**.

5. Use the buttons on the Picture Tools Format tab to apply your choice of picture effects to format the picture.

6. View the slide show.

7. Save the presentation and leave it open for the next Step-by-Step.

Finding and Replacing Text on Slides

To find and replace text, on the Home tab of the Ribbon, in the Editing group, use the Find and Replace commands. The Find command locates the word or phrase you type in the Find what text box. The Replace command locates the word or phrase you type in the Find what text box and replaces it as directed with the word or phrase you have typed in the Replace with text box. See Figure 2-15. Click Find Next to find the next occurrence, Replace to replace the next occurrence, and Replace All to replace all occurrences.

FIGURE 2-15
Replace text box

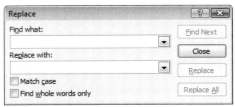

You can replace all text that is formatted with one font with another font. On the Home tab in the Editing group, click the Replace list arrow, and then click Replace Fonts. You select a current font that you want to replace, and then you click the With arrow and find the font you want to replace it with. Click Replace and all the text will be reformatted with the replacement font.

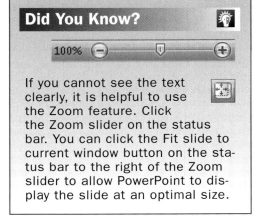

Did You Know?

If you cannot see the text clearly, it is helpful to use the Zoom feature. Click the Zoom slider on the status bar. You can click the Fit slide to current window button on the status bar to the right of the Zoom slider to allow PowerPoint to display the slide at an optimal size.

S TEP-BY-STEP 2.8

1. On the Home tab in the Editing group, click the **Replace** button.

2. In the Find what text box, type **Staff**, and then press the **Tab** key. In the Replace with text box, type **Personnel**, and then click **Find Next**. PowerPoint finds the word "Staff" on slide 9.

3. Click **Replace**, click **OK** to confirm that there are no more occurrences of "Staff" in the presentation, and then click **Close** to close the Replace dialog box. The word Staff is replaced with the word Personnel.

4. Save the presentation and leave it open for the next Step-by-Step.

Adding Text to Slides

Working with Placeholders

The slide layouts create placeholders on the slides that reserve a space in the presentation for the type of information you want to insert. To replace a text placeholder, click the text. A box with a hashed-line border appears around the text. You can then select the existing text and type whatever you like. You can work on the Slide pane to enter text to a slide; this way you can see the text you enter and the placement on the slide.

Did You Know?

You can also add a text box to a slide. A text box is created by clicking the Insert tab on the Ribbon, and then, in the Text group, clicking the Text box button.

STEP-BY-STEP 2.9

1. Click **slide 10**.

2. Click the **Click to add title** placeholder, and then type **Cardiopulmonary Resuscitation**.

3. In the left content placeholder, click **Click to add text,** type **Begin rescue breathing**, press the **Enter** key, type **Begin chest compressions**, press the **Enter** key, and then type **Call 911**.

4. With **slide 10**, *Cardiopulmonary Resuscitation* selected, on the Ribbon, click the **Home** tab, click the **New Slide** button arrow in the Slides group, and then click the **Title and Content** layout.

5. On the new **slide 11**, click **Click to add title**, and then type **Why Study First Aid?**.

6. Click **Click to add text**, type **Injury and illness occur daily**, press the **Enter** key, type **Basic knowledge can help if you are first on the scene of an accident or serious illness**, press the **Enter** key, and then type **Your reaction may improve the victim's chance of recovery**.

7. In the Slides group, click the **New Slide** button to insert another new slide with a **Title and Content layout**.

8. Click the **Click to add title** placeholder, and then type **Emergencies** as the title of this slide.

STEP-BY-STEP 2.9 Continued

9. Click **Click to add text**. Refer to Figure 2-16 as you type the following and press the **Enter** key after each line:

- ■ **Bleeding**
- ■ **Shock**
- ■ **Fractures and Dislocations**
- ■ **Poisoning**
- ■ **CPR**

FIGURE 2-16
New slide 12

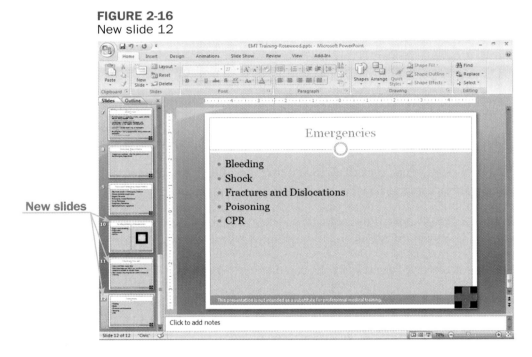

10. Save the presentation and leave it open for the next Step-by-Step.

Using Outline Tab to Enter Text

You have learned how to enter text by typing it directly on the slide in the Slide pane. You can enter the rest of the presentation using the Outline tab. When you enter text using the Outline tab, pressing the Tab and Enter keys doesn't work the same way as when you work in the Slide pane.

STEP-BY-STEP 2.10

1. Click the **Outline** tab in the left pane and click **slide 12** *Emergencies*, if necessary.

2. On the Ribbon, click the **Home** tab, and then click the **New Slide** button in the Slides group to insert a new slide with a **Title and Content layout**.

3. On the Outline tab, type **Bleeding** as the title of the new slide 13. You did not have to click the title placeholder.

4. Press and hold the **Ctrl** key, and then press the **Enter** key. The insertion point is now in the Content placeholder on the Bleeding slide.

> **Did You Know?**
>
> If you press the Tab key, the text will become a bullet on the previous slide.

5. Type the following as the content on the slide, pressing the **Enter** key after each line:

- **Apply pressure to wound**
- **Use a clean bandage**
- **Elevate injured extremity**
- **Apply pressure to slow bleeding**
- **Call 911**

6. Press and hold the **Ctrl** key, and then press the **Enter** key to insert a new slide. Type **Shock** as the title for this slide.

7. Press and hold the **Ctrl** key, and then press the **Enter** key to move the insertion point into the content placeholder.

8. Type the following as the content on the slide, pressing the **Enter** key after each line:

- **Lay the patient down**
- **Elevate patient's legs**
- **Maintain patient's body temperature**
- **Monitor breathing**
- **Provide fresh air**
- **Call 911**

9. Insert another new slide with the **Title and Content layout** using any method. Using either the Outline tab or the Slides tab, type **CPR** as the title of this slide.

10. Type the following as the content on the slide:

- **Airway**
- **Breathing**
- **Circulation**

STEP-BY-STEP 2.10 Continued

11. Compare your slides with Figure 2-17. Save the presentation and leave it open for the next Step-by-Step.

FIGURE 2-17
The Outline tab

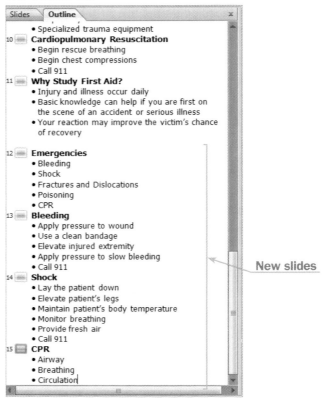

New slides

Entering Text in Text Boxes

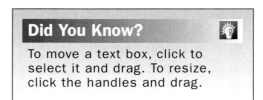

You have learned how to enter text by typing it directly on the slide in the Slide pane. You also learned that you can enter text using the Outline tab. These methods enter text, using placeholders. There are times when you want to enter text in a text box or shape. Use the Text Box tool to add text to a slide without using a content or text placeholder. On the Ribbon, on the Insert tab, in the Text group, click the Text Box button.

> **Did You Know?**
>
> To move a text box, click to select it and drag. To resize, click the handles and drag.

STEP-BY-STEP 2.11

1. In the Slides/Outline pane, click the **Slides** tab, and then click **slide 15**, *CPR*, if necessary. On the Ribbon, click the **Insert** tab, and then click the **Text Box** button in the Text group.

2. Click in the middle of the slide.

3. Referring to Figure 2-18, type **If the patient does not respond, call 911**.

STEP-BY-STEP 2.11 Continued

FIGURE 2-18
Creating a text box

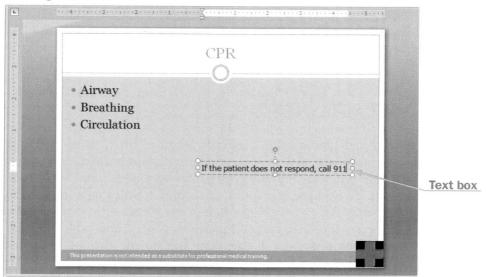

4. Click **slide 3**, *Emergency Medical Service Providers*, drag **may be provided by a:** to select the text in the text box, and then type **is essential!**.

5. Move the mouse to the **border of the box** around the text box so the pointer becomes the move pointer, click to select the **text box**, and then drag the **text box** below the text **Or a combination of the above**, as shown in Figure 2-19.

FIGURE 2-19
Editing and moving a text box

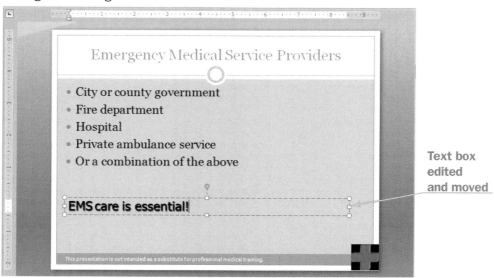

6. Click the **Save button** on the Quick Access Toolbar to save the presentation.

STEP-BY-STEP 2.11 Continued

7. Click the **Slide Show** button on the status bar and then click the mouse to advance through the presentation.

8. Click the **Normal** button to return to Normal view, save the presentation, and then leave the presentation open for the next Step-by-Step.

Adding Notes to Slides

 A good PowerPoint presentation generally contains brief, main points about the subject. You want your audience listening to you rather than reading large amounts of text on slides. Use the speaker notes to remind yourself of any additional information you need to include in your speech. To add speaker notes, click in the Notes pane below the slide and begin typing, or switch to Notes Page view. Notes Page view shows an image of a slide and the notes you entered in the Notes pane. You can add pictures, charts, and tables to your notes. You can also format the text of the notes. Click the View tab on the Ribbon and, in the Presentation Views group, click the Notes Page button. If the text is too small to read in Notes Page view, you can increase the size by using the Zoom feature on the status bar.

STEP-BY-STEP 2.12

1. Click the **Normal** button on the status bar to return to Normal view, if necessary.

2. Click **slide 10**, *Cardiopulmonary Resuscitation*.

STEP-BY-STEP 2.12 Continued

3. In the Notes pane, click **Click to add notes**, and then refer to Figure 2-20 as you type **Remember the ABC's of CPR: Airway, Breathing, Circulation**.

FIGURE 2-20
Adding notes

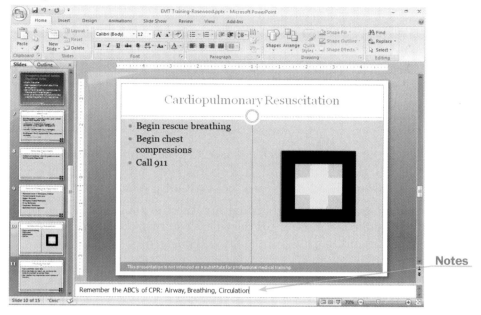

4. On the Ribbon, click the **View** tab, and then click the **Notes Page** button in the Presentation Views group to see the Notes Page for slide 10.

5. Save the presentation and leave it open for the next Step-by-Step.

Changing Text Alignment, Spacing, Case, and Tabs

To change text alignment, select the text and click one of the alignment buttons in the Paragraph group on the Home tab of the Ribbon, as shown in Figure 2-21. To change spacing, select the text, click the Line Spacing button, and then select the line spacing.

FIGURE 2-21
Font and Paragraph groups on the Ribbon

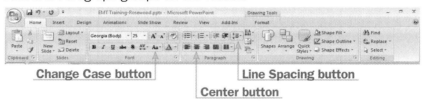

To change the case of text, first select the text. On the Ribbon, on the Home tab, in the Font group, click the Change Case button, and then choose one of the five options: Sentence case, lowercase, UPPERCASE, Capitalize Each Word, or tOGGLE cASE.

Set a tab by selecting the text and clicking the Tab button at the left of the horizontal ruler. Clear a tab by dragging the tab marker off the ruler. You turn the rulers on and off by clicking the View tab on the Ribbon and working in the Show/Hide group.

FIGURE 2-22
Tabs on the ruler

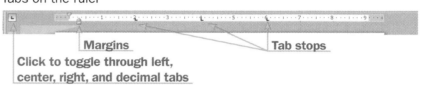

S TEP-BY-STEP 2.13

1. On the Ribbon, click the **Home** tab, and then click the **Normal** button on the status bar.

2. Click **slide 15**, *CPR*, click the **New Slide** button in the Slides group, and then type **Web Resources** as the slide title.

3. Type **American Red Cross** as the first bullet, type **American Heart Association** as the second bullet, and then type **Kid's Health** as the third bullet.

4. On the Ribbon, on the **Home** tab, click the **Center** button in the Paragraph group. The third bullet, Kid's Health, is centered on the slide.

5. Click to select the **content placeholder border** so it becomes a solid line.

6. In the Paragraph group, click the **Line Spacing** button to display the Line Spacing options, and then click **2.0**.

STEP-BY-STEP 2.13 Continued

7. Select the text **American Red Cross**, in the Font group, click the **Change Case** button, and then click **UPPERCASE**.

8. Select the text **American Heart Association**, and then click the **Align Text Right** button. Your slide should look similar to Figure 2-23.

FIGURE 2-23
Slide with case and alignment changes

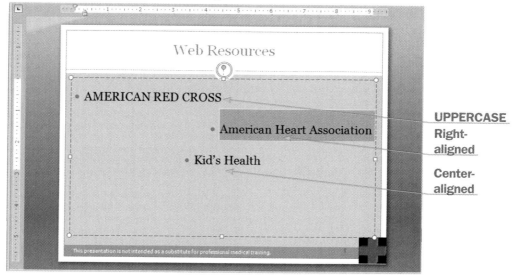

9. Save the presentation and leave it open for the next Step-by-Step.

Working with Bullets

Bullets define each line in the Content placeholder on a slide. To have special formatting that is different from that which the theme provides on a slide, you can format the bullets by selecting the text or placeholder and then clicking the Bullets button list arrow on the Mini toolbar to display the Bullets gallery. Default bullets are determined by the theme. The Bullets button is also on the Home tab on the Ribbon in the Paragraph group. Click Bullets and Numbering to open the Bullets and Numbering dialog box, as shown in Figure 2-24. To change all the bullets in a bulleted list, select the entire list. On the Bulleted tab, you can select a preset bullet or add a graphical bullet by clicking the Picture button. You can also change the color or the bullet size in relation to the text.

You can customize a bulleted list after it has been created. You can change the appearance of the bullets—such as their shape, size, or color—and you can also adjust the distance between the bullets and the text. To change the appearance of the bullets throughout a presentation, make the changes on the slide master. You cannot select a bullet to make changes; you must select the associated text.

FIGURE 2-24
Bullets and Numbering dialog box

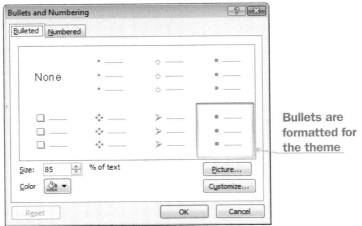

Bullets are formatted for the theme

STEP-BY-STEP 2.14

1. On the Ribbon, click the **View** tab, and then click the **Slide Master** button in the Presentation Views group.

2. Click the **Civic slide master**, the first thumbnail in the left pane.

3. Click **Click to edit Master text styles** in the Content placeholder.

4. On the Ribbon, click the **Home** tab, click the **Bullets Button** list arrow in the Paragraph group, and then click **Bullets and Numbering**.

Did You Know?

If your list is numbered rather than bulleted, choose the Numbered tab in the Bullets and Numbering dialog box to customize the list.

STEP-BY-STEP 2.14 Continued

5. In the Bullets and Numbering dialog box, click the **Bulleted** tab if necessary, click the **Star Bullets** icon, type **125** in the Size text box, and then click **OK**. The bullet style and size changes on the slide master, as shown in Figure 2-25.

FIGURE 2-25
Bullet style and size changed

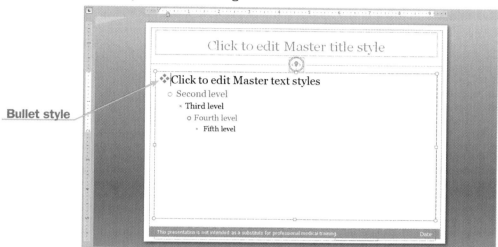

6. Click the **Normal** button on the status bar to close the slide master, click **slide 1** in the Slide pane, and then press the **PgDn** key to advance through the presentation to view the changes on each slide.

7. Save your work and leave the presentation open for the next Step-by-Step.

Did You Know?

You can format the Second, Third, Fourth, and Fifth level bullets to be any combination of styles, pictures, colors, or characters.

Did You Know?

Press Tab to demote a bullet one level.

Changing Font Attributes

 If you use a theme, the format of the text for body text, titles, and bullets on your slides is predetermined so that the layout, color scheme, font, size, and style are consistent throughout the presentation. You can alter the format by making changes to individual slides. You change the font, style, size, effects, and color using the buttons on the Home tab in the Font group.

To make changes to words, you select the word. To make changes to a line of text, you can drag to select the line. When you select text in a placeholder, the border of the placeholder is a dashed line. If you want to format all of the text in one placeholder, you can click the border of the placeholder so it becomes a solid line. Any formatting to a selected placeholder will affect all of the text in the placeholder.

You can also use the Mini toolbar, shown in Figure 2-26, as a shortcut to changing the font, font size, font style, and font color. The Increase Font Size and Decrease Font Size buttons allow you to change the font size quickly in preset increments.

FIGURE 2-26
Formatting text using the Mini toolbar

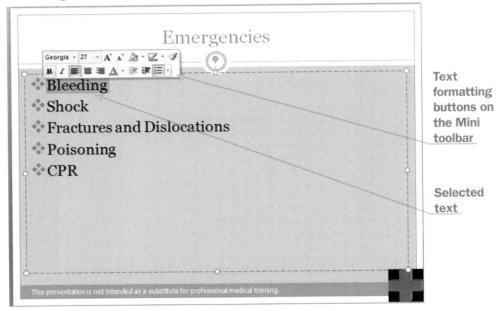

Text formatting buttons on the Mini toolbar

Selected text

S TEP-BY-STEP 2.15

1. Click **slide 12**, *Emergencies*, and then drag to select the text *Bleeding*.

2. On the Ribbon, click the **Home** tab, and then click the **Font Color** list arrow in the Font group. A palette of colors opens, organized into Theme colors and Standard colors. You can also click More colors to open the Colors palette.

3. Point to several **colors** and watch how the Live Preview shows the effect on the selected text, and then click any color.

4. Double-click **Shock**, on the Ribbon on the **Home** tab, click the **Font list arrow** in the Font group to display a list of installed fonts.

5. Point to several **font styles** and watch how the Live Preview shows the effect on the selected text, and then click any font.

6. Double-click **Poisoning**, on the Ribbon on the **Home** tab, click the **Font size** list arrow in the Font group to display a list of font sizes beginning with 8 pt and extending beyond 96 pt.

STEP-BY-STEP 2.15 Continued

7. Point to several sizes, watch how the Live Preview shows you the effect on the selected text, and then click **36**.

8. Save your work and then leave the presentation open for the next Step-by-Step.

An effective presentation should be consistent, error-free, and visually appealing. PowerPoint helps you determine if your presentation conforms to the standards of good style. For instance, title text size should be at least 36 points and the number of bullets on a slide should not exceed six. You should try to limit the number of words in each bullet to six. This is called the 6 by 6 rule, although sometimes you have to make exceptions.

Checking Spelling, Style, and Usage

Automatic spell checking identifies misspellings and words that are not in PowerPoint's dictionary by underlining them with a wavy red line immediately after you type them. To correct a misspelled word, right-click the underlined word. A shortcut menu appears with a list of suggested correctly spelled words. Click the suggestion that you want, and PowerPoint replaces the misspelled word. You can turn the automatic spell checker on or off, or change the way that it checks your document by clicking the Office Button, clicking the PowerPoint Options button, then clicking Proofing.

You can also check the spelling in a presentation after it is complete. Click the Review tab on the Ribbon, then, in the Proofing group, click the Spelling button. The Spelling dialog box contains options for ignoring words, making changes, or adding words to your own custom dictionary.

Another useful PowerPoint tool is the Thesaurus. Click the Review tab on the Ribbon, and then click the Thesaurus button in the Proofing group. The Research task pane appears and offers a selection of alternative words with the same or similar meanings.

STEP-BY-STEP 2.16

1. Click **slide 1**, *When You Call 911*, on the Ribbon click the **Review** tab, and then click the **Spelling** button in the Proofing group. If spelling errors are in the presentation, the Spelling dialog box opens, as shown in Figure 2-27.

FIGURE 2-27
Spelling dialog box

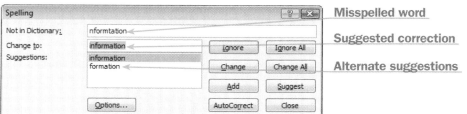

STEP-BY-STEP 2.16 Continued

NOTE: Depending on how accurately you typed the text during these steps, you will have different words selected. If you typed all the text correctly, you will not have any spelling errors in your presentation. When you click the Spelling button a dialog box will open with the message "The Spelling Check is complete!"

2. Review the suggestions in the dialog box.

3. Click **Change** to replace any incorrect spellings, or click **Ignore** to skip the words that are correct.

4. When the spell checker is finished, click **OK** in the spelling check is complete message box.

5. Select **slide 6**, *Emergency Medical Service Dispatcher Duties*, in the first bullet, double-click the word **Calm**, on the Ribbon, click the **Review** tab, and then click the **Thesaurus** button in the Proofing group.

6. Scroll through the words in the Research task pane and hover over the word **Soothe** until it is outlined with a box, click the **down arrow** next to the word, click **Insert**, and then notice that the word *Soothe* replaces the word *Calm*.

7. Save the presentation and leave it open for the next Step-by-Step.

Formatting Slides

Deleting Placeholders and Text from Slides

To change or delete text on an existing slide, scroll to display the slide you want to change. Then, as in other Office programs, select the text you want to change so that it is highlighted. Press the Delete key, the Backspace key, or type the new text to replace the selected text.

To delete a placeholder, simply click the text inside a placeholder so that a dashed line box appears around it. Click the placeholder box so that it is a solid line, and then press the Delete key. The text within the placeholder is replaced with the default placeholder text "Click to add text." Select the placeholder, then press Delete again to remove the placeholder from the slide.

Changing Slide Layouts

When you want to change the layout of text or graphics on slides easily, you can use the program theme's preset layouts. PowerPoint includes many layouts that you can choose from to create a new slide or change the layout of an existing slide. The different layouts include placeholders for text and content. Text includes paragraphs and bulleted lists. Content can be clip art, tables, organization charts, SmartArt graphics, objects, graphs, movies, and media clips. Just click a placeholder icon and replace it with your own information. You can choose the layout that best fits the need of a particular slide.

To change the layout for an existing slide, select the slide or slides. You can change more than one slide at a time. On the Home tab, in the Slides group, click the Layout button, and then scroll to view the available layouts.

S TEP-BY-STEP 2.17

1. Click **slide 8**, *Emergency Departments*, then on the **Home** tab in the Slides group click the Layout button. The Slide Layout gallery appears.

2. Scroll down to the view all layouts for the Civic slide master theme, and then click **Content with Caption** to apply it to the slide. The existing text adjusts to the new layout. You want to try a few other choices.

3. Click the **Layout** button in the Slides group, click **Picture with Caption,** view the results, and then click **Content with Caption** to apply it to the slide. See Figure 2-28.

FIGURE 2-28
Content with Caption layout

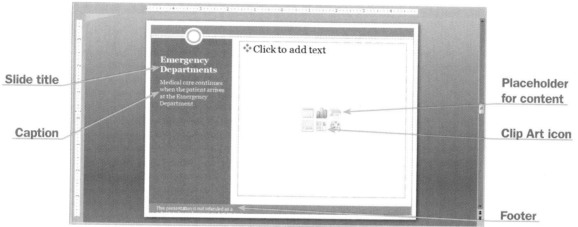

4. Click the **footer** text box, drag the right sizing handle to the right so the entire footer appears on one line.

5. Save the presentation and leave it open for the next Step-by-Step.

Adding Clip Art and Sounds to Slides

If a content placeholder appears on a slide, you can choose from six objects: table, chart, SmartArt graphic, picture from file, clip art, and movie. When you click the Insert Clip Art icon, the Microsoft Clip Art Gallery task pane appears. See Figure 2-29. You find clips based on a keyword search. You can also import clips from other sources into the Clip Art Gallery and connect to the Web to access more clips. A keyword is a phrase or a word that describes the item you want in the Search text box. Click the Go button to show the results. You will work with tables, charts, and SmartArt graphic objects in Lesson 3.

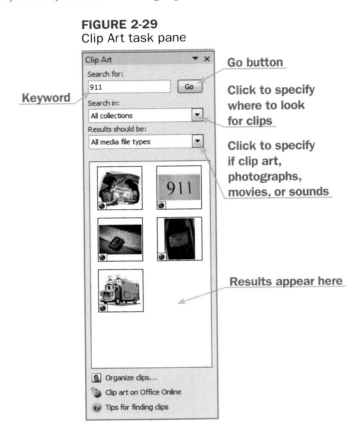

FIGURE 2-29
Clip Art task pane

Working with Clip Art

If there is no content placeholder, you can still insert clip art on a slide. On the Ribbon, on the Insert tab, click the Clip Art button. The Clip Art task pane opens. This task pane offers several options for finding the item you want to insert. To find an item, type one or more words into the Search for text box that might help identify the item. You can narrow your search by selecting from the two drop-down menus under the Search in and Results should be options. The Search in options enable you to narrow your search by selecting the collections that you want to search. Clicking the plus sign next to an item allows you to narrow your search further. In the Results should be box, you specify the media types. In addition to clip art, you can also search for photographs, movies, and sounds. You can narrow this search by clicking the plus sign and selecting from the list of the typical formats for each category. Once you have determined the search filters, click the Go button to show the results.

The results appear in the task pane. An arrow for a drop-down menu appears to the right of the item. Click Insert to insert the image in the slide at the location of your insertion point. Click Preview/Properties to view the image and its properties without adding it to your document. To see similar clips, click Find Similar Style.

STEP-BY-STEP 2.18

1. Click **slide 8**, *Emergency Departments*, if it is not already selected.

2. Click the **Clip Art** icon on the Content placeholder to open the Clip Art task pane, click the **Results should be** list arrow, and then click next to **All media types**, **Photographs**, **Movies**, and **Sounds** to remove the check marks so only the Clip Art check box is selected.

3. In the Search for text box, type **911**, click **Go**, review the results, and then click a **thumbnail of the clip** to insert a clip of your choice. Note: if you do not get results, try different key words such as "emergency."

4. Click the **Close** button on the Clip Art task pane to close the task pane. The clip art you chose is inserted on the slide in the placeholder.

> ### Did You Know?
>
> To move clip art, click the object and drag. To resize, click the handles and drag.

5. Save the presentation and leave it open for the next Step-by-Step.

Adding Sound to Slides

You can add sound effects to any slide by inserting a sound. Click the Insert tab on the Ribbon, then, in the Media Clips group, click the Sound button. You can insert a sound from a file that is stored on your computer or a disk, you can insert a sound from the Clip Organizer, you can play a CD Audio Track, or you can Record a Sound and attach it to the file. Recorded sound is good for narration. When a sound is on a slide, you will see the sound icon on the slide.

STEP-BY-STEP 2.19

1. Display **slide 10** *Cardiopulmonary Resuscitation*.

2. On the Ribbon, click the **Insert** tab, and then click the **Sound** button in the Media Clips group. The Insert Sound dialog box opens.

3. Click the sound file **911.wav** in the folder where you store the Data Files, click **OK** to insert the sound file, and close the Insert Sound dialog box.

   You must choose to have the sound play automatically or only when the sound icon is clicked during the slide show.

STEP-BY-STEP 2.19 Continued

4. In the dialog box shown in Figure 2-30, click **Automatically**. The sound icon appears on the slide, and the sound will play automatically during the slide show.

FIGURE 2-30
Choosing how sound is played

5. Click the **sound** icon, click the **Sound Tools Options** tab, and then click **Preview** in the Play group. If your computer has a sound card and speakers, you should hear the 911 sound file.

6. Save the presentation and leave it open for the next Step-by-Step.

Inserting Hyperlinks

Ⓒ A hyperlink allows you to jump to another slide, file, or to a Web site if you are connected to the Internet. You can add a hyperlink to go to another slide within your presentation, a different presentation, or to another Office document. You can also add a hyperlink that opens a message window for an e-mail address.

To insert a hyperlink in a presentation, select the text you want to make a hyperlink. On the Ribbon, click the Insert tab; in the Links group, click Hyperlink. The Insert Hyperlink dialog box opens, as shown in Figure 2-31. In the Link to section, choose where you want the link to go. The Look in section allows you to specify the Current Folder, Browsed Pages, or Recent files. You can also specify a ScreenTip to help the person using the slide show. When you click OK, a hyperlink is inserted in the document. The text you selected is displayed in a special color and underlined. The hyperlink formatting is part of the theme colors. Click it to go to the linked location. You can also link to an Internet site by typing the Web address in the Address box in the Insert Hyperlink dialog box.

FIGURE 2-31
Insert Hyperlink dialog box

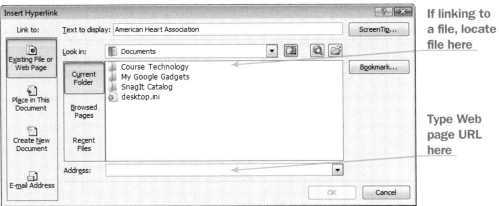

STEP-BY-STEP 2.20

1. Click **slide 16**, *Web Resources*.

2. Select the text **AMERICAN RED CROSS**, on the Ribbon, click the **Insert** tab, and then click **Hyperlink** in the Links group. The Insert Hyperlink dialog box opens.

3. Type **www.redcross.org** in the Address box, and then click **OK**. The text is underlined in the slide, indicating that it is a hyperlink.

4. Select the text **American Heart Association**, on the Ribbon, click the **Insert** tab, click **Hyperlink** in the Links group, type **www.americanheart.org** in the Address box, and then click **OK**.

5. Select the text **Kid's Health**, and then create a hyperlink to **www.kidshealth.org**.

6. Save the presentation, and then click the **Slide Show** button. The Web Resources slide fills the screen in Slide Show view.

7. Point to the **AMERICAN RED CROSS** hyperlink so your arrow pointer changes to a hand pointer, indicating that you are pointing at a link.

8. Click the **AMERICAN RED CROSS** link to open your Web browser and display the Web page (you must have an Internet connection).

9. Close your Web browser, and then press the **Esc** key to exit the slide show.

10. Save the presentation and leave it open for the next Step-by-Step.

> **Did You Know?**
>
> When you type an e-mail address on a slide, such as myaddress@mailbox.com PowerPoint automatically creates a hyperlink that opens a new message window addressed to that e-mail address.

Using Custom Animation

You can add select animation effects to any of the objects on a slide. Animation is what makes slide shows fun and interesting to watch. You can have a lot of fun creating animations on slides. When you animate an object, text, or slide, you add a visual effect. Animation enhances your presentation and increases audience interest.

On the Ribbon, click the Animations tab; in the Animations group, click Custom Animation. The Custom Animation task pane appears, as shown in Figure 2-32. Click the Add Effect button to open the menu of many effects. Effects are organized into Entrance, Emphasis, Exit, and Motion Paths. Entrance and Exit define the animation for the entry and exit of an object. Emphasis defines the animation of an object that is already placed in the slide. **Motion Paths** allows you to use predefined paths for the movement of an object. You can also draw a customized path for an object. As you hover over each option, a new menu appears with the last nine animations used. You can click the More Effects option on any of the submenus to display a dialog box containing all the animation features.

FIGURE 2-32
Custom Animation task pane

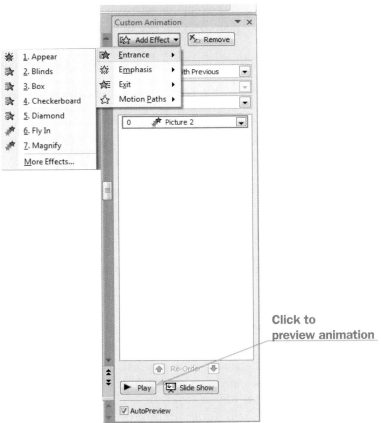

Each animated object is assigned a number on the slide, and the corresponding number is listed in the task pane. The objects that are not assigned an animation effect do not have numbers. When you click an object in the task pane, the properties assigned to that object display in the task pane. You can select how an object is animated, arrange animation order, determine whether to display the animation manually or automatically, and adjust the speed of the animation. If an object is already animated, you can change or remove the animation by clicking the object listed in the task pane, and then clicking the Change or Remove button.

To the right of each animated object, an arrow opens the animation drop-down menu, which contains the commands that determine how you want to trigger that animation for the object. You can set the object to animate three ways: when you click your mouse, with the previous object, or after the previous object. You may also make adjustments to the effects by clicking Effects Options. In this dialog box, you can select how the text enters the screen. You can also choose a sound to accompany it. You have the option of dimming the object after it has been animated. The text can appear all at once, by the word, or by the letter, and you can increase or decrease the delay percentage. The Timing tab allows you to adjust the timing of the animation and determine the trigger for the animation. When animating text, the Text Animation tab allows you to animate the text as a group or by individual levels.

> **Did You Know?**
>
> The Show Advanced Timeline feature displays the time of the animation as a horizontal line graph. This allows you to easily see the timing of each object all at once.

Adding or Changing Slide Animation

You can apply an animation to the current (displayed) slide. Select the placeholder to apply animation to all text items on the placeholder. You can also individually animate text boxes, pictures, and transitions into the slide. The two buttons at the bottom of the task pane allow you to preview the animation. Play activates the animation in the current screen. The Slide Show button shows the slide in full screen, as it would appear in a slide show.

S TEP-BY-STEP 2.21

1. Click **slide 8**, *Emergency Departments*.

2. Select the **clip art** you inserted in the previous Step-by-Step.

3. On the Ribbon, click the **Animations** tab, and then click the **Custom Animation** button in the Animations group to open the Custom Animation task pane.

4. Click **Add Effect** in the task pane, point to **Entrance**, click **More Effects**, click **Magnify** in the Exciting section, and then click **OK**.

5. In the Custom Animation task pane, click the **Speed list** arrow, click **Fast**, click the **Start list** arrow, and then click **With Previous**.

6. In the Custom Animation task pane, click **Play** to view the animation.

7. Save the presentation and leave it open for the next Step-by-Step.

Using Slide Transitions

When you run a presentation, slide transitions determine how one slide is removed from the screen and how the next one appears. You can set the transitions between slides. On the Ribbon, click the Animations tab, then, in the Transitions to this Slide group, click any of the transitions. You can click the More button to view additional transitions, as shown in Figure 2-33.

FIGURE 2-33
Slide transitions

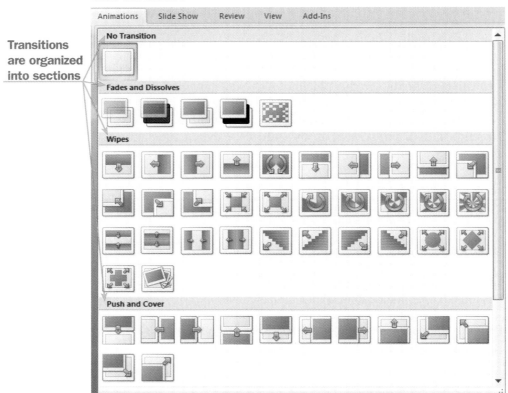

Transitions are organized into sections

The Ribbon includes commands for a list of effects. The best view to use when you work on the transitions is Slide Sorter. You can see all the slides in the presentation in one view. You can select the speed at which a slide displays and add a sound by clicking the Transition Sound button. You can choose a sound effect that will play while the slide transition occurs. In the Advance slide section you determine whether to advance the slides manually by clicking the mouse or

Did You Know?

PowerPoint is a useful teaching tool. Many instructors use PowerPoint because it provides a visual outline of the content and helps students focus their attention on what is being said.

set the timing to advance slides automatically. To set slides to advance automatically, click Automatically After and enter the number of seconds you want the slide to be displayed on the screen. If you click Apply to All, the selections you made affect all slides in the presentation. You can apply a transition to several slides by holding the Control (Ctrl) key down, and clicking the slides in the Outline/Slide pane.

S TEP-BY-STEP 2.22

1. Click the **Slide Sorter** button on the status bar.

2. Click **slide 1**, *When You Call 911*, on the Ribbon click the **Animations** tab, and then click several of the **transitions** in the Transitions to this Slide group to see the effects.

3. Click the **transition** that you like best, click the **Transition Speed** button, and then click **Medium**. A transition icon beneath the slide indicates that a transition is applied to the slide.

4. In the Advance Slide section of the Transitions to this Slide group, **On Mouse Click** should have a check mark in the check box, and **No Sound** should be selected in the Sound section.

5. Click **slide 2**, *Emergencies*, select a different transition, and then set **Slow** as the speed.

6. Click **slide 3**, *Emergency Medical Service Providers*, press and hold the **Shift** key, and then click **slide 16**, *Web Resources*. You selected slides 3-16.

7. Click a transition of your choice for these slides, and then set **Fast** as the speed. Your screen should look similar to Figure 2-34.

FIGURE 2-34
Completed presentation in Slide Sorter view

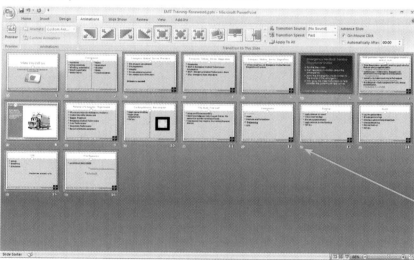

Transition icon

8. Add your name as a footer to the Handouts page, save the presentation, and then view the presentation to see the final presentation.

STEP-BY-STEP 2.22 Continued

9. Click the **Office Button**, click **Print**, click the **Print what list arrow**, click **Handouts**, click **Slides per page**, click any **6**, and then click **OK** to print the handouts at six slides per page.

10. Close the presentation, and then exit PowerPoint.

Did You Know?

If you want to print the whole presentation, but don't want to use a lot of paper, you can print handouts or notes.

SUMMARY

In this lesson, you learned how to:

■ Use PowerPoint to create new presentations using blank presentations or templates.

■ Insert headers and footers in a presentation.

■ Apply themes and color schemes.

■ Use the slide, notes, and handout masters.

■ Change presentations in PowerPoint by applying slide layouts.

■ Edit pictures.

■ Add slides to an existing PowerPoint presentation.

■ Find and replace text.

■ Add text to slides.

■ Add notes to slides in PowerPoint.

■ Change the appearance of text and bullets in PowerPoint.

■ Check spelling, style, and usage.

■ Change slide formatting.

■ Add clip art and sounds.

■ Insert hyperlinks on slides.

■ Apply custom animation to slides.

■ Use slide transitions.

VOCABULARY *Review*

Define the following terms:

Animation	Handout master	Notes master
Blank presentation	Hyperlink	Placeholder
Design template	Layout master	Slide master
Effects options	Motion Paths	Slide transitions

REVIEW *Questions*

MATCHING

Write the letter of the term in the right column that best matches the description in the left column.

Column 1

_____ 1. Controls formatting for all slides in a presentation

_____ 2. Allows you to make adjustments to an animation

_____ 3. Determines where content and objects are placed on a slide

_____ 4. Determines how one slide is removed from the screen and the next one appears

_____ 5. Predesigned graphic styles that can be applied to your slides

Column 2

A. Template

B. Slide transition

C. Effect Options

D. slide master

E. Themes

F. Outline view

G. animate

H. slide layout

WRITTEN QUESTIONS

Write a brief answer to each of the following questions.

1. What option would you use to create a presentation from scratch, using the layout, format, colors, and style you prefer?

2. What types of content can you add to a Content layout using the icons?

3. How do you insert clip art if a placeholder for clip art is not included on the slide?

4. What can you use to animate an object?

5. How do you insert a hyperlink?

PROJECTS

PROJECT 2-1

1. Start PowerPoint.

2. Open the presentation EMT Advanced Class.pptx from the drive and folder where you store the Data Files for this lesson.

3. Save the presentation as **EMT Advanced Class-Fall Session**, followed by your initials.

4. View the presentation.

5. In Normal view on slide 2, change the slide layout to Two Content. Add relevant clip art or a photograph to the slide, using the placeholder.

6. Apply a theme of your choice to the presentation.

7. Apply a different theme to the World Wide Web slide.

8. Enter notes on at least two slides, using the Notes pane. Then, add text to at least two of the slides that have titles.

9. Insert at least two new slides and add text to the placeholders.

10. Add Web page addresses to the Web slide. Add clip art, photographs, or any sounds to several of the slides.

11. Use the Custom Animation task pane to create at least two animations in the slide show; animate any objects or text.

12. Switch to Slide Sorter view and add at least two different transitions to the slide show.

13. Use the Thesaurus to replace at least one word with a synonym. Run the spelling checker.

14. Adjust all of the text in the presentation so that it appears correctly on each slide.

15. Switch to Slide Show view and run the presentation on your computer.

16. Add your name as a footer to the Notes and Handouts pages, and then print the handouts at 6 slides per page.

17. Save the presentation, then exit PowerPoint.

PROJECT 2-2

1. Start PowerPoint. Click the Office Button, click Open to open the Open dialog box, and click once on the EMT Advanced Class-Fall Session.pptx file you created in Project 2-1.

2. Click the Open button list arrow, and then click Open as Copy. Save the presentation as **EMT Advanced Class-Fall Session – Copy.pptx**, followed by your initials.

3. Switch to Outline view.

4. Insert a new slide after the last slide with the layout Title and Text.

5. On the last slide type **Prices** as the title of the slide.

6. Below Prices, Type the following:
   Beginning Class — $100
   Intermediate Class — $125
   Advanced Class — $150

7. Print the last slide and then leave the presentation open for the next project.

PROJECT 2-3

1. In Normal view, go to slide 1 and type the following in the Notes pane: **Be sure everyone has a handout.**

2. Print slide 1 using the Notes Pages print options.

3. Enhance the slide show, adding any additional objects or animations that you want. Check spelling. Save and print the entire presentation as handouts with six slides on a page.

4. Close the presentation and then exit PowerPoint.

CRITICAL*Thinking*

 ACTIVITY 2-1

Use a template, either installed or from the Microsoft Office Web site, and the skills you learned in this lesson to create a presentation for an organization to which you belong. Be sure to check your presentation for correct spelling, punctuation, and grammar usage. Include clip art, at least one image from a file, and add animations and transitions to the slide show. Include one hyperlink to a favorite Web site. Save and print the entire presentation as handouts with six slides on a page.

 ACTIVITY 2-2

Create a presentation using the ideas you organized in Critical Thinking Activity 1-2 in Lesson 1. Choose a theme. Add sound and clip art. Include slide transitions and animation. Run the presentation for your class.

WORKING WITH VISUAL ELEMENTS

OBJECTIVES

Upon completion of this lesson, you will be able to:

- Insert a SmartArt graphic.
- Convert text to a SmartArt graphic.
- Change the style of a SmartArt graphic.
- Add and format an organization chart.
- Enter text into a SmartArt graphic.
- Create and format WordArt.
- Build and format charts.
- Create a table.
- Modify a table's style and layout.
- Draw, select, manipulate, and format an object.
- Scale and size an object.
- Copy, move, and group objects.
- Create a text box on a shape.
- Animate shapes.
- Order visual elements on a slide.
- Insert objects on a slide.
- Add a header or footer.

Estimated Time: 1.5 hours

VOCABULARY

Adjustment handle

Cell

Chart (graph)

Column

Datasheet

Grouping

Handle

Organization chart

Rotate handle

Row

SmartArt graphic

Table

WordArt

Working with SmartArt Graphics

When you have to present information to an audience, text is not always the best way to present content. Graphics are a much more powerful way to visually convey information about flow, sequence, process, and organization, or even to make simple points. SmartArt graphics, dynamic and exciting graphics, are available for you to use on your slides in PowerPoint.

PowerPoint includes over 80 basic styles of SmartArt graphics that are organized into seven categories: List, Process, Cycle, Hierarchy, Relationship, Matrix, and Pyramid (see Figure 3-1).

FIGURE 3-1
Choose a SmartArt graphic

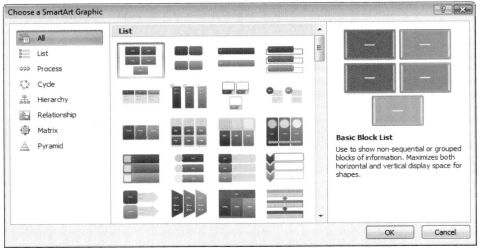

You can insert a SmartArt graphic on a slide by clicking the SmartArt icon on a content placeholder. To create a SmartArt graphic on a slide using the SmartArt dialog box, click the Insert tab on the Ribbon, and then click SmartArt to open the Choose a SmartArt Graphic dialog box gallery. You can also convert existing text into a SmartArt graphic by clicking the Convert to SmartArt Graphic button on the Ribbon, on the Home tab in the Paragraph group.

STEP-BY-STEP 3.1

1. Open the presentation file **Cotton.pptx** from the drive and folder where you store the Data Files for this lesson.

2. Save the presentation as **Cotton Report**, followed by your initials.

3. Click the **Slide Show** button on the status bar to run the slide show, press the **spacebar** to advance the slides, and then press the **Esc** key after the last slide. Because the slide show is partially completed, some slides just have titles. You will work on these slides in this lesson to add visual elements and complete the slide show.

4. Click the **Home tab** on the Ribbon if it is not already selected, click **slide 4**, *Types of Cotton*, to select the slide, click anywhere in the content placeholder, and then in the Paragraph group click the **Convert to SmartArt Graphic** button to open the SmartArt gallery.

5. Move the pointer over the different **SmartArt thumbnails** in the gallery, view the Live Preview effect on the text, and then click the **Pyramid List SmartArt** style (see Figure 3-2).

STEP-BY-STEP 3.1 Continued

FIGURE 3-2
Text converted to SmartArt graphic

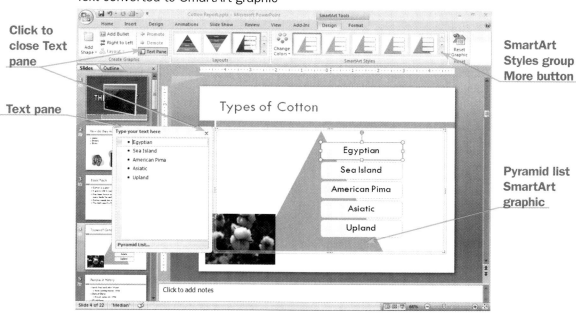

6. Save the presentation and leave it open for the next Step-by-Step.

Each SmartArt graphic style can be altered in countless ways to give you artistic control over how the graphic looks on the slide. Work with the SmartArt Tools tab on the Ribbon to change layouts, styles, and colors. You can add additional shapes or bullets. You can work using the features available through the buttons on the SmartArt Tools Format tab to change the way the text looks on each shape. You can use the Text pane to add text or edit and delete existing text. The Text pane provides an easy way to enter text in a SmartArt graphic. You can enter text either in the Text pane or directly in the SmartArt graphic.

STEP-BY-STEP 3.2

1. Click the **Text pane close** button to close the Text pane, if it is open.

2. Click the **SmartArt Tools Design** tab. In the SmartArt Styles group, click the SmartArt Styles group **More** button to open the gallery, move the pointer over the different SmartArt styles to see the Live Preview effect, and then in the 3-D group click the **Cartoon** icon.

STEP-BY-STEP 3.2 Continued

3. In the SmartArt Styles group click the **Change Colors** button, move the pointer over the different styles in the gallery, as shown in Figure 3-3, and then click **Colored Fill – Accent 2** in the Accent 2 section.

FIGURE 3-3
Changing colors

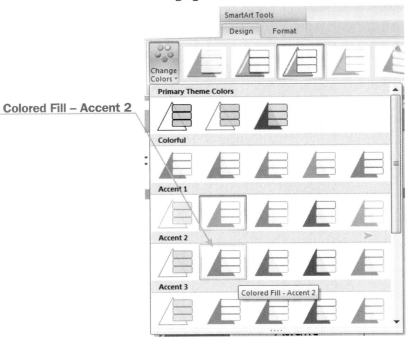

4. Click the **triangle shape** in the SmartArt graphic, click the **SmartArt Tools Format** tab on the Ribbon, and then in the Shape Styles group click the **Shape Fill** button.

5. In the Theme Colors section, click **Olive Green, Accent 3**. You have formatted the SmartArt graphic to present the different types of cotton in a very dramatic way.

6. Save the presentation and leave it open for the next Step-by-Step.

Working with Organization Charts

Organization charts are useful for showing the hierarchical structure and relationships within an organization. An organization chart is a way to graphically explain the structure of an organization in terms of rank. You can also use an organization chart to show relationships among objects, animals, or things that are related in a structured way. For a company or organization, the chart usually shows the managers and subordinates who make up its workforce. The graphics, such as boxes or ovals, will each contain the name of a person, position, or object. Vertical lines

Did You Know?

In many large companies the organization chart can be large and complicated, so companies often break the chart into several smaller charts for different departments.

drawn between the graphics show the direct relationships among superior and subordinate items in the chart. A horizontal line shows a lateral or equal relationship on the same level.

To add an organization chart to a slide, you can apply a Content layout to a slide and then click the SmartArt Graphic icon in the content placeholder. The Hierarchy category of SmartArt Graphics provides many different layouts for you to use as you create the organization chart on the slide.

To fill in the chart, click in a text box and type the text. Use the SmartArt tools on the Ribbon to add more boxes to the organization chart. Graphic elements are grouped with the text boxes to enhance the chart. Graphics can include shapes as well as pictures or clip art.

STEP-BY-STEP 3.3

1. Scroll down the Slides pane, click **slide 19**, *Products and Byproducts of Cotton*, click the **Home** tab on the Ribbon, in the Slides group click the **Layout** button, and then click **Title and Content**. The slide displays a content placeholder with the six icons. An organization chart is a SmartArt graphic.

2. Click the **Insert SmartArt Graphic** icon in the content placeholder. The Choose a SmartArt Graphic dialog box opens.

3. In the left pane, click **Hierarchy**, click the **Hierarchy** icon in the center pane, as shown in Figure 3-4, and then click **OK**. The Hierarchy chart appears on the slide with text placeholders, and the SmartArt Tools Design tab appears on the Ribbon. You can change the layout and style of the organization chart at any time.

FIGURE 3-4
Hierarchy SmartArt graphic selected

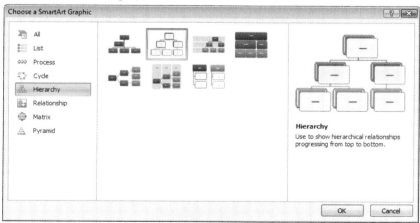

4. Save the presentation and leave it open for the next Step-by-Step.

Entering Text in a SmartArt Graphic

You can type text directly in the graphic or you can open the Text pane to the left of the SmartArt graphic to enter text. You click the Text Pane button to open and close the Text pane. Each text box in a SmartArt graphic can be formatted to meet your needs for the slide.

SmartArt graphics consist of text boxes and graphic elements that are grouped together. As you enter text in the text box, the font size will adjust so the text is visible in the graphic.

S TEP-BY-STEP 3.4

1. Click the top box **Text placeholder**, and then type **Cotton**.

2. Click the left **Text placeholder** on the second level, and then type **Lint**.

3. On the second level, click in the right **Text placeholder**, and then type **Cotton Seed**.

4. On the third level, click the left **Text placeholder**, and then type **Fabric, Yarn**. You can add and delete shapes and text boxes. You can promote and demote shapes and text boxes. Continue to work with the SmartArt graphic to create the levels and shapes as needed.

5. On the third level, click the middle **Text placeholder**, and then press the **Delete** key. The third level now has two shapes.

6. On the third level, click the right **Text placeholder**, and then type **Cotton Seed Oil**.

7. Click the **SmartArt Tools Design** tab. In the Create Graphic group, click the **Add Shape** button arrow, click **Add Shape After**, and then type **Hulls**. There are two subordinate shapes for Cotton Seed and one subordinate shape for Lint.

8. Click the **Cotton Seed Oil** text box. On the SmartArt Tools Design tab, in the Create Graphic group, click the **Add Shape** button arrow, click **Add Shape Below**, and then type **Refined Cooking Oil**.

9. Click the **Hulls shape**. On the SmartArt Tools Design tab, in the Create Graphic group, click the **Add Shape** button arrow, click **Add Shape Below**, and then type **Soap, Cosmetics**.

10. Continue to add shapes before and after and type text so that the SmartArt graphic looks similar to Figure 3-5.

> **Did You Know?**
>
> Use the Promote and Demote buttons in the Create Graphic group to move shapes in the SmartArt graphic to different levels.

> **Did You Know?**
>
> If you make a mistake, you can press the Ctrl+Z keys to undo your previous actions.

STEP-BY-STEP 3.4 Continued

FIGURE 3-5
Cotton organization chart

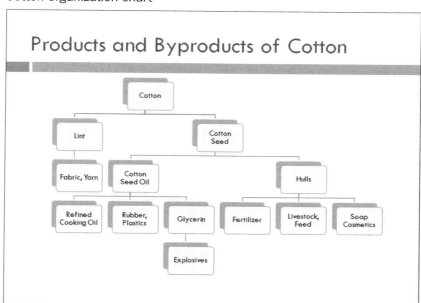

11. On the SmartTools Design tab on the Ribbon, in the Create Graphic group, click the **Right to Left** button, view the change, and then click the **Right to Left** button again.

12. Save the presentation and leave it open for the next Step-by-Step.

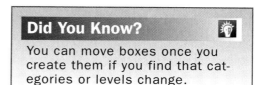

Did You Know?

You can move boxes once you create them if you find that categories or levels change.

You can animate a SmartArt graphic just as you do other slide objects. Click the Animations tab on the Ribbon, click the Custom Animation button, and then in the Custom Animation task pane, click the Add Effect button. Choose how you want to introduce the elements of the SmartArt graphic. You can select entry or exit animations, or have a segment animated for emphasis. If you want to add sound, click the Animation list arrow in the Custom Animation task pane, and then click Effect Options.

Creating and Formatting WordArt

WordArt is decorative text that you can insert on a slide. You can work with QuickStyles, predetermined combinations of color, fills, fonts, and effects, to create dramatic graphics from text. WordArt can also be shaped so the text fits a shape such as an arc, arrow, or oval. You can create new text as WordArt or change existing text into WordArt. To insert WordArt, click the Insert tab on the Ribbon; in the Text group, click the WordArt button. If you have text selected, click the Drawing Tools Format tab on the Ribbon, and, in the WordArt Styles group, click the More button to open a gallery of QuickStyles (see Figure 3-6), or click the Text Fill, Text Outline, and Text Effects buttons to create your own personal style. To create a shape from the text, in the WordArt Styles group, click the Text Effects button, point to Transform, and then click the shape you want (see Figure 3-7).

FIGURE 3-6
WordArt Styles gallery

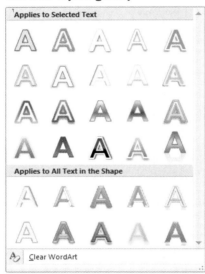

FIGURE 3-7
WordArt Transform text shapes

Transformation styles are grouped

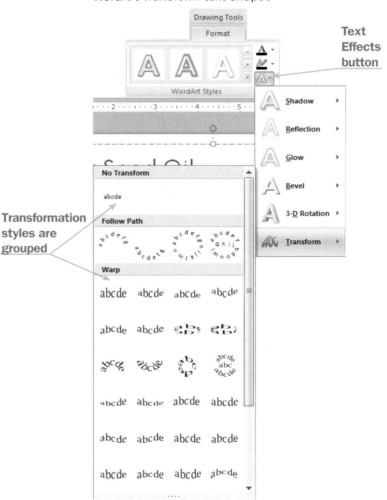

S TEP-BY-STEP 3.5

1. Click the **Home** tab on the Ribbon, in the Slides tab click **slide 13**, *Bales*, drag to select the text **Wrapped for protection**, and then in the Clipboard group, click the **Cut** button.

2. Click **slide 14** (the next slide with the full picture). In the Clipboard group, click the **Paste** button to paste the text as a text box on the slide.

3. Click the **Drawing Tools Format** tab on the Ribbon, click the WordArt Styles group **More** button to open the WordArt Styles gallery, and then in the Applies to All Text in the Shape section, in the last row click **Fill – Accent 2, Matte Bevel**.

4. In the Shape Styles group, click the **Shape Effects** button, point to **Glow**, and then in the last row click **Accent color 2, 18pt glow**.

5. In the WordArt Styles group, click the **Text Effects** button, point to **Transform**, and in the Warp section click **Ring Outside**. The text is a little difficult to read, so you can enlarge it.

6. Using the **Resize Pointer**, drag down the **middle bottom sizing handle** to enlarge the box so you can read the letters, and then use the **Move Pointer** to drag the WordArt shape to the sky part of the photograph so that the WordArt on the slide looks like Figure 3-8.

FIGURE 3-8
WordArt resized and moved

WordArt

7. Save the presentation and leave the presentation open for the next Step-by-Step.

Working with Charts

Charts, also called **graphs**, provide a visual way to display numerical data in a presentation. When you create a chart in PowerPoint, you are working in a program called Microsoft Excel. If you do not have Microsoft Excel installed, you can use a program called Microsoft Graph to create and edit the chart. Microsoft Graph is much less powerful than Excel, but for simple graphing it does the job just fine. When you are building and modifying a chart, Microsoft Excel (or Graph) features, commands, and buttons become available to help you.

If you have an existing chart in an Excel worksheet, you can include that chart on a slide by linking or embedding the worksheet as an object in the slide. You will learn about linking and embedding objects in Lesson 4.

Building a Chart

To create a chart in a presentation, choose a slide layout that contains a content placeholder for a chart. Click the content placeholder Insert Chart icon to open the Insert Chart dialog box, as shown in Figure 3-9. To create a chart on a slide that does not have the Insert Chart icon on the Content Layout placeholder, on the Ribbon click the Insert tab, and in the Illustrations group click the Chart button.

FIGURE 3-9
Insert Chart dialog box

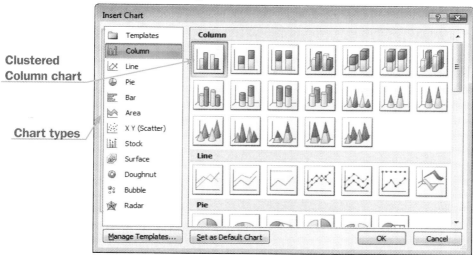

Once you select a chart type, the chart appears on the slide with default data. The screen splits into two, with PowerPoint and Excel windows open side-by-side. The data for the chart is in the Excel window. This is the datasheet, a worksheet that appears with the chart and has the numbers for the chart. You replace the sample data with your own. The chart changes to reflect the new data. When you are ready to return to the presentation, click to close the Excel window and you will see the chart on the PowerPoint slide.

A worksheet is made up of columns and rows. The intersection of each column and row is a cell. You identify the cells by their column letter and row number. The cell that is at the intersection of column C and row 3 would be cell C3.

STEP-BY-STEP 3.6

1. Click **slide 7**, *Where Does Cotton Grow?* This slide has a Title and Content slide layout.

2. Click the **Insert Chart** icon on the content placeholder.

3. In the Insert Chart dialog box, click **Column** in the left pane, click the **Clustered Column** icon (first icon, first row), and then click **OK**.

STEP-BY-STEP 3.6 Continued

The window splits so that you have PowerPoint open in a window on the left side of the screen and Excel open in a window on the right side of the screen (see Figure 3-10). The sample data in the Excel window is shown as a sample chart in the PowerPoint window. Excel displays the data in a worksheet. To enter data in an Excel worksheet, you click the cell and then type the numbers or text. You press the Enter key after you type the data in each cell. You can also press the Tab key to move from cell to cell. You have to replace the data with meaningful numbers for your chart. For this lesson, you can leave the numbers alone and simply enter the labels (the text) for the chart, to learn how charts work.

FIGURE 3-10
Excel and PowerPoint windows

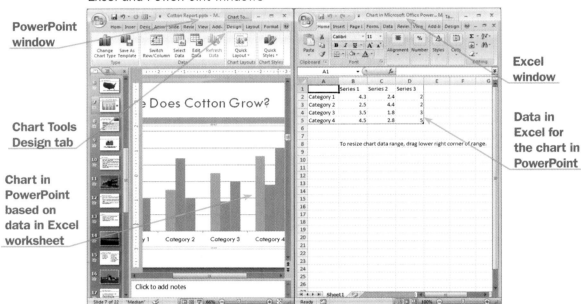

4. Click cell **A2**, and then type **Texas**.

5. Click cell **A3**, and then type **Missouri**.

6. Click cell **A4**, and then type **Virginia**.

7. Click cell **A5**, and then type **Alabama**.

STEP-BY-STEP 3.6 Continued

8. Click cell **B1**, type **2007**, press the **Tab** key, type **2008**, press the **Tab** key, type **2009**, and then press the **Enter** key. The data is entered in the worksheet, as shown in Figure 3-11.

FIGURE 3-11
Data in Excel

The chart changes to reflect the new data. The states are listed on the horizontal axis, the values in the worksheet are the numbers on the vertical axis, and the legend shows each year in a different color for each column in the chart.

9. Click the Microsoft Excel **Close** button and return to the presentation, and then maximize the PowerPoint window if necessary.

10. Save the presentation and leave it open for the next Step-by-Step.

Formatting a chart

The chart gives a visual representation of numeric data. Any text you add to the chart helps your audience understand the data by identifying what each number refers to. A legend identifies the data series or bars in a column chart. A title gives the chart a name. To format and edit the chart, you can use the Ribbon commands on the Chart Tools Design tab, the Chart Tools Layout tab, and the Chart Tools Format tab, as shown in Figure 3-12.

FIGURE 3-12
Chart tools

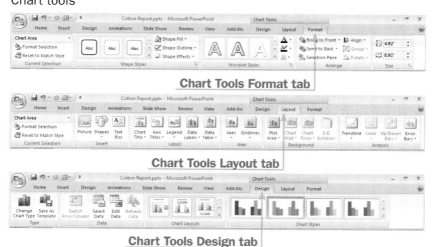

If you need to modify a chart at any time, click the chart to select it and open the Chart Tools tab on the Ribbon. You can change the type of chart by clicking the Change Chart Type button in the Type group on the Chart Tools Design tab. The Change Chart Type dialog box that opens is basically the same as the Insert Chart dialog box shown in Figure 3-9. Choose a chart type and subtype.

STEP-BY-STEP 3.7

1. Click the **chart** to activate it and display the Chart Tools Design tab on the Ribbon.

2. Click the **Chart Tools Layout** tab on the Ribbon, in the Labels group click the **Chart Title** button, on the menu click **Centered Overlay Title**, and then type **Top Cotton Producing States**.

3. On the Chart Tools Layout tab on the Ribbon, in the Labels group, click the **Data Labels** button to open the menu, and then click **Inside End**.

4. Click the **Chart Tools Design** tab on the Ribbon, in the Chart Styles group click the Chart Styles **More** button, and then click **Style 26**. Your chart should look similar to Figure 3-13.

FIGURE 3-13
Column chart formatted

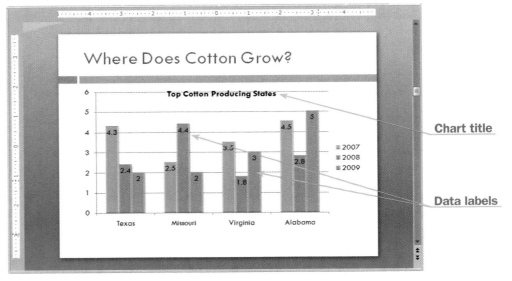

5. Click the **Chart Tools Design** tab on the Ribbon, in the Type group click the **Change Chart Type** button, in the Change Chart Type dialog box, in the left pane click **Pie**, in the Pie section click **Pie in 3D** (second chart icon), and then click **OK**. The chart is now a 3-D pie chart.

6. Click the **Chart Tools Design** tab on the Ribbon, in the Type group click the **Change Chart Type** button, in the Change Chart type dialog box, and then in the left pane click **Column**, in the last row of the Column section click **3-D Pyramid**, and then click **OK**. Your chart should look similar to Figure 3-14.

STEP-BY-STEP 3.7 Continued

FIGURE 3-14
3-D pyramid chart

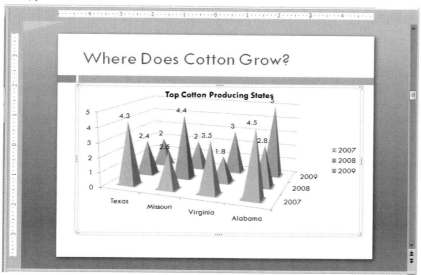

7. Save the presentation and leave the presentation open for the next Step-by-Step.

Working with Tables

Tables are useful when you need to organize information that can be displayed in **rows** and **columns**. Each intersection of a row and column is a **cell**. You enter text or numbers in each cell. Tables can be formatted to enhance their appearance. A table can have column headings to identify each item in each column and row headings to identify the rows. A sample table for a club appears in Figure 3-15. The column headings are the days of the week. The row headings are the assignments. Each cell has the name of a club member.

FIGURE 3-15
A sample table

	Monday	Tuesday	Wednesday	Thursday	Friday
Breakfast	Jennifer	Emily	Michael	David	Simon
Lunch	Emily	Michael	David	Simon	Jennifer
Dinner	Michael	David	Simon	Jennifer	Emily

Creating a Table

To include a table on a slide, you can use the Content slide layout and click the Insert Table icon to open the Insert Table dialog box. Type the number of columns and rows you want, and then click OK, and a table is inserted on the slide. You type the text in the table; you can move between cells by pressing the Tab key. If you prefer to use the Ribbon and you want to drag a table, click the Insert tab on the Ribbon, and then in the Tables group, click the Table icon. You drag to specify the number of rows and columns, as shown in Figure 3-16.

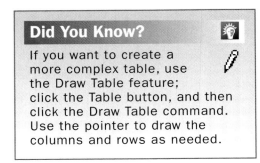

Did You Know?

If you want to create a more complex table, use the Draw Table feature; click the Table button, and then click the Draw Table command. Use the pointer to draw the columns and rows as needed.

FIGURE 3-16
Dragging to create a table

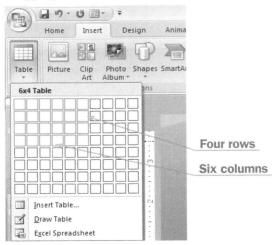

Four rows

Six columns

STEP-BY-STEP 3.8

1. Click **slide 18**, *Cotton Production in Millions of Bales*, in the Slides pane. Slide 18 is selected. The slide layout is Title and Content, and the Insert Table icon is on the slide. For this theme, there is also a slide layout for Title and Table.

2. On the content placeholder click the **Insert Table** icon to open the Insert Table dialog box, as shown in Figure 3-17.

FIGURE 3-17
Insert Table dialog box

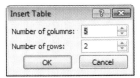

STEP-BY-STEP 3.8 Continued

3. In the Number of columns text box, type **4**, and then press the **Tab** key.

4. In the Number of rows text box, type **9**, and then click **OK**.

PowerPoint inserts a table with four columns and nine rows on the slide. The table is formatted according to the Median theme. You can change the formatting at any time. The Table Tools Design tab appears on the Ribbon. The insertion point is in the first cell, ready for you to type the data. The table style applied by the theme on the slide includes a different style for column headings. You do not want column headings.

5. On the Table Tools Design tab, in the Table Style Options group, click the **Header Row** check box to remove the check mark.

6. Type the data as shown in Figure 3-18, click the cell or press the **Tab** key to move from cell to cell. Do not worry if the text does not seem to fit. You will adjust the table later.

FIGURE 3-18
Table data

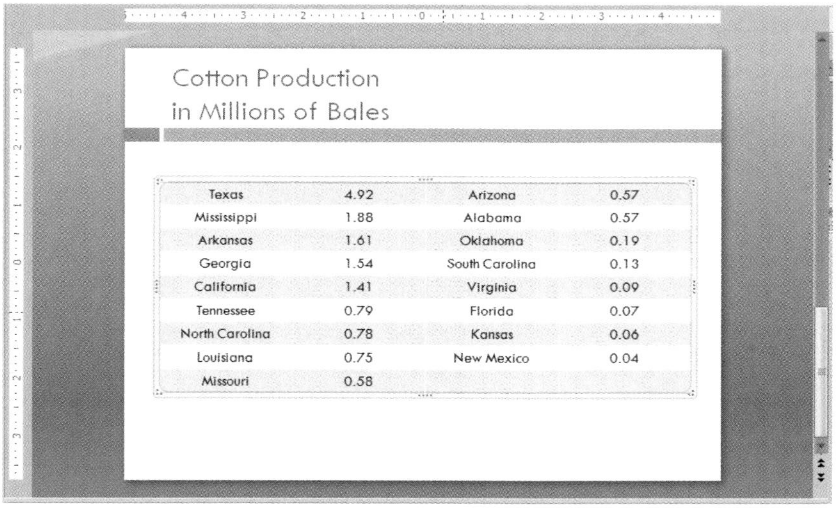

7. Save the presentation and leave it open for the next Step-by-Step.

Modifying Table Styles

To modify a table's borders, fill, or text boxes, select the table to open the Table Tools Design tab on the Ribbon, shown in Figure 3-19. You can apply a table style to format the table elements at once. If you want to work on individual elements, you can click the different buttons to change the shading, borders, and effects to give the table a unique look.

FIGURE 3-19
Table Tools Design tab on the Ribbon

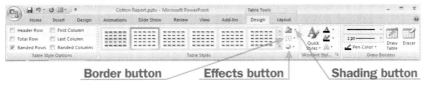

STEP-BY-STEP 3.9

1. Click the table to select it and open the Table Tools Design tab.

2. Click the **Table Tools Design** tab on the Ribbon, and then click the Table Styles **More** button to open the gallery, as shown in Figure 3-20. The Table Styles gallery is organized into sections: Best Match for Document, Light, Medium, and Dark.

FIGURE 3-20
Table Styles gallery

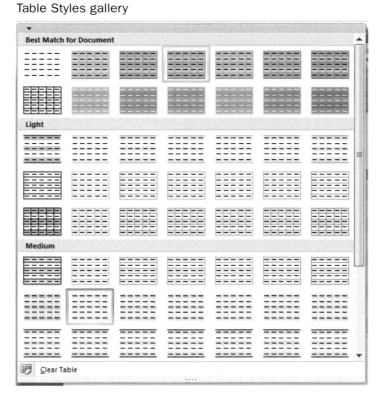

STEP-BY-STEP 3.9 Continued

3. Move the pointer over the different table styles in the gallery and watch as Live Preview shows the effect on the table.

4. In the Light section, click **Light Style 1 – Accent 5**.

5. Save the presentation and leave it open for the next Step-by-Step.

Modifying Table Layout

You can insert or delete columns and rows, merge or split cells, and change the alignment. You can add gridlines, distribute content among cells, rows, and columns, and even change the direction of text in a cell. You work using the Table Tools Layout tab on the Ribbon (see Figure 3-21). To change the width of a column or row, you can also click and drag a border.

> **Did You Know?**
>
> If all the text in each column in a table doesn't fit in the cell, you can double-click the column border to widen the entire column so all text in any cell in that column fits on one line.

FIGURE 3-21
Table Tools Layout tab on the Ribbon

STEP-BY-STEP 3.10

1. Click and drag the **table** using the Move pointer so that the table is in the center of the slide below the blue horizontal graphic.

2. On the Table Tools Layout tab, in the Alignment group, click the **Center** button.

3. Click the **Texas** cell. In the Rows & Columns group, click the **Insert Above** button, and then in the Merge group, click the **Merge Cells** button. A new row with one cell is in the top row of the table.

4. In the new top row, type **Data from the US Department of Agriculture**, in the Cell Size group, click the **Height** text box, and then type **.75**.

5. Click the **Table Tools Design** tab on the Ribbon, and then in the Table Style Options group, click the **Header Row** check box. The new row is now a header row and has header row formatting.

STEP-BY-STEP 3.10 Continued

6. In the Table Styles group, click the **Shading button** list arrow, point to **Texture**, and then click the **Canvas texture** icon. The texture fills the row, see Figure 3-22.

FIGURE 3-22
Designed table

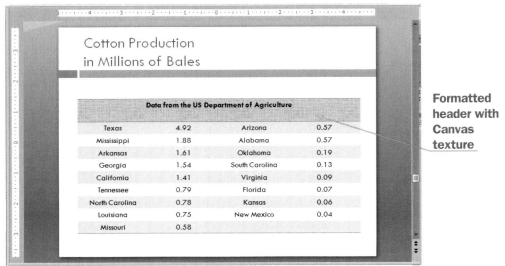

Formatted
header with
Canvas
texture

7. Save the presentation and leave the presentation open for the next Step-by-Step.

Creating Shapes and Objects

You can add shapes and other drawing objects to your presentation to add interest to a slide. Shapes include arrows, circles, cones, and stars. On the Insert tab, you can click the Shapes button to display a gallery of available shapes, as shown in Figure 3-23. The Shapes button is also available by means of the shapes and drawing tools on the Home tab in the Drawing group. There are also a variety of other shapes you can add, including equation shapes, connectors, flow chart shapes, banners, and other kinds of objects that help draw the shape you want. Click the slide to insert the shape with a predefined size.

FIGURE 3-23
The Shapes gallery

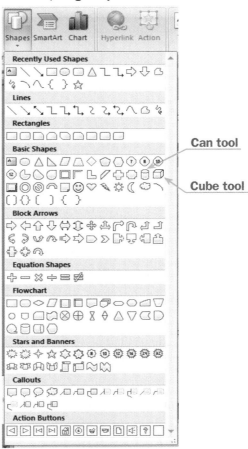

Can tool

Cube tool

Drawing an Object

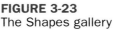 The Shapes gallery contains buttons for drawing objects such as lines, circles, arrows, and squares. Click the corresponding button to activate the tool. The Rectangle tools draw rectangles and squares. The Oval tool draws ovals and circles. To use a tool, click and hold the mouse button, and then drag to draw. To create a perfect circle or square, hold down the Shift key as you drag.

Selecting an Object

When you click an inserted object to select it, little squares appear at the edges of the graphic. These small squares are called **handles**. They indicate that the object is selected, and they allow you to manipulate the object. You drag handles to resize the object. The yellow boxes are **adjustment handles**. The green circle is the **rotate handle**. You will learn more about selecting and manipulating objects later in the lesson.

S TEP-BY-STEP 3.11

1. Click **slide 20**, *Cotton Seed Oil*, in the Slides pane, on the Home tab in the Slides group click the **Layout** button, and then click the **Title Only** layout.

2. In the Drawing group, click the **Shapes** button to open the Shapes gallery.

3. In the Basic Shapes section, click the **Cube** icon, as shown in Figure 3-23.

4. Click in the left side of the slide just below the blue bar. A cube is drawn and handles appear on the object.

> **Did You Know?**
>
> Depending on the resolution of your computer, the Shapes button may appear as a gallery of shapes or as the Shapes button in the Drawing group on the Ribbon. If the Shapes button is on the Ribbon, click the Shapes More button to view the Shapes gallery.

5. In the Drawing group, click the **Shapes** button to open the Shapes gallery. In the Recently Used Shapes section, click the **Cube** icon, and then click the right side of the slide just below the blue bar to create another cube.

6. Create one more cube near the bottom of the slide, below the cube on the right side of the slide. Refer to Figure 3-24 for placement.

7. In the Drawing group, click the **Shapes** button to open the Shapes gallery. In the **Basic Shapes** section, click the **Can** icon, and then click near the bottom of the slide, below the left cube, to create a can similar to the one in Figure 3-24.

8. In the Drawing group, click the **Shapes** button to open the Shapes gallery. In the Block Arrows section, click the **Right Arrow** icon.

9. Click to the right of the left cube, and then drag to the right to draw an arrow to the right of the first cube you created.

10. In the Drawing group, click the **Shapes** button to open the Shapes gallery, in the Block Arrows section, click the **Left Arrow** icon, and then draw a left arrow in the middle of the screen, about twice as long as the one you drew in Step 9. Your slide should look similar to Figure 3-24.

STEP-BY-STEP 3.11 Continued

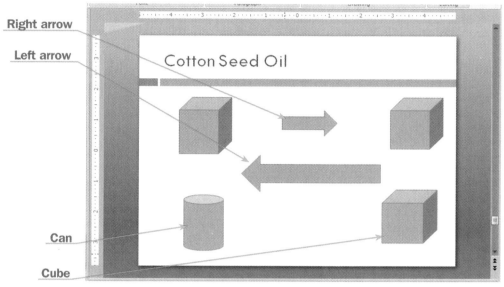

FIGURE 3-24
Six drawn objects

Right arrow

Left arrow

Can

Cube

Cotton Seed Oil

11. Save the presentation and leave it open for the next Step-by-Step.

Manipulating Objects

Once you have created an object, there are many ways of manipulating it to achieve the final effect you want. You can rotate, fill, scale, or size an object, as well as change its color and position.

As you learned earlier in the lesson, when you select an object, square handles surround it. To select an object, simply click it. The selection handles appear around the object, allowing you to manipulate it. You can move the object, resize the object, rotate the object, or change the key features of the shape. To deselect an object, click another object or anywhere in the window.

Selecting More Than One Object

Sometimes you will want to select more than one object. PowerPoint gives you several ways to select more than one object using the mouse. One method is to shift-click; another is to draw a selection box around a group of objects. You can also click the Select button in the Editing group on the Home tab on the Ribbon to open the Selection and Visibility task pane.

Shift-Clicking

To shift-click, hold down the Shift key and click each of the objects you want to select. Use this method when you need to select objects that are not close to each other, or when the objects you need to select are near other objects you do not want to select. If you select an object by accident, click it again to deselect it, while still holding down the Shift key.

Drawing a Selection Box

Using the Select Objects tool, you can drag a selection box around a group of objects. On the Home tab on the Ribbon, in the Editing group, click the Select button and then click Select Objects. Use a selection box when all of the objects you want selected are near each other and can be surrounded with a box. Be sure your selection box is large enough to enclose all the selection handles of the various objects. If you miss a handle, the corresponding item will not be selected.

Combining Methods

You can also combine these two methods. First, use the selection box, and then shift-click to include objects that the selection box might have missed.

Rotating an Object

One way of modifying an object is to rotate it. The three rotate commands on the Arrange menu are Rotate Right 90°, Rotate Left 90°, and More Rotation Options. The Rotate Right command moves a graphic in 90-degree increments to the right. The Rotate Left command rotates the graphic in 90-degree increments to the left. You can also drag the rotate handle, the green circle on a selected object, to rotate a graphic to any angle. You can flip an object by choosing the Flip Horizontal or Flip Vertical command on the Rotate submenu, as shown in Figure 3-25.

FIGURE 3-25
Rotate commands

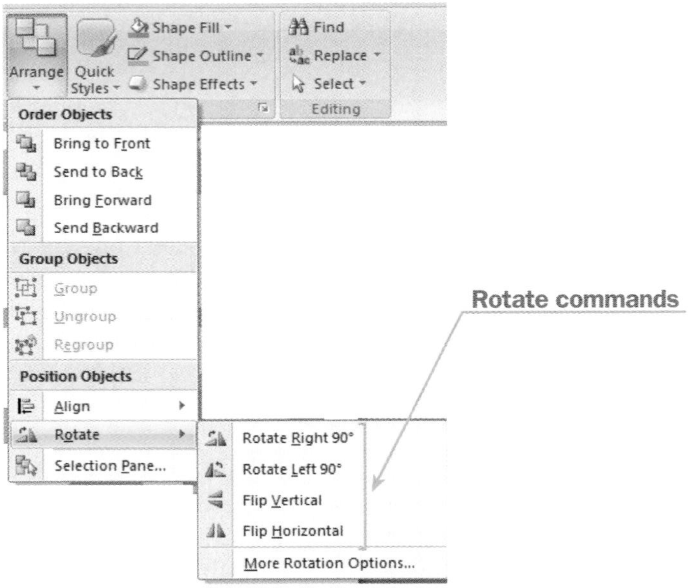

STEP-BY-STEP 3.12

1. Click the **left arrow** in the middle of the screen. Sizing handles appear around the perimeter of the shape, two adjustment handles appear at the prominent features—the arrow head and the arrow body—and a rotate handle appears near the top of the shape, as shown in Figure 3-26.

STEP-BY-STEP 3.12 Continued

FIGURE 3-26
Selected Left Arrow

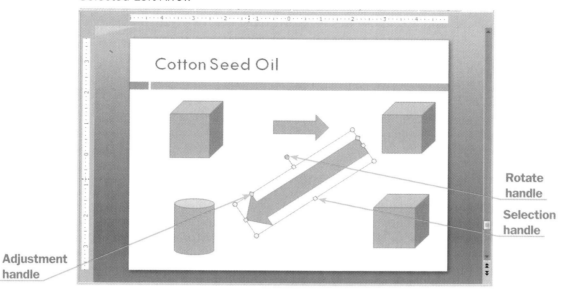

Rotate
handle

Selection
handle

Adjustment
handle

2. Drag the green **rotate handle** in a counterclockwise direction until the arrow points to the can.

3. Click the **right arrow** you created on the slide.

4. On the Home tab in the Drawing group, click the **Arrange** button, in the Position Objects section point to **Rotate**, and then click **Rotate Left 90°**. The arrow is now pointing up.

5. Drag the green **rotate handle** counterclockwise 270 degrees so that the arrow points to the right again.

6. Save the presentation and leave it open for the next Step-by-Step.

Did You Know?

As you rotate an object, the pointer will appear as a **rotate pointer**.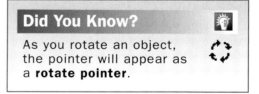

Applying Formatting

The Drawing Tools Format tab on the Ribbon, shown in Figure 3-27, contains various ways to apply formatting to visual elements in a presentation. You can change the fill, line, or font color. You can apply Shape Styles or WordArt Styles, or arrange objects for added effects.

FIGURE 3-27
Drawing Tools Format tab on the Ribbon

Filling a Shape and Changing Shape Effects

Filling an object can help add interest to your drawing objects. Select the object you want to fill and click the Shape Fill button in the Shape Styles group on the Drawing Tools Format tab. You can fill a shape with theme or standard colors, or click More Fill Colors to open a full color palette in the Colors dialog box. You can also use a picture, gradient, or texture to fill a shape (see Figure 3-28).

FIGURE 3-28
Formatting the shape fill

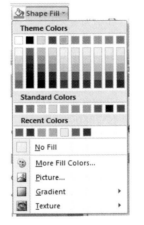

Changing Line Color

Another way to apply formatting to a drawing object is to change the line color. Click the Shape Outline button in the Shape Styles group on the Drawing Tools Format tab, and then click a theme or standard color in the palette, or click More Outline Colors to open a full color palette in the Colors dialog box. Other Outline options include changing the weight or thickness of the outline or creating dashes or a designed line. Refer to Figure 3-29.

FIGURE 3-29
Formatting the outline of a shape

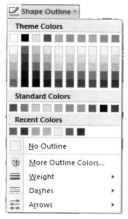

Changing Shape Effects

Another way to apply formatting to a drawing object is to change the shape effects. Click the Shape Effects button in the Shape Styles group on the Drawing Tools Format tab. Shape effects include Shadow, Reflection, Glow, Soft Edges, Bevel, and 3-D Rotation.

To work on the shape and design your shape you can use the Format Shape dialog box, shown in Figure 3-30. To open the Format Shape dialog box, click the Shape Styles dialog box launcher in the Shape Styles group.

FIGURE 3-30
Format Shape dialog box

STEP-BY-STEP 3.13

1. Click the **upper-left cube object**. On the Drawing Tools Format tab, in the Shape Styles group, click the **Shape Fill** button, and then click **Picture**. The Insert Picture dialog box opens.

2. Locate the folder that contains the Data Files for this lesson, click the **Cotton Gin.jpg** picture file in the Data Files, and then click **Insert**. The picture of the cotton gin appears on the cube.

3. Click the **lower-right cube object**. On the Drawing Tools Format tab, in the Shape Styles group, click the **Shape Fill** button, and then click **Picture**. The Insert Picture dialog box opens.

4. Click **Potato Chip Plant.jpg**, and then click **Insert**. The picture of the potato chip plant appears on the face of the cube.

5. Click the **can object**. On the Drawing Tools Format tab, in the Shape Styles group, click the **Shape Fill** button, and then click **Orange Accent 2** in the Theme Colors section.

6. Click the **upper-right cube object**. On the Drawing Tools Format tab, in the Shape Styles group, click the **Shape Effects** button, point to **Glow**, and then in the Glow Variations section, click **Accent color 4, 18 pt glow** in the last row.

7. The **upper-right cube** should still be selected. On the Drawing Tools Format tab, in the Shape Styles group, click the **Shape Outline** button, in the Theme Colors section click **Orange Accent 2**, click the **Shape Outline** button, point to **Dashes**, and then click **Square Dot**. Your shapes should look similar to Figure 3-31.

FIGURE 3-31
Formatted shapes

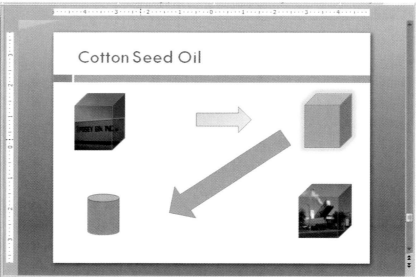

8. Save the presentation and leave it open for the next Step-by-Step.

Working with an Object

Handles do more than indicate that an object is selected. They make it easy to resize an object that is too large or too small. Select the object to make the handles appear, and then drag one of the handles inward or outward to make the object smaller or larger.

To scale an object, hold down Shift and drag a corner handle. This maintains an object's proportions. You scale and size clip-art graphics just as you do objects. Many shapes have a yellow diamond adjustment handle that you can drag to change the appearance of the object.

Copying or Moving an Object

To move an object, first select it and then drag it into place. You can cut, copy, and paste objects the same way you do text. The Cut and Copy commands place a copy of the selected image on the Office Clipboard. Pasting an object from the Office Clipboard places the object in your drawing. You can then move it into position.

Did You Know?

You can size an object more precisely by using the height and width text boxes on the Drawing Tools Format tab in the Size group to specify a height and width.

Grouping Objects

As your drawing becomes more complex, you might find it necessary to "glue" objects together into groups. Grouping allows you to work with several items as if they were one object. To group objects, select the objects you want to group, then in the Home tab on the Ribbon, in the Drawing group click the Arrange button to open the menu shown in Figure 3-32, and then click Group. You can ungroup objects using the Ungroup command.

FIGURE 3-32
Arrange menu

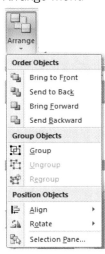

STEP-BY-STEP 3.14

1. Click the **upper-left cube**, press and hold the **Ctrl** key, click the **upper-right cube,** click the **lower-right cube**, and then release the **Ctrl** key. The three cube objects are selected.

2. On the Drawing Tools Format tab, in the Arrange group click the **Group** button, and then click **Group**. The three cubes are now grouped into one object. Sizing handles and the rotate handle affect all three objects at once. Any formatting changes will affect all objects in the group.

3. Move the pointer over the **upper-left sizing handle** until it becomes a two-headed diagonal arrow.

4. Click and drag the **diagonal resize pointer** up and to the left to enlarge the three cubes. On the Drawing Tools Format tab in the Arrange group, click the **Align** button, and then click **Align Center**. The objects are larger and centered on the slide, as shown in Figure 3-33.

FIGURE 3-33
Grouped objects

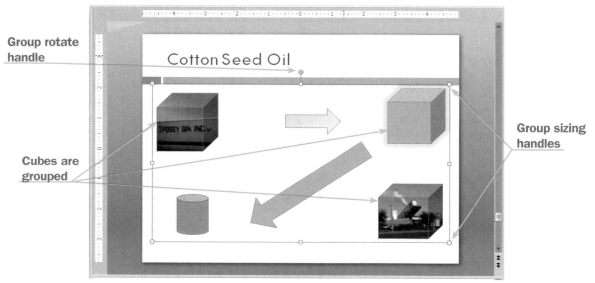

5. Click the **can object**, and then drag the yellow **adjustment handle** down slightly so it is even with the two middle sizing handles. You changed a feature of the object by dragging the yellow adjustment handle.

6. Right-click the **right arrow object** between the two top cubes, and then click **Copy**. A copy of the right arrow is pasted on the Office Clipboard.

7. Right-click a blank area of the slide, and then click **Paste**. The arrow is pasted from the Office Clipboard into the slide, just offset from the original arrow.

8. Use the Move pointer to drag the **arrow object** to a new position between the can and the lower-right cube, press and hold the **Ctrl** key, click the original **right arrow object** so both arrows are selected, release the **Ctrl** key, on the Home tab on the Ribbon in the Drawing group, click the **Arrange** button, point to **Align** on the menu, and then click **Align Center**.

STEP-BY-STEP 3.14 Continued

9. Right-click the **can object**, click **Copy**, right-click a blank area of the slide, click **Paste**, right-click a blank area of the slide, and then click **Paste** again to add two new cans to the slide.

10. Move the **diagonal left arrow** as needed, and then arrange the cans as shown in Figure 3-34.

FIGURE 3-34
Shapes copied, moved, and aligned

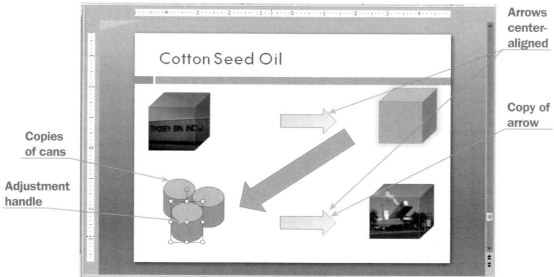

11. Save the presentation and leave it open for the next Step-by-Step.

Create a Text Box on a Shape

To place text inside a shape, simply click the shape and then begin to type. A text box will appear on the shape. You can wrap text or change the alignment of text in a shape by working in the Format Shape dialog box. Right-click any shape, and then click Format Shape to open the Format Shape dialog box. You cannot type text on an object that is part of a group. You can ungroup the object to add special formatting or text, and then regroup it to make it part of the original group again.

STEP-BY-STEP 3.15

1. Click any **cube** to select the cube group. On the Home tab on the Ribbon, in the Drawing group, click the **Arrange** button, and then click **Ungroup**. The three cubes are no longer grouped.

2. Click a blank area of the slide to deselect the three cubes, and then click the **upper-right cube** that does not have a picture.

3. Type **Cottonseed Oil Mill** inside the text box. Notice how the text wraps in the shape.

STEP-BY-STEP 3.15 Continued

4. Drag to select the text **Cottonseed Oil Mill** you just typed in the cube. On the Ribbon click the **Drawing Tools Format** tab, click the WordArt Styles **More** button, move the pointer over the different WordArt styles to see the effects, and then click **Fill – Text 2**, **Outline – Background 2** in the first row.

5. If the shape is not big enough to fit the text, drag the lower-right sizing handle to resize the cube so all the text fits on two lines.

6. On the Ribbon, on the Drawing Tools Format tab, in the Arrange group, click the **Group** button, and then click **Regroup**. You made changes to the one cube, and then regrouped it with the other two cubes. The three objects are grouped again, and are treated as one object by PowerPoint.

7. Click the front **can**, and then type **Cottonseed Oil**.

8. Drag a **selection box** around the three cans to select the three objects, right-click the selected objects, on the shortcut menu point to **Group**, and then click **Group** from the shortcut menu.

9. Resize the grouped can object so the text Cottonseed Oil fits on two lines, as shown in Figure 3-35.

FIGURE 3-35
Text added to objects

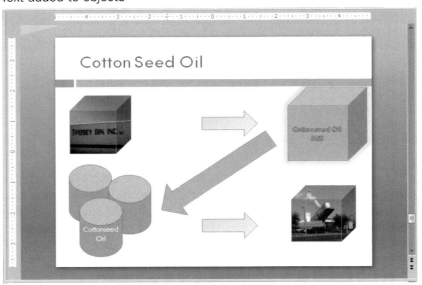

10. Save the presentation and leave it open for the next Step-by-Step.

Animating Shapes

Ⓒ **W**hen you create shapes on a slide, often you want to add animation to the shapes to help the slide to tell a story. Grouped objects will animate as a single object. If you want the individual objects in a group to animate separately, you have to ungroup them.

Ⓢ TEP-BY-STEP 3.16

1. Click any **cube** on the slide, click the **Drawing Tools Format** tab, in the Arrange group click **Group**, click **Ungroup**, and then click a blank area on the slide.

2. Click the **upper-right cube**, click the **Animations** tab on the Ribbon, click the **Custom Animation** button to open the Custom Animation task pane, click the **Add Effect** button, point to **Entrance**, click **More Effects**, click **Appear**, and then **click OK**. The effect is set to be triggered by Start On Click.

3. Click the **top arrow** between the two cubes, click the **Add Effect** button, point to **Entrance**, click **More Effects**, scroll to the **Exciting** group, click **Glide**, and then click **OK**. This effect is also set to be triggered by Start On Click.

4. Select the **upper-left cube**, click the **Add Effect** button, point to **Entrance**, click **More Effects**, scroll to the **Exciting** group, click **Bounce**, click **OK**, click the **Start** list arrow in the Custom Animation task pane, and then click **After Previous**.

5. Select the **arrow** that points to the cans in the middle of the slide, click the **Add Effect** button, point to **Entrance**, click **More Effects**, click **Spinner**, click **OK**, click the **Speed** list arrow, click **Medium**, and then set the animation to **Start On Click**.

6. Click the **cans group**, add the **Appear Entrance** effect, and then set it to be triggered by **Start On Click**.

7. Click on the **upper-left cube**, press and hold down the **Shift** key, click the **top** and **middle arrows**, click the **upper-right cube**, click the **Add Effect** button, point to **Exit**, click **More Effects**, in the Basic section click **Diamond**, click **OK**, click the **Start** list arrow in the Custom Animation task pane, and then click **After Previous**.

8. Click the **bottom arrow**, click the **Add Effect** button, point to **Entrance**, click More Effects, scroll to the **Exciting** section, click **Pinwheel**, click **OK**, click the **Start** list arrow, and then click **On Click**.

9. Click the **last cube** on the lower-right corner of the slide, click the **Add Effect** button, point to **Entrance**, click **Appear**, click the **Start** list arrow in the Custom Animation task pane, and then click **After Previous**.

10. Click the **Insert** tab on the Ribbon, in the Text group click the **Text Box** button, click anywhere on the slide, and then type **Cottonseed is separated from the lint at the cotton gin.**

11. Click the **Animations** tab on the Ribbon. In the Custom Animation task pane, click the **Add Effect** button, point to **Entrance**, click **Appear**, click the **Start** arrow in the Custom Animation task pane, and then click **With Previous**. The new text box is now animated.

STEP-BY-STEP 3.16 Continued

12. With the **text box** still selected, in the Custom Animation task pane, click the **Re-Order up** arrow so that the Text box animation is second on the list.

13. With the **text box** still selected, click the **Add Effect** button, point to **Exit**, click **Checkerboard**, click the **Start** arrow in the Custom Animation task pane, click **After Previous**, and then click the **Re-Order up** arrow so that the exit Text box animation is third on the list.

14. Move the **text box** to the middle of the slide. The slide should look similar to Figure 3-36.

FIGURE 3-36
Objects are animated

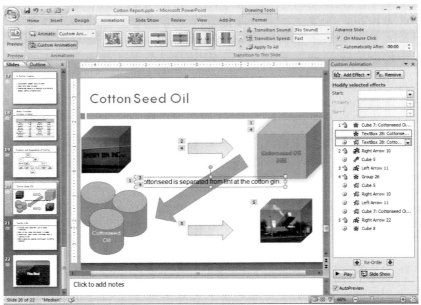

15. Close the Custom Animation task pane.

16. View the presentation, save it, and leave it open for the next Step-by-Step.

> **Did You Know?**
>
> Animation is one of the most interesting and creative features in PowerPoint. You should continue to experiment with animating objects until you get the effects you want for a slide.

Ordering Visual Elements

If you add an object to a slide that already contains other objects, the last object is stacked on top of the other objects. To bring an object forward or send it backward, select the object you want to move, and click the Bring to Front, Send to Back, Bring Forward, or Send Backward command in the Arrange group on the Drawing Tools Format tab. These commands are also available in the Picture Tools Format tab on the Ribbon. You can also access this feature by right-clicking the object, then making a selection from the shortcut menu.

S TEP-BY-STEP 3.17

1. Click **slide 21**, *Textile Mills*, click the **Home** tab on the Ribbon, in the Slides group click the **New Slide** button arrow, and then click the **Blank layout**.

2. Click the **Insert** tab on the Ribbon, and then, in the Illustrations group, click the **Picture** button to open the Insert Picture dialog box.

3. Locate the folder that has the Data Files for this lesson, click the file **Sky.jpg**, and then click **Insert**. The picture of a blue sky appears on the slide.

4. Drag the **corner sizing handles** so that the picture fills the entire slide.

5. Click the **Insert** tab on the Ribbon, and then, in the Illustrations group, click the **Picture** button to open the Insert Picture dialog box.

6. Locate and insert the picture **Truck.jpg** on the slide, and then move the truck down to the lower portion of the slide.

7. Click the **Insert** tab on the Ribbon. In the Illustrations group, click the **Picture** button, locate and insert the picture **Highway.jpg** on the slide, and then resize and position the **Highway.jpg** picture so that it covers the bottom half of the slide and covers the Truck.jpg picture.

8. On the Picture Tools Format tab, in the Arrange group, click the **Send to Back** arrow, and then click **Send Backward**. The truck appears again. The stacking order of the pictures should be sky, highway, and then truck. You should see all three images.

9. Click the **Truck.jpg** picture on the slide and resize the picture so that it is proportional to the cars in the Highway.jpg picture, and then move the **Truck.jpg** picture so that it is positioned on the left side of the overpass, slightly off the slide (see Figure 3-37).

FIGURE 3-37
Pictures inserted on a slide

STEP-BY-STEP 3.17 Continued

10. Click the **Truck.jpg** picture so it is selected. On the Picture Tools Format tab on the Ribbon, in the Adjust group, click the **Recolor** button, and then click **Set Transparent Color**. The pointer changes to show that the Transparent tool is selected.

11. Carefully click the **white color** in the Truck.jpg picture and notice that it becomes transparent.

12. With the **Truck.jpg** picture selected, click the **Animations** tab on the Ribbon, click the **Custom Animation** button to open the task pane, click the **Add Effect** button, point to **Motion Paths**, point to **Draw Custom Path**, click **Line**, and then draw a line from the left side along the overpass in the picture and off the slide on the right side of the overpass.

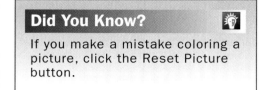

> **Did You Know?**
>
> If you make a mistake coloring a picture, click the Reset Picture button.

13. Set the animation to be triggered by **Start On Click**, and then change the speed to **Very Slow**. The truck appears to travel along the motion path on the slide. Your slide should look like Figure 3-38.

FIGURE 3-38
Pictures ordered and animated on a slide

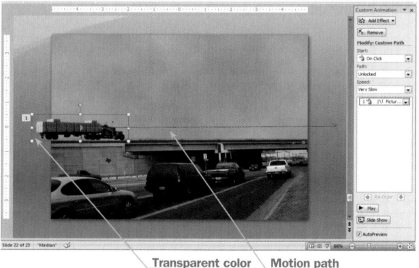

Transparent color Motion path

14. In the Custom Animation task pane, click **Play** to view the slide to see the new animation, and then close the task pane.

15. Save the presentation and leave it open for the next Step-by-Step.

Inserting Objects on a Slide

Objects can include Excel charts, media clips, bitmaps, or almost any other media file that can be embedded into a PowerPoint presentation. To insert an object on a slide, click the Insert tab on the Ribbon. To insert a movie, click the Movie button in the Media Clips group. To insert a sound, click the Sound button in the Media Clips group. To insert an object, click the Object button in the Text group. The Insert Object dialog box opens, as shown in Figure 3-39. Scroll through the list of objects that are compatible with PowerPoint, and click the type of object you want to insert. If you are inserting an object that has already been created, click Create from file. The dialog box changes to allow you to locate the file you want to insert. Click OK to close the Browse dialog box, and click OK again to embed the file. You will learn more about embedding files in the next lesson.

FIGURE 3-39
Insert Object dialog box

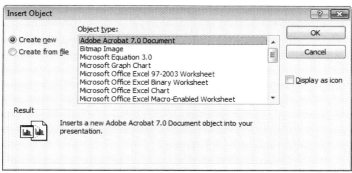

STEP-BY-STEP 3.18

1. Select **slide 2**, *How do they make…?*, click the **Insert** tab on the Ribbon, and then in the Media Clips group, click the **Movie** button.

2. In the Insert Movie dialog box, locate and click **cribbedding.mpg** from the Data Files for this lesson.

3. Click **OK**, and then click **Automatically**.

4. Resize and center the video on the slide, and then reposition the other images as necessary.

5. Click the **Slide Show** tab on the Ribbon, click the **From Beginning** button to view the presentation, and then view the short video.

6. Save the presentation and leave it open for the next Step-by-Step.

Adding a Header or Footer

You can add a header or footer on the slide master or by using the Header and Footer dialog box. Click the Insert tab on the Ribbon; in the Text group, click the Header & Footer button. The Header and Footer dialog box opens on the screen, as shown in Figure 3-40. You can add the date and time, slide number, and any text you want to the footer of the slide. When you click the Notes and Handouts tab, you also have the option of creating a header. Some items that you might include in a header or footer are the presenter's name, e-mail address, Web site address, or phone number.

FIGURE 3-40
Header and Footer dialog box

STEP-BY-STEP 3.19

1. Click the **Insert** tab on the Ribbon, and then, in the Text group, click the **Header & Footer** button. The Header and Footer dialog box opens.

2. Click the **Notes and Handouts** tab in the Header and Footer dialog box.

3. Click the **Footer** check box, and then type **The Story Of Cotton**.

4. Click the **Date and Time** check box, if it is not already selected. It is set to Update automatically.

5. Click the **Header** check box. In the Header text box, type your name.

6. Click **Apply to All**.

7. Click the **Office** Button, click **Print**, click the **Print what** list arrow, click **Handouts**, click the **Slides per page** list arrow, click **4** slides per page, and then click **OK**.

8. Save and close the presentation, and then exit PowerPoint.

SUMMARY

In this lesson, you learned:

- You can insert and modify SmartArt graphics to give special effects to text and graphics on a slide.

- You can add organization charts to a presentation and format them.

- You can enter text into a SmartArt graphic.

- You can create and format WordArt.

- You can build and format charts in a presentation using Microsoft Excel.

- You can create a table on a slide and then modify it, using the commands available on the Table Tools Design and Table Tools Layout tabs on the Ribbon.

- You can add shapes and objects to your presentation to add effects to the text.

- You can rotate, fill, scale, or size an object as well as change its fill or line color.

- You can copy, move, and group objects on a slide.

- You can add text on a slide or inside a shape by creating a text box.

- You can animate shapes on slides.

- You can order visual elements on a slide and make parts of pictures transparent.

- You can insert objects on slides, including worksheets, sounds, and videos.

- You can add a header or a footer to slides in a presentation.

VOCABULARY *Review*

Define the following terms:

Adjustment handle	Grouping	Row
Cell	Handle	SmartArt graphic
Chart (graph)	Organization chart	Table
Column	Rotate handle	WordArt
Datasheet		

REVIEW *Questions*

TRUE / FALSE

Circle T if the statement is true or F if the statement is false.

T   F   1. The shapes of an organization chart must be on the same level and cannot be moved or changed once created on the slide.

T   F   2. When you insert a table on a slide, you have to specify the number of rows and columns.

T   F   3. Using the Select Objects tool, you can drag a selection box around a group of objects.

T   F   4. To change the color in a picture so that the background appears, use the Set Transparent Color command.

T   F   5. To place text inside a shape, click the Insert Object button.

MULTIPLE CHOICE

Select the best response for the following statements.

1. Pie, line, bar, and column are types of _____.
   A. SmartObjects
   B. textures
   C. charts
   D. effects

2. The small squares surrounding a selected graphic are called _____.
   A. buttons
   B. handles
   C. tabs
   D. boxes

3. Which command do you use to turn a graphic, such as an arrow, from facing right to facing down?
   A. Rotate Left 90°
   B. Rotate Right 90°
   C. Flip Vertical
   D. Flip Horizontal

4. You can fill an object with _____.
   A. gradients
   B. texture
   C. color
   D. all of the above

5. If you want to create an organization chart from a bullet list on a slide, you click the
   _____ button.
   A. Convert to SmartArt
   B. Insert SmartArt
   C. Convert to WordArt
   D. Insert WordArt

PROJECTS

PROJECT 3-1

1. Start PowerPoint, open the Animals.pptx presentation from your Data Files, and then save it as **Animal Shelter**, followed by your initials.

2. Display slide 4, and then convert the text to a SmartArt graphic of your choice.

3. Insert a new slide, draw five different objects on the slide, and then enter text on at least three of the objects. Group two of the objects.

4. Create a table on a slide. Enter the text of your choice, and then format the table using a style.

5. Create a chart on a slide with the title **Funds Raised This Year**. Enter data for at least four rows and four columns in the data sheet.

6. Add your name to the handouts, print the presentation handouts, and then save the presentation.

PROJECT 3-2

1. Open the Animal Shelter.pptx presentation you created in Project 3-1.

2. Display the slide with the chart, On the Chart Tools Design tab, in the Type group, click the Change Chart Type button and then choose a Chart Type. Apply a new chart type to the chart.

3. Change two of the data points. Add a chart title to the chart.

4. Insert a new slide, and then add two pictures of your choice, from your computer or from a search on the Internet. Order the photos on the slide, and then animate one of the photos using a motion path.

5. Add your name as a footer on the notes page. Save the presentation. View the presentation, and then note any changes you want to make.

6. Make changes to your presentation based on your notes.

7. Save the presentation, print the handouts with four slides per page, and then exit PowerPoint.

CRITICAL*Thinking*

 ## ACTIVITY 3-1

Use the Internet to research a company. Use the information you find to create a presentation about the company that includes an organization chart, a graph, a table, and at least one other SmartArt object.

■ Apply a theme to the presentation.

■ Include your name in the header of the handouts.

■ Use the spelling checker to make sure you have no spelling errors in the presentation.

■ Save the presentation using the name of the company.

 ## ACTIVITY 3-2

You want to make some changes to some graphics on several slides. Use the Microsoft Office PowerPoint 2007 Help system to find out how to do the following:

■ Change the shape of any drawn object, such as a star or arrow, on a slide.

■ Display text vertically instead of horizontally in a table cell.

■ Change the various features in a chart.

 ## ACTIVITY 3-3

Think about a company that you want to start. Use a template from Microsoft Office Online to create several slides in a new presentation to let people know about your company. The presentation should include at least four slides:

■ A title slide with the name of your company

■ A slide with a chart

■ A slide with two drawn objects

■ A slide with a SmartArt graphic

■ A slide with a formatted table

■ Include your name in the slides footer

■ Save the presentation as MyCompany

EXPANDING ON POWERPOINT BASICS

OBJECTIVES

Upon completion of this lesson, you will able to:

- Integrate PowerPoint with other Office programs.
- Create a new master.
- Create new layout masters.
- Format text and objects.
- Align text and pictures.
- Insert comments.
- Set up a slide show.
- Package a presentation.
- Save a presentation to view on the Web.
- Send a presentation via e-mail.
- Create output.

Estimated Time: 2 hours

VOCABULARY

Action button

Comment

Custom show

Destination file

Document Inspector

Document properties

Embed

Format Painter

Grid

Guides

Link

Linked object

Package for CD

Snap to

Source file

Integrating PowerPoint with Other Office Programs

As you learn to work with the different computer applications, you will begin to develop preferences for using certain programs for various tasks. You may find that you have created a chart or have data in a spreadsheet program that you want to include in a slide presentation in PowerPoint. You may also find that you have written text using a word processor such as Microsoft Word and want to include that text in the presentation. You do not have to recreate that work to use it in a presentation. You can easily insert objects and link or embed text or data from other programs into slides.

Inserting Text from a Word Outline

If you have a lot of text that you want to use in a presentation, you may find it easier to type the text using a word processor, such as Microsoft Word. You can then import text from Word to create a new presentation or add slides to an existing presentation. A Word outline is the easiest kind of document to import because it is formatted with styles, and each heading level is translated into a corresponding level of text in PowerPoint. For example, Heading 1 text is converted to slide titles. If the Word document does not have heading styles applied, PowerPoint uses the paragraph indentations to create an outline structure.

STEP-BY-STEP 4.1

1. Start Microsoft Word, and then open the **Planet Facts.docx** Data File. Notice that the document is formatted as an outline.

2. Click the **Microsoft Office** button, and then click **Exit Word** to close the file and exit Word.

3. Start PowerPoint, to open a new blank presentation.

4. In the new presentation title slide, click the **Click to add title** placeholder, type **The Solar System**, click the **Click to add subtitle** placeholder, and then type your name on the title slide to identify this presentation as yours.

5. In the Slides group, click the **New Slide** button arrow, and then click **Slides from Outline** at the bottom of the Layout gallery. The Insert Outline dialog box opens and displays the Data Files for this lesson. If not, you can click the **Folders** button and locate the Data Files for this lesson.

> **Did You Know?**
>
> To start Microsoft Word, click the Start button on the task bar, type Microsoft Word in the Search box, and then click Microsoft Office Word 2007 on the Programs menu.

> **Did You Know?**
>
> If the document file Planet Facts.docx does not open in Outline view in Word, click the View tab on the Ribbon, and then click the Outline button in the Document Views group.

6. In the Insert Outline dialog box, click the document file **Planet Facts.docx**, and then click **Insert**.

PowerPoint imports the Word document text into a presentation and formats it as slides. Nine new slides appear. There is one slide for each level 1 head. The way the outline was created set up the slide show so that the planet name is the title of the slide. See Figure 4-1.

FIGURE 4-1
Slides created from Microsoft Word outline

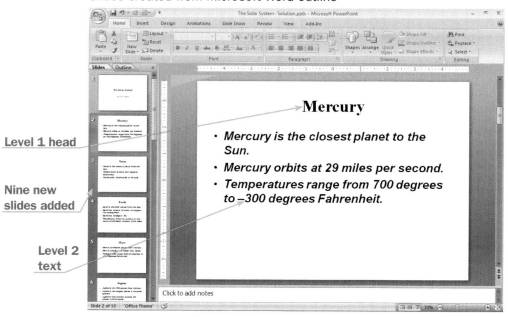

STEP-BY-STEP 4.1 Continued

7. Click the **Save** button on the Quick Access toolbar, locate the folder where you store the Data Files for this lesson, and then save the presentation as **The Solar System**, followed by your initials.

8. Leave the presentation open for the next Step-by-Step.

Applying a Design Theme

The outline was inserted into a new blank presentation. The Office theme is applied to the presentation by default. Now that you have the text in the slides, you can begin to work on the design and graphics to enhance the presentation.

STEP-BY-STEP 4.2

1. Click the **Design** tab on the Ribbon. In the Themes group, click the **More** button to open the Themes gallery, and then in the gallery click the **Flow** theme.

Did You Know?

The themes are in alphabetical order in the Themes gallery.

2. Click the **Slide Show** button on the status bar to run the slide show, and then press the **spacebar** to advance the slides.

3. Press the **Esc** key after you view the last slide, to return to Normal view.

4. Save the presentation and leave it open for the next Step-by-Step.

Understanding Embedding, Linking, and Paste Special

When you work with more than one file, it is often convenient to refer to the files as source or destination files. Since you are creating a presentation in PowerPoint, the presentation file is the destination file. The source file is where you have the text, chart, numbers, or whatever data it is you want to bring into the presentation.

Remember that the main difference between linking and embedding is where you store the data and how you update the data after you place it in the destination file.

When you move data among applications by cutting or copying and pasting, Microsoft Office changes the format of the data you are moving so that it can be used in the destination file. When it is easier to edit the information using the original application, you can embed the data as an object, using the Insert Object dialog box. You can create a new object, or you can insert an object from an existing file. See Figure 4-2 and Figure 4-3.

FIGURE 4-2
Insert Object Create new

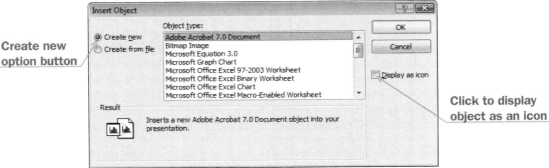

FIGURE 4-3
Insert Object Create from file

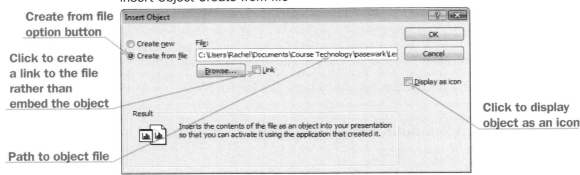

The embedded information becomes part of the new file, but as a separate object that can be edited using the application that created it. For example, if a table from a Word document is embedded into a PowerPoint presentation, PowerPoint enables the table to be edited using Word. If you insert an object from a file, you can choose to link the object. If you link the

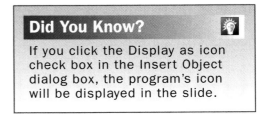

Did You Know?

If you click the Display as icon check box in the Insert Object dialog box, the program's icon will be displayed in the slide.

object, a connection is retained between the source and destination files. With a linked object, if you update the source file, the data in the destination file is also updated. It is a way to always have the most recent data on the slides.

Using Paste Special

Data from one application can be embedded into another application, using the copy and paste commands. The Paste Special command has several options that provide you with flexibility in how you copy data from a source file to a destination file. The Paste Special dialog box is shown in Figure 4-4. If you choose to paste a link, you will link rather than embed the data, so you will retain the connection between the source and destination files. Table 4-1 explains the different Paste Special options.

FIGURE 4-4
Paste Special dialog box

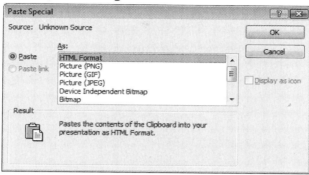

TABLE 4-1
Paste Special options

OPTION	PASTES THE CONTENTS OF THE CLIPBOARD INTO THE PRESENTATION AS:
HTML Format	HTML format; HTML is the format that can be read by a browser, the format of Web pages
Microsoft Office Word Document Object	A document that you can edit using Microsoft Word
Picture (Enhanced Metafile)	An enhanced metafile picture, so you can edit the contents using Picture Tools
Picture (Windows Metafile)	A metafile picture, so you can edit the contents using Picture Tools
Formatted Text (RTF)	Formatted text in Rich Text Format, retaining coding and formatting
Unformatted Text	Unformatted text, with all coding removed

S TEP-BY-STEP 4.3

1. Click **slide 6**, *Jupiter*, in the Slides tab. Click the **Home** tab on the Ribbon, in the Slides group, click the **New Slide** button arrow, and then click the **Blank** slide layout.

2. Click the **Start** button on the task bar, click **Microsoft Office Word 2007** to start Word, click the **Microsoft Office** button, click **Open**, locate the drive and folder where you store the Data Files for this lesson, and then open the document file **The Moons of Jupiter.docx**. Notice that the document is one page.

3. In the Editing group on the Ribbon, click the **Select** button, and then click **Select All**.
   All of the text in the document is selected.

4. In the Clipboard group on the Ribbon, click the **Copy** button to copy the text to the Clipboard.

STEP-BY-STEP 4.3 Continued

5. Click the **Microsoft Office** button, and then click **Exit Word** to close the file and exit Word. Slide 7, a blank slide, should be in the PowerPoint window on your screen.

6. In the Clipboard group on the Ribbon, click the **Paste** button arrow, and then click **Paste Special**.

7. In the Paste Special dialog box, click **Microsoft Office Word Document Object**, and then click **OK**. Your slide should look similar to Figure 4-5.

FIGURE 4-5
Word text pasted as an object on a slide

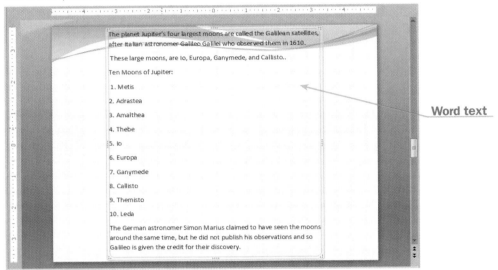

Word text

8. Save the presentation and leave it open for the next Step-by-Step.

Editing Embedded Data

To make changes to the Word file embedded in the PowerPoint presentation, double-click the text you want to edit. Word, the application in which the file was created, opens so that you can edit the text. When you finish and return to PowerPoint, the presentation includes the changes you made to the text. You can also resize and reposition the borders of the object box to place the pasted object as you want on a slide.

STEP-BY-STEP 4.4

1. Display **slide 7**, if it is not already displayed in the Slide pane.

2. Double-click inside the **Word object box** anywhere on the text, to activate Word for editing the text. The Word Home tab on the Ribbon appears above the slide on the screen. You have full access to all the Word editing features. See Figure 4-6.

STEP-BY-STEP 4.4 Continued

FIGURE 4-6
Editing the slide in Word

Word Home
tab on the
ribbon

Word object

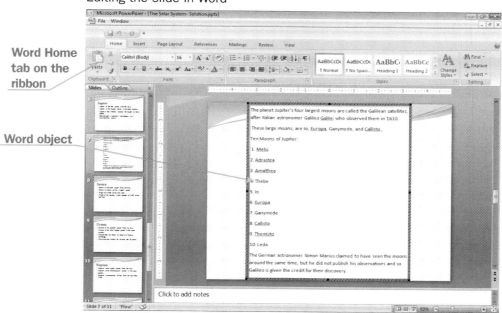

3. In the first paragraph, add a comma after "Galileo Galilei". In the second paragraph, click to the right of the second period after the word Callisto, press the **Backspace** key to delete the extra period, and then delete the **comma** after "large moons".

4. Click to the right of the word **Ten** just above the list of moons, and then type **of the**.

5. In the list of moons double-click **Io**, press and hold the **Ctrl** key, double-click **Europa**, double-click **Ganymede**, and then release the **Ctrl** key so that all three moons are selected.

6. In the Font group click the **Font Color** list arrow, and then click the **Red, Accent 2** swatch in the Theme Colors palette.

7. Drag to select from **1. Metis** to **10. Leda** to select the entire list of moons. On the Ribbon click the **Page Layout** tab, in the Page Setup group click the **Columns** button, and then click **Three**.

STEP-BY-STEP 4.4 Continued

8. Click outside the Word object to exit Word. Notice that the changes you made are now part of the presentation. See Figure 4-7.

FIGURE 4-7
Edited slide

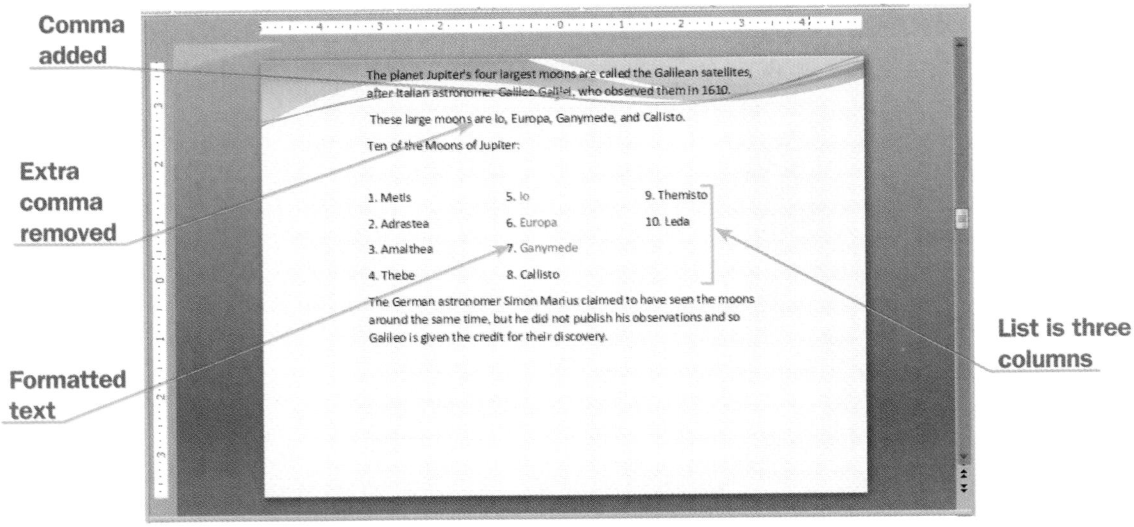

Comma added

Extra comma removed

Formatted text

List is three columns

9. Save the presentation and leave it open for the next Step-by-Step.

Importing an Excel Worksheet into a Presentation

You learned how to build and modify a chart on a slide and use Excel to edit and change the chart and data on the slide. You can also import data from an existing Excel worksheet.

STEP-BY-STEP 4.5

1. Click **slide 11**, *Pluto*, in the Slides tab. In the Slides group, click the **New Slide** button arrow, and then click the **Blank** slide layout to insert a new slide with a blank layout.

2. The new **slide 12** is selected.

3. On the Ribbon click the **Insert** tab, and then in the Text group click **Object** to open the Insert Object dialog box.

4. Click the **Create from file** option button, click **Browse**, locate the folder where you store the Data Files for this lesson, double-click the Excel file **Planets.xlsx**, and then click **OK** to close the Insert Object dialog box. Your screen should look similar to Figure 4-8.

STEP-BY-STEP 4.5 Continued

FIGURE 4-8
Excel worksheet inserted on a PowerPoint slide

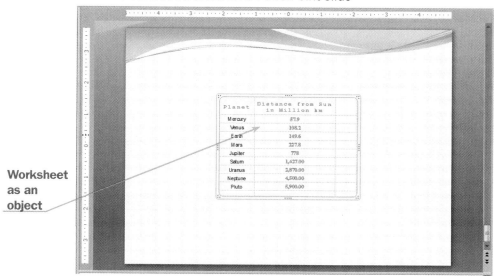

Worksheet
as an
object

5. Drag the corner of the Excel worksheet object to enlarge it so you can better see the contents on the slide, and then double-click the **Excel worksheet object** to open it for editing in Microsoft Excel.

6. Click **cell A1** and drag to **cell B10**. You selected the cells from A1 to B10.

7. Click the **Insert** tab on the Excel Ribbon. In the Charts group, click the **Line** button, and then click the **Line with Markers** chart type button. A chart is created in Excel. See Figure 4-9. You can continue to use the Excel chart-formatting features to enhance the chart, or you can change the data in the worksheet as needed using the Excel features.

FIGURE 4-9
Excel chart in a PowerPoint slide

Chart Tools
Design tab
on the
Excel Ribbon

Line chart
with markers

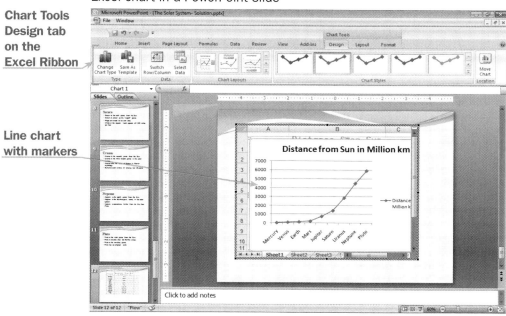

STEP-BY-STEP 4.5 Continued

8. Click a blank area of the slide to exit Excel and return to the slide in PowerPoint.

9. Save the presentation and leave it open for the next Step-by-Step.

Reusing Slides from Other Presentations

Slides often take time to create. If you have presentations with slides that work well, you can certainly use them in more than one presentation. There are different methods for reusing slides. You can copy and paste slides from one presentation to another. Open the presentation that has the slides you want to copy. Switch to Slide Sorter view. Click to select the slides you want to reuse, and then on the Home tab on the Ribbon, in the Clipboard group, click the Copy button. Open the new presentation or the presentation in which you want to paste the slides, switch to Slide Sorter view, and then click after the slide that you want the new slides to follow. On the Ribbon, in the Clipboard group, click Paste.

You can also use a Slide Library to store favorite slides that you want to reuse again and again. To use the Reuse Slides task pane, click the New Slide button, and then click Reuse Slides. You browse to find the PowerPoint file that has the slides or the Slide Library. See Figure 4-10.

Did You Know?

To duplicate a slide, in Slide Sorter view, click to select the slide you want to duplicate, click the Paste button arrow, and then click Duplicate.

FIGURE 4-10
Reuse Slides task pane

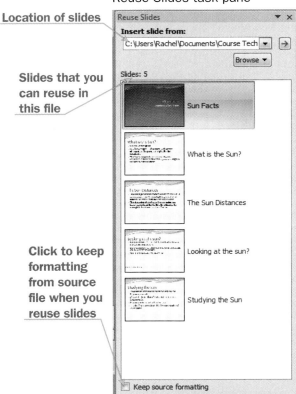

Location of slides

Slides that you can reuse in this file

Click to keep formatting from source file when you reuse slides

S TEP-BY-STEP 4.6

1. Click the last slide in the presentation, if it is not already selected, and then click the **Slide Sorter** button on the status bar.

2. Click the **Home** tab on the Ribbon. In the Slides group click the **New Slide** button arrow, and then click **Reuse Slides** at the bottom of the gallery. The Reuse Slides task pane opens.

3. In the Reuse Slides task pane, click **Browse**, and then click **Browse File** to open the Browse dialog box.

4. Locate the folder where your Data Files are stored for this lesson, click the presentation file **Sun Facts.pptx**, and then click **Open**. The five slides appear in the Reuse Slides task pane.

5. In the Reuse Slides task pane, point to each slide to see an enlarged version of each of the slides from the Sun Facts presentation. See Figure 4-11.

FIGURE 4-11

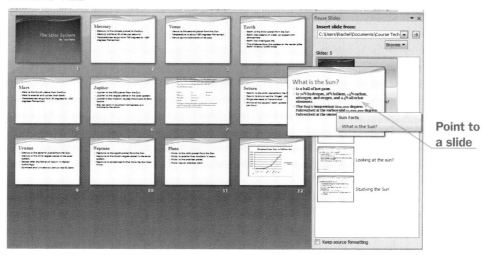

STEP-BY-STEP 4.6 Continued

6. In the Reuse Slides task pane, click the **Sun Facts** slide, click the **What is the Sun?** slide, click the **The Sun Distances** slide, click the **Looking at the Sun?** slide, click the **Studying the Sun** slide, and then click the Reuse Slides task pane **Close** button to close the task pane. Each slide is inserted into the current presentation. The slides have taken on the Flow theme of the current presentation. See Figure 4-12.

FIGURE 4-12
Slides reused

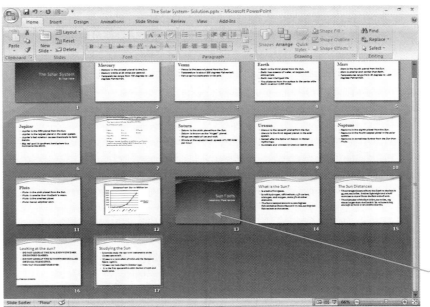

Five new slides take on theme of presentation

7. Save the presentation and leave it open for the next Step-by-Step.

Sending a Presentation to Word

 You can save a presentation as a Word document to use as a handout, or create other documents using the text and slides from the presentation.

To save the presentation in Word format, click the Microsoft Office button, point to Publish, and then click Create Handouts in Microsoft Office Word. The options in the Send To Microsoft Office Word dialog box can send your presentation to Word in several different formats. See Figure 4-13.

FIGURE 4-13
Send To Microsoft Office Word dialog box

STEP-BY-STEP 4.7

1. Click the **Microsoft Office** button, point to **Publish**, and then click **Create Handouts in Microsoft Office Word**. The Send To Microsoft Office Word dialog box opens.

2. Click the **Blank lines next to slides** option button in the dialog box.

3. Click **OK**. The presentation is exported into Word and formatted as a document.

4. Click the **Document1** button on the task bar, and then scroll through the document to view all the pages. See Figure 4-14.

FIGURE 4-14
Presentation as a Word document

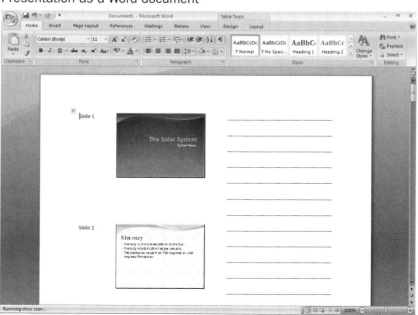

STEP-BY-STEP 4.7 Continued

5. Drag to select the first line of the first page in the document next to slide 1, The Solar System, type your name, click the **Save** button on the Quick Access toolbar, and then save the document as **The Solar System**, followed by your initials.

6. Click the **Microsoft Office** button, point to **Print**, and then click **Print**.

7. Click the **Current page** option button, and then click **OK** to print the first page of the document.

8. Click the **Microsoft Office** button, and then click **Exit Word** to close the document and exit Word.

9. The presentation file is on the screen in a PowerPoint window in Slide Sorter view.

Creating New Masters

PowerPoint will allow you to apply more than one slide master to a presentation. This is useful if your presentation will contain slides with more than one theme or any other features that are controlled by the slide master. This saves time as you are creating presentations, because you can choose which master to apply to each slide.

There are several ways that you can create a new master. Display the slide masters by clicking the View tab on the Ribbon, and then clicking the Slide Master button. In the Edit Master group, click the Insert Slide Master button. (See Figure 4-15.)

FIGURE 4-15
Inserting a new slide master

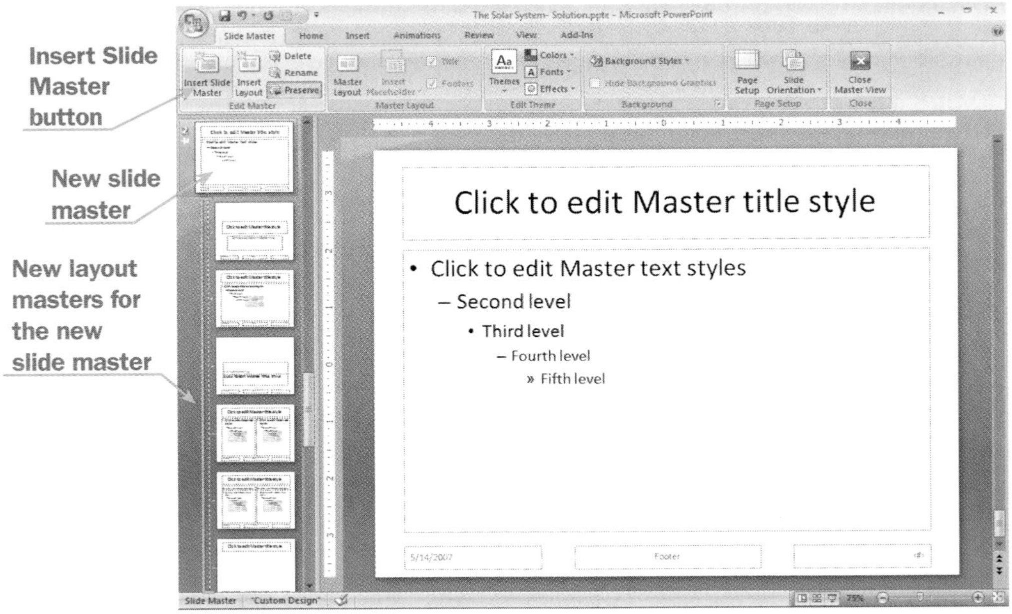

Insert Slide Master button

New slide master

New layout masters for the new slide master

Click to edit Master title style

• Click to edit Master text styles
   – Second level
      • Third level
         – Fourth level
           » Fifth level

Another way to create a slide master is to apply a new theme. Each theme will generate a new slide master and the corresponding layout masters.

Creating New Layout Masters

PowerPoint will allow you to create a new layout master for any theme or slide master. When you click the New Slide button, you are presented with a series of layouts for that slide master. There may be times when you want to place objects and text on a slide and the existing masters do not quite work for you. PowerPoint allows you to create a custom slide layout and then add the placeholders as needed.

STEP-BY-STEP 4.8

1. Click **slide 1**, *The Solar System*, in Slide Sorter view to select the first slide.

2. Click the **View** tab on the Ribbon. In the Presentation Views group, click the **Slide Master** button to switch to Slide Master view.

3. Click the **Slide Master** thumbnail in the left pane. The ScreenTip tells you that the Flow slide master is used by all 17 slides in the presentation. See Figure 4-16.

FIGURE 4-16
Slide Master view

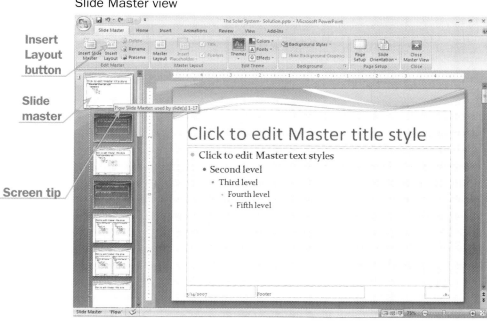

4. On the Slide Master tab on the Ribbon, in the Edit Master group, click the **Insert Layout** button. A new layout is added to the bottom of the left pane as part of the Flow slide master. It has a Title placeholder, a Date, Footer, and Slide number placeholder.

5. On the Slide Master tab on the Ribbon, in the Master Layout group, click the **Insert Placeholder** button. You can select from a list of placeholders and place them anywhere on the layout master.

STEP-BY-STEP 4.8 Continued

6. Click **SmartArt**, point to the upper-left corner of the slide below the lower-left corner of the Click to edit Master title style placeholder, press and hold the left mouse button, and then drag to draw a box in the center of the slide to just above the Slide number placeholder as shown in Figure 4-17.

FIGURE 4-17
Drawing a placeholder

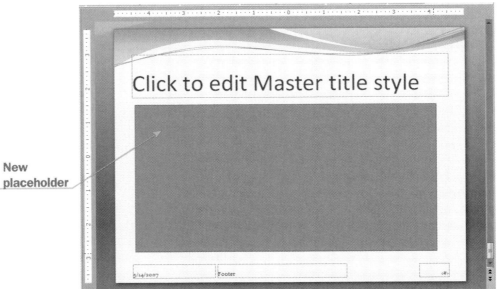

7. Release the mouse button. A SmartArt graphic placeholder appears centered on the slide. Click the **Close Master View** button on the Ribbon to return to Slide Sorter view.

8. Click the **Home** tab on the Ribbon. In the Slides group, click the **New Slide** button arrow to open the Layout gallery, and then click the **Custom Layout thumbnail**. A new slide is inserted with the new custom layout that you just created.

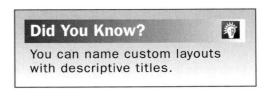

Did You Know?

You can name custom layouts with descriptive titles.

9. Double-click the new **slide 2** to open it in Normal view, and then click the **Insert SmartArt Graphic** icon in the new slide to open the Choose a SmartArt Graphic dialog box.

10. Click **List** in the left pane, click the **Vertical Box List** icon, and then click **OK**. You added a Vertical Box List SmartArt graphic.

11. Click the first **Text** placeholder and type **The Sun**, click the second **Text** placeholder and type **The Planets**, and then click the third **Text** placeholder and type **Moons**.

12. Click **Click to add title**, and then type **Overview** as the title for the slide. Your completed slide should look like Figure 4-18.

STEP-BY-STEP 4.8 Continued

FIGURE 4-18
New slide using custom layout

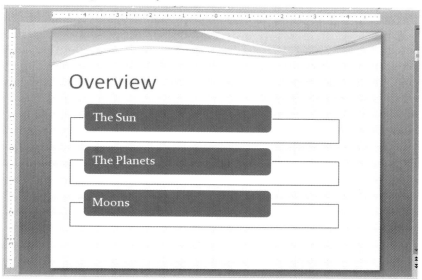

13. View the presentation as a slide show.

14. Save the presentation and leave it open for the next Step-by-Step.

Formatting Text and Objects

You have learned the basics of formatting text and objects. PowerPoint has several helpful features to make formatting easier.

Replacing Text Fonts

You can change a font throughout your presentation to another font. On the Home tab on the Ribbon, click the Replace list arrow, and then click Replace Fonts. The Replace Font dialog box opens, as shown in Figure 4-19. In the Replace box, choose the font you want to replace. In the With box, choose the font you want to use as a replacement, and then click Replace. Any text in the presentation that has the Replace font will now have the font you designated in the With box.

FIGURE 4-19
Replace Font dialog box

Current font

New font

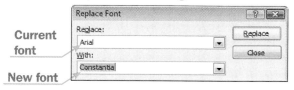

Using the Format Painter

If you format an object with certain attributes, such as fill color and line color, and then want to format another object the same way, use the Format Painter. Select the object whose attributes you want to copy, click the Format Painter button, and then click the object you want to format. You can use the same process to copy text attributes, such as font, size, color, or style, to other text. To copy attributes to more than one object or section of text, select the object whose attributes you want to copy, double-click the Format Painter button, and then click each of the objects or sections of text you want to format. When you are finished, click the Format Painter button. The Format Painter button is located on the Mini toolbar, as well as on the Home tab on the Ribbon in the Clipboard group.

STEP-BY-STEP 4.9

1. Click **slide 3**, *Mercury*, and then click **Mercury** in the body text.

2. On the Home tab on the Ribbon, in the Editing group, click the **Replace** list arrow, and then click **Replace Fonts**.

    The Replace Font dialog box opens. The body text on the slides for each planet is in the Arial font. In the Replace box, Arial is selected.

3. Click the **With** list arrow, click **Constantia**, and then click **Replace**. All the text in Arial font throughout the presentation is replaced with the Constantia font.

4. Click **Close** to close the Replace Fonts dialog box.

5. Click **slide 4**, *Venus*, and then drag to select the words **900 degrees Fahrenheit** in the second bullet.

6. In the Font group, click the **Font Color** list arrow, and then click the **Orange** color swatch in the Standard Colors palette.

7. With **900 degrees Fahrenheit** still selected, in the Clipboard group click the **Format Painter** button.

8. The pointer changes to ![brush pointer].

9. In the Slides tab click **slide 3**, *Mercury*, and then click and drag the pointer over the words **700 degrees to -300 degrees Fahrenheit**.

    You have painted the formatting. The format of the text changed so it is the same as 900 degrees Fahrenheit in the second bullet point on the Venus slide.

10. View the presentation.

11. Save the presentation and leave it open for the next Step-by-Step.

Aligning Text and Pictures

A good presentation uses short phrases, pictures, and graphs to convey its point. Out-of-alignment text or pictures can distract from the point of a presentation. To align a text box or picture, you can add grid lines and picture guides to the slide as you are creating it. Click the View tab on the Ribbon, and then, in the Show/Hide group, click the Gridlines check box to turn on the grid. To turn on Grids and Guides, you can right-click any blank area of a slide (do not click inside a place-holder) and click Grid and Guides. The Grid and Guides dialog box opens, as shown in Figure 4-20. The Snap to option Snap objects to grid moves an object to the closest gridline on a slide and snaps it to the line. The line appears to be "magnetic," which is very useful when you want to place objects exactly in position. The Grid settings section sets the spacing between the intersections of the gridlines. You can also choose to display the grid by clicking the check box. The Guide settings area displays a set of crosshairs on the screen to help you align an object in the center, left, right, top, or bottom of the slide, as shown in Figure 4-21.

FIGURE 4-20
Grid and Guides dialog box

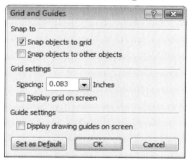

FIGURE 4-21
Slide with grid and guides

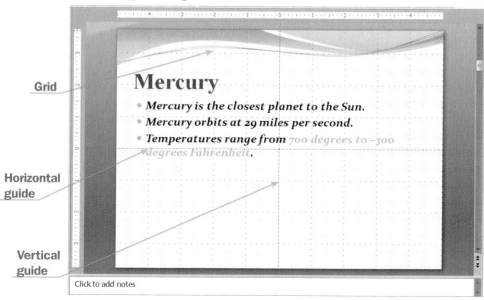

STEP-BY-STEP 4.10

1. Click **slide 5**, *Earth*, in the Slides tab to select the slide, right-click any blank area of the slide, and then, on the shortcut menu, click **Grid and Guides**. The Grid and Guides dialog box opens.

2. Click the **Display grid on screen** check box to insert a check mark, click the **Display drawing guides on screen** check box insert a check mark, and then click **OK**.

3. Click the **Insert** tab on the Ribbon, and then, in the Text group, click the **Text Box** button.

4. To the right of the vertical guide and below the horizontal guide, click in a blank area of the slide, and then type **Our home planet**.

5. Use the Move pointer to drag the **text box** so that the top sizing handles are on the second gridline from the bottom of the slide, and then drag the **text box** so that the green rotation handle and the middle sizing handles are on the vertical guide of the slide. See Figure 4-22.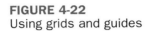

FIGURE 4-22
Using grids and guides

New text box

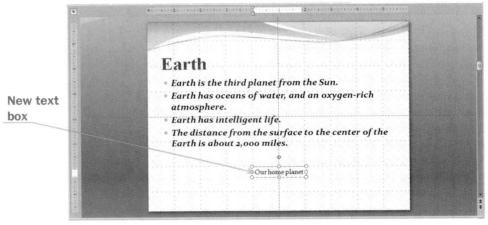

6. Click **slide 6**, *Mars*. On the Insert tab, in the Text group, click the **Text Box** button. To the right of the vertical guide and below the horizontal guide, click in a blank area of the slide, and then type **Our nearest neighbor**.

7. Use the same process as in step 5 to center the text box on slide 6 *Mars*, below the second gridline from the bottom.

   Did you notice how the box snapped to the grid and guides, because you had the Snap objects to grid option active?

8. View the presentation to make sure the changes look correct.

9. Right-click any blank area of any slide, on the shortcut menu click **Grid and Guides**, click the **Display grid on screen** check box to remove the check mark, click the **Display drawing guides on screen** check box to remove the check mark, and then click **OK**. You turned off the grid and drawing guides.

10. Save the presentation and leave it open for the next Step-by-Step.

Inserting Comments

Working with friends or coworkers on a project is a way to collaborate to get the best presentation. Sometimes you want to ask a question about the content or design of a particular slide, or you may have a question or comment on the entire presentation. You do not have to be present with the slide show to pass along comments. You can insert comments in the slide for others to see. You use the Comment features in the Review tab on the Ribbon, in the Comments group. You can insert, review, and edit comments. Each user's comment will have a different color or initial, so you can identify who originated each comment.

STEP-BY-STEP 4.11

1. Click **slide 6**, *Mars*, click the **Review** tab on the Ribbon, and then, in the Comments group, click the **New Comment** button. A new comment opens. The letters identifying the source of the note will vary, depending on whom the computer is registered to.

2. Type **This slide needs clip art.** in the comment box.

3. Click **slide 8**, *Jupiter Moons*. In the Comments group, click the **New Comment** button, and then type **This slide needs a new layout.** in the comment box. See Figure 4-23.

FIGURE 4-23
Review tab on the Ribbon

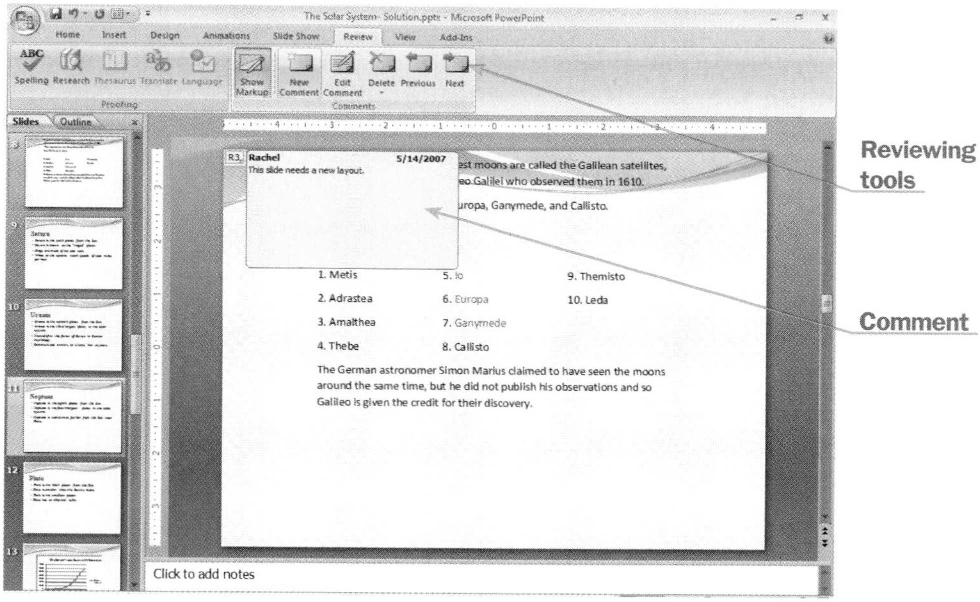

4. In the Comments group, click the **Previous** button to review the last comment. You can click the Previous and Next buttons to review all the comments in a presentation.

5. Save the presentation and leave it open for the next Step-by-Step.

Delivering a Presentation

To start a slide show, click the Slide Show button on the status bar. You can start the slide show on any slide by displaying or selecting the slide you want to begin with before clicking the Slide Show button. You can also begin to view the slide show by clicking the buttons using the Slide Show tab on the Ribbon. See Figure 4-24.

FIGURE 4-24
Slide Show tab on the Ribbon

Creating Custom Shows

If you want a particular slide to be hidden when you run your presentation, click the Hide Slide button. Rather than hide a specific slide, you may want to create a custom show. A custom show is a way to limit the slides in any slide show for a particular audience. Click the Slide Show tab on the Ribbon, click the Custom Slide Show button in the Start Slide Show group, and then click Custom Shows. The Custom Shows dialog box allows you to select an existing custom show or create a new one. Click New to open the Define Custom Show dialog box in which you select the slides you want in a show and then name the show. See Figure 4-25.

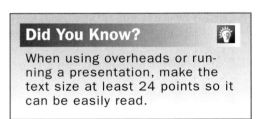

Did You Know?

When using overheads or running a presentation, make the text size at least 24 points so it can be easily read.

FIGURE 4-25
Define Custom Show dialog box

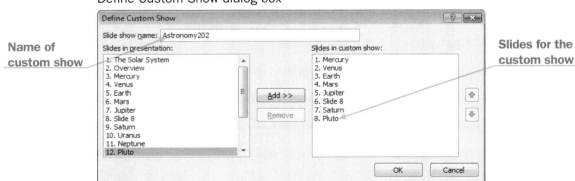

Name of custom show

Slides for the custom show

Using On-Screen Tools

There are on-screen navigation tools you can use to control a presentation while presenting it. When you run the presentation, a navigational toolbar appears in the lower-left corner of the screen. Click the rectangle button and a Slide show menu is displayed, as shown in Figure 4-26.

FIGURE 4-26
Slide show menu

When you click the mouse, the slides advance in order. You can choose the Previous or Next button to display the slide before or after the current one. To go to another slide, choose Go to Slide from the menu that is displayed and Slide Navigator from the submenu. Click the slide you want to display. To exit the slide show, choose End Show from the menu.

The Slide show menu (also available if you right-click the screen in Slide Show view) has many useful features. To make the screen appear blank, point to Screen, and then click Black Screen or White Screen. Switch Programs displays the Windows toolbar to give you access to other programs that you may want to display during a presentation.

> **Did You Know?**
>
> You display a hidden slide by choosing it in the Slide Navigator dialog box. Parentheses around the slide number indicate that it is hidden.

> **Did You Know?**
>
> PowerPoint files have different file extensions. A filename that ends with .pptx is a PowerPoint 2007 presentation file, .ppt is a PowerPoint97-2003 presentation file, .potx is a PowerPoint 2007 template file, and .ppsx is a PowerPoint 2007 presentation file that displays the Slide Show view in Internet Explorer.

Creating Action Buttons

Another on-screen tool is the Action button. **Action buttons** are buttons that are inserted on a slide. They enable you to jump from slide to slide, even to slides in another slide show, or to other documents. Action buttons are assigned hyperlinks to direct the actions. You can insert an Action button using one of two methods. Click the Shapes button, and then click the Action button you want in the Action Buttons group. The Action Setting dialog box opens automatically. If you want to insert an Action button that is a shape not in the Action buttons group, use the Shapes gallery to draw the shape that you want as the button, click the Insert tab on the Ribbon, and then, in the Links group, click the Action button. You work to create the Action button in the Action Settings dialog box, as shown in Figure 4-27.

FIGURE 4-27
Action Settings dialog box

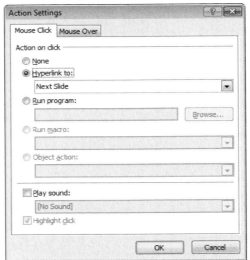

STEP-BY-STEP 4.12

1. Click **slide 3**, *Mercury*, in the Slides tab to display it in the Slide pane.

2. On the Home tab in the Drawing group, click the **Shapes** button. In the Basic Shapes section, click the **Sun** icon, and then drag to draw a sun shape on the lower-right corner of the slide.

3. Click the **Insert** tab on the Ribbon, and then click the **Action** button in the Links group. The Action Settings dialog box opens. The Sun shape is selected. You will apply an action to this drawn shape.

4. Click the **Hyperlink to** option button, and then click the **Hyperlink to** list arrow, scroll down, and then click **Slide**. The Hyperlink to Slide dialog box opens.

5. Click **slide 18**, *Studying the Sun*, click **OK**, and then click **OK** again. The Action button on slide 3 is hyperlinked to slide 18.

6. Click **slide 18**, *Studying the Sun*, in the Slides tab to display it, click the **Shapes** button on the Insert tab in the Illustrations group, click the **Action Button: Back or Previous** icon in the Action Buttons section, and then drag to draw a **box** on the lower-right corner of the slide. The Action Settings dialog box opens, the Hyperlink to option button is selected, and Previous Slide is selected.

7. Click the **Hyperlink to** list arrow, scroll down, click **Last Slide Viewed**, and then click **OK**.

You have created a return button in the lower-right corner of the slide that hyperlinks back to the last viewed slide. If you view slide 18 by clicking the hyperlink on slide 3, and then click the Action button on slide 18, you will return to slide 3.

STEP-BY-STEP 4.12 Continued

8. Click the **Slide Show** tab on the Ribbon, click the **From Beginning** button in the Start Slide Show group, and then press the **spacebar** two times. View slide 1 and slide 2.

9. When you get to slide 3, click the **sun** action button. The presentation jumps to slide 18, *Studying the Sun*.

10. Click the **return** Action button to return to **slide 3**, *Mercury*.

11. Finish viewing the presentation.

12. Save the presentation and leave it open for the next Step-by-Step.

Hiding Slides

If you need to limit the number of slides you are showing to a particular audience, you can quickly hide slides. This is faster than creating a custom show.

STEP-BY-STEP 4.13

1. Click the **Slide Sorter** button on the status bar to switch to Slide Sorter view, and then click **slide 14**, *Sun Facts*.

2. On the Ribbon click the **Slide Show** tab, and then, in the Set Up group, click the **Hide Slide** button.

3. Click **slide 13**, *Distance from Sun in Million km* chart, and then, in the Set Up group, click the **Hide Slide** button.

Notice that the slide number in the lower-right corner of the hidden slides has a box and a slash though it, showing that it is a hidden slide. See Figure 4-28.

FIGURE 4-28
Hidden slides

4. Click **slide 11**, *Neptune*, on the Slide Show tab on the Ribbon, and then, in the Start Slide Show group, click the **From Current Slide** button. The presentation begins on slide 11.

5. Click to advance through the slide show. Notice that you did not see slides 13 and 14 during the show.

STEP-BY-STEP 4.13 Continued

6. Click **slide 13**, *Distance from Sun in Million km* chart. In the Set Up group, click the **Hide Slide** button, click **slide 14**, *Sun Facts*, and then, in the Set Up group, click the **Hide Slide** button. These slides are no longer hidden.

7. Save the presentation and leave it open for the next Step-by-Step.

Annotating a Show

As you are presenting the slide show to the audience, you can use the on-screen annotation tools to emphasize specific text or graphics on a slide. You have several pointer options. When you move your mouse during the slide show, an arrow appears so that you can point out parts of the slide. Right-click the screen, point to Pointer Options, point to Arrow Options, and then select from: Automatic, Visible, and Hidden. Automatic displays the arrow as you move it around a slide, but hides it if you do not move the mouse for a short period of time. Visible displays the arrow all of the time during a presentation, and Hidden hides the arrow during a presentation. The Ball Point Pen, Felt Tip Pen, and Highlighter are tools that allow you to write or highlight features on the screen. You can choose the colors from the Ink Color menu. The Eraser tool erases any ink it touches, and Erase All Ink on Slide deletes all ink marks.

STEP-BY-STEP 4.14

1. Click **slide 1**, *The Solar System*. On the Slide Show tab on the Ribbon in the Start Slide Show group, click the **From Current Slide** button. The presentation begins on slide 1.

2. Right-click the **title slide** screen, point to **Pointer Options** on the on-screen navigation tools menu, and then click **Felt Tip Pen**.

3. Right-click the **title slide** screen again, point to **Pointer Options**, point to **Ink Color**, and then click the **Red** color swatch in the Standard Colors section of the palette.

4. Press the **spacebar** to advance the show to **slide 2**, *Overview*, and then use the pointer to draw a circle around the words The Sun. See Figure 4-29.

STEP-BY-STEP 4.14 Continued

FIGURE 4-29
Annotating a slide

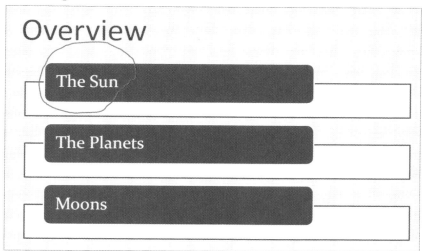

5. Right-click the **slide** on the screen, point to **Pointer Options** on the on-screen navigation tools menu, and then click **Arrow**. The pen changes to a pointer.

6. Right-click the **slide** screen, and then click **End Show** from the menu to exit the slide show. You will be prompted by a dialog box asking if you want to keep or discard your ink annotations.

7. Click **Discard**.

8. Save your work and then leave the presentation on the screen for the next Step-by-Step.

Setting Up a Slide Show

PowerPoint has many features to help you make a presentation interesting and effective. There are several options for delivering a presentation. A presentation can be set up to be self-running, for viewing at a trade show booth, for example. An individual can view a presentation over a company intranet or on the Web. However, the most common method is to run a presentation with a speaker who directs the show.

To set up the slide show, on the Slide Show tab on the Ribbon, click the Set Up Slide Show button. The Set Up Show dialog box appears (Figure 4-30). It has six sections. See Table 4-2.

FIGURE 4-30
Set Up Show dialog box

TABLE 4-2
Understanding Set Up Show

OPTION	DESCRIPTION
Show type	Determines how the show will be viewed
Show slides	Allows you to choose which slides you are showing
Show options	Allows you to choose features that you want to include when making your presentation
Advance slides	Determines whether you advance the slides manually or automatically
Multiple monitors	Sets up your computer when you are using a secondary monitor or projector
Performance	Adjusts your computer's settings to give the best picture at the fastest speed

STEP-BY-STEP 4.15

1. Click the **Slide Show** tab on the Ribbon, and then click the **Set Up Show** button. The Set Up Show dialog box opens.

2. In the Show type section, click the **Presented by a speaker option** button, if it is not already selected.

3. In the Show slides section, click **From**. The first box should be 1. Press the **Tab** key, and then type **18** in the To text box.

4. In the Advance slides section, click **Using timings**, if present, if it is not already selected.

5. Click **OK**.

STEP-BY-STEP 4.15 Continued

6. View the presentation.

7. Leave the presentation on the screen for the next Step-by-Step.

Rehearsing Timing

PowerPoint can automatically advance the slides in your presentation at preset time intervals. This is helpful in the case of an unattended presentation at a kiosk or sales booth, or if you must make a presentation within a specific time limit.

To rehearse timing for a presentation, in the Slide Show tab in the Set Up group, click the Rehearse Timings button. The slide show automatically starts, and the Rehearsal toolbar (See Figure 4-31), with a timer for the slide and a timer for the presentation, appears on the screen. When you think enough time has passed for a slide to appear on the screen, click the Next button. The presentation advances to the next slide, and the slide timer starts over. You can pause the timer by clicking the Pause button. The Repeat button resets the slide timer back to zero and the presentation timer back to the time that has elapsed, through the previous slide. When you get to the end of the show, a dialog box appears, asking if you want to keep the slide timings for the presentation.

FIGURE 4-31
Rehearsal toolbar

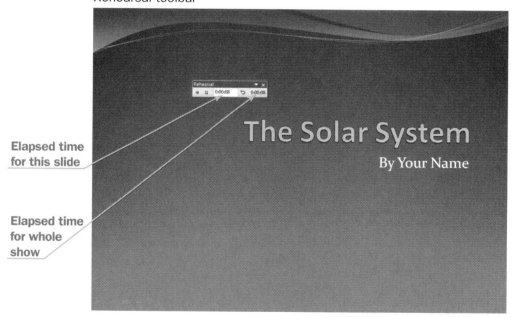

Elapsed time
for this slide

Elapsed time
for whole
show

To view rehearsal times for each slide, view the presentation in Slide Sorter view. The time allotted to each slide is listed at the lower-left corner of each slide. You can further edit the timing of each slide by opening the Slide Transition dialog box and changing the time below the Advance slide area of the dialog box.

STEP-BY-STEP 4.16

1. Switch to **Slide Sorter view** if it is not the current view.

2. Click the **Slide Show** tab on the Ribbon, and then, in the Set Up group, click the **Rehearse Timings** button. The slide show starts, and the timers for the slide and the slide show begin.

3. Click the **Next** button every four to five seconds. Don't worry if you make a mistake.

   When you reach the end of the slide show, a dialog box appears, asking if you want to keep the timings.

4. Click **Yes**. The presentation returns to Slide Sorter view.

5. Click the **Animations** tab on the Ribbon. In the Transition to This Slide group, click the **Automatically After up arrow** to add 1 second to the first slide.

   You can continue to adjust the time for each slide using the Advance slide section in the Transition to This Slide group. You can also apply different transition effects to each slide.

6. Click the **Slide Show button** on the status bar. The slides will automatically advance at the rate you set for each slide.

7. Save the changes to the presentation and then leave the presentation on the screen for the next Step-by-Step.

Inspecting a Document and Viewing Document Properties

Before you send a presentation out for review, or even submit it as final, it is a good idea to inspect the document for personal information or anything that you might not want to "travel" with the presentation file. The Document Inspector is a feature that can get this job done easily. To use the Document Inspector, click the Microsoft Office button, point to Prepare, and then click Inspect Document. The Document Inspector dialog box gives you choices as to what you want to look for. See Figure 4-32.

Careers

Many people use PowerPoint to sell their products at trade shows. Customers watch automated presentations about the product, delivered in a kiosk or self-running computer in a booth, while the sales reps are busy with other customers.

FIGURE 4-32
Document Inspector dialog box

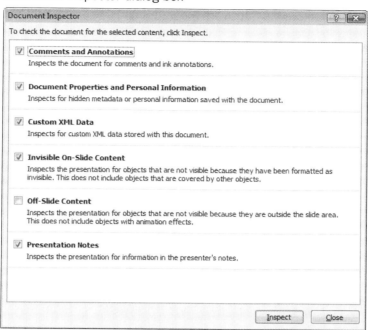

The Document Properties pane stores information about the document, the document properties, that can be helpful as you develop the presentation. Document properties include the author name, document title, subject, keywords, category, and status. You may choose to remove this information before you pass a file along. You may also choose to modify the default information that is added when you create a document. To view the Document Properties pane, click the Microsoft Office Button, point to Prepare, and then click Properties. See Figure 4-33.

FIGURE 4-33
Document Properties

STEP-BY-STEP 4.17

1. Click the **Microsoft Office** button, point to **Prepare**, and then click **Inspect Document**.

The Document Inspector dialog box opens.

2. Verify that all the boxes have check marks, and then click **Inspect**.

Review the inspection results. The document should have comments and personal information.

3. Click **Remove All** to remove the Comments and Annotations.

STEP-BY-STEP 4.17 Continued

4. Click **Remove All** to remove the Document Properties and Personal Information.

5. Click **Reinspect**, click **Inspect**, and then click **Close** to close the Document Inspector.

Embedding Fonts

Not all computers have every font style installed on them. If you are giving your presentation on a computer other than your own, your presentation text might not look exactly as it did when you created it. PowerPoint can embed fonts into your presentation so that your text appears exactly as you originally created it.

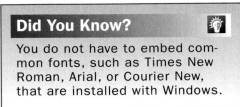

Did You Know?

You do not have to embed common fonts, such as Times New Roman, Arial, or Courier New, that are installed with Windows.

To embed fonts in your presentation, click the Microsoft Office button, and then click PowerPoint Options to open the PowerPoint Options dialog box. Click Save in the left pane. The Customize how documents are saved pane appears, as shown in Figure 4-34. Click the Embed fonts in the file option button, and then click Embed only the characters used in the presentation option button. Click OK to close the PowerPoint options dialog box.

FIGURE 4-34
Customize how documents are saved

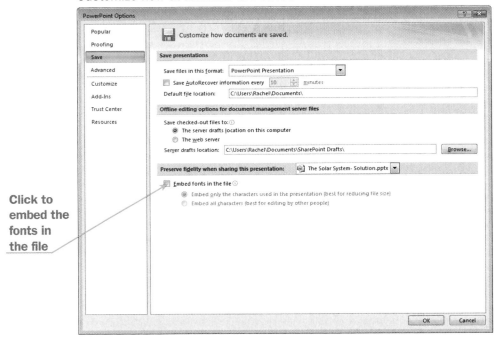

Click to embed the fonts in the file

STEP-BY-STEP 4.18

1. Click the **Microsoft Office** button, and then click **PowerPoint Options** to open the PowerPoint Options dialog box.

2. Click **Save** in the left pane. The Customize how documents are saved pane opens.

3. Click the **Embed fonts in the file** option button, and then click **Embed only the characters used in the presentation (best for reducing file size)** option button.

4. Click **OK** to close the PowerPoint Options dialog box.

5. Click the **Save** button on the Quick Access toolbar to save the file. Notice the green progress bar on the status bar indicating that the fonts are being embedded in the file.

6. Leave the presentation on the screen for the next Step-by-Step.

Using Package for CD and Copying Presentations to Folders

Note: You must have a CD burner installed to complete this exercise.

If you are giving your presentation on another computer, you can use Package for CD to compact all your presentation files into a single, compressed file that fits on a CD. You can then unpack the files when you reach your destination computer.

To use this feature, click the Microsoft Office button, point to Publish, and then click Package for CD. The Compatibility message box appears, as shown in Figure 4-35.

FIGURE 4-35
Compatibility message

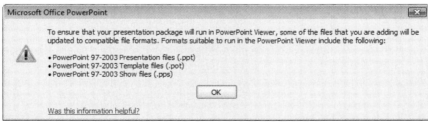

The Package for CD dialog box is shown in Figure 4-36. The dialog box gives several options for preparing your presentation. The Add Files button selects the presentation you want to package. The Copy to Folder button allows you to choose the destination folder for your files. The Options button opens another dialog box where you can choose the linked files and fonts you want to package. If the computer on which you are giving your presentation does not have PowerPoint installed, you can download a PowerPoint Viewer. This dialog box will also allow you to include a password on your PowerPoint file.

FIGURE 4-36
Package for CD dialog box

STEP-BY-STEP 4.19

1. Click the **Microsoft Office** button, point to **Publish**, and then click **Package for CD**.

2. Read the Compatibility message, and then click **OK**.

3. In the Package for CD dialog box, in the Name the CD box, type **Solar System**, and then click the **Copy to Folder** button. The Copy to Folder dialog box opens.

4. Click the **Browse** button, locate the folder where you store your Data Files, click the **Organize** button in the Choose Location dialog box, click **New Folder**, type **Package Solar System – Your Name**, and then click **Select**. The folder location appears in the Location section of the Copy to Folder dialog box.

5. Click **OK**, and then click **Yes** to copy the linked files to the package. The files are copied to the folder.

6. Click the **Options** button. The Options dialog box opens. This presentation does not include any linked files, and you embedded the fonts and checked for private information in the previous Step-by-Step.

7. Deselect both the **Linked files** and **Embedded TrueType fonts** check boxes.

8. Click **Viewer Package** in the Package type section, if it is not already selected, and then click **OK**.

9. Insert a blank CD in the CD burner of your computer.

10. Click **Copy to CD**, and the files are copied to the destination CD burner.

11. Save the presentation and leave it on the screen for the next Step-by-Step.

Saving Presentations to View on the Web

As with other Office applications, PowerPoint also helps you easily create Web documents, by either creating a new presentation or converting an existing presentation. Click the Microsoft Office button, point to Save As, and then click Other Formats. If you are converting an existing presentation to a Web page, click the Save as type list arrow, and then click Web Page in the Save As dialog box as shown in Figure 4-37.

FIGURE 4-37
Saving a file as a Web page

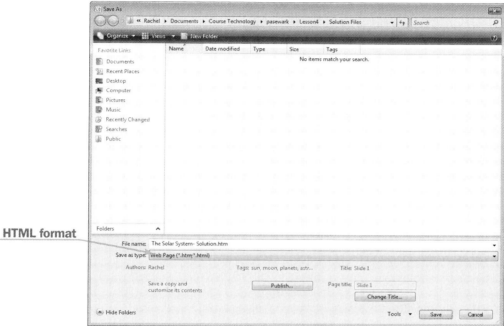

HTML format

Making a presentation available on the Web is also known as "publishing a presentation." When you choose Web Page or (*.htm or *.html) or Single File Web Page (*.mht, *.mhtml) in the Save As dialog box, the Publish option appears. Click Publish to open the Publish as Web Page dialog box, as shown in Figure 4-38. You can preview a presentation in your browser.

FIGURE 4-38
Publish as Web Page dialog box

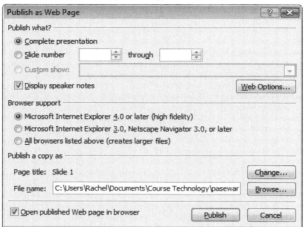

STEP-BY-STEP 4.20

1. Click the **Microsoft Office** button, point to **Save As**, and then click **Other Formats**.

2. Click the **Save as type** list arrow, and then click **Single File Web Page** in the Save As dialog box.

3. Click the **Publish** button. The Publish as Web Page dialog box opens.

4. In the Publish what? box, click the Complete presentation option button, if it is not already selected.

5. Click the **Browse** button, click the **Organize** button in the Publish As dialog box, click **New Folder**, type **Solar System Web page – Your Name**, and then click **Open**.

6. Click **OK** in the Publish As dialog box, and then click **Publish** in the Publish as Web Page dialog box.

7. You may get a security warning at the top of your browser window. If so, click the **bar** at the top of the browser, click **Allow Blocked Content**, and then click **Yes**.

Your browser opens, and the presentation is displayed as a Web page. Your screen should look similar to that in Figure 4-39. Each slide title is a link in the left pane.

STEP-BY-STEP 4.20 Continued

FIGURE 4-39
Presentation as a Web page

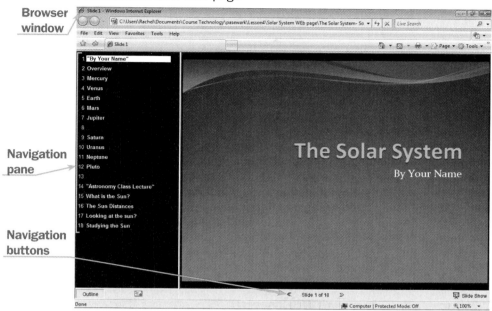

8. Click the **slide titles** in the left frame to view each slide.

9. When you are finished, close the browser.

10. Leave the presentation on the screen for the next Step-by-Step.

Sending a Presentation via E-mail

There are several ways you can use e-mail in conjunction with PowerPoint. You can send a presentation as an e-mail attachment or e-mail it to a recipient for review.

Open the presentation you want to send, click the Office Button, point to Send, and then click E-mail. PowerPoint automatically opens your e-mail editor, and the presentation is inserted into the e-mail as an attachment, as shown in Figure 4-40.

FIGURE 4-40
Send a presentation via e-mail

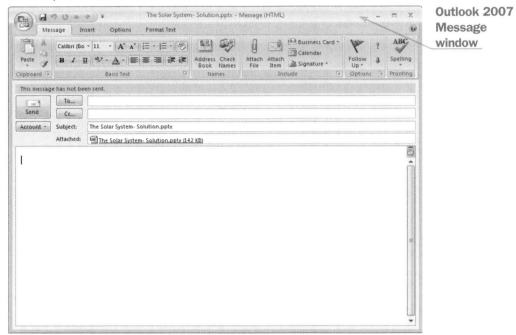

Fill in the recipient information, type a message, and click Send. A copy of the presentation is e-mailed, but the original stays open so you can continue working on it..

To complete this next Step-By-Step, arrange with a friend to exchange presentations via e-mail.

STEP-BY-STEP 4.21

1. Click the **Office** button and point to **Send**, and then click **E-mail**.

   Your e-mail program will open a new message window with the presentation as an attachment

2. Enter the e-mail address of a friend, click in the **message body**, type **This is the presentation I told you about**, and then click **Send** to exchange your presentations.

3. Close the e-mail program if it is open.

Creating Output

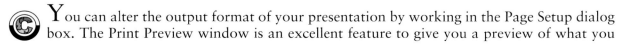

You can alter the output format of your presentation by working in the Page Setup dialog box. The Print Preview window is an excellent feature to give you a preview of what you are printing before you print and waste paper. See Figure 4-41. You can change the orientation of your slides or notes, handouts, and outline.

FIGURE 4-41
Print Preview

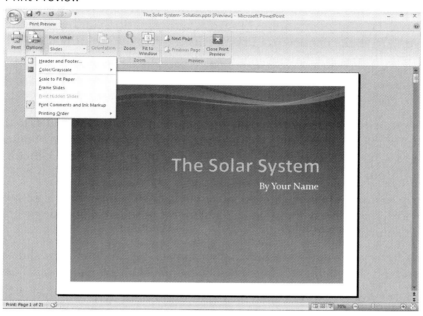

STEP-BY-STEP 4.22

1. Click the **Microsoft Office** button, point to **Print**, and then click **Print Preview**.

2. Click the **Options** button, click **Header and Footer**, click the **Notes and Handouts** tab, click the **Header** check box, type **your name** in the Notes and Handouts Header text box, and then click **Apply to All**.

3. Click the **Print What** list arrow, click **Handouts (6 Slides Per Page)**, click the **Orientation** button, click **Landscape**, and then click **Print**.

4. Click **OK**.

5. Print the presentation as handouts with nine slides per page.

6. Save and close the presentation.

7. Exit PowerPoint.

Did You Know?

You can mark a presentation as final so other people can look at the presentation but cannot make any changes to it. Click the Microsoft Office button, point to Prepare, and then click Mark as Final. You can also password-protect your presentation file if you want to safeguard who can and cannot look at the slide show. Click the Microsoft Office button, point to Prepare, and then click Encrypt Document. You will be asked to create a password and then confirm a password. Be sure you remember the password or write it down in a safe place. If you forget the password, you will not be able to open the presentation again.

SUMMARY

In this lesson, you learned:

■ You can embed or link data from other applications such as Microsoft Excel and Microsoft Word into PowerPoint presentations. Embedded information can be edited using the original application. To make changes to an embedded object, double-click on it to open the application that created it. Changes made when editing are reflected in the destination file.

■ Text can be imported from Word to create a new presentation or add slides. It is easiest for PowerPoint to convert the text to slides when the Word document is in outline form.

■ Slides can be copied and pasted from one presentation to another. You can also use a Slide Library to store favorite slides that you want to reuse again and again. You can also save a presentation as a Word document to use as a handout, or create other documents using the text and slides from the presentation.

■ You can apply multiple slide masters to a presentation. This can help you save time if you are creating a presentation containing slides with more than one theme or any other features that are controlled by the slide master.

■ PowerPoint allows you to create a new layout master for any theme or slide master. You can also create custom slide layouts and then add the placeholders as needed.

■ To replace fonts throughout an entire presentation, use the Replace Font dialog box.

■ You can copy the formatting of an object or text by clicking the Format Painter button. Use the Format Painter to apply the same format to another object or text.

■ To align a text box or picture, you can add grid lines and picture guides to slides.

■ Comments can be inserted in a slide for others to see.

■ A custom show can be created to limit the slides displayed in any slide show for particular audiences.

■ Action buttons are the buttons inserted on a slide that enable you to jump from slide to slide, even to slides in another slide show, or to other documents.

■ When presenting a slide show, you can use on-screen annotation tools to emphasize specific text or graphics on a slide. The Ball Point Pen, Felt Tip Pen, and Highlighter tools allow you to write or highlight features on the screen. The Eraser tool erases any ink it touches, and Erase All Ink on Slide deletes all ink marks.

■ A presentation can be set up to be self-running, so that it automatically advances the slides at preset time intervals.

■ You can inspect a presentation for personal information or anything that you might not want to "travel" with the presentation file, using the Document Inspector.

■ If you are giving your presentation on another computer, you can use Package for CD to compact all your presentation files into a single, compressed file that fits on a CD. You can then unpack the files when you reach your destination computer.

■ PowerPoint helps you easily create Web documents, either by creating a new presentation or by converting an existing presentation. Making a presentation available on the Web is also known as "publishing a presentation."

- You can send a presentation as an e-mail attachment to a recipient for review.

- You can alter a presentation's output format depending on the target audience.

- The Print Preview window previews what you are printing. You should use Print Preview prior to printing slides.

VOCABULARY *Review*

Define the following terms:

Action button	Embed	Linked object
Comment	Format Painter	Package for CD
Custom show	Grid	Snap to
Document Inspector	Guides	Source file
Document properties	Link	

Review *Questions*

FILL IN THE BLANK

Complete the following sentences by writing the correct word or words in the blanks provided.

1. If you want to place objects in the same place on more than one slide you can use _____ and _____.

2. If you format an object with certain attributes, such as fill color and line color, and then want to format another object the same way, use the _____.

3. When importing text from Word, a(n) _____ is the easiest document for PowerPoint to convert.

4. In order to be sure the Excel chart in the slide always has the most up-to-date numbers, you should _____ it rather than embed it in the presentation.

5. When you save a presentation as a Web page, it is saved using the _____ format.

MATCHING

Write the letter of the term or phrase from Column 2 that best matches the description in Column 1.

___ 1. Used when you want a presentation to contain only certain slides

___ 2. Button to click if none of the layouts for the theme works for you

___ 3. Where you specify the output format of a presentation

___ 4. Copy attributes of text or objects

___ 5. Dialog box you access to embed information

A. Format Painter

B. Insert Layout

C. Print Preview

D Slide Sorter

E. Insert Object

F. Slide Navigator

G. Custom Show

PROJECTS

PROJECT 4-1

For an astronomy club meeting, you need to create a custom slide show presentation about the solar system. After the presentation, the club members ask you for a file so that they can post the presentation to their Web site.

1. Start PowerPoint and open the The Solar System presentation file you worked on earlier in this lesson. Save the presentation as **Astronomy Class**, followed by your initials.

2. Change the theme to a new theme of your choice.

3. Replace the current font throughout the presentation with a font of your choice.

4. Select the title The Solar System on slide 1.

5. Change the font to 40-point Franklin Gothic Book.

6. Insert a text box on slide 7 with a new fact about Jupiter, format the text box using a new font, fill, and color. You can also apply a shape effect.

7. Insert a new text box on slide 9, Saturn, with a new fact about Saturn. Use the Format Painter to apply the same format as the text box on slide 7 to the text box on slide 9.

8. Inspect the document, and then view the document properties.

9. Publish the presentation as a Web page, and preview it in a browser.

10. Save, print the presentation as handouts with four slides per page, and then close the presentation.

PROJECT 4-2

You decide to create another presentation about the moons around each planet.

1. Open a new blank presentation. Enter the title on the title Slide as **Many Moons**, and then type **By Your name** as the subtitle.

2. Save the presentation as **Many Moons.pptx**.

3. Insert a new slide with a blank layout.

4. Start Word and view the Planet Number of Moons.docx Data File that has a Word table containing the following information:

Planet	Number of Moons
Mercury	0
Venus	0
Earth	1
Mars	2
Jupiter	16
Saturn	18
Uranus	15
Neptune	8
Pluto	1

5. Embed the Word table in the Many Moons presentation file that is open.

6. Center the text box on the slide. Open the file in Word and format the text as you see fit.

7. View the presentation.

8. Create a custom layout using a SmartArt graphic and a clip art placeholder.

9. Create a slide using the new custom layout.

10. Add another slide using this text, and format the text:

Planet	Time to Rotate Around Sun
Mercury	88 Earth days
Venus	224.7 Earth days
Earth	365.3 days
Mars	687 Earth days
Jupiter	12 Earth years
Saturn	29.5 Earth years
Uranus	84 Earth years
Neptune	165 Earth years
Pluto	248 Earth years

11. Add as many slides as you want to create a presentation. Apply a theme and use graphics and design elements to enhance the presentation.

12. Inspect the file, and then check the document properties.

13. Save, print the presentation as handouts with two slides per page, and then close the presentation.

CRITICAL *Thinking*

 ACTIVITY 4-1

Your supervisor wants you to insert a chart into the presentation you are editing for him. You decide to use a Microsoft Excel chart that you will create on your own. Use the Excel Help system to find out how to enter data in a worksheet, and then create a chart using Excel. Use the features on the Chart Tools Layout tab to add titles, gridlines, and data labels. Embed the chart in a new presentation.

 ACTIVITY 4-2

Create an outline in Word using heading styles. Use at least three Heading 1 styles so your presentation has at least three slides. Import the text into PowerPoint to create a new presentation. Convert the presentation into a Web page and view it with your browser.

INTRODUCTION TO MICROSOFT POWERPOINT

REVIEW *Questions*

TRUE/FALSE

Circle T if the statement is true or F if the statement is false.

T   F   1. When viewing a slide in Normal view, you can see graphics and text for each slide on the Outline tab.

T   F   2. The View Shortcuts are buttons on the status bar that you click to change between Normal, Slide Sorter, and Slide Show view.

T   F   3. The Zoom Slider adjusts the font size on the slide.

T   F   4. When you view a slide show, each slide fills the screen.

T   F   5. A PowerPoint presentation is a file with a .pptx file extension.

MULTIPLE CHOICE

Select the best response for the following statements.

1. Which method will not let you view the presentation as a slide show?
   A. Click the Office Button, then click Slide Show.
   B. Click the Slide Show button on the status bar.
   C. Click the View tab on the Ribbon, then in the Presentation Views group, click the Slide Show button.
   D. Click the Slide Show tab on the Ribbon, then in the Start Slide Show group, click the From Beginning button.

2. What reserves space on a slide for text, graphics, or an object?
   A. Master
   B. Placeholder
   C. Template
   D. Object box

3. The way a new slide appears on the screen is called the slide _____.
   A. transition
   B. scheme
   C. animation
   D. effects

4. Which feature should you use to show hierarchical structure and relationships in a company on a slide?
   A. Microsoft Word Table
   B. Microsoft Excel Graph
   C. SmartArt graphic organization chart
   D. PowerPoint Text box

5. You can apply formatting or design changes to all the slides in the presentation using the
   _____.

   A. Notes master
   B. Handout master
   C. Header and Footer dialog box
   D. Slide master

PROJECTS

PROJECT 1

1. Use the Foundry Installed theme to create a new presentation.

2. Type **My Favorite States** as the slide title, then type **by your name** as the subtitle.

3. Save the presentation as **My Favorite States Project 1.pptx**, followed by your initials.

4. Insert a new slide with a Title and Content layout.

5. Type the name of the state you live in as the title of the slide. (*Note*: If you do not live in one of the United States, type the name of a state you want to learn more about.)

6. Type four facts about the state in the content placeholder.

7. Insert a third slide with a Title and Content layout.

8. Type the name of a state you want to visit as the title of the third slide. Enter three facts about that state in the content placeholder.

9. Use the Outline tab to add two more slides to the presentation. Enter state names as the title and three facts for each state.

10. Change the font color for the facts on slides 3, 4, and 5 to different colors of your choice.

11. View the presentation in Slide Sorter view.

12. Figure 1 shows an example of what your presentation might look like.

13. Add your name to the handouts header. Print the presentation as handouts with four slides per page.

14. View the presentation as a slide show. Save and close the presentation.

FIGURE UR-1
Presentation in Slide Sorter view

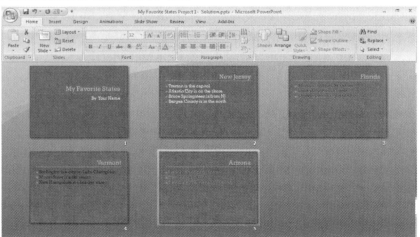

PROJECT 2

1. Open the **My Favorite States.pptx** presentation file you created in Project 1, and then save the presentation as **My Favorite States Project 2.pptx,** followed by your initials.

2. Add two more slides, and then add content for two more states.

3. Change the layout of the third slide to Two Content.

4. Replace the right placeholder with a picture that is relevant to the state you chose.

5. Add a speaker's note to slide 4: **Remember to show the flags for all states.**

6. Change the theme for the presentation to **Metro,** and then change the style of the bullets for all slides in the presentation to a different color and style of your choice.

7. Change the font attributes for the Master title style for the Title and Content to a different theme color and font style.

8. Insert a graphic image (a picture from your computer or clip art) on all the slides.

9. Insert a last slide with hyperlinks to www.usa.gov and www.whitehouse.gov. Give the slide a meaningful title. Format and design the slide as you see necessary.

10. Apply custom animation to at least two slides.

11. Apply slide transitions to all the slides.

12. Check the spelling.

13. Print the presentation as audience handouts with six slides per page.

14. Refer to Figure 2 for a sample of what the printout might look like.

15. Save and close the presentation.

FIGURE UR-2
Handouts six slides per page

PROJECT 3

1. Create a new presentation file from a template (you can use an installed template or one from Microsoft Office Online). Templates include content, so you can select a template with a topic that is of interest to you. Save the presentation as **Project 3 Template Presentation.pptx**, followed by your initials.

2. Insert a SmartArt graphic on one slide, then convert any existing text on another slide to a SmartArt graphic. If the template does not have enough slides to complete the follow steps, add additional slides.

3. Create and format WordArt on two slides.

4. Create a line chart on a slide, then format the chart. Add an appropriate slide title.

5. Create a table with three columns and three rows. Enter text in all the cells. You can enter any text that is relevant to the presentation topic.

6. Use a Table Style to modify the table's style and layout.

7. Insert a new slide, give the slide a meaningful title, draw and format a star and an arrow shape, then scale and size the shapes. Group the shapes into one object.

8. On a new slide, draw five shapes. Format the shapes with colors and fills. Enter a descriptive title on the slide.

9. Insert an oval object on the slide with five shapes, then type **This is an oval.** to create a text box on the oval shape.

10. Animate the drawn objects.

11. Add a footer with your name and the current date to all slides.

12. Apply transition effects to the slides.

13. Save your work. View the slide show, then print the presentation in any view.

14. Refer to Figure 3 for a sample of what the presentation might look like in Slide Sorter view.

15. Save and close the presentation.

FIGURE UR-3
Presentation in Slide Sorter view

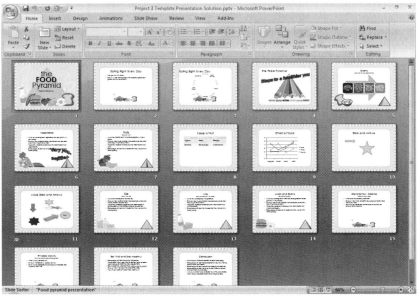

PROJECT 4

1. Open the **Project 3 Template Presentation.pptx** presentation that you created in Project 3, and then save the presentation **Project 4 Template Presentation.pptx**, followed by your initials.

2. Switch to Slide Master view, then create a new layout master that includes a picture and text placeholder. Refer to Figure 4 for a sample of what the new layout might look like. You can format the text or change the bullets.

FIGURE UR-4
New layout master with text and picture placeholders

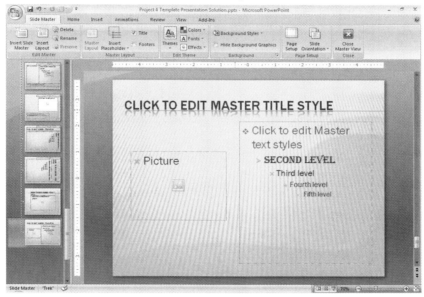

3. Change the theme of the presentation. Work the design and objects until you are happy with the design of the presentation.

4. Align text and pictures on any of the slides using the Arrange commands.

5. Insert comments on three of the slides.

6. Use the Rehearsal toolbar to set up the timing for the slide show.

7. Send the presentation via e-mail to a friend or colleague.

8. View the presentation, return to Slide Sorter view, hide a slide, then view the presentation again.

9. Save and print the presentation as handouts with four slides per page.

10. Save the presentation as a Web page, preview it in your browser, and then close the browser.

11. Save and close the presentation.

12. Exit PowerPoint.

SIMULATION

 JOB 1

The Java Internet café is working to increase the number of members who visit the café. The manager asks you to create a presentation to show to all new members so they can learn about all the benefits of coming to the cafe.

1. Start PowerPoint and open **Internet Basics.pptx** from the Data Files. Save the presentation as **Internet Basics.pptx**, followed by your initials.

2. Convert the text on **slide 2:** *Welcome* into a **Basic Venn** SmartArt graphic. You can change the formatting as you see fit.

3. Change the layout of **slide 3:** *Introduction* to **Two Content layout** and insert a clip art picture relevant to the slide.

4. Create WordArt on **slide 4:** *Agenda* using the text **Have Fun!**

5. On **slide 5:** *Overview*, draw and format three shapes, 2 arrows and 1 other shape, then cut and paste the text **Good for you!** onto one shape. Animate the shapes using custom animation.

6. Insert a new slide after slide 2 with a **Title and Content** layout. Type **Sample Coffee Pricing** as the title. Insert the Microsoft Excel worksheet Data File, **Coffee Prices.xlsx**, as an embedded object. Search for clip art using the keyword "coffee". Insert an appropriate clip art on the slide.

7. On **slide 8:** *Vocabulary*, add a hyperlink on the text **Google** to www.google.com. Preview the page and test the hyperlink.

8. Add clip art images to two other slides.

9. Insert a sound file for clapping from the Clip Organizer to the last slide. It should play automatically.

10. Add your name as a footer to the handout master.

11. Add transitions and timings to all the slides.

12. View the slide show.

13. Save and print the presentation as handouts with nine slides per page.

14. Close the presentation and then exit PowerPoint.

MICROSOFT OUTLOOK

Unit

Estimated Time for Unit: 3 hours

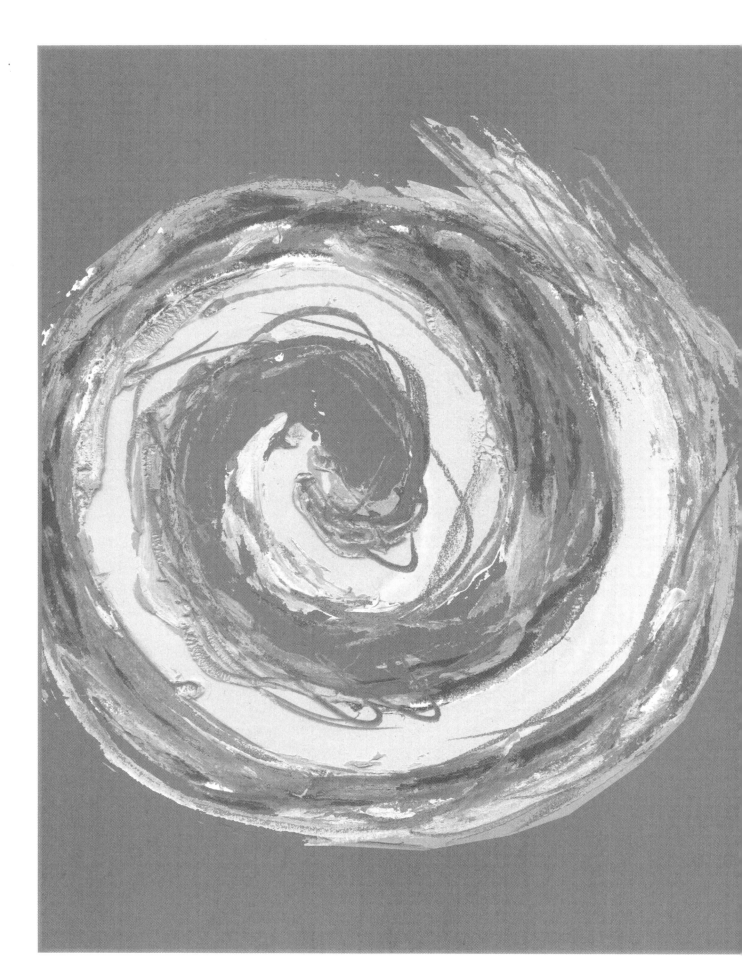

Outlook Basics and E-Mail

OBJECTIVES

Upon completion of this lesson, you will be able to:

- Start Outlook.
- Create a list of contacts and add contacts.
- View, sort, and print the Contacts list.
- Send, receive, and print e-mail messages.
- Create and use an Address Book.
- Create a distribution list.
- Create a signature.
- Attach files to e-mail messages.
- Create, move, and archive folders.
- Search, save, and delete e-mail messages.

Estimated Time: 1 hour

VOCABULARY

Address Book

Archive

Bcc

Contact

Distribution list

E-mail

Keyword

Ribbon

Signature

Spam

To-Do Bar

Introducing Outlook

Outlook is a desktop information manager that helps you organize information, communicate with others, and manage your time efficiently. You can use the various features of Outlook to send and receive e-mail, schedule events and meetings, store information about business and personal contacts, create to-do lists that integrate with your appointments, record information about interactions, create reminders, and subscribe to online content feeds. You can use these tools to group together information for easy access and maximum productivity. For example, you may want to create a category named Key Customers for your most important clients. You can also arrange Outlook to show your activities, appointments, and messages for the day.

Outlook is integrated with other Office 2007 programs, which makes it easy to share information for different tasks. For example, you can open an Outlook e-mail Message window from other Office applications, use an Outlook Contacts list to create a mail merge in Word, or move a name and address from a Word document into your Outlook Contacts list.

Starting Outlook

To start Outlook, click the Start button on the taskbar. Click All Programs on the Start menu, click Microsoft Office on the submenu, and then click Microsoft Office Outlook 2007. The Outlook window opens with the Outlook Today pane opened, as shown in Figure 1-1.

FIGURE 1-1
Outlook Today

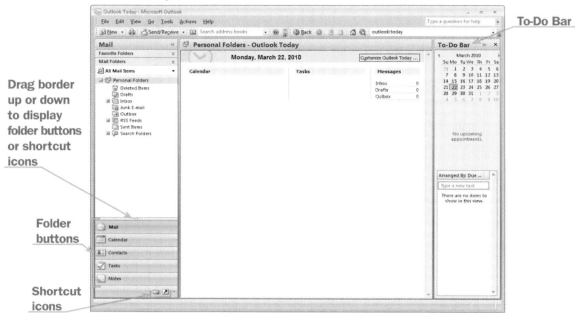

The Navigation Pane is located on the left side of the Outlook window and provides centralized navigation to all parts of Outlook. It includes folder buttons and shortcut icons you can use to quickly access the information you need. From the Navigation Pane you can access Mail, Calendar, Contacts, Tasks, Notes, Folder List, and Journal, or create a new shortcut. Table 1-1 describes each of these elements. You can drag the folder buttons border up or down to show a button in the list or a shortcut icon at the bottom of the pane.

TABLE 1-1
Navigation Pane options

ICON	NAME	DESCRIPTION
	Mail	Contains e-mail messages that you have sent and received.
	Calendar	Schedules your appointments, meetings, and events.
	Contacts	Lists information about those with whom you communicate.
	Tasks	Creates and manages your to-do lists.
	Notes	Keeps track of anything you need to remember.
	Folder List	Lists all of your folders.
	Shortcuts	Provides quick access to folders in any Outlook view.
	Journal	Records entries to document your work.

Outlook Today gives you a summary of your day's activities: appointments, tasks, and e-mail messages. The **To-Do Bar**, located on the right side of the Outlook window, includes a Date Navigator, Appointments section, Task Input section, and a task list. You can view a specific component by clicking its icon in the Navigation Pane. Once open, you can rearrange your view of any component, such as Mail, Calendar, or Tasks, by clicking View on the menu bar, pointing to Current View, and then clicking a view option.

> **Did You Know?**
>
> You can hide/show or customize options in any section of Outlook. To customize the Navigation Pane, right-click a component, click Navigation Pane Options, and then select or move options as desired.

STEP-BY-STEP 1.1

1. Click the **Start** button on the taskbar.

2. Click **All Programs** on the Start menu and then click **Microsoft Office** on the submenu. Click **Microsoft Office Outlook 2007**. (*Note*: You may be prompted to set up a personal account.)

> **Important**
>
> If the Navigation Pane is not visible, click View on the menu bar, point to Navigation Pane, and then click Normal.

3. The Outlook window opens with the Navigation Pane and Outlook Today Pane open, as shown in Figure 1-1. Leave this pane open for the next Step-by-Step.

Creating a Contacts List

You can store information about the people or organizations with whom you communicate by creating a Contacts list. A **contact** is any person or company in your Address Book. Your Contacts list can contain e-mail, address, phone, and other information. You can create contacts in several ways. Using the Navigation Pane, click the Contacts button to display the Contacts Pane, as shown in Figure 1-2. You can also create a contact from an e-mail message that you open or preview, or from an electronic business card you receive.

FIGURE 1-2
Contacts Pane

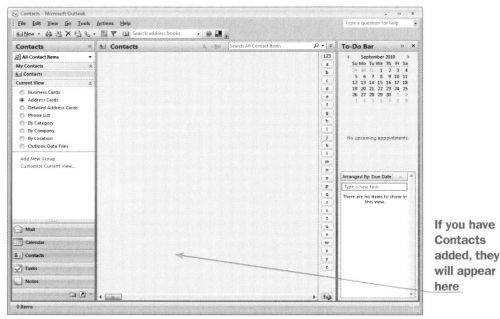

If you have Contacts added, they will appear here

Adding a Contact

To add a contact, click the Contacts folder button in the Navigation Pane and then click the New Contact button on the Standard toolbar. A new Contact window opens with the title Untitled – Contact, as shown in Figure 1-3. When you finish adding information about the contact, on the Ribbon, in the Actions group, click the Save & Close button to return to the Contacts Pane, or click the Save & New button to add another contact.

Did You Know?

You can store information for both individuals and companies by manually entering the data or by grabbing information from an open e-mail message. Right-click the sender's e-mail address on the From line, and then click Add to Outlook Contacts.

FIGURE 1-3
New Contact window

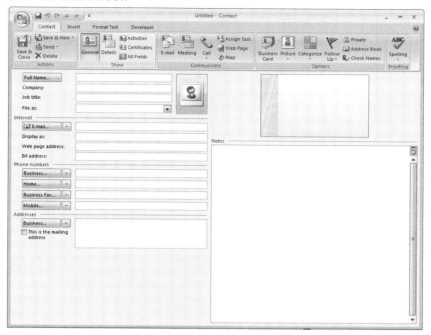

The top of the Contact window contains the Ribbon. The Ribbon is organized into four tabs and contains commands for working with the Outlook element you've selected. The Contact tab contains tools for customizing what information appears and for communicating with your contact. Once you've entered some information about the contact, you can add display details, set up a meeting with or e-mail the contact, add a photograph, categorize the contact, even find a map to their address. The Insert tab allows you to attach files or e-mail messages to the entry, or insert illustrations, tables, different media, or text in the Notes section of the Contact window. The Format Text tab allows you to modify the font layout and style attributes of the contact information as it appears in the Contact window. The Developer tab contains advanced options for customizing contact information.

> **Did You Know?**
>
> To update information about a contact, double-click the contact's name in the Contacts list. Make your changes and then, on the Ribbon, in the Actions group, click the Save & Close button.

S TEP-BY-STEP 1.2

1. Click the **Contacts** folder button in the Navigation Pane. The Contacts Pane appears, similar to Figure 1-2.

2. Click the **New Contact** button on the toolbar. A new Contact window opens, as shown in Figure 1-3.

3. In the *Full Name* box, type **Sofia Acosta**.

STEP-BY-STEP 1.2 Continued

4. Press the **Tab** key or the **Enter** key. The title of the Contact window automatically changes to Sofia Acosta – Contact, but the surname is automatically placed first in the File as box.

5. In the *Company* box, type **El Flamenco Realty** and then press the **Tab** key or the **Enter** key.

6. In the *Job title* box, type **President** and then press the **Tab** key or the **Enter** key.

7. For the remaining boxes, type the information shown in Figure 1-4. On the Ribbon, in the Contact tab, in the Options group, click the **Categorize** button, and then click **Red Category** for the contact. The contacts are color-coded for easy identification. (*Note*: If prompted to rename the color category, click **No**.)

FIGURE 1-4
Completed contact information

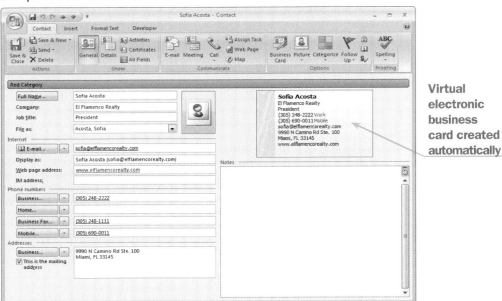

Virtual electronic business card created automatically

8. When you have completed entering the contact information, on the Ribbon, in the Actions group, click the **Save & New** button. The contact information is saved, and a blank Contact window opens.

9. Add two more contacts using the information shown in Figure 1-5. When you finish, on the Ribbon, in the Actions group, click the **Save & Close** button to return to the Contacts list.

Important

Notice that after you type the e-mail address, the full name and e-mail address automatically appear in the Display As box, and a virtual business card showing the contact information is visible.

STEP-BY-STEP 1.2 Continued

FIGURE 1-5
Add two more contacts

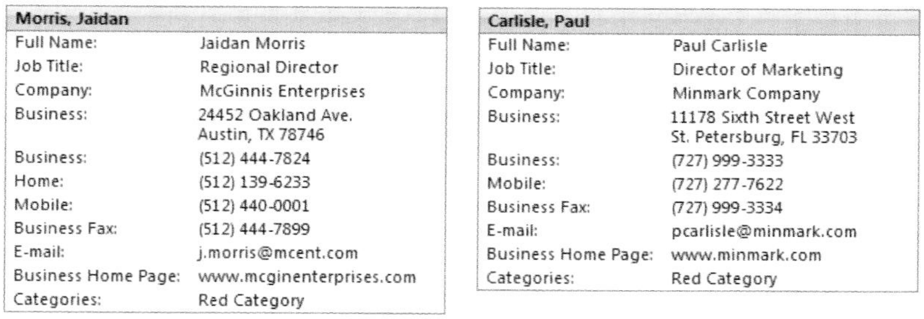

Morris, Jaidan	
Full Name:	Jaidan Morris
Job Title:	Regional Director
Company:	McGinnis Enterprises
Business:	24452 Oakland Ave. Austin, TX 78746
Business:	(512) 444-7824
Home:	(512) 139-6233
Mobile:	(512) 440-0001
Business Fax:	(512) 444-7899
E-mail:	j.morris@mcent.com
Business Home Page:	www.mcginenterprises.com
Categories:	Red Category

Carlisle, Paul	
Full Name:	Paul Carlisle
Job Title:	Director of Marketing
Company:	Minmark Company
Business:	11178 Sixth Street West St. Petersburg, FL 33703
Business:	(727) 999-3333
Mobile:	(727) 277-7622
Business Fax:	(727) 999-3334
E-mail:	pcarlisle@minmark.com
Business Home Page:	www.minmark.com
Categories:	Red Category

10. In the *Contacts* list, double-click **Sofia Acosta**. The Contact window for Sofia Acosta opens.

11. In the *Job title* box, delete **President** and type **Owner**. On the Ribbon, in the Actions group, click the **Save & Close** button to save your changes. Leave the Contacts list open for the next Step-by-Step.

> **Extra Challenge**
>
> Add five more contacts to your Contacts list, using fictitious information.

Viewing, Sorting, and Printing the Contacts List

To change how you view your contacts, click the Navigation Pane, and then click a view option in the Current View section. View options for the Contacts list are described in Table 1-2. When you click Contacts, Address Cards is the default view in the Contacts Pane.

TABLE 1-2
View options for Contacts list

VIEW	DESCRIPTION
Business Cards	Displays company logos, layouts, designs, photos, or other images.
Address Cards	Default view; displays general information on individual cards.
Detailed Address Cards	Displays detailed information about contacts on individual cards.
Phone List	Lists contacts in a table with all phone numbers included.
By Category	Groups contacts in a list according to category.
By Company	Groups contacts in a list according to company.
By Location	Groups contacts in a list according to country or region.
Outlook Data Files	Groups contacts by the data file that stores items and folders, such as by project or archived file.

To sort your Contacts list for the table views, click View on the menu bar, point to Arrange By, and then click a field or column, such as date, subject, or attachment. You can also click Custom and then click Sort or another category in the Custom View dialog box. To sort your Contacts list for the card views, click View on the menu bar, point to Current View, click Customize Current View, and then click Sort in the Custom View dialog box. The available sorting options for the Contacts list include sorting by full name, last name, company, business address, job title, and so on.

To print your Contacts list in the current view, click File on the menu bar and then click Print. The Print dialog box opens. The Print style box provides different options depending on the selected view. For example, from a card view, you can print your contacts as cards, booklets, or a phone list.

> **Did You Know?**
>
> When using either Address Cards view or Detailed Address Cards view, you can click a letter on the bar on the right to quickly display contacts whose last names begin with that letter.

STEP-BY-STEP 1.3

1. With the Contacts Pane open, click the **Detailed Address Cards** option in the Current View section. Your screen should look similar to Figure 1-6.

FIGURE 1-6
Viewing Contacts in Detailed Address Cards view

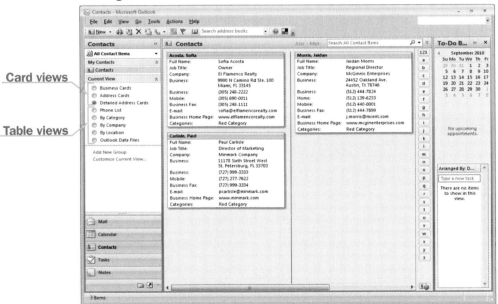

2. Click the **Phone List** option in the Current View section. Notice how the contact information displays in a phone list table style.

3. Click **View** on the menu bar, point to Current View, and then click **Customize Current View**. The Customize View dialog box opens.

STEP-BY-STEP 1.3 Continued

4. In the Customize View dialog box, click the **Sort** button. The Sort dialog box opens, as shown in Figure 1-7.

FIGURE 1-7
Sort dialog box

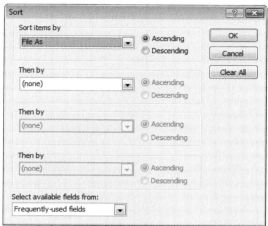

5. In the Sort dialog box, click the **arrow** under the Sort items by option box to view the available sorting options, scroll down, and then click **Company**. Click **OK** to close the Sort dialog box. Click **OK** again to close the Customize View dialog box. Your contacts are now sorted by company in ascending order.

6. Click the **Print** button on the Standard toolbar. The Print dialog box appears.

7. In the Print style box, make sure Table Style is selected. Click **OK**. The Contacts list will print as a phone list, which is the currently selected view. Leave Outlook open for the next Step-by-Step.

Did You Know?

To preview a Contacts list before printing, click File on the menu bar and then click Print Preview. You can adjust the magnification by clicking the magnifying glass pointer.

 Careers

Contacts lists in Outlook are helpful in any project in which you have many colleagues and associates. For example, salespeople can create a Contacts list to store detailed information on each of their clients. They can organize this information by assigning a category to each client. A Contacts list can also make it easy to communicate with clients. To send an e-mail message to a contact from any view, simply drag the contact to the Mail folder button or to the Mail shortcut icon in the Navigation Pane. A new Message window opens with the contact's name in the To box. Type your message and click the Send button. You will learn more about sending e-mail messages later in this lesson.

Using E-Mail

One of the most common and useful Internet services is **e-mail** (electronic mail), which uses a computer network to send and receive messages. E-mail has become an essential global communications tool. It is fast, paperless, and accessible from many different devices. In addition to your computer, you can use e-mail from portable devices, such as pocket PCs or smartphones, such as Blackberries.

To use electronic mail, you need an e-mail address that includes your name; your host, server, or domain name; and an extension that tells whether the account is at a school, business, government location, or in another country. No one else has your unique e-mail address. E-mail addresses are composed of a user name to the left of the @ symbol, and a domain name, which is the text equivalent of an Internet address. Examples include:

yourteacher@yourschool.edu

tickets@comedycentral.com

president@whitehouse.gov

Using Outlook, you can send e-mail messages to others connected by your intranet. If you have an Internet connection, you can send messages to anyone around the world who also has an Internet connection. E-mail has transformed business and personal communication and is the preferred way to communicate with clients, co-workers, friends, and family. Your software needs to be configured with the appropriate profile and service settings to send and receive e-mail.

> **Net Tip**
>
> E-mail was used on the Internet many years before Web pages even existed. Since 1971, billions and billions of e-mail messages have been sent. Some estimate the percentage of **spam**, electronic junk mail, to be up to 50 percent of all e-mail.

Setting E-Mail Options and Assigning Categories to Messages

Click the New Mail Message button on the Standard toolbar, and a new Message window opens, as shown in Figure 1-8. To help you manage your e-mail messages, Outlook provides several settings that you can modify when sending and receiving messages. For example, you can set a message's importance. On the Ribbon, in the Options group, you can modify the default importance setting, Normal, by clicking the High Importance button or the Low Importance button. On the Ribbon, click the Options tab to modify additional settings, such as delivery options. You can access all of these settings at once by opening the Message Options dialog box, as shown in Figure 1-9. You can open this box in several ways. In an open Message window, on the Ribbon, click the Message tab, and then, in the lower-right corner of the Options group, click the dialog box launcher; or, on the Ribbon, click the Options tab, and then, in

> **Important**
>
> Because your e-mail account may have a limited amount of space available for messages, it is important to manage the number of messages you store. You can delete any unnecessary e-mail messages by selecting them and then clicking the Delete button on the toolbar.

the lower-right corner of the Tracking group or the More Options group, click the dialog box launcher. You can access both the Contacts list and the Categories dialog box by clicking the options at the bottom of the dialog box.

FIGURE 1-8
New Message window

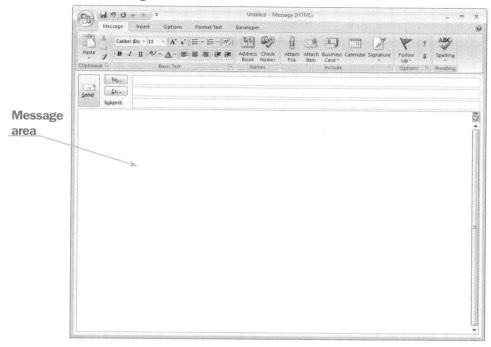

Message area

FIGURE 1-9
Message Options dialog box

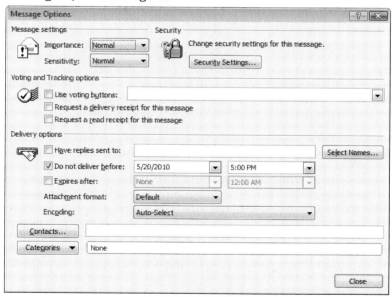

STEP-BY-STEP 1.4

1. On the Navigation Pane, click the **Mail** icon at the bottom of the page. If necessary, click the **Inbox** folder in the Mail section of the Navigation Pane to display the Inbox.

2. Double-click the **message** from Microsoft or another message if you have one in your Inbox. Scroll through and read the message. Notice all the formatting features used in the message.

3. Click the **Office Button** and then click **Close**, or click the **Close** button in the upper-right corner of the Message window to close the message.

4. Click the **New Mail Message** button on the toolbar. The new Message window opens, similar to Figure 1-8.

5. In the Message window, on the Ribbon, in the Options group, click the **launcher**. The Message Options dialog box opens, similar to Figure 1-9.

6. In the *Message settings* section, click the **arrow** next to the Importance box and change the setting to **Low**.

7. In the *Voting and Tracking* options section, click the **check box** for the Use voting buttons option. A check mark appears in the box, indicating it is selected.

8. In the *Delivery options* section, click the **check box** next to the Have replies sent to option. Your name and e-mail address will appear in the field.

9. Click the **Categories** arrow at the bottom of the dialog box and then click **Red Category**.

10. Change the settings back to the original defaults, using Figure 1-9 as your guide.

11. Click **Close** to close the Message Options dialog box. Click the **Close** button in the Message window. A message box will open asking you to save changes. Click **No** and leave Outlook open for the next Step-by-Step.

Sending, Receiving, and Printing E-Mail Messages

The Mail section of the Navigation Pane contains mail folders, such as the Drafts folder, in which unsent items are stored, and the Junk E-mail folder, in which messages identified as spam are stored. The Inbox folder contains incoming mail, and the Outbox folder stores outgoing mail. The Sent Items folder stores the e-mail messages you've sent, and Deleted Items stores the messages you've deleted. You can use Search Folders to view e-mail messages matching specific criteria, such as containing certain **keywords**, or messages flagged as important. You can open any folder by clicking it in the Navigation Pane. The folder contents display in the center pane.

To create and send an e-mail message, open a new Message window, as shown in Figure 1-8. In the To box, type the e-mail address of the person to whom you are sending the message. You can send a copy of the message to someone by typing his or her e-mail address in the Cc box. You can also send a **Bcc** (blind carbon copy) of the message to someone, which means that person's

> **Did You Know?**
>
> To add the Bcc field to a Message window, on the Ribbon, click the Options tab, and then in the Fields group, click the Show Bcc button.

name will not be visible to the other recipients when they open the message. In the Subject box, type the subject of your message and then in the message body area, type your message.

You can modify the basic formatting features of your message, such as the font, size, color, and text alignment. On the Ribbon, in the Basic Text group, click the attribute you want to change. To modify the Theme, Theme Fonts, Theme Colors, Theme Effects, and Page Color, on the Ribbon, click the Options tab, and then in the Themes group, click the feature you want to change. You can also save the message, check its spelling, print the message, and attach a file to the e-mail message. When you're finished writing your message, you can send it by clicking the Send button.

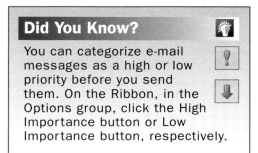

Did You Know?

You can categorize e-mail messages as a high or low priority before you send them. On the Ribbon, in the Options group, click the High Importance button or Low Importance button, respectively.

To open an e-mail message, double-click the message in the Inbox. The message opens. After reading a message, you can reply to it or forward it to someone else. To reply to it, on the Ribbon, in the Respond group, click the Reply button. To forward it, on the Ribbon, in the Respond group, click the Forward button. You can also print the message, or go on to read the next message.

S TEP-BY-STEP 1.5

1. Click the **New Mail Message** button on the Standard toolbar. A blank Message window opens, as shown in Figure 1-8.

2. In the *To* box, type your **e-mail address** or one provided by your instructor.

3. In the *Subject* box, type **Test**.

4. In the message area, type **This is a test**.

5. Click the **Send** button. Your mail is sent, and if Outlook is set up correctly for intranet e-mail, you should receive the message in a few moments. (*Note*: If you do not receive the message shortly, click the **Send/Receive** button on the toolbar.)

Did You Know?

To reply to the sender in an open message, on the Ribbon, in the Respond group, click the Reply button. To respond to all the recipients listed in the message, click the Reply to All button. To forward a message to another recipient, click the Forward button, insert the person's address, and then click the Send button.

6. Double-click the **e-mail message** with the subject "Test" to open the message.

7. Click the **Office** button, point to **Print**, then click **Quick Print** to print the message. Close the message.

8. Click the **Sent Items** folder in the Mail section of the Navigation Pane to display the list of sent messages. The message you sent to yourself appears at the top.

9. Click the **Outbox** folder in the Mail section of the Navigation Pane. If the message is still waiting to be sent, it appears in this folder. (*Note*: You may need to scroll down in the All Mail Items section to find the Outbox folder.) Leave Outlook open for the next Step-by-Step.

Creating an Address Book

Most of the time, you will be sending e-mail messages to the same people. To make sending an e-mail message easier, you can access names and addresses from the **Address Book**, a collection of personal and professional contact information. Outlook creates Address Book information automatically when you add a new contact with an e-mail address to your Contacts list. The Address Book contains the contact's name and e-mail address.

To display the Address Book, make sure the Mail Pane is open and then click the Address Book button on the toolbar. The Address Book window opens, as shown in Figure 1-10. To add a new contact from the open Address Book, click File on the menu bar, and then click New Entry. The New Entry dialog box opens, as shown in Figure 1-11. Make sure that New Contact is selected and then click OK. The new Contact window opens, as shown in Figure 1-12. When you are done adding information about the contact, on the Ribbon, in the Actions group, click the Save & Close button to return to the Address Book window. The new contact appears in the Address Book.

FIGURE 1-10
View contacts in the Address Book window

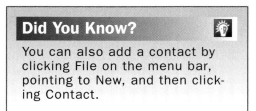

To display the more detailed information about a contact listed in the Address Book, double-click the contact's name to open the Contact window.

Did You Know?

You can also add a contact by clicking File on the menu bar, pointing to New, and then clicking Contact.

FIGURE 1-11
New Entry dialog box

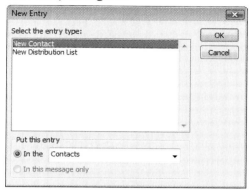

FIGURE 1-12
New Contact window

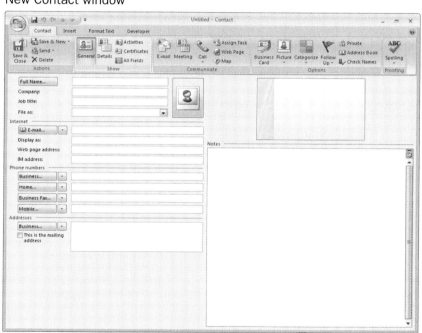

S TEP-BY-STEP 1.6

1. Click the **Inbox** folder in the Mail section of the Navigation Pane to display the Inbox.

2. To display the Address Book, click the **Address Book** button on the toolbar. The Address Book dialog box opens, as shown in Figure 1-10.

3. Click **File** on the menu bar and then click **New Entry**. The New Entry dialog box opens, as shown in Figure 1-11.

4. In the *New Entry* dialog box, if not already selected, click **New Contact**, and then click **OK**. The new Contact window opens, as shown in Figure 1-12.

5. In the *Full Name* box, type your first and last name and then press the **Tab** key or the **Enter** key. Your name appears as Last name, First name in the File as box.

6. In the *E-mail* box, type your e-mail address or one provided by your instructor.

7. On the Ribbon, in the Actions group, click the **Save & Close** button. The Address Book dialog box reappears with your name added to the list.

8. Double-click either listing for **Paul Carlisle**. The Contact window opens, showing detailed information about Paul Carlisle.

9. When finished viewing, on the Ribbon, in the Actions group, click the **Save & Close** button to close the Contact window. Close the Address Book dialog box to return to the Inbox. Leave Outlook open for the next Step-by-Step.

Using an Address Book

To open the Address Book while creating a new e-mail message, click the To button in the Message window. The Select Names dialog box opens with names from your Contacts list, as shown in Figure 1-13. Select the contact to whom you want to send the message, and then click the To button at the bottom of the dialog box. The contact's name appears in the To box. Click OK and the contact's name appears in the To box in the Message window as the recipient of the e-mail message. When you finish your e-mail message, click the Send button.

FIGURE 1-13
Select Names window

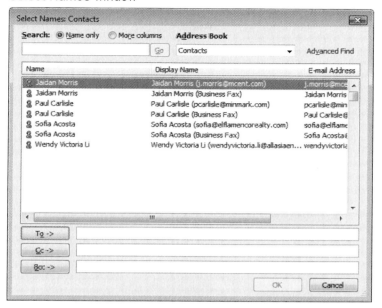

S TEP-BY-STEP 1.7

1. From the Inbox, create an e-mail message by clicking the **New Mail Message** button on the Standard toolbar. A blank e-mail Message window opens.

2. Click the **To** box. The Select Names dialog box opens, as shown in Figure 1-13.

3. Select **your name** from the list of contacts and then click the **To** button. Your name appears in the To box.

4. Click **OK**. The new Message window reappears, and your name appears in the To box as the recipient of the e-mail message.

5. In the *Subject* box, type **Tomorrow's meeting**.

6. In the *Message* area, type **Don't forget tomorrow's meeting at 1:30 pm**.

7. Click the **Send** button.

8. Click the **Sent Items** folder in the Mail Folder section of the Navigation Pane to see the sent message. (*Note*: If you do not receive the message shortly, click the Send/Receive button on the toolbar.) Leave Outlook open for the next Step-by-Step.

Creating a Distribution List

You can use your time more efficiently by creating distribution lists. Distribution lists are collections of contacts that provide an easy way to send messages to everyone within a group or department. They eliminate the need to individually select e-mail recipients.

To create a distribution list, click File on the menu bar, point to New, and then click Distribution List. A new Distribution List window opens with the title Untitled – Distribution List. In the Name box, type a unique name for the distribution list. On the Ribbon, in the Members group, click the Select Members button. The Select Members window opens, where you can select members for your distribution list from any address book, including your Contacts list. Select the names you want to include in your distribution list by typing them in the Search box or by selecting them in the list, and then click the Members button. When you are finished, click OK. To view the new distribution list name in your Address Book, on the Standard toolbar, click the Address Book button.

STEP-BY-STEP 1.8

1. Click **File** on the menu bar, point to **New**, and then click **Distribution List**. A blank Distribution List window opens.

2. In the Distribution List window, in the Name box, type **El Flamenco Project**.

3. On the Ribbon, in the Members group, click the **Select Members** button. The Select Members window opens.

4. In the Search box, type **Sofia**, and then click the **Members** button at the bottom of the window.

5. In the Search box, type **Morris**, and then click the **Members** button at the bottom of the window.

6. When finished adding names, click **OK**. The El Flamenco Project–Distribution List window has Sofia Acosta and Jaidan Morris listed as members.

7. Click the **Office Button**, point to **Print**, and then click **Quick Print** to print the distribution list.

8. On the Ribbon, in the Actions group, click the **Save & Close** button.

9. Click the **Address Book** button on the Standard toolbar. The Address Book window opens, and the El Flamenco Project distribution list name appears in the list.

10. Close the Address Book window to return to the Inbox Pane. Leave Outlook open for the next Step-by-Step.

> **Did You Know?**
>
> To edit a distribution list, open the Address Book window and then double-click the distribution list name to open it. You can edit, add, or delete contacts.

Creating a Signature

You can create a signature to add to the end of each of your messages, which adds a professional or unique look and feel to your messages. To create a signature, open a new Message window, then, on the Ribbon, in the Include group, click the arrow at the bottom of the Signature button, then click Signatures. In the Signatures and Stationery dialog box, on the E-mail Signature tab, click New. In the New Signature dialog box, type a name for the signature and then click OK. In the Edit Signature box, type the text for your signature. Format the text, add images, electronic business cards, or hyperlinks as desired, and then click OK.

STEP-BY-STEP 1.9

1. Click the **New Mail Message** button on the Standard toolbar and then, on the Ribbon, in the Include group, click the **arrow** at the bottom of the Signature button, then click **Signatures**. The Signatures and Stationery dialog box opens.

2. In the Signatures and Stationery dialog box, on the E-mail Signature tab, in the Select signature to edit section, click **New**. In the New Signature dialog box, type **your name** and then click **OK**. A new signature is added to the list, and the Signatures and Stationery dialog box looks similar to Figure 1-14.

FIGURE 1-14
Signatures and Stationery dialog box

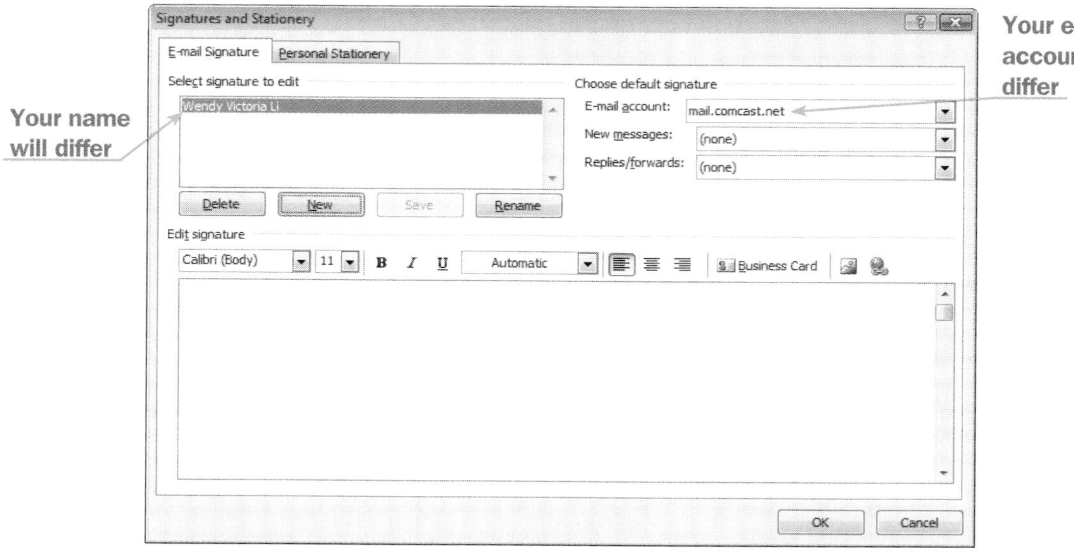

3. In the Edit signature section, click the **Italic** button. Click the **Font arrow**, scroll down, and then click **Cambria**. Click the **Font Size arrow** and then click **12**.

4. In the Edit signature box, type your name. In the Select signature to edit section, click the **Save** button.

STEP-BY-STEP 1.9 Continued

5. In the Choose default signature section, click the New messages **arrow**, and then select your name. Click **OK** to close the Signatures and Stationery dialog box. Your signature is saved for new messages.

6. Close the new Message window, and then click the **New Mail Message** button on the Standard toolbar. Your signature appears at the bottom of the message area. Leave Outlook open for the next Step-by-Step.

> **Did You Know?**
>
> To select a different signature for your e-mail messages, open the Signatures and Stationery dialog box. In the Choose default signature section, click the New messages arrow, and then click the signature name you want to include.

Attaching Files to E-Mail Messages

Outlook enables you to attach a variety of files to e-mail messages and send them to others. After you have created and addressed a new message, on the Ribbon, in the Include group, click the Attach File button. The Insert File dialog box opens, showing the folders and files in the Documents folder, similar to Figure 1-15. Browse to the location where the file is located. At the bottom of the dialog box, click the Insert button. In the Message window, the attached file appears in the Attached box.

> **Did You Know?**
>
> To attach another e-mail message to a message, on the Ribbon, in the Include group, click the Attach Item button.

FIGURE 1-15
Insert File dialog box

Your location will differ

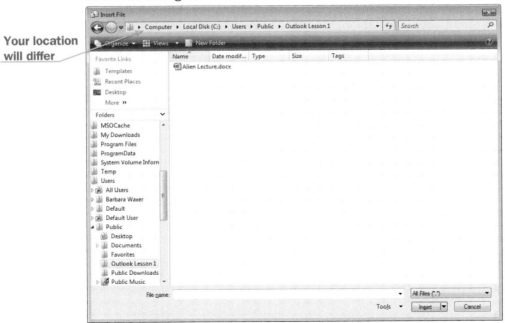

S TEP-BY-STEP 1.10

1. Click the **New Mail Message** button on the Standard toolbar.

2. Click the **To** button. The Select Names window opens.

3. In the Select Names window, click your **name** from the list of contacts and then click the **To** button. Your name appears in the To box.

4. Click **OK**. Your name appears as the recipient in the new e-mail.

5. In the *Subject* box, type **See planetarium attachment**.

6. On the Ribbon, in the Include group, click the **Attach File** button. The Insert File dialog box opens, as shown in Figure 1-15.

7. In the Insert File dialog box, locate the folder where your Data Files are stored, click the **Alien Lecture.docx** Word document, and then click the **Insert** button at the bottom of the dialog box. The document name appears in the Attached box in the Message window.

8. Click the **Send** button. You are the recipient of the e-mail and the attachment. Leave Outlook open for the next Step-by-Step.

> ### Did You Know?
>
> You can attach many different file types to your messages, including photographs, illustrations, sound, video, text, and spreadsheet files.

Creating, Moving, and Archiving Folders

At times it is necessary to clean off your desk and discard accumulated documents. There will be times when your Outlook mailbox also needs to be reorganized. The process of organizing, storing, and saving old documents is called archiving. Outlook can archive all items, including attachments.

You can create new folders to organize documents from the Inbox Pane. Click File on the menu bar, point to New, and then click Folder. The Create New Folder dialog box opens, as shown in Figure 1-16. In the Name box, type the name of the folder you want to create. In the Folder contains box, select Mail and Post Items. In the Select where to place the folder box, click the location where you want to place the new folder. Click OK, and the new folder appears in the list of folders in the Navigation Pane.

FIGURE 1-16
Create New Folder dialog box

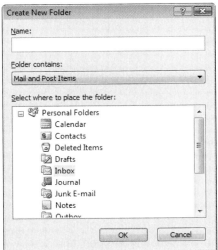

You can transfer old files to a storage file by clicking Archive on the File menu. The Archive dialog box opens, as shown in Figure 1-17. Select the option to Archive this folder and all subfolders and then select the folder to be archived. In the Archive items older than box, click the arrow and select a date from the calendar. Click OK, and all of the files in your folder with dates prior to the date you selected are archived.

Did You Know?

To view items in an archived folder, in the Navigation Pane, click Archive Folders. To specify when AutoArchive runs or to turn it off, click Tools on the menu bar, click Options, click the Other tab, click the AutoArchive button, and then adjust settings as desired.

FIGURE 1-17
Archive dialog box

Your name and
path will differ

STEP-BY-STEP 1.11

1. Click **File** on the menu bar, point to **New**, and then click **Folder**. The Create New Folder dialog box opens.

2. In the Create New Folder dialog box, in the *Name* box, type **Test**. In the *Folder contains* box, make sure that **Mail and Post Items** is selected.

3. In the *Select where to place the folder* box, select the location where you want to place the new folder and then click **OK**. The Test folder appears in the list of Inbox folders in the Navigation Pane.

4. In the Inbox, select the message named **Test**. Place the pointer on the selected message and then drag the Test message to the Test folder in the Navigation Pane. When finished, click the **Test** folder to view its contents; the Test message appears.

5. Click the **Sent Items** folder in the Navigation Pane. Select the **Test** message you previously sent to yourself.

6. Click **File** on the menu bar and then click **Archive**. The Archive dialog box opens with the Sent Items folder selected. Make sure the Archive this folder and all subfolders check box is selected.

7. In the Archive dialog box, click the **Archive items older than arrow**. A calendar opens. Choose a date approximately three months prior to today's date and then click **OK**. Your messages with dates prior to the date you selected are archived.

8. Click the **Inbox** folder in the Navigation Pane. Leave Outlook open for the next Step-by-Step.

> ### Did You Know?
>
> You can visually organize your e-mail by color coding messages you send and receive, just as you can color code contacts. Select the message you want to categorize by color, click the Categorize button on the Standard toolbar, and then click a color.

Saving, Searching, and Deleting E-Mail Messages

There are many occasions when you deem e-mail messages important enough to save them for future reference. To save a message as a document or HTML (Web page) file, click File on the menu bar and then click Save As. Click the Address bar arrow and navigate to the location where you want to save the message. By default, the file name is the message's subject line. To search for a particular message, click the Inbox, type one or more keywords in the Instant Search box on the right side of the Inbox Pane, and then press Enter. A keyword is a significant word or phrase used to search a database as small as a Contacts list or as large as the Internet. The keywords are highlighted in the search results. To expand your search capabilities, click the Expand the Query Builder arrow next to the search box. To delete a message, select the message to be deleted in the Inbox and then click the Delete button on the Standard toolbar. The message is moved to the Deleted Items folder, where you can later retrieve or permanently delete it.

In addition to using Instant Search to find e-mail messages, you can also locate tasks and appointments that match your search criteria. To find contacts, type contact information in the Find a Contact box. See Figure 1-18.

> **Did You Know?**
>
> By default, Outlook searches all folders for the keywords. To restrict the search to the currently selected folder, click the Show Instant Search Pane Menu list arrow next to the Instant Search box, click Search Options, and then in the Instant Search Pane section, click the Only the currently selected folder option.

FIGURE 1-18
Instant Search box

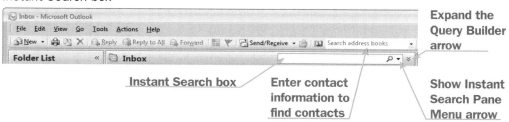

Expand the Query Builder arrow

Instant Search box

Enter contact information to find contacts

Show Instant Search Pane Menu arrow

STEP-BY-STEP 1.12

1. Click the **New Mail Message** button on the Standard toolbar. A new Message window opens.

2. In the *To* box, type **your e-mail address** or one provided by your instructor.

3. In the *Subject* box, type **To Be Deleted**.

4. In the *Message* area, type **Delete this message**.

5. Click the **Send** button. After receiving the e-mail, double-click the **message** to open it.

6. Click the **Office Button**, point to **Save As**, and then click **Save As**. The Save As dialog box opens.

STEP-BY-STEP 1.12 Continued

7. Navigate to the folder where you save files for this course. The title of the e-mail message appears in the File name box.

8. Click **Save**, and the message is saved as an HTML document in the folder you selected.

9. Click the **Office Button** and then click **Close** to close the message.

> **Did You Know?**
>
> To save this message as a text document, in the Save As dialog box, click the Save as type list arrow and then click Text Only (.txt).

10. In the Inbox Pane, click the **Instant Search** box beneath the Standard toolbar, type **Delete this message**, and then press **Enter**. (*Note*: The Instant Search box has a magnifying glass icon in it.) See Figure 1-18.

11. Click the **message** to select and then click the **Delete** button on the toolbar. The message is sent to the Deleted Items folder.

12. Click the **Close** button in the upper-right corner of the window to close Outlook. The Outlook window closes and the Microsoft Windows desktop appears.

SUMMARY

In this lesson, you learned:

■ Outlook is a desktop information manager that helps you organize information, communicate with others, and manage your time. You can use the various features of Outlook to send and receive e-mail, schedule events and meetings, store information about business and personal contacts, create to-do lists that integrate with your appointments, record information about interactions, create reminders, and subscribe to online content feeds.

■ The Contacts list is a useful tool where you can store mail, phone, and other information about people and companies. You can view or print your contacts in several ways, including as address cards or as a phone list.

■ E-mail has become an essential global communications tool, accessible from many different devices. In addition to your computer, you can use e-mail from portable devices, such as smartphones and pocket PCs.

■ Most of the time you will be sending e-mail messages to the same people. To make sending an e-mail message easier, you can use an Address Book, listing the addresses that you use most often.

■ Using distribution lists to send the same message to several people is efficient and allows you to use or modify the list however you need.

■ Adding an electronic signature to your e-mail messages helps set the right tone for your contacts and correspondence. Outlook allows you to attach photos and logos for a distinctive touch.

■ Using Outlook, you can send e-mail messages to others connected to your network or to anyone around the world with an Internet connection. Outlook enables you to attach a variety of files to e-mail messages and send these files to others. You can view and organize your messages in a variety of ways, as well as archive them and save them to your computer.

VOCABULARY *Review*

Define the following terms:

Address Book	Distribution list	Signature
Archive	E-mail	Spam
Bcc	Keyword	To-Do Bar
Contact	Ribbon	

REVIEW *Questions*

TRUE/FALSE

Circle T if the statement is true or F if the statement is false.

T F 1. The Navigation Pane contains a calendar.

T F 2. The default view for Contacts is Detailed Address Cards.

T F 3. In the Contact window, you can add a photograph or a nickname to the contact's listing.

T F 4. You can create multiple distribution lists, but you cannot edit one after you create it.

T F 5. You can create multiple signatures for your messages.

WRITTEN QUESTIONS

Write a brief answer to the following questions.

1. What is a contact?

2.   Name two different devices on which you can use e-mail.

3.   Name three types of contact information included in the Contact window.

4.   Explain the importance of creating distribution lists.

5.   Explain what an e-mail signature is and how it is useful.

PROJECTS

PROJECT 1-1

You recently met two people you want to add to your Contacts list.

1.   Display the Contacts pane.

2.   Add the two contacts using this information. Save and close when you finish.

Name: **Austin Parker**	Name: **Allie Hunter**
Job Title: **Associate Professor**	Job Title: **Head Pro**
Company: **Clark Junior College**	Company: **Litchfield Tennis Club**
Address: **1880 Orchard Road**	Address: **34 Segalla Lane**
Berkshire, VT 53217	**Litchfield, PA 60211**
Business Phone: **(420)555-7642**	Home Phone: **(709)555-0901**
Mobile: **(420)544-7666**	Mobile: **(709)919-3779**
Business Fax: **(420)555-7644**	E-mail: **hunter@spoloc.org**
E-mail: **a_parker@cjc.edu**	Category: **Personal**
Category: **Personal**	

3.   View the Contacts list as Business Cards.

4.   View the Contacts list as a Phone List.

5.   Print a copy of your Contacts list as a Phone List.

6. Delete the contacts you typed.

7. Leave Outlook open for the next project.

PROJECT 1-2

Create and send an e-mail message to your staff concerning the monthly staff meeting.

1. Display the Inbox Pane.

2. Create a New Mail Message and type your **e-mail address** or the e-mail address of a class-mate in the To box.

3. Type **Monthly Staff Meeting** as the subject.

4. In the message area, type **Meeting held in Conference Room A from 2:00 to 3:30 p.m. Be prepared to give an update on projects.**.

5. Click the High Importance button to identify the message as high priority.

6. Send the message.

7. Open the Sent Items folder to see the sent message. (*Note*: It might take a few minutes for your message to arrive.)

8. Open the message and then print it.

9. Delete the e-mail message.

10. Leave Outlook open for the next project.

PROJECT 1-3

Create and send an e-mail message to yourself about the promotion of a staff member.

1. From the Inbox Pane, edit your signature by changing its font style and color.

2. Create a new e-mail message and send it to yourself. Access your e-mail address from the Address Book.

3. Type **Congratulations to Amy Jenkins** as the subject.

4. In the message area, type **Please join me in congratulating Amy Jenkins, who has been pro-moted to Sales Manager. This promotion is well deserved!**.

5. Send the message.

6. Open the Sent Items folder to view the sent message.

7. Print this e-mail message.

8. Delete this e-mail message.

9. Open the File menu and click Exit to close Outlook.

CRITICAL*Thinking*

ACTIVITY 1-1

Use the Help system to find out how to focus your search for items in Outlook by using additional fields and adding keywords to Live Search. Click the Expand the Query Builder arrow next to the Live Search box. Perform a search using the additional fields. If necessary, first create and then send yourself various e-mail messages you find using Live Search.

CALENDAR

OBJECTIVES

Upon completion of this lesson, you will be able to:

- View Calendar.
- Schedule and change appointments.
- Schedule, change, and delete events.
- Schedule a meeting and respond to a meeting request.
- Customize the Calendar.
- Print a calendar.

Estimated Time: 1 hour

VOCABULARY

Appointment

Date Navigator

Event

Meeting

Resources

Tasks

Introducing Calendar

Outlook Calendar is designed to help you stay organized and coordinate your activities with others. Calendar lets you enter your activities, or actions, in four different ways. An **appointment** is an activity that involves only you at a set date and time (although you have the option to invite or involve other people if you wish). A **meeting** is similar to an appointment, in that it has a scheduled date and time, but includes other people and a place, even if it is a virtual location, such as a conference call. By default, appointments and meetings block out time in your calendar and Outlook warns about conflicting actions. An **event**, such as a conference or school orientation, lasts all day long over one or more days, but does not block out time in your calendar. You can still schedule other actions on that day. The last item, **task**, also involves only you and does not block out scheduled time in your calendar. You'll learn more about tasks in the next lesson.

Calendar can help you stay organized by allowing you to schedule your activities on a weekly, monthly, or yearly basis. To help you anticipate and prepare for your upcoming appointments, meetings, events, and tasks, Calendar can create reminders and categorize your activities so you can view them quickly and easily. You can schedule meetings using Calendar and, because Outlook is an integrated program, you can receive responses to planned meetings through e-mail.

Viewing the Calendar

The Calendar, shown in Figure 2-1, allows you to enter your appointments, meetings, events, and tasks. You can display the Calendar by clicking the Calendar folder button or the Calendar icon on the Navigation Pane, or by clicking a date in the Date Navigator.

You can view the Calendar in various time periods or by type of action. In Figure 2-1, the Calendar is displayed in Day/Week/Month view, showing appointments, meetings, events, and tasks for a work week. To change the view option, click View on the menu bar, point to Current View, and then select an item in the list, such as recurring appointments or annual events. You can change the Calendar to a daily, weekly, or monthly view and select a work week or full week by clicking the appropriate option button. (*Note*: A work week is typically Monday–Friday.) Cells in the Calendar display the scheduled activities for the time frame you choose.

Use the Date Navigator, the monthly Calendar at the top of the To-Do Bar, to change dates by clicking the date you want to view. You can change months by clicking the Back or Forward arrows next to the month. A boldface date on the Date Navigator indicates that an action is scheduled for that day.

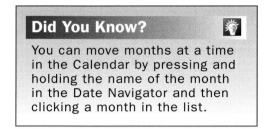

Did You Know?

You can move months at a time in the Calendar by pressing and holding the name of the month in the Date Navigator and then clicking a month in the list.

FIGURE 2-1
Viewing the Calendar

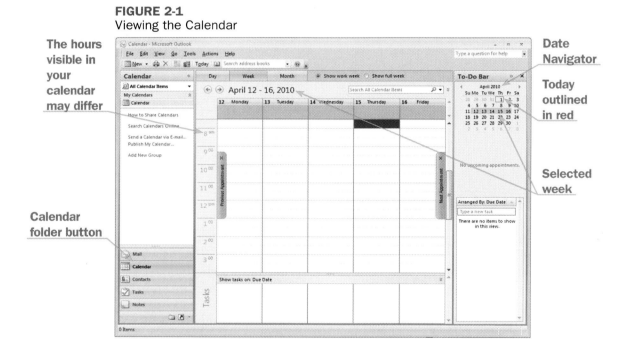

The hours visible in your calendar may differ

Date Navigator

Today outlined in red

Calendar folder button

Selected week

STEP-BY-STEP 2.1

1. Start Outlook, click **View** on the menu bar, point to **To-Do Bar**, and then click **Normal** to make sure the To-Do Bar is visible.

2. On the Navigation Pane, click the **Calendar** button and then click the **Week** button at the top of the Calendar, if necessary. The Calendar opens, similar to Figure 2-1.

3. Click the **Day** button at the top of the Calendar. On the To-Do Bar, in the Date Navigator, click **tomorrow's date**. Notice that the date changes automatically in the Calendar. If you have appointments scheduled, they appear in the appropriate time cell.

STEP-BY-STEP 2.1 Continued

4. Click the **Month** button at the top of the Calendar to display the month. Notice that today's date is outlined in red in the Date Navigator.

5. Click the **Week** button at the top of the Calendar to return to Week view.

6. Click the **Forward** button next to the date to display next week's schedule. Notice that the highlighted week in the Date Navigator changes as you scroll to the next week. Leave the Calendar open for the next Step-by-Step.

Scheduling an Appointment

To add an appointment to your Calendar, select the day for which you want to set up the appointment, and then on the Standard toolbar, click the New button. A new Appointment window opens, with the title Untitled – Appointment, as shown in Figure 2-2. On the Ribbon, on the Appointment tab, in the Actions group, you can determine how to proceed with the appointment. In the Show group, you can click the Scheduling button to view the free and busy times of optional participants, which is helpful for determining meeting times. The Insert tab allows you to insert files, signatures, images, media, and other formatted objects. If visible, the Developer tab contains advanced options for customizing appointment information.

Did You Know?

When you invite participants to an appointment, it becomes a meeting.

FIGURE 2-2
New Appointment window

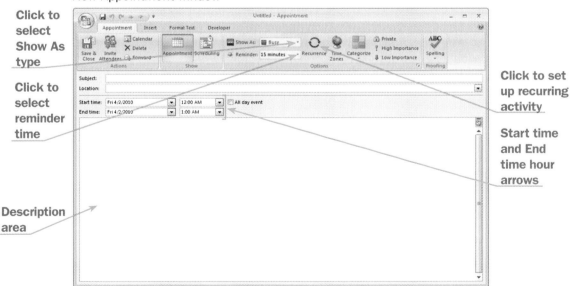

In the Options group, in the Show As box, you can designate how an appointment appears in the Calendar. You can show an appointment as busy, free, tentative, or out of office. In the Reminder box, you can set up a reminder of how often and when Outlook notifies you of an appointment. You can choose not to be reminded, or to be reminded any time from when the appointment actually starts to two weeks ahead of time. You can also select a custom reminder sound if you wish. When it is time for the reminder, the sound plays, and a dialog box opens, where you can dismiss the reminder, click the Snooze button to be reminded again later, or open the appointment to review the details. You can click the Recurrence button to set up an appointment to occur repeatedly, which is an effective tool to make sure you never miss an activity, no matter how busy you are. The Categorize button allows you to color-code your appointments. The Private button prevents other users on an intranet from viewing your appointment information. When Private is selected, a key icon appears next to the appointment on the Calendar. You can also rate an appointment's importance as High or Low.

Type the subject and location of the appointment in the appropriate boxes. Click the up and down arrows to change the Start time or End time, if necessary. Select the All day event check box if the appointment is scheduled for the entire day.

When you have entered all the necessary information about the appointment, on the Ribbon, in the Actions group, click the Save & Close button to return to the Calendar. You'll see the appointment in the designated time.

> **Did You Know?**
>
> Some work or school policies may prevent you from completely restricting access to your Calendar, which means that using the Private option will not be totally effective. To have a truly private activity, create a new calendar by clicking File on the menu bar, pointing to New, and then clicking Calendar.

S TEP-BY-STEP 2.2

1. At the top of the Calendar, click the **Day** button, and then in the Date Navigator, click tomorrow's date, if necessary. The date is selected in the Calendar.

2. Click the **New Appointment** button on the toolbar. The Appointment window opens, as shown in Figure 2-2.

3. In the Subject box, type **Lunch with Zach Anderson**.

4. In the Location box, type **Tortilla Flats**.

5. In the Description area, type **Bring latest draft of proposal.**

6. Click the **hour arrow** next to Start time and then click **11:30 AM**.

7. Click the **hour arrow** next to End time and then click **1:00 PM**. Notice that the end time options also tell you how long the appointment is scheduled to last, in this case, 1.5 hours.

8. On the Ribbon, in the Options group, click the **arrow** next to Show As, and then click **Out of Office**.

9. Click the **arrow** next to Reminder and then click **30 minutes**.

> **Did You Know?**
>
> You can quickly enter an appointment in Day or Week view by positioning the pointer over a time, clicking the cell when prompted, and then typing the details. Or, you can pre-select the appointment time by dragging over the desired time in the Calendar, and then clicking the New Appointment button on the Standard toolbar.

STEP-BY-STEP 2.2 Continued

10. Click the **Private** button.

11. In the Actions group, click the **Save & Close** button. The appointment information and key icon appear in the appointment. The key icon indicates that the appointment is private. Leave the Calendar open for the next Step-by-Step.

Changing an Appointment

To simply move the start or end times of an appointment, click the top or bottom border and drag to a new time. To move an appointment to an entirely new time, drag it to a new time or day. To delete an appointment, click to select it, and then press the Delete key or click the Delete button on the Standard toolbar.

To edit an appointment in Day or Week view, double-click the appointment. The Appointment window opens, where you can make changes.

> **Did You Know?**
>
> You can set the date and time for an appointment by typing natural spoken language, such as "this Friday" or "midnight" in the date and time fields of the Appointment window; Outlook automatically converts the words into the correct date and time.

STEP-BY-STEP 2.3

1. At the top of the Calendar, click the **Day** button, and then double-click the **Lunch with Zach Anderson** appointment. The Appointment window opens.

2. Change the Location to **Trotsky's Deli**.

3. In the Description area, press the **Enter** key after the word *proposal*, and then type the following: **Have Brad make reservations, see if Katie can join us, and call Zach about changes.**

4. Click the **Private** button to turn it off.

5. In the Actions group, click the **Save & Close** button. The appointment no longer contains the key icon.

STEP-BY-STEP 2.3 Continued

6. Press and hold the **Lunch with Zach Anderson** appointment, and then drag it down so the top border aligns with 12 pm, as shown in Figure 2-3. The appointment times are now 12:00 pm to 1:30 pm.

FIGURE 2-3
Modified appointment

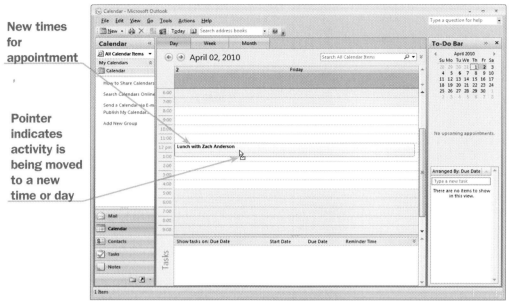

New times for appointment

Pointer indicates activity is being moved to a new time or day

7. Click the **Lunch with Zach Anderson** appointment to select it, position the pointer over the bottom appointment handle, and then when the pointer changes to a sizing pointer, drag the border to **2 pm**. The appointment times are now 12:00 pm to 2:00 pm.

8. Position the pointer over the appointment until the subject, location, and times appear, similar to a ScreenTip. Notice that you can easily see the important details about the appointment. Leave the Calendar open for the next Step-by-Step.

> ### Extra Challenge
>
> Add four more appointments with varying settings to the Calendar for this month. Add each appointment as a different Show As type and notice how they appear in the Calendar.

Scheduling an Event

An event is an activity that usually lasts an entire day. Because it does not have an assigned time, it appears in the Calendar, but does not by default block out time in it. Instead, an event appears as a banner message at the top of the day or days affected. Other scheduled activities on those days appear normally. An annual event occurs every year on the same date, such as a birthday, or every year at a different time, such as a vacation or some holidays. A recurring event occurs at the same time every day, week, or month, such as a day-long managers' meeting that is scheduled every quarter (every three months). You can use your Calendar to schedule any type of event.

Use the Date Navigator to locate the date of the event, click Actions on the menu bar, and then click New All Day Event. A new Event window opens with the title Untitled – Event, as shown in Figure 2-4. Tabs on the Ribbon are the same as for appointments, although events have different default settings, such as showing the event as free instead of busy. Fill in basic information about the event, such as subject, location, and description. Choose the Reminder option if you would like to be reminded of the event. For example, you could be reminded two days ahead of time to buy a birthday card for someone.

Did You Know?

You can quickly open the Event window in Day or Week view by double clicking the darker shaded area between the day heading and time row. In Month view, just double-click the day cell.

FIGURE 2-4
Event window

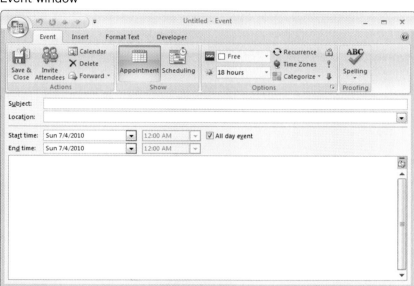

If the event repeats at the same time, on the Ribbon, on the Event tab, in the Options group, click the Recurrence button to open the Appointment Recurrence dialog box. You can choose a recurrence pattern and your event will appear on the Calendar every day, week, month, or year. Type a range of recurrence or a beginning and end date for how long the

Did You Know?

If you deselect the All day event check box in the Event window, the event automatically becomes an appointment.

event should appear in the Calendar. Choose OK to return to the Event window, and notice that the title bar now identifies the event as a "Recurring Event." On the Ribbon, in the Actions group, click the Save & Close button. The event appears as the top entry in any Calendar view.

STEP-BY-STEP 2.4

1. In the Date Navigator, find and click **July 4**.

2. Click **Actions** on the menu bar and then click **New All Day Event**. A new Event window opens.

3. Type the event information shown in Figure 2-5. On the Ribbon, in the Options group, be sure to change the Show As and Reminder settings.

FIGURE 2-5
All day event settings

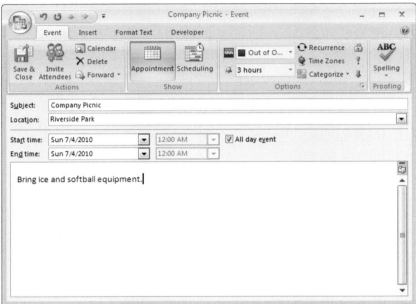

4. When finished, in the Actions group, click the **Save & Close** button.

5. In the Date Navigator, click the **back arrow**, and then click **June 10**.

6. On the menu bar, click **Actions**, and then click **New All Day Event**. A new Event window opens.

7. In the Subject box, type **Brittany's Birthday**.

8. On the Ribbon, in the Options group, click the **Recurrence** button. The Appointment Recurrence dialog box opens, similar to that shown in Figure 2-6.

STEP-BY-STEP 2.4 Continued

FIGURE 2-6
Appointment Recurrence dialog box

Times and duration settings

Recurrence pattern settings

Range settings

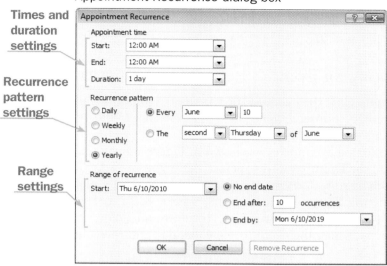

9. In the Recurrence pattern section, click the **Yearly** option button, and then click **OK**.

10. In the Options group, click the **arrow** next to Reminder, and then click **1 day**.

11. In the Actions group, click the **Save & Close** button. Click the **Day** button at the top of the Calendar, if necessary. The event appears at the top of the day's actions, as shown in Figure 2-7.

FIGURE 2-7
Viewing a recurring event in Day view

Event appears above daily actions

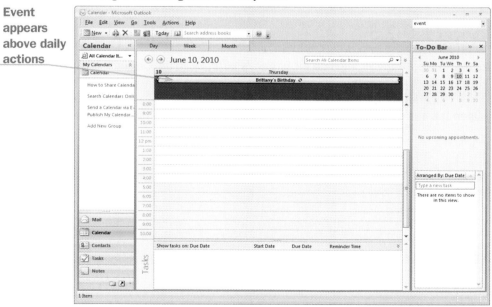

STEP-BY-STEP 2.4 Continued

12. At the top of the Calendar, click the **Week** button, and then click the **Show full week** option button. Notice how the event appears in Week view. Leave the Calendar open for the next Step-by-Step.

Changing and Deleting an Event

To edit an event, double-click the event at the top of the Calendar. If the event is nonrecurring, the Event window opens. If the event is marked as one that recurs, the Open Recurring Item dialog box opens, as shown in Figure 2-8. When you select the Open this occurrence option button, the Event window opens, where you can edit specific settings that affect that individual event, such as start and end times or location. When you select the Open the series option button, the Recurring Event window opens, where you can edit settings that affect the series of recurring actions, such as when it recurs. To delete an event, click the Delete button on the Standard toolbar, or right-click the event in the Calendar and then click Delete.

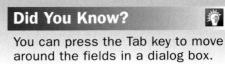
Did You Know?

You can press the Tab key to move around the fields in a dialog box.

Extra Challenge

Add five more annual events to your Calendar, such as birthdays and anniversaries of family members and friends.

FIGURE 2-8
Open Recurring Item dialog box

STEP-BY-STEP 2.5

1. You realize that you have the wrong date for Brittany's birthday. In the Calendar, double-click the event **Brittany's Birthday**. The Open Recurring Item dialog box opens, as shown in Figure 2-8.

2. Click the **Open the series** option button and then click **OK**. The Recurring Event window opens.

STEP-BY-STEP 2.5 Continued

3. On the Ribbon, in the Options group, click the **Recurrence** button.

4. In the Recurrence pattern section, make sure the **Every** option button is selected, click the **arrow** next to the month box, click **May**, click the **day** text box, and then type **22**.

5. In the Range of recurrence section, click the **arrow** next to the Start box, in the pop-up calendar, click the **back arrow** to go to May, then click **22**. Click **OK**. The Recurring Event window opens with the new recurrence date on the Recurrence line.

6. In the Actions group, click the **Save & Close** button.

7. In the Date Navigator, click the **back** button to go to **May** (or the previous month), and then click **22**. In the Calendar, click the **Day** button. The Brittany's Birthday event appears at the top of the Calendar. (*Note*: Your month may vary when you click the back button.)

8. Click **Brittany's Birthday** to select it and then click the **Delete** button on the Standard toolbar. In the Confirm Delete dialog box, click **Delete the series**, and then click **OK**. The Brittany's Birthday event for May this year and all its occurrences are removed from the Calendar.

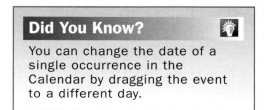

Did You Know?

You can change the date of a single occurrence in the Calendar by dragging the event to a different day.

9. Click the **Today** button on the Standard toolbar to go back to today's date. Leave the Calendar open for the next Step-by-Step.

Scheduling a Meeting and Responding to a Meeting Request

If you and your co-workers use Outlook and are connected by an intranet, you can use your Calendar to schedule meetings and resources. A meeting is an appointment to which you invite people and for which you schedule resources. Resources are rooms, materials, and/or equipment needed for a meeting, such as a conference room, computer, or large plasma screen.

Use the Date Navigator to choose a date for the meeting. To preset the meeting times, click a start time in the Calendar and then drag to an end time. Click File on the menu bar, point to New, and then click Meeting Request. A new Meeting window opens with the selection times and the title

Untitled – Meeting, as shown in Figure 2-9. The Meeting window lets you select meeting details and send a notice of the meeting to attendees. On the Ribbon, on the Meeting tab, in the Actions group, you can determine how to proceed with the meeting. The Show and Options groups function the same as for events and appointments. Specific to meetings is the Attendees group. Windows SharePoint users can select an online workspace using the Meeting Workspace feature. All users can access the Address Book and the Check Names feature, and select the type of response to receive from attendees. Click the To button and select contacts to add as attendees, and then type a subject, location, and description.

FIGURE 2-9
New Meeting window

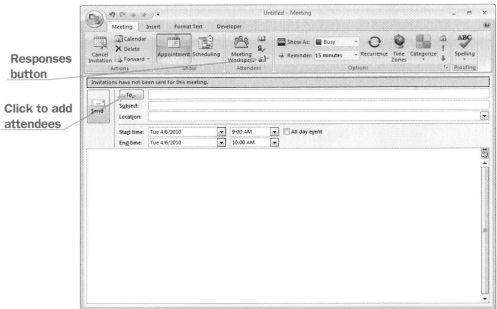

If your attendees share their Calendars, you can adjust for any meeting conflicts and find the best time for everyone to meet. In the Show group, click the Scheduling button to open a grid indicating the availability of attendees.

Once attendees open a meeting invitation, they can perform several actions specific to the meeting. On the Ribbon, in the Respond group, they can accept, accept tentatively, or decline the invitation. They can also delete, reply, reply to all, or forward the meeting message. The responses to the meeting requests appear in your Inbox.

S TEP-BY-STEP 2.6

1. In the Date Navigator, choose a date. Click and hold **9 am** and then drag to **10 am**.

2. On the menu bar, click **File**, point to **New**, and then click **Meeting Request**. The Meeting window opens, as shown in Figure 2-9.

3. Click the **To** button. The Select Attendees and Resources window appears, as shown in Figure 2-10.

FIGURE 2-10
Select Attendees and Resources window

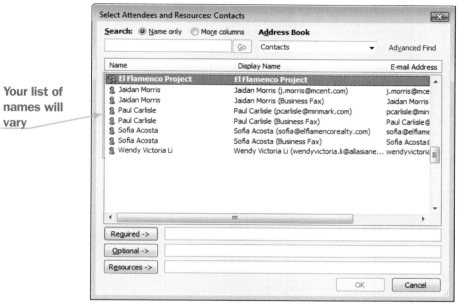

Your list of names will vary

4. Press and hold the **Ctrl** key and then click each individual name in the list. (If the same name appears more than once, select the first instance.) Be sure to click your name, as well. When finished, click **Required**. Click the beginning of the Required box, type the e-mail address of a classmate or an address given to you by your instructor, and then click **OK**.

5. In the Subject box, type **Contract Negotiations**.

6. In the Location box, type **Algonquin Conference Room**.

7. On the Ribbon, in the Attendees group, click the **Responses** button, and then make sure that both **Request Responses** and **Allow New Time Proposals** have check marks next to them.

STEP-BY-STEP 2.6 Continued

8. In the Description area, type **Please let me know as soon as possible if you can't make it.** Compare your Meeting window to Figure 2-11.

FIGURE 2-11
Completed Meeting window

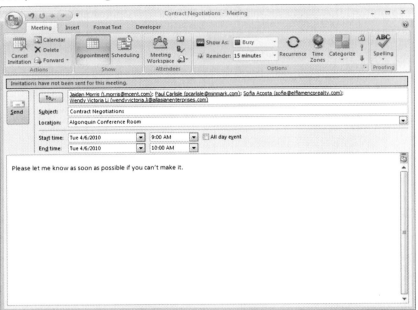

9. Click the **Send** button. Outlook sends the e-mail message to you and the attendees. The meeting appears in your Calendar at 9:00 am.

10. Click the **Mail** folder button on the Navigation Pane to see the meeting e-mail message you received. If necessary, click the Inbox folder in the Mail section of the Navigation Pane to display the Inbox view.

11. A meeting e-mail message has a calendar icon next to it, indicating that it is a meeting message. Double-click the meeting e-mail message you sent to yourself to open it. As the organizer, you receive a message that resembles Figure 2-12.

STEP-BY-STEP 2.6 Continued

FIGURE 2-12
Organizer meeting e-mail

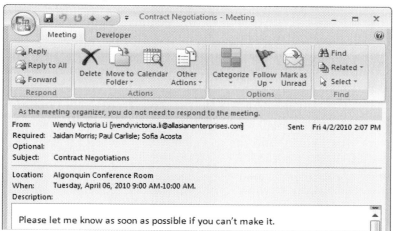

12. If possible, open the meeting e-mail message you sent to a classmate or other e-mail address on another computer. An attendee will receive a message that resembles Figure 2-13.

FIGURE 2-13
Attendee meeting e-mail

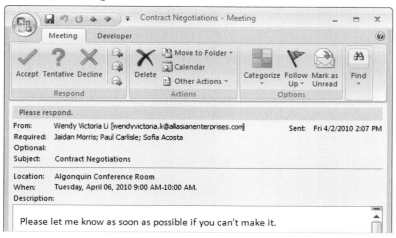

13. On the Ribbon, in the Respond group, click the **Accept** button. Outlook sends the acceptance back to the organizer.

14. On the Navigation Pane, click the **Calendar** folder button to return to today's date in Calendar view. Leave the Calendar open for the next Step-by-Step.

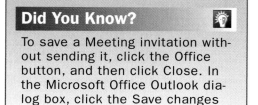

Did You Know?

To save a Meeting invitation without sending it, click the Office button, and then click Close. In the Microsoft Office Outlook dialog box, click the Save changes but don't send option button, and then click OK.

Customizing the Calendar

You can modify many settings in the Calendar to adjust its appearance and how it displays time. For example, in Month view, you can adjust the amount of detail that is visible by clicking option buttons in the Details section at the top of the Calendar. The Low setting shows events in a calendar cell, but meetings and appointments are not visible. Under the Medium setting, meetings and appointments appear as a solid blue line in a calendar cell. Under the High setting, the subject line for appointments, events, and meetings all appear in a calendar cell. Note that a summary of any scheduled meeting always appears on the To-Do Bar.

To customize a calendar's appearance, click Tools on the menu bar, and then click Options to open the Options dialog box, then click the Calendar Options button in the Calendar section to open the Calendar Options dialog box, as shown in Figure 2-14. You can change the start and end days of a work week, the color of the Calendar, and other settings.

> **Did You Know?**
>
> To format Calendar fonts or change the time scale of the grid, right-click a blank cell, click Other Settings, and then click the setting you'd like to change.

FIGURE 2-14
Calendar Options dialog box

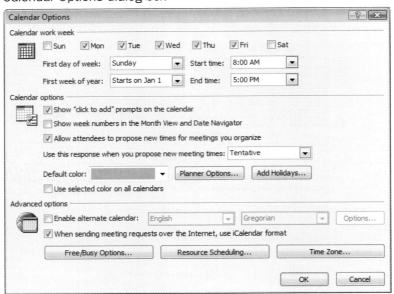

STEP-BY-STEP 2.7

1. In the Date Navigator, click the **date** when you scheduled the contract negotiations meeting. At the top of the Calendar, click the **Month** button, and then in the Details section, alternately click the **Low**, **Medium**, and **High** option buttons. Notice changes in the level of detail as you click each option button.

2. On the menu bar, click **Tools**, and then click **Options**. The Options dialog box opens, where you can adjust settings for all of Outlook's features. Make sure the Preferences tab is selected.

STEP-BY-STEP 2.7 Continued

3. In the Calendar section, click **Calendar Options**. The Calendar Options dialog box opens, similar to that shown in Figure 2-14.

4. In the Calendar work week section, click the **Friday** box to deselect it. The work week is now Monday–Thursday.

5. Click the **arrow** next to the Start time box and then click **7:30 AM**.

6. Click the **arrow** next to the End time box and then click **5:00 PM**.

7. Click the **arrow** next to the Default Color box and then click the **yellow** color in the list.

8. Click **OK** twice to return to the Calendar.

9. The new color is applied to the Calendar. Click the **Week** button at the top of the Calendar to view the new work week format.

10. Click the **Show full week** option button, if necessary, and then click the **Show work week** option button. The adjusted work days and work hours appear in the Calendar, as shown in Figure 2-15. Leave the Calendar open for the next Step-by-Step.

FIGURE 2-15
Modified Calendar

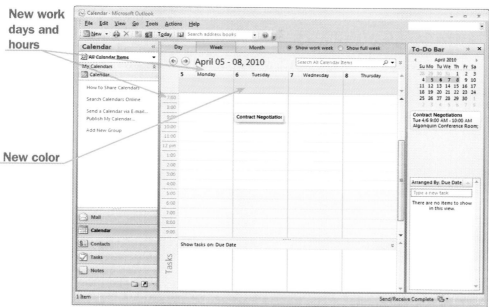

Printing a Calendar

Outlook provides several options for printing your Calendar. You can select from the following styles: daily, weekly, monthly, tri-fold (which separates the daily Calendar, tasks list, and weekly Calendar), and calendar details (which includes the description area). Click File on the menu bar and then click Print. The Print dialog box opens, as shown in Figure 2-16. Select a style from the options in the Print style section and then click OK. You can print a more specific range of dates by selecting Start and End dates in the Print range section.

To preview a calendar before printing, click File on the menu bar, and then click Print Preview, or in the Print dialog box, click Preview. The pointer changes to a magnifying glass that you can click to zoom in or out when previewing the page.

FIGURE 2-16
Print dialog box

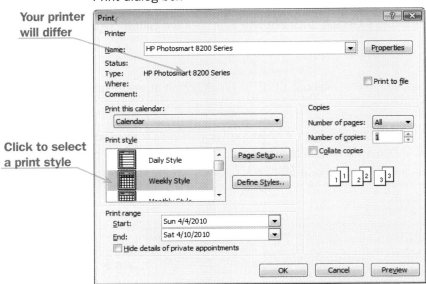

Your printer will differ

Click to select a print style

Careers

An office manager can use Outlook to keep a busy healthcare practice running efficiently. For example, the Calendar can be used to schedule and reschedule patient appointments. Recurring appointments can be made on a daily, weekly, monthly, or annual basis. Resources, such as an examination room or a piece of equipment, can also be scheduled. Appointments can be color-coded so that certain types of appointments or appointments with a specific physician are easily recognized. A patient's information can be entered into the Contacts list. Then, when an appointment is made with that patient, you can link the appointment to the patient's information in the Contacts list.

STEP-BY-STEP 2.8

1. In the Calendar, click the **Day** button, and then in the Date Navigator, click the date where you scheduled the contract negotiations meeting.

2. On the menu bar, click **File**, and then click **Print**. The Print dialog box opens, as shown in Figure 2-16.

3. In the Print style box, make sure that Weekly Style is selected, and then click **Preview**. View the layout and then on the toolbar, click the **Print** button.

4. In the Print style box, click **Monthly Style**, and then click **Preview**. View the layout and then click the **Print** button.

5. In the Print style box, click **Daily Style**.

6. Click **OK** to print a daily Calendar.

7. When you finish printing, click the **Contract Negotiations** appointment to select it, and then press the **Delete** key. The Meeting window opens. Because you already sent out invitations for the meeting, Outlook requires that you send a cancellation message. Click **Send Cancellation**. The appointment is deleted from the Calendar.

8. Click the **Close** button in the upper-right corner of the window to close Outlook. The Outlook window closes and the Microsoft Windows desktop appears.

SUMMARY

In this lesson, you learned that:

- The Calendar is used to schedule appointments, events, meetings, and tasks. You can view the Calendar in daily, weekly, or monthly format. If you use the Reminder option, Outlook notifies you before each activity.

- Using Calendar, you can schedule a meeting and invite other people to the meeting. You can also use Calendar to respond to meeting requests.

- The Appointment Recurrence dialog box makes it easy to schedule events that occur annually.

- You can customize the Calendar by altering days, time, and color.

- You can print the Calendar information in a variety of styles.

VOCABULARY *Review*

Define the following terms:

Appointment	Event	Resources
Date Navigator	Meeting	Tasks

REVIEW *Questions*

TRUE/FALSE

Circle T if the statement is true or F if the statement is false.

T F 1. It is possible to set a work week to begin on a Thursday.

T F 2. You can set a reminder option to notify you months before an appointment.

T F 3. It is impossible to make changes to an annual event once it is placed into the Calendar.

T F 4. You can modify a single instance of a recurring event.

T F 5. An event is an activity that has a set start and end time.

WRITTEN QUESTIONS

Write a brief answer to the following questions.

1. What activity always appears in the To-Do Bar?

2. Where do events appear on the Calendar Weekly view?

3. What is the difference between an appointment and an event?

4. What icon appears next to an appointment on the Calendar to indicate that it is private?

5. Describe the difference between deleting an event or an appointment and deleting a meeting that has been sent to attendees.

PROJECTS

PROJECT 2-1

1. Open Outlook, display the To-Do Bar, select tomorrow's date in the Date Navigator, and then display the Calendar in Day view.

2. Open a New Appointment window.

3. Select the appointment time from 9:00 to 11:00 am.

4. Add an appointment with **Long-Term Goals Training** as the subject.

5. Add the location of the appointment as **Atrium Training Room**.

6. Add description of the appointment as **Training with staff and management**.

7. Set a reminder for one hour before the appointment.

8. Set the Show As option as Busy. Save and close the Appointment window.

9. Add another appointment from 8:00 to 8:30 am with **Coffee with Dylan** as the subject and **Daily Grind Coffee Shop** as the location.

10. Do not set a reminder. Show the time as Out of Office, and use the Private option.

11. Add a description of the appointment: **Ask him about kayaking this weekend.** Save and close the Appointment window.

12. Leave the Calendar open for the next project.

PROJECT 2-2

1. Move the time of the Long-Term Goals Training appointment to 10 am to noon.

2. Change the location to **Conference Room 4**.

3. Add a new line to the end of the description: **Make copies of new office policy for tuition reimbursement.**

4. In the Date Navigator, select this Sunday for an event.

5. Add **My Best Friend's Birthday** as an annual event.

6. Set a reminder for one day before the event date. Save and close the Event window.

7. Leave the Calendar open for the next project.

PROJECT 2-3

1. Display the Calendar with today's date.

2. Create a new meeting for a week from today from 2:00 pm to 4:30 pm. Do not add any attendees to the To box.

3. Type **Computer Upgrade** as the subject and **Conference Room A** as the location.

4. Label the meeting with the High Importance option.

5. Set a reminder for 18 hours before the meeting.

6. Add a description to the meeting: **Take extra copies of agenda and handouts.**

7. Close the Meeting window and save changes. Move to next week and notice the meeting in the Calendar.

8. Close Outlook.

CRITICAL *Thinking*

ACTIVITY 2-1

Create your personal Calendar for this month. Be sure to include class and social activities, recurring events such as sports or exercise, and single events, such as concerts, movies, or plays. You can also schedule medical or dental appointments and your work hours. When you are finished, print your Calendar in the style of your choice, and then delete all the entries for this activity.

WORKING WITH OTHER OUTLOOK TOOLS

Using Outlook Today and the To-Do Bar

Outlook Today and the To-Do Bar gather and summarize information about the day's activities in different ways. You can display either or both depending on your personal preference.

Outlook Today gives you a quick summary of the day's activities. Divided into three sections, Calendar, Tasks, and Messages, you have a clear snapshot of your day's appointments, meetings, tasks, and the number of new e-mail messages you have in your folders.

The To-Do Bar includes the Date Navigator, a summary of your appointments, a Task Input Panel, where you can create new tasks, and a list of tasks.

In Outlook Today, the Calendar section displays the appointments for the day. The next appointment is flagged with an arrow, and appointments earlier in the day are displayed in a lighter type. The Tasks section lists previously entered tasks. Outlook shows completed tasks by including a check mark in the task box and striking through text. When marked Completed, a task no longer appears in the To-Do Bar task list. The Messages section contains the number of messages in the Inbox, Drafts, and Outbox. To move around Outlook quickly from Outlook Today, simply click a section heading. Figure 3-1 shows activities as they appear in both Outlook Today and the To-Do Bar.

FIGURE 3-1
Viewing activities in Outlook Today and the To-Do Bar

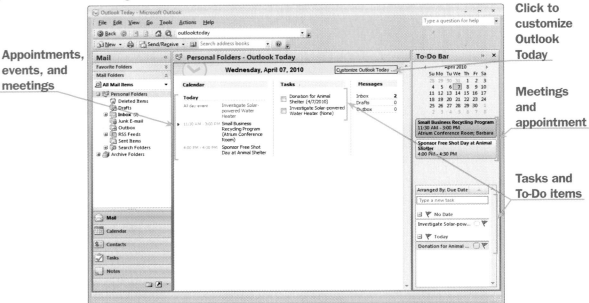

To turn on Outlook Today, on the Navigation Pane, click the Mail Folders button, and then click the Outlook Today icon at the top of the Mail Folders section. To customize the Outlook Today pane, click Customize Outlook Today above the Messages section. A list of options for customizing Outlook Today appears, as shown in Figure 3-2. To automatically open Outlook Today when you start Outlook, in the Startup section, click the check box next to When starting, go directly to Outlook Today. In the Messages section, you can also select which message folders appear. In the Calendar section, you can select how many days of the week appear. In the Tasks section, you can display and sort all tasks or only the tasks for the day. Finally, you can select different styles in the Styles section. When you have completed your selections, click Save Changes.

FIGURE 3-2
Customize Outlook Today

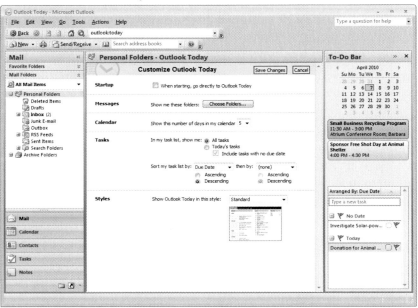

In the To-Do Bar, you can show multiple calendars by dragging the left border of the To-Do Bar. To customize the To-Do Bar, click View on the menu bar, point to To-Do Bar, and then click Options. The To-Do Bar Options dialog box opens, as shown in Figure 3-3. You can click check boxes to show or hide the Date Navigator, Appointments, and the Task List. To show multiple months vertically, click the box next to Number of month rows, and then type a number from 1 to 9. You can adjust the number of tasks that appear by typing a number in the box next to Number of appointments.

FIGURE 3-3
To-Do Bar Options dialog box

STEP-BY-STEP 3.1

1. Click the **Mail Folders** button on the Navigation Pane and then click the **Outlook Today** icon at the top of the Mail Folders section. Outlook Today appears. Your screen will be similar to Figure 3-1, but may show differences, depending on items that have been previously added or deleted, or the current style selected for your installation of Outlook.

2. Click **Customize Outlook Today** at the top of the pane. The Customize Outlook Today dialog box opens, as shown in Figure 3-2.

3. In the *Startup* section, click the **check box** next to When starting, then go directly to Outlook Today (if necessary). Outlook Today will automatically appear every time you start Outlook.

4. Click **Save Changes** in the upper-right corner of the window to go back to Outlook Today.

5. Click **View** on the menu bar, point to **To-Do Bar**, and then click **Options**. The To-Do Bar Options dialog box opens, as shown in Figure 3-3.

6. Make sure that check marks appear in every box. In the *Show Date Navigator* section, click the **box** next to the Number of month rows, type **2**, and then click **OK**. The next month appears in the Date Navigator, as shown in Figure 3-4.

7. Click **View** on the menu bar, point to **To-Do Bar**, and then click **Options**. In the *Show Date Navigator* section, click the **box** next to the Number of month rows, type **1**, and then click **OK**. Leave Outlook open for the next Step-by-Step.

FIGURE 3-4
Modified To-Do Bar

Creating a Tasks List

You can use Tasks view in Outlook to create and manage your tasks. A task is any activity you want to perform and monitor to completion. A to-do item is any Outlook entry, such as a contact or e-mail message, that you have flagged for follow-up. You can assign tasks to color categories, specify start and due dates, check the status of and prioritize tasks, and set reminders.

A simple way to create a task in the To-Do Bar is to type a subject in the Task Input Panel. You can also click File on the menu bar, point to New, and then click Task. A new Task window opens with the title Untitled – Task, as shown in Figure 3-5. You can choose a subject, specify start and due dates, and set a percentage indicating how much of the task is completed. On the Ribbon, in the Show group, you can click the Details button to view record statistics. In the Manage Task group, you can assign the task, send a status report about the task, or mark the task as complete. As with other Outlook activities, in the Options group, you can mark a task as recurring, categorize or mark it for follow-up, or identify it as private. When you are done creating the task, in the Actions group, click the Save & Close button.

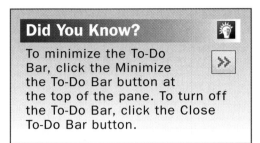

Did You Know?

Note that any time you flag an e-mail message or a contact using the Follow Up button, the item is automatically added to the task list in the To-Do Bar.

Did You Know?

To minimize the To-Do Bar, click the Minimize the To-Do Bar button at the top of the pane. To turn off the To-Do Bar, click the Close To-Do Bar button.

You can view tasks no matter what other activities you are managing in Outlook. Tasks are visible on the To-Do Bar in the To-Do List, visible when you select Tasks in the Navigation Pane; and in the Daily Task List, located at the bottom of the Calendar in Day or Week view. To view and sort the complete list of active and completed tasks, in Outlook Today, click Tasks at the top of the pane, or on the Navigation Pane, click the Tasks folder button or Tasks icon.

STEP-BY-STEP 3.2

1. Click **View** on the menu bar, point to **To-Do Bar**, then click **Normal** to make sure To-Do Bar visible.

2. Click **File** on the menu bar, point to **New**, and then click **Task**. The Task window opens, as shown in Figure 3-5.

FIGURE 3-5
New Task window

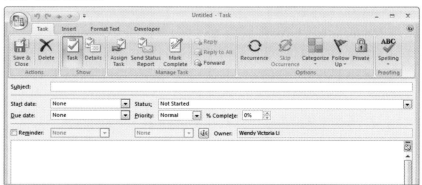

STEP-BY-STEP 3.2 Continued

3. In the *Subject* box, type **Buy new desk supplies**.

4. In the *Start date* box, click the **arrow** next to the box, and then click the first Friday in the Calendar.

5. In the *Due date* section, click the **arrow** next to the box, and then click the third Friday in the Calendar.

6. In the *Status* box, click the **arrow** next to the box, and then click **In Progress**.

7. In the *Priority* box, click the **arrow** next to the box, and then click **High**.

8. In the *% Complete* box, click the **up arrow** next to the box until **50%** appears.

9. In the *Reminder* section, click the **check box** to select it, click the **arrow** next to the date box, and then click the second Friday in the Calendar. Click the **arrow** next to the time box, and then click **10:00 A.M.**

> **Did You Know?**
>
> You can also turn on Outlook Today by clicking View on the menu bar, pointing to Toolbars, clicking Advanced, and then clicking the Outlook Today button on the toolbar.

> **Did You Know?**
>
> You can select new colors for the Categorize feature by clicking the Categorize button, clicking All Categories, and then clicking the Color arrow in the Color Categories dialog box.

10. In the Description area, type **Buy desk and drawer organizers, trays, sorters, lamps, etc. Check that phone lines and cable lines are active.**

11. On the Ribbon, in the Options group, click the **Categorize** button, click **Green Category**, and then type **Office Annex** as the new name in the Rename Categories dialog box. (*Note*: If the Color Categories dialog box does not prompt you to name the color category, double-click the **Green Category bar**, select the **Green Category**, click **Rename**, type **Office Annex**, and then click **OK**.)

12. Click the **Private** button. Your Task dialog box should appear similar to Figure 3-6.

FIGURE 3-6
Buy new desk supplies task

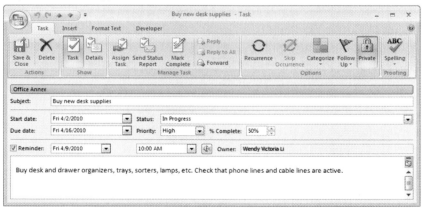

13. In the Actions group, click the **Save & Close** button.

STEP-BY-STEP 3.2 Continued

14. Create three more tasks using the information shown in Figures 3-7, 3-8, and 3-9, respectively. (*Note*: Enter your own dates.) Leave Outlook open for the next Step-by-Step.

FIGURE 3-7
Buy computer and other equipment task

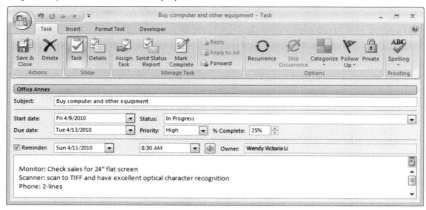

FIGURE 3-8
Ergonomic chair upgrades task

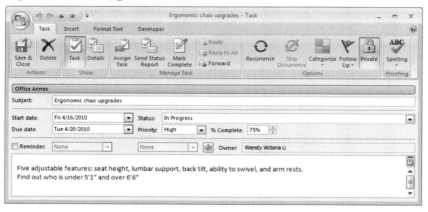

FIGURE 3-9
Painting and finish work task

Managing Tasks

You can sort and group tasks, move tasks up and down the list, add and delete tasks, edit a task, or mark a task off when you complete it.

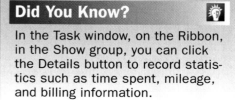

Did You Know?

In the Task window, on the Ribbon, in the Show group, you can click the Details button to record statistics such as time spent, mileage, and billing information.

To sort or group tasks, on the Navigation Pane, click the Tasks folder button, and then click an option in the Current View section, as shown in Figure 3-10. Simple List view is selected as default view and tasks are displayed in the To-Do List. In the To-Do Bar, click the Arranged By button above the Task Input Panel, and then select an option, as shown in Figure 3-11.

FIGURE 3-10
To-Do List

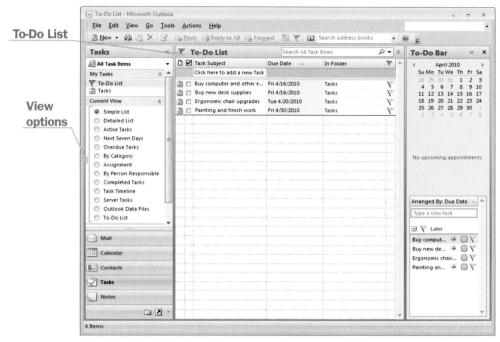

FIGURE 3-11
Task arrange options in the To-Do Bar

To mark a task complete, double-click the task to open it, and then click the up arrow next to the % Complete box until 100% appears in the box. When a task is complete, it is no longer visible in the To-Do Bar. However, in the To-Do List and in the Daily Task List in Day or Week view in the Calendar, a line appears through the task and a check mark appears in the corresponding box. To delete a task, right-click the task and then click Delete. To edit a task, double-click it, make your changes, and then on the Ribbon, in the Actions group, click the Save & Close button.

S TEP-BY-STEP 3.3

1. On the Navigation Pane, click the **Tasks** folder button. The tasks appear in the To-Do List, as shown in Figure 3-10. In Simple List view, basic task information such as Subject, Due Date, and Folder is visible.

2. On the Navigation Pane, click the **Detailed List** option button. Additional task information, including the task's status, the percent complete, and its category is visible. The tasks are arranged by Due Date. (*Note:* If necessary, adjust the columns so you can read your entries in the Subject, Status, Due Date, % Complete, and Categories columns.)

3. In the To-Do Bar, click the **Arranged By** button above the Task Input Panel, as shown in Figure 3-11, and then click **Start Date**. The tasks are arranged by Start Date. Notice that rearranging tasks in the To-Do Bar does not affect their arrangement in the To-Do List.

4. In the To-Do List, double-click the **Ergonomic chair upgrades** task. In the % Complete section, click the **up** arrow until **100%** appears in the box, and then on the Ribbon, in the Actions group, click the **Save & Close** button. In the To-Do List, the check box is selected, the subject is grayed out, and the task has a strikeout line running through it. In the To-Do Bar, the task no longer appears in the list, as shown in Figure 3-12.

> ### Did You Know?
>
> To quickly create a task from an e-mail message, on the Navigation Pane, click the Mail folder button, open the Inbox, and then drag a message from the Inbox to the top of the Tasks folder button on the Navigation Pane.

FIGURE 3-12
Completed task in the To-Do List

5. Make sure the **Ergonomic chair upgrades** task is selected in the To-Do List, and then click the **Delete** button on the Standard toolbar. The task is deleted from the To-Do List. Leave the To-Do List open for the next Step-by-Step.

 Careers

Managers can use the Tasks list to keep track of their employees' workloads. A manager can assign and delegate tasks to each employee. To do this, the manager creates a Task Request and sends it to the employee. The employee responds to the Task Request by either accepting or declining the request. When finished with the task, the employee marks the task as complete.

Assigning Tasks

At times, you need to delegate tasks to others. You can create a new task and assign it to someone, or you can assign an existing task to someone. To assign a task to someone else, double-click an existing task or create a new task. In the Task window, on the Ribbon, in the Manage Tasks group, click the Assign Task button. The To section appears, just as in a new e-mail Message window, where you can enter e-mail addresses for one or more recipients. Click the Send button to deliver the task to the recipient or recipients.

STEP-BY-STEP 3.4

1. Click **File** on the menu bar, point to **New**, and then click **Task**. A new Task window opens.

2. In the *Subject* box, type **Task assignment**.

3. In the *Start date* section, click the **arrow** next to the box, and then click next Wednesday in the Calendar.

4. In the *Due date* section, click the **arrow** next to the box, and then click next Friday in the Calendar.

5. On the Ribbon, in the Manage Task group, click the **Assign Task** button.

> **Did You Know?**
>
> To customize tasks, open the Customize View dialog box by clicking View on the menu bar, pointing to Current View, and then clicking Customize Current View.

6. Click the **To** button and the Select Task Recipient dialog box opens. Click a classmate's name or one assigned by your instructor from the list of contacts, click the **To** box at the bottom of the dialog box, and then click **OK** to close the dialog box.

7. Click the **Send** button to send the message to your classmate.

8. In the To-Do List, in the Tasks list, double-click the **Buy computer and other equipment** task. The Buy computer and other equipment – Task window opens.

9. In the *Due date* section, click the **arrow** next to the box, and then click a day **12 days** from the Start date.

> **Did You Know?**
>
> You can reverse the sort order of any column by clicking the column head.

10. In the *% Complete* section, click the **down arrow** until **0%** appears in the box.

11. On the Ribbon, in the Manage Task group, click the **Assign Task** button.

12. Click the **To** button and the Select Task Recipient dialog box opens. Click a classmate's name or one assigned by your instructor from the list of contacts. Click the **To** box at the bottom of the dialog box, and then click **OK** to close the dialog box.

13. Click the **Send** button to send the task message to your classmate. Assume a classmate is sending you a task request at the same time. If a dialog box opens reminding you that you are no longer the owner of the task, click **OK**.

STEP-BY-STEP 3.4 Continued

14. On the Navigation Pane, click the **Mail folder** button and then click the **Inbox** folder, if necessary. On the Standard toolbar, click the **Send/Receive** button. When the task request arrives from your classmate, double-click the **message** to open it. The Task window opens, similar to Figure 3-13.

FIGURE 3-13
Task window

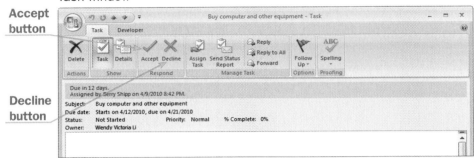

15. On the Ribbon, in the Respond group, click the **Decline** button. The Declining Task dialog box opens.

16. Make sure the **Decline without comment** option button is selected, and then click the **Send the response now** button. The message is sent to your classmate.

> **Did You Know?**
>
> To mark a task completed, you can also right-click the task and select Mark Complete from the shortcut menu.

17. On the Navigation Pane, click the **Tasks** icon at the bottom of the pane and leave the Tasks list open for the next Step-by-Step.

Viewing and Printing the Tasks List

You can easily change your view of tasks by clicking an option in the Navigation Pane. The view options are listed in the Table 3-1. You can print your Tasks list in the current view of the To-Do List. To print your Tasks list, click File on the menu bar, and then click Print. The Print dialog box opens. Depending on the current view, you can print your tasks in a table style, which looks similar to the To-Do List, or in a memo style, which places each task on its own page.

> **Did You Know?**
>
> You can quickly assign a task to someone by clicking File on the menu bar, pointing to New, and then clicking Task Request.

TABLE 3-1
View options for the Tasks list

VIEW	DESCRIPTION
Simple List	Lists tasks by check box, task, due date, and folder.
Detailed List	Lists active and completed tasks by Simple List fields and by priority, status, percent completed, and categories.
Active Tasks	Lists active tasks only in a Detailed List.
Next Seven Days	Lists tasks due in the next seven days in a Detailed List.
Overdue Tasks	Lists only overdue tasks in a Detailed List.
By Category	Lists tasks grouped by category and sorted by due date in a Detailed List.
Assignment	Lists tasks assigned to others.
By Person Responsible	Lists tasks by the requestor or owner.
Completed Tasks	Lists only completed tasks.
Task Timeline	Presents tasks chronologically across a visual timeline.
Server Tasks	Lists tasks assigned from a SharePoint site
Outlook Data Files	Lists tasks in different data files.
To-Do List	Lists the active tasks in the To-Do List.

STEP-BY-STEP 3.5

1. On the Navigation Pane, in the Current View section, click **Active Tasks**.

2. Click **File** on the menu bar and then click **Print**. The Print dialog box open.

3. In the *Print style* box, click **Memo Style**, and then click **Preview**. The currently  selected task appears in memo format. In the Print Preview dialog box, click the **Print** button on the toolbar. The Tasks list prints in memo format.

4. In the *Print style* box, click **Table Style**, and then click **OK**. The Tasks list prints in table format. Leave Outlook open for the next Step-by-Step.

> **Extra Challenge**
>
> Create a Tasks list that includes at least five things you need to do this week.

Using the Journal

You can use the Journal to record entries and document your interactions with contacts. You can create journal entries manually to keep track of phone calls and other activities, or you can choose to record e-mail, meetings, and tasks automatically.

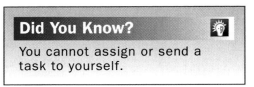

Did You Know?

You cannot assign or send a task to yourself.

To open the Journal, click Go on the menu bar, and then click Journal. In the Microsoft Office Outlook dialog box, click No. The Journal appears as a timeline, as shown in Figure 3-14. To add a new Journal entry, click File on the menu bar, point to New, and then click Journal Entry. A new window opens with the title Untitled – Journal Entry, as shown in Figure 3-15. Here you can set the type and time of the Journal entry. You can set the duration by selecting a preset time or by recording the actual time you spend on the interaction. On the Ribbon, in the Timer group, you can click the Start Timer button and the Pause Timer button to capture the time you spend on an activity, as if you were using a stopwatch. When you are finished with the Journal entry, on the Ribbon, in the Actions group, click the Save & Close button.

FIGURE 3-14
View the Journal

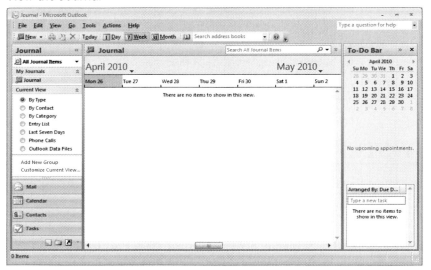

FIGURE 3-15
New Journal Entry

Start Timer button

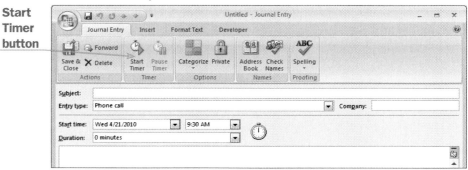

You can rearrange your view of the Journal by clicking View on the menu, pointing to Current View, and then clicking a view option.

STEP-BY-STEP 3.6

1. Click **Go** on the menu bar and then click Journal. If you are prompted to turn on the Journal, click **No**. The Journal appears, as shown in Figure 3-14.

2. Click **File** on the menu bar, point to **New**, and then click **Journal Entry**. The Journal Entry window opens, as shown in Figure 3-15.

3. In the *Subject* box, type **Interview keynote speaker for conference**.

4. In the *Entry type* box, make sure that **Phone call** is selected.

5. In the *Duration* box, choose **15 minutes**.

6. In the *Description* area, type **Presentation can be no longer than 30 minutes**.

7. On the Ribbon, in the Actions group, click the **Save & Close** button. The journal entry appears on the timeline.

8. On the Navigation Pane, in the Current View section, click the **Phone Calls** option button. The journal entry appears in a list. Your screen should appear similar to Figure 3-16. Leave Outlook open for the next Step-by-Step.

> ### Did You Know?
>
> To record journal entries automatically, click Tools on the menu bar, and then click Options to open the Options dialog box. In the Contacts and Notes section, click Journal Options to open the Journal Options dialog box. You can select the items, contacts, or files you want to automatically record. When finished, click OK.

FIGURE 3-16
View a Journal entry

Using Notes

The Notes feature is the electronic equivalent of using paper sticky notes as reminders. You can use notes to type anything you need to remember, such as an errand, a great idea, or a question to ask a co-worker. You can assign contacts from your Address Book to your notes, and, just as you can with e-mail and Calendar, you can also assign categories to notes.

At the bottom of the Navigation Pane, click the Notes icon to display Notes. To add a note, click the New Note button on the Standard toolbar. A blank note opens, as shown in Figure 3-17. Outlook automatically adds the date and time. Click the Close button on the note to save and close it.

FIGURE 3-17
View note

New note

STEP-BY-STEP 3.7

1. At the bottom of the Navigation Pane, click the **Notes** icon. (*Note*: If the Notes icon is not visible, click the **Configure buttons** icon, point to **Add or Remove Buttons**, and then select **Notes** in the pop-up submenu.)

2. Click the **New Note** button on the Standard toolbar. Your screen should appear similar to Figure 3-17.

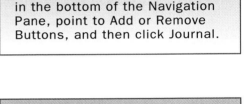

3. Type **Fax lunch order to Gourmet in a Box** and then click the **Close** button at the top of the note. The note appears in Notes.

4. Click the **New Note** button on the Standard toolbar and then type **Download ringtones for company phones**.

5. Click the **Note** icon in the upper-left corner of the note, point to **Categorize**, and then click **Orange Category**. The note color changes to orange. (*Note*: If prompted to rename the color category, click No. Click another color if orange is already renamed.)

6. Click the **Close** button to close the note.

7. Click the **New Note** button on the Standard toolbar and then type **Call bank to arrange for direct deposit**.

8. Click the **Note** icon in the upper-left corner of the note and then click **Contacts** to open the Contacts for Note dialog box.

9. In the Contacts for Note dialog box, click **Contacts** to open the Select Contacts dialog box.

STEP-BY-STEP 3.7 Continued

10. In the Select Contacts dialog box, in the Items section, click **Acosta, Sofia** (or another contact) and then click **OK**. In the Contacts for Note dialog box, click **Close**.

11. Click the **Note** icon in the upper-left corner of the note, point to **Categorize**, and then click **Blue Category**. The note color changes to blue. (*Note*: If prompted to rename the color category, click No. Click another color if blue is already renamed.)

12. Click the **Close** button to close the note.

13. Click the **Small Icons** button on the Standard toolbar. The notes appear in smaller icons.

14. On the Navigation Pane, in the Current View section, click the **Notes List** option button. The notes appear in Detailed List view in Notes, as shown in Figure 3-18.

> **Did You Know?**
>
> You can change a note's default color, size, and font by clicking Tools on the menu bar, and then clicking Options. In the Options dialog box, in the Contacts and Notes section, click Notes Options, and then change settings in the Notes Options dialog box.

FIGURE 3-18
View Notes List

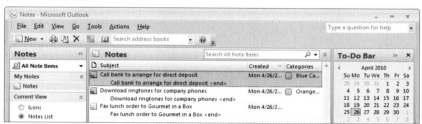

Exiting Outlook

You can exit Outlook by opening the File menu and then clicking Exit.

STEP-BY-STEP 3.8

1. Click the **Mail** folder button in the Navigation Pane.

2. Open the **File** menu and then click **Exit**.

3. The Outlook window closes.

> **Did You Know?**
>
> You can also click the Close button on the Outlook title bar to exit Outlook.

SUMMARY

In this lesson, you learned:

■ Outlook Today and the To-Do Bar gather information about activities from Calendar, Tasks, and Mail and summarize the information in one window.

■ You can create tasks from several views, including Outlook Today and the To-Do Bar. You can assign categories, specify start and end dates, check the status of tasks, prioritize, and set reminders. You can also move tasks up and down the list, sort by subject or due date, add or delete tasks, edit a task, assign or delegate a task, or mark a task off when you complete it. In addition, you can view a Tasks list from different views and print a Tasks list in different styles.

■ The Journal is used to record entries and document your work. You can set Outlook to record entries automatically or use the Journal Entry dialog box to record entries manually.

■ Notes is similar to using paper sticky notes as reminders. The date and time are automatically added. You can change the color of a note and view notes according to color.

■ When you've completed your work in Outlook, you can exit the program.

VOCABULARY *Review*

Define the following terms:

Daily Task List	Task	To-do item
Journal	Task Input Panel	To-Do List
Notes		

REVIEW *Questions*

TRUE/FALSE

Circle T if the statement is true or F if the statement is false.

T   F   1. Making Journal entries in Outlook is similar to using sticky paper notes.

T   F   2. You can view tasks in the Calendar in the Daily Task List.

T   F   3. You can view multiple calendars in the Date Navigator.

T   F   4. You can view both active and completed tasks in Outlook.

T   F   5. A note is usually an activity you want to perform and monitor to completion.

WRITTEN QUESTIONS

Write a brief answer to the following questions.

1. Where do tasks appear on the To-Do Bar?

2. How do you create a task in the To-Do Bar?

3. What is the default appearance of a note in Notes?

4. In what window can you time your activity as if you had a stopwatch?

5. What happens to a completed task in the To-Do Bar?

PROJECTS

PROJECT 3-1

1. Open Outlook and display Tasks view.

2. Mark all existing tasks as complete.

3. Add a new task with **Paint bathroom** as the subject and a due date of this Saturday.

4. Set a reminder at 3 P.M. on Friday.

5. In the text box, type **Get another drop cloth.** Save and close the Task window.

6. Add another new task with **Pick up carpet samples** as the subject and a due date of this Thursday.

7. Set a reminder at 10 A.M. on Wednesday. Set the priority as High. Save and close the Task window.

8. View the tasks in Detailed List view.

9. Sort the tasks by Due Date.

10. Print the Tasks list in Table view. Leave Outlook open for the next project.

PROJECT 3-2

1. Display the Journal.

2. Create a new journal entry with **Phone interview** as the subject.

3. Use Phone call as the Entry type.

4. Type **Rocky Mountain Press** as the Company.

5. Choose a duration of 30 minutes.

6. In the text box, type **Will send photographer Monday**.

7. Categorize the entry as purple. Save and close the Journal Entry window. Leave Outlook open for the next project.

PROJECT 3-3

1. Display Notes.

2. Add a red note that says **Order flowers for Aunt Kate's birthday**.

3. Add a green note that says **Send an e-card**.

4. Add a yellow note that says **Call Tracey (668-3113) about white water rafting**.

5. View the notes by Category.

6. Exit Outlook.

CRITICAL *Thinking*

ACTIVITY 3-1

Pick a type of small business that you would like to own. Describe in paragraph form how you would use the Calendar, Tasks, and Journal features of Outlook to organize information, communicate with others, and manage time. Make a list of four or more categories for grouping all of the information.

ACTIVITY 3-2

Your supervisor asks you to change the default settings for Journal tracking or the automatic recording of Outlook activities. Use the Help system to search for the steps to change the defaults. Write down the steps.

ACTIVITY 3-3

Design an Outlook Today view for your supervisor using the customizing options. Explain in a short paragraph why you chose those particular options.

MICROSOFT PUBLISHER

Unit

Lesson 1
Publisher Basics

1.5 hrs.

Lesson 2
Enhancing Publisher Documents

1.5 hrs.

Estimated Time for Unit: 3 hours

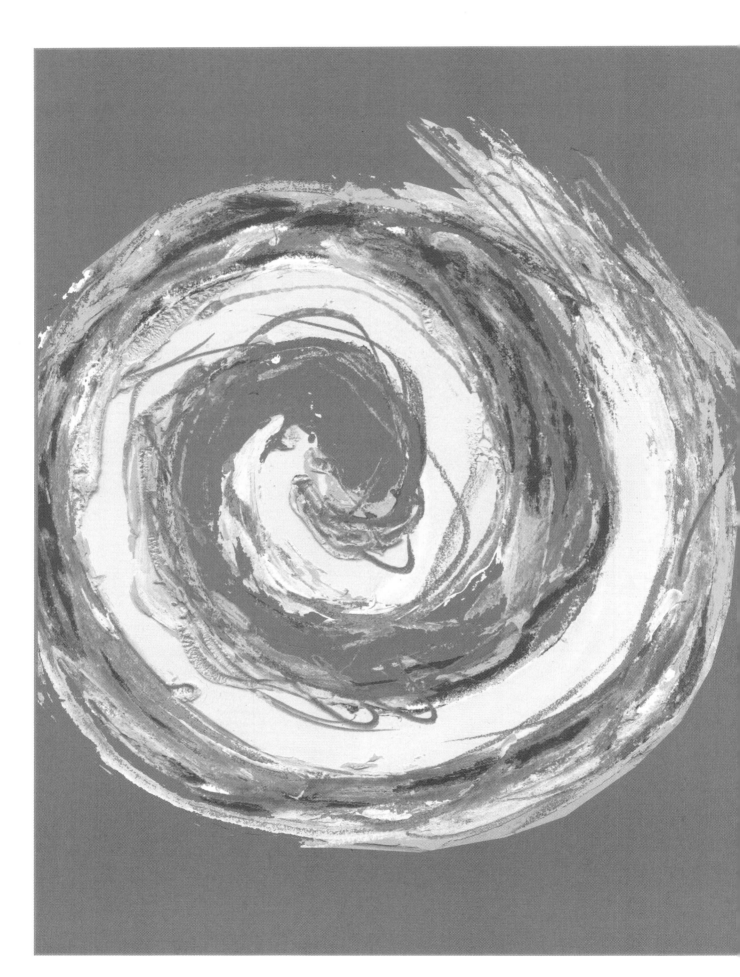

PUBLISHER BASICS

VOCABULARY

Business information set

Design gallery object

Design Checker

Logo

Publication Types list

Task pane

Template

Introduction to Publisher

Publisher is a desktop publishing program that you can use to create a wide assortment of publications, such as newsletters, brochures, business cards, and restaurant menus. Publisher contains hundreds of predesigned layouts called templates that you can use as the basis for professional-looking projects. All you have to do is add your own custom touches.

Starting Publisher

To start Microsoft Office Publisher 2007, click the Start button, point to All Programs, click Microsoft Office, and then click Microsoft Office Publisher 2007. The Microsoft Publisher window opens with the Getting Started category selected, as shown in Figure 1-1. The Microsoft Publisher window consists of three panes that can help you to create a new publication or open an existing publication. The left pane includes the Publication Types list—a list of template categories from which to choose. For example, clicking the Newsletters category will display all of the available newsletter templates in the middle pane. The Getting Started category, which is chosen by default, displays Popular Publication Types in the middle pane. These publication types represent those that are used often, such as Flyers and Brochures. The right pane, Recent Publications, lists Publisher files that have been opened recently.

FIGURE 1-1
Microsoft Publisher window

STEP-BY-STEP 1.1

1. Click the **Start** button to open the Start menu.

2. Point to **All Programs** to open the All Programs menu.

3. Click **Microsoft Office**.

4. Click **Microsoft Office Publisher 2007** to start the program, then leave the program open for the next Step-by-Step.

Did You Know?

If you do not see a file in the Recent Publications list, click From File, then navigate to its location on your computer.

Choosing a Template

Publisher makes it easy for you to get started on a project right away. If you know the type of publication you want to create, simply click a category in the Publication Types list, then click a template in the middle pane. Templates may fall into one or more subcategories, such as Classic Designs or Newer Designs. Notice also that you can choose Blank Sizes from many of the categories. When you choose a template, you will see a thumbnail image of it in the top-right corner of the window, with options for customizing the template before you click Create. Figure 1-2 shows the Appreciation 8 template selected from the Classic Designs subcategory of the Award Certificates category. You are not limited to using a template from this window. You can simply click File on the menu bar, and then click Open to open an existing publication.

FIGURE 1-2
Choosing the Appreciation 8 Award Certificate template

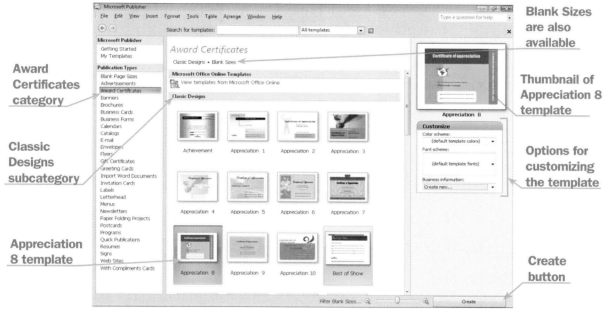

Understanding the Publisher Window and Task Panes

Once you create a publication by clicking the Create button, the publication will appear in the document window. Above the document window you will see the title bar, menu bar, and the Standard and Formatting toolbars. The current task pane is located

Did You Know?

You can choose not to customize your template at this point. You will have access to the same customization options in the Format Publication task pane after you create the publication.

to the left of the publication. **Task panes** contain options for modifying your publication. Task panes are categorized by function, such as Clip Art. For example, the Clip Art task pane is used to add clip art to the open publication. The Format Publication task pane is the first task pane that appears when a new publication is created. The Format Publication task pane allows you to change the color scheme, font scheme, and page size of a publication. You can even choose another template to replace the one you are currently working with. The options in the Format Publication task pane will differ depending on which template is chosen. To change from one task pane to another, you can click the Other Task Panes list arrow, then choose the task pane that you want. Figure 1-3 shows the Appreciation 8 Award Certificate template in the document window, with the Format Publication task pane open.

FIGURE 1-3
Appreciation 8 Award Certificate in document window

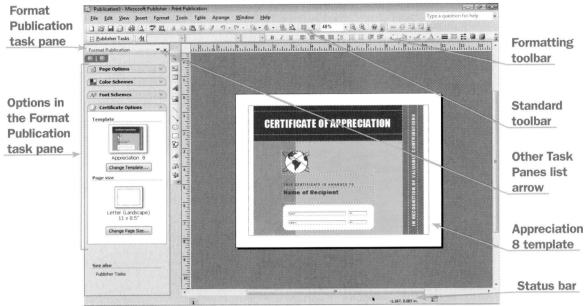

Format Publication task pane

Options in the Format Publication task pane

Formatting toolbar

Standard toolbar

Other Task Panes list arrow

Appreciation 8 template

Status bar

Creating Business Information Sets

A business information set is a collection of information about an individual, such as name, company name, address, telephone number, e-mail address, and so on. Business information sets are stored in Publisher and are associated with templates; the information in the set is automatically plugged into templates that call for them. For example, imagine you are creating a brochure that requires your return address. The required information for your return address is pulled from the business information set and plugged into the template, saving you time and effort. You can create business information sets using the Business Information command on the Edit menu or the Business Information task pane. Figure 1-4 shows the Create New Business Information Set dialog box. If you create more than one set, it might be a good idea to assign a descriptive name to each, such as "Personal" or "Work." When you choose a new template, you can pick from a list of business information sets (if you have created more than one) in the Microsoft Publisher window before clicking Create.

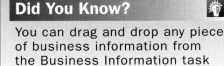

Did You Know?

The status bar at the bottom of the document window displays the object size and position of a selected object

Did You Know?

You can drag and drop any piece of business information from the Business Information task pane to a publication.

FIGURE 1-4
Create New Business Information Set dialog box

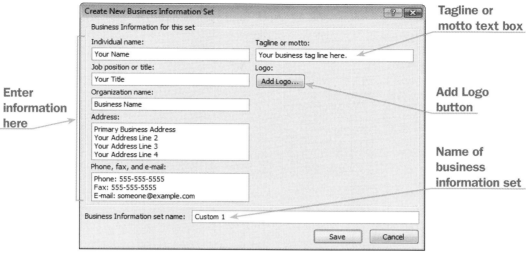

Enter information here

Tagline or motto text box

Add Logo button

Name of business information set

S TEP-BY-STEP 1.2

1. Select the **Business Cards** category in the Publication Types list, and then click **PhotoScope** in the Newer Designs subcategory, as shown in Figure 1-5.

FIGURE 1-5
Business card templates

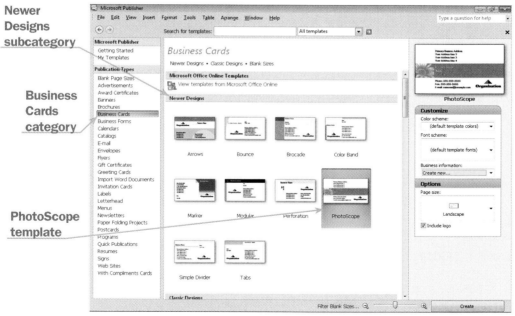

Newer Designs subcategory

Business Cards category

PhotoScope template

2. In the Customize section, click the Color scheme **arrow**, and then click **Cavern**.

3. Click **Create**.

STEP-BY-STEP 1.2 Continued

4. In the Format Publication task pane, click the Font Schemes **arrow**, click **Module**, and then compare your screen to Figure 1-6.

FIGURE 1-6
PhotoScope business card

Font
Schemes
list arrow

Module

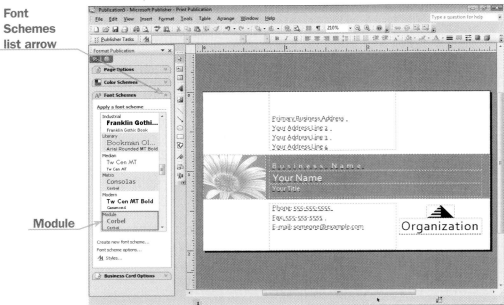

5. Click the Other Task Panes list **arrow**, and then click **Business Information**.

6. In the Business Information task pane, click the Individual name **arrow**, and then click **Change Business Information**.

7. In the Individual name text box of the Create New Business Information Set dialog box, type **Maryann Lockhart**.

8. In the Job position or title text box, type **Technician**.

9. In the Organization name text box, type **Lawson Electronics**.

10. In the Address text box, type
1218 Albany
Anderson, IN 46011

11. In the Phone, fax, and e-mail text box, type
Phone: 812-555-9213
Fax: 812-555-9211
Email: mlockhart@lawson.com

STEP-BY-STEP 1.2 Continued

12. In the Business Information set name text box, type **Work Information**, then compare your dialog box to Figure 1-7.

FIGURE 1-7
Create New Business Information Set dialog box

13. In the Create New Business Information Set dialog box, click **Save**, click **Update Publication**, then leave the file open for the next Step-by-Step.

Saving a Publication

The first time you save a publication, the Save As dialog box appears in which you name the publication. Once a publication has been saved, the Save command will update the latest version. The publication may also be saved by clicking the Save button on the Standard toolbar.

STEP-BY-STEP 1.3

1. From the menu bar click **File**, and then click **Save As**. The Save As dialog box appears.

2. Type **New Card**, followed by your initials, in the File name text box.

3. Click **Save**. Leave the file open for the next Step-by-Step.

Modifying a Publication

Choosing a template is often a good starting point in creating a publication. Publisher offers numerous ways to modify a publication to customize it to meet your needs. You can add, delete, move, rotate, and scale text boxes and graphics. Publisher supplies you with basic shape tools and clip art so that you can create simple graphics from scratch. You can also add your own graphics and photographs to a publication. Modifications are made using the task panes and the toolbars. Most companies use their logo on all business publications for consistency and brand recognition. A logo is a symbol that is designed to help customers remember a business and its products. In Publisher, you can create your own logo from scratch, from clip art, or use one created in another software program.

> ### Did You Know?
>
> You can add your own company logo and tagline or motto in the Create New Business Information Set dialog box.

STEP-BY-STEP 1.4

1. Right-click the logo in the bottom-right corner of the business card, then click **Delete Object**.

2. Click the Other Task Panes list **arrow**, and then click **Clip Art**.

3. In the Clip Art task pane, click the Results should be list **arrow**, then make sure that the **All media types check box** is checked.

4. In the Clip Art task pane, type **Electronics** in the Search for text box, then click **Go**.

5. Scroll down in the task pane until you see the green television image, as shown in Figure 1-8, and then click the **green television** image. If you do not see the green television image, feel free to choose another similar image that you like. The clip art image is centered horizontally and vertically on the business card and remains selected.

STEP-BY-STEP 1.4 Continued

FIGURE 1-8
Clip Art Task Pane

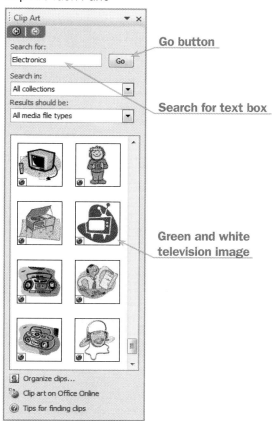

Go button

Search for text box

Green and white
television image

6. Right-click the **green television** image, then click **Format Picture**.

7. In the Format Picture dialog box, click the **Size tab**.

STEP-BY-STEP 1.4 Continued

8. Click the **Lock aspect ratio** check box if it is not already checked. Type **25** in the Height text box in the Scale section, as shown in Figure 1-9, then press the **Tab** key to move to the Width text box. Note that when you select the Lock aspect ratio box, the Width value will automatically change to match any adjustments made to the Height value.

FIGURE 1-9
Format Picture dialog box

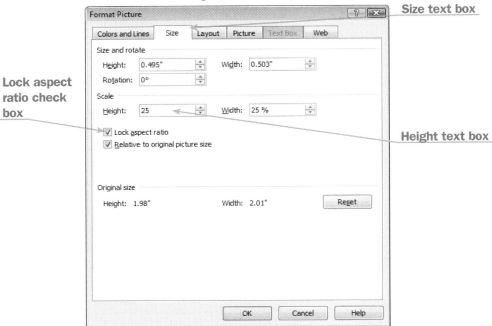

9. Click **OK**, and then drag the image to the lower-right corner of the business card so that your business card resembles Figure 1-10.

FIGURE 1-10
Modified buiness card

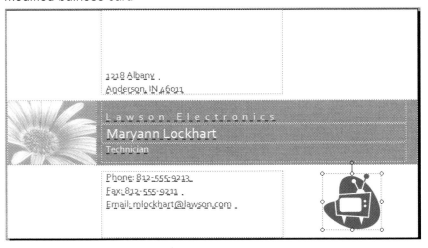

STEP-BY-STEP 1.4 Continued

10. On the Standard toolbar, click the **Save** button, then leave the file open for the next Step-by-Step.

> **Did You Know?**
>
> You can also resize a graphic by selecting it then dragging a resizing handle.

Inserting a Design Gallery Object

Just as Publisher provides a collection of templates for creating publications, the Design Gallery provides a collection of designs and text placeholders that can be used to further enhance a publication's appearance and functionality. As shown in Figure 1-11, the left pane of the Design Gallery dialog box displays categories and the right pane provides the available options for the currently selected category. In this example, the Attention Getters category is selected. Items from the Design Gallery are referred to as Design Gallery Objects. To use a Design Gallery Object, you first need to click the Design Gallery Object tool on the Objects toolbar. When you find the Design Gallery Object you would like to use, click Insert Object in the Design Gallery.

> **Did You Know?**
>
> When a picture is selected, as the television image is in Figure 1-10, the Picture Toolbar appears. The picture toolbar includes tools for formatting pictures, such as setting transparency and adjusting brightness and contrast.

FIGURE 1-11
Design Gallery

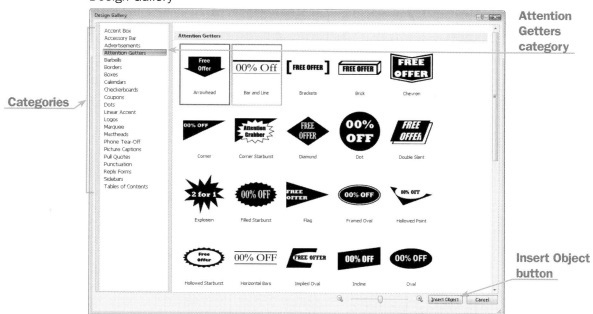

*S*TEP-BY-STEP 1.5

1. Right-click the **green television** image, then click **Delete Object**.

2. Right-click the **flower** image on the left side of the business card, then click **Delete Object**.

3. From the menu bar click **View**, point to **Toolbars**, and then click **Objects**, if it is not already checked.

4. On the Objects toolbar, click the **Design Gallery Object** button.

5. In the Design Gallery, click the **Linear Accent** category, then click **Tri-shape**, as shown in Figure 1-12.

FIGURE 1-12
Choosing the Tri-shape Linear Accent

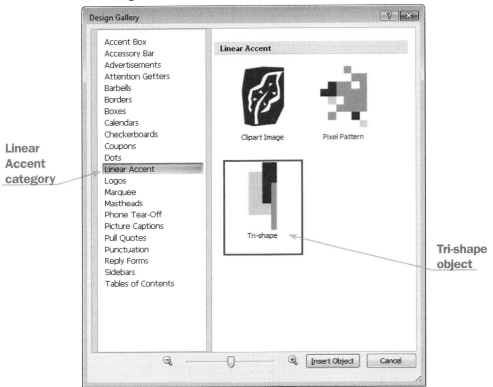

6. At the bottom of the Design Gallery dialog box, click **Insert Object**, then drag the Tri-shape object to the approximate location shown in Figure 1-13.

STEP-BY-STEP 1.5 Continued

FIGURE 1-13
Completed buiness card

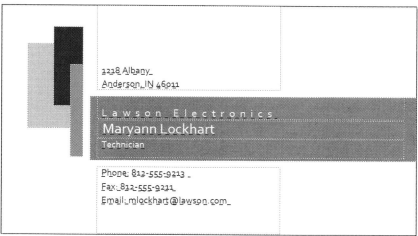

7. Click another area of the publication to deselect the object.

8. On the Standard toolbar, click the **Save** button. Leave the file open for the next Step-by-Step.

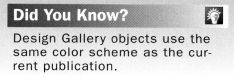

Using Design Checker

When you are working long and hard on a publication, especially a multipage publication, you might not catch all of your errors. For example, your publication may have overflow text or an object that is not positioned properly on the page. The Design Checker task pane finds and lists potential design problems associated with your publication. Using the Design Checker task pane, you can select from four different check types: general design, commercial printing, Web site, and e-mail. Publisher creates a list of errors that you can opt to fix or leave as is. Some errors can be fixed automatically, while others must be fixed manually.

STEP-BY-STEP 1.6

1. Click the Other Task Panes list **arrow**, and then click **Design Checker**.

2. In the Design Checker task pane, make sure that a check mark only appears next to **Run general design checks**, so that your Design Checker task pane matches Figure 1-14.

FIGURE 1-14
Design Checker

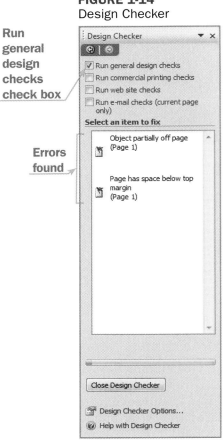

3. In the Design Checker task pane, click **Object partially off page (Page 1)**. The Tri-shape object is selected, showing that this is the item that is partially off the page.

4. Click the **arrow** next to Object partially off page (Page 1) to view options for fixing this problem, as shown in Figure 1-15, then release the pointer. This problem can only be fixed manually. For the purposes of this exercise, we will leave it alone.

STEP-BY-STEP 1.6 Continued

FIGURE 1-15
Options for fixing problems

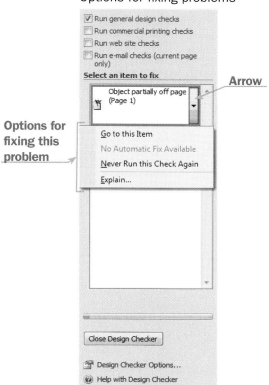

Arrow

Options for fixing this problem

5. Close the Design Checker task pane, then leave the file open for the next Step-by-Step.

Printing a Publication

You may print your publication by clicking File from the menu bar, then clicking Print, which will access the Print dialog box. As shown in Figure 1-16, many options are provided in the Print dialog box. You can choose the number of copies and the page range to print. For some types of publications, such as business cards, you have the option to print one copy or multiple copies per page. The Preview window allows you to see how your publication will print before you click the Print button. If you are working in a classroom or lab setting, you may need to click the Printer name arrow to choose a specific printer. To print a publication using your computer's default settings, you can simply click the Print button on the Standard toolbar. The Print dialog box will not be displayed when this print option is used.

FIGURE 1-16
Print dialog box

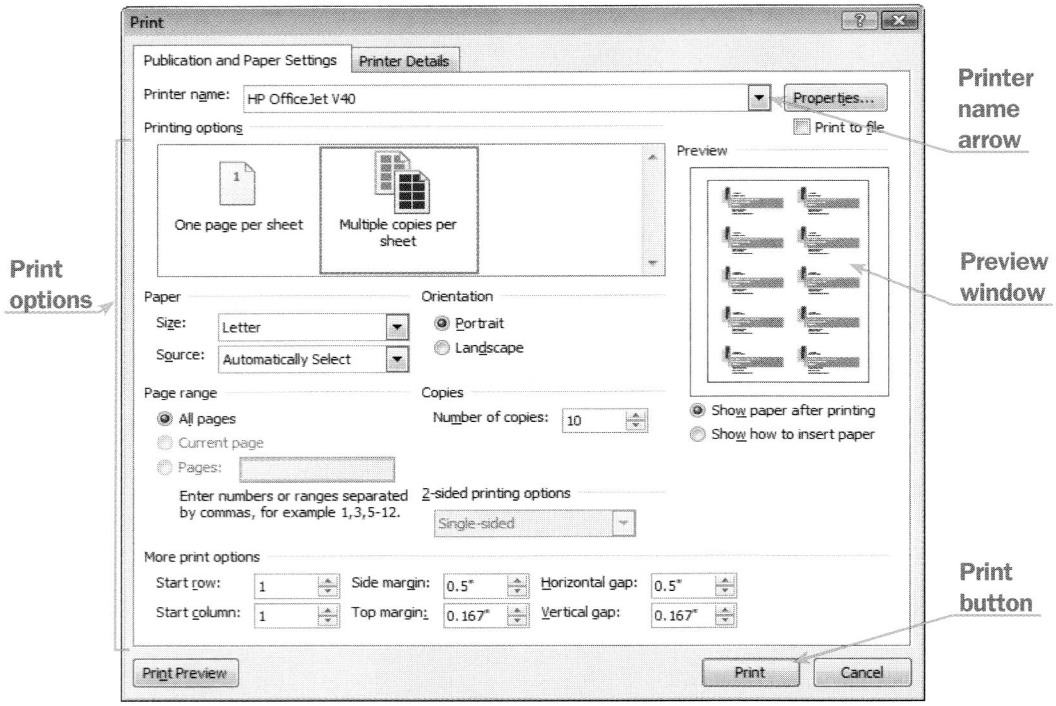

Closing a Publication

Unlike other Microsoft Office 2007 programs, the Publisher program does not have a Close Window button in the top-right corner, only a Close button, which will close the entire Publisher program. To close your publication, but not the entire Publisher program, click File from the menu bar, then click Close.

STEP-BY-STEP 1.7

1. On the Standard toolbar, click the **Save** button to save the publication. Your business card should look similar to the one shown in Figure 1-17.

FIGURE 1-17
Finished publication

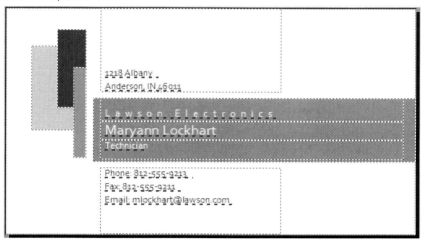

2. From the menu bar click **File**, then click **Print**.

3. In the Print dialog box, keep the current settings, and then click **Print**.

4. From the menu bar click **File**, and then click **Close**.

SUMMARY

In this lesson, you learned:

■ Microsoft Publisher is a program that allows you to produce professional-looking publications in almost any format imaginable. Publisher makes this process even easier with the use of templates and design gallery objects.

■ You can modify a template using the Format Publication task pane. You can change the color scheme and the font scheme of a publication as well as the page size. The options in the Format Publication task pane will differ depending on which template is chosen. Templates can also be modified by moving, adding, deleting, and resizing graphics and text boxes.

■ A Design Gallery Object is a design or text placeholder that can be added to a publication. Design Gallery Objects are stored in the Design Gallery.

■ Business information sets are collections of information about individuals. They are stored in Publisher and used with templates.

- It is important to save your work often. The first time you save a publication, the Save As dialog box opens so that you can name and save your file.

- The Design Checker is a task pane that helps you find potential design problems in your publication. Some problems can be fixed automatically; others can only be fixed manually.

- When you are finished with your publication, you can print the publication using the Print dialog box and then close Publisher.

VOCABULARY *Review*

Define the following terms:

Business information set	Logo	Task pane
Design gallery object	Publication Types list	Template
Design Checker		

REVIEW *Questions*

TRUE/FALSE

Circle T if the statement is true or F if the statement is false.

T   F   1. To create a blank publication, choose a template, and then remove any items on it.

T   F   2. The Design Checker is used to add design gallery objects to your publication.

T   F   3. In the Print dialog box, you can print a range of pages instead of the entire publication.

T   F   4. You can change the color scheme of a publication in the Format Publication task pane.

T   F   5. Newsletters is a category in the Design Gallery.

WRITTEN QUESTIONS

Write a brief answer to each of the following questions.

1. List two ways to open an existing publication.

2. List at least one change that you can make to a template before you click the Create button.

3. Which task pane allows you to create a collection of information about an individual?

4. Once a publication is created, what are at least three ways that you can modify it?

5. What happens the first time you save a new publication?

PROJECTS

PROJECT 1-1

1. Start Publisher, if necessary.

2. From the menu bar click **File**, and then click **Open**.

3. Navigate to the location of the data files for this lesson, click **Yoga**, and then click **Open**.

4. Save the file as **Yoga**, followed by your initials.

5. Change the color scheme to **Cherry** in the Format Publication task pane.

6. Change the font scheme to **Casual**.

7. Right-click the **Organization** logo, then click **Delete Object**.

8. Right-click the **Number** text box, then click **Delete Object**.

9. Type your name after "Authorized by" in the text box. (Depending on the setup of your classroom, your publication may or may not show a business information set. Leave all other text boxes as they are.)

10. Save and print your publication, then close the file.

PROJECT 1-2

1. Start Publisher, if necessary.

2. From the menu bar click **File**, and then click **Open**.

3. Navigate to the location of the data files for this lesson, click **Coupon**, and then click **Open**.

4. Save the file as **Coupon**, followed by your initials.

5. On the Objects toolbar, click the **Design Gallery Object** button.

6. Click the **Coupons** category, click **Tilted Box**, and then click **Insert Object**.

7. In the Format Publication task pane, change the font scheme to **Aspect**.

8. Replace "Name of Item or Service" with **Car Wash**.

9. Replace the Organization name and location, or landmark, with your own school name and town. Do not change the telephone number.

10. Change the expiration date to one of your choice.

11. Save and print your publication, then close the file.

CRITICAL *Thinking*

 ACTIVITY 1-1

Use a Business Card template to create a business card for yourself that you can use for babysitting services or dog-walking services. Use any of the skills that you have learned in this lesson to customize your business card. As you design your card, think about colors, fonts, and graphics that will work well to represent your image. Enter your own information or use an existing business information set. Feel free to remove any unnecessary business information, such as the fax number. Save the business card as My Card, followed by your initials, print one copy, and then close the file.

 ACTIVITY 1-2

Open **Gift Certificate** from the location of the data files for this lesson. Show the Design Checker task pane, and notice that no problems are found with the general design. Click the next two check boxes in the Design Checker task pane (Run commercial printing checks and Run Web site checks). For each problem, click the arrow, and then click Explain. After reading about each problem, choose two that you feel familiar with. Write a few sentences as to why these problems cropped up in Publisher. If you do not know or do not understand the explanation, write what you think might have caused the problem. Use a word-processing program or sheet of paper. Save your explanations as Gift Certificate, followed by your initials, print a copy of your answers, and then close all files.

 ACTIVITY 1-3

Use a template from the Publications Types list to create a birthday card. (*Hint*: Look under Greeting Cards.) Add a personalized message to the inside of the card. (*Hint*: To display the inside page of your card, use the page navigator at the bottom of the window.) Save your card as Birthday Card, followed by your initials, print your card, and then close Publisher.

ENHANCING PUBLISHER DOCUMENTS

OBJECTIVES

Upon completion of this lesson, you will be able to:

- Understand guides.
- Enter text.
- Insert pictures.
- Work with objects.
- Use the Content Library.
- Insert text from a Word document.
- Use Find and Replace.
- Check the spelling in a publication.

Estimated Time 1.5 hours

VOCABULARY

Content Library

Layout guides

Master page

Object

Page navigator

Panel heading

Enhancing Your Publisher Documents

The use of business information sets, templates, and design gallery objects helps you get a jump start on creating publications. Enhancing Publisher projects with your own pictures and text is fun, easy, and provides a way for you to create attractive and professional-looking publications tailored to meet your school, business, and personal needs.

Beginning a Brochure

STEP-BY-STEP 2.1

1. Start Microsoft Office Publisher 2007, if necessary, and then click **Brochures** in the Publication Types list.

2. In the middle pane, scroll down to the Classic Designs section, keep scrolling until you see the Price List subcategory, and then click **Accent Box**, as shown in Figure 2-1.

FIGURE 2-1
Choosing the Accent Box template

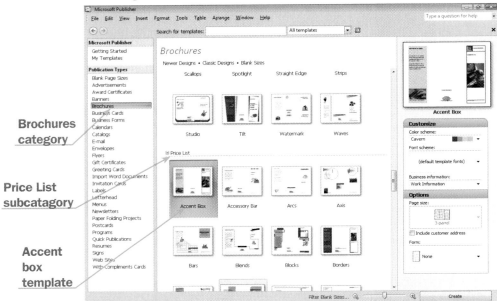

3. Make sure you see "Work Information" in the Business Information section under Customize, and then click **Create**.

   Work Information is the name of the business information set that you created in Lesson 1. If you did not create a business information set in Lesson 1, feel free to create a new set with your own information.

4. Save the file as **Brochure**, followed by your initials, and then leave the document open for the next Step-by-Step.

Understanding Guides

Publisher has many types of **layout guides** to help you position objects in a publication. Each template has guides already in place, depending on the type of template you are using, including margin guides, grid guides, column guides, row guides, and baseline guides. When viewing publication pages, you'll quickly realize that the default guides cannot be moved manually. However, you can change guide settings in the Layout Guides dialog box. To access the Layout Guides dialog box, you click Arrange on the menu bar, and then click Layout Guides. As shown in Figure 2-2, the Layout Guides dialog box has three tabs: Margin Guides, Grid Guides, and Baseline Guides. The Column Guides and Row Guides settings can be found in the Grid Guides tab.

FIGURE 2-2
Layout Guides dialog box

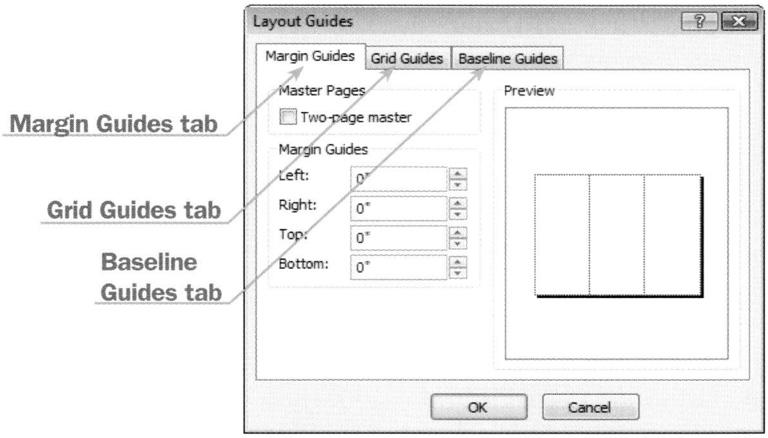

Finally, you can create your own guides by simply placing the pointer over the horizontal or vertical ruler. The pointer becomes a double arrow pointer. To create a guide, drag the pointer from the ruler onto the page and release the pointer wherever you want to position the new guide. Once positioned, ruler guides can be moved freely on the page.

To temporarily hide guides, click View on the menu bar, and then click Boundaries and Guides.

Did You Know?

If you do not see rulers in the publication window, click View on the menu bar, and then click Rulers. As you drag to create a Guide from one of the rulers, you can position it accurately by viewing the object location coordinates in the status bar. These two numbers display the horizontal and vertical locations of the guide.

Understanding Master Pages

If you want to drag layout guides manually, you must switch to the master page for the current publication. The **master page** is a background page that includes placeholders for text and graphics as well as layout guides. Simply press the Ctrl+M keys to switch to the master page. On the master page, you can drag guides to new locations with ease. To return to the publication pages, press the Ctrl+M keys again.

Entering Text

When developing newsletters, brochures, flyers, or postcards, you will need to add your own information to your project. Using Publisher templates, you can add text directly into text boxes or panel headings. A **panel heading** is the area provided for the title or heading of a project or section of a project. Once an area for adding text has been selected, you can zoom in for better viewing and editing and, with Microsoft Publisher, you always have the option to resize and reposition text boxes. The **page navigator**, located in the lower-left side of the window, allows you to move quickly from one page to another when you are adding text to your publication. You can also insert text from a Microsoft Word document, something that you'll learn about later in this lesson.

STEP-BY-STEP 2.2

1. The Brochure file should be open from the previous Step-by-Step. Close the Format Publication task pane.

2. Display page **1** by using the page navigator, if necessary, and then click the **Zoom In button** on the Standard toolbar to zoom to **75%**.

3. Click inside the text box that reads *Back Panel Heading,* then type **Our Mission**.

4. Click three times anywhere in *Our Mission* to highlight the phrase.

5. On the Formatting toolbar, click the **Center button** to center the text in the text box.

6. Click in the text box below *Our Mission* to select it, and then type:
It is our mission to provide students with a quality computer education in a timely manner. Students will be better prepared for their future and obtain knowledge that will help them further their careers and personal lives.

7. Select the text that you just typed, center it, and then change the font size to **16**.

8. In the same panel, click the caption below the photograph of the keyboard, and then type **A Happy Student**.

9. Save your work, compare your first panel to Figure 2-3, and then leave the document open for the next Step-by-Step.

FIGURE 2-3
First pane of page 1

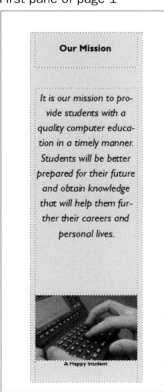

Inserting Pictures

One of the best ways to personalize a flyer or brochure (and to make it look more professional) is to add artwork and photographs. This can be done easily by adding clip art or your own photographs and illustrations. You can insert pictures as new objects in Publisher, or you can replace existing pictures with newly inserted pictures in the same location. To insert a picture, simply click Insert on the menu bar, point to Picture, and then click From File. You'll be prompted to navigate to the place where you have stored your pictures, select the picture, and then click Insert. Pictures are automatically centered horizontally and vertically on the page, unless they are replacing an existing picture. To replace an existing picture, right-click the picture, point to Change Picture, and then click From File. The new picture appears in the same location as the original picture. Once a picture is inserted into a publication, it can be resized, rotated, or flipped to fit your needs. When you select a picture, the Picture toolbar automatically appears, offering you tools for manipulating the picture such as cropping it, adjusting its brightness and contrast, and even creating transparent areas in the picture.

Did You Know?

You can insert pictures directly from your scanner or digital camera using the Insert Picture from Scanner or Camera dialog box. Make sure your device is connected to your computer, click Insert on the menu bar, point to Picture, and then click From Scanner or Camera.

S TEP-BY-STEP 2.3

1. Click the image in the first pane of page 1 (hands at the keyboard), then click the **Ungroup Objects** button below the picture.

The picture and the caption were grouped together.

2. Click another point on the page to deselect all, right-click the **keyboard picture**, point to **Change Picture**, and then click **From File**.

3. Navigate to the location where you store your Data Files, click **William.tif**, and then click **Insert**.

The new picture replaces the keyboard picture.

4. Click outside the picture to deselect it, click **View** on the menu bar, and then click **Boundaries and Guides** to remove the check mark and view your publication without guides.

5. Save your work, compare your first page to Figure 2-4, and then keep the document open for the next Step-by-Step.

FIGURE 2-4
First pane with new picture inserted

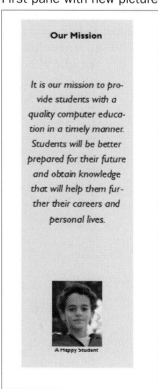

Working with Objects

Text boxes, shapes, clip art, and pictures are all **objects**. Objects are any items that can be modified in Publisher using the provided tools and features. When you right-click an object, a menu appears that includes the "Format" command. When you right-click a text box, the command is called Format Text Box; when you right-click a graphic, the menu command changes to Format Object or Format AutoShape. The Format dialog box includes many options for formatting the selected object. For example, you can enter specific values for an object's height and width. This is much easier than trying to draw a shape with a specific width or height from scratch.

The Arrange menu has many important features for manipulating objects, all of which add to making your publication look professional. For example, using the Align and Distribute commands, you can align objects by their tops, bottoms, centers, and left or right sides. Distributing objects means to place the same distance horizontally or vertically between objects. Once you have aligned or distributed the objects to your liking, it's a good idea to group them together to ensure that they are not moved or deleted by accident. You'll find the Group, Ungroup, and Regroup commands on the Arrange menu.

In Publisher, you also have the ability to stack or layer items using the Order commands. Imagine that you want to create an illustration of a dartboard using circles, each one smaller than the last and of a different color. You could "stack" the circles perfectly using any combination of the four Order commands on the Arrange menu. The Send to Back command sends the selected object to the back of the stack, and the Bring to Front command brings the selected object to the top of the stack. The Send Backward and Bring Forward commands send the selected object back or forward one level at a time. Rotate or Flip is another helpful set of commands found on the Arrange menu. You can rotate an object left or right 90° or use the Free Rotate tool. You can also flip an object horizontally or vertically.

S TEP-BY-STEP 2.4

1. Click **View** on the menu bar, and then click **Boundaries and Guides** to view your publication with guides in view.

2. If you do not see the rulers, click **View** on the menu bar, and then click **Rulers**.

3. Position the pointer on the horizontal ruler, drag the double arrow pointer down to the 2-inch mark on the vertical ruler, and then release the pointer.

Your screen should resemble Figure 2-5.

FIGURE 2-5
Adding a horizontal guide

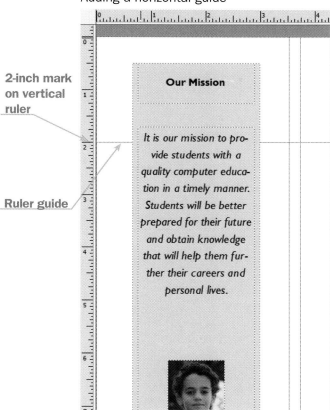

4. On the Objects toolbar, click the **Rectangle tool**, and then draw a rectangle of any size in the middle panel.

5. Right-click the **rectangle**, and then click **Format AutoShape**.

STEP-BY-STEP 2.4 Continued

6. In the Format AutoShape dialog box, click the **Size tab**, as shown in Figure 2-6.

The Width and Height values of your rectangle will differ from the figure.

FIGURE 2-6
Format AutoShape dialog box

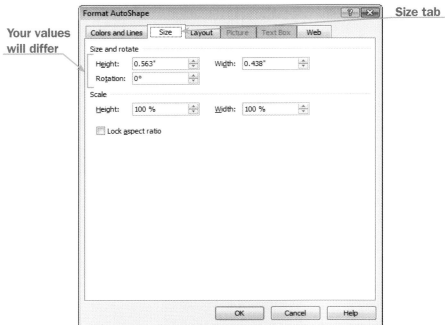

7. Select the contents of the Height text box, type **.5**, press **[Tab]**, type **.5** in the Width text box, and then click **OK**.

8. Press and hold **[Ctrl]**, drag the rectangle to the right, release the pointer, then release [Ctrl] to make a duplicate of the rectangle.

STEP-BY-STEP 2.4 Continued

9. Repeat Step 8 to create a third rectangle.

You should have three rectangles in the middle pane, as shown in Figure 2-7. Do not worry about their exact location in the pane at this time.

FIGURE 2-7
Three rectangles

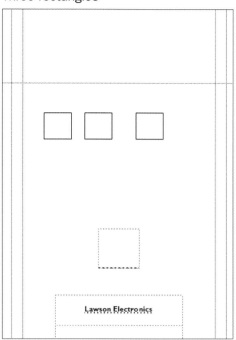

Lawson Electronics

10. Click the **first rectangle**, press and hold **[Shift]**, click the next **two rectangles**, and then release [Shift].

11. On the menu bar, click **Arrange**, point to **Align or Distribute**, and then click **Distribute Horizontally**.

12. With the rectangles still selected, on the menu bar, click **Arrange**, and then click **Group**.

13. Drag the group up toward the green guide, and snap the group to the guide.

14. With the group still selected, on the Formatting toolbar, click the **Fill Color arrow**, and then click **Accent 2 (RGB (153, 153, 204))**.

Did You Know?

If your objects do not seem to snap to guides, click Arrange on the menu bar, point to Snap, then click To Guides to add a check mark.

STEP-BY-STEP 2.4 Continued

15. Save your work, compare your screen to Figure 2-8, then keep the document open for the next Step-by-Step.

FIGURE 2-8
Viewing the new group

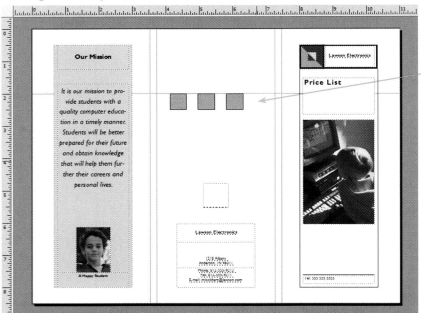

Three rectangles, distributed and grouped

Using the Content Library

The Content Library is a task pane used for storing text and graphics for future use. Imagine that you design brochures for a summer camp. Each year you use the same camp logo as well as specific information, such as vaccine requirements. You can store the elements that you'll reuse each year in the Content Library. Storing items in the Content Library will save you lots of time and energy and, more important, will ensure that your brochures have a consistent look and feel to them each year. You can also be certain that important text is intact. This is very important for any information, such as legal requirements, that must be perfect. You can add items to the library and use items from the library in your publication. To get started, you simply right-click an object, then click Add to Content Library. The Add Item to Content Library dialog box opens. Here you can assign a descriptive name to your content and place it in one of the three available categories: Business, Personal, or Favorites. To use an item from the Content Library, drag the item to the page or click the content arrow, then click Insert.

STEP-BY-STEP 2.5

1. On the menu bar, click **View**, and then click **Task Pane**.

2. On the current task pane, click the **Other Task Panes list arrow**, and then click **Content Library**.

3. In the middle pane of the brochure, right-click the **bottom text box** that contains the Telephone, Fax, and E-mail information, and then click **Add to Content Library**.

4. In the Add Item to Content Library dialog box, select the contents of the Title text box, and then type **Contact Information**.

5. Click the **Business check box**, and then compare your dialog box to Figure 2-9.

FIGURE 2-9
Add Item to Content Library dialog box

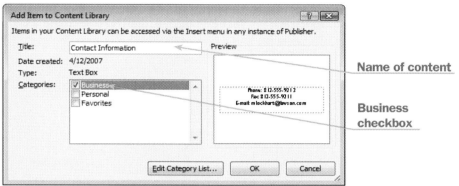

Name of content

Business checkbox

6. Click **OK**, then view the newly added content in the Content Library task pane.

7. In the Content Library task pane, click the **arrow** next to the Contact Information item, and then click **Insert**. A copy of the Contact Information item is added to the page.

8. On the menu bar, click **Edit**, then click **Undo Paste**.

9. Save your work, and leave the document open for the next Step-by-Step.

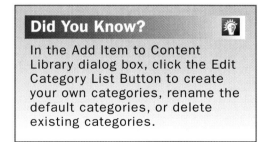

Did You Know?

In the Add Item to Content Library dialog box, click the Edit Category List Button to create your own categories, rename the default categories, or delete existing categories.

Inserting Text from a Word Document

When your publication calls for a large amount of text, it is sometimes easier to create it in Microsoft Word and then insert it into Publisher. Once in Publisher, the text can still be edited and formatted to your liking. It's easy to insert text from a Word document. Create a text box as a placeholder to put your text into. Click Insert on the menu bar, and then click Text File. Once you find the text file you want, click OK, and the text falls right into place. If there is too much text to fit the text box, you can resize the text box or link the overflow text to additional text boxes in the publication using the Create Text Box Link tool on the Standard toolbar.

S TEP-BY-STEP 2.6

1. In the middle pane, right-click the object directly below the group of rectangles and above the Lawson Electronics text box, and then click **Delete Object**.

2. On the Objects toolbar, click the **Text Box button**, then drag to create a text box in the middle pane that is approximately the same size of the text box shown in Figure 2-10.

FIGURE 2-10
Creating a text box in the middle pane

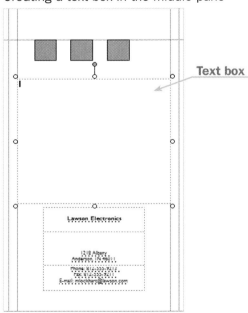

STEP-BY-STEP 2.6 Continued

3. On the menu bar, click **Insert**, and then click **Text File**.

4. Navigate to the location where you store your Data Files, click **New Classes.doc**, and then click **OK**.

5. Press **[F9]** to zoom in, then format the text using fonts and sizes that you like.

6. Click the **page 2 icon** on the page navigator, then delete the large text box that includes a list of prices in the middle pane.

7. On the Objects toolbar, click the **Text Box button**, and then create a text box in the middle pane that fills approximately the top half of the pane.

8. On the menu bar, click **Insert**, and then click **Text File**.

9. Navigate to the location where you store your Data Files, click **Prices.doc**, and then click **OK**.

10. Format the text using the fonts, sizes, and colors of your choice.

11. Save your work, and then compare your middle pane to Figure 2-11.

FIGURE 2-11
Inserting the price list

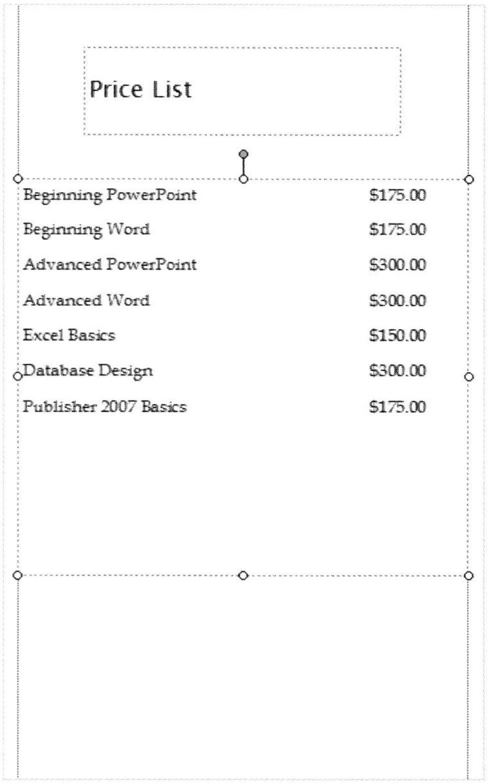

Price List	
Beginning PowerPoint	$175.00
Beginning Word	$175.00
Advanced PowerPoint	$300.00
Advanced Word	$300.00
Excel Basics	$150.00
Database Design	$300.00
Publisher 2007 Basics	$175.00

12. Keep the document open for the next Step-by-Step.

Using Find and Replace

One of the most powerful features in Publisher is the Find and Replace task pane. This feature searches your publication for a specific word or phrase and replaces it with a new one. Remember the example of creating camp brochures earlier in this lesson. Imagine that the name of the camp was changing from Camp Arrowhead to Campers Dream. Instead of searching each paragraph of your brochure for the camp name in order to change it, you could simply type Camp Arrowhead in the Find what text box and type Campers Dream in the Replace with text box of the Find and Replace task pane, as shown in Figure 2-12. You can find and replace a word or phrase one at a time using the Find Next and Replace buttons or replace them all at once using the Replace All button. Using Find and Replace not only saves you time but it also eliminates the possibility of misspellings and inconsistencies in your publication.

Did You Know?

In the Find and Replace task pane, you can check the Match case checkbox to make sure that Publisher only searches for uppercase or lowercase text. You can also click the Match whole word only checkbox when you are looking for text that may be found within larger segments. For example, if you need to search for every instance of "on", Publisher will find "on" in words such as upon, iron, son, and so on. To avoid this, click the Match whole word only checkbox, then click Find Next.

FIGURE 2-12
Find and Replace task pane

Find what text box
Replace with text box

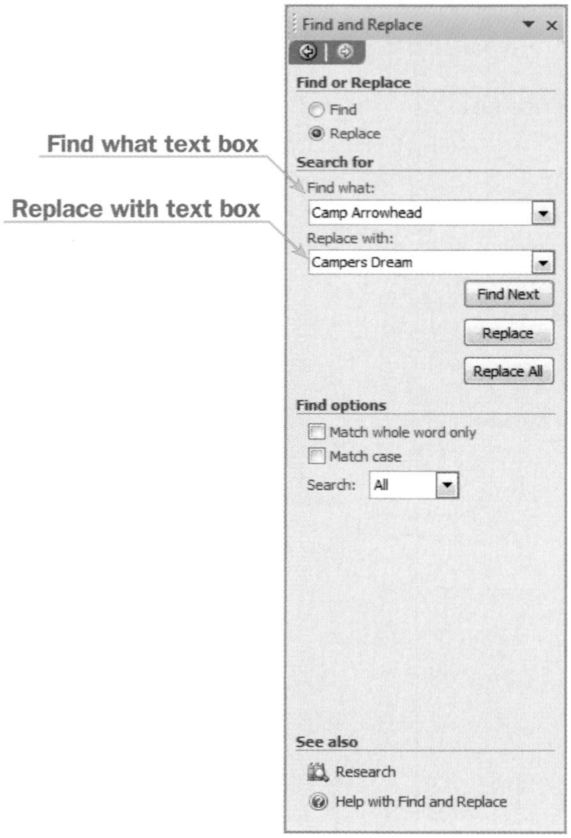

Checking the Spelling in a Publication

Spelling checkers have become standard features in most software applications. You are probably familiar with using spelling checkers in your work and rely on them each time you finish an assignment. However, you should not solely rely on spelling checkers alone to proof your work. Sometimes you may use the wrong word by mistake, such as "their" instead of "they're." Since "their" is spelled correctly, the spelling checker won't flag it as a problem. Therefore, make sure you always read your work carefully after you check the spelling to increase the likelihood of finding content errors. To check the spelling in Publisher documents, click Tools on the menu bar, point to Spelling, then click Spelling. For each misspelled word, Publisher offers a list of suggestions to replace the misspelled word. Since proper names are not stored in Publisher's electronic dictionary, they are often flagged as misspellings. In this case, simply click Ignore in the Check Spelling dialog box.

> **Did You Know?**
>
> The Spell checker will not flag proper names found in the business information sets as being misspelled.

S TEP-BY-STEP 2.7

1. Click the **Other Task Panes list arrow**, and then click **Find and Replace**.

2. On the Find and Replace task pane, click the **Replace option button**, if necessary.

3. On the Find and Replace task pane, in the Find what text box, type **Lawson Electronics**.

4. In the Replace with text box, type **Lawson Computers**, click **Replace All**, and then click **OK** in the dialog box stating that the search is complete.

5. Right-click the text box in the third pane, and then click **Delete Object**.

STEP-BY-STEP 2.7 Continued

6. Select the remaining information in the third pane, and then center it in the pane, as shown in Figure 2-13.

FIGURE 2-13
Completed page two of the publication

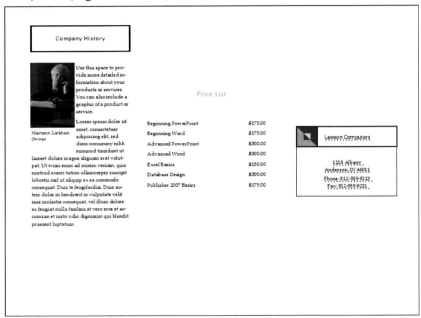

7. In the middle pane, drag the price list heading and price list down so that the two text boxes are more centered in the pane.

8. In the first pane, assign a fictitious title and caption for the photo, and then apply any formatting to any of the text boxes.

9. Hide the guides, save your work, and then compare your finished page two to Figure 2-13.

10. Print one copy, close the publication, and then exit Publisher.

SUMMARY

In this lesson, you learned:

- Layout guides include column, row, baseline, and margin guides. All guides help you to align objects on the publication page. You can change guide settings in the Layout Guides dialog box. Ruler guides are dragged from the horizontal or vertical rulers.

- Publisher templates come with text box placeholders that you can customize by entering your own text. You can add text directly into text boxes or panel headings. When you have entered text, it's best to zoom in on the text so that you can easily modify it.

- In addition to using the provided clip art in Publisher, you can insert your own photographs and illustrations using the Insert command. Pictures can be modified using the Picture toolbar.

- Publisher provides many ways to work with objects. The Arrange menu offers a large collection of commands for manipulating objects—all of which lend to creating a professional-looking page. You can align and distribute objects, layer objects, rotate and flip objects, and group them together. Grouping allows you to treat a group of objects as one object.

- The Content Library task pane allows you to store text and graphics so that they can be used over and over. You can add objects to the Content Library and assign them a descriptive name as well as categorize them. Then, when you need to use an item from the Content Library, you can drag it from the task pane onto the page.

- Inserting text from a Word document is easy and saves time. To insert text, you simply create a text box, then, using the Insert menu, click Text File and navigate to the location of the text file on your hard drive. Once the text is inserted, you can format it in Publisher.

- The Find and Replace task pane is used for replacing specific characters, words, or phrases with new ones. This is a powerful feature that ensures accuracy within a publication and saves time.

- Publisher offers a standard spelling checker that examines your publication for any misspelled words, offers a list of suggested replacements, and lets you fix a misspelling by choosing one of the suggestions. If a word is not misspelled, you can ignore the entry. In addition to using the spell checker, it is always best to proofread a document for content and accuracy.

VOCABULARY *Review*

Define the following terms:

Content Library	Master page	Page navigator
Layout guides	Object	Panel heading

REVIEW *Questions*

TRUE/FALSE

Circle T if the statement is true or F if the statement is false.

T   F   1. The Send Backward command sends the selected object to the backmost layer of the page.

T   F   2. The Content Library is actually a task pane.

T   F   3. If you right-click a picture, point to Change Picture, then click From File, the newly inserted picture is centered horizontally and vertically on the publication page.

T   F   4. You should not rely on the spelling checker alone to proof a document.

T   F   5. The page navigator is an example of a Publisher object.

WRITTEN QUESTIONS

Write a brief answer to each of the following questions.

1. Why is it sometimes important to group items?

2. Is it possible to create your own categories in the Content Library and, if so, how do you do this? Why would you want to create a category (give an example)?

3.   What types of objects can be added to the Content Library?

4.   How would go about arranging four pictures so that they were stacked in the following order from bottom to top: bed, blanket, pillow, stuffed bear?

5.   Which type of guide can be moved freely?

PROJECTS

PROJECT 2-1

1. Start Publisher, if necessary.

2. On the menu bar, click File, and then click Open.

3. Navigate to your Lesson 2 folder, click Ballet Classes, and then click Open.

4. Save the file as **Ballet Classes**, followed by your initials.

5. Right-click the cloud image, and then click Delete Object.

6. Change the color scheme to **Garnet**.

7. Display the Clip Art task pane, and then search for an image of a ballerina.

8. Place the ballerina image on top of the dark gray rectangle (which is on top of the larger pink rectangle), then resize it, if necessary, so that the dark gray rectangle frames the image.

9. Click the image, press and hold [Shift], and then click the dark gray rectangle.

10. On the menu bar, click Arrange, point to Align or Distribute, and then click Align Center.

11. On the menu bar, click Arrange again, point to Align or Distribute, and then click Align Middle.

12. On the menu bar, click Arrange, and then click Group.

13. Type an appropriate caption under your ballerina image.

14. Position the cursor after "9" in the Monday column of the April calendar, press [Enter], then type **Ballet class**.

15. Repeat Step 14 to place "Ballet class" on the next three Mondays (16th, 23rd, and 30th).

16. Save and print your document, and then close the document.

PROJECT 2-2

1. Start Publisher, if necessary.

2. On the menu bar, click File, and then click Open.

3. Navigate to your Lesson 2 folder, click Flyer, and then click Open.

4. Save the file as **Flyer**, followed by your initials.

5. Click the text box that is on top of the light blue rectangle.

6. On the menu bar, click Insert, click Text File, and then insert **Publisher.doc** from the drive and folder where you store your Data Files.

7. Press [F9] to zoom in on the text.

8. On the menu bar, click Tools, point to Spelling, and then click Spelling.

9. Change the first misspelled word "brochurs" to "brochures".

10. Change the second misspelled word "informasion" to "information".

11. Click Yes to search the rest of the document, and then click OK.

12. Click the Other Task Panes list arrow, then click Find and Replace.

13. In the Find and Replace task pane, click the Replace option button, if necessary, to display the Replace with text box.

14. In the Find and Replace task pane, type **requirements** in the Find what text box.

15. Type **prerequisites** in the Replace with text box, and then click Find Next.

16. In the Find and Replace task pane, click Replace, and then click OK in the dialog box stating that the search is complete.

17. Click the Other Task Panes list arrow, and then click Content Library.

18. Right-click the newly inserted text, and then click Add to Content Library.

19. In the Add Item to Content Library dialog box, change the title to Publisher description, click the Business check box, and then click OK.

20. Replace the cloud image with a photograph from the Clip Art task pane. (Try to find a picture of a student or students at a computer.) Type **school**, **computer**, or **learning** in the Search for text box of the Clip Art task pane.

21. Position the new image wherever you like on the page.

22. Format the Publisher class description text any way that you like, and then save your work.

23. Print one copy of the document, and then exit Publisher.

CRITICAL *Thinking*

 ACTIVITY 2-1

Start Publisher, click Blank Page Sizes under Popular Publication Types in the middle pane, click Letter (Portrait) 8.5 x 11", and then click Create. Save the publication as **Guides,** followed by your initials. Create three vertical ruler guides at the 3", 4", and 5" marks. Create four horizontal ruler guides at the 4", 5", 6", and 7" marks. On the menu bar, click Arrange, and then click Layout Guides. Change the four margin guides to .5" each. Create a text box in the top-left corner that snaps to the inside of the top and left margin guides. Type **Guide Template** in the text box, and then change the font size to 16 pt. Right-click the text box, and then click Format Text Box. Change the height of the text box to 1" and the width to 2.5". Save your work, and then exit Publisher.

 ACTIVITY 2-2

Open Layers from your Lesson 2 Data Files folder, and then save it as **Layers,** followed by your initials. Right-click each rectangle from smallest to largest, click Format AutoShape, and then change their widths and heights to 1" x 1", 2" x 2", 3" x 3", and 4" x 4". Use commands on the Arrange menu so that the four squares are stacked on top of each other, with the largest at the bottom of the stack and the smallest at the top. Place the star on top of the smallest square. Select all five objects, and then align their centers and their middles. Group the five objects together, and then add the grouped item to the Content Library. Name it **Star Logo** and assign the Personal category to it. Position the grouped item in the approximate center of the page, save your work, print one copy, and then exit Publisher.

ACTIVITY 2-3

Did you know that there are paper airplane templates in Publisher? Start Publisher, and from the Publication Types list, click Paper Folding Projects. Choose Airplanes and select the plane of your choice. Save the publication as **Airplane**, followed by your initials. Create and print the project, and then follow the directions to fold and shape the airplane. Exit Publisher.

CAPSTONE SIMULATION

GREEN WAY LAWN CARE SERVICE

Introduction

In this book, you have learned to use Word, Excel, Access, PowerPoint, Outlook, and Publisher. In this business simulation, you will apply the skills you learned in each Office 2007 program, following a realistic schedule for the month of May.

First, you will modify a PowerPoint presentation, and then you will use Word to create a form letter to advertise the services of Green Way Lawn Care Service. You will create a calendar using Outlook. You will use Access to maintain customer address and billing information and Excel to calculate and maintain earnings and expenses data. You will use Access and Word to integrate data to create an invoice that will be delivered to customers. Finally, you will use Publisher to create an advertising flyer.

BACKGROUND

You started Green Way Lawn Care Service last spring. Over the spring and summer you cared for ten lawns in the neighborhood using environmentally friendly methods and products. You offered the following services:

- Mowing

- Edging

- Hedge trimming

- Fertilization and weed control

Your current tasks are preparing for the upcoming spring season and contacting current customers. You are also thinking of ways to attract new customers.

As you increase the number of lawns you maintain, you will need some extra help to finish each job more quickly. Because you own two lawn mowers, an edger, a weed eater, and a hedge trimmer, you realize that the potential exists to have several machines operating at the same time. You also realize that if you hire additional workers, you could complete each job faster than you could by working alone.

MAY 1

You are thinking of asking two friends, Marcus and Julia, to help you with Green Way Lawn Care Service. You created a PowerPoint presentation to give them an overview of the business. You decide to make a few modifications to the presentation.

1. Start PowerPoint and open the **Presentation.pptx** file from the Data Files.

2. Save the file as **GWPresentation** followed by your initials.

3. Insert a new slide with the Title and Content layout after slide 6. Enter the title and text on the slide, as shown in Figure CS-1. (*Hint:* After typing the Advantages, press **Shift+Tab** to move the text back one level.)

FIGURE CS-1

Option #2

- I can ask Marcus and Julia to join the business
  - Advantages
    - Together we can complete jobs faster
    - We would share the profits and work
  - Disadvantages
    - Are there enough lawns to mow?
    - Who would keep accurate customer records?

4. Change the title of slide 8 to **Option #3**.

5. Change the title of slide 6 to **Option #1**.

6. Display the first slide, and then use Slide Show view to view the presentation.

7. Print the presentation as handouts with six slides per page.

8. Save and close the presentation, and then exit PowerPoint.

Marcus and Julia agree to join your business. The three of you will work together and split the profits. You will earn a greater share of the profit because everyone will be using your equipment. You brainstorm to solve the anticipated problems of the new business and decide that you can use Microsoft Office to create documents for advertising the business, create bills for customers, and calculate profits.

MAY 3

The three of you compile addresses for potential customers and estimated weekly fees into a text file named Potential Customers.txt. Names are available for some of the addresses because they were your customers from the previous year. Other contacts are from referrals, people whom you have met, and the addresses of your clients' neighbors. When names are unavailable, the word "Resident" is used. All addresses are in the city of Chesapeake, VA 23322. The weekly fee is an estimate based on the size of the potential customer's yard.

You will import this information into a database that will supply addresses and fees for an advertising letter and an invoice, should these contacts become customers.

1. Start Access and use the Blank Database template to create a new database named **Neighbors.accdb.** Close the Table1 table that opens.

2. On the Ribbon, on the External Data tab, in the Import group, click the **Text File** button. Import the **Potential Customers.txt** file into a new table in the current database. Note that the first row contains column headings, and you should not use the Import Spreadsheet Wizard to set the data types for fields. Be sure to choose the ID field as the table's primary key, and make sure that the table name is Potential Customers. Do not save the import steps.

3. Open the **Potential Customers** table in Design view. Use the information in Table CS-1 to set the field properties for the Potential Customers table.

TABLE CS-1

FIELD NAME	DATA TYPE	FIELD PROPERTIES
ID	Text	Field Size: 3 Primary key
Title	Text	Field Size: 10
Last Name	Text	Field Size: 20
First Name	Text	Field Size: 20
Address	Text	Field Size: 40
City, State, Zip	Text	Field Size: 50
Fee	Currency	

4. Save the table.

5. Switch to Datasheet view, and then resize all columns to best fit.

6. Save and close the table. Leave Access open.

MAY 4

Marcus wrote the form letter shown in Figure CS-2 to advertise the services available through Green Way Lawn Care Service. First, you will design a letterhead template. You will also personalize the letter by merging the names and addresses of potential customers in the Potential Customers table with the form letter.

FIGURE CS-2

> May 4, 2010
>
>
> Dear
>
> Green Way Lawn Care Service would like to add you to our growing list of clients who rely on us to provide environmentally friendly lawn services. We can create a custom plan to suit your individual needs, or you can sign up for our standard weekly package that includes:
>
> - Mowing
> - Edging and weeding
> - Trimming hedges
> - Fertilization and weed control
>
> The estimated fee for our weekly standard package is based on the size of your lawn, and you will be billed monthly. We guarantee all of our work, and can provide references in your neighborhood.
>
> If you would like to consider using our services, or if you have any questions, please contact us at 757-555-3894.
>
> Sincerely,
>
>
> *Student's name*   Marcus Reider   Julia Perez

1. Start Word.

2. Design a letterhead template for Green Way Lawn Care Service that you can use with the letter shown in Figure CS-2. Include the company's name and the following address and telephone number in the letterhead template:

   221 Kentwick Avenue
   Chesapeake, VA 23322
   757-555-3894

   Add an appropriate logo to the letterhead template using a clip art image or the drawing tools in Word. Save the document as a template in the Templates folder using the name **Letterhead Template.dotx**. Close the file.

3. Create a new Word document based on the Letterhead Template. Save the new document as **Form Letter.docx** followed by your initials. Type the form letter shown in Figure CS-2. (You will add the merge fields later.)

4. Save the document and leave it open.

MAY 5

You plan to visit potential customers you do not yet know. You will print the form letters for potential customers with the word "Resident" in the Title field of the Potential Customers table.

1. Save the Form Letter document as **Resident Letters.docx**.

2. Close the Resident Letters document, and then exit Word.

3. In Access, click the **External Data** tab, click the **More** button in the Export group, and then start the mail merge with Word. Link your data to the **Resident Letters** document.

4. Apply a filter to the recipient list to merge records that contain the word *Resident* in the Title field. (There should be four records.)

5. Add an address block to the letter, below the date.

6. On the line that includes the word *Dear*, type a space, and then insert the Title field. Type a comma after the merge field you just inserted.

7. Merge, print the first page, and save the **Resident Letters**.

8. Save and close the document. Leave Word open.

MAY 6

Anticipating a response to the letters, Julia suggests creating the billing information file for May.

You will create a workbook that you can use to calculate and track billing. Create columns to show the amount due for each customer for each week. For example, the Week 3 column will contain the amount due for the third week in May. The May Bill column will contain the total amount due for each customer for the month of May. The May Paid column will contain the amount paid for each customer for the month of May.

1. Start Excel.

2. Save the workbook as **Billing.xlsx** followed by your initials.

3. In cell A1, type **Week 3**.

4. In cell B1, type **Week 4**.

5. In cell C1, type **May Bill**.

6. In cell D1, type **May Paid**.

7. Enter a formula in cell C2 to calculate a total for the bills for the third and fourth weeks in May. (*Hint*: The total is the sum of the amounts in the Week 3 and Week 4 columns.)

8. Copy the formula you added in cell C2 down to cells C3 through C31.

9. Save and close the workbook. Leave Excel open.

MAY 7

The three of you decide to create a flyer that will advertise your services. Use Publisher to create the flyer using a template. You can use the logo and some of the information from the previously created form letter in your flyer. Save the publication as **GWFlyer.pub** followed by your initials. Put your name somewhere on the flyer. Print and close the publication.

MAY 8

The following people (mostly former customers) have notified you that they would like to hire Green Way Lawn Care Service:

Carver, Alton	Levine, Heather
Cash, H. J.	Phillipston, Paul
Guy, D. P.	Rigby, Eddy
Harper, G. H.	Strayer, L. T.

In addition, based on the flyer you created, the residents at 209 Kentwick (Mr. Tom Alfreds) and 213 Fordham (Ms. Lillian Spears) have decided to hire Green Way.

1. Switch to Access.

2. Open the **Potential Customers** table in Design view. Add two new fields to the table using the information provided in Table CS-3.

TABLE CS-3

FIELD NAME	DATA TYPE
Current Customer	Yes/No
Amount Due	Currency

3. The names of the residents at 209 Kentwick and 213 Fordham were unknown when the database was created. Edit the Title, Last Name, and First Name fields to update these records.

4. Add a check mark to the Cust field for people who have hired Green Way. You might want to use the Find command or sort the records alphabetically by last name to help you find customer records.

5. Leave the table and Access open.

MAY 9

In anticipation of billing new customers, Julia writes a draft of the invoice shown in Figure CS-3. She will create the invoice using Word.

FIGURE CS-3

June 2, 2010

Charges for the month of May

We have calculated your May invoice based on our contract amount of $ per week. The amount due for May is $.

Please make your check payable to "Green Way Lawn Care Service." Payment is due by June 30.

Thank you for your business.

1. Switch to Word.

2. Use the Letterhead Template file to create a new document. Save the document as **Invoice.docx** followed by your initials.

3. Create the invoice shown in Figure CS-3. You will insert the merge fields later.

4. Save and close the document. Leave Word open.

MAY 10

In response to your advertising, the following people have notified you that they would like to hire Green Way Lawn Care Service for the summer:

Mata, Ricardo	Goldberg, Richard
Novack, D. K.	Torres, Raul
Lake, Jasmine	Sanchez, Mercedes
Mueller, Anne	Aslam, Ritu
Keung, Yi	Johnson, Virginia
Robinson, T. R.	Roberts, Chad
Lauer, Corey	Page, Misha

Switch to your table in Access and edit the records for the new customers to show that they are current customers.

Leave the database open.

MAY 11

For planning purposes, you decide to create a calendar showing the May schedule.

1. Start Outlook and change to Calendar view.

2. Display the month of May 2010 in Month view.

3. Insert the information shown in Figure CS-4 into the calendar by clicking the day and entering each task as an all-day event.

FIGURE CS-4

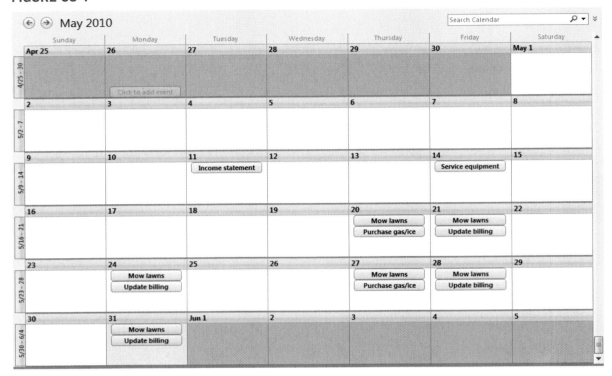

4. Print the monthly calendar. Be sure to choose the dates **5/1/10** to **5/31/10** in the print range.

5. Close Outlook.

MAY 12

Julia prepares a monthly income statement to report the profits of Green Way Lawn Care Service. Figure CS-5 shows a draft of the income statement for May. All three partners agree that this income statement will provide information to evaluate the progress of their business venture.

FIGURE CS-5

	A	B	C
1	**Green Way Lawn Care Service**		
2	Income Statement		
3	For the month ending May 31, 2010		
4			
5	REVENUES		
6			
7	Collected lawn care revenues		
8	Uncollected lawn care revenues		
9			
10	TOTAL REVENUES		
11			
12	EXPENSES		
13			
14	Gasoline		
15	Mower repair and maintenance		
16	Trailer repair and maintenance		
17	Drinks and ice		
18	Office supplies		
19	Miscellaneous		
20			
21	TOTAL EXPENSES		
22			
23	NET INCOME		

1. Switch to Excel. Create a new workbook and set up an income statement, as shown in Figure CS-5, for May.

2. Save the workbook as **Income Statement.xlsx** followed by your initials. You will add the values and formulas later. Leave the workbook open.

MAY 14

The following people have notified you that they want to hire Green Way Lawn Care Services for the summer:

Dye, Allen	Liu, Lin-Ji
Richardson, Delia	Gibb, H. R.

The residents at 208 Picnic (Ms. Regina Hinkle) and 213 Picnic (Ms. Jeanne Garland) have also decided to hire Green Way.

1. Switch to Access.

2. The title and names of the residents at 208 Picnic and 213 Picnic were unknown when the database was created. Edit these records to update the information.

3. Add a check mark to the Cust field for people who have hired Green Way.

4. Leave the table open.

MAY 16

You want to be sure your equipment is in good working order before the summer begins, so you take it to the local mower repair shop for servicing. The cost of servicing is $185.37. You also buy a new tire and brake light for your trailer. The total cost for these items is $99.75.

1. Switch to the **Income Statement** workbook in Excel. Record the expenses for mower repair and maintenance and for the trailer repair and maintenance in the appropriate cells.

2. Format the cells in column B using the Accounting format and two decimal places. Display a dollar sign as the symbol.

3. Save the workbook. Leave the workbook open.

MAY 21

Green Way serviced the lawns of the following customers:

Aslam	Mueller
Dye	Novack
Goldberg	Page
Johnson	Roberts
Keung	Robinson
Lake	Sanchez
Mata	Torres

1. Switch to the **Potential Customers** table in Access.

2. Use the AutoFilter option to create a filter to display current customers. (*Hint*: Current customers have a check mark—a "Yes" value—in the Cust field.)

3. Sort the records in ascending order using the Last Name field. Save the table.

4. Switch to Excel and open the **Billing.xlxs** workbook you created on May 6. Insert three new columns to the left of column A.

5. Switch to the **Potential Customers** table in Access. Move the Address and Fee columns in the datasheet so they are to the right of the Last Name field. Select the **Last Name, Address, and Fee** columns, and then copy the data in these three columns to the Clipboard.

6. Click **cell A1** in the workbook, and then click the **Paste** button in the Clipboard group on the Home tab.

7. Adjust the row height and column widths in the Billing workbook to display the data.

8. In the Billing workbook, format the cells in columns D, E, F, and G with the Accounting format, two decimal places, and the dollar sign as the symbol.

9. Enter the amount due (listed in the Fee column) in the Week 3 column for the customers whose lawns have been serviced.

10. Change the column headings in row 1 to bold and centered. Change the fill color to no fill. Delete the borders from all cells. Resize all columns in the worksheet to best fit.

11. Save the workbook.

12. Switch to the **Income Statement** workbook and enter the following expenses: **$17.31** for gasoline and **$13.97** for drinks and ice.

13. Save the workbook and leave it open.

MAY 24

Green Way has serviced the lawns of the following customers:

Alfreds	Lauer
Carver	Levine
Cash	Liu
Garland	Phillipston
Gibb	Richardson
Guy	Rigby
Harper	Spears
Hinkle	Strayer

1. Switch to the **Billing** workbook and enter the amount due for each customer in the Week 3 column.

2. Save the workbook and leave it open.

3. Switch to the **Income Statement** workbook and add the following expenses to the worksheet: **$7.39** for gasoline and **$6.56** for drinks and ice. (*Hint*: Replace the value $17.31 in the Gasoline row with the formula =17.31+7.39.)

4. Save the workbook and leave it open.

MAY 28

Green Way has serviced the lawns of the following customers:

Aslam	Mata
Cash	Mueller
Dye	Novack
Garland	Page
Goldberg	Richardson
Hinkle	Sanchez
Johnson	Spears
Lake	Torres

1. Switch to the **Billing** workbook and enter the amount due for each customer in the Week 4 column.

2. Save the workbook and leave it open.

3. Switch to the **Income Statement** workbook and modify formulas as necessary to add the following additional expenses to the worksheet: **$10.18** for gasoline and **$6.78** for drinks and ice.

4. Save the workbook and leave it open.

MAY 30

During May, Green Way spent $32.79 on paper and $21.56 on miscellaneous expenses.

1. Record the amounts for office supplies and miscellaneous expenses in the Income Statement workbook in the appropriate cells.

2. Save the workbook and leave it open.

MAY 31

Green Way has serviced the lawns of the following customers:

Alfreds	Levine
Carver	Liu
Gibb	Phillipston
Guy	Rigby
Harper	Roberts
Keung	Robinson
Lauer	Strayer

1. Switch to the **Billing** workbook and enter the amount due for each customer in the Week 4 column. Save the workbook and leave it open.

2. Switch to the **Income Statement** workbook and add the following additional expenses to the worksheet: **$19.76** for gasoline and **$9.80** for drinks and ice.

3. Save the workbook and leave it open.

JUNE 2

Julia is preparing the monthly bills for May. She will print the bills and distribute them in person.

1. Switch to Access and the **Potential Customers** datasheet.

2. With the filter still applied to display current customers, sort the records in alphabetical order by last name, if necessary.

3. Switch to the **Billing** workbook. Copy the amounts in the May Bill column (cells F2 through F31) to the Clipboard.

4. Switch to Access. Click the **Amount Due** field selector in the Potential Customers table to select the entire field, and then press **[Ctrl][V]**. When the message box opens and asks if you want to paste the records, click **Yes**.

5. In Word, open the **Invoice** document you created on May 9, and then save it as **SNInvoice.docx** followed by your initials. Close the document and leave Word open.

6. Switch to the **Potential Customers** datasheet in Access, and then save and close the table. Use the Microsoft Word Mail Merge Wizard to merge the SNInvoice document with data from the Potential Customers table. Edit the recipient list to print the records for the customers with the last names Spears and Novack.

7. Use the Insert Merge Field button in the Write & Insert Fields group on the Mailings tab to insert the merge fields shown in Figure CS-6 in the document. Make sure to insert the proper spacing between merge fields.

FIGURE CS-6

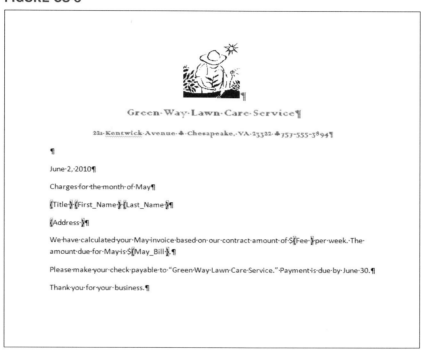

8. Merge the document.

9. Save and close the document, and then exit Word.

JUNE 3

When Julia delivers the invoices, the following customers are at home and promptly pay the amount due in full:

Alfreds	Lauer
Aslam	Levine
Cash	Mata
Dye	Novack
Garland	Page
Goldberg	Rigby
Guy	Roberts
Hinkle	Robinson
Lake	Sanchez

Switch to the Billing workbook and record the amount collected in the May Paid column. Save the workbook and leave it open.

JUNE 8

The following customers sent payments to Green Way Lawn Care Service to pay the amount due in full:

Gibb	Phillipston
Harper	Spears
Johnson	Strayer
Liu	

1. Record the collection of these amounts in the May Paid column of the Billing workbook.

2. Save the workbook and leave it open.

JUNE 9

Julia wonders about the unpaid bills. She wants to calculate the amounts billed to the customers and the amounts paid.

1. In cell A33 of the Billing workbook, type **TOTALS** and change the text to bold.

2. Enter a formula in cell F33 to calculate a total for the May Bill column. Make sure that the cell's format uses the Accounting format, two decimal places, and the dollar sign as the symbol.

3. Copy the formula in cell F33 to cell G33.

4. In cell A34, type **Uncollected**.

5. In cell B34, enter a formula to subtract the total in the May Paid column from the total in the May Bill column. Make sure that the cell's format uses the Accounting format, two decimal places, and the dollar sign as the symbol.

6. Sort the records in the May Bill column so the records for the five customers with unpaid invoices appear at the bottom of the list.

7. In cell A35, type your first and last names, and then resize the column to best fit. Save, print, and close the workbook.

JUNE 10

Green Way Lawn Care Service has now compiled the data for the first month of operations. The partners want to know if they made a profit in May. They want copies of the May income statement to assess their progress.

1. Switch to the **Income Statement** workbook. This file already contains updated expenses for May.

2. In cell B7, type **1856** and in cell B8, type **332**.

3. In cell B10, enter a formula to calculate the total revenues (collected revenues plus uncollected revenues).

4. In cell B21, enter a formula to calculate the total amount for all expenses.

5. In cell B23, enter a formula to calculate the net income for the month (total revenues minus total expenses).

6. Make sure that column B uses the Accounting format, two decimal places, and the dollar sign as the symbol.

7. Save, print, and close the workbook. Close Excel.

8. Close all other Office programs.

APPENDIX A

COMPUTER CONCEPTS

What Is a Computer?

A computer is a machine that is used to store, retrieve, and manipulate data. A computer takes input, uses stored instructions to process and store that data, and then produces output. You enter the data into the computer through a variety of input devices, such as a keyboard or mouse. The processor processes the data to produce information. Information is output or presented in many ways such as an image on a screen or a monitor; printed pages from a printer, or sound through speakers. Computer software is the stored instructions or programming that runs the computer. Memory inside the computer stores the programs or instructions that run the computer as well as the data and information. Various storage devices are used to transfer or safely store the data and information.

A computer system is made up of components that include the computer, input, and output devices. Computer systems come in many shapes, sizes, and configurations. The computer you use at home or in school is often called a personal computer. See Figure A-1. Desktop computers often have a 'computer case' or a system unit, which contains processing devices, memory, and some storage devices.

FIGURE A-1
Example of a computer system

Input devices such as the mouse and keyboard are attached to the system unit by cables or wires. Output devices, such as the monitor, speakers, and printer are also attached to the system unit by cables or wires. Wireless technology makes it possible to eliminate wires and use the airwaves to connect devices. Laptop or notebook computers have all the essential parts in one unit.

The operating system is the main software or system software that runs a computer and often defines the type of computer. There are two main types or platforms for personal computers. The Macintosh computer, or Mac, is produced by Apple Computer, Inc. and runs the Mac operating system. The PC is a Windows-based computer produced by many different companies, but which runs the Microsoft Windows operating system.

Hardware

The physical components, devices, or parts of the computer are called hardware. The main parts are the central processing unit (CPU), the monitor, the keyboard, and the mouse. Peripherals are additional components, such as printers and scanners. Peripherals are not essential to the computer but enhance the computer.

Input Devices

There are many different types of input devices. You enter information into a computer by typing on a keyboard or by pointing, clicking, or dragging a mouse. A mouse is a hand-held device used to move a pointer on the computer screen. Similar to a mouse, a trackball has a roller ball that turns to control a pointer on the screen. Digital tracking devices, such as a touchpad, are an alternative to the trackball or mouse. Situated on the keyboard of a laptop computer, they allow you to simply move and tap your finger on a small electronic pad to control the pointer on the screen.

Tablet PCs allow you to input data by writing directly on the computer screen. Handwriting recognition technology converts handwritten writing to text. Many computers have a microphone or other sound input device which accepts speech or sounds as input and converts the speech to text or data. For example, when you telephone a company or bank for help and have the option to say your requests or account number, this is speech recognition technology at work!

Other input devices include scanners and bar code readers. You can use a scanner to convert text or graphics from a printed page into code that a computer can process. You have probably seen bar code readers being used in stores. These are used to read bar codes, such as the UPC (universal product code), to track merchandise or other inventory in a store. See Figure A-2.

FIGURE A-2
Examples of input devices

Processing Devices

Processing devices are mounted inside the system unit of the computer. The **central processing unit (CPU)** is a silicon chip that processes data and carries out instructions given to the computer. The **data bus** includes the wiring and pathways by which the CPU communicates with the peripherals and components of the computer. The CPU is stored on the motherboard of the computer. The **motherboard** is where the computer memory and other vital electronic parts are stored. See Figure A-3.

FIGURE A-3
A motherboard

Storage Devices

A storage device is used to store data on a computer. Storage devices are both input and output devices. Most computers have more than one type of storage device. The main storage device for a computer is the hard disk drive that is usually inside the system unit. See Figure A-4. It is fixed storage, not removable from the computer. External and removable hard disk drives are available that can plug into the USB port on the system unit. The hard disk drive reads and writes data to and from a round magnetic platter, or disk. The data is digitally encoded on the disk as a series of 1s and 0s. A byte stands for a single character of data. At the time this book was written, typical hard drives for a computer system that you might buy for your personal home use range from 80 gigabytes (GB) to 250 gigabytes. The prefix "giga" means a billion. A gigabyte (GB or Gbyte) is approximately one billion bytes.

FIGURE A-4
A hard disk drive

The floppy disk drive is an older technology that is no longer available on new computers. Some older computers still have a floppy disk drive which is mounted in the system unit with access to the outside. A floppy disk is the medium that stores the data. You put the floppy disk into the floppy disk drive so the computer can read and write the data. The floppy disk's main advantage was portability. You can store data on a floppy disk and transport it for use on another computer. A floppy disk can hold up to 1.4MB (megabytes) of information. A Zip disk is similar to a floppy disk. A Zip disk is also a portable disk contained in a plastic sleeve, but it will hold 100MB or 250MB of information. A special disk drive called a Zip drive is required to read and write data to a Zip disk.

Another storage device is the CD drive or DVD drive. These drives are typically mounted inside the system unit, although external versions of these devices are also available. Most new computers are equipped with CD/DVD burners. That means they have read and write capabilities. You use a CD/DVD drive to read and write CDs and DVDs. A CD is a compact disc, which is a form of optical storage. Compact discs can store 650MB. These discs have a great advantage over other forms of removable storage as they can hold vast quantities of information—the entire contents of a small library, for instance. They are also fairly durable. Another advantage of CDs is their ability to hold graphic information, including moving pictures, with the highest quality stereo sound. A DVD is also an optical disc that looks like a CD. It is a high-capacity storage device that can contain up to 4.7GB of data, which is a seven-fold increase over a CD. There are two variations of DVDs that offer even more storage—a 2-layer version with 9.4GB capacity and double-sided discs with 17GB capacity. Newer versions store even more data. These highest-capacity discs are designed to store large databases. A DVD holds 133 minutes of data on each side, which means that two two-hour full-length feature movies can be stored on one disc. Information is encoded on the disk by a laser and read by a CD/DVD drive in the computer.

Solid state storage is another popular storage technology. A USB flash drive is a very portable small store device that works both as a drive and medium. It plugs directly into a USB port on the computer system unit. You read and write data to the flash drive. Solid state card readers are devices that can read solid state cards. Solid state storage is often used in cameras.

Magnetic tape is a medium most commonly used for backing up a computer system, which means making a copy of files from a hard drive. Although it is relatively rare for a data on a hard drive to be completely lost in a crash (that is, for the data or pointers to the data to be partially or totally destroyed), it can and does happen. Therefore, most businesses and some individuals routinely back up files on tape. If you have a small hard drive, you can use DVDs or CD-ROMs to back up your system. Figure A-5 shows removable storage media and devices.

FIGURE A-5
Removable storage

Output Devices

The monitor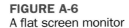 on which you view your computer work is an output device. It provides a visual representation of the information stored in or produced by your computer. The typical monitor for today's system is a flat-screen monitor similar to a television. See Figure A-6. It provides a very sharp picture because of the large number of tiny dots, called pixels, which make up the display as well as its ability to present the full spectrum of colors. Resolution, the term that tells you how clear an image will be on the screen. is measured in pixels. A typical resolution is 1024 × 768. A high-quality monitor may have a resolution of 1680 × 1050. Monitors come in different sizes. The size of a monitor is determined by measuring the diagonal of the screen. Laptops have smaller monitors than desktop computers. A laptop monitor may be 13", 15", or 17". Desktop monitors can be as large as 19"- 24" or even larger.

FIGURE A-6
A flat screen monitor

Printers are a type of output device. They let you produce a paper printout of information contained in the computer. Today, most printers use either inkjet or laser technology to produce high-quality print. Like a copy machine, a laser printer uses heat to fuse a powdery substance called toner to the page. Ink-jet printers use a spray of ink to print. Laser printers give the sharpest image and often print more pages per minute (ppm) than ink jet printers. Ink-jet printers provide nearly as sharp an image, but the wet printouts can smear when they first are printed. Most color printers, or photo printers for printing photographs, are ink jet printers. Color laser printers are more costly. These printers allow you to print information in a full array of colors, just as you see it on your monitor. See Figure A-7.

FIGURE A-7
Typical printers

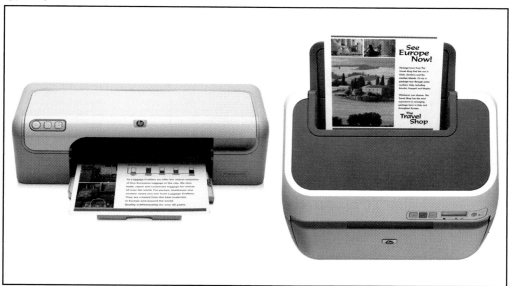

Laptop or Notebook Computer

A laptop computer, also called a notebook computer, is a small folding computer that can literally fit in a person's lap or in a backpack. Within the fold-up case of a laptop is the CPU, data bus, monitor (built into the lid), hard drive (sometimes removable), 3.5-inch floppy drive, CD/DVD drive, and trackball or digital tracking device. The advantage of the laptop is its portability—you can work anywhere because you can use power either from an outlet or from the computer's internal, rechargeable batteries. Almost all laptops have wireless Internet access built into the system. The drawbacks are the smaller keyboard, smaller monitor, smaller capacity, and higher price, though newer laptops offer full-sized keyboards and higher quality monitors. As technology allows, storage capacity on smaller devices is making it possible to offer laptops with as much power and storage as a full-sized computer. See Figure A-8.

FIGURE A-8
A laptop or notebook computer

Personal Digital Assistants (PDA)

A Personal Digital Assistant is a pocket-sized electronic organizer that helps you to manage addresses, appointments, expenses, tasks, and memos. The common input devices for PDAs include touch-senstive screens that accept input through a stylus pen or small keyboards that are either built in to the PDA or available as software on the screen. PDA data and information can be shared with a Windows-based or Macintosh computer through a process called synchronization. By placing your PDA in a cradle or through a USB port attached to your computer, you can transfer data from your PDA's calendar, address book, or memo program into your computer's information manager program and vice versa. The information is updated on both sides, making your PDA a portable extension of your computer. PDAs are becoming more and more functional. Newer PDAs include cameras and have cell phone capability. Depending on the amount of memory in the specific PDA, they can include many of the same programs found on a personal computer.

FIGURE A-9
A Personal Digital Assistant

How Computers Work

All of the input, processing, storage, and output devices function together to make the manipulation, storage, and distribution of data and information possible.

Data and Information Management

Data is information entered into and manipulated or processed within a computer. Processing includes computation, such as adding, subtracting, multiplying, and dividing; analysis planning, such as sorting data; and reporting, such as presenting data for others in a chart or graph.

Memory

Computers have two types of memory—RAM and ROM. RAM, or random access memory, is the silicon chips in the system unit that temporarily store information when the computer is turned on. RAM is what keeps the software programs up and running and provides visuals that appear on your screen. You work with data in RAM up until you save it to a storage media device such as a hard disk, CD, DVD, or solid state storage such as flash drive.

Computers now have sophisticated application programs that tend to include a lot of graphics and data. In order to run these programs, computers require a lot of memory. Therefore, computers have at least 512MB of RAM to start. Many computer systems are expandable and you can add on RAM after you buy the computer. The more RAM available for the programs, the faster and more efficiently the machine will be able to operate. RAM chips are shown in Figure A-10.

FIGURE A-10
RAM chips

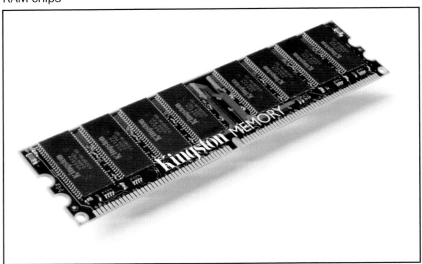

ROM, or read-only memory, is the memory that stays in the computer when it is turned off. It is ROM that stores the programs that run the computer as it starts or "boots up." ROM holds the instructions that tell the computer how to begin to load its operating system software programs.

Speed

The speed of a computer is measured by how fast the computer processes each instruction. There are several factors that affect the performance of a computer: the speed of the processor, or the clock speed, the front side bus speed—the speed of the bus that connects the processor to main memory—the speed in which data is written and retrieved from the hard drive or other storage media, and the speed of the graphics card if you are working on programs that use a lot of graphic images. These all factor into a computer's performance.

The speed of a computer is measured in megahertz (MHz) and gigahertz (GHz)

Processors are sold now by name, and each brand or series has its own specifications. Processor manufacturers include Intel, Motorola, and AMD. When you research processors and computers you might see names such as Intel® Core™2 Extreme Processor QX6800, Intel® Core™2 Duo Processor E6700, Pentium® 4 Processor Extreme Edition supporting Hyper-Threading Technology for PCs, or AMD Mobile Athelon or Turion 64 X2. For Macs you might see PowerPC G5 or Xeon 5300.

Networks

Computers have expanded the world of communications. A **network** is defined as two or more computers connected to share data. **LANs (local area networks)** connect computers within a small area such as a home, office, school, or building. Networks can be wired or wireless. The **Internet** is the largest network in the world connecting millions of computers across the globe. Using the Internet, people can communicate across the world instantly.

Networks require various communication devices and software. **Modems** allow computers to communicate with each other by telephone lines. Modem is an acronym that stands for "MOdulator/DEModulator." Modems convert data in bytes to sound media in order to send data over the phone lines and then convert it back to bytes after receiving data. Modems operate at various rates or speeds. **Network cards** in the system unit allow computers to access networks. A **router** is an electronic device that joins two or more networks. For example, a home network can use a router and a modem to connect the home's LAN to the Internet. A **server** is the computer hardware and software that "serves" the computers on a network. Network technology is sometimes called "client-server." A personal computer that requests data from a server is referred to as a **client**. The computer that stores the data is the **server**. On the Internet, the computer that stores the Web pages is the **Web server**. Figure A-11 shows a network diagram.

FIGURE A-11
Diagram of a network

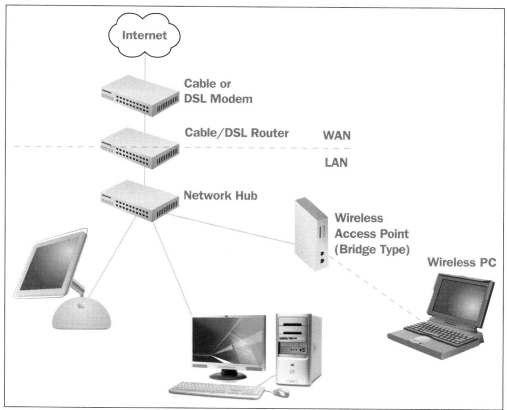

Networks have certain advantages over stand-alone computers: they allow communication among the computers; they allow smaller capacity computers to access the larger capacity of the server computers on the network; they allow several computers to share peripherals, such as one printer; and they can make it possible for all computers on the network to have access to the Internet.

Connect to the Internet

To connect to the Internet you need to subscribe to an Internet Service Provider (ISP). There are several technologies available. Connection speeds are measured in bits per second. Upload speeds are slower than download speeds. Dial-up is the oldest, and the slowest, Internet access technology and offered by local telephone companies. To get access to the Internet, your computer has to dial out through a phone line. Many people have moved to always-on connection technologies. The computer is always connected to the Internet if you turn the computer on, so you don't have to dial out. These always-on faster technologies, known as Digital Subscriber Line (DSL), include cable connections, satellites, and fiber optic. They are offered by telephone companies, cable television companies, and satellite service providers. It can be noted that satellite Internet access is the most expensive, dialup is the cheapest. Table A-1 shows a brief comparison of these technologies.

TABLE A-1
Comparing Internet access options

FEATURE	DSL INTERNET	CABLE INTERNET	SATELLITE INTERNET	FIBER OPTIC (FIOS)
Max. High Speed	Up to 1.5 Mbps	Up to 3 Mbps	Up to 1 Mbps	Up to 20 Mbps
Access is through	Existing phone line	Existing TV cable	Satellite dish	Fiber optic phone lines
Availability	Generally available in populated areas	Might not be available in rural areas	Available in all areas; note that satellite service is sensitive to weather conditions	Might not be available in all areas as fiber optic lines are just being installed in many areas

Software

A program is a set of instructions to the computer. Software is the collection of programs and other data input that tells the computer how to operate its devices, how to manipulate, store, and output information, and how to accept the input you give it. Software fits into two basic categories: systems software and applications software. A third category, network software, is really a type of application.

Systems Software

Systems software refers to the operating system (OS) of the computer. The OS is a group of programs that is automatically copied in from the time the computer is turned on until the computer is turned off. Operating systems serve two functions: they control data flow among computer parts, and they provide the platform on which application and network software work—in effect, they allow the "space" for software and translate its commands to the computer. The most popular operating systems in use today are the Macintosh operating system, MAC OS X and several different versions of Microsoft Windows, such as Windows 2000, Windows XP, or Windows Vista. See Figure A-12 and Figure A-13.

FIGURE A-12
The Windows Vista operating system

FIGURE A-13
The Mac OS X operating system

Since its introduction in the mid-1970s, Macintosh has used its own operating system, a graphical user interface (GUI) system that has evolved over the years. The OS is designed so users "click" with a mouse on pictures, called icons, or on text to give commands to the system. Data is available to you in the WYSIWYG (what-you-see-is-what-you-get) format; that is, you can see on-screen what a document will look like when it is printed. Graphics and other kinds of data, such as spreadsheets, can be placed into text documents. However, GUIs take a great deal of RAM to keep all of the graphics and programs operating.

The original OS for IBM and IBM-compatible computers (machines made by other companies that operate similarly) was DOS (disk operating system). It did not have a graphical interface. The GUI system, Windows™, was developed to make using the IBM/IBM-compatible computer more "friendly." Today's Windows applications are the logical evolution of GUI for

IBM and IBM-compatible machines. Windows is a point-and-click system that automatically configures hardware to work together. You should note, however, that with all of its abilities comes the need for more RAM, or a system running Windows will operate slowly.

Applications Software

When you use a computer program to perform a data manipulation or processing task, you are using applications software. Word processors, databases, spreadsheets, graphics programs, desktop publishers, fax systems, and Internet browsers are all applications software.

Network Software

Novell™ and Windows NT are two kinds of network software. A traditional network is a group of computers that are hardwired (connected together with cables) to communicate and operate together. Today, some computer networks use RF (radio frequency) wireless technology to communicate with each other. This is called a wireless network, because you do not need to physically hook the network together with cables. In a typical network, one computer acts as the server, which controls the flow of data among the other computers, called nodes, or clients on the network. Network software manages this flow of information.

History of the Computer

Though various types of calculating machines were developed in the nineteenth century, the history of the modern computer begins about the middle of the last century. The strides made in developing today's personal computer have been truly astounding.

Early Development

The ENIAC, or Electronic Numerical Integrator and Computer, (see Figure A-14) was designed for military use in calculating ballistic trajectories and was the first electronic, digital computer to be developed in the United States. For its day, 1946, it was quite a marvel because it was able to accomplish a task in 20 seconds that normally would took a human three days to complete. However, it was an enormous machine that weighed more than 20 tons and contained thousands of vacuum tubes, which often failed. The tasks that it could accomplish were limited, as well.

FIGURE A-14
The ENIAC

From this awkward beginning, however, the seeds of an information revolution grew. Significant dates in the history of computer development are listed in Table A-2.

TABLE A-2
Milestones in the development of computers

YEAR	DEVELOPMENT
1948	First electronically stored program
1951	First junction transistor
1953	Replacement of tubes with magnetic cores
1957	First high-level computer language
1961	First integrated circuit
1965	First minicomputer
1971	Invention of the microprocessor (the silicon chip) and floppy disk
1974	First personal computer (made possible by the microprocessor)

The invention of the silicon chip in 1971 and the release of the first personal computer in 1974 launched the fast-paced information revolution in which we now all live and participate.

The Personal Computer

The PC, or personal computer, was mass marketed by Apple beginning in 1977, and by IBM in 1981. It is this desktop device with which people are so familiar and which, today, contains much more power and ability than did the original computer that took up an entire room. The PC is a small computer (desktop size or less) that uses a microprocessor to manipulate data. PCs may stand alone, be linked together in a network, or be attached to a large mainframe computer. See Figure A-15.

FIGURE A-15
Early IBM PC

Computer Utilities and System Maintenance

Computer operating systems let you run certain utilities and perform system maintenance to keep your computer running well. When you add hardware or software, you make changes in the way the system operates. With Plug and Play, most configuration changes are done automatically. The drivers, software that runs the peripherals, are installed automatically when your computer identifies the new hardware. When you install new software, many changes are made to the system automatically that determine how the software starts and runs.

In addition, you might want to customize the way the new software or hardware works with your system. You use utility software to make changes to the way hardware and software works. For example, you can change the speed at which your mouse clicks, how quickly or slowly keys repeat on the keyboard, and the resolution of the screen display.

Virus and Spyware Protection

Certain maintenance should be performed regularly on computers. Viruses are software programs that can damage the programs on your computer causing the computer to either stop working or run slowly. These programs are created by people, called hackers, who send the programs out solely to do harm to computers. Viruses are loaded onto your computer without your knowledge and run against your wishes. Spyware is also a form of a program that can harm your computer. There are utilities and programs that protect your computer from spyware and viruses.

You should install and update your antivirus and spyware protection software regularly, and scan all new disks and any incoming information from online sources for viruses. Some systems do this automatically; others require you to install software to do it.

Disk Maintenance

From time to time, you should run a program that scans or checks the hard drive to see that there are not bad sectors (areas) and look for corrupted files. Optimizing or defragmenting the hard disk is another way to keep your computer running at its best. Scanning and checking programs often offers the option of "fixing" the bad areas or problems, although you should be aware that this could result in data loss.

Society and Computers

The electronic information era has had global effects and influenced global change in all areas of people's lives. With the changes of this era have come many new questions and responsibilities. There are issues of ethics, security, and privacy.

Ethics

When you access information—whether online, in the workplace, or via purchased software—you have a responsibility to respect the rights of the person or people who created that information. Digital information, text, images, and sound is very easy to copy and share, however, that does not make it right to do so. You have to treat electronic information with respect. Often images, text, and sound are copyrighted. Copyright is the legal method for protecting the intellectual property of the author—the same way as you would a book, article or painting. For instance, you must give credit when you copy information from the Web or another person's document.

If you come across another person's personal information, you must treat it with respect. Do not share personal information unless you have that person's permission. For example, if you happen to pass a computer where a person left personal banking information software open on the computer, or a personal calendar available, you should not share that information. If e-mail comes to you erroneously, you should delete it before reading it.

When you use equipment that belongs to your school, a company for which you work, or others, here are some rules you should follow:

1. Do not damage computer hardware.

2. Do not add or remove equipment without permission.

3. Do not use an access code or equipment without permission.

4. Do not read others' e-mail.

5. Do not alter data belonging to someone else without permission.

6. Do not use the computer for play during work hours or use it for personal profit.

7. Do not access the Internet for nonbusiness related activities use during work hours.

8. Do not install or uninstall software without permission.

9. Do not make unauthorized copies of data or software or copy company files or procedures for personal use.

10. Do not copy software programs to use at home or at another site in the company without permission.

Security and Privacy

The Internet provides access to business and life-enhancing resources, such as distance learning, remote medical diagnostics, and the ability to work from home more effectively. Businesses, colleges and universities, and governments throughout the world depend on the Internet every day to get work done. Disruptions in the Internet can create havoc and dramatically decrease productivity.

With more and more financial transactions taking place online, identify theft is a growing problem, proving a person's online identity relies heavily upon their usernames and passwords. If you do online banking, there are several levels of security that you must pass through, verifying that you are who you claim to be, before gaining access to your accounts. If you divulge your usernames and passwords, someone can easily access your accounts online with devastating effects to your credit rating and to your accounts.

Phishing is a criminal activity that is used by people to fraudulently obtain your personal information, such as usernames, passwords, credit card details, and your social security information. Your social security number should never be given out online. Phishers send e-mails that look legitimate, but in fact are not. Phishing e-mails will often include fake information saying that your account needs your immediate attention because of unusual or suspected fraudulent activity. You are asked to click a link in the e-mail to access a Web site where you are then instructed to enter personal information. See Figure A-16. Phishing e-mail might also come with a promise of winning some money or gifts. When you get mail from people you don't know, the rules to remember are "you never get something for nothing, and if it looks too good to be true, it's most likely not true."

FIGURE A-16a
Fake e-mails for phishing

Message header doesn't include a recipient

A company like PayPal would not use a yahoo.com e-mail address; the sender is NOT PayPal

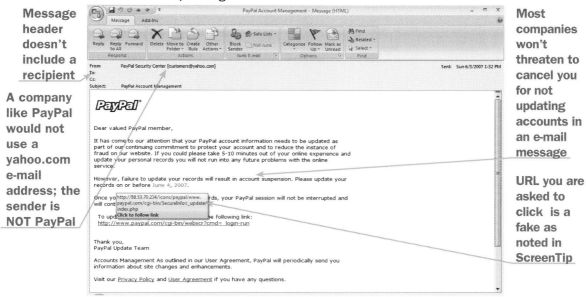

Most companies won't threaten to cancel you for not updating accounts in an e-mail message

URL you are asked to click is a fake as noted in ScreenTip

FIGURE A-16b
Fake e-mails for phishing

No To: address and From is NOT a ncua.gov address

Never click a link and then type your SSN

Never type or tell your credit/debit card PIN number to anyone

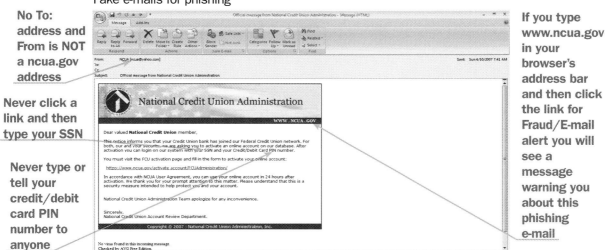

If you type www.ncua.gov in your browser's address bar and then click the link for Fraud/E-mail alert you will see a message warning you about this phishing e-mail

Whatever the ruse, when you click the link provided in the phishing e-mail, your browser will open a Web site that looks real, perhaps like your bank's site, eBay, or PayPal. But, in fact, this is a fake site set up to get you to give up your personal information. Phishing sites are growing. You should never click a link provided in an e-mail to get to sites such as your bank, eBay, or PayPal. Your bank or any other legitimate Web site will never ask you to type personal information on a page linked from an e-mail message. Always type the Web page address directly in the browser. Banks and Web sites have been trying to stop phishing sites through technology. Other attempts to reduce the growing number of reported phishing incidents include legislation and simply educating users about the practice.

Just as you would not open someone else's mail, you must respect the privacy of e-mail sent to others. When interacting with others online, you must keep confidential information confidential. Do not endanger your privacy, safety, or financial security by giving out personal information to someone you do not know.

Career Opportunities

In one way or another, all of our careers involve the computer. Whether you are a grocery store clerk using a scanner to read the prices, a busy executive writing a report that includes charts, graphics, and detailed analysis on a laptop on an airplane, or a programmer writing new software—almost everyone uses computers in their jobs. Most scientific research is done using computers.

There are specific careers available if you want to work with computers in the computer industry. Schools offer degrees in computer programming, computer repair, computer engineering, and software design. The most popular jobs are systems analysts, computer operators, and programmers. Analysts figure out ways to make computers work (or work better) for a particular business or type of business. Computer operators use the programs and devices to conduct business with computers. Programmers write the software for applications or new systems. There are degrees and jobs for people who want to create and maintain Web sites. Working for a company maintaining their Web site can be a very exciting career.

There are courses of study in using CAD (computer-aided design) and CAM (computer-aided manufacturing). There are positions available to instruct others in computer software use within companies and schools. Technical writers and editors must be available to write manuals on using computers and software. Computer-assisted instruction (CAI) is a system of teaching any given subject using the computer. Designing video games is another exciting and ever-growing field of computer work. And these are just a few of the possible career opportunities in an ever-changing work environment. See Figure A-17.

FIGURE A-17
Working in the computer field

What Does the Future Hold?

The possibilities for computer development and application are endless. Things that were dreams or science fiction only 10 or 20 years ago are now reality. New technologies are emerging constantly. Some new technologies are replacing old ways of doing things; others are merging with those older methods and devices. Some new technologies are creating new markets. The Internet (more specifically, the Web), cell phones, and DVD videos are just a few inventions of the past decades that did not have counterparts prior to their inventions. We are learning new ways to work and play because of the computer. It is definitely a device that has become part of our offices, our homes, and our lives.

Social networking has moved from the streets and onto the Web. People meet and greet through the Internet using sites such as myspace.com and facebook.com.

Emerging Technologies

Today the various technologies and systems are coming together to operate more efficiently. Convergence is the merging of these technologies. Telephone communication is being combined with computer e-mail and Web browsing so users can set a time to meet online and, with the addition of voice technology, actually speak to each other using one small portable device.

The Web, now an important part of commerce and education, began as a one-way vehicle where users visited the Web to view Web pages and get information. It has evolved into sites where shopping and commerce takes place and is now evolving into a technology where users create the content. Web 2.0 and sites such as facebook.com, flickr.com, wikipedia.com, and youtube.com have content generated by the people that visit the Web sites. See Figure A-18.

FIGURE A-18
Content generated by the people that visit Web sites

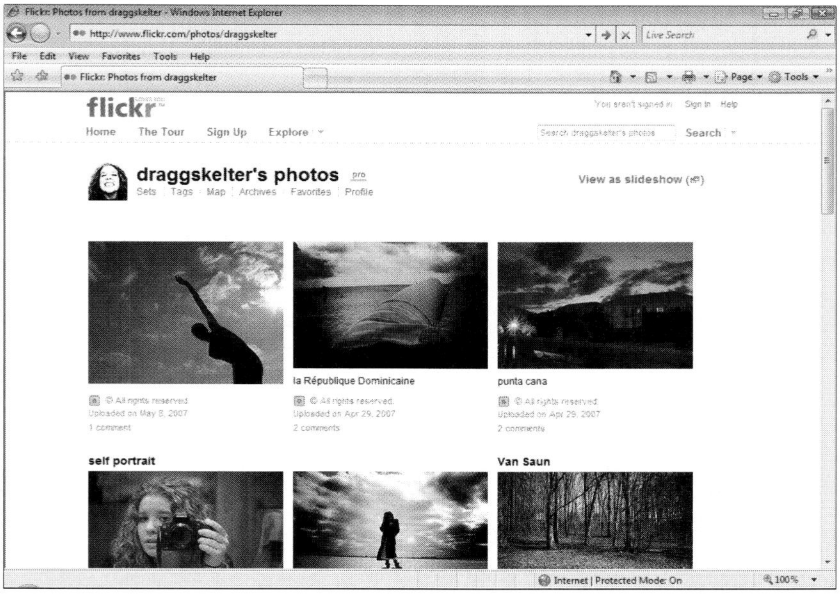

Used with permission by Emily C. Bunin

Computers have radically changed the way the medical profession delivers health care. Through the medical community, computers have enhanced medicine and healthcare throughout the world.

Trends

There are many trends that drive the computer industry. One trend is for larger and faster storage. From megabytes, to gigabytes, to terabytes, storage is becoming less an issue as the cost of storage is also dropping. RAM today is increasing exponentially. The trend is to sell larger blocks of RAM with every new personal computer. Newer processors also operate at speeds that are faster than the previous generation processors.

The actual size of computers is decreasing. Technology is allowing more powerful components to fit into smaller devices—laptops are lighter, monitors take up less space on the desktop, and flash drives can fit in your pocket and store gigabytes of data.

Home Offices

More and more frequently, people are working out of their homes—whether they are employees who are linked to a place of business or individuals running their own businesses. Telecommuting meets the needs of many industries. Many companies allow workers to have a computer at home that is linked by network to the office. Employees can use laptop computers to work both at home and on the road as they travel. A laptop computer, in combination with a wireless network, allows an employee to work from virtually anywhere and still keep in constant contact with her or his employer and customers.

Business communication is primarily by e-mail and telephone. It is very common for serious business transactions and communications to occur via e-mail rather than through the regular mail. Such an arrangement saves companies workspace and, thus, money.

Home Use

More and more households have personal computers. The statistics are constantly proving that a computer is an essential household appliance. Computers are used to access the Internet for shopping, education, and leisure. Computers are used to maintain financial records, manage household accounts, and record and manage personal information. More and more people are using electronic banking. Games and other computer interactions also offer a more reasonable way of spending leisure dollars. The convergence of television, the Internet, and the computer will find more households using their computers for media such as movies and music.

The future is with computing. It's clear that this technology will continue to expand and provide us with new and exciting trends.

APPENDIX B

KEYBOARDING TOUCH SYSTEM IMPROVEMENT

Introduction

- *Your Goal – Improve your keyboarding skills using the touch system so you are able to type without looking at the keyboard.*

Why Improve Your Keyboarding Skills?

- To be able to type faster and more accurately every time you use the computer

- To increase your enjoyment while using the computer

> **Did You Know?**
>
> You will type faster and more accurately when using the touch system instead of looking from the copy and then to the keyboard and pressing keys with one or two fingers—the "hunt and peck" system.

Getting Ready to Build Skills

In order to get ready you should:

1. **Prepare your desk and computer area.**
   a. Clear your desk of all clutter, except your book, a pencil or pen, the keyboard, the mouse, and the monitor.
   b. Position your keyboard and book so that you are comfortable and able to move your hands and fingers freely on the keyboard and read the book at the same time.
   c. Keep your feet flat on the floor, sit with your back straight, and rest your arms slightly bent with your finger tips on the keyboard.
   d. Start your Word processor, such as Microsoft Office Word, or any other text editor. You can use any simple program such as the Microsoft Works word processor or WordPad that is part of the Windows operating system. Ask your teacher for assistance.

2. Take a two-minute timed typing test according to your teacher's directions.

3. Calculate your words a minute (WAM) and errors a minute (EAM) using the instructions on the timed typing progress chart. This will be your base score you will compare to future timed typing.

4. Record today's Date, WAM, and EAM on the Base Score line of the writing progress chart.

5. Repeat the timed typing test as many times as you can.

6. Record each attempt on the Introduction line of the chart.

Skill Builder 1

Your Goal – Use the touch system to type the letters j u y h n m and to learn to press the spacebar.

Keys (J) (U) (Y) (H) (N) (M) (SPACEBAR)

What to Do

1. Place your finger tips on the home row keys as shown in Figure B-1.

FIGURE B-1
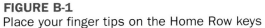
Place your finger tips on the Home Row keys

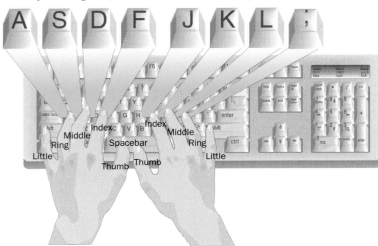

2. Look at Figure B-2. In step 3 you will press the letter keys j u y h n m. To press these keys, you use your right index finger. You will press the spacebar after typing each letter three times. The spacebar is the long bar beneath the bottom row of letter keys. You will press the spacebar with your right thumb.

FIGURE B-2
Pressing the j u y h n m keys

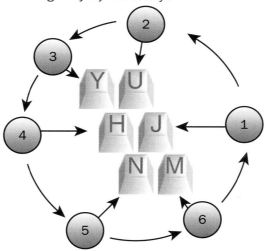

3. Look at your keyboard. Repeat the letters silently to yourself as you move your right index finger from the j key to press each key three times, then press the spacebar. Start typing:

   jjj uuu jjj yyy jjj hhh jjj nnn jjj mmm

   jjj uuu jjj yyy jjj hhh jjj nnn jjj mmm jjj

4. Repeat the same drill as many times as it takes for you to reach your comfort level.

   jjj uuu jjj yyy jjj hhh jjj nnn jjj mmm

   jjj uuu jjj yyy jjj hhh jjj nnn jjj mmm jjj

5. Close your eyes and visualize each key under each finger as you repeat the drill in step 4.

6. Look at the following two lines and type:

   jjj jjj jjj juj juj juj jyj jyj jyj jhj jhj jhj jnj jnj jnj jmj jmj jmj

   jjj jjj jjj juj juj juj jyj jyj jyj jhj jhj jhj jnj jnj jnj jmj jmj jmj

7. Repeat step 4, this time concentrating on the rhythmic pattern of the keys.

8. Close your eyes and visualize the keys under your finger tips as you type the drill in step 4 from memory.

Did You Know?

- Ignore errors.
- To complete the following exercises, you will type text that is bold and is not italicized and looks **like this**.
- If you have difficulty reaching for any key, for example the y key, practice by looking at the reach your finger tips make from the j key to the y key until the reach is visualized in your mind. The reach will become natural with very little practice.
- You may want to start on a new line by pressing the Enter key.

9. Look at the following two lines and type these groups of letters:

j ju juj j jy jyj j jh jhj j jn jnj j jm jmj j ju juj j jy jyj j jh jhj j jn jnj j jm jmj

jjj ju jhj jn jm ju jm jh jnj jm ju jmj jy ju jh j u ju juj jy jh jnj ju jm jmj jy

10. You may want to repeat Skill Builder 1, striving to improve typing letters that are most difficult for you.

Skill Builder 2

The left index finger is used to type the letters f r t g b v. Always return your left index finger to the f key on the home row after pressing the other keys.
Your Goal – Use the touch system to type f r t g b v .

Keys

What to Do

1. Place your finger tips on the home row keys as you did in Skill Builder 1, Figure B-1.

2. Look at Figure B-3. Notice how you will type the letters f r t g b v and then press the spacebar with your right thumb.

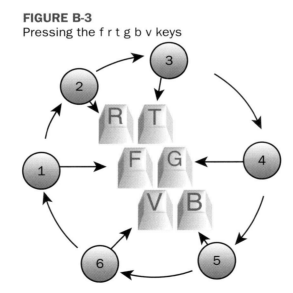

FIGURE B-3
Pressing the f r t g b v keys

3. Look at your keyboard. To press these keys, you use your left index finger. You will press the spacebar after typing each letter three times. The spacebar is the long bar beneath the bottom row of letter keys. You will press the spacebar with your right thumb.

After pressing each letter in the circle, press the home key f three times as shown. Don't worry about errors. Ignore them.

fff rrr fff ttt fff ggg fff bbb fff vvv

fff rrr fff ttt fff ggg fff bbb fff vvv fff

4. Repeat the same drill two more times using a quicker, sharper stroke.

   fff rrr fff ttt fff ggg fff bbb fff vvv

   fff rrr fff ttt fff ggg fff bbb fff vvv fff

5. Close your eyes and visualize each key under each finger as you repeat the drill in step 4.

6. Look at the following two lines and key these groups of letters:

   fff fff fff frf frf frf ftf ftf ftf fgf fgf fgf fbf fbf fbf fvf fvf fvf

   fff fff fff frf frf frf ftf ftf ftf fgf fgf fgf fbf fbf fbf fvf fvf fvf

7. Repeat step 6, this time concentrating on a rhythmic pattern of the keys.

8. Close your eyes and visualize the keys under your finger tips as you type the drill in step 4 from memory.

9. Look at the following two lines and type these groups of letters:

   fr frf ft ftf fg fgf fb fbf fv fvf

   ft fgf fv frf ft fbf fv frf ft fgf

10. You are about ready to type your first words. Look at the following lines and type these groups of letters (remember to press the spacebar after each group):

    jjj juj jug jug jug rrr rur rug rug rug

    ttt tut tug tug tug rrr rur rub rub rub

    ggg gug gum gum gum mmm mum

    mug mug mug hhh huh hum hum hum

11. Complete the Keyboarding Technique Checklist.

Skill Builder 3

Your Goal – Use the touch system to type k i , d e c.

Keys ⬚K⬚ ⬚I⬚ ⬚,⬚ *(comma)*

What to Do

1. Place your finger tips on the home row keys. The home row key for the left middle finger is d. The home row key for the right middle finger is k. You use your left middle finger to type d, e, c. You use your right middle finger to type k, i, , as shown in Figure B-4.

FIGURE B-4
Pressing keys k i , d e c

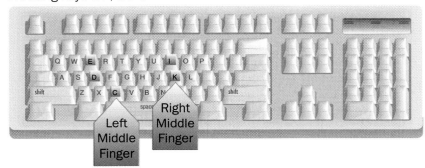

2. Look at your keyboard and locate these keys: k i , (the letter k key, the letter i key, and the comma key).

3. Look at your keyboard. Repeat the letters silently to yourself as you press each key three times and put a space between each set of letters and the comma to type:

   kkk iii kkk ,,, kkk iii kkk ,,, kkk iii kkk ,,, kkk iii kkk ,,, kkk iii kkk ,,, kkk

4. Look at the characters in step 3 and repeat the drill two more times using a quicker, sharper stroke.

5. Close your eyes and repeat the drill in step 3 as you visualize each key under each finger.

6. Repeat step 5, concentrating on a rhythmic pattern of the keys.

Keys ⬚D⬚ ⬚E⬚ ⬚C⬚

1. Place your finger tips on the home row keys.

2. Look at your keyboard and locate these keys: d e c (the letter d key, the letter e key, and the letter c key).

3. Look at your keyboard. Repeat the letters silently to yourself as you press each key three times and put a space between each set of letters to type:

  ddd eee ddd ccc ddd eee ddd ccc ddd eee ddd ccc ddd eee ddd ccc ddd

4. Look at the letters in step 3 and repeat the drill two more times using a quicker, sharper stroke.

5. Close your eyes and repeat the drill in step 3 as you visualize each key under each finger.

6. Repeat step 5, concentrating on a rhythmic pattern of the keys.

7. Look at the following lines of letters and type these groups of letters and words:

fff fuf fun fun fun ddd ded den den den

ccc cuc cub cub cub vvv vev vet

fff fuf fun fun fun ddd ded den den den

ccc cuc cub cub cub vvv vev vet

8. Complete the Keyboarding Technique Checklist.

Skill Builder 4

*Your Goal – Use the touch system to type l o . s w x
and to press the left Shift key.*

Keys Ⓛ Ⓞ Ⓒ *(period)*

What to Do

1. Place your finger tips on the home row keys. The home row key for the left ring finger is s. The home row key for the right ring finger is l. You use your left ring finger to type s w x. You use your right ring finger to type l o . as shown in Figure B-5.

FIGURE B-5
Pressing keys l o . s w x

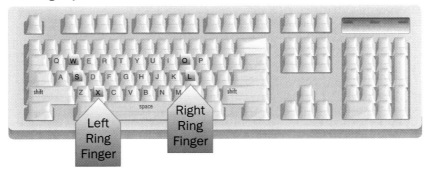

2. Look at your keyboard and locate the following keys: l o . (the letter l key, the letter o key, and the period key).

3. Look at your keyboard. Repeat the letters silently to yourself as you press each key three times and put a space between each set of letters and the periods to type:

    lll ooo lll ... lll ooo lll ... lll ooo lll ... lll ooo lll ... lll ooo lll ... lll ooo lll ... lll

4. Look at the line in step 3 and repeat the drill two more times using a quicker, sharper stroke.

5. Close your eyes and repeat the drill in step 3 as you visualize each key under each finger.

6. Repeat step 5, concentrating on a rhythmic pattern of the keys.

Keys Ⓢ Ⓦ Ⓧ

1. Place your finger tips on the home row keys.

2. Look at your keyboard and locate the following letter keys: s w x

3. Look at your keyboard. Repeat the letters silently to yourself as you press each key three times and put a space between each set of letters to type:

    sss www sss xxx sss www sss xxx sss www sss xxx sss www sss xxx sss

4. Look at the line in step 3 and repeat the same drill two more times using a quicker, sharper stroke.

5. Close your eyes and repeat the drill in step 3 as you visualize each key under each finger.

6. Repeat step 5, concentrating on a rhythmic pattern of the keys.

Key (SHIFT) *(Left Shift Key)*

You press and hold the Shift key as you press a letter key to type a capital letter. You press and hold the Shift key to type the character that appears above the numbers in the top row of the keyboard and on a few other keys that show two characters.

Press and hold down the left Shift key with the little finger on your left hand while you press each letter to type capital letters for keys that are typed with the finger tips on your right hand. See Figure B-6.

FIGURE B-6
Using the Shift keys

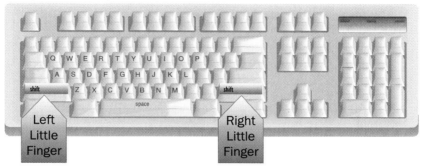

1. Type the following groups of letters and the sentence that follows.

   jjj JJJ jjj JJJ yyy YYY yyy YYY nnn NNN nnn NNN mmm MMM

   Just look in the book. You can see well.

2. Complete the Keyboarding Technique Checklist.

Skill Builder 5

*Your Goal – Use the touch system to type a q z ; p /
and to press the right Shift key.*

Keys (;) *(semi-colon)* (P) (/)

What to Do

1. Place your finger tips on the home row keys. The home row key for the left little finger is a. The home row key for the right little finger is ;. You use your left little finger to type *a q z* . You use your right little finger to type *; p /* as shown in Figure B-7.

FIGURE B-7
Pressing keys a q z ; p / and the right Shift key

2. Look at your keyboard and locate the following keys: ; p / (the semi-colon, the letter p, and the forward slash).

3. Repeat the letters silently to yourself as you press each key three times and put a space between each set of characters to type:

    ;;; ppp ;;; /// ;;; ppp ;;; /// ;;; ppp ;;; ///

    ;;; ppp ;;; /// ;;; ppp ;;; /// ;;; ppp ;;; /// ;;;

4. Look at the lines in step 3 and repeat the drill two more times using a quicker, sharper stroke.

5. Close your eyes and repeat the drill in step 3 as you visualize each key under each finger.

6. Repeat step 5, concentrating on a rhythmic pattern of the keys.

Keys (A) (Q) (Z)

1. Place your finger tips on the home row keys.

2. Look at your keyboard and locate the following keys: a q z (the letter a, the letter q, and the letter z).

3. Look at your keyboard. Repeat the letters silently to yourself as you press each key three times and put a space between each set of letters and type:

aaa qqq aaa zzz aaa qqq aaa zzz aaa qqq aaa zzz aaa qqq aaa zzz aaa

4. Look at the line in step 3 and repeat the same drill two more times using a quicker, sharper stroke.

5. Close your eyes and repeat the drill in step 3 as you visualize each key under each finger.

6. Repeat step 5, concentrating on a rhythmic pattern of the keys.

Key ⌐SHIFT⌐ *(Right Shift Key)*

Press and hold down the right Shift key with the little finger on your right hand while you press each letter to type capital letters for keys that are typed with the finger tips on your left hand.

1. Type the following lines. Press and hold down the right Shift key with the little finger of your right hand to make capitals of letters you type with the finger tips on your left hand.

sss SSS rrr RRR

Press each key quickly. Relax when you type.

2. Complete the Keyboarding Technique Checklist.

Skill Builder 6

You will probably have to type slowly at first, but with practice you will learn to type faster and accurately.
Your Goal – Use the touch system to type all letters of the alphabet.

What to Do

1. Close your eyes. Do not look at the keyboard and type all letters of the alphabet in groups of three with a space between each set as shown:

aaa bbb ccc ddd eee fff ggg hhh iii jjj

kkk lll mmm nnn ooo ppp qqq rrr sss

ttt uuu vvv www xxx yyy zzz

2. Repeat step 1, concentrating on a rhythmic pattern of the keys.

3. Repeat step 1, but faster than you did for step 2.

4. Type the following sets of letters, all letters of the alphabet in groups of two with a space between each set as shown:

aa bb cc dd ee ff gg hh ii jj kk ll mm nn oo pp qq rr ss tt uu vv ww xx yy zz

5. Type the following letters, all letters of the alphabet with a space between each letter as shown:

   a b c d e f g h i j k l m n o p q r s t u v w x y z

6. Continue to look at this book. Do not look at the keyboard, and type all letters of the alphabet backwards in groups of three with a space between each set as shown:

   zzz yyy xxx www vvv uuu ttt sss rrr

   qqq ppp ooo nnn mmm lll kkk jjj iii

   hhh ggg fff eee ddd ccc bbb aaa

7. Repeat step 6, but faster than the last time.

8. Type each letter of the alphabet once backwards:

   z y x w v u t s r q p o n m l k j i h g f e d c b a

9. Think about the letters that took you the most amount of time to find the key on the keyboard. Go back to the Skill Builder for those letters, and repeat the drills until you are confident about their locations.

Timed Typing

Prepare to take the timed typing test, according to your teacher's directions.

1. **Prepare your desk and computer area.**
   a. Clear your desk of all clutter except your book, a pencil or pen, the keyboard, the mouse, the monitor, and the computer box if it is placed on the desk.
   b. Position your keyboard and book so that you are comfortable and able to move your hands and finger tips freely.
   c. Keep your feet flat on the floor, sitting with your back straight, resting your arms slightly bent with your finger tips on the keyboard.

2. Take a two-minute timed typing test according to your teacher's directions.

3. Calculate your words a minute (WAM) and errors a minute (EAM) scores using the instructions on the timed typing progress chart in this book.

4. Record the date, WAM, and EAM on the Skill Builder 6 line.

5. Repeat the timed typing test as many times as you can and record each attempt.

Skill Builder 7

Your Goal – Improve your typing techniques—which is the secret for improving your speed and accuracy.

Did You Know?

You may want to ask a class-mate or your teacher to record your scores.

What to Do

1. Rate yourself for each item on the Keyboarding Technique Checklist.

2. Do not time yourself as you concentrate on a single technique you marked with a "0." Type only the first paragraph of the timed typing.

3. Repeat step 2 as many times as possible for each of the items marked with an "0" that need improvement.

4. Take a two-minute timed typing test. Record your WAM and EAM on the timed typing progress chart as 1st Attempt on the Skill Builder 7 line. Compare this score with your base score.

5. Looking only at the book and using your best techniques, type the following technique sentence for one minute:

   .   **2**   .   **4**   .   **6**   .   **8**   .   **10**   .   **12**   .   **14**   .   **16**

   Now is the time for all good men and women to come to the aid of their country.

6. Record your WAM and EAM on the 7 Technique Sentence line.

7. Repeat steps 5 and 6 as many times as you can and record your scores.

Skill Builder 8

Your Goal – Increase your words a minute (WAM) score.

What to Do

You can now type letters in the speed line very well and with confidence. Practicing all of the other letters of the alphabet will further increase your skill and confidence in keyboarding.

1. Take a two-minute timed typing test.

2. Record your WAM and EAM scores as the 1st Attempt.

3. Type only the first paragraph only one time as fast as you can. Ignore errors.

4. Type only the first and second paragraphs only one time as fast as you can. Ignore errors.

5. Take a two-minute timed typing test again. Ignore errors.

6. Record only your WAM score as the 2nd Attempt. Compare only this WAM with your 1st Attempt WAM and your base score WAM.

Get Your Best WAM

1. To get your best WAM on easy text for 15 seconds, type the following speed line as fast as you can, as many times as you can. Ignore errors.

   . **2** . **4** . **6** . **8** . **10**

   Now is the time, now is the time, now is the time,

2. Multiply the number of words typed by four to get your WAM (15 seconds x 4 = 1 minute). For example, if you type 12 words for 15 seconds, 12 x 4 = 48 WAM.

3. Record only your WAM in the 8 Speed Line box.

4. Repeat steps 1-3 as many times as you can to get your very best WAM. Ignore errors.

5. Record only your WAM for each attempt.

Skill Builder 9

Your Goal – Decrease errors a minute (EAM) score.

What to Do

Did You Know?
How much you improve depends upon how much you want to improve.

1. Take a two-minute timed typing test.

2. Record your WAM and EAM as the 1st Attempt.

3. Type only the first paragraph only one time at a controlled rate of speed so you reduce errors. Ignore speed.

4. Type only the first and second paragraphs only one time at a controlled rate of speed so you reduce errors. Ignore speed.

5. Take a two-minute timed typing test again. Ignore speed.

6. Record only your EAM score as the 2nd Attempt. Compare only the EAM with your 1st Attempt EAM and your base score EAM.

Get Your Best EAM

1. To get your best EAM, type the following accuracy sentence (same as the technique sentence) for one minute. Ignore speed.

   Now is the time for all good men and women to come to the aid of their country.

2. Record only your EAM score on the Accuracy Sentence 9 line.

3. Repeat step 1 as many times as you can to get your best EAM. Ignore speed.

4. Record only your EAM score for each attempt.

Skill Builder 10

Your Goal – Use the touch system and your best techniques to type faster and more accurately than you have ever typed before.

What to Do

1. Take a one-minute timed typing test.

2. Record your WAM and EAM as the 1st Attempt on the Skill Builder 10 line.

3. Repeat the timed typing test for two minutes as many times as necessary to get your best ever WAM with no more than one EAM. Record your scores as 2nd, 3rd, and 4th Attempts.

> **Did You Know?**
>
> You may want to get advice regarding which techniques you need to improve from a class-mate or your teacher.

Assessing Your Improvement

1. Circle your best timed typing test for Skill Builders 6-10 on the timed typing progress chart.

2. Record your best score and your base score. Compare the two scores. Did you improve?

	WAM	EAM
Best Score	____	____
Base Score	____	____

3. Use the Keyboarding Technique Checklist to identify techniques you still need to improve. You may want to practice these techniques now to increase your WAM or decrease your EAM.

Timed Typing

Every five strokes in a timed typing test is a word, including punctuation marks and spaces. Use the scale above each line to tell you how many words you typed.

```
          .    2    .         4    .         6    .
If you learn how to key well now, it
   8    .       10    .       12    .       14    .       16
is a skill that will help you for the rest
       .       18    .       20    .       22    .       24    .
of your life.  How you sit will help you key
26    .       28    .       30    .       32    .       34    .
with more speed and less errors.  Sit with your
   36    .       38    .       40    .       42    .       44
feet flat on the floor and your back erect.
       .       46    .       48    .       50    .       52
To key fast by touch, try to keep your
       .       54    .       56    .       58    .       60
eyes on the copy and not on your hands or
       .       62    .       64    .       66    .       68    .       70
the screen.  Curve your fingers and make sharp,
       .       72    .
quick strokes.
          74    .       76    .       78    .       80    .
Work for speed first. If you make more
       82    .       84    .       86    .       88    .       90
than two errors a minute, you are keying too
       92    .    94    .       96    .       98    .       100
fast. Slow down to get fewer errors. If you
       .       102    .       104    .       106    .       108
get fewer than two errors a minute, go for
   .       110
speed.
```

Timed Typing Progress Chart

Timed Writing Progress Chart

Last Name: _____   *First Name:* _____

Instructions

Calculate your scores as shown in the following sample and footnotes (a) and (b). Repeat timed writings as many times as you can and record your scores for each attempt.

Base Score: *Date* ____   *WAM* ____   *EAM* ____   *Time* ____

Skill Builder	Date	(a) WAM	(b) EAM	WAM	EAM	WAM	EAM	WAM	EAM
		1st Attempt		2nd Attempt		3rd Attempt		4th Attempt	
Sample	9/2	22	3.5	23	2.0	25	1.0	29	2.0
Introduction									
6									
7									
8					-----				
9				-----					
10									
7 Technique Sentence									
8 Speed Line			-----		-----		-----		-----
9 Accuracy Sentence		-----		-----		-----		-----	

(a) Divide words keyed (44) by 2 (minutes) to get WAM (22)

(b) Divide errors (7) by 2 (minutes) to get EAM (3.5)

Keyboarding Technique Checklist

Last Name: ———————————   *First Name:* ———————————

Instructions

1. Write the Skill Builder number, the date, and the initials of the evaluator in the proper spaces.

2. Place a check mark (✓) after a technique that is performed satisfactorily. Place a large zero (0) after a technique that needs improvement.

Skill Builder Number:	Sample										
Date:	9/1										
Evaluator:	SL										
Technique											
Attitude											
1. Enthusiastic about learning	✓										
2. Optimistic about improving	✓										
3. Alert but relaxed	✓										
4. Sticks to the task; not distracted	✓										
Getting Ready	✓										
1. Desk uncluttered											
2. Properly positions keyboard and book	✓										
3. Feet flat on the floor	✓										
4. Body erect, but relaxed	0										
Keyboarding											
1. Curves fingers	0										
2. Keeps eyes on the book	✓										
3. Taps the keys lightly; does not "pound" them	0										
4. Makes quick, "bouncy," strokes	0										
5. Smooth rhythm	0										
6. Minimum pauses between strokes	✓										

GLOSSARY

3-D reference A reference to the same cell or range in multiple worksheets that you use in a formula.

A

Absolute cell reference A cell reference that does not change when copied or moved to a new cell.

Action button An interactive button that performs instructions such as going to a specific slide or other object that you can create by drawing from the Shapes gallery.

Active cell The cell in the worksheet in which you can type data.

Active worksheet The worksheet that is displayed in the work area. Also called active sheet.

Address bar An area in a window that contains the path to the current folder.

Address Book A directory of personal and professional contact information.

Adjustment handle A yellow diamond-shaped handle that appears on a selected object. Drag the handle to change the appearance of the object.

Alignment The position of text between the margins. (Word)

Alignment The position of data within a cell. (Excel)

Alphanumeric data Data that contains numbers, text, or a combination of numbers and text.

Always-on connection An Internet connection method, such as DSL or cable, where the computer is always connected to the Internet as long as the computer is on.

And operator An operator used in a query that selects records that match all of two or more conditions in a query.

Animation Adding motion to an object.

Applications software A program used to perform a job or task; examples include word processors, databases, graphics programs, and spreadsheets.

Appointment An Outlook activity that the user will attend at a set date and time.

Archive An electronic repository that organizes, stores, and saves old files.

Argument The value a function uses to perform a calculation, including a number, text, or a cell reference that acts as an operand.

Ascending sort A sort order that arranges records using the values in a specific field or column from A to Z, from smallest to largest, or from earliest to latest.

Aspect ratio The relationship of an object's height to its width.

Attribute A formatting feature that affects how a font looks, such as a style, the color, or an effect.

AutoComplete A feature in Word that guesses names of calendar items, such as the days of the week and months, as you type them, and then suggests the complete word.

AutoCorrect A feature in Word that corrects errors as you type.

AutoFilter A menu that opens when you click the arrow on the right side of a field selector. The menu contains options for sorting data and for applying and clearing filters. (Access)

AutoFilter A menu that opens when you click a filter arrow. The menu lists all the values that appear in that column along with additional criteria and color filtering options. (Excel)

AutoFit An automatic determination of the best width for a column or the best height for a row, based on its contents.

AutoFormat An optional predefined set of colors, fonts, and design elements that you can apply to a form or report to change its appearance.

AutoFormat As You Type A feature in Word that applies built-in formats as you type.

Automatic grammar checking A feature in Word that checks your document for grammatical errors as you type, and flags them with a green, wavy underline.

Automatic page break A page break Excel inserts whenever it runs out of room on a page.

Automatic spell checking A feature in Word that checks your document for spelling errors as you type, and flags them with a red or blue wavy underline.

AutoNumber A data type that automatically adds a unique field value to each record in a table.

Axis A horizontal or vertical line that establishes the relationship between data in a chart.

B

Background The area behind the text and graphics on a slide.

Bar code readers Devices used to read printed codes such as the UPC (universal product code) to track merchandise or other inventory in a store.

Best fit The term used when a column in a datasheet is resized to the best width for the data contained in the column.

Blank Database template A template that creates a database that contains no objects.

Blank presentation A new presentation that does not have theme elements, text, or objects.

Blind Carbon Copy (Bcc) Including someone in an e-mail message without their name being visible to the other recipients.

Border A line around the edges of a cell.

Bound control A control in a form or report that is connected to a field in the record source and is used to display, enter, and update data.

Building block Document parts that you can store in Word and reuse.

Bullet Any small character that appears before an item in a list.

Business information set A collection of information about an individual, including name, company name, address, telephone number, e-mail address, and more.

Button An icon you click to choose a command, which gives the program instructions about what you want to do.

Byte A single character of data such as a letter which is composed of eight bits.

C

Calculated field A field in a query, form, or report that displays a value that is calculated using the values in other fields.

Callout A special type of label in a drawing that consists of a text box with an attached line to point to something in the drawing.

CD (compact disc) A durable form of removable optical storage in the form of a round flat disk that can hold 750MB.

CD drive A device used to read and write data to CDs.

Cell The intersection of a column and a row in a table or worksheet.

Cell reference A unique identifier for a cell, which is formed by combining the cell's column letter and row number.

Cell style A collection of formatting characteristics you apply to a cell or range of data.

Center To position text so that it is centered between the left and right margins.

Central processing unit (CPU) A silicon chip, stored on the motherboard, which processes data and carries out instructions given to the computer.

Chart A graphical representation of data.

Chart area The entire chart and all other chart elements.

Chart layout An arrangement that specifies which elements are included in a chart and where they are placed.

Chart sheet A separate sheet in a workbook that stores a chart.

Chart style Formatting applied to a chart based on the colors, fonts, and effects associated with the workbook's theme.

Clear To remove all of the formatting applied to a cell or range of cells.

Client A personal computer that requests data from a server.

Clip art Graphics that are stored in the Clip Organizer or available online that you can insert in any presentation.

Clipboard A temporary storage place in the computer's memory, available to all the programs on your computer, which can hold only one selection at a time; to place items on the Clipboard, you use the Cut or Copy command. An item on the Clipboard can be pasted into the file. Also called system Clipboard.

Clock speed The speed of the processor.

Close button Window button that closes the open window or application.

Color palette A coordinated set of colors available for use in a document.

Column A vertical stack of cells in a table or worksheet.

Column chart A chart that uses bars of varying heights to illustrate values in a worksheet.

Comma-separated values (CSV) A file format in which commas separate the field values of each record in the data source and paragraph marks separate individual records.

Comment A small note or annotation.

Common field A field that appears in two or more tables in a database and that has the same data type and field values. A common field (also called a matching field) is used to relate tables and usually has the same field name in the related tables.

Compacting A process that rearranges the way a database is stored on disk and optimizes the performance of the database.

Computer folder In Windows Vista, provides access to hard disk drives, removable drives and media, CD and DVD drives, network locations, and other removable media such as cameras and scanners.

Computer system Includes the system unit of a computer, and all peripheral input and output devices.

Condition In a query, a condition specifies which data to display in the query results. Also called a criterion.

Conditional formatting Formatting that highlights worksheet data by changing the look of cells that meet a specified condition.

Contact A person, organization, or business in the Outlook Address Book.

Content control A special placeholder designed to contain a specific type of text, such as a date or the page number.

Content Library A task pane used for storing text and graphics for future use.

Contextual spell checking A feature in Word that checks your document for words that are spelled correctly, but that might be misused, and flags them with a blue, wavy underline.

Contextual tab A tab that appears on the Ribbon only when you select certain items in a file, and contains commands related to that item.

Control An object in a form or report, such as a label or text box, that displays data from the record source on which the form or report is based.

Control layout A "container" that groups together the controls in a form or report so that you can change the formatting of and move these controls as a group.

Control Panel The command center for configuring Windows settings.

Copy To place a copy of selected text on the Clipboard or the Office Clipboard.

Copyright The legal method for protecting the intellectual property of the author or creator. Images, text, and sound files can be copyrighted.

Criteria A term that indicates that a query contains two or more conditions. A condition specifies which data to display in the query results.

Crop To remove part of a picture.

Custom show A feature that allows you to create presentations for different audiences by selecting specific slides from a presentation.

Cut To remove selected text and place it on the Clipboard or the Office Clipboard.

D

Daily Task List Tasks visible in Calendar in Day or Week view.

Data Information entered into and manipulated or processed by a computer.

Data and information management Organizing and storing of data in a company or organization using computers.

Data bus The wiring and pathways by which the CPU communicates with the peripherals and components of the computer.

Data label Text or numbers that provides additional information about a data marker.

Data marker A chart symbol (such as a bar, line, dot, slice, and so forth) that represents a single data point or value from the corresponding worksheet cell.

Data series A group of related information in a column or row of a worksheet that is plotted on a chart.

Data source The file that contains the records or fields used in another document or file; could be a Word document, an Excel workbook, or an Access database. In Excel, a range of cells that stores the data plotted on a chart.

Data table A grid that displays the data plotted in a chart.

Data type The property of a field that determines the type of data that you can enter into the field, such as numbers or text.

Database A collection of objects that work together to store, retrieve, display, and summarize data and also to automate tasks.

Database management system (DBMS) A program that you use to store, retrieve, analyze, and print information.

Datasheet Displays the data for a chart, table or query in rows and columns, with records in rows and fields in columns.

Datasheet selector The box in the upper-left corner of a datasheet that when clicked selects all fields and records in a datasheet.

Datasheet tool An Access tool that creates a form that looks like a datasheet.

Datasheet view The view of a database table that displays data in rows and columns.

Date and time functions Functions that convert serial numbers to a month, a day, or a year, or that insert the current date or the current date and time.

Date Navigator The monthly calendar shown at the top of the To-Do Bar in Outlook.

Default Value property An optional description of a field that specifies the value to enter into each record in a table.

Delimited data Data that is stored in text format and separated by delimiters, such as commas.

Descending sort A sort order that arranges records using the values in a specific field or column from Z to A, from largest to smallest, or latest to earliest.

Description property An optional field property that you can use to describe the data to store in the field.

Design Checker A task pane that locates potential design problems associated with a publication.

Design gallery object Graphics and text placeholders found in the Design Gallery that can be used to enhance a publication's appearance and functionality.

Design grid The top half of the Table window in Design view that displays the name, data type, and optional Description property for each field in a table.

Design view (table) The view of a table that lets you add, delete, and rearrange fields. You can also use Design view to make changes to the way that fields store data.

Desktop The main screen and workspace that opens with Windows is started.

Desktop computer A personal computer that includes a system unit, keyboard, and mouse that is not portable.

Destination file The file that an object is embedded in or linked to. *See also* Source file.

Detail query A query that shows every field in each record in the query results.

Detail section The section in Design view for a form or report that contains the detail records from the record source.

Diagram A visual representation of data to help readers better understand relationships among data.

Dialog box An interactive message window that appears when more information is required before the command can be performed.

Dial-up The oldest, slowest, and cheapest Internet access technology, where your computer has to dial out through a local phone line to get access to the Internet.

Digital Subscriber Line (DSL)   Always-on broad-band Internet connection that is faster than dialup or satellite but not as fast as cable or fiber optic.

Disk Cleanup   A Windows Vista utility that deletes temporary files from the hard disk and improves computer performance.

Distribution list   Collection of contact e-mail addresses that can be used to send a message to a group.

Document Information Panel   A pane that you can display at the top of the document window in which you can view or add properties to a document.

Document Inspector   A feature that enables you to check for hidden meta-data or personal information in a presentation.

Document properties   Information about the presentation file including title, author, and keywords.

Documents folder   Stores the files you use for your projects, such as documents, presentations, spread-sheets, and other files.

Draft view   A way of viewing a document on screen that shows only the text of a document; you don't see headers and footers, margins, columns, or graphics.

Drag   To select text by positioning the I-beam pointer to the left of the first character of the text you want to select, holding down the left button on the mouse, dragging the pointer to the end of the text you want to select, and then releasing the button.

Drag-and-drop   To drag selected text from one place in a file to another.

Drivers   Software that runs peripheral hardware devices; or facilitates other programs; may install automatically when new hardware is detected by your computer, or you may have to install a driver yourself.

DVD   A high-capacity, optical disc that can store up to 4.7GB of data.

DVD drive   A device used to read and write data to CDs and DVDs.

E

Editing mode   The mode with insertion point placed within the cell contents, so you can edit and format text directly in the cell.

Effects options   The Entrance, Exit, and Emphasis animation features such as pinwheel, diamond, and fly effects that you can use to animate objects.

E-mail   An electronic message sent using a computer network.

Embed   To place an object that was created in another application such as Microsoft Word or Excel in a slide. When you select the object, the original program will open for editing.

Embedded chart   A chart is inserted in the center of the worksheet.

ENIAC (Electronic Numerical Integrator and Computer)   One of the earliest computers; designed for military use in 1946, and could accomplish a task in 20 seconds that normally would took a human three days to complete.

Event   An Outlook activity that lasts at least one day, but does not block out time in a calendar.

Exact match condition   A condition in a query that specifies the exact condition that a record must satisfy to be displayed in the query results.

Exploded pie chart   A pie chart with one or more slices pulled away from the pie to distinguish them.

Explorer windows   Vista windows that are used to modify computer settings and navigate to items.

Export   A term used when data is saved into a different file format.

Expression   The term given to the calculation used in a calculated field that identifies the fields and operators to use in the calculated field.

F

Field   A single characteristic in a table's design that appears in a datasheet as a column.

Field List pane   A pane in Design view for a form or report that displays the tables and other objects in the database and the fields they contain.

Field name   The name of a column in a database table.

Field Properties pane   The bottom half of the Table window in Design view that displays properties for the selected field in a table.

Field property An additional description of a field beyond the field's data type that specifies how to store data in the field, such as the number of characters the field can store.

Field selector The top of a column in a datasheet that contains the field name. Clicking a field selector selects the column.

Field Size property The property that identifies the number of characters that a Text, Number, or AutoNumber field can store.

Field value The specific data stored in a field for a record.

File extension A series of letters Office adds to the end of a file name that identifies in which program that file was created.

Fill The background color of a cell.

Fill To copy a cell's contents and/or formatting into an adjacent cell or range.

Fill handle The black square in the lower-right corner of the active cell or range that you drag over the cells you want to fill.

Filter To display a subset of the data that meets certain criteria and temporarily hide the rows that do not meet the specified criteria.

Filter arrow An arrow that appears in a column heading cell that opens the AutoFilter menu.

Filter By Form A filter that you can apply to a datasheet that rearranges the records based on one or more field values that you select from a list.

Filter By Selection A filter that you can apply to a datasheet that rearranges the records based on a selected field value or part of a field value.

Financial functions Functions that are used to analyze loans and investments.

Find A command that lets you specify how to locate data in a file.

First-line indent A description of the indent in a paragraph when only the first line of text in the paragraph is indented.

Floating object An object in a document that acts as if it were sitting in a separate layer on the page and can be repositioned anywhere on the page.

Floppy disk drive An outdated removable magnetic storage technology that came in many formats including the 3?-inch HD which was capable of storing 1.4 megabytes (MB) of information.

Folder An electronic directory containing files or other folders.

Font The design of text.

Font effect Similar to a font style, helps you enhance or clarify the look of text.

Font size The height of characters in points.

Font style Emphasis added to cells, such as bold, italics, and underlining.

Footer Text that is printed at the bottom of each page.

Foreign key When two tables in a database are related, the common field in the related table is called a foreign key.

Form A database object that displays data from one or more tables or queries in a format that has a similar appearance to a paper form.

Form Footer section The section in Design view for a form that contains the information that is displayed at the bottom of the form.

Form Header section The section in Design view for a form that contains the information that is displayed at the top of the form.

Form letter A document that contains merge fields to indicate where to print data from a data source, such as an Access database or an Excel workbook.

Form tool An Access tool that creates a simple form that includes all the fields in the selected table or query.

Form view A view of a form that displays the data in the record source in a form.

Form Wizard An Access wizard that creates a form based on a record source and using options that the user specifies to select the form's layout and style.

Format To change the appearance or look of text.

Format Painter A feature that copies format attributes such as colors, borders, and fill effects from an object, text, or cell in order to apply the same formatting to another object, text, or cell.

Format property A property for a field that specifies how to display numbers, dates, times, and text.

Formula An equation that calculates a new value from values currently in a worksheet.

Formula AutoComplete A feature to help you enter a formula with a valid function name and arguments.

Formula Bar The box to the right of the Name Box that displays a formula when the cell of a worksheet contains a calculated value (or the results of the formula).

Freeze panes To keep selected rows and/or columns of the worksheet visible on the screen as the rest of the worksheet scrolls.

Front side bus speed The speed of the bus that connects the processor to main memory.

Full Screen Reading view A way of viewing a document on screen that shows text on the screen in a form that is easy to read; the Ribbon is replaced by a small bar called a toolbar that contains only a few relevant commands.

Function A shorthand way to write an equation that performs a calculation.

G

Gadget A tool available on the Windows sidebar.

Gallery A list of options available for a command.

Gigahertz (GHz) One billion cycles per second.

Go To To jump to a specific location in a file.

Graphic A picture that helps illustrate the meaning of the text and make the page more attractive; graphics include predefined shapes, diagrams, charts, as well as photographs and drawings.

Grid settings Vertical and horizontal lines that appear on the Slide pane and help you place text and objects.

Gridline The lines in a table that form the rows and columns.

Group The organization for related commands on a tab of the Ribbon.

Grouping A feature that allows you to move, format, or resize several objects as if they were one object.

Grouping level An option for reports that organizes data based on one or more fields into groups.

Guides Vertical and horizontal lines that you can display on the Slide pane to help place objects on the slide.

Gutter margin See inside margin.

H

Hackers People who create and send programs such as viruses in order to do harm to other computers.

Handles Appear when an object is selected and are used to drag to resize the object.

Handout master The master view for the audience handouts; includes placeholders for the slides, a header, footer, and the date and slide number.

Hanging indent A description of the indent in a paragraph when the first line of text is not indented but all of the following lines in the paragraph are.

Hard disk drive The main storage device for a computer; reads and writes data to and from a round magnetic platter, or disk.

Hardware The physical components, devices or parts, of the computer such as the central processing unit (CPU), the monitor, the keyboard, and the mouse.

Header Text that is printed at the top of each page.

Help and Support The Windows system where information can be found using topic lists or by searching using keywords.

Home page The first page that opens when you start your browser. Also called start page.

Hyperlink Text, cell, or an object that when clicked "jumps to" another location, such as another file location or a Web site. Also called a link.

I

Icon A small graphic image that represents a file, folder, program, or program shortcut.

Identify theft Using person's identity without their permission.

Import A term used when data is copied from a file into a different location.

Indent The space between text and the margin. (Word)

Indent To shift data within a cell and insert space between the cell border and its content. (Excel)

Inline object An object in a document that can be repositioned as if it were a character in the line of text.

Input   Data entered into the computer through a variety of devices, such as a keyboard, microphone, or mouse.

Input Devices   Devices used to enter information into a computer and interact with the user; for instance, a keyboard, microphone, or pointing device.

Insertion point   A blinking vertical line that shows where text will appear when you begin typing.

Inside margin   The right margin on a left page and the left margin on the right page when a document is set up with mirrored margins. Also called gutter margin.

Internet   The largest network in the world connecting millions of computers worldwide.

Internet Service Provider (ISP)   A company that provides connection to the Internet by subscription.

J

Join line   The line that connects tables that have a relationship; the join line connects the matching fields and indicates the relationship type.

Journal   An Outlook tool used to record entries and document interactions with contacts.

Justify   To format a paragraph so the text is distributed evenly across the page between the left and right margins and both the left and right edges of the paragraph are aligned at the margins.

K

Keyword   A word or phrase used in a search.

L

Label Wizard   An Access wizard that creates a report of mailing labels or custom labels.

LAN (local area network)   Connected computers within a small geographical area such as a home, office, school, or building.

Landscape orientation   A page or worksheet rotated so it is wider than it is long.

Laptop computer   A small lightweight computer that includes monitor, keyboard, hard disk drive, CD/DVD storage drives, and a pointing device as one unit that folds for easy portability. Also called notebook computer.

Laser printer   A fast, high-quality printer that uses heat to fuse a powdery substance called toner to the page.

Layout   The way content and text placeholders are placed on the slide.

Layout guides   Margin guides, grid guides and baseline grid guides that help you position text and objects on a page.

Layout master   In the slide master, the individual layouts that determine the location of content and text placeholders for the slides.

Layout view   A view of a form or report that displays data from the record source and that lets you make certain types of changes to the form or report, such as increasing the size of a text box control.

Leader   A solid, dotted, or dashed line that fills the blank space before a tab stop.

Left-align   To position text so that it is aligned along the left margin.

Legend   A list that identifies patterns, symbols, or colors used in a chart.

Line chart   A chart that uses points connected by a line to illustrate values in a worksheet.

Line spacing   The amount of space between lines of text.

Line tool   An Access tool that you can use to add a line to a form or report.

Link   See Hyperlink.

Linked object   A file, chart, table or other object that is created in another application such as Excel, stored in a source file, and inserted into a destination file, such as a PowerPoint slide, while maintaining a connection between the two files.

Live Preview   The Office 2007 feature that lets you point to the various choices in a gallery or palette and see the results before applying.

Logical functions   Functions that display text or values if certain conditions exist.

Logo   A symbol that represents a business and its products.

M

Magnetic tape Removable, sequential storage medium commonly used for backing up a computer system, used by most businesses.

Mail merge A process that combines a document with information that personalizes it.

Main document The file used in a mail merge that contains the information that does not vary from one document to the next.

Manual calculation The option that lets you determine when Excel calculates formulas in the worksheet.

Manual page break A page break you insert to start a new page.

Margins Blank spaces around the top, bottom, and sides of page.

Master page A background page that includes layout guides and placeholders for text and graphics.

Matching field A field that appears in two or more tables in a database and that has the same data type and field values. A matching field (also called a common field) is used to relate tables and usually has the same field name in the related tables.

Mathematical functions Functions that manipulate quantitative data in a worksheet.

Maximize button Window sizing button that enlarges a window to the full size of the screen.

Meeting An Outlook activity that it has a scheduled date and time and includes other people and a place.

Megahertz One million cycles per second.

Memory The chips that store data and programs while the computer is working. Often called RAM or Random Access Memory.

Menu A list of related commands.

Merge To combine multiple cells into one cell.

Merge field A placeholder in the main document in a mail merge that is replaced with data from the data source when you perform the merge.

Mini toolbar A floating toolbar that appears in the work area after you drag the pointer over text while holding down the left mouse button.

Minimize button Window sizing button that reduces the window to an icon on the taskbar.

Mirrored margins Margins on left and right pages that are identical—"mirror" each other—when facing each other; usually used in books and magazines.

Mixed cell reference A cell reference that contains both relative and absolute references.

Modem Device that allow computers to communicate by converting data in bytes to sound media in order to send data and then convert it back to bytes after receiving data.

Monitor A standard output device that includes the screen on which you view your work.

Motherboard Located inside the system unit, a circuit board where the computer memory, power supply, the processor, and other vital electronic parts are housed.

Motion Path A way to animate an object by drawing the path on the slide.

Mouse A hand-held device used to move a pointer on the computer screen.

Multilevel list A list with two or more levels of bullets or numbering. Also called outline numbered list.

Multiple Items tool An Access tool that creates a form that lists all the fields in the record source in a datasheet format.

Multitable query A query that is based on the data in two or more tables.

N

Name Box The cell reference area located below the Ribbon, which displays the cell reference of the active cell.

Navigation pane An area in a window that contains links to folders, searches, objects, or more.

Negative indent A description of an indent in a paragraph in which the left indent marker is past the left margin. Also called outdent.

Network Two or more computers connected to share data, either by wires or using wireless technology.

Network card A device in the system unit that allow computers to access networks.

Network software Software used to run a network server, such as Novell™ and Windows NT.

Normal view The view in PowerPoint that includes the Slides/Outline tabs on the left, the Slide pane showing the selected slide in the center, and the Notes pane beneath the Slide pane. Commonly used to place objects on the slide. (PowerPoint)

Normal view The worksheet view best for entering and formatting data in a worksheet. (Excel)

Notebook computer See laptop computer.

Notes In Outlook, an electronic equivalent of a sticky note.

Notes master The master view for the notes pages. Includes placeholders for the slide, notes, header, footer, date, and slide number.

Notes Page view A view in PowerPoint for working on the speaker notes page; includes placeholders for the slide notes.

Number format Formatting option that changes the way data looks in a cell.

O

Object Anything that appears on the screen that you can select and work with as a whole, such as a shape, picture, or chart.

Office Button A button that opens a menu with commands for working with files, including commands for opening, saving, printing, and creating new files.

Office Clipboard (Clipboard) A temporary storage area for up to 24 selections you copy or cut.

One-to-many relationship A relationship between two tables in a database in which one record in the primary table can match many (zero, one, or many) records in the related table.

Operand A number or cell reference used in a formula.

Operating system Software such as Windows Vista that controls the basic operations of a computer.

Operator A symbol that indicates what mathematical operation to perform on the operands, such as a plus sign (+) for addition.

Or operator An operator used in a query that selects records that match at least one of two or more conditions in a query.

Order of evaluation The sequence used to calculate the value of a formula.

Organization chart A SmartArt graphic used to show hierarchy and relationships of people or objects.

Orientation The rotation of cell contents to an angle or vertically.

Orphan The last line of a paragraph at the top of a page.

Outdent See negative indent.

Outline numbered list See multilevel list.

Outline tab A tab used to enter text in Normal view, located on the left side of the window in the same pane as the Slides tab.

Outline view A way of viewing a document on screen that displays headings and text in outline form so you can see the structure of your document and reorganize easily; headers and footers, page boundaries, graphics, and backgrounds do not appear.

Output The results of data processing; can be presented in many ways such as an image on a screen or a monitor; printed pages from a printer, or sound through speakers.

Output device Device that displays the results of computer processing; for example, a monitor, printer, or speaker.

Outside margin The left margin on the left page and the right margin on the right page when a document is set up with mirrored margins.

P

Package for CD A feature that allows you to save a presentation to a CD to be viewed on a computer that does not have PowerPoint installed.

Page break The place where one page ends and another begins.

Page Break Preview The worksheet view for adjusting page breaks in a worksheet.

Page Layout view The worksheet view that shows how the worksheet will appear on a printed page.

Page navigator Located in the lower left side of the window, and allows you to move quickly from one page to another.

Panel heading An area provided for the title or heading of a project or section of a project.

Paragraph spacing The amount of space between paragraphs.

Paste To copy an item stored on the Clipboard or the Office Clipboard to a location in a file.

Paste Options Commands that appear below and to the right of pasted text; you can click the Paste Options button to open a menu of options for formatting the pasted text.

Peripheral Additional hardware, such as printers and scanners that are not essential to the computer but increase its functionality.

Personal computer The computer you use at home or in school.

Personal Digital Assistants (PDA). A pocket-sized electronic organizer that helps you to manage addresses, appointments, expenses, tasks, and memos. Many have cell phone capability.

Personal folder Stores your most frequently used folders and is labeled with by the computer user account name.

Phishing A criminal activity that is used by people to fraudulently obtain your personal information, such as usernames, passwords, credit card details, and your social security information.

Picture A digital photograph or other image file.

Pie chart A chart that shows the relationship of a part to a whole.

Pixels A single point in a graphic image. It is from picture element, using the abbreviation "pix" for "picture."

Placeholder A boxed outline on a slide that can be used to insert text or an object when clicked.

Plot area The graphical representation of all of the data series.

Point The unit of measurement for fonts.

Point-and-click method In a formula, to click a cell rather than type its cell reference.

Pointer The tip of a pointing device as it appears on the screen.

Pointing device A device that allow users to navigate and interact with a computer.

Points The measurement unit for font size.

Portrait orientation A page or worksheet rotated so it is longer than it is wide.

PowerPoint presentation A computer slide show created in PowerPoint.

Primary key The field in a database table that contains a unique field value for each record in the table.

Primary table In a one-to-many relationship, the table that contains the records on the "one" side of the relationship.

Print area The cells and ranges designated for printing.

Print Layout view The most common way of viewing a document on screen; it shows how a document will look when it is printed, and you can work with headers and footers, margins, columns, and graphics, which are all displayed.

Print Preview A way of viewing a document on screen that enables you to see the document as it will appear when printed.

Print title Designated rows and/or columns in a worksheet that print on each page.

Printers A type of output device that produces a paper printout of information.

Processing device Electronic chips inside the system unit that are used to provide results of data input or user commands.

Program A set of instructions to the computer.

Program window The rectangle that contains the open program, tools for working with the file, and the work area.

Property Identifying information about a file that is saved along with the file, such as the author's name and the date the file was created.

Public folder Used to store the files you want to share with other users on the same computer or who are connected through a network.

Publication Types list A list of template categories found in the Microsoft Publisher window.

Publishing Placing a presentation in a format for others to use; published presentations include handouts, Package for CD, and presentations on a document management server, in a document workspace, and on the Web.

Pull quote Text copied from a document and set off in a text box.

Q

Query A database object that lets you ask the database about the data it contains.

Quick Access Toolbar A small customizable toolbar at the top of the screen with buttons for common commands such as Save and Undo.

Quick Part A building block stored in the Quick Parts gallery and available when you click the Quick Parts button in the Text group on the Insert tab.

Quick Style A predefined format that you can apply by clicking a button in the Styles group on the Home tab.

R

Random Access Memory (RAM) Memory that temporarily stores programs and data when the computer is turned on but does not retain the contents when the computer is turned off.

Range A group of selected cells.

Range reference The unique identifier for a range, which is the cell in its upper-left corner and the cell in its lower-right corner, separated by a colon.

Range-of-values condition A condition in a query that specifies a range of values that a record must satisfy to be displayed in the query results.

Read-only A term used to describe data that can be viewed but not changed.

Read-only memory (ROM) Permanent memory that stores the instructions that tell the computer how to begin to load its operating system and programs.

Record The collection of field values for a complete set of data.

Record selector The box to the left of a record in a datasheet that when clicked selects the entire record.

Record source The tables or queries that contain the data used in a form or report.

Recycle Bin Wastebasket icon on the Windows Vista desktop where items are deleted and from which they can be restored before the Recycle Bin is emptied.

Redo To reverse an action that you undid.

Referential integrity A set of rules that a DBMS follows to ensure that there are matching values in the common field used to create the relationship between related tables and that protects the data in related tables to make sure that data is not accidentally deleted or changed.

Related table In a one-to-many relationship, the table that contains the records on the "many" side of the relationship.

Relationship The feature of a DBMS that lets you connect the data in the tables in the database so you can create queries and other objects using the data from two or more tables.

Relative cell reference A cell reference that adjusts to its new location when copied or moved.

Repeat To repeat the most recent action.

Replace To search a file for each occurrence of a specific word or phrase that you specify and then replace the word or phrase with another word or phrase that you specify.

Report A database object that displays data from one or more tables or queries in a format that has an appearance similar to a printed report.

Report selector The box in the upper-left corner of a report where the horizontal and vertical rulers intersect that selects the entire report.

Report tool An Access tool that creates a simple report that includes all the fields in the selected table or query, uses a simple columnar format, and includes a title with the same name as the record source.

Report Wizard An Access wizard that you can use to create a report by specifying a record source, layout, style, and grouping level.

Required property A field property that specifies whether a value must be entered into the field.

Research task pane A task pane that provides access to information typically found in references such as dictionaries, thesauruses, and encyclopedias.

Resolution The clarity of an image on the screen, measured in pixels. The higher resolution, the more pixels and clearer the image.

Resources In Outlook, materials and/or equipment that can be reserved for a meeting, such as a conference room, projector, or plasma screen.

Restore Down button Window sizing button that returns the window to the size it was before the Maximize button was clicked.

Ribbon An area at the top of an Office program window that contains commands for working with the open file; the commands are organized under tabs.

Right-align To position text so that it is aligned along the right margin.

Rotation handle A green circle that appears connected to a selection rectangle around an object and that you can drag to rotate the object.

Router An electronic device that joins two or more networks and directs the flow of information across the network.

Row The horizontal placement of cells in a table or worksheet.

Run The term given to the act of opening a query and displaying the query results.

S

Scale To resize a worksheet to print on a specific number of pages.

Scanner A device that converts text or graphics from a printed page into code that a computer can process.

Scatter chart A chart that shows the relationship between two categories of data; sometimes called an XY chart.

ScreenTip A box that appears when you point to a button; contains the button's name and a description of its function as well as a link to more information and a keyboard shortcut if available.

Scroll arrows Located at either side of a scroll bar; used to move the window contents up or down.

Scroll bar A bar that appears on the edge of a window when there is more content than can appear in the window at its current size.

Scroll box A slider that can be dragged to change position in a scroll bar.

Section A part of a document where you can apply a layout, headers and footers, page numbers, margins, orientation, and other formatting features different from the rest of the document.

Select To highlight a block of text.

Selection box The marker that surrounds a selected chart element.

Selection rectangle The box that appears around an object when it is selected.

Server Computer hardware and software that stores and delivers data to the other computers on a network.

Sheet tab The worksheet identifier that appears at the bottom of the workbook window.

Shortcut menu A menu that appears when you right-click something in the program window; contains a list of commands you are most likely to use with the item or text you right-clicked.

Show/Hide ¶ A command that allows you to see hidden formatting marks in a document.

Sidebar Text set off from the main body of text in a text box that provides additional information for the reader.

Signature An electronic identifier inserted in e-mail messages that can contain text, hyperlinks, pictures, or an Electronic Business Card

Simple Query Wizard The wizard in Access that lets you create a query and indicate what you'd like to see in the query results by selecting options in dialog boxes.

Sizing button A button you click to change the size of the program window or exit the program.

Sizing handle A square, circle, or set of three dots that appears on a selection rectangle around an object and that you can drag to resize the object.

Slide layout The placement of placeholders or objects on a slide that determines how all of the objects on a slide are arranged.

Slide master Determines the graphics and layout for the slides in a presentation. Each theme has a slide master, and slide masters include layout masters.

Slide pane The main work area for the selected slide in Normal view.

Slide Show view A view in PowerPoint that shows the slides on the full screen with the animations and transitions.

Slide Sorter view A view in PowerPoint that displays a thumbnail of each slide in the order in which they appear in the presentation; used to rearrange slides, check timings, and view slide transitions.

Slide transition The animated way in which a slide appears and leaves the screen during a slide show.

Slides tab In Normal view the tab on the left side of the PowerPoint window that displays thumbnails of each slide.

SmartArt graphic A graphic diagram that visually illustrates text and includes formatted graphics.

Snap to When an object is drawn to the guide or grid as though it was magnetic; used for exact placement of objects.

Software The programs or code that run on a computer; includes programs that tells the computer how to operate its devices, how to manipulate, store, and output information, and how to accept the input you give it.

Solid state card reader Devices that can read solid state memory cards, such as those used by digital cameras.

Sort To arrange a list of words or numbers in ascending or descending order.

Sound input device A microphone or other device that accepts speech or sounds as input for processing on a computer.

Source The location data is being transferred from.

Source file The file in which a linked or embedded object is stored in a presentation.

Spam Unsolicited or junk e-mail.

Speech recognition technology Software that converts speech or sounds to data.

Speed How fast the computer processes each instruction; measured in megahertz (MHz) and gigahertz (GHz).

Spell checker A feature used to locate and correct spelling errors.

Split To divide the work area into two or four panes that scroll independently.

Split Form tool An Access tool that creates a form using all the fields in the selected record source and splits the window into two panes, with one displaying the form in Form view and the other displaying the form in Datasheet view.

Spreadsheet A grid of rows and columns in which you enter text, numbers, and the results of calculations.

Spyware A program that can harm a computer by gathering user information through the user's Internet connection without his or her knowledge, usually for advertising purposes.

Statistical functions Functions that are used to describe large quantities of data.

Status bar A bar at the bottom of the program window that provides information about the current file and process.

Storage device Device such as disk drive, CD/DVD drive, flash drive, or tape drive that is used to store and retrieve data on a computer.

Style A set of formatting options that have been named and saved.

Subdatasheet When two tables are related, the datasheet for the primary table contains expand indicators for each record. Clicking an expand indicator in the primary table displays the records in the related table in a subdatasheet.

Sum button A button on the Ribbon that inserts the SUM function to add long columns or rows of numbers.

Summary query A query that summarizes relevant data, such as adding the field values in a column that displays price data, in the query results.

SuperScript A text format where text is raised and smaller than surrounding text.

System Clipboard See Clipboard.

System unit A computer case that contains the CPU, power supply, , memory, and some storage devices.

Systems software The operating system (OS) of the computer; controls data flow among computer parts, and provides the platform on which application and network software work.

T

Tab A section of the Ribbon that contains related commands.

Tab stop An indicator in a paragraph that marks the place where the insertion point will stop when you press the Tab key. Also called *tab*.

Table Text or graphics organized in columns and rows.

Tablet PC Small portable computers that allow you to input data by writing directly on the computer screen.

Task An Outlook activity involving the user that can be monitored to completion.

Task Input Panel Area in the Outlook To-Do Bar where you input a new task.

Task pane A window along the left side of the program window that contains options and commands.

Taskbar The area at the bottom of the Windows screen that contains the Start button as well as program or window buttons for open programs.

Telecommuting When employees use computer technology to work from home or during business travel and are linked by network to the office.

Template A predesigned file that you can use to create a new file.

Text box A shape specifically designed to hold text.

Text functions Functions that are used to format and work with cell contents.

Theme A preset collection of design elements, including fonts, colors, and other effects.

Thesaurus A built-in reference for finding synonyms for words in a document.

Thumbnail Small graphic image.

Title bar The bar at the top of the program window with the names of the program and the current file.

To-Do Bar Part of the Outlook window that contains the Date Navigator, Appointments section, Task Input section, and a task list.

To-Do Item An Outlook entry, such as a contact or e-mail message, that has been flagged for follow-up.

To-Do List Tasks visible in the To-Do Bar in Outlook.

Toggle To switch between two options or to turn a feature on or off.

Toggle command A command that you can select or deselect to switch between two options or to turn a feature on or off.

Toner A powdery substance used by laser jet printers instead of ink to create printed output on paper.

Toolbar An area in a window that contains buttons used to execute a function or open a command menu.

Total row The optional row in a datasheet that counts of the number of values in a column. When a field contains numeric data, you can use the Total row to calculate the total, average, minimum, or maximum value in a column.

Touchpad A digital tracking device on the keyboard of a laptop computer that allows you to control the pointer by moving your finger on a small electronic pad.

Track Changes A tool in Word that keeps a record of any changes you or a reviewer makes in a document by formatting inserted text in a color and underlined, and deleted and moved text in a balloon in the right margin.

Trackball A digital tracking device that has a roller ball that turns to control a pointer on the screen.

Transition See Slide transition.

Trigonometric functions Functions that manipulate quantitative data in a worksheet.

Truncate To hide text that does not fit in a cell from view.

U

Unbound control A control in a form or report that is not connected to a record source, such as a line, rectangle, or picture.

Undo To reverse a recent action.

Uniform Resource Locator (URL) The address of a Web page on the Web.

USB flash drive A very portable, small solid state storage device that plugs directly into a USB port on the computer system unit and that can read and write data.

Utility software Programs that allow you to make changes to the way hardware and software works, such as changing the screen resolution, or improving the way disk drives read and write data.

V

Vertical alignment The position of text on a page between the top and bottom margins.

View buttons In an Office program window, buttons that you can click to change views quickly.

Virus Malicious software program written by a hacker that can damage the programs on your computer causing the computer to either stop working or run slowly.

W

Web browser Special software used to view Web pages.

Web Layout view A way of viewing a document on screen that simulates the way a document will look when it is viewed as a Web page; text and graphics appear the way they would in a Web browser, and backgrounds are visible.

Web server A computer that stores and delivers the Web pages on the Internet.

Widow The first line of a paragraph at the bottom of a page.

Wildcard A special character that represents other characters in a search.

Window A work area in Windows Vista containing a user interface.

Windows Aero Windows Vista graphic interface that includes transparent windows and dialog boxes.

Windows Security Center Windows Vista utility that monitors the status of a computer's security components.

Windows Sidebar A transparent panel attached to one side of the Vista desktop screen that contains gadgets.

Wireless network technology Technology that uses the airwaves to connect devices and computers.

Word processing The use of a computer and software to enter and edit text and produce documents such as letters, memos, forms, and reports.

Word wrap A feature in Word that automatically wraps words around to the next line when they will not fit on the current line.

WordArt Stylized text that is treated as an object.

Work area The workspace that displays the file you are working on.

Workbook The file used to store worksheets; usually a collection of related worksheets.

Workgroup collaboration The process of working together in teams, sharing comments, and exchanging ideas for a common purpose.

Worksheet A computerized spreadsheet in Excel.

Worksheet range A group of adjacent worksheets.

World Wide Web (Web) A system of computers that share information by means of links on Web pages.

Wrap text To move data to a new line when the cell is not wide enough to display all the contents.

Z

Zip disk A portable disk that will hold 100MB, 250MB, or 750MB of data.

Zoom The percentage the file is magnified or reduced on the screen; 100% zoom represents the normal size; percentages higher than that mean the document appears larger on screen; percentages lower than that mean the document appears smaller on screen.

Zoom slider A bar in the lower-right corner of an Office program window that you can use to increase or decrease the size of the document on screen.

INDEX

Windows Vista Basics = WIN; Office 2007 Basics = OFF; Word Unit = WD; Excel Unit = EX;
Access Unit = ACC; PowerPoint Unit = PPT; Outlook Unit = OL; Publisher Unit = PUB;
Capstone Simulation = CAP; Appendix A = CC; Appendix B = KEY

1